The Victor
❧ Bible ❧
Background
Commentary:
New Testament

THE VICTOR BIBLE BACKGROUND COMMENTARY

New Testament

LAWRENCE O. RICHARDS

VICTOR BOOKS

A DIVISION OF SCRIPTURE PRESS PUBLICATIONS INC.
USA CANADA ENGLAND

Copyediting: Ben Unseth, Robert N. Hosack
Cover Design: Scott Rattray

Library of Congress Cataloging-in-Publication Data

Richards, Larry, 1931–
    The Victor Bible background commentary: New Testament / Lawrence O. Richards.
        p.   cm.
    ISBN 0-89693-507-8
    1. Bible. N.T.—Criticism, interpretation, etc.   I. Title.
BS2361.R44   1994
225.7—dc20   93-27863
                                                                                  CIP

---

1   2   3   4   5   6   7   8   9   10   Printing/Year   98   97   96   95   94

CONTENTS

INTRODUCTION

Commentaries are among the most important books any Christian can own, for commentaries are dedicated to helping the reader better understand the Bible.

Yet commentaries vary in focus. The writers of some commentaries are primarily concerned with solving technical textual problems. The writers of other commentaries are most interested in drawing devotional insights from the text, while still other authors emphasize tracing the argument of a passage. Some commentaries emphasize the cultural and social background of events or teachings, while others are intended simply to give the reader a quick overview of the meaning of the passages treated.

What Is a Bible Background Commentary?

Because the word "commentary," as attractive as it rightfully is, is not clear in itself, it's important to explain just what a *Bible Background Commentary* is and why it might deserve a place in the libraries of preachers, teachers, Sunday School and home Bible study group leaders, and intelligent laypersons. Simply put, *The Victor Bible Background Commentary: New Testament* is *intended to provide enrichment information for the communicator of God's Word.*

In so doing I draw on a variety of sources to provide background which illuminates the text and guides its application to people today. And, because my goal is to serve the lay Bible teacher and the preacher, special attention is paid to those passages which are most teachable and preachable.

The plan of the book is simple. Each chapter opens with *Exposition,* a feature intended to give an overview of a longer or shorter segment of the NT. The *Exposition* attempts to show how the teachable passages explored in the rest of the chapter fit together in the thought of the author and how they serve to develop his theme.

This is followed by *Word Studies,* which pick up key terms and phrases. Here too the intent is not simply to explain meaning, but to show the contribution of words to the author's theme and to do so in a preachable and teachable way. For instance, one brief entry picks up on Matthew's comment on the Triumphal Entry, "the whole city was *stirred* (21:10)." The entry continues, "The word *eseisthe* is 'shaken,' as by an earthquake. A wave of wild enthusiasm swept Jerusalem when Jesus entered the city. The fact that in just a few days cries of 'Crucify Him' echoed in the same streets alerts us. Enthusiasm is no substitute for commitment."

The third element found in each chapter is *The Passage in Depth.* This feature explores discrete teachable and preachable events or teachings found in the larger section. Here the goal is to provide information which can help keep preaching and teaching fresh, interesting, and relevant. Most of the entries in this section have three elements: *Background,* which gives information on some key historical, archaeological, cultural, or grammatical element of the passage discussed; *Interpretation,* which examines the intent of the writer and what he intended to communicate; and *Application,* which suggests how the passage might be developed in a sermon or lesson.

There is a fourth element found in some, but not all, of the chapters. This element is set off by a box and contains quotes from primary historical sources or relevant research. For instance, in the chapter that covers Matthew 23, an extended quote from Josephus' *Antiquities* provides a first-century Jew's view of the Pharisees.

By providing this blend of information, I hope to offer the reader a source of ideas and illustrations for effective teaching and preaching of God's Word.

I might also note the relationship of this two volume *Bible Background Commentary* to an earlier work, *The Teacher's Commentary*. That book provides a general commentary on the whole Bible, broken into 174 "teachable units." The unique contribution of *The Teacher's Commentary* is that it includes a lesson plan for each of these units, plus a number of *Link-to-life* teaching ideas for those teaching children as well as ministering to adults. In organizing the present works I followed the organizational plan of *The Teacher's Commentary*. So chapters in *The Victor Bible Background Commentary: New Testament* and the forthcoming *Old Testament* cover virtually the same passages as those of the earlier work.

While each work stands on its own, many will want to work with both these tools. *The Teacher's Commentary* shows *how* to teach. And the two *Bible Background Commentaries* provide that *extra* information which can enrich sermons and lessons, fascinate learners, and so give the teacher and preacher a very special edge.

It has been a special privilege to work with Victor Books to develop each of these tools and a very special joy to be able to spend the years devoted to their writing in personal study of the Word of God.

Lawrence O. Richards
Hudson, Florida

MATTHEW 1–2
The Birth of Jesus

EXPOSITION

Matthew has a story to tell. It is the story of Jesus, a story that does not begin "Once upon a time . . . " but "Now, at long last. . . ."

This realization is the key to understanding the structure of Matthew's Gospel and the key to the significance of these first two chapters of his work. Matthew, once a despised tax collector but nevertheless a Jew, writes to show his own people that Jesus of Nazareth truly was the Messiah promised by the Old Testament seers. Matthew also writes to answer a question that must have burned in the heart of every first-century Jew. If Jesus was the Messiah, what happened to the glorious kingdom foretold in the Scriptures? The answer, like the evidence of Jesus' messiahship, will unfold gradually as Matthew tells his story. But from the very first Matthew understands what he must do to reach the Jewish community. So he looks back and, as he begins, roots his account in the glorious history of the ancient and beloved people of God.

Matthew begins with an answer to the first question any ordinary Jew, as well as a rabbi, would ask. What basis exists to support Jesus' claim of messiahship? The first evidence Matthew presents is Jesus' genealogy: Jesus is a descendant of Abraham and a descendant of David (1:1-17). Matthew then tells the story of Jesus' conception, weaving into it several additional lines of evidence (1:18-25): Christ's birth was miraculous, the fulfillment of a prophecy made 700 years earlier by Isaiah. And, His birth was announced by the Angel of the Lord, a divine manifestation of Yahweh's personal involvement in events that occurred only infrequently in Israel's history (cf. Gen. 16:7-14; 22:9-18; Ex. 3:1–4:17). The full weight of the past thus affirms Jesus' right to David's throne, and an aura of the supernatural shines around His birth. This is evidence indeed!

But there is more. Magi from the East saw and recognized a supernatural sign in the heavens and came seeking the "King of the Jews" (2:1-12). Here again mystical elements are woven into the story along with references to OT prophecy. Strikingly, the context of each prophecy referred to in this chapter emphasizes the royal mission and destiny of the Messiah (cf. 2:2 with Jer. 23:5; 2:6 with Micah 5:2; 2:23 with Hosea 11:1). Again a combination of prophecy and the uncanny creates an aura of the supernatural and supports Matthew's argument that from the very beginning Jesus was marked out as special, identified by God as the One chosen to be His Messiah.

As Matthew continues, he answers other questions sure to be raised by Jewish leaders. If Jesus was David's heir, born in Bethlehem, why did He not grow up there?

The answer is that the family fled into Egypt to escape the murderous jealousy of Herod (2:13-18)—and in so doing fulfilled God's Word, "Out of Egypt I called My Son" (2:15). And, when the family returned, God directed Joseph to settle in Nazareth (2:19-23)—and in so doing fulfilled another word of God, "He will be called a Nazarene" (2:23). Thus God set His own mark on these events, directing Jesus' family to acts which fulfilled predictions and whose significance was only revealed later on.

Thus Matthew lays the foundation of his argument. The story he has to tell about Jesus is not the story of an ordinary man, or even of an exceptional Jewish rabbi. It is the story of Israel's Messiah, who is also God's Son, who has become the Savior of the world.

WORD STUDIES

A *record of the genealogy* of Jesus Christ the Son of David, the son of Abraham (1:1). The Greek *biblos geneseos* means a "record of the origins." This Greek phrase is used in the Septuagint, a Greek translation of the OT, in Gen. 6:9, 10:1, 11:10, and 11:27. (The NIV reads, "This is the record.") In the OT the phrase often indicates a new turn in God's plan, a new beginning. Thus Matthew alerts us: The birth of Jesus marks a new beginning, not just for Israel, but for the human race!

Joseph, the husband of Mary, of whom was born Jesus (1:16). Matthew purposely fails to define the relationship between Joseph and Jesus. Legally, Jesus was the son of Joseph, and thus His claim to David's throne is firmly established. Biologically, Jesus was born of Mary. Joseph, as Matthew goes on to explain, did not father this One who was to be the Messiah. Jesus is not only God the Son, but also the Son of God.

Was the *father of* (1:2, etc.). The Greek word *egennesen,* translated "begat" in older versions and "was the father of" in the NIV, does not indicate immediate parentage, but does claim direct descent. Jesus is firmly placed in the line of the great men of sacred history. This is an important reminder for us. We cannot sever the NT from the OT, the fulfillment from the promise, the age of the New Covenant from the age of the Old Covenant. The Jesus we worship is that descendant of David who came as Israel's Messiah. In Jesus, Old and New, Jew and Christian, are inseparably linked. [See box, page 13.]

Fourteen generations . . . (1:17). It is well known that Hebrew genealogies do not include all ancestors, but are highly selective in nature. Why then does Matthew select and organize his genealogy into three groups of fourteen? The best answer is that he uses a familiar rabbinic device called *gematria,* which builds an argument on the numerical value of the Hebrew letters that make up a word. The letters in David's name add up to 14 (D=4, W=6, D=4). Thus Matthew's organization may well reflect a then familiar way of subtly emphasizing Jesus' descent from David.

Because Joseph her husband was a *righteous man* and did not want to expose her to public disgrace (1:19). This text gives us wonderful insight into what it means to be "righteous" [*dikaios*]. Under Jewish custom Mary was bound to Joseph as a wife, even though they had not had intercourse. The betrothal was legally binding. Discovery that Mary was pregnant gave Joseph a basis for breaking the contract and recovering the bride-price he had already paid. Many a man, finding his betrothed pregnant, would have demanded public exposure, not only to silence any gossip about him but also to recover his money. And in so doing would have considered himself fully justified (and thus righteous)! Joseph, although he must have felt betrayed, considered Mary and made a very different choice. Under the law he could give Mary a bill of divorce, without public trial, but would also have to return any dowry he had received, as a fine. Joseph chose this option, despite the financial as well as emotional cost. Let's never mistake "making the other person pay" for righteousness. In doing what is right we are to show compassion, even to those who wrong us.

You are to *give Him the name* Jesus (1:21). It is significant that the angel addressed this to Joseph. It was the father's privilege to name an infant, and by naming a baby the father formally acknowledged the child as his own. Thus the Angel of the Lord was instructing Joseph not only to fulfill the marriage contract with Mary, but also to bring Jesus up as his own child. Undoubtedly, the neighbors in Nazareth never suspected the truth of Jesus' birth.

***They will call* Him Immanuel (1:23).** Jesus' name, as the text says, means "God [is] with us." Here, "they will call" does not so much mean "name" as "acknowledge." Jesus claimed that the one seeing Him had seen the Father (John 14:9). Only those who acknowledge Jesus as God, born to take a stand with and for us, have grasped the truth Matthew is so intent on sharing.

Bethlehem (2:6). The name means "house of bread." In biblical times "bread" stood for "food," essential to sustain biological life. As the "Bread of heaven," born in this "house of bread," Jesus sustains eternal, spiritual life.

We saw His star *in the east* (2:2). The star was not in the east. It was the Magi who were in the east when they saw the star, and they traveled west following it.

He *asked them* where the Christ was to be born (2:4). The imperfect tense (*epunthaneto*) suggests repeated inquiries. Herod was frantic to know where this One he saw as a rival would be born and grilled everyone who might know.

He will be called a *Nazarene* (2:23). The verse is puzzling, for no verse predicts the Messiah would grow up in Nazareth. The reference may be intended to link the fact that Nazareth was looked upon with contempt in the first century as a backwater (John 7:42, 52)

JEWS ON JESUS

It is popular these days for Jewish scholars to argue that Jesus stands squarely in the tradition of first-century rabbis and sages. They suggest that Christians are mistaken about supposed differences in His teachings from the teachings of His contemporaries. In a letter to the *Bible Review* (June 1991, p. 9), an outstanding Jewish scholar, Jacob Neusner, who is Graduate Research Professor of Religious Studies at the University of South Florida, writes:

What makes a Christian is that he or she believes Jesus is Christ, unique, God, Son of God, risen from the dead. To these profound, Christian beliefs the issue of whether or not Jesus taught this or that which Judaism also taught is simply, monumentally irrelevant. . . . This does not mean that we cannot be friends, work together, respect, and admire and even love one another. It does mean that we have a major theological problem to address, since both of us—Judaism, Christianity—cannot be right, and if (as I believe) we are right, then Christians are wrong, and if (as most Christians believe) Christianity is right about Jesus Christ, then we Jews are wrong. Characterizing Jesus as a Galilean charismatic is not merely childish and trivial, it is irrelevant to the life of the lived faiths, Christianity and Judaism; and characterizing Jesus as some sort of rabbi, or as a Jew among Jews (as though nothing happened on or after first Easter) is simply an evasion and an irrelevance.

Matthew, who so clearly grasped this issue, makes it clear from the beginning of his Gospel that this is the issue his own people must confront. Who is Jesus? Is He Christ, unique, Son of God, risen from the dead? Matthew's answer is an unequivocal, unmistakable "Yes!"

with the many OT prophecies that the Messiah would be despised (Ps. 22:6-8; Isa. 49:7; 53:2-3). If so, we are surely reminded that Jesus totally changes man's point of view. Nazareth, once despised, is honored today as the childhood home of the Savior.

They opened their *treasures* (2:11). The Greek phrase is *thesaurous auton* and refers to the containers in which valuables were kept. The fact that three valuables are mentioned

has led to the unjustified assumption that there were "three kings" in the party that found Jesus.

Slew *all the male children* that were in Bethlehem (2:16). Archaeological surveys of remains dating from the first century suggest, on the basis of the population of the area, that probably some 15-18 children were killed by Herod's soldiers.

THE PASSAGE IN DEPTH

The Genealogy (1:1-17). See the parallel passage in Luke 3:23-38 for a discussion of the differences between the two genealogical records.

The Genealogy's Four Women (1:3, 5-6). One of the distinctive features of Matthew's genealogy is his specific inclusion of four women. The critical question here is: Why?

Background. Hebrew culture was patriarchal, and genealogies usually listed only men. There were, however, two typical reasons in the east to include a woman or two. (1) The woman was greatly admired, and her inclusion enhanced the reputation of the family. (2) The husband had more than one wife, in which case the name of the wife is typically given with the name of her son. This practice is often followed in the OT when naming the kings of Israel and Judah.

However, we can appeal to neither of these practices to explain why Matthew included the four women he chose to name. They were hardly admired. Nor is there any confusion in the OT concerning whose children their sons were. So we are led to seek another reason for Matthew's decision to name these particular four.

Interpretation. The explanation must hinge on what we know of the four. Tamar, a Canaanite woman, seduced the father-in-law who had wronged her, and bore him two sons (Gen. 38). Rahab, also a Canaanite, made her living as a prostitute before giving her allegiance to the Lord and helping Israelite spies escape Jericho (Josh. 2, 6). Ruth, though morally pure, was a Moabitess, a race whose origins were in incest (Gen. 19:30-37) and which, according to Deut. 23:3, was banned

from the Lord's assembly. Bathsheba is best known for her (forced?) adultery with David. Although born into a Jewish family (1 Chron. 3:5), she may have been classified as a Hittite because of her marriage to Uriah (2 Sam. 11:3; 23:39).

The four women seem to have two things in common. They were flawed morally. And they were outside the OT Covenant community, with no native right to claim God or to expect Him to deal with them in grace. What then moved Matthew to include these four women in the line of Jesus the Messiah?

One possibility is that, as a tax collector, looked on with contempt by his neighbors, Matthew knew what it meant to be a sinner and then redeemed. Matthew identifies with these four women and includes them as illustrations of the transforming power of God who has now sent the Messiah to "save His people from their sins" (1:21).

Another possibility, Matthew may be thinking of the universality of the mission of Jesus. God's covenant with Abraham included the promise, "all peoples on earth will be blessed through you" (Gen. 12:3). The four women demonstrate God's commitment to keep that promise, which receives its ultimate fulfillment in the Christian Gospel's invitation to all to believe in Jesus and be saved.

A third possibility is that Matthew is subtly reminding his readers, who looked for a Messiah who would appear in glory and power, that history shows God working in strange and mysterious ways. We cannot say how God will or must act. All we can do is recognize His handiwork and worship Him.

Application. There is no reason to rule out any of the three interpretations above. In fact, they blend together in a wonderful way. Our God is the God of the unexpected. He remains concerned for those "outside," as well as for you and me. As each of the four women illustrates, God reaches out in grace for the sinner and by His transforming power God cleanses sinners and makes them vital, contributing members of the community of faith.

The Birth of Jesus Christ (1:18-25).

Background. Perhaps the first things a person should note in this passage are the miraculous elements. The fathering of the child by the Holy Spirit. An angelic visitation to announce the birth to Joseph. The promise of ancient prophecies about to be fulfilled. These all support Matthew's thesis that Jesus truly is Israel's Messiah and the Son of the Living God.

Yet we need to note something else. God carefully, graciously, guarded Joseph's love for Mary and prepared him to love her child.

Marriage customs in Jewish culture were very unlike those in our day. The marriage was negotiated by a girl's parents and involved the payment of a bride-price by the husband when an agreement was reached. At this point the girl was "pledged" (1:18), betrothed, and was considered the wife of her husband-to-be, even though she still lived in her parents' home and had no marital relations with him.

It was not unusual for older men to arrange to marry girls of nine or ten, often in order to protect property rights when a father died, or because orphan girls in the ancient Middle East had no means of support. In such cases a child bride would live in the home of her husband, but remain a virgin till she reached marriageable age. Of course, if she were found not to be a virgin when the marriage was consummated, the husband could obtain an annulment and the bride-price would be returned.

Interpretation. It is perhaps significant that an ancient tradition suggests Joseph was an older man and Mary a very young girl. If this is the case it is possible that, as a child bride, Mary had lived in Joseph's home, and that he had developed a deep affection for her. We can imagine his dismay when Joseph discovered Mary was pregnant—a discovery he could hardly have made if Mary still lived in her parents' home. That affection, and his own righteous character, led Joseph to contemplate a self-sacrificial step. He would not "expose her to public disgrace." Instead he would divorce her quietly and suffer the loss of the bride-price he had paid. We can only imagine the anger and hurt Joseph must have felt. But we can surely admire this man of character and compassion, who although seemingly betrayed, still put Mary's needs and reputation before his own.

It was only then, the decision made, that God intervened. Only then did God reveal the miracle of Mary's pregnancy and what that miracle would mean. The child had been conceived by the Holy Spirit. He would be "God with us." And He was the One God intended to use to "save His people from their sins." Joseph is not to hesitate consummating the relationship when the child has been born.

Note: The NIV translation seems to rule out examining this possibility by translating *paralabe* in v. 20 as "take Mary home." But the word means simply to "take to oneself" and need not imply that Mary was not already living with Joseph as a virgin child bride.

Application. How fascinating that God's angel appeared to Joseph only after he had discovered Mary was pregnant. God could have spared Joseph much pain by telling him beforehand—as He told Mary beforehand (Luke 1:26-31). But the pain served a beautiful purpose. When tested, Joseph displayed his "righteous" character. In that display of righteousness, Joseph teaches us. It is important to do what is morally correct. But as we do, it is just as important to act with compassion and concern.

The incident also reminds us of something else. God was deeply concerned with the relationship which was to exist between Mary and Joseph. This was not only for their own sake, but also for the sake of Jesus and the other children they would parent. The angel visitor removed any suspicion which might have tainted the relationship and restored not only the affection but also the trust so vital to growth in any couple's marriage.

Yes, the miraculous in this story is a vital element. But nearly as wonderful is that common touch which reminds us that God is concerned about our ordinary lives—about preserving the love we have for others and shaping a home where warmth and trust create that climate in which children can grow.

The Visit of the Magi (2:1-12).

Background. The Magi in OT times were a class of scholarly, priestly individuals who served as advisers to Babylonian and Persian rulers. This class persisted in Persia and was influential in the Parthian empire into NT times. Little, however, is known of the specific role or background of these Eastern visitors to little Judea.

Some have suggested these men recognized the star because they were familiar with Num. 24:17: "A star will come out of Jacob; a scepter will rise out of Israel." Certainly there was a significant Jewish population in the East at this time, and the massive scholarly work known as the Babylonian Talmud was located there. It is surely possible that the Magi had access not only to the OT Scriptures but also to extensive Jewish writings on them.

The nature of the star reported by Matthew has been debated, and a variety of natural explanations have been offered. But all of these miss the point. The timing of the appearance of the star was supernatural.

The other details are most natural. For instance, in desert countries of the East nomads find their way over the sands by following stars. "Take that star in your hand" is a common way of giving directions. It would not be unusual at all for God to guide the Magi to the Christ Child by, in essence, telling them "Take that star in your hand and follow it until you come to the One born King of the Jews."

What the Prophet Has Written (2:6ff).

Background. Matthew's "quote" does not follow either the Massoretic (Hebrew) nor Septuagint (Greek) text of Micah 5:2. Despite the furor over this fact, there is a simple explanation. Matthew, moved by God, gives us an inspired interpretation of the original text, modified only slightly in order to emphasize its original point. He also links the Micah quote with 2 Sam. 5:2.

What is more significant is that this is an example of Matthew's great care in linking Jesus to OT prophecy. In his Gospel, Matthew quotes the OT 53 times, drawing from 25 of the 39 OT books, and alludes to many additional OT passages. Matthew is determined to explain Jesus—His Person, His ministry, His destiny—within a framework already established by the Jewish Scriptures.

It is particularly fascinating to explore these quotes to see just what Matthew's use implies. Strikingly, the OT contexts emphasize the kingly role of the coming Messiah. Although Jesus failed to meet the expectations of His generation, Jesus is the promised Messiah King. The suffering Savior and the glorious Ruler of OT prophecy are one and the same.

Observation. To sense this emphasis, let us examine the context of two passages referred to in Matthew 2:

■ Underlying Matt. 2:2, Jer. 23:5: " 'The days are coming,' declares the Lord, 'when I will raise up to David a righteous Branch, a King who will reign wisely and do what is just and right in the land. In His days Judah will be saved and Israel will live in safety. This is the name by which He will be called: The Lord Our Righteousness.' "

■ Underlying Matt. 2:6, Micah 5:2, 4: "But you, Bethlehem Ephrathah, though you are small among the clans of Judah, out of you will come for me One who will be ruler over Israel, whose origins are from of old, from ancient times. . . . He will stand and shepherd His flock in the strength of the Lord; in the majesty of the name of the Lord His God. And they shall live securely, for then His greatness will reach to the ends of the earth."

Application. Matthew's use of quotes is undoubtedly evangelistic, in that his intent is to show his own Jewish brothers and sisters that Jesus is the Christ. But that use is a vital reminder to Christians today. Our understanding of who Jesus is, of His mission, and of God's intended future for Christ's rule on earth, must be formed only after a careful study of the OT, as well of the NT.

The Escape to Egypt (2:13-23). Great attention has rightly been paid to Herod's character, so cruelly displayed in the pursuit of Jesus and the murder of the innocent children of Bethlehem. But this need not be the focus of our exposition.

Commentators have also puzzled over the relevance of Matthew's use of Jeremiah 31:15. The best answer is that Jeremiah's message of the New Covenant was given at the moment of Judah's greatest suffering: the fall of Jerusalem and deportation of the Jewish survivors to Babylon. Yet at that same moment in history God's word through Jeremiah gave birth to hope. Similarly, the moment that the Bethlehem mothers experienced their most anguishing loss, God's intervention saved the Christ Child, who is the fulfillment of the New Covenant and the true hope of the world.

These themes are present in the text, and yet there is another theme that overrides them all—the theme of providence.

The Magi bring gifts—and so finance the travel of Jesus, Mary, and Joseph to Egypt at the very moment when they must escape. Herod dies, and Joseph leads his family home, but at the last moment turns away from Beth-lehem to settle in Nazareth. Each happening is marked as the leading of God: by the dream that directed it, and by a word from Scripture which, unexpectedly, proves prophetic.

Thus the entire sequence of events is evidently guided and directed by God, and we are reminded that the Lord never removes His hand from His Son.

We are encouraged.

We are children of this same Lord. And He will not remove His hand from you or me.

MATTHEW 3–4
Jesus' Preparation

EXPOSITION

Matthew is intent on revealing Jesus as Israel's Messiah, the One who is Savior and King. As Matthew continues to build his case, he moves now to two key strands of evidence and skillfully weaves them into his narrative. Jesus met the conditions established in the OT (3:1-12). And Jesus personally was qualified to serve as Israel's Messiah (3:13–4:25).

The fact that there were conditions for Messiah to meet was believed by commoner and rabbi alike. Before Messiah, Elijah must come. The appearance of Elijah, first-century Israel believed, would mark the end of the age and precipitate the appearance of Messiah. That condition was met by John the Baptizer, a man whose rough dress and fierce character, whose strident call for repentance clearly modeled Elijah's ministry. Looking back at the ministry of John, Matthew's readers must acknowledge that God did send an Elijah (3:1-12; 11:1-19).

Matthew then shows that Jesus Himself was personally qualified for the role of Messiah. God acknowledged Jesus as "My Son, whom I love," and said, "with Him I am well pleased" (3:13-17). Jesus was also qualified in His humanity, for as man He triumphed over Satan's temptations (4:1-11). Thus in His Person deity bonded with sinless humanity, uniquely qualifying Jesus to serve as Israel's Messiah. But there is more. Jesus was qualified by power. He preached, and His word transformed ordinary people, who became followers of His (4:12-22). He spoke, and at His word sickness fled and demons cowered. Every act demonstrates that Jesus not only met the conditions imposed by OT prophecy, but that He was fully qualified by a unique character and power to claim Israel's throne. And to claim the throne of every heart.

WORD STUDIES

Repent (3:2). Our English word unfortunately suggests being sorry for sin. This clouds the emphasis of the Greek original. There *metanoeite* calls for a radical change of heart and mind; a change which will issue in a radically different lifestyle. Thus John's emphasis:

"Produce fruit in keeping with repentance" (3:8).

All too often we make the mistake of focusing on feelings. John did not. His call to repent was no invitation to tears, but a demand for decision.

F.B. MEYER ON THE CALL TO REPENT

John the Baptist is sadly needed today. Much of what we call Christianity is but Christianized heathenism. It glosses over covetousness, luxurious self-indulgence, compliance with fashion and worldliness; it admits into its high places men who thrive on the oppression of the poor; it condones the oppression of the native races, the sale of opium and spirits, and shameless traffic in impurity; it rears the ideals of the world in the place of the changeless cross of the slain Christ with its divine sorrow and blood. Ah, we need that John the Baptist should come with his stern words about the axe, the winnowing-fan, and the fire. Nothing less will avail to prepare the way for a new coming of Christ.

Each age has had its John the Baptist. Now St. Bernard; now Savanarola; now John Knox. With sonorous, ringing voice the herald has prepared the way of the King: "He cometh to judge the world!"

—from Great Verses Through the Bible

"Repent, for the *kingdom* of heaven is near" (3:2). In Scripture a "kingdom" is not so much a place as a sphere of influence; a realm in which the will of the king had dynamic force.

The "kingdom of heaven" thus stands for the dynamic force of God's will breaking into the world and working His mighty transformations.

While many in the first century expected that God's dynamic force would take political shape and free the Jews from the power of Rome, we must remember that God's kingdom takes many forms. This is key to understanding Matthew's Gospel.

More important, this is key to our own present relationship with God. We find ourselves in God's kingdom when we commit ourselves to Jesus, the King. In Jesus, God's dynamic force takes spiritual shape and frees us from the power of sin. And we continually

experience that dynamic force in our lives as we give daily allegiance to Him as King, responding gladly to His will.

Repent, for the kingdom of *heaven* is near (3:2). Some have argued for a distinction between the "kingdom of God" in the other Gospels and the "kingdom of heaven" in Matthew.

A more likely explanation is that Matthew is being careful not to give offense to the Jews he is trying to reach. It was common Jewish practice to use a circumlocution like "heaven" to refer to God.

One who is more powerful than I, *whose sandals I am not fit to carry* (3:11). The Aramaic text reads "to remove," thus agreeing with Mark 1:7 and Luke 3:16. In the East shoes are removed when entering a house. Most visitors in John's time removed their own shoes; servants removed the shoes of their master or an important guest. The owner himself would stoop to remove the shoes only of a truly illustrious visitor. John, whom some speculated was himself the Messiah, denied this claim and exalted Jesus by insisting that he was not even worthy to handle Jesus' sandals.

What an example for us. May we have as clear an understanding of the significance of Jesus, and as earnestly turn the attention of others from ourselves to Him.

He will baptize you *with the Holy Spirit and with fire* (3:11-12). John baptizes only with water for (because of) repentance. The coming Messiah baptizes with the Holy Spirit (1 Cor. 12:13; also Ezek. 36:25-27; Joel 2:28) and fire. Some take "fire" here as a symbol of judgment (as Isa. 34:10; 66:24; Jer. 7:20), while others see it as a symbol of purification (as Isa. 1:25; Zech. 13:9; Mal. 3:2-3). As both the Spirit and fire are controlled by the same preposition, *en*, which is not repeated in the text, the second view is preferable.

The saying reminds us of the superiority of Jesus. John preached repentance, but his baptism with water could only acknowledge the expressed intent of a man or woman to change. Jesus preached repentance, but His baptism of the Spirit actually provides the sanctifying fire that purifies and transforms.

Let's not be satisfied with the water. What we need is the Spirit's fire.

Jesus was led by the Spirit into the desert to be *tempted* by the devil (4:1). The Greek word is *peirazo*, which means both "tempt" and "test." Whichever English word we use to translate the Greek, and this varies according to context, it is clear that testing or temptation places us in situations that produce intense stress. Under this stress, we frequently jump to the conclusion that our temptations or tests are divine punishment, or at the very least are "bad." Matthew corrects our impression. God has just affirmed His love for His Son (3:17). Yet immediately Matthew says Jesus was "led" out to the place of temptation "by the Spirit." Clearly, love was intimately involved in the testing of God's Son!

How important in our own moments of stress to remember that we are loved by God. When He leads us into temptations—something we are told not to ask for—it is not evidence of abandonment, but simply further proof of His love.

Worship the Lord Your God, and *serve Him* only (4:10). The Greek word here is *latreuo. The Expository Dictionary of Bible Words* (Zondervan) notes "every occurrence of the latreuo group in the NT carried the religious sense of worship, or serving God." (Words in this group are found in Matt. 4:10; Luke 1:74; 2:37; 4:8; John 16:2; Acts 7:7, 42; 24:14; 26:7; 27:23; Rom. 1:9; 9:4; 12:1; Phil. 3:3; 2 Tim. 1:3; Heb. 8:5; 9:1, 6, 9, 14; 10:2; 12:28; 13:10; Rev. 7:15; 22:3.)

We can hardly claim to be worshipers of God without offering Him our wholehearted service.

Come, *follow* Me (4:19). Following Jesus involved more than trailing along after Him, although this the Twelve surely did. Most important, to follow Christ meant then, as now, to enroll in His school as trainees, that an understanding of Jesus' teaching and His way of life might infuse the disciple's personality.

THE PASSAGE IN DEPTH

John the Baptist Prepares the Way (3:1-12). In-depth discussion of this theme is found in the parallel passage, Luke 3:1-20. See also Mark 1:1-8.

The Baptism of Jesus (3:13-17). The baptism of Jesus has been a focal point of much debate. Why, if Jesus was sinless, did He choose to be baptized by John "for repentance"? Why did John seek to restrain Jesus? And what did Jesus mean when He said it was "proper" in order to "fulfill all righteousness"? The answer to these questions suggests several fascinating and important truths.

Background. John the Baptist's baptism was a true religious innovation. The Jewish world knew two types of baptisms or washings with water. There was the baptism required of proselytes on conversion, and there was the more frequent washings of cleansing that were rooted in biblical tradition.

Rabbinic writings indicate three things were required of a first-century male Gentile wishing to become a Jew: circumcision, sacrifice, and baptism. In his classic work, *The Life and Times of Jesus the Messiah,* Edersheim writes, "The baptism was to be performed in the presence of three witnesses, ordinarily Sanhedirsts (Yebam. 47 b), but in case of necessity others might act. The person to be baptized, having cut his hair and nails, undressed completely, made fresh profession of his faith, before what were designated the 'fathers of baptism,' and then immersed completely, so that every part of the body was touched by the water" (pp. 745-46). Clearly there is no direct parallel here with John's public baptism of Jews, not as a rite of conversion but as a sign of repentance.

Similarly there is no direct parallel with the Jewish cleansing rituals. *The Revell Bible Dictionary* says of these acts, "In the time of Jesus, the Jewish people used ritual bathing pools for personal purification. Archaeologists have found such baths not only on the Temple Mount but also in the remains of wealthy homes in Jerusalem, and even at the Khirbet Qumran, the headquarters of the Dead Sea Scrolls sect. Each bath, or *mikvah,* had a reserve pool that was filled from rain water because rabbinic law dictated flowing ('living') water for use in purification" (pp. 126-27). Again there is no direct parallel between this private ritual and John's call for a public act of baptism as a sign of repentance and renewed commitment to God.

What John did, then, was to create a new symbol from elements of the old: a baptism in living (flowing) water that did not promise renewal, but that instead symbolized commitment to an inner renewal that could only be accomplished by complete dedication to God, as personal preparation for the impending eschatological kingdom.

Interpretation. Our interpretation of this brief passage hinges on understanding John's reluctance and Jesus' insistance.

First, we cannot explain John's reluctance by supposing that the Baptizer recognized Jesus as the Messiah. John's own words, found in John 1:31, 33 make this plain. There the Baptizer is reported to have told his followers, "I myself did not know Him . . ." and, "I would not have known Him, except

that the One who sent me to baptize with water told me, 'The Man on whom you see the Spirit come down and remain is He. . . .' " Thus John did not realize Jesus was the Messiah until after His baptism! Why then was John reluctant to baptize Jesus?

The conclusion we must draw is surprising. John was convinced that Jesus did not need to be baptized. This suggests that John knew Jesus personally. In fact, this is not all that unlikely. Mary and Elizabeth, John's mother, were very close (cf. Luke 2:39ff). Surely the two families would have gotten together, especially at those holiday times when Joseph and Mary traveled from Galilee to Judea. The two boys, so close in age and in early spiritual commitment, would have played and talked together. Undoubtedly the spiritual insights which Jesus showed at age 12, when He amazed the teachers of Judaism who ministered on holy days in the temple courts (cf. Luke 2:41-51), would have had great appeal for the ascetic John, already filled with zeal for the Lord. Thus when John insisted, "I need to be baptized by You" — and in the Greek the pronouns "I" and "you" are most emphatic — he was expressing an informed opinion that Jesus, surely, had no need to repent!

But Christ insisted. Some suggest the "now" is important and that Jesus' act was intended to confirm the eschatological element so prominent in John's preaching of a messianic kingdom near at hand. But perhaps it is better to emphasize what Jesus did: that it was a proper thing for Him to do to "fulfill all righteousness." One recent suggestion posits that since it was God's will that Jesus be baptized, it was proper for John and Jesus (the "us" in the verse) to fulfill that will. But this does not explain why it was God's will for Christ to undergo the rite.

Perhaps a simple solution is in order. Perhaps Jesus chose to be baptized, even though He personally had no need to repent, in order to publicly identify Himself with John's ministry. Thus Jesus added Messiah's "Amen!" to all that John taught and did.

Application. There are two thoughts here that can be readily applied to us and those we teach.

First, although John deeply respected Jesus, he was amazed to learn that his childhood friend was actually the Messiah. Somehow he never expected it! Could the fun-loving, hard-working Jesus, that attractive and yet "ordinary" person, be God's Messiah? He just doesn't fit the mold. The Messiah should be awesome—distant; someone you look up to who is overwhelming—different.

John's failure to suspect that Jesus was the Messiah calls us to reexamine our own notions of spirituality. Must the truly spiritual person be distant, overwhelming, far removed from ordinary life? Or is the secret of true spirituality simply living a truly human life, as Jesus did, in union with God? Laughter, hard work, warm friendships, caring, fun—all of these things are at least as likely to characterize the spiritual person as a grim visage, sunken eyes, and self-imposed distance from other women and men.

Jesus, history's one truly spiritual man, was criticized by His contemporaries for "eating and drinking" and being a "friend of tax collectors and sinners" (Matt. 11:19). He enjoyed parties and loved all kinds of people. And even His close friend, John, did not suspect who He really was.

Let's not let distorted notions of how a "spiritual" person behaves lead us to miss the dedication to God of those who don't fit into our pigeonholes. And let's not let a distorted notion of spirituality keep us from that freedom to enjoy life and relate to others that Jesus so beautifully displays.

Second, the fact that Jesus had no personal need to repent, and thus was not required to be baptized, should challenge us. Jesus was baptized because it was the right thing for Him, as a righteous person, to identify Himself with John and his message. It's so easy for us today to stand on the sidelines and let others fight God's battles. For example, think of the campaign some are waging to limit the showing of sex and violence on TV. Perhaps, we say, we don't permit such shows to be seen in our home. So why should we become involved? Why indeed? Perhaps simply because those who seek to influence advertisers and networks are doing the right thing. And, if they are, then we should publicly ally ourselves with them. As Jesus did when He chose to be baptized with John.

The Temptation of Jesus (4:1-11). See also the parallel passages in Mark 1:12-13 and Luke 4:1-13.

Background. While there are significant passages on testing/temptation in the NT (see commentary on Heb. 2:18; James 1:13-15), we must seek to understand the temptation of Jesus against the backdrop of OT thought. God's Spirit led God's Son into the wilderness, not to punish Him or expose His weaknesses, but that in the crucible of testing, certain essential qualities might be displayed and shown to be genuine.

Testing, or temptation, is an infrequent theme in the OT. Three Hebrew words are translated "test" in the NIV and NASB. *Nasah* is found 36 times in the OT and indicates an attempt to prove the quality of someone or something (Ex. 16:4; Deut. 8:16). *Sarap,* which means to smelt or refine, suggests a process of purification. Seven times in the OT this word is translated as "test" (Ps. 17:3; 119:140; Jer. 9:7). *Bahan* is a test intended to demonstrate the existence of some quality. This word is found 29 times in the OT (Gen. 42:15-16; Ps. 7:9; Prov. 17:3; Jer. 6:27; Mal. 3:10, 15).

Strikingly, the Greek word *periazo,* which is translated both tempt and test in the NT, is used in the Septuagint to render the Hebrew *nasah.* This may well explain why Matthew, writing with the Jewish reader in mind, selected *periazo* to describe the temptation of Jesus rather than the more appropriate, to the Greek, *dokimazo; periazo* clearly indicates testing with the intent of proving genuine rather than exposing as false.

Interpretation. Once we agree that the intent of Jesus' temptation was to prove the existence of qualities essential to His mission as Messiah, we note a number of significant things about Matthew's text.

■ There were three temptations. This seems obvious, but is nevertheless significant. Each of the three represents a distinctive avenue of attack used by Satan. And just as clearly, each of the three reveals some essential quality that was a necessary qualification for Jesus' ministry.

■ "If" in 4:3 does not mean "if." In English "if" generally suggests doubt. The Greek construction (*ei* plus the indicative) assumes that Jesus is the Son of God. Thus Satan's challenge to Jesus was to act in character, as God, and solve the problem raised by the 40-day fast by performing a miracle and turning the stones into bread.

■ Jesus responds in the first instance by quoting a passage which emphasizes His humanity: "Man does not live by bread alone" (Deut. 8:3). Thus Jesus announced His intention to meet Satan's challenges in His human nature, without appeal to the independent prerogatives of deity which He had willingly set aside in the Incarnation.

■ Jesus responds to each test by appealing to Scripture. In each instance the quote is from Deuteronomy, which is not as important as the way in which Christ used the Scripture. What He did in fact was to draw from each passage a principle—and choose to act on that principle. Thus we are reminded that the freeing power of God's Word is not released simply by our knowing it, but only by our applying it.

■ There is significance in the sequence in which the three temptations were presented. Interestingly, the Greek text of Matthew indicates a definite sequence, using the temporal connectors "then" (4:5) and "again" (4:8). In contrast, Luke, who records the sequence in a different order, uses no such connectors and thus does not require us to assume a specific order. What is perhaps most significant is that the offer of "all the kingdoms of the world and their splendor" (4:8) is the culminating temptation. Rightly so, for it is ultimately the kingdom that is at issue in Matthew. The King has come. But what has happened to the kingdom?

■ We can only understand and apply this passage when we determine the nature of the temptations, the quality that each test was intended to display, and how each quality related to Jesus' messianic mission.

■ The First Temptation (4:1-4). The first temptation grew out of the hunger Jesus felt after a 40-day fast. He was challenged by Satan to act in His essential nature as God's Son to satisfy His human need. Jesus refused, affirming that "man shall not live by bread alone."

Jesus faced this test as a man. But more significantly, the test rested on the reality of His humanity. As a human being, Jesus was subject to hunger. He was subject to pain. He was, in the words of the Prophet Isaiah, "a Man of sorrows, and familiar with suffering"

(53:3). If Jesus was to fulfill the mission of the Servant of Yahweh as that mission is described in the OT, He must suffer. And despite suffering, Jesus must choose to submit completely to the will of God. In refusing to act independently to relieve His own intense suffering, Jesus showed He possessed the strength of character required of the Messiah.

■ The Second Temptation (4:5-7). The second temptation also grew out of Jesus' humanity and again features the preamble, "If You are the Son of God." But here the Greek construction differs. Now Satan raises a real question, seeking to introduce an element of doubt.

We can see why doubt might exist. Would God treat His own Son so shabbily? Was it really the Spirit's leading that took Jesus into the wilderness, or was it some other voice, perhaps the whisper of ambition or misplaced zeal? And now we hear Satan's voice, quoting Scripture itself to show how easy it would be to settle every doubt! Just leap from the corner of the temple wall into the valley below. God's angels will catch You—and then You'll know.

Jesus' response confirms this understanding, for He refers to a moment in history when the Exodus generation demanded proof that God was among them. In essence, Jesus commits Himself to live a life of total trust, however dark the circumstances may be.

How much Jesus would need this quality as He faced His own dark night of the soul. How often, ridiculed and tormented by the Pharisees, doubted by the common man, deserted at last even by His disciples, Jesus had many a reason to feel deserted and alone. How much of His experience echoed the words of Psalm 22:1, acknowledged to be messianic even in the first century, we cannot know. Yet, however often Jesus cried out within—"My God, My God, why have You forsaken Me? Why are You so far from saving Me, so far from the words of My groaning?"—He never faltered in His trust in God.

■ The Third Temptation (4:8-10). The third temptation relates directly to Jesus' mission. As Messiah, He is ultimately to become Ruler of all. And suddenly Satan comes with an offer to give Jesus "all the kingdoms of the world and their splendor."

It is likely that if Jesus was tempted, it was

not by the splendor of earth's kingdoms but by the good His rule could do. The OT prophets give us many vivid images of a world revitalized by Messiah's beneficent rule. Extended lifetimes, prosperity and peace, even nature tamed so that "the wolf and the lamb will feed together" (Isa. 65:25), are all outcomes of Messiah's coming rule.

Wouldn't it be "good" for all those generations since the Incarnation that have lived and died—often in pain—if over these past centuries Jesus had ruled? And all this could be had without the cross! Humanity would be blessed, and the Savior would achieve His kingly destiny without pain. Why not then accept Satan's offer?

The problem is, God's purpose could be served only if the path to the kingdom led first to the cross. Suffering must come before glory; redemption must precede renewal. How-

ever "good" Satan's offer may have seemed on its face, God's Messiah must be fully committed to do the will of God, and God's will alone.

Application. Much in this passage has direct application to our lives. Like Jesus, we are susceptible in our humanity to temptation along each avenue Satan used here.

Like Jesus, we must choose to live by principles established in God's Word. As the following chart suggests, there are lessons we can learn from Christ's experience, and these lessons will help us overcome our temptations.

In fact, if you and I hope to fulfill God's purpose in our lives, we must make the choices Jesus made and nurture those qualities which He so beautifully displayed.

Like Jesus, we are susceptible to pressures from the physical, spiritual, and social universe in which we live. We too have needs—a need

Analysis of Jesus' Temptation

The Temptation	The focal relationship	Its avenue	The basic human need	Lessons learned
Turn stones to bread	Self	The physical	Survival	Surrender self
Leap from temple	God	The spiritual	Security	Trust God completely
Accept all earth's kingdoms	Others	The social	Significance	Choose always to do God's will

for survival, a need for security, a need for a personal significance that comes not only from recognition by others but also from a sense of fulfilling our own destiny in life. Each of these needs is strong, and our desire to meet each need will at times create intense stress. When we experience that stress, we must recognize the situation for what it is: a temptation, a test. How wonderful to find in this experience of Jesus the keys that will enable us to pass the test as He did, and go on to a deeper life.

The Calling of the First Disciples (4:18-22). See also the parallel passages in Mark 1:16-20; Luke 5:1-11.

Background. In first-century Judaism the training of persons for spiritual leadership was well-defined. Rather than relying on schooling,

Judaism required that learners serve as apprentices of recognized masters, becoming their "disciples" in a technical sense of that word.

A rabbi's disciple literally lived with his teacher, accompanying him everywhere. He learned not only by listening to his Master's teaching but also by observing his actions. We see reflections of this process in passages like Mark 3:14, "He appointed twelve . . . that they might be with Him," and Luke 6:40, "everyone who is fully trained will be like his teacher." Mark reveals the process; Luke the goal of discipleship training. The disciple hoped not only to learn all that his master knew, but also to develop piety of character.

It is clear that becoming a particular teacher's disciple was a life-shaping decision. And it was just as important to the teacher to carefully select his disciples. For while the disciple expected the relationship with his master to shape as well as equip him, the master would be honored for the piety of his students, and he would have to depend on them to pass on any distinctive teachings of his own to future generations.

How then can we explain the almost casual description Matthew gives of Jesus choosing the Twelve? It would seem He was simply walking along the sea, happened to see Peter and Andrew, and on the spur of the moment said, in effect, "Hey, strangers! Come follow Me!" And the two fishermen, on the spur of the moment, decided to drop their life work and tag along with the stranger!

But the fact is, it didn't happen that way at all. And discovering how it did happen gives us important insights into how to attract others to Jesus Christ.

Interpretation. This is one of those issues that must be dealt with by comparison of the Gospel accounts. No Gospel writer distorts events. But each writer has his own agenda—his own purposes in including some material and leaving other material out. At times it is necessary to look at every Gospel in order to construct an accurate sequence of events. For instance, we have to look at each Gospel to reconstruct Jesus' "seven words from the cross," or the sequence of events on that first resurrection morning. Similarly, to see the dynamics of the relationship between Jesus and the disciples, we need to look at other Gospels—in this case, the Gospels of John and Luke.

■ John 1:35-51. Andrew, Peter's brother, had abandoned the family fishing business when the word of John's preaching reached Galilee. He hurried on the 90-mile journey, and was there when John baptized Jesus. The next day Andrew, hearing John identify Jesus as the Son of God, followed the Nazarene and spent the day with Him. The very next day Andrew found Peter, who had also come to hear John. Announcing that he had found the Messiah, he took Peter to meet Jesus.

Other disciples, particularly Philip and Nathaniel, also met Jesus just after His baptism, and when Christ turned toward home, these Galileans went with Him.

■ John 2:1-11. When the companions arrived, they went together to a wedding feast at Cana, and there witnessed Jesus' first miracle.

■ John 2:12-23. Peter, Andrew, John, and James were partners in a fishing business. It had prospered so much that its headquarters was moved from little Bethsaida (1:44) to Capernaum. The new friends stayed together for several days (John 2:12), and since it was time for one of the Jewish festivals when all were to go worship at God's temple, they went up to Jerusalem. There they witnessed Christ's first, stunning public act: an angry cleansing of the temple by driving out those who bought and sold there.

The future disciples had now seen many sides of the Savior: they had known Him as a friend, joined Him in joyful celebration at a wedding, seen Him burn with fury as He drove the money changers from the temple. In Jerusalem they witnessed other miracles Jesus performed (2:23).

■ Luke 5:1-11. Thus it was that Peter and the others knew Jesus quite well when one day He returned to the Sea of Galilee, and found them washing their nets. Pressed by crowds, Jesus got into His friend Peter's boat and taught from it. Then Jesus turned to Peter and told him to go out into the lake again and let down his nets.

This was not a usual thing, for in Galilee then as now fishermen plied their trade at night. But Peter, knowing Jesus, did as He said. And "they caught such a large number of fish that their nets began to break" (5:6).

At this point Peter fell to his knees before Jesus, and begged Him: "Go away from me, Lord; I am a sinful man!" (5:8) Instead, Jesus called Peter and his friends to become disciples. And they did.

Application. It is important for us to have this picture of the relationship between Jesus and His disciples. Otherwise we might have the mistaken impression that the bonding of the Twelve to Christ was totally miraculous. In fact, it was—and it was not.

Jesus was no stranger to the disciples when He called them on the shore of the Sea of Galilee. He had spent weeks with them! He had stayed in their homes, gone with them to parties, familiarized Himself with their business. In the process He had made sure they had gotten to know Him as a person. They had seen His sensitivity as He turned water into wine; they had seen His fierce zeal for God at the temple; they had listened to His teaching and even seen Him perform public miracles. When Jesus called them to be His disciples, He did not expect them to make a blind decision! Jesus made sure that the disciples knew very well just who it was that was calling them to follow—a Teacher, a Healer, a Zealot for God, who was fully committed to doing God's will.

What a lesson for us. Sharing the Gospel is not a matter of passing out a tract and passing on, but of cultivating relationships. It is a matter of being willing to take time, to let others come to know Jesus gradually. This is how Jesus fished for people. And this is how we must fish for them as well.

There is another lesson in these passages as well. We discover it when we hear Peter say, "Master. . . . Because You say so, we will let down the nets" (Luke 5:5), and then a few moments later, to hear him cry out, "Go away from me, Lord; I am a sinful man!" (5:8)

"Master" here is *epistates,* a word we could translate as "chief." Peter recognizes Jesus as One with authority, but still addresses Him somewhat casually. Then something happens. The sudden appearance of the great shoal of fish, contradicting everything the skillful fisherman Peter knows about fish behavior, seems to bring sudden realization. Peter drops to his knees and cries out, "Lord!" Overwhelmed with the realization of who Jesus truly is, he is gripped by a sense of his own sinfulness.

In Peter, as in us, a sense of sin at first causes him to shrink back from Christ, fearful and ashamed. But Jesus quiets Peter's fears and, wonder of wonders, tells His suddenly shaken friend, "From now on you will catch men" (Luke 5:10).

How often it happens that Jesus makes Himself known to us gradually. We learn more and more about Him—perhaps in church or Sunday School, perhaps from parents, and although we respect Him, we still treat Jesus casually. And then suddenly the realization of who Jesus is and of who we are breaks into our consciousness. Suddenly we fall on our knees, and with Peter cry out, "Lord!"

Conversion is just this kind of blend of the natural and supernatural: the gradual process of getting to know another person, and the Spirit-given, sudden burst of insight that leads us to realize who Jesus really is. How important it is for you and me to remember that both the natural and supernatural have a part in our own fishing. And what a comfort, as we minister to those who are coming to know Jesus but still treat Him casually, to realize the moment is coming when the Spirit will work, and Jesus will be recognized as Lord.

Jesus Begins to Preach (4:12-25). The initial temptations are over. Jesus has displayed those qualities essential to His ministry. And so that ministry begins. In a few brief words Matthew introduces themes that will be developed throughout his book. Jesus joins John in announcing that the kingdom is at hand and in calling for repentance. Some respond to His preaching and become His followers. And any who come to Jesus for healing find a physical release that mirrors the ultimate freedom from sin's impact—the freedom that is mankind's through relationship with heaven's King.

MATTHEW 5
The Beatitudes

EXPOSITION

Matthew has demonstrated that Jesus met all the conditions established in the OT for the Messiah. He has also shown that Jesus is personally qualified to fill that role. Now Matthew relates the core of the stunning teaching of this One who came preaching "Repent, for the kingdom of heaven is near" (4:17). That teaching begins with the significant announcement, "Blessed are the poor in spirit, for theirs is the kingdom of heaven" (5:3). The kingdom which is "near" can be experienced as a reality, now!

Thus we must understand Matthew's report of Jesus' "Sermon on the Mount" as at least one part of his answer to those Jews who ask, "If Jesus of Nazareth is the Messiah, what has happened to the kingdom?"

Matthew makes a variety of points as he organizes and relates teachings which Jesus must have repeated again and again during three years of itinerant ministry. These points can be summarized as follows: First, the kingdom of heaven can be experienced now, but only by those whose values and attitudes are attuned with spiritual reality (5:1-12).

Second, heaven's kingdom is revealed in individuals whose commitment to God enables them to serve as society's salt and light (5:13-16).

Third, Jesus' teaching on the kingdom does not deny the Scriptures. In fact, Jesus has come to unveil the true meaning of God's Law and its relationship to the kingdom (5:17-20).

Fourth and finally, that Law rightly understood calls for an inner transformation, not outward conformity (5:21-48). The commandments, such as "Do not murder" and "Do not commit adultery," are as much against the hostility and lust that motivates the acts as they are against the acts themselves. The rulings, which permit divorce and make some but not all oaths binding, do not really release anyone from the obligations of faithfulness in marriage and honesty in every relationship. The principles, such as "an eye for an eye," which limits retaliation, and the call to love one's neighbor, which has been taken to limit responsibility to others, simply do not apply in the kingdom of heaven that Jesus now describes.

In brief, stunning images, the words of Jesus shift the attention of those who dream of heaven's kingdom on earth from the outer to the inner, from physical manifestation to spiritual expression, from pomp to humility, from worldly power to a spiritual dynamic that transforms the human heart.

And so we are now introduced to at least part of Matthew's answer to his own people's questions about heaven's kingdom. Yes, Matthew says, Jesus is the Messiah, the Ruler of the kingdom of heaven. But the kingdom over which Jesus rules is a spiritual kingdom. And the dynamic power of heaven's King operates within the human heart. For proof that Jesus is Lord, we must first of all look within.

WORD STUDIES

Theirs is the *kingdom of heaven* (5:3). In our last study we noted that in ancient thought the central notion underlying the idea of "kingdom" was not territorial, but rather that of a sphere of influence. Thus the "kingdom of heaven" stands for the dynamic force of God's will operating in the world.

In *Jesus and the World of Judaism,* the respected Jewish scholar Geza Vermes points out that the concept of the kingdom of God had distinct formulations in rabbinic and intertestamental literature. Vermes, on pages 32-35, notes first that every formulation "relates to God's sovereignty itself rather than to the realm over which He governs." In the kingdom era, God's sovereignty was a counterpart of earthly kingship and operated through the king as His representative. After the Babylonian captivity, "Israel looked for a new David to reestablish God's visible and institutional rule over Jews liberated from foreign empires, and to impose this rule over mankind as a whole." During the following intertestamental period the belief developed that "the kingdom of God was to ensue from the victory on earth of heavenly angelic armies over the hosts of Satan."

Finally, there was another concept, attested in Isaiah, that the pagans would suddenly realize that "Israel's God is the only Savior" and would flock to Jerusalem to worship Him. By acceptance of the "yoke of the Torah" the Jewish people could manifest God's sovereignty "through personal obedience to God's Law." Then "a pure and sanctified Israel was to draw the Gentiles to God."

Jesus' teaching in His Sermon on the Mount fits none of these four contemporary formulations. Rather, Jesus announces an expression of God's sovereignty that operates so powerfully within the human heart that a righteousness exceeding that called for by the Law is produced. The "kingdom of heaven" as Jesus presents it is a call to repent; a call to examine our attitudes as well as our acts; a call to focus on being rather than doing; a challenge to rely totally on God rather than self-effort.

In none of this does Jesus explicitly deny the prophets' vision of a future, visible, and

---

100 YEARS LATER

Justin Martyr, born in A.D. 100, wrote *His Apology,* a defense of Christianity, when he was about 50 years old. He had this to say about the impact of God's kingdom on the Christian's commitment:

And when you hear that we look for a kingdom, you suppose, without making any inquiry, that we speak of a human kingdom; whereas we speak of that which is with God, as appears also from the confession of their faith made by those who are charged with being Christians, though they know that death is the punishment awarded to him who so confesses. For if we looked for a human kingdom, we should also deny our Christ, that we might not be slain; and we should strive to escape detection, that we might obtain what we expect. But since our thoughts are not fixed on the present, we are not concerned when men cut us off; since also death is a debt which must at all events be paid.

institutional rule of heaven on earth. But He does clearly call His listeners, and He calls us, to seek a present, hidden, and deeply personal experience of heaven's rule.

Blessed (5:3). The word so often repeated here is *makarious,* a word the Septuagint uses to render the Hebrew interjection *'asre,* "Oh the blessedness of . . . !" Despite the TEV translation and a popular book on the *Be Happy Attitudes, makarious* does not mean "be happy." Rather, it is an exclamation of approval, an affirmation of God's gracious praise. Jesus does not promise us happy feelings, but the approval of God, which is a far greater reward.

The *poor in spirit* (5:3). Perhaps this includes the economically destitute, but surely those whose learned the futility of hoping in anything but God. The danger in wealth is the insulation it provides from the ordinary person's vulnerabilities; it may make the rich insensitive to their desperate need to rely on God.

Those who *mourn* (5:4). To feel deep sorrow, having recognized that misery is a consequence of personal and institutionalized sin.

The *meek* (5:5). Meek, *praus,* is a complex term suggesting gentleness, an absence of ostentation, a willingness to respond. The Greeks viewed meekness as contemptible, confusing it with servility. In biblical thought meekness is beautiful, for the meek relate to others without hostility, without malice, and without arrogance or pride.

Who *hunger and thirst* for righteousness (5:6). The two express powerful desire.

The *peacemakers* (5:9). The idea of peace found in the OT is not simply an absence of strife. Rather peace, *shalom,* is a positive, dynamic term which implies both health and wholeness. There is no limit to the aspect of "peace" implied in this verse: peace with God, inner peace, interpersonal peace, or international peace. There is, however, a clear denunciation of those who would "fight" injustice with violence. There is the clear implication that the person equipped to bring healing and wholeness is poor in spirit, meek, merciful, and pure in heart.

The *salt of the earth* (5:13). Salt was so valuable in NT times that Roman soldiers were often paid their wages in salt. It was used as flavoring, as a preservative, as a fertilizer, and even as medicine. Here Jesus speaks of mined rock salt, which deteriorated under high heat, and from which minerals were leached by moisture. This analogy, like the following reference to the "light of the world," reminds us that the kingdom of heaven expresses itself through individuals. Unless we remain committed to its kingdom norms, Jesus' rule will remain unrecognized in our society.

The *light* of the world (5:14-16). Ancient cities were built of white limestone, and thus glistened brightly in the sun. Lamps were kept burning in the home all night long, placed on raised lampstands. Both images remind us that "light" is not to be hidden. Christ makes His analogy clear. The righteous acts of heaven's citizens are lights which make that kingdom visible to all. Again we see that the kingdom of heaven is an inner kingdom, which can be seen and must be looked for in its citizens.

Do not think that I have come to abolish the Law or the Prophets; I have not come to abolish them but *to fulfill them* (5:17). The meaning of "fulfill" has been much debated. One suggestion is that Jesus came to confirm or validate the Law. A more common view is that Jesus completes what the OT revelation introduced. Others suggest that Jesus "fills up" the Law by expanding its demands. Probably the most common interpretation is that Jesus intends to present Himself as the fulfillment of the prophecies, types, and foreshadowings found in the OT.

Yet a better explanation, although one which requires us to ascribe an unusual meaning to *pleroo,* "fulfill," puts Jesus' sermon in sharp perspective. What Jesus means is that He accomplishes what every rabbi yearned to do: to "fulfill" the Law in the sense of providing a true, accurate, and authoritative explanation of the Law's real meaning.

With this understanding, we see new force in all that follows. Even the least of the commandments is not to be broken; participation in the kingdom of heaven calls for a righteousness that "surpasses that of the Pharisees and the teachers of the Law" (5:20). This is significant, for the Pharisees and experts in the Law were known for their scrupulous compliance with even the most obscure biblical injunction.

At this point Jesus turned the attention of His listeners to familiar commandments and practices. In each of the six illustrations that follow, Jesus shows that the Law which prohibited an act in reality condemned the attitude which gave rise to the act!

The righteousness the Law actually calls for is a surpassing righteousness—an inner purity which cleanses so completely that not the slightest desire to do wrong exists within.

Thus the real meaning of the Law, the "fulfilled" meaning, is seen in its revelation of a righteousness which rests on an inner transformation, a righteousness which no mere observance of rules and regulations can confer. To participate in this expression of the kingdom of heaven a person must be changed within!

This in no way abolishes the Law, which regulates acts. Instead it fulfills the Law, by showing how the Law's commands and rulings testify to the ultimate requirement of God: a flawless and transformed moral character.

"Anyone who says to his brother, 'Raca,' is answerable to the Sanhedrin. But anyone who says 'You fool!' will be in danger of the fire of hell" (5:22). "Raca" is from the Aramaic word *rak,* which means "to spit." Most quarrels in the Middle East are started by spitting, a most insulting act. Strikingly, the epithet "you fool" was less insulting.

There is a fascinating reverse progression here. Calling a person a fool leads to the insulting act of spitting, which leads to murder. Murder requires society to act in judgment; quarrels call for the Sanhedrin to intervene; just calling a person "fool!" requires that God act in judgment! Why? While society is concerned with crime, and civil leadership with those conflicts which might result in a crime, God is concerned with the heart attitude that leads to both conflict and killing! The fact that such an attitude places one "in danger of the fire of hell" makes it clear that God judges the heart, not simply the actions, of humankind.

Anyone who looks at a woman *lustfully* has already committed adultery with her in his heart (5:28). This teaching does not, as

some commentators have suggested, "make the Law more stringent." Instead it follows naturally on Jesus' promise to "fulfill," in the sense of revealing the true meaning, of that Law which Israel honored from Moses' day. Adultery is, on the one hand, unfaithfulness to the marriage covenant. On the other hand it is a violation of personhood: the treatment of a human being as an object. A person is used as a thing might be used, and this is a denial of the basic value and worth of the individual.

What then is the "lustful look" which Jesus sees as the precipitate cause of adultery? It is simply looking at a person not as a being formed in the image of God, but as a "sex object."

It is not necessary for a man to bed a woman to violate the intent of the commandment against adultery. All that is necessary is to look at her lustfully, as a sex object rather than as an individual.

Adultery, like murder, is a sin of the heart, as real in its earliest intent as in its commission.

If your right eye causes you to sin, gouge it out and throw it away (5:29). Jesus' powerful imagery indicates the seriousness of sin and urges human beings to deal with sin in a radical way. Origen, an early church father, took this injunction so literally he had himself castrated. But the problem is that the sin ultimately is not in the eye, but in the imagination. The imagination calls the physical eyes to rest on the object of temptation and so feeds itself.

Surgery is required—an internal operation that will cut away our bent toward evil and transplant goodness.

Do not swear at all (5:34). Cussing is not in view here. Instead, Jesus comments on the practice of binding oneself to keep a promise by swearing an oath. In the first century a whole system had developed that differentiated between binding and nonbinding oaths. Thus a person was bound if he swore "toward Jerusalem"; but not if he swore "by Jerusalem." A person was bound if he swore by "the gold on the altar," but not if he swore by "the altar" itself.

Jesus dismisses this as sophistry. A person should be so honest that his yes means yes and his no means no at all times. The very practice of swearing oaths provided proof that the one swearing was dishonest and could not be trusted to keep his word! God is not pleased by wrangling over binding and nonbinding oaths. God is pleased by simple honesty.

Eye for eye, and tooth for tooth (5:38). This principle was not intended to encourage revenge, but rather, to limit it. Many a feud began with a simple offense, repaid by a greater offense, which stimulated an even fiercer reaction. The escalation of a word or minor injury into interfamily warfare was a very real and present danger in the ancient Middle East.

God's Law simply said that a person who was damaged one "eye's worth" could not re-quire any more from the offender than what that eye was worth! And the same with a tooth or any other member of the body.

But what ultimately did that ruling in OT Law reveal? Simply that God's people were vengeful. Rather than suffer injustice and leave the issue up to God, they became vindictive and hostile, eager to hurt others for revenge.

Again, the Law as "fulfilled" by Jesus reveals our need of an inner transformation. A truly righteous person, a citizen of the kingdom of heaven that Jesus brings, will respond even to injustice in a loving way.

Today too we do not need more rules, or a more stringent application of biblical moral law. What we need is to be renewed, that we might be the kind of people God desires.

THE PASSAGE IN DEPTH

The Beatitudes (5:1-12). See also the parallel passage in Luke 6:20-26.

Background. The Beatitudes serve as the introduction to Jesus' Sermon on the Mount. Like a modern preacher, Jesus begins in a way that literally compels attention. He does not begin with a homey illustration or a joke. No, what Jesus begins with is an absolutely stunning series of affirmations.

And the Beatitudes are stunning. They were in direct conflict with the popular wisdom of Jesus' age as well as of our own. In a society where the "beautiful people" are envied for wealth, pride, and popularity, Jesus hailed the poor, the hungry, and the humble. The first group enjoys the good things of this world. The second, says Jesus, enjoys the blessings of heaven's kingdom, now!

To sense the reaction of the crowd just imagine a modern TV preacher who, rather than teaching that God wants His children to be healthy and rich, cries out that the destitute and the infirm even now enjoy God's blessing! That message would hardly be popular. Nor would it bring in a flood of contributions. Nor was this message popular in Jesus' time. But it did shock. It did cause some to listen, and to cry, "What!" And perhaps it led some to ask, "Why?"

Interpretation. In *The Teacher's Commentary* I sum up various views of the Sermon on the Mount, and thus, of the Beatitudes which launch that discourse. Some believe Jesus is showing the way of salvation. Some insist His words are the constitution of the coming messianic kingdom, to be inaugurated when Jesus returns. Some think His message is for the church, and outlines a higher standard to which believers in the church age will be held. Another view says simply that this is Jesus' exposition of ethical standards — an exposition rooted in and clarifying the OT's authoritative word. But *The Teacher's Commentary* (p. 540) goes on:

> To these traditional interpretations we need to add a fifth. *The Sermon on the Mount describes the way in which men are freed to live when they commit themselves to the kingdom of Jesus!* When men and women of any age realize that *in Jesus* the kingdom is "near" to them, they are free to abandon themselves totally to God's will, confident that, as they obey, He will act to shape events.

What the author means is simply that God's sovereign rule is realized, and His kingdom becomes a present reality, when God's people trust themselves to Him and adopt the lifestyle described in Jesus' Beatitudes.

This interpretation hinges on a fascinating interplay between the present and future tense in Jesus' words. The kingdom is the possession of the poor in spirit, and the meek will inherit the earth. Tasker points out the significant fact that the Greek present tense can include the future and that the future tense can indicate certainty. In being God's kind of person we experience now the rich blessings of heaven's kingdom, and we guarantee our participation in their fullest expression when Jesus comes. Heaven breaks into our life, and whoever participates in God's present kingdom work within will surely have a place when that kingdom takes its final, visible form.

The question that Jesus' Beatitudes raises, and the question they answer is: Who can experience God's kingdom now? Most simply put, only those who reject the values of the world and adopt the values of God can even begin to catch a glimpse of God's kingdom. Thus the poor in spirit are blessed, for in their humility they have rejected the worldly values of arrogant self-confidence and self-reliance. Those who mourn are blessed, for they have rejected the ways of a world caught up in a hedonistic drive for pleasure. Those who are meek are blessed, for they have rejected pride, power, and self-importance. Those who hunger for righteousness are blessed, for they will not settle for the satisfactions offered by this world. Those who are merciful, pure in heart, peacemakers, and persecuted because of righteousness, do not "fit" in the world, but fit perfectly in that kingdom of heaven which now, as when Jesus spoke, is "near."

Application. Israel made a basic error in assuming God would bring His end-of-the-world kingdom to them. What Jesus taught is that God must be permitted to bring us into God's kingdom. Entering God's kingdom is a supernatural event, accomplished by the Lord for those who put their trust in Jesus. Just entering the kingdom, however, is no guarantee we will live in it.

That depends not so much on our faith in Christ as on our decision to follow Him. Will we surrender the old values and the priorities that motivate men and women of the world? Will we adopt the values Jesus emphasizes in the Beatitudes? If we will, we shall be blessed indeed. For wherever we go, God's kingdom will be there, and His mighty power will be unleashed on our behalf.

The Fulfillment of the Law (5:17-48). See also the parallel passage in Luke 6:20-49.

Background. It is tempting to look at Jesus'

remarks about murder, adultery, and especially divorce, in isolation from the introduction found in vv. 17-20. As noted in the preceding word study on "fulfill," Jesus clearly indicates that He is about to expose the true meaning of OT Law. To do this Jesus uses a familiar approach: He presents case studies.

The biblical roots of this approach go back to Exodus. There Moses recorded the Ten Commandments (Ex. 20), which are statements of general principle, and immediately after he provides numerous case-law illustrations, which apply the principles to typical situations. For instance, the Law says "You shall not murder" (20:13). The case-law illustrations make a distinction, already implied in the Hebrew word translated "murder," between intentional and unintentional homicides (21:12-14). Case law also examines a situation in which someone's animal kills a person (21:28-29). Strikingly, case law also demonstrates that "You shalt not murder" has a positive corollary. The commandment against actively doing harm also implies a positive responsibility to guard others' well-being. One who digs a pit must not fail to cover it, lest even an animal fall in it and suffer harm (21:33-34). And so Deut. 22:8 says, "When you build a new house, make a parapet around your roof so that you may not bring the guilt of bloodshed on your house if someone falls from the roof."

The use of case law to explain the implications of a general principle is thus nothing new. So when Jesus states a general principle, it is completely natural for Him to give a variety of illustrations which will make His point perfectly clear.

What is the principle? The righteousness expected of one entering the kingdom of heaven must surpass "the righteousness of the Pharisees and the teachers of the Law" (5:20). Somehow Law itself must be reinterpreted to display the nature of the righteousness which heaven must, and does, require.

Interpretation. A distinct pattern appears in the six illustrations which Jesus gives. Introducing each illustration, He says, "You have heard that it was said," and then goes on "But I tell you. . . ."

Rabbinic literature often uses the "You have heard it said" formula. Typically, this was done either when raising a theoretical, but soon-to-be-rejected point, or to mark out an interpretation about to be extended by further analysis. This is exactly what Jesus is about to do, and so His opening phrase has the force of "You have understood." That is, Jesus introduces each illustration by saying that the Law quoted was thought by the rabbis to have a particular meaning—such as, murderers must be judged (5:21), or, adultery is a physical act (5:27-28).

In saying "But I tell you" Jesus then indicates that He is about to expose a deeper, truer meaning of the Law.

It is important to note that Jesus is not criticizing OT Law. He is saying, however, that the true meaning of the Law has been misunderstood by contemporary teachers.

The following chart summarizes the common points made in each illustration and illuminates the truth that Jesus was intent on driving home: Righteousness is not a matter of what we do, but of what we are. Righteousness is a matter of the heart. Only a heart so pure that anger or lust never even arises can meet the standard that God has unveiled for us in His Law—a standard that was misunderstood by His chosen people.

That misinterpretation was fatal. Israel failed to use the Law as a mirror which revealed mankind's hopeless condition, and instead, tried to use the Law as a stairway to heaven. In so doing, all too many of God's ancient people failed to throw themselves completely upon His grace. As Paul later writes, in their zeal Israelites "sought to establish their own [righteousness], they did not submit to God's righteousness" (Rom. 10:3).

Application. Taking these illustrations out of the context of Jesus' argument has led some to assume that Christ is laying down a stricter law for His people than God did for Israel. This seriously misses the point.

This can be demonstrated in several ways: (1) From the flow of Jesus' argument. Contemporary understanding of OT law limited its application to outward behavior. Jesus extends understanding of OT law by pointing

Verse	The Law	Contemporary understanding	Jesus' reinterpretation
v. 21	Do not murder (Ex. 20:13)	Killers must be punished by society	Hostility toward others must be judged by God
v. 27	Do not commit adultery (Ex. 20:14)	Adultery is a physical act	Even considering a member of the opposite sex is adulterous
v. 31	A husband must give a wife a legal writ when he divorces her (Deut. 24:1)	A husband who gives his wife such a paper has no more obligation to her	Marriage is a commitment that cannot be treated so lightly
v. 33	Keep oaths you make to the Lord	Only oaths sworn in God's name are binding	Be completely honest so that binding oaths are unnecessary.
v. 38	"Eye for eye" Ex. 21:24; Deut. 19:21	It is appropriate to get back at those who harm you	Respond generously to those who harm you rather than seek retribution
v. 42	"Love your neighbor" Lev. 19:18	Treat others as they treat you—love neighbors, hate enemies	Treat others as God treats His enemies—He loves us and meets our needs

out that Law demonstrates God's concern with man's heart. Righteousness is not simply a matter of what one does or does not do, but a matter of intent and motive, of desire and attitude. If Law is understood in this way, it becomes clear that no one can claim to be righteous before God. If anger is the same as murder in God's eyes, and lust the same as adultery, then clearly all have sinned.

(2) From the development of Jesus' theme in NT Epistles. Paul will drive this point home later, quoting the OT to establish the fact that "There is no one righteous, not even one" (Rom. 3:9-18). He then goes on to point out that "Whatever the law says, it says to those who are under the law, so that every mouth may be silenced and the whole world held accountable to God." Law does not define the stair one climbs to achieve righteousness. "Through the Law we become conscious of sin" (Rom. 3:20).

(3) From the obvious absurdity of treating what Jesus says as "advanced legislation." Is society or even the church to treat anger as murder? Is an angry shouting match the legal equivalent of homicide? Under OT Law adultery was a crime that called for stoning. Are we to try the man who gazes at a *Playboy* centerfold for adultery?

It is obvious that while anger and lust are the "moral equivalents" of murder and adultery in God's eyes, they cannot be the legal equivalents of these crimes. Jesus is not telling us to legislate these standards. He is telling us what God's standards are so that we might recognize our sinfulness and hurry to the Lord for salvation, the inner transformation which alone can make us righteous.

It should be noted that this argument leads us to the conclusion that Matt. 5:31-32 cannot be used to require a no-divorce standard in the Christian community. Surely, if the first two illustrations are not and cannot be legislative in intent, this third illustration cannot be so applied either. What Jesus is doing here is exactly what He is doing in each of the other cases He studies. He is pointing out that God now and always has called His people to a lifetime marital commitment. Moses' Law permitted divorce (Matt. 19), but that permission did not make divorce right. This did not free a man who divorced his wife and remarried from the stain of committing adultery. The "legal" divorce, although lawful, and although accepted in fact and principle in first-century Judaism, was a testimony to the failure of a couple to live up to God's ideal. Therefore, lawful divorce, when followed by remarriage, involved the couple in sin.

How then are we to apply these illustrations of Jesus to our own lives? First, we are to let them deliver us from the false and foolish belief that, if we only try, we can live up to the standards of righteousness God's kingdom requires. We cannot—for God judges the heart, and not only the act.

Second, we can accept the testimony of these illustrations and humbly cry to God, first for forgiveness, and then for cleansing. Jesus' preaching undoubtedly was intended not only to confront Israel with God's true demands, but also to prepare them for the Cross. Since we have fallen short, the Messiah must die and, in dying as a sacrifice, carry away our sins. This teaching was also intended to prepare Israel and us for the Resurrection. Only the resurrection power that God exhibited in Jesus, flowing into our lives, can give us that surpassing righteousness of which Jesus spoke, and make us truly good.

Finally, we can grasp the truth Jesus was conveying to His first-century listeners. The kingdom of God exists within. God's rule in a human life reshapes the believer's very personality—a reshaping that finds expression in a transformed life.

MATTHEW 6–7
Kingdom Lifestyle

EXPOSITION

Jesus has come! In the Person of the King, the kingdom of God which John announced truly is "near" (3:2). Now, in the Sermon on the Mount, Jesus explains the nature of His kingdom and the impact of God's rule. Rather than finding expression in a visible, institutional kingdom, God's rule will take a deeply personal form. God will not impose righteousness on society, but will create a surpassing righteousness within human beings—a righteousness which the Law, rightly understood, has always required (chap. 5).

Now, as the Sermon on the Mount continues, Jesus goes on to describe life in God's kingdom of the heart. First, citizenship brings a striking new "in secret" relationship with God as Father. Citizens seek to please the unseen God, not to win the approval of people (6:1-18). So too citizens care nothing for material possessions, but value the invisible treasures stored up for them in heaven (6:19-24). Citizens freely put kingdom obligations first because, secure in the knowledge that Father God knows and will meet every need, they are not anxious even about life's necessities (6:25-34).

Second, citizenship brings a new freedom in relationships with other persons. Citizens are freed from the frustrating sense of obligation to judge others (7:1-6). Rather than depend on others to meet their needs, citizens depend on God (7:7-12). Citizens are also freed from that insecurity which leads so many to submit to peer pressure (7:13-14) or to leaders whose only goal is to exploit their followers (7:15-23).

Finally, in the familiar story of the wise and foolish builders, Jesus gives us the key to life in the present, hidden, and inner kingdom of God. One who would live as a citizen of God's kingdom must hear Jesus' words—and do them (7:24-29).

WORD STUDIES

Your *Father* in heaven (6:1). Just how striking was Jesus' encouragement to think of and to approach God as "Father"? In the Bible God is called the Father of the Israelites (Isa. 63:16; Mal. 2:10). But here "Father" is used in the sense of source or originator. Psalm 89:26 uses Father in a deeply personal vein, but this Messianic verse has God saying of David's de-scendant, "He will call out to Me, 'You are My Father, My God, the Rock My Savior.'"

Familiar invocations in ancient Jewish prayers do refer to God as "Father," with the title preceded by "Lord" or followed by "Ruler" or "God." But Geza Vermes admits, "Where synagogal prayer is concerned, with its frequent use of 'Our Father,' I must confess that it is not possible to prove that even the earliest form extant represents anything actually current during the age of Jesus" (*Jesus and the World of Judaism,* p. 40).

Thus, some have argued that Jesus' invitation to His listeners to think of and to approach God as Father in an intimately personal way was a stunning innovation. This is not completely true. For instance, the book of Ben Sira, a Jewish wisdom teacher who ministered between 200 and 175 B.C., invokes God as "Lord, my Father, and the Master of my life" (23:1a; 51:1a,10a). This suggests that the pious Jew of intertestamental times had some sense of relationship with God as Father.

Yet, Jesus' emphasis in this sermon on the Father/child relationship to be experienced by citizens of His kingdom is strikingly new. Jesus describes no corporate, synagogal prayer, but an intimate, personal "in secret" relationship between the individual and his or her Father-God. Strikingly too that prayer we know as the Lord's Prayer lacks the string of honorifics common in Jewish prayers: "O sovereign King, Most High, Almighty God"— and only afterward "Father" (cf. 3 Maccabees 6:2-4). Instead Jesus seems to picture us as children, rushing into the house and, without even knocking, bursting into our father's study, sure of our welcome.

How we need to cultivate the realization that God truly is our Father now, and that we are His beloved children. Not only will we find new freedom in prayer. We will also find freedom from anxiety, from materialism, and the freedom to do God's will.

When you *give to the needy* (6:2). In Judaism giving to the poor was a religious duty, not philanthropy (Deut. 15:7-11; Ps. 112:9). No one in Jesus' time, seeing a person give to the poor, would think, "Isn't he generous?" but rather, "Isn't he pious?" Jesus does not criticize this view; it is rooted in biblical command. What Jesus criticizes is people giving to the poor in order to make others think they are pious. Truly pious people do what is right simply to please God, whom they love.

As the *hypocrites* do in the synagogues and on the streets, to be honored by men (6:2). The word *hypokrites* is the Greek word for stage-player or actor. For more information, see the Matthew 23 discussion.

Then your Father, who sees what is done *in secret,* will reward you (6:4). The phrase "in secret" or "hidden" (to *krupto*) is significant in this context, being repeated in 6:6 and 6:18. It is the believer's invisible personal relationship with God that is to have priority in our lives. Two things are repeated in each context. God is an unseen reality. And, God will reward those who act out of love and loyalty to Him.

Don't settle for popularity and the empty applause of the crowd. Seek to please God, earnestly desire His approval, and you will surely receive treasures in heaven.

When you pray, do not keep on *babbling like pagans* (6:7). The thought may not so much emphasize the repetitious nature of pagan prayer as the value given to ritual. Official Roman state worship required rote memorization of religious formulas. Should a single mistake be made by the officiating priest, the entire service had to be repeated.

In contrast, Jesus reminds us that prayer is an expression of personal relationship, not a religious rite. Pagans rely on ritual; God's people spontaneously enter the presence of One they know as Heavenly Father.

Give us this day our *daily bread* (6:11). Most people in the Palestine of Jesus' day either worked their own fields or served others as day laborers. A worker was paid a denarius for his work at the end of each day. With that denarius he bought food for his family, oil for the household lamp, and other necessities. That denarius, which was a typical day's wage, was just barely enough to cover those daily expenses.

Thus, the prayer Jesus taught His followers was poignant indeed. Believers are to rely on God on a daily basis for their bread. Relationship with God promises no lottery win, no vast savings account. Indeed, what we are to ask for is daily bread, a prayer which reminds us that aside from God we can rely on nothing in this world, but that with Him as Father we truly have all we need.

When you *fast,* do not look somber (6:16). Only one fast day is commanded in the OT, the Day of Atonement (Lev. 16:29-31; 23:27-32). Still, fasting was part of the social and religious life of Israel. Individuals and groups

---

Proverbs 30:7-9

Two things I ask of You, O Lord; do not refuse me before I die:

Keep falsehood and lies far from me; give me neither poverty nor riches, but give me only my daily bread.

Otherwise, I may have too much and disown You and say, "Who is the Lord?"

Or I may become poor and steal, and so dishonor the name of my God.

---

fasted as a sign of humility and confession (Ps. 35:13; Isa. 58:3, 5; Dan. 9:2-19; Jonah 3:5), or as an indication of desperation in prayer (2 Sam. 1:12; Ezra 8:21-23; Esther 4:16). After the Babylonian exile commemorative fasts were introduced (Zech. 7:3-5; 8:19).

In Jesus' time, the Pharisees voluntarily fasted twice a week (Luke 18:12), each Monday and Thursday. However, many who fasted made sure that others knew they were performing this pious act, by looking downcast, sprinkling ashes on their heads, or going about unwashed and with their hair un-oiled.

Interestingly, those in the post-apostolic church who chose to fast were encouraged not to follow the Jewish practice—but to fast on Tuesdays and Wednesdays!

Yet all this misses the point. Jesus is neither discouraging nor encouraging fasting. He is simply reminding us that when a person fasts, he should do so as an act of worship, not for self-promotion.

This is a good principle to apply in all our "religious" activities. Whatever we do, let's do it out of a desire to please God, rather than out of concern for what other people will think of us.

Do not store up for yourselves *treasures* on earth (6:19). The Greek reads, *me thesaurizete humin thesaurous,* a play on words which might be translated, "Stop treasuring your treasures." The wisdom of this edict is seen when we consider three things. First, earthly treasures are corruptible or perishable (6:19b). Second, earthly treasures are corrupting (6:22-23). And third, material things compete with total allegiance to God (6:24).

You cannot *serve* both God and money (6:24). We know what it means to serve God.

But how can a person serve Money? The Greek word for "serve," *douleuein,* emphasizes the subjection of the will. It has the same root as "slave."

We might paraphrase this verse, "No one can slave for Money and still serve God."

Jesus is stating a profound spiritual and psychological truth. We may be able to compartmentalize our thoughts, so that work and home and play and church are all kept separate. Underneath, however, there will be an orienting value by which every choice is measured. For some that orienting value is popularity, and such persons will do anything to win the approval of the crowd. For many the basic value is wealth, and every choice is ultimately measured by the bottom line. Jesus tells us that the orienting value of the kingdom is God's will, and God must have priority in our lives. If we do not choose to serve God, and make pleasing Him the most important thing in our lives, we will surely be enslaved to something of no ultimate value at all.

Only the service of God pays eternal riches.

I tell you, do not *worry* about your *life* (6:25). "To worry" is *merimnao,* to be anxious, distracted by fears. In a weaker sense it may mean simply, to be concerned about. Life is *psuche,* a word which reflects the meaning of the Hebrew *nephish* and draws attention to our nature as beings who live in the material world.

Because we exist in bodies, we need food and drink and shelter to maintain biological life. Some see themselves as beings with only biological life, and see life itself as no more than a struggle to gain material things. The modern bumper sticker captures this outlook well: "The one with the most toys when he dies, wins."

Jesus does not challenge the fact that human beings need food and clothing and shelter. But He reminds us that human beings are not essentially biological in nature. We have a share in the image of God, and the spiritual has more ultimate meaning to us than the material.

As for our *psuche* needs, we have the Father who will provide for us. Thus, we citizens of God's kingdom are free from worry about mundane needs, free to give priority to the spiritual.

Do not *judge*, or you too will be judged (7:1). The word *krino* has both the sense of "evaluate, distinguish," and of "pass judgment on, condemn." Here "Stop judging!" refers to a critical, caustic attitude toward others. Why? Jesus makes three powerful points.

First, the way we treat others will set the tone for the way they treat us (7:2). Second, keeping alert to our own flaws is a big enough job (7:3-5). And third, if others do not value what you value ("Do not throw your pearls to swine" [7:6]), your condemnation will tend to enrage them rather than convict them of sin.

We are given the clear impression that setting ourselves up as the judge of others' behavior is not only wrong (James 4:11-12), but counterproductive as well!

When a person goes fishing for men, there's not much value in using a distasteful bait!

If you, then, though you are *evil*, know how to give good gifts to your children (7:11). The "if" clause is a first-class conditional in Greek, which assumes that the condition is fulfilled. The original text undoubtedly means "since you are evil." The Greek word, *poneroi*, pictures human beings as actively hostile and malevolent, self-centered, and thus indifferent to the welfare of others. This is the same word always used when Satan and his kingdom are described as evil (Eph. 6:12).

When Jesus points out that even evil human beings can be caring parents, He is not identifying any redeeming virtue in mankind. He is challenging His listeners to examine their view of God. Surely, a person who admits that a parent will give good gifts to his children, although that parent is sinful, must agree completely that God—who is truly and wholly good—will give only good gifts to His children. And we are His children!

What a blessed confidence we can have when we bring any need to our Heavenly Father.

Enter through the *narrow gate* (7:13-14). The imagery is clearer in the original text. We must choose between two pathways. The one path is "difficult" (*tethlimmene*, not "narrow"), and the gate it leads to is "narrow" (*stene*). So few choose it. On the other hand, crowds flock to the way that seems broad and easy, that leads to a wide, easily entered gate. Here as always the crowds are wrong, for it is the difficult path and the narrow gate that lead to life.

If it looks easy, and is popular with the crowd, it's probably the wrong choice.

Many will say to Me on that day, "*Lord, Lord. . . .*" Then I will tell them plainly, "I never knew you" (7:22-23). During Christ's ministry on earth the title "Lord" is usually to be understood as "teacher." Only later did the disciples and the early church come to use this title in its fullest sense.

THE PASSAGE IN DEPTH

The theme of the believer's "in secret" relationship with God (6:1-18) is developed under three NIV headings: Giving to the Needy; Prayer; and Fasting. For an in-depth study of the Lord's Prayer (Matt. 6:9-13), see Luke 11:2-4.

Background. Jesus' exposition of the true meaning of OT Law (Matt. 5:17-48) shifted His listeners' attention from behavior to the inner disposition from which behavior springs.

Jesus now continues to develop His thesis, with a careful examination of three religious behaviors which the Jews of that day considered especially pious: alms-giving, prayer, and fasting.

The contemporary attitude toward alms-giving, firmly rooted in OT calls to generosity, is reflected in Tobit 4:7-11, an apocryphal book dating from the second century B.C.

Give alms from your possessions to all who live uprightly, and do not let your eye begrudge the gift when you make it. Do not turn your face away from any poor man, and the face of God will not be turned away from you.

If you have many possessions, make your gift from them in proportion; if few, do not be afraid to give according to the little you have. So you will be laying up a good treasure for yourself against the day of necessity.

For charity delivers from death and keeps you from entering the darkness; And for all who practice it, charity is an excellent offering in the presence of the Most High.

Reading Tobit, we can sense how important giving was in the religion of Israel. And we can see why generosity was taken as evidence of true piety in Jesus' time.

In the same way, prayer and fasting were viewed as especially pious acts, and as visible measures of one's dedication to God. In a society noted for its zeal for God, it is no wonder that a person who consistently gave to the poor, prayed, and fasted was considered to be especially close to the Lord.

Interpretation. It is important to note that Jesus does not criticize giving, praying, or fasting. What Jesus does is show that each of these acts can spring from base motives. Some make a public show of giving, praying, and fasting, in order that others may think of them as especially pious. Jesus remarked dryly, "They have received their reward in full" (6:2).

There is more here, however, than the exposure of hypocrisy, and making the rather obvious point that motives count. Jesus challenges the assumption that actions can serve as a measure of piety.

There are two implications of this challenge. First, the best way to ensure that our own acts are pious is to do them secretly, making them acts of worship seen by God alone. Thus, Jesus says of giving, "Do not let your left hand know what your right hand is doing, so that your giving may be in secret" (6:4); and "When you pray, go into your room, close the door and pray to your Father, who is unseen. Then your Father, who sees what is done in secret, will reward you" (6:6).

The believer's relationship with God is in-

tensely personal and private. This does not mean that there is no valid corporate affirmation or experience of faith. It does mean that corporate expressions of faith must flow from faith-community members' vital and real "in secret" relationships with the living God.

The second implication of Jesus' challenge is this: no public actions can ever serve as a measure of the reality of an individual's personal relationship with God.

The reason for this is simple. We have no way to judge what motivates a person's public acts. Of course, if a person sends servants ahead of him to blow a trumpet and attract a crowd when he dispenses charity, we may assume there are mixed motives. But the fact is that we can never really know.

God's kingdom is a hidden, in-secret working of His will in the lives of kingdom citizens. The most pious-seeming act may be totally self-serving. A suspicious act, however, can be an expression of intimate relationship with God.

When Gib Martin, now a pastor in Seattle, was a schoolteacher in Ohio, he used to drop into a bar for a beer after school. Each time, Gib noticed an older man, sitting quietly by himself. After some weeks they began to talk and Gib, an agnostic, was invited to go to hear an evangelist. Although hostile to the message, he was unable to sleep and finally, about 4 A.M., Gib surrendered to Christ. The next day he hurried to the bar after work and told his older friend what had happened. The man responded, "I know. My wife and I were praying for you all night, until about 4 o'clock the Lord told us we could stop."

Later Gib urged his friend to go with him to church, but the older man sadly refused. "I'm not welcome in the churches here," he said. "I go to a bar."

Application. Perhaps the first thing we learn from Jesus' teaching here is the importance of cultivating our own "in secret" relationship with God. We need to spend time alone with Him in our "inner room." We need to serve God and others anonymously. There is very little more dangerous to a vital spiritual life than the praise of others for our pious acts.

The second thing we learn from Jesus is to avoid defining certain acts as "pious" and others as "impious." The lists we create and use to classify others are bound to be wrong! The bare fact that a person comes to every church meeting, teaches Sunday School, serves on committees, and even tithes, means nothing in and of itself. On the other hand, discrediting the person who smokes, takes a social drink now and then, buys a lotto ticket, or is involved in other "don'ts" of some Christian communities, is just as wrong. Neither observing our do's nor refraining from our don'ts can measure an individual's "in secret" relationship with God.

None of this contradicts something Jesus says later: people, as trees, are known by the fruit their lives produce (7:16). What it does contradict is the mistaken notion some of us hold that pious acts are fruit.

The fruit of an "in secret" relationship with God is a transformed heart—a heart that is responsive to the words of Jesus and responsive to the needs of one's fellow human beings.

Treasures in Heaven (6:19-24) and Judging Others (7:1-6). On judging, see also the discussion of Romans 14 and James 4:11-12.

Interpretation. At first it seems strange to link these two passages. Their subject matter is admittedly diverse. The first passage begins "Do not store up . . . treasures" and the second "Do not judge." Surely there is no link between treasures and judging.

On closer examination, however, we find that there are links. First, each passage has to do with personal values, those inner priorities which set the direction of each individual's life. Jesus has been talking about our "in secret" or hidden, inner relationship with God. And each of these passages is related to this theme.

Second, each passage is made up of three sayings, whose linkage is superficially unclear. Thus, the structure of the two sets of sayings is parallel, even though the subject matter seems diverse.

To appropriately interpret each set of sayings we must take into account both their common focus on values and their parallel structure.

The first sequence begins with the command, "Stop treasuring your earthly treasures" (6:19, author's paraphrase). It would be enough for us to know that Jesus spoke the command. But Jesus graciously goes on to explain why obeying this command is essential.

Earthly things are corruptible, perishable (6:19-21), so it is foolish to set our hearts on that which has no ultimate value.

Earthly things are corrupting (6:22-23). If we fix our gaze on earthly possessions our "eye," here a metaphor for heart, will be "bad." Here the word is *diplous,* which means "double." Unable to see the issues of life clearly, our confused perception of what is really important in life will lead us into trouble.

Earthly things compete for our allegiance with God. We cannot be completely committed to God if we love money. Love for God and love of wealth are incompatible, for each struggles to determine the choices we make. The path that love for God directs us to take is very different from the path we will take if we make our choices out of love for money.

These three sayings, then, are links in a single argument. It begins with visible, earthly treasure. And it ends with the inner self, with the commitment to God which will and must be the determining value in our lives.

The second sequence is similar, although the topic is not relationship with God but relationship with others. It too begins with a command, "Stop judging!" (7:1, author's paraphrase) Here too Jesus goes on to provide an explanation. And again Jesus begins with the external, and concludes with the internal. To trace the argument, we must note an interesting truth: When values are externalized, they are expressed as standards. This is dangerous, because values externalized as standards will be misunderstood (7:1-2), misapplied (7:3-5), and misused (7:6).

A value is misunderstood when it is externalized as a standard, for then it will be used as the basis for judging another person's actions (7:1-2). It is all right to say that citizens of Jesus' kingdom will "hunger and thirst for righteousness" (5:6). But it is not all right to say that such a hunger can be identified by the external standard: The citizen of God's kingdom will go to church frequently.

Not only is it inappropriate to transform values into standards, it is dangerous—even to the person who does it! If this is the approach you and I take to evaluating others' relationships with God, others will take the same approach to evaluating our relationships with Him. And you can be quite sure that we will come up short of whatever standards they devise!

A value is trivialized and misapplied when it is externalized as a standard (7:3-5). As a standard, an externalized value only enables us to identify the specks of dust in another's eye. But if we hold on to values as values rather than externalize them as standards, they perform the important function of enabling us to discern the planks (literally, "log") in our own eyes.

We will be able to look at everything we do and ask ourselves, "Is this loving?" or "Does this honor God?" If we, however, externalize kingdom values, we will likely conclude that "Love is giving at the office"; we will soon become blind to the obligation to measure all that we do by Jesus' call to love.

Finally, a value when externalized as a standard will be misused (7:6). The citizen of God's kingdom will attempt to communicate the meaning of relationship with God by affirming his understanding of kingdom standards. It is wrong to get drunk and drive. It is right to let the unborn live. It is wrong of the media to present pornography as "adult." It is right to present Creationism in school as a scientific alternative to Evolution. These may well be pearls—beautiful, valuable truths. Strangely, the people of the world, rather than receiving our insights with delight, become hostile and "turn and tear you to pieces."

Externalized standards of kingdom values do not reveal the good news of Jesus' kingdom to the unconverted. The good news of Jesus' kingdom is summed up in the Person of the King. The first and only issue for the unconverted is, "What is your relationship with Jesus Christ?"

It is not wrong to stand for righteousness in our society. But we are not to use kingdom values, externalized as standards, as the basis for relating to others, whether they be fellow believers (7:3-5) or the unsaved (7:6).

Application. These two passages, seemingly different in subject matter, each teach us the same truths. Ultimately, relationship with God is an "in secret" and intimately personal thing. We must be so committed to God and His hidden kingdom that earthly treasures have no hold on our hearts.

Also, we must be committed to kingdom values, avoiding every temptation to externalize them as "standards," which we would then use to blame others—and to excuse ourselves.

Kingdom living is a matter of the heart.

And to live today in Christ's kingdom, we must ever keep our hearts in tune with Him.

Ask, Seek, Knock: Jesus on Prayer (7:7-12). See also the discussion of the Lord's Prayer in the commentary on Luke 11:2-4.

Background. Prayer is a motif that appears and reappears in Jesus' teaching on kingdom lifestyle. Jesus speaks of private prayer as an expression of the believer's "in secret" relationship with the Lord (6:6-7). He teaches a prayer which models filial respect, submission, and dependence (6:9-13). Later He reminds His listeners that God, as Father, knows and will meet every need, freeing the children to concentrate their efforts on His kingdom and His righteousness (6:25-34).

Now in 7:7-11, Jesus picks up the motif of prayer again, and encourages His hearers to ask, seek, and knock.

Interpretation. Two observations are key to our interpretation. Jesus is speaking these words as encouragement. Jesus is speaking of petition, not of other forms of prayer.

We know Christ's words are to be taken as encouragement rather than as command, because each exhortation is accompanied by a promise:

Ask—and it will be given.

Seek—and you will find.

Knock—and the door will be opened.

This leads to the immediate question: Why would we need to be encouraged to bring our petitions to God?

The answer may be suggested in the total context of Jesus' teaching. Relationship with God truly is an "in secret" thing. Unbelievers cannot see, touch, or measure "God." Neither can we! When we pray, we take a leap of faith, relying on an unseen Being to act on our behalf in the material universe. As we begin to practice prayer, we need the reassurance provided by Jesus' promises. Even later, when we have experienced answers to prayer, we need to be reminded again and again that what happens cannot be dismissed as "coincidence" but truly is evidence of divine intervention on our behalf.

There is another reason why we need encouragement. Often answers to prayer are delayed, and delay may lead to doubt. We may not doubt the ability of God to answer our prayers. But we may very well doubt His willingness. Perhaps we're conscious of some sin or failure, and feel we do not deserve God's care. Perhaps our view of God is so exalted we feel ashamed to "bother" Him with our situation. Thus as part of His encouragement to prayer Jesus reminds us that the relationship we have with God is not merely that of creature to Creator. We are related to God as child to Father!

If human parents, who are evil, give good gifts to their children, God, who is wholly good, will surely give good gifts to those who ask Him.

This is encouragement indeed. God will not only answer our prayers, but His response will grow out of His Father-love for us, and be a truly "good gift."

Second, the kind of prayer Jesus is teaching about is petition. This is not praise, or thanksgiving, or contemplation. It is asking God for something that is of vital importance to us.

We know this because Jesus describes prayer as asking, seeking, and knocking. "Ask" is the act of prayer in its simplest form. "Seek" conveys intensity, an "earnest sincerity." And "knock" pictures persistence. We knock on the door of heaven and keep on knocking!

It is important not to mistake what Jesus is saying as laying down conditions which, if met, will move God to respond to us. Jesus is not saying if you ask ardently enough, and are persistent enough, then God will answer your prayer. He is simply saying that when we feel a need so intensely that it drives us to the Lord again and again, we need not be discouraged even if the answer seems delayed. God really does care about those things that matter to His children. And God responds to our requests by giving us good gifts.

Application. What a wonderful freedom Jesus' words offer as we consider prayer. From them, we know that if something matters to us, it matters to God! And we know that God is never "put off" when we keep on bringing such matters to Him.

A Tree and Its Fruit (7:15-23). For an in-depth discussion of this imagery, see the commentary on Matthew 12:33-35. See also the parallel passage in Luke 6:43-45.

The Wise and Foolish Builders (7:24-27). For an in-depth discussion of this story, see the commentary on Luke 6:47-49.

MATTHEW 8–11
The Authority of the King

EXPOSITION

Jesus' Sermon on the Mount (Matt. 5–7) established Christ's intent to rule a hidden kingdom. This kingdom's foundation of surpassing righteousness requires that its citizens experience an inner, "in secret" transformation. Now Matthew records a sequence of miraculous acts which prove Jesus' royal power (8:1–9:34). Then, in a stunning demonstration, Jesus actually gives authority to His disciples! (9:35–10:42)

Even so, Jesus is not the Messiah that Israel expected. Despite the evidence of Jesus' works, even John the Baptist now has doubts. The cities where Jesus has performed His most spectacular miracles remain unmoved. Although His nation is deaf to Jesus' call, He invites individuals to turn to Him for rest (11:1-30).

Within the flow of these chapters, the sequence of events is particularly important. Jesus' miracles follow an ascending order, demonstrating His power over illness (8:14-17), over nature (8:23-27), over the supernatural (8:28-32), over sin (9:1-8), and over death itself (9:18-26). This is stunning enough, but in the next sequence Jesus gives His twelve disciples "authority to drive out evil spirits and to heal every disease" (10:1, 8). Jesus' power as King is so great that He can imbue mere humans with supernatural ability to serve others. The power of the King flows into and through the citizen of His kingdom!

Despite this evidence the population of His Jewish homeland hesitates. Jesus is not the type of King they expected! Even John the Baptist, who knows that Jesus is the Son of God (John 1:32-34), is uncertain. He sends his disciples to ask if Jesus is the expected King, "or should we expect someone else?" (11:3) The hope of Israel has been so focused on the appearance of One who would reestablish David's visible and institutional rule on earth that, despite every demonstration of Jesus' power, the people cannot bring themselves to accept Him as the Messiah. Nor will they settle for an inner, "in secret" rather than an earthly kingdom.

Jesus responds graciously to John's followers and simply tells them to report His healing acts to John (11:4-6). Christ is confident that His cousin will remember Isaiah's description of Messiah's works (Isa. 35:5-6; 61:1) and believe. Yet Jesus is harsh in His denunciation of the cities where most of His miracles had been performed (11:20-24). The most wicked of pagan peoples would have fallen to their knees in repentance if they had seen such works, but not God's own people.

The sequence ends with a beautiful statement of salvation's paradox. Only those to whom God reveals the hidden kingdom can possibly see it. Yet it is visible to all in Jesus, who invites the weary to reach out and take His hand (11:25-30).

WORD STUDIES

Lord, if You are *willing*, You can make me clean (8:2). The Greek words used to express the idea of "will" or "willing" (*thelo* and *boulomai*) can each represent inclination and choice. The leper did not doubt Jesus' power. The only question remaining was whether Jesus would be inclined to use His power on the leper's behalf. What Jesus did is a healthy reminder to us. Our God is always inclined to respond to the prayers of those who trust in Him.

Offer the gift Moses commanded as a *testimony* to them (8:4). The phrase *eis martyrion,* "for a witness," occurs eight times in the synoptic Gospels. Here, however, Matthew adds *autois,* "to them." This addition brings into clearer focus the question we must ask: Why did Jesus send the cleansed leper to the priests, only to follow a procedure called for in Lev. 14 that was intended to confirm a leper's restoration to health?

Perhaps the answer lies in the fact that *autois* in this construction can just as well be translated "against them" as "to them." The very religious leaders who were among Jesus' harshest critics were forced to examine the healed leper and pronounce him clean!

Today too Christ's work in another's life is *eis martyrion autois.* The very admission "Yes, I can see a difference in her life" is a witness to, and against, the observer.

The fever left her, and she got up and began to wait on Him (8:15). The imperfect tense *diekonei* is rightly translated as "began to serve" Him. Matthew's point is that the healing of Peter's mother-in-law was completely effective: she was fully and instantly restored.

Many who were *demon-possessed* were brought to Him, and He drove out the spirits with a word (8:16). Demons and evil spirits are mentioned frequently in these chapters (cf. 8:31-32; 9:32-34; 10:1, 8). Most identify these beings with the angels that followed Satan in his rebellion against God. The Bible portrays demons as actively hostile to human beings, tormenting men and women with disease (Matt. 4:24; 12:22; 15:22; Luke 4:33-35) and madness (Mark 5:2-20; Luke 8:27-39).

Wherever Jesus confronted the works of demons He first expelled them from the personality of the human being they had possessed. Then He repaired the damage they had done. We flee to Jesus not only for protection but for restoration of wholeness.

This was to *fulfill* what was spoken through the prophet Isaiah (8:17). The quote reflects Matthew's personal paraphrase of Isa. 53:4, a rendering which does not follow exactly either the original Hebrew text or its Greek translation, the Septuagint.

Dodd rightly notes that when a brief OT passage is quoted in the NT, the entire context is implied. Thus, we must read Isaiah's emphasis on God's Suffering Servant taking all man's infirmities upon Himself in His suffering and death into Matthew's brief mention of healing. It is also important to remember that the Jews, and Scripture itself, view all sickness as a consequence either directly or indirectly of sin.

What was Jesus demonstrating then in healing people? It was more than an act of power. It was a witness to His intent, through His suffering and death, to provide a salvation which will ultimately destroy all sickness.

In the healing miracles of Jesus, we can see between the lines the fulfillment of the prophet's promise of ultimate healing of sin's every impact on us all.

Lord, first let me go and *bury my father* (8:21). Jesus' response, with its concluding "let the dead bury their own dead" (8:22) grates on us. We do not expect such a brief, harsh statement from our Lord.

First, however, we must note that the man's father was not dead at the time. In Jesus' day people were buried the same day they died, as quickly as possible. If the father were already dead, the son would have been organizing the funeral, and Jesus would have been expected to join the mourners, for this was considered a religious duty in the first century.

Thus, what the young man meant was, "I am obligated to take care of my aging father. With this obligation met, then I can follow You." To first-century listeners, Jesus' response was just as plain as the request. "Your first obligation is to follow Me."

Jesus' teaching here is not comfortable. The obligation to care for aged parents was very real in first-century Jewish society. It may well have been an obligation the speaker wanted to fulfill out of an honest affection for his dad. Yet the rest of Jesus' disciples had abandoned parents, and even wives, to follow Jesus, and in so doing had entrusted their care to God and the believing community.

You and I must often face decisions like the one which confronted this early follower of Jesus. Will we put Jesus first, before even the most important of our other obligations? If Jesus calls, will we trust our loved ones into His hands, and unhesitatingly follow Him?

Jesus replied, "You of *little faith,* why are you so afraid?" (8:26) The Greek word, *oligopistoi,* tells the quality as well as quantity of the disciples' faith. There was some faith; the disciples did appeal to Jesus to "do something!" But their fears revealed the flaw in their faith. Circumstances, the storm, so dominated their thinking that they failed to see that Christ's presence guaranteed their safety. First, as Jesus was the Messiah, God would hardly let Him perish in a storm. Second, as Jesus' earlier miracles demonstrated, His personal power was unlimited. No storm could threaten Him or those with Him.

Frightening circumstances still all too frequently dominate our thoughts, as generations of commentators have noted. When this happens, Jesus' question, "O you of little faith, why are you so frightened?" (paraphrased) calls us to reflect. We are safe with Jesus. And He is with us always.

So that you may know that the Son of

Man has authority on earth to *forgive* sins (9:6). The word "forgive," *aphiemi,* primarily means "send away." Another Greek word also translated "forgive," *charizomai,* simply means to "be gracious to." You and I can be gracious and overlook another's faults. Only God can deal decisively with sin by sending it away.

Those who stumble need caring people who will accept and encourage them. But most of all, we stumblers need that total cleansing available only from the God who can send away our sin.

Why does your master eat with tax *collectors and "sinners"*? (9:11) We can hardly sense the devastating nature of this criticism. In calling Matthew, a tax collector, to be His disciple, and in actually going to a dinner party at Matthew's house attended by many tax collectors and "sinners," Jesus utterly shocked not only the religious but ordinary people as well.

Rabbinic literature dating from near the time of Christ contains several lists of despised trades. Prominent among the social outcasts were tax collectors, who won their positions by bidding for the right to collect taxes and who then extorted more money than due in order to enrich themselves. The Mishnah says that "for herdsmen [who had the reputation of picking up others' property as they wandered with their sheep], tax collectors, and publicans, repentance is hard." The reason? These folk would be hard put to identify each person they had cheated or harmed, and thus could not make the restitution the Law required! (Ex. 22:3)

The general condemnation of tax collectors is reflected in phrases found in rabbinic literature, as well as the NT, that link them with other despised classes. Phrases from rabbinic sources link "tax collectors and robbers," "tax collectors and Gentiles," and "murderers, robbers and tax gatherers." The same linguistic patterns are found in the NT, which links "tax collectors and 'sinners'" (Mark 2:15; Luke 5:30), and "robbers, evildoers, adulterers" and, of course, "tax collector(s)" (Luke 18:11).

Shocked and repelled, and yet undoubtedly delighted to have something with which to accuse Jesus, the Pharisees asked Christ's disciples, "Why . . . ?" Why would Jesus, who claims a special relationship with God, debase Himself by keeping company with such scum?

Christ's answer echoes through the ages as a challenge to Christians. "It is not the healthy who need a doctor, but the sick" (9:12).

I have not come to *call* the righteous, but sinners (9:13). When Jesus uses "call," *kalesai,* it has the force of "invite." His enigmatic saying makes an important point. First-century Jews expected the Messiah to appear and, after purging Israel of sinners, establish an earthly kingdom for the righteous. Here Jesus reminds us that His mission is one of grace; He has come to pursue the lost. Those who classify themselves as "the righteous" not only have misunderstood His mission, but have placed themselves outside the circle of those who stand in need of God's grace.

No one is more difficult to reach with the Gospel message than the person convinced its Good News is desperately needed by someone else.

Neither do men pour *new wine* into old wineskins (9:17). "New wine" was unfermented grape juice. "Wineskins" were the skins of goats sewn to form leather bottles. Fresh skins were used with the new crop, for as the wine fermented and gasses formed, old skins would burst.

The metaphor communicates important truth. Jesus' teaching about the kingdom, like His revelation of Himself as Messiah, simply does not fit the categories contemporary Judaism had developed in its study of the Old Testament. Jesus' teaching is new, and it requires Israel to develop new ways of thinking to contain it. Unless the old categories are abandoned, they will be shattered, and Jesus' teaching will be spilled on the ground. Then neither the old skins nor the new wine will do Israel any good.

There is a lesson here for us too. Our theological categories must never be given the same authority as Scripture. As each generation faces new challenges, we must return to God's Word, asking the Spirit to open our hearts and minds to new ways of understanding and applying His truth.

Have mercy on us, *Son of David!* (9:27) The name is a title—the title of the expected Messiah. How often the Gospel writers portray the blind as having spiritual insight.

There is nothing *concealed* that will not be disclosed (10:26). The word is *kekalummenon,* from *kalupto,* "to hide," or "cover over." The saying cuts two ways. On the one hand, the corrupt motives and acts of those who persecute the followers of Jesus will be exposed. On the other hand, the faithfulness of the disciples despite persecution will one day win them praise from all.

There is another contrast in this context. Those who kill the body are all too visible. But what they cannot kill is the essential personality, the "soul," *psyche.* One day the unseen will be revealed as the real, and the visible will be known as illusory.

Whoever *acknowledges* Me before men, I will also acknowledge before My Father in heaven. But whoever *disowns* Me before men, I will disown him before My Father in heaven (10:32-33). These verses reflect two sides of the same coin. Jesus is saying that the choice anyone makes in this world affects his or her destiny in the next. In this context of warning, Jesus' words are solemn indeed. We are not to fear people, but God (10:28), and God's attitude toward us depends entirely on our response to Jesus Christ.

It's not unusual for a Christian to ask another person "Are you saved?" More than one person has come back with the quip, "From what?" This passage reminds us that there is really only one compelling answer. "Saved from God."

We must choose Jesus, for only through Him can we avoid the coming wrath of God.

From the days of John the Baptist until now, the kingdom of heaven has been *forcefully advancing,* and *forceful* men lay hold of it (11:12). This puzzling verse has garnered a host of interpretations. Once again context may provide the key to help us understand it. The verb *biazetai* is used in contradictory senses, a construction called "antanclasis." From the very beginning the kingdom message has had to force its way, beating back the power of darkness. And from the very beginning forceful (used here with the sense of "violent") men have desperately resisted its advance.

John had been puzzled because the King, Jesus, had not swept all opposition away and easily established His visible, earthly rule. But Jesus had gone about establishing a kingdom based on light, not fiery destruction. And the world's violent men have resisted desperately, with ridicule (11:16-19) and with unbelief (11:20-24).

History has taught us that the Gospel message creates opposition as well as stimulating faith. We have to come to grips with this reality, and with the fact that God gives each human being the freedom to accept or reject His Son. But in the first century this was new wine indeed, certain to burst the old wineskin of contemporary messianic expectations.

THE PASSAGE IN DEPTH

Jesus Heals a Leper (8:1-4). For an in-depth discussion, see the commentary on Mark 1:40-45.

The Faith of the Centurion (8:5-13). See also the parallel passage in Luke 7:1-10.

Background. The Roman army was organized into legions, each with 6,000 men when at full strength. Legions were made up of six cohorts, each with 60 "centuries" of 100 men each. These 100-man units were led by "centurions," of whom *The Revell Bible Dictionary* says, "Centurions were the working officers on whom the effectiveness of the Roman army depended. Intelligent, well paid and highly motivated, they typically stayed in the army beyond the normal 20-year enlistment.

On discharge a centurion received a large bonus. Many became influential citizens of the cities in which they retired."

It is perhaps surprising that the NT displays a universally positive attitude toward these military men. Luke reports that the centurion whose story we read here was viewed in the Jewish community as one who "loves our nation and has built our synagogue" (7:5), and on this basis the Jewish leaders of Capernaum urged Jesus to respond to his request (Luke 7:1-10). Other centurions are also portrayed as men who were spiritually sensitive. The officer in charge of the squad that executed Jesus did not ridicule Him, but at the end confessed, "Surely this man was the Son of God" (Mark 15:39). The first Gentile to hear and respond to the Gospel was a centurion named Cornelius, whom Luke describes in Acts 10 as "devout and God-fearing," and one who "gave generously to those in need and prayed to God regularly" (10:2). Finally, the centurion who was assigned to take Paul to Rome saved the life of the prisoners on the journey, because he "wanted to spare Paul's life" (Acts 27:43).

While some have suggested that the Gospel writers purposely slanted their accounts to flatter Rome, this is not likely in Matthew, whose Gospel is directed to his own people, the Jews, whose hostility to Rome was intense when he wrote his Gospel.

Interpretation. In the story recorded here we meet a centurion more likely "posted to" than "retired in" Capernaum, at that time the administrative center of Galilee. When the centurion asks help for a servant, Jesus volunteers to go and heal him. It was then that the centurion displayed a reasoned faith, the like of which Christ had not found in anyone in Israel (8:10).

Why do we say the faith of the centurion was "reasoned"? Simply because his words to Jesus reveal a penetrating analysis of the meaning of the miracles Jesus has already performed, and reveal the centurion's willingness to commit to his conclusions.

That reasoned faith is expressed in the centurion's explanation, "For I myself am a man under authority" (8:9). As an officer in the Roman army, the centurion was aware that his orders were obeyed because his power flowed from the Emperor himself. The central reality in being "under authority" was not subordination, but power. For power in Rome ultimately derived from the Emperor, so that a soldier in obeying the centurion's orders was in effect obeying Emperor Augustus. The centurion could command others only because as an army officer he was a channel of imperial authority.

Thus, the centurion's explanation indicates that he realized Jesus too was a channel, whose acts were possible only because He derived His power from God. It was divine power, flowing from God through Jesus, that enabled Christ to command the obedience of sickness, nature, and even demons.

In a sense this inference is obvious. And so is the centurion's conclusion: "Just say the word, and my servant will be healed" (8:8).

But Jesus' words, "I have not found anyone in Israel with such great faith" (8:10), not only commend — they condemn. The simplicity of the choice confronting human beings, recognized so clearly by the centurion, was somehow missed by Israel, as God's people ignored the significance of Jesus' works and debated His identity.

Is Jesus God's spokesman? Does He really speak and act for God in man's world? The centurion would say, "Of course! His works prove it." And he believed.

Application. The centurion's simple yet reasoned faith, in such contrast to the uncertainty, doubt, and endless theological debate we read about in the following chapters of Matthew's Gospel, teaches us several lessons.

First, we are reminded that Jesus has all power. However distant from us His physical presence, Christ's word of power is able to transform our situation.

Second, we are reminded that the central issue in the Christian life is not theology but faith in Jesus. Rather than debate beliefs, let us encourage each other to hold on to the conviction that Jesus is the Son of God, the one channel through which God's power flows to meet human need today.

Jesus Heals Peter's Mother-in-Law (8:14-15). See Luke 4:38-39 and the commentary on Mark 1:24.

Jesus Calms the Storm (8:23-27). See Luke 8:22-25, and the commentary on Mark 4:35-41.

Jesus Heals the Demoniac (8:28-34). See Luke 8:26-39 and the commentary on Mark 5:1-20.

Jesus Heals the Paralytic (9:1-8). See Mark 2:2-12 and the commentary on Luke 5:17-26.

Jesus Calls Matthew (9:9-13). See the commentary on Mark 2:13-17.

Jesus Is Questioned about Fasting (9:14-17). See Mark 2:18-22, Luke 5:33-39, and the Word Study on Matt. 6:16.

A Dead Girl and a Sick Woman (9:18-26). See Mark 5:22-43 and Luke 8:41-56.

Jesus Heals the Blind and Mute (9:27-34). See Luke 18:35-43.

Jesus Sends Out the Twelve (10:1-42). See also parallel passages in Mark 6:8-11, Luke 9:1-10 and 10:1-16.

Background. It would be a mistake for us to think of the rabbis of Jesus' day as wealthy men. References in Jewish literature of the era suggest that many rabbis lived in extreme poverty. Hillel, perhaps the most famous rabbi of the era, was born in a poor family in Babylonia. He walked to Jerusalem, and worked as a day laborer for only half a denarius, paid a quarter of that as school fees, and cared for his family on the quarter denarius left. One story about him tells of a winter when he could not find work. Unable to pay the school entrance fee, Hillel listened outside the window and nearly froze. Only after he himself became a celebrated teacher did he escape the most bitter poverty.

Jesus too came from a poor family (Luke 2:24; Lev. 12:6-8). Matthew quotes Jesus warning a would-be follower that the Son of Man Himself "has no place to lay His head" (8:20). Christ Himself carried no cash (Mark 12:13-15; Luke 20:20-24) and depended on charity (Luke 8:1-3). Like other rabbis, Jesus must be counted among the poorer people of the Holy Land.

We must realize, then, that Jesus' command to the Twelve to take no gold, or even copper, and to take no "bag" [of food] for the journey (10:9-10) is no religious innovation. It is part of a continuing tradition which calls for those who teach about God to demonstrate their dependence on the Lord by their indifference to material things.

This tradition carried over into the apostolic and early church. Paul and Barnabas worked as laborers to support themselves, but also received gifts from the church to help them travel from city to city. And as churches were established throughout the Roman world, itinerant Christian teachers crisscrossed the empire. The Third Letter of John refers to such persons in vv. 5-8, giving us a vivid picture of their lives and ministries:

Dear friend, you are faithful in what you are doing for the brothers, even though they are strangers to you. They have told the church about your love. You will do well to send them on their way in a manner worthy of God. It was for the sake of the Name that they went out, receiving no help from the pagans. We ought therefore to show hospitality to such men so that we may work together for the truth.

The same theme is reflected in the *Didache,* one of the earliest of Christian writings, which indicates an itinerant teacher should be given enough provisions to reach his next destination (11:6).

Even in Hellenistic society the attitude toward the itinerant "philosophers" in every city who sought to gather a few students was shaped by their attitude toward money. The truly wise man would take no money for his wisdom while cynics were motivated by avarice. So Paul writes in 2 Cor. 2:17, "Unlike so many, we do not peddle the Word of God for profit. On the contrary, in Christ we speak before God with sincerity, like men sent from God."

Thus, Matthew 10 should not be viewed as a set of unusual instructions, applicable only to one brief training trip taken by the Twelve in the little Jewish province of Galilee. In fact, Jesus' guidelines reflect the unexpressed but deeply held convictions of Jewish society that one who teaches about God must be indifferent to worldly wealth. The guidelines also reflect Christ's own utter dependence on His Father. And the guidelines that Jesus gave the Twelve helped form the early church's view of ministry as well.

Interpretation. While Matt. 10:5-16 fits the immediate situation in Galilee, the rest of the chapter seems to envision a time when Jesus' followers would minister throughout the world (10:18). Thus Matthew relates the story of the sending out of the Twelve, and goes on to show us how that early adventure provides a pattern for ministry throughout the church age.

The passage can be broken down as follows:

■ Specific instructions (10:5-15). At this stage of Jesus' mission He is presenting Himself to Israel as that nation's Messiah. The disciples are told to preach only to Israel; why offend Israel by prematurely extending ministry to the hated Samaritans or Gentiles? The issue is Jesus' claims, and nothing must distract the people of Galilee from making a decision about Him.

Thus, the Twelve are to preach and teach,

depending on God alone to meet their needs through those who respond to their ministry.

■ General principles (10:16-42). At verse 16 an important shift takes place, and Christ's teachings lay down general principles that apply not only to the immediate task but to the future mission of His church.

Shrewd but innocent (10:16). Jesus' imagery balances the serpent against the dove. In relating to unbelievers Christ's followers must be shrewd enough to avoid attack where possible, yet innocent enough that caution does not become fear and drive them into isolation.

Guarded but confident (10:17-20). Believers can expect persecution, but can also be confident that when they are challenged God Himself will speak for them. In NT times the wealthy used professional orators to represent them in court. Christ promises His followers that they will have the best counsel available — the Holy Spirit Himself, who will be "speaking through you" (10:20).

Hated but delivered (10:21-23). Commitment to Christ will arouse an antagonism that can split families and stimulate hatred, making our lives in this world constantly stressful and sometimes even calling for flight. Yet before we exhaust every refuge, Jesus will come and deliver us.

Abused but unafraid (10:24-33). Jesus was condemned as the prince of demons; we can hardly expect kinder treatment. When persecution comes, we are to remain unafraid. Why? The truth will ultimately be revealed, humans can touch only our bodies not our souls, and God is totally committed to our care. We who acknowledge Christ here on earth can rest assured that He acknowledges us before His Father in heaven.

At war but victors (10:34-39). Life for those who follow Jesus is to be marked by conflict with others and conflict within. But in the decision to follow Jesus we gain rather than lose, for we find a new life that is only possible in Him.

The passage closes with a statement that had special meaning in the world of the first century. In that era a person's agent was to be received as the man himself (Luke 10:16; John 12:44-45; Acts 9:14). In honoring the servant, one honored the master who sent him.

How much better to be honored by God's people for serving Jesus than to have all the wealth and popularity the world can offer.

Application. The passage as a whole gives us a sobering description of ministry. It seems that the person sent by Jesus must be ready to surrender most things that people hold dear.

The passage reminds us that Jesus faced hostility and persecution, and so may those who choose to live as He lived in this world. It also reminds us that commitment to Christ may even cost us the love of family members. Perhaps the most significant message to the church, in our materialistic age, is Jesus' call to consciously abandon dependence on wealth, and to live as the poor.

One commentator from the Middle East notes that in Eastern countries wealthy men tended to wear a number of shirts and jackets, and carry an extra pair of shoes. This made them a target for robbers, who took the extra clothing and beat them if they resisted. So, this commentator suggests, Jesus' instruction to His disciples to wear only one cloak and carry no bag of provisions or coins, was intended to protect them from brigands.

The interpretation is culturally acute. But it misses the point entirely.

Those who represent Jesus must depend entirely on God to meet their needs. They must demonstrate their trust in God by going out as though poor, willing to count on the generosity of strangers. In choosing this way of life the rabbis, Jesus, and the early Christian missionaries proved their commitment to the message they proclaimed: God cares, and that as a child of the Heavenly Father, the believer can be content.

I suspect that the world still rightly judges those who claim to speak for God by their attitude toward money. How easy it is to feel a call to serve in the beginning — but to become mere peddlers for profit, purveyors of a Gospel shaped to comfort the affluent rather than challenge the comfortable.

The hostile and self-pitying poor surely have no right to claim spiritual superiority. Yet those who set out through life, as the Twelve set out through Galilee, determined to take nothing extra along for the journey, may be the wisest, and the richest, of us all.

Jesus and John the Baptist (11:1-30). See also Matt. 3 and John 1:19-28.

Background. Malachi closed the last book in

the OT canon with this prediction: "See, I will send you the prophet Elijah before that great and dreadful day of the Lord comes" (4:5). And so the question is raised even today: Was John the Baptist that Elijah?

John himself denied that he fulfilled the prophecy (John 1:21). But Jesus plainly said to His contemporaries, "If you are willing to accept it, he is the Elijah who was to come" (Matt. 11:14). Two things help us resolve the apparent conflict.

First, it was commonly believed in first-century Judaism that Elijah, who had been caught up into heaven (2 Kings 2), would return personally to usher in the messianic age. John quite rightly denied that he was the actual Elijah.

Second, Jesus conditioned His identification of John as Elijah by saying, "If you are willing to accept it. . . ." This remark implies that John could fulfill the prophecy of Malachi, but does not necessarily do so. The explanation is found in what is sometimes called "multiple reference." The *Revell Bible Dictionary* notes:

A predicted event may foreshadow a series of events rather than a single event, just as Ezekiel's prophecies of the imminent invasion of Judah by Babylon mirrors another, greater invasion launched from the north at history's end (compare Ezek. 38, 39). In addition, some prophecies may be partially fulfilled in an event, while still awaiting complete fulfillment in the distant future. For example, Joel's prophecy of the Day of the Lord was partially fulfilled when the Spirit came on the day of Pentecost (Acts 2:14-21), but other elements of this prophecy have yet to happen (p. 822).

Thus, what Jesus seems to be saying is that Malachi's prophecy of a coming Elijah is partly fulfilled in John—so much so that should Israel accept her Messiah, John can fulfill that prediction completely.

It is important to understand this point, because it provides a key to our interpretation of the entire passage. It tells us that Jesus is in fact defending John, and in the process is making His own role in salvation history perfectly clear. For if John is Elijah, then Jesus must surely be the Messiah.

Interpretation. The passage contains several difficult verses, which we can understand if we trace the argument, the flow of thought, of the passage.

John sends to Jesus to ask if He is the coming one (the Messiah), or if Israel should expect someone else (11:1-3). John has been imprisoned for about a year at this time, and he is puzzled why the One he pointed to has not acted to first judge and then bless the land.

Christ tells John's messengers to report the acts of healing they have witnessed (11:4-6). His words allude to OT passages (Isa. 35:5-6; 61:1) that describe both the blessing and the judgment, and promise "Your God will come . . . with vengeance; with divine retribution He will come to save you" (35:4). The blessings prove that Jesus is the Messiah; the Scriptures reassure John that judgment, though delayed, will surely come.

When John's disciples leave, Jesus speaks to the crowd about John (Matt. 11:7-15). First, John is "more than a prophet" (11:9). For one thing, John is also the subject of prophecy (11:10). Of no other Old Covenant prophet can this be said.

Second, John is greater than any who have come before him. Other prophets have looked far ahead and described the Messiah at a distance. John has seen the Messiah, and announced, "Look, the Lamb of God" (John 1:29, also 1:30-34). John alone was privileged to identify Jesus in a decisive way.

John's privileged position in salvation history moved Christ to say of him, "Among those born of women there has not risen anyone greater than John the Baptist" (Matt. 11:11). We can understand Jesus' next remark, that "he who is least in the kingdom of heaven is greater than [John]" (11:11) in this context. Today we see Jesus from the perspective of His cross and resurrection; even the least in God's present kingdom can give a clearer witness to Jesus and the meaning of His life than John was able to.

John had failed to understand that, rather than sweeping away all opposition, Jesus "in secret" kingdom was "forcefully advancing" against intense opposition. Yet John's ministry did fulfill the Elijah prophecy, and Jesus is the Messiah of whom the OT prophets spoke (11:12-15).

Now Jesus turns from the issue of John's role in salvation history to describe the lax attitude of the Jewish people toward John and

Jesus (11:16-19). In style John and Jesus were strikingly different, even though each called for repentance and announced that God's kingdom was at hand. Jesus' imagery is of children playing at "wedding" and "funeral" in the marketplace. The trouble is, whatever tune is played, John's and Christ's listeners sit on the sidelines and refuse to join in. Instead of responding to the music, they complain and criticize musicians!

The result is that the unrepentant cities of Galilee will suffer a judgment more severe than ancient towns known for their wickedness (11:20-24). If the works performed by Jesus had been done in them, their citizens "would have repented long ago" (11:21).

The passage closes with words of reassurance and invitation (11:25-30). The failure of the nation to respond is no more evidence that the kingdom is not coming than was the delay of the judgments predicted in the OT. In fact, the hidden kingdom can only be seen by those "children" to whom the Father and Son reveal themselves.

And so, Jesus concludes with an invitation. The weary and burdened are invited to abandon self-effort and to come to Jesus for rest.

They are to take Christ's yoke upon them and learn from Him, for it is in Him that they will find rest.

The reference to a "yoke" returns our attention to the central theme of the chapter. It was common in Judaism to speak of the "yoke of the Law," a phrase which implied intense study of the Torah and obedience to it as a means of gaining acceptance with God. Now Jesus offers every weary person a rest to be found, not in scholarly study of Torah, but in adopting Christ's own teaching. What Israel can learn from Jesus, not from the rules the scholars have drawn from Torah, promises human beings rest.

Application. Perhaps the most significant thing to note is that while this passage is ostensibly about John, it is, in fact, about Jesus.

We understand the significance of John the Baptist only by understanding his relationship to Jesus and his role in salvation history. In a similar way, each of our stories is the story of Jesus. The role He plays in our lives determines our destinies. And the role we play in God's kingdom gives our lives on earth their meaning and purpose.

MATTHEW 12–15
Hardening Opposition

EXPOSITION

The message of Jesus has been spread throughout the Jewish homeland by Jesus and His disciples. The common people have stood by, uncommitted despite being deeply impressed by Jesus' teachings and healings. But Matthew now focuses our attention on the hardening opposition of the religious leaders, and an unexpected response—a dramatic shift in Jesus' teaching about the kingdom of heaven.

Opposition crystalizes around two issues. The first issue was Sabbath-keeping (12:1-21). This central tenet of Judaism had been so rigidly defined by rabbinical tradition that even Jesus' healings are considered to violate the Sabbath rest. In response, Jesus lays claim to being Lord of the Sabbath, the Servant of Yahweh promised in Isaiah. The second issue is linked to the unusual flurry of demonic activity that seemed to break out wherever Jesus went (12:22-45). When Jesus' power over demons is displayed, and some begin to wonder aloud if Christ might be the Messiah, the Pharisees charge that Jesus is actually in league with the devil. Jesus ridicules this idea, but warns that attributing the works the Spirit performs through Him to Satan is an unforgivable sin. The charge demonstrates the character of Jesus' enemies, who demand miracles — but then reject the evidence of the miracles He has already performed.

This hardening opposition stimulates a dramatic shift in Jesus' teaching (13:1-58). Rather than continue to speak clearly about the kingdom, Jesus begins to use parables whose meaning is disguised so that those who hear without faith will not understand. The parables develop contrasts between the visible, institutional kingdom expected by Israel and the hidden kingdom of the heart which Jesus will establish in His death and resurrection. A final incident underlines the need: those in Christ's own hometown jealously refuse to even consider Him a prophet (13:53-58).

The turning of the tide against Jesus is further illustrated by the execution of John the Baptist, a witness to Jesus' deity (14:1-12). Yet Jesus continues to exercise His power: He feeds 5,000 who follow Him into the wilderness (14:13-21) and, witnessed only by the disciples, walks on water (14:22-36). When the Pharisees once again attack Jesus, raising traditional rabbinical "cleanness" as an issue, Jesus makes it clear that mere ritual is meaningless, for God is concerned with a clean heart (15:1-20). Jesus then meets a Canaanite woman who begs for healing for her daughter (15:21-28). The strange incident is a foreshadowing: a striking indication that the benefits Christ brings to Israel will soon be available to all through faith. Not that Christ is finished with His own people — He heals the crowds who come to Him, and when they hunger, He miraculously provides them with food (15:29-39). God's door stands open. But to enter it, even the Jews must come by faith.

WORD STUDIES

A *bruised reed* He will not break (12:20). Rabbis recognized this and other Servant Song passages of Isaiah as messianic, and looked forward eagerly to the One who would "lead justice to victory" and make even the Gentile world subject to God. Jesus, however, highlights other images embedded in the prophecy: the Servant/Messiah will be unwilling to snap a bruised reed, or discard a smoldering wick, "till" He appears in judgment.

The bruised reed is the shepherd's pipe, a simple flute made by gently *tap-tapping* a supple twig until the bark was loosened and slid off as a single piece. If the bark was bruised, the flute was ruined and the reed, now good for nothing, was snapped and thrown away. In the same vein the wick used in an oil lamp smoldered when covered with carbon and soot and became useless. The imagery is powerful: God's Servant will not appear first as a Conqueror, sweeping away all sinners before Him; He will come as One so moved by compassion He is unwilling to discard even the broken and useless in Israel's society. Till the day of judgment dawns.

Out of the overflow of the *heart* the mouth speaks (12:34). In Hebrew culture the heart (Heb. *leb*, Gk. *kardia*) was used to identify internal organs and the inner person. Hebrew thought did not divide the individual into separate functions, such as spiritual, rational, intellectual, emotional, and volitional. Hebrew thought tended to look at the person as a whole.

51

Thus, "heart" refers to the entire inner person, the true self, including every function that makes a person a human being. Jesus is simply saying that what a person expresses in words and acts exposes one's essential character.

Men will have to give account on the day of judgment for every *careless* word they have spoken (12:36). The Greek word is *argon,* and refers here to seeming inconsequential remarks. When we think carefully about what we say, it's easy to put a good face on our words. It is the careless word, the word uttered without thought, that unveils character. Thus, the Pharisee who muttered about healing on the Sabbath (12:10) was so concerned with tradition that he never realized how his remarks displayed his deep lack of compassion for a human being in need. And what about those who charged Jesus with being in league with Satan? They were so intent on countering rumors of Jesus being the Messiah that they never thought how clearly their words revealed vindictive unbelief.

Which has priority, right knowledge or right actions? While rabbinical writings call for doing meritorious deeds, some indicate that a study of the Torah has priority over good works. Here are two quotes:

Rabbi Abbahu sent his son, Rabbi Hani-nah, to Tiberias to study Torah. People came and reported to him: He spends his time performing deeds of kindness. Whereupon he sent this message to his son: Are there no graves in Caesarea? For they (long ago) decided in the upper chamber of Beth Arus in Lod, that learning is to be given priority to action [Yer. Pes. III: 30b; Yer. Hag. I: 6c].

and

Once, as Rabbi Simeon ben Yohai went about visiting the sick, he found a certain man afflicted and laid up with bowel sickness, uttering blasphemies against the Holy One blessed by He. Wretch, the Rabbi said, you should be praying for mercy instead of cursing. The man replied, (Very well then), may the Holy One remove the sickness from me and lay it on you. Rabbi Simeon said: That serves me right, for I

forsook the study of Torah and engaged in activities that use the time up (*The Fathers According to Rabbi Nathan*).

He told them many things in *parables* (13:3). The Greek word means "set alongside." Thus, a parable communicates truth by comparison, whether it is a story, proverb, simile, or metaphor. Most often parables are intended to unveil. But the parables found in Matt. 13 are intended to conceal what Jesus calls "secrets of the kingdom of heaven" (13:11) from everyone but His disciples.

Why would Jesus want to conceal His teachings about the form of God's kingdom He intended to establish? Perhaps to focus attention on the real issue: His own Person. Only by submission to Christ as King can anyone enter the kingdom of heaven. And surely that kingdom is truly known only from within.

When the wheat sprouted and formed heads, then the *weeds* also appeared (13:26). The "weeds" in this familiar parable are zizania, which we know today as bearded darnel (*lolium temulentum*). It is almost impossible to discriminate between this weed and the wheat plant when the two are young. But another characteristic of darnel is even more important. The roots of darnel become so entangled with the roots of the wheat plant that it is impossible to pull up the one without destroying the other.

The application is important to us today. We're not to try to "purify" the church by ripping out those we think are weeds. In the first place, we can't be sure whose faith is real and whose faith is counterfeit. In the second, even when we are right, our efforts to expel the false are likely to harm the real.

Our role is to love unstintingly and let both "grow together." God is able to tell the false from the true, and He will surely do so on judgment day.

Though it [the mustard seed] is the *smallest of all your seeds,* yet when it grows, it is the largest of garden plants (13:32). Some have foolishly taken this as a general botanical statement and claimed Jesus was wrong because there are plants with smaller seeds. Yet not only did the black mustard have the smallest seed of any plant cultivated in Palestine, but among first-century Jews it was proverbial as the smallest substance that could be weighed using a balance scale. The mustard seed is an idiom suggesting insignificance, something so small as to be worthless.

The point Jesus was making is thus made clear. The kingdom that Jesus introduces may seem insignificant to His contemporaries. But like the mustard plant, which grew into a plant often reaching 10 feet in height, Christ's kingdom will also grow to become a great movement.

The king was *distressed*, but because of his oaths and his dinner guests, he ordered that her request be granted (14:9). The Greek word is *lupetheis*, which means to become sad, sorrowful, filled with grief. Here we see a powerful description of a troubled conscience, urging Herod to do what he knows is right. How tragic when we, like Herod, let concern for what others might think move us to act against our consciences.

You give them something to eat (14:16). The word "you" is used emphatically in the Greek. The disciples were concerned about the hungry crowd but wanted to send the people away to fend for themselves. Jesus shifted responsibility for the crowd to them: "you" give them something to eat. When they protested that they had "only" five loaves and two fish, Jesus multiplied their resources and fed the crowd.

What important lessons for us. We do need to feel concern for others. We need to accept responsibility to meet others' needs. But this is possible only when we surrender our resources to Jesus for Him to multiply.

For God said, "*Honor* your father and mother" (15:4). In Judaism the "honor" due to fathers included material support. Rabbis held that a son's obligation to his father was so great that if necessary he should beg in the streets to meet his father's needs. This was true both of one's spiritual father, a rabbi giving a student instruction, and one's biological father. Despite this, they permitted anyone to declare goods or money *corban,* or set aside for the temple treasury. A person could continue to use something he had "donated" in this way, but he had a "lawful" basis for withholding it from his parents! As Jesus scornfully points out, this is sheer hypocrisy, and an illustration of how "tradition" can set aside the Law and will of God.

Thus you *nullify* the Word of God for the sake of your *tradition* (15:6). The word translated "nullify" is a form of *akyroo,* a common legal term used when speaking of a canceled debt, or a void will. The image is of the rabbis stamping "canceled" on laws expressing God's intention by using the instrument of tradition.

"Tradition" is *paradosin,* and refers to the oral law, or mass of comments and interpretations which even in the first century had been handed down for generations as authoritative. Rather than hold tradition in awe, as rabbinical Judaism continues to do, Jesus rejected it in favor of an interpretative approach to Scripture which emphasized "original intent." Where the original intent is clear, it is blatant hypocrisy to use man's interpretations to avoid doing what is clearly God's will.

THE PASSAGE IN DEPTH

Lord of the Sabbath (Matt. 12:1-21). See also parallel passages in Mark 2:23-28, 3:1-6, and Luke 6:1-11.

Background. The centrality of the Sabbath in first-century Judaism is illustrated by a simple fact: no writing of the era, whether Jewish, Christian, or pagan, fails to mention the Sabbath when speaking of the Jews.

Yet the host of rulings that governed Jewish observance of this holy day was generated from a single, simple command: "Observe the Sabbath day by keeping it holy, as the Lord your God has commanded you. Six days you shall labor and do all your work, but the seventh day is a Sabbath to the Lord your God" (Deut. 5:12-14). A record of the rulings on Sabbath observance is preserved for us in the Mishnah (see p. 54), and helps us sense the religious zeal of men intent on keeping the Law down to its last detail. The Mishnah also gives us insight into how tradition developed, how interpretation built on interpretation, defining and refining, gaining in time an authority equal to that of the original biblical command. The great Jewish scholar Geza Vermes, in *Jesus and the World of Judaism,* explains. The "prime concern" of the scribes "was to invest all religious doctrine with the sanction of tra-

---

THE MISHNAH ON SABBATH

The Mishnah is an important, six-part code of rules intended to govern the daily life and worship of the Jewish people. It is in the form of sayings of rabbis from the late first and second century A.D., and reflects the approach taken by teachers of the Law in the time of Jesus. The following quotes some of the Mishnah's many intense discussions of Sabbath and Sabbath-keeping:

7:2 A. The generative categories of acts of labor [prohibited on the Sabbath] are forty less one:

B. (1) he who sews, (2) ploughs, (3) reaps, (4) binds sheaves, (5) threshes, (6) winnows, (7) selects [fit from unfit produce or crops], (8) grinds, (9) sifts, (10) kneads, (11) bakes;

C. (12) he who shears wool, (13) washes it, (14) beats it, (15) dyes it;

D. (16) spins, (17) weaves;

E. (18) makes two loops, (19) weaves two threads, (20) separates two threads;

F. (21) ties, (22) unties;

G. (23) sews two stitches, (24) tears in order to sew two stitches;

H. (25) he who traps a deer, (26) slaughters it, (27) flays it, (28) salts it, (29) cures its hide, (30) scrapes it, and (31) cuts it up;

I. (32) he who writes two letters, (33) erases two letters in order to write two letters;

J. (34) he who builds, (35) tears down;

K. (36) he who puts out a fire, (37) kindles a fire;

L. (38) he who hits with a hammer; (39) he who transports an object from one domain to another—

M. lo, these are the forty generative acts of labor less one.

6:3 A. A woman should not go out with (1) a needle which has a hole, (2) with a ring which has a seal, (3) with a cochleae brooch, (4) with a spice box, or (5) with a perfume flask.

B. "And if she went out, she is liable to a sin offering," the words of R. Meir,

C. And sages declare [her] exempt in the case of a spice box and a perfume flask. . . .

6:5. A. A woman goes out in hair ribbons, whether made of her own hair or of the hair of another woman or of a beast;

B. and with (1) headband, (2) head bangles sewn [on the headdress], (3) a hair net, and (4) false locks,

C. in the courtyard;

D. (1) with wool in her ear, (2) wool in her sandals, (3) wool she has used for a napkin for her menstrual flow;

E. (1) pepper, (2) a lump of salt, and (3) anything she puts into her mouth,

F. on condition that she not first put it there on the Sabbath.

G. And if it fell out, she may not put it back.

H. A false tooth and a gold tooth—

I. Rabbi permits.

J. And the sages prohibit.

dition as being part of a strictly defined chain of transmission originating — in fact, or by means of exegetical ingenuity — in Scripture, and preferably in the Pentateuch" (p. 31).

Michael A. Fishbane, in *Judaism,* adds this explanation:

> In a strict historical sense, the revelation at Sinai was a "once and only" time for Jewish religious destiny. But as we have seen, this event has also been something more than a one-time occurrence for Jews and Judaism: it has been something of a mythic moment, recurring "always and again" whenever the Torah is studied and its teachings interpreted. Thus the divine voice heard at Sinai does not cease, according to the traditional Jewish self-understanding, but is authoritatively developed through the human words of the sages (p. 15).

This attitude of awe at the words of the sages, combined with those worthies' intense efforts to explore every possible implication of God's Law, helps us understand the shock of the Pharisees. Jesus' disciples actually picked heads of grain and ate them on the Sabbath! (see Mishnah 7.2 B [3] on p. 54) To the Pharisees, the disciples' act was tantamount to breaking the Law of God, and they were shocked that Jesus would permit it.

In our passage Jesus responds by claiming to be Lord of the Sabbath. Thus He alone has the right to determine what is and what is not Sabbath-breaking.

In another confrontation, recorded in Matt. 15, Jesus challenges the view of tradition held by the Pharisees and teachers of the Law. There He demonstrates that not only are the sages without authority, but their teachings in fact both contradict and corrupt Scripture.

It is no wonder, then, that the crowds were amazed at Jesus' teaching. Instead of relying on formal justification for His words — that is, on the sayings of earlier rabbis — Jesus "taught as one who [Himself] had authority, and not as their teachers of the Law" (Matt. 7:29). It is no wonder that the religious leaders both resented and hated this bold young teacher, who openly disdained the interpretation of the OT upon which their entire theology was based!

Interpretation. Jesus responded to the claim that His disciples' act was "unlawful" by first referring to a time when David violated a law actually found in the Pentateuch — without punishment (12:3-4). Two things are implied. The *halakah* (lifestyle rules) of tradition are less significant than Scripture. And, while David's act might possibly be excused on the basis of David's famished condition or greatness, one greater than David is now present.

Jesus goes on to note that every Sabbath the priests serving in the temple must "work," but are excused on the basis that the significance of temple worship provides them with an exemption (12:5-6). He now makes His claim explicit: now "One greater than the temple is here." The phrase "One greater" is neuter, allowing it to refer either to a person or thing. Some suggest Jesus means the kingdom of God is here, and the disciples who serve the kingdom are now exempt. It is more likely, however, that Jesus refers to Himself: the disciples serve Him, and their exemption from Sabbath *halakah* is based on who He is.

Jesus' final statement is a criticism of the rabbinical approach to Scripture itself (12:7-8). The rabbis have missed the essential meaning of the OT revelation — "If you had known what these words mean . . ." — and their condemnation of the innocent disciples reflects the error of their method of interpreting the Word. And if they wonder on what basis Jesus makes this claim, He makes it as one who is Himself Lord of the Sabbath.

Matthew now reports another Sabbath incident (12:9-14). Jesus is challenged to say whether or not it is right to heal a man with a shriveled hand on the Sabbath. In general, the rabbis agreed that if a man was in mortal danger, it was lawful to provide medical treatment on the Sabbath. But if not, one should wait until the next day to give any aid.

Jesus replied with a form of argument known as *qal wahomer,* "the light and the weighty." If the lesser were true, the greater must be. Thus if the rabbis permitted helping an animal out of a pit on the Sabbath as "lawful," even if the animal was not in mortal danger, it surely must be "lawful" to help a human being, who as a person made in God's image is much more important than an animal.

Jesus then stated a principle that cut through the whole of Sabbath *halakah:* "It is lawful to do good on the Sabbath" (12:12). And He healed the man's shriveled hand.

Matthew states the reaction of the Pharisees.

They "went out and plotted how they might kill Jesus" (12:14).

The headings added to our NIV and other versions might lead us to think that this is where the flow of the passage ends, and that Matthew moves on to a new, unrelated matter. Not so. Jesus quotes from one of Isaiah's "Servant Songs," clearly understood in the first century to be messianic. The scribes and Pharisees have not only distorted the meaning of God's Law by their approach to biblical interpretation, they have misunderstood its central message. They have rejected Him because He too failed to fit their system, and ignored those prophecies which portray the Messiah as compassionate, gentle, and harmless—until the day of judgment dawns.

This is the ultimate issue, and the ultimate tragedy of Jesus' day. Although zealous for God, Israel has misunderstood and corrupted God's revelation—a misunderstanding so great that when Messiah came, rather than welcome Him, the religious leaders determined that He must die.

Application. We must balance our appreciation for the great and influential persons in our theological tradition with an awareness of human fallibility. As a consequence, we continually seek fresh insights into Scripture, guided not only by the Spirit, but also by Jesus' example. How simply and beautifully Jesus cuts through legalism to remind us that our do's and don'ts must be measured against simple, basic principles. God desires mercy, not simply sacrifice (i.e., ritual observance). Thus, it is always "lawful" to do what is good, and like Jesus Himself, to have compassion on those society dismisses as the most useless of people.

Jesus and Beelzebub (12:22-50). For an in-depth discussion, see the commentary on Mark 3:7-30. Also see Luke 11:14-28.

Parables of the Kingdom (13:1-56). See also Mark 4:1-34 and Luke 8:4-18; 13:18-21.

Background. As noted earlier (see Word Study on Matt. 13:3), a "parable" is a simile, story, object, or metaphor set "alongside" a spiritual truth to illuminate its significance or meaning.

It is important, then, to explore how the original listeners would have understood the metaphor if we are to accurately understand

the meaning of the parable. Joachim Jeremias, writing on *The Message of the Parables of Jesus,* is helpful in defining the import of parables found in Matt. 13. Concerning the parables of the leaven and the mustard seed, Jeremias observes:

> The occasion of the utterance of the two parables may be taken to be some expression of doubt concerning the mission of Jesus. How differently the beginnings of the Messianic Age announced by Jesus appeared than was commonly expected! It is not the purpose of either parable merely to describe a process: that would be the way of the western mind. The oriental mind includes both beginning and end in its purview, seizing the paradoxical element in both cases, the two successive, yet fundamentally differing, situations. . . . The seed is the image of the resurrection, the symbol of mystery of life out of death. The oriental mind sees two wholly different situations; on the one hand the dead seed, on the other, the waving cornfield, here death, there, through the divine creative power, life. . . . The modern man, passing through the ploughed field, thinks of what is going on beneath the soil, and envisages a biological development. The people of the Bible, passing through the same plough-land, look up and see miracle upon miracle, nothing less than resurrection from the dead. Thus did Jesus' audience understand the Parables of the Mustard Seed and the Leaven as parables of contrast. Their meaning is that out of the most insignificant beginnings, invisible to human eye, God creates His mighty Kingdom, which embraces all the peoples of the world (pp. 148-49).

> The feature common to all four parables is that they contrast the beginning with the end, and what a contrast! The insignificance of the beginning and the triumph of the end! But the contrast is not the whole truth. The fruit is the result of the seed; the end is implicit in the beginning. . . . Those to whom it has been given to understand the mystery of the Kingdom see already in its hidden and insignificant beginnings the coming glory of God (pp. 152-53).

This extended quote helps us grasp the most significant thing about these parables. They concern the form of the kingdom of heaven that is being introduced by Jesus. And they are intended to contrast this form of the kingdom with the visible, institutional kingdom described by the prophets and expected by Jesus' contemporaries.

When we keep this clearly in mind, we find it relatively easy to understand what each parable is intended to teach.

We also understand why Jesus speaks of His parables as disguising rather than revealing truth about the kingdom (13:11-15). The parables disguise, not because they are obscure, but because listeners are blinded by their refusal to accept Jesus as Messiah. The opponents of Jesus are so intent on their own vision of King and kingdom that "though seeing, they do not see; though hearing, they do not hear" (13:13).

If we accept the simple proposition that Jesus' parables draw contrasts between the ex-pected and unexpected forms of the kingdom of heaven, we have a clear basis for interpreting them. And, if we then ask how the *oriental* mind approached the parables, we find each is relatively easy to understand.

Interpretation. The following chart sums up the specific contrast implicit in each parable, and shows how complete a picture of Jesus' kingdom the parables of Matthew 13 actually do draw. While each parable is a rich source of teaching and preaching, their greatest impact is gained when we look at them together and see some sense of what it means for us to be a part of the present working of our Lord in this world.

Application. Today, as in the first century, it is easy to miss what God is about in this world. We wonder at the inability of the church to affect society. We yearn for the power to challenge wickedness and injustice. And we wonder why Christianity seems to have so little local, national, or international influence. Some have been so concerned that, as in

Parables of the Kingdom

The Parable	Expected Form	Unexpected Characteristic
1. Sower 13:3-9, 18-23	Messiah turns *Israel* and all *nations* to Himself	*Individuals* respond differently to the Word's invitation.
2. Wheat/tares 13:24-30, 37-43	The kingdom's righteous citizens *rule over* the world with the King.	The kingdom's citizens are *among* the men of the world, growing together till God's harvesttime.
3. Mustard seed 13:31-32	Kingdom *begins* in *majestic glory.*	Kingdom *begins in insignificance;* its greatness comes as a surprise.
4. Leaven 13:33	Only righteousness enters the kingdom; other "raw material" is excluded.	The kingdom is implanted in a different "raw material" and grows to fill the whole personality with righteousness.
5. Hidden treasure 13:44	Kingdom is *public* and for all.	Kingdom is *hidden* and for individual "purchase."
6. Priceless pearl 13:45-46	Kingdom *brings all valued things* to men.	Kingdom demands *abandonment* of all other values (cf. 6:33).
7. Dragnet 13:47-50	Kingdom begins with initial separation of righteous and unrighteous.	Kingdom ends with final separation of the unrighteous from the righteous.

South America today, whole theologies have been developed that justify even the use of force to win "liberation" for the poor and powerless.

The parables of Matthew 13 guard us against distorting the Gospel message. And guard us against despair. They remind us, as do the NT letters, that God is at work in and through His people. The persecution Christians experience, and our sufferings here on earth, cannot touch Christ's inner, hidden and secret kingdom of the heart.

In this kingdom God is still vitally at work, taking sinners as raw material and making them righteous individuals, transforming values, calling for commitment, all the while scattering believers among the men of the world so that they might influence yet other individuals to come to Jesus. One day these things, which seem so insignificant to many today, will fill a renewed and transformed earth, when Christ returns to judge and separates the citizens of His kingdom from the lost.

John the Baptist Beheaded (14:1-12). For in-depth discussion, see the commentary on Mark 6:14-29. See also Luke 9:7-9 and Matt. 11:1-24.

Clean and Unclean (15:1-20). See also Mark 7:1-23.

Background. See the discussion of "tradition" in the background segment of the discussion of Matthew 12:1-21, pp. 53-55.

Interpretation. The particular tradition which Jesus deals with in 15:1-6 is one which sets *corban,* an act of dedicating possessions or money to the temple, over against the fifth commandment, which calls on children to honor their parents. The rabbis had given a most strict interpretation to the fifth commandment. In fact, commenting on this commandment the Talmud says, "A son is bound to feed his father, to give him drink, to clothe him, to protect him, to lead him in, and to conduct him out, and to wash his face, his hands, and his feet." So Jesus' criticism does not suggest that the rabbis ignored the implications of the fifth commandment. His criticism is based on the fact that they gave corban, which itself is only a rabbinic interpretation of the laws on vows, more weight than the commandment of God! In doing so, they actually

nullified the Law, making it of no practical effect for anyone wishing to avoid his obligation to parents.

Jesus' conclusion was stated in a quote from Isaiah. The teachers of the law are hypocrites, for while they give God lip service, their "rules taught by men" show their hearts are far from Him (15:7-9).

At this point Jesus moved to an even more open confrontation, returning to the original challenge raised by the Pharisees against His disciples: "They don't wash their hands before they eat" (15:3). This washing was ritual rather than hygienic, prescribed by the elders rather than Scripture, and given religious force by tradition. Thus, on Halakic tradition in the treatise on "hands" (Yadaim) says, "If a man poured water over the one hand with a single rinsing, his hand is clean; but if over both hands with a single rinsing, R. Meir declares them unclean unless he pours over them a quarter-log or more" (2:1).

Jesus dismissed this concern as totally irrelevant to one's relationship with God. Cleanness and uncleanness are matters of the heart, not of externals like washing. In fact, Jesus says, even eating the ritually "unclean" foods proscribed in Scripture itself (Lev. 11) does not concern God. What God cares about is a person's heart (see Word Study on Matt. 12:35)! The implication is clear. The religious in Israel occupy themselves with irrelevancies. They are blind to spiritual realities, stumbling along in the dark as they pretend to lead others just as blind as themselves. Rather than finding the kingdom of God, these men will "fall into a pit" (15:14).

The Pharisees, Matthew tells us, were "offended" when they heard what Jesus said to the crowd (15:12). "Offend," *skandalizo,* means to cause anger, shock, or repulsion. Jesus not only rejected the whole structure of their faith but ridiculed their reputation, and these were the most important things in their lives.

We need to see 15:1-9 as perhaps a last effort at evangelization. These religious leaders had not responded to earlier, gentler invitations of the King. His teaching of love, His miracles of healing, all underscored the fact that here was a Man who threatened no one, and in fact offered hope to all. Now, in the face of hardening opposition, Jesus more and more openly confronts the Pharisees and teachers of the Law. He must show them reality. He must reveal to them the emptiness of their religion, and turn their hearts to God for forgiveness.

But when the Pharisees take offense, Jesus turns to the crowd and warns them (15:10-11). The way taken by the Pharisees may seem "religious," but it is empty of meaning and of hope. And so Jesus says, "Leave them" (15:14). Let go of their hands! Only by turning from tradition to Jesus can Israel discover the light and deal with sinfulness of the human heart.

Application. On the one hand this passage may challenge us. Normally we witness to the kingdom by acts of kindness and words of God's love. But sometimes the one who witnesses to the kingdom of Jesus may be called to confront. Often confrontation is a last desperate attempt to open blind eyes. Usually it is futile.

On the other hand, Jesus calls us to self-examination. Is our faith essentially a matter of the heart, or have we fallen into the same pit and treated citizenship in God's kingdom as a matter of "do" and "don't" rather than an issue of personal relationship with Jesus? Are we being responsive to Him, or simply living by rules laid down by men that purport to show how we please God? Questions like these must be asked—and answered—by every generation. And by each individual believer as well.

The Faith of the Canaanite Woman (15:21-28). See also Mark 7:24-30.

Background. Paul graphically describes the position of the Gentile before Christ came in Ephesians 2:12: "Remember that at that time you were separate from Christ, excluded from citizenship in Israel and foreigners to the covenants of the promise, without hope and without God in the world." To the pious Jew, the Gentile was unclean, a *goy* (dog), in many ways beneath contempt. Few Jews would be surprised that Jesus rejected outright the appeal of the Canaanite woman who tearfully appealed to him as the "Son of David," the Jewish Messiah. Few would have been shocked that Jesus likened her to a dog, while likening the Jews to children of the household. But certainly we may be surprised and shocked. Until we sense the marvelous lesson that this incident teaches, coming as it does immediately after Jesus' painful confrontation with the Pharisees and teachers of the Law.

Interpretation. Jesus' mission was first of all to God's covenant people. His response to the Canaanite woman underlined this. The interplay also establishes vital principles. Although as a Canaanite the woman had no right to appeal to the Jewish Messiah, her "great faith" (15:28) led to her participation in the blessings promised to Israel!

Faith in the Messiah is the key to blessing. The Messiah brings enough to satisfy the deepest hunger of "the children" and also of all those peoples Israel then dismissed as *goyim.*

"The children" without faith would reject the Messiah and would themselves be rejected. But every individual, Gentile or Jew, who approaches God's Christ with faith, will be filled indeed.

MATTHEW 16–17
The Turning Point

EXPOSITION

Matthew has carefully developed his theme. That Jesus is the expected messianic King is shown by the unique events associated with His birth (Matt. 1–2). It is demonstrated in His baptism, His victory over Satan, and the healings He performed (Matt. 3–4). But the kingdom Jesus announced is an inner one, characterized by an "in secret" relationship with God which transforms people's hearts (Matt. 5–7). In a series of bold images, Matthew reports incidents that prove Jesus had royal authority—over sickness, nature, demons, and even death (Matt. 8–11). Despite the evidence, however, hostility shown to the young Teacher by the religious leaders hardened into open opposition (Matt. 12–15).

With chapter 16 we come to a vital historical and theological turning point. The leaders have rejected the claims of Jesus and refused to submit to His authority. When Jesus sends His disciples to circulate through the crowds, it becomes clear that the general population, while willing to accept Jesus as a prophet, is also unwilling to acknowledge Christ for who He really is. The nation is unwilling to affirm, with Peter and the disciples, "You are the Christ, the Son of the living God" (16:16).

Many things demonstrate that this confession and the events leading up to it are pivotal, both historically and theologically. "From that time on Jesus began to explain to His disciples . . . that He must be killed and on the third day be raised to life" (16:21). Now too the focus of Jesus' teaching shifts; He speaks primarily to the disciples rather than the crowds. Jesus no longer preaches a "Gospel of the kingdom" to Israel, but rather instructs His own on how to live in the hidden kingdom of the heart to be established after His resurrection. And the geographical movement of the book is one of inexorable progress toward Judea, Jerusalem, and the cross.

We see shift clearly in these two chapters. The "Pharisees and Sadducees" represent the Sanhedrin, the official ruling council of the Jews. They demonstrate official unbelief by demanding yet more proof from Jesus (16:1–12). The crowds, although in awe of Jesus, do not acknowledge Him as Messiah (16:13–15). Only the disciples, represented in Peter's confession, accept the truth: Jesus is "the Christ [Messiah], the Son of the living God" (16:16). Their faith commissions them, and a great assembly of those who believe will be founded on the reality Peter confessed, and built by those who teach it (16:17–20).

But to found His kingdom the King must die and be raised again (16:21–23). To live in Jesus' kingdom, a citizen must surrender his old self in order to be made new (16:24-28). Is that surrender worthwhile? Three of the disciples accompany Jesus up a mountain, where they are given the opportunity to see Jesus' glory as He is transformed before them (17:1-13). Like the King, the kingdom is initiated in humility, but culminates in splendor.

Back in the valley Jesus finds frustrated disciples who are unable to heal a demon-possessed boy (17:14-23). The incident emphasizes the importance of faith; God, though unseen, can and will act in the world as Jesus' followers trust in Him. And very soon faith in the hidden God will be desperately needed by the disciples. Jesus will be betrayed and killed. And will be raised again (17:22).

The chapter closes with an object lesson. Does all this mean a change in Israel's relationship with God? No, Israel has always paid the half-shekel temple tax. And everyone knows that rulers do not tax their children, but "others." Under the Old Covenant as under the New, personal relationship with the Lord was a matter of personal faith in the saving grace and power of God.

WORD STUDIES

"The *Pharisees and Sadducees* came to Jesus" (16:1). When linked in this way, the phrase does not simply mean that members of these two first-century religious parties "came to Jesus." When linked, "Pharisees and Sadducees" implies an official delegation representing the Sanhedrin, the Jewish spiritual and civil governing council.

Tested Him by asking Him to show them a *sign from heaven* (16:1). The demand is for a miracle "from heaven" so definitive that

---

SADDUCEES

The Sadducees (Heb. *saiqim*; "righteous ones") were one of the two major religious parties in Judaism between the second century B.C. up until the destruction of the temple. Information on the Sadducees comes from about a dozen brief mentions in the NT and hostile sources such as Josephus and the Talmud. Following Roman suppression of the Jewish rebellions of A.D. 68-70 and 135, the Pharisee party alone survived. Thus that view of and approach to Scripture alone is reflected in rabbinic Judaism. But in the NT era the Sadducees was the party of the well-to-do, representing the aristocratic priesthood. Although charged in later writings with attempting to corrupt Jewish life by introducing Greek ways, the Sadducees maintained a large block of members in the ruling Sanhedrin (Acts 23:6-11).

While no writings of the Sadducees exist, and nothing certain can be said of the ideals or motives of members of this movement or their role in first-century society, our sources do agree in their description of Sadducean doctrines. *The Revell Bible Dictionary* summarizes:

The Sadducees denied the possibility of life after death and scoffed at the common belief in resurrection (Mark 12:18). They also rejected the existence of angels or spirits (Acts 23:8). The Sadducees believed in the total freedom of the human will, uninfluenced by fate or God's providence. The Sadducees held that only the five books of Moses were authoritative, and rejected the traditional interpretations of the Law so dear to the Pharisees (p. 885).

there will be no possible doubt about who Jesus is. Some early commentators have taken this demand literally: the leaders required Jesus to make the sun stand still, or turn the moon red. This view is supported by Jesus' response: the Pharisees can read weather signs reflected in the sky. They cannot, however, read the significance of things happening right before them on earth, a clear reference to the many miracles Jesus has already performed among them.

Miracles are an encouragement to faith. But they cannot create faith. We believe first; then we see.

None will be given it except the *sign of Jonah* (16:4). God did give Israel a definitive sign, unmistakably authenticating Jesus as God's Son. The "sign" is explained in Matt. 12:40: "For as Jonah was three days and three nights in the belly of a huge fish, so the Son of Man will be three days and three nights in the heart of the earth."

And when Jesus was raised, did the members of the Sanhedrin believe? Not at all. They devised a plan: they gave the soldiers a large sum of money telling them, "You are to say, 'His disciples came during the night and stole Him away while we were asleep.' " Faith is a matter of being willing to submit to God, not a matter of being convinced that God has acted in Jesus.

Be on your guard against the *yeast* of the Pharisees and Sadducees (16:6). Jesus explains that the reference is to the "teaching" of the Pharisees and Sadducees. The combination is unique, for these two parties were characterized by dramatically different teachings! What then can Jesus mean?

In context, both Pharisees and Sadducees demanded to be shown a "sign" (16:1). Thus the teaching (doctrine) at issue is refusal to believe in Jesus without absolutely compelling proof. The problem with this approach is obvious: relationship with God, from the time of Abraham on, has been a matter of faith (Gen. 15:6). Now Jesus has shown Himself to be both Messiah and Son of God, but neither Pharisee nor Sadducee will accept His word unless compelled to do so.

How much we too must guard ourselves against the tendency to withhold faith until we have proof of God's involvement in our lives.

Jesus is Lord. Let us put our complete confidence in Him.

I tell you that you are Peter, and on this *rock* I will build My church (16:18). The verse has stimulated endless debate. Was Jesus making a play on the name "Peter" by addressing him as *petros,* "rock," and calling him a *petra,* "stone"? If He originally spoke in Aramaic, this distinction does not exist. Thus, the church fathers claimed by the Roman Catholic church argued:

■ Peter is the rock, and the naming constitutes his commission as pope, and the church will be built on his authority as vicar, personal representative, of Christ on earth.

Others have offered different interpretations:

■ Peter is a stone; the rock is Peter's confession of Christ, and the church will be built of those who make a similar confession of faith in our Lord.

■ Peter is a stone; the rock is the truth which Peter recognized and affirmed, and the church will be founded on the reality of Christ's nature as Son of God and Savior.

The issue will surely be debated on and on, until Christ returns. Yet there is no doubt that Peter, always mentioned first in any NT listing of the Twelve, played the most prominent role in the earliest years of the church, as seen in Acts 1–12. There is also no doubt that our confidence of security in Christ rests not on the fact that Peter believed, but on the great reality that Christ Himself is the firm foundation on which the church rests (1 Cor. 3:11).

And the *gates of Hades* [hell] will not overcome it [the church] (16:18). The phrase has been interpreted in two ways. One is based on the popular usage of phrases like "gates of death" in the Bible (Job 17:16; Ps. 9:13), in Jewish literature (Macc. 5:5), and even in pagan literature (Iliad 9. 312). This approach suggests that "gates of Hades" refers to death and dying: Christ is saying that even the powers of death will not triumph over His church.

The other interpretation takes "gates of Hell" (KJV) to refer to Satan's powers, since "gates" can represent fortifications and military strength (Gen. 22:17 [KJV]; Ps. 127:5; and see below Qumran Hymn 6:25-30, from one of the Dead Sea Scrolls).

In reality, both interpretations reflect the wonderful truth that we are secure in Christ, now and forevermore.

> But I shall be as one who enters a fortified city, as one who seeks refuge behind a high wall until deliverance; I will [lean on] Your truth, O my God, For You will set the foundation on rock and the framework by the measuring cord of justice; and the tried stones by the plumb line [of truth], to [build] a mighty [wall] which will not sway; and no man entering there shall stagger. For no enemy shall ever invade it, since its doors shall be doors of protection through which no man shall pass; and its bars shall be firm, and no man shall break them. No rabble shall enter in with their weapons of war until all the [arrows] of the war of wickedness have come to an end. And then at the time of judgment the sword of God shall hasten, and all the sons of His truth shall awake to overthrow wickedness; all the sons of iniquity shall be no more. The hero shall bend his bow; the fortress shall open on to endless space, and the everlasting gates shall send out weapons of war.

I will give you the *keys of the kingdom* of heaven (16:19). In biblical times "keys" frequently served as a symbol of a steward's authority in a master's household (Isa. 22:15, 22). There seems no doubt from the text that these keys are given to Peter. Yet many commentators argue that the other disciples, and Jesus' followers today, exercise the same authority. Clearly, as the subsequent dispute over who would be greatest in the kingdom of heaven shows (Matt. 20:20-28), the disciples did not understand Jesus' pronouncement as a special anointing or appointment of Peter to primacy in either church or kingdom.

Many commentators see Peter's exercise of the keys, described immediately following, as opening the door of faith to invite others to enter Christ's kingdom. Historically, of course, this is just what happened. Peter was the first after the resurrection to preach Christ to the Jews (Acts 2) and to the Gentiles (Acts 10).

Whatever you *bind* on earth will be bound in heaven, and whatever you *loose* on earth will be loosed in heaven (16:19). The terms "binding" and "loosing" were used in two ways in Jesus' day. The rabbis debated precisely when a person was bound to keep a vow, and under what conditions he might be released, or loosed, from it. The saying also related to the competence of rabbis to make other decisions concerning ritual and law. Thus Rabbi Nehuyna ben Hakanah's prayer:

> May it please You, Lord my God and God of my fathers, that I loose not my temper regarding my colleagues, and visa versa, so that we will not declare as defiled what is pure, or purse what is defiled, that we will not loosen what is bound [permit what should be forbidden] or bind what is loosened [prohibit what should be permitted]; lest I be ashamed in this and the future world (yBerakhot 4:2, 7d).

From this we might suppose that binding and loosing relate to teachings. The Greek *ho,* being neuter, also suggests that Jesus means whatever "things" are bound or loosed by Peter on earth "have been bound" (lit.) or loosed in heaven. This is also suggested in Luke 11:52, where the teachers of the law are condemned for taking away the "keys to knowledge," so that they not only fail to enter the kingdom of heaven themselves, but "have hindered those who were entering."

If this is correct, and salvation itself is at issue in the use of the keys, it becomes apparent that what Jesus delivers to Peter is the Gospel itself—that message which opens the door of salvation. This message both looses and binds, permits and prohibits, for those who respond to it with faith are welcomed into God's kingdom, while those who reject are excluded. Why then the contrast between heaven and earth? Because how a person responds on earth will indeed be bound or loosed in heaven, now and forevermore.

Did Peter use the keys? Yes, indeed, for he was granted the privilege of proclaiming first, to the Jews on Pentecost (Acts 2), and to Cornelius, representing the other major biblical division of mankind, the Gentiles, some time later (Acts 10).

There He was *transfigured* among them

(17:2). The Greek word *metamorphoo* means to transform, to change. It implies an inner change that may be either visible outwardly or invisible. Jesus momentarily set aside the veil of flesh that disguised His essential deity and displayed His glory to the three disciples. What Jesus had been before the Incarnation, and what He was about to become after the Resurrection, was momentarily visible to His followers.

Many point out that expressions such as "after six days" (17:1), which set the time exactly, are rare in the Gospels. What we have in the Transfiguration is the fulfillment of Jesus' promise that some of the disciples would see the Son of Man in His kingdom glory.

The experience should have led the three to marvel that Christ, so splendid in essential nature, should willingly set aside awesome power to live and die as a human being. The experience of the three is a reminder to us today too, even though we look back from the vantage point of the Resurrection. One day Christ will return in glory, and we will be glorified with Him. However humdrum or ordinary our lives may seem today, the return of Christ will transform our experience forever.

Because you have so *little faith* (17:20). The Greek word is *oligopistian*. While this is the only occurrence of the word in the NT, its adjectival form is also found in Matt. 6:30; 8:26; 14:31 and 16:8. In each case it refers to the disciples rather than the crowds.

But what is this "little faith" that all too often characterizes Jesus' followers? The word does not refer to the amount of faith, but rather to its character. Even a small amount of faith can "move mountains," a proverbial expression meaning to overcome great difficulties (Isa. 40:4; Matt. 21:21-22; Luke 17:6). But a faith that is defective is powerless.

This was the reason the disciples had been unable to cast out the demon that troubled the epileptic boy (Mark 9:17-19, 29). They firmly expected to be able to perform the miracle, but seem to have treated the spiritual authority given them (Matt. 10:1, 8) as if it was their power. That confidence was misplaced and their faith defective because they did not rely totally on the God who promised, in Jesus, to work through them.

Our faith too is flawed and defective when we expect that, because God has worked through us in the past, we ourselves are able to perform spiritual works today. Only constant awareness of our dependence on God, and unshaken confidence in the availability of His power to those who trust in Him, keeps our faith pure.

THE PASSAGE IN DEPTH

The Demand for a Sign (16:1-4). See Word Study on "sign from heaven" and Mark 8:11-13.

The Yeast of the Pharisees and Sadducees (16:5-12). See Word Study on "yeast" (16:6).

Peter's confession of Christ (16:13-20). See parallel passages in Mark 8:27-29 and Luke 9:18-20, and word studies on "rock" (16:18), "gates of Hades [Hell]" (16:18), "keys of the kingdom" (16:19), and "bind and loose" (16:19).

Jesus predicts His death (16:21-28). See parallel passage in Mark 8:31–9:1.

Interpretation. Jesus' sudden introduction of the cross shocked and horrified His disciples. They were comfortable with the way things were, secure in Jesus' presence. No wonder Peter blurted out his objection, "Never, Lord!" (16:22)

Peter's objection, and Christ's blunt rebuff, reaffirms the cross as God's will. It also sets up Christ's explanation of the implications of discipleship.

The impact of what Jesus said is blurred in older English versions of v. 25, which translate psyche as "soul." Without self-denial and acceptance of His cross, the disciple seemed to be threatened with the loss of "his soul." The interplay of losing one's soul and finding it was confusing to say the least. The NIV helps, leaving the meaning merely fuzzy rather than blurred. But it remains difficult to understand how a disciple saves "his life" in following Jesus, and how by losing "his life for Me" a person can "find it."

The solution is found when we remember that the language in which Jesus conversed with His disciples was undoubtedly Aramaic. In this tongue as in Hebrew, the word *nepesh,* variously rendered as "life," "person," "self," "being," "I," etc., is used as a reflexive pronoun meaning the person himself. In translating into Greek the Hebraism was retained, and the Greek word *psyche* was used to translate *nepesh.*

Jesus was then simply saying this: The decision to follow Jesus and take up one's cross means the loss of the old self. It also means the gain of a new self! How clearly the NT shows us that the "I" we leave behind is wisely abandoned, while the "I" we become is the person we have always yearned to be. A person we can only become as God works His grace in our hearts.

What then does Jesus present as the key to this personal renewal? "He must deny himself and take up his cross and follow Me" (16:24). The first phrase and the last are easy to understand. Self-denial is simply a refusal to respond to the promptings of the sin nature within us. And following Jesus is acting on His words and responding to the Spirit's promptings. But what about "take up his cross"?

While on the one hand the cross is a symbol of Christ's sufferings for us, we must remember that for Jesus the cross was a symbol of God's will. Jesus chose the cross, saying "Yet not as I will, but as You will" (26:39). We must also remember that Jesus did not say we were to take up His cross, but that we are to each to take up our own cross. Simply put, my cross represents the will of God for me. We take up our cross when we make the same decision Jesus made: to do the will of God, daily, whatever the cost or wherever God's will may lead us.

We can sense then the interrelationship between Jesus' sharp rebuke of Peter, whose "Never" was an invitation to turn away from God's will, and Christ's instruction to His disciples. We dare not turn away from the will of God. Only by denying ourselves and by committing ourselves to God's will can we find personal renewal.

Application. How often persons hesitate to accept Christ for fear they will have to "give up" something they enjoy. And how often Christians hold back from full commitment for the same reason.

Jesus shifts the focus of our concern from "What will I lose if I commit fully?" to "What will I lose if I do not make a total commitment to Christ?" To drive the question home Jesus asks us to imagine a balance scale. On the one side Jesus places the old self and adds the whole world! On the other side Jesus places just one thing, the new self. Then, looking at the scales tilt, He asks, "What good will it be for a man if he gains the whole world, and forfeits the self he could become?" (16:26, author's paraphrase)

And immediately He shifts the focus of our gaze to history's end. The Son of Man is going to come in His Father's glory. Not only does becoming the person we yearn to be outweigh this world, but in choosing to take up our cross and follow Jesus we win eternal rewards as well.

The Transfiguration (17:1-13). See the in-depth commentary on Mark 9:2-8 and the parallel passage in Luke 9:28-36.

Elijah must come first (17:10-13). See also the parallel passage in Mark 9:9-13.

Background. Christians have tended to assume that this passage implies that the Jews believed Elijah must appear before the Messiah comes. There is, however, no compelling evidence that the coming of the Messiah was linked in contemporary Jewish thought with Elijah's appearance. The verses in Malachi which predict Elijah's appearance simply state that the prophet will reappear "before the great and dreadful day of the Lord comes" (Mal. 4:5).

Most rabbinic texts which mention Elijah's return see his role as one of resolving questions of *halakah,* and is expressed in the literature in the term *teyqu,* which means "The Tishbite will resolve difficulties and problems." This notion that when Elijah appeared, unresolved questions would be answered is in complete harmony with rabbinic preoccupation with matters of law and interpretation.

There are, however, one or two references that link Elijah's appearance to the coming of the Messiah. One talmudic midrash reads, "Assuming that as Elijah would not come the Messiah also would not come, why should not [the drinking of wine] be permitted on Sabbath eve?" (in b. Erubin 43b). In an undated commentary on Deut. 30:4 (Targum Ps.-Jonathan) the author writes, "If you dispersed ones will be unto the end of heaven, from there the *memra* of the Lord your God shall gather you by the hand of Elijah, the high priest, and from there He shall bring you near by the hand of the King Messiah."

Even so, it is not at all clear that in the time of Jesus there was a general belief that Elijah's coming heralded the appearance of the Messiah. What is clear is that Elijah was expected. There is undoubtedly linkage between Elijah and the Messiah, for both are associated with the end of the age. But it is not at all clear that the coming of the Messiah was thought to depend on the preceding appearance of Elijah as His forerunner.

Interpretation. In view of the above, what were the disciples really asking Jesus? They had just seen His glory on the mountain. Why, as they followed the path down from its peak did the three raise the issue of Elijah?

The answer is that Jesus' disciples' eyes were still filled with visions of splendor. What they were really asking was: When are You going to establish Your glorious kingdom? When is Elijah going to appear, so that Israel's heart will be turned to You? When will purging judgments strike the Gentile world and purify our people?

Christ's answer must have stunned them. John the Baptist would have fulfilled the prediction of Elijah — if God's people had accepted him (11:13-14). But the people of Israel were not willing to accept John or his Elijah-like ministry. They killed "Elijah." "In the same way the Son of Man is going to suffer at their hands" (17:12).

The disciples are not to expect the kingdom, but the cross.

Application. Like the disciples, we often look for the glory and shut our eyes to the suffering which necessarily precedes it. Yes, Jesus will establish God's kingdom here on earth. But not now. Here and now Christ's disciples are called to a life of commitment to God's will — a life of self-denial, of taking up one's cross daily, and of following Jesus.

It is right and good that we should look forward to Christ's return. It is essential that we also realize the Christian's calling now: to serve God and others, and gladly to pay whatever loving God and others may cost.

Healing the Epileptic Boy (17:14-23). See the in-depth commentary on Mark 9:14-32,

and the parallel passage in Luke 9:37-45.

The Temple Tax (17:24-27).
Background. The "temple tax" was a half-shekel or its equivalent, sent to Jerusalem annually by every Jew in and beyond Palestine. The funds were used for the temple and its sacrifices, but also went for maintenance of Jerusalem's walls, repair of the aqueduct that brought the city water, and for other city needs.

Philo, the famous first-century Jewish philosopher of Alexandria, eloquently describes the solemn ceremony involved in collecting the half-shekel, choosing the messengers who would convey it to Jerusalem, and seeing it off. Contribution toward this tax was viewed as a great *mitzvah,* or good deed, and the Jews outside Palestine often fought for the right to make the contribution against Gentiles who attacked the practice, arguing that it constituted "payment of a tax to a foreign country."

Josephus in his *Antiquities* (XIV: 7:2 [115]) reports an incident in Cyrenaean Lybia during the reign of Augustus when the Greeks of the city "were persecuting [the Jews] to the extent of taking their sacred monies away from them." A delegation was sent to Rome, and Agrippa wrote a letter to the city fathers reminding them that Augustus had specifically instructed the governor not to permit the annual contribution to be blocked.

Against this background we can sense some surprise in the question several Jews asked Peter, Jews given the privilege of collecting the half-shekel tax in Capernaum. "Doesn't your Teacher pay the temple tax?" (16:24) The form of the negative here expects a "yes" answer: "Your Teacher pays the temple tax, doesn't He?" The fact the question was asked at all implies that payment was probably overdue.

Peter, without any hesitation, blurted out, "Yes." It was the answer any pious Jew would give, surely the answer the collectors expected.

Why then does Jesus seem to gently rebuke Peter, and what does His dialogue with His disciple mean? The question Jesus asks, Peter's response, and Jesus' summary, are in fact quite clear. And the implications are stunning. Look at the dialogue here:

> When Peter came into the house, Jesus was the first to speak. "What do you think, Simon? From whom do the kings of the earth collect duty and taxes — from their

own sons or from others?"

"From others," Peter answered.

"Then the sons are exempt," Jesus said to him.

The dialogue with Peter establishes a central point: Kings do not tax family members. What happens when we apply this principle to the practice of paying the annual temple tax? We note the following critical points:

The tax is paid to God (for His temple).

The tax is paid by the Jewish people.

Jesus has not paid the tax.

The conclusion we draw is stunning. If kings do not tax family, and God is the One to whom the temple taxes are paid, then clearly the very existence of the temple tax is a repeated, annual witness to the fact that the Jewish people are not, by virtue of race alone, the children of God!

And Jesus' failure to pay it is a similarly silent but clear affirmation that He Himself is God's Son.

The Jews are God's chosen people, yes. But they are not, as a people, God's family. Family relationship with God for human beings, from the time of Abraham himself, has been established only by faith.

Application. Neither religion nor race can provide personal relationship with God. Our heritage may well offer some great advantage in terms of available knowledge of God. But this can be as great a disadvantage as it is an advantage. Unless an individual responds to what can be known of God with simple faith, even the clearest revelation will be distorted and misunderstood. How strange that the temple tax, viewed in first-century Judaism as evidence of the scattered community's link with God and as a privilege to be fought for was, in fact, a witness to each individual's estrangement from the Lord!

MATTHEW 18–20
The Way to Greatness

EXPOSITION

Matthew now records a series of incidents that are linked by a theme which is introduced in 18:1 and culminates in 20:34. That theme is: "Who is the greatest in the kingdom of heaven?" (18:1) Taken together, these chapters constitute Jesus' basic teaching on spiritual achievement for His disciples.

In answer to the question "Who is the greatest?" Jesus calls a child, who responds immediately and comes to stand by our Lord (18:2-5). How unlike Israel, which has held back, demanding the right to pass judgment on Christ rather than simply respond to His word! Jesus then underlines the importance of retaining this "little child" characteristic (18:6-9) and tells three stories intended to show how believers can encourage "little childness" in each other and in the church. Remembering that, like sheep, we human beings tend to go astray, we must be quick to restore each other, with rejoicing, and not recriminations (18:10-14). Because the children in any family "sin against" each other, we are to take the initiative when harmed and actively seek reconciliation. This calls for acknowledgment of the hurt and an extending of forgiveness (18:15-20). A brief interchange with Peter makes it clear we are to keep on extending forgiveness, again and again (18:21-22). If this seems difficult, we are to remember how much God has forgiven us, and accept the fact that we who have been forgiven an unpayable debt ought to forgive others, who surely owe us less than we owed God (18:23-35).

Matthew now reports a series of three incidents which illustrate paths religious people have taken in a quest for spiritual achievement.

■ The Pharisees took the way of Law, assuming that if they were more rigorous than others in their do's and don'ts they would achieve spiritual superiority. Jesus uses a question about divorce to establish that the Law actually was a lowered standard, which demonstrates God's willingness to accommodate Himself to the weakness of sinful humanity rather than demand total conformity to His ideal (19:1-15).

■ A rich young man who has taken the way of philanthropy then asks Jesus how he can gain eternal life. Jesus tells him to give his wealth away, forcing the young man to choose between his wealth and the command of One who is his God. The young man leaves, and in departing reminds us that "doing good" is not necessarily evidence of spiritual achievement.

■ Jesus then tells the story of a man who deals with his workers on the basis of grace rather than merit. The story reminds us that even working harder likewise is no proof of spiritual achievement (20:1-16).

What then does make for greatness in God's kingdom? Respond to Jesus as a "little child" — and this is enabled by living together as sheep, as siblings, as a forgiving and forgiven people. Jesus goes on to reveal the attitude that is God's final key to true greatness. Jesus Himself is about to be betrayed and condemned to death — for us (20:17-19). When the mother of James and John begs Jesus to grant her sons the highest positions in His coming kingdom, Jesus asks if they can drink His cup — that is, live as He has lived and experience what He must experience (20:20-23). Then Jesus explains to all the Twelve what greatness requires: not ruling over God's people, but living among them as servants, willing to give oneself as Jesus has and will give Himself for the benefit of others (20:24-28).

A final incident illustrates. As Jesus leaves Jericho to go up to Jerusalem and the cross, He hears two blind men, almost drowned out by the crowd (20:29-34). Despite the heaviness of His own heart as Jesus takes what He knows will be His last journey, Christ stops. And He asks the blind men, "What do you want Me to do for you?"

This is greatness in Jesus' kingdom: to serve God's little ones, our fellow believers, and live with them in such a way that we encourage them to eager, spontaneous responsiveness to the voice of our Lord.

WORD STUDIES

Who is the *greatest* in the kingdom of heaven? (18:1) The Greek word *meizon* is the comparative, "to a greater degree," rather than the superlative, "greatest." It is translated "greatest" in our versions because it was frequently used as a superlative in ordinary speech in the first century. What is tragic here, however, is that the disciples were evidently thinking about which of them would have the greater office when Jesus' kingdom came. What Jesus goes on to do is what each of us must do in our own lives: He shifts the focus from public to personal achievement, from office to character. How different our priorities are to be from the priorities of people of the world!

Whoever *humbles* himself like this child (18:4). The Greek verb is from the root *tapeinos.* In Greek culture the "humble" were the powerless, and to be powerless was a shameful thing. In the NT, however, *tapeinos* is nearly always used in a positive sense, to represent our proper estimate of ourselves in relation to God. We acknowledge our dependence and our powerlessness before Him, and humbly submit to His words. It is this the incident illustrates. Christ has presented Himself to Israel as her Messiah. But the crowds hold back, taking it upon themselves to stand in judgment on the Son of God. What a contrast with the child, who simply heard and responded. Both a childlike sense of dependence and a willingness to respond are to mark our relationship with God.

But if anyone *causes* one of these little ones . . . *to sin* (18:6). In this verse and in verses 8 and 9, the Greek word "cause to sin" is *skandalon*; it simply means something that trips a person up. The NIV and RSV actually paraphrase *skandalon* as "cause to sin." This is too narrow, for as one commentator observes, "One can be 'tripped up' as much by a disparaging attitude, a lack of concern . . . or a refusal to forgive, as a 'temptation to sin.' "

While Jesus' references to the hand, foot, and eye are figurative (5:29-30), the mention of eternal fire adds intensity here. Jesus is not saying that the saved are in danger of being lost, but that living with others in such a way as to trip them up spiritually is no minor offense! It is bad enough to send a person into hellfire!

How carefully we must guard the quality of "little childness" in our brothers and sisters in the Lord.

Again, I tell you that if two of you on earth agree about *anything you ask for* (18:19). The Greek phrase *peri pantos pragmatos* is, literally, "concerning any matter." In this context this verse is not a prayer promise; in fact, it is not about prayer at all. Jesus has called for conflict between disciples to be resolved by a reconciliation process defined in 18:15-17. When reconciliation is impossible because the person at fault "refuses to listen" the case is to be submitted to binding arbitration (18:18). The "two or three of you" in 18:19-20 are those set aside by the church to investigate the case and make a determination. The presence of Jesus in this process is assured, and the determination of the "court" will be ratified, "done for you," by Christ's Father in heaven.

Not seven times, but *seventy-seven times* (18:22). The rabbis had come to the conclusion that a person should be forgiven three times for a repeated sin. But not a fourth! Thus Peter's offer of forgiving up to seven times was generous indeed! Christ's use of 77 times (or perhaps 70 x 7) is not intended as a limit on forgiveness, but to show that forgiveness should be extended without limit or restraint.

If you want to be *perfect,* go, sell your possessions (19:21). The wealthy young man who asked Jesus about what he could do to obtain eternal life was sincere. We know this because the Greek construction "If you want" assumes the condition to be true: "Since then you want to be perfect."

But what does it mean to "be perfect"? The Greek word, *teleios,* means "to be complete, to reach a goal, to be mature." Its OT cognates, *tamim* and *kalil,* do not suggest sinlessness but do imply legal blamelessness and moral uprightness. The thought here is that if the young man wishes to be completely faithful to the Old Covenant, he must give away his wealth.

Why this strange demand? Note that Jesus' reply to the initial question lists commands on the "second tablet" of the Law—those which have to do with a man's relationship with other human beings. Christ's command shifts the focus to the "first tablet" — to commands that have to do with man's relationship with God. The first of those commands is "You shall have no other gods before Me" (Ex.

20:3). Yet when Jesus, Israel's God enfleshed, says " 'Sell your possessions and give to the poor.' . . . The young man . . . went away sad" (19:21-22).

Just because a person is thoughtful, kind, and generous is not evidence that God is first in his life. The real test comes when we are asked to surrender, not our surplus, but everything!

The rulers of the Gentiles lord it over them, and their high officials *exercise authority* over them (20:25). Jesus does not reject the right of secular authority to rule over ordinary citizens. He does, however, mean that the structures utilized to govern in the secular world cannot be transferred and applied by Christian leaders to relationships within the body of Christ.

THE PASSAGE IN DEPTH

The Greatest in the Kingdom of Heaven (18:1-9). See the in-depth commentary on Mark 9:33-50, and the parallel passage in Luke 9:46-50.

The Parable of the Lost Sheep (18:10-14). See the Word Study of Luke 15:7.

A Brother Who Sins against You (18:15-19). See the Word Study on Matt. 18:19, above.

The Parable of the Unmerciful Servant (18:21-35). See the Word Study on Matt. 18:22, above.

Divorce (19:1-15). See also relevant passages Matt. 5:31-32 and 1 Cor. 7.

Background. This passage has been the focus of much study, for two reasons. First, it touches on an issue of great significance for individuals and those with pastoral responsibilities. Second, the passage contains terms whose meanings are debated not only in our time but in Jesus' day as well.

The debate in Jesus' time hinged on the meaning of two Hebrew words appearing in Deut. 24:1, the lone OT verse that deals directly with divorce: "If a man marries a woman who becomes displeasing to him because he finds something indecent about her, and he writes her a certificate of divorce, gives it to her, and sends her from his house."

Separately the two Hebrew words are relatively easy to understand. The first, *'erwat*, indicates some unchastity, while the second, *dabar*, simply means "way" or "thing." One major group of interpreters, the Shammaites, understood the two words to form an inseparable phrase and so took Deut. 24:1 to indicate that divorce was appropriate only for "some

[morally] unseemly thing."

The other major group of interpreters, the Hillelites, argued that the words must be considered separately. Thus, divorce was appropriate in the case of unchastity or if any of a wife's "ways" (*dabar*) were displeasing to her husband.

It is important to realize that neither of these schools of thought was primarily concerned with making divorce either "easy" or "hard." The sages were deeply interested in understanding just what Deuteronomy implied, and in developing *halakah*, "rules of conduct" that reflected and expanded on its meaning. Also, there were other mechanisms in OT times that discouraged divorce, and divorce was not in fact a major social problem in the first century.

The two major deterrents to divorce in the first century were (1) social pressure, and (2) cost. Socially, divorce in first-century Judaism carried a stigma for both wife and husband. Economically, divorce could carry a terrible price. When a husband divorced his wife, he had to give her a sum of money prescribed in the marriage contract. In addition the husband had to add to this amount, and assume liability for any perishable goods his wife brought into the marriage. During the marriage all these goods were under the husband's control, and an economic asset. Upon divorce, they were to be restored to her, along with any gifts from the husband or the father which had been given unconditionally to the wife and thus were classified as property "over which the husband has no control."

Because in Judaism the husband alone was able to write a writ of divorce, some husbands who were unwilling to return the wife's assets simply refused to live with them — and refused to return their property. In such cases first-century rabbinical courts pressured the husband to grant the required writ.

Interestingly, a recent article in the February 10, 1990 issue of the *Jerusalem Post* decried the fact that "thousands of women are trapped because of abuses of Halakah and flaws in the rabbinical courts which have jurisdiction over marriage and divorce." According to the article by Beth Uval some 8,000 to 10,000 Israeli women are trapped and cannot remarry because their husbands refuse to grant them a divorce. By withholding consent, some men in Israel blackmail their wives for thousands of dollars to agree to a divorce.

Divorce, then and now, in first-century Judaism and modern Israel, was a right of the husband, although the woman's interests were (theoretically at least) protected by the cost of dissolving the marriage partnership and by social pressure.

However we understand the interaction between Jesus and the Pharisees who came to question Him, we must not read the issue in contemporary debate as one hinging on "easy" vs. "difficult" divorce. Instead the issue was strictly one of interpretation of a Scripture on which important *halakah* was based.

Interpretation. Two elements of context are vital if we are to understand what is being said here. The first is the biblical context. Matthew is developing the theme of greatness in God's kingdom. In this context, the Pharisees represent the view that spiritual superiority is a matter of keeping, in every detail, the Law of God revealed by Moses and interpreted over the ages by the sages.

The second element is the historical context. The Pharisees who came to Jesus were not asking about divorce per se, but were raising an issue of interpretation. By keeping these two points in view, we can trace the argument of the passage and be protected from the tendency to interpret not the passage as a whole but verses or phrases taken out of context.

What emerges when we view the passage in keeping with these two contextual issues? The Pharisees come to Jesus and ask, "Is it lawful for a man to divorce his wife for any and every reason?" (19:3) The question clearly is technical, one which will force Jesus to identify either with the school of Shammai or of Hillel. The question also is typical, for to the Pharisee "lawfulness" is the key to greatness in God's sight.

Strikingly, Jesus ignores the issue of lawfulness, and goes back to Creation to establish a principle (19:4-6). God's original intent was that marriage be a lifelong union, a covenant relationship. When a couple unites in marriage they become "one flesh," joined in such a way that they share everything in their journey together through life. It follows then that the "lawfulness" of divorce is not really at issue, in so far as understanding God's will is concerned. It also follows that the sages, who established themselves as rabbinical courts "which have jurisdiction over marriage and divorce" in fact have no jurisdiction. In this context it is clear that Jesus' words, "Let man not separate," are not directed to a couple contemplating divorce. They are directed instead to those Pharisees who assume that the sages must interpret the Scriptures and rule on the validity of what is in fact a private issue, to be determined by those who are involved in the marriage.

This answer did not please the Pharisees, who misunderstood and blurted out, "Why then . . . did Moses command that a man give his wife a certificate of divorce?" (19:7) Christ's answer is significant: God permitted divorce, although it clearly is not His will that marriages be dissolved. The reason Jesus gives is that God in effect gave Israel a law through Moses which represented a lower standard than His ideal "because your hearts were hard" (19:8). That is, God knew that sinful human beings would at times so distort a relationship He intended to be healing and constructive that it would become destructive and harmful.

It follows then that divorce and remarriage (for subsequent remarriage was always assumed in ancient and first-century Judaism) fall short of God's ideal and thus involve sin, at least in the "falling short" sense implied by the Hebrew *hata'* and the Greek *hamartia*. So remarriage does involve adultery—and yet God's Law itself provides for a divorce which leads to remarriage! While it remains unclear what the so-called "exception clause"—"except for marital unfaithfulness [*porneia*]" (19:9)—may mean, it clearly does not change Jesus' main point. Divorce and remarriage involve "sin," and yet God provides for them in His own Law.

Remembering that the issue here is not really divorce but of the Pharisees' view of religion, we need to ask what Jesus' response does to their position. What Jesus has done is, very simply, to show (1) that God's intent and will cannot be discerned by the painful process of analyzing and reanalyzing the Law to develop rules of conduct. In fact, using this approach the Pharisees asked the wrong question about divorce, and missed entirely the truth that the Pentateuch reveals about God's will. (2) In fact, Jesus rejects the whole "rule focused" approach of the Pharisees, and shows them decisively that the way of legalism is not a path that leads to spiritual superiority.

The disciples, like many Christian interpreters through the ages, missed the point and

thought that Jesus was issuing a new rabbinical ruling: "No divorce" (Matt. 19:10-12). Jesus simply points out that there are a variety of reasons for remaining single, but His teaching reaffirms a difficult standard that "The one who can accept this [singleness] should accept it." Marriage is to be a lifelong relationship and must be approached in this way. Yet, if for reason of the hardness of heart of one or both parties the relationship becomes destructive, it is Jesus Himself who explains the rationale on which the option to divorce may be exercised (19:8).

A final incident included here by the Evangelist Matthew drives his central message

	Adultery	**Prostitution (Fornication)**
OT	*nā' ap*	*zānâh*
NT	*moicheia*	*porneia*
differences	usually refers to men	usually refers to women
	relations with a married person not spouse	relations outside of marriage
	not a professional prostitute	often a professional prostitute
	death penalty appropriate	death penalty not appropriate
similarities	both are forbidden by God	
	both are used figuratively to represent spiritual and moral unfaithfulness in God's people	
	both merit and will receive divine punishment	

home (19:13-15). Jesus welcomes "little children" and announces that "the kingdom of heaven belongs to such as these." Even the most rigorous Pharisee would never imagine that "little children" were subject to Moses' Law, much less to the strict interpretation of that Law which they imposed on themselves. Little children did not relate to God through the Law, but in a much more direct and personal way.

And, Jesus proclaims, it is to "such as these" that the kingdom of heaven belongs: not those who approach God as the Pharisees and sages, by diligent attempts to keep rules drawn from Scripture but made by men. Rather, those who exercise personal faith and commitment to Jesus become children of the King.

Much confusion exists over the exact meaning of *porneia*, rendered "marital unfaithfulness" in the NIV's version of Matthew 19:9's so-called "exception clause." The chart on page 72 summarizes the OT's and NT's most basic use of this term and its OT cognate.

Application. This passage is an important one. It deals with an issue which brings pain to many in our day, for divorce and remarriage are much misunderstood in the modern Christian community. No one wants to promote "easy" divorce; surely Jesus' words cannot be understood in this way. Yet too often Jesus' words are interpreted in a Pharisaical manner, as if Christ was imposing more rigid restrictions than those imposed by rabbinical courts. How tragic when our ecclesiastical courts hurl Jesus' words, "Let man not separate," at a hurting couple rather than realize that those words are addressed to religious leaders, denying them the right to stand in judgment on what is undoubtedly one of the most painful and personal ordeals we humans can experience. Surely, if others were to stand in judgment on a couple contemplating divorce, some process would have been provided in OT law. Instead, the Law simply called for the husband to write a bill of divorce. This written bill was proof the marriage had ended, and that the wife was free to marry again.

It was totally unnecessary for the sages of Israel to intrude in this private process, although it could be and at times was perverted and used against the innocent. The fact that they did intrude, with the intent not of ministering to the hurting couple or saving the marriage but rather with the intent of determining

what was "lawful," reveals the very mind-set toward the spiritual realm which Jesus so often confronted and rejected out of hand.

Perhaps the most important thing we can learn from this passage is the terrible danger posed by legalism, which slinks into our fellowships too in the guise of piety, and robs us of that sense of God's forgiving and restoring grace which is central in our faith.

The Rich Young Man (19:16-30). See the in-depth commentary on Mark 10:17-31, and the parallel passage in Luke 18:18-30.

The Parable of Workers in the Vineyard (20:1-16).

Background. In NT times many Jews earned their living by working on land owned by others. Various categories of such workers are mentioned in the literature of the first and second centuries A.D. There was the *'aris*, who gave the landowner about half of what the land produced as his share. The *hokker* was also a tenant, but one who gave the landlord a fixed fee rather than a share of the corp. The *sokher* paid a cash rental; the *shattal* was a hired planter who received half the crop and a percentage of any improvements he made on the owner's land. The *shkhir* was a hired hand who received room and board, and was paid when he left after a period of time which extended from a week to seven years, although three years was the normal period. The *ikkar* was also an employee, but apparently an indentured farm worker who was considered in some sense part of the family.

The workers we meet in this parable of Jesus are *po'el*, day laborers who worked from sunrise to sunset, and were given food plus a day's wage by the landowner. The closest modern equivalent is the migrant worker, who follows the harvest from place to place, hoping for enough seasonal work to keep himself and his family alive.

While the religious in Israel lived up to their obligation to the *po'el*, and some even provided both food and wage in advance, land owners were not noted for their generosity. This is reflected in an interesting incident reported in the Mishnah (B.M. VII:1):

It happened once that Rabbi Johanan ben Mathia said to his son: go out and hire us some po'alim. He went and made an agreement with them that he would provide them their meals. When he came back, his father said to him: My son, even if you prepare them a banquet worthy of Solomon in all his glory you will not have discharged your duty, for they are the sons of Abraham, Isaac and Jacob. So (if you want to protect yourself) go to them before they start work and get them to stipulate that they will not hold you responsible for anything more than bread and pulse [vegetables].

Surely everyone who heard Jesus tell the Parable of Workers in the Vineyard was familiar both with the lot of the *po'el* and the attitude of wealthy landowners to them. Thus Jesus' story must have made an even greater impact on them than the story does on us today.

Interpretation. As the familiar story unfolds, we see some workers hired at sunrise and sent to work in the vineyard. The pay agreed on, a denarius, was a silver coin that under Rome had a stable value for decades. It was equivalent to one day's wage for a laborer.

As the day passed the owner of the vineyard returned again and again to the marketplace, and each time enlisted a few more workers. These he promised to pay "whatever is right" (20:4).

When the workday ended at sunset, the owner set up a table and doled out the day's wage. The workers around the table must have been stunned as they saw men who had worked only an hour or two given a full day's wage! This was totally out of character with the way landowners treated *po'el*.

At the same time, the owner's generosity raised the expectations of those who had worked the full day. Surely if it were "right" to pay those who hardly contributed a full day's pay, they, who had worked through the heat of the day, would surely receive much more than a mere denarius. But when their turn came, all they received was the single, silver coin they had agreed on with the owner

that morning. We can surely understand why they began to complain (no doubt loudly, as is common in that culture!) that the owner was being unfair.

The point of the parable is summed up in Jesus' report of the owner's words: "Don't I have the right to do what I want with my own money? Or are you envious because I am generous?" (20:15)

If we take the owner in the parable to represent God, which Jesus surely intends (20:1), the point Christ makes is clear. God relates to human beings on the basis of His generosity, not on the basis of what a man or woman deserves.

The stunning implication in this parable is that in doing this God is right.

Jesus' hearers, even His disciples, would hardly have understood how this could be. Only after the cross and resurrection would Christ's followers look back and realize that through His death Jesus paid the price of sin, and so freed the Father to be righteous and yet act toward human beings in complete generosity and grace.

Application. This story is particularly valuable to those of us who fall into the trap of seeking to please God by working harder than others. It is not that zeal to serve God is wrong. It is simply that "working harder" is no path to greatness in the kingdom of heaven.

In everything in our Christian lives, we are dependent on the grace and generosity of God. When we truly understand and experience that grace, we will dedicate ourselves to serve the Lord. But we will never assume, as the workers in Jesus' parable, that we deserve anything from the hands of our loving God.

A Mother's Request (20:20-28). See the in-depth commentary on Mark 10:32-45 and the parallel passages in Luke 18:31-34 and Luke 22:24-30.

Two Blind Men Receive Sight (20:29-34). See the in-depth commentary on Mark 10:46-52, and the parallel passage in Luke 18:35-43.

MATTHEW 21–23
Confrontation

EXPOSITION

Jesus is welcomed by the Jerusalem crowds, and hailed as the Messiah. But the accolades of common people incense the religious/political leaders, who are threatened by His popularity. They renew their attacks, desperately trying to trap Christ into some statement that will erode His popularity or incriminate Him with their Roman overlords. Jesus not only silences each challenge, but turns on His accusers. His parables expose their selfish motives and their fate. In a powerful summary, Jesus pronounces woes on the Pharisees and teachers of the Law who hypocritically emphasize religious externals that mask the greed, wickedness, and selfishness which mar their own character. Each of the events in this section moves toward Christ's culminating denunciation of the Pharisees, and His tears for a Jerusalem so blinded by legalism that it cannot — will not — recognize Him as the Savior.

The sequence begins with the triumphal entry (21:1-11). Jesus, fulfilling a prophecy of Zechariah, enters the city to shouts acclaiming Him the "Son of David," a messianic title. Proceeding to the temple, Jesus drives out the money changers and merchants who operate there under license from the high priest (21:12-17). In a strongly symbolic act Jesus curses a fig tree which, like contemporary Israel, appears vital and alive and yet is fruitless (21:18-22).

When Jesus returns to Jerusalem the aroused leaders confront Him. These men, who lay claim to the right to interpret and apply Moses' Law to Jews everywhere, demand that Christ explain the source of His authority. Instead, Jesus poses a question the leaders are afraid to answer, thus exposing the emptiness of their claim to be the interpreters of God's Word (21:23-27). Now comes a series of devastating parables. In the first, Jesus affirms that the despised "tax collectors and prostitutes" who responded to the ministry of John the Baptist will enter the kingdom of God, leaving the "respectable" spiritual leaders behind (21:28-32). In the second, Jesus exposes the true motives of the leaders: they want to administer Israel not for God's glory, but for their own profit and power. They are so grimly determined to resist God's rightful claim to His people's allegiance that they will gladly kill God's own Son (21:33-46). In the third parable, Jesus looks into the future. Israel, whom God first invited to His banquet, has rejected Him and will in turn be rejected by the Lord, in favor of "anyone" who is willing to respond (22:1-14).

Jesus' attack on the religious elite moves them to frantic action. The Pharisees attempt to force Jesus either to express support for the right of the hated Romans to collect taxes—and thus turn the crowds against Him—or to speak out against taxes—in which case the Romans might arrest and condemn Him. Christ deftly avoids this most famous of the traps set for Him (22:15-22). He then shows up the shallowness of the Sadducees' grasp of Scripture when this group tries to trip Him up with a theological puzzler long used to confuse those who believed in the resurrection (22:23-33).

Suddenly the focus shifts from intellectual game playing to truly significant issues. What is the greatest command? To love God completely, and to love others as yourself (22:34-40). And, whose Son is the Christ prophesied in the OT? He is—He must be—the very Son of God (22:41-46).

The parables of chapter 21 indicted the Pharisees and teachers of the Law. The crude traps set by the Pharisees and Sadducees, reported in chapter 22, displayed their superficial approach to faith. Now, in chapter 23, Jesus pronounces the divine verdict on these religious pretenders. In grim, severe tones Jesus enumerates seven "woes"— seven exclamations denouncing the religious leaders for attitudes and actions that will exclude them forever from the kingdom of God's dear Son (23:1-36). The denunciation is emphatic. And yet the last few verses reveal that Christ's heart is breaking for the city and for the people He is driven to condemn (23:37-39).

WORD STUDIES

Daughter of Zion (21:5). The idiomatic phrase simply means "Zion," a poetic name for the city of Jerusalem. For other uses of the idiom see Isa. 22:4; 47:1; Ps. 45:12.

Hosanna to the Son of David! (21:9) *Hosanna* is an exclamation and prayer meaning "Save!" which had become an exclamation of praise. The phrase "Son of David" is a messianic title, making it clear that in the Triumphal Entry Jesus was being acclaimed as coming king, with the expectation that He would deliver the Jews from Roman rule.

The whole city was *stirred* (21:10). The word *eseisthe* is "shaken," as by an earthquake. A wave of wild enthusiasm swept Jerusalem when Jesus entered the city. The fact that in just a few days cries of "Crucify Him!" (27:22) echoed in the same streets alerts us. Enthusiasm is no substitute for commitment.

They *discussed it among themselves* (21:25). The single word translated by this phrase is *dielogizonto,* they "reasoned with themselves." The imperfect tense implies an ongoing process, a continuous debate about how to answer Jesus' challenge. Two things are significant. Men who claimed religious authority in Israel did not seek God's guidance,

but reasoned "with themselves." And, their unwillingness to accept the responsibility of the authority they claimed to answer difficult civil and religious questions, showed how hollow their claims were.

He *changed his mind* and went (21:29). The word *metameletheis* means to be sorry. The verb is found only five times in the NT: Matt. 21:29, 32; 27:3; 2 Cor. 7:8; and Heb. 7:21. It is very different from a similar word, *metanoia,* which is repentance as a change of mind and direction. The phrase "and went" is key, for this sorrow did lead to action. He was sorry— and went to the vineyard as his father had told him to do! Compare this with Judas, who was sorry (27:3), but rather than turn to Jesus for forgiveness remained mired in self-pity and remorse. Feeling sorry is good. But unless a person adds "and went," the sorrow is essentially meaningless.

Sent his servants *to those who had been invited* to the banquet *to tell them to come* (22:3). The Greek phrase is *kalesai tous keklemoneous,* "to call the called." It reflects the Jewish custom of sending a second invitation to persons who had already been invited to a celebration. How appropriate. In Abraham God had invited Israel to be His chosen people. Now in Christ God called the invited to Him again—and they stubbornly refused! It's the same today. In Christ God has invited the entire world to come to Him. When the Spirit makes that invitation personal, convicting an individual and calling him or her to salvation, he *must not* reject God's call.

They *paid no attention* . . . mistreated them and killed them (22:5-6). The verse describes two reactions to God's invitation. *Amelesantes* means to neglect or to be unconcerned, while *hubrisan* means to insult, to treat in an arrogant, spiteful manner intended to publicly insult and humiliate. When you and I give God's "second invitation" to others, some will respond. But we can also expect two other reactions: indifference and hostility. Each of these responses is an insult to the One who invites all humanity to a banquet paid for by the blood of His Son.

Which is *the greatest commandment* in the Law? (22:36) The *entole megale* is "the great commandment." The question is significant because the Jewish scribes had identified 248 positive commands and 365 negative commands in the OT, for a total of some 613 separate and distinct commands. The question thus was, "Jesus, which of the many commands in the Law comes first with You?" Christ's identification of love for God as first, and love for others second, lays the foundation of Paul's developed theology of Law and Love. In Romans Paul will say the Christian's sole obligation to others is to "love one another." As a person who loves his neighbor will do nothing to harm that neighbor, love fulfills the Mosaic Law, for that law rules against actions which do others harm (Rom. 13:8-10). St. Augustine sums up this same point, saying, "Love God, and do what you please."

Jesus' answer reminds us that in our own walk with God we must not major on the minors, as the religious leaders of Christ's time did. Let's love God, and others. And let these great principles shape our motives, our character, and our daily lives.

Whose *Son* is He? (22:41) The word *huios*, son, is often used in extended ways. Here it is used in the sense of "descendant"—but with the added significance of "heir." The OT promised that God would exalt a particular

descendant of David and give Him an everlasting rule over an Israel restored to her ancient glory (2 Sam. 7:11-16; Isa. 9:6-7). This is this person whom the Jewish people expected and referred to as "the son of David." But in Jewish thought a descendant was considered dependent on and thus inferior to his father/ancestor. So custom demanded that a son show appropriate respect by addressing his father/ancestor as "lord." Christ's puzzler points to Ps. 110:1, long acknowledged as a messianic psalm, in which David reverses this entrenched tradition and addresses the Messiah—his own descendant—as "Lord." The necessary conclusion is that David's messianic heir is greater than David, which lends direct scriptural support to Jesus' oft-stated claim to be the Son of God!

The religious authorities refused to reply when Christ challenged them to explain how David's Son and Heir could be greater than David. They knew the answer; the Scripture and its implications were clear. They refused to reply because they *did not like* the answer. How tragic today too when people understand but simply do not like what the Bible says.

Nor are you to be called *"teacher"* (23:10). The word *kathegetai* is found only in this verse in the NT. Some take it to distinguish between a "master teacher" and an ordinary teacher; a teacher with the highest authority, and one who instructs others in the master's interpretations. If so, this leaves room for you and me, who seek not to be authorities ourselves, but to share as accurately as we can the authoritative Word of "the Teacher," Jesus Christ.

You *hypocrites* (23:13, 15, 23, 25, 27, 29). The word *hupokritai* originally meant to play a part on the stage. Soon it took on the implications of conscious fraud: a hypocrite pretends to be something he isn't; he wears a mask; he hides his real self by words and actions intended to deceive. There was no more devastating accusation the Lord Jesus could make against the religious leaders who paraded their piety to win the praise of men. There is only one antidote to the nagging sin of hypocrisy. We must care supremely for the approval of God. When we are truly committed to Him, the person others see will be the person we truly are.

Woe (23:13, 15-16, 23, 25, 27, 29). The word *ouai* is an exclamation, a cry both of grief and of denunciation.

To win a single *convert* (23:15). The word *proseluton,* or proselyte, comes from a root that means alien or newcomer. The first century knew two kinds of Jewish proselytes: one, "of the gate," admired Judaism and its moral vision, and is often spoken of in the NT as a "God fearer." The other, "of righteousness," was circumcized and bound himself to keep the Law, thus actually becoming a Jew. But here Jesus speaks of the Pharisees as driven to win converts to *Phariseeism!* They were motivated by *party spirit.* What a reminder. Our mission isn't to win others to a denomination or our congregation, but to Jesus.

Woe to you, *blind* guides (23:16). The Pharisees are condemned as "blind" five times in this chapter (23:16-17, 19, 24, 26). The Greek word *typhos* like the Hebrew *'iwwer* is used both literally and metaphorically. The prophets especially use "blind" to indicate spiritual insensitivity. Spiritual blindness is both an evidence of sin and a divine judgment imposed on sinners (Isa. 29:9-10). Yet the prophets look ahead to a time of conversion for the humble, when "the deaf will hear the words of the scroll, and out of gloom and darkness the eyes of the blind will see" (Isa. 29:18).

The Pharisees were "blind guides" because they refused to accept the clearly visible evidence of Christ's Messiahship. As a result of their refusal to see, their ability to see is also taken away from them. Those who will not believe, all too soon find themselves unable to believe.

THE PASSAGE IN DEPTH

The Triumphal Entry (21:1-11). In-depth discussion in parallel passage, Luke 19:28-40. See also Mark 11:1-10; John 12:12-19.

Jesus at the Temple (21:12-17). In-depth discussion in parallel passage, Luke 19:45-48. See also Mark 11:15-19.

The Fig Tree Withers (21:18-22). See also Mark 11:12-14, 20-25.

Background. In Palestine cultivated trees produced fruit for some ten months of the year, and were so important the ideal called for every family to have its own fig tree as well as its own vineyard (1 Kings 4:25). Even so, at Passover time when Jesus saw and approached a leafed-out fig tree as He traveled toward Jerusalem, "it was not the season for figs" (Mark 11:13). Why approach the tree when it was not fig season? Because in early varieties, the fruit often emerges even before the leaves, and in all varieties fruit appears *within* the leaves.

Interpretation. In Matthew the fig tree incident occurs directly *after* the cleansing of the temple. In Mark's account the incident brackets the cleansing of the temple: Jesus predicts the withering of the fruitless tree on the way to the temple, and the next day when the little company returns to the city the tree has already shriveled and died. It's clear in both accounts that the two events are closely linked.

That linkage is made clear by the "law of the fig tree," noted above. Leaves and fruit appear together. If we apply that law to Israel, we see that God intends spiritual fruit to be produced by true religion. Thus Jesus says, "My house shall be called a house of prayer for all nations" (Mark 11:17). But instead of such fruit the greed of Israel's leaders had made the temple Court of the Gentiles a marketplace; indeed a "den of robbers" (11:17). Worship at the temple, so famous throughout the world, so bustling and apparently vital, was as void of spiritual fruit as the green-leafed tree was empty of figs.

As in Isaiah's time, God "looked for good grapes" but found the yield only "bad." Although the Lord delighted in Israel, when He "looked for justice, [He] saw bloodshed; for righteousness, but heard cries of distress" (Isa. 5:7).

There is another parallel between Isaiah and the fig tree incident. God warned through the prophet that He would make His fruitless vineyard a wasteland (5:6). Just so, as the fig tree withered, all too soon the city which rejected Jesus would rebel against Roman rule, and in A.D. 70 suffer complete destruction. The temple would lie in ruins, and the people who worshiped there not only were driven from the site, but forbidden by Rome even to approach it.

As far as interpretation is concerned, then, the fig tree represents first-century Israel; its fruitless state the emptiness of its legalistic approach to religion; its withering the doom of the nation that would not welcome its Deliverer with faith.

Application. The disciples looked at the withered fig tree with amazement, impressed by the power Jesus displayed, but ignoring the meaning of the act. They were not concerned about the symbolism, but about the power. They did not ask, "What does this act mean?" but "How did the fig tree wither so quickly?" (21:20) — in essence, "How can *we* do such marvels too?"

Jesus uses a familiar figure in His answer: that of a mountain cast into the sea (Matt. 17:20). In essence Jesus dismisses the marvel of the fig tree by suggesting an even greater marvel, and so suggests that *all* answers to prayer are marvels, for they depend on the power of God rather than on anything intrinsic in man. Thus "if you believe, you will receive whatever you ask for in prayer" (21:22).

But doesn't this make the marvel dependent on *our belief?* Not at all. What Christ is doing is expanding on the theme of faith — a faith lacking in Israel, and demonstrated in the withering of the fig tree. For "faith" and "believing" in the NT are expressions that indicate a sincere trust in God, and a genuine relationship with Him. Christ's relationship with the Father made the miracle of answered prayer not only a possibility, but a certainty. And when our prayers grow out of a genuine relationship with the Lord, our prayers too can be expressions not of uncertain hope, but of real confidence that we "will receive."

Why then does Mark in telling of this same incident add "and when you stand praying, if you hold anything against anyone, forgive him, so that your Father in heaven may forgive you your sins"? (Mark 11:25) For the same reason that fig trees in leaf must bear fruit. A genuine faith-relationship in Jesus will bear fruit in our lives, and we will treat others as God treats us — in grace and forgiveness. The genuineness of our faith is displayed in the fruit that relationship with God produces in our lives. Power in prayer grows out of this fruit-filled relationship with the Lord.

The Parable of the Two Sons (21:28-32).

Background. Jesus told this parable immediately after being challenged by Israel's religious leaders to explain the source of His authority. He then posed a question which the leaders refused to answer, thus in effect abdicating the authority they themselves claimed as the interpreters of God's will for Israel (21:23-27). In this parable Jesus presses the leaders further. They not only lack *authority* in Israel. They have no *personal relationship* with God!

Interpretation. The two sons in Jesus' story represent the "tax collectors and prostitutes" who responded to the call of John the Baptist to repent, and "you," the leaders of Israel. The Father here is, of course, God. It is important that in a religious state, as Israel was, tax collectors and prostitutes were considered the dregs of society. They were despised by the majority, and especially by the very religious. A truly pious Jew in first-century Jerusalem would move out of the way so that he might not be touched even by the shadow of a known tax collector or prostitute! Thus the religious/social gap between the two groups Jesus refers to in His parable was truly vast.

The first son in the story, by refusing to respond to the father's command to go into the vineyard, repudiated his authority. But later, by changing his mind and going into the vineyard, he actually submitted to his father. The second son responded to the father's command by saying, "I will." Thus he professed to recognize the authority of the father. But when "he did not go," he showed his profession was meaningless.

The chief priests and elders professed to be sons of God. But when John came calling them to turn from legalism to real righteousness, they refused. Even when they saw sinners converted, they themselves refused to respond. The inescapable conclusion is that even the worst sinners who respond to God's call are far closer to God than Israel's religious leaders!

This is one of the most devastating of Jesus' attacks on the leadership. They not only have no authority *from* God. They have no relationship *with* Him!

Profession without obedience is proof of alienation.

Application. There are four different possibilities concerning relationship with God.

(1) A person can profess relationship with

God, and submit to Him. This is the ideal toward which we all want to work. (2) A person can profess relationship with God, but in daily life fail to submit to Him. This was the condition of the spiritual leaders of Jesus' time. We would call this kind of person a hypocrite, whose concern is to look pious rather than to be holy. (3) A person can make bad decisions, and choose to sin despite knowing God's will. But that person has the option, like the "tax collectors and prostitutes" of Jesus' time, of changing his mind and submitting to the Lord. (4) A person can refuse throughout his or her life to submit to God.

Perhaps 2 and 3, the kind of person highlighted in Jesus' stories, have the most relevance to us today. A churchgoer may profess by his involvement in religious affairs to have a relationship with God. But be warned. Unless profession is accompanied by a submission to God that is expressed in obedience, a person is no child of the Father's.

But how wonderfully the first son speaks to our heart. In the past we may have rejected God. But the door to sonship remains open. We can decide, now, to submit to Him. And in submitting to Him and claiming the promises God gives us in Christ, the worst of sinners can become a child of God.

The Parable of the Wedding Banquet (22:1-14). See Luke 14:16-24 for a similar, but not quite parallel, parable.

Background. Banquets were an important social occasion, and in the first century were defined by a fixed etiquette. The wealthy employed an expensive cook—who would have to return his fee plus a penalty if his cooking embarrassed the host. Guests might drink undiluted wine from real glass vessels. Guests were invited well in advance, and informed of who else was invited. A second invitation was brought by a messenger, who brought a personal summons to the banquet the day before or even on the day of the feast (see Word Study, Matt. 22:3). Often banquets began early in the day and continued late into the night, or even for several days. This was the case in Jesus' parable: what the king prepared was not "dinner" but *ariston,* "breakfast." As v. 4 shows, the banquet was intended to be a truly significant affair, begun early, and celebrated late into the night and undoubtedly for days to come.

There is evidence that Herod the Great did provide special clothes for guests at some of his banquets. Thus some have seen in rejection of the man "not wearing wedding clothes" (22:11) a metaphor for the righteousness that God must provide if any human being is to stand in His presence. But there is no evidence that it was *common practice* for a host to provide wedding clothes. So it's best to understand this simply as a reference to a person who came unprepared to the wedding, wearing his old or work clothes to the feast—an indication he was indifferent to the significance of the event and unprepared to take part.

There is an interesting parallel in the king's decision to invite "all the people" to fill his banquet hall. At Passover the poor of Jerusalem might be invited to a public feast. And on the death of his father Herod, Archelaus invited "the whole populace" to a banquet.

In first-century Jewish society then, a banquet was a most significant social occasion. This makes the rejection of a king's invitation to such a celebration even more of a rebuff than it might be in our time. To refuse the invitation then was to reject the king and to show contempt for his son, in whose honor the banquet was held.

Interpretation. In the parable, the invited guests represent Israel, while the king who spreads the banquet in honor of his son is God. The parable is divided into two parts. The first part describes the reaction of the invited guests, and the king's response. Some guests (the general population) are indifferent (22:5), and others (the religious leaders) are hostile (22:6). Note that each response constitutes rebellion against the king, and like any monarch of that era, the king sends an army to "destroy those murderers" and he burns their city.

This response has dual historical significance. The OT portrays the Assyrians as God's army, which He leads to discipline His people Israel (Isa. 10:1-5). This image from history past must have been familiar to Jesus' hearers, and some may have sensed a foreshadowing of what was to come. Within a generation God sent another army, the Roman army under Titus, and in A.D. 70 did just what Jesus predicted: "destroy those murderers and burn their city."

The second half of the parable has been viewed as a figure of the Gospel era itself.

Since the invited guests—the people and leaders of Israel—refuse to respond to God's summons, God will summon those who have long traveled the highways of this world, both the good and the bad. But the person not wearing wedding clothes reminds us of an important truth. When we come to God's banquet, we must be prepared to stay. We are not asked to drop in and look around. The tragic fact is that not everyone who shows up at church will have truly responded to God's invitation. The curious still poke their heads in as they pass by. Only those who are committed and who demonstrate commitment by showing up in wedding garments may stay.

Application. The immediate application to Jesus' hearers was a warning of judgment: reject the summons of the King and face His wrath. The extended application for us is bright with hope. God's servants are to stand at the crossroads of their society, inviting all who pass by to the banquet God has prepared for all. We are to extend the invitation to good and bad alike, for God's grace is great enough to encompass all.

The words, "For many are invited, but few are chosen" (22:14), are often listed among the "hard sayings of Jesus." However, the "for" (*gar* in Greek) makes it clear that the saying is intended to sum up the teaching of the whole parable. In context, it indicates that the invitation God extends to humanity is broad: as John 3:16 says, "whoever will" is free to come. But again as Christ's parable, and His experience with Israel and church history itself make clear, far more whosoevers *won't* rather than *will!* The company of the elect—a term used often in Scripture of the aggregate of those who believe—is smaller than the sum of the lost.

Seven Woes Spoken against the Teachers of the Law and the Pharisees (23:1-37). Parallel passages: Mark 12:38-40; Luke 20:45-47.

Background. Jesus introduces this extended denunciation of the "teachers of the law and Pharisees" by making a critical observation: these men "sit in Moses' seat." In the Judaism of Jesus' time, this meant they were obeyed by the common people as Israel's religious authorities.

In this phrase the "and" is *kai*, and here should be understood as "even." Thus "Phari-

see" indicates a theological position, rather than persons. Jesus is speaking of teachers of the Law who operate from the theological stance adopted by the Pharisees.

Moses' seat was the stone seat at the front of the synagogue. It was from this seat that a person recognized in Judaism as an expert in the Law, in NT terms a "rabbi" and in modern Jewish terms a "sage," gave his judgment concerning the application of OT Law and tradition to specific legal and social cases.

In *Foundations of Judaism* (Fortress, 1989) a contemporary Jewish scholar, Jacob Neusser, points out that in Judaism the sage participates in the process of revelation. The Torah (the OT) is *interpreted* in the Mishnah (the oral, but now recorded, commentary on and interpretation of Torah), and the two are *applied* by the sage. Thus Torah, Mishnah, and sage are all necessarily involved in the process of discerning God's will. In Neusser's words, "Scripture, the Mishnah, the sage—all three spoke with equal authority" (p. 119). It is this approach to faith that Jesus indicates when He says "the teachers of the law, even Pharisees, sit in Moses' seat." A radical transformation of OT faith had begun a century or so before Christ, took a distinct form a century after Him, and shaped what we know today as Judaism into a religion that is very different from the faith of the OT.

Jesus' critique points to the weakness of this theological position. Teachers of the Law are in fact fallible, sinful human beings like all others. Yet Neusser rightly observes that developing Phariseeism placed the sage in a unique position. Neusser says, "So in the rabbi, the word of God was made flesh. And out of the union of man and Torah, producing the rabbi as Torah incarnate, was born Judaism, the faith of the Torah: the ever-present revelation and always-open canon" (p. 121). Imposing the burden on mere humans of being "Torah incarnate," Phariseeism produced not humble believers but hypocrisy. No wonder Jesus says to His disciples, "You are not to be called 'Rabbi' " and adds, "nor are you to be called 'teacher,' for you have one Teacher, the Christ"! (23:10)

Many of the Pharisees of Jesus' time were undoubtedly sincere men. But the very essence of their approach to religion made them vulnerable to the weaknesses Christ exposes so starkly in Matt. 23.

Pressured by the necessity to seem more than any human can be, those accepting this position soon do everything "for men to see" (Matt. 6:1-18), and soon become hypocrites: play-actors, masked actors on the religious stage.

But did these teachers of the laws and Pharisees *actually have* spiritual authority? It is best to interpret vv. 2-3a as heavy irony, and translate the aorist *ekathisan* ("sit") as "have sat down" in Moses' seat. God did not give them the position they enjoyed in first-century Judaism: they took it! Thus the words "you must obey and do everything they say" is irony: it reflects the exalted view of the teachers themselves as to their role. In fact, Jesus tells His listeners *not* to do as they do—and they did rigorously keep their own rules—because their teachings bind rather than release men, keeping them from entering the kingdom of God.

JOSEPHUS' DESCRIPTION OF THE PHARISEES

For the present I wish merely to explain that the Pharisees had passed on to the people certain regulations handed down by former generations and not recorded in the laws of Moses, for which reason they are rejected by the Sadducean group. . . . And concerning these matters the two parties came to have controversies and serious differences, the Sadducees having the confidence of the wealthy alone but no following among the populace, while the Pharisees have the support of the masses.

Antiquities 13:297-298

The Pharisees simplify their standard of living, making no concession to luxury. They follow the guidance of that which their doctrine has selected and transmitted as good, attaching the chief importance to the observance of those commandments which it has seen fit to dictate to them. They show respect and deference to their elders, nor do they rashly presume to contradict their proposals.

Though they postulate that everything is brought about by fate, still they do not deprive the human will of the pursuit of what is in man's power, since it was God's pleasure that there should be a fusion and that the will of man with his virtue and vice should be admitted to the council-chamber of fate. They believe that souls have power to survive death and there are rewards and punishments under the earth for those who have led lives of virtue or vice; eternal imprisonment is the lot of evil souls, while the good souls receive an easy passage to a new life.

Because of these views they are, as a matter of fact, extremely influential among the townsfolk; and all prayers and sacred rites of divine worship are performed according to their exposition. This is the great tribute that the inhabitants of the cities, by practicing the highest ideals both in their way of living and in their doctrine, have paid to the excellence of the Pharisees.

Antiquities 18:12-15

Interpretation. Each of the seven woes gives us insight into the effect of lifting up mere men as "living torahs," and into the nature of religious hypocrisy. The word "woe" should be understood as a compassionate but strong judicial condemnation.

■ The first woe (23:13-14): "You shut the kingdom of heaven in men's faces." Chapters 21–22 have revealed these leaders' refusal to accept clear evidence that Jesus is the Messiah—and that they expended every effort to keep the populace from believing in Him (9:33-34; 11:19; 12:1-14, 23-24; 21:15). Unwilling to surrender their positions of power, the teachers of the Law reject the testimony of the Law that points to Jesus as the Christ.

■ The second woe (23:15): "You travel . . . to win a single convert . . . and make him twice as much a son of hell as you." The zeal of first-century Pharisees to win adherents is illustrated in the zeal of the Judaisers, men who later followed Paul everywhere he went and tried to subvert new Christians from the Gospel of grace to a Gospel of law. Christ points to the results: those they win to their position become "twice as much a son of hell." The hypocrisy and legalism of the convert exceeds that of the teacher.

■ **The third woe (23:16-22):** "You, blind guides." The Pharisees clearly misunderstand the Scriptures they claim authority to interpret. In what Jewish scholars have pointed out was an attempt by the rabbis to correct the abuse of oaths and vows, the sages distinguished between binding and nonbinding oaths. Not only were the distinctions they made foolish, but the result was to encourage the use of evasive oaths!

■ **The fourth woe (23:23-24):** "You have neglected the more important matters of the law." The spices here were typically grown in tiny plots in the courtyard of Jewish homes and used to flavor foods. Phariseeism demanded careful attention to tithing every product of the land—even household spices. But Jesus charges these rigorously careful men with a monumental misunderstanding of God's will. To God the central issues of faith are concerned with justice, mercy, and faithfulness, and these the Pharisees ignore.

Jesus sums up in a fascinating and perceptive illustration. Both gnat and camel are unclean animals according to the food laws found in Lev. 11. In effect the Pharisees carefully strain out gnats, but swallow camels—and fail to see the inconsistency! Their misunderstanding of Scripture and of God's will is fundamental and basic.

■ **The fifth woe (23:25-26):** "You clean the outside of the cup and dish." The Pharisees are intent on the externals of religion, and ignore the inner man. In the first century there was a debate between the school of Shammai and the school of Hillel concerning how a dish should be ritually cleansed. Jesus calls this spiritual blindness, for what must be cleansed is not just the cup, but the person who drinks from it. The true spiritual issue is that of inner cleansing from the greed and self-centeredness that make a person morally unacceptable to God.

■ **The sixth woe (23:27-28):** "You are like whitewashed tombs . . . full of hypocrisy and wickedness."

■ **The seventh woe (23:29-32):** "You are the descendants of those who murdered the prophets." Like their forefathers, who rejected and killed the prophets God sent to Israel, this generation too is murderously intent on rejecting God's Word and God's Son.

There is a fascinating V-shaped pattern to Jesus' seven woes, with the point of the V the fourth woe, charging a fundamental failure to understand the central message of Scripture.

Reject Christ	**1**			**7**	Reject prophets
Zeal, but do harm not good	**2**		**6**		Zeal, but do harm not good
Misapply Scripture		**3**	**5**		Misapply Scripture
		4 Misread Scriptures' central message			

Application. The Pharisees and teachers of the Law not only allowed themselves to be exalted as "the authorities" in Judaism, they loved their power and position. They became more concerned with the trappings of faith and with appearances than with personal holiness and personal relationship with God. As a result, they could not hear, or rightly understand, or respond to God's Word when He spoke. And so Jesus' condemnation echoes across the centuries: "Woe to you, teachers of the law, even Pharisees, you hypocrites!" And how that condemnation speaks to us today.

Have we permitted hypocrisy to infect our spiritual life? Do we want spiritual authority for the position and praise and power it brings us? Do we concentrate on externals, so that we can seem more spiritual to others? Is what others think of us so important that we find ourselves pretending a piety we do not feel? If it is, be sure that your own inner corruption will prevent you from hearing and rightly understanding God's Word.

But it need not be so! Jesus in this chapter shows us His better way, in these words: "You are not to be called 'Rabbi,' for you have only one Master and you are all brothers. And do not call anyone on earth 'father,' for you have one Father, and He is in heaven. Nor are you to be called, 'teacher,' for you have one Teacher, the Christ. The greatest among you will be your servant. For whoever exalts himself will be humbled and whoever humbles himself will be exalted (23:8-12).

That better way? Put Jesus first, see others as brothers, and humble yourself to serve them. With Christ exalted, and our brothers' welfare our primary concern, there will be nothing in us to block our hearing, our rightly understanding, and our responding to, God's holy Word.

MATTHEW 24–25
The Future of the Kingdom

EXPOSITION

Matthew has built a strong case. Jesus' birth and miracles show Him to be the Messiah promised by Old Testament prophets and, stunningly, God come in the flesh! But this descendant of David has not fulfilled Israel's expectations. Rather than exercise His power to overthrow Rome and set up a visible, institutional kingdom on earth, Jesus has used that power only to heal the sick. What's more, in His teaching Jesus has spoken only of a hidden kingdom of the heart, marked by an "in secret" relationship with God the Father. This teaching puzzled the crowds. Christ's radical approach to the Scriptures had aroused the fierce hostility of the religious leaders. This hostility peaked in a series of confrontations over Sabbath-keeping and tradition, and ultimately led to Christ's open denunciation of the Pharisees and teachers of the Law as hypocrites.

Before this, however, Christ called on the Twelve who were His disciples to make the critical decision that the Jewish people as a whole had refused to face: Who is this One who has come as the Son of Man? Peter spoke for them all when he answered, "You are the Christ, the Son of the living God!" From this point on the thrust of Jesus' ministry changed. He began to speak of His coming death. And He began to teach His disciples, the future leaders of His church, about greatness and leadership in the secret kingdom to be established at His death.

This flow of Matthew's argument leaves unanswered at least one vital question that His Jewish readers are sure to ask. Christ's parables have set the secret kingdom over and against the institutional kingdom envisioned by the prophets. What, then, has happened to the kingdom the prophets describe? Is that kingdom permanently set aside? And if it is, has not God gone back on His word? Or, perhaps, have the prophets been misunderstood? Is the kingdom described in such graphic, realistic terms simply a metaphor for the hidden kingdom that Jesus will initiate by His death and resurrection?

We come now to a passage that has been understood by some to provide the answer to those questions, although in fact it does not deal directly with a future earthly kingdom. What this passage does deal with is history's end, and the visible, personal return of Jesus to our earth. Certainly many early Christian commentators saw in this passage a way to harmonize OT and NT kingdom revelations. The secret kingdom is initiated by the Resurrection; the visible, institutional kingdom will be initiated by Christ's return. But even here, in these chapters, the focus is not really on the future but rather on how we are to live our lives in view of Christ's certain return.

When Jesus spoke of a coming destruction of the temple, the disciples raised three questions about the future (24:1-3). The questions are answered in reverse order in this chapter. The three questions are: What will be the sign of the end of the age? answered in 24:4-25; What will be the sign of Your coming? answered in 24:26-35; and When will this happen? answered in 24:36-41. Jesus' answers can be summarized. The end of the age will be marked by intense tribulation that will be initiated by the fulfillment of the Daniel 9:27 prophecy of "the abomination that causes desolation" (Matt. 24:15). His own coming will be visible to all, for He will return openly with an army of angels. But as for just when this will happen, no one knows.

The rest of Matthew 24 and all of chapter 25 develop a single theme. Until Jesus does return, God's people are to keep watch, always ready, since Christ may come at any moment (24:42-44). Like servants responsible for the welfare of others, we are to be faithful till Jesus comes (24:45-51). Like bridesmaids waiting to escort the groom to the bride's home, we are to watch, prepared and ready (25:1-13). Like those given resources by an absent master, we are to use what we are and have for His benefit until He returns (25:14-30). One day the King will return. Then the righteous will be welcomed into His presence, while the unrighteous will be rejected, forever (25:31-46).

WORD STUDIES

What will be the sign of Your coming and of *the end of the age*? (24:3) The phrase "end of the age" is used six times in the NT, five of them in Matthew (13:39-40, 49; 24:3; 28:20; Heb. 9:26). In Matthew the phrase clearly refers to the transition from a present state of affairs to the consummation of God's plans for His people.

Three Hebrew phrases current in the first century provide background that helps us understand what the disciples were thinking of when they asked this question. Second-century B.C. Jewish writings portray that which is to follow the "present age," *olam hazzeh.* The next period, beginning with the "days of the Messiah," is the "coming age," *atid labho,* which leads into the "world to come," *olam*

habba. Various views of the length of the messianic period were proposed, ranging from 3 generations to 7,000 years. There is little doubt that when Matthew reports that the disciples asked about the "end of the age" they were in fact referring to Israel's messianic expectations, and were inquiring when Christ intended to fulfill them.

There is also no doubt that these images of the future were rooted in the predictions of the biblical prophets as recorded in the sacred Scriptures, although the prophets' visions were frequently expanded upon. Jewish convert Alfred Edersheim describes some of the views current then in the following excerpt from his classic *The Life and Times of Jesus the Messiah,* p. 443.

CONTEMPORARY JEWISH VIEWS OF THE MESSIANIC AGE

At last, when these distresses have reached their final height, when signs are in the sky, ruin upon earth, and the unburied bodies that cover the ground are devoured by birds and wild beasts, or else swallowed up by the earth, would God send "the king," who would put an end to unrighteousness. Then would follow the last war against Jerusalem, in which God would fight from heaven with the nations, when they would submit to, and own Him. But while in the Book of Enoch and in another work of this same class the judgment is ascribed to God, and the Messiah represented as appearing only afterwards, in the majority of these works the judgment or its execution is assigned to the Messiah.

In the land thus restored to Israel, and under the rule of King Messiah, the new Jerusalem would be the capital, purified from the heathen, enlarged, nay, quite transformed. This Jerusalem had been shown to Adam before his Fall, but after that both it and Paradise had been withdrawn from him. It had again been shown to Abraham, to Moses, and to Ezra. The splendor of this new Jerusalem is described in most glowing language. Of the glorious Kingdom thus instituted, the Messiah would be King, although under the supremacy of God. His reign would extend over the heathen nations. The character of their submission was differently viewed, according to the more or less Judaic standpoint of the writers. Thus, in the book of Jubilees the seed of Jacob are promised possession of the whole earth; they would "rule over all nations according to their pleasure; and after that draw the whole earth unto themselves, and inherit it for ever." In the Assumption of Moses this ascendency of Israel seems to be conjoined with the idea of vengeance upon Rome, although the language employed is highly figurative.

So when you see standing in the holy place "the *abomination that causes desolation*" (24:15). The reference is clearly to an event predicted by Daniel, and mentioned no less than four times in his book (8:13; 9:27; 11:31; 12:11). It has been argued that Daniel was referring to the desecration of the temple by Antiochus Epiphanes, who erected an altar to Zeus in the Jewish temple and sacrificed a pig there in 168 B.C. But clearly Jesus treats the prediction as if its ultimate fulfillment still lies ahead.

Two theories predominate. The first assumes that Jesus is speaking about the fall of Jerusalem to the Romans which took place in A.D. 70. Proponents observe that the Jewish Christians abandoned that city about A.D. 68, and argue that this was in response to Christ's caution to flee (24:16-18). It is very difficult, however, to take the Roman siege, set up outside the city of Jerusalem, as a sacrilege which desecrates the holy place — especially when the Romans had for decades maintained a military garrison in the Fortress Antonia which cast its shadow over the temple itself.

This leaves us with yet another alternative. Jesus is in fact speaking to the issue implied in the disciple's questions about the end of the age. The "great distress" He mentions is in fact the culminating tribulation, which according to the OT prophets is to mark history's end. And the "abomination that causes desolation" is an act yet to be performed, by a person the NT calls the "Antichrist" or the "man of sin," and Daniel describes as a "king" who "will do as he pleases" (11:36).

While students of prophecy seem to enjoy debating the interpretation of this passage, we must remember that everything Christ says here leads up to a single conclusion. Jesus will be gone for a time. In His absence His people are to keep watch and remain committed.

We must never forget that while interpretation of prophecy can be debated, there is no debate at all that we are to live as faithful servants of the Son of God. And we must never forget that personal commitment to readiness for Jesus' imminent return is far more important than being "right" about what form that return will take.

HOW EARLY CHRISTIANS VIEWED OLD TESTAMENT PROPHECY

Since, then, we prove that all things which have already happened have been predicted by the prophets before they came to pass, we must necessarily believe also that those things which are in like manner predicted, but are not yet come to pass, shall certainly happen. For as the things which have already taken place came to pass when foretold, and even though unknown, so shall the things that remain, even though they be unknown and disbelieved, yet come to pass. For the prophets have proclaimed two advents of His; the one, that which is already past, when He came as a dishonored and suffering man; but the second one, according to prophecy, He shall come from heaven with glory, accompanied by His angelic host, when also He shall raise the bodies of all men who have lived, and shall clothe those of the worthy with immortality, and shall send those of the wicked, endured with eternal sensibility, into everlasting fire with the wicked devils. And that these things also have been foretold as yet to be, we will prove. By Ezekiel the prophet it was said, "Joint shall be joined to joint, and bone to bone, and flesh shall grow again" (Ezek. 37:7-8); and "every knee shall bow to the Lord and every tongue shall confess Him" (Isa. 45:23). . . . And what the people of the Jews shall say and do, when they see Him coming in glory, has been thus predicted by Zechariah the prophet: "I will command the four winds to gather the scattered children. I will command the north wind to bring them, and the south wind, that it keep not back. And then in Jerusalem shall be great lamentation, not the lamentation of mouths or of lips, but the lamentation of the heart; and they shall rend not their garments, but their hearts. Tribe by tribe they shall mourn, and then they shall look on Him whom they have pierced; and they shall say, Why, O Lord, hast Thou made us to err from Thy way? The glory which our fathers blessed, has for us been turned into shame" (Zech. 2:6; 12:3-14; Isa. 63:17; 64:11). Justin Martyr (A.D. 100-167), *Certain Fulfillment of Prophecy*, Chapter 52, p. 231

Let no one *on the roof of his house* go down to take anything out of the house (24:17). How were persons to react when the "abomination that causes desolation" takes place? Jesus' warning communicates a strong sense of urgency. The flat rooftops of houses in Palestine frequently served as extra rooms, especially in summer. The stairway leading to the roof was built on the outside of the house. In cities, the rooftop of one house might abut the rooftop of its neighbor. A person startled into flight might run across the rooftops to the edge of town. But if he or she did have to go downstairs, that person was not even to hesitate long enough to slip inside and collect valuables.

For then there will be *great distress* (24:21). The Greek word is *thlipsis,* meaning distress or tribulation. The fact that this distress is "unequaled" in past or future makes it very clear in our time, when Hitler's holocaust is so well remembered, that Jesus must be speaking of that terrible period at history's end referred to so frequently in the prophets. For OT images, see: Deut. 4:30; Isa. 2:12, 19; 13:6, 9; 24:1-6, 19-21; 26:20-21; Jer. 30:7; Ezek. 13:5; 30:3; Dan. 9:27; 12:1; Joel 1:15; 2:1-2, 11, 31; 3:14; Amos 5:18-20; Zeph. 1:14-18; and Zech. 14:1.

False Christs and false prophets will appear and *perform great signs and miracles* to deceive even the elect—if that were possible (24:24). The Bible records three historic periods when miracles and signs were given frequently. The time of the Exodus and Conquest, when God brought Israel out of captivity and gave her the land. The time of Elijah and Elisha, when God turned back the threat of a virulent form of Baalism to the biblical faith. And the time of Jesus and the early apostolic church. Each of these periods marked a spiritual and religious crisis and the introduction of fresh, dramatic revelation. Strikingly, a fourth time of miracles is predicted. But this time, the signs given and the miracles performed will be counterfeit, satanic in origin and intended to "deceive even the elect" if this were possible (cf. also Rev. 13:13; 16:14; 19:20).

What a reminder for us. We do walk by faith rather than by sight. We have the completed revelation of God in our Old and New Testaments. We need no miracles to convince us to trust Him fully—and no claim of miracles by others can shake our faith.

I tell you the truth, *this generation* **will certainly not pass away until all these things have happened (24:34).** This phrase is puzzling and its meaning is still debated. Those who believe that Jesus' warnings of coming great tribulation refer to the destruction of Jerusalem in A.D. 70 find an easy solution. Those who link the tribulation reference to the end times have a more serious problem, and suggest two possible solutions. (1) Christ intends the generation living when the "abomination of desolation" takes place. This generation He is speaking of will survive the turmoil and not be wiped out before Christ comes. Or (2) Matthew uses the word "generation," *genea,* in one of its other possible senses. These senses include "family," "race," and even "age." If *genea* is used in one of these senses, Jesus may intend the Jewish people, and mean that they will be preserved as a distinct race until the end foreseen by the OT prophets. Or He may intend by "this generation" to characterize that class of people who are unbelieving and perverse—a class which will persist through history until Jesus returns, despite the supernatural power of the Gospel message.

Two **men will be in the field; one will be taken and the other left.** *Two* **women . . . (24:40-41).** In the East work was typically a social affair. Two would plow, a son leading the ox and the father holding the plow; two women would sit together in the courtyard and talk as they ground grain. The emphasis is not on the unexpectedness of Jesus' coming,

but on the fact that no matter how close the relationship between persons, Christ's return will mean the sudden disruption of the most intimate human relationships.

What a powerful reminder that the relationship which is most critical to us is our relationship with the Lord.

Therefore keep *watch,* **because you do not know on what day your Lord will come (24:42).** The Greek verb is *gregoreo,* which means to "keep alert and watchful." This word provides the key to the rest of chapter 24 and all of chapter 25. Each of the five parables here stresses some aspect of watchfulness. A person ever aware of the imminence of Jesus' return will remain on guard (24:42-44); will actively serve God's people rather than his own interests (24:45-51); will plan ahead and be prepared for delay (25:1-13); will use every resource in the service of his absent master (25:14-30); and true disciples will express the reality of their faith in the way they treat those who represent Jesus here on earth (25:31-46).

You who are cursed, into the *eternal fire* **prepared for the devil and his angels (25:41).** The "eternal fire" image of judgment is common in Scripture (cf. Matt. 3:12; 5:22; 18:8; Rev. 20:10-15). The image was also familiar to the Jews of Jesus' time and, significantly, the recorded sayings of Jesus include seven times as many references to hell as to heaven.

This is a critical verse for those who object that a "loving God" could never condemn anyone to such a terrible hell. In fact, God did not create the realm of eternal fires for human beings, but for Satan and his fallen angels.

God's love for human beings is so great that He took the punishment our sins deserve on Himself, in order that we might be spared eternal fires. God does not condemn any human being to hell. Those persons who fail to respond to God's revelation of Himself in Creation and in Christ condemn themselves (Rom. 1).

THE PASSAGE IN DEPTH

Signs of the End of the Age (24:1-35). See the in-depth commentary on Mark 13:5-37 for more information.

The Parable of the Ten Virgins (25:1-13).
Background. The Parable of the Ten Virgins is drawn from everyday life, and every detail is

true to life not only in Bible times but also to life in Palestinian villages up to the last century.

Weddings were typically celebrated during the fall or winter months when few agricultural duties enabled the community to participate in the joyous occasion. That weddings were truly times of delight is reflected in Jeremiah's description, found in 7:34, of "the sounds of joy and gladness and . . . the voices of bride and bridegroom in the towns of Judah and the streets of Jerusalem." It was surely appropriate to liken the eschatological coming of the kingdom to a wedding.

But our attention is focused on ten young women waiting to "meet the bridegroom." A typical wedding saw friends of the bride waiting at her home. They waited for the bridegroom, who must come to get the bride and bring her to his home. The description of a Jerusalem wedding published in 1909 tells how guests met in the bride's home. As they waited for hours, messengers repeatedly announced the bridegroom was at hand. The guests hurried out to meet him, only to return home. Finally, near midnight, the groom arrived with his friends, all brightly lit by carried lamps and candles. Then the two groups of friends merged and the whole party moved off in a blaze of light to escort the couple to the groom's home.

In our parable, ten young women among the bride's friends are singled out. Each has a lamp, but only five have brought oil to fuel their lamps. Since light is a symbol of happiness, candles and oil lamps were essential equipment for the wedding party. Normally visitors from out of town purchased oil or candles in the town where the wedding took place, although some brought such supplies with them. It is likely that the five unprepared virgins expected to obtain oil at the last minute, but fell asleep, and when they awoke it was too late.

By the time they were able to "go to those who sell oil and buy some for yourselves" (25:9) the wedding procession had moved on through the streets and reached the groom's home. As was customary after the invited guests had entered the home, the door was locked. The five knocked loudly, but it was too late for the unprepared virgins to join the festivities.

Interpretation. Like the other parables in this section, the emphasis is on watchfulness and readiness. Like the others, it also implies a long delay in Christ's return.

However, in the Middle East a delay on the part of the bridegroom is expected. Typically this is caused by last-minute negotiations over presents the groom is to bring the bride's relatives. If the bride is surrendered too cheaply, it implies that she is lightly regarded; if the groom ignores this process he is thought to display little regard for the relatives. Whatever the reason, delay in the bridegroom's appearance is an expected thing. And so we can understand why five of the virgins did not seem too concerned about obtaining oil, and instead joined their friends in happy conversation — until sleep overtook them.

The failure to take steps necessary to be ready for the bridegroom's coming proved disastrous for the five without oil! The message of the parable is simple: Don't wait, but make your preparations now for His coming.

One of the greatest dangers in interpreting images drawn from daily life is "making the illustration walk on all fours." That is, rather than keep the main point of the story in view, the interpreter looks for meaning in every detail — and in the process often misses the point.

For instance, oil is a frequent symbol of the Holy Spirit. Thus some see in Jesus' story a warning that mere professing Christians lack "oil," and thus will be shut out of the kingdom.

Others assume that the five foolish virgins had brought some oil but not enough. Thus the parable has been taken to suggest that some believers foolishly rely on yesterday's spiritual experiences, rather than seek daily resupplies of grace.

However attractive these flights of fancy may be, they distract us from the emphasis of this parable within the set of five images Jesus uses to explain His command to the disciples: Watch. The lesson it teaches is a simple one: Watchfulness means to let nothing distract us from being prepared for Christ's return.

Application. Weddings were times of great delight in the ancient world. They were one of the major social occasions that drew friends from surrounding villages and towns. No wonder the girls were distracted, captivated by the opportunity to gossip and enjoy each other's company. No wonder finalizing preparations for the bridegroom's coming was completely driven out of their minds until they were overtaken by drowsiness.

It's not surprising when we too are distracted from preparing for Jesus' return by the delights or troubles of this world. And so Jesus' story speaks to us as well, reminding us that the Bridegroom is coming. We do not know when. But we must make sure that we are ready, now.

The Sheep and the Goats (25:31-46).

Background. Both sheep and goats were familiar in Bible times, and each was important to the economy. While sheep were more important economically, goats were valued for their meat, milk, and cheese. Goat skins were used to make water and wine bottles, and their hair was woven into ropes and fabric. Goats, as ritually clean animals, were acceptable sacrifices (Lev. 1:10; 4:28). It would thus be wrong to read into this parable any notion that sheep and goats stand in any strong natural contrast to each other, as would be the case if Jesus had spoken of separating sheep from pigs.

Interpretation. That this is one of the most difficult of NT passages to interpret is illustrated by the plethora of views that have been advanced by commentators. The interpretations hinge on several key issues:

■ Who are "the least of these brothers of mine"? (25:40, 45) Most scholars tend to see these as the needy, who are oppressed by society but are precious to God. This view reflects the emphasis in Judaism on the merit of giving to the poor. But it is not at all in harmony with the rest of the NT, which while reflecting compassion for the poor does not make poverty the criteria for a family relationship with God. Nor does the rest of the NT make salvation hinge on caring for the unfortunate.

Another view holds that Jesus' brothers are the disciples and apostles who carry the Gospel. One's reaction to them is not the basis of salvation, but serves as an indicator of faith. A similar interpretation extends the "brothers" to all who openly confess Christ.

■ Who is intended by the "nations" (20:31) who are subject to this judgment? Those who see Jesus' "brothers" as the poor assume that Jesus is describing the last judgment, and equate all nations with all persons, including Christians! Dispensationalists place this judg-

ment in a tribulation context. They suggest that it determines who may enter the earthly millennial kingdom to be ruled by Jesus as the promised Davidic king. The "brothers" are Jews who have come to faith during those terrible times; the sheep and goats are Gentile nations or individuals, who are judged on the basis of how they treated the believing Jews.

■ How many groups are involved? Are there three—sheep, goats, and brothers of Jesus? Several interpretations seem to imply this: the one which identifies Jesus with the poor; and the dispensational approach, which identifies the brothers as racial brethren, Jews converted during the Tribulation period. It is likely however that only two groups are here, and the "least of these brothers of mine" refers to the sheep who demonstrate their faith by loving compassion for one another (John 13:34-35).

In a sense, however, it is not essential to understand every detail. Instead we need to see the role this parable has in the sequence of five stories emphasizing the importance of watching for Christ's return. Certainly this parable adds an important dimension to what "watching" means. To watch for Jesus' coming means to show compassion for the needy among God's sheep, a theme found in the second illustration as well (24:45-51). Perhaps the surprise reflected by the sheep and the goats at this criteria is an indicator of how little value we place on loving concern for others— and how great a value is placed on compassion by God.

But this parable does more than add to our understanding of watching. It reminds us that when Jesus comes, blessing comes with Him! We cannot overemphasize the import of the words "you who are blessed by My Father" (25:34). The Greek word is *eulogemenoi,* not *makarioi* as in the Beatitudes (5:3). The blessedness awaiting the saved is not the hidden blessing of the kingdom's counter-values, but rather the realized blessings to be found in the full establishment of God's eternal rule!

Application. It is always an error to attempt to interpret or to apply verses, events, or teachings in isolation from their context. It is particularly important to keep the context in view when dealing with the Parable of the Sheep and Goats.

Two repeated elements in the five parables deserve special consideration. Each of the five parables adds to our understanding of what it means to "watch," or be alert to the imminent return of Jesus. Watching means that while Jesus is absent we are to be constantly on guard (24:42-44), to serve our fellow servants faithfully (24:45-51), to make preparation rather than be distracted by earthly affairs (25:1-13), to use every resource we have as stewards of our absent Master (25:14-30), and to show practical compassion toward those among us who are in need (25:31-46).

The other repeated element is most disquieting. Four of the five parables strongly suggest severe judgment, and even eternal condemnation, for those who fail to watch! If a servant exploits his fellow servants, God will "cut him to pieces and assign him a place with the hypocrites" (24:51). The five virgins who neglected to obtain oil are shut out of the wedding party (25:10-13). The person who hid rather than used his talent was thrown outside, "into the darkness, where there will be weeping and gnashing of teeth" (25:30). And the goats "will go away to eternal punishment, but the righteous to eternal life" (25:46). While watching is not a condition of salvation, it is clear that those who do watch are "the righteous." For only those who grasp who Jesus is, and who confidently expect Him to return, order their lives in view of this reality.

These parables do not grant us the right to judge the relationship of others to Christ. But they surely challenge us to examine ourselves, and see how real our faith in the Lord may be. Those with a true and abiding faith in Jesus will watch.

MATTHEW 26–27
Jesus' Trial and Death

EXPOSITION

Nearly a third of each Gospel is devoted to the last week of Jesus' life on earth. And, as the days of this last week speed by, events are more and more carefully chronicled.

The catalog of culminating events is basically the same in each book. Judas volunteers to betray Jesus for money. The little company of disciples meets for a final Passover supper. Jesus speaks of His betrayal, and Judas slinks away into the dark. Alone with the faithful eleven, Jesus utters the words of institution that convey the meaning of His death and establish the church's practice of Communion. When Jesus speaks again of His death Peter reaffirms his commitment, only to be told that very night he will deny the Lord. The company moves out to Gethsemane, where Jesus prays in deep emotional agony. There a hostile mob led by Judas finds Jesus and drags Him away to an illegal nighttime trial. That night Peter does betray Jesus. Christ reaffirms His identity as the Son of God, only to be condemned by the Sanhedrin.

Early the next morning Pilate, the Roman governor, succumbs to intense pressure and condemns Jesus to death. Christ is mocked, flogged, and led away to Golgotha where, around noon, He is crucified with two brigands. As even the sun hides its face, Christ suffers there. At last, surrendering His spirit, He dies. As the shadows begin to fall, Jesus' body is buried in a borrowed tomb. The bright promise He offered seems to have ended in tragedy and injustice. While His friends depart, crushed by grief, His self-satisfied enemies prepare to lead the nation in the worship of the God whose Son they have successfully conspired to kill.

A STUDY NOTE

The thesis is the same in each Gospel: Jesus' suffering and death were real events; events on which history itself turns. While the events reported are the same, each Gospel places delicate emphasis on its own unique themes. Matthew pays special attention to human frailty—a frailty reflected in the utter rejection of Jesus by Judas and in Peter's denial of Him. Mark provides the bare-bones structure of key events. Luke highlights the sufferings Jesus underwent for us. John focuses on Jesus' trials before the Sanhedrin and before Pilate. Each of these themes is developed in "The Passage In Depth" section of the appropriate Gospel.

WORD STUDIES

Not *during the feast* . . . or there may be a riot among the people (26:5). The population of Jerusalem multiplied some five-fold during Passover week. This created a volatile situation; Jerusalem seethed with religious fervor during these days. Unable to tell which way popular opinion might swing, the religious leaders hesitated to try getting rid of Jesus during the feast. They need not have. While emotionalism about our faith is good, it tends to be shallow and fickle. Soon the crowds that cheered Christ's entry into Jerusalem joined in the shout, "Crucify Him!"

I tell you the truth, *wherever* this Gospel is preached throughout the world, what she has done will also be told, in memory of her (26:13). Alabaster jars of perfume were so valuable in the first century they were often purchased as investments. The woman's gift truly was a rich one. Yet she is not remembered for her generosity, but for her insight. While the disciples refused to hear what Jesus said about His coming crucifixion, this woman understood and acted to "prepare Me for burial" (26:12). The Greek word *hopou* (26:13) normally means "wherever." But it

can also mean "when." As the Gospel is preached throughout the world we honor a woman who realized that Christ was destined to die, and remember that only by grasping the meaning of that death can we be saved.

So they counted out for him *thirty silver coins* (26:15). This is hardly a princely price, equivalent to about a month's wages for a day laborer. More significant symbolically, 30 pieces of silver is the price that Exodus 21:32 sets as the indemnity to be paid the owner when his slave is gored to death by someone's ox. The price is a tragic commentary on how terribly Judas misjudged Jesus. And a continuing commentary on those who dismiss Christ's claims today.

***The one who* has dipped his hand into the bowl with Me will betray Me (26:23).** The Greek has an aorist participle, *ho embapsas*. Rather than indicate a specific individual, the Greek phrase emphasizes that Christ's betrayer would be someone close; close enough to share a meal. This is particularly significant in Eastern culture, where participation in a shared meal implies both intimacy and mutual obligation.

Participation in the Christian community brings us close to Christ. But closeness isn't enough. There must be personal commitment as well.

Even if I have to die with you, I will never *disown* you (26:35). The word is *aparneomai*, often used interchangeably with the stronger *arneomai*. Zondervan's *Expository Dictionary of Bible Words* says, "When used in a context in which a person must make a decision, these Greek words indicate rejection. But when the subject of the verbs is a person who has an established faith in Jesus, denial means unfaithfulness in the relationship, an abandoning of fellowship" (p. 219).

My Father, *if it is possible,* may *this cup* be taken from Me. Yet not as I will, but as You will (26:39). What is "this cup"? Some assume the "cup" refers to Christ's coming suffering and death. Others see a deeper meaning, for in the OT and in Revelation "cup" (Gk. *poterion*) is often associated with divine judgment (Ps. 60:3; Isa. 51:19, 22; Hab. 2:16; Rev. 14:10; 16:19). Jesus did not fear the physical suffering, but was in anguish at the thought that the contaminating touch of the sins He bore must necessarily turn the Father against Him.

Of particular note is the use of a first-class conditional in the phrase "if it is possible" (26:39). This normally suggests that the condition is assumed to be fulfilled—that is, that it was possible to avoid the "cup" Jesus had in mind. This interpretation is supported by Hebrews 5:7 which notes that when Jesus "offered up prayers and petitions with loud cries and tears to the One who could save Him from death, and He was heard because of His reverent submission."

What then did Christ request, and how did God answer? Jesus did not ask to avoid the cross, but rather that after dying He might be released from spiritual and physical aspects of "death." Three days later this prayer was answered! Christ rose from the dead, completely transformed in resurrection, and restored at last to the glory He had possessed from the beginning as God the Son.

Biological death held no terrors for Jesus. It holds no terrors for us. Because Jesus bore our sins and experienced the wrath of God in our stead, we too have been released. Neither biological nor spiritual death has any permanent hold on those who through Christ have been given eternal life.

One of Jesus' companions reached for his *sword,* drew it out and struck the servant of the high priest, cutting off his ear (26:51). The incident has been used to argue *for* Christian pacificism—Jesus rejected the use of the sword—and to argue *against* Christian pacificism—Jesus did say, "Put your sword back in its place" (26:52) and not, "Throw it away!"

This argument overlooks the fact that the same Greek word is used for "sword" and for "knife." Indeed, the type of sword used in Israel was a straight, triangular blade, primarily used for thrusting. The fact that the disciple swung his blade and cut off an ear suggests the blade was probably a knife rather than a sword, perhaps one of the knives commonly used by fishermen in plying their trade. The incident has nothing to say about pacificism, pro or con.

How then can we apply this passage? Perhaps simply to note how totally inappropriate it is to use force in the defense of Christ. The Gospel is a message of grace, better characterized by Jesus' act in restoring the severed ear (Luke 22:51) than by the violence involved in cutting it off.

In the future you will see the Son of Man *sitting at the right hand of the Mighty One* and coming on the clouds of heaven (26:64). Jesus not only affirmed His deity, but warned the Sanhedrin. He stood before them in weakness, a prisoner whom they claimed the right to judge. But the ultimate right of judgment belongs to God. When Jesus' Sanhedrin judges see Him again, He will be standing in the place of authority (at God's "right hand"). Then Jesus will judge them.

Today too human beings evaluate the claims of Christ and decide for or against Him. When they do, how important to remember that ultimately Christ is mankind's Judge as well as Savior.

Your *accent* gives you away (26:73). Even though Palestine is a tiny land, the people of Galilee had a distinctly different accent from those who lived in Judea.

Surely, however, not every Galilean in Jerusalem at Passover was a follower of Jesus! It takes more than an accent to give us away as those who belong to Him. In fact, if there is nothing in our way of life or talk that marks us as Jesus' followers, there is something wrong in our relationship with Him.

Judas . . . was seized with *remorse* and returned the thirty silver coins (27:3). The Greek verb is *metamelomai.* It expresses sorrow, and makes it clear that Judas was deeply pained after betraying Jesus. But being sorry afterward does not undo any act, nor does it in

---

PSALM 22

This great prophetic psalm contains many phrases that clearly refer to Christ's experience on the cross. The powerful emotion expressed by the psalmist also provides some insight into what Jesus experienced as He died for us.

My God, My God, why have You forsaken me?
 Why are You so far from saving me,
 so far from the words of my groaning?
O my God, I cry out by day, but You do not answer,
 by night, and am not silent.

But I am a worm and not a man,
 scorned by men and despised by the people.
All who see me mock me;
 they hurl insults, shaking their heads;
"He trusts in the Lord;
 let the Lord rescue him.
Let Him deliver him,
 since he delights in Him."
Yet You brought me out of the womb;
 You made me trust in You
 even at my mother's breast.
From birth I was cast upon You;
 from my mother's womb You have been my God.
Do not be far from me,
 for trouble is near and there is no one to help.

I am poured out like water,
 and all my bones are out of joint.
My heart has turned to wax;
 it has melted away within me.
My strength is dried up like a potsherd,
 and my tongue sticks to the roof of my mouth;
 You lay me in the dust of death.
Dogs have surrounded me;
 a band of evil men has encircled me,
 they have pierced my hands and my feet.
I can count all my bones;
 people stare and gloat over me.
They divide my garments among them
 and cast lots for my clothing.
But You, O Lord, be not far off;
 O my Strength, come quickly to help me.

vv. 1-2, 6-11, 14-29

itself indicate a change of heart.

Being sorry is not wrong, but inadequate. Being sorry has value only when that sorrow leads to a radical change of heart and life.

They offered Jesus wine to drink, mixed with *gall* (27:34). This offer by the members of the military detail assigned to crucify Jesus was no act of compassion. Rather than being a narcotic, gall (identified as "myrrh" in Mark 15:23) is extremely bitter. After struggling through the city, weak from His beating and forced to drag the crossbar to which He was to be nailed, Jesus' thirst must have been intense. By mixing the wine offered to Jesus with a strong dose of gall, the soldiers made it undrinkable. Jesus' reaction must have amused the soldiers, who earlier had played other cruel games with the Savior (27:27-31).

Two *robbers* were crucified with Him, one on His right and one on His left (27:38). The word here is *lestai*, a term also applied to Barabbas (John 18:40). Robbery, even robbery with violence, was not punished by crucifixion in the first century. It is most likely the term implies insurrection against the government; in modern terms a person involved in "guerilla warfare" who tried to overturn the social order by destroying property as well as by killing.

My God, My God, why have You *forsaken* me? (27:46) The mystery of the crucifixion is only intensified by this cry. The Greek word translated as "forsaken," *enkataleipo*, is a powerful word that expresses terrible emotional anguish caused by abandonment. Christ was not abandoned to the grave (same word, Acts 2:27), but on the cross He was abandoned by the Father.

How could the Godhead itself be torn apart on Calvary? In what sense was the Son abandoned there? Was that momentary isolation, or a deeper severing? We are not told, and if we were we could hardly understand. We do know, however, that it was this agony which Jesus feared; this agony was so terrible that in a single, endless moment, what Christ suffered more than paid for the sins of humankind from Adam to history's end.

Surely He was *the Son of God* (27:54). The centurion's confession need not imply that this non-Jewish army officer recognized Jesus as the Jewish Messiah. It is much more likely that he used the phrase (which in the Greek lacks "the") in a Hellenistic sense to mean "a divine being," a pagan god. Certainly the unusual events of that day—the darkness and earthquake, and the words from the cross —made a deep impression on the centurion.

THE PASSAGE IN DEPTH

See the chart of parallel passages (below). Verses in boldface indicate where each listed topic is discussed in depth.

Topic	Matthew	Mark	Luke	John
The plot against Jesus	**26:1-5**	14:1-11	22:1-6	
Anointing at Bethany	26:6-13	**14:3-9**		
Judas agrees to betray Christ	**26:14-16**			
The Last Supper	**26:17-30**	14:12-25	22:14-23	**13–17**
Peter's denial predicted	**26:31-35**	14:27-31	22:31-38	13:31-38
Gethsemane	26:36-46	14:32-42	**22:39-46**	
Jesus' arrest	**26:47-56**	14:43-52	22:47-53	18:1-12
Before the Sanhedrin	26:57-68	14:53-65	22:63-71	**18:13-23**
Peter denies Jesus	**26:69-75**	14:66-72	22:54-62	18:25-27
Judas hangs himself	**27:1-10**			
Jesus before Pilate	27:11-26	15:1-15	23:1-25	18:28–19:16
The soldiers mock Jesus	27:27-31	15:16-20		
The crucifixion	27:32-56	15:21-41	**23:26-49**	19:17-37
Jesus' burial	27:57-61	15:42-47	23:50-56	19:38-42
Guard placed at the tomb	**27:62-66**			

Judas and the conspiracy to kill Jesus (26:1-5, 14-30, 47-56; 27:1-10). See chart on p. 95 for parallel passages.

Background. It is clear that Jesus quickly aroused extreme hostility among the religious leaders of His time. Matthew describes a number of confrontations, and after one encounter focusing on Sabbath-keeping remarks, "the Pharisees went out and plotted how they might kill Jesus" (12:14). Jesus continued to reject the leaders' approach to religion (15:1-11) and even openly charged them with hypocrisy (23:1-36). All this further intensified the leaders' hostility, so that as the Passover drew near the "chief priests and the elders" (other members of the Sanhedrin) actively plotted how to arrest Jesus "in some sly way and kill Him" (26:3-4).

We can understand the motivation of these leaders. Jesus' teachings threatened not just their place in society, but challenged the very basis of their approach to faith. Rather than acknowledge, even to themselves, that they had been "blind guides" (15:14) and hypocrites (23:13, 15, etc.), the leaders were fiercely determined to rid themselves of Jesus and the threat that He posed to them, their approach to religion, and indeed to their society as a whole.

While we can understand the motivation of the chief priests and elders, it is more difficult to understand why Judas chose to betray Jesus. Judas had been one of the Twelve from the beginning. As treasurer of the little company (John 12:6), Judas had been given a post of responsibility—more responsibility than most of the others whose names are hardly mentioned in the NT.

John dismisses Judas with some contempt and seems to ascribe his motive for staying with Jesus as long as he did to the opportunity his position gave him to filch a few coins for himself. Judas rebuked Mary of Bethany when she anointed Christ with expensive ointment rather than donate it to the poor not "because he cared about the poor but because he was a thief; as keeper of the money bag, he used to help himself to what was put into it" (John 12:6).

This aside, however, tells us much about Judas' character. He was a person who cared for *things* more than *persons.* Judas was a materialist, whose values reflect an ultimate concern with this world rather than the next.

This is an absolutely vital insight. It helps us sense the absolute turmoil that Judas must have experienced as Christ's ministry took a direction that he, like the other disciples, had never foreseen. Like others in first-century Judaism, the popular expectation was that Messiah would establish a visible, institutional kingdom. Certainly, becoming a powerful person in such a kingdom would have tremendous appeal for a materialist like Judas. Yet as the months passed it became more and more clear that Jesus was moving in a different direction. His Sermon on the Mount announced His intention to set up an "in secret" kingdom of the heart. Although possessing supernatural power, Jesus did not use it against His or Israel's enemies, but only to heal the sick and demon possessed. After His initial popularity peaked, it became more and more clear that the truly influential people in Judea—those with wealth as well as power—were ranged against Jesus. And, as Christ spoke with increasing frequency about the cross and predicted His approaching death, Judas must have realized that he had thrown in his lot with the losing side!

We do not know how long Judas resisted the tremendous internal turmoil he must have experienced. We do know that unlike Peter and the others, Judas never made a full commitment to the person of Jesus. Judas had been committed to the image of Conquerer/ Messiah, and that out of expectation of some material reward. Unless we make a commitment to Jesus as a person, rather than follow Him because of what we expect He will do for us in the here and now, our "faith" rests on shaky ground.

Judas' "faith" could not survive the stress. As Passion Week progressed and it appeared Jesus Himself would not survive, Judas made his choice. He would leave the sinking ship, and in the process make whatever profit he could.

Perhaps Judas imagined that the enemies of Jesus would welcome him as one of them, and out of gratitude give him a place among them. If he could not have wealth and power in the kingdom of the Messiah, he would settle for wealth and power in a Judea that bowed under the yoke of Rome.

But Judas was not welcomed with respect or gratitude. He was treated as what he was—a traitor, willing to violate the special bonds that linked a disciple with his teacher, for money. Judas was not even offered an amount commensurate with the worth of the betrayal. They bargained with Judas. In the end he had to settle for a paltry 30 pieces of silver, hardly enough to buy food and shelter for a month.

How deceptive is materialism. How it blinds our eyes to that which is really important. How worthless the little we gain in the end.

Interpretation. Three events are described in some depth in Matthew.

■ The betrayal (26:47-50). Judas not only agreed to tell where Jesus was, he led an armed mob to the spot and personally identified the Savior. Although Jesus was well known, in the dark, in a society where no photographs were available to confirm identity, someone else might easily take His place. So Judas climbed up the hill to the enclosed olive garden where he knew Jesus would be, followed by the armed crowd.

The description in Matthew is filled with irony. Eager to be finished with his dark deed Judas went "at once" to Jesus and kissed Him (26:49). The word for kiss is intensive; Judas flung his arms around Jesus and kissed Him enthusiastically.

In crying out his greeting, Judas violated a protocol which demanded that a disciple not speak before his master. Judas has clearly cut every tie with Jesus and cloaked himself in an assumed superiority.

The words, "Greetings, Rabbi!" like the kiss, were intended for the mob and not for Jesus. But Christ's reply, "Friend," was for Judas alone. The Greek word here is *hetaire.* While warm, it is not an intimate greeting nor does it express great affection. Even so, it suggests that Jesus still holds the door open for Judas. Judas has rejected Christ. But Christ has not yet rejected him.

■ The remorse (27:1-10). After the deed was done Judas was consumed with a sense of guilt. The text says he felt remorse (see the Word Study on *metamelomai,* Matt. 27:3, above). But rather than face his guilt and appeal to Jesus for mercy, Judas did something very different. He tried to return the money, and when the chief priests and elders would not accept it, he "threw the money into the temple" (27:5). What was the meaning of this

act that Matthew describes so carefully?

The Mishnah describes an interesting custom that dates from before Jesus' time. A seller had twelve months to revoke the sale of a house. But at times the buyer would hide so that the money could not be repaid. M. Arak. ix. 4 states,

> If a man sold a house . . . he may redeem it at once at any time during twelve months. . . . If the last day of the twelfth month was come and it was not redeemed, it became the buyer's forever. . . . The buyer used to hide himself on the last day of the twelve months so that the house might be his forever; but Hillel the elder ordained that he that sold it could deposit his money in the Temple chamber, and break down the door and enter, and that the other, when he would, might come and take his money.

We appear to have in Matthew 27 an attempt by Judas to revoke his sale of Jesus. But the priests and elders refuse to take the money back. In a last, vain attempt to rid himself of his guilt, Judas takes the stained coins and throws them violently on the temple floor.

But Judas cannot go back. The return of the 30 coins cannot break his compact with hell, nor free him of the terrible burden of his guilt. As Judas stumbles out of the temple the weight of the silver coins is gone, but the weight on his conscience is unrelieved.

Even then Judas cannot see the significance of Jesus' greeting, "Friend," or the implications of the cold and unfeeling words of men who were commanded to have compassion on the weak and offer sacrifices on their behalf (27:4b). There is no help for him from Israel's priesthood, but there might still be mercy for him at the hand of the One he had betrayed.

But Judas cannot see. And the priests gather round the spilled coins, and debate how they might be "lawfully" used — unconcerned for the guilt-ridden man who has run from the temple, or the innocent Man they are about to condemn to death.

Judas tried to rid himself of guilt. He tried to take back the terrible sin he had committed. But neither of these choices was possible. Only when we face our guilt, and come humbly, as sinners, to the Savior, can we find relief.

■ Judas' suicide (27:5; Acts 1:18-19). Judas could not live with his guilt. So, ever the materialist, he committed suicide. There is no real conflict between the description here and in Acts. Some postulate that Judas hanged himself, the rope broke, and in tumbling down the rocky hillside on which the tree grew his intestines were spilled out—and ironically his body came to rest in the very field later purchased with the silver he had received.

There is no escape, in this world or the next, from the consequences of the choices we make. No escape—but there is redemption. To Christ, crucified for our sins as well as by the sins of Judas, we must appeal.

Application. Judas is an important subject for study. Like Esau in the OT, Judas is the NT's prime example of the materialist, who is totally insensitive to spiritual realities.

As Judas' story unfolds, we realize that the spiritual is far more real than the material. Judas chooses to betray Jesus for money. Although he cared nothing for the spiritual kingdom of the heart that Christ announced, his own heart is crushed with an unbearable burden of guilt. A guilt that cannot be touched, or seen, or heard—or washed away. This guilt drove a now frantic Judas to abandon entirely the material world that had been the focus of all his hopes.

How many, like Judas, stumble through life with total, permanent spiritual blindness! How desperately they need to hear Jesus say to them "Friend," even at the moment they betray God by some fresh sin. How desperately they need the Gospel's good news, which promises relief from guilt, spiritual renewal, and life evermore.

Peter's denial of Christ (Matt. 26:31-35, 69-75; John 21:15-19). See also parallel passages indicated on the chart on page 95.

Background. These chapters contain, in a sense, profiles of three individuals.

Jesus is the Son of God and perfect Man, who with resolute courage and complete commitment to the will of God strides toward the cross. He is human, torn at times by anguish and yearning for emotional support from His friends (26:36-46). And yet He is at the same time serene, completely in charge, totally devoted to God and to His disciples.

Judas is the materialistic man, blind to spiri-

tual things, intent on gaining power and wealth in the here and now. He attaches himself to Jesus not because he shares Christ's vision, but because he assumes Jesus will take him where he, Judas, wants to go. When Christ disappoints him, Judas rejects Jesus as well as His vision of a spiritual kingdom, and chooses to betray the Lord.

Peter is the opposite of Judas. He is deeply committed to Jesus as the Christ, the Son of the Living God. He does not understand everything Jesus says, and only now and then catches a glimpse of the kingdom his Lord describes. But Peter cannot be outdone in his fierce loyalty, or his firm intent to give himself fully to serve his Master.

We expect Judas to be flawed and to fail when put to the test. But somehow we expect Peter to pass every test with flying colors. After all, isn't his commitment complete? Isn't he absolutely honest in his protestations of love for the Lord?

Peter is committed. He is loyal. Peter really does love his Lord. But Peter is also flawed. Like every human being Peter can fall short of his own ideals, to say nothing of falling short of God's perfection. What we learn from Judas is that the thorough-going materialist has hope of redemption. What we learn here from Peter is that even the spiritually sensitive individual, who knows and loves the Lord, will fall short at times and must ultimately rely on the forgiving grace that God has made available to us in Jesus Christ.

Interpretation. Matthew provided us with a report of three significant events relating to Judas during Christ's last twenty-four hours. The Gospels also provide us with a description of three significant events relating to Peter during this same time span.

(1) Peter's promise (26:31-35). Just after the meal, as the company moved down into the Kidron Valley on the way to the Mount of Olives and Gethsemane, Jesus remarked, "This very night you will all fall away on account of Me" (26:31). Even though Christ stated that this would happen as a fulfillment of prophecy, Peter blurted out his objection. Others might fall away. "I never will" (26:33).

We can leave aside for the moment the foolishness of contradicting Christ. Instead we need to focus on the utter conviction with which Peter spoke. Others might fall.

"I never will."

With absolute sincerity Peter declared, "Even if I have to die with You, I will never disown You." (See Word Study on "disown," Matt. 27:35, above.)

The problem that Peter had and that many of us share is that, like Judas, even the most ardent believer is flawed. Sin is a reality with which we all must live. No amount of faith or of love for Christ can make us immune to failure, or guarantee that we will not sin. Only continual, humble dependence on the Lord growing out of a deep sense of our personal inadequacy can keep us from disowning Jesus by some word or deed.

(2) Peter's fall (26:69-75). When Jesus was taken away, Peter alone followed. He truly was, at that time, more committed than the others.

But waiting outside in the courtyard of Caiaphas, Peter must have been near despair. He, like Judas, had been unwilling to accept the notion that Jesus could die (cf. Matt. 16:21-23). Shaken and uncertain, terribly frightened for his Lord, Peter must have felt unbearably alone.

It was there, in the dark, that Peter was challenged three times with being a follower of the Nazarene. And three times, the last time violently (26:74), Peter disowned the Lord.

Before the oaths of denial ceased echoing in the courtyard, a cock crowed. And Peter realized what he had done.

Again like Judas, Peter was swept away with feelings of grief and anguish. Utterly crushed, Peter stumbled outside and "wept bitterly" (26:75).

Here the paths of Judas and Peter diverge. Unlike Judas, Peter truly had been committed to Jesus, even though he too had not yet grasped Christ's vision of the future. Judas, blind to spiritual realities, abandoned hope. Peter, suddenly aware of his own weakness, continued to believe.

(3) Peter restored (John 21:15-19). When resurrection morning came, Peter, humbled and undoubtedly ashamed, was still with the disciples. He was the first to stoop and peer into the empty tomb. And now, on the shore of the familiar Sea of Galilee, although he hangs back uncertain, Peter still fixes his gaze on Jesus' face, and he hopes.

How glad we are to see Christ single Peter out, to ask, "Do you truly love [*agapao*] Me?"

(21:15) The word Christ chose was a rather bland term in Koine (everyday) Greek. But the NT fills it full of new meaning, by using *agape* to describe the love God has for humankind—a love He chose to show in sending His Son to die for us. Peter answers, "Yes Lord, You know I love [*phileo*] You." Peter's word is a much less significant one, indicating a fond affection. Many theories have been advanced for the use of the two verbs by Christ and Peter. Perhaps the best explanation is that Peter has, at last, learned how weak and untrustworthy even his best instincts are.

Agape is a word of firm conviction: it expresses a wonderful reality. God has chosen to love us, even though we sinners are unlovable in ourselves and are in fact hostile to God and godliness. Peter had felt that his will was strong enough to affirm that he had the same kind of love for Christ that Jesus had for him. That his commitment to Christ was as firm as Jesus' commitment to him. Now, however, Peter knows better.

And so Peter chooses a weaker term, in effect saying, "Lord, You know how deep my affection is for You. But Lord, I am unable to love You as You love me. Lord, hold tight to me forever. For I now know that I am not strong enough to hold tight to You."

Jesus accepted Peter's love, as He accepts ours. Uncertain, often weak, all too often inadequate to keep us from disowning Jesus by some careless word or deed, Jesus still accepts our love as He accepts us.

Peter quickly learned how wonderful that acceptance is. For Jesus not only restored His humbled follower, but commissioned him to "Feed my lambs" (21:15).

Application. Only Jesus is perfect. The sooner we face this reality the more quickly we will learn the open secret of living in fellowship with our Lord. We must not, cannot, depend on ourselves. Like Peter, we will surely fail ourselves and Him.

What we can do is accept our weakness, and learn to rely completely on His love for us. And when we do fail, we can turn to Him again and, like Peter, experience again Jesus' forgiving love.

The Guard at the Tomb (27:62-66). The guard was set because the Sanhedrin remembered what Jesus had said about rising the third day. It's hard to say whether doubts and fears stirred in their hearts. Could this Man who had performed so many miracles really rise again?

Publicly they refused to express any doubt. "His disciples may come and steal the body," they announced (27:64). What a deception that would be!

Pilate gave them a military guard. Perhaps he too felt uneasy, eager to make the tomb secure. How futile their efforts were. God's power would soon burst forth within that closed tomb. And as the great stone that blocked its door was jolted from its tracks, humankind was given unmistakable proof of God's overcoming love. The Resurrection is the grand testimony.

MATTHEW 28
Alive, Forevermore!

EXPOSITION

As the first day of the week dawned, two heartbroken women trudged beyond Jerusalem's walls toward the tomb where the disciples had laid Jesus' body. Each of the Gospel accounts adds more detail to the events of that morning (see chart, below). Yet all these details are mere backdrop to the central reality the Gospels portray. Jesus is no longer in His tomb. He is risen from the dead.

Matthew focuses our attention on the angelic announcement of the Resurrection to the women and their first meeting with the risen Lord (28:1-10), on the fiction invented by the religious leaders in their desperate attempt to explain the Resurrection away (28:11-15), and on that meeting of Jesus with His disciples at which He challenged them with what we know as the Great Commission (28:16-20). His message for us is simply that Jesus' resurrection is real—and that Christ's rising from the dead has continuing meaning for His church and for the world.

RESURRECTION MORNING EVENTS

Three women start for the tomb	Luke 23:55–24:1
They find the stone rolled away	Luke 24:2-9
Mary Magdalene leaves to tell the disciples	John 20:1-2
Mary, the mother of James, sees the angels	Matt. 28:1-5
Peter and John arrive, and look in the tomb	John 20:3-9
Mary Magdalene returns, sees angels and Jesus	John 20:10-18
Mary, the mother of James, returns with others	Luke 24:1-4

These women see the angels	Luke 24:5; Mark 16:5
The angel tells them Jesus is risen	Matt. 28:6-8
As they leave they are met by Jesus	Matt. 28:9-10

LATER APPEARANCES OF JESUS

To Peter, the same day	Luke 24:34; 1 Cor. 15:5
To two disciples on the Emmaus road	Luke 24:13-31
To the apostles (Thomas is absent)	Luke 24:36-45; John 20:19-24
To the apostles (Thomas is present)	John 20:24-29
To seven by the Lake of Tiberius	John 21:1-23
To about 500, in Galilee	1 Cor. 15:6; Matt. 28:16-20
To James in Jerusalem and Bethany	1 Cor. 15:7
To many at the Ascension	Acts 1:3-9
To Stephen when he is stoned	Acts 7:55
To Paul near Damascus	Acts 9:3-6; 1 Cor. 15:8
To Paul in the temple	Acts 22:17-19; 23:11
To John on Patmos	Rev. 1:10-18

WORD STUDIES

An angel of the Lord . . . rolled back the stone and sat on it (28:2). In NT times burial practices were much different than today. Tombs were hewn in the sides of cliffs. These were sealed with heavy, carved, wheel-like stone slabs that rolled in a track carved into the base of the rock.

Why did the angel roll back the stone? Not to release Jesus, but to enable His followers and others to see that the tomb really was empty!

The guards were so afraid of him that they shook and became like dead men (28:4). The phrase simply suggests that they were so terrified by the supernatural apparition that they fainted dead away!

Then go quickly and tell His disciples: "He has risen" (28:7). Here is a most interesting event. The word translated "tell" is the most ordinary of terms. What is exceptional is that the angel commissioned women to report the news of resurrection to the disciples. Why is this exceptional? The testimony of women could not be accepted in Jewish courts!

What powerful symbolism. Even in His resurrection Christ chooses to minister through "the foolish things of the world to shame the wise. God chose the weak things of the world to shame the strong. He chose the lowly things of this world and the despised things"

(1 Cor. 1:27-28). This is a graphic example of the upside-down kingdom of Jesus.

God's choice of women to be the first to carry word of the Resurrection despite the prejudices of that age should encourage us. The effectiveness of the Gospel does not rest on the status of the messenger, but on the wonderful truth we are commissioned to share.

They came to Him, clasped His feet and worshiped Him (28:9). The Greek word is *prosekynesane,* and means to "kneel down to." Before the Resurrection such an act might simply have expressed the deep respect one felt for Jesus. Now it is an instinctive reaction—respect transformed by the Resurrection to worship and awe. Jesus is not a mere rabbi, but Lord of heaven and earth. He is worthy of worship by all men and women.

When the chief priests had met with the elders and devised a plan, they gave the soldiers a large sum of money, telling them, "You are to say, 'His disciples came during the night and stole Him away while we were asleep' " (28:12-13). The Greek word is *symboulion.* It means to consult, to plan, to reach a decision.

The plan finally arrived at is foolish on its face. For one thing, sleeping on duty was a capital offense in the Roman army. No guards would voluntarily make that admission. For another, if sleeping they could not possibly have known that "His disciples came during the night and stole Him away." A person can hardly testify to what happened while he slept, for he could not have witnessed it! For a third, an ordinance promulgated by Caesar and preserved in what is known as the "Nazareth Inscription" makes molesting graves a dire offense, which could in certain cases call for the death penalty. The demoralized and crushed disciples could hardly have mustered the courage to rob the grave that holy week. And if there were any evidence to support the charge, the Sanhedrin surely would have tried to suppress the Christian movement by charging the Eleven with grave robbing!

Despite the obvious flaws in the story trumped up by the Sanhedrin, the story was quickly accepted by those Jews unwilling to accept the claims of Christ. The story persisted, and is argued against by the early church fathers, and within the last twenty years has been resurrected yet again in a book by a modern Jewish scholar. As our Lord taught in the story of the Rich Man and Lazarus (Luke 16:19-31), "If they do not listen to Moses and the prophets, they will not be convinced even if someone rises from the dead."

The Sanhedrin had rejected the testimony of the OT to Christ. It had rejected the witness of His miracles. It had rejected His own clear claim to be the Son of God and promised Messiah. Now that Christ had risen, the Sanhedrin still refused to believe the truth, and chose instead to create a fiction that is absurd on its face.

Josephus on Jesus' Resurrection

The Jewish historian Josephus, who lived from A.D. 37 to 95, wrote about the administration of Pilate in his *Antiquities*. Here is what he had to say about Jesus in XVIII.3.3.(63): There was about this time Jesus, a wise man, if indeed it be right to call Him a man; for He was a doer of marvelous works, a teacher of men who received the truth with pleasure; and He won over to Himself many Jews and many of the Greek [race] also. This one was the Christ. And when, upon accusation of the leading men among us, Pilate had condemned Him to the cross, those who had loved Him at the first did not cease; for He appeared to them alive again on the third day, as the divine prophets had spoken these and ten thousand other wonderful things concerning Him. And even until now the "sect" of Christians, named after this one [man], has not ceased.

When *they* saw Him, they worshiped Him; but some *doubted* (28:17). Our understanding of this surprising verse hinges on the question of who the "they" are that Matthew refers to. It is best to link this appearance of Jesus in Galilee to the event mentioned in 1 Cor. 15:6. In this case, while the Eleven are most prominent in the Gospel resurrection accounts, the "brothers" the women were sent to tell (28:10) include a larger company of those who remained loyal to Him. And the group that gathered to meet Jesus in Galilee included the much larger company Paul mentions in 1 Cor. 15 along with the eleven apostles.

This theory helps us understand Matthew's remark, "but some doubted" (28:17). The word translated "doubted" is *edistasan,* found only here and in 14:31. It does not suggest that those who knelt before Jesus at that time did not believe, but rather suggests that they felt some hesitation. The fact of the Resurrection was simply too overwhelming to take in so quickly.

It is unlikely that this word describes the reaction of the Eleven, for the apostles have met with Jesus several times before (see chart on p. 101). But surely both the fact of the Resurrection, and its implications, began to dawn on the little company of 500 that must have formed the core of what became the apostolic church.

For thoughts of the early church fathers on the Resurrection, see the passages from Justin

Martyr's *First Apology*, written about A.D. 158-159, and Athenagoras, who wrote his *Plea for Christians* between A.D. 176 and 180.

All authority *in heaven and on earth* has been given to Me (28:18). The thought is not that in His resurrection Jesus became greater than before, or possessed more authority. Instead the thought is that while on earth the sphere in which Jesus' authority was exercised was limited to the little land in which He lived and ministered. Resurrected, Christ's authority can now be exercised universally.

No wonder our text says, "Therefore go." We go, confidently, expectantly, knowing that wherever we travel Christ is present in power.

Go and make disciples of all nations, *baptizing* them in the name of the Father and of the Son and of the Holy Spirit, and *teaching* them to obey everything I have commanded you (28:19-20). The only verb in the Great Commission is the imperative, "make" in "make disciples." The three italicized terms, although translated as if they had verbal force, are participles in the original Greek. While some have argued that the participles describe the means by which disciples are made, it is better to say simply that these elements characterize the way in which Christ's command is fulfilled. Where the church has accepted the responsibility our Lord lays on us as His followers, believers have reached out aggressively (fulfilling "go"), baptized new believers, and led them into the way of life portrayed in Jesus' words (fulfilling "teach"). The Great Commission is the church's mandate.

Justin Martyr on the Resurrection

The resurrection possible:

To any thoughtful person would anything appear more incredible, than, if we were not in the body, and some one were to say that it was possible that from a small drop of human seed bones and sinews and flesh be formed into a shape such as we see? For let this now be said hypothetically; if you yourselves were not such as you now are, and born of such parents, and one were to show you human seed and a picture of a man, and were to say with confidence that from such a substance such a being could be produced, would you believe before you saw the actual production? No one will dare to deny [that such a statement would surpass belief].

In the same way, then, you are now incredulous because you have never seen a dead man rise from the dead. But as at first you would not have believed it possible that such persons could be produced from the small drop, and yet now you see them thus produced, so also judge ye that it is not impossible that the bodies of men, after they have been dissolved, and like seeds resowed to earth, should in God's appointed time rise again and put on incorruption. For what power worthy of God those imagine who say, that each thing returns to that from which it was produced, and that beyond this not even God Himself can do anything, we are unable to conceive; but this we see clearly, that they would not have believed it possible that they could have become such and produced from such materials, as they now see both themselves and the whole world to be.

And that it is better to believe even what is impossible to our own nature and to men, than to be unbelieving like the rest of the world, we have learned; for we know that our master Jesus Christ said, that "what is impossible with men is possible with God" (Matt. 19:26) and, "Fear not them that kill you, and after that can do no more; but fear Him who after death is able to case both soul and body into hell" (10:28). And hell is a place where those are to be punished who have lived wickedly, and who do not believe that those things which God has taught us by Christ will come to pass.

Athenagoras on the Resurrection

Bearing of the doctrine of the Resurrection on the practices of Christians:

Those who have set up a market for fornication, and established infamous resorts for the young for every kind of vile pleasure—who do not abstain even from males, males with males committing shocking abominations, outraging all the noblest and comeliest bodies in all sorts of ways, so dishonoring the fair workmanship of God (for beauty on earth is not self-made, but sent hither by the hand and will of God)—these men, I say, revile us for the very things which they are conscious of themselves, and ascribe to their own gods, boasting of them as noble deeds, and worthy of the gods. These adulterers and pederasts defame the eunuchs and the once-married (while they themselves live like fishes; for these gulp down whatever falls in their way, and the stronger changes the weaker; and, in fact, this is to feed upon human flesh, to do violence in contravention of the very laws which you and your ancestors, with due care for all that is fair and right, have enacted), so that not even the governors of provinces sent by you suffice for the hearing of the complaints against those, to whom it even is not lawful. . . . But it is incumbent on us to be good and patient of evil. It is reasonable to suppose that those who think they shall have no account to give of the present life, ill or well spent, and that there is no resurrection, but calculate on the soul perishing with the body, and being as it were quenched in it, will refrain from no deed of daring; but as for those who are persuaded that nothing will escape the scrutiny of God, but that even the body which has ministered to the irrational impulses of the soul, and to its desires, will be punished along with it, it is not likely that they will commit even the smallest sin. But if to anyone it appears sheer nonsense that the body which has mouldered away, and been dissolved, and reduced to nothing, should be reconstructed, we certainly cannot with any reason be accused of wickedness with reference to those that believe not, but only of folly; for with the opinions by which we deceive ourselves we injure no one else.

THE PASSAGE IN DEPTH

The Resurrection (28:1-10). See also Luke 24 and John 20–21.

The actual, physical resurrection of Jesus Christ is foundational to our Christian faith. As the Apostle Paul says in 1 Cor. 15:17, "If Christ has not been raised, your faith is futile; you are still in your sins." In fact, a variety of lines of evidence make it very clear that Jesus did rise from the dead. As is often the case, we are called to accept the Gospel message by faith—and then discover that our faith is indeed most reasonable. What are some of the lines of evidence that give us confidence that the Resurrection is no myth, or an event that took place in "sacred history" but not in space and time?

■ Jesus predicted the Resurrection. In Deut. 18 the OT establishes a principle: prophets are authenticated as God's messengers when the things they predict actually—and always—happen. Thus prophecy and fulfillment together constitute a divine sign, a clear and unmistakable indication of God's involvement in our world. A prediction without fulfillment is meaningless; an event that has not been foretold may be mere happenstance. But when prediction and fulfillment are linked, there is no mistaking the hand of God. True prophets never erred.

Thus the fact that the Gospels record frequent statements by Jesus that He would be killed by His enemies and would rise again after the third day is significant. In fact, each time Christ spoke of His death He also promised that He would rise again. Thus the Resurrection is a foretold event, and a clear link between prediction and fulfillment is established, giving added credibility to the resurrection report.

Where did Jesus predict His death and resurrection? Matthew 12:38-40; 16:21; 17:9; 17:22-23; 20:18-19; 26:32; 27:63; Mark 8:31-9:1; 9:10, 31; 10:32-34; 14:28, 58; Luke 9:22-27; John 2:19-22; 12:34; 14–16.

■ The Old Testament predicts Christ's resurrection. If the link between prophecy and fulfillment rested only on the Gospel writers' reports of Jesus' words, some might argue that they ascribed words to Jesus that He had not spoken and then closed the link by describing a resurrection that did not take place.

But predictions of Messiah's resurrection can be found in the OT as well, in passages dating many hundreds of years before the time of Christ. Thus Ps. 16:10 says, "You will not abandon me to the grave, nor will you let your Holy One see decay." And Isaiah reports that after the Servant of the Lord suffers and dies He will be restored: "Though the Lord makes His life a guilt offering, He will see His offspring and prolong His days, and the will of the Lord will prosper in His hand. After the suffering of His soul, He will see the light of life and be satisfied" (53:10-11).

■ The transformation of the disciples. One of the most powerful reasons for accepting the Resurrection as a fact of history is the reaction of Jesus' disciples to Christ's death and resurrection. Jesus' death stunned His followers, dashed their hopes, and left them in despair. Despite what Christ had told them, they never really accepted the notion that their Master was destined to die.

Then, suddenly, we see a group of men who with great enthusiasm and conviction announce that Christ is risen, and who dedicate their lives to bringing this message to the world. If these men became rich or famous by proclaiming Christ, as some who have invented religions, we might question their motives. But instead of fame the apostles of Jesus gave up hope of worldly wealth, suffered rejection and persecution, and despite the most terrible hardships felt only delight in their privilege of serving Jesus. It is simply unimaginable that this could have taken place unless the disciple were totally convinced that Jesus was truly the Son of God, and was truly risen from the dead.

■ The reaction of Jesus' enemies. Clearly, if the members of the Sanhedrin who had arranged Christ's death could have disproved the Resurrection, they surely would have. How? Simply produce the body! If the Sanhedrin really thought the disciples had "stolen" Christ's corpse, as the rumor they started suggests, they were fully empowered to arrest the disciples and to force them to reveal where the body lay. Yet there was no attempt to do anything of the sort!

■ The utter failure of the Jewish leaders to stifle the resurrection report—and they surely must have struggled to find some way to do so—makes it clear that they could not disprove the report.

JOHN CHRYSOSTOM ON THE EVIDENCE

This fourth-century Archbishop of Constantinople argued that in their efforts to squelch the Jesus movement, Christ's enemies instead add powerful testimony to the resurrection story! See, at any rate, these words bearing witness to every one of these facts. "We remember," these are the words, "that that deceiver said, when He was yet alive," (He was therefore now dead), "After three days I rise again. Command therefore that the sepulchre be sealed," (He was therefore buried), "lest His disciples come and steal Him away." So that if the sepulchre be sealed, there will be no unfair dealing. For there could not be. So then the proof of His resurrection has become incontrovertible by what ye have put forward. For because it was sealed, there was no unfair dealing. But if there was no unfair dealing, and the sepulchre was found empty, it is manifest that He is risen, plainly and incontrovertibly. Seest thou, how even against their will they contend for the proof of the truth?"

In view of the eagerness of the Jewish leaders to squelch the Jesus movement, we must take their failure to show the Resurrection to be a hoax as strong evidence that it was not a hoax at all, but actually happened.

■ The Gospels are a late invention anyway. There is unmistakable evidence that the Gospels were written within a few decades of the events the authors describe, well within the lifetimes of those who claim to have been eye-witnesses. And well within the lifetimes of others, both friend and foe, who would surely have known if the reports of Jesus' activities were false! The notion that the story of Jesus and His resurrection could be a fable is absurd on its face, for without a basis in fact, the stories would have been immediately contradicted within Palestine, no vital church would have been formed there and in nearby Samar-

FALSE EXPLANATIONS OF THE EMPTY TOMB

1. Swoon Theory Jesus did not die, but only fainted. Later He left the tomb, and retired into obscurity.	2. Theft Theory Jesus' body was stolen by His followers. Later they lied and said that He was still alive.	3. Removal Theory The Jews themselves removed Jesus' body and hid it to keep the disciples from stealing the body.	4. Hallucination Theory Jesus' followers were hallucinating, and only thought that they saw their Friend alive after His crucifixion.
The soldiers who crucified Jesus attested to His death. This was "expert testimony" indeed!	Jesus' demoralized disciples would not have mounted such an effort.	If the Jews had removed the body, they could have produced it when the disciples announced the resurrection just seven weeks after the crucifixion. The fact that they did not do so makes it clear that no one in authority [in Judaism, or in Rome] had any idea where the body might be.	The psychological makeup of the witnesses, and their various moods when seeing Jesus, do not fit the profile of those who are subject to hallucinations.
Those who wrapped His body would have known if He still lived.	The soldiers on guard would have easily fought off such an attempt.		Too many people saw Jesus at one time for this theory to offer any reasonable explanation for the resurrection report.
After His terrible sufferings Jesus could hardly have survived 3 days on a cold, stone slab.	The Sanhedrin would have arrested the disciples and forced them to reveal where the body was hidden.		The disciples were able to touch Jesus, and saw Him eat. Hallucinations are hardly solid enough for this!
Even if alive He could not have moved away the sealed stone.	Recent Roman law decreed the death penalty for grave robbing.		

ia. And, because we know that Jewish communities throughout the world kept in close touch with the homeland, the temple, and the sages of the land, Paul's mission which went first to the synagogues of Jewish communities in the Roman Empire, would have been countered by simple ridicule and a denial that Jesus had ever lived, performed miracles, died, or been raised from the dead.

But no such ridicule or denial of facts very well known in Palestine and in the Jewish communities of the world took place. Instead there was simply the denial that Jesus was the Savior, and an insistence that somehow the disciples had stolen His body.

This too is strong testimony to the reliability of the Gospel accounts. And a striking attestation of the resurrection of our Lord.

The Guard's Report (28:11-15). Would a military guard unit (typically made up of four men) have willingly admitted sleeping on duty? Certainly not without strong promises of protection as well as payment from the High Priest! The guards assigned by King Herod to watch Peter in prison were summarily executed after the apostle was supernaturally released from prison by an angel (Acts 12:19). Justian's *Digest* [of laws] lists some 18 offenses for which Roman soldiers were liable to the death penalty. Here are the offenses mentioned in the *Digest:* A scout remaining with the enemy (3.4); desertion (3.11; 5.13); going over the wall or rampart (3.17); starting a mutiny (3.19); refusing to protect an officer or deserting one's post (3.22); a drafted man hiding from service (4.2); murder (4.5); laying hands on a superior or insulting a general (6.1); taking flight when the example would influence others (6.3); betraying plans to the enemy (6.4; 7); wounding a fellow soldier with a sword (6.6); disabling self or attempting suicide without reasonable excuse (6.7); leaving the night watch (10.1); breaking a centurion's staff or striking him when being punished (13.4); escaping the guard house (13.5); and disturbing the peace (16.1).

Certainly "sleeping on duty" while an unknown group of men broke the seal on a tomb the soldiers were assigned to guard fits several of the categories!

The Great Commission (28:16-20). The Great Commission provides the driving force for Christian missions. It also reminds us of a vital reality. Christ had "all authority" as He walked the dusty roads of Palestine in His incarnation. But the Incarnation did, in effect, limit Christ's exercise of His power. After the resurrection Christ, now at the right hand of the Father, is again everywhere present, this time as the God-Man. Thus He reminds His followers "all authority in heaven and on earth" is His and, "therefore," we are now enabled to make disciples "of all nations."

Because Christ has been raised from the dead, and lives indeed, there is no place in this world where His power does not reach. Wherever we go, in all the nations of our planet, Jesus' followers go with confidence to present a Gospel that can save and transform the lives of those who believe.

EXPOSITION

Mark's Gospel is marked by rapid movement. Jesus is portrayed as a Man of action, in such a way that His nature as "the Son of God" (1:1) shines clearly through. The vivid and fresh nature of Mark's brief Gospel is created by frequent use of the historical present, by details that could only be provided by eyewitnesses (1:27, 41; 3:5; 7:34; 9:5-6; etc.), and by some 41 uses of the adverb *euthys,* "immediately." Traditionally, Mark's habit of transliterating Latin words into Greek, and his frequent use of Latin grammatical constructions, has led most commentators to suggest that this Gospel was directed primarily to those whose Roman cultural orientation gave them a practical outlook on life.

What impression of Jesus does Mark intend to communicate to the Roman world? Mark intends to demonstrate that Jesus is a unique Person, whose deeds and words establish Him as the Son of God. Mark thus bypasses Christ's birth, barely mentions John's ministry and Christ's baptism (1:1-13), and the calling of the disciples (1:14-20), to move quickly to describe acts that reveal Jesus' divine authority. The supernatural source of Jesus' authority is established in Mark's first report: Jesus is confronted by and drives out an evil spirit (1:21-28). A series of incidents establishes the fact that Christ's authority is complete. Christ not only expels demons, but also is able to heal the most devastating of diseases and even to forgive sins (1:29–2:17). As far as Judaism is concerned, Christ's healing on the Sabbath demonstrates that as Son of God He also holds supreme religious authority: an authority which surpasses that of those who claimed to be the authentic interpreters of Moses (2:18-27).

Jesus appoints Twelve as apostles (3:12-19), and Mark reports a series of significant incidents. The leaders of the Jewish people reject Jesus—even though Christ's acts show He not only is Satan's enemy but is greater than the prince of demons (3:20-30). Even Christ's mother and brothers fail to realize what His miracles imply (3:31-35). Christ now begins to speak in parables, intending that only those willing to do the will of God (and believe in Him) will understand what He teaches about the nature of God's present work in the world (4:1-34).

Yet the one basic, vital truth which humankind must acknowledge is clearly demonstrated by what Jesus then does. He stills a storm, showing His authority over the natural world (4:35-41). He drives out a legion of demons, showing His authority over massed supernatural forces (5:1-20). He cures a woman suffering from a chronic, incurable disease (5:21-34), and even raises the dead (5:35-43). The conclusion is inescapable. The Man who did these things is more than a mere man. He is, as Mark announced in the opening verse of his Gospel, the very Son of God!

WORD STUDIES

Jesus Christ, the Son of God (1:1). Many believe this Gospel was written around A.D. 65-67. At that time the church in Rome was undergoing severe persecution stemming from the fire that devastated the city in A.D. 64, which Nero blamed on Christians. If this is the setting for Mark's Gospel, we can understand why his emphasis on the deity and authority of Jesus would serve to comfort the church as well as evangelize the unreached. The historian Tacitus tells what was happening in Rome at this time, in words recorded in his *Annals* (15:44):

> But neither human help, nor imperial munificence, nor all the modes of placating Heaven, could stifle scandal or dispel the belief that the fire had taken place by order. Therefore, to scotch the rumour, Nero substituted as culprits, and punished with the utmost refinements of cruelty, a class of men, loathed for their vices, whom the crowd styled Christians. Christus, the founder of the name, had undergone the death penalty in the reign of Tiberius, by sentence of the procurator Pontius Pilatus, and the pernicious superstition was checked for a moment, only to break out once more, not merely in Judaea, the home of the disease, but in the capital itself, where all things horrible or shameful in the world collect and find a vogue. First, then, the confessed members of the sect were arrested; next, on their disclosures, vast numbers were convicted, not so much on the count of arson as for hatred of the human race. And derision accompanied their end: they were covered with wild beasts' skins and torn to death by dogs; or they were fastened on crosses and, when daylight failed were burned to serve as lamps by night. Nero had offered his Gardens for the spectacle, and gave an exhibition in his Circus, mixing with the crowds in the habit of a charioteer, or mounted on his car. Hence, in spite of a guilt which had earned the most exemplary punishment, there arose a sentiment of pity, due

to the impression that they were being sacrificed not for the welfare of the state but to the ferocity of a single man.

Preaching a *baptism of repentance* for the remission of sins (1:4). The genitive suggests the repentance preceded or accompanied the baptism: the deliberate change of heart was reflected in the act. The end result ("for" or *eis*) was forgiveness of sins. There is a hint in Scripture of superficial conversion. Faith in any era is expressed in personal commitment and in a transformed life which testifies to the reality of forgiven sins.

All the people of Jerusalem *went out to Him* (1:5). The imperfect tense here suggests a constant flow of persons: they "kept on going out" to hear John. The Jewish people, weary of life under Rome and the Herods, were eager for the prophesied deliverer. How tragic that, as events showed, they were unready to accept the Deliverer God sent them: a deliverer from sin rather than from present political oppression.

He [Jesus] went to her, took her hand and helped her up (1:31). Many focus on the fact that the person healed was Peter's mother-in-law, and use this verse, with 1 Corinthians 9:5, as a proof text against the Roman Catholic doctrine of a celibate clergy. In context, Mark is making a very different point. The healing Jesus brought was immediate and effective. She was not only cured, but at once "began to wait on them."

He also drove out many *demons* (1:34). These beings, identified by most as the angels who fell at the time of Satan's original defection, play a significant role in Mark's Gospel. Concerning their activity and relationship with Jesus, the *Zondervan Expository Dictionary of Bible Words* says,

> Gospel references to demons show them possessing or oppressing human beings (Matt. 8:16, 28, 33; 9:32; 12:22-28; Mark

1:32; 5:16-18; Luke 4:33-35; 8:27-29, 36; 9:42). Such demonic influence was expressed in various sicknesses and in madness. When some observers argued that Jesus was mad or in league with Satan, others said, "Can a demon open the eyes of the blind?" (John 10:21). The Gospels also show Jesus driving out demons whenever He met them (Matt. 9:33; 17:18; Mark 7:26, 29-30; Luke 11:14). Jesus' own defense against the charge is based on this fact. How could Satan's kingdom stand if Jesus drove out demons by demonic powers? Any divided kingdom must soon fall (Luke 11:14-22).

So the Gospels do picture demons as living beings with malignant powers. Demons are personal beings, not impersonal influences (Matt. 8:31). Jesus demonstrated His total mastery of demons, expelling them with a word. He is the "stronger" being of His own illustration, able to "attack and overpower" the demons in their own realm (Luke 11:21-22). However fearsome demons may be, the person who walks with Jesus has nothing to fear (p. 218).

They made an opening in the roof above Jesus, and after *digging* through it (2:4). It was not unusual for sages to travel from town to town to teach the Law, although by the second century some tried to confine study of Torah within the walls of schools. Material reflecting conditions in the first century appeals to householders to welcome traveling sages, saying, "Let your house be a meeting house for the sages" and "Sit amidst the dust of their feet" (Aboth 1:4).

What is striking about this story is the faith that motivated the paralyzed man's friends to dig through the hardened dirt roof formed of layers of branches and mud. Belief in Jesus compels us to come to Him when we're in need, whatever the obstacle.

Why does this fellow talk like that? He's *blaspheming!* Who can forgive sins but God alone? (2:7) The Greek word means to slander or to utter abusive, damaging words. The point expressed by the "teachers of the Law" is that by claiming a prerogative that belongs to God alone, Jesus injured or demeaned God.

Shortly Jesus turned the charge against His critics, when they murmured that the works the Spirit performed through Jesus were energized by Satan (3:20-30). They did blaspheme, for they slandered God Himself. Jesus did not, for the simple reason that, as the Son of God, He had a divine right to forgive sins—and proved His authority by healing the paralytic!

It is not the healthy who need a *doctor*, but the sick (2:17). As late as the third century B.C., popular opinion in Judaism held physicians in suspicion. Disease was linked to sickness and sin; therefore it was appropriate to seek help from a man of God like Elijah or Elisha. Going to a physician displayed a lack of faith.

This attitude began to change in the second century B.C., as reflected in the writings of Ben Sira. After praying, repenting, and making contributions to the temple, the sick person was encouraged to see a physician, but only a godly individual who would seek God's wisdom to understand and prescribe for the ailment. As Ben Sira writes,

> Make friends with the physician, for he
>   is essential to you;
> him also God has established in his
>   profession.
> From God the doctor has his wisdom . . .
>   (38:1, 2).

By the time of Jesus doctors were common in the Holy Land, and ordinarily called in when a person was seriously ill.

But here Jesus uses a metaphor, going back to the imagery linking sickness and sin. This imagery is well established in the prophets (Isa. 1), where physical disorders often stand for spiritual maladies. Christ's observation that the healthy do not need a doctor does not imply that the "teachers of the Law who were Pharisees" (2:16) are spiritually healthy, but rather that they fail to recognize their true condition. Today too, only those who realize they are lost sinners are likely to turn to Jesus. The religious, who feel they are all right, are the hardest to reach with the Gospel.

He looked around at them in anger and, deeply distressed at their *stubborn hearts* (3:5). The Greek word is *porosis,* used of a kind of marble and of hardened bone. The callousness of these opponents of Jesus was revealed when they watched Jesus "closely" to see if He would heal a man on the Sabbath. These religious leaders were not concerned about the man who was suffering, but only about using him to get at Jesus!

Christ's reaction is fascinating. He glared at them in momentary anger (suggested by the aorist tense of the participle) and continued looking around with deep, continuing grief (indicated by Mark's shift to the present participle).

Those whose hearts are so hardened may well deserve to be condemned. But we must grieve when attitudes like theirs characterize those who claim to honor God's name.

The *secret* of the kingdom of God has been given to you" (4:11). Here as elsewhere in the NT (21 times in Paul's writings!) "secret" identifies something previously unknown but now revealed. Why did Jesus limit knowledge of secrets about His kingdom to His disciples? Despite the suggestions of some, the *mysterion* is not that in Jesus the promised eschatological kingdom is now at hand. Christ's words and deeds made it unmistakably clear who He claimed to be. No, the "secret" of Jesus' kingdom is the form it will take (cf. commentary on Matt. 13).

By limiting His revelations about the form of the kingdom to His disciples, Jesus in effect maintained public focus on the real issue: the question of His identity as Messiah and Son of God.

Today too, when dealing with the unconverted, it's wise to keep the focus of our sharing on the real issue: who Jesus is, and what His identity as Son of God means to those who believe in Him.

Don't you put it [a lamp] on its stand? (4:21) Only in this report of the familiar parable is the definite article placed before "lamp," thus indicating "the" lamp rather than "a" lamp. Here the suggestion may be that Jesus, although unrecognized at the moment, is the lamp who will in the future be placed on its stand. His light will be "brought out into the open" (4:22).

No wonder the next image encourages careful listening to Jesus now! (4:24)

The *seed sprouts and grows* (4:27). This parable, like that of the Sower and the Mustard Seed, focuses our attention on the power of the seed. Whether the man who scatters the seed "sleeps or gets up," the dynamic of the seed is at work, and it grows. Surely the Gospel message will have a rich harvest! And, even though Christ's kingdom seems to be launched in insignificance — His appearance as trifling an event as a mustard seed — His kingdom ultimately will fill the whole world.

How important this is for us to remember today. All too often we are enamored by the super-church, and discouraged by the apparent feebleness of our own efforts. Yet it is the seed of the Gospel word that sprouts and grows. If we continue to be faithful we will see God's rich harvest.

At once Jesus realized that power had gone out from Him (5:30). According to OT Law the woman with an issue of blood was "unclean," and would contaminate anyone whom she touched. Similarly, a dead body, like that of the 12-year-old girl in this story, would make the person touching her ritually unclean. As had been established in Haggai 2:10-14, holiness cannot be transmitted by touch, but ritual uncleanness can. And the striking thing is that in the religion of Israel ritual uncleanness prevented an individual from approaching God in worship or participating in the worship celebrations of God's people!

Thus the story of Jesus' healing of the sick woman and raising of the dead girl are especially significant. Christ was not cut off from God by the touch of either the woman or the girl! Instead the power of God flowed from Him, to conquer illness and overcome death! In the case of this one Man the flow was reversed. This one Man's power was not only unscathed by ritual contamination, but the power going "out from Him" was so great that the very cause of uncleanness itself was removed.

Perhaps the method of healing here, which involved touching the dead, is the cause of the "strict orders" that Jesus gave "not to let anyone know about this" (5:43). The "this" here is far more likely to be the fact that Jesus took the dead girl's hand and lifted her up than the fact of her restoration to life. That could hardly be kept secret, for the home was already surrounded by mourners who knew very well that the "little girl" was dead.

Jesus may have had in mind the fact that the religious leaders would surely focus on Christ's act in touching the girl rather than on the miracle, and use that touch as an excuse to criticize Him and cloud the issue.

Let's not make that same mistake when we see Christ work in lives today. It matters little whether or not others do it our way. What matters is the power of Jesus to heal body and soul.

THE PASSAGE IN DEPTH

John the Baptist Prepares the Way (1:1-8). See the Commentary on John 1:19-34, and parallel passages in Matt. 3:1-12, Luke 3:3-20.

The Baptism and Temptation of Jesus (1:9-13). See the Commentary on Matt. 4:1-11, and parallel passages in Matt. 3:13-17 and Luke 4:1-13.

The Calling of the First Disciples (1:14-20). See Mark 3:13-19.

Jesus Heals Many (1:29-34). See the Commentary on Mark 3:20-30, and parallel passages in Matt. 8:14-17 and Luke 4:31-37.

A Man with Leprosy (1:40-45). See parallel passages in Matt. 8:1-4 and Luke 5:12-16.

Background. The disease called leprosy, *lepros* here, is identified by the Hebrew word *sara'at* in the OT. The NIV correctly renders it as "infectious skin disease," for it included any sickness that caused sores or eruptions on the skin.

The most significant thing about such diseases is that they made a person ritually "unclean," and meant that he or she was to be isolated from others. Both of these elements, the uncleanness and the isolation that was experienced by a person with "leprosy," play a significant role in Mark's story.

According to the OT a person with any visible outbreak was to present himself or herself to a priest, who was responsible to diagnose the problem (Lev. 13). When the eruptions subsided the individual was to return to the priest, who certified him or her ritually clean (Lev. 14). This did not imply that the priest had a medical function, but instead reflected the priests' role in OT religion of maintaining the ritual standards for participation in Israel's worship and community life.

Interpretation. The man who came to Jesus was convinced that Christ could heal him

(1:40). But he was not certain that Jesus would be willing to act for someone "unclean."

The text says that Jesus was "filled with compassion" (1:41). The word here is *splanchnizomai.* Much more common are *eleos,* also translated "mercy," and *oiktirmos,* expressing pity. But our word is especially important, and indicates a powerful surge of emotion. It is the word chosen by the Gospel writers to describe Jesus' response to persons in need (Matt. 9:36; 14:14; 15:32; 18:27; Mark 6:34; 8:2; Luke 7:13; 10:33; 15:20).

Moved by this outpouring of love and concern Jesus reached out and touched the leper, announcing at the same moment, "Be clean!" The act was stunning, for any other person would have been ritually contaminated by contact with a leper. Instead Jesus' touch cleansed the unclean by healing the disease which caused his isolation.

Many have pointed out that leprosy serves at times as a metaphor for sin, which causes human beings to be isolated from God. Thus in Jesus' act they see a symbolic affirmation of His power to cleanse mankind of sin itself. Very likely. Perhaps even more clearly the incident shows that attitude which most sharply distinguished Jesus from the religious leaders of His day. Jesus cared about human beings, and by touching the leper He showed that in God's sight human need takes precedent over ritual and regulation.

Why then did Jesus send the leper to a priest, in compliance with that OT law He seems to have violated? The text says Jesus commanded him to "show yourself to the priest and offer the sacrifices . . . as a testimony to them" (1:44). There must be no question in the mind of the man or of the leaders that Jesus had truly healed the leper, and so displayed His authority over ritual defilement.

Why then warn the leper to tell no one? We see the reason in the result: Jesus could no longer enter a town openly. Rather than aid Jesus in His ministry, reports of His miracles brought crowds who came not to hear His message, but to be healed or simply to see Him work His wonders.

Application. Christ's response to the leper provides a powerful example for believers today. The "untouchables" in our own society may believe that God is able to help them, but like the leper they doubt His willingness to do so. Only by responding to those in need as Jesus did—with a surge of compassion that causes us to reach out, to touch, and to help—can we convince them that our God does care.

Jesus heals a paralytic (2:1-12). See the commentary on Luke 5:17-26, and the parallel passage in Matt. 9:1-8.

Jesus calls Levi (2:13-17). See parallel passages in Matt. 9:9-13 and Luke 5:27-32.

Background. It is difficult for us to grasp the social position of the "sinners" and tax collectors in first-century Judaism. While the "sinners" may simply refer to those who failed to maintain the Pharisees' high standards of ritual observance, the "tax collectors" undoubtedly were despised and ostracized by all. Not only could no tax collector hold public office or even serve as a witness in a civil or criminal case, money from the wallets of tax gatherers was so tainted that it could not be accepted at the temple even as alms for the poor. Nor could their money be exchanged.

Yet Jesus not only called Levi (identified in Matt. 9:9 as the Apostle Matthew himself), but accepted his invitation to a banquet he held for many of his fellow "tax collectors and 'sinners.' "

It is no wonder the Pharisees, committed to a way of life that required them to separate from any person or thing that bore the slightest taint of uncleanness, were incensed. Jesus actually ate with sinners. In that day, sharing a meal signified mutual acceptance! Surely the coming Messiah would crush sinners and succor the righteous. Here this supposed Teacher and Prophet scorned the righteous to identify Himself with sinners. To them, Christ's actions were incomprehensible, and were evidence that whoever He claimed to be, He simply could not have come from God.

Interpretation. Both Mark and Luke report Christ's observation that it is the sick rather than the healthy who need a doctor (see Word Study, Mark 2:17). Christ clearly understood His mission as one to sinners. The Pharisees did not grasp the nature of His mission, in part because they did not realize that they were sinners, in need of spiritual healing and renewal.

Matthew adds another phrase to Christ's response. "Go and learn what this means: 'I desire mercy, not sacrifice' " (9:13).

This was a stunning statement, for the phrase "go and learn" was a rabbinic formula, used to dismiss those who need further study of text! The Pharisees, who prided themselves on their conformity to OT law, had actually misunderstood God's message.

The verse Jesus quoted is found in Hosea 6:6. In this particular form, "mercy, not sacrifice," the Semitic antithesis means "mercy is more fundamental than sacrifice."

Thus Jesus is correct in giving priority to the needs of sinners for restoration to right relationship with God. And the Pharisees are wrong in giving priority to ritual over human need.

Implications. It is tragic when Christians today, like the Pharisees of Christ's time, are so zealously committed to the less important implications of faith's lifestyle that they ignore that which has priority with God. How often our commitment to our particular doctrinal distinctives seems more important to us than fulfilling Christ's command to love our brothers and sisters in the Lord (John 13:34-35). How often our fear of contamination makes us uncomfortable with today's "sinners," when we ought instead to be so filled with compassion that we reach out to touch them.

In His formulation of His own mission, "I have not come to call the righteous, but sinners" (Mark 2:17), Christ reminds us of God's priority for our time as well.

May we experience the freedom Christ knew to respond to sinners, whatever the reaction of those among us who also need to "go and learn."

Jesus Questioned about Fasting (2:18-22). See parallel passages in Matt. 9:14-17 and Luke 5:37-39.

Lord of the Sabbath (2:23–3:6). See the Commentary on Matthew 12:1-21, and the parallel passage in Luke 6:1-11.

Crowds follow Jesus (3:7-12). See the Commentary on 3:20-30 for Christ vs. demons.

The Appointing of the Twelve Apostles (3:13-19). See parallel passages (cf. chart below). The word "apostle" is used of representatives commissioned by a high-ranking person, and implies that they speak and act under, and with, His authority. Four lists of

the Twelve are found in Scripture. In each list, Peter is mentioned first, and the same four hold the top four places, although in different orders. The second group of four begins in each case with Philip, and the third group of four lists James first. Judas Iscariot is always mentioned last. Note that Thaddaeus in Matthew and Mark is called Judas, son of James, in Luke and Acts.

Matthew	Mark	Luke	Acts
1. Simon Peter	1. Simon Peter	1. Simon Peter	1. Simon Peter
2. Andrew	2. James, son of Zebedee	2. Andrew	2. John
3. James, son of Zebedee	3. John	3. James	3. James
4. John	4. Andrew	4. John	4. Andrew
5. Philip	5. Philip	5. Philip	5. Philip
6. Bartholomew	6. Bartholomew	6. Bartholomew	6. Thomas
7. Thomas	7. Matthew	7. Matthew	7. Bartholomew
8. Matthew	8. Thomas	8. Thomas	8. Matthew
9. James, son of Alphaeus	9. James, son of Alphaeus	9. James, son of Alphaeus	9. James, son of Alphaeus
10. Thaddaeus	10. Thaddaeus	10. Simon the Zealot	10. Simon the Zealot
11. Simon the Zealot	11. Simon the Zealot	11. Judas, son of James	11. Judas, son of James
12. Judas Iscariot	12. Judas Iscariot	12. Judas Iscariot	12. Judas Iscariot

Jesus and Beelzebub (3:20-30). See also parallel passages in Matt. 12:22-37 and Luke 11:14-26.

Background. Jesus had already clearly and unmistakably demonstrated His authority over demons, driving them out of the ill and insane (1:34; 3:11-12). He had even given His disciples authority to preach, and drive out demons as well (3:15). There was only one question remaining. Where did Jesus get such authority?

This question had only two possible answers. Either Jesus drove out demons by the power of God, or by the prince of demons, Beelzebub. The origin of the name is uncertain, but may be constructed on the Hebrew *zebul,* "house," and *baal,* "master." There is no doubt, however, that in Jesus' day it was a name for Satan.

On the one hand there were exorcists in Israel, who were welcomed rather than viewed with suspicion. Why then wasn't Jesus honored by these leaders whose own followers (literally, "sons") practiced exorcism? It was undoubtedly due to the fact that Jesus scandalized them by eating with sinners (2:13-17)

and violating their interpretation of the Sabbath (2:23–3:6). How could they acknowledge God as the source of Jesus' works, without at the same time questioning their most dearly held beliefs.

In fact, Christ's miracles were evidence that compelled belief. The teachers of the Law made a conscious and willful choice to reject that evidence when they accused Jesus of being "possessed by Beelzebub."

Interpretation. Christ's response to the charges was to point out the obvious. No ruler acts against the interests of his own kingdom. It is obvious that Satan would not empower Jesus to make war on his own!

There is another obvious implication of Christ's success against demons. Jesus must be more powerful than the one He overcomes! Thus Christ's authority over demons is unmistakable proof that God is the source of His power.

With this established, Jesus warns His accusers. Their accusation is a blasphemy against the Holy Spirit, which is an "eternal sin" and will "never be forgiven."

The context enables us to define this "unforgivable sin." People may doubt the Gospel and blaspheme against Christ, but they may also change their minds, believe, and be forgiven. The sin of these teachers of the Law is that they knew the truth, and realized that Christ's exorcisms must have been done by the power of God. Their accusation was a hardened, deliberate and conscious rejection of the Spirit's work through Christ even though there could be no other explanation of His works.

It is the deliberateness of the rejection, its conscious and willful rejection of known truth, that makes the sin unforgivable. It is unforgivable not because God is unwilling to accept those who repent, but because the choice these men made shows that they are beyond repentance.

Application. J.C. Ryle notes that "there is such a thing as a sin which is never forgiven. But those who are troubled about it are most unlikely to have committed it." There is perhaps a corollary. Those who adopt the view of the teachers of the Law are so hostile to Christ that they are not at all likely to be troubled by the thought of possible judgment.

Jesus' Mother and Brothers (3:31-35). See parallel passages in Matt. 12:46-50, Luke 8:19-21.

The Parable of the Sower (4:1-34). For a discussion of the parables see the Commentary on Matthew 13:1-58 and the parallel passages in Luke 8:4-18 and 13:18-21.

Jesus Calms the Storm (4:35-41). See also the parallel passages in Matt. 8:23-27 and Luke 8:22-25.

Background. The Sea of Galilee lies in a shallow basin surrounded by hills. The lake is subject to sudden, furious squalls, which Luke calls *lailaps anemou,* "a windstorm of wind." We can gauge the fury of this blow by the disciples' terror, for several of them were fishermen who must have weathered many a storm on this very sea in the years they had plied their trade here.

Interpretation. A number of commentators have looked for some hidden spiritual lesson in this story. Tertullian saw the boat as the church, and felt that the storm was a threat to it rather than the disciples. Others see in it an indication that those who follow Jesus (Matt.

8:23) will experience fearful storms, but will surely be protected by Jesus' presence. While there may be merit in drawing such applications, in Mark's sequencing of events this launches a series of "great miracles." These are structured to show the reader that Jesus truly does have all power. Calming the storm reveals His control over nature; the healing of a demon-possessed man shows His authority over all the spirit realm; the healing of a sick woman and raising of a dead girl demonstrate His ability to conquer every power which holds man captive. Jesus not only claimed to be the Son of God, He demonstrated it in every realm.

Application. The terror of the disciples who failed to realize that despite the storm they were perfectly safe in Jesus' presence surely spoke to Mark's readers. Recalling the report in the *Annals of Tacitus* quoted at the beginning of this study, we can sense something of the comfort this story must have brought early Christians. Whatever the dangers, whatever the pain, Jesus was present, and in the most significant eternal sense of the word, the believer was and is "safe."

The Healing of a Demon-possessed Man (5:1-20). See also parallel passages in Matt. 8:28-34 and Luke 8:26-39.

Background. This account follows that of calming the storm in each of the Synoptic Gospels. In each it forms part of a series demonstrating the unlimited extent of Jesus' powers.

This sequence, as well as such details as casting the demons into a herd of swine, make it clear that each writer describes the same incident. Yet Matthew speaks of two demon-possessed men, while Luke and Mark mention only one. And Luke places the incident in Garasa rather than Gadara. This has been widely pointed to as an "error" in Scripture. However, the new Revell *Bible Difficulties, Solved!* points out a simple explanation.

The most likely location of the event is Gadara. Most believe Garasa reflects a scribal error, involving the substitution of an "r" for a "d," letters which look similar in Aramaic.

What then about the "two" versus "one" maniacs? Is this a contradiction? Not necessarily. After all, Matthew and Mark do not suggest there was only one maniac. They simply concentrate attention on one. Suppose you told a friend, "Jim was at the party but came late," while another person told the same friend, "Jim and Carl came late to the party." Should you be charged with an "error" because you failed to mention Carl when telling about Jim? Of course not! Why then should the NT be charged with an error because Matthew and Mark only mention one of the two maniacs, while Luke mentions two?

Especially since each writer agrees on the central elements of the story. Jesus demonstrates His power over demons by casting them out of their human victims and permitting them to go into a herd of pigs, which dash into the water and are drowned. To insist that Matthew and Mark or Luke made an error, simply because they fail to agree on the number of maniacs, hardly seems reasonable under the circumstances.

Interpretation. Perhaps the most striking element in this story is the transformation of the attitude displayed by the demons. When we meet them they seem then in total control of the man they possess, terrorizing the neighborhood. When Jesus appears, however, they shout out His identity, "What do You want with me, Jesus, Son of the Most High God?" (5:7)

Immediately they are transformed from tyrants who dominate into supplicants who grovel before Jesus, begging Him not to torment them.

Why did Jesus permit them to enter the herd of pigs? It would be wrong to assume that Jesus felt any sympathy for those malevolent beings. What this unique event did, however, was to prove to the man who had been demon-possessed and to all observers that the demons had really been driven out. And the herd's subsequent rush to destruction made it very clear that those who house demons are sure to be destroyed rather than benefited.

Application. Let's never underestimate the authority of Jesus over the powers of darkness. And let us never mistake the danger in seeking help from the satanic and occult.

MARK 6:1–8:30
Jesus' Conflicts

EXPOSITION

The reports of miracles that fill the first chapters of Mark's Gospel have clearly established the authority of Jesus. The frustrated Pharisees have suggested that Jesus' power over demons comes from Satan—an attack Jesus easily deflects. Jesus then went on to show that His authority extended to power over nature, sickness, and even death, as well as demons.

Now Mark reports a new cycle of events, revealing a variety of reactions to Jesus' ministry. The people of Nazareth reject Jesus because they think they know Him (6:1-6). Yet He is able to give His disciples authority over evil spirits! (6:6-13) About this time John the Baptist is executed by Herod, who preferred to kill a man he knew was innocent rather than suffer possible embarrassment before dinner guests (6:14-29).

Then comes a fascinating double sequence of events. Each begins with the feeding of a hungry multitude, suggesting Jesus' ability to meet the most basic needs of humankind. After crossing a sea, Jesus engages in a sharp conflict with the Pharisees and teachers of the Law. He has a conversation about bread and performs a miracle of healing, which leads to an expression of wonder by the crowds, and finally of faith by the disciples.

Jesus Clashes with Pharisees	7:1-23	8:11-13
Jesus Arouses Awe, Faith	7:37	8:27-30

It is fascinating in these chapters to trace the variety of reactions to Jesus.

■ His neighbors at Nazareth seem almost insulted that one of their own should gain fame.

■ The 5,000 Jesus fed wanted to acclaim Him king "by force" (John 6:14-15).

■ The Pharisees and teachers of the Law held rigidly to their traditions despite Jesus' devastating critique of their theology.

■ A pagan woman saw clearly who He was, and her faith was rewarded.

■ Other crowds were deeply impressed with Jesus' powers of healing, but rather than respond with faith were simply "overwhelmed with amazement" (7:37).

■ His disciples continued to be confused about the meaning of what they had seen, but despite their lack of understanding they grasped the one central and essential truth: Jesus is the Christ, the Son of God.

Today, as in the first century, men and women must make a decision about Jesus. Mark reminds us that the evidence is in, and each of us must choose. Will we simply be amazed and awed or will we trust ourselves to Jesus as the Christ, the Son of the living God?

WORD STUDIES

Isn't this the *carpenter*? (6:3) In Israel carpentry was an insignificant occupation. While working in metals was considered an art, carpentry was a part-time trade. The carpenter used a few crude tools, fixed broken doors or plows, made wooden spoons and wooden door keys, and shaped rude tables and chairs. In the East houses were constructed of stone or mud bricks, and most household dishes were of pottery. There was little need for the skilled work done by modern carpenters.

Thus, to call Jesus "the carpenter" was to dismiss Him as one who followed an insignificant trade, as today one might say, "Oh, he's just a day laborer." How completely Isaiah's prediction was fulfilled: "He had no beauty or majesty to attract us to Him, nothing in His appearance that we should desire Him. He was despised and rejected by men" (Isa. 53:2-3).

Isn't this *Mary's son,* and the brother of James, Joseph, Judas and Simon? (6:3) The Jews normally identified a man by naming his father rather than his mother—even when the father had died. Why then did the neighbors call Jesus "Mary's son"? This verse may indicate that rumors persisted that Jesus was born before the marriage of Mary and Joseph was consummated, and He was thought to have been illegitimate. On the one hand this may help to explain why Christ's neighbors "took offense" at Him. On the other, it is perhaps subtle support for Scripture's teaching of Christ's virgin birth.

"He could not do any miracles there, except lay hands on a few sick people and heal them" (6:5). The Greek phrase is *ouk edynato,* "not able to." Typically the verb looks to the inherent physical, spiritual, or supernatural power of individuals. The challenging question here is: how could the attitude of Jesus' neighbors limit His inherent power to perform *dynamis,* "powerful acts"?

While Mark tends to show situations in which Jesus performed miracles in response to faith, we should not conclude that the failure of Jesus' neighbors to believe did in fact limit Christ's essential power. Instead Jesus was unable to act because of moral responsibility to His unbelieving neighbors. He was not able to perform miracles because the people of Nazareth would have rejected this evidence as well, and so been hardened in their unbelief.

It is striking that at this time Jesus' own brothers did not believe in Him (John 7:5). Christ's failure to perform miracles in their hometown may have actually given them time for faith to be born and to grow (Acts 1:14).

He sent them out *two by two* (6:7). The Sanhedrin also sent out the rabbis it commissioned as special messengers in pairs. The well established Jewish custom apparently reflects the requirement that any testimony must be established "on the testimony of two or three witnesses" (Deut. 17:6).

***You* give them something to eat (6:37).** "You" is an emphatic personal pronoun, added despite the fact that the verb form already indicated whom Jesus was speaking to. The disciples were sensitive to the needs of the crowd, and this was good. In saying "You give them something to eat," Jesus taught three lessons. First, where there is need, Christ's followers are responsible to respond. Second, in ourselves we have no ability to help. And third, if we commit our resources to Jesus He will multiply what we do have and enable us to meet others' needs.

The number of the men who had eaten was *five thousand* (6:44). Matthew adds that there were also "women and children." The number gathered is phenomenal, for archeological surveys have shown that at the time the population of the nearby cities of Capernaum and Bethsaida was only two to three thousand!

Not only did the disciples lack funds to buy bread for over 5,000 people. There would not have been enough bread available in the area to feed them!

About the *fourth watch of the night* He went out to them, walking on the lake (6:48). Mark uses the Roman system of marking time. The fourth watch would fall between 3 and 6 A.M. As it was already "late" (6:35) when Jesus fed the 5,000, "evening" here means late at night.

"Eating food with hands that were 'unclean,'—that is, [ceremonially] unwashed" (7:2). Alfred Edersheim describes the practice Mark refers to in his *Life and Times of Jesus the Messiah:*

It was the practice to draw water out of these with what was called a natla, antila, or antelaya, very often of glass, which must hold (at least) a quarter of a log—a measure equal to one and a half "egg-shells." For, no less quantity than this might be used for affusion. The water was poured on both hands, which must be free of anything covering them, such as gravel, mortar, etc. The hands were lifted up, so as to make the water run to the wrist, in order to ensure that the whole hand was washed, and that the water polluted by the hands did not again run down the fingers. Similarly, each hand was rubbed with the other (the fist) provided the hand that rubbed had been affused; otherwise, the rubbing might be done against the head, or even against a wall. But there was one point on which special stress was laid. In the "first affusion," which was all that originally was required when the hands were not

Levitically "defiled," the water had to run down to the wrist (*chuts lappereq,* or *ad happereq*). If the water remained short of the wrist, the hands were not clean. Accordingly, the words of St. Mark can only mean that the Pharisees eat not "except they wash their hands to the wrist" (Vol. 2, p. 11).

How tragic to be concerned about such details! After Christ has performed such miracles, it is utterly clear that the one issue that every person must face is who He is.

For from within, out of men's *hearts,* come evil thoughts (7:21-22). Here, as often in the Bible, the "heart" stands for the essential character of the individual. True righteousness can be achieved only by a change of heart, not by ritual practices, ascetic commitment, or attempts at self-reformation.

Even the *dogs* under the table eat the children's crumbs (7:28). The Greek word that Mark chooses is *kynarioi,* "puppies" that were household pets. Obviously, the needs of children in the house are of greater concern than the needs of mere pets, so the children will be fed "first." But the woman asked in faith for the "crumbs" left over. She rightly saw that there was no limit to God's supply of blessings.

Afterward the disciples picked up seven *basketfuls* of broken pieces that were left over (8:8). On the surface it might appear that after feeding the 4,000 there was less food left over than after the earlier feeding of the 5,000 ("twelve basketfuls," 6:43). In fact, the opposite is the case. The baskets at the first miracle were *kophinos,* wicker containers in which an individual carried food when on a journey. But here the baskets are *spyris,* giant storage baskets large enough to hold the Apostle Paul when he was lowered from the walls of Damascus (Acts 9:25). Christ's ability to supply our needs truly is unlimited.

Why does this generation ask for a *miraculous sign?* (8:12) The Greek word here is *semeion.* It views a miracle as an authenticating mark, rather than looking at it as a demonstration of power. Jesus had shown the full extent of His authority in a variety of miracles that showed His power over nature, demons, sickness, and even death. Yet the Pharisees demanded some sign "from heaven" that would authenticate His claim to have come from God!

Jesus refused their demand. They had already rejected the overwhelming evidence of His many miracles. Without faith, they would reject whatever wonder He performed.

Interestingly, Matthew 16:4 adds, "None will be given it except the sign of Jonah," referring to His coming resurrection. When that utterly compelling confirmation of Christ's claims took place, the leaders of Israel still refused to believe.

Even miracles are powerless to change the minds of those who simply refuse to believe.

Watch out for the yeast of the Pharisees and that of Herod (8:15). The rabbis used yeast as a metaphor for evil dispositions within human beings. Reference to "Herod" is found only in Mark. Luke 12:1 says "Pharisees" and Matt. 16:6 says "yeast of the Pharisees and Sadducees," identifying the "yeast" with their teachings (16:12). The approach to Scripture of these religious parties contains an evil disposition which in time will corrupt the very Word they are so intent on understanding!

Why then does Mark add Herod? Perhaps because Herod too wanted a sign (Luke 23:8). More likely, because Herod, like the Pharisees, failed to realize the meaning of Christ's miracles (Mark 6:14), and refused to heed Jesus' words concerning who He was. If the Pharisee stands here for the individual blind to Jesus because of his religious faith, Herod stands for the secular man who, although burdened by a sense of guilt for actions he knows full well are wrong, remains blind to who Jesus is, and blind to the hope He offers every man.

THE PASSAGE IN DEPTH

A Prophet Without Honor (6:1-6). See the Commentary on Luke 4:14-30, and also the parallel in Matt. 13:54-58.

Jesus Sends Out the Twelve (6:6-13). See the Commentary on Matt. 10:1-34, and also Luke 10:1-24.

John the Baptist Beheaded (6:14-29). See also Matt. 14:1-12 and Luke 9:7-9.

Background. Herod Antipas, the son of Herod the Great, was actually a tetrarch. For some 30 years he had been permitted by Rome to rule Galilee and Perea. The title "king" is a courtesy title only.

John had been preaching primarily in Perea, "on the other side of the Jordan" (John 1:28), while Jesus' ministry was focused on Galilee. Technically both John and Jesus operated within Herod's jurisdiction, and the ruler would undoubtedly have had agents watch the crowds that gathered to hear the two popular preachers.

In this situation John's open condemnation of Herod for taking "your brother's wife" (6:18) created a problem for the wicked but weak ruler. Herod's first wife was the daughter of the king of Nabateans, whose land lay next to Herod's. Earlier a border war had broken out, and Herod was saved only by Roman intervention. Now Herod had thrown out his wife and lived openly with Herodias, who was married to Herod Philip, another son of Herod the Great and Antipas' half brother. To further complicate the matter, Herodias was also Herod's own niece, the daughter of another half brother, Aristobulus. While marriage to a niece was acceptable at the time, marrying a half-brother's wife was considered to be incest (Lev. 18:16; 20:21). Matthew tells us that John kept on denouncing Herod continually. Matthew uses the imperfect *elegen,* which means "used to say repeatedly."

This harassment was dangerous to Herod on two counts. It might well stir up the further animosity of Herod's ex-father-in-law, Aretas. And it might very well stimulate an uprising among religious Jews, scandalized by Herod's behavior and impassioned by the messianic expectation John's preaching had aroused.

Thus we can understand why Herod acted to imprison John, and why he feared the reaction of the people if he had John executed (Matt. 14:5). Herod was also apparently fascinated by the "righteous and holy" John (6:19-20), whom he protected from the violent hatred of Herodias.

We sense something of Herodias' character not only from reports of that time of her scandalous morals, but also from the fact that she cast her daughter, then probably between 12 and 14, as a dancing girl. While nothing in the text indicates Salome's dance was sensual, the low status and poor reputation of dancing girls may suggest it. The dance pleased Herod, who foolishly promised her any reward in his power to give.

Interpretation. The story Mark tells turns on the foolish promise Herod made, and the hostility of Herodias. After Herod uttered his foolish oath, the girl asked her mother what to request. Then she told the king, "I want you to give me right now the head of John the Baptist on a platter" (6:25).

Mark tells us that the king was "greatly distressed" (6:26) at the request. He knew it was wrong to execute the "righteous and holy" John. But he was more concerned about how he appeared to his guests.

It is interesting that his promise, "Whatever you ask I will give you, up to half my kingdom" (6:23), follows a formula used by the ancient Persian rulers. Herod, a minor ruler at best, was consciously aping the powerful great kings of the past! How hard it is for little men, desperate to appear greater than they are, to admit they have done something foolish!

What might Herod have done? He might have rebuked Salome and Herodias as well, and truly acted as a king. Instead he chose to do what he knew was wrong, merely to preserve the false image he tried so desperately to project to the sycophants who attended his banquet. And so John died, because of the weakness of a wicked, foolish man.

Application. Herod's act that night provides us with an important mirror to use in examining ourselves. Are we moral heroes, like John, who confronted evil in the powerful? Or are we moral cowards, like Herod, more concerned about what others will think than about doing what is right?

When we make Herod's choice we are sure to harm others. But, more importantly, we are sure to trap ourselves. Others may pretend to admire us, but moral cowards who act in order to appear strong are always known for what they are—and laughed at behind their backs.

Jesus Feeds the Five Thousand (6:30-44). See the Commentary on Mark 8:1-13 below.

Jesus Walks on the Water (6:45-56). See the parallel passages in Matt. 14:22-36 and John 6:16-24.

Background. The Gospel accounts agree on the occasion, the prevailing winds which made the disciples' progress so slow, and the appearance of Jesus walking on the water. Only Matthew tells us of Peter's courageous leap over the side to walk toward Jesus, and the sudden failure of his faith.

There may be several reasons for Mark's reticence. For one thing, it is not necessary to the pattern he develops (see Exposition, above). For another, Mark may display Peter's own hesitation to tell this story. Not because it reflects negatively on Peter, but because in fact it reflects so positively!

Why would what Mark wrote display Peter's point of view? Clement of Alexandria (ca. A.D. 150-203) reports an early tradition that "the [Gospel] according to Mark had this occasion: When Peter had preached the word publicly in Rome and had declared the Gospel by [the] Spirit, those who were present—they were many—besought Mark, since he had followed him [Peter] for a long time and remembering the things that had been spoken, to write out the things that had been said; and when he had done [this], he gave the Gospel to those who [had] asked him. When Peter learned of it later, he neither obstructed nor commended [it]."

Interpretation. Matthew tells us that when Jesus identified Himself to the terrified disciples, Peter cried out to Him. "Lord, if it's You, tell me to come to You on the water" (14:28). When Christ answered, "Come," Peter "got down out of the boat" and "walked on the water" (14:29).

It is common to focus on the next verse; it tells us that when Peter "saw the wind" he became frightened and began to sink. It may seem a strange phrase, to "see the wind." But, as F.F. Bruce has noted, "It is one thing to see a storm from the deck of a stout ship, another to see it in the midst of the waves." The phrase tells us that suddenly Peter became aware of the storm, while before he had been aware only of Jesus! Only when his gaze shifted from Jesus to the circumstances did he plunge into the waters.

Yet the danger served to remind him of Christ, and he cried out urgently, "Lord, save me!" Jesus did, reaching out His hand, and asking why he behaved as a "little faith" and began to doubt.

There was reason enough in the circum-

stances to create doubt! But the fact that Peter left the safety of the boat in response to Jesus' invitation should have erased his fears. As long as we act in obedience to Jesus' call, we are safe, whatever winds rage around us.

How then does this incident reflect to Peter's credit? Simply in this. Only Peter had enough courage to leave the boat in the first place. Only Peter was so eager to be with Jesus that he begged our Lord to call him to Him. It is this, Peter's courage and his commitment, that made him the first of the Apostles. And it is these qualities that make him a person believers today might well emulate.

Application. There are many lessons here for us. But perhaps the most important one is that those who seek to be close to Jesus, and who respond courageously to His call, are still vulnerable to doubts. Yet when we keep our eyes on Christ, we are safe. And even if we momentarily take our eyes off the Lord, He is close by, to reach out His hand and lift us up.

Clean and Unclean (7:1-23). See the Commentary on Matt. 15:1-20.

The Faith of a Syrophonecian Woman (7:24-30). See the Commentary on Matt. 15:21-38.

The Healing of a Deaf and Dumb Man (7:31-37). See also Matt. 16:13-15.

Background. The response of the people to Jesus' miracle of healing has a fascinating resemblance to that of the crowds as reported in Matt. 16. "He has done everything well" (Mark 7:37) is the same kind of praise the disciples recounted by identifying Jesus with one of the great prophets of times past.

The trouble is, the response is inadequate. It might be enough if Jesus were merely another man. But Christ was the Son of God. Instead of amazement, His acts should have generated faith.

Jesus Feeds the 4,000 (8:1-13). See also Matt. 14:13-21, 15:29-39, Mark 6:30-44, Luke 9:10-17, and the Commentary on John 6.

Background. While the bread of the wealthy was made of wheat, and the poor made do with that made from ground barley, bread was viewed as the most basic of foods. Frequently "bread" served as a metaphor for food itself, and so it was bread that sustained biological life. Thus when Jesus said "man does not live on bread alone" (Matt. 4:4), He was affirming that human beings, although material, are also spiritual beings, not to be dominated by physical urges or even needs.

Jesus' miracles of feeding the 5,000, and later the 4,000, were dramatic evidence to all Israel that Christ was concerned with every human need. It also, however, stimulated a most revealing response. Matthew 14:20 says, "They all ate and were satisfied," and John 6:15 tells us that the crowd "intended to come and make Him king by force." The crowd was more excited by the possibility that Jesus might feed them than by the possibility that He might save them from their sins.

Interpretation. The miracles of feeding thousands with only minimal resources are reported in Matthew, Mark, and John. In John the miracle serves as the occasion for Jesus preaching on the Bread of Life. It is clear from John that the crowds who ate the food Jesus provided were challenged to see in His miracles evidence that He Himself was the "true bread" (John 6:32) sent by God from heaven to sustain not merely physical but more importantly spiritual life. It is also clear that the crowds rejected Christ's explanation of the meaning of His miracle. They "began to grumble" (6:41) and because Jesus' words constituted a "hard teaching" (6:60), many early adherents of His movement "turned back and no longer followed Him" (6:66).

Mark and Matthew tell us none of this. Instead, they ask us to simply look at what Jesus did and draw our lessons from that. It is only when we read John that we find in Christ's discourse the deeper meaning of this important sign.

What then can we learn from the synoptics' accounts? Placing the accounts side by side, we note their similarities.

FEEDING THE 5,000

Matthew 14:13-21
When Jesus heard what had happened He withdrew by boat privately to a solitary place. Hearing of this, the crowds followed Him on foot from the towns. When Jesus landed and saw a large crowd, He had compassion on them and healed their sick.

As evening approached, the disciples came to Him and said, "This is a remote place, and it's already getting late. Send the crowds away, so they can go to the villages and buy themselves some food.

Jesus replied, "They do not need to go away. You give them something to eat."

"We have here only five loaves of bread and two fish," they answered.

"Bring them here to Me," He said. And He directed the people to sit down on the grass. Taking the five loaves and the two fish and looking up to heaven, He gave thanks and broke the loaves. Then He gave them to the disciples, and the disciples gave them to the people. They all ate and were satisfied, and the disciples picked up twelve basketfuls of broken pieces that were left over. The number of

Mark 6:30-44
The apostles gathered around Jesus and reported to Him all they had done and taught. Then, because so many people were coming and going that they did not even have a chance to eat, He said to them, "Come with Me by yourselves to a quiet place and get some rest."

So they went away by themselves in a boat to a solitary place. But many who saw them leaving recognized them and ran on foot from all the towns and got there ahead of them. When Jesus landed and saw a large crowd, He had compassion on them, because they were like sheep without a shepherd. So He began teaching them many things.

By this time it was late in the day, so His disciples came to Him. "This is a remote place," they said, "and it's already very late. Send the people away so they can go to the surrounding countryside and villages and buy themselves something to eat."

But He answered, "You give them something to eat."

They said to Him, "That would

those who ate was about five thousand men, besides women and children.

take eight months of a man's wages! Are we to go and spend that much on bread and give it to them to eat?"

"How many loaves do you have?" He asked. "Go and see."

When they found out, they said, "Five—and two fish."

Then Jesus directed them to have all the people sit down in groups on the green grass. So they sat down in groups of hundreds and fifties. Taking the five loaves and the two fish and looking up to heaven, He gave thanks and broke the loaves. Then He gave them to His disciples to set before the people. He also divided the two fish among them all. They all ate and were satisfied, and the disciples picked up twelve basketfuls of broken pieces of bread and fish. The number of the men who had eaten was five thousand.

FEEDING THE 4,000

Matthew 15:29-39
Jesus left there and went along the Sea of Galilee. Then He went up on a a mountainside and sat down. Great crowds came to Him, bringing the lame, the blind, the crippled, the mute and many others, and laid them at His feet; and He healed them. The people were amazed when they saw the mute speaking, the crippled made well, the lame walking and the blind seeing. And they praised the God of Israel.

Jesus called His disciples to Him and said, "I have compassion for these people; they have already been with Me three days and have nothing to eat. I do not want to send them away hungry, or they may collapse on the way."

His disciples answered, "Where could we get enough bread in this remote place to feed such a crowd?"

"How many loaves do you have?" Jesus asked.

"Seven," they replied, "and a few small fish."

He told the crowd to sit down on the ground. Then He took the seven loaves and the fish, and when He had given

Mark 8:1-13
During those days another large crowd gathered. Since they had nothing to eat, Jesus called His disciples to Him and said, "I have compassion for these people; they have already been with Me three days and have nothing to eat. If I send them home hungry, they will collapse on the way, because some of them have come a long distance."

His disciples answered, "But where in this remote place can anyone get enough bread to feed them?"

"How many loaves do you have?" Jesus asked.

"Seven," they replied.

He told the crowd to sit down on the ground. When He had taken the seven loaves and given thanks, He broke them and gave them to His disciples to set before the people, and they did so. They had a few small fish as well; He gave thanks for them also and told the disciples to distribute them. The people ate and were satisfied. Afterward the disciples picked up seven basketfuls thanks, He broke them and gave them to the disciples and they in turn to the people. They all ate and were satisfied. Afterward the disciples picked up seven basketfuls of broken pieces that were left over. The number of those who ate was four thousand, besides women and children. After Jesus had sent the crowd away, He got into the boat and went to the vicinity of Magadan.

Comparing, we note a number of similarities.

■ The crowds came to Jesus uninvited, but were not turned away. Despite Christ's own need for solitude, He gave of Himself and healed their sick.

■ The crowds had failed to make provision for themselves.

■ The disciples did not want the responsibility of caring for the needs of the crowd, and urged Jesus to send them away.

■ Jesus was moved by compassion for the crowds to meet their needs (see the Word Study of Mark 1:41).

■ Jesus used the resources the disciples had. The disciples were appalled at how little they had, unaware of Jesus' ability to multiply those resources.

■ Each report tells us the people "ate and were satisfied." Christ met their needs fully.

■ In each case, basketfuls were left over. There was not only enough, there was more than enough.

Application. While we can draw lessons from each of the similarities noted above, perhaps the most significant lesson for us comes from the nature of the need and Christ's response to it.

The need for food is one of the most basic of human needs. Jesus was not only con-

of broken pieces that were left over. About four thousand men were present. And having sent them away, He got into the boat with His disciples and went to the region of Dalmanutha.

cerned about the people's spiritual condition, He was moved by compassion for physical hunger as well. We cannot represent Jesus adequately if we are moved only by the need to win lost souls. To represent Jesus we must be as concerned for the hungry, the homeless, and the oppressed as our Lord was for the hungry multitudes.

There is also a lesson for us in the disciples' reaction to the crowds. Understandably, they simply did not want to accept responsibility for the needs of thousands. Their feeling that the crowds should take care of their own needs—perhaps mixed with some resentment—is certainly something most of us have felt as well. Certainly too, we are as deeply aware of our own lack of the resources needed to meet the vast needs that exist in our society. Yet Jesus said, "You give them something to eat" (6:37). And then Jesus took what the disciples provided, those few small loaves and fishes, and so multiplied them that they were able to satisfy everyone.

Let's open our hearts to those in need, accept responsibility, step out in faith—and trust God to multiply what little we have.

The Yeast of the Pharisees and Herod (8:14-21). See the Word Study of 8:15, and the parallel passage in Matthew 16:6-12.

The Healing of a Blind Man of Bethsaida (8:22-26). See Exposition.

Peter's Confession of Christ (8:27-30). See the Commentary on Matt. 16:13-20, and the parallel passage in Luke 9:18-20.

MARK 8:31–10:52
Teaching His Disciples

EXPOSITION

Mark, like Matthew and Luke, sharply distinguishes a turning point in Christ's ministry. Each reports His early demonstrations of messianic authority, and each traces the intensifying hostility of the religious leaders. The turning point comes when Jesus asks the Twelve who people say He is, and then ask who they say He is. Peter answers for them. The crowds see Jesus as a prophet: His disciples know Him as the Son of God (8:27-30).

From this point on Jesus begins to speak of His approaching death and resurrection. And the events and words are more for the benefit of the crowds than of the disciples.

Jesus predicts His death, and tells His disciples each of them must "deny himself" (8:31-37). When three of the disciples witness the Transfiguration, the message is clear: self-sacrifice leads ultimately to glory (8:38–9:13). But the disciples' failure to heal a child with an evil spirit emphasizes the need for prayer and continual dependence on the Lord (9:14-32).

A dispute among the disciples about who will be greatest creates a teachable moment, and allows Jesus to emphasize the importance of seeing Christian leadership as servanthood (9:33-50). Jesus' rejection of the claims of the Pharisees to be arbiters of God's Word on divorce reinforces the importance of personal response and responsibility to God—and His teaching that leaders are servants, not masters, in God's kingdom (10:1-16). Then Christ's word to a rich young man reminds the disciples that the values of the kingdom are not the values held by this world (10:17-31).

Another sequence of events mixed with teaching sums up the message of these chapters. James and John appeal to Jesus for the chief places in His kingdom, and foolishly insist they can drink from Christ's cup (share His sufferings and commitment) (10:35-40). The other disciples are angry at the two brothers. Again Jesus says that the "first" in His kingdom do not have power "over" God's people, and explains that greatness is expressed in a servanthood patterned on His own willingness to give His life for others (10:41-45). Christ then shows exactly what this means. Deeply burdened as He turns toward Jerusalem and His impending death, our Lord still stops to heed the request of a blind beggar, asking, "What do you want Me to do for you?" (10:45)

It is only when we are able to set aside our own needs to make this response to others that we will have grasped what it really means to be a follower of Jesus—and a leader in Christ's church.

WORD STUDIES

He then began to teach them that the *Son of Man* **must suffer many things (8:31).** Jesus is the only person who refers to Himself as "Son of Man," and does so some 81 times in the Gospels! In the Psalms the phrase simply means "man," or "human being." In Ezekiel it is simply the way God refers to the prophet. But in Dan. 7:13-14 the phrase clearly refers to Messiah, the ruler of God's eschatological kingdom. In Mark 8:31 and again in 9:9, 12 Son of Man is also a messianic title. Jesus, the Messiah, will suffer but will be raised again.

How appropriate is the "Son of Man" title. Jesus died as a human being, that through His death He might transform every human being who believes in Him.

Get behind Me, *Satan!* **(8:33)** Jesus uttered this stern rebuke publicly as He "turned and looked at His disciples," although He spoke to Peter individually. Apparently Peter expressed the reaction of the entire group when he urged Christ to avoid the cross. But in what way was Peter "Satan"?

Simply in that he was taking Satan's side, tempting Jesus to turn away from doing God's will, even as Satan had tempted Jesus at the first (Matt. 4:1-11). If we are truly Christ's disciples, nothing is to have higher priority for us—or others we love—than doing the will of God, whatever the cost.

He must *deny himself.* **. . . What good is it for a man to gain the whole world, yet forfeit his** *soul?* **(8:34, 36)** Self-denial is nothing more or less than choosing God's will when that will conflicts with what some part of ourselves wants to do. The phrase "forfeit his soul" is a Hebraism. In Hebrew the word *nephes* is often used as a reflexive pronoun, to indicate the "man himself." The Greek equivalent, *psuche,* is used here in this same sense. What believers forfeit by failing to choose God's will is not some immaterial "soul," but rather their very selves; the new people they would become if only their lives were fully committed to Jesus.

Jesus reminds us that the whole world cannot tip the balance against the importance of following Jesus and being the persons that God's Spirit can help us become.

Why do the teachers of the law say that *Elijah* **must come first? (9:11)** For a discussion of the Elijah prophecy and the place of John the Baptist, see the commentary on Matt. 17:10-13.

Salt is good, but if it looses its *saltiness,* **how can you make it salty again? Have salt in yourselves, and be at peace with each other (9:50).** Salt was as vital a mineral in ancient times as it is today. It was used to flavor foods, spread lightly as a fertilizer on the soil, and salt solutions were used medicinally. In NT times the Roman army provided a salt allowance, the *salarium,* to its soldiers. If that word looks familiar it should: it is the root of our word "salary."

In Israel salt was mined from a great ledge of rock salt lying near the Dead Sea and evaporated from that Sea's waters. The rock salt deteriorated in high temperatures, and moisture could leach the salt from the rock. Thus this important product could lose its saltiness—and become absolutely worthless.

In context, the disciple's saltiness is preserved only by complete commitment to the Lord. Without this trait, followers of Christ lose their value not only to the Lord but to the world as well.

No one who has *left home* **or brothers or sisters or mother or father or children or fields for Me and the Gospel (10:29).** Jesus may be referring to the familiar practice of servants living and eating in their masters' homes, and maintaining a separate home for their own families. Servants, or apprentices of skilled craftsmen, who lived in their own homes were viewed with some suspicion. Unless they were available at any hour they might be needed, servants might be resented for a failure to put the master and his family first. And, an apprentice who did not live with the master craftsman was often viewed as a possible future competitor, and was not taught all the master's secrets.

Jesus' remarks may well have been understood by the disciples to mean simply that disciples must put His interests first, even before those of their own families. Christ's accompanying promise is striking. Whatever "loss" this involves, our gain will be far greater.

Jesus said to them, "**You will drink the cup I drink**" **(10:39)**. The image of a cup is found frequently in OT and NT, and indicates an experience that an individual or group must undergo. Jesus' cup was the suffering He was about to experience in performing God's will. But Christ's cup was also the glory of the resurrection that awaited just beyond the cross. In choosing Christ's cup you and I elect to do God's will, whatever the cost. We choose intelligently, fully aware that beyond any cross we may have to bear lies an eternity filled with joy and glory.

He shouted all the more, "*Son of David, have mercy on me!*" **(10:48)** "Son of David" is a messianic title. Bartimaeus appealed to Jesus as Israel's deliverer and begged for personal deliverance.

Although the nation as a whole rejected Jesus' messianic claims (John 1:11), Jesus never turned away an individual who acknowledged Him as Savior. Whatever others may say, we can be sure that if we recognize Christ for who He is, He will listen to us and meet our needs.

THE PASSAGE IN DEPTH

Jesus Predicts His Death (Mark 8:31-38). See the commentary in Matt. 16:21-28, and the parallel passage in Luke 9:22-27.

Jesus' Transfiguration (Mark 9:1-13). See also parallel passages in Matt. 17:1-13 and Luke 9:28-36.

Background. In the first century, as in orthodox Judaism today, the "kingdom" theme is tightly interwoven with Israel's confidence that one day God's Messiah would appear. Many pressures in first-century Judaism made the yearning for God's kingdom intense. Roman domination meant heavy taxes, imposed by foreigners who had no historic right to the land given Israel by God. Pilate, then Rome's governor of the land, was cruel and unconcerned with the deeply held religious convictions of the Jews. And perhaps the greatest pressures were created by the appearance of Jesus Himself, for His miracles and teachings aroused even greater messianic fervor.

As later events make clear, Jesus' disciples themselves expected our Lord to establish an earthly kingdom—and eagerly jockeyed for roles of greater power (10:35-45).

While the Transfiguration was undoubtedly a wondrous revelation of Jesus' essential nature, in context it was also a powerful demonstration of the nature of the kingdom our Lord intended to establish through His death.

Interpretation. The key to understanding the intended meaning of the Transfiguration found in 9:2 is in the phrase "after six days." What had happened six days earlier? Jesus had spoken of His cross and the glory to follow, and given a specific promise: "I tell you the truth, some who are standing here will not taste death before they see the kingdom of God come with power" (9:1).

It is not Mark's habit to indicate precise time relationships between events. Clearly the phrase "after six days" binds the Transfiguration intimately to Christ's prediction of His death and resurrection—and to the promise He made to the disciples that some would "see the kingdom of God come with power."

Of the two, the second relationship is the more significant. While the Transfiguration provided visible confirmation of Christ's deity, the disciples before whom He displayed His glory had already recognized Him by the eyes of faith (8:29). What they did not recognize was the nature of His kingdom; they did not understand the implication of taking up the cross and following Jesus in order to become new.

Then Jesus was transformed before them, and in that transformation they saw "the kingdom of God come with power" (9:1). They saw One who appeared in His incarnation as an ordinary man suddenly shine with overpowering radiance. What they saw was truly a Transfiguration—a revolutionary transformation from one state of being to another. A state of being which unmistakably displayed the glory and the power of God.

It is in this that Jesus' transfiguration redefines the kingdom for His disciples. When, after Christ's death and resurrection "the kingdom of God comes with power," the mark of the kingdom will not be angelic armies marching to crush the power of Rome. The kingdom of God comes with power in order to change ordinary human beings who choose to follow Jesus. The kingdom, at least until Jesus reappears, is about transformation, not conquest!

Why the appearance of Moses and Elijah with Christ on the Mount of Transfiguration? Some have suggested that Moses was the first revealer of the Messiah, and Elijah was to be the last, as forerunner of the Messiah. But perhaps more significant is the fact that both Moses and Elijah ended their time on earth mysteriously (Deut. 34:5-6; 2 Kings 2:11). Despite the accomplishments of these great men of faith, they appeared as ordinary human beings—until the end!

Certainly there will be evidence in our daily lives when God's kingdom comes to us with power. In our life and death many who look on will see only the ordinary. Until the end!

When Jesus comes again, we will shine with a glory like His. Then we will be fully like Him, completely transformed, "for we shall see Him as He is" (1 John 3:2).

Application. It is good to be concerned with society and its ills. As Christians we are to care for the poor and the oppressed, and do all we can to establish righteousness. But we must never forget that the kingdom Christ has established for today is concerned first of all with the transformation of individuals. And that God's power is available to bring each human being personal, inner renewal.

The Healing of a Boy with an Evil Spirit (Mark 9:14-29). See also parallel passages in Matt. 17:14-23 and Luke 9:37-45.

Background. Two things which have been already established in Mark constitute the significant background to this story. First, Christ has demonstrated His authority over evil spirits (1:23-25, 34; 3:20-30; 5:1-20). In fact, Mark 9 contains this Gospel's last report of casting out a demon, not its first.

The second thing that has been established earlier is that Christ has already delegated authority over demons to His disciples—and they have used that authority successfully (6:7; 6:13).

Thus, this story is told in the context of Christ's established power over the demonic, a power which the disciples had, at least briefly, shared.

Interpretation. While two other Gospels report this same story, Mark's account is the

longest and provides the most detail. Mark graphically portrays the confusion and disorder as "the teachers of the Law" who were monitoring Jesus' activities seize the opportunity to launch a loud attack when the disciples fail to heal an epileptic boy. Jesus' return interrupts the argument, and the crowd rushes to meet Him.

As the father blurts out his story, Jesus utters two puzzling sayings, and then talks with the father about faith. Christ then casts out the demon, leaving the child limp and exhausted, but free at last. After helping the child up, Jesus withdraws with His disciples and answers their anxious questions about why they were unable to perform the exorcism.

Interpretive questions focus on three issues.

First, who was Jesus speaking of when He said, "O unbelieving generation" (9:19), and what do the two following exclamations mean?

Most commentators believe Jesus was expressing frustration and disappointment with His disciples in the remark about the "unbelieving [*apistos,* "without faith"] generation." Although the characterization surely fits the nation as a whole, if applied to the disciples it provides an additional key to interpreting the third interpretive question.

The next two questions are best understood as exclamations. Some suggest that "How long shall I stay with you?" reflects frustration at the brief time remaining to Christ. If the disciples had not learned in the years past, how could anything be accomplished in the next few weeks? On the other hand, "How long shall I put up with you?" expresses frustration at the disciples' spiritual dullness.

Second, what is the meaning of the exchange between Jesus and the boy's father about faith? The father's "If You can" (9:22) clearly expresses doubt. In response Jesus demands belief, and says that "everything is possible for him who believes" (9:23). The point here is not that the believer's faith enables God to work. God is not limited by our lack of faith. The point is that our ability to receive is limited by the absence of faith.

The father's response reveals a struggle that goes on in all of us. "I do believe, help me overcome my unbelief!" (9:24) is the honest confession of a person who has believed enough to bring his son to Jesus, yet whose doubts and fears continue to trouble him. It is important here to note that despite the man's confession of his inner struggle, Jesus did heal the son. Christ does not demand that we have an unwavering faith in order to act for us. He does require that we have enough faith to be open to the possibility of God's miraculous intervention in our lives, however dark the doubts that swirl within our hearts.

Third, there are the interpretive questions aroused by Jesus' later, private instruction of the disciples who had failed so completely to cast out the demon themselves. Here most commentators see the solution as relatively simple. The disciples had assumed that they still possessed the power once granted to them by Christ. Yet no spiritual authority is inherent in God's gifts: every spiritual authority is exercised *by* God *through* His chosen vessels.

Thus the significance of prayer, not as a ritual, but as an expression of conscious, humble dependence on God. The disciples had approached this healing without this kind of faith, as Christ's first exclamation reveals (9:19).

Application. As we resolve the interpretive questions, we clearly see that the entire event focuses our attention on the nature and role of faith in our lives. It teaches us at least two profound truths.

The first is that, while Jesus has all power, it requires faith to open up our lives to an experience of that power. This does not mean that we must have a perfect faith. In all of us, faith and unbelief remain in tension. But we must have enough faith to come to Jesus and appeal to Him if He is to act for us.

The second truth is that, if we are to be used by God in the lives of others, our faith must be focused on God rather than on any gifts He may have granted us. Faith which exists as continual dependence on the Lord—a faith often expressed by Jesus Himself in prayer—can make us channels of blessing to others.

How important then that we remain rooted in the simple conviction that "Jesus can" and that "Only Jesus can." If we build our relationship with God on these two realities, we will have sufficient faith to experience God's working in our lives, and to be His agents of ministry to others.

Jesus on Greatness (Mark 9:33-50). See the Commentary on Matt. 18–20, and parallel

passages in Luke 9:46-50.

Jesus on Divorce (Mark 10:1-12); Jesus and the Little Children (Mark 10:13-16). See the Commentary on Matt. 19:1-15 and a parallel passage in Luke 18:15-17.

The Rich Young Man (Mark 10:17-31). See parallel passages in Matt. 19:16-30 and Luke 18:18-30.

Background. In every society any person given the choice will more likely choose wealth than poverty. In Judaism wealth was considered a double blessing from God. Not only was the wealthy person blessed by his prosperity, but such a person had the opportunity to use his wealth to benefit others, thus earning much merit.

Intertestamental Jewish writings, as does the Bible, make it clear that riches are not an unmixed blessing. Humans can be entrapped by their desire for gold, and put their confidence in riches rather than God. In fact, a wicked person who has wealth has the ability to follow his evil tendencies, and thus may be far worse off than one whose poverty limits his ability to run after sins.

Yet the wealthy person who was also a good man was especially admired in Judaism, and his wealth considered an unmixed blessing. Thus Ben Sira, writing a century and a half before Christ, describes a person very like the young man who now comes to our Lord:

Happy the rich found without fault,
 who turns not aside after wealth!
Who is he, that we may praise him?
He, of all his kindred, has done wonders,
For he has been tested by gold and come off safe,
 and this remains his glory;
He could have gone wrong but did not,
 could have done evil but would not,
So that his possessions are secure,
 and the assembly recounts his praises.

All those commandments which govern man's relationship with man this rich young man had carefully kept "since I was a boy" (10:20). He had not used his wealth to do harm, but rather was fully committed to good. That he was sincere is confirmed by Mark, who alone observes that "Jesus looked at him and loved him" (10:21).

Interpretation. The utter honesty of the wealthy young man's reply and Jesus' warm love is the key to understanding this event.

Some have focused on Christ's question, "Why do you call Me good?" (10:18) and argued that here Christ overtly rejected the church's later claim that He was God enfleshed. Instead the opposite is intended: Don't address Me as "good" unless you are ready to follow through on the implication of this title, and confess that I am also your God. This point is vital to our interpretation. But it is only relevant because the youthful rich man truly was committed to the commandments in his relationship with other men. He was by every human test a "good" man himself!

Then Jesus stuns the supplicant and His listeners as well when He says, "Go, sell everything you have and give to the poor, and you will have treasure in heaven. Then come, follow Me" (10:21). Why should Jesus make this particular demand of this particular individual?

Briefly, the answer is that Christ's command is loving, intended to show the young man who has lived such a good life that he is in fact a sinner in need of a Savior. How? The first command of the Law is that the individual put God first and love Him completely. In making His demand Jesus spoke as Israel's God (thus the question in 10:18). And when the young man's face fell, and he "went away sad" (10:22), a terrible hidden reality was revealed. Despite all his good works, in the last analysis this young man's wealth was more important to him than God!

Jesus' subsequent remark, "How hard it is for the rich to enter the kingdom of God!" (10:23) unveils the true deceitfulness of riches. It is not that riches may further corrupt the wicked. The real danger is that riches may corrupt the good man! The real danger is that a good person may come to so depend on the good he can do with his wealth that he or she will fail to depend utterly on the Lord. The real danger is that the good person may fail to realize he is a sinner, and be blind to the flaw in his personal relationship with God.

Application. According to history, some have taken Christ's words to the rich man as a general command to all to surrender all worldly wealth. Not at all. Christ's words were spoken to one special individual, and while they contain a lesson for all of us, the command was directed to him alone.

So what is the lesson that can be drawn for the rest of us? Certainly that neither humanitarianism nor benevolence can substitute for a personal relationship with God. Certainly too that wealth is no sure sign of God's favor.

Perhaps the most important lesson is more subtle. Even those whom Jesus loves can mistake doing good for loving God. And while love for God will move us to do good, it is undoubtedly wrong to assume that doing good in itself is evidence that we serve God. In tragic fact we, like the rich young man, may unconsciously be serving ourselves—and only a demand that we surrender what we do not realize we love more than God will bring this reality home.

The Request of James and John (Mark 10:32-41). See also the parallel passages in Matt. 20:17-28 and Luke 18:31-34.

Background. The most significant treatment of this incident is given in Matt. 20, and it is this Gospel which best describes its context. In that Gospel we see that the event described here is one element in Christ's teaching to His disciples about greatness. For background, see the Exposition tracing the argument of those chapters, pp. 67–68.

Briefly, this incident in which James and John manipulated their mother to ask Jesus for the principle places of power in His coming kingdom, created a teachable moment and allowed Jesus to provide pointed instruction on what leadership in His kingdom really involves.

Interpretation. Despite Christ's earlier instruction, the disciples still envision an earthly kingdom over which Christ rules as Messiah/King. For one of the eager brothers to "sit at Your right and the other at Your left" (10:37) means to have power second only to the ruler Himself.

Christ's response (10:38-40) stresses the fact that those who are significant in the kingdom as these disciples are about to experience it must share His cup and baptism. They will and must experience what He has experienced, of commitment and obedience. But power in the coming age, the age of the kingdom's final full expression on earth, is not something Jesus is prepared to commit.

Word of the two brothers' attempts to win personal advantage upsets the other disciples and creates an ideal setting for Jesus' instruction concerning spiritual leadership. Unlike the "rulers of the Gentiles" (10:42) who exercise a coercive power "over" their subjects, a spiritual leader in the hidden kingdom Christ is about to establish must live "among" (10:43) its other citizens as a "servant" (10:43) and "slave" (10:44). Rather than use others, as secular powers do, those with authority in Jesus' kingdom must model themselves on the Lord, and serve rather than be served, even giving their very lives to benefit others.

Application. This passage makes a most significant contribution to the NT's teaching on church leadership. It contrasts two models—a secular model and a model derived from Christ's behavior.

The secular model is traditional and hierarchical. The ruler is above others, his will and purposes central, and other persons are used by him to win him greater glory. In contrast, Christ, although endowed with all authority by the Father, lived among human beings as a servant, and used His power to meet the needs and heal the diseases of others. Rather than exercise His power to win personal glory, Christ used it for the benefit of others, and in so doing revealed the loving heart of God.

In view of this clear contrast, it is difficult to understand how Christians can exalt their priests or pastors to a role "over" the flock. Or how priests and pastors can assume that their role gives them the right to enlist others to serve their visions or promote their own personal prominence. Instead, spiritual leaders are to subordinate their interests to the needs of the flock, and rather than use, to permit themselves to be used as Christ was used by the hurting and the lost.

How difficult this is for us to grasp, and how difficult to work out in practice. Yet Christ's command regarding worldly leadership is clear: "Not so with you" (10:43). The church is different, and its leaders must model their leadership on Christ the Servant rather than on the powerful of this world.

Blind Bartimaeus Receives His Sight (Mark 10:46-52).

See the parallel passages in Matt. 20:29-34 and Luke 18:35-43.

Background. The Gospels, and later John in his Epistles, frequently relate situations in which sight and blindness serve as contrasting metaphors. How often the person without physical sight sees Jesus clearly and recognizes Him as the Son of God, while those whose eyes see Jesus' form are blind to the significance of His words and works.

Here another blind man hears that Jesus is passing by, and his cry, "Jesus, Son of David" (10:47) makes it very clear that Bartimaeus acknowledges Jesus as the Messiah destined to spring from David's line.

But here the story is not intended to underline the distinction between physical and spiritual sight. It explores the implications of Christ's teaching (discussed earlier) on servant leadership.

Interpretation. Jesus is on His way through Jericho toward Jerusalem. His earlier predictions (8:31-33; 10:32-34) make it clear that Jesus is fully aware of the significance of this journey. Very soon tears shed in Gethsemane will reveal how great the stress is under which He now lives. And so as Jesus passes through Jericho His mind is filled with thoughts of what lies ahead, swirling with joy at fulfillling the will of God, and anguishing with awareness of what that will for Him involves.

Surely, if any person ever had a right to be concerned about His own affairs, it was Jesus as He passed through Jericho that day.

Yet, although the crowd shushed the blind man, Jesus stopped and said, "Call him." And suddenly, we realize that the contrast Mark seeks to draw is not between the blind and the sighted, but between the reaction of the crowd and of Jesus to the blind man.

To the crowd the blind man was a person of no consequence, a nonentity to be rebuked and silenced. Every eye was on Jesus, the one around whom controversy swirled, whose name was on every person's lips. As measured by the crowd, Jesus was important, the blind man utterly insignificant.

And in one sense they were correct. Jesus, God incarnate, is undoubtedly the heart and center not only of our faith but of the history of the universe itself. And yet, in that moment, Jesus turned everything upside down. For Jesus set aside His own concerns, His vision of the cross, the anguish of His soul, His sense of purpose and unshakeable commitment to do God's will in the coming stressful days—and stopped for a blind man. He asked, "What do you want Me to do for you?"

In this, in showing His willingness to serve this most inconsequential person, Jesus turned everything upside down. In an amazing display, the Master of the Universe became a servant of Bartimaeus, making Himself subject to the useless blind man's need.

And so we begin to sense what it means for the significant in God's kingdom to take the role of servants, and for its leaders to become its citizens' slaves. Like Christ, we freely choose to set aside our own concerns — although they seem to be of far greater significance — and choose to respond to the hurts of the humble. We become the servants, not making ourselves subject to the will of mere humans, but rather by the will of God making ourselves subservient that we might meet their deepest needs.

It is not the person whom all hold in awe for mighty buildings or grand accomplishments that is great in the kingdom of our Lord. It is that person with a mission, who realizes that the pain and hurt suffered by the insignificant is so important to God that he pauses on his mission to meet a human need.

MARK 11–13
The Last Week

EXPOSITION

We now move into the realm of the very familiar. Jesus has reached Jerusalem, and the events of His last week here, as well known as an intimate friend, quickly unfold.

Each of the Gospel writers devotes nearly a third of his biography to this one week. Since Jesus ministered some three or more years, it is clear that what happened during this week is of overarching significance. During these few days Jesus' claim of messiahship is uniquely advanced, challenged, and ultimately rejected by His people. At week's end the dark specter of the cross is raised, and in a stunning display of irony the One who entered Jerusalem in triumph just a few days before is nailed to a tree, to hang midway between the darkening heavens and the blood-stained earth. All that happens now is prelude, moving toward those final moments.

What does occur? Jesus enters Jerusalem to the cheers of crowds who have assembled for the annual Passover festival (11:1-11). The next day He returns, drives out those who do business in the temple's outer courts, and teaches the crowds there before returning to Bethany at evening (11:12-19). Returning the next morning, Jesus' companions see the results of Christ's earlier curse of a fruitless fig tree (11:12-14, 20-25). This event prepares us for a series of confrontations with the leaders of Israel, whose sterile approach to religion is symbolized in the barren and withered branches. When the leaders challenge Christ's authority (11:27-33), Christ tells a parable that reveals their motives for rejecting Him—they want for themselves that glory which belongs only to God (12:1-12). Furious and frustrated, Christ's enemies try to trap Him with questions about taxes and the resurrection (12:13-27). But one "teacher of the Law" acknowledges the rightness of Christ's answer, reminding us that there were godly men in Israel in the first century as in every age (12:28-34). Christ then poses a question about Ps. 110:1, a question whose answer clearly required the admission that the Messiah had to be God incarnate, an answer that the leaders were clearly unwilling to give (12:35-40). Mark now relates a final incident which again has symbolic significance. Jesus observes worshipers placing voluntary offerings in the temple treasury and points out a poor widow whose offering, though tiny, is all she has. What an image of complete surrender—and what a contrast to the leaders of Israel who were unwilling to surrender their position and so coldly rejected Christ's call to acknowledge Him as Lord.

Mark (13:1-37) now gives a brief summary of a theme that is given extended treatment by Matthew. When the disciples comment on the wonders of the temple, Jesus remarks that every stone will be thrown down. This stunning information raises a vital question. What really lies ahead for Israel? God's people, represented by their leaders, have decisively rejected Christ's every claim. What will the future now hold? And how will Christ establish His kingdom on earth?

WORD STUDIES

Hosanna! (11:9) The word literally means "Save now," but in the first century was uttered as an exclamation of praise.

Blessed is He who comes in the name of the Lord! (11:9) This phrase from Ps. 118:25-26 served as a greeting used to joyfully welcome pilgrims who entered Jerusalem to worship during the Festivals of Tabernacles and Passover. Its link here with what is clearly a messianic shout, "Blessed is the coming kingdom of our father David!" (11:10) suggests that the psalm also had messianic implications.

What seems clear as the week unfolds, however, is that the crowds expected Jesus to act as Messiah, not that their Hosannas were evidence of their willingness to submit to His authority. How often people seek God on their terms, for what He will do for them, rather than seeking God on His terms, as creatures eager to submit to their Creator.

Jesus entered the *temple area* and began driving out those who were *buying and selling* there (11:15). The "temple area" referred to here is the outer court, apparently the "court of the Gentiles." Buying and selling there was allowed by the priests, who supervised the merchants who sold sacrificial animals and exchanged foreign coins for "temple currency."

These businessmen were permitted to charge a fee of 1/24th of the value of any money exchanged, to cover wear on the coinage. But the high priestly family which controlled the temple at that time was remembered by later generations for its rapacity and greed. Jesus' characterization of the market as a "den of robbers" (11:17) certainly suggests that the reasonable limits tradition decreed were far exceeded in practice.

The most fascinating insight is gleaned from Christ's quote of Isa. 56:7; God's house is to be "a house of prayer for all nations" (11:17). Even the court of the Gentiles, not considered by Israel part of the temple proper, was in fact holy, for God intended from the beginning to gather all nations to Himself.

How careful we must be not to define others out of the circle of God's love. And how careful we must be that, wherever we are, whatever we do must honor our Lord.

If anyone says to this mountain, "Go, throw yourself into the sea," and does not doubt in his heart but believes that what he says will happen, it will be done for

him (11:23). In the first century a "mountain" frequently served as a symbol of a great difficulty. Most believe that Christ was speaking metaphorically, and that His words are intended to remind us that prayer is a resource to the person of faith, who trusts God and firmly expects Him to act on our behalf in this present world.

Forgive him, so that your Father in heaven *may* **forgive you your sins (11:25).** Some, like A.T. Robertson, assume that "evidently God's willingness to forgive is limited by our willingness to forgive others." To Robertson, "this is a solemn thought for all who pray."

Undoubtedly there is a close connection in our text between prayer and forgiveness. But we should not assume that our failure to forgive limits God. Instead, what an unforgiving spirit does is limit us. An unforgiving spirit so closes our hearts that we ourselves are not open to receiving the forgiveness God so freely extends. Furthermore, in closing our hearts to God, we shut ourselves off from that awareness of God's presence that is essential if we are to believe without doubt.

Let's not conclude that what we do can cut God off from us. But let's never forget that the choices we make can cut us off from God!

They *feared* **the people, for everyone held that John really was a prophet (11:32).** What irony each of the Gospels expresses in this description of Israel's fearful, hesitant leaders. The leaders resent Christ's bold words and actions, and demand He justify His implicit claim to authority. As for themselves, the leaders feel secure in their claim to sit in Moses' seat (Matt. 23:2) as the recognized interpreters of God's Word and His contemporary will.

That claim is reflected in this dictum from the Torah, found in Sanhedrin 11:3, which reads:

> 11:3 A. A more strict rule applies to the teachings of scribes than to the teachings of Torah.
>
> B. He who rules, "There is no requirement to wear phylacteries," in order to transgress the teachings of the Torah, is exempt.
>
> C. [But if he said,] "There are five parti-

tions [in the phylactery, instead of four]," in order to add to what the scribes have taught, he is liable.

How fascinating the reaction of these scribes when Jesus asks them a question that they are afraid to answer. Suddenly their claim of "authority" appears hollow indeed. If they really possessed an authority like Moses', an authority that came from God, they surely must know whether or not John the Baptist was a prophet. And they would be duty bound to instruct the people.

How ironic. Persons who most resent those who do have spiritual authority are themselves pretenders. They want to be important, but in fact are empty and hollow. Jesus' question about John exposed that hollowness, as all pretenders must ultimately be exposed.

Then he *rented* **the vineyard to some farmers (12:1).** This story, as so much of Jesus' imagery, drew on the familiar. By the first century large royal and private estates had forced many family farmers off their land, and the owners either leased the lands to tenants or hired day laborers to work their fields.

There were various categories of tenants: the *aris,* who paid a rent of one-half or one-third of the harvest; the *sokher,* who paid a fixed amount in money, and the *hoker,* who paid a fixed amount in produce. There was also the *shatla,* who developed land while paying half the produce in rent, and when it became profitable, he received part of it. What is important is that each class of tenants who lived and worked the land owed rent to the person who owned it.

Jesus' parable does not specify the type of tenant involved here, although from 12:1 it is clear that the owner (God) had invested His own resources to prepare the land for fruitfulness. What Jesus argues is that God, as owner of the Promised Land and its people, deserves at least "some of the fruit" (12:2) of His own vineyard! But when God attempts to collect His due, His representatives are rejected and brutalized by tenants, for they want everything for themselves.

Then, in a final attempt to reach His tenants, God sends His Son "whom He loved" (12:6). *Agapatos,* translated "whom He loved" or "beloved," is most likely used here in the Septuagint sense of "only" Son.

It was clear to all of Jesus' listeners that the allegory was both a bold claim by Jesus of special relationship with God, and an attack on the religious leaders' claim to serve God's interests. In fact, Jesus charges that they deny God even "some of the fruit" which is His due.

But Jesus knew their *hypocrisy* (12:15). Hypocrisy is masking one's real intent, playing a part to look good to others. The Pharisees' hypocrisy is evident in their initial, insincere compliments. It is also evident that their question was not asked as part of a search for truth, but with the intent of trapping Jesus into a pronouncement which would either alienate the people or provide a basis for lodging a charge against Him with the Roman authorities.

The incident can serve as a warning to us. When those who are hostile to us approach with lavish compliments, they probably intend us harm. But more importantly, we are warned to check our own motives, and be sure that in our relationship with others we are honest in our own search for truth and in our commitment to love.

They will be *like the angels* in heaven (12:25). The Greek of Mark and Matthew says literally "as angels in heaven." Luke 20:36 has *isanggeloi,* "equal unto angels." This does not mean that the saved become angels, but when resurrected, like those angelic beings directly created by God, will neither marry nor procreate.

There is an important message in this. The Pharisees, who believed in resurrection, assumed that life in the future world would be very like life in this one. Jesus' response reminds us that we do not really know what the True World will be like, or have any notion of what wonders await us. We can, however, be sure of this. When death comes, we continue to live with God, and we will be raised to bodily, eternal life. Surely He who designed the wondrous world in which we now live has planned even greater wonders for that coming day.

I *am* the God of Abraham (12:26). As many have observed, Jesus' interpretation here of Ex. 3:6 hinges on the tense of a verb. God did not announce Himself to the forefathers as He who *was* the God of Abraham, but He who *is* the God of Abraham. Thus Abraham must still live in God's presence, although he died long ago.

How trustworthy are the Scriptures, which unveil hidden realities in every phrase and passage.

Of all the commandments, which is the *most important?* (12:28) See the word study of "greatest commandment" (Matt. 22:36).

David himself calls Him "Lord." How then can he be His *Son?* (12:37) See the word study of "son" (Matt. 22:41).

She, out of her *poverty,* put in everything (12:44). Mark describes the widow as "poor" (12:42). The Greek word in v. 42, *ptoche,* indicates a pauper, not just a person whom we might call poor. Just how destitute she was is indicated by the fact that all she possessed was two coins which Mark and Luke identify as "lepta."

A great variety of coin denominations circulated in first-century Palestine. The basic unit was a "denarius," a small silver coin which represented a day's pay for an ordinary laborer. The "as" was worth approximately 1/25 of a denarius, and at that time might buy one person's lunch. However, even the as was broken into smaller units; the half-piece (semis) and quarter-piece (quadrans). What were two lepta worth? About one quadrans.

While it is foolish to attempt to translate ancient monetary units into modern equivalents, for the sake of illustration we might value the denarius at $20. This would make the widow's mite worth about 25 cents. But the real impact is felt only if we compare what these amounts would purchase in the first century. When we do this, we come up with a 2-dollar price tag for a loaf of bread. Even a sparrow would have cost about 50 cents! Our widow, with only two lepta to her name, was destitute indeed.

Yet to God her gift counted for more than all the coins poured by the well-off into temple coffers. Because she gave all.

How foolish we are in the ways we measure value and worth. And how many unknowns will wear crowns larger and brighter than the famous among us when Jesus distributes our rewards.

His disciples said to Him, "Look, Teacher! What *massive stones! What magnificent buildings!*" (13:1) For some 2,000 years a stone that once capped an arch linking Robinson's Arch to the western wall of the temple mount has been exposed to wondering eyes. That stone weighs approximately 20 tons, at least 5 tons more than the heaviest stone in Egypt's pyramids. Yet recently another stone, part of the foundation of the western retaining wall that supported the temple mount, has been uncovered. And that stone weighs some 415 tons! No wonder the disciples looked around with awe, and felt confident of the permanence of that magnificent temple dedicated to the glory of Israel's God.

How stunning Jesus' remark, "Not one stone [of all these great buildings] here will be left on another" (13:2).

Like the disciples, we too often mistake the transient as permanent. The large, the massive, the impressive—whether a building or an organization or an institution—seems so solid. So impressive. So real. Yet in reality all that the eye sees is by its nature impermanent, and will swiftly pass off history's stage. What is real is the world we cannot see. And what remains is the stamp of God's working on the hearts of believers—our own hearts, and the hearts of those we serve and love.

When you see the *abomination that causes desolation* standing where it does not belong . . . let those who are in Judea flee (13:14). For a discussion of this event, see the Word Study at Matt. 24:15.

Those will be *days of distress* unequaled from the beginning, when God created the world (13:19). For a discussion of this time of great tribulation, see the Word Study at Matt. 24:21.

For *false Christs* and false prophets will appear and perform signs and miracles (13:22). For a discussion of this theme, see the Word Study at Matt. 24:24.

THE PASSAGE IN DEPTH

The Triumphal Entry (11:1-11). See the commentary on Luke 19:28-44, and the parallel passage in Matt. 21:1-11.

Jesus Clears the Temple (11:15-19). See the commentary on Luke 19:45-48, the parallel passage in Matt. 21:12-17, and a similar event reported in John 2:12-25.

The Withered Fig Tree (11:12-14, 20-26). See the commentary on Matt. 21:18-22.

Jesus' Authority Questioned (11:27-33). See the Word Study of Mark 11:32, above, and parallel passages in Matt. 21:23-27 and Luke 20:1-8.

The Parable of the Tenants (12:1-12). See the Word Study of Mark 12:1, above, and parallel passages in Matt. 21:33–22:14 and Luke 20:9-19.

Paying Taxes to Caesar (12:13-17). See the parallel passages in Matt. 22:15-22 and Luke 20:20-26 for other accounts of this early church-state question.

Marriage and the Resurrection (12:18-27). See the Word Study of Matt. 12:25, above, and parallel passages in Matt. 22:23-33 and Luke 20:27-40.

Whose Son Is the Christ? (12:35-40) See the Word Study of "son" at Matt. 22:41, and parallel passages in Matt. 22:41–23:39 and Luke 20:41-47.

The Widow's Offering (12:41-44). See the Word Study of Mark 12:42, above, and the parallel passage in Luke 21:1-4.

Signs of the End of the Age (13:1-37). See also parallel passages in Matt. 24–25, and Luke 21:5-38.

Background. In examining each of these passages one thing is clear. The focus of Christ's teaching is on what we may call "the Interim"—that period between the end of His life on earth and His return in glory and power to judge humankind.

Those who delight in using prophetic materials to piece together Scripture's puzzling images of the future search these passages for information they can use to construct their charts and timelines. Certainly much material in these reports does have relevance to such an effort. If we take the overall vision of the future as portrayed by the OT prophets, we quickly see references to major eschatological themes. Jesus foresees a future fulfillment of Daniel's warning concerning an "abomination that causes desolation" (13:14) to be set up in the Jerusalem temple at history's end, and warns of a great tribulation ("distress" [13:19, 24]) to follow hard on that event. Yet, while temporal words such as "at that time" (13:21), and "in those days, following that distress" (13:24) do occur in the text, it would be a mistake to suppose that the primary purpose of Jesus' instruction is to provide material for a prophetic timeline.

This is especially clear in Matthew, who gives us a much fuller account than Mark, and in so doing emphasizes the lessons Christ Himself drew from His teaching. That emphasis, explored in this commentary's notes on Matt. 25–26, is simply this: Until Jesus returns, His people are to expectantly watch for Him—and live accordingly.

Thus as Jesus speaks of this period I have called "the Interim," the glimpses of the future which He does provide are intended to shape our lives now, not to serve as data for prophetic speculation, however attractive to us that may seem to be.

For this reason, we can gain the most from an exploration of this passage if we concentrate on implications of Jesus' teachings for our own lives in these days in which we live—the Interim between Jesus' resurrection and His return.

Interpretation and Application. In taking an approach to this chapter which emphasizes its Interim nature, we note several themes that Jesus develops.

THEME 1: MARK 13:5-8
■ The Interim is to be marked by suffering.

It is impossible to guess how often throughout the Interim believers, overwhelmed by tragedy and suffering, have cried out in desperation, "This must be the end! The Lord must be about to return."

The events Jesus mentions here are terrible indeed. "Wars and rumors of wars. . . . Nation rising up against nation" (13:7-8). What images we have from war! Refugees in flight, strung out along a highway, as warplanes dip overhead and dive to strafe them. Jews, packed together in a square, guarded by black-clad troops, waiting for freight cars that will take them away to "resettlement" camps where millions met their doom. Napalm, raining globules of fire on screaming villagers. Restaurants exploding, shattering the limbs of innocent bystanders as terrorists fight their battles against the innocent, complaining that they are victims.

But even this is not all: nature itself seems to conspire to burden a suffering humanity. Earthquakes shatter our communities, burying infant and grandparent alike. Famine stalks first one continent and then another, and hollow-cheeked, bulging-bellied children stare dully at emaciated parents drained of every drop of hope.

How easily we mouth the familiar words and phrases. "Wars and rumors of wars." "Earthquakes . . . and famines" (13:8). And yet it is only the fortunate who have so far escaped such massive disasters who fail to sense the terror these words convey.

What does Jesus mean when He Himself seems to dismiss them lightly, saying, "These are the beginning of birth pains"? (13:8) Simply that such terrors must never be confused with the judgments that lie ahead for humankind. Simply that we are utterly mistaken if we confuse the agonies of war and natural disaster with judgment!

These are no more judgments than early twinges felt by expectant mothers are "birth pains."

What then can these things be? What they are is vivid, continuing evidence of the corruption sin introduced into our race and into nature itself. As we live our lives in the Interim, we must see suffering not as evidence of the indifference of God, or even as His judicial verdict, but rather as grim, continuing testimony to the fact that sin has consequences far beyond our ability to imagine.

We live in a society and a world so corrupted by sin that even the innocent suffer. The man with faith is just as vulnerable as the man without faith. But at least we understand the why. At least we realize that suffering is the sure and certain unfolding of the results of our rebellion against God. Because we recognize this fact, we retain our trust in God, and we are filled with thankfulness that through

Christ we are not victims locked into history's dark present, but victors, destined for the joyous eternity that lies ahead.

THEME 2: MARK 13:9-13

■ The Interim is to be marked by interpersonal conflict.

Jesus' next words picture the three major social contexts in which human beings relate to one another: the local community, the broader society and, most intimate of all, the family. In each of these social contexts that Jesus describes, the believer's experience during the Interim is to be one of conflict rather than harmony with others.

There is a simple reason for this: the believer has, through faith in Christ, made peace with God. Yet during the Interim, believers must live in a world that remains in rebellion. There is no way that the committed Christian can live in harmony with both God and a world at war with God.

In warning the disciples that they will be handed over to "local councils and flogged in the synagogues" (13:9) Jesus focuses our attention on the local community. In the first century the "supreme court" of Judaism was the Sanhedrin, a council that met in Jerusalem. But each community had its local courts, made up of the community's elders, which considered and settled local disputes. If a matter of Law rather than of fact was in dispute, recognized "teachers of the law" were available to hand down the authoritative rulings based on the earlier interpretations of the sages.

Neither OT nor first-century Jewish law provided for imprisonment. The most severe punishment that could be ordered by a local court was a flogging, and this itself was limited to a maximum of 40 strokes with a supple pole or simple whip. In practice the local court ordered only 39, a tradition intended to protect against the possibility that someone might miscount and administer 41 strokes, and thus inadvertently break God's Law.

What is important here, however, is to note that beatings were ordered only for the most unresponsive and unruly in the local community. These were a last, rather than first, resort in a local court's attempt to cause a person to conform to community norms.

The message is clear. However godly a life the believer lives, he or she will be unable to conform to the standards of the local community in which he or she lives. The believer will find himself always at odds, in some way or other, with unbelievers who demand conformity to standards which the believer simply cannot accept.

We see this in our own times, as police and judges refuse believers the right to peacefully protest the massacre of the unborn, as an elderly Christian woman in San Francisco is told that she cannot refuse to rent a room to a homosexual, and as teenagers are told that their Christian club is forbidden to meet on school property even though a witchcraft club may.

Jesus then moves on to the larger society and speaks of believers standing before governors and kings. Here the tension that exists is not between the believer and his community, but the believer and government itself.

The final arena Jesus mentions is perhaps the most painful of all. During the Interim, commitment to Christ may be in such great conflict with secular values and society that the family itself will be torn apart. The natural love of brother for brother, of parent for child, and children for parents, may be lost in a hostility so intense that one family member brings about the other's death.

Jesus' point is not that this will always happen. His point is simply that commitment to Jesus has the potential of introducing conflict into every relationship. We must not suppose that the Gospel message alone will somehow bring peace and usher in an era of good will on earth. It will not, and cannot. Many during this Interim period will reject the claims of Christ. And that rebellion not only eliminates every hope for world peace, but also excludes the hope of the kind of just, loving community of which we all yearn to be a part.

The Interim holds no hope for peace of any kind. The only hope we have of peace is linked to the return of the Prince of Peace, our Lord Jesus Christ.

THEME 3: MARK 13:14-31

■ History remains on God's intended course despite the confusion that exists during the Interim.

This section of Jesus' discourse begins with the word "when." Despite the seemingly random rise and fall of civilizations, the rise to dominance and the subsequent destruction of world powers, the flow of events during this time of the Interim has not moved history one degree off God's intended course.

There is no "if" in Jesus' teaching. There is only "when."

When. When you see what the prophets have prophesied taking place.

When. When the time of worldwide "distress" (*thlipsis,* tribulation) comes.

When. When, in the days following that distress, "the sun will be darkened, and the moon not give its light; the stars will fall from the sky and the heavenly bodies will be shaken" (13:24-25).

When. When, at that time, "men will see the Son of Man coming in clouds with great power and glory" (13:26).

While these words excite the developers of eschatological charts, they should provide even more comfort and delight to the average believer. We are not compelled to make sense out of the history of the Interim. We have no need to puzzle over how God's plan is being worked out in the rise and fall of the Byzantine or British Empires, in Communism, or in the past and future of our own democratic land. The endless struggle of human beings to build Interim civilizations apart from God are destined to fail, however noble the ideals on

which they are constructed. And every failure testifies simply to the fact that the meaning and purpose of human history is to be sought not in any society's "now," but rather in God's fast-approaching "when."

We Christians are citizens of a kingdom whose full expression on earth awaits the return of the King. And, until that time, we must first of all be loyal to Him, and live each day as strangers and pilgrims far from our true home.

THEME 4: MARK 13:32-37

■ Because we do not know when the Interim will end, we are to "Be alert!" or "Watch" (13:33).

The word for "Be alert!" calls for vigilance. During the Interim we believers, like servants of a first-century household, each have our "assigned task" (13:34). The simple fact is that we do not know the moment that God's "when" will be transformed into "now." God's when may be today, tomorrow, or lie in the distant future long after we have completed our sojourns here on earth. But these options make no difference to us at all. What is important is that as we wait expectantly, we "watch," using every gift and opportunity to serve the Lord.

MARK 14–16
Jesus' Death and Resurrection

EXPOSITION

In a very real sense, the few hours that passed between Jesus' anointing in Bethany and His trial and death serve as the fulcrum of history. All that happened before looked forward to these moments; all that has happened afterward looks back to them.

Because these moments in time are treated so thoroughly by each Gospel writer, rather than be repetitive in treating the chapters that report them I have chosen to focus attention on different themes found in each Gospel's record of these hours. Thus, in the study of Matthew we looked at the conspiracy, at Judas' betrayal, and at Peter's denial of Christ. In Luke we closely examine Jesus' sufferings. In John, we examine Jesus' trials. In Mark we take yet another approach, required by the fact that each Gospel writer goes into considerable detail about the events that took place during these hours. Yet each writer reports particulars that others leave out. This raises questions about timing and sequence. How do the Gospel accounts fit together? What happened, and when?

The best way to deal with these questions is to attempt to construct a time line, and as well as we can, list the occurrences reported by the Gospel writers in their most likely order. The chart below attempts to reconstruct the last events in the life of our Lord. And later, in The Passage in Depth, we look closely at Jesus' Seven Last Words from the cross.

JESUS' LAST DAY

Time	Place	Event	Matt.	Mark	Luke	John
Evening	Bethany	Jesus anointed by Mary	26:6-13	14:3-9		12:2-8
Night	Caiaphas' house	Judas agrees to betray	26:14-16	14:10-11	22:3-6	
Morning	Jerusalem	Preparation for Passover	26:17-19	14:12-16	22:7-13	
6 P.M.	Upper Room	Passover Supper observed	26:20	14:17	22:14-16, 24-30	
		Jesus washes disciples' feet				13:1-17
		Jesus predicts His betrayal	26:21-25	14:18-21	22:21-23	13:18-30
		Jesus predicts Peter's denial	26:31-35	14:27-31	22:31-38	13:37-38
		"Communion" established	26:26-30	14:22-26	22:17-20	
8 P.M.	Upper Room	Last Supper Discourse				13:31–16:33
10 P.M.	Upper Room	Jesus' "High Priestly" prayer				17:1-26
11 P.M.	Gethsemane	Jesus prays in the Garden	26:36-46	14:32-42	22:39-46	18:1
12 P.M.	Gethsemane	Jesus arrested	26:47-56	14:43-52	22:47-53	18:2-12
	Annas' house	Jesus examined by religious authorities				18:12-14, 19-23
	House of Caiaphas	Jesus examined by Sanhedrin	26:57-68	14:53-65	12:54	18:24
	Caiaphas' Courtyard	Peter denies Jesus	26:69-75	14:66-72	22:55-62	18:15-18, 25-27
Dawn	Sanhedrin	Jesus condemned by Sanhedrin	27:1	15:1	22:63-71	
	Outside Jerusalem	Judas kills himself	27:3-10			

6:30 A.M.	Pilate's Palace	Jesus taken to Pilate	27:2	15:2-5	23:1-5	18:28-38
	Herod's Palace	Jesus sent to Herod			23:6-12	
	Pilate's Palace	Jesus tried by Pilate and condemned	27:11-26	15:6-15	23:13-25	18:39–19:16
	Soldiers' Quarters	Jesus mocked and beaten	27:27-30	15:16-19		19:2-3
9 A.M.	Golgotha	Jesus led out to execution	27:31-34	15:20-23	23:26-33	19:16-17
9 A.M.– 12 P.M.	Golgotha	Jesus crucified: The first three hours	27:35-44	15:24-32	23:33-43	19:18-27
		First words from the cross			23:34	
		Second words from the cross			23:43	
		Third words from the cross				19:26-27
12-3 P.M.	Golgotha	Jesus on the cross: The next three hours— darkness	27:45-50	15:33-37	23:44-46	19:28-30
		Fourth words from the cross	27:46	15:34		
		Fifth words from the cross				19:28
		Sixth words from the cross				19:30
		Seventh words from the cross			23:46	
3 P.M.	Golgotha	Jesus' death and accompanying signs	27:51-56	15:38-41	23:44-49	
5 P.M.	Garden Tomb	Jesus is buried in a borrowed tomb	27:57-61	15:42-47	23:50-56	19:31-42
6 P.M.	Garden Tomb	The tomb is sealed and a guard is set	27:62-66			

For a sequence of Resurrection events, see Exposition, Matt. 28.

WORD STUDIES

In the home of a man known as Simon the Leper (14:3). Both the Pharisees and the Essenes, the two first-century Jewish groups most concerned with purity, feared and were utterly repelled by lepers. It is likely they were influential in establishing the rule that each Jewish city must establish some area outside it where lepers might live, so they would not defile the community. It is striking that the Temple Scroll, one of the manuscripts recovered with the Dead Sea Scrolls, indicates that lepers were isolated from others "east of the city" of Jerusalem. And it is there, just east of Jerusalem, that the town of Bethany lay!

The outstanding Jewish archaeologist Yigal Yadin concludes that "Jesus had not happened by chance to find Himself in the house of a leper, but had deliberately chosen to spend the night before entering Jerusalem in this leper colony, which was anathema both to the Essenes and the Pharisees."

What a significant choice. The "religious" drew back from those in need for fear of ritual contamination. Jesus sought them out, aware of the cleansing, transforming power that would be released in His death and resurrection.

Where I may eat the *Passover* with My

disciples (14:14). Commentators have debated as to whether or not the meal Jesus shared with His disciples was a Passover, or a meal eaten on the "day of Preparation of Passover Week" (John 19:14). It is best to understand this phrase to mean simply "the Friday of Passover week."

Harold Hoener (*Chronological Aspects of the Life of Christ,* Zondervan, pp. 76-78) summarizes 14 arguments that indicate the Last Supper truly was a Passover meal.

In summary form, scholars list the following arguments for a Passover meal: (1) The Synoptics explicitly state that the Last Supper was a Passover (Matt. 26:2, 17-19; Mark 14:1, 12, 14, 16; Luke 22:1, 7-8, 13, 15). (2) It took place, as required by the Law (Deut. 16:7), within the gates of Jerusalem even though it was so crowded at the time. (3) The Upper Room was made available without difficulty in keeping with the Passover custom. (4) The Last Supper was eaten at night (Matt. 26:20; Mark 14:17; John 13:30; 1 Cor. 11:23) which was an unusual time for a meal. (5) Jesus limited Himself to the Twelve rather than eating with the large circle of followers (which corresponds to the Passover custom). (6) A reclining posture at the table was for special occasions only. (7) The meal was eaten in levitical purity (John 13:10). (8) Jesus broke the bread during the meal (Matt. 26:26; Mark 14:22) rather than as customarily done at the beginning of the meal. (9) Red wine was drunk which was only for special occasions. (10) Some of the disciples thought that Judas left (John 13:29) to purchase items for the feast which would not have been necessary if the Last Supper was a day before the Passover since he would have had the whole next day (Nisan 14) available for this purpose. (11) Some of the disciples thought that Judas left to give to the poor (John 13:29), which was customary on Passover night. (12) The Last Supper ends with the singing of a hymn which would have been the second half of the Passover hallel. (13) Jesus did not return to Bethany which was outside of Jerusalem's limit but went to spend the night on the Mount of Olives which was within the enlarged city limits for the purpose of the Passover feast.

(14) The interpretation of special elements of the meal was a part of the Passover ritual.

The significance of this is found in the symbolism of the Passover lamb in Israel's deliverance from Egypt. When the death angel saw the blood of the lamb on the doorposts of God's people, he passed over that household, and all in the family lived. In the same way the blood of Jesus, our Passover Lamb, is sprinkled on us. Through Him and His shed blood we are spared death, and welcomed into eternal life.

Watch and pray so that you will not *fall into temptation.* The spirit is willing, but the body is weak (14:38). The phrase means "give in" to temptation. The Greek makes it clear that the words "watch" and "pray" are addressed to all the disciples, not just Peter. While the specific weakness of the body in view here is simply physical exhaustion, many commentators take *sarx* ("body" here but literally "flesh") in a theological sense, to indicate flawed human nature itself.

What is important to us is that watching (keeping alert) and prayer (remaining constantly dependent on the Lord) are imperative for us too, if we are to overcome our temptations.

A *young man,* wearing nothing but a linen garment, was following Jesus. When they seized him, he fled naked, leaving his garment behind (14:51). Most commentators assume that the young man was Mark himself. The text indicates he wore only a *sindon,* without the normal undergarment, a *chiton.* The fact that the *sindon* was of linen rather than wool tells us he was wealthy.

Why is this incident reported here? Perhaps it is Mark's quiet way of letting us know that he too was a witness to the events he describes. Or perhaps he takes this way of symbolizing how deserted Jesus was—even the children fled. Yet there is another implication. In his terror the young man was stripped of every bit of clothing and his nakedness fully exposed. In the same way the flight of His disciples stripped their self-delusions.

How eagerly James and John had insisted they were able to drink Jesus' cup and share His baptism (10:37-39). And how quickly

Peter swore he would follow Jesus to the death (14:31). Now, as they too deserted Jesus, they must have felt as exposed and naked as young John Mark. And perhaps realized how helpless they were in themselves to do anything for the Lord.

As Jesus had said just moments before, the flesh is weak. Only by watching and by prayer are we enabled by God to do anything at all.

And they *crucified* Him (15:24). For a discussion of this method of execution that the Roman's deemed too cruel for any but slaves and rebels, see the study of Jesus' sufferings found in this commentary's discussion of Luke 23.

Joseph of Arimathea, a *prominent* mem- **ber of the Council (15:43).** The Council, of course, is the Sanhedrin, the governing body in Judaism. The word translated "prominent" is *euschemon*. This word is used in the many papyri of the era to designate a wealthy landowner (Matt. 27:57). Joseph's land holdings would be near his home city of Arimathea. The fact that the tomb was still in the process of being hewn from a rocky hillside suggests this property probably had not been his for very long.

How fascinating to think of Joseph, buying a plot of land near Jerusalem in preparation for his own burial, never imagining that this transaction would make possible the fulfillment of a messianic prophecy uttered some 700 years earlier: "He was assigned a grave with the wicked, and [yet lay among] the rich in His death" (Isa. 53:9).

THE PASSAGE IN DEPTH

THE SEVEN WORDS FROM THE CROSS

The Gospels report seven utterances by Jesus as He hung on the cross. Three of these can be assigned to the first three hours, between 9 A.M. and 12 noon. Four can be assigned to the next three hours, 12-3 P.M., during which the scene was shrouded in darkness.

It is traditional during Good Friday services to meditate on these seven utterances. Surely there is much here for us to ponder.

THE FIRST WORDS

■ *"Father, forgive them, for they do not know what they are doing" (Luke 23:34).*

It's easy to recapture the attitude of the Roman soldiers assigned to the execution detail.

"Just doin' our duty, sir. Nothin' personal, you understand."

And of course, it was nothing personal. Oh, perhaps they grumbled about having to get up earlier than usual. But soldiers always grumble. And besides, those assigned to an execution detail did get to sell the clothing of the victims, so it wasn't all loss.

To the Roman soldiers the executions scheduled for this morning must have seemed no different than any other. Oh, one of the criminals was someone who had excited the hopes of the Jews. But the ordinary Roman soldier neither knew nor cared about local re-

ligion or politics. Such soldiers, undoubtedly non-Roman auxilliaries recruited from the western empire and transferred far away from their homelands, kept to themselves. Especially in a land where the poorest citizen considered the soldiers not only foreign oppressors but pagans, unworthy to associate with even the lowliest Jew.

Centurions might very well make an effort to understand the peoples in whose lands they were posted. But not ordinary soldiers in a land as inhospitable as the Jewish homeland.

So executing three more Jews was undoubtedly a matter of indifference to the soldiers. They just went about their duty in a businesslike manner. Hammering home the nails that fixed the victim's hands to the crossbars. Roughly lifting up the bar, tearing the flesh as they fixed the crossbars to the posts already embedded in the earth. Then hammering home spikes that held the feet fast, and added agony to each arching movement of the body that was necessary to catch another breath.

Just doing our duty, sir.

Just another execution detail.

Just more bodies, warm and pulsing with life, to be fastened to blood-drenched wood where they will twist and turn until the muscles can no longer twitch, the lungs suck no more air, and life slowly slips away. And while they die the soldiers pass the time in gambling, unmoved by sob or sigh, until death relieves them of their duty and they take down cold, clammy remains.

Just doing our duty, sir. Nothing personal, you understand.

And then one of the victims speaks and instead of cursing His executioners simply says, "Father, forgive them, for they do not know what they are doing."

Certainly they did not understand who Jesus was. But Christ's words imply far more about their ignorance. These soldiers who so casually carried out their officer's orders to kill other men had no sense of the sanctity of human life. They had no vision of humanity as a special creation of God, and no sense of the image and likeness of God the victims bore. No, it is not wrong for the state to impose the death penalty. But it is tragic for even a murderer to be executed with casual disregard.

It was this terrible ignorance, the ignorance of those who viewed other human beings and even themselves merely as animals, and so treated others in this way, that so troubled Jesus. Through His pain Jesus watched the soldiers. Jesus saw their profound unawareness of the eternal significance of the duty they carried out. And moved by compassion for them He spoke His first words from the cross.

Let us make no mistake. Ignorance does not absolve anyone. We still need forgiveness. But like Jesus we must have compassion on those who simply do not know what they are doing. And like Jesus we are to pray that God may instruct them, and that they may learn—and be forgiven.

THE SECOND WORDS
■ "I tell you the truth, today you will be with Me in paradise" (Luke 23:43).

The focus now shifts from the soldiers to the two "thieves" crucified with Jesus. The word for thieves indicates brigands or guerilla fighters who were in open conflict with the established order.

At first both these men "heaped insults" on Jesus (Matt. 27:44). Unlike the soldiers, whose contempt had been aroused by the charge that Jesus was "a king," these men knew of our Lord's claim to be the Christ, the Jewish Messiah (Luke 23:39).

Finally one of the two rebuked the other. His words (Luke 23:40-42) reveal the process of his spiritual transformation. This man acknowledged his guilt. He recognized Jesus' purity. And he appealed to Jesus in faith: "Remember me when You come into Your kingdom."

What a faith the criminal on the cross expressed! It is easy for us, looking back on the Resurrection, to see that Jesus truly is the Son of God. But the man on the cross saw an apparently helpless Jesus, suffering as He was suffering, and despite the cold perspiration that stood out on Jesus' brow, and the blood that stained His hands and feet, the criminal on the cross believed.

And in response to this amazing faith, Jesus replied, "I tell you the truth, today you will be with Me in paradise."

"Paradise," a Persian word meaning "garden" or "beautiful place," was adopted into Semitic languages as a euphemism for heaven, and the comfort and bliss to be experienced there.

It is probably a mistake to place the comma in the Greek or English verse before today. Jesus very likely used a more common Aramaism and said, "I tell you the truth today, you will be with Me in paradise." The figure of speech was used to confirm a promise, for in that culture a promise made and associated with a certain day would surely be kept.

Thus Jesus did not imply that either He or the thief would be in paradise on that day. Instead Jesus made a firm commitment to the thief that his faith guaranteed him a place, not simply in Christ's kingdom, but in eternity.

THE THIRD WORD
■ "Dear woman, here is your son. . . . Here is your mother" (John 19:26-27).

The circle now expands again beyond the brow of the hill to encompass weeping witnesses who stand nearby. There Jesus' mother and several women stand bowed in grief, perhaps leaning on the disciple John.

Jesus looks up and notices them, feeling their pain more deeply than He feels His own. Mary and John are linked by the anguished sense of their loss, perhaps felt more deeply by them than by any of the others, for they were undoubtedly even emotionally closer than the others to our Lord.

Seeing their pain Jesus gives them each a unique gift: to Mary He gives the sensitive, caring John to take the place of the Son she is about to lose. To John He gives Mary, to love and to take care of as an expression of His undying love for her Son.

It is not as if Mary had no other sons to care for her. She did. And it is not as if John were alone. He was not. Instead Jesus redirects the love each has for Him to the other, that in the opportunity each will have to express care for the other each will find fulfillment gradually replacing their sense of loss.

There is a beautiful message here for us. Our love is to be first of all for Jesus. But until we are present with Christ and Christ is present with us, we are to direct our love for Christ toward others. It is in loving others that we not only express our love for Christ, but also in such loving that we experience Jesus' love for us.

THE UNSPOKEN WORDS
■ Matt. 27:41-43

The first three sayings from the cross are linked directly to witnesses of the crucifixion. Jesus asked God to forgive the soldiers, whose casual attitude revealed their ignorance not only of Jesus' Person but of the value of human life itself. Jesus gave the believing thief a binding promise of paradise. And Jesus gave both His grief-stricken mother and the Apostle John a unique gift, redirecting their love for Him toward each other, in order that by giving and receiving love they might experience Jesus' presence in a unique way.

But there were other witnesses to the crucifixion, who came not to grieve, but to gloat. Matthew describes them. "In the same way the chief priests, the teachers of the Law and the elders mocked Him. 'He saved others,' they said, 'but He can't save Himself! He's the king of Israel! Let Him come down now from the cross, and we will believe in Him. He trusts in God. Let God rescue Him now if He wants Him, for He said, "I am the Son of God" ' " (27:41-43).

Their taunts provoked no response. Everything that could be said to them had been said, and had evoked no response of faith but only bitterness and persistent, antagonistic unbelief. Even when God would speak three days hence in that awesome act of Resurrection which confirmed Jesus as His Son, these men would refuse to believe. And for such persons no words of forgiveness, of promise, or of love will suffice.

Oh, there will be a word addressed to the men who hated and rejected the Son of God. But it will be a word of judgment—a word which they will be forced to hear, no matter how hard they press their hands against their ears. Yet the cross is no place for that word to be spoken. For the cross is the ultimate symbol of God's forgiveness, of paradise won, of rediscovered love. And such words unbelief will always choose not to hear.

And so the silence from the cross speaks as loudly to us as any of the seven words.

THE FOURTH WORDS
■ *"My God, My God, why have You forsaken Me?" (Matt. 27:46)*

The first three words from the cross were spoken while bright morning light exposed Christ's suffering to witnesses. Each of these three words was either to or about those witnesses—the indifferent soldiers, the believing criminal, the grieving loved ones. But now two dramatic shifts take place.

First, the sun seems to dim, and the dreadful scene is shrouded in darkness. For nearly three hours the darkness deepens. Although the text does not indicate it, I suspect the religious who taunted Jesus from the road that passed Golgotha began to scurry home as the darkness deepened.

For almost all those hours Christ suffered in silence. Then, as the moment of death approached, the last four sayings burst from Christ's lips. None are addressed to the witnesses, squinting to pierce the darkness. Instead each reflects Christ's own inner struggle and His intimate relationship with the Father.

The first of these four sayings, "My God, My God, why have You forsaken Me?" The words express distressed astonishment, the emotion of utter desolation. The fact that they are first found in Psalm 22 reminds us that these emotions are common to men. Yet the fact that it is only during this extended moment that Christ knows this sense of total isolation and loss is deeply significant.

As God the Son our Lord had spent eternity past in the unbroken fellowship of love that pulsed steadily within the Godhead. Father, Son, and Holy Spirit were at one, and were one. Even in the Incarnation Jesus lived a life of unbroken fellowship with the Father.

But now the Son of God was dying on the cross—dying that He might take upon Himself the burden of our sins, and suffer death in our place. For this awesome moment Jesus, who knew no sin, was "made . . . sin" for us (2 Cor. 5:21). And at that extended moment, stretching over three darkened hours, God the Father forsook the Son, turning away from Him, and Christ experienced spiritual death—isolation from God.

In an awesome sense which we cannot begin to grasp the Godhead itself was ripped and torn, and the anguish Jesus felt was deeper and more real than all the anguish felt by our sin-cursed race. All this, all of history's sin and suffering, was suddenly, stunningly shouldered by the Son of God, and in the resultant sundering of that intimate tie that bound Father, Son, and Spirit together, Christ suffered more than we can ever imagine or begin to know.

THE FIFTH WORDS

■ *"I am thirsty"* (*John 19:28*).

The first word out of the darkness impresses us with the deity of Jesus. This second word out of the darkness reminds us of His humanity.

Christ's suffering was both spiritual and physical; both a tearing of His spirit and an assault on His body.

Psalm 22:15 describes this dimension of Jesus' sufferings: "My strength is dried up like a potsherd, and my tongue sticks to the roof of my mouth." Physically the cross not only drained what strength remained in Jesus' body after the brutal whipping He had received back in Jerusalem, but had also instigated a raging fever that further dried out His body tissues. This may suggest a reason why Christ called for a drink. It was not to alleviate the thirst or relieve the suffering. Most likely it was to momentarily relieve the dryness that His next, triumphant words might be uttered clearly and triumphantly.

Despite the limits imposed by taking on our human nature, Christ prevailed.

THE SIXTH WORDS

■ *"It is finished"* (*John 19:30*).

John adds, "With that He bowed His head and gave up His spirit" (30:31). The last, shouted prayer of Jesus, which occurs between vv. 30 and 31, is not recorded by John, who wants us to understand fully the relationship between our salvation and Jesus' death.

Jesus came into our world not simply to reveal God to humankind, but to die as our substitute, paying the price that justice demands for our sins. In those final, dark hours on the cross Jesus experienced that awesome isolation from the Father which is the essence of spiritual death. And in that moment of time the finite and infinite coalesced, and the Son of God paid in full a penalty imposed for the sin of every human being from Adam to history's end—a penalty which those who refuse to believe can never pay although they suffer for eternity. When at last Jesus cried, "It is finished," He had suffered more than all our race together. And He suffered there for you and me.

The word translated "gave up" His spirit is *paredoken,* and the emphasis is on the fact that Jesus surrendered His spirit voluntarily. The implication of this is striking. Throughout His suffering Jesus had the ability to choose to live or die. Earlier Jesus had said, "No one takes it [My life] from Me, but I lay it down of My own accord. I have authority to lay it down and authority to take it up again" (John 10:18). Now He proved His determination to complete His mission of salvation, for He held on to life until all our sins were paid for, and the penalty had been paid in full.

We will never know how desperately Christ yearned for release from His spiritual suffering before full payment was made. But at last the moment came. And only then Jesus "gave up His spirit."

THE SEVENTH WORDS

■ *"Father, into Your hands I commit My Spirit"* (*Luke 23:46*).

The words are from yet another psalm, Ps. 31:5, and were used in Israel as an evening prayer. The psalm is a beautiful expression of unshakable confidence. It reminds us that, although Christ accepted death as the Father's will, His suffering in no way threatened the loving bond of trust that existed between them.

The words of that psalm, penned by David, remind us that even in the darkest of times God is our refuge too. Jesus' willingness to suffer for us is unshakable proof that as He committed His spirit into the Father's hands, so can we.

EXPOSITION

Luke begins his Gospel with a special claim: he has himself "carefully investigated everything [about Jesus' life] from the beginning" (1:1-4). Thus Luke's Gospel is a careful, historically accurate report of Jesus' birth, ministry, death, and resurrection. Yet as we read Luke we realize that his work is no dry repetition of dates and doings. Luke's writing is vivid, drawing us into the events he describes. Luke's writing also displays an ardent sensitivity to intimate personal details. He tends to dwell on Christ's unusual concern for the poor, for the helpless, for the outcasts of society, and for women. Luke also emphasizes Christ's own dependence on prayer and the Holy Spirit. Luke's writing displays another quality as well. It is energized by vibrant hope in and praise of God. We can hardly read a chapter of this Gospel without being caught up in the conviction that, in Jesus, God has brought salvation to humankind.

Each of these strengths, the historian's care and the true believer's abounding joy, are seen in these opening chapters of Luke's Gospel. More than any other Gospel writer, Luke delves into a variety of unique events that are associated with Jesus' birth. He tells us of the unusual circumstances of the birth of John the Baptist (1:5-25, 57-80); of the relationship between Mary and Elizabeth, and the two women's exultant joy when they realize God is about to work wonders through their offspring (1:26-56). Luke tells about the angelic visit to the shepherds (2:8-20), about the revelation given to Simeon and Anna that the infant Jesus is in reality God's Christ (2:21-40), and about Jesus' childhood visit to the temple (2:41-52).

Where did Luke discover these stories? Many believe that Luke, who was Paul's constant companion, took advantage of the two years that Paul was held in Caesarea by Roman governors (Acts 23–26) to travel the Holy Land and interview many informants who were eyewitnesses. So we are deeply indebted to Luke for this background that only he shares, before taking up the subject that intrigues the other Gospel writers as well — the "forerunner" ministry of John the Baptist. This ministry would soon propel John's cousin Jesus of Nazareth to sudden prominence (3:1-22).

WORD STUDIES

It seemed good *also* to me to write an orderly account for you (1:3). Why another Gospel? Luke clearly is aware that Matthew and Mark have given us their accounts of Jesus' life. The answer is best provided by noting distinctive features of this Gospel as compared to others. Luke, like the others, wants us to see Jesus from his special perspective. Walter L. Liefeld's commentary, *Luke* (Zondervan), sums up some of these distinctives for us.

Among these are Jesus' concern for all people, especially those who were outcasts — the poor, women, and those who were known as "sinners"; Luke's universal scope; his alteration of some of the terminology of Mark to facilitate the understanding of Luke's readers — e.g., the Greek term for "lawyer" (*nomikos*) instead of the Hebrew term "scribe" (*grammateus*); an emphasis on Jesus' practical teaching (e.g., chs. 12 and 16 deal with finances); Luke's sense of purpose, fulfillment, and accomplishment; his sense of joy and praise to God for His saving and healing work; Jesus' strong call to discipleship; Jesus' dependence on the Holy Spirit and prayer; and many examples of God's power.

In the first century, when pagans had not only long since turned from the traditional gods but had also wrestled unsuccessfully with issues of luck and fate and had turned to the false hopes of the so-called Eastern or mystery religions, such a narrative as Luke's doubtless had a genuine appeal. Here was a "Savior" who actually lived and cared about people. He was here among people; He was crucified and actually raised from the dead. And Luke tells all this with a conviction and verisimilitude that brought assurance to Theophilus and continues to bring assurance down to our day.

I myself have carefully investigated everything from the beginning (1:3). Luke pays closer attention to events that took place before Jesus' birth than any other Gospel. The following list gives the sequence of events concerning Christ's birth, developed by integrating Luke's and Matthew's Gospels.

TIMELINE OF CHRIST
THE ETERNAL SON OF GOD

Christ's Preexistence	John 1:1-18

Events Associated with Jesus' Birth

John's Birth Announced	Luke 1:5-25
Jesus' Birth Announced to Mary	Luke 1:26-38
Mary Visits Elizabeth	Luke 1:39-45
Mary's "Magnificat" of Praise	Luke 1:46-56
John Born	Luke 1:57-80
Jesus' Birth Announced to Joseph	Matt. 1:18-25
Jesus Is Born	Luke 2:1-7
Announcement to the Shepherds	Luke 2:8-20

Events Associated with Jesus' Infancy and Childhood

Jesus Is Circumcised	Luke 2:21
Jesus Is Presented at the Temple	Luke 2:22-38
The Wise Men Seek Out Jesus	Matt. 2:1-12
The Family Flees to Egypt	Matt. 2:13-18
The Family Returns to Nazareth	Matt. 2:19-23; Luke 2:39
Jesus Grows Up	Luke 2:40
Jesus Visits the Temple	Luke 2:41-50
Jesus Continues to Grow	Luke 2:51-52

Zechariah belonged to the *priestly division* of Abijah (Luke 1:5). When we read of "priests" in the Gospels, we need to distinguish between the priestly aristocracy and "ordinary" priests. The aristocracy was limited to several priestly families, who dominated the offices in the hierarchy that controlled temple finances and ritual. These families had homes in Jerusalem. They were extremely wealthy and exercised political as well as economic and religious power. Early Jewish writings tend to portray them as greedy and corrupt. One writer complains that "their sons are treasurers . . . and their servants smite the people with sticks."

On the other hand "ordinary" priests resided outside Jerusalem, in either Judea or Galilee. It was their task to officiate at the sacrifices and other ceremonies that took place daily at the temple. The organization of these ordinary priests into groups of 24 is mentioned as early as 1 Chron. 24:1-10, and while the names of these groups changed over the years, the system of 24 groups of priests, each of which served in Jerusalem for one week, from Sabbath to Sabbath, persisted to the time of Christ. Early Jewish writings show that in the first century these 24 weekly "clans" were further divided into some 156 "families" who undertook the daily priestly duties. The "division" Luke mentions is most likely this daily "family," whose members drew lots to determine who would enter the temple at the time of the morning or evening sacrifice to offer incense.

Some authorities indicate that there were so many of these "ordinary" priests that an individual could only perform this particular sacred duty once in his lifetime. Whether or not this is true, it is clear that God was at work in the "chance" assignment of Zechariah to this ministry.

When Zechariah saw him, he was *startled* and was gripped with *fear* (1:12). *Etarachthe,* "startled," indicates an intense emotional disturbance, which Luke defines as fear. In one sense the reaction is typical, for others responded in the same way in the presence of the supernatural (5:8-10). Yet there is a lesson here for us.

Zechariah was entering the temple where the God of Israel dwelt—a God known for His supernatural acts in history on behalf of His people. A God whose miracles were recounted in festivals of praise. And yet Zechariah never dreamed that God would act for him. No wonder he was startled. Despite the awe he must have felt in entering the holy place, Zechariah had expected a comfortable, quiet approach to a silent, rather passive God! Let's not make this same assumption. God can and does work in our lives today. Let us approach Him with a sense of awe, but also a sense of expectancy.

He is never to *take wine or other fermented drink* (1:15). The description suggests that John was to be subject to a Nazarite vow throughout his life (Num. 6:1-12). The only other person so described in the Bible is Samson (Jud. 13–16). The contrast between the two men, the one physically strong and the other a spiritual giant, reminds us that what makes the difference is not external symbols of religion, but our personal, inner commitments to God.

Samson lived with the symbols of commitment. John lived out the reality that the symbols were intended to represent.

Mary was greatly *troubled* at his words and wondered what kind of greeting this might be (1:29). The Greek word is *dietarachthe,* which means "perplexed," "confused." What a different reaction this simple country girl makes, probably still in her early teens, from that of Zechariah, who was deeply shaken and terrified at Gabriel's appearance.

None of this is a criticism of Zechariah. His reaction at the appearance of Gabriel is understandable, and Luke describes him as "blameless" (one who lived in full accordance with the Mosaic Law). What the contrast in reactions does do is redound to Mary's praise, and remind us of the simplicity and sincerity of her faith in the Lord—a simplicity and sincerity we might well emulate.

Trust in God is a beautiful quality, one not dependent on age, rank, or position. Often the simplest believer is graced with more of this kind of responsive faith than those with some status.

"How will this be," Mary asked the angel, "since I am a *virgin?*" (1:34) We might fasten on this term "virgin," and note that it does not simply mean "unmarried young woman," but one who has had no sexual intercourse with a man.

But consider first what it is she asks. Not, "How could I explain to Joseph?" Not, "How could I face the shame of being unmarried and pregnant?" Not, "What will happen to me?" Instead she simply wonders, "How will God perform this miracle and make me, a virgin, mother of the Messiah?"

When Gabriel explains the miracle, Mary's immediate response is, "I am the Lord's servant" (1:38).

How remarkable a person this country girl has proven to be. A "servant" is one who does the will of his or her master and sets aside personal concerns in order to fulfill any commission. In saying, "I am the Lord's servant," Mary commits herself fully to do God's will, whatever the personal cost.

On the eighth day they came to *circumcise* the child, and they were going to *name Him* (1:59). The birth of a son was an occasion of rejoicing, launching what was known as the "son's week." For seven days friends came to the home in the evenings. Then on the eighth a great crowd gathered to celebrate the boy's circumcision. The circumcision marked the child's official initiation into the Covenant God made with Abraham, and marked him forever as a member of the chosen people. Of note in Luke's description is the fact that his is the only reference in first-century literature to naming a child on the eighth day—a practice well attested to later in Jewish history.

Of note too, the Jews viewed celebrating a person's birthday as a pagan practice. Their joy marked the festivities associated with a boy's circumcision. The significance of one's relationship with God was far greater than even the beginning of biological life itself. Today too, our "second birthday," when we establish a relationship with Christ through faith, is an event that is worthy of greater celebration than our first!

In those days Caesar Augustus issued a decree that a *census* should be taken of the entire Roman world (2:1). It was the practice under Augustus to take a census, which not only counted individuals but also recorded their possessions, as a basis for taxation of the lands controlled by Rome. In v. 2 Luke mentions a census that took place while Quirinius was governor of Syria. This census was especially notable, because it nearly caused an open rebellion against Rome in Judea. Judas of Gaulanitis and the Pharisee Saddok aroused the general population by crying out that it symbolized enslavement by Rome and must surely lead to heavier taxes. Luke's mention of this census creates difficulty, however, in that it is known to have taken place in A.D. 6, a decade or so after the birth of Jesus!

This has led some to argue that Luke is guilty of an obvious mistake, leading them to question the accuracy of other information found in his Gospel and in Acts.

The best solution to this apparent historical contradiction rests on the meaning of the word *prote*. While one meaning is "first," as in the NIV of Luke 2:2, *prote* can also mean "previous" or "former." If we use this meaning, Luke 2:1 indicates that "a census," the one that brought Mary and Joseph to Bethlehem, "happened before Quirinius was governor of Syria."

In adopting this translation we see that Luke is actually careful to distinguish the census he is writing about from the more recent census ordered by Quirinius, which the reader might otherwise have assumed to be the census Luke had in mind.

Today in the *town* of David (2:11). In Scripture the "town" of David is Bethlehem, while Jerusalem is the "city" of David.

Glory to God in the highest, and on earth peace to men *on whom His favor rests* (2:14). How did the *King James* translators render this verse as "on earth, peace to men of good will"? The answer lies in a single letter, the Greek sigma, "s." The Greek texts available in 1611 had the nominative *eudokia*. Later discoveries of earlier texts have the genitive *eudokias*. The presence of that single letter shifts the meaning of the angelic announcement from a proclamation of peace to "men of good will" to a proclamation of peace to all mankind, on whom, through the birth of the Savior, God's favor now rests.

Similar constructions found in early church hymns, and in an Aramaic text found among the Dead Sea Scrolls, makes it clear that the NIV rendering is correct.

Of course, biblical theology makes it just as clear. God's favor does not rest on "men of good will," for we all fall short. But in providing us with a Savior, God has made it clear that His favor rests on all of us. How can we not respond to such grace with worship and praise!

A pair of *doves or two young pigeons* (2:24). Old Testament law required a woman to offer a lamb to God a certain number of days after the birth of a child (Lev. 12:1-8). However, this regulation includes a special provision: "If she cannot afford a lamb, she is to bring two doves or two young pigeons, one for a burnt offering and the other for a sin offering."

The fact that Mary brought this alternate sacrifice indicates that she and Joseph were poor indeed.

How intriguing that God did not choose to place His Son in the home of some well-to-do couple. Instead He chose to place Jesus with a family poor in material things but rich in faith and love.

Surely our own drive to provide a better life materially for our children is understandable. But perhaps it is also unwise. We have much to ponder and to learn from God's placement of His Son with the humble Mary and Joseph.

Didn't you know I had to be in *My Fa-*

ther's **house? (2:49)** At age 13 a Jewish boy became a "son of the commandment" and was required to journey to Jerusalem to participate in major annual religious festivals. However, the rabbis of the era called for a boy to be brought up to Jerusalem two years earlier to observe the festive rights. Thus Jesus was very likely as young as eleven when the events described here took place.

We also know from rabbinic writings that Luke's picture of the boy Jesus discussing the Law with famous adult teachers accurately reflects the custom of the time. On feast days and Sabbaths the sages not only taught publicly, but ordinary folk freely engaged in asking questions and debating with the lecturers. Anyone who knew the Scriptures in Hebrew could engage in these discussions — as the boy Jesus did.

The reason that Luke tells this story, however, is that the boy Jesus identified the temple as the house of "My Father." This was not the way the average Jew thought of God, although He was the "Father" — the source — of the Hebrew race. Luke wants us to understand that even at this early age Jesus was aware of His unique relationship with the Lord — a claim which His parents "did not understand" (2:50).

He [John] went into all the country around the Jordan, preaching (3:3). For a discussion of the ministry of John the Baptist, see John 3:22-36, Matthew 11:1-19, and Mark 1:1-8.

He will *baptize* you with the Holy Spirit and with fire (3:16). For a discussion of this phrase, see the Word Study of Matt. 3:11.

THE PASSAGE IN DEPTH

These chapters of Luke's Gospel report monologues uttered by three persons who are significant in his story of Jesus' infancy. The first is in the form of praise uttered by Mary (1:46-55). The second is in the form of prophecy uttered by Zechariah, the father of John the Baptist (1:67-79). And the third is in the form of a prayer uttered by the aged Simeon, who has seen and recognized the infant Jesus as the promised Savior (2:29-32).

Each monologue shares an important trait: each looks ahead with expectant joy to what God will do, while at the same time interpreting that future in terms of God's revelation of His purpose for Israel through Moses and the prophets. The past saw the planting of the seed. The present is to each a time of sprouting. And surely the future will yield God's intended fruit.

Each of these three powerful monologues is worthy of careful scrutiny.

MARY'S MAGNIFICAT
■ The Virgin's Prayer (1:46-55)
Background. One of the most impressive elements of Mary's praise poem is its saturation with Old Testament phrases and concepts. Even the construction of thoughts clearly echoes patterns found in the Hebrew psalms and their contemporary Greek translation in the Septuagint. Mary's thrill at her privilege to "magnify" (glorify, make great) the Lord is expressed first by the psalmists. They too cry "Glorify the Lord with me; let us exalt His name together" (Ps. 34:3) and "I will praise God's name in song and glorify Him with thanksgiving" (Ps. 69:30).

As Mary moves to direct worship, praising God for specific attributes (1:49-50), parallels become even more striking. For instance, the phrase "the Mighty One has done great things for me" picks up the thought and language of Ps. 71:19, and may reflect the image of God as a warrior/hero seen in Isa. 42:13, "The Lord will march out like a mighty man, like a warrior He will stir up His zeal; with a shout He will raise the battle cry and will triumph over His enemies."

One commentator, tracing through Mary's praise line by line, has linked her thoughts and terms to some twelve different OT passages.

Some have questioned whether a young girl, probably in her early teens at the time, could have spontaneously produced a poem of such depth and so filled with biblical allusion. Yet there are at least two things to remember. The Jews in the first century remained at heart a theocratic community. It was their relationship with God that gave them not only their identity as a people, but also was the foundation of their hope for the future. These were truly a people of the Book, and biblical phrases and images were woven into daily speech, memorized and sung, and discussed in the synagogue every Sabbath.

The second thing to remember, of course, is that Mary was a young woman of deep faith and spiritual insight. She was truly an exceptional person, as we quickly learn as we see her response to the announcement by the Angel Gabriel (1:38). Not every young woman in first-century Galilee could have composed the Magnificat. But as Mary traveled to visit her cousin Elizabeth in Judah's hill country, a journey of some three to four days on foot, Mary pondered her experience and Mary did compose these wonderful words of praise.

What a challenge to us in our day. If we expect to be used by God, we need not be great in the eyes of the world. But we must saturate ourselves with the Scriptures, till the thoughts and concepts revealed by God become an integral part of our hearts and minds too.

Interpretation. Mary's Magnificat, so named because of its first word when translated into Latin, has four divisions. (1) Verses 46-48 praise God for what He has done for Mary and reflect her own awe at being chosen to give birth to the Messiah. (2) Verses 49-50 focus our attention on attributes of God. Israel's Mighty One is powerful, holy, and merciful. (3) Verses 51-53 reflect God's eschatological commitment—a commitment foreshadowed by His choice of the "humble" Mary to bear the Messiah. That eschatological commitment is also revealed in history, as God has "brought down rulers from their thrones" and has "lifted up the humble." Yet the past is merely prelude to what God will do in the Messiah, turning this world upside down and rejecting the rich and welcoming the hungry.

In a significant sense Mary's lyric hymn of praise is an affirmation of foundational truths taught in the older revelation. God is concerned with the individual, for He is the God of power, holiness, and mercy. He will not forget His covenant promises to Abraham. Instead, in the Messiah who now grows in Mary's womb, God intends to fulfill His commitment to the humble, and when Messiah has executed judgment and brought down the powerful of this world, the Lord will comfort Abraham's offspring forever.

Application. It is important to note that Luke has not chosen material that divorces Jesus from the OT's vision of the Messiah, but rather material which affirms Jesus of Nazareth as the very individual the prophets describe. Today the church rightly focuses on the first verses of Mary's psalm of praise. We rejoice in God as "my Savior," and acknowledging our "humble state" we point others to Christ for deliverance.

Yet the power unleashed to bring us salvation will one day accomplish the devastating judgments envisioned by the prophets of old. When that day comes our world will be turned upside down. The mighty will fall—and the weak be lifted up. God will keep every promise, as in the day of judgment He remembers to be merciful to His own.

Let's consider how swiftly the day of grace may be passing away. And commit ourselves to doing His will.

THE BENEDICTUS
■ Zechariah's Prophecy (Luke 1:67-79)
Background. Zechariah's prophecy, even more clearly than Mary's praise, expresses thoughts that are fully defined by OT texts and contemporary Jewish expectations. The prophecy has two major divisions: vv. 68-75 focus on the meaning for Israel of the birth of Christ, while vv. 76-79 focus on the role in God's plan to be fulfilled by Zechariah's own son, John.

While modern Christian commentators spiritualize OT prophecy, and see in the vivid images of a land, a kingdom, and prosperity for God's OT people spiritual blessings for NT believers, this approach was not taken by Jewish commentators in the first century. They expected a real descendant of David to appear. They expected Him to break the yoke of foreign domination under which the Jews had been forced to bow for centuries, and to establish an earthly kingdom whose capital would be Jerusalem. The Jewish people were convinced that as God's chosen ones they would serve Him and His Messiah by ruling Gentile nations whose people had at last been forced to acknowledge and submit to God.

This was a grand vision of a world at peace under the benevolent but firm rule of God's Servant the Messiah—one in which the specialness of the Jews would at last be acknowledged by the other races of humankind.

All this is implied, and even more than implied — mandated — in Zechariah's exulting, prophetic cry. And again we are reminded. Even Luke, most likely himself a "Gentile" Christian, makes it clear that to understand the ultimate role of Jesus Christ in God's plan we must take into account not only the NT's teaching, but that of the OT as well.

Interpretation. The first section (1:67-75) of Zechariah's prophecy, which Luke reminds us is uttered when this priest is "filled with the Holy Spirit" (1:67), praises God "because He has come and has redeemed His people" (1:68).

This theme is picked up and amplified in the following verses: "He has raised up a horn of salvation" (1:69). Thus the present time has become the locus in which the messianic visions of "His holy prophets of long ago" are at last being fulfilled.

Zechariah moves on to praise God as if the envisioned salvation were already accomplished! The deliverer has come

■ to remember His holy covenant (1:72)

■ to rescue us from the hand of our enemies (1:74)

■ to enable us to serve Him without fear in holiness and righteousness before Him all our days (1:74-75).

Zechariah speaks this way because he sees in the seed of God's present act the fruit that will be produced when that present act matures. It is as if the planting of an acorn guarantees the development of a mighty oak, or the laying of the keel makes certain the launching of the ship. All that God has promised to accomplish at history's end is made certain and sure, for it is implicit in His act of raising up the Deliverer.

The key term in this prophetic psalm of Zechariah's is "salvation" (1:69), a salvation which the OT links with the Deliverer to descend from David. Here, as in the majority of its OT occurrences, "salvation" is not primarily a spiritual salvation that comes through the forgiveness of our sins. It is, rather, a deliverance from those hostile nations which oppress God's people. Salvation is "from our enemies" (1:71), and is that "rescue . . . from the hand of our enemies" (1:74) which will "enable us to serve [God] without fear, in holiness and

righteousness before Him all our days" (1:74-75).

The second part of Zechariah's prophetic hymn (1:76-79) focuses on John, the infant who lies before them, just eight days old, about to be circumcised. The description of John's destiny in v. 76, to be that prophet who "will go on before the Lord to prepare the way for Him" undoubtedly reflects Isa. 40:3 and Mal. 3:1; 4:5, clearing linking John with Elijah, the forerunner of the Messiah. Here at last we have a reference to "the knowledge of salvation through the forgiveness of their sins" (Luke 1:77), a clear reference to John's future preaching of repentance. Here too, however, Zechariah is speaking within the context of OT rather than NT truth. When Messiah accomplishes the deliverance of God's people, it will be on behalf of a redeemed Jewry, which has turned wholeheartedly to the Lord for forgiveness and renewal (Jer. 31:33-34).

Interpretation. It is significant that Luke so faithfully reports Zechariah's prophetic utterance, just because the context in which that utterance fits is so completely "Old Testament" in nature. Jesus is the One the prophets predicted would come. Jesus is the One who will accomplish Israel's deliverance from her oppressors. Jesus is the One who will fulfill the covenant promises made to Abraham and David.

Zechariah, steeped in OT lore, understood Christ's mission in the context of that revelation, and had no notion at all of the present Gospel age in which a salvation from personal sins is offered to persons of every family, race, and nation who put their trust in Israel's crucified and risen Savior.

Some, noting this seeming discrepancy in expectations, assume either that the OT vision of the future or the Christian conviction that Jesus is the prophesied Christ must somehow be wrong. But this assumption is unwarranted. It must be clear that Luke, who looks back and writes from a distinctively Christian perspective, sees no discrepancy in fully reporting Zechariah's prophecy. To Luke, and to us, Zechariah's words should first of all imply the unity of OT and NT as parts of one whole. Second, Zechariah's words should remind us that God's plans and purposes are more complex than we may imagine. Should we assume a "discrepancy" when we discover that this Gospel Age, an interim period between the

First Coming and the Second Coming of Christ, was unrevealed to OT saints? Or are OT predictions concerning the Holy Land and Israel's future in it under the Messiah some "error" that needs to be excused by proposing a spiritual fulfillment of promises given God's OT people? Or is it possible that God's plan, and the purposes He intends to accomplish in Christ, is more complex that we imagine?

Perhaps for us this is the most important and practical message to be found in the Benedictus. Let's not try to simplify what God intends, to make everything fit in our categories. Let's remember that God's purposes are complex, and that we should not expect to comprehend all that is in His mind. Instead of debating what the future holds, let us realize as Zechariah did that in Christ, the future is now. All God's purposes are and will be summed up in the one that we present to the world as Savior and Lord. How important then that we share Him with everyone we know.

THE FAREWELL

■ Simeon's Prayer (Luke 2:29-32)

Background. The temple was the focal point of OT religion, the place where God's presence dwelt, the only place where sacrifices of atonement or praise were to be offered. Luke tells of two godly individuals who meet Mary and Joseph when they bring the Baby Jesus to the temple—and guided by the Holy Spirit recognize Him as the Messiah.

Interpretation. Each of the two individuals who recognizes Jesus' significance, one a man and one a woman, is aged. In a sense each represents the end of the then present era. Each has outlived his or her contemporaries, and the long decades that Anna had lived without a husband, worshiping in the temple, speak of both waiting and unfulfillment. Yet the hope of each throughout the years was fixed in God. And so these two representative OT saints were chosen to see the Baby Jesus and recognize Him as the Messiah.

Luke records the prayer of Simeon, the elderly man who has been told by the Spirit that he would not die before he had seen the Lord's Christ (2:26). Simeon's prayer, much more than Zechariah's prophecy, marks a transition from the era of the OT to that of the NT. If we see Simeon as a representative of

his era, there is great symbolic as well as personal significance in his words.

Now dismiss Your servant in peace (2:29). This statement reflects Simeon's sense of personal fulfillment and readiness to die. He is old now, and his age weighs heavily on him. Now that he has witnessed the coming of the Savior he is ready to pass away. Similarly the birth of the Savior meant the passage of an era in Israel's history. For centuries God's people had been weighed down, as first one and then another foreign world power oppressed them. Surely life itself weighed heavily on God's people as Rome's ever-heavier yoke pressed upon them. And then at last God acted, sending His own Son as Bethlehem's Babe.

My eyes have seen Your salvation (2:30). Enlightened by the Holy Spirit, Simeon sees in the person of the Baby Your [God's] salvation. This is a striking insight. When Jesus was grown, teaching and performing miracles, Christ's contemporaries refused to acknowledge Him for who He was. But Simeon recognized and acknowledged Him when He was just a helpless Babe.

In a real sense Simeon represents the link between the OT and NT eras—a link which exists not in the external religious practices of Israelite or Christian, but a link which exists as simple faith in God and in His Christ. The eyes of faith do see God's salvation, for they recognize the Savior.

A light for revelation to the Gentiles and for glory to Your people Israel (2:31). Here we find an insight which is greater than that granted to Zechariah. Zechariah's vision of the meaning of Christ's coming was focused by those prophecies which dealt with the future of Israel. Simeon's vision incorporated the less frequent references of the prophets to the Messiah's mission to bring salvation to all humankind.

In the old era Israel was the center of God's attention. In the new that was about to replace it, Israel's Messiah would be revealed as the Savior of all mankind, a light to the Gentiles (Isa. 42:6; 49:6), who brings glory to Israel from which He sprang.

Application. Simeon's prayer represents a transition that is graciously and gratefully experienced. Simeon is ready to die, comfortable with his vision of a future which is different from and yet a fulfillment of the past.

Simeon reminds us that our own time on earth is limited and that we too must soon let go, and release our own vision's fulfillment to others. Let us do so graciously, confident that God will work through them as He has through us, and even though the future may be different than we suppose, all remains in God's hands.

LUKE 3:23–4:44
Overcoming Temptation

EXPOSITION

Luke continues to introduce Jesus to his intended Hellenistic audience. The miraculous events associated with Jesus' birth mark Him as special. But unlike the Greek and Roman deities who, according to pagan tales, briefly took on human appearance, Jesus was a true human being whose lineage can be traced back to Adam (3:23-38).

Jesus was unlike pagan deities in yet another way. The stories of the gods and goddesses of mythology portray them as subject to all the sinful passions that surge in humankind: lust, pride, selfish ambition, and covetousness. Yet before Jesus launches into a public ministry in which He will present Himself as God's solution to sin, Jesus is Himself tempted. And what a stunning revelation this is. Rather than think first of Himself, Jesus resists His own fierce hunger and chooses submission to the will of God (4:1-4). Unmoved by the ambition that moved Hellenistic gods and goddesses to scheme and compete for position, Jesus rejects Satan's offer of all this world's kingdoms out of His loyalty to God (4:5-8). In a final temptation Jesus refuses to leap from the temple walls and, by surviving, prove His unique relationship with the Father (4:9-13).

But now Luke introduces another, surprising theme. When this unique person returns to His hometown, He announces Himself as the Messiah, the subject of centuries-old prophecy (4:14-27). Suddenly everything fits—His birth, His lineage, His victory over temptation. But as Jesus continues to speak, His neighbors suddenly become hostile—and not only reject His claim, but attempt to kill Him!

Could His neighbors have been right? After all, they were in a position to know Him best. No, Luke quickly demonstrates that they were wrong. For the public ministry Jesus now begins is marked by supernatural authenticating signs. He drives out demons, who acknowledge Him as "the Holy One of God!" (4:31-37) And as He preaches the good news of the kingdom of God, He heals "each one" who comes to Him for help, whatever their complaint (4:38-44).

This ends Luke's introduction of Jesus—an introduction which answers many questions his Hellenistic readers might ask, and yet an introduction which raises many others. Jesus is One whose birth was marked by supernatural signs, yet He is a true human being. Jesus is the selfless Servant of God, yet He is Himself the fulfillment of the prophets' hopes and dreams. Jesus dominates demons and can cure the sick, yet He is reviled by His neighbors. As Luke's history continues, his readers will see how these themes are woven together to tell salvation's story. Together they help us grasp the meaning of Jesus' life—and the meaning for us of His death and His resurrection.

WORD STUDIES

The *son* of Heli (3:23). The word "son" is a flexible term even as used in genealogies. It indicates descent rather than immediate offspring. As other biblical genealogies, this one selects representative individuals within the family line rather than attempt to include every male in the line.

For a discussion of the differences between Luke's genealogy of Jesus and that provided by Matthew, see The Passage in Depth.

Jesus . . . *was led* by the Spirit in the desert (4:1). Usually when we think of God's leading we imagine the Spirit leading us into blessing. But Luke tells us Jesus was led by the Spirit into a desert place. There, in the unceasing heat, without food and surely with little water, Jesus waited 40 days. Finally, when on the verge of exhaustion, Satan appeared and pressured our Lord.

The first thing this teaches us is not to be confused about our tragedies and trials. God can lead us into our desert places too, where we, like Jesus, will become exhausted and experience temptations that we find difficult to bear.

But there is another lesson in this verse. The verb translated "was led" is in the original an imperfect passive, a construction that means "was continuously led." The Spirit never left our Lord during His time of trial, but guided Him every step of the way. Even so the Spirit is with us as we pass through those "desert" times in our lives.

Worship the Lord your God and *serve* Him only (4:8). One Christian tradition attempts to make a distinction between "worship," *proskyneo,* and "serve," *latreuo.* Thus God alone is to be worshiped, but it is acceptable to pray to Mary and the saints, for this is merely

"service." However, every form of *latreuo* in the NT is used in the religious sense of worshiping or serving God.

In context, of course, Jesus makes a different point. Those who claim to worship God must surely demonstrate their commitment by actively serving Him and carrying out His purposes. Here, as in so many areas it is not our theology but our daily commitment to Jesus that makes the real difference.

He taught in their *synagogues* (4:15). The synagogue was perhaps the most important institution in first-century Judaism. Literary sources make it clear that there were many synagogues in Galilee in Jesus' time, as well as many synagogues in the Jewish quarter of Alexandria in Egypt and Rome itself. Typically schools, tribunals, and guest-houses (these particularly in Jerusalem) were associated with the synagogue. Later Roman law indicates that the "head of the synagogue" was viewed as the leader and representative of the Jewish population. Interestingly, the head of the synagogue had an assistant (a *hazzan*) who supervised the practical details of running a synagogue. The person referred to in 4:20 as the "attendant" (*uperetes*) was probably the *hazzan.*

Sabbath worship at the synagogue typically lasted for hours, and involved not only prayers and the reading of Scripture but also a public discussion of Scripture in which any man who wished to might take part. Thus it was not at all surprising that Jesus "stood up to read" (4:16)—words which suggest taking the initiative in coming forward rather than being invited to speak by the leadership.

It seems clear from v. 14 that Jesus initiated the strategy adopted later by Paul and other Christian missionaries of contacting the Jewish community first at the synagogue, where

He would have access to the entire community and where custom allowed any [biblically] educated man to speak.

Amazed at the *gracious words* that came from His lips (4:22). The phrase can refer either to Jesus' gentle way of speaking, or to the content of His message. The near parallel in Acts 14:3 may suggest the latter: they were amazed at the words Jesus spoke about the grace of God.

The word "amazed" is neutral, suggesting neither acceptance nor rejection of the message. At first what Jesus said simply seemed to be a great wonder. All too soon, however, a decision was made, and the crowd turned against Jesus.

Don't be surprised when words you speak about the grace of God first amaze others—and then bring angry rejection. Many people resent the notion that they need to rely on God's grace, supposing that God simply must give them credit for their good deeds!

"Be quiet," Jesus *said sternly*. "Come out of Him!" Then the demon threw the man down before them all and came out without injuring him (4:35). We are so familiar with the NT's portraits of Jesus' domination of demons that we can hardly imagine how stunning this was to the first-century Jew.

It is not that exorcism was unknown. In fact there was a well-established tradition, and the literature contains many incantations used against demons by exorcists on behalf of clients who paid well for their service. Take, for instance, the magical incantation, reported by J.A. Montgomery (*Aramaic Incantation Texts from Nippur*), used by Joshua bar Perahya intended to divorce his clients from demons. It reads:

I bind, tie and suppress all demons and harmful spirits that are in the world, whether male or female, from the greatest of them to the least, from the young to the old, whether I know his name or do not know his name. In case I do not know the name, it has already been explained to me at the seven days of creation. What has not been disclosed to me at the time of the seven days of creation, was discovered to me in the get that came here from across the sea, which was written and sent to Rabbi Joshua bar Perahya. Just as there was a

Lilith who strangled people, and Rabbi Joshua sent a ban against her, but she did not accept it because he did not know her name; and her name was written in the get, and an announcement was made against her in heaven by a get that came here from across the sea; so you are bound, tied and suppressed all of you beneath the feet of the said Marnaqa son of Quala. In the name of Gabriel, the mighty hero, who kills all heroes who are victorious in battle, the name of Yah, Yah, Yah, Sabaoth. Amen, Amen, Selah.

In this incantation the get is a "bill of divorce" freeing the client from the demon. The Lilith in the incantation is a demon who refused to acknowledge the validity of the get because she was not identified by name. The incantation argues that heaven intervened, and miraculously supplied the name of the get. Thus the exorcist is explaining (to the demon!) that his exorcism has legal force, since heaven inserts the correct name even though the exorcist does not know it, thus giving the get legal force and driving out the demon.

Thus while the first-century Jew was familiar with exorcism, it was viewed as a complicated process, involving magical incantations and also involving legal niceties in order to be effective.

How stunned then were the witnesses who saw Jesus cast out demons simply by commanding, "Come out of him!" (4:35) Here was a person with no need to rely on magical words or legalities; a person whose authority over the spiritual world was total and complete. When the text reports that "all the people were amazed" (8:36) there is no exaggeration. The people were truly amazed at the "authority and power" with which "He gives orders to evil spirits and they come out!"

It would be well if you and I, reading what have become such familiar stories, were able to recapture the awe felt by those who heard Jesus speak and saw demons obey. Jesus is Lord. His Word is the ultimate authority in our universe. How confidently we can place our future—and our present—in His hands.

All the people were *amazed* (4:36). This is the second time Luke uses the word "amazed" to describe a group's reaction to Jesus. The first crowd was amazed at His message. The second was amazed at His power, as He cast out demons. Sadly, in neither case was amazement translated into faith. It is not enough to wonder at Christ's words and works. We must respond to them, and to our Lord.

The people brought to Jesus all who had various kinds of sickness, and laying His hands *on each one,* He healed them (4:40). This simple description of Jesus' ministry picks up the emphasis of the Isaiah quote which Jesus read in the synagogue (4:18-19). Jesus' healing of "each one" indicates He was deeply aware that He truly had been anointed "to preach good news to the poor" and to proclaim "recovery of sight for the blind, to release the oppressed, to proclaim the year of the Lord's favor."

One major theme of Luke's Gospel is Jesus' concern for the sick and the poor. We see it here. We see it later, when Jesus responds to questions of John the Baptist by pointing to this healing, caring ministry: "Go back and report to John what you have seen and heard: The blind receive sight, the lame walk, those who have leprosy are cured, the deaf hear, the dead are raised, and the good news is preached to the poor" (Luke 7:22; see also 14:21). In a series of teachings that drive home Jesus' point by referring to banquets, Christ again emphasizes God's concern for the poor. "At the resurrection of the righteous" God will surely repay those who care for the handicapped and the poor (14:12-14). It is also Luke who tells the story of Lazarus the beggar and the rich man who neglected the poor (16:19-31).

This sensitivity to others must have seemed strange in Hellenistic society, where the ideal of *arete,* excellence, called for each person to develop his own potential, whatever the cost to others. Yet as Luke's story of Jesus unfolds, it becomes more and more clear that Jesus is a far better example of what human beings are to be than the proud and selfish "beautiful people" of society. In Jesus, a poor man Himself who constantly displayed compassion for others, an entirely new standard of *arete* is about to be established. A standard which will forever change mankind's view of "excellence."

He bent over her and *rebuked* the fever, and it left her (4:39). The word here, *epetimesen,* is used only by Luke. It portrays Jesus' effective power over sickness and over demons (4:41). But there is more here than ridding a sufferer of that which plagues him or her. Luke continues, "She got up at once and began to wait on them" (4:39).

Normally when a raging fever breaks we are left weak and nearly helpless. But Jesus' rebuke restores even as it heals! And so we are invited to see Peter's mother-in-law bustling happily about her kitchen, vital and active once again.

We are invited by this image to remember that, whatever the ruin of our life, at Jesus' rebuke of sin spiritual health and vitality most surely will be restored. We are saved from the consequences of sin. Through Christ we are also saved from the very power of sin in our daily lives. How wonderful it is to rely on Him.

THE PASSAGE IN DEPTH

The Genealogy of Jesus (Luke 3:23-38). See Matt. 1:1-17 for a discussion of the women that evangelist identifies as Jesus' line.

Background. It is immediately apparent that there are significant differences in the line of Jesus as reported by Matthew and by Luke. Matthew launches his book with a genealogy; Luke waits until Jesus' uniqueness has been established. Matthew links Jesus firmly to Abraham and to David, thus forging an unbreakable link between OT history and Jesus' story. Luke traces Christ's line back to Adam, and then takes pains to show us that despite the supernatural events surrounding His birth, Jesus is a true human being. Matthew groups his names, Luke lists his. Matthew includes several women; Luke, despite the sensitivity to women shown throughout his Gospel, restricts his genealogy to men. Most significant, the two lines reported in these genealogies diverge after David, with Luke's line following the offspring of the great king's son Nathan, while Matthew's follows the traditional royal line that passes through Solomon and the subsequent kings of Israel.

While there is debate over the reason for

this last, major difference in the genealogy, there is no lack of plausible explanations.

(1) Some suggest Matthew gives Joseph's genealogy, while Luke gives Mary's. This is supported by Jer. 36:30, which reports a divine curse that interrupts the royal line: "This is what the Lord says about Jehoiakim king of Judah: He will have no one to sit on the throne of David; His body will be thrown out and exposed." Since both Joseph and Mary were from David's family, the line of Jesus' stepfather Joseph would establish His legal right to the throne, while the descent through Mary's line would establish the biological link required of the Messiah.

(2) A second option, suggested in the third century A.D. by Africanus, suggests that Heli and Jacob were half brothers with the same mother but fathers with different names. If one died, the widow of a childless man could marry his brother's widow. In this case the first son would be legally considered the son of his mother's first husband. If this had happened, one genealogy could validly trace the legal line, and the other the biological line, which would explain the differences in the genealogies.

There are other explanations as well. Taken together they remind us of an important point. We do not lack a valid explanation of the differences. We simply do not know which of several valid explanations is the right one!

Interpretation. It is significant that Luke begins his genealogy with a disclaimer: "He [Jesus] was the son, so it was thought, of Joseph" (3:23). In fact, while Jesus was legally the son of Joseph, Jesus had no biological relationship with the husband of Jesus' mother, Mary. Whatever Christ's neighbors in Bethlehem supposed, Jesus was in fact the unique Son of God, even as He had been identified by the voice of heaven when He was baptized (3:22).

It took the church centuries to arrive at a final definition of the Person of Christ (see boxes). Yet the fact that Jesus Christ was at one and the same time fully God and a real human being is clearly implied in the carefully drawn words with which Luke closes the account of Christ's baptism, and begins the genealogical record.

There is one other interpretive issue in the genealogy that calls for comment. When the line of Jesus finally arrives at Adam, Luke calls him the "Son of God." We noted in the word study of 3:23 that in Hebrew usage "son" is a very flexible term that can convey a variety of meanings and idiomatic uses. The *Zondervan Expository Dictionary of Bible Words* observes:

> "Son" is often used idiomatically. The "sons of Israel" are simply the Israelites, members of that group.
>
> "Son" can also imply other things. One is the close relationship of God and Israel, indicated by God's announcement to Pharaoh:
>
> "Israel is my firstborn son" (Ex. 4:22).
>
> Likewise, "Son" may indicate membership in a group, as in the phrase "sons of the prophets" (1 Kings 20:35), a phrase that may simply denote prophets or a prophets' guild. The phrase "Sons of God" seldom occurs in the OT (KJV: Gen. 6:2, 4; Job 1:6; 2:1; 38:7); it usually indicates heavenly beings.
>
> The imprecision of "son" can be illustrated by the fact that to designate a particular king as the "son of" another king may indicate only succession, not family line.
>
> "Son," then, is a flexible term in Hebrew, suggesting but not defining precisely a descendant relationship.

What Luke's use of "son" indicates, then, is simply that as Seth owed his existence to Adam his father, Adam owed his existence to God, his Creator.

But is it possible that Jesus is the "son" of God in this creation sense? No, for Scripture guards against this misunderstanding. Not only is Jesus presented as the eternal Son, preexistent with the Father from the beginning (see the commentary on John 1, page 212ff.), where Jesus is called God's "one and only Son." Other passages which portray the unique Sonship of Jesus are John 3:16-21, 32-36; 5:19-27; Rom. 1:3-4; Heb. 1; 1 John 4:9-15; 1 John 5:11-13.

Application. Our confidence in Jesus rests ultimately on our conviction that He is no mere man, but the God incarnate.

As Luke goes on to report Jesus' teachings and His miracles, the conviction grows that this Man truly was unique. As the final act unfolds, and Luke traces Jesus' journey through death and the grave to triumphant Resurrection, we are utterly convinced. Jesus

---

THE ORTHODOX DEFINITION OF THE PERSON OF JESUS

The orthodox definition of the Person of Jesus was given "final" form in a Creed formulated at Chalcedon in A.D. 451. The relevant paragraph reads as follows:

> Therefore, following the holy fathers, we all with one accord teach men to acknowledge one and the same Son, our Lord Jesus Christ, at once complete in Godhead and complete in manhood, truly God and truly man, consisting also of a reasonable soul and body; of one substance (*homoousios*) with the Father as regards His Godhead, and at the same time of one substance with us as regards His manhood like us in all respects apart from sin; as regards His Godhead, begotten of the Father before the ages, but yet as regards His manhood begotten, for us men and for our salvation, of Mary the Virgin, the God-bearer (*theotokos*); one and the same Christ, Son, Lord, Only-begotten, recognized in TWO NATURES, WITHOUT CONFUSION, WITHOUT CHANGE, WITHOUT DIVISION, WITHOUT SEPARATION; the distinction of natures being in no way annulled by the union, but rather the characteristics of each nature being preserved and coming together to form one person and substance (*hupostasis*), not as parted or separated into two persons, but one and the same Son and Only-begotten God the Word, Lord Jesus Christ; even as the prophets from earliest times spoke of Him, and our Lord Jesus Christ Himself taught us, and the creed of the Fathers has handed down to us.

---

is Lord. Jesus is God incarnate; God become Man to be our Savior.

The Temptation of Jesus (Luke 4:1-13). See the commentary on Matt. 4:1-11 and the parallel passage in Mark 1:12-13.

Jesus Rejected at Nazareth (Luke 4:14-30). See the parallel passages in Matt. 13:53-58; Mark 6:1-6.

Background. Luke provides an important clue to the context of Jesus' presentation of Himself as Messiah in His hometown of Nazareth. He tells us that the "news about Him [Jesus] spread throughout the whole countryside" (4:14). John adds more detail. He tells us that when Jesus "arrived in Galilee, the Galileans had welcomed Him. They had seen all that He had done in Jerusalem at the Passover Feast, for they also had been there" (John 4:45).

Thus that Sabbath morning when Jesus entered the familiar synagogue at Nazareth, the whole community was watching Him. What could this be? The quiet carpenter, who for most of His thirty years had lived in Nazareth as one of them, a wonder-worker? We could understand if they were skeptical. But skepticism hardly explains their irate reaction to the words Jesus spoke that morning.

Interpretation. Our understanding of this event hinges on an analysis of the two separate speeches of Jesus which Luke reports, and the very different response of Christ's neighbors to each.

The first speech and reaction: 4:16-22. It was customary in the synagogue to invite a visitor to read the day's Scripture and comment on the passage. As the lengthy service continued, any man might rise and offer a comment or exhortation. Luke does not say whether Jesus was invited to read (cf. Acts 13:15), or stood up voluntarily. Nor does the passage indicate whether Jesus chose Isaiah 61 or whether it was that day's scheduled reading. However, what Jesus read is significant—and even more significant is what He did not read. The Isaiah passage was clearly understood by the Jews of that time to be a messianic prophecy. Not only are these verses discussed in the Midrash on Lam. 3:49, but vv. 5 and 9 of this chapter are also applied to Messianic times (see Yalkut, vol. i, Pa. 212p, p. 64a and the Midrash on Ecc. 3:7). Thus when Jesus read these words and announced, "Today this Scripture is fulfilled in your hearing" (4:21), He clearly and unequivocally presented Himself to His neighbors as the Messiah.

OTHER AFFIRMATIONS OF JESUS' DEITY AND HUMANITY

Here is an earlier statement, by Irenaeus, who wrote some two and a half centuries before Chalcedon, and a later statement by John Wesley.

Now it has been clearly demonstrated that the Word which exists from the beginning with God, by whom all things were made, who was also present with the race of men at all times, this Word has in these last times, according to the time appointed by the Father, been united to His own workmanship and has been made passible man. Therefore we can set aside the objection of them that say, "If He was born at that time it follows that Christ did not exist before then."

For we have shown that the Son of God did not then begin to exist since He existed with the Father always; but when He was incarnate and made man He summed up in Himself the long line of the human race. (Irenaeus)

I believe that He is the proper, natural Son of God, God of God, very God of very God' and that He is the Lord of all, having absolute, supreme, universal dominion over all things. . . .

I believe that He was made man, joining the human nature with the divine in one person; being conceived by the singular operation of the Holy Ghost, and born of the Virgin Mary. (Wesley)

It is striking that while the claim seems to have confounded Jesus' neighbors, it did not arouse their hostility. In fact, Luke says "all spoke well of Him" (4:22). Even the question "Isn't this Joseph's Son?" should be understood in a positive sense. In a land where one's ancestry was valued, Joseph's neighbors would surely have realized He was one of David's line. Thus being Joseph's son would strengthen, not weaken, Jesus' claim.

But it is also clear that the listeners had not realized the significance of the words Jesus failed to read. For Isaiah 61:2 concludes, ". . . to proclaim the year of the Lord's favor and the day of vengeance of our God." Today we understand: Jesus quoted that part of the passage which relates to the ministry performed at His first coming. The "day of vengeance of our God" is associated with the Second Coming, and thus was not relevant to the dawning day of grace. Yet it was the very nature of this grace which was soon to turn Jesus' neighbors against Him.

The second speech and reaction: 4:23-30. Jesus sat silently for a time, listening to the buzz of approving conversation that swept the synagogue. Then He spoke again, and here we can sense a deeply pessimistic tone. We can sense the gloom in His voice as Jesus suggests that the present approval will soon turn to doubt, and His listeners will demand miraculous signs to prove His claim (4:23). But it was His next words that turned the town against Him. For Jesus went on to suggest that when historically Israel displayed unbelief, God extended His blessings to Gentiles! It was no Jewish widow Elijah miraculously supplied with food during a lengthy famine, but a Syrophoenician woman, a widow in Zarephath in Sidon. And Elijah rid a Syrian general of leprosy, even though there were plenty of lepers in Israel in his time.

Those "gracious words" (words about God's grace) which Jesus had spoken were intended for the Gentile as well as Jew! And now Nazareth becomes a microcosm representing all Israel.

Will God's people accept the Messiah on faith? Will they accept a Savior who offers God's grace to all—to believing Gentile as well as believing Jew?

The answer is reflected in the fury Jesus' words stimulated. To understand it, we need to remember that for centuries the Jewish people had been persecuted in their own homeland. They resented and hated their Gentile oppressors, and longed for God to send the Messiah to punish the pagan world. That attitude is expressed in the comment on Isa. 61:5 found in Yalikut vol. 1, noted above. When asked what would become of the nations in the days of Messiah, the sage replies that every nation and kingdom which had persecuted and mocked Israel would be confounded, and have no share in life. On the other hand every nation and kingdom which had not persecuted Israel would come to the land in the days of Messiah to serve Israel as farmers and vinedressers.

So we can understand. In His first speech Jesus identified Himself as Messiah. Yet in His second He promised to extend God's grace even to Gentiles. What's more, by failing to finish the Isaiah passage Jesus implicitly rejected, for the present, that dream of vengeance which had, with faith, sustained Israel for so long. It was this that aroused in Jesus' neighbors a murderous wrath so intense that they attempted to kill Him.

Although they took Jesus to the edge of a cliff, intending to throw Him down to His death, Luke tells us our Lord simply "walked right through the crowd and went on His way" (4:30).

Application. Jesus' treatment of Isa. 61:1-2 has long been recognized as a major example of the difficulty of interpreting OT prophecy. Here in a single verse events related to the First and Second Comings of Jesus are described. Yet, even though some 2,000 years intervene between "favor" and "and" in that ancient text, no hint of this gap is found in the Hebrew original.

But surely more important to us now is a great truth that the description of the Nazareth events drives home. Christ came to His hometown as Messiah. The initial response was favorable. But when Jesus announced His kingdom agenda, His words were met with anger and rejection.

What a strange thing. If Jesus was the Messiah appointed by God, surely He must be allowed to set His own agenda, especially when that agenda is rooted in Scripture. If Jesus is Lord, the proper response is to obey and follow His lead.

Yet how often do we who acknowledge Jesus as Lord find ourselves reacting as His Nazareth neighbors did? How often do we insistently demand that God follow our agenda—meet our needs, satisfy our desires, proceed according to our schedule—rather than humbly seek to understand and then do His will?

The angry mob tried to force Jesus up that hill because it was unthinkable that He should offer God's grace to Gentiles. It may be that what God intends to do in our lives is something we too may find unthinkable at first. When Christ makes His will known, we must resist the impulse to rebel. For every rebellion is a symbolic effort to force Jesus up that hill and cast Him from the throne of our heart.

Jesus is Lord and God. And, wonderfully, His agenda is one of overflowing grace. Surely we can trust our God of love, and gladly submit to His will.

Jesus Drives Out an Evil Spirit (Luke 4:31-37). See the commentary on Mark 1:21-28, and the Word Study on 4:36.

Jesus Heals Many (4:38-44). See parallel passages in Matt. 8:14-17 and Mark 1:29-34. See also the index to the various discussions of "healing" found in this commentary.

LUKE 5:1–7:17
The Choice

EXPOSITION

Luke has now completed His introduction of Jesus. The supernatural events associated with Jesus' birth make it clear He is special. Then, though claimed by God as His own Son, Luke provides a genealogy which proves Jesus is also truly human. Victory over the Tempter proves that although fully human, Jesus is without sin and totally committed to do the will of God. Who is this Jesus? In His hometown synagogue Jesus identifies Himself as the Messiah predicted by the Old Testament prophets. And, although His neighbors angrily reject His claim when He indicates He will extend God's grace to Gentile as well as Jew, Christ subsequently performs authenticating exorcisms and miracles of healing.

With this foundation laid, Luke moves on to provide a series of vignettes which, together, drive home a critical point. In sending Jesus, God made known His choice to treat humankind with grace. Yet in sending Jesus, God requires each human being to make a choice as well: a choice for, or against, His Son.

The interplay of choices is illustrated in the first vignette: Jesus chooses Peter to become a "fisher of men." Peter, although deeply aware that he is a sinner, puts aside His fear and chooses to follow the Lord (5:1-11). The interplay continues: a leper chooses to come to Jesus and affirms "if You are willing, You can make me clean." Jesus answers, "I am willing," and heals the man (5:12-16). When a delegation of Pharisees and teachers of the Law come to pass judgment on Jesus, He chooses to pronounce forgiveness of a paralytic's sin—and proves His right to do so by restoring the crippled limbs (5:17-26).

Next Jesus chooses to associate with "sinners," even as a tax collector named Levi chooses to associate himself with Christ (5:27-32). In another demonstration of His authority, Jesus chooses to heal a man with a crippled hand on the Sabbath, and in so doing affirms His lordship of this holy day set aside for the worship of God (6:1-11). Then, after choosing the Twelve who will become His apostles (6:12-16), Jesus begins to announce choices that those who opt to follow Him must make in daily life.

These choices that the follower of Jesus must make deal with the most basic issues of our lives. In Christ's Beatitudes we see that God calls us to live by His rather than mankind's values (6:17-26). In Christ's call to love our enemies (6:27-36) and to forgive rather than judge (6:37-42), we see that God calls us to a new kind of relationship with our fellowmen; a relationship possible only to those whose hearts

163

have been transformed by Him (6:43-45). How is this new life possible even for those whose hearts have been renewed? Only by building one's life on the solid foundation of Jesus' Word, choosing not only to hear what Christ says, but also to put His words into practice (6:46-49).

What then is the prospect for those who choose Jesus? The story of a centurion who appeals to Jesus shows that the prospect for any person with faith is bright; the army officer's faith is rewarded and his servant healed (7:1-10). And what about those beyond hope? In His great compassion Jesus responds to the pain of a widow who has lost her only son, and brings him back to life (7:11-17). What assurance this story brings. God does care. Through Jesus He reaches out to us in our need, to bring new life and restore even what seems now to have been lost without possibility of recall. Surely we are wise to choose Jesus as our Savior. And when we have, we are wise to commit ourselves to hear and obey His Word.

WORD STUDIES

Simon answered, "*Master, we've worked hard all night*" (5:5). The word used here, *epistata,* is found only in Luke. It was familiar to his Hellenistic readers and replaces the "teacher" or "rabbi" of parallel passages in Mark and Matthew. *Epistata* might be loosely translated "boss" and was addressed by workers to their supervisors or overseers. In using it Peter acknowledges Jesus' authority, but clearly doubts the wisdom of Jesus' command. After all, Peter is the authority on fishing! But then the nets are filled with a shoal of fish—and a stunned Peter drops to his knees and blurts out, "Lord" (*kyrios*).

Never should we doubt that Christ's way is best, we must follow Peter's example and obey, however reluctantly. It is in obedience that we discover, as Peter did, that Jesus truly is Lord of all.

Go away from me, Lord; I am a *sinful man* (5:8). The Greek word here is *hamartolos,* "sinner." As Peter grasped the fact that the One speaking to him was Lord, he was suddenly overcome with the awareness of how far short he fell of what he knew he should be. But, while this Greek word for sin indicates falling short of a mark, Luke does not use it in a condemning way. Instead Luke reminds us constantly that God has compassion on sinners, and that we who fall short are objects of His love.

Jesus does not "go away from" Peter the sinner. Rather than isolate Himself from such persons, as the religious in Judaism did, Christ called Peter closer. "Don't be afraid," our

Lord says, "from now on you will catch men."

Whenever you or I feel as Peter did, unworthy because of our failures to associate with Jesus Christ, we need to remember what Christ said. He is not shocked by what we were, or what we are. What counts to Him, and should count to us, is that "from now on" we will experience Christ's power to change and renew.

When he saw Jesus, he fell with his *face to the ground* and begged Him (5:12). Peter "fell at Jesus' knees" (5:8) when overcome with guilt. But this leper falls with his "face to the ground." Why? In Israel a leper was considered unclean, or filthy. The leper did not feel guilt, but he surely felt shame, and it is shame that the "face to the ground" indicates.

How did Jesus respond? Not by turning away in disgust or contempt. Instead Jesus actually reached out His hand and touched the leper. Here too is an image we need to keep vivid in our mind. Shame, like guilt, is a powerful emotion that keeps many from turning to Jesus. Yet if when we feel shame we visualize Jesus reaching out to touch the trembling leper, we will find the courage to turn to Him and, like the leper, experience His cleansing power.

Pharisees and *teachers of the Law,* who had come from every village . . . and Jerusalem (5:17). These "teachers of the law" were rabbis or sages, whose mastery of traditional interpretations of the OT gave them a unique religious authority in first-century Judaism. These men were there as an official or semi-official investigating committee, assembled to listen to Jesus and judge whether or not His teaching was acceptable. As the passage develops, it is clear that they are both suspicious and hostile. After all, who in the "establishment" welcomes a bright young star who appears from nowhere and threatens to undermine their authority?

We must beware of a similar attitude in our approach to Scripture. We are to approach God and His Word as eager learners, not to discover what we like and do not like, but rather to joyfully welcome what we find without standing in judgment on it. We are not to judge the Word, but to obey it.

They went up on the roof and lowered him on his mat through the *tiles* (5:19). Mark pictures these men "digging through" the roof. This suggests a mud-and-stick construction of the roof. But Luke describes the paralyzed man being lowered through "tiles."

One possibility is suggested by the construction of houses in areas of Syria-Palestine where wood was not readily available. To roof such homes arches were placed in the walls at three-foot intervals. Then thin slabs of limestone, some three feet long, were laid on the arches, and a lime-based "cement" spread over these slabs. The story in Luke suggests this method of construction for the house in question. If so, the paralytic's friends "dug through" the thin layer of cement and then lifted the slab "tiles" to let the paralytic down into the room where Jesus was teaching.

Who is this fellow who speaks *blasphemy*? Who can forgive sins but God alone? (5:21) On what basis did the teachers of the Law assume that Jesus' words of forgiveness were blasphemy? Cunningham Geikie, in his classic *The Life and Words of Christ* (vol. 1, New York: Appleton, 1893), explains:

> The Law knew no such form as an official forgiving of sins, or absolution. The leper might be pronounced clean by the priest, and a transgressor might present a sin offering at the Temple, and transfer his guilt to it, by laying his hands on its head and owning his fault before God, and the blood sprinkled by the priest on the horns of the altar, and toward the Holy of Holies,

was an atonement that "covered" his sins from the eyes of Jehovah, and pledged His forgiveness. But that forgiveness was the direct act of God; no human lips dared pronounce it. It was a special prerogative of the Almighty, and even should mortal man venture to declare it, he could only do so in the name of Jehovah, and by His immediate authorization. But Jesus had spoken in His own name. He had not hinted at being empowered by God to act for Him. The Scribes were greatly excited; whispers, ominous head-shakings, dark looks, and pious gesticulations of alarm, showed that they were ill at ease. "He should have sent him to the priest to present his sin offering, and have it accepted; it is blasphemy to speak of forgiving sins, He is intruding on the divine rights." The blasphemer was to be put to death by stoning, his body hung on a tree, and then buried with shame. "Who can forgive sins but One, God?"

It is foolish of some to argue that Jesus never claimed to be God. In this and many other words and actions He affirmed His deity, and was clearly understood by His contemporaries to do so!

One *Sabbath* Jesus was going through the grainfields (6:1). Frequent controversy over Sabbath observance marked Jesus' relationship with the Pharisees. For a discussion of the origin and nature of the Jewish approach to Sabbath-keeping, see the commentary on Matt. 12:1-14. Because the Sabbath was so significant in Judaism, the differences between Jesus' approach to relationship with God and that of the religious establishment could be sharply defined in these controversies, most of which Jesus Himself stimulated!

The passages which describe these conflicts (Matt. 12:1-21; Mark 2:23-28; 3:1-6; Luke 6:1-11) establish several important points:

■ Jesus is Lord of the Sabbath, and He (not tradition) determines what is "lawful" to do on that holy day.

■ The Sabbath was established for our benefit, not to burden mankind (Mark 2:27).

■ The overriding principle is that the Sabbath is for doing good. That which is a response to human need graces rather than violates the Sabbath principle.

■ Finally, even as God is active on the Sabbath, so Jesus has the right to do His good works on that holy day (John 5:17).

These principles might well be applied by Christians today seeking guidelines for what is "right" or "wrong" to do on Sunday. Like Jesus we best honor God by affirming positive acts rather than by imposing restrictions.

Jesus went out to a mountainside to pray, and *spent the night praying* (6:12). The Gospels frequently picture Jesus at prayer. But this is the only incident in which He "spent the night" (*en dianuktereyon*). This underlines the importance of Christ's final choice of the Twelve as His apostles. It also contains a vital message for us. If Jesus felt a need for prayer when making this critical choice, how much more do we need to pray when we are faced with significant decisions?

He went down with them and stood on a *level place* (6:17). This phrase has led some to call the following teaching of Jesus His "Sermon on the Plain" to set it off from Matthew's "Sermon on the Mount." Others argue the two are reporting one and the same incident, despite several significant differences in the accounts.

What is often ignored is the fact that Jesus undoubtedly repeated this "keynote" sermon again and again as He taught throughout Galilee. It would hardly be surprising to find the variations reflected in the two accounts, as any public speaker who uses the same address a number of times would know.

What is undoubtedly most significant is not the differences between the accounts, but their essential consistency. Those who heard Jesus were so deeply impressed that when Luke interviewed them years later, they remembered His teachings with great clarity.

Blessed are you who are *poor* (6:20). The first-century Jew viewed the poor as of special concern to God. Giving to the poor was one way in which a wealthy person might commend himself to God. In fact, the destitute might even take pride in the fact that by begging he could contribute to the holiness of the community!

But there was no such tradition in Hellenism, and Christ's affirmation of the blessedness of the poor must have stunned Luke's intended readership. The upper classes were dedicated to increasing their personal fortunes. Those few who engaged in "good works" might endow a library, a school, a bath, or establish a fund that would pay for an annual banquet to be enjoyed by a town's entire population. But rather than reflect the donor's generosity, they were more likely ostentatious displays.

In the Roman Empire society viewed the poor man, who had to work for hire, with disgust rather than pity or respect. Even those who were able to gain wealth by their own efforts were viewed by the upper-classes with disdain, and treated with condescension. In fact, one of classical literature's most biting parodies is Petronius' description of Trimalchio, a slave who worked as his master's financial agent and subsequently inherited much of his master's wealth. The fact that he made his profits by investing in commerce rather than by purchasing land emphasized society's contempt not only for the working poor, but for anyone who might earn money by his own effort.

Against this background we can perhaps better understand the difficulty of the choice that Jesus' words call Luke's readers to make. If one is to follow Jesus, the values of human society truly must be rejected, and replaced with those appropriate to citizens of the kingdom ruled by God.

But woe to you who are *rich* (6:24). How then do the rich inherit "woe" while the poor are blessed? Wealth in Hellenistic society made its possessor self-centered and indifferent to others. It led to an attitude of contempt which is the opposite of that loving concern which we are called to display toward others. The present verse suggests that the rich are so satisfied with the pleasures they experience now that they have no concern for the future. In another passage Luke portrays the rich as indifferent to spiritual realities (12:15-21). Wealth thus tends to insulate the wealthy from that sense of inadequacy which leads us to realize our need for God. And, tragically, it tends to insulate us from that concern for others which God Himself displays, and which He expects to be reproduced in those who own Christ as Lord.

Be merciful, *just as your Father is merci-ful* **(6:36).** Jesus' call to imitate God is not unique. The OT commanded, "Be holy because I, the Lord your God, am holy" (Lev. 19:2). A second-century Rabbi, Abba Shaul, comments on the command: "Oh, be like Him! As He is merciful and gracious, you also must be merciful and gracious." An anonymous commentator on Exodus 34:6 refers to Joel 2:32 (Joel 3:5 in the Hebrew OT, the Tanakh, which reads "But everyone who invokes the name of the Lord shall escape") and asks, "How can a man be called by the name of the God? As God is called merciful, you too must be merciful. The Holy One, blessed be He, is called gracious, so you too must be gracious. . . . God is called righteous, so you too must be righteous." Finally a paraphrase of Lev. 22:28 in the Targum (Ps.-Jonathan) says, "My people, children of Israel, as your Father is merciful in heaven, so you must be merciful on earth."

We must never suppose that Christianity alone has insight into what God wills. But we must never imagine, as some do, that *knowing* what is right is the issue. The issue has always been *doing* what is right. And what makes

Christianity unique is that Jesus not only forgives our sins, but comes into our life and infuses us with an ability no unaided human being has — the ability to serve God, and please Him by doing His good and perfect will.

Do not *judge* **(6:37).** The following phrase is typical of Hebrew parallelism, which frequently strengthens thoughts by repeating a critical instruction using a synonym. Here, then, "judging" is not exercising our ability to distinguish between right and wrong, but rather condemning another for violating our moral sensibilities. This important topic is explored in the discussion of several passages dealing with judging. To locate them, see the Index.

When Jesus had finished saying all this *in the hearing* **of all the people (7:1).** Jesus made His teaching available to all. Yet how fascinating that Luke goes on immediately to mention a centurion — a Roman officer — who "heard of Jesus" (7:3) and who immediately sent to Him for help.

All too often when the message Jesus has for us is delivered "in the hearing" of all — only a few truly hear Him.

THE PASSAGE IN DEPTH

The Calling of the First Disciples (5:1-11). See the commentary on Matt. 4:18-22, and the parallel passage in Mark 1:16-20.

The Man with Leprosy (5:12-16). See the commentary on Mark 1:40-45 and the parallel passage in Matt. 8:1-4.

Jesus Heals a Paralytic (5:17-26). See the commentary on Sabbath disputes in Matt. 12:1-21, and the parallel passages in Matt. 9:1-8 and Mark 2:1-12.

Background. Luke immediately alerts us to the significance of the story he is about to relate. He does this by stating that "teachers of the Law" had come not only from Galilee but also Judea and from Jerusalem, which was often spoken of as a separate district from the province Judea in which it lay.

One of the duties of "teachers of the Law" in first-century Judaism was to serve as judges, who heard civil, criminal, and religious cases and passed judgment on them. The assembly

of so many sages from every part of the Holy Land suggests an official delegation, gathered to observe Jesus and pass judgment on His ministry.

The dramatic story of the paralytic brought to Jesus by such dedicated friends is familiar to every Sunday School student, and many a sermon has been preached on the role of the faith those friends displayed in the Savior. Yet in Luke's account there is a different and dual emphasis: an emphasis on the very personal spiritual transaction that took place between Jesus and the paralytic, and the shocked reaction of that delegation of sages to Christ's announcement of forgiveness.

Interpretation. The personal spiritual transaction takes place when Jesus says to the paralytic, "Friend, your sins are forgiven" (5:20). Surely the paralytic had been driven to Jesus by the desperate hope that the Lord might meet his physical need. That need was overwhelming: it bound him in total helplessness and made him utterly dependent on the goodness of others. I suspect that as the paralytic was being carried to Jesus neither he nor his friends gave a single thought to his sins.

There is no way to gauge how often a similar acute sense of need drives human beings to Jesus. The appearance of a cancer, the loss of a job, a devastating disappointment, and in desperation a person appeals to God for help. At first there is no sense of sin. But in the process of turning to God for help awareness grows that Christ offers forgiveness, and in sudden joy faith floods a heart with the realization that although the cancer may persist, life's deepest need has been met.

Thus it was with Jesus and the paralytic. With the words, "Your sins are forgiven," Jesus both unveiled and met the paralytic's deepest need. And all there witnessed that intimate moment of faith's transaction between Jesus and the paralytic.

It was, however, just this that aroused the hostility of the teachers of the Law. Jesus' pronouncement of forgiveness was the exercise of a prerogative belonging to God alone. Every one of them immediately thought "blasphemy," a sin that merited death.

Luke does not say how Jesus "knew what they were thinking" (5:22). But the fact that they were "thinking these things in [their] hearts" suggests something more than a mere reading of shocked or horrified expressions. Christ's response was to demonstrate His authority by telling the cripple to "get up, take your mat and go home" (5:24). While the teachers of the Law might deny the validity of Christ's pronouncement of forgiveness, they could never deny the power of His word to heal. For everyone would actually see the paralyzed man rise and walk.

And this the paralytic did, and Luke tells us he did it "immediately" (*parachrema*) (5:25).

The result? The man "went home praising God" (5:25). And the crowd, utterly amazed, joined him in giving glory to God for the wonder they had observed.

Application. There are so many lessons for us in this fascinating story. In context the events Luke relates demonstrated the extent of Jesus' authority: His act of healing was proof that He had the right to forgive sins. Jesus has power to transform the inner and outer man.

As we meditate on the story we realize how often it is not awareness of sin but some other pressing sense of need that first brings a person to turn to God. Perhaps we make a mistake in our evangelism to begin with a presentation of those "four spiritual laws" which seek first of all to convict of sin before affirming "your sins are forgiven."

Yet perhaps the most important message of this story is in its reminder that there is always an external witness to the reality of that inner spiritual transformation forgiveness brings. Jesus said, "that you may know that the Son of Man has authority on earth to forgive sins . . ." (5:24) and then commanded, "Get up, take your mat and go home." And "Immediately he stood up in front of them" (5:25).

What is that visible, external witness? No, it is not necessarily, or even often, physical healing. It is far more compelling than that!

The truly compelling evidence of Christ's power to forgive is conveyed in the moral transformation of the believer.

This is the significance of the next words in our passage: "After this . . ." (5:27). After this Luke tells us Jesus called a tax collector named Levi to become His follower. We know him better as that disciple who later wrote the Gospel which launches our New Testament: Matthew. Levi/Matthew did follow Jesus. He abandoned the post of tax collector, a post which in that society labeled him a flagrant "sinner," and leaving everything committed himself to follow Jesus.

Can Jesus really forgive sins? Yes. He visibly demonstrated His authority over the spiritual as well as the material universe when He made the paralytic walk. And He has continued to demonstrate that authority throughout history as men and women, like Matthew, have left their sins behind and chosen to follow Him.

The Calling of Levi (5:27-32). See the commentary on Mark 2:13-17 and the parallel passage in Matt. 9:9-13.

Jesus Questioned on Fasting (5:33-39). See the parallel passages in Matt. 9:14-17 and Mark 2:18-20, and the Word Study of Matt. 6:16 and 9:17.

Lord of the Sabbath (6:1-11). See the commentary on Matt. 12:1-21, and the parallel passage in Mark 2:23–3:6.

The Twelve Apostles (6:12-16). See the

commentary on Mark 3:13-19.

Blessings and Woes (6:17-36). See the commentary and Word Studies on Matthew 5–7.

Judging Others (6:37-42). See the parallel passage in Matt. 7:1-6, and references in the Index on "judging."

The Tree and its Fruit (6:43-45). See the commentary on Matt. 7:15-23; 12:33-35.

Wise and Foolish Builders (6:46-49). See the parallel passage in Matt. 7:24-29.

Background. Palestine is a dry land. Yet during certain times of the year heavy rains create raging torrents that rush down usually dusty wadis (gullies), and stream along every dip and down every hillside. It is important to the point of Jesus' story to note that neither builder is criticized for his poor choice of building site. Each location looks secure. And, until the storms come, each house appears sturdy enough. In Palestine, as in life itself, only the ability to survive storms will reveal the quality of construction.

Interpretation. Earlier Luke has used several stories to make an important point. Jesus has authority to forgive. And, while forgiveness is by its nature intangible, Jesus' exercise of His authority nevertheless has tangible results! Thus the healing of the paralytic gave tangible evidence of Christ's power. But so did the transformation of Levi the tax collector into Matthew the disciple.

This emphasis is followed in Luke's telling of Jesus' story by our Lord's description of the lifestyle expected of those who experience forgiveness, and through forgiveness become citizens of the kingdom of God. Thus the forgiven person is expected to give tangible expression to the inner transformation he or she has experienced by commitment to a new set of values (6:17-26) and a new way of relating to others (6:27-42) that will, like the good fruit that forms on a healthy tree, demonstrate the goodness of the believer's transformed heart.

The thrust of this sequence in Luke is to affirm that forgiveness will make a difference. Our experience of the intangible will find tangible expression in the way we live our lives.

But now the story of the two builders introduces yet another vital thought. We must never confuse hearing of Jesus' words — here equivalent to an intellectual assent to His pronouncement of forgiving grace — with a saving response to those words. It is not enough to say, "Lord, Lord." The person who has actually experienced forgiveness is the one who comes to Christ, who hears Christ's words, and who puts them into practice. In other words, when that inner transformation has well and truly taken place we will be drawn to Jesus, continually looking and turning to Him. We will be eager listeners to His Word. And we will be obedient practitioners of His Word.

And, when the storms come, the cloak of the one who pretends to have faith, whose commitment is merely intellectual, and who enjoys dabbling in Christianity as long as he isn't forced to take it too seriously, will be stripped away. He and all around will suddenly realize what God knew all the time — that his claim to belong to God was empty and insincere.

Application. For those of us who do believe, Jesus' story of the wise and foolish builders brings both challenge and comfort. Challenge, in that we sense again the importance of full commitment to our Lord. Comfort, in that we are reassured. The storms of life will come. But when they do the relationship that we have built with Jesus Christ will enable us not only to survive, but to triumph. And in that triumph we will not only witness to the reality of the forgiveness we enjoy, but will also bring glory to our God.

The Faith of the Centurion (7:1-10). See the commentary on Matt. 8:5-13.

Jesus Raises a Widow's Son (7:11-17).

Background. In his *Life and Times of Jesus the Messiah* (pp. 554-55), Alfred Edersheim gives the following moving portrait of the funeral of the widow's only son.

The last sad offices have been rendered to the dead. The body has been laid on the ground; hair and nails have been cut, and the body washed, anointed, and wrapped in the best the widow could procure; for, the ordinance which directed that the dead be buried in "wrappings" (*Takhrikhin*), or, as they significantly called it, the "provision for the journey" (*Zevadatha*), of the most inexpensive linen, is of later date than our period. It is impossible to say, whether the later practice already prevailed, of covering the body with metal, glass, or salt, and laying it either upon earth or salt.

And now the mother was left *Oneneth* (moaning, lamenting) — a term which distinguished the mourning before from that after burial. She would sit on the floor, neither eat meat, nor drink wine. What scanty meal she would take, must be without prayer, in the house of a neighbour, or in another room, or at least with her back to the dead. Pious friends would render neighborly offices, or busy themselves about the near funeral. If it was deemed duty for the poorest Jew, on the death of his wife, to provide at least two flutes and one mourning woman, we may feel sure that the widowed mother had not neglected what, however incongruous or difficult to procure, might be regarded as the last tokens of affection. In all likelihood the custom obtained even then, though in modified form, to have funeral orations at the grave. For, even if charity provided for an unknown wayfarer the simplest funeral, mourning-women would be hired to chant in weird strains the lament: "Alas, the lion! Alas, the hero!" or similar words, while great Rabbis were wont to bespeak for themselves a warm funeral oration (*Hesped,* or *Hespeda)*. For, from the funeral oration a man's fate in the other world might be inferred; and, indeed, the "honor of the sage was in his funeral oration." And in this sense the Talmud answers the question, whether a funeral oration is intended to honor the survivors or the dead.

But in all this painful pageantry there was nothing for the heart of the widow, bereft of her only child.

Interpretation. Edersheim's description drives

home the critical point. As the body of the widow's son was being carried out of the hamlet of Nain toward the burial ground that lies east of the town, all hope was gone. The son was firmly held in death's terrible grip, and the widow, without a man to support her, would in that society likely become destitute.

It was at this moment, when all hope was gone, that Jesus met the procession and, seeing the stooped form of the mother, "His heart went out to her" (7:13). Going over to the "coffin" (*sorou,* actually a litter on which the body was carried), Jesus called the lost son back to life and "gave him back to his mother" (7:15).

This event has been called the ultimate kind of miracle; a work which will certify Jesus as the Messiah. Surely it is that. Just as surely, Luke's emphasis is on the anguish of the weeping widow and the sympathy that it aroused in Jesus' heart. This miracle was no calculated act, engaged in for the effect it might have on others. It was a spontaneous act of compassion. And, as such, it perhaps sums up the whole meaning of Christ's coming.

Why did God's Son enter the stream of humanity and cast His lot among us? Unless Christ acted decisively all hope was gone. And seeing us, lost and helpless, God cared. "His heart went out" to us.

In compassion Jesus touches us even now in our deadness, and His touch makes us alive.

Application. It is well to stand in awe as we see this expression of Jesus' power. What should cause us to fall on our knees and praise God — as the crowd did that afternoon near Nain — is the realization that our God cares. We can understand that He who formed the material universe has all power. But what we will never understand is the depth of that love that moved Jesus to reach out, to touch us, and to give us life.

LUKE 7:18–10:24
Decision Time

EXPOSITION

Luke has identified Jesus, and described the choices our Lord has made, and the choices some have made to trust or reject Him. Now in a further series of stories, Luke continues to drive home the importance of making a decision concerning Jesus Christ.

God has sent this generation two messengers: John, the powerful preacher in the mold of Elijah, and Jesus, whose ministry is marked by gentleness and miracles of healing. Yet the "experts in the law" (7:30) rejected both John and Jesus (7:18-35). Immediately Luke introduces us to a woman identified as a "sinner" (a prostitute) (7:39). Unlike the Pharisee who is hosting Jesus, this woman has grasped Jesus' message of forgiveness and responded with love (7:36-50). Luke then retells the familiar Parable of the Sower, but here shifts its focus significantly. In Matthew the emphasis is on the power of the Word; here Luke, in keeping with the theme of decision, places his emphasis on the kind of person who responds to the Word (8:1-15). That same emphasis on decision and its implications is seen in three brief, familiar images which are also found in the other synoptics: a lamp (8:16-18), Jesus' mother and brothers (8:19-21), calming the storm (8:22-25). The three culminate with a specific statement of the issue that must be faced: "Who is this?" (8:26)

Christ's healing of a man possessed by a legion of demons answers the question, "Who is this?" It also begins Luke's exploration of the difference that a decision for or against Jesus makes. Only Luke describes in any detail the impact of demon possession. Without Jesus, man is helpless before hostile spiritual powers (8:26-39). Luke goes on to describe the healing of a woman suffering from a chronic issue of blood and the raising of a dead girl (8:40-56). Without Jesus, man is helpless before the powers of sickness and death. Thus one who decides for Jesus is no longer a helpless victim. He has cast his lot with One who is in every sense Victor over those forces so inimical to humankind!

Now Jesus sends His disciples on a mission. They are to carry the Good News throughout the land (9:1-9). Although the disciples are inadequate in themselves to meet the needs of others, Jesus can miraculously multiply their meager resources and so satisfy the thousands who are drawn to Him (9:10-17). This is possible because, as Peter confesses, Jesus is "the Christ of God" (9:18-27), whose true nature is revealed in the Transfiguration (9:28-36) and whose power is again displayed in the healing of a

171

boy possessed by an evil spirit (9:37-45).

The disciples still do not understand. They argue over who will be greatest when Jesus establishes His kingdom (9:46-50) and are angry when some Samaritans refuse them hospitality (9:51-56). But the decision to acknowledge Jesus as Lord must be reflected in a commitment to follow Him, and "No one who puts his hand to the plow and looks back is fit for service in the kingdom of God" (9:57-62). And so, once again, Jesus sends out followers to bring both healing and the kingdom message to Israel. Some receive the message, and some reject it. Blessed are those who do see, and who gladly come to the Father through the Son (10:1-24).

WORD STUDIES

Go back and report to John *what you have seen and heard* (7:22). John, like others in Israel, expected Jesus to quickly establish the prophesied messianic kingdom. John, languishing in prison, became uncertain when Jesus did not act as he anticipated, and sent his followers to ask Christ if He really were the Messiah.

Jesus showed no anger when John doubted Him despite God's earlier revelation to John that Jesus was the Christ (John 1:29-36). Instead Jesus understood the pressures that John, imprisoned and fearing for his life, must have felt. Even as Jesus understands the doubts we may feel when difficult circumstances lead us to wonder where our God can be.

Jesus simply told the messengers to report miracles of healing. John would realize that the healings were messianic works—works the OT predicted that the coming Deliverer would perform (4:17-19).

In reality Jesus' response was a wonderful vote of confidence in John, for His response demonstrated trust that John would understand. It may well be that this demonstration of Jesus' confidence did more to encourage and strengthen the beleaguered prophet than the answer itself. And it may also be that when doubts and fears assault us, the silence of heaven may speak more of God's confidence in you and me than of any abandonment. God knows our hearts. He knows full well that despite the uncertainty that troubles us at times, we do believe. And that our faith will triumph in the end.

The one who is *least* in the kingdom of God is *greater* than he [John] (7:28). For an explanation of this puzzling verse, see the Word Study of Matt. 11:11.

These women were *helping to support* them [Jesus and the disciples] out of their own means (8:3). It was considered a good deed to provide funds that enabled a rabbi to carry on his teaching mission or support his disciples. Here Luke mentions several women who performed this service for Jesus and the Twelve. It is characteristic of Luke to be aware of women and to give them credit for their good works and abilities.

It is interesting to see how often Luke holds up women as model Christians. The "sinful woman" of 7:36-50 serves as a model of the power of forgiveness to evoke love, the "persistent widow" of 18:1-5 as a model of prayer, the "poor widow" of 21:1-4 as a model of giving. If we were to search through all of Scripture we would find few clearer models of "liberated women." Note how carefully Luke notes that these women helped Jesus "out of their own means." Although Mary was apparently single, Joanna was married, yet each had the freedom to act on her own convictions and to use her own funds as she chose.

But the seed on good soil stands for those with a *noble* and *good* heart, who hear the word, retain it, and by persevering produce a crop (8:15). "Noble and good" (*kale kai agathe*) is a common Greek phrase, here given unique Christian definition. Luke's point is that the noble and good heart characterizes the person who hears, retains, and by patience ultimately brings forth the fruit of a righteous and good life.

There is an important distinction here. Some might say that "if you persevere you will become good." Christ's parable teaches that "if you are good you will persevere." Actions cannot change our nature. But when

God in grace has changed our hearts, that inner transformation will be displayed in the choices we make and the way in which we act.

My *mother and brothers* are those who hear God's word and put it into practice (8:21). Jesus does not reject family, but instead grants those who hear and do God's Word family status.

Many times it had *seized* him (8:29). Luke alone gives a detailed description of the horrors of demon possession (8:27-29). Under the influence of the demon the man was degraded (naked), isolated from others, homeless, and without control of his own voice or limbs. Perhaps this last, the complete loss of self, is the most terrifying.

Today, as in the first century, most who turn to the occult do so in the hope of somehow using supernatural forces to reach their own ends. The appalling reality is that these forces are utterly malevolent, as completely hostile to human beings as they are hostile to God. What a terrible risk is taken by anyone who dabbles in the occult.

A large *herd of pigs* was feeding there (8:32). To the Jew pigs were unclean, revolting beasts. They were by far more appropriate hosts for the demons than a human being, who was made in the image of God.

The story is, however, filled with irony. When the demons entered the pigs, these animals rushed headlong into the sea and destroyed themselves. The demons had controlled the man. But did the demons drive the herd into the waters, or did the despised animals experience such revulsion at the demons' touch that they were driven to destroy themselves?

Perhaps the greatest irony, however, is seen in the hostility of the region's population. They were amazed to see the demoniac restored, clothed, and rational. But they were so upset at the financial loss of their herds that they begged Jesus to leave.

How easy it is for us to place an economic value on things, and how hard to measure the human value. Yet as this familiar story reminds us, the human value is the measure we must use — even when the economic cost may be high.

A woman was there who had been subject to bleeding for twelve years, but *no one could heal her* (8:43). How often, in very human ways, the writers of the Scriptures are glimpsed through the inspired words. Luke, many believe, was himself a physician, and merely notes the difficulty of the case. Mark, who typically gives briefer descriptions of the events he reports, adds a note that Luke (carefully?) leaves out: "She had suffered a great deal under the care of many doctors and had spent all she had, yet instead of getting better she grew worse" (Mark 5:26). Doctors then as now were apparently not eager to openly criticize their colleagues! Laymen, like Mark, are less reticent.

She came up behind Him and touched the edge of His cloak, and immediately her bleeding stopped (8:44). Mark 5:28 explains why the woman touched Jesus' cloak: "She thought, 'If I just touch His clothes, I will be healed.' "

The notion, although popularized by modern media preachers who urge listeners to send for blessed handkerchiefs or to lay their hands on the radio, has a pagan rather than biblical origin. The notion that power could be magically transmitted by touch was a common Hellenistic superstition.

Why, then, did it work? The woman was healed when she touched Christ's clothing, and Jesus knew that "power has gone out of Me" (8:46).

The best answer is found in Jesus' last remark to the woman. "Daughter, your faith has healed you. Go in peace" (8:48). The woman's actions were based on a mistaken idea, but those actions did in fact express a real faith in Jesus. And it is faith in Jesus that enables Christ's power to flow freely to human beings.

How tragic when we lose sight of this basic truth, and teach others that they must do things in the right way if God is to bless them. They must pray as we teach them (speak in tongues or not speak in tongues), interpret this passage this way and that passage that, if God is to respond to them in their need.

In fact, we are all limited in our understanding of God. And, undoubtedly, we all at times approach God in inappropriate ways. How wonderful that our God is a God of grace, who asks only one thing: that we come to Him in trust and faith, expecting Him to work.

I beheaded John. *Who, then, is this* I hear such things about? (9:9) Poor Herod. He had at last rid himself of John the Baptist. And suddenly the perplexed ruler hears of another messenger of God, not only preaching, but sending out followers to do miracles and preach "everywhere" (9:6). Somehow, no matter how they try, people simply cannot get rid of God. His name continues to come up, no matter what they do. Shut Him out of their lives in one area, and He will suddenly appear in another, just as insistent, just as demanding that they make a decision for or against Him.

"Who, then, is this" indeed! It's God confronting us again. There is no way any person can be rid of Him, or of the necessity to decide.

The people there did not welcome Him, because He was *heading for Jerusalem* (9:53). The Samaritans were a semi-pagan people whose worship of God involved a corrupted form of Judaism. The Jews were actively hostile toward them, and the Samaritans resented the contempt in which their interpretations of religion were held.

Even so, the manners of the East made the offer of hospitality to a group of travelers almost mandatory. Yet this Samaritan village re-fused the request of Jesus and the Twelve to stay among them. Luke's phrase "because He was heading for Jerusalem" explains the hostility. The little party of Jews was heading up to the temple for one of the required religious festivals. This was more than the Samaritans could endure.

James and John were angry and eager to punish the Samaritans, whom they undoubtedly despised as bigots. Their attitude won them Jesus' rebuke.

How do we handle those heated disputes over issues that are as vital to us as religion was to Jews and Samaritans? We follow the example of Jesus, and as the company He led "went to another village" (9:56) we remove ourselves from the situation, and go on.

[Jesus] replied, "I *saw* Satan fall like lightning from heaven" (10:18). This verse is taken by many to allude to Isaiah 14:4-11, and may in fact describe Satan's fall. At the same time it has a special application in context.

When the 72 Jesus sent out to preach returned, they were elated that "even the demons submit to us in Your name" (10:17). Jesus' remark may simply indicate that He has seen something far greater. But it also links the casting out of demons in first-century Galilee with that earlier disaster. In each case, evil is defeated, and the victorious power of God revealed.

THE PASSAGE IN DEPTH

Jesus and John the Baptist (7:18-35). See the commentary on Matt. 11:1-30 and the parallel passage in John 1:19-20.

Jesus Anointed by a Sinful Woman (7:36-50).
Background. At first it may seem surprising. Jesus eating with a Pharisee? Normally we think of the Pharisees standing by, judgmental and hostile, while Jesus enjoys a meal with the outcasts of society. Luke indicates, however, that it was not uncommon for Jesus to associate socially with Pharisees as well as with ordinary people. In fact, this is only one of three incidents Luke reports which find Jesus sharing a meal with Pharisees (11:37; 14:1).

Jeremias, in his exploration of the parables of Jesus, identifies this meal as a banquet (*kateklithe*) held in Christ's honor. He also suggests that, since it was considered a good deed to invite a traveling teacher to a meal after he had preached in the synagogue, this was a Sabbath meal and that the Pharisee was at least undecided whether or not Jesus was a prophet.

If this is the case, we can suppose that not only the Pharisee, but also his invited guests and the woman who slipped in uninvited had heard Jesus' teaching. The Pharisee responded by urging Jesus to eat at his home, evidently that he might more carefully examine this itinerant preacher. But the woman responded wholeheartedly. When she learned where Jesus would be, she rushed home and, seizing a jar of expensive ointment that undoubtedly represented her life savings, hurried to the home of the Pharisee and anointed Jesus' feet.

The woman is identified in the text as a "sinner" [*hamartolos*] (7:39), meaning either that she was a prostitute or the wife of a man whose employment was considered dishonorable. As v. 47 reports that Jesus spoke of "her" many sins, it is apparent that the first possibility is to be preferred.

But how, we wonder, could a known prostitute enter the house of the Pharisee? We must not imagine that she knocked on the door of his great house, told the butler of her mission, and was permitted to pass through a series of halls to the private dining room. In that day when hospitality was viewed as a great virtue, the host often set tables in an open area and left the gate open, so others might see how generously he had provided for his guests. Some passers-by might even stand in the courtyard, admiring the food provided, an act which honored rather than embarrassed the host. And so the woman could easily have slipped in, to crouch at Jesus' feet and moisten them with a flood of tears.

Interpretation. As the woman sits, bent double at Jesus' feet, she suddenly becomes the focus of every person's attention. How each interprets her actions, and the conclusions each one draws, teaches us more about that person than about the woman.

The Pharisee, Simon, quickly fits the woman into a well-worn pigeon hole. She is a "sinner." From this the Pharisee draws a series of quick, apparently logical conclusions. If Jesus were a prophet, He would know the kind of person she is. And, if Jesus were one of God's prophets, surely He would not allow a sinner to touch Him. The inescapable conclusion, for the Pharisee, is that Christ is not a prophet, and surely cannot speak or act for God.

The problem with his logic is the problem with many of our arguments. It is based on unspoken assumptions. Those assumptions must be examined before we allow reason to lead us to any conclusion.

Here the Pharisee's assumption is rooted in his own approach to religion. Like all in his movement, Simon believes in total commitment to the laws of ritual purity which generations of rabbis had derived from OT proscriptive laws. Ritual purity demanded that the person who was separated to God be separated from all that was impure. And so Simon automatically assumed that, since the woman was a sinner, the only appropriate way to relate to such a woman was to reject her and withdraw, or else be contaminated.

Jesus operated on a completely different set of assumptions. He saw the woman as a person, not an object. He viewed her with compassion and love, not scorn and condemnation. To Jesus, holiness was no negative thing, but a positive, dynamic power. This woman's present actions demonstrated a response to Him that promised an inner transformation—a transformation that would make her past irrelevant and her future bright.

In the woman now kneeling at Jesus' feet two essentially opposing approaches to religion came into conflict. And yet Christ's words to Simon the Pharisee, while bluntly rejecting his view, are in the form of gracious instruction.

Who will love more, a person who is aware of a gigantic debt or one whose debt seems smaller? The Pharisee rightly answers that, even though neither person can pay, the one with the greatest debt will be more grateful. Christ then goes on to compare the response of the woman and of Simon to Jesus.

When Christ came to the banquet the Pharisee omitted the courtesies usually shown to an honored guest. The slight may have been small, but in that culture it was significant. The lack of these touches of hospitality were Simon's way of signaling to his other guests that he had not yet decided how worthy this traveling preacher was. He had also made it subtly but unmistakably clear that although the feast was given in Christ's honor, Simon considered his guest to be below him socially and spiritually.

In contrast, this woman whom Simon dismissed as a "sinner" has from the moment of her entrance displayed overwhelming love and gratitude. Jesus thus saw her in a totally different perspective than the Pharisee. Her actions displayed a true and transforming faith. And so Jesus concluded His lesson to Simon with words she must have longed to hear; words which confirmed the understanding which had first awakened her love: "Your sins are forgiven" (7:48).

And as the other guests murmured in amazement, Jesus spoke to the woman again. "Your faith has saved you; go in peace" (7:50).

175

Application. There is so much in this simple story for us. First, let's not miss the point of Jesus' story. The woman undertook these acts of love because she had already grasped and appropriated God's forgiving grace. She was not forgiven because she loved, but loved because she was forgiven.

The Pharisee, unconscious of his sins, sought to approach God in a totally different way—a way of works. While that way enabled him to take pride in his supposed righteousness while condemning the woman as a sinner, it blinded him to the nature of grace.

Second, we need to learn to see others as Jesus saw them, not as the Pharisee saw them. The Pharisee placed people in pigeon holes. He classified them, and then was able to dismiss them: this woman is a "sinner," that man a "tax collector," this group over here merely one of the "crowd" who does not know the fine points of God's Law. In contrast Jesus saw the woman as an individual rather than as a member of a class. What was important to Him was how she, as an individual, responded to His message of grace. Whatever she had been was unimportant in view of what she was now and would become as a forgiven person. She who had once sold herself for money was now eager to give away all she had in gratitude to the Savior.

What a truth to remember and to live by. It is not what a person has been that is important. What a person can become through an experience of God's forgiving grace is what counts. The overflowing generosity of this woman of the street stands as a permanent reminder of the power of Christ's forgiveness to utterly transform.

The Parable of the Sower (8:1-15). See the commentary on Matt. 13:1-23 and the parallel passage in Mark 4:1-20.

A Lamp on a Stand (8:16-18). See the Word Study of Mark 4:21 and the parallel passage in Matt. 5:14-16.

Jesus' Mother and Brothers (9:19-21). See the parallel passages in Matt. 12:46-50 and Mark 3:31-35.

Jesus Calms the Storm (9:22-25). See the commentary on Mark 4:35-41 and the parallel passage in Matt. 8:18, 23-27.

The Healing of a Demon-Possessed Man (9:26-39). See the commentary on Mark 5:1-20 and the parallel passage in Matt. 8:28-34.

A Dead Girl and a Sick Woman (8:40-56). See the parallel passages in Matt. 9:18-26 and Mark 5:21-43. See also the Word Study of Luke 8:43 and 8:48.

Jesus Sends Out the Twelve (9:1-9). See the commentary on Matt. 10:1-42, and parallel passages in Matt. 14:1-12 and Mark 6:6-29.

Jesus Feeds the Five Thousand (9:10-17). See the commentary on Mark 8:1-13, and the parallel passages in Matt. 14:13-21 and Mark 6:30-44.

Peter's Confession of Christ (9:18-27). See the Word Studies on Matt. 16:18-19, and the parallel passages in Matt. 11:2-19 and 16:13-20.

The Transfiguration (9:28-36). See the commentary on Mark 9:1-13 and Matt. 16:21-28; 17:1-8.

The Healing of a Boy with an Evil Spirit (9:37-45). See the commentary on Mark 9:14-32 and the parallel passage in Matt. 17:14-23.

Who Will Be the Greatest? (9:46-50) See the commentary on Mark 9:33-41 and the parallel passage of Matt. 18:1-6.

Samaritan Opposition (9:51-56). See the Word Study of Luke 9:53, above.

The Cost of Following Jesus (9:57-62). See a parallel in Matt. 8:19-22.

Background. Luke has carefully developed the theme of choice in chaps. 5–9 of his Gospel. Now he briefly reports a series of three incidents that invite us to ponder the implications of choosing to trust Jesus as Lord. If Christ is who He claims to be, and we accept those claims, then surely we must commit ourselves to follow Him faithfully.

The word "follow" is *akoloutheo.* This is a common verb, found often in narrative passages, used in its common, descriptive sense. Yet at times "follow" serves as a technical theological term. When thus used it is closely linked in the Gospels with discipleship, and expresses the disciple's essential commitment to make his or her daily choices in obedience to the Lord.

Interpretation. Against this background we realize that these three incidents are truly important, and in a sense serve as the culmination of the development of this major theme in Luke's Gospel. What then are we to learn from these three incidents?

Perhaps the first thing we note is that to follow Jesus means more than personal commitment to Christ as a person. It also means commitment to carry out Christ's purposes in the world. The one who follows Jesus must "go and proclaim the kingdom of God" (9:60), and gladly give himself "for service in the kingdom of God" (9:62). To follow Jesus means to identify ourselves with His purposes in the world, and give ourselves fully to them.

At the same time, each of Luke's stories makes it very clear that following Jesus involves a surrender of things which human beings find important.

■ To a man who volunteers to follow Him, Jesus says simply "the Son of Man has no place to lay His head" (9:57-58). One who follows Jesus must be willing to surrender material comforts and all that "home" implies.

■ Jesus calls another man, saying "Follow Me" (9:59). While the man calls Jesus "Lord," he begs Christ to "first let me go and bury my father" (9:60). We must understand here that the father is not dead. What the candidate for discipleship means is, "Let me live at home until my father has died, and I will have fulfilled a son's obligation." Jesus' answer is blunt and clear. One who follows Jesus must be willing to surrender even the dearest of relationships to give complete allegiance to the Lord.

■ A third man makes the verbal commitment, "I will follow You," but begs to be allowed to first go say good-bye to his family. This is a very different request than the one just before. That request suggested that family responsibility outweighs commitment to the Lord. This request suggests only that commitment to Christ need not exclude other obligations.

Jesus answers with an image drawn, as so many of His illustrations are, from the ordinary and familiar. The plows of Palestine were very light. While they could be guided by one hand, usually the left, that hand had to keep the plow upright, constantly adjust its depth, and avoid the rocks and stones which might break off or blunt its delicate point. At the same time the plowman had to drive his oxen, usually using an iron-tipped, six-foot goad held in his right hand. And all the time the plowman had to concentrate on keeping his furrows straight.

While light and apparently simple, the plow of the ancient Middle East required the farmer's total and absolute concentration.

And so Jesus gave His answer. One who chooses to follow Jesus has no choice but to give the same total and absolute attention to "service in the kingdom of God" (9:62) that was required of a farmer when he plowed.

Application. Taken together these three incidents sum up what our decision to follow Jesus as His disciples involves. We choose His will over our own comfort or even our material security. We choose His will over even the most intimate of personal and family relationships. And we give our total, absolute attention to serving Him.

Jesus Sends Out the 72 (10:1-24). See the commentary on Matt. 10 and the parallel passage in Mark 6:8-13.

LUKE 10:25–12:3
Spiritual Detours

EXPOSITION

Luke has gradually led his readers to see Jesus not only for who He is, but also to the point of decision. He has confronted us with a Christ who has chosen to enter our world and display God's love. This very act confronts each of us with the necessity of making a choice for or against Jesus as Savior. Luke has also reminded us that if we respond to Jesus as Savior, we must also acknowledge Him as Lord, and follow Him in full and complete commitment. Now, as Luke's story of Jesus continues, the beloved physician invites us to explore with him an alternative to commitment to Jesus as God's Christ.

That alternative is introduced in the Parable of the Good Samaritan. The key figures in this incident are the "expert in the Law" (10:25), who gave an answer that any educated Jew would to Christ's question, "What is written in the Law?" concerning eternal life, and the priest and Levite in the Samaritan story whose indifference to the suffering of the man attacked by robbers denies the most basic principal of that Law (10:25-37). The only real alternative to Jesus, then, is a "religion of the Book" represented by first-century Judaism, which had lost sight of mercy while seeking, as the expert in the Law did, to "justify himself" (10:29) by his interpretations of God's Law.

The story of Mary and Martha represents a warning. The followers of Christ will fare no better than the first generation who followed Moses if, like Martha, they place priority on "doing." Like Martha, we must emphasize the disciple's duty to maintain an intimate personal relationship with God (10:38-42). Jesus' teaching on prayer (11:1-13) brings the quality of that relationship into clear focus. We approach and rely on God as our Father (11:1-4). We know He will respond, as surely as a neighbor fulfills a social obligation (11:5-10), or a father gives good gifts to children who ask for his help (11:11-13).

Luke then returns to the basic question. If a person does not choose Jesus, what will he or she choose? Can anyone imagine that Jesus' works were energized by Satan, as some in the crowd charged? (11:14-28) Surely a person who accepts this notion actually takes sides with demons—and becomes vulnerable to them!

What choice then does a person have? Either accept Jesus by faith—with far more evidence of who He is than the people of Nineveh had in Jonah's day or the Queen of Sheba had in Solomon's (11:29-32)—or continue in spiritual blindness (11:33-36).

Luke's next reported incident makes unmistakably clear the condemnation of contemporary religion implied in Jesus' Parable of the Good Samaritan. Jesus is again eating a meal at a Pharisee's home. When Christ fails to follow tradition and go through the ritual washing the Pharisees performed, the guests are shocked. In response Christ uttered a series of "woe's" against them and against the experts in the Law (11:37-54). The Pharisees are self-centered, unclean hypocrites (11:39-44), while the "experts in the Law," like their forefathers who murdered God's prophets, burden rather than help God's people, and have stolen the "key to knowledge" through which God's people might enter the kingdom of heaven (11:45-54).

What then is the alternative to accepting Christ as Savior and Lord? There is no viable alternative at all. Oh, we can choose to be "religious." We can attempt to commend ourselves to God through works and ritual observance. But this path will only lead us farther from God, not closer. Ultimately this choice will lead us to take sides with Satan, not God, and we too will in the end hear Jesus pronounce, "Woe!"

WORD STUDIES

The one who had *mercy* on him (10:37).

We do not often find the word "mercy" in the OT of our English versions. Typically the Hebrew words related to this concept are translated by other English terms. The root idea, however, is expressed in two important Hebrew words. *Raham* indicates the love of a superior for an inferior. This love is deep, and moves the superior to help when his friend is in need. This Hebrew word is most frequently rendered as "love" or "compassion."

The other Hebrew word is *hanan*. It focuses our attention on the response of a person who is able to help another who is in need. Although the needy person has no "right" to expect help, the other is moved spontaneously by his feelings to give aid. This Hebrew word is most frequently translated "grace" or "loving-kindness."

Thus the expert in the Law with whom Jesus was speaking clearly understood what he was saying when he admitted that "the one who showed mercy" to the victim in Christ's story was acting the part of neighbor to him.

As we come into the NT we find the concept of "mercy" brought into sharper focus. The Greek word, *eleos,* is more precise and better defined. Mercy is compassionate response: it involves feeling with a sufferer and being moved to help him. We see this echoed in the words of sufferers who desperately appealed to Jesus, "Have mercy" (Matt. 15:22; 17:15). And we see mercy in Christ's consistent, immediate response to such pleas.

Perhaps mercy's most important aspect, however, is the role it is given in the developed theology of the New Testament epistles. There we realize that "mercy" depicts not only the attitude of God toward us sinners, but also explains the purpose of Christ's incarnation. He came that He might have mercy on us. As the *Zondervan Expository Dictionary of Bible Words* recaps:

> The NT continues to affirm that mercy has been provided for the believer: God, "who is rich in mercy, made us alive with Christ even when we were dead in transgressions" (Eph. 2:4-5). "In His great mercy He has given us new birth into a living hope" (1 Peter 1:3). And "He saved us, not because of righteous things we had done, but because of His mercy" (Titus 3:5).

One of the great purposes of the story of the Good Samaritan is to warn us. In its dependence on doing righteous things, rabbinic Judaism had lost sight of the central role of mercy in an individual's relationship with God. We depend on His mercy, for we are sinners who fall far short of being able to please Him. And, as those who have received mercy and understand human frailties, we must be quick to extend mercy to our fellow men.

Martha was *distracted* by all the preparations that had to be made (10:40). The Greek verb is *periespato.* Martha's attention was drawn from Jesus to the meal she was preparing. How easy it is to be so busy serving Jesus that we have no time to spend with Him.

Only *one thing* is needed (10:42). There is no agreement by commentators on what this enigmatic saying means. The three most likely translations are (1) "One thing is needed," (2) "Few things are needed," or (3) "Few things are needed — or only one." Even this, however, leaves the issue unclear. Is Jesus talking about the dinner itself, and encouraging Martha to simplify the meal rather than put on a more impressive spread? Or is the "one thing" Jesus calls for a commitment to Him like that displayed by Mary?

Whatever the specific reference here, it is clear that the incident contrasts priorities. Mary's priority was listening to and responding to Jesus. Martha's way was to immerse herself in service. Surely the message of the story is clear. Our relationship with Jesus — our desire to spend time with Jesus and listen to His Word — is to take priority even over loving service.

The warning here is clear as well. Unless we give relationship priority, the loving service we now provide may well deteriorate into the sterile religion of the priest and Levite of the Good Samaritan story.

The door is already locked, and my children are with me in bed. I can't get up (11:7). When night fell, most families in Palestine slept in the same room. A long sleeping mat was unrolled, and the mother lay down at one end and the father at the other, with the children stretched out between them. When the knock came at the door late at night, the irritated householder at first refused to open the door, complaining in effect that it would disturb his whole family to do so. In fact, however, the "I can't get up" here really means "I won't," or "I don't want to." When a person doesn't want to do something, he or she can usually find some reason why "I can't."

Let's always keep in mind that, as Christ's disciples, we are called to be merciful. Our response to others in need is to be "I can," and "I will."

Yet because of the man's *boldness* he will get up and give him as much as he needs (11:8). It is most likely that *anaideia* here has a different meaning than "boldness." The word can mean "avoidance of shame," and that is most certainly the meaning here.

Several other things in our English version cloud the meaning of this illustration. One is that the "suppose" in v. 5 fails to catch the impact of the Greek *tis ex humon*. We would better render it "Can you imagine?" with the clear implication that the answer is, "Never! Such a thing is unthinkable."

Another problem in our English version is the paragraph break at 11:7. This is not really a break, but rather a continuation of the question posed in v. 5. And so to understand what Jesus is really teaching about prayer, we need to paraphrase these verses and recast the illustration.

> Then He said to them, "Can you imagine that one of you has a friend, and he goes to him at midnight and says, 'Friend, lend me three loaves of bread, because a friend of mine on a journey has come to me, and I have nothing to set before him.' Now, can you imagine that the one inside would answer, 'Don't bother me. The door is long since locked, and my children are with me in bed. I can't get up and give you anything.' Can you imagine that? Of course not! Why, even if he would not get up and give him the bread because he is his friend, yet to avoid the shame he will get up and give him as much as he needs."

What is the impact of Christ's illustration? Simply that in that time, in a land without hotels, travelers typically stayed with friends. A common proverb notes, "Today he is my guest, tomorrow I will be his." The obligation of hospitality was not laid only on the householder, but on the whole community. It would shame the community if the neighbor refused the request for bread, and he himself would be ashamed before his neighbors.

Thus the point of the illustration is not that persistence will ultimately force God to answer our prayers. The point is rather that it is as unthinkable that God would not respond to the prayer of one of His own, as it is unthinkable that a neighbor would not respond to an appeal for bread to feed an unexpected guest.

No wonder Christ concludes with the promise, "Ask and it will be given to you; seek and you will find; knock and the door will be opened to you" (11:9).

It goes through *arid places* seeking rest

and does not find it (11:24). Here Jesus uses imagery that reflects the popular belief that demons (evil spirits) inhabited the desert. But evil spirits are not at home in arid places. They are drawn to human beings, where they can express their nature by causing human beings harm. The mention of "seven" is idiomatic, a common symbol of totality. The point of the saying is made clear in v. 25. If the house (person) is "swept clean" and empty, that individual has no defense. Only when we are indwelt by Christ and His Spirit are we safe.

It asks for a miraculous sign, but none will be given it except the *sign of Jonah* (11:29). The word translated "sign" is *semeia,* and means as the NIV translates a "miraculous" sign. Here the "sign of Jonah" is Jonah himself, whose prophetic word caused repentance in Nineveh. Jesus' point is that He Himself is God's miraculous sign to His generation—a sign far greater than Jonah was in his day. The failure of Jesus' listeners to repent guarantees their condemnation.

How foolish to ask God for more evidence of His love and grace than He has already provided us in Jesus. There is no greater revelation of God than He has given us in His Son. One who does not respond to Jesus will not respond, whatever wonder God might perform.

When your *eyes are good,* your whole body also is full of light (11:34). Here "good" is *haplous,* "sound" or "healthy." Jesus' point is that whether or not a person receives light depends not on the light's brightness but on the health of the eye. Only as we open our eyes to God's light shed in Jesus and let it shine in, can we be full of light. As Christians we are called to walk in the light.

Woe (11:42-44, 46-47, 52). The word is an exclamation, expressing grief or denunciation.

This generation will be held *responsible for the blood* of all the prophets (11:50). Old Testament law made the community responsible to put murderers to death. The specific responsibility for exacting this penalty belonged to the "avenger of the blood," a near relative of the murder victim (Num. 35). Under no circumstances was a murder to be overlooked, lest the whole land become guilty before God.

Now Jesus warns that this generation is about to be held accountable for the blood of all the prophets murdered by earlier generations. Why? Because in rejecting Christ and in causing His fast approaching death, this generation has taken sides with the murderers of the prophets, rather than with the God who demanded their punishment. Just as one who refuses to execute the murderer becomes as guilty as the killer, those who rejected Christ took upon themselves the mantle of those who murdered the prophets, and so share fully in their guilt.

Woe to you experts in the law, because you have taken away the *key to knowledge* (11:52). We might render the phrase, "have taken away the key, even knowledge." The key to relationship with God is that knowledge of the Lord revealed in Scripture. Yet the "experts in the Law" whose boast is in their superior knowledge of God's Law, have not simply lost the key but have taken it away, so distorting the Scriptures by their legalism that the people of God no longer know Him.

We must come to God's Word seeking Him. If we do not grow closer to the Lord through our study of the Word, then we have tragically misunderstood its basic message.

THE PASSAGE IN DEPTH

The Parable of the Good Samaritan (10:25-37).

Background. The Parable of the Good Samaritan is undoubtedly one of the most familiar stories in the whole of Scripture. Like other stories Jesus told, it grew out of the familiar and carried the stamp of everyday realities.

The narrow, 21-mile route between Jericho and Jerusalem was notoriously insecure. It was not a road normally used by commercial travelers, but more often by pilgrims. During the days before and after one of the great religious festivals it was crowded. At other times those who traveled it were more likely to be like the priest and Levite of Jesus' story: residents of Jericho whose duty demanded service for two weeks each year at the temple. Jeremias notes, however, that when on their way to serve, priests and Levites traveled in groups. He suggests that each one's traveling alone is evidence that neither was on his way to serve at the temple. This is important, because if they had been reporting for temple duty the pious Jew might argue that responsibility to God took priority over responsibility to neighbor, and the thrust of Jesus' story would have been blunted.

The fact that none of the travelers journeyed with a guard may reflect the commitment of Rome to root out and execute brigands. Yet the route, laid through a rocky wasteland, was known to be dangerous, and most often people hoped to travel through it in a group for protection. It is not only possible but likely that the priest and the Levite abandoned their fellow-countryman and hurried on for fear that the men who had attacked him might be lying in wait to assault them.

Jesus' listeners would certainly have grasped all this immediately, and while they felt sympathy for the robber's helpless victim, would also have understood the fears of the priest and the Levite who hurried by when they saw him lying, beaten and bloody, by the side of the narrow road.

In essence Jesus' story immediately created a moral dilemma. Of course one feels compassion for the hurt and helpless. But how much is a person obligated to risk for the sake of another? His possessions? His very life? Whatever we might say about the setting Jesus sketched in such a few descriptive terms, we must admit that His listeners — and the expert in the Law to whom He was talking — would hardly give a glib or superficial answer.

Against this background, then, we can explore just what message Jesus intended to convey to His questioner, and through Luke's report, to you and me.

Interpretation. To understand the story we need to understand something of the dynamics of the interaction that led up to it. Our text tells us that "an expert in [OT] law" (10:25) raised a question, "What must I do to inherit eternal life?" This led Jesus to ask how this expert "read" (understood) (10:26) the OT.

■ The opening dialogue (10:25-29). First we note that the local expert asked his question to "test" (*ekpeirazon*) Jesus (10:25). We should not see this as an expression of hostility: the

man accepts Jesus as a teacher (*didaskale*), and most likely sought to engage Him in one of those lengthy discussions about the Law in which his class took such delight.

The question, "What must I do to inherit eternal life?" was in fact not unusual. The Gospels tell us that a rich young man asked the same question (Matt. 19:16). The question displays a basic flaw in the approach of rabbinic Judaism to relationship with God: there is always the implicit assumption that eternal life is a reward earned by the believer for his good works. The real question was: Which good works can a person do that will merit God's favor?

A later rabbinic writing reports a discussion on this point between a rabbi and a merchant, and resolves the question by quoting Psalm 34:12-14: "Whoever of you loves life and desires to see many good days, keep your tongue from evil and your lips from speaking lies. Turn from evil and do good; seek peace and pursue it." Yet Edersheim argues that when Jesus asked the expert in the law how he read the Scripture, that man's answer expressed the conviction of most persons of his time. The paramount obligation in the Law, found in Deut. 6:5, was to love God completely.

At the same time the rabbis frequently discussed Lev. 19:18 and the duty to love one's neighbor. As Hillel expressed, "What is hateful to thee, that do not to another. This is the whole Law; the rest is only commentary."

What is striking is that these two principles, keeping the Law and loving one's neighbor, are not linked in any known writings of the ancient sages. And so Jesus commends the rabbi, saying, "You have answered correctly. Do this and you will live" (10:28).

■ The roles of principle and practice (10:29). There is something very comfortable about a discussion of theology. We can discuss on a totally theoretical level, enjoy ourselves tremendously, and after a stimulating interchange feel a great deal of satisfaction in the conviction that we certainly were "right" in everything we said. We can do this without ever being forced to explore the practical implications of what we have affirmed.

This is exactly what was happening until, suddenly, Jesus changed the focus of the dialogue. " 'You have answered correctly,' Jesus said. 'Do this and you will live.' "

Just as suddenly, the comfort of that familiar rabbinic debate was dissolved in the uncomfortable realization that being right was not enough: it is doing right that counts.

All this is expressed in the discomfort of the expert in the Law, who asks, "Who is my neighbor?" in the hope of "justifying himself" (10:29). This is an evasive tactic which one simply must take if he or she hopes to be justified by the Law. Either one must whittle down the Law's demands by redefining them to achievable terms, or one must prop himself or herself up by pretending to be better than he or she really is. When principle is applied to practice, it immediately becomes clear that principle must be redefined!

And so the writings of the rabbis contain several discussions of the question this expert in the law hopefully asked Jesus Christ, "Who is my neighbor?" Edersheim refers to a passage, Ab Zar 26a, which "directs that idolators [e.g., Gentiles] are not to be delivered when in imminent danger, and that apostates are to be led into it." He also notes an exposition on Ex. 23:5 in Babha Mets 32b. The Exodus verse reads, "If you see the donkey of someone who hates you fallen down under its load, do not leave it there; be sure you help him with it." That rabbinic commentary says that the burden need only be unloaded — unless not helping to reload would provoke hostility. In addition, the principle applies only to Jewish and not Gentile enemies.

It was not at all unusual then that Jesus' questioner sought Jesus' interpretation of "neighbor" — or that his motive was to justify himself by restricting the implications of what appears on its face to be a universal principle.

"Who is my neighbor?" (10:29) The Parable of the Good Samaritan which Jesus told in answer to this question is no allegory. Against the background of contemporary rabbinic thought, as sketched above, it is a pointed condemnation of an approach to religion which, rather than bringing God's people closer to Him, had led them away. The priest and the Levite represent the best of the old economy. The priest represented God to man and man before God, while the Levite was dedicated to service and to worship. Yet each turned his eyes, and quickly passed by the fellow Israelite!

Then a hated Samaritan came along. A Samaritan was viewed as an apostate by the orthodox, and thus should actually be "led into" danger. This Samaritan, an "enemy," was moved by compassion at the victim's plight.

In one brief, incisive story Jesus had cut through all the rabbinic dialectic dedicated to defining "neighbor" and "enemy." Then Jesus asked His questioner, "Which of these three do you think was a neighbor to the man who fell into the hands of robbers?" (10:36)

There could be only one answer, and the expert in the Law was forced to reply, "The one who had mercy on him" (10:37).

Application. How quickly Jesus' story cut through the clutter of religious debate. What do you read in the Scriptures? Human beings are to love God and love others. How clear and how simple this is. What does loving others entail? Why, simply having compassion when we see another human being in need, and reaching out to help.

What of all the debate over who is and who is not a person's neighbor? What of all the argument over how to treat an enemy? It is not only useless, but terribly wrong, for by defining others out of the circle of those we are to love we do violence not only to God's Word, but also to His very nature. For the one essential reality that our faith affirms is that God is love and that, since all men are sinners, God's love must by its very nature encompass those who are His enemies.

And so this simple, familiar story challenges you and me today. God's command to love our neighbor is His call to imitate Him in His attitude toward our kind. When our path brings us to another human being in need, that person is our neighbor, and love will create within us a compassion that moves us to help.

At the Home of Mary and Martha (10:38-42). See the Word Studies of 10:39 and 10:42.

Jesus' Teaching on Prayer (11:1-13). See the Word Studies on Matt. 6:11 and Luke 11:7 and 11:8, the commentary on Matt. 7:7-12, and the parallel passage in Matt. 6:9-14.

Background. Prayer formed a rich tapestry in first-century Judaism. Along with the conviction that the simplest cry of the poor for help was a prayer that God would surely hear, there developed some of the most beautiful and complex expressions of praise to be found in any culture. Many of these are gathered in the

Siddur, the Jewish book of common prayer, which contains prayers for every day of the week and for Sabbath. Its contents include personal and congregational prayers, and prayers that fit every religious need and situation of the pious Jew.

While the first Siddur was compiled in the Rabbinic Academy of Sura in Babylonia, during the Byzantine Age, many of the prayer traditions go back well into the era of the second temple and reflect practice in the time of Christ. For instance, the Mishna records this difference between the first-century Rabbis Gamaliel and Aqiba over what is perhaps the most famous of the ancient prayers, the Eighteen Benedictions.

4.3 A. R. Gamaliel says, "Each day a man should pray the Eighteen."

B. R. Joshua says, "An abstract of the Eighteen."

C. R. Aqiba says, "If one's prayer is fluent he prays the Eighteen. But if not, an abstract of the Eighteen."

It is not surprising then that since prayer was so important in the life of Israel, the rabbis gave careful attention to defining rules and conditions under which it might be offered efficaciously. For instance, the Mishna also gives the views of the rabbis concerning what is to be done if a person makes a mistake in reciting one of the liturgical prayers during public worship.

We see this in Berakhot 5:3:

A. One who comes before the ark [in the synagogue, to recite the liturgy] and erred — let another go before [the ark] in his place.

B. And [the one designated as a replacement] may not decline at that time.

C. Whence does [the replacement] begin?

D. At the beginning of the blessing in which the [previous] one erred.

In a similar fashion, even the answers to private prayer were thought to depend on the facility [correctness] with which they were uttered. Thus Berakhot 5:5 in the Mishna says:

A. One who prays and errs — it is a bad sign for him.

B. And if he is a communal agent [who prays on behalf of the whole community], it is a bad sign for them that appointed him.

C. A man's agent is like himself.

D. They said concerning R. Haniniah b. Dosa, "When he would pray for the sick he

would say 'This one shall live' or 'That one shall die.' "

E. They said to him, "How do you know?"

F. He said to them, "If my prayer is fluent, then I know that it is accepted."

G. "But if not, I know that it is rejected."

In His Parable of the Good Samaritan Jesus cut through the clutter of rabbinic interpretations and reaffirmed the original simplicity of God's call to His people to love. Now, in His teaching on prayer, Jesus again challenges the approach to the religion of the Rabbis of His day and affirms a similar simplicity to the practice of prayer.

Interpretation. The passage has a single message. When a disciple asks Jesus to teach them to pray, our Lord gives them the spare, simple "Lord's Prayer" (11:1-4). Christ then uses two images to assure His followers that God not only hears but is eager to answer their prayers. It is as unthinkable that God would fail to answer their prayers as it is that anyone would fail in the duty of hospitality to a stranger (11:5-10; see the Word Study of Luke 11:8). And, it is as unthinkable that God would not give supplicants what is good as it is that a father would give a snake or a scorpion to a child who begged him for bread (11:11-13).

All this rests on one great truth. God is a Father to those who believe in Him. Prayer is an expression of our family relationship with Him. And the answers to prayer do not depend on whether or not one has made an error in reciting appropriate ritual words. Instead, answers to prayer are an overflow of that unfailing love which God has for us, His children.

This great reality gives us the key to understanding what we call the Lord's Prayer (11:2-4).

■ **Father.** We approach God as Father, deeply aware of His love and His commitment to us, even as we respect and love Him.

■ **Hallowed be Your name.** We exalt God, praising Him for who He is. We savor the privilege of approaching this One who is Lord of the Universe with our thanksgiving and praise.

■ **Your kingdom come.** We affirm our submission to God as ruler of a universal kingdom in which we are citizens. We commit ourselves to live here and now in obedience to the Lord, as though His kingdom were already established here on earth.

■ Give us each day our daily bread. We acknowledge our dependence on the Lord, and gladly place our entire trust in Him. We ask not today for enough to meet tomorrow's needs, for we know that God is Father to us, and we can rely fully on Him.

■ Forgive us our sins. We acknowledge our flaws and frailties, and depend not on any supposed merit in our works but on God's willingness to forgive us. We demonstrate this attitude by our willingness to treat others as we are treated by God, and thus "we also forgive everyone who sins against us."

■ And lead us not into temptation. As God does not tempt anyone to sin (James 1:13), the word must be understood here in the sense of "test." This request does not indicate doubt that God will enable us to overcome, but rather demonstrates faith. Some people are so uncertain in their relationship with God that they seek temptations to overcome, and so reassure themselves that they do belong to the Lord. God will permit us to undergo tests, and will provide a way to escape when He does (1 Cor. 10:13). Because we are confident this is true, we need not seek proof, but rather express our faith by asking the Lord not to lead us into temptation.

As we review this model prayer we sense more about the nature of prayer, and more about the relationship that makes prayer vital and real. There is trust in God as Father. There is worship and appreciation of God for who He by nature is. There is an expressed commitment to do His will, along with reliance on Him to meet our needs daily. And underlying it all is the wonderful awareness that God deals with us in grace; that forgiveness of sins assures us of His continuing favor and of access to Him when we are in need.

Application. Jesus' teaching on prayer is intended to strip away the false trappings of "religion" and remind us that what our faith provides is an intimate, personal relationship with God.

How terribly we err when we imagine all sorts of "conditions" we must meet before

God will hear or answer our prayer. We are His children and deeply loved by Him. If we remember this always, we will find release from that hesitancy and fear which plague so many. Many who would never imagine that salvation depends on works, somehow mistakenly suppose that answers to prayer do.

Jesus and Beelzebub (11:14-28). See the commentary on Mark 3:7-30 and the parallel passage in Matt. 12:22-50.

The Sign of Jonah (11:29-32). See the parallel passage in Matt. 12:38-42 and the Word Study of Luke 11:29.

The Lamp of the Body (11:33-36). See the word study of Luke 11:34.

Six Woes (11:37-54). See the commentary on Matt. 23 and the Word Study of Luke 11:52.

Background. The Parable of the Good Samaritan and Jesus' teaching on prayer exposed the fallacy of the contemporary rabbinic approach to the religion of the Old Testament. Yet the Pharisees, the most zealous practitioners of all the requirements of that tradition, clearly failed to see the implications of what Christ said.

We see this immediately as Luke moves on to describe another incident. Jesus is again eating with a Pharisee. Christ goes in and sits down to eat, but does not perform the ritual washing that tradition required. The Pharisee's failure to understand is expressed in his "surprise" at this "failure" of the now famous young rabbi.

At this point Jesus speaks bluntly, in clear condemnation of that tradition and those prescribed actions which the Pharisees viewed as commending them to God. They are "foolish people" (11:40). They carefully scrutinize externals, but ignore the greed and wickedness within their own hearts.

Interpretation. Jesus pronounces a series of "woes" against the Pharisees (11:42-44). These woes are pronounced because they faithfully followed their rituals. The problem is they neglect "justice and the love of God" (11:42), for they are not motivated by a concern for God but by a concern for status and public opinion. The comparison of the Pharisees to "unmarked graves, which men walk over without knowing it" (11:44) was perhaps

185

the ultimate insult. According to the OT merely touching the dead ritually defiled the individual, and disqualified him from worship or participation in the life of the community until such time as he or she had undergone purification. The Pharisees scrupulously avoided touching even a grave, lest they be subject to this contamination. Yet Jesus' words charge Pharisaism not only with distorting the worship of God, but also condemned the Pharisees as being so corrupt within that they actually defiled those who came in contact with them.

One of the "experts in the Law" who was at the meal realized that Jesus' condemnation of Pharisaism was an insult to the entire rabbinical tradition represented in rabbi and sage. Christ responded by making explicit His charges against this group as well (11:46–52).

The traditions in which the rabbis set such store were in fact unbearable burdens. What is more, the attitude of the religious leaders of Christ's day reflects the attitude of those who murdered the prophets. As Israel's recognized interpreters of Scripture, the source of all knowledge of God, the experts in the Law have actually taken that knowledge away from Israel. They do not use the key themselves, and their traditions and interpretations actually hinder those who are entering.

How tragic this all is. And how devastating was Christ's critique of the form of Judaism practiced in His day.

When that criticism was heard and at last fully understood, the Pharisees and experts in the Law "began to oppose Him fiercely" (11:53). Here we see a final confirmation of the accuracy of Jesus' assessment of these men and their approach to religion. Jesus spoke the truth to them, and rather than pause to evaluate themselves, they "fiercely" rejected His words and set themselves to oppose Him. Anyone can be wrong. But only a person who is open to God and others will be willing to judge himself, and if wrong, to repent.

Application. How do you and I respond when we are challenged about some dearly held belief or practice? If we react angrily, and refuse to engage in self-examination, we are just like those who cast themselves as Jesus' enemies so long ago.

Because we are as sure of God's love as we are of our own fallibility, we have the freedom to listen carefully and open our lives to the scrutiny of others and of our Lord. By opening ourselves in this way His Spirit can have free access to our hearts, and He will correct, cleanse, and lead us in the way we should go.

LUKE 12:4–16:31
Life's Illusions

EXPOSITION

We are now deep into a section of Luke which has few direct parallels in either of the other synoptics or in John. There are reflections of familiar themes, but even these are cast uniquely. Yet these chapters contain some of the most familiar of all the stories that Jesus told. Here we find the Parable of the Rich Fool and the Parable of the Great Banquet. Among the familiar images are those of a Lost Sheep, a Lost Coin, and a Prodigal Son. Here too we find the puzzling Parable of the Shrewd Manager and the striking Parable of the Rich Man and Lazarus, a beggar.

While story follows story, and one briefly described incident leads us quickly into yet another, common issues appear and reappear. All around us life presents attractive alternatives that vie for our commitment. Yet how many of these are illusions! The admiration of others is meaningless if to gain it we sacrifice the approval of God (12:1-12). Riches cannot meet life's greatest needs, or even release us from anxiety (12:13-34). The hedonistic individual who lives for the pleasures of the present moment fails to realize that human beings are placed here to serve God, and must give an account when Christ returns (12:35-59). One day every illusion will be stripped away; how great then is man's need to repent, and enter God's kingdom through the narrow door that contrasts so greatly with Broadway's brightly lit and seductive signs (13:1-35).

Yet there is hope. God invites all who will come to choose that way which leads, ultimately, to His banquet hall (14:1-24). His attitude toward us sinners is beautifully described in Jesus' pictures of the Lost Sheep, the Lost Coin, and the Prodigal Son, lost through his own willful abandonment of his father (15:1-32). With these stories Jesus returns to the theme with which He began: that of wealth.

Money has no value in itself, but only if it is used to prepare for our eternal future (16:1-18). It is eternity that counts. Measured by eternity, we realize that the beggar Lazarus was far more blessed than the rich man outside whose gate he lay (16:19-31). For perhaps the greatest illusion of all is time, and our foolish notion that what really counts is what happens to us today or tomorrow. Soon time itself will be set aside. We will step into eternity, and then at last we will grasp what is truly real.

WORD STUDIES

Be on your guard against the yeast of the Pharisees, which is *hypocrisy* (12:1). This familiar charge was often laid by Jesus against the Pharisees. The word "hypocrisy" comes from the theater and the masks of characters in a play that actors held in front of their faces. Here with the charge Jesus adds a special note of warning. "There is nothing concealed that will not be disclosed" (12:2). It may be possible to disguise motives and values now under a cloak of piety. But one day every mask will be torn away, and the real person exposed to every view.

"But he who disowns Me before men will be disowned before the angels of God" (12:9). The terms "acknowledge" (*homolgesei*) (12:8) and "disown" (*arnesetai*) are opposites. They contrast those who publicly identify themselves with Jesus with those who repudiate Him. The warning also contrasts two times: the present and the eschatological future. We must make our decision about Jesus today, for our choice determines our eternal future.

Then Jesus said to His disciples: "Therefore I tell you, *do not worry* about your life" (12:22). The command not to worry is addressed to the disciples, not to the crowd. "Worry" here is *merimnate*, a word which in classical Greek described a condition of being "raised up" or "suspended in air." It is a graphic image of a person who feels totally insecure. But Jesus' disciples are never left "up in the air." We may not know how our needs will be met, yet we are secure because we know that we are valuable to God.

This is the first of the "do not" words of warning and encouragement Jesus gives disciples here. The others? "Do not set your heart on" material things (12:29). "Do not worry" about them (12:29). And "do not be afraid" of the future (12:32).

Your Father has been pleased to give you the kingdom (12:32). Jesus reminds us that we have the kingdom; He does not simply promise that one day we will inherit it. In that age a "kingdom" was primarily understood not as a geographical or ethnic district, but by the primacy of its ruler. To live in God's present kingdom means to live daily in the awareness that God rules, and controls every circumstance in our lives.

What difference does it make for the believer to realize that he lives, now, in that kingdom in which God's will is supreme? Jesus suggests several implications. We will be freed from fear (12:32). And we will be freed to respond generously to those in need (12:33).

Jesus adds one more thought. Our attitude toward and use of money not only shows our confidence in God, but also where our heart is.

Be *dressed ready* for service (12:35). To be "dressed ready" to travel or work, a person in first-century Palestine wrapped a belt around his waist, and tucked in his long robe so it would not be in the way.

If we really are living in God's kingdom today, let's be about His work!

Do you think I came to bring peace on earth? No, I tell you, but *division* (12:51). The Greek word is *diamerismon,* to divide. All human beings belong to one class — sinners, who by nature are enemies of God. Then Jesus appeared, and humankind was given a choice.

The fact that family members are portrayed as divided against each other is significant, and underlines the fact that each person makes the decision for or against Christ by himself or herself. There is no way to avoid accepting this responsibility, for even refusal to choose is itself a choice.

Try hard to be *reconciled* to [your adversary] on the way [to the magistrate] (12:58). There is some debate over the meaning of the verb found here, *apellachthai,* the perfective passive infinite of *apallasso.* In Acts 19:12 the NIV translates the same verb as "left" in, "The evil spirits left them." Older versions render the phrase in Luke as "be quit of him," taking it as a legal phrase suggesting a final settlement of the dispute. J.B. Phillips has it, "Do your best to come to terms with him while you have the chance."

However the word is translated, the point of Jesus' story is clear. Each of us speeds through life toward God's judgment day. How important it is to make life's vital decision about Jesus before life ends.

Do you think that these Galileans were *worse sinners* than all the other Galileans because they suffered this way? (13:2) Jesus refers to one of those incidents in which the brutal Pilate ordered the murder of Galileans suspected of rebellion, and another incident in which 18 perished "accidentally" when a stone tower collapsed on them (13:4). Ordinary folks would have assumed there was no difference between the judicial murder and the "accident": each of these deaths was viewed as a divine judgment, and thus proof that the person killed had sinned.

Jesus contradicts this popular view in order to drive His point home. Their guilt was no greater than anyone living in Jerusalem! How vital then that each person repent, for all who fail to repent will perish.

For *three years* now I've been coming to look for fruit (13:6). According to Lev. 19:23 three years had to pass before a fig tree's fruit was ritually "clean," and could be eaten. Thus the landowner had planted the tree some *six* years before. Every indication was that the tree was permanently barren.

The problem is that fig trees drain the land of extremely large amounts of minerals, thus starving other plants. It was only prudent for the landowner to order the removal of a useless tree that depleted the land without providing any return.

Jesus' illustration reflects an interesting folk tale that had been already told for centuries. "My son," a father once said to his son, "you are like a tree which yielded no fruit, although it stood by the water, and its owner was forced to cut it down. And it said to him, 'Transplant me, and if even then I bear no fruit, cut me down.' But its owner said to it, 'When you stood by the water you bore no fruit, how then will you bear fruit if you stand in another place?'"

How striking then that Jesus changes this familiar story, and has the gardener say, "Leave it alone for one more year, and I'll dig around it and fertilize it" (13:8).

The use of vine and tree imagery in such OT passages as Isa. 5:1-7 makes Christ's meaning plain. God has sentenced unfruitful

188

Israel, yet in grace He has done far more than anyone had a right to expect. If His people fail to respond now, they must surely be cut down (cf. Paul's use of similar imagery in Rom. 11:11-24).

Leave this place and *go somewhere else* (13:31). Commentators debate whether the Pharisees who urged Jesus to go somewhere else were sincerely concerned for His safety, or tired of being "humiliated" (13:17) and simply intent on being rid of the embarrassment. There may very well have been some danger from Herod, who not long before had executed John the Baptist. But Herod was certainly not a "clear and present" threat to Jesus' well-being.

How like the Pharisees' reaction to Jesus is that of many in our society. One can hardly turn the radio dial without hearing the name of Jesus. Yet how quickly most people turn on past, hoping to ignore Christ's demand for a decision about relationship with God. Hoping He will simply "go somewhere else" and leave them alone.

But they remained *silent* (14:4). Luke often reports questions that the Pharisees and "experts in the Law" asked Jesus. Here he has Jesus asking them a question.

There is a significant difference. Those who questioned Jesus sought to elicit His opinion, usually in order to evaluate or criticize it. But "experts in the Law" identifies those who were accepted authorities in the interpretation of the OT. In fact, they claimed to "sit in Moses' seat" (cf. Word Study of Matt. 23:2); that is, they claimed the right to make judgments about the Law which were then binding on their fellow Jews. Thus when Jesus asks a question, He is asking for a ruling from those who claimed that right in all matters of faith and practice.

So the phrase "but they remained silent" is significant. Rather than risk further humiliation (13:17) these proud rulers of God's people chose to abdicate the role they so haughtily claimed (Matt. 21:23-27). Even though by remaining silent they revealed the emptiness of their claim.

They may invite you back and so you will be *repaid* (14:12). This concept is not new with Jesus. Proverbs 19:17 says, "He who is kind to the poor lends to the Lord, and He will reward him for what he has done." Jesus is attending a dinner at the house of a Pharisee, sitting with the Pharisee's friends. His remark draws attention to the fact that despite their strict adherence to ritual, the social practices of the Pharisees revealed that they are more concerned with the good opinion of their equals than the good opinion of God.

Then the master told his servant, "Go out to the roads and country lanes and *make them come in*" (14:23). Much theological debate has been stimulated by this phrase, which in older versions reads "compel them to come in." Does the verse imply human beings have no free will—does it teach "irresistible grace"?

The answer is, there are no theological implications here at all! Instead, the parable is rooted in the etiquette of first-century Jewish society, and the phrase's power depends on understanding those customs. For instance, it was customary not only to invite intended banquet guests well ahead of time, but also to send a subsequent invitation to inform them that the banquet was ready. For the invited guests to offer excuses at the time of the final invitation was a great insult to the host. Thus Jesus' listeners would expect the host to be angry.

His hearers would also have understood what Jesus meant when He told of seeking guests in the streets (*plateri*) and alleys (*rhyme*). The former were well traveled paths where a wide variety of persons might be found. The latter were narrow paths between the homes of the poor. There the host's servants would find the lower classes and outcasts of society.

But what then about the command to "make them" come to the festive meal? In that region it is considered polite to appear reluctant when urged to accept another's hospitality. The sincere host will continue to urge the person who has been invited. This enhances the host's reputation for hospitality, and enhances the guest's status by displaying the host's desire for his company. So the host's command meant, simply and surprisingly, "Servants, treat the poor and the outcasts as honored guests, and show them respect by urging them to accept my hospitality."

This parable was spoken while Jesus shared a meal at the Pharisee's house, just after exhorting the Pharisees to invite the poor and crippled who cannot repay, rather than to invite their social equals who will invite them in return. But the parable does have theological implications. The people of Israel were the guests long ago invited to God's eschatological banquet. But when the banquet was ready, when the Messiah appeared and extended the final invitation, the invited guests refused to attend!

What then will God do? He will go out into the streets and alleys of the world, and He will extend to the Gentiles that same honor which He extended to Israel when He invited them. And God will treat these despised people with respect.

How wonderfully gracious our God is. We do not deserve His invitation, yet He not only extends it, but He honors us by letting us know that we are precious objects of His love!

In the same way, any of you who does not give up everything he has cannot be My disciple (14:33). The Greek word here is *apotassetai*. It means "say farewell" when used of a person or "renounce" when applied to things. Note that Jesus does not say "sell" or "give away" but renounce. His point is that as disciples of Jesus, we surrender to Him the title deed to all we possess. From now on we live as those conscious that we are stewards of our Lord, and that all we have belongs ultimately to Him.

There was a rich man whose *manager* was accused of wasting his possessions (16:1). The manager was an *oikonomos*, an agent, responsible for the management of funds or property. In this case the *oikonomos* learned his accounts were about to be audited—and his dishonesty discovered.

The story has puzzled many, for Jesus commends this dishonest man for "shrewdly" rewriting contracts with several of his master's debtors. The solution is that Jesus did not commend the guilty steward for his dishonesty, but for the steward's realization that money is not an end in itself, and his readiness to sacrifice it to prepare for his future. Some have made this lesson even more pointed by suggesting that in rewriting the contracts, the manager did not defraud his master, but rather reduced the debt only by excessive interest charges he had intended to keep for himself.

The application of this parable to us is simple and direct. We are to value "worldly wealth" (16:9) only as something to be used in God's service, and not for itself. Jesus drove His point home by stating that we must view worldly wealth in this way, for either the love of money will drive out love for God as the central motivation in our life, or love for God will drive out love for money.

What is highly valued among men is *detestable* in God's sight (16:15). The Greek term here is extremely strong: *bdelugma*, "abominable." The word expresses the meaning of the Hebrew *siqqus*, a word always linked with idolatry and immoral practices in the OT. It in fact represents the most wicked of religious sins!

What was Jesus saying then? When the Pharisees heard Jesus apply His story about the Shrewd Manager and warn against the love of money, they sneered at Him. For they "loved money," and yet loudly proclaimed their love for God. In saying that a love for money is "detestable" Jesus accused the Pharisees of the most hateful of religious crimes—idolatry—and of all the corruption that the OT associates with that sin.

Luke records much that Jesus had to say about money. Yet here we have the most damning words of all. Worldly wealth, if seen as a means we can use to the end of serving God, is morally neutral. But if we value worldly wealth for itself, we become idolaters, and wealth turns our hearts away from the Lord.

THE PASSAGE IN DEPTH

Warnings and Encouragement (12:1-12). See the Word Study of Luke 12:1 and 12:9, and the commentary on Mark 3:20-30.

The Parable of the Rich Fool (12:13-21). *Background.* In NT times rabbis served as judges to settle all sorts of civil disputes. Since in the popular mind Jesus was Himself an expert in the Law, it is not surprising that a man in the crowds might call on Him to pass judgment on an older brother who was illegally withholding the one-third share of an inheritance the two received when their father died.

Jesus refuses to become involved in this dispute, but rather comments on the motivation of those who care so much for money that they are unwilling to do what is right.

Interpretation. The story, at face value, is simple, yet like all of Christ's illustrations it is also profound. Jesus tells of a wealthy farmer whose lands produced plentiful crops. The complacent farmer contemplates a future made secure by the abundance of his possessions—and orders new barns constructed to hold the overflow.

Then Jesus portrays God, observing it all, saying to the rich farmer, "You fool!" (12:20)

It is important to understand that the word "fool" here has little relationship to "foolish." Foolishness is a result of ignorance or a senseless act. But the biblical term in both Testaments has a moral dimension. Here *aphron* is used in an OT sense, to portray one who has rejected God and His precepts as life's guiding principles.

What principles has the rich fool violated? He has focused all his attention on this life rather than on the eschatological future. And he has selfishly concentrated on personal gain rather than on serving God.

Application. Christ's point is stated clearly in 12:15, "A man's life does not consist in the abundance of His possessions."

The rich farmer would never have been able to consume all the food and drink he had stored up for future years, even if he had lived to be very old. Greed drove him because he refused to adopt God's perspective on what life is all about. We are just as "foolish" when we permit a desire to pile up possessions to control our lives. The meaning of life cannot be found in possessions—we must not simply "believe" that, we must live this way.

Do Not Worry (12:22-34). See the commentary on Matt. 6:25-34.

Watchfulness (12:35-48). See the commentary on Matt. 24:36–25:46.

Not Peace, but Division (12:49-53). See the Word Study on Luke 12:51, above.

Interpreting the Times (12:54-59). See the parallel passage in Matt. 16:1-4.

Repent or Perish (13:1-9). See the Word Studies on Luke 13:2 and 13:7, above.

A Crippled Woman Healed on the Sabbath (13:10-17). See the commentary on Matt. 12:1-14.

The Parables of the Mustard Seed and the Yeast (13:18-21). See the parallel passage in Matt. 13:31-35.

The Narrow Door (13:22-30). See also Matt. 7:13-14.

Jesus' Sorrow for Jerusalem (13:31-35). See also Matt. 23:37-39.

Jesus at the Pharisee's House (14:1-14). See the Word Study of 14:4 and 14:12 above.

The Parable of the Great Banquet (14:15-24). See the Word Study and discussion of Luke 14:23, above.

The Cost of Being a Disciple (14:25-35). See the Word Study of Luke 14:33, above.

Three Parables: the Lost Sheep (15:1-7), the Lost Coin (15:8-10), and the Lost Son (15:11-32). See also Matt. 18:10-14.

Background. These three familiar parables told by Jesus constitute a single response to some Pharisees and teachers of the Law who reproach Jesus because He "welcomes sinners and eats with them" (15:2). Together they portray God's attitude toward sinners—an attitude in stark contrast to that displayed by Jesus' critics.

To understand each, we need to realize the great value of each "lost" object to its owner— a value Jesus' hearers would have immediately perceived.

■ **The Lost Sheep.** Sheep were an important economic asset. Most clothing worn by ordinary people in Israel was made of wool. The skins of sheep were tanned and used as leather. Sheep were also the most desirable of sacrificial animals, and their meat was served at the feasts and banquets which infrequently brightened the life of the average person.

While shepherds in the first century had a typically low social status, all were familiar with the care with which a good shepherd

191

guarded his flock. At night a shepherd carefully counted his sheep to make sure none was missing. If one was, he would not leave the others alone, but would find another person to watch them for him. Yet Jesus pictures this shepherd hurriedly leaving his flock to find the one sheep that was lost. Somehow the shepherd felt a terrible urgency, and when he found the sheep, he picked it up in his arms and brought it back to the fold rejoicing.

■ **The Lost Coin.** Most commentators assume that this lost coin was part of the woman's dowry. In biblical times such coins were attached to a headband and worn even at night. These were particularly important to the woman, for they symbolized her personal rights and independence.

The Revell Bible Dictionary explains the custom reflected here:

> In the Middle East a man was expected to make a gift to his bride's father (Ex. 22:17). Such compensation to the father was not always paid in money. Jacob worked for seven years in order to marry Laban's daughter Rachel (Gen. 29:18). . . .
>
> Yet it would be a mistake to conclude that women were merely property to be purchased. The bride was also given gifts by her father, which she brought into the marriage. But these remained hers if there should be a divorce. . . .
>
> In NT times the gifts given the bride by her father often took the form of coins, with holes drilled in them so they could be worn on a string or headdress. It is likely that the woman in Jesus' parable who was distraught when she lost one of the ten silver coins was so upset because the coins were her dowry (Luke 15:8-10).

But why was she so distraught? Because bringing her dowry into the marriage symbolized her partnership in the relationship, setting her apart from slave or servant, and giving her the dignity of a personhood she enjoyed apart from her identity as her husband's wife.

The fact that she had only ten coins suggests that she and her husband were poor. But her frantic search reflects the fact that it was far more precious to her for its symbolic than monetary value.

Once again we see that Jesus with a simple parable has made it perfectly clear to His listeners that the lost truly are precious to God.

■ **The Lost Son.** Jesus now relates a story which shifts its focus from the preciousness of what was lost to the deep concern and love for us felt by God. Christ's listeners would need no special setting to convince them that a man's son is precious to him; everyone viewed children and especially sons as gifts from God.

The first story emphasized the helplessness of the lost, for sheep are notably prone to go astray and once lost, typically lie down in hopeless confusion. The second story emphasizes the preciousness of the lost, and draws a vivid picture of the frantic search undertaken by the woman who lost the coin. The third story emphasizes the love of the father, who cares deeply for his son, even though the boy abandoned his home and family and spent his inheritance in immoral and profligate living. Taken together the stories represent a single answer to the Pharisees' condemnation of Jesus' involvement with sinners. Human beings like sheep tend to become lost. Yet because human beings are precious to God, God will actively search for the lost. And, because God is the loving Father, He will surely welcome anyone who repents and returns to Him.

Interpretation. The message of the stories is unmistakably clear, and an appropriate refutation of the criticism of the Pharisees. Their theology made small place for the penitent, but God deeply loves the lost and actively seeks them.

While the third story emphasizes the forgiving love of the Father, it also makes another point. The prodigal son had an older brother. Jewish law decreed that the older brother would receive two-thirds of the father's estate, and the younger son one-third. According to custom the property could be distributed either by a will upon the father's death, or as a gift made during the father's lifetime. If land is passed to the next generation, the younger son would receive title to his third, but could not dispose of the land until his father's death. Apparently this son asked for his share in cash, intending to leave the area and seek his fortune, perhaps in one of the great trade centers of the East.

The father grants the son's request, and the young man hurries away from home. But he is both young and foolish, and spends his inheritance in the pursuit of sinful pleasures. Only when everything is spent and the boy is destitute does he "come to himself" and choose to return to his father.

Note the difference in this parable. In each of the others the owner actively and frantically searched for the sheep and the coin that were lost. But the father in the parable does not search: he waits at home, patiently looking down the road, looking eagerly for the slightest sign that his son is returning. What is the reason for this difference? The sheep and coin are not persons, but objects. But the lost son is a person, and as such he must make the choice to return. The father loves him intensely, but he will not force his son to return to him. The father respects the right of his son to choose.

There is one more fascinating aspect to this story. When the prodigal son returns, the focus shifts to his older brother. Jesus shows the father and the servants filled with joy at the younger son's return. Yet the older son is bitter and jealous. He is completely indifferent to the welfare of the brother for whom his father cares as deeply as the father cares for him. Just so, the Pharisees and teachers of the Law revealed a hostile indifference to the "sinners" that Jesus came to seek and to save.

Application. The message of each parable is utterly clear: God cares for the lost. While like the prodigal son's father the Lord waits for the lost to come to their senses and return to Him, there is no question at all about the welcome a returning sinner will receive.

The concluding criticism of the elder brother reminds us that you and I are to model our attitude toward others on God's. We are to seek them as lost sheep, and care about them as intently as the woman cared about the dowry coin that affirmed her significance as a person. And we are to be as willing to rejoice over the repentant as the Father in Jesus' story was to welcome His returning son.

The Parable of the Shrewd Manager (16:1-18). See the Word Study of Luke 16:1 and 16:15.

The Rich Man and Lazarus (16:19-31).

Background. The NIV note on v. 23 reminds us that while the text pictures the rich man in "hell," the Greek word is "Hades." In NT times "Hades" (Heb. *sheol*) was a general term for the place/state of the dead as they awaited final judgment. Popular opinion held that the righteous rested in Gan Eden, while the wicked observed from Gehinnom. In contrast to Jesus' story, which portrays Abraham compassionately addressing the tormented rich man as "son," in Jewish legend the righteous rejoice as they observe the suffering of the wicked.

Edersheim reports a Jewish legend that is a close parallel with this story of Jesus. Two wicked companions died. One died penitent, the other did not. When the man in Gehinnom saw the blessedness of his friend, and was told it was because of his friend's penitence, he begged for the opportunity to repent too. The answer came, this life is the eve of the Sabbath. (On the eve of the Sabbath the pious Jew prepared the food he would eat the next day, so he would not have to "work" on the holy day and thus violate it. The point is that one must prepare for eternity while he or she lives, for afterward there is no chance for change.)

The Parable of the Rich Man and Lazarus reflects contemporary Jewish views of the afterlife in other ways as well. Not only was Hades thought to be divided into two compartments, popular belief held that conversations could be held between persons in Gan Eden and Gehinnom. Jewish writings also picture the first as a verdant land with sweet waters welling up from numerous springs, while Gehinnom is not only a parched land, but the waters of the river that separate it from Gan Eden recede whenever the desperately thirsty wicked kneel and try to drink.

These roots in the popular theology of first-century Judaism help us answer a difficult question about the story. Is Jesus' story a parable or, as some have argued, is Jesus describing the literal fate of two actual persons who were known to His original audience? Those who adopt the second view see the story as a confirmation by Christ of the details of the popular theology concerning the afterlife. Those who see the story as a parable agree that it teaches personal, self-conscious existence after death, but argue (correctly) that it is not appropriate to build a theology of the nature of the afterlife on this story.

Why then do some classify this story as "true" rather than as a parable? In part because

Jesus does not introduce the story as a parable. In part because in other stories Jesus does not use a specific name, as He does here in identifying the destitute beggar as "Lazarus." This last argument, however, is weak in view of the fact that "Lazarus" was a common abbreviation for Elazar, which in the Hebrew means "God is his help," or "God help him!" In Christ's story God was the beggar's only source of help, for the rich man was certainly not going to do a single thing for Him!

Overall, then, it is best to take this story as a parable, and to focus our interpretation and application on the lesson Jesus intended to drive home to those who heard it from His lips.

Interpretation. It is important to see this parable of Jesus as a continuation of His conflict with the Pharisees over riches. Christ has said, "You cannot serve God and Money" (16:13). When the Pharisees sneered, Jesus responded, "What is highly valued among men is detestable in God's sight" (16:15).

There's no doubt that the Pharisees remained unconvinced, and continued to smirk and ridicule the young prophet whose poverty was as apparent as His idealism. And so Christ told a story intended to underline the importance of what He had just said.

The Pharisees had ridiculed Jesus when He warned that God detests what men value. Jesus responds with a story which contrasts the experience of a wealthy and a destitute Jew—during this life and after it.

During this life the wealthy man would surely have been featured on the 1980s TV program, "Lifestyles of the Rich and Famous." The cameras would have focused on his marble mansion with its decorative wrought iron gates, his silks—a fabric which in the first century was worth its weight in gold—and the fabulous feasts he held for his important friends.

As the TV equipment was taken into the rich man's home, a cameraman might have stumbled over the dying beggar, destitute and abandoned just outside the rich man's house. But no one would have interviewed or photographed him. Surely he was beneath the notice of the homeowner, who never gave a thought to the starving man just outside, though all Lazarus yearned for was just a crumb from the overladen tables.

If we look only at this life, the rich man seems to be both blessed and fortunate, and the poor man, rejected and cursed. There is no question which state people would highly value, and which they would find detestable.

But then, Jesus says, both men died. And suddenly their situations are reversed! Lazarus is by "Abraham's side," a phrase which pictures him reclining in the place of honor at a banquet that symbolizes eternal blessedness. But the rich man finds himself in torment, separated from the place of blessing by a "great chasm" (16:26). Even though he begs for just one drop of water, Abraham sadly shakes his head. No relief is possible—or appropriate! In life the rich man "received your good things" while Lazarus "received bad things" (16:25).

There is a subtle but very real note of judgment here. The rich man had received his good things, and had used them selfishly for his benefit alone. Despite frequent injunctions in the OT for the rich to share their good things with the poor, this rich man's indifference to Lazarus showed how far his heart was from God and how far his path had strayed from God's ways. They were his riches, and he would use them only for himself. Ah, how well the rich man depicts those Pharisees who "loved money" and who even then were sneering at Jesus!

And so Jesus' first point is driven home. You Pharisees simply cannot love God and Money. Love for Money is detestable to God, for you will surely be driven to make choices in life which are hateful to Him. A love of money may serve you well in this life. But in the world to come, you will surely pay.

But Jesus does not stop here. He portrays the rich man as appealing to Abraham to send Lazarus to warn his brothers, who live as selfishly as he did. Again Abraham refuses. They have "Moses and the Prophets" (16:31), that is, the Scriptures. If they do not heed the Scriptures they will not respond should one come back from the dead. While this statement surely foreshadows Christ's resurrection and the religious leaders' response to that great miracle, Christ's point must not be lost. The Word of God is a sufficient revelation to call men to belief and commitment.

In essence then Christ makes a stunning charge: the hardness and unwillingness of the Pharisees and teachers of the Law to respond to Jesus' words reflect a hardness to the Word of God itself, which these men pretend to honor.

Application. This life is "the eve of the Sabbath." It is a time for us to prepare for eternity. This entire chapter calls us to realize that if we take this reality seriously, it will affect the way we view and use money, and the way we respond to the poor and the oppressed.

LUKE 17:1–19:44
Only Believe

EXPOSITION

Luke has made it clear to his readers: every individual who meets Jesus Christ must make a decision about Him. Christ must be received or rejected. His claims must be denied or believed. With this established, Luke now moves on to explore something of the nature of faith in this Man who has presented Himself to Israel as Messiah, and to all as Savior.

A fascinating story reminds Jesus' disciples that, to those who do believe, the issue shifts from "faith" to obedience (17:1-10). What is more, a faith which truly makes a person whole is characterized by a continuing relationship with God expressed in gratitude and praise (17:11-19). One day God will intervene directly and visibly in human affairs; until then there is a hidden kingdom of God which is experienced through our relationship with Christ (17:20-37). What enables this kind of faith is our realization that God does respond to those who appeal to Him (18:1-8), and that He relates to sinners in mercy (18:9-14), as any adult would relate to a helpless babe (18:15-17). When a rich ruler asks what he must "do" to inherit eternal life, Christ's response shows how impossible a works-based relationship with God is (18:18-30). Then Jesus predicts His death—the means through which God will win salvation for us all (18:31-34). Christ's response to a blind beggar again underlines the fact that those who approach God must do so in the conviction that God is merciful and able, and trust only in Him.

But how will trust in God be expressed? Luke returns to a theme that runs throughout his Gospel—money. One who believes will demonstrate his commitment ,expressed financially, as illustrated by the "chief tax collector" Zacchaeus (19:1-10). That same theme is seen in the Parable of the Ten Minas (19:11-27). One committed to God will faithfully use his or her resources for the Master's benefit.

And now Luke brings us to the gates of Jerusalem itself. There crowds, gathered for the Passover festival, enthusiastically hail Jesus as "the king who comes in the name of the Lord" (19:28-44). Although commonly called the "Triumphal Entry," Luke is deeply aware that the cheering multitudes have no real faith in or commitment to Jesus. They cheer because they expect Him to serve them by establishing Messiah's kingdom. Soon the same crowds will jeer as Jesus is led to the cross. In contrast, a true faith in God is expressed in our willingness to serve Him, and so promote a kingdom of God which has not come visibly (17:20), but which to us is vital and real.

WORD STUDIES

It would be better for him to be thrown into the sea with a millstone tied around his neck than for him to cause one of these *little ones* to sin (17:2). As in the parallel passage in Matt. 18:1-6, Jesus refers to adult believers as "little ones." The millstone was the heavy top stone turned, typically by an ox, when grinding grain. From Luke 16:4 on Jesus was addressing the Pharisees, but these words are addressed to His disciples. They underline the importance of the instruction on forgiveness about to be given. Only a life of mutual repentance and forgiveness can protect the believing community from "things that cause people to sin" (17:1).

If your brother sins, *rebuke* him, and if he repents, forgive him (17:3). The word here is *epitimeson*. The verb *epitimeo* occurs 29 times in the NT and indicates a strong reproof or stern warning. In essence Jesus here lays on us the obligation to care enough to confront.

We Christians tend to be sloppy in our thinking about forgiveness. Too many of us mistake "overlook" or "ignore" for "forgive." Forgiveness is an essential element in a process of reconciliation which Jesus defines here. That process can be diagrammed: Sin — Rebuke — Repentance — Forgiveness. Forgiveness can bring reconciliation only when it is part of this total process.

Strikingly, the believer who observes or is the victim of another's sin has two obligations, while the sinner has one. The first obligation the observer has is to rebuke. The only obligation the sinner has is to repent. When he or she does repent, then the observer has a second obligation — to forgive.

Let's not burden ourselves or others with guilt by demanding "forgiveness" when there is no evidence of repentance on the part of the guilty. Forgiveness simply cannot operate in this circumstance. But, let us not excuse ourselves for failing to forgive if we have been unwilling to confront and rebuke.

Then He said to him, "Rise and go; your faith has *made you well*" (17:19). The word here is *sesoken,* a word which expresses complete healing. There is an interesting contrast here with the earlier word, *ekatharisthesan,* "cleansed" (17:14, 17), which is not as sweeping a term.

We can assume, as all 10 lepers did as Jesus said, and set out to show themselves to the priest before they were actually healed, that all had faith. Note that they were cleansed "as they went" (17:14).

Yet only one returned to express praise and gratitude. Only one sought a continuing relationship with Jesus expressed by gratitude and praise.

Faith in Christ as Savior is enough to cleanse you and me of our sins. But for that complete healing which Christ offers we must return to Him and build a continuing relationship in which we gratefully offer Him our praise.

The kingdom of God does not come [*visibly*] with your careful observation . . . because the kingdom of God is *within you* (17:20-21). The NIV translation is unfortunate in both these phrases. "Come visibly" is *meta paratereseos,* "with observation." The most likely meaning here is that the kingdom's coming cannot be observed or predicted from visible signs. It is a secret kingdom, although one day God will burst unexpectedly into history (cf. commentary on Matt. 6).

"Within you" is *entos hymon,* "among you." How true this was! The ruler of God's kingdom, Jesus Himself, stood at that moment among His critics. Intent on seeking visible signs, they recognized neither King nor kingdom, and thus were surely doomed.

"*Where, Lord?*" they asked (17:37). The Pharisees had asked "when" the kingdom was coming, not realizing that Christ the King stood among them (17:20). After hearing Jesus speak of the "day that the Son of man is revealed" (17:30), the disciples ask, "Where?" The obtuse answer means, "The place of slaughter." The disciples would have understood this as a reference to OT prophecy concerning history's end: the "where" is the Holy Land itself, destined to be overrun by God's enemies, who will then be destroyed by God Himself.

When Jesus heard this, He said to him, "You still lack one thing. *Sell everything* you have and give to the poor" (18:22). Earlier (14:33) Christ called on every disciple to "give up," *apotassetai* (surrender personal rights to) their possessions. Here the same word is used. But it has a different meaning, for Jesus tells this particular individual to not only give up his rights to his wealth but to distribute it to the poor.

Why? This particular wealthy individual thought to merit a place in God's kingdom by the benevolence he admittedly showed in his treatment of others. His very "goodness" masked a reality which Christ's command exposed. In fact the wealthy ruler's choice to keep his possessions rather than to obey and follow Jesus revealed he had unknowingly violated the very first commandment in the Decalogue: to love God with his whole being.

How easily we deceive ourselves! How important to realize that the essential nature of sin is to put self first rather than God.

It is easier for a camel to go through the eye of a needle than for a rich man to enter the kingdom of God (18:25). Some have assumed the image is of a camel going through a narrow, low "needle gate" in the wall of Jerusalem. However, the term used here, *belone,* is a medical term for a surgical needle rather than the ordinary term for needle, *rhaphis* (Matt. 19:24; Mark 10:25). The

clear implication is that Jesus has in mind the literal eye of a needle. The point then is to emphasize the impossibility of the rich entering God's kingdom.

The saying stunned the disciples, who assumed that the rich were both blessed by God, and had the advantage of being able to do good deeds and so gain merit with God. While the Jews were aware that a love for wealth could be detrimental, the notion that wealth was in itself dangerous was foreign. And the notion that a truly generous and benevolent young man could be harmed by his wealth was unthinkable.

BEN SIRA ON WEALTH (11:14-26)
Good and evil, life and death,
    poverty and riches, are from the Lord.
The Lord's gift remains with the just;
    His favor brings lasting success. . . .
My son, hold fast to your duty,
    busy yourself with it,
    grow old doing your task.
Marvel not how sinners live,
    but trust in the Lord and wait for
    His light
For it is easy, as the Lord sees it,
    suddenly, in an instant,
    to make the poor man rich.

Because you have been trustworthy in a *very small matter*, take charge of ten cities (19:17). The word *elachistos* is a superlative: "a very small," "the very least" thing. Jesus is not saying that the servant's dedication to his master was unimportant, but rather that compared to the reward, the ten minas (three months wages) were truly insignificant.

How foolish we are if we deem material possessions important. Compared to the rewards that await those who dedicate what they have to Christ's service, the wealth of the whole world is insignificant.

THE PASSAGE IN DEPTH

Sin, Faith, and Duty (17:1-10). See the Word Studies on Luke 17:2 and 17:3, above.

Background. The word translated "servant" in Jesus' story is *doulos*, a slave, or bond-servant. Paul frequently refers to himself as a bond-servant or slave of Jesus (Rom. 1:1, NASB) to emphasize a fact displayed in this

story reported by Luke. The believer who owns Jesus as Lord voluntarily surrenders his or her own will in order to serve Jesus and do the will of God. This is in fact the defining nature of slavery as understood in biblical times. The servant no longer lives for himself, but lives to serve his or her master.

It is also important to realize that a servant's status in the ancient world hinged somewhat on the identity of his master and the closeness of the servant to his master. Many of the most important bureaucrats in the Roman Empire were slaves. Their closeness to the Emperor and role as his agents made them powerful and influential men. Other slaves achieved renown and even riches for outstanding ability as scholars, physicians, and teachers.

We must not, then, assume that the slave in Jesus' illustration is demeaned by his role in life. Instead, we need to focus on the nature of slavery itself, as a state in which the slave is dedicated to doing the will of his master.

Interpretation. While some commentators have called this passage "disjointed," there is in fact a clear and distinct argument. Jesus warns disciples against "things that cause people to sin" (17:1-2), and immediately emphasizes the importance of rebuke, repentance, and forgiveness. This pattern must become so much a part of the lifestyle of the believing community that even repeated sins and repeated repentance will not staunch the flow of forgiving love (17:3-4). Here, as in Matt. 18, the purity of that community of faith which is made up of God's little ones can be maintained only by living together conscious of our weaknesses and willingness to forgive.

The disciples are daunted by what Jesus has said and beg Him, "Increase our faith!" (17:5) In essence they say, "Lord, to do what You've said we need more faith!"

The thought behind the rest of this passage is often missed as commentators focus on the image of faith casting a mulberry tree (or mountain) into the sea (17:6). In fact, Christ's remark about the mulberry tree, along with the story of the servant (17:7-10), is intended to dismiss the disciple's plea for greater faith.

What does Jesus say? He talks about a servant who works in the field, comes in, and then prepares his master's meal. Is the servant to be thanked when he has done everything required? Not at all. In fact, the servant does not even expect thanks, for he has simply done his duty. Jesus concludes, "So you also, when you have done everything you were told to do, should say, 'We are unworthy servants; we have only done our duty' " (17:10).

One commentator suggests that the word translated "unworthy" probably would be *batiley,* "idle," in Aramaic. In the East hired servants are not employed to work a specific number of hours a day, but rather are expected to be available to their masters at all times, day or night. The servant who tells his master that he is "idle" displays a positive attitude, for he is simply saying, "I am ready to do more."

How then does the passage fit together? Jesus, whom the disciples affirmed as their Lord, had not asked them if they felt like confronting and forgiving. He had commanded them to do so. Their request for more faith was thus inappropriate! Faith might be suitable for moving mulberry trees. But faith is not the issue when Jesus utters a command. Then the sole issue is: will Jesus' servants obey?

What disciples are to do when Jesus says "forgive" is say, "Yes, Lord, and what else can we do"!

Application. All too often we use our "lack of faith" as an excuse. "If only I had more faith, I'd speak out at work." "If only I had more faith, I'd give what I believe God wants me to give." "If only I had more faith, I'd go to this person who has hurt me."

All such excuses duplicate the mistake Jesus' disciples made so long ago. They misunderstand the role of faith in the Christian's life. And they avoid the responsibility of the person who does believe to say, "Yes, Lord," and obey.

Faith is important in the Christian life.

But faith is no substitute for obedience.

Each of us needs to carefully examine his or her life and become aware that the real issue in many a Christian's life is not that he fails to believe, but that he fails to obey.

Ten Healed Lepers (17:11-19). See the Word Study of Luke 17:19, above.

The Coming of the Kingdom of God (17:20-37). See the Word Study of Luke 17:20-21 and 17:37, and the parallel passages in Matt. 24 and Mark 13.

The Parable of the Persistent Widow (18:1-8).

Background. This parable and the story of the Pharisee and Tax Collector which follows it focus our attention on the character of God. Faith is not something which we generate by screwing up our eyes and concentrating completely on "believing." Instead, faith is our response to God as He reveals Himself to us. Thus it is appropriate for Luke to include in these stories which explore the nature of belief in God two which remind us just who it is that invites us to trust Him.

Interpretation. The Parable of the Unjust Judge teaches about God by contrast. The argument is: if a human judge with no compassion or concern for what is right responded to the widow's plea (because not to respond in that society would appear to be a blot on his character), how much more can we expect God, who does have compassion and cares about what is right, to respond to us when we cry out in our need.

Verse 5 is the key to interpreting this story. In the NIV it reads, "yet because this widow keeps bothering me, I will see that she gets justice, so that she won't eventually wear me out with her coming!"

This is another of those few incidents where the NIV translation is regrettable. Edersheim translated the Hebrew "eventually wear me out" much more literally, and argues that it means "lest in the end she bruise me," and indicates the judge was afraid the angry widow would eventually attack him physically. It is true that the Greek *hypopiaze me* does literally mean "strike under the eye." But it is much better to understand this as a metaphor. In fact, we have a similar metaphor in our culture, and we all understand "to give someone a black eye" means to damage a person's reputation. The judge seems to be saying that if the persistent widow keeps on confronting him at every street corner and crying out for justice, soon people will wonder why he has not acted on her behalf. And so, even though the unjust judge feared neither God nor man, he did care about his reputation. And so finally he acted to grant the tenacious widow's request.

Now Jesus draws an inescapable conclusion. If a dishonest judge, who respects neither God nor his fellowman, cares so much about his reputation, how can anyone imagine that God, who is committed to compassion and to justice, would not care about His reputation? How could anyone imagine that God would not see to it that His chosen one receive justice, and quickly?

God's reputation is precious to Him, and His very commitment to doing right for His own makes it certain that He will hear and

answer our prayers.

Why then the description of His chosen ones as those who "cry out to Him day and night"? (18:7) Not to encourage us to be persistent, but to describe the sense of urgency that drives us to Him with our requests. In essence Jesus is saying that when your sense of need is so overwhelming that you are driven to God day and night, you can be assured He will answer, and quickly.

What then about the concluding remark: "However, when the Son of Man comes, will He find faith on the earth?" (18:8) suggests a negative answer. Despite God's clear revelation of His character, and the faith that this stimulates in God's chosen ones, most remain blind to the character of God and live devoid of faith.

Application. The story invites us to review our own images of God. Do we see Him, as Christ knew the Father, as the God of compassion and the God committed to doing justice? Do we see Him as the One whose very reputation rests on His readiness to fulfill His obligations to His chosen ones?

If we understand God in this way, we will approach Him freely in prayer, and we will approach Him confidently. We will know, and not simply "believe," that our God hears and will surely answer us when we cry out to Him with our deepest needs.

The Parable of the Pharisee and the Tax Collector (18:9-14).

Background. This parable continues the theme introduced in the story of the Unjust Judge. How are we to understand God, and how are we to relate to Him?

To understand this parable, and the truly shocking impact it must have had on Jesus' first-century listeners, we must understand something of the religious attitudes and beliefs of the time.

The basic attitude is underlined in another prayer that dates from the first century A.D.: a prayer recorded in the Talmud [b. Ber.28b].

I thank thee, O Lord, my God, that thou hast given me my lot with those who sit in the seat of learning, and not with those who sit at the street-corners; for I am early to work, and they are early to work; I am early to work on the words of the Torah, and they are early to work on things of no moment. I weary myself, and they weary themselves; I weary myself and profit thereby, while they weary themselves to no profit. I run and they run; I run towards the life of the Age to Come, and they run toward the pit of destruction.

In this prayer, as in the Pharisee's prayer in our text, the worshiper compares himself with others, and finds great satisfaction in the way of life that he has chosen. Each thanks God, and thus credits the Lord for the favored role in life that is his. Neither would change places with those he looks down on, for each is convinced that his way will surely win life in "the Age to come."

It is important to realize that all of Jesus' listeners would agree with the Pharisee and with the Talmud's anonymous worshiper. Those who committed themselves to study and keep the Law, and who were rigorous in performing their religious duties, were surely candidates for eternal blessing. Their works commended them to God, and their dedication would surely win His favor.

It is also important to remember that the tax collector was classified by society as a whole, just as he was viewed by the Pharisee—as a fit companion only for rogues, swindlers, and adulterers. Interestingly, Jewish tax collectors had no civil rights; they could not even testify before a rabbinical court.

Today we can scarcely imagine the impact of Jesus' pronouncement that the tax collector returned from the temple justified before God, while the Pharisee did not. There is no doubt that in every listener's mind one question was uppermost: How can this be?

Interpretation. Luke answers that question when he introduces Jesus' parable. Christ's words were addressed to "some who were confident of their own righteousness and looked down on everybody else" (18:9). Many of Jesus' listeners evaluated their spiritual condition by comparing themselves with other human beings. By this measure, some of us do look pretty good!

The problem is, other human beings are not the yardstick by which God measures righteousness. You or I, at two inches tall on the morality yardstick, may seem vastly superior to others who measure only a quarter or a half inch in moral height. But if only we were to look to God, we would realize that com-

pared to His infinite moral height, the best of us falls immeasurably short.

The Pharisee's prayer, the Talmud's first-century parallel, and most rabbinic literature, make it clear that the religious leaders of Israel had in fact fallen into this spiritual trap. Like the Pharisee, they "were confident of their own righteousness."

We can pinpoint this basic misunderstanding in another way as well. The Pharisee takes pride in being able to say, "I fast twice a week and give a tenth of all I get" (18:12). Old Testament law established only one day a year on which the pious Jew was to fast—the day of atonement (Lev. 16:29). The Pharisee went far beyond what was required, and fasted twice a week! Similarly, OT law commanded that tithes be paid by a landholder on whatever his land produced. The Pharisee tithed what he purchased, unwilling to risk eating food on which God's tithe had not been paid. In this too he went far beyond what the Law required. Surely a person who not only kept the requirements of the Law, but did even more than the Law prescribed, must be justified by God and welcomed by Him in the age to come.

Thus Jesus' description of the Pharisee portrayed an individual every listener immediately recognized, and admired!

His description of the tax collector was also easily recognizable. No one would expect a tax collector to enter the temple confidently. Aware of his many failings, such a person "surely stood at a distance" (18:13). Normally the worshiping Israelite lifted up his hands when praying (Ps. 28:2; 63:4). Instead he beat his breast, a symbolic act expressing grief and guilt, and uttered only one word of appeal: "God, have mercy on me, a sinner" (18:13).

After these brief, yet vivid descriptions of two representative human beings, Jesus gave His verdict. The tax collector went home justified; the Pharisee did not.

It may be that no single story so clearly puts the Gospel in perspective. The basic message of Jesus' life, death, and resurrection is that God has chosen to have mercy on sinners who appeal to Him for mercy. Yet who is it that is ready to put his relationship with God on such a basis? Only the individual who realizes that he is a sinner, lost and hopeless, with absolutely no basis on which to commend himself to God. The problem with the Pharisee, who represents all those who are "confident of their own righteousness," is that the very "righteousness" of all such people blinds them to their spiritual bankruptcy. And, because they rely on their works rather than on God's mercy, the end result is that they are lost.

Application. The Christian is called to do good works as an expression of gratitude to God. Works are a response to mercy received. How tragic that the perspective of many is so warped that they neither see God as merciful, nor themselves as spiritually destitute.

Little Children and Jesus (18:15-17). See the parallel passages in Matt. 19:13-15 and Mark 10:13-16.

The Rich Ruler (18:18-30). See the Word Study of Luke 18:22, above, and the Word Studies of Matt. 19:21 and 19:24. See also the commentary on Mark 10:17-31.

Jesus Again Predicts His Death (18:31-34). See the commentary on Luke 18:31-45 and the parallel passage in Mark 10:32-45.

A Blind Beggar Receives His Sight (18:35-43). See the parallel passage in Matt. 20:29-34 and the commentary on Mark 10:46-52.

Zacchaeus the Tax Collector (19:1-10).
Background. Zacchaeus is identified by Luke as an *architelones,* a "chief tax collector." In the Roman system the right to collect taxes was sold to men who bid for the privilege. These men then hired others to do the actual work, and at each level of this operation, profit depended on how much the local population could be overcharged. Since the collection of taxes was enforced by the Roman army, the purchase of a tax concession was in effect a license to steal. In Jewish territory, where many believed intensely that only God had a right to tax His people, tax collectors were despised and hated. The hatred was even more intense because it was Jews who manned the system and some, who like Zacchaeus were high up in the system, became very rich.

Stambaugh and Balch, in *The New Testament in its Social Environment,* report that the major fixed taxes in the era of Augustus were the *tributum soli* and the *tributum capitis.* The first was a tax on property, which was assessed in Syria/Palestine at the rate of 1 percent a year. The second was a head tax on adults, set at one denarius a year. In Syria/Palestine this applied to every person between the ages of 14 and 65.

But the most painful taxes may have been collected in the form of customs duties set at about 2½ percent. These were collected at the borders of provinces and districts, and additional taxes might be collected at the juncture of major highways. At the gates of cities even produce or firewood was taxed, supposedly to collect Augustus' 1-percent sales tax.

While these taxes seem low to us, we must remember two things. Most of the land was owned by the state, the king, or large land owners, so the average person paid some 40 percent of his income in rents. In addition a head tax and tithe were owed to God, and paid to the temple. And the local ruler, one of Herod's offspring in our period of study, also collected his due. Taken together all these expenses laid an unimaginably heavy burden on the average working man, and help to further explain the hostility toward men like Zacchaeus.

Jericho, where Jesus met Zacchaeus, was a frontier city between the provinces of Judah and Perea. As chief tax collector he admittedly became wealthy by overcharging at least some of those whose taxes he collected (19:8). So we can perhaps understand why Zacchaeus was unable to push through the crowds to find a spot where he could see Jesus. He was not only short but, recognizing him, the people were undoubtedly unwilling to part to let him through.

Interpretation. In the story of Zacchaeus, Luke draws together a number of familiar themes. Zacchaeus, another in a long line of social outcasts and sinners, responds to Jesus while the religious leaders do not. Jesus chooses to identify Himself with this "sinner" by eating with him, exposing Himself to severe criticism. And Christ explains, using a familiar saying which has been called the key verse of this Gospel: "The Son of Man came to seek and to save what was lost" (19:10).

Yet there is another theme here which is emphasized again and again in Luke. A person's spiritual condition will be indicated by his attitude toward and use of possessions. Thus the announcement of Zacchaeus that he will give half of all he has and repay anyone he has defrauded fourfold is solid evidence that Jesus is correct in saying, "Today salvation has come to this house" (19:9). Old Testament law did specify restitution. The general principle was to make restitution and add 20 percent (Lev. 5:16; Num. 5:7). However, the Law required a thief to pay back double (Ex. 22:4, 7, 9). In promising to repay those he had defrauded fourfold, Zacchaeus is doing far more than the Law requires.

Zacchaeus' salvation is explained by Jesus in the saying, "This man, too, is a son of Abraham" (19:9). Like Abraham, Zacchaeus has responded to God's voice with faith, and so demonstrated that he is in that spiritual, rather than simply physical, line. The converted tax collector's sudden generosity is not the basis of his salvation, but rather is the chief indicator that he truly has been saved.

Application. The story of Zacchaeus is the final story in a series of sayings and parables concerning wealth. It stands in contrast with the story of the rich ruler (18:18-30), who when commanded to sell his possessions and follow Jesus, made his choice and so demonstrated that his money was more important to him than his God. Unlike him, Zacchaeus has chosen to follow Jesus, and suddenly his possessions are no longer important. His heart overflows, and he unhesitatingly commits himself to give half of all he has to the poor, and to use the rest to repay those he has cheated.

How fascinating it would be if we applied the yardstick Luke suggests to measure our own commitment to the Lord. What would this admittedly major indicator of spirituality in Luke tell us about our own relationship with Jesus?

While it would not be appropriate for the church to apply this yardstick to every member, it is appropriate for every one of us to use this yardstick to reevaluate ourselves and our own way of life. As Christ's Parable of the Shrewd Manager (16:1-15) reminds us, we can use our material possessions to prepare for eternity. Any other use of wealth is essentially meaningless. And if we permit Money to become our master, the desire for wealth will surely draw our hearts away from the Lord.

The Parable of the Ten Minas (19:11-27).
See the parallel passage in Matt. 25:14-30, and the Word Study of Luke 19:17.

Background. In the East nobles and rulers of the smaller districts into which provinces were often subdivided received no salary. With the population already heavily burdened by taxes (see the background to the Zacchaeus story, above), many engaged in business, but only indirectly. Since it would be demeaning for a nobleman to buy and sell himself, such persons worked through servants or stewards. The money might be loaned to merchants, or used to buy sheep in the country for resale at a profit in the city, or invested in trading ventures, etc.

In this parable the amount entrusted to stewards is only a few minas, a very small amount of money equivalent to about three month's wages for an ordinary laborer. In setting this amount Jesus makes sure we realize that it is not the sum that is significant, but the faithfulness of the servant in using what he has for his master's benefit.

Interpretation. Luke's introduction of this parable makes it clear that the parable is significant on several levels. Luke tells us that it was "while they were listening" (19:11) to what Christ said about Zacchaeus that Jesus told this story. Thus the story picks up the theme of wealth, and adds further commentary.

Jesus also spoke of a "man of noble birth" who "went to a distant country to have himself appointed king and then to return" (19:12). Every listener would have been very familiar with the trip of Archelaus, a son of Herod the Great, to Rome in order to gain the Emperor's permission for him to reign over part of his father's domain as a client-king of Rome. Although a delegation of Jews hurried to Rome to oppose his request, it was granted, and Herod was confirmed, not as king, but as tetrarch.

The analogy helps us understand this parable on another level. Jesus has presented himself to the Jews as Messiah. But soon He will be killed at the instigation of the leaders of His own people. What then will happen to the kingdom the OT prophets predicted Messiah will rule?

The answer is that Jesus will travel to the courts of the Emperor of the Universe, His own Father. There He will be confirmed as King, despite the opposition of the Jews, and when He returns He will reign.

What then are Jesus' servants to do while their master is away? The parable makes it clear. We are to use every resource which He has committed to us, no matter how insignificant our resources may appear to be, in His service. When He returns He will reward us, far beyond what we might expect for the "very small matter" (19:17) in which we have been engaged.

Application. Matthew takes two chapters (24–25) to develop concepts Luke establishes by reporting this parable of Jesus. And in doing so he not only urges us to "watch," but encourages our hearts as well.

How often the thing we find we can do for our Lord is a "very small matter." How insignificant we often feel our opportunities and even ourselves to be. Yet to Jesus each "very small matter" is important indeed, and faithfulness will win us rewards far out of proportion to what we have been able to do.

Perhaps most important is the reminder that Jesus will return. And He will return as King, confirmed in this role by God the Father, and ready at last to execute that royal authority which is His by right. The return of Christ and the kingdom He will establish then is, and must become to us, far more real than the transitory world in which you and I live today. When Christ and His coming kingdom are truly real to us, we will serve Him with our whole heart.

The Triumphal Entry (19:28-44). See the Word Studies on Matt. 21:5, 9-10, and the parallel passages in Matt. 21:1-11, 14-16; Mark 11:1-11; and John 12:12-29.

Background. Jesus' entry into the city was a fulfillment of prophecy: Israel's King came to the city "gentle and riding a donkey, on a colt, the foal of a donkey" (Matt. 21:5; Zech. 9:9).

Each of the Gospels sketches the familiar scene, the ecstatic crowds and delighted shouts of welcome. But as the story of the next few days continues, we realize how much of the acclaim was due to men and women being caught up in the thrill of the moment with no underlying commitment to Jesus at all.

Luke concludes his account even before Jesus enters the city. He makes it very clear that Christ Himself knows how little the cheers of the crowds mean. And so as Christ approaches He pauses to weep over the city and its people. Enemies will soon encircle and destroy the holy city, causing its people unmatched suffering, "because you did not recognize the time of God's coming to you" (19:44).

Today we as Christ's people are privileged to present Him to a doomed world. May our generation prove wiser than those in first-century Jerusalem, and recognize in the Gospel the time of God's coming to them.

LUKE 19:45–24:53
The Price

EXPOSITION

Like the writers of the other Gospels, Luke now describes in great detail the last few hours of Jesus' life. As incident follows incident, we sense again that the suffering and death of Jesus Christ were historical events — events on which time and eternity hinge.

While the events reported in each Gospel are essentially the same, each writer selects and emphasizes those details which help him develop his own particular themes. Matthew pays special attention to human frailty, reflected in his study of the plot against Jesus, of Judas' betrayal of his Lord, and in Peter's denial. Mark provides the bare-bones structure of key events. Luke highlights the sufferings that Jesus underwent. John focuses on Christ's trials before the Sanhedrin and before Pilate. Each of these areas is developed in "The Passage in Depth" section of its respective Gospel.

The major last-week events discussed in the Gospels are indicated on the chart below. Verses in boldface indicate where each topic is most carefully explored. In addition, a listing of every last-week event, with cross references, is found in The Passage in Depth for Matt. 26–27. Christ's "seven words from the cross" are discussed in the study of Mark 14–16.

Topic	Matthew	Mark	Luke	John
The plot against Jesus	**26:1-5**	14:1-11	22:1-6	
Anointing at Bethany	26:6-13	**14:3-9**		
Judas agrees to betray Christ	**26:14-16**			
The Last Supper	**26:17-30**	14:12-25	22:14-23	**13–17**
Peter's denial predicted	**26:31-35**	14:27-31	22:31-38	13:31-38
Gethsemane	26:36-46	14:32-42	**22:39-46**	
Jesus' arrest	**26:47-56**	14:43-52	22:47-53	**18:1-12**
Before the Sanhedrin	26:57-68	14:53-65	22:63-71	18:12-40
Peter denies Jesus	**26:69-75**	14:66-72	22:54-62	18:17-27
Judas hangs himself	**27:1-10**			
Jesus before Pilate	27:11-26	15:1-15	23:1-25	**18:28–19:16**
The soldiers mock Jesus	27:27-31	15:16-20		
The crucifixion	27:32-56	**15:21-41**	**23:26-49**	19:17-37
Jesus' burial	27:57-61	15:42-47	23:50-56	19:38-42
Guard placed at the tomb	**27:62-66**			

WORD STUDIES

I will send my son, *whom I love;* perhaps they will respect him (20:13). The Greek *agapeton* had a technical meaning in the ancient Near East. It identified the person so indicated as the primary heir, and may serve as a synonym for *monogenes,* "one and only" (John 3:16), "only begotten" (KJV).

God not only gave us His best, He gave all He had to give in the person of His beloved Son, Jesus Christ.

Some of the teachers of the law responded, "*Well said, teacher!*" (20:39) It may appear from this remark either that not all of the experts in the Law were hostile to Christ, or that His clever argument from Exodus 3:6 won even His enemies' grudging admiration.

There is, of course, another possibility. Mark tells us that the "Pharisees and Herodians" had tried to trip Jesus up with their famous question about taxes (12:13-17). And that the Sadducees then posed the hypothetical case of multiple Leverite marriages, intended to ridicule the notion of resurrection (12:18-27). Christ's response answered their riddle completely and silenced them, which would have delighted the Pharisees against whom this same trick question had been used again and again. It is most likely that the words "Well said!" slipped from the mouths of teachers associated with the Pharisee party, who despite their hostility to Jesus were delighted to see their traditional opponents put down.

How fascinating that people who are willing to use Jesus for their ends are totally unwilling to submit themselves to serve His purposes. Even though serving Him means winning an eternal reward.

While all the *people* were listening, Jesus said to His disciples (20:45). Luke is the only one of the Gospel writers to draw a careful and consistent distinction between the response of several different groups to Jesus. Like the others he portrays disciples who were committed to Christ as Lord. He also precisely portrays the spiritual leaders (teachers of the Law, experts in the Law, rabbis) and the members of the religious parties who were so hostile toward Christ's teaching. But Luke goes on to add two other terms which he also uses very precisely. These are "the people" (*laoi*), whom Luke describes as responsive to Jesus (21:38), and who hear Him with some delight or approval, and "the crowds" (*ochloi*) who were not responsive to Him. When we read either of these phrases in Luke's Gospel we are to understand that "the people" indicates a large group that to some extent at least approves of Christ, and that "the crowds" indicates a large group which does not approve of Him.

Ultimately, of course, humankind must be divided into two groups: those who believe, and those who do not. The claims of Christ require we not simply approve of what Jesus says, but fully commit ourselves to Him as Lord.

Watch out that you are not *deceived*. For many will come in My name, claiming, "I am He" (21:8). The Greek word *planethete* was commonly used in the NT and early Christian church to describe the efforts of false prophets and heretics. Nothing is to draw our eyes away from Jesus and the promise of His return during the long interim between Christ's departure and His return.

This extended passage in Luke 21 is notable for nine separate exhortations, which are intended to guide us as we wait for Jesus' Second Coming. These are:

(1) Don't be deceived by false teachers (21:8).

(2) Don't be frightened by disasters that are similar to those predicted to take place at history's end (21:9-11).

(3) Don't be anxious when subjected to legal action because of your witness to Christ (21:12-15).

(4) Do stand firm when betrayed by those dearest to you and when hated by all (21:16-19).

(5) Do stay away from Jerusalem when you see the city under siege by enemy armies (21:20-24).

(6) Do be encouraged when the events associated with final judgment begin to take place (21:25-28).

(7) Do recognize them as evidence that God's eschatological kingdom is about to appear (21:29-31).

(8) Do have confidence that during this time of tribulation Christ's words remain sure (21:32-34).

(9) Do watch and pray, during the interim and during the dreadful time of the end, so that when Christ comes you may win His endorsement for your faithfulness (21:35-38).

While only the first four have direct application to believers today, the others remind us that during any time of difficulty we are to remain positive and hopeful in our faith.

Then *Satan* entered Judas (22:3). Luke alone reports Satan's role in the betrayal of Jesus. This simple verse supports two important observations. A person who holds back in his or her commitment to Jesus becomes vulnerable to hostile spiritual influences. And, Satan is not as powerful or wise as some fearfully suppose. Satan would hardly have participated actively in his own defeat at Calvary, unless he had supposed that causing Christ's death would defeat rather than accomplish God's purposes.

Let's always remember that God is able to so order His universe that even acts intended to harm Him or His own actually accomplish His good purposes. How foolish we are to fear Satan or our human enemies.

I have *eagerly desired* to eat this Passover with you before I suffer (22:15). This phrase, and the unusual grammatical structure in the original of Christ's words "I will not eat" (22:16) and "I will not drink" (22:18) indicate strong emotion and intense feeling. While like the other Gospel writers Luke does not provide the kind of gory crucifixion detail we might expect from modern TV or news reporters, Luke is particularly sensitive to the stress Jesus was under and the emotions which surge under the surface.

Also a *dispute* arose among them as to which of them was considered to be greatest (22:24). Luke contrasts the intensity of Jesus' feelings with the insensitivity of the disciples, who continue a running dispute which the other Gospel writers place in other settings as well.

As we read in the account each writer is so careful to provide of the passion of Christ, let's set aside our personal concerns, and consider all that Jesus suffered for you and me.

The kings of the Gentiles lord it over them: and those who exercise authority over them *call themselves Benefactors* (22:25). In the first century *euergetes,* "benefactor," was a title rather than a description. This is appropriately indicated by the capital "B" in the NIV. But what is interesting is the verb *kalountai,* "call themselves." Ancient rulers, who unmercifully exploited their citizens, wanted the name of Benefactor without the cost of truly serving others.

How different Jesus is! And how different you and I, servants of others for Christ's sake, are called to be.

He said to them, "But now if you have a purse, take it, and also a bag; and if you don't have a *sword,* sell your cloak and buy one" (22:36). This is one of the most surprising sayings in Scripture, for it seems to contradict earlier instructions that Christ gave to His disciples as they set out on preaching missions (9:1-3; 10:1-3). The question this raises is important. Are we to follow the earlier guidelines, or is this normative for us during the Church Age?

The larger context makes it clear that no reversal of the earlier principle is implied. Christ reminds His disciples that God had earlier supplied all their needs (22:35). He shrugs off the statement of the disciples, who obviously took Him literally, when they say they already have two swords (22:36). And later, when Peter drew a weapon to defend Christ from the mob that had come to arrest Him, Christ not only said, "No more of this!"

but even restored the man whose ear Peter had cut off (22:51).

But if this seemingly clear instruction to the disciples does not mean what it seems to say, what did Jesus mean? The best answer seems to be suggested by the strong contrast expressed in the phrase, *alla nun,* "but now" (22:36). In the present emergency, and the interim between Christ's death and resurrection, the disciples would need to fend for themselves.

But what of the reference to a sword? We must remember that Hebrew and Aramaic are picture languages, tongues in which mountains stand for strength, towers stand for security, and the sword for times of intense danger and crisis. To "buy a sword" may well be a literal instruction in some contexts. In this context it is intended symbolically, as a warning of imminent catastrophe.

The Lord turned and *looked straight* at Peter (22:61). This phrase represents a single Greek word, *emblepto.* The word makes it clear that this was more than a glance, and certainly not a glare. Instead Jesus focused a look of love and concern on Peter—a look that reached that faithful disciple's heart and broke it. That look, directed toward Peter at the very moment of the disciple's denial, told Peter that despite what he had done Jesus still cared and remained concerned about him.

How wonderful if you and I, at the moment of our greatest failure, could sense the Savior's loving gaze on us. How quickly our hearts too would break, and we would return to Him in cleansing, grateful tears.

They all asked, "Are you then the Son of God?" He replied, "You are right in *saying I am*" (22:70). The Greek phrase is literally, "You say that I am." The NIV adds "are right" because the reaction of the counsel makes it clear they understood the phrase as a clear affirmation of deity.

How tragic the scene. How many say Jesus is the Son of God, but in their hearts do not really believe. What counts is not saying Jesus is the Son of God. What counts is committing ourselves totally to Him in the absolute conviction that these words are true.

Father, forgive them, *for they do not know* what they are doing (23:34). The "they" here are the Roman soldiers, for their ignorance of the significance of their act was real and perhaps excusable. Both the OT and the NT view most spiritual ignorance as inexcusable. The *Zondervan Expository Dictionary of Bible Words* explains:

> The problem in spiritual ignorance is a misunderstanding that comes from a wrong perception of available data. Jesus' listeners heard what He told them, but could not understand its meaning for them (Mark 9:32; Luke 9:45). Ignorance lies at the core of pagan worship (Acts 13:27) and explains the failure of all the lost to realize that it is God's kindness only, designed to lead them to repentance, that delays God's judgment (Rom. 2:14).

What is the Bible's antidote to an ignorance that comes from failure to perceive spiritual realities? Romans 12:2 says, "Be transformed by the renewing of your mind" (*nous,* the mind as the organ of perception). It is by listening to God's will expressed in His Word and putting that will into practice that we will have a totally new outlook on life's issues. But inner transformation requires both a grasp of what the Word says and an obedient response to the Word. Only by a commitment to obedience to God can our ignorance be replaced by firm knowledge.

Christ's prayer surely has been answered. God stands ready to forgive, despite the distorted way in which we have perceived Him and His Son. We must, however, abandon the way we have viewed Jesus, acknowledge Him as the Son of God, and trust ourselves to Him. Then our ignorance will be replaced by knowledge, and we will experience the forgiveness of our loving God.

The centurion, seeing what had happened, praised God and said, "Surely this was a *righteous man*" (23:47). The other Gospels report that he also expressed the belief that Jesus was "Son of God" (Matt. 27:54; Mark 15:39). Why did Luke use this expression instead of the other? Most likely because the Hellenistic audience for whom he wrote might have assumed that the centurion was using the expression "son of God" in its pagan rather than Christian sense. At the same time by reporting the phrase a "righteous man" Luke maintained a basic emphasis of his Gospel: that Jesus represents not only God in the flesh, but also ideal humanity.

***Remember* how He told you, when He was still with you (24:6).** There may be an implied rebuke in this statement. Most importantly, there is the reminder that from the beginning Jesus was aware of the suffering as well as the triumph that lay before Him. Just before we look in depth at the sufferings of Christ, let's read His prophetic words.

■ Luke 9:22. "The Son of Man must suffer many things and be rejected by the elders, chief priests and teachers of the law, and He must be killed and on the third day be raised to life."

■ Luke 18:31-33: "We are going up to Jerusalem, and everything that is written by the prophets about the Son of Man will be fulfilled. He will be handed over to the Gentiles. They will mock Him, insult Him, spit upon Him, flog Him and kill Him. On the third day He will rise again."

THE PASSAGE IN DEPTH

Any exploration of the sufferings of Christ must reflect an awareness that Jesus suffered as a man and as the Son of God. His suffering as a man involved a vulnerability to both physical and psychological torment—a vulnerability which we share. His suffering as Son of God was, however, unique, involving a mystery which we may dimly sense but are not competent to fully comprehend. We need to examine each of these aspects of Jesus' suffering and death separately, yet always aware that He was and is the God/Man, truly God and yet fully human, so that the various aspects of His final torment cannot actually be isolated from each other.

Truly, as we visit Christ's last hours, we tread softly and with awe.

THE PSYCHOLOGICAL TORMENT
Throughout His years of ministry Jesus suf-

fered psychologically. John tells us, "He came to that which was His own, but His own did not receive Him" (John 1:11). The crowds flocked to hear Jesus and viewed Him as a prophet (Matt. 16:14). But they were unwilling to accept Him for who He truly was, their long-awaited Messiah and Son of God. The religious leaders frowned on His teachings, and finally recognizing Him as a threat to their pretense of spiritual authority, plotted to kill Him. And even those disciples who were fully committed to Him remained insensitive to His pain and unaware of the meaning of His most significant teachings.

You and I know something of the raw misery of being rejected. We know something of the pain that comes when no other human being seems to care how we feel, and yet demand that we be sensitive to their hurts. We know something of the ache of that loneliness which strikes in moments when we realize that no other human being really understands us.

All this pain was Christ's constant companion as He ministered among us, the Son of God, unacknowledged and unrecognized by those who were by Creation and Covenant His own.

All this constant, inner pain is focused and exposed for us in an incident each of the synoptic Gospels portrays—Christ's prayer at Gethsemane. (Note: Matthew's and Mark's accounts are essentially the same. Matthew's and Luke's words are reproduced in the box on this page.)

We note particularly the words in boldface, and realize that each in the original represents overwhelmingly powerful emotion. That anguish which Christ knew throughout His years of ministry is suddenly exposed, as even His iron control is broken in the stress of that terrible hour.

CHRIST'S ANGUISH AT GETHSEMANE

Matthew 26:36-41/Mark 14:32

Then Jesus went with His disciples to a place called Gethsemane, and He said to them, "Sit here while I go over there and pray." He took Peter and the two sons of Zebedee along with Him, and He began to be **sorrowful** and **troubled.** Then He said to them, "My soul is **overwhelmed with sorrow** to the point of death. Stay here and keep watch with Me."

Going a little farther, He fell with His face to the ground and prayed, "My Father, if it is possible, may this cup be taken from Me. Yet not as I will, but as You will."

Then He returned to His disciples and found them sleeping. "Could you men not keep watch with Me for one hour?" He asked Peter. "Watch and pray so that you will not fall into temptation. The spirit is willing but the body is weak."

Luke 22:39-47

Jesus went out as usual to the Mount of Olives, and His disciples followed Him. On reaching the place, He said to them, "Pray that you will not fall into temptation." He withdrew about a stone's throw beyond them, knelt down and prayed, "Father, if You are willing, take this cup from Me; yet not My will, but Yours be done." An angel from heaven appeared to Him and strengthened Him. And being **in anguish,** He prayed more earnestly, and His **sweat was like drops of blood** falling to the ground.

As the Jewish court had no authority to condemn Christ to death, Jesus was taken before the Roman governor, Pilate. After Pilate had reluctantly condemned Jesus, He was subjected to even more serious abuse.

Mark 15:16-20 takes us into the garrison courtyard, and describes the cruel sport He was subjected to by the soldiers.

The soldiers led Jesus away into the palace (that is, the Praetorium) and called together the whole company of soldiers.

They put a purple robe on Him, then twisted together a crown of thorns and set it on Him. And they began to call out to Him, "Hail, King of the Jews!" Again and again they struck Him on the head with a staff and spit on Him. Falling on their knees, they paid homage to Him. And when they had mocked Him, they took off the purple robe and put His own clothes on Him. Then they led Him out to crucify Him.

Matthew adds to this report a vitally significant detail. He says, "He [Pilate] had Jesus flogged, and handed Him over to be crucified" (27:26). The whip that the soldiers used to prepare a victim for crucifixion was called a flagellum. It was composed of a number of strips of leather, into which pieces of bone, lead, or glass had been woven. The person to be flogged was tied to a post and struck repeatedly with this terrible instrument. As the flesh was ripped and torn, bone was often exposed, and blood flowed copiously. Flogging alone killed many. As a preparation for crucifixion, it was intended to weaken the victim so that his hours or days suspended from the cross would be even more excruciatingly painful.

Beaten, flogged, and ridiculed, Christ was then forced to hoist the wooden crossbeam on His torn shoulders. Staggering under its weight and the intolerable pain, Jesus was herded along the narrow streets and out of the city to the public execution grounds.

Now we come to the ultimate physical horror. For this is how ancient peoples universally viewed this means of execution. It was, in fact, considered so terrible that it was reserved for slaves, brigands, and rebels against the imperial power and was never to be used on a Roman citizen.

What was so terrible about the cross? And how did it kill? The victim was tied or nailed to a cross bar that was set atop or nailed to a pole fixed in the ground. A report published in the September 1985 issue of the *Biblical Archeologist* (pp. 190-91) provides this description in a discussion of the remains of part of a first-century Jewish man who, like Jesus, was executed by crucifixion.

It is important to remember that death by crucifixion was not caused by the traumatic injury of nailing; rather, hanging from the cross resulted in a painful process of asphyxiation, in which the two sets of muscles used for breathing—the intercostal muscles and the diaphragm—became progressively weakened. In time, the victim expired as a consequence of the inability to continue breathing properly.

The feet of the condemned man were nailed laterally to the upright piece of the cross, so that he straddled it. . . . When the feet were nailed to the cross, an olive wood plaque was put between the head of each nail and the foot, probably to prevent the condemned from pulling free of the nail.

Again and again Jesus must have pulled Himself up in order to gasp just one more breath, straining against the pain in His nail-pierced hands and feet. Even though weakened and in anguish, the victim might live on for days until the loss of blood and intense pain made it impossible to lurch up for even one more breath, and the victim died of suffocation or cardiac arrest.

THE SPIRITUAL TORMENT

As terrible as the physical suffering was, it did not compare with the spiritual anguish that Jesus experienced. That anguish is foreshadowed in several Old Testament passages. Psalm 22, long acknowledged as messianic, powerfully expresses Christ's feelings: "My God, My God, why have You forsaken Me? Why are You so far from saving Me, so far from the words of My groaning? O My God, I cry out by day, but You do not answer, by night, and am not silent" (22:1-2).

Not only do these words describe Christ's experience, Christ shouted them out as He hung suspended that dark day: "My God, My God, why have You forsaken Me?" (Matt. 27:46) This is indeed the ultimate mystery. How could it be that in this awesome moment the Godhead itself was torn apart, Son separated from Father, and spiritual death experienced by He who is the source of eternal life?

Whatever we may say about the physical sufferings of Christ, we must realize that they pale in comparison to the spiritual. The union of God with man made it possible for the theanthropic person to die, and thus Paul writes in Colossians that "[God] has reconciled you by Christ's physical body through death to present you holy in His sight" (Col. 1:22). Commenting, the *Zondervan Expository Dictionary of Bible Words* notes:

> In view of the varied and terrible meanings that Scripture ascribes to death, it would be wrong to think of Jesus' death as a mere biological event. When the Bible teaches that Jesus suffered death and tasted death (Heb. 2:9), a full experience of all that death involves is implied. That this extends even to the awful separation from God that tears the heart of the godly is revealed in Jesus' cry from the cross: "My God, My God, why have You forsaken Me?" (Matt. 27:46)

In the anguish of the moment the cry of "Why?" was torn from Christ's lips. Yet from eternity past the reason why was known by Father, Son, and Holy Spirit. The why is expressed throughout the New Testament in words like these:

> Therefore, just as sin entered the world through one man, and death through sin, and in this way death came to all men, because all sinned—for before the law was given, sin was in the world. But sin is not taken into account when there is no law. Nevertheless, death reigned from the time of Adam to the time of Moses, even over those who did not sin by breaking a command, as did Adam, who was a pattern of the One to come.
>
> But the gift is not like the trespass. For if the many died by the trespass of the one man, how much more did God's grace and the gift that came by the grace of the one Man, Jesus Christ, overflow to the many! Again, the gift of God is not like the result of the one man's sin: The judgment followed one sin and brought condemnation, but the gift followed many trespasses and brought justification. For if, by the trespass of the one man, death reigned through that one man, how much more will those who receive God's abundant provision of grace and of the gift of righteousness reign in life through the one Man, Jesus Christ.
>
> Consequently, just as the result of one trespass was condemnation for all men, so also the result of one act of righteousness

was justification that brings life for all men. For just as through the disobedience of the one man many were made sinners, so also through the obedience of the one Man the many will be made righteous (Rom. 5:12-21).

> But we see Jesus, who was made a little lower than the angels, now crowned with glory and honor because He suffered death, so that by the grace of God He might taste death for everyone. . . . Since the children have flesh and blood, He too shared in their humanity so that by His death He might destroy him who holds the power of death—that is, the devil—and free those who all their lives were held in slavery by their fear of death (Heb. 2:9, 14-15).

> When you were dead in your sins and in the uncircumcision of your sinful nature, God made you alive with Christ. He forgave us all our sins, having canceled the written code, with its regulations, that was against us and that stood opposed to us; He took it away, nailing it to the cross (Col. 2:13-14).

RESURRECTION: SUFFERING'S MEANING ASSURED

The report of Jesus' resurrection spread quickly that first Easter. Luke's story of the two disciples on the road to Emmaus emphasizes the uncertainty and puzzlement of Christ's followers. This is displayed in the variety of terms Luke uses to describe their excited conversation as they walked along the way. They "were talking," *homiloun* (24:14-15), "discussed," *suzetein* (24:15), and as another word translated "discuss" (*antiballete*) suggests, were literally "throwing ideas back and forth."

It was then that Jesus joined them, unrecognized. As they walked on, Christ "explained to them what was said in all the Scriptures concerning Himself" (24:27), showing them that the Christ had to "suffer these things" and only then enter His glory (24:26).

You and I will never fully understand what Jesus experienced here on earth, or begin to grasp what anguish that moment of spiritual death caused our God. But what we do know is that Christ had to suffer.

Not because we deserved redemption. No, the necessity existed because of who He is, not because of who we are.

JOHN 1:1-18
The Deity of Jesus

EXPOSITION

John has been called the "universal Gospel." It is distinctly different from the synoptics. Although Matthew, Mark, and Luke are each shaped for a different audience, each of the three traces Jesus' public ministry more or less chronologically. Each tends to describe events with a minimum of commentary. And each tends to focus on Galilee, where most of Christ's public ministry took place. Who Jesus is — whether cast as the Rejected Messiah of Matthew, God's Man of Action of Mark, or the Ideal Human Being of Luke — shines through each of the synoptics. Yet while Christ's parallel identity as Son of God and Savior is affirmed and fully demonstrated in Jesus' reported miracles and teachings, none of the three synoptics "theologize."

As we begin John's Gospel we immediately realize that this account is different. John's very first words draw us into the central mysteries of faith, as John challenges us to look back to, and beyond, the beginning — and to find there a Jesus who exists not as the supposed carpenter's son of Nazareth, but as God, distinct from and yet with and equal to God.

As we read on we find great structural differences between John and the synoptics. They record the flow of Christ's earthly history; John selects seven miracles and uses these as the setting for reporting deeply theological discourses of the Savior. The three synoptics concentrate on events in Galilee; John focuses our attention on Judea. Most significantly, again and again John casts Jesus' teaching in universal categories: light vs. dark, life vs. death, truth vs. falsehood, love vs. hate, belief vs. unbelief.

These contrasts have led some to argue that the fourth Gospel was only ascribed to, rather than written by, the Apostle John. Yet each argument advanced against Johannine authorship has been fully answered by scholars, and the traditional view demonstrated to be the best. What is that view? We know that the Apostle John long outlived the other members of Jesus' inner circle. As the decades passed John saw the need for a Gospel account which met the need of the developing Christian church — an account which answered challenges to its understanding of Jesus mounted from both Jewish and secular/philosophical sources. So, sometime between A.D. 90 and 100, though some argue for a date as early as A.D. 80, John set down his own most vivid memories of Jesus' acts and teachings which showed Christ to be both God and Man, and set Him sharply apart from every contemporary distortion.

And so in John's Gospel we have a unique portrait of our Lord. It is fully as accurate as the other Gospel portraits, despite its differences in structure and purpose. And it reminds us that in Jesus Christ God not only revealed Himself to the Jews as their Messiah, to the Romans as their ideal Man of Action, and to the Greeks as the true Model of Humanity. In Jesus Christ God revealed Himself in His Son, as the one and only answer to the deepest, universal needs of a lost mankind. In Jesus the light shines and reveals the darkness in which we once walked. Through Jesus we are given a vital, dynamic life that breaks forever the power of death over our present and future. By Jesus we are at last able to measure truth and falsehood. With Jesus God's love swallows up the animosity that we once felt toward God and others. And everything hinges on a single issue: belief vs. unbelief.

The clear, wonderful message of this most theological of the Gospels is that God invites us to believe in His Son. When we do, light, life, truth, love—all God's greatest gifts—become ours.

WORD STUDIES

In the beginning was *the* Word (1:1). The Greek term is *logos,* which usually focuses attention on the spoken word, but on the meaning rather than simply the sound. In Greek philosophical thought *logos* was used of the rational principle or Mind that ruled the universe. In Hebrew thought "the word of God" was His active self-expression, that revelation of Himself to humanity through which a person not only receives truth about God, but meets God face-to-face.

A.T. Robertson sums up the significance of *logos* in his *Word Pictures of the New Testament* (vol. 5, p. 3):

> *Logos* is from *lego,* old word in Homer to lay by, to collect, to put words side by side, to speak, to express an opinion. Logos is common for reason as well as speech. Heraclitus used it for the principle which controls the universe. The Stoics employed it for the soul of the world (*anima mundi*) and Marcus Aurelius used *spermatikos logos* for the generative principle in nature. The Hebrew *memra* was used in the Targums for the manifestation of God like the Angel of Jehovah and the Wisdom of God in Prov. 8:23.

Early Christian writers had more to say about the Gospel of John than about any of the others. And most early writers focused on the theme introduced in John's opening statement: Jesus is the preexistent Word of God. John's use of the term *logos,* "word," with its deep roots in both Greek philosophy and in Hebrew thought, immediately enrolled this Gospel in a realm of speculation that had long fascinated religious thinkers.

Here are a number of comments on this Gospel and its opening words penned by early Christian writers.

IRENAEUS (ca. A.D. 125–200)
And all the presbyters, who associated in Asia with John, the disciple of the Lord, testify that John handed down [these things]. For he remained with them until the times of Trajan [A.D. 98–117]. And also the church in Ephesus founded by Paul—John having remained with them until the times of Trajan—is a true witness of the tradition of the Apostles.

Now Matthew published also a book of the Gospel among the Hebrews in their own dialect, while Peter and Paul were preaching the Gospel in Rome and founding the Church. After their death, Mark, the disciple and interpreter of Peter, he too handed down to us in writing the things preached by Peter. Luke also, the follower of Paul, put down in a book the Gospel preached by that one. Afterwards John, the disciple of the Lord who also leaned upon His breast, he too published a Gospel while residing in Ephesus in Asia.

And all these have handed down to us [the doctrine that there is] one God, maker of heaven and earth, proclaimed by the Law and the Prophets, and one Christ, the Son of God. If a person does not assent to these, he surely rejects the followers of the Lord; he rejects even Christ the Lord

Himself; he rejects indeed also the father and is self-condemned, resisting and fighting against his own salvation—which thing all the heretics do.

John, the Lord's disciple, proclaims this faith and desires, by the proclamation of the Gospel, to remove that error which had been disseminated among men by Cerinthus and much earlier by those who are called Nicolaitans who are an offshoot of that knowledge falsely so called, that he might confound them and persuade that there is one God who made all things through His Word, and not as they say that the Creator was surely one, and the Father of the Lord another; and that the Son of the Creator was surely one, but the Christ from higher spheres another, that He lived impassible to the end, descended on Jesus the Son of the Creator, and returned again to His Pleroma; and that the Only-begotten was indeed the beginning, but that the Word was the true Son of the Only-begotten; and that the world in which we "live" has not been made by the Supreme God, but by some power lying far below Him, and excluded from communion with things invisible and ineffable. . . . Thus he began "with" the teaching of the Gospel: "In the beginning was the Word. . . ."

THEOPHILUS (ca. A.D. 170–180)

But when God determined to do the things which He had purposed, He brought forth this utterable Word, the first-born of all creation; He Himself was not emptied of the Word but bringing forth [the] Word He always had consort with His Word. Hence the Holy Scriptures and all the inspired writers teach us as one of these, John, says: "In the beginning was the Word, and the Word was with God"; showing that at the first God was alone and the Word was in Him. Then he says: "And the Word was God; all things were made by Him and without Him not a thing was made." Therefore, the Word, being God and proceeding by nature from God, whenever the Father of the universe determines, He sends Him to a certain place; coming He is both heard and seen; being sent by Him, He is also found in [that] place.

TERTULLIAN (A.D. 155–235)

He appeared among us, whose coming to renovate and illuminate man's nature was preannounced by God—I mean Christ, that Son of God. And so the supreme Head and Master of this grace and discipline, the Enlightener and Trainer of the human race, God's own Son, was announced among us, born—but not so born as to make Him ashamed of the name Son or of His paternal origin. It was not His lot to have as His father, by incest with a sister, or by violation of a daughter or another's wife, a god in the shape of serpent, or ox, or bird, or lover, for His vile ends transmuting Himself into the gold of Danaus. They are your divinities upon whom these base deeds of Jupiter were done. But the Son of God has no mother in any sense which involves impurity; she, whom men suppose to be His mother in the ordinary way, had never entered into the marriage bond. But first, I shall discuss His essential nature, and so the nature of His birth will be understood. We have already asserted that God made the world, and all which it contains, by His Word, and Reason, and Power. It is abundantly plain that your philosophers, too, regard the Logos—that is, the Word and Reason—as the Creator of the universe. For Zeno lays it down that He is the creator, having made all things according to a determinate plan; that His name is Fate, and God, and the soul of Jupiter, and the necessity of all things. Cleanthes ascribes all this to spirit, which he maintains pervades the universe. And we, in like manner, hold that the Word, and Reason, and Power, by which we have said God made all, have spirit in their proper and essential substratum, in which the Word has inbeing to give forth utterances, and reason abides to dispose and arrange, and power is over all to execute. We have been taught that He proceeds forth from God, and in that procession He is generated; so that He is the Son of God, and is called God from unity of substance with God. For God, too, is a Spirit. Even when the ray is shot from the sun, it is still part of the parent mass, the sun will still be in the ray, because it is a ray of the sun—there is no division of substance, but merely an extension. Thus

Christ is Spirit of Spirit, God of God, as light of light is kindled. The material matrix remains entire and unimpaired, though you derive from it any number of shoots possessed of its qualities; so, too, that which has come forth out of God is at once God and Son of God, and the two are one. In this way also, as He is Spirit of Spirit and God of God, He is made a second in manner of existence — in position, not in nature; and He did not withdraw from the original source, but went forth. This ray of God, then, as it was always foretold in ancient times, descending into a certain virgin, and made flesh in her womb, is in His birth God and man united. The flesh formed by the Spirit is nourished, grows up to manhood, speaks, teaches, works, and is the Christ.

ATHANASIUS (A.D. 298–373)

1. But one cannot but be utterly astonished at the Gentiles, who, while they laugh at what is no matter for jesting, are themselves insensible to their own disgrace, which they do not see that they have set up in the shape of sticks and stones.

2. Only, as our argument is not lacking in demonstrative proof, come let us put them also to shame on reasonable grounds — mainly from what we ourselves also see. For what is there on our side that is absurd, or worthy of derision? Is it merely our saying that the Word has been made manifest in the body? But this even they will join in owning to have happened without any absurdity, if they show themselves friends of truth.

3. If then they deny that there is a Word of God at all, they do so gratuitously, jesting at what they know not.

4. But if they confess that there is a Word of God, and He ruler of the universe, and that in Him the Father has produced creation, and that by His Providence the whole receives light and life and being, and that He reigns over all, so that from the works of His providence He is known, and through Him the Father — consider, I pray you, whether they be not unwittingly raising the jest against themselves.

5. The philosophers of the Greeks say that the universe is a great body, and rightly so. For we see it and its path as objects of our senses. If, then, the Word of God is in the Universe, which is a body, and has united Himself with the whole and with all its parts, what is there surprising or absurd if we say that He has united Himself with man also.

6. For if it were absurd for Him to have been in a body at all, it would be absurd for Him to be united with the whole either, and to be giving light and movement to all things by His providence. For the whole is also a body.

7. But if it beseems Him to unite Himself with the universe, and to be made known in the whole, it must beseem Him also to appear in a human body, and that by Him it should be illumined and work. For mankind is part of the whole as well as the rest. And if it be unseemly for a part to have been adopted as His instrument to teach men of His Godhead, it must be most absurd that He should be made known even by the whole universe [Chapter XLI].

"In the beginning was the Word" (1:1). John, in all likelihood consciously, duplicates the words of Genesis 1:1, "In the beginning God." The "beginning" in each case carries us back beyond Creation into an eternity inhabited by God alone. Before God's utterance of that first, formative word which called the universe into existence and fashioned from raw matter the habitable world on which we live, that Person destined to be God's active agent in all things existed as and with God.

This is emphasized in the text by the use of *en*, "was." Three times in this verse John uses this term, the imperfect tense of the verb *eimi*, rather than a form of the verb *egeneto*. *Eimi* and *en* simply describe continuing existence; *egeneto* indicates becoming. In the beginning the Word, as God, already enjoyed a timeless existence, without beginning and without end. Knox's translation displays the sense of this verb, when he translates the next phrase, "God had the Word abiding with Him."

We cannot begin to grasp how God can exist without beginning. Scripture does not attempt to explain, or even to argue the point. Scripture simply affirms that God is, was, and always will be. And John reminds us as he begins his Gospel that we must never forget that Jesus, carpenter of Nazareth, teacher and miracle worker of Israel, crucified and risen Savior, is also God enfleshed. Eternal, immutable, immortal, the only wise God, to whom we owe honor and praise for ever and ever more.

And the Word was God (1:1). One contemporary cult, reflecting a theological position adopted by ancient heretics, points out that in the Greek the definite article "the" is found with "Word" but not with "God." On this basis cultists argue that John teaches Jesus was "a" God, but surely not God. A lesser deity, yes. But God from eternity? Never.

The fallacy in this argument is that it rests on English rather than Greek grammar. As the article "Qualitative Anarthrous Predicate Nouns" in the *Journal of Biblical Literature* (March 1973) points out, in Greek the absence of the article with "God" emphasizes quality. Thus John is clearly stating that the Word has the *same* quality as God, and is God!

Far from detracting from a high view of Jesus' nature, John strongly affirms the full deity of this Man who was the Word made flesh!

Through Him all things were *made*; without Him nothing was made that has been made (1:3). Here there is a distinct shift in verb, from the imperfect of *eimi* in vv. 1-2 to the aorist of *ginomai*, "to become." Here, as throughout Scripture, John envisions a beginning for the material universe, and for those created beings who populate the spiritual universe. And John now presents Christ as the active agent in that Creation.

Here is a New Testament passage which also affirms this truth: "He is the image of the invisible God, the firstborn over all creation. For by Him all things were created: things in heaven and on earth, visible and invisible, whether thrones or powers or rulers or authorities; all things were created by Him and for Him. He is before all things, and in Him all things hold together" (Col. 1:15-17).

And here is an Old Testament passage, which foreshadows the clearer revelation of Christ's role in the making of all things: "By the word of the Lord were the heavens made, their starry host by the breath of His mouth. . . . Let all the earth fear the Lord; let all the people of the world revere Him. For He spoke, and it came to be; He commanded, and it stood firm" (Ps. 33:6, 8-9).

In Him was *life,* and that life was the light of men (1:4). The Greek word here is *zoe,* which can indicate the life-principle that vitalizes the body, or more often refers to spiritual life and vitality. Here John portrays the Word, Jesus, as the source of all life, who vitalizes the living and gives eternal, spiritual life to men.

"Life" is one of John's favorite themes; the word occurs some 36 times in his Gospel. The article on "life and death" in the *Zondervan Expository Dictionary of Bible Words* comments on this passage:

Human sin was the source of death. God alone is the source of life, for God "has life in Himself" (5:26). All other life is derived. As Creator, God is the source of biological life. John 1 presents Jesus as the active agent in creation and the source of life in the universe. "Through Him all things were made; without Him nothing was made that has been made. In Him was life, and that life was the light of men" (John 1:3-4).

God is also the source of eternal life, the spiritual dynamic that shatters the power of death in human personality. John reports Jesus' words: "I tell you the truth, whoever hears My word and believes Him who sent Me has eternal life and will not be condemned; He has crossed over from death to life. I tell you the truth, a time is coming and has now come when the dead will hear the voice of the Son of God and those who hear will live. For as the Father has life in Himself, so He has granted the Son to have life in Himself" (5:24-26).

Jesus is also the source of vitality for the believer's experience of eternal life here on earth. As Paul writes, "I have been crucified with Christ and I no longer live, but Christ lives in me. The life I live in the body, I live by faith in the Son of God, who loved me and gave Himself for me" (Gal. 2:20; cf. Phil. 1:21). At every turn, the Bible's teaching on life points us to Jesus. As the Mediator sent from God, Jesus is the source in which the eternal life from God can be found (1 John 1:1-2).

How is "that life the light of men"? Only by seeing a glimmer of hope and turning to the Savior can we human beings lay hold on eternal life.

The light shines in the darkness, but the darkness has not *understood it* (1:5). The Greek verb *katelaben* is difficult to translate here. It can mean "overtake" or "overcome," as well as "apprehend" or "attain." The problem is discerning which meaning applies here, and how it fits in with what John is saying about the light shining in the darkness.

"Light" and "darkness" are another pair of opposites which are found frequently in John's writings. In a real way "darkness" represents the world dominated by Satan, whose lost inhabitants are energized by those same passions which led to Satan's fall, and who thus "loved darkness instead of light" (3:19). Only by following Jesus' words and walking in the light can a human being avoid the "darkness overtak[ing] you" (again *katelambano* [12:35]).

Perhaps this gives us the best clue for understanding the sense of John 1:5. The life that throbbed in Jesus shed light as He lived among us in this world, this world that is Satan's realm. The forces of darkness crowded around: Satan, demons, and even the religious leaders of God's people, struggling to put that light out. Yet the darkness was unable to extinguish or overcome the light.

In Jesus God's light continues to shine. And no matter what forces array themselves against the Savior, the darkness will never triumph over the light!

He came as a witness to *testify* concerning that light (1:7). On the surface it appears strange. Why in the world would anyone have to "testify" (*marturesei*, bear witness, to make clearer) concerning a "light"? If there is anything that is obvious in a dark place, it is a light shining there!

But we must remember one thing. The light shining in the darkness is obvious only to those with sight! The blind cannot see the light, no matter how clearly it shines.

John was sent by God, in fulfillment of prophecy, to cry out to a generation blinded by sin that the Redeemer had indeed come. Because of John's testimony, many groped after Him. And those who heard Jesus' own words, and believed, saw!

It is much the same today. Jesus is still the light of the world. And those blinded by sin still need us to testify concerning Him, that they too may believe—and see.

The true light that *gives light to every man* was coming into the world (1:9). If man is lost in sin and blind to spiritual realities, as Jesus shows in 9:39-41, what does John mean by speaking of the Word as the "true light" and saying that He "gives light to every man"?

One solution is to argue for an alternative translation that links the participle "coming" with "light" rather than "man." Thus the verse would mean that Christ, the genuine light, "illuminates every man as He comes into the world." Rather than implying that every man has light, the verse is understood to say that genuine light is shed on all in Christ's coming.

While the above is probably the best rendering of the verse, the NIV translation has interesting implications. We know from a study of comparative religions that many of the world's faiths share a high moral vision. What human beings ought to be really is not disputed in what are known as the "higher" religions. The difference is that Christianity alone affirms that nothing man can do can commend him to God or merit salvation, but that God's love for the lost is so great that He sacrificed His own Son for us.

But where, then, do human religions gain the moral insights they display? John may be saying that all genuine light is shed by Christ, and that the glimpses of truth the lost do have are themselves sourced in His matchless grace.

He was in the world, and though the world was made through Him, the world did not recognize Him (1:10). In the original, "world," *kosmos,* comes first in all three phrases, each of which displays a different aspect of the relationship of the Word to His universe and its inhabitants.

The Word was "continually" (for so the imperfect indicates) in the world. Here John wants us to understand that the Incarnation was a special involvement of the Word with His creation, but that at no time before the Incarnation had the Word failed to maintain a presence among us. In nature's revelation of God, in the Law of Moses, and in the voices of the prophets, the Word made His presence known.

The Word made the world. Its very existence depended on His creative and sustaining act. It was and is His world, in the deepest sense.

Yet the world refused (or failed) to recognize the Word when He came to live among us. And here we have a delicate shift in the connotation of *kosmos*. In its theological sense *kosmos* in the NT portrays human society apart from God, a web of relationships and institutions energized by those same passions that led to Satan's rebellion against the Lord. When used without this theological tint, *kosmos* focuses our attention on the earth, not as a planet, but as a biosphere, an infinitely well organized system designed by God that with animate and inanimate life incorporates humanity as an essential element. And so John reminds us that as the Word Christ has always been involved in this planet's complex weaving. As the Word, Christ is indeed its Creator. But when the Word appeared on earth in Jesus Christ, humanity—the crown of creation—refused to acknowledge Him.

All the universe gives testimony to the Word. Man alone refuses to acknowledge His role or worship Him.

He came to that which was *His own,* but *His own* did not receive Him (1:11). In the first phrase "His own" is neuter plural: His own things, or creation. The second phrase differs: now "His own [people]" are in view. In the first instance John is probably thinking of the Jews, God's chosen, who not only refused to acknowledge their Messiah but decisively rejected Him. In the second, however, this verse encompasses all humankind, for all belong to Him by right of creation, and He calls all His own in His universal offer of grace.

Yet to all who *received* Him, to those who *believed* in His name (1:12). "Believe" is perhaps the most important word in John's Gospel. As he nears the end of his unique account of Jesus, the apostle concludes, "These are written that you may believe that Jesus is the Christ, the Son of God, and that by believing you may have life in His name" (20:31).

But what does "believe" mean? In 1:12 John provides a preliminary definition by equating "believe" with "receive." How clear an image this is. What can you or I do to obtain a gift? Simply reach out our hands and take what is offered. In responding to an offer, in reaching out to take, we express our confidence in the giver, and our reliance on his promise. Unlike Lucy in "Peanuts," who convinces Charlie Brown that this time she'll really hold the football for him to kick, and then jerks it away, God's promise of salvation through Christ is no prank.

Children of God—*children* born not of natural descent, nor of human decision or a husband's will, but born of God (1:12-13). John here portrays an amazing change of status. Belief transforms us from being mere creatures of God to being His children: members of His family, sons and daughters of the Heavenly Father. The verse goes on to make it very clear that this relationship does not depend on any accident of birth or biological relationship. It is spiritual, a relationship that depends on an inner rebirth that is itself a supernatural work of God. J.B. Phillips paraphrases, "These were men who truly believed in Him, and their birth depended not on natural descent nor on any physical impulse or plan of man, but on God."

The theme of a new birth is introduced here. It is developed further in Jesus' conversation with Nicodemus (chap. 3).

The Word *became flesh* and made His dwelling among us (1:14). There is an important transition here. John began by asserting that from the very beginning the Word was God. Now John tells us that this Word became flesh. Note that there is no suggestion here that the Deity temporarily entered an existing human being. No, the great mystery of the ages is stated here: the eternal Word became a human being, accepting the limitations under which we live, subject to the conditions nature and history impose on ordinary men. John frequently alludes to these limitations, as in 3:17, 6:38-42, 7:29, 8:23, 9:5, 10:36, and 16:28, reminding us that the reality of the Incarnation is no abstract philosophical concept, but was for Jesus an experiential reality.

As for John, he bears witness, and in the Incarnation saw God's glory revealed in the Person of His one and only Son.

Who came from the Father, full of *grace and truth* (1:14). This significant phrase, "grace and truth," is repeated in v. 17, where the grace and truth brought by Jesus are placed in contrast with the Law given through

Moses. John's point is not that the Law was something other than a divine gift. His point is that while the Law displayed God's righteousness for all, Christ displays God's grace. And the truth revealed in Jesus has an authority that surpasses that of the truth given through Moses.

Later Paul thoroughly explores the relationship between Law and Grace (see Index). Here John simply affirms that through Christ a new revelation of God's character and plan has taken place, a revelation that takes precedence over all that has been given before.

No one has ever *seen God,* but God the

One and Only, who is at the Father's side, *has made Him known* (1:18). "God" is an anarthrous *Theon,* which might be better translated "deity." John's point is that man's limited capacity makes it impossible for human beings to perceive the essential nature of God. But the Son, the Word become flesh, has "explained" or "interpreted," *exgesato,* God to us through the Incarnation. The teaching and the acts of Jesus are adequate to not only communicate to us who God is, but also to bring us into His very presence.

In and through Jesus, human beings still meet the Living God, and those who respond with belief are given eternal life.

JOHN 1:19–4:42
The New Has Come

EXPOSITION

John has launched his Gospel with a series of bold affirmations (1:1-18). The eternal Word became flesh and lived for a time among men as a real human being. In that Incarnation the eternal Son of God has revealed the true nature of the Deity, and offers a stunning new relationship with God to all who receive Him by faith. God had spoken earlier to humankind through Moses, but now a new revelation "full of grace and truth" supersedes the former message of God to man. Later the writer of Hebrews will pick up this theme, and point out that although Moses was a faithful servant in God's house, the Son is the owner and architect. It follows that when the Son reveals His ultimate authority, His authority will rightly supersede that of the former message. Now, with this foundation laid, John goes on to explore the new that has come in Christ, the Word Incarnate, the Son and Revealer of the Living God.

John marshals his evidence carefully, first of all describing witnesses that give testimony to the new (1:19-51). These witnesses include John, the forerunner of OT prophecy (1:9-28); the Holy Spirit, who appeared in the form of a dove at Jesus' baptism (1:29-34); and both Andrew and Philip, who after the briefest moments with Jesus recognized and acknowledged Him (1:35-51).

John then recounts two incidents which illustrate the superiority of the new (2:1-25). At a wedding in Cana Jesus turns water into wine (2:1-11). The ordinary drink of the people is transmuted to become the liquid associated with celebration and joy—the liquid linked in both Testaments with the banquet that initiates the coming eschatological kingdom of God. Then Jesus stuns observers by driving money changers from the Jerusalem temple (2:12-25). This act is an expression of divine judgment on corrupt worship, and is also a promise. The new has come, and the positive implications of Jesus' acts are made explicit in Matt. 21:13: "My house will be called a house of prayer."

But what is the nature of the new? John now introduces Nicodemus, a leading member of the Sanhedrin, who comes to Jesus for a private discussion of the young Rabbi's teaching (3:1-36). Through the dialogue between Jesus and this ruler of Israel (3:1-21), John reveals that the "new" Jesus brings is "new birth," a spiritual renewal so fundamental that it produces an absolute change in an individual's relationship with God and in his or her eternal destiny. A renewal whose implications John takes pains to explain after reporting the conversation (3:22-36).

Finally John tells us another story—the familiar story of a Samaritan woman Jesus meets and speaks with beside a well (4:1-42). This story shows us that the impact of the new is destined to be felt beyond ancient boundaries, bringing hope to Gentile as well as Jew.

Yes, in the Incarnation of Jesus Christ the new has come. In Christ the joy of celebration, the glory of worship, the vitality of spiritual renewal, and the certainty of eternal life, all become ours.

WORD STUDIES

When the Jews of Jerusalem sent priests and Levites to ask Him who He was (1:19). John uses the phrase "the Jews" in a distinctive way. In John's Gospel the phrase is neither an ethnic nor religious description, but John's way of distinguishing between the Jewish people and the Jewish religious leaders who actively opposed Jesus (10:24, 31; 18:14, 31, 36, 38). Even here it is not pejorative but descriptive.

Let's never imagine that the New Testament is anti-Semitic, even though most first-century Jewish leaders were increasingly anti-Christian. Paul expresses the appropriate attitude of believers toward the Jewish people in Rom. 10:1: "Brothers, my heart's desire and prayer to God for the Israelites is that they may be saved."

Are you *Elijah?* . . . Are you *the Prophet?* (1:21) Both questions reflect beliefs common in first-century Judaism and rooted in the OT. The first question reflects the popular belief that Elijah would anoint Messiah, and this act would reveal His identity. John's denial re-flects his self-understanding and should not be taken to contradict Jesus' teachings about John (Matt. 11:7-15).

The second question is based on the expectation that a prophet fulfilling the promise of Deut. 18:15, 18 would appear and duplicate the Exodus miracles and so reconquer the Promised Land. Here John's "no" again reflects his self-understanding, although some see in his response a rejection of the popular theology.

The fact is that few of us understand the role we are playing in God's great plan. John was more significant than he suspected, even though he recognized his commission to call Israel back to God in preparation for the coming of the Messiah. You and I as well may be more significant in accomplishing God's purposes than we suspect!

I have *seen and I testify* that this is the Son of God (1:34). Throughout biblical history the prophets were granted visions of spiritual reality unseen by others. Now this last of the OT prophets is given the most stunning vision of all: he has seen Jesus as Son of God.

In this we share John's vision and his mission. The reality of who Jesus is remains hidden to a world that uses His name so casually. But we have seen, and so we must testify. Jesus is the Son of God.

"Come," He replied, "and *you will see."* So they went and saw where He was staying, and spent that day with Him (1:39). That experience was enough to convince Andrew. The text tells us that "the first thing Andrew did" (1:41) was to find Peter and excitedly announce, "We have found the Messiah."

How wonderful it is when you and I can say to anyone, "Come, and you will see." Jesus is in heaven, but through His body here on earth He maintains a living presence in our lost world. When our congregations are filled with the love and presence of our Lord, we can gladly invite inquirers to come, knowing that in the warmth of the loving relationships which marks people in whom Jesus now dwells, they will see—and find—Him.

"Nazareth! Can anything good come from there?" Nathanael asked (1:46). We need to take this remark as an exclamation. It was surely unlike the cruel contempt the religious leaders displayed in dismissing ordinary folk with the remark, "This mob that knows nothing of the law—there is a curse on them" (7:49).

In fact, the exclamation reflects a surprise that would have been shared by most in Judea at the idea that Galilee, lying south of Judea, should be the origin of any significant religious movement. This attitude is reflected in the Sanhedrin's later rebuke of Nicodemus (7:52), but also in remarks attributed to sages of our era. Rabban Johanan ben Zakkai is supposed to have said, "O Galilee! O Galilee! You hated the Torah! In the end you will be fated to fall into the hands of the *mesiquin."* In another traditional dialogue Rabbi Simlai is supposed to have visited Rabbi Jonathan to discuss some *haggadah.* The latter rabbi is supposed to have replied,

I have a tradition from my forebears that discourages teaching haggadah to Babylonians or to Southerners [e.g., the people of Galilee], for they are gross in spirit and wanting in Torah, and you, sir, qualify on both counts: you come from Hehardea and live in the South.

Given the prevalent view of those who lived in Judea, which was admittedly the intellectual heart and center of Jewish thought in the time of Christ, Nathanael's surprise is perhaps understandable.

How easy it is for our thinking to be colored by popular opinion. And how often that popular opinion is wrong!

I saw you while you were *still under the fig tree* before Philip called you (1:48). An interesting suggestion is offered by an Arab Christian commentator, who takes this phrase as an idiomatic expression, meaning "I know you very well." But the phrase "before Philip called you" seems to define a specific setting in the then present. Jesus is simply stating a matter of fact: although out of sight, Jesus knew the place where the two met and was aware of that incident. The OT contains precedents. Elisha knew what was happening in the councils of the king of Syria though he was in Israel (2 Kings 6:8-12); Ezekiel in Babylon was fully aware of events that took place at the same time in Jerusalem (Ezek. 8). Nathanael, a man of sincere faith, undoubtedly saw in Jesus' statement the same divine stamp of approval that evidenced itself in the ancient prophets, and unhesitatingly accepted this confirmation of the testimony of his brother Philip.

This response is also evidence that Jesus knew Nathanael well when He said, "Here is a true Israelite, in whom there is nothing false," *oude estin en to stomatai autou dolos.* The Greek phrase says literally, "There is no deceit in his mouth," and suggests not simply that Nathanael is not deceitful himself, but that in his utter honesty he does not look for deceit in others. A Pharisee hearing Jesus speak of seeing him under some distant fig tree would have pondered, puzzled, and wondered what trickery Jesus used to gain His knowledge. Nathanael accepted Jesus' testimony, and believed.

How we need Nathanaels today! To take Jesus at His word, and respond in faith, is the key to spiritual growth and power.

Dear woman, why do you involve Me? (2:4) The Greek phrase, *ti emoi kai soi,* means literally "what to me and to you." Its ambiguity has led to a variety of explanations. One commentator suggests that Jesus means, "What concern is this of ours?" He suggests that, following contemporary custom, the guests took turns purchasing the wine to be drunk by all to the health of the bride and groom. He thinks Mary, in telling Jesus the wine was about to run out, was urging Him to perform a guest's duty, and buy the next round. Jesus' response would simply mean, "It's not my turn!"

Although an interesting insight in the culture, there are probably better renderings of the phrase. For instance, Christ may be gently asking Mary why she speaks to Him about a need He already understands and intends to meet. In this case Mary's instructions to the servants are more understandable. Jesus has not rejected her request, but intended to meet the need without His mother's prompting. (This version is bound to have more appeal to Protestants, who tend to resent the Roman Catholic use of this story as a basis for addressing prayers to the Virgin Mary. After all, so that line of reasoning goes, Jesus will surely grant any request of hers today, as He did in Cana of Galilee!)

But there is still another possibility. Jesus is about to perform the first of His miraculous signs: a sign that will reveal His glory and move His disciples to "put their faith in Him" (2:11). Long ago, as a child, Jesus had insisted that "I had to be in My Father's house" (Luke 2:49). Yet Jesus returned to Nazareth, and lived as a child in Mary and Joseph's house. But now, at last, He is about to set out on the Father's business, even though the final hour of that service lies far off in the future. Gently Jesus rejects Mary's importunity: Woman, what to Me and to you? Woman, now no earthly relationship can bind Me, for at last I am setting out on My Father's business.

Mary bows now to her son, and says to the servants, "Do whatever He tells you" (2:5). Jesus is now subject to the Father alone, and because of that, all humankind is subject to Christ as Lord.

There comes a time for us too when we affirm the ties of a duty to God that supersedes every relationship we hold dear. When that time comes we realize that we are called, as Jesus was, to put God's will first and serve Him all our days.

To those who sold *doves* He said, "Get these out of here! How dare you turn My Father's house into a market!" (2:16) Doves were the sacrifices that God, in grace, permitted for those too poor to bring a lamb to the temple altar. A fascinating study of the economic circumstances of the people of first-century Jerusalem notes that fruit prices were as much as three to six times higher in the city than in the country! But this cannot compare to the inflated prices demanded in Jerusalem for sacrificial doves, which was as much as 100 times that charged in rural areas! God's house was not only turned into a marketplace by those tradesmen who bought and sold there under the aegis of the chief priests. It was turned into a marketplace where the poor whom God's Law provided for became victims of extortion!

Many people saw *the miraculous signs He was doing* and believed in His name (2:23). The imperfect tense of "did" indicates continuing action. What the original suggests is that as long as Jesus continued to perform miraculous signs, His acts continued to support a certain level of belief. The fact that this was no settled commitment to Jesus as Lord is clearly indicated by the next verse: "Jesus would not entrust Himself to them" (2:24).

A faith that rests only on the visible is unlikely to survive.

Men loved darkness instead of light because their deeds were evil (3:19). Both those who respond to Christ and those who reject Him have lived in darkness. But the radical difference between the lost and the saved is increasingly displayed in the response of each group to the light. The lost scurry away, crouching in ever deepening darkness, not simply because their deeds are evil, but because they are unwilling and ashamed to be exposed for what they are. The saved increasingly put evil behind them; they respond to the light because they are aware that what they do "has been done through God" (3:21). How wonderfully freeing it is to welcome light. How frightening to be driven deeper into darkness.

He must become greater; I must become *less* (3:30). Exalting Christ rather than ourselves is a true measure of greatness!

Whoever rejects the Son will not see life, for God's *wrath* remains on Him (3:36). This is the only passage in John's writings where "wrath," the conscious, determined hostility of God toward sin, is mentioned. A distinctive wrath of God is, however, taught in other OT and NT passages.

The Bible maintains a positive view of God's anger. It is aroused only by sin, and most frequently by sins which either are direct affronts (Ex. 32:7-12; Num. 32:10; Deut. 11:16-17) or involve unjust treatment of others (Ex. 22:22-24). Thus God's anger is not only righteous, but expressly in harmony with His compassion, love, commitment to justice, and eagerness to forgive. Thus God is portrayed in Scripture as "slow to anger"

(cf. Ex. 34:6; Ps. 86:15).

Given all this, God remains committed to express His wrath against sin. He does so in the careful, considered, and fair judgment of sinners, which will take place when Christ returns. As 2 Thes. 1:9 says, "They will be punished with everlasting destruction and shut out from the presence of the Lord and from the majesty of His power."

John 3 is rightly best known for its great affirmation that "God so loved the world that He gave His one and only Son" (3:16). But, in the gratitude that wells up within us as we contemplate God's great gift, we must not forget that this same chapter warns those who will not respond to love that they must then fear the wrath of our God.

THE PASSAGE IN DEPTH

John the Baptist Denies Being the Christ (1:19-34). See also the commentary on Matt. 3:13-17, 11:1-30, and the parallel passage in Mark 1:1-8.

Background. The questions asked by the delegation of religious leaders from Jerusalem focus on a vital issue (1:19). John had burst suddenly out of the wilderness, dressed as a latter-day Elijah, and cried out warnings that echoed the holy fervor of God's ancient prophets. He quickly attracted excited crowds, for he announced that God's kingdom was at hand, about to break into history. And he urged the people of God to a radical change of heart, that they might be ready to enter that kingdom when it came.

The answer demanded by the Jerusalem delegation was simply, "Who are you? What is your role in God's plan?" John rejected suggestions that he might himself be the Christ, or the prophet that popular belief expected to usher in the messianic age (see Word Study of John 1:21, above). Instead John identified himself as the "voice of one calling in the desert, 'Make straight the way for the Lord'" (1:23). This response is a quote from the Prophet Isaiah (40:3), a quote nestled among the words of "Comfort my people" (40:1) that initiate the second half of that great prophetic work.

As that passage unfolds, Isaiah says,

You who bring good tidings to Zion,
    go up on a high mountain.

You who bring good tidings to Jerusalem,
    lift up your voice with a shout,
    lift it up, do not be afraid;
    say to the towns of Judah,
    "Here is your God!"
See, the Sovereign Lord comes with power,
    and His arm rules for Him.
See, His reward is with Him,
    and His recompense accompanies Him.
He tends His flock like a shepherd:
    He gathers the lambs in His arms
    and carries them close to His heart;
He gently leads those that have young (Isa. 40:9-11).

What is significant here is the fact that Isaiah's emphasis is not on the coming of messianic times, but on the coming of the messianic Person; the "Sovereign Lord" who despite His awesome power will, like a Shepherd, stoop to gather the lambs in His arms.

The Baptist himself was later unable to separate these two themes, as his questioning of Jesus displays (Matt. 11:3). But in this Gospel, John unquestionably emphasizes the testimony of the Baptist as a witness to the Person of the Messiah, who did "testify that this [Jesus] is the Son of God" (1:34).

How then are we to understand the preaching reported in the other Gospels that constitutes such a clear, urgent call for repentance? Since the ministry of the voice in Isaiah is to prepare the way for the Person of the Messiah rather than the Age of the Messiah, we need to see that preaching as pre-evangelism. As preaching intended to strip away those defenses which insulate us from the awareness of our own sin and need, and in doing so ready us to hear God's message of a full and free forgiveness of sin.

Interpretation. While John does not give a summary of the Baptist's preaching, other Gospel writers do. And it is appropriate to look at their descriptions here.

John's clothes were made of camel's hair, and he had a leather belt around his waist. His food was locusts and wild honey. People went out to him from Jerusalem and all Judea and the whole region of the Jordan. Confessing their sins, they were baptized by him in the Jordan River.

But when he saw many of the Pharisees and Sadducees coming to where he was baptizing, he said to them: "You brood of vipers! Who warned you to flee from the coming wrath? Produce fruit in keeping with repentance. And do not think you can say to yourselves, 'We have Abraham as our father.' I tell you that out of these stones God can raise up children for Abraham. The ax is already at the root of the trees, and every tree that does not produce good fruit will be cut down and thrown into the fire.

"I baptize you with water for repentance. But after me will come one who is more powerful than I, whose sandals I am not fit to carry" (Matt. 3:4-11).

And so John came, baptizing in the desert region and preaching a baptism of repentance for the forgiveness of sins. The whole Judean countryside went out to him. Confessing their sins, they were baptized by him in the Jordan River. John wore clothing made of camel's hair, with a leather belt around his waist, and he ate locusts and wild honey. And this was his message: "After me will come one more powerful than I, the thongs of whose sandals I am not worthy to stoop down and untie" (Mark 1:4-7).

John said to the crowds coming out to be baptized by him, "You brood of vipers! Who warned you to flee from the coming wrath? Produce fruit in keeping with repentance. And do not begin to say to yourselves, 'We have Abraham as our father.' For I tell you that out of these stones God can raise up children for Abraham. The ax is already at the root of the trees, and every tree that does not produce good fruit will be cut down and thrown into the fire."

"What should we do then?" the crowd asked?

John answered, "The man with two tunics should share with him who has none, and the one who has food should do the same."

Tax collectors also came to be baptized.

"Teacher," they asked, "what should we do?"

"Don't collect any more than you are required to," he told them.

Then some soldiers asked him, "And what should we do?"

He replied, "Don't extort money and don't accuse people falsely—be content with your pay."

The people were waiting expectantly and were all wondering in their hearts if John might possibly be the Christ. John answered them all, "I baptize you with water. But one more powerful than I will come . . ." (Luke 3:7-16).

Comparing these passages we note important common elements:

■ The Baptist bluntly identifies sins. John does not hesitate to identify sin as sin and sinners as sinners. Modern euphemisms, such as "adult literature," "alternate lifestyles," and "a woman's right to her own body," had no place in the Baptist's vocabulary. In our day John would speak boldly, naming the "adult" as immoral, the "alternate lifestyle" as sexual depravity, and abortion as murder of an unborn person whose uniqueness is stamped in the chromosomal pattern of every cell. There was no way to disguise sin, for John unhesitatingly named every act for what it was.

It is, however, important to note here that John's words were spoken to the crowds, rather than to individuals. In speaking out as he did, he forced his society to confront God's standards of righteousness, refusing to let them hide behind words that disguised the true nature of their acts. When individuals asked John what they should do, his answers pointed them to principles long established in Mosaic Law.

■ The Baptist challenges religious assumptions. It was common in first-century Judaism to suppose that biological descent from Abraham was enough to secure standing before God. John not only denied this assumption, but directly confronted those who based their expectation of God's favor on their faithfulness to tradition.

In our day people adopt similar blinders, supposing that if God exists He is so "good" that He must overlook human failures, and eagerly welcome anyone who professes even a nodding acquaintance with religion of any sort. The God of the Bible, who demands total allegiance to Himself as He has revealed Himself is both strange to our population, and repelling. As the Baptist reminded the people of his time, human beings must seek a relationship with God on grounds that God establishes. How foolish to insist that God accept our conditions, as though relationship with God was a favor we offer Him rather than a grace gift that He offers to us.

■ The Baptist warns of approaching judgment. Many who recognize their actions as wrong simply shrug and say, "So what?" John the Baptist preached to people in a society who believed in divine blessing and judgment. Yet even in that society judgment seemed so distant as to be irrelevant to everyday decisions. "Perhaps someday God will call us to account, but surely not now" undoubtedly insulated many from the fear of just retribution for sinful acts. John the Baptist preached an imminent judgment: the "coming wrath" is near, for "the ax is already at the root of the trees" (Luke 3:7, 9).

How fascinating our society's reaction to those who view the scourge of AIDS as an expression of divine judgment—of God's ax, already striking at the root of sin in our society. Even to suggest such a thing is met with outraged charges of insensitivity or prejudice. Never mind that the majority of cases are consequences of the choices of victims to engage in immoral or illegal activities. Our society desperately attempts to deny the principle of personal responsibility for one's acts and its

consequences, and just as desperately denies the truth with which the Baptist confronted his listeners: this is a moral universe, and God does and will most surely judge.

■ The Baptist points men to Christ. Each Gospel drives this point home. When the Baptist spoke, he pointed his listeners to the One coming after him; the One he identifies in John's Gospel as "Lamb of God" (1:29) and "Son of God" (1:34).

This is the goal of all pre-evangelism. To awaken human beings to the reality of their condition so that they will be ready to hear, and respond to, Jesus Christ.

Application. A study of the Baptist's ministry reminds us how many misconceptions exist in any society that blind men to the Gospel's Good News. The Baptist's preaching is not intended to serve as a model for our personal evangelism. But it is a reminder that Christians, individually and united as the church, must confront those in our society with those unpopular yet vital truths that prepare men and women to respond to the Gospel of Jesus Christ.

Jesus Changes Water to Wine (2:1-11). See the Word Study of John 2:4, above.

Background. The fact that the large jars John mentions were of stone (2:6) is significant. It indicates that the water they contained was most likely used for ritual purification, as stone containers unlike those of clay or metal did not contract "uncleanness." Thus, transformation of this water into wine has symbolic significance: the water representing OT religion was transmuted by Jesus into a wine that represented the abundant blessing of God. The validity of this symbol is established in Scripture, which often pictures God's eschatological kingdom as a banquet (Matt. 5:6; 8:11-12; Mark 2:19; Luke 22:15-18), a primary feature of which was a profusion of wine (cf. Isa. 25:6).

A similar symbolism is found in the first-century Jewish philosopher Philo's comments on Melchizedek. In his Leg. Alleg. 3.79 Philo writes that Melchizedek "shall bring forth wine instead of water and give our souls a pure draught, that they may become possessed by that divine intoxication that is more sober than sobriety itself."

In turning the water of representative of the old economy into a wine that represents the coming of God's kingdom, Jesus "revealed His glory, and His disciples put their faith in Him" (2:11).

A NOTE ON WINE

One of the most fruitless of all arguments is one advanced by those who are determined to transform wine into unfermented grape juice. Granting that drunkenness and alcoholism are scourges of our age, there is enough direct testimony against them in Scripture to support the position of the most passionate prohibitionist without the necessity of denying the role of wine in first-century celebrations and in biblical symbolism. The *Zondervan Expository Dictionary of Bible Words* provides a good overview of this issue. Part of the article on wine found there says:

> There are two Hebrew words translated "wine" in the NIV and the NASB: *tiros* and *yayin*. Tiros is "new wine," the unfermented product of grape vines. It is associated in the OT with blessing (e.g., Deut. 7:13; 11:14; 2 Kings 18:32) and was an important product for the agricultural economy. *Yayin* is fermented wine, which in Bible times contained about seven to ten percent alcohol. In the NT era the rabbis called for dilution of this wine when it was used at the Passover. But fermented wines were drunk at feasts, given as gifts (1 Sam. 25:18; 2 Sam. 16:1), and used in offerings to God (Ex. 29:40; Lev. 23:13; Num. 15:7). Yet the OT calls for moderation and rejects both drunkenness and a love for drink (Prov. 20:1; 21:17; 23:20). The two sides of the use of wine—abuse and proper use—are both seen in Amos: God's people were condemned for sins associated with wine (Amos 2:8, 12; 5:11; 6:6) and, in the later chapters, which are filled with promises of restoration, they were promised that wine would "drip from the mountains" (Amos 9:13) and that they would "plant vineyards and drink their wine" (v. 16).
>
> The Greek word for wine is *oinos*. References in the NT show the same appreciation of wine and the same condemnation of its abuse as the OT.

Jesus Clears the Temple (2:12-25). See the Word Study in Mark 11:15, and the parallel passage in Matt. 21:12-17.

Jesus Teaches Nicodemus (3:1-21).
Background. The text identifies Nicodemus as "Israel's teacher" (*ho didaskalos tou Israel*, literally, the teacher of Israel). This indicates that Nicodemus was no ordinary rabbi, but was a member of the Sanhedrin and held a significant, although difficult in our day to define, place in the theological hierarchy. The fact that the interview took place at night need not imply secrecy, as some have suggested, but rather that Nicodemus chose a time when he could speak with Jesus in private. What is most revealing may be Nicodemus' opening remark, "Rabbi, we know You are a Teacher who has come from God. For no one could perform the miraculous signs You are doing if God were not with Him" (3:2). This should not be dismissed as mere courtesy. Instead it indicates that, from the beginning of Jesus' ministry, the religious elite knew that Christ spoke with an authority granted Him by God.

Nothing in Nicodemus' words suggests hostility. Instead there seems to be an honest desire to hear from Jesus' own lips just what God's message through this new Rabbi may be. In this Nicodemus was unlike most of his fellows. They knew that the miracles Jesus performed were signs which fully authenticated Him as God's messenger. Yet they consciously closed their hearts and minds against Jesus, seeing Him not as God's bright hope for tomorrow but as a threat to their position and authority today.

In comparison Nicodemus' stature grows. We are hardly surprised to see Nicodemus attempt to speak a word on Jesus' behalf (7:50), or to find early traditions which suggest he later became a Christian.

Questions about Nicodemus are, of course, less significant than the wonders Jesus revealed to him. Yet we need to see in the dialogue that follows the earnest attempt of an honest man to grapple with concepts that, despite his deep religious commitments or perhaps because of them, Nicodemus clearly did not understand.

Interpretation. The account divides into two distinct parts: John's report of the gist of the two men's discussion (3:1-15), and John's thoughtful meditation on its meaning (3:16-36).

■ The dialogue. Jesus makes a series of assertions that stun Nicodemus. A person must be "born again" (*anothen*, lit., born from above) to even see the kingdom of God (3:3).

When Nicodemus exclaims in amazement, Jesus explains. To be born from above means to be "born of water and the Spirit" (3:5). Here Jesus uses the familiar terminology introduced by John the Baptist: water, symbolizing repentance and a turning from the old; the Spirit, symbolizing that supernatural gift to be given by the One John is sent to announce. While flesh gives birth to flesh, only God's Spirit can provide that spiritual rebirth necessary for a person to function in a kingdom whose essence is spiritual rather than biological and material (3:4-7).

This new birth is inner, not outward, and cannot be assessed by those external acts on which first-century Judaism set such store (3:8).

Nicodemus still struggles to understand and begs Jesus to explain further. Jesus' rebuke is mild, but real. Surely Israel's instructor in spiritual things must understand this utterly basic principle (3:10). In fact, the principle of essential inner renewal is taught in the OT, a vital element in Jeremiah's vision of the New Covenant God will make with Israel (Jer. 31:33-34; Ezek. 36:26).

Mildly Jesus assures Nicodemus: He speaks with authority. He knows, for He has come from heaven, and although He has spoken using earthly analogies of water and wind, what He describes is solid, absolute reality (3:10-13). All Nicodemus needs to know now is that Christ Himself is destined to be an object of faith which, when lifted up, will bring healing and health to all who look to Him in faith (3:14-15).

That symbol too was surely well known to Nicodemus. The story, told in Numbers 21:4-9, is strikingly appropriate. The Israelites of that time were disobedient, unthankful, and hostile to God's messenger. God condemned their acts and decreed punishment: a plague of serpents. The bite was deadly, and there was no hope of recovery. Yet in mercy God commanded Moses to "lift up" on a pole a bronze serpent, an emblem of their judgment. And then the people were told that if they would only look, they would be healed.

The parallels are immediately clear. God's people, and all mankind, were disobedient, unthankful, and hostile to the Lord, condemned by Him to death. Yet in mercy God sent His Son, commanded that He be lifted up, an emblem of the judgment which sin requires. And we are told that if we but look to Him in faith, we will be forgiven and healed.

■ **The meditation.** Looking back, with the perspective provided by the cross, resurrection, and the explosive growth of the church, John pens his own meditation on this now famous meeting between the Savior and the honest Pharisee.

"God so loved the world that He gave His one and only Son, that whoever believes in Him shall not perish but have eternal life" (3:16). The Savior was lifted up, and in that decisive act light burst on mankind's dark world. All who respond to that light with faith have passed from death to life. All who scurry back deeper into darkness show that they are condemned already, their destiny to experience the unending wrath of God.

Application. Never suppose that there is more than one way of salvation. The issue is utterly clear. There is one light; all else is darkness. There is one way to eternal life; all else is endless death.

Jesus Talks with a Samaritan Woman (4:1-42). See the Index on "Samaritans."

Background. We know so much about the woman at the well. In the East, drawing water was the time when the women of a community gathered to talk, chattering eagerly as they walked to and from the well and waited while each jug of water was drawn. Yet the woman in our story comes alone. Clearly something had alienated the other women of the town and made her a social outcast.

We know more. No woman in that culture would speak to a man without her husband present. Jesus knew this as well, so His request to "Go, call your husband" (4:16) was intended to confront. But there were no cultural clues to the fact that she had had five men, and was now living unwed with yet another. And so we understand her amazement that He, a Jewish man, would stoop to talking with a Samaritan. And the disciples were surprised to find Him in dialogue with an isolated woman.

Interpretation. The story of the woman at the well is often suggested as a model for personal evangelism. Jesus initiated conversation. He asked her to do something for Him, thus assuming a humble and nonthreatening position. He quickly introduced the theme of eternal life as a gift from God. When the woman expressed a desire for what Jesus offered, Christ confronted her more directly. Although she tried to avoid the issue of sin by raising a theological question, Jesus did not dispute. He simply spoke of who God is, and assured the woman that God seeks worshipers. And then Jesus presented Himself as the long-promised Messiah.

The woman responded with belief, and hurried to tell the news in her community. This led many to hurry down to the well where they too met Jesus, and believed when they heard His words. There, in that Samaritan village, a little community of faith was established of persons who had heard Jesus "for ourselves" (4:42), and who had come to "know that this man really is the Savior of the world."

Application. Many a person shunned by others is waiting for one of us to approach him or her. Like Jesus, we can recognize the sin in others without accusing or condemning.

This is an important concept. If we pretend not to be aware of another's flaws, they may hide themselves behind a mask, and be unwilling to admit a need. If we condemn, that person will draw back behind walls. We only need to show, as Jesus did, that we know others as they really are, and that God still cares.

There are many other insights we can gain from this story. We keep the offer of God in plain sight. We focus on Jesus — not theology. And we invite others, as the woman of long ago, to respond to Him.

JOHN 4:43–6:71
The Power of the New

EXPOSITION

John opened his Gospel with a powerful affirmation. In Jesus the eternal Word was made flesh, bringing a new revelation to humankind. The grace and truth which come by Jesus supersede the Law given by Moses (1:1-14), for as John saw and testified, Jesus is the Son of God (1:15-51). Through a series of stories John has displayed something of the nature of the new: the old ritual waters are transformed into the wine of kingdom promise; the temple is purified and again becomes a house of worship (chap. 2). This is possible because in its essential nature the "new" involves rebirth, a work of God's Spirit infusing human beings who were spiritually dead with eternal life (chap. 3). What is more, this new work of God bursts through old boundaries and brings God's grace to Samaritan as well as Jew (4:1-42). And if the "official" in 4:43-54 is, as many suspect, a Gentile, God's life-giving grace extends to all humankind.

With this established, John goes on to further illustrate the power of the Person who extends God's grace-gifts to all. *Jesus heals an official's son with a word* (4:43-54). *He heals a helpless cripple beside a pool in Jerusalem* (5:1-15), and explains His powers by defining His relationship with God the Father (5:16-30), pointing out that the miraculous works He performs testify to the truth of His claims (5:31-47). *Jesus continues to display His power by miraculously feeding the 5,000* (6:1-15), *and then walks at night on the waters of Galilee* (6:16-24).

It is important to note that this portion of Scripture contains four of the seven miracles, indicated in italics, that John designates as "signs" (*semeia*). The seven are distinctive because they show Jesus is fully able to deal with life's emergencies, not simply for Himself, but for others. Several of the signs also became the occasion of major teachings by Jesus. The seven signs are:

1. Turning water into wine (2:1-11)
2. Healing an official's son (4:43-54)
3. Healing a paralytic (5:1-15)
4. Feeding the 5,000 (6:1-14)
5. Walking on the waters (6:16-21)
6. Curing a man born blind (9:1-41)
7. Raising Lazarus (11:1-44)

We can understand, noting that three of these miracles were performed in public, that by now Jesus would be at the height of His popularity, a fact reflected in the eagerness of many to "make Him king" (6:15). Yet Jesus uses the occasion of the feeding of the multitudes to announce that He Himself is the Bread of heaven. To have eternal life His listeners must eat His flesh and drink His blood, a powerful yet, to the Jews, repelling metaphor suggesting full appropriation of Jesus Himself (6:25-59).

At this point many who have followed Him, enthralled by His power to perform miracles, and excited by the prospect of having a ruler who can miraculously provide them with food, begin to drop away (6:60-71). Jesus' "hard teachings" (6:60) have begun to force the crowds to realize that they must take Him on His own terms, not on theirs. The new has come. Only a settled and continuing confidence that Jesus is "the Holy One of God" (6:69) makes it possible for the new to come to us.

WORD STUDIES

And there was a certain *royal official* whose son lay sick at Capernaum (4:46). The Greek word is *basilikos,* and likely indicates a member of Herod's staff. Some suggest he was a Gentile, for it is known that Herod preferred to employ Gentiles in administrative posts.

Unless *you people* see miraculous signs and wonders you will never believe (4:48). At the time Jesus spoke these words, He was in fact popular because of the miracles He had performed (4:45). What's wrong with a faith that is rooted in miracles? Simply that a fasci-

nation with the miraculous is no substitute for a settled confidence in the Person of Jesus, or for obedience to His Word.

Jesus replied, "You may go. Your son *will live*" (4:50). While the NIV may express the sense of what Jesus said, this is interpretation rather than translation. The original reads *ho huios sou ze,* "Your son is living."

Jesus' words forced the royal official to make a difficult decision. When he left Capernaum his son had been at the point of death. Jesus had said "Go," and informed him, "Your son lives." Jesus did not promise that the boy would keep on living. What then should the official do? Return, as Jesus had commanded? Or keep on urging Christ to come and heal his son?

The official's choice revealed the kind of belief that 4:48 suggests Jesus longed for. He chose to trust Christ and obey, knowing only that Jesus was aware of his need and had asserted that, at least for now, his son was living.

When he returned home he learned that his son was recovering, and that the fever had broken at just the time Christ had announced, "Your son lives." And that initial faith expressed in obedience blossomed into total trust in the Savior.

Often we have to be satisfied with just what Jesus offered that royal official. At this moment we live. All we can do is commit ourselves to do His will and realize that Jesus knows our deepest needs. This is enough for now. Tomorrow, when we realize that Christ has acted for us, our faith will be strengthened and renewed.

Some time later, Jesus went up to Jerusalem for a feast of the Jews (5:1). John's Gospel is not organized chronologically. A similar phrase is found in 6:1: "Some time after this." While each Gospel writer selects and organizes his material to forward his theme, this is more apparent in John than in the synoptics.

My Father is always *at His work* to this very day, and I, too, am working (5:17). What an answer to the attacks against Jesus for healing on the Sabbath! God doesn't halt the processes of nature because it is the Sabbath! On Sabbath white blood cells still rush to fight infection; a cut begins to heal; tears flow to wash a speck of dust out of the eye. Since the Father performs His healing works on the Sabbath, how can the Son be criticized for doing the same thing!

Let's be careful that our convictions about do's and don'ts are based on better insight into the nature and works of God than were those of Jesus' first-century opponents!

He was even calling God His own Father, making Himself equal with God (5:18). Jesus' listeners clearly understood Him to claim equality with God. As the passage goes on, we see that rather than correct the Jewish leaders Jesus went on to claim for Himself other prerogatives of deity.

■ Like the Father, Jesus raises the dead and gives them life.

■ The Father has "entrusted all judgment" to the Son, in order that Jesus and the Father might be shown equal respect by all humankind.

■ Like the Father, Jesus has "life in Himself." That is, the existence of neither the Father nor the Son depends on another, as our existence depends on the act of our biological father and mother.

It is popular in some circles to insist that Jesus never claimed to be God, that deity was thrust upon Him by the apostles and the early church. There is no way that this view can be upheld by anyone who in any way places reliance on the accounts of Jesus' life given us in the four Gospels.

If I testify about Myself, My testimony is not valid (5:31). This verse does not mean that Christ's words about Himself are mistaken or are lies. All Jesus means is that under Jewish, Roman, or Greek law, no witness could testify on his own behalf (Deut. 19:15). Later Jesus argues that His testimony is valid despite the legal technicality, because the Father Himself speaks through the Son and corroborates what He says (8:12-18).

The very *work* that the Father has given Me to finish, and which I am doing, testifies that the Father has sent Me (5:36). The word here is *erga,* "works." Typically *erga* is used of miracles. Here the use seems to be more encompassing, involving everything that Jesus says and does while performing this mission on which He has been sent by God.

Don't judge Jesus simply on reports of His miracles. Look at the nature of the miracles—most performed in response to some human need and thus revealing God's commitment to His creatures. Listen to His words, which promise eternal life. Watch how He exposes the rigid, empty religion imposed on Israel by traditions which fail to reflect the spirit of God's Word. Everything Jesus said and did reveals what God is like, and in revealing the Father proves His claim to be the Son.

Jesus, knowing that they intended to come and *make Him king by force,* withdrew again to a mountain by Himself (6:15). What John describes is a popular movement, urging rebellion against Rome and Herod, with the popular young prophet to be acclaimed sole ruler of the Jews. The fact that the instigators planned to make Him king "by force," *harpazein,* is revealing. It suggests that they realized Jesus would not willingly take this step and assume the political role. How strange. If the crowd was truly willing to submit to Christ's will, how could they ever have thought of using force to gain something they wanted, but He did not? Yet how often do we try to bend Christ to our will, rather than simply saying "Your will be done on earth as it is in heaven"? (Matt. 6:10)

There is, however, an interesting historical parallel in the way that, not too much time later, Claudius became emperor of Rome. After the assassination of his nephew Caligula, Claudius was found hiding in a closet by a group of soldiers in the Praetorian Guard. Quickly seizing on him as their candidate, the imperial guard proclaimed Claudius Emperor and forced the Roman Senate to confirm their action. As expected, the somewhat reluctant but now imperial Claudius rewarded the Praetorians with a generous distribution from the public treasury.

Then Jesus declared, "I *am* the bread of life" (6:35). One of the distinctives of the Gospel of John is its series of "I am" sayings of Jesus. Their significance is underlined in 8:58, in which Jesus announces that "before Abraham was born, I am!" His hearers understood the implicit claim, for they knew full well that "I am" (*ego eimi*) is the Greek equivalent of YHWH, Yahweh, the revelatory and personal name of God that vitalizes the Old Testament.

What are the "I am" statements in John, and how do they display the deity that Jesus claimed?

■ "I am the bread of life" (6:35). Jesus is the One who sustains physical and spiritual life.

■ "Before Abraham was born, I am!" (8:58) Jesus is the preexistent One, the witness to and source of sacred history.

■ "I am the Gate for the sheep" (10:7). Jesus

provides access to God and salvation.

■ "I am the Good Shepherd" (10:11). Jesus lays down His life for us, His sheep.

■ "I am the Resurrection and the Life" (11:25). Jesus is the source and giver of life eternal.

■ "I am the Way and the Truth and the Life" (14:6). Jesus alone provides access to God the Father and all of the Father's good gifts to humankind.

■ "I am" the true vine (15:1). Jesus is the source of spiritual vitality. By remaining close to Him we are enabled to bring forth fruit and so glorify God.

No one can come to Me, unless the Father who sent Me *draws* him (6:44). This is why I told you that *no one can come* to Me unless the Father has *enabled* him (6:65). These verses raise a question that has troubled many an individual. Do they teach an irresistible grace that compels a person against His will? Even more troubling, do they suggest that the Gospel's "whoever" is a fiction, and only those specially selected and empowered by God have any hope of salvation?

There is some help in the original language. The word translated "draws" is *helkuo,* which is unlike the similar word *suro,* "to drag." *Helkuo* here may very well indicate an inner moral response to an outer force, such as of a piece of metal to a magnet. This view seems to find some support in the next verse, which turns our attention to the Scriptures. It is here we have the teaching of God, and it is to this Word that the responsive individual listens.

In verse 65, the original reads *ean me e dedomenon auto.* The verb is the periphrastic perfect passive subjunctive of *didomai,* "to give." The problem is that this verb is found over 400 times in the NT—with a wide range of meanings! J.B. Phillips translates the verse, "No one can come unto Me unless My Father puts it in his heart to come." His translation maintains a nice balance between the theological "rock and a hard place." It affirms the initiating work of God in the human heart. But it also preserves human responsibility. God puts it in the heart. Yet the individual still must choose to come.

Ultimately the position a person adopts on

questions of free will and election will not rest on word studies or on Greek grammar, for neither decisively answers the questions we may want to ask.

Ultimately what we must decide to do is simply, to trust. Jesus is the great I AM: the Bread of Life; the Good Shepherd; the Way, Truth and Life; the Vine on whose vitality we are privileged to draw. Even as the works He performed in the first century revealed His and His father's nature, so it is that nature, who God is, that is the foundation of our faith. On that foundation we must, and can, find rest.

THE PASSAGE IN DEPTH

Jesus Heals the Official's Son (4:43-54). See the Word Studies of John 4:46, 48, and 50, and the similar story in Matt. 8:5-13.

The Healing at the Pool (5:1-15). See the Word Study of John 5:1.

Background. The pool John describes probably lay under what is today the Church of Saint Anne, in northwest Jerusalem. Its name is debated; various mss. suggest Bethzatha ("house of bubbling up"), as well as Bethesda ("house of mercy"). The first name may imply it was fed by an intermittent spring, which caused a bubbling up of the waters when it began to flow.

It is important to note that the Bible does not assert that an angel stirred the waters (see NIV footnote). Nor does the passage suggest that healing was guaranteed to the first to slip into the pool after the waters were stirred. John simply quotes the paralyzed man, who undoubtedly reflects the popular superstition.

While there is no hint in OT or NT of similar healing pools, Edersheim points out that "holy wells" seem to have been "very common in ancient times," and are mentioned on Babylonian cuneiform tablets.

Interpretation. The miracle of healing (5:1-15) provides the occasion for a lengthy sermon by Jesus (5:16-47). We see here a pattern that John frequently follows. The feeding of the 5,000 is the background of Christ's discourse on the Bread of Life; the healing of a man born blind the background against which Jesus warns of spiritual blindness. Even so, there is much for us to reflect on in this account of the event itself. First, it is fascinating to consider what we are told about the man himself in this brief account. He has been an invalid for 38 years. During those long, empty decades those who had once been close to him left or died, for he says, "I have no one to help me" (5:7). He has apparently become reconciled to his situation, for Jesus asks him, "Do you want to get well?" (5:6)

This is a deeply perceptive question. Our first inclination might be to say, "Of course he wanted to get well!" But on reflection, we realize that many truly do not want healing. For some 38 years this invalid had undoubtedly supported himself by begging. Once healed, he would have to become responsible for himself and find work. If we are invalids, we have every excuse for our failures, every reason to avoid taking responsibility for ourselves. Healed, those excuses are stripped away, and we become accountable.

And so when Jesus asked, "Do you want to get well?" the invalid equivocated. Unwilling to say "yes" or "no," he excused himself: "I have no one to help me."

Despite this, Jesus commanded the man to pick up his mat and walk. John says, "At once the man was cured; he picked up his mat and walked" (5:9). There is an interesting difference in this account and in Luke's story of the Healing of Ten Lepers. There Luke says, "And as they went, they were cleansed" (17:14). They did as Jesus said, and it was through their response of faith (17:19) that healing came. Here John places the cure before the response. We cannot infer any role that faith may have played in the healing of the invalid of Bethesda.

Nevertheless the invalid felt strength surge through his wasted limbs, and so as Jesus commanded he did pick up his mat—and walked away. Later, when confronted by "the Jews" (see Word Study of 1:19), we note that the healed man quickly shifts responsibility to "the man who made me well."

What is even more fascinating is what happens when, later, Jesus finds him at the temple, and warns him, "Stop sinning" (5:14). Most take this as an indication that his lengthy illness had been divine discipline! The man's next action, to hurry off and tell the Jewish leaders that it was Jesus who made him well, suggests at the least a lack of gratitude. From the harsh criticism the one-time invalid himself had experienced from the religious leaders, he simply must have known that they were actively hostile to Christ. It is hard to see anything in this betrayal of Jesus to them other than latent antagonism or terrible personal weakness.

No matter how we might try to excuse the invalid of Bethesda, we cannot avoid the conclusion that he was of a most disagreeable character. Weak, unwilling to accept responsibility, ungrateful, even betraying one who had done so much for him by pandering to those in authority.

Second, then, we must be equally fascinated by Jesus' decision to select this particular man for healing. We might argue that in selecting a "hopeless case," Christ's miracle-working powers would appear even more wonderful. Yet there is no indication Jesus intended to exploit this healing. He healed, and then slipped away into the crowds, and even the man who was healed did not know who He was. Later He found the man, but it was to warn him rather than to solicit his testimony.

Why, then? Why heal a man who has no hope, who is isolated from others, who displays no faith or gratitude, whose illness is a divine judgment for some earlier sin, and who was all too ready to identify Jesus to the Savior's enemies? Perhaps because only this kind of person could adequately represent you and me. Perhaps because Jesus comes to us in our hopelessness. Comes as we live under the judgment of God for our sins, without faith or gratitude, hostile toward God and already betraying Him by denying what we do know of His nature.

When Jesus comes to us, His question rightly is: "Do you want to get well?" Do we want to hold on to our sins, our anger, our selfishness, our excuses? Or do we want to be made well, knowing that when we are we must accept responsibility for ourselves and our future choices? The issue has never been whether God can heal us. The issue has always been, and still is, do we want to get well?

Life through the Son (5:16-47). See the Word Studies of John 5:17, 5:18, 5:31, and 5:36 above. Also see other passages in which Sabbath controversies are discussed, such as Matt. 12:1-14; Mark 2:23–3:6 and Luke 6:1-11.

Background. Jesus healed the invalid on the Sabbath. This occasioned another of those intense controversies over the Sabbath which heighten the ever-developing hostility of the religious leaders for Jesus.

Christ meets the criticism head on. He argues that God works on the Sabbath; thus it is appropriate for the Son to work. Then comes a passage which can be fully understood only by reference to cultural background. That passage reads: "Jesus gave them this answer: 'I tell you the truth, the Son can do nothing by Himself; He can do only what He sees His Father doing, because whatever the Father does the Son also does. For the Father loves the Son and shows Him all He does' " (5:19-20).

In the East great emphasis was placed by artisans on trade secrets. The metal worker, the glass worker, the maker of dyes—all guarded their processes and skills jealously. Typically these were family secrets, passed on from one generation to the next. While apprentices outside the family might be employed, even those who served loyally for years were unlikely to be taught all the family secrets, lest they leave and establish a competing establishment. In contrast the son works with his father from childhood. The son watches the father mix his compounds or add distinctive finishing touches to work done in his shop. As they work together day by day the father teaches his son all his secrets. Such a son can "do nothing by himself" but instead can do "only what he sees his father doing." In time the work of the father and the son becomes indistinguishable, because the father "loves the son and shows him all he does."

In the context of Jesus' time, then, these verses serve as a powerful affirmation of Jesus' unique position, and explain His right to give authoritative interpretation of Sabbath Law. As the Son of God, Jesus' healings bear the unmistakable mark of being God's Word—even as the work of an artisan bears his own unmistakable stamp, clear to all who examine his work closely!

Interpretation. The above is the key to interpreting the rest of this lengthy passage, as well as to understanding the nature of Jesus' response to the leaders' criticism of His Sabbath healing.

Christ goes on in the passage to indicate "greater things" (5:20) than His recent healing that God has entrusted into the Son's hands. Raising the dead (5:21), judging human beings (5:22), and having "life in Himself" (5:26) (see Word Studies, above), are all "works" that Christ has learned from the Father and that have been turned over to Him. Jesus is no religious "apprentice." Instead, His actions are so fully in harmony with the Father's nature and will that what Jesus says and does are "works" which are indistinguishable from Father's own.

There is another implication, which Christ develops in John 5:36-40. If the religious leaders of Israel are unable to recognize the stamp of God's work in the healings Jesus has performed, then the inescapable conclusion is that they must not know the Father! You have never heard His voice or seen His form, nor does His word dwell in you, for you do not believe the One He sent (5:37-38).

The religious "diligently study the Scriptures" (5:39) in the hope of finding eternal life. But, although the Scriptures testify about Jesus, they "refuse to come to Me to have life" (5:40).

Application. Perhaps the most important question we can answer as we study the Scriptures and meditate on the life of Christ is simply this: What is God like?

The religious leaders of Judaism had lost sight of the God of forgiveness and mercy, whose grace is displayed in the OT as well as the NT. Somehow they saw Him as a Rule Maker. As One who could only be pleased by rigorous observance of ritual, and unfailing observance of requirements that tradition rather than biblical law decreed. They could not recognize Jesus, because their vision of God had become distorted and unclear.

We must always seek to understand the Scriptures better, and seek to apply biblical principles as guides for daily life. But the most important single principle in interpretation remains this: Is my understanding in full harmony with the character of God as He Himself is unveiled in the written and living Word.

Jesus Feeds the Five Thousand (6:1-15). See the commentary on Mark 8:1-13, and the parallel passages at Matt. 14:13-21; Mark 6:30-

44; Luke 9:10-17.

Jesus Walks on the Water (6:16-24). See the commentary on Mark 6:45-56 and Matt. 14:22-36.

Jesus the Bread of Life (6:25-71).

Background. The *Zondervan Expository Dictionary of Bible Words* notes that bread was the primary food in Bible times. Bread was baked from a variety of grains, and often the flour was mixed with beans or lentils. The bread was baked flat, perhaps a half-inch thick, in wide loaves. Bread has special significance in the Bible: it represents the sustenance of life in the world. The significance of bread as a sustainer of life underlies the metaphorical uses of "bread" in the Scriptures (p. 140).

Interpretation. This extended passage contains three distinct segments: Jesus' dialogue with the crowd; Jesus' debate with "the Jews"; and Jesus' "disciples' " response.

JESUS' DIALOGUE WITH THE CROWD (6:25-40)

The thousands that Jesus fed by miraculously multiplying a few loaves and fishes (6:1-15) were distraught when He left without telling them (6:22-24). Crowding into some of the 330 fishing boats Josephus tells us worked the waters at the north end of the Sea of Galilee, many of them crossed the waters in search of our Lord.

Jesus responded by confronting them: they looked for Jesus because He had fed them. Rather than be concerned about ordinary bread, they should be concerned "for food that endures to eternal life" (6:27). There is a direct parallel here to Jesus' dialogue with the woman at the well (chap. 4). At that time He asked for well water, but quickly turned the conversation: "The water I give him will become in him a spring of water welling up to eternal life" (4:14). In both settings Jesus asserts that He is the one able to "give" that which provides "eternal life."

But here the two stories take very different twists. The Samaritan woman simply asks: "Sir, give me this water" (4:15). The crowd around Jesus says instead, "What must we do to do the works God requires" (6:28). This response reflects the great flaw in rabbinic Judaism—a flaw that the Apostle Paul sharply defines in Rom. 10:2-3: "For I can testify

233

about them that they are zealous for God, but their zeal is not based on knowledge. Since they did not know the righteousness that comes from God and sought to establish their own."

The question reveals the belief that human beings must "work" to please God and the misplaced belief that members of the covenant community are capable of doing what is required to please the Lord.

But Jesus had said He would give the "food that endures to eternal life" (6:27). The only "work" God requires is "this: to believe in the One He has sent" (6:29).

Now, however, we see again that the crowd was in fact motivated by materialistic rather than spiritual concerns. What counts with the crowd is the now, not the hereafter; biological life, not eternal spiritual life. For immediately they ask for a "miraculous sign" (6:30) and shrewdly suggest that the appropriate sign would be that which Moses performed in providing manna for the Exodus generation.

Some commentators suggest that the crowds have already forgotten the miraculous feeding of the 5,000. Not at all! They remember it very well. Their point is that Moses provided manna for 40 years! If Jesus were to continuously provide bread, they would certainly believe in Him.

We can almost see Jesus sadly shaking His head. God's gift is the "true bread" (literally, "genuine," "authentic"), which is the source of life in this world, and Jesus Himself is this Bread of Life. (See Word Study of 6:35, above.) "My Father's will is that everyone who looks to the Son and believes in Him shall have eternal life, and I will raise Him up at the last day."

JESUS' DEBATE WITH "THE JEWS" (6:41-59)

In John "the Jews" is a term applied to the religious leaders of the nation. They now begin to "grumble" about Jesus' teaching. The Greek word is *egogguzon,* which indicates a buzzing or murmuring. How could someone known (supposed!) to be the son of Mary and Joseph have come down from heaven?

Rather than answer directly Jesus points out that even as the Scriptures have a drawing power for those who listen to the Father, so Christ also draws men — and the one listening to the Father will come to Him. (See Word

Study of John 6:44, 65 above.) There is no use dealing with the leaders' objections, for no one can be argued into faith. Faith is a response of those who hear God speak and recognize His voice.

Now, instead of making it easier for His opponents, Jesus seems to make it even more difficult! Not only is He the Living Bread that came down from heaven, but a person must "eat" this bread — His very "flesh, which I will give for the life of the world" (6:51). Then Jesus made the analogy even more extreme, and promised that "whoever eats My flesh and drinks My blood has eternal life" (6:54).

The imagery not only shocked the Jewish leaders, but repelled them. According to Leviticus 17:11, "The life of a creature is in the blood." Blood may be shed in sacrifice, but drinking blood was specifically forbidden, with the penalty of expulsion from covenant relationship. While clearly Jesus could not be speaking literally, even the image was repulsive to the Jews.

This imagery has been misunderstood by Christians as well. Some have taken Jesus' words in a literal sense and supposed that He refers to the elements in Communion, which in Roman Catholic tradition are supposedly changed into the very body and blood of Christ, and in Lutheran tradition become one substance with the body and blood of Christ.

This, however, ignores the metaphorical use of "bread" here and in the rest of Scripture, and ignores Jesus' own statement: "The Spirit gives life; the flesh counts for nothing. The words I have spoken to you are spirit and they are life" (6:63). Thus even the church fathers see here a powerful metaphor of faith, appropriating Christ, entering into union with Him, and sharing in His life. Thus Augustine calls this "a figure, bidding us communicate in the sufferings of our Lord, and secretly and probably treasure in our hearts the fact that His flesh was crucified and pierced for us." Thus Augustine's dictum was *Crede et manducasti,* "Believe, and you have eaten." To the devout monk, Bernard of Clarvaux, eating Christ's flesh and drinking His blood meant simply this: "He who reflects on My death, and after My example mortifies his members which are on earth, has eternal life."

It is important to note that the Greek text uses different tenses in the several references to "eating" Christ's flesh. Verses 51, 53 have the aorist tense of *esthio,* consuming, implying an initial act of acceptance. But vv. 54, 56 have the present tense of *trogo,* to gnaw. The relationship with Christ symbolized by eating His flesh is initiated and sustained by faith's participation in all that Jesus is and all He has done for us.

JESUS' "DISCIPLES" DESERT (6:60-71)
This sermon on the Bread of Life marks the height of Jesus' popularity. From this point on, the "Jesus movement" went into decline. While we cannot correlate this sermon exactly with events reported in the synoptics, it is significant that each of the other three Gospels portrays a turning point shortly after reporting stories of Jesus walking on the water and feeding a multitude, which would correlate with John.

Here John describes "many of His disciples" (6:60) complaining because of Jesus' "hard teaching." Even though Jesus clearly stated that "the words I have spoken to you are spirit" (6:63), from that point in time "many of His disciples turned back and no longer followed Him" (6:66).

It is important here to note that the word "disciple" in the Gospels does not always imply belief. The *Zondervan Expository Dictionary of Bible Words* notes that

the word *mathetes* is used in several different ways in the Gospels. First, it designates the Twelve whom Jesus chose to be with Him. The Twelve are unique in that Jesus chose and trained them to both teach and serve. . . .

Second, *mathetes* identifies followers of various schools or traditions. There were disciples of the Pharisees (Matt. 22:16; Mark 2:18; Luke 5:33) and the disciples of John the Baptist (Matt. 11:2ff.; Mark 2:18;

Luke 5:33; John 1:35-37; 3:34). Used in this sense, "disciple" does not identify a student in a traditional teacher-learner relationship; rather, it identifies persons who are adherents of a movement.

Third, our NT describes a much wider circle beyond the Twelve who are also called disciples. These are adherents of the movement associated with Jesus. At times the word "disciple" may seem to carry the sense of "believer" (cf. John 8:31; 13:35; 15:8). But it would be a mistake to think that all those who were called disciples in the Gospels were persons who made a firm commitment to Jesus. In fact many were only initially attracted to Jesus. When they found His teachings difficult, as after His discourse on the Bread of life, "many of His disciples turned back and no longer followed Him" (John 6:66). [pp. 226-27]

Jesus, noting the flow of loose adherents away from His movement, turned to the Twelve. "You do not want to leave too, do you?" (6:67)

Peter answered for them all, and for us. "You have the words of eternal life. We believe and know that You are the Holy One of God" (6:68-69). The perfect tense is used in the original, so what the disciple actually said was, "We have believed and come to know." We have made our decision about who You are— and that decision remains as fixed and firm today as it was the day we chose to believe.

Application. By faith we do participate in Jesus' death and His resurrection. We have partaken of His body and blood, and received His gift of eternal life. However difficult His words may be to understand, with the Twelve we affirm "we have believed and come to know." Jesus has the words of eternal life, and we will never abandon our allegiance to Him.

JOHN 7–9
Light and Darkness

EXPOSITION

Jesus' popularity has peaked. Now as the annual Feast of Tabernacles approaches, enthusiasm continues to wane. John opens this section of his book with the note that "the Jews there [in Judea] were waiting to take His life" (7:1), and that "even His own brothers did not believe in Him" (7:5).

In the Holy City the crowds are divided, some insisting He is a good man and others that He is a deceiver (7:1-13). Even so, Jesus appears at the feast and begins to teach openly. This fuels the debate. The hostility of the leaders is well known, yet they seem powerless to silence the Galilean preacher. Against this backdrop of open hostility and uncertainty, Jesus calls upon the crowds to believe in Him. Boldly He promises that "living water" will well up within those who do (7:25-52).

At this point John's report of Jesus' preaching is interrupted by a story not found in the earliest Greek manuscripts of this Gospel (7:53–8:11). Still, the story fits the flow of John's thought, for it underlines the fact that all have sinned, and that Jesus has not come to condemn but to save. Unless God's people believe He is the One He claims to be, they will die in their sins (8:12-30). Christ, the Light of the world, has come to reveal the Father and His grace. The Jews' unbelief is proof positive that whatever their physical lineage, spiritually they are not related to that great man of faith, Abraham — or to God! In fact, rejection of Jesus shows that they are related to Satan (8:31-47).

At this point Jesus makes an unmistakable claim. Before Abraham, Jesus existed as the I AM (Yahweh) of the OT. The Man speaking to them is the God they profess to worship, but have in fact rejected and slandered. Underlining this rejection, the infuriated religious leaders pick up stones, intent on killing Jesus, who slips away from them (8:48-59).

There is no break in the action here. As Jesus "went along" (9:1) He sees a man born blind, and gives him sight (chap. 9). The miracle stuns everyone. When the man is brought to the Pharisees, the debate intensifies. Desperate to condemn Jesus, the Pharisees fasten on the fact that the miracle was performed on the Sabbath and charge Christ with Sabbath-breaking. Yet they are unable to explain how a sinner could "do such miraculous signs" (9:16). Now comes John's point. The man born blind clearly sees the implications of Christ's act, and believes. But the sighted Pharisees and the religious elite willfully shut their eyes and refuse to believe. He who is Light is in the world, but so is darkness. And men still choose the darkness rather than the light.

236

WORD STUDIES

No one who *wants to become a public figure* acts in secret (7:4). The tone is sarcastic, as indicated by John's observation that even His brothers did not yet believe in Him (7:5). Most whose goal is to glorify God will at some time or other find others questioning their motives.

How did this man get such learning *without having studied?* (7:15) The reference is to the fact that in the first century only an ordained scholar had a right to be called "Rabbi," and that this status could only be achieved by undergoing a long apprenticeship with an acknowledged "expert in the Law." This status was based on possession of what was, in fact, "secret knowledge." The scribe not only had mastered the Scriptures but the traditional interpretations of the OT which had at least as much weight as the OT itself. In fact the sacred books themselves were accessible only to scholars, for they were written in Hebrew rather than the language of the people, Aramaic. Even Rabbi Gamaliel I, around A.D. 30, who is celebrated for his liberal views, had a copy of the Book of Job which had been transcribed into Aramaic, buried in a wall (b. Shab. 115a). This is just one indication of the well-known fact that in the first century, the leading scribes were fighting the spread of Aramaic translations of the OT.

This helps us understand the amazement of Jesus' enemies, these very experts in the Law, that Christ displayed "such learning" in His allusions and references to the Old Testament and in the forms of His arguments.

If anyone *chooses to do God's will,* He will find out whether My teaching comes from God or whether I speak on My own (7:17). The choice Jesus speaks of here is a firm commitment to do God's will. Understanding God's truth depends on our commitment to obey the Lord.

I did *one miracle* and you are all astonished (7:21). Jesus has performed a number of miracles. But the one that His opponents focus on is the Sabbath healing of the invalid (5:1-15). The word translated "astonish" is *thaumazo.* John uses this word in a distinctive way, to describe the general impact of Christ's miracles and teachings. Here *thaumazo* indicates hesitation and doubt; the miracle has confronted Jesus' opponents and the crowds, and all seem momentarily immobilized by the puzzle.

Finally some shout out that Jesus must be demon-possessed, a charge that Jesus responds to with one of those typically rabbinical arguments that so surprised the sages who observed Him (see 7:15 above). The argument hinges on the fact that the Law of Moses called for circumcising a child on the eighth day—and this was done even when the eighth day was the Sabbath. If a surgical procedure that affects only one part of the body can be performed on the Sabbath, how can the establishment criticize Jesus for making a man's entire body whole on that same day?

This is in fact a point made by other rabbis, but applied by them only to cases where an individual's life is threatened. In T. Sabb. 15-16 Rabbi Eliezer (ca. A.D. 90) argues that one must perform circumcision on the Sabbath, and notes "does not that justify a conclusion from the less to the greater? If one supersedes the Sabbath on account of one of his members, should he not supersede the Sabbath for his whole body?" On the same subject Rabbi Eliezer ben Azariah (ca. A.D. 100) argues in Yoma 85b, "If circumcision, which affects one of man's two hundred and forty-eight members, supersedes the Sabbath, how much more must his whole body supersede the Sabbath?"

The innovation Jesus introduces is that He does not limit healing on the Sabbath to life-threatening situations. God's compassion is far greater than man's.

On the last and greatest day of the Feast, Jesus stood and said in a loud voice, "If anyone is thirsty, let him come to Me and drink. Whoever believes in Me, as the Scripture has said, streams of living water will flow from within him" (7:37-38). The "last day" was the seventh (Deut. 16:13) or possibly an added eighth day (Lev. 23:36). The Feast of Tabernacles was itself a celebration recalling God's provision for the Exodus generation as they journeyed in the wilderness to the Promised Land.

Edersheim describes a special service that was a highlight of the festival, and provides the background we need to understand the symbolism behind Jesus' stunning offer.

To the sound of music a procession started from the Temple. It followed a Priest who bore a golden pitcher, capable of holding three log [note, a little over three quarts]. . . . When the Temple-procession had reached the Pool of Siloam, the Priest filled his golden pitcher from its waters. Then they went back to the Temple, so timing it that they should arrive just as they were laying the pieces of the sacrifice on the great Altar of Burnt-offering, toward the close of the ordinary Morning-Sacrifice service. A threefold blast welcomed the arrival of the Priest, as he entered through the "water-gate," which obtained its name from this ceremony, and passed straight into the Court of the Priests.

There, Edersheim relates, the water was poured into a silver funnel that led to the base of the altar, as psalms of praise were sung and Isa. 12:3 was recited: "With joy you will draw water from the wells of salvation." Edersheim goes on:

We can have little difficulty in determining at what part of the services of "the last, the Great Day of the Feast," Jesus stood and cried, "If anyone thirst, let him come unto Me and drink!" It must have been with special reference to the ceremony of the outpouring of the water, which, as we have seen, was considered the central part of the service. Moreover, all would understand that His words must refer to the Holy Spirit, since the rite was universally regarded as symbolical of His outpouring. The forthpouring of the water was immediately followed by the chanting of the Hallel [praises]. But after that there must have been a short pause to prepare for the festive sacrifices (the *Musaph*). It was then, immediately after the symbolic rite of water-pouring, immediately after the people had responded by repeating those lines from Psalm cxvii [117] — given thanks, and prayed that Jehovah would send salvation and prosperity, and had shaken their *Lulabh* [bundled branches that were supposed to fulfill Lev. 23:40] toward the altar, thus praising "with heart, and mouth, and hands," and then silence had fallen upon

them — that there rose, so loud as to be heard throughout the Temple, the Voice of Jesus. He interrupted not the services, for they had for the moment ceased: He interpreted, and He fulfilled them.

The meaning is even more powerful when we realize that "living water" is a term that identifies a flowing, bubbling spring of water flowing out of the earth. And that symbolism was deeply imbedded in first-century Jewish consciousness. Sukk. 5:1 says, "He who has not seen the joy of the place of water-drawing has not seen joy in his whole lifetime."

Against this symbolic background deeply embedded in the Feast of Tabernacles Jesus promised those who believed in Him that the ever-living Holy Spirit, symbolized in that morning's service, would take up residence in them, providing everlasting, eternal life.

"No one ever spoke the way this man does," the guards declared (7:46). The temple guards had been sent to arrest Jesus. They returned empty-handed with an excuse that our version does not quite capture. The Greek places "man," *anthropos,* in the emphatic position, at the end of the sentence. The structure suggests we understand the awed guards as hesitating because "no mere man has ever spoken in this way." Without committing themselves to the belief that Jesus was the Christ, the guards certainly imply that Jesus may at least be the Prophet destined to come and supersede Moses as a revealer of God's will (Deut. 18:15).

In their frustration the Pharisees reveal their contempt for the people for whom their position makes them responsible: "This mob that knows nothing of the Law — there is a curse on them" (7:49). No one claiming to be a shepherd, with such an attitude toward God's sheep, could possibly possess spiritual understanding. Thus the fact that none of the "rulers or of the Pharisees believed in Him" (7:48) is a point in Jesus' favor — not a point against Him.

How often we are known as much by our enemies as by our friends!

I am the Light of the world. Whoever follows Me will never walk in darkness, but will have the light of life (8:12). Light and darkness are expressive symbols frequently contrasted in John's Gospel. But John, like the OT, is not thinking of intellectual enlightenment or ignorance. Instead light and dark are soteriological terms, images which contrast the bright joy the saved experience in the presence of the Lord, with the fearful gloom through which those separated from Him must trudge. As Ps. 44:3 exults, "It was not by their sword that they won the land, nor did their arm bring them victory; it was Your right hand, Your arm, and the light of Your face, for You loved them."

Just as Jesus' saying about living water grew out of the ritual of the Feast of Tabernacles, so did His proclamation of Himself as the Light of the world. Each night of the feast a joyous celebration was held in the light shed by lamps set in the temple court. The tractate Sukk. 5 describes the scene:

> Towards the end of the first day of the feast of Tabernacles, people went down into the court of the women, where precautions had been taken [to separate the men from the women]. Golden lamps were there, and four golden bowls were on each of them, and four ladders were by each; four young men from the priestly group of youths had jugs of oil in their hands containing about 120 logs and poured oil from them into the individual bowls. Wicks were made from the discarded trousers of the priests and from their girdles. There was no court in Jerusalem that was not bright from the light of the place of drawing [water]. Men of piety and known for their good works danced before them with torches in their hands, and sang before them songs and praises. And the Levites stood with zithers and harps and cymbals and trumpets and other musical instruments without number on the 15 steps, which led down from the court of the Israelites into the court of the women and which corresponded to the 15 songs of the steps in the psalms.

We can imagine the joy of the dancing and the singing that lasted through the night. The rabbis were careful to distinguish these nightly celebrations from pagan revelry. During that ceremony two priests with trumpets descended the steps, turned to the temple, and proclaimed, "Our fathers who were in this place turned their backs to the temple of God and their faces eastward and threw themselves down eastward before the sun; but we direct our eyes to Yahweh." God was the light of Israel, the Source of salvation, of hope, and of joy.

And it was at this celebration, perhaps at the very moment the crowd fell silent to hear the affirmation of the priests, that Jesus stood and shouted, "I am the Light of the world. Whoever follows Me will never walk in darkness, but will have the light of life."

Even if I testify on My own behalf, My testimony is valid, for I know where I came from and where I am going (8:14). Earlier Jesus argued that His claims were not unsupported, but were in fact endorsed by the Father and the miracles He performed. Here He makes a different point. Perhaps a Jewish court would refuse to accept self-testimony, assuming that evidence offered by a person bringing a case would be biased in his own favor. But in this case Jesus' testimony is valid: first, because He has unique knowledge not available to those who "judge by human standards" (8:15), and second, because it is corroborated by the Father.

There is no way to argue those who will not believe into faith. The supernatural cannot be probed by any means available to mortal man. We must accept Christ's testimony on faith, simply because, as Morris has noted, "No human witness can authenticate a divine revelationship."

It is important, however, to not assume that taking Jesus' words "on faith" means to accept what He says "against reason." In fact, it is patently reasonable to believe. In view of the miracles Jesus performed it was in fact unreasonable for Jesus' opponents not to believe in Him. Even as it is unreasonable for moderns not to believe the testimony of Scripture and of millions of Christians who, through some 20 centuries, have experienced the joy of the salvation that Jesus Christ brings to those who follow Him in obedience.

When you have lifted up the Son of Man, then you will know that I am the One I claim to be (8:28). The phrase "lifted up," *huposo,* refers to the cross (3:14). These last words, *ego eimi,* appear three times in this lengthy interchange (8:24, 28, 58) and identify

Jesus as the I AM of the Old Testament, Yahweh Himself.

What is so significant about this saying, directed as it is to those very men who are so intent on seeing Jesus killed, is the indication that "when you have lifted [Him] up," then these very persons "will know" that Jesus is the I AM. The Resurrection will settle the question once and for all, and then those who plotted Christ's death will know who He was.

Yet, as we complete the Gospels, and read on in Acts and the Epistles, we make a frightening discovery. The religious leaders still refuse to believe, and in fact persecute the church even as they persecuted its founder.

There is an important lesson here. "Knowing" who Jesus is is not the critical issue. The critical issue is whether, knowing, we choose to throw ourselves on His mercy, and accept the forgiveness He won for us on the cross.

If you hold to My teaching, you are really My disciples. Then you will *know the truth,* and the truth will set you free (8:31-32). These words are addressed to those who believe in Jesus and make a vital point. Holding to Christ's teaching is not giving intellectual assent, but putting Jesus' words into practice. J.B. Phillips renders the phrase, "If you are faithful to what I have said."

Despite the misuse of this verse by one of our major newspapers, "knowing the truth" is not a matter of having information. One meaning of both the Hebrew and Greek words for "truth" is "in harmony with reality." When later John writes, "Sanctify them by the truth, Your Word is truth" (17:17), his point is that God's Word provides an accurate portrayal of reality, as God knows reality. Here, when a person "hold[s] to My teaching" (8:31) he orders his or her life by it, and in doing so begins to experience reality! It is this, the experience of that reality portrayed in the words of our Lord, that makes us free. We are free from the shadowy world of illusion through which men stumble, grasping at phantoms that appear desirable but which in fact bring only suffering and pain. We are freed by Christ's words to know what is right and good, and by choosing the right and good we discover that which is best for us and for others. The greatest freedom of all is freedom from sin and its effects.

"I tell you the truth, everyone who sins is a slave to sin. Now a slave has no permanent place in the family" (8:34-35). A slave in the first century enjoyed some protections under the law, but was not considered a "person" in a legal sense. Without ability to claim family ties, no one has any obligation toward him, while the slave does have an obligation to his master. The phrase "everyone who sins" is a present participle in the Greek, and indicates a continual habit rather than an infrequent slip. Human beings are sinners, trapped by an inner disposition toward sin that is as heartless as slavery. Only the Son can grant a person freedom, and make him or her a member of the family of God.

You belong to your father, the devil, and you want to carry out your father's desire (8:44). Christ's opponents argue that as descendants of Abraham, and thus members of the covenant community, they have a secure relationship with God. Jesus replies that mere physical descent is not sufficient: individuals must exercise the same faith in God that Abraham displayed.

At this point Jesus introduces a devastating teaching. Mankind can be divided into two groups. The members of one group love Jesus and have God for their Father. The others are "unable to hear" (*ou dunasthe*: inherently unable, without the capacity), because their "father" is the devil—a being who loves lies and murder, even as do Jesus' opponents.

It is important to understand the meaning of "father" in this context. In Hebrew thought "father," *'ab,* could indicate biological descent. But it also served as a title, indicating respect for a governor or spiritual leader, and to indicate the founder of a tribe or family group. It is in this last sense that Jesus uses "father" in condemning His opponents. Their actions show that they are in that group of rebels against God and godliness that was founded by Satan when he fell.

In some ways all of us display our spiritual family relationship. We either love God, and show His qualities in our relationships with others. Or we display characteristics of Satan, and so demonstrate our membership in that class of renegades who resist the Lord.

There is no in-between.

"I tell you the truth," Jesus answered, "before Abraham was born, I am!" At this,

they picked up stones to stone Him (8:58-59). This is the third time in this chapter that Jesus affirms His identity as Yahweh of the OT. As the I AM, Jesus existed before Abraham was born, and as the I AM Jesus was known by that great man of faith. It is clear from the response of Jesus' enemies that they had no doubt about what Christ was affirming. They "picked up stones to stone Him" (8:59) for the sin of blasphemy.

The *Reference Guide to the Steinsaltz Edition of the Talmud* explains the *Halakhic* principle that must have been applied, a principle called "the zealous may attack him."

There are a number of transgressions for which Torah law does not require that capital punishment be administered by a court of law. Nevertheless, if a "zealous person" apprehends an individual committing one of these transgressions, he may kill him. These transgressions are: the theft of sacred utensils; cursing God by using the name of a false god; public sexual relations with a non-Jewish woman; and serving in the Temple while ritually impure. If a "zealous person" witnessed one of these transgressions and then went to ask advice of a court, the court could not advise him to slay the offender. Permission to do so was only granted if the "zealous person" acted while the offender was actually committing the transgression (Vol. 1, 254).

It seems clear that Jesus infuriated opponents, and assuming His claim to be false, they chose to act as "zealous persons" and kill Jesus without any trial.

He saw a man blind from birth. His disciples asked Him, "Rabbi, who sinned, this man or his parents, that he was born blind?" (9:1-2) The miraculous healing is vivid evidence of the truths Jesus has affirmed. He is the Light of the world, able to bring sight to the blind. Those like the blind man, whose sight was restored, recognize and acknowledge Him and walk in the light. But those who claim to see, and yet cannot recognize God's confirmation of the Savior in His miracles, prove that they are blind spiritually, and will die in their sins.

There is something special for us here too. The disciples, upon seeing the man born blind,

were moved to raise an interesting theological question. Popular belief suggested that this man's disability was due to sin in his life. But, since he was born blind, how could he have merited this punishment? Was he punished for some sin of his parents? Or perhaps some sin God foreknew the man himself would commit?

What is important here is not the answer Jesus gave—that the blindness was not a punishment for sin at all, but would serve as an occasion to glorify God. What is important is that when the disciples saw suffering—their curiosity rather than their compassion was aroused.

The light Jesus brings, and in which we are to walk, must radically change our priorities. Solving theological puzzles, and even being "right" in our interpretations of Scripture, should be less important to us than displaying the compassion and concern for others that Jesus' own actions constantly reveal.

"Nobody has ever heard of opening the eyes of a man born blind. If this man were not from God, He could do nothing." To this they replied, "*You were steeped in sin at birth;* how dare you lecture us!" and they threw him out (9:32-34). How fascinating! The investigating Pharisees dragged out their old argument that Jesus could not be from God because He had performed the healing on the Sabbath (9:13-14). After being totally frustrated in their attempt to show that the healing was fraudulent, the religious leaders had to admit that the man really had been born blind. But they could not admit to the conclusion that must logically be drawn from this fact.

They seem almost desperate as they urge the now sighted individual to let God have the credit, thus implicitly ignoring the role Jesus had played (9:24). The man, however, remains firm: he is a committed disciple of his Benefactor. Finally all the frustrated leaders can do is to insult and mount a personal attack against the man whose sight has been restored.

Don't be surprised when those who reject Christ display anger or hostility at His witnesses. The Gospel message is a message of hope to those who believe. But for those who reject the light, it is a dark threat that may move them to strike in hatred and fear at the messenger.

THE PASSAGE IN DEPTH

The Woman Caught in Adultery (7:53–8:11). Most believe that this passage, which is not found in those early Greek manuscripts scholars consider the most reliable, was probably not in John's original text. At the same time most also view this story as authentic, displaying clearly the spirit of Jesus and the spirit of His antagonists as well.

Because this story is so familiar, and so often finds a place in our teaching and preaching, it remains worthy of careful study.

Background. The Babylonians, Assyrians, and Hittites all viewed adultery as a capital crime. In these cultures adultery was seen as a crime against the husband's property rights, and the husband retained the right to exact the ultimate penalty, a lesser penalty, or to forgive the wife entirely. In contrast, biblical law approached adultery as a moral affront rather than as an injury to the husband. Israel was called by God to be holy, a community whose moral tone reflected the righteousness of the God who claimed this people as His own.

Thus in biblical law no provision is made for a ransom or for a husband's forgiveness of the crime. And the death penalty is called for, in order to underline the seriousness of a crime which strikes at the family foundation of the society. It is important to note that in the OT the man and woman are considered equally guilty, and so the Scripture says that "both the adulterer and the adulteress must be put to death" (Lev. 20:10).

Rabbinic law follows the OT in its treatment of adultery. The husband's "rights" were not an issue. Instead rabbinic writings contain extensive discussions of just how a person guilty of adultery should be put to death. The forms adopted by the rabbis included stoning, burning, and strangling, and there is much discussion of which manner of execution should be used with the various forms of adultery that the rabbis distinguished. These four were: (1) Adultery with a married woman; (2) Adultery with a married woman who is a priest's daughter; (3) Adultery with a betrothed virgin; and (4) Adultery with a betrothed virgin, discovered by the husband on their wedding night not to be a virgin.

Despite the extensive discussion, and the formulation of case histories to define how the complex rulings of the rabbis should be applied, the rabbis intended their discussion of capital punishment to remain theoretical! It was not in practice applied by any rabbinical court. It is fascinating to note that, in practice, the rabbis strenuously attempted to avoid ordering capital punishment for any crime. For instance, rabbinical courts required that the criminal be warned, in the presence of witnesses, of the seriousness of his crime before committing it. And that the criminal can only be executed if he says, using these exact words, "I know and I do not care; I will take the consequences."

In practice, then, other penalties—usually whipping—were substituted for execution of an adulterer by first-century Jewish courts. This makes the situation described in John 8 most fascinating. By bringing a woman caught in the very act of adultery before Jesus, and challenging Him to either uphold or reject the Law of Moses, Christ's opponents were attempting to force Him to apply what they themselves viewed as merely theoretical law to an actual case! If Jesus failed to condemn the woman, He could be charged with denying the Law of Moses, which Jesus claimed to honor. If Jesus did condemn the woman, this Man whose Sabbath healings had portrayed the "teachers of the law and Pharisees" as heartless and merciless, would Himself be shown to have less compassion than the rabbis!

Against the background of first-century culture we sense the real nature of the trap that now closed on Jesus and, unexpectedly, on His accusers!

Interpretation. The account of this incident is fascinating in many ways. How would the average person know where to go to find an adulteress? If you did know where to go, how would you catch a woman "in the act of adultery"? (8:4) And there's another problem. Where is the man who was involved? Old Testament law is specific: both adulterer and adulteress are guilty and to pay the penalty. In that case, why didn't the "teachers of the law and the Pharisees" bring in the guilty man as well as the woman?

The only thing we can conclude is that this was no spontaneous discovery, but rather a carefully crafted plot to discredit Jesus in the eyes of the people. If this is so, it is clear that what we call entrapment was involved, and that the religious leaders actually conspired to catch her in the act.

The text says that Jesus knelt down and began to write on the ground. This is the only report in the Gospels of Jesus writing, and many have speculated as to just what words He scratched there in the dust. Some have suggested that He wrote down by the name of each accuser a listing of his own hidden sins. It hardly seems necessary. Perhaps we can see here not so much a counterattack on opponents, but rather evidence of the depth of Christ's dismay at their heartlessness. How could those to whom God had given such wondrous covenant promises, the privilege of knowing Him through the Word and worshiping Him at the temple, "use" another human being so shamelessly?

The rabbis and Pharisees kept up their verbal attack, confident now of victory. But Jesus stood up, and His words stunned them into silence. "If any one of you is without sin, let him be the first to throw a stone at her." Suddenly Jesus' accusers were faced with a dilemma. Deuteronomy 17:7 states: "The hands of the witnesses must be the first in putting him to death, and then the hands of all the people."

But if the witnesses were present and did not stop the act, they in effect condoned it and would be considered partners in it. If they created the situation to trap Jesus, then too they were guilty. It might be possible that one person might stumble on such an intimate scene. But how likely was it that several in this crowd of religious leaders, who normally would have nothing to do with commoners, should accidentally discover the adultery?

Suddenly realizing that their trap had made them terribly vulnerable, not one of the woman's accusers dared step forward and present himself as a witness.

When they were gone, Jesus spoke to the woman. While our Lord did not condemn her, He did not pronounce her innocent either. In fact, Christ's words make it clear that she was, in fact, a prostitute: "Go now, and leave your life of sin" (8:11). Undoubtedly the religious leaders had arranged the adultery in an attempt to discredit Jesus, never realizing that instead they would spring the trap on themselves, and reveal not some flaw in Jesus but their own sin and guilt.

Application. The story once again displays both the wisdom and the compassion of Jesus. Yet its most stunning revelation is of the character of Christ's opponents.

Before we criticize them, however, we need to remember that religious conviction can be as corrupting morally as lasciviousness. The person who is so totally convinced that he is right, so convinced that he or she is driven to destroy those who disagree, is in terrible danger. Let's be careful that, while we remain fully committed to Christ and His Word, we never fall into the trap of using others to make our point or forget compassion in our passion for truth.

JOHN 10–12
The Choice

EXPOSITION

John's account of Jesus' ministry now reaches the critical stage. Christ has presented Himself to Israel not only as the promised Messiah, but also as the Revealer and Son of God. The religious elite, represented by the teachers of the Law and the Pharisees, have openly attacked Jesus. The common people, although awed by Christ's miracles, seem confused by the bold claims Jesus has made. Yet as John's story continues, it becomes increasingly clear that all simply must choose whether to accept or reject Jesus' assertions.

These critical chapters are launched with Jesus' public announcement that He is the Shepherd of God's sheep (10:1-21). The imagery is rooted in Ps. 23 and the prophecies of Jeremiah and Ezekiel. Jesus is the fulfillment of God's promise, "I Myself will tend My sheep" (Ezek. 34:15). Israel's leaders are mere hirelings, who care nothing for the sheep. The sermon receives mixed reviews: "the Jews" ridicule it, but many ordinary folk are impressed. Shortly afterward Jesus is surrounded by a crowd of His opponents, who demand to know if He claims to be the Christ (10:22-42). Jesus affirms His claim, and also asserts His authority to give eternal life to those who respond to His voice, for Jesus is One with God the Father.

But how can Jesus' professed ability to "give them eternal life" (10:28) be proven? When Mary and Martha desperately appeal to Jesus to heal their brother, Jesus delays until Lazarus is dead and buried (11:1-16). When Jesus does arrive the grieving sisters are asked to reaffirm their faith that Jesus Himself is "the Resurrection and the Life" (11:17-37). Although they do believe, the two sisters and all the gathered mourners are stunned when Jesus calls to Lazarus in his grave—and brings him back to life (11:38-44). The miracle forces the hand of Jesus' opponents. They must decide what to do, before His notable miracles convince all Israel that He truly is the Christ. Rather than choose to believe, members of the ruling council agree that Jesus must die (11:45-57). The people remain uncertain on the sidelines. But the religious leaders are now fully committed.

Back in Bethany, as the chief priests continue to plot, Jesus is anointed by Mary during a feast given in honor of Lazarus (12:1-11). The very next day Jesus enters Jerusalem, riding on a donkey, and is acclaimed as King by enthusiastic crowds (12:12-19). But Jesus knows very well how fleeting His popularity will be. Troubled, Jesus speaks of His coming death, and reaffirms His commitment to do the Father's will

(12:20-36). At the same time the ruling council and chief priests are hardened in their refusal to believe and direct intense pressure against any of their number who do believe (12:37-49). Sadly Jesus describes the consequences of their choice: "that very word which I spoke will condemn [them] in the last day" (12:48).

Today too we have freedom of choice. We can choose to believe in Jesus, or we can refuse to believe in Him. But we have no freedom at all to avoid the consequences of our choice. We who believe have eternal life. Those who will not believe stand condemned before God. The choice is ours.

WORD STUDIES

The man who does not enter the sheep pen by the gate . . . is a *thief and a robber* (10:1, 8). A "thief," *kleptes,* uses trickery, while a "robber," *lestes,* relies on violence. But both are intent on exploiting others for their own benefit. How often so-called "religious leaders" are intent on victimizing rather than serving others.

Then the wolf attacks the flock and *scatters* it (10:12). Jesus' parable or analogy is based on the accurate knowledge of sheep and shepherds that most in Galilee or Judea would have shared. This is just one illustration. If a flock of goats is attacked, the goats huddle together, horns at the ready for defense. But sheep scatter, making them even more vulnerable. Their only hope is a shepherd who is committed to defend them, even though by doing so he must endanger himself.

I have other sheep that are *not of this sheep pen* (10:16). Most commentators believe that "this sheep pen" refers to Israel, while the "other sheep" are those Gentiles who will recognize Christ's voice in the Gospel and respond to Him.

Then came the *Feast of Dedication* at Jerusalem (10:22). The festival was Hanukkah, which celebrated the cleansing and rededication of the Jerusalem temple by Judas Maccabeus some 200 years before. The temple had been profaned at the order of the Syrian Antiochus IV, and a pig sacrificed on its altar. After a three-year rebellion stimulated by this and other acts intended to stamp out Judaism, the Maccabees liberated the Jewish people and recaptured Jerusalem.

The Jews *gathered around* Him (10:24). The verb *ekuklosan* means "to surround." The image it suggests is of a threatening crowd of religious leaders (see Word Study of John 1:19) encircling Jesus, intent on forcing Him to "tell us plainly" if He was the Christ. We can almost sense Jesus shaking His head in wonder: "I did tell you," He replied (10:25). And moreover, "The miracles I do in My Father's name speak for Me."

We shouldn't be surprised. How often do we keep praying for some sign that God will permit us to do something we know is not in His will? The problem is not that we need to know "plainly." The problem is that all too often we do not want to accept what we have been told!

If we approach life fully committed to do God's will as He reveals it to us, most of our uncertainty will disappear. But if we approach life hoping that the Lord will permit what we want to do, we will experience many moments of terrible uncertainty (James 1:5-8).

My sheep listen to My voice; I know them, and they follow Me (10:26). The flocks of several shepherds were often kept in the same fold at night. In the morning each shepherd would call his flock, using a distinctive word or phrase. Even if another person called to the sheep using the same word or phrase, the sheep did not respond. The sheep recognized the specific tone and timbre of their own shepherd's voice, and responded only to him.

God's flock recognizes the voice of Jesus and responds to Him. As the Gospel call comes, His sheep lift up their heads and turn their eyes toward the Savior. And, recognizing Him, they obediently follow Him where He leads.

We cannot argue others into faith. We can

only speak the words of Jesus, knowing that those who are God's sheep will recognize and acknowledge His inner voice.

I and the Father are one (10:30). The Greek "one" is the neuter pronoun, *hen.* Its use here indicates equality or an identity of natures. Once again the Jews knew exactly what Jesus claimed, and once again they reacted as "zealous persons" (see Word Study of John 8:58-59) and sought to stone Jesus for the blasphemy of "claim[ing] to be God" (10:33).

Again we see that the issue was never one of uncertainty. The demand to "tell us plainly" (10:24) was never sincere, never an expression of a desire to know or understand. At best the demand was a frustrated effort to force Jesus to deny His calling. At worst it was an effort to trap Him into an admission which could provide an excuse to stone Him—exactly as the crowd intended to do now.

Jesus answered them, "Is it not written in your Law, 'I have said you are gods'?" (10:34) This enigmatic statement has generated a number of confusing interpretations. Some have assumed that these words imply a denial that Christ's words in 10:30 were in fact a claim to be equal with God. Not at all. Instead Jesus' reference to Psalm 82:6 strengthens His claim of equality. The argument is simply this: if the Lord addressed as *elohim* (gods) mere human beings who served as judges charged with applying God's Law, how much more does Jesus, "the One whom the Father set apart as His very own and sent into the world" (10:36), deserve to be considered equal with God? The charge of blasphemy is foolish, in view of God's demonstrated commitment to the Son.

Then Thomas (called Didymus) said to the rest of the disciples, "Let us also go, that we may die with Him" (11:16). When Jesus did not hurry to Bethany in response to the message from Mary and Martha, the disciples concluded that Jesus feared His opponents. Bethany lay just two miles from Jerusalem; at that time Christ and His disciples were some 20 miles distant in Perea and relatively safe. So when Jesus finally stirred Himself and said, "Let us go back to Judea" (11:7), the disciples were surprised.

The disciples were correct in their evaluation of the temper of Jesus' enemies. And they were convinced that should Jesus return He would surely be killed.

Two things stand out in this statement by Thomas. First, Thomas and the disciples completely misunderstood Jesus' motivation. He did not act out of fear, but out of compassion and a fixed determination to glorify God. Let's remember that in whatever God asks us to do, His motives are always both positive and good.

Second, Thomas displayed a praiseworthy commitment. He did not understand why Jesus was ready to return, but he was determined to go with the Lord even if it cost him his life.

Discipleship still requires two qualities: A commitment to follow Jesus, whatever the cost. And a conviction that whatever the Lord asks us to do is intended for good.

Lazarus had already been in the tomb for *four days* (11:17). Rabbinical literature suggests that the burial place should be visited for three days to make sure that person was really dead (Sem. 8), while Gen. Rab. 100 (64a) says, "Bar Qappara taught, The whole strength of the mourning is not till the third day; for three days long the soul returns to the grave, thinking that it will return [to the body]; when however it sees that the color of its face has changed then it goes away and leaves it."

Jesus waited to appear on the fourth day so that there would be no question in anyone's mind that Lazarus was truly dead when called forth from the grave.

When Jesus saw her weeping, and the Jews who had come along with her also weeping, He was *deeply moved* in spirit and troubled (11:33). The Greek word here is *embrimaomai,* which normally indicates an angry outburst. Most translators, however, take it here as some strong emotion such as grief or sympathy.

It is, however, fascinating to speculate. Did Jesus feel a surge of anger as He heard the wailing of the crowd, and sensed a despair that cast doubt on their belief in everlasting life? Or perhaps did Jesus feel anger at the very fact of death, and its grim, unnecessary grip on humankind? As this same verb is found in v. 38, this is perhaps possible.

But it is more likely that "deeply moved" is an appropriate rendering here. For of all men Jesus must have understood the importance of grieving; of facing the pain of rejection and loss that we all feel, and by bringing this grief to God, to ultimately know peace.

Then the Romans will come and take away both *our place and our nation* (11:48). The saying reflects the fear that Jesus might stimulate a spontaneous religious revolution. If this happened, it was likely that the Romans would strip the Jews of their last vestiges of national identity and self-rule. It seems significant that the first concern expressed was that the Romans would take away "our place." Like politicians of every era, there was a tendency for the leaders to think of themselves first, and their nation second.

You do not realize that it is better for you that one man die for the people than that the whole nation perish (11:50). Caiaphas' statement was unintentional prophecy (11:51). But the high priest's words reflect a lengthy debate that had engaged the attention of the rabbis.

The debate grew out of the OT story of Sheba (2 Sam. 20:1), who after leading a revolt against David fled to the city of Abel Beth Maacah. When David's forces attacked the city, a "wise woman" (10:16) persuaded the citizens to cut off the head of Sheba and throw it over the wall to David's general, Joab. The story raised the question: When is it right to give a fellow Jew up to death?

Gen. Rab. 91.58a and 94.60a admit the principle: "It is better that one life be in uncertain danger of death than all in (danger of) certain death," and "It is better that this man be killed than the totality be punished on his account." Even so, the rabbis were not satisfied with that, and tried to specifically define the conditions under which it would be permissible to give up one person in order to save the many. The developed consensus ruled that if a group of thugs or heathen authorities demanded "one of" a company of Jews or else the whole group would be killed, all should die. But if heathen authorities demanded a named individual, he should be given up for the benefit of the whole.

This, however, was not entirely satisfying, and so a further qualification was suggested.

Noting that Sheba was called a "troublemaker" (2 Sam. 20:1), Resh Laqish argues that even a named individual should be given up only if he was really deserving of death.

All the fine sensibilities displayed in this extended rabbinic discussion, however, are irrelevant here. The Romans had not demanded that Jesus or any Jew be surrendered to them. Caiaphas had in fact reinterpreted the ancient debate, and the high priests and Sanhedrin were about to manipulate the Romans into putting Jesus to death. Jesus was to be offered to the pagan rulers by His own people, rulers who had not demanded Him by name or indeed that any Jew be surrendered.

And so while Caiaphas' use of an even-then familiar saying, "It is better for you that one man die for the people," was completely at odds with the usual context in which it was discussed. No rabbi in examining the implications of Sheba's surrender ever imagined the principle some derived from it would be used to justify the betrayal of the Messiah.

You will always have the poor among you, but you will not always have Me (12:8). It is possible to twist this verse so that the words seem cold and heartless. We know that such an interpretation does twist the truth, for these words were spoken by Jesus, who throughout His ministry has shown deep compassion for the oppressed.

How then are we to take them? In their plain sense. Jesus would not be with His followers much longer. But if Judas' concern for the poor were sincere, he need not worry. There would always be poor whom he could help.

Jesus was right. There still are plenty of poor. And too few are sincerely concerned about them.

I, when I am lifted up from the earth, will draw *all men* to Myself (12:32). John only uses the verb "lifted up," *hupsoo,* to describe Jesus' coming death (3:14; 8:28; 12:32, 34). This verse does not suggest that somehow every human being will ultimately be saved through the Cross. The phrase "all men," *pantas,* teaches us that Christ's death was for all without regard to race or nationality, without regard to wealth or poverty, without regard to status or power. Jew, Samaritan, and Gentile alike are called by the Cross to Jesus Christ, to find in Him a life that apart from Him no one has.

Even after Jesus had done all these miraculous signs in their presence, they still *would not* believe in Him (12:37). Jesus invites all. But each individual must make his or her own choice. Everyone who wills, may come. Everyone who will not, cannot be saved.

There is a judge for the one who rejects Me and does not accept My words (12:48). God is still in Christ, speaking to lost humanity through the Gospel. His voice is heard today. And the choice each person makes has eternal consequences.

THE PASSAGE IN DEPTH

The Shepherd and His Flock (10:1-21).

Background. Much has been written on the analogies this passage develops between the ways of the Oriental shepherd and the way Christ relates to His own. This is of course appropriate, for Jesus expected His listeners, familiar with the ways of the shepherd with his sheep, to understand what He was saying. At the same time, it is important to understand the biblical background to what Jesus said. Surely the well-established biblical imagery was at least as important in what Jesus said as was the agricultural.

The biblical imagery is rooted in two facts. God is often represented as Shepherd and Israel as His sheep. And human leaders are also cast as shepherds, responsible for the well-being of the people in their care.

The most familiar passage casting God as Shepherd is, of course, Ps. 23. There are, however, many other passages. Psalm 80, a hymn used in public worship, begins, "Hear us, O Shepherd of Israel, You who lead Joseph like a flock; You who sit enthroned between the cherubim, shine forth before Ephraim, Benjamin and Manasseh. Awaken Your might; come and save us."

Ezekiel emphasizes the tenderness of the shepherd, and uses this image to convey God's love for His people: "I Myself will tend My sheep and have them lie down, declares the Sovereign Lord, I will search for the lost and bring back the strays. I will bind up the injured and strengthen the weak, but the sleek and the strong I will destroy. I will shepherd the flock with justice" (Ezek. 24:15-16).

Jeremiah, warning against false shepherds who care nothing for God's flock, makes a promise the Messiah will one day fulfill: "I myself will gather the remnant of my flock out of all the countries where I have driven them and will bring them back to their pasture, where they will be fruitful and increase in number" (Jer. 23:3).

Thus when Jesus claimed, "I am the Good Shepherd," His listeners, steeped in the OT, should have immediately realized that He was once again presenting Himself as Israel's Messiah and as her God.

At the same time, Jesus' references to "hired hand[s]" (10:12-13) who care nothing for the sheep, was an unmistakable attack on the "teachers of the law" who claimed spiritual authority over God's people. There is no question that the OT refers to Israel's leaders as shepherds (Num. 27:15-16). And there is no question that the OT sternly condemns leaders who fail to care, as God does, for the covenant people. A few passages illustrate: " 'Woe to the shepherds who are destroying and scattering the sheep of My pasture!' declares the Lord. Therefore this is what the Lord, the God of Israel, says to the shepherds who tend My people: 'Because you have scattered My flock and driven them away and have not bestowed care on them, I will bestow punishment on you for the evil you have done,' declares the Lord" (Jer. 23:1-2).

"My people have been lost sheep; their shepherds have led them astray and caused them to roam on the mountains" (50:6).

"This is what the Sovereign Lord says: Woe to the shepherds of Israel who only take care of themselves! Should not shepherds take care of the flock? You eat the curds, clothe yourselves with the wool and slaughter the choice animals, but you do not take care of the flock. You have not strengthened the weak or healed the sick or bound up the injured. You have not brought back the strays or searched for the lost. You have ruled them harshly and brutally. So they were scattered because there was no shepherd, and when they were scattered they became food for all the wild animals. My sheep wandered over all the mountains and on every high hill. They were scattered over the whole earth, and no one searched or looked for them" (Ezek. 34:1-6).

How clearly Ezekiel describes the indifferent Pharisees, who cared nothing for the sick Jesus healed on the Sabbath, or for the "sinners" that they bitterly criticized Jesus for associating with! And so these OT passages provide the most significant background against which to read Jesus' claim to be "the Good Shepherd," and against which to hear His words about "hired hands" who "care nothing for the sheep" (John 10:13).

There is also value, of course, in learning about the ways first-century shepherds cared for their sheep. We need to visualize the "sheep pen" Jesus spoke of (10:1, 9): a cave, or stone-walled corral topped with briars, which featured a single entrance, at which the shepherd slept in order to protect the flock inside. In saying "I am the gate" (10:7, 9) Jesus made an emphatic claim to be the only way to be saved (10:9).

We have noted in the Word Study of 10:23 that the Oriental shepherd leads rather than herds his flock, which responds to the shepherd's voice and trustingly follows him. All these analogies do have possible application to us in our relationship with Jesus today. But it is the OT background of the imagery of sheep and shepherd, and of false shepherds who care nothing for the sheep, that is key to understanding the impact of Christ's words as they were proclaimed in Jerusalem that fateful year.

Interpretation. We need to read this passage in view of the OT's use of the sheep and shepherd image. Against this background, what Jesus is saying is simple, sharp, and clear. We can sum up as follows:

Christ's announcement that He is the "Shepherd of the sheep" (10:2) is a clear affirmation that He is the Messiah, God come in the flesh to care for His flock. As the "Good Shepherd," Jesus will willingly lay down His life for His flock. In this He is totally different from the "hired hands" who care nothing for the flock, and in fact exploit God's people for their own benefit.

Not all in Israel will acknowledge Him, but those who are His sheep will recognize His voice and follow Him.

Application. On the one hand, the extended metaphor sharply contrasts the attitude of God and Jesus to human beings with the attitude of the religious leaders of Christ's day. Anyone who accepts a leadership role in the church must be willing to closely examine his or her own motives and attitudes. Unless we have that same concern for others that moved Jesus, our ministry is sure to be flawed.

On the other hand, we are reassured. Despite the prevalence of false shepherds, God's people do recognize the voice of Jesus. We can have confidence as we teach the Word of God that its truth will be heard and responded to by those who are God's own.

The Death and Raising of Lazarus (11:1-57).

Background. See the Word Study of 11:17 for the significance of Jesus' arrival four days after Lazarus' death and burial. Remember that the Jews buried an individual the very day he died, without the delay that marks our burial practices.

Interpretation. John develops this story with four distinct parts: Jesus' delay; Jesus' dialogue; and Jesus' decisive act. This is followed with a description of the reaction to this most notable of Christ's miracles.

JESUS' DELAY

When Lazarus fell sick in Bethany, Jesus was in Perea, about a day's journey away. But even as the messenger hurried down the road, rushing to tell Jesus that "the one You love is sick" (11:3), Lazarus died. Before the messenger could arrive, Lazarus was wrapped in the graveclothes and placed in his grave.

It was the next day that the messenger arrived and told Jesus, only to be reassured, "This sickness will not end in death" (11:4). The words were carefully chosen. Death might intervene. But, as with you and me, even our final sickness will not end in death, but in new life.

John is careful to tell us that Jesus did love Martha and Mary and Lazarus (11:5). He tells us this, because Jesus' next actions do not seem to express love. For, when He heard, "He stayed where He was two more days" (11:6). This verse is a special one, one we should memorize and hold close. It reminds us that God loves us even when He seems silent, even when He seems unresponsive to our prayers.

Jesus "stayed where He was," and made no move to hurry to the side of His loved ones. Yet His inaction was not evidence of unconcern. Nor did it mean that Jesus hesitated to do what was best for Mary, Martha, and their brother. In fact, Christ's delay was intentionally designed to bring them stunning blessing which would strengthen their faith and glorify God. It is the same with us. The pains we experience, the anguished doubts that make us wonder, "Could this have happened if Jesus were here?" will one day dissolve in the joy of the greater miracles Christ intends to perform for us.

And then, after two days, with Lazarus three days buried, Jesus told His disciples, "Let us go back to Judea" (10:7). Some have misunderstood the words "Our friend Lazarus has fallen asleep; but I am going there to wake him up" (10:11). However, "sleep" is a frequent biblical euphemism for death. The *Zondervan Expository Dictionary of Bible Words* notes:

> There is an obvious similarity between a person who is asleep and one who is dead. Neither is aware of or responds to what happens around him. But in the NT there is a theological similarity that carries us beyond the obvious. In the two passages in which this word is used several times (1 Thes. 4; 1 Cor. 15), the NT speaks of our resurrection. The joyous affirmation of Scripture is that death, which seemed so final to the pagans, takes on a new meaning in Christ. Robbed of its dread, death wears the face of untroubled rest; and so the believer today can say with the deeper meaning the ancient words of David: "I lie down and sleep; I wake again, because the Lord sustains me" (Ps. 3:5). [p. 571]

And so Jesus speaks here of the sleep of death; a sleep from which He intended to awaken Lazarus, and demonstrate for us the power He has over death's authority.

The disciples did not understand. Even when Jesus told them plainly (11:14-15), there is no indication they even dreamed what they would soon witness. Rather than arouse the excitement of expectation, Jesus' words had the opposite effect, and Thomas felt certain the little company was returning to Judea to meet their own deaths rather than to see death flee before Jesus' command.

Let us listen more carefully to Jesus, and take His words to heart. Biological death is still our enemy. But it is an enemy which has met defeat. Even when we face death, we look beyond it, and see there the bright and glowing countenance of eternal life.

JESUS' DIALOGUE WITH THE SISTERS

When Jesus finally arrived at Bethany, Lazarus had been in the grave four days. There was no doubt now that he was truly dead.

Martha hurried out and met Jesus first. Her first words were words of faith, not, as some have suggested, of rebuke. If Jesus had been there, her brother surely would not have died. Christ had the power to hold that grim reaper off. But Martha seems to expect even more of Jesus: "Even now," she says, "God will give You whatever You ask" (11:22).

Yet when Jesus promises that "your brother will rise again" (10:23), Martha thinks forward to the resurrection of the last day.

In this Martha, and Mary as well (11:32), are very like you and me. We are convinced that Jesus has miracle-working power. We are convinced that He can do anything. We know and are convinced that He died and rose for us, and that when Jesus returns He will restore the believing dead to endless life. Yet how much of our faith in Jesus' power to act limits His work to the distant past or that yet future? How much of our faith is focused on now? How often do we expect Him to work in and for us in our today?

When Jesus told Martha, "I am the Resurrection and the Life" (11:25), He used a verb of timelessness. There has never been a moment in history past when Jesus' power to vitalize was limited. There will never be a moment in history future when He will be unable to act. Just as nothing limits Jesus right now—in our present, as in Martha's, Jesus is the Resurrection and the Life, the ultimate Power and Authority in all this universe.

This does not mean that Jesus will act to answer every prayer of ours. Not every sickness will be healed. Not every tragedy averted. But if they are not, we can be sure that when Jesus waits, He loves. And when at last Jesus does act for us, we will discover love's blessing in those painful moments of delay.

John wants us to know that Jesus really does care when, like Martha and Mary, we are stricken with pain. Jesus was "deeply moved in spirit and troubled" at their sorrow (11:33). And Jesus too wept (11:35). It is never easy for God to permit us to experience pain. He not only loves us; He suffers with us. He permits our suffering, but only because He knows that through our suffering both good and joy will come.

JESUS' DECISIVE ACT

When Jesus came to the tomb He commanded them to take away the stone that blocked its entrance. Martha objected. The body would already have begun to decompose. Jesus insisted, and uttering a prayer of thanks to the Father, Christ called out, "Lazarus, come out!" (11:43)

Lazarus' body had doubtless been prepared in the normal way. It was wrapped in a single large linen sheet, doubled around the body, and then wrapped with linen strips. When the dead man came out, "His hands and feet [were] wrapped with strips of linen, and a cloth around his face" (11:44). Lazarus did not stride out into the light. He must have come stumbling, still bearing the symbols of death. But his appearance, alive again, was a supreme demonstration of the power of life to triumph over death, and of Christ's preeminence.

REACTIONS

Finally John describes the various reactions to this notable miracle Jesus performed. Some believed (11:45). But the Sanhedrin was blind to the hope implicit in the raising of Lazarus. In their jealousy and fear all they saw was the likelihood that Jesus would become even more popular, and so they became more determined than ever to kill Him.

How blind. As if death could ever overcome the source of life. Or darkness put out the light.

Application. The story of the raising of Lazarus is so encouraging. It reminds us that God loves us and has a good purpose even when He permits us to suffer. It reminds us that Jesus is not limited in His ability to act in our today. And it assures us that we are forever safe in the One who triumphs over death.

Jesus Anointed at Bethany (12:1-11). See the similar story discussed in Luke 7:36-50, and parallel passages in Matt. 26:6-13 and Mark 14:3-9.

The Triumphal Entry (12:12-19). See the commentary on Luke 19:28-44, and parallel passages in Matt. 21:1-11, 14-17 and Mark 11:1-11.

Jesus Predicts His Death (12:20-36). See additional predictions in Matt. 16:21-28, Mark 8:31-38, and Luke 9:22-27.

The Jews Continue in Their Unbelief (12:37-50). See the Word Studies on John 12:37 and 12:48.

JOHN 13:1–15:17
Jesus' Last Words

EXPOSITION

Each of the Gospels speaks briefly of a Last Supper that Jesus shared with His disciples. But only John invites us to join the Twelve who gathered around Christ that momentous night, to hear the last words that our Lord addressed to His closest followers. Those words are summarized for us in John 13–17. The passage has been called the "seed bed of the Epistles," for nearly all major doctrines developed in the NT letters are seminally present in Jesus' Last Supper instruction. This discourse is so important that two separate chapters in this Commentary are devoted to it, and to the key themes developed here by our Lord.

John's account begins as the meal is being served. Jesus shocks His disciples by taking the role of a woman or household slave and washing His disciples' feet. In this He modeled for them the servant attitude they will have to display as leaders of His church (13:1-17). When Jesus predicts His betrayal, Judas slips out into the night, leaving Christ alone with the faithful Eleven (13:18-30). It is to them that Jesus gives His "new commandment" to love one another "as I have loved you" (13:31-38); it is the Eleven Christ encourages with the promise that He will return after preparing a place for them (14:1-4); it is the Eleven Jesus reminds that He Himself is the only way by which any human being can approach God the Father (14:5-14). Then, for the first time, Jesus begins to explain how believers will be able to continue a personal relationship with Him after His resurrection (14:15-31). This possibility exists because Jesus will send the Holy Spirit to take up residence in the believer. Through the Spirit, the believer who loves Jesus and obeys His teaching will actually experience Christ's presence and know a peace that only Jesus can give.

How important is it that we remain close to Jesus? It is just as important for us as it is that a branch remain united to its vine. The vine is the source of vitality and life; without an intimate union which enables the life-giving fluids to flow from vine to branches, the branch is dry and useless, unable to produce fruit. By loving Jesus and being responsive to His words, the Christian maintains this essential union and will produce the fruit that God desires. And, moreover, will experience the joy that a fruitful union with the Lord provides.

The Last Supper discourse, then, opens with a clear and distinctive focus. Jesus is not physically present with us as we live our lives in the world. Yet through the Spirit His spiritual presence is utterly real. When love for our Lord is expressed in obedience to Him, we experience that real presence and are spiritually productive as well. No wonder walking close to the Lord produces both peace and joy.

WORD STUDIES

It was just *before* the Passover Feast (13:1). There is debate whether the Last Supper was in fact the Passover meal, or a meal traditionally eaten the night before Passover. Matt. 26:19, however, says that the disciples "prepared the Passover." It has been argued that since John 13:29 indicates that the disciples thought Jesus told Judas to hurry out and buy something for the feast, this could not have been the Passover meal. If they were even then eating the Passover, they would hardly need to buy ingredients for it! On the other hand, they might have needed more food to continue the feast. If Passover really were the next day, there would have been no need to hurry. Actually, however, the phrase "or to give something to the poor" (13:29) establishes this as the Passover feast indeed. Why? It was customary to give alms to the poor on that night, and beggars gathered at the temple gates till midnight to accept gifts from those who wished to perform this good deed.

Actually, then, Jesus' disciples had entered the city around noon on Thursday, the 14th of Nisan. They obtained the room, took the lamb to the temple where it was killed, and made the other arrangements for the evening meal. Then they assembled after nightfall (the 15th by Jewish reckoning), and were joined by Jesus to celebrate the ancient ceremony. The next afternoon, still the 15th, the Passover symbolism was fulfilled as Jesus died on the cross, sheltering by His shed blood all those who believe.

As we read on, we remember that these truly are Jesus' "last words" to His disciples — words that express what was closest to His heart as death approached.

He . . . began to *wash His disciples' feet*, drying them with the towel that was wrapped around Him (13:5). Foot-washing was considered among the most menial of tasks in the first century. Rabbinical literature suggests just how demeaning. According to Mekh Exod 21:2.82a Jewish slaves should not be required to wash another's feet; this was a job only for Gentile slaves, wives, and children. One interesting story about foot-washing is told in Pe'a 1.15c. 14. The story reports that Rabbi Ishmael would not permit his mother to wash his feet when he returned from the synagogue because the work was too demeaning. She, however, asked a court of rabbis to rebuke him for not allowing her the honor. While the story is intended to suggest the exalted place granted the sages in rabbinic Judaism, it underlines why the disciples reacted as they did when Jesus began to wash their feet. Christ's act, then, within the context of first-century Judaism, was truly shocking — an absolutely stunning example of humility that must have made a deep, lasting impression on His followers. We can imagine no more powerful way that Jesus could have left His disciples "an example" (13:15) of the attitude they must develop to effectively lead the people of God.

A person who has had a *bath* needs only to *wash* his feet (13:10). Many interpreters have noted, first, that this verse uses the imagery of bathing and washing metaphorically. Here "bathe" is *louo*, while "wash" is *nipto*, which means to wash or rinse.

The context for this remark is Peter's shocked refusal to permit Jesus to wash his feet. The Greek of v. 8 is emphatic: "You wash my feet? NEVER!" But consider. The rinsing that cleansed Peter's feet with water was nothing compared to the washing of Peter's personality with the very blood of the Savior! One who has been completely cleansed within: his heart is "washed" and

thus fit for God's kingdom. But even those cleansed by God's Word are imperfect. As the man who ventures from the bath to a neighbor's banquet picks up grime and dirt as he walks through the streets, so believers need to be cleansed from every fault they may fall into as they travel through this world.

Perfection escapes us. But the forgiving love of God keeps on cleansing us as we confess our sins to Him who has purified us within (1 John 1:9).

I have set you an example that you should do as I have done for you (13:15). Some during the Reformation took this verse literally, and so added "foot-washing" to the ordinances or sacraments they observed. John Calvin, who saw in Jesus' act symbolic self-humbling for the sake of others, was particularly critical of those who took pride in their foot-washing services and looked down on Christians who observed the practice. Calvin wrote,

> Every year they hold a theatrical feet-washing, and when they have discharged this empty and bare ceremony they think they have done their duty finely and are then free to despise their brethren. But more, when they have washed twelve men's feet they cruelly torture all Christ's members and thus spit in the face of Christ Himself. This ceremonial comedy is nothing but a shameful mockery of Christ. At any rate, Christ does not enjoin an annual ceremony here, but tells us to be ready all through our life to wash the feet of our brethren.

It surely is not wrong to practice the actual washing of other's feet if we so choose. But the ceremony is at best a symbol of an attitude toward self and others that must be lived every day of our lives.

Jesus said, "Now is the Son of Man *glorified* and God is *glorified in Him*" (13:31). For a discussion of this term and its use by John, see the discussion of John 17:1.

A new command I give you: Love one another. As I have loved you, so you must love one another. By this all men will know that you are My disciples, if you love one another (13:34-35). The Greek word here is *kainen,* a word that indicates quality. Here "new" does not mean "more recent," but rather "superior, new and better in quality." Certainly the call to love is an old one, deeply embedded in the first Testament (Lev. 19:18, 34). What is superior to that old command in Jesus' new expression of it? At least three things:

■ There is a new relationship. The OT called on God's people to "love your neighbor as yourself" (Lev. 19:18). Jesus calls on us to "love one another," a phrase which reminds us that in Christ's new community we are not simply neighbors, but family: bonded to each other by our common relationship to the God we now acknowledge as Father.

■ There is a new standard. The OT command was to love your neighbor as you love yourself. Jesus' superior commandment calls on us to love one another "as I have loved you." As Jesus placed our welfare above His own, even surrendering up Himself to save us, so we are to likewise sacrifice ourselves for the brothers and sisters we are charged to love.

■ There is a new outcome. The purity of the OT community of faith was intended to display God's righteousness. Now Jesus says that, as we do love one another as He has loved us, "all men will know that you are My disciples" (13:35). Love in the Christian community is compelling proof to a lost world that Jesus is real and among us. When they see our love, they know that the only explanation is: we are Jesus' people, and Jesus' disciples.

So Christ's commandment is new indeed. It is not that God has never before called His people to love. Instead it is that, in Christ, love becomes an even more dynamic and powerful expression of the relationship we have with one another and with our Lord.

***Do not let* your hearts be troubled (14:1).** The Greek construction, *me tarassestho,* really means "stop being troubled." How easy it is to become discouraged or fearful when things go wrong. Yet the solution is near at hand. We put our trust in God, and in Jesus. Focusing on who God is, and on the great love Jesus has for us, brings peace.

In My Father's house are *many rooms*

(14:2). The *King James* translated *monai pollai* as "many mansions." This was unfortunate, for the image this English phrase conveys is that of large, imposing but impersonal estate homes. A totally different image was created for the first-century reader. They envisioned just what our NIV describes, a single, beautiful home with many rooms laid out around a central courtyard where the family would gather in the warm afternoons. A beautiful home where every member of the family had his or her own apartment, and all lived in close proximity to the Father all loved.

The heaven we yearn for, and that Jesus prepares for us even now, is not a place where we can be alone, but one where we will truly belong. And a place where we will truly be close to our God.

I tell you the truth, anyone who has faith in Me will do what I have been doing. He will do *even greater things than these,* because I am going to the Father (14:12). On its surface this is an amazing statement. How could any disciple—whether one of the Eleven or a believer today—do "greater things" than Jesus did? This just couldn't be true! Yet Jesus said it, and so it must be that the "even greater things" than Jesus had been doing are expected of us.

The context provides the clues we need to understand. Jesus spoke of the Father, living in Him, doing His work through the Incarnate Son (14:10). This is not really surprising, for the Father and Son were one, and the sinless Jesus lived His life in complete, unbroken union with the Father.

Yet in these "last words" Jesus looks forward to a future in which He Himself is physically absent, yet spiritually present with believers. As He lived in union with the Father, we will live in union with Him. And as the Father acted through the Son, so the Son will act through us, who are His body here on earth.

And this is the reason why "anyone who has faith in Me" will do "even greater things." It was not surprising that the Father could work through the Son. But it is totally amazing that we sinful human beings should become the avenue through which our Holy God will work and express Himself in the world.

The works are greater, not because they are

greater in power or degree, but because God will express His power through sinful agents rather than a sinless agent. When God works through you or me—this is a miracle indeed!

You may ask Me for anything *in My name,* and I will do it (14:14). In Hebrew thought and in the NT as well, the "name" is intimately linked with the identity and essential character of the person named. The *Zondervan Expository Dictionary of Bible Words* observes:

> When Jesus encouraged the apostles to pray in His name (John 14:13-14; 15:16; 16:23-24, 26), He was not referring to an expression tacked on to the end of a prayer. To pray "in Jesus' name" means (1) to identify the content and the motivations of prayers with all that Jesus is and (2) to pray with full confidence in Him as He has revealed Himself. Jesus promised that prayer in His name would be answered (p. 454).

This promise is no blank check against which we can draw to satisfy selfish desires. It is instead a promise that when we make Christ's goals our own He will make all the resources of heaven available to achieve them.

Peace I leave with you; *My peace* I give to you. I do not give to you as the world gives. Do not let your hearts be troubled and do not be afraid (14:27). Jesus' promise is rooted in the OT concept expressed in the word *shalom.* That concept is complex, suggesting wholeness, unity, harmony, completeness, soundness. Although essentially a relational concept in the OT, *shalom* has overtones of prosperity, health, and fulfillment.

The OT makes it very clear that the source of real peace is one's relationship with God, and is experienced only by "they who love Your law" (Ps. 119:165). In contrast, "The wicked are like the tossing sea, which cannot rest, whose waves cast up mire and mud. 'There is no peace,' says my God, 'for the wicked' " (Isa. 57:20-21).

The only peace that the world can offer is a cessation of external strife. The peace that Jesus brings is an inner calm and security that persists however stormy our circumstances.

If anyone does not remain in Me, he is like a branch that is thrown away and withers; such branches are picked up, *thrown into the fire and burned* (15:6). This verse has struck fear in many a believer's heart. Is this Christ's warning that unless we abide in Him, God will reject us and consign us to eternal punishment?

One of the most important hermeneutic principles that must be followed if we hope to understand any passage in Scripture is to ask first: What is the subject of the passage we're reading? That is: What is the passage talking about?

In this case, Jesus is not talking about salvation, but about fruitfulness. In dealing with this subject, Jesus draws on the common practices of those who tended the grape orchards so familiar in Israel's high country. In this verse He simply underlines the uselessness of any branch that fails to produce fruit. The fibrous grapevine cannot be shaped, like pine or oak, to form any useful object. Good for nothing, it is discarded by the vinedresser and burned.

Christ's observation here is not to be taken as a threat. We are not in danger of being lost if we fail to bear fruit. But we are in danger of living an essentially empty, useless life. God has chosen us to bear fruit. To do this we must stay close to Jesus, and respond obediently to His words. There is no use telling ourselves that any other goal to which we dedicate ourselves has lasting value. Christians are branches, and our only value to God is to be found in producing the fruit that He desires.

THE PASSAGE IN DEPTH

Jesus Washes His Disciples' Feet (13:1-17). See the Word Studies of John 13:5 and 13:10, above.

Jesus Predicts His Betrayal (13:18-30). See the commentary on Matt. 26:17-30, and the parallel passages in Mark 14:18-21 and Luke 22:21-23.

Jesus Predicts Peter's Denial (13:31-38).

See the commentary on Matt. 26:31-35, and the parallel passages in Mark 14:27-31 and Luke 22:31-38.

Jesus Comforts His Disciples (14:1-4). See the Word Study of John 14:2, above.

Jesus the Way to the Father (14:5-14). See the Word Studies of John 14:12-13 above.

Background. The ancient Middle East was a land of many gods and goddesses. Two elements were common in ancient religions. First, the various gods and goddesses of a people were thought to play different roles—such as god of war, goddess of hearth and home, etc. And second, most lands were viewed as owned by one or more of the people's deities. Thus if a person moved from, say Persopolis to Damascus, he or she might continue to worship his own deities, but also considered it wise to worship the gods who owned Syria as well.

The God of the OT is strikingly different from contemporary deities. God is One. He alone has every attribute of Deity, and controls every aspect of His people's destiny. While Israel is uniquely His land, on loan to the Covenant people, the Lord is the Creator and Owner of all lands on earth; the sole Master of the Universe.

This conviction held by the pious Jew that the God of the OT alone is God, and all the deities of the pagans empty idols or masks for demons, set Judaism apart from all the world's religions. The rest were marked by the superstitious assumptions that there were many gods, a belief that led to a general tolerance of all religions of others. In contrast Judaism was considered intolerant; its exclusive claims went against the grain of every contemporary culture. By the first century, however, Judaism was accepted in the Roman Empire as a legitimate religion. This was not because anyone accepted its theological presuppositions, but instead because of Judaism's antiquity. It seemed to the Romans that any religion which was ancient had much to commend it, and similarly a religion which was new was viewed with great suspicion.

What is important to us as we look at John 14:5-14 is to understand that biblical faith has always been essentially intolerant of other religions and has always maintained that it alone promises a relationship with God. It is not surprising then to hear Jesus, who presents Himself as the fulfillment of the OT prophet's visions, make a similar exclusive claim.

Interpretation. Jesus' statement is blunt and plain. "I am the way and the truth and the life. No one comes to the Father except through Me" (14:6).

When Christians assert this truth today we too are likely to be charged with intolerance. God is known by many names, others will tell us. And religious men and women will insist that there are many roads, but all lead to God. Some, especially concerned with the Jews, argue today for a "two covenant" approach to biblical faith. The first Covenant (the OT) is still in force for the Jew, who is accepted on the basis of his commitment to the God of the OT, while the second Covenant (the NT) is in force for the Christian, who is accepted on the basis of his faith in Jesus Christ. The Jew need not believe in Jesus to be acceptable to God, for the New Covenant does not really supersede the Old.

Others will tell you that God is so good and loving that He could not possibly condemn anyone to eternal punishment, and thus logically all men and women will surely be saved. They can believe in Allah or Buddha or nothing at all. It makes no difference. In the end they will all be gathered up by God as His own. But Jesus says simply, "No one comes to the Father except through Me."

Today each person certainly is free to believe what he or she chooses. He can believe that all will be saved. She can argue that OT faith is as acceptable to God as Christianity. Great emotional appeals can be advanced for the "sincere" believer who seeks to approach God through Hinduism or Shinto. But whatever human beings may say, Jesus said, "No one comes to the Father except through Me."

Application. The person who believes in the God of the Bible has always borne the burden of giving witness to a God who insists that He be approached His way, not man's way. This is still our challenge: to give witness to Him, and to share the Good News that all can come to the Father—but only through Jesus the Son.

Jesus Promises the Holy Spirit (14:15-31).
Background. This passage contains some of the clearest teachings in Scripture that the Holy Spirit is both a divine Person, and at the

same time with the Father and the Son constitutes the One God of the OT and NT Scriptures. When Jesus said I will give you "another Counselor" (14:16), He used the Greek word *allos,* which means "another of the same kind." The *Zondervan Dictionary of Christian Literacy* sums up the biblical evidence for the personhood and deity of the Spirit.

Some people have suggested that the Holy Spirit should be understood simply as the "divine influence" or as God's "animating power." Such attempts to rob the Holy Spirit of personhood and deity fail simply because they are so clearly contradicted by Scripture.

When Jesus spoke of the Holy Spirit, our Lord chose the personal pronoun "He," even though "spirit" in Greek is a neuter word (John 14:17, 26; 16:13-15). Christ promised to send His disciples "another Comforter" when He returned to heaven, and He identified the Spirit as the promised one. The word in Scripture for "another" is *allos,* a Greek term meaning "another of the same kind" in distinction to *heteros,* meaning "another of a different kind." Christ, the second person of the Godhead, was to send the Spirit, equally God, to live within those who believe.

There are many other indications that the Spirit is a Person and not a force or influence. The Holy Spirit knows and understands (Rom. 8:27; 1 Cor. 2:11). The Holy Spirit communicates in words (2 Cor. 2:13). The Holy Spirit acts and chooses (1 Cor. 12:11). The Spirit loves (Rom. 15:30), can be insulted (Heb. 10:29), can be lied to (Acts 5:3), can be resisted (Acts 7:51), and can be grieved (Eph. 4:30). The Holy Spirit teaches (John 14:26), intercedes (Rom. 8:26), convicts (John 16:7-8), bears witness (John 15:26), and guides (John 16:13). Each of these activities testifies to the fact that the Spirit is a person, not an impersonal influence.

The Holy Spirit is also a divine person. The Bible clearly identifies the Spirit as God by the titles it gives Him. He is the eternal Spirit (Heb. 9:14), the Spirit of Christ (1 Peter 1:11), the Spirit of the Lord (Isa. 11:2), the Spirit of the Sovereign Lord (Isa. 61:1), the Spirit of the Father (Matt. 10:20) and the Spirit of the Son (Gal. 4:6).

No other being apart from God bears such divine titles.

The deity of the Spirit is shown in other ways. He is omnipresent, as only God can be (Ps. 139:7; 1 Cor. 12:13). He is all powerful (Luke 1:36; Rom. 8:11). He was an agent in Creation (Gen. 1:2; Ps. 104:30) and has power to work miracles (Matt. 12:28; 1 Cor. 12:9-11). The Spirit is the one who brings us new birth (John 3:6; Titus 3:5). It was the Spirit who raised Jesus from the dead and who brings God's resurrection life to you and me (Rom. 8:11). The Holy Spirit can be blasphemed (Matt. 12:31-32; Mark 3:28-29), and lying to the Holy Spirit is said to be lying to God (Acts 5:3-4). The biblical testimony is clear. The Holy Spirit is a person. And the Holy Spirit is God (p. 186).

Interpretation. This passage does more than introduce the NT's teaching on the Holy Spirit as a Person. It introduces the theme of the Spirit's personal presence with and within the believer. This has many implications for the Christian's life and experience, some of which are explored in the Commentary on Rom. 8 and Gal. 5. Here the particular issue in view is the believer's personal experience of the presence of an absent Christ.

In making His promise of the Spirit, Jesus said, "I will not leave you as orphans; I will come to you" (14:18). Our first thought is, of course: Jesus will return. But the next words make it clear that Jesus is not speaking of the Second Coming. "Before long," Jesus went on, "the world will not see Me anymore, but you will see Me" (14:19).

But how will we be able to "see" Jesus? It is clear from the phrase "the world will not see Me any longer" that "see" is not intended in its natural sense. The world will not "see" Jesus because He will not be here physically; physical sight will not serve them. Yet Jesus says, "You will see Me." You and I will "see" Jesus, and thus know His presence with us, despite the fact that He is physically present with the Father (14:2-3).

It is obvious in the context of Christ's remarks that Jesus is speaking of a spiritual presence with us. It is also clear Jesus intends this spiritual presence to be as real to His disciples as His physical presence. Somehow we will see Him. Somehow we will know Him.

Somehow we will experience Him as real and vital, as if He were by our side.

It is clear from this chapter's emphasis on the Holy Spirit that He is the One who establishes the link between Christ and the believer which makes our experience of the Lord possible. The question that remains, however, is: What must we do to actually experience Jesus' presence?

Jesus answers this question clearly. Note these verses in our chapter:

"Whoever has My commands and obeys them, he is the one who loves Me. He who loves Me will be loved by My Father, and I too will love him and show Myself to him" (14:21).

And, "If anyone loves Me, he will obey My teaching. My Father will love him, and We will come to him and make Our home with him. He who does not love Me will not obey My teaching" (14:24).

Each of these verses notes that love for Christ motivates obedience to Christ's teaching. And each states that Jesus shows Himself to the one whom love motivates to respond.

This is why the world will never sense the reality of Jesus. The world does not love Jesus, and thus will not be moved from the heart to obey Christ's words. But you and I, who do love Jesus, and who want to please Him, will sense His presence—as we obey.

Implications. There are times when the Lord may not seem real to believers: Times when we pray, and heaven seems closed. Times when we doubt, and hear no voice of reassurance. Times when we fear, and struggle hopelessly for inner peace. Yet here we have Christ's own promise of His personal presence with us, and Christ's own guidelines for "seeing" Him—even in the most difficult of times.

There is no call here for us to have an overcomer's faith. Or a scholar's knowledge. Or a sage's wisdom. Or a saint's self-denial. All that we need to do is love Jesus and, as love motivates us, respond to the words He leaves us. Augustine said it best: "Love God, and do what you please." What he meant, of course, was that if you truly love God, you will do what pleases Him.

So when the dry times come, focus on Jesus. Consider who He is, and what He has done for you. Rekindle the love that has burned so brightly in the past. Then, as love is

renewed, travel step by step down the path Jesus' words mark out. And suddenly, unexpectedly, you will sense Jesus there with you. You will surely see Him by your side.

The Vine and the Branches (15:1-17).
Background. A number of OT passages portray God's people as a vine, and fruit as the consequences or outcomes of human actions. This figurative use of "fruit" is the most common, found some 11 times in the Psalms and 10 times in the Proverbs. Undoubtedly the principle example is found in Isa. 5:1-7, where the prophet describes Israel as God's vineyard. Although the Lord did everything to prepare the land and protect the young plants, the results were more than disappointing. Here is Isaiah's vision of God's vineyard—a vision which helps us understand as Jesus' disciples would have, Christ's extended analogy of His own vine/branches relationship with believers.

I will sing for the one I love
  a song about his vineyard:
My loved one had a vineyard
  on a fertile hillside.
He dug it up and cleared it of stones
  and planted it with the choicest vines.
He built a watchtower in it
  and cut out a winepress as well.
Then he looked for a crop of good grapes,
  but it yielded only bad fruit.
"Now you dwellers in Jerusalem and men of Judah,
  judge between Me and My vineyard.
What more could have been done for My vineyard
  than I have done for it?
When I looked for good grapes,
  why did it yield only bad?
Now I will tell you
  what I am going to do to My vineyard:
I will take away its hedge,
  and it will be destroyed;
I will break down its wall,
  and it will be trampled.
I will make it a wasteland,
  neither pruned nor cultivated,
  and briers and thorns will grow there.
I will command the clouds
  not to rain on it."
The vineyard of the Lord Almighty
  is the house of Israel,
and the men of Judah

are the garden of His delight.
And He looked for justice, but saw
bloodshed;
for righteousness, but heard cries of
distress.

Against the well-known background of this
image Jesus now announces, "I am the Vine;
you are the branches" (15:5). Just as God
looked for fruit from His OT planting, Israel,
so God now looks for fruit from His NT
investment, the church. Unlike the OT vine
which produced bitter fruit, God expects the
branches united to Jesus to "bear much fruit."

One question often asked is what does
"fruit" mean here. The meaning is established
in the OT imagery and reinforced in NT imagery. Isaiah portrays fruit as justice and righteousness. Paul, in Gal. 5:22-23, portrays fruit
as that "love, joy, peace, patience, kindness,
goodness, faithfulness, gentleness and self-
control" which the Holy Spirit produces in
the converted person's life. Both OT and NT
focus our attention on character: "fruit" are
those good and right acts which are produced
by a person whose heart is in tune with God's
own character and nature (Matt. 7:15-23).

What Jesus tells His disciples, then, is that
as the true Vine He will produce in His
branches that fruit which God has always
sought in those who are His own.

Interpretation. Two themes dominate this
critical NT passage: the theme of the Vine and
its branches, and the command of Jesus to His
disciples to love one another.

The first theme is developed as Jesus stresses that a believer must "remain in" (15:4-10)
Him, as a branch must remain in intimate
union with the vine. This is essential because
"no branch can bear fruit by itself; it must
remain in the Vine. Neither can you bear fruit
unless you remain in Me" (15:4). And, "apart
from Me, you can do nothing" (15:5). Thus

to "remain in" means something very different than to continue believing in Jesus; it
means to live in union with Him.

Only in union is fruit-bearing possible. And
only in fruit-bearing can God's purpose for us
be achieved. The important thing for us to
realize is that whatever prominence we may
achieve—in our church or in the larger Christian world—God's goal for us is to be fruitful.
Unless we are living in union with our Lord
and seeing His fruit produced in our lives, all
else is meaningless (see Word Study of 15:6,
above).

How do we live in that union with the
Lord that bonds us to Him as closely as a
branch is bonded to its vine? Christ again, as
in John 14, emphasizes obeying His commands and thus remaining in His love. And
He emphasizes a specific command: "Love
each other as I have loved you" (15:12).

God has chosen us to bear fruit. If love for
Christ moves us to love one another, we will.

Application. While John 15:1-17 is normally
treated as a separate unit, it is in fact part of a
single argument begun in 14:15. Jesus has sent
the Holy Spirit to bond us to Himself. We
experience Jesus' real presence when love for
Him moves us to obey His teachings. What is
more, as we live in intimate union with Jesus
He produces fruit in our lives. Again the key
to living in union is a love that moves us to
obedience, this time to a specific command:
love each other. Why this command? Because
the fruit identified in the OT—righteousness
and justice—and the fruit identified in the
NT—love, patience, goodness, etc.—must be
expressed in interpersonal relationships. As we
love one another those beautiful qualities of
our God which He seeks to express through
us will be realized in our lives. Without love
for one another, there can be no fruit. With
love for Christ and love for one another,
God's fruit will bud and grow.

JOHN 15:18–17:26
Jesus' Last Words (Continued)

EXPOSITION

The Last Supper discourse continues. Jesus has encouraged His disciples with Good News. Even after Christ returns to the Father, His followers will be linked to Him by the indwelling Holy Spirit. Those who love Jesus and are thus moved to obey Him, will "see" Jesus in a way that the world cannot. They will experience His presence and find both peace and joy. And, by "remaining in" Jesus, as a branch remains united to its vine, His followers will be enabled to bear much fruit.

As the discourse continues Jesus tells His disciples more about what will happen when He is gone. He has spoken about the believer's intimate though hidden future relationship with Him. He has also emphasized His "new commandment," and explained the importance of loving one another. Now He warns the disciples: the world which has hated Him will hate them as well, but despite persecution Christ's followers must testify about Him (15:18–16:4). This is another reason why the Holy Spirit's coming is so essential. We are to testify, but the One who drives home the message of Jesus and convicts the world is the Spirit Himself (16:5-16). The disciples remain puzzled, uncertain of what Jesus is saying to them. But the day is coming when the grief that Christ's followers will experience at His departure turns to joy, as they begin to experience the wonderful new relationship Jesus has won for them with the Father (16:17-33). The world may remain hostile, but we have peace, for Jesus has overcome the world.

With no word of transition John then records what has been called Christ's "high priestly" prayer. The NIV outlines this as a three-part prayer. Jesus prays for Himself (17:1-5), Jesus prays for His disciples (17:6-19), and Jesus prays for all believers (17:20-26). In Christ's prayer for Himself, we discover our duty and our destiny. In Christ's prayer for the disciples, we find the secret of our security and sanctification. And in Christ's prayer for all believers, we learn the real meaning of Christian unity.

WORD STUDIES

If the *world* hates you, keep in mind that it hated Me first (15:18). The Greek word here is *kosmos,* the most significant of the words rendered by "world" in the NT. It is found nearly 200 times in the NT, with a variety of meanings. In one sense "the world" is all created things. In another, it is the biosphere, where human beings live and work. In a third sense, "the world" is humanity itself. But *kosmos* is also a theological term. The *Zondervan Expository Dictionary of Bible Words* says that here *kosmos*

> portrays human society as a system warped by sin, tormented by beliefs and desires and emotions that surge blindly and uncontrollably. The world system is a dark system (Eph. 6:12), operating on basic principles that are not of God (Col. 2:20; 1 John 2:16). The entire system lies under the power of Satan (1 John 5:19) and constitutes the kingdom from which believers are delivered by Christ (Col. 1:13-14). Its basic hostility to God is often displayed (1 Cor. 2:12; 3:19; 11:32; Eph. 2:2; James 1:27; 4:4; 1 John 2:15-17; cf. John 12:31; 15:19; 16:33; 17:14; 1 John 3:1, 13; 5:4-5, 19).

What we have here, then, is a clear warning. We must not expect a lost world, driven by motives and drives that are corrupt and ungodly, to gladly embrace Christ or Christian beliefs and standards. The individual who imagines that the Gospel will one day usher in utopia fails to realize that humanity wanders in a dark world of illusion, not only unable to see the light, but hostile and resentful to any hint that its ways lie under the judgment of God. Christians who live by Christ's teachings and share the message of Christ stand against the world. And the world responds to God's modern messengers as it responded to Christ Himself: "They will treat you this way because of My name" (15:21). It is sometimes hard to grasp the reason for the open hostility of the world to Christians who seek to live by and who openly affirm God's standards. Jesus gives two reasons: "They do not know [*ouk oidasin*] the One who sent Me" (15:21), and in His incarnation Jesus revealed righteousness and thus rebuked sin (15:22). The first phrase suggests that the world lacks an adequate conception of God. With a distorted view of God the world has no way to correctly judge the messengers or message.

But the problem is not simply conceptual; it is moral. In Jesus' incarnation and through His words the world has been given a clear vision of righteousness. Measured against the standard of Jesus' perfect life, as against the standard of His words, every shred of false pride and every excuse is stripped away, and the world stands exposed as guilty before God. It is this that makes the world so hostile toward Christ and Christians. If all that were involved in "Jesus' name" was some philosophical concept about God's nature, the world could simply ignore Christ and Christians. It is the moral message implicit in the name of Christ that arouses hatred, for that moral message exposes every human being as guilty of sin.

He will *testify* about Me. And you also must testify, for you have been with Me from the beginning (15:26-27). The concept underlying "witness" or "testify" (the same word in Greek) in both Testaments involves making a strong statement or offering evidence based on direct personal knowledge.

The theme of testimony to Jesus is found frequently in the Gospel of John. The Baptist testified to the fact that Jesus was "the Son of God" (1:34; 5:33). The miracles that Jesus performed testified to the fact that Christ truly was sent by the Father (5:36). The Father Himself testifies through Jesus' miracles (5:37), and the Scriptures add their testimony as well (5:39). Later Jesus argued that His own testimony about Himself was valid, for He alone had personal knowledge of His origins (8:14). And again Jesus asserts that His testimony about Himself is confirmed by the Father (8:18).

In our passage Jesus informs His disciples that the Holy Spirit whom He will send "will testify about Me" (15:26), but adds "you also must testify, for you have been with Me from the beginning" (15:27). The Holy Spirit will testify, but He must testify through the words and actions of believers.

This is still true today. The world responds to Christ and Christians with hostility. But we are to respond to the world with a love that reflects the character of Christ, and with a message that offers forgiveness and hope.

But I tell you the truth: It is for your *good* that I am going away. Unless I go away, the Counselor will not come to you; but if I go, I will send Him to you (16:7). Neither of the two common words translated "good" is found in this passage. Instead the Greek has *sumpherei,* which means something is advantageous and therefore better.

It would have been hard to convince the disciples, who had come to love and depend on the Lord in all things, that His departure was "good." They would not "enjoy" Christ's absence, but they would benefit from it!

The reason, of course, is that while Christ was here physically the disciples had to be with Him to enjoy His presence. This severely limited their ministry. But with Christ spiritually present with every believer in the person of the Holy Spirit, the Lord would be able to guide and empower each of them at all times and in all places!

It is encouraging for us to remember, when we long for the presence of Jesus, that He is here with us now. In the person of the Spirit who has taken up residence in our lives, we are united with Jesus wherever we are. Whatever our circumstance or need, He is with us now and always.

But when He, the Spirit of truth, comes, He will *guide you into all truth* (16:13). The word translated "guide" is *hodegeo.* The translation is fortunate; it appropriately conveys the image of someone leading a stranger into an unknown realm.

This verse has troubled some, who have wondered why, if the Spirit guides believers into "all truth," Christians differ on many points of theology. Such persons, however, misunderstand the verse, assuming that "truth" here means "doctrinal agreement." Underlying the biblical concept of "truth" is the conviction that God alone knows reality, and that He has revealed reality to us in His Word. God alone knows what is truly right and good, what is truly beneficial and helpful. This is truth: that moral and spiritual reality which God knows and has revealed to us in Christ and in Scripture.

All mankind wanders in a swirling fog of illusions, unwilling and unable to accept those revealed standards and values which are rooted in the very nature of God. But the believer, guided by the Holy Spirit, will be enabled to find his way through the fog and make those choices which are in harmony with truth.

Christians of various traditions may very well disagree on minor points of doctrine. But whatever our differences, as we follow the Spirit's leading, we will come to know by personal experience what it means to live in that realm of reality which is portrayed in Scrip-

ture as God's Truth (see commentary on John 17:17).

In that day you will no longer *ask* Me anything. I tell you the truth, My Father will give you whatever you *ask* in My name. Until now you have not *asked* for anything in My name. *Ask* and you will receive, and your joy will be complete (16:23-24). The passage is confusing because the meaning of the verb "ask" shifts. The first "ask" here means "ask a question," not "request a favor." After Jesus' resurrection the disciples' confusion over what Jesus meant will be resolved. By then too the disciples will have a relationship with the Father, based on Christ's work and Person, which enables them to appeal directly to the Father and be assured that He will respond to them. This wondrous thought is continued in 16:26-27: "I am not saying that I will ask the Father on your behalf. No, the Father Himself loves you because you have loved Me and have believed that I came from God."

What assurance we have in prayer. We come confidently, not because we deserve answers, but because we know that God loves us in Jesus Christ, and is moved by love to provide for us whatever is best.

Sanctify them by the truth; Your Word is truth (17:17). Three critical theological concepts meet in this one verse. "Truth," "Sanctify," and God's "Word."

To "sanctify" means to make holy, and/or set apart for sacred use. "Truth" is reality as God understands and reveals it through Scripture and the Son. God's "Word" is the means, written and incarnate, through which He pierces the veil of human confusion and reveals reality as He—as Creator and Redeemer—knows it to be.

As we put our trust in and act on God's revelation we move into the realm of reality, where we experience transformation and are made useful to the Lord.

My prayer is not that You take them *out of the world* but that You protect them from the evil one. They are not of the world, even as I am not of it (17:15-16). It would seem that these verses should be treated before verse 17. But verse 17 provides the key to understanding Jesus' point here.

In the OT that which is sanctified was set apart from the common, isolated for service. It was literally "taken out of" the ordinary world, and could be defiled by the mere touch of anything that was ritually unclean. Now Jesus says that He will not take believers "out of" the world, but will leave us in it. While we are protected from the evil one, Satan, we still must live in daily contact with a corrupt and corrupting society. We daily find ourselves subject to influences which vie with each other to distort our thinking, our desires, our emotions, our motives, our relationships with others.

This introduces us to the dramatic difference between "sanctify" as it is conceived in OT and NT. In the OT, sanctification was a matter of isolation. In the NT, sanctification is a matter of transformation—a dynamic, purifying work of the Holy Spirit within us which enables us to live holy lives even while playing our part within a society which is essentially corrupt and hostile to God.

This is an important truth for us to grasp and live by. We need to throw off the siege mentality that has led some Christians to pursue holiness by a retreat behind separatistic do's and don'ts. Instead we are to be actively involved in the world, but as Jesus was. Not as participants in the follies of a lost society, but as beacons of light, who shine because we are fully committed to living by God's Truth.

JESUS AS THE WORD (17:17)

There are a number of correspondences between John's vision of Jesus as the Incarnate Word, and David's great psalm of appreciation for the written Word (Ps. 119). Here are a few:

PSALM 119	JOHN'S GOSPEL
THE WAY	
Blessed are they whose ways are blameless, who walk according to the law of the Lord. (v. 1)	I am the way and the truth and the life. (14:6)
How can a young man keep his way pure? By living according to Your word. (v. 9)	Whoever has My commands and obeys them, he is the one who loves Me. (14:21)
I run in the path of Your commands, for You have set my heart free. (v. 32)	
THE TRUTH	
Your righteousness is everlasting and Your law is true. (v. 142)	I am the way and the truth and the life. (14:6)
I have chosen the way of truth. I have set my heart on Your laws. (v. 30)	If you hold to My teaching, you are really My disciples.
All Your commands are trustworthy. (v. 86)	Then you will know the truth, and the truth will set you free. (8:31-32)
The statutes You have laid down are righteous; they are fully trustworthy. (v. 138)	Sanctify them by the truth; Your Word is truth. (17:17)
All Your words are true; all Your righteous laws are eternal. (v. 160)	For the law was given by Moses; grace and truth come through Jesus Christ. (1:17)
THE LIFE	
Turn my eyes away from worthless things; preserve my life according to Your Word. (v. 37)	In Him was life, and that life was the light of men. (1:4)
Let Your compassion come to me that I may live, for Your law is my	The Son of Man must be lifted up, that everyone who believes in Him may have eternal life. (3:14-15)

delight. (v. 77)
Sustain me according to Your
promise, and I will live; do
not let my hopes be dashed. (v. 116)
Your statutes are forever right; give me
understanding that I may live. (v. 144)

Jesus said . . . "I am the resurrection and the life. He who believes
in Me will live, even though
he dies; and whoever lives and
believes in Me will never die."
(11:25)

THE LIGHT

Your word is a lamp to my feet
and a light to my path. (v. 105)

I am the light of the world.
Whoever follows Me will never
walk in darkness, but will have
the light of life. (8:12)
I have come into the world as
a light, so that no one who
believes in Me should stay in
the darkness. (12:46)

LOVE

I delight in Your commandments
because I love them. I lift up my
hands for Your commandments, which
I love, and I meditate on Your
decrees. (vv. 47-48)
Oh, how I love Your law! I meditate
on it all day long. (v. 97)
Your promises have been thoroughly
tested, and Your servant loves them.
(v. 140)
See how I love Your precepts,
preserve my life, O Lord, according
to Your love. (v. 159)

Now remain in My love. If you
obey My commands, you will remain
in My love, just as I have obeyed
My Father's commands, and remain
in His love. (15:9-10)
If anyone loves Me, he will
obey My teaching. My Father will
love him, and We will come to him
and make Our home with him. He
who does not love Me will not
obey My teaching. (14:23-24)

JOY

Your statutes are my heritage forever;
they are the joy of my heart. (v. 111)

I will see you again and you
will rejoice, and no one will
take away your joy. (16:22)

THE PASSAGE IN DEPTH

**The World Hates the Disciples (15:18–
16:4).** See the Word Studies of 15:18, 15:21,
and 15:26 above.

The Work of the Holy Spirit (16:5-16).
Background. In the first part of this discourse
Jesus promised the disciples He would send
them the Comforter, the third Person of the
Trinity, and outlined some of the ministries of
the Holy Spirit to believers.

In this section of the Last Supper discourse
Jesus now defines ministries of the Holy
Spirit to "the world." Here, as frequently in
John's writings, "the world" is both that cul-
ture shaped by a lost humanity's sinful

passions, and the men and women who make
it up. In introducing this theme Jesus says that
"the Spirit of truth who goes out from the
Father, He will testify about Me" (15:26), and
adds that "you also must testify [about Me]"
(15:27).

As Christians give testimony to Jesus by life
and by word, the Holy Spirit speaks through
us.

Interpretation. What is critical about this passage is its definition of the ministry of the
Spirit to the world. Unfortunately, this definition is sometimes distorted in our English versions (see the three versions reproduced here).
To understand what the text is saying, we

need to approach this passage in view of something the Apostle Paul says in His second letter to the Corinthians. There Paul notes that those who spread the knowledge of Jesus are "the aroma of Christ among those who are being saved and those who are perishing. To the one we are the smell of death; to the other, the fragrance of life" (2 Cor. 2:15-16). To those who are being saved, the ministry of the Holy Spirit is freeing, bringing vitality and life. To the world that rejects Jesus, the ministry of the Holy Spirit crushes, condemns, and destroys every false hope.

So we must not take the critical verses that describe the Spirit's ministry to the world as elements in a saving, purifying process. Rather they are aspects of God's judgment of "everything in the world." Everything which John later characterizes as "the cravings of sinful man, the lust of his eyes and the boasting of what he has and does" (1 John 2:16).

With this said, we can look more carefully at what Jesus says here about the ministry of the Spirit to the world that hated Him, and which hates and persecutes those who represent Him.

THREE TRANSLATIONS OF JOHN 16:8-11

NEW INTERNATIONAL VERSION
When He [the Counselor] comes, He will convict the world of guilt in regard to sin and righteousness and judgment; in regard to sin, because men do not believe in Me; in regard to righteousness, because I am going to the Father, where you can see Me no longer; and in regard to judgment, because the prince of this world now stands condemned.

THE LIVING BIBLE
And when He has come He will convince the world of its sin, and of the availability of God's goodness, and of deliverance from judgment. The world's sin is unbelief in Me; there is righteousness available because I go to the Father and you shall see Me no more; there is deliverance from judgment because the prince of this world has already been judged.

J.B. PHILLIPS
When He comes, He will convince the world of the meaning of sin, of true goodness and of judgment. He will expose their sin because they do not believe in Me; He will reveal true goodness for I am going away to the Father and you will see Me no longer; and He will show them the meaning of judgment, for the spirit which rules this world will have been judged.

In order to judge which of the three translations best captures the meaning of the original, we need to examine the significance of four words, each of which is introduced in verse 8: convict, sin, righteousness and judgment.

■ Convict. The Greek word here is *elegcheo*. The *Theological Dictionary of the New Testament* (2:473-474) says:

In Homer *elegcheo* signifies "to scorn, to bring into contempt"; in later literature it means (a) "to shame" by exposure, opposition, etc.; (b) "to blame"; (c) "to expose,"

"to resist"; (d) to "interpret, expound"; (e) "to investigate." In the NT the usage is more restricted; basically it means "to show someone his sin and summon him to repentance."

However, in John this word conveys the first element of this meaning, "to show someone his sin," without the second, "and summon him to repentance." Thus in John 3:20 John points out that the evil person hates the light and avoids it "for fear that his deeds will be exposed." The reaction of the evil person to exposure is to scurry further into the shadow

265

in an attempt to escape the light! A similar emphasis is seen in John 8:46, where Jesus asks His adversaries, "Can any of you prove Me guilty of sin?" This verse asks: Can anyone expose Jesus as a sinner?

Here then we have John using *elegcho* in its usual sense. The Holy Spirit's ministry in the world is to expose: to unmask, to show up its error, to strip away its pretense. And here in this verse we have a clear definition of those specific errors which the Holy Spirit will expose. The Spirit will demonstrate the error with reference to sin, to righteousness, and to judgment.

But *elegcheo* has even greater import. In the first century this word was also a legal term, one used of a judge pronouncing the verdict which establishes the guilt of one who is accused of a crime. The Holy Spirit not only exposes the sin of the world; the Holy Spirit strips away every shred of pretense and every excuse, and publicly announces God's verdict.

How fascinating it is. The world announced its verdict concerning Jesus, rejecting and crucifying the Son of God. Now the world itself stands before a heavenly court, to be convicted by the Holy Spirit.

Jesus is careful not to leave us in doubt when He says the Spirit will expose the world with regard to sin, righteousness, and judgment. He carefully explains each point.

■ Sin. "In regard to sin, because men do not believe in Me" (16:9). The central sin of humanity is unbelief. Again and again this thought is emphasized in John's Gospel. "Whoever believes in Him," John writes, "is not condemned, but whoever does not believe stands condemned already because He has not believed in the name of God's one and only Son" (3:18). Unbelief is not a sin of ignorance. It is and always was a willful rejection of God (Rom. 1; Ps. 19), a rejection which is now made unmistakable since Jesus came and in His life and death unveiled the forgiving love of God.

Human beings might once have mouthed excuses. They might have (wrongly) argued that Nature revealed only the power and not the character of God (Rom. 1:18-20), and so fear of the unknown kept them from belief in Him. But now God in Christ has stripped away that excuse. In the person of the Son the love, the grace, and the glory of God have been fully displayed. To refuse to believe now unmistakably exposes the sinfulness of those who would reject so great a salvation offered by so wonderful a God.

■ Righteousness. "In regard to righteousness, because I am going to the Father, where you can see Me no longer" (16:10). Christ had been condemned to the cross as a sinner—a blasphemer to the Jew, a threat to the social order of the Roman. Yet the very cross to which Christ was condemned by the world was the means of His return in glory to the Father, having won our salvation there, and being fully vindicated by the Resurrection. The return of Jesus to the Father proved Christ righteous, and established Him as the standard by which we are to determine what righteousness is. The judgment of the world that Jesus was a sinner was reversed by God when He welcomed Christ home, exposing the "righteousness" of the world as sin and the "sinner" as the standard of righteousness for humankind.

Jesus' return to the Father exposed the guilt of the world in yet another way as well. After the Resurrection, the disciples' grief at Jesus' crucifixion turned to joy as they realized He was now with the Father. But, unable to see Jesus, the world rejoiced in the mistaken notion that it was rid of the Lord! (16:20) The joy of the saved that rests on a clear vision of the absent Christ stands in stark contrast to the joy of the damned. And even as the disciples' grief turned to joy, the world's joy will one day soon be transformed into anguish and remorse.

■ Judgment. "In regard to judgment, because the prince of this world now stands condemned" (16:11). The cross revealed unmistakably that God is committed to judge sin and sinners. There is now no possible hope that Satan and those who follow him will escape divine justice. Earlier, approaching the cross, Jesus announced, "Now is the time for judgment on this world; now the prince of this world will be driven out" (12:31). In the Cross and Resurrection God proclaims the end of sin's grip on our universe. In the Cross and Resurrection, the "prince of this world," Satan, has been judged—and a world which has gladly submitted to the rule of this prince is judged with him!

Application. This important passage on the ministry of the Holy Spirit to the world is not a message of hope. There is no thought here that the Spirit's work of "convicting" the world is a "saving" work, despite the impression that is left by one of the translations — actually a paraphrase — above. The Spirit's convicting work is rather a work of judgment, exposing the sin so deeply embedded in the world as a system and in its citizens as individuals.

In a real sense, the Spirit's work of exposing the guilt of the world is a ministry performed for the benefit of believers. We must never let ourselves grow accustomed to this world or its ways. We must instead always be on our guard, for the Holy Spirit exposes everything about this world as corrupt, breathing a spirit of unbelief, unrighteousness, and commitment to the ways of a "prince" who stands under the judgment of God. The wonderful news is that even as the Holy Spirit exposes the guilt of the world, He also "will guide you into all truth" (16:13). As we look to the Spirit and depend on Him to guide us, He will enable us to walk in the light.

The Disciple's Grief Will Turn to Joy (16:17-33). See the Word Study on 16:23, above.

Jesus Prays for Himself (17:1-5).
Background. Key words in John's Gospel are "glory" and "glorify." The NT usages reflect an OT concept expressed in the Hebrew word, *kabod.* That word expresses God's active presence with His people, thus disclosing who He is and enabling us to praise Him for His essential nature and character.

In secular usage *doxa,* the Greek word, focused attention on the opinion others held of a person based on actions or achievement. Thus in ordinary speech *doxa* was quite close in meaning to "fame." But in the NT "glory" expresses the very different, distinctive theological thought established in the OT. God's glory is rooted in who He by nature is, and to glorify God is to display His nature in acts which take place in space and time.

Interpretation. As the Last Supper ends Jesus turns to the Father in prayer, fully aware that "the time has come" (17:1) Christ's first concern as He prays is, rightly, not for Himself but for God's glory. Thus He prays "glorify

Your Son, that Your Son may glorify You" (17:1). He adds, "I have brought You glory on earth by completing the work You gave Me to do" (17:4), and again prays, "Glorify Me in Your presence with the glory I had with You before the world began" (17:5).

Jesus brought God glory on earth by completing the work assigned, for in all that Jesus did and said He displayed the nature and character of God. It is striking that the ultimate act of glorification is the cross itself, for it is the most stunning display in all of history of the love and grace of our God (7:39; 11:4; 12:16, 23; 13:31).

The cross is also a doorway. Passing through it Jesus will experience resurrection, a decisive event by which He is "declared with power to be the Son of God" (Rom. 1:4). In the Resurrection His own identity and nature are fully established, and the meaning of His crucifixion firmly established. All this underlies Jesus' prayer for Himself: that in what He has done, and is about to do, Jesus will glorify God and be glorified.

Application. As Jesus glorified God by doing His work in the world, so can we. What we display as we love and serve others is not our own goodness, but the transforming grace of a God who can work through human beings. Our good works are performed for God's glory, not our own, for we gladly admit that He is the source of all that is good within us.

Jesus Prays for His Disciples (17:6-19). See the Word Studies of John 17:17 and 17:15-16 above.

Jesus Prays for All Believers (17:20-26).
Background. There may be no passage in Scripture whose message has more frequently been distorted in the last few decades. Many a sermon has been preached, arguing that Jesus' prayer that believers "be brought to complete unity" (17:23) demands we confess our sins for the division represented by denominational differences, and seek organizational unity. Yet all such preaching is based on an absolute and total misunderstanding of Jesus' words!

Interpretation. The key to understanding this part of Christ's prayer, which contains Jesus' specific request for Christians throughout the church age, is found in the words "that all of them may be one, Father, just as You are in Me and I am in You" (17:21). The "complete unity" that we are to experience is a oneness like that experienced by the Father and the Son.

A number of passages in John's Gospel help us understand the nature of that unity, as experienced by Jesus in His life on earth.

■ John 5:19-20. "I tell you the truth, the Son can do nothing by Himself; He can do only what He sees His Father doing, because whatever the Father does the Son also does. For the Father loves the Son and shows Him all He does."

■ John 6:38. "I have come down from heaven not to do My will but to do the will of Him who sent Me."

■ John 8:28-29. "I do nothing on My own but speak just what the Father has taught Me. The one who sent Me is with Me; He has not left Me alone, for I always do what pleases Him."

■ John 12:44-45. "When a man believes in Me, he does not believe in Me only, but in the One who sent Me. When he looks at Me, he sees the One who sent Me."

■ John 14:9-11. "Don't you know Me, Philip, even after I have been among you such a long time? Anyone who has seen Me has seen the Father. How can you say, 'Show us the Father'? Don't you believe that I am in the Father, and that the Father is in Me? The words I say to you are not just My own. Rather, it is the Father, living in Me, who is doing His work. Believe Me when I say that I am in the Father and the Father is in Me."

In essence, Jesus' unity with the Father enabled Him to live His human life in the world in complete harmony with the Father's will.

Note the correspondence of this language with what we read in John 17:21. Earlier Jesus spoke of being in the Father and the Father being in Him. Now He prays that "just as You are in Me and I am in You, may they also be in Us." And before asking that believers be brought to "complete unity" He defines that unity by asking again "that they may be one as We are one: I in them and You in Me" (17:22-23).

The complete unity that Jesus prays for is not an organizational union of churches, but rather a spiritual union of individual believers with the Father and the Son. A union in which we submit to and do the Father's will. A union which enables Christ to act through us, and thus "let the world know that You sent Me and have loved them even as You have loved Me" (17:23).

Thus, John 17 picks up the theme of John 15. There Christ spoke of Himself as the Vine and believers as Branches, and stressed the importance of remaining in Him by choosing to express our love for Him by an ever-obedient response to His teachings. Here Jesus prays to the Father, asking that what is potential in the union faith creates between the believer and the Lord might be actual in our experience.

Application. You and I can have close and warm personal relationships with believers from other traditions. This is possible, not because we dot the same doctrinal "i" or cross the same theological "t," but because as children of the same Father through faith in Jesus we are brothers and sisters, called to love rather than debate one another. This distinctive "spiritual family" unity does exist, and it exists independently of organizational union.

But here Jesus prays not about the union you and I have with each other, but about the union that we are to experience with Him and with the Father! That union exists because we are linked forever to Christ by the Holy Spirit. That union is experienced when we, like Jesus, commit ourselves to do the Father's will, and ever be responsive to Him.

When we do commit ourselves to doing the Father's will, God works through us as He did through Jesus. As we remain with Him, we see His glory. And the glory of God is expressed through our lives.

JOHN 18–21
Grace and Glory

EXPOSITION

Here in the fourth Gospel we again find a careful account of the events associated with the crucifixion and resurrection of Jesus. Because the four accounts so closely parallel each other, our treatment of each Gospel emphasizes a different theme. Since Matthew seems to pay such close attention to human frailty, the in-depth treatment of Matthew focuses on Jesus' rejection by Judas and His denial by Peter. Mark, the briefest of the Gospels, provides a survey of events in sequence, and so in treating Mark we examine that sequence, and also look at Jesus' "seven last words from the cross." Luke highlights the sufferings of Christ. So in exploring Luke's account of Jesus' last hours we focus attention on the physical, the psychological, and the spiritual torment experienced by Jesus on the cross. Here, in John, we look at another theme mentioned in each of the four Gospels: the trials of Jesus before the Sanhedrin, before Herod, and before the Roman governor, Pontius Pilate.

The chart below gives additional information on specific passages that are developed in treatments of each Gospel.

Topic	Matthew	Mark	Luke	John
The plot against Jesus	**26:1-5**	14:1-11	22:1-6	
Anointing at Bethany	26:6-13	**14:3-9**		
Judas agrees to betray Christ	**26:14-16**			
The Last Supper	**26:17-30**	14:12-25	22:14-23	**13–17**
Peter's denial predicted	**26:31-35**	14:27-31	22:31-38	13:31-38
Gethsemane	26:36-46	14:32-42	**22:39-46**	
Jesus' arrest	**26:47-56**	14:43-52	22:47-53	18:1-12
Before the Sanhedrin	26:57-68	14:53-65	22:63-71	**18:12-40**
Peter denies Jesus	**26:69-75**	14:66-72	22:54-62	18:17-27
Judas hangs himself	**27:1-10**			
Jesus before Pilate	27:11-26	15:1-15	23:1-25	18:28–19:16
The soldiers mock Jesus	27:27-31	15:16-20		
The crucifixion	27:32-56	15:21-41	**23:26-49**	19:17-37
Jesus' burial	27:57-61	15:42-47	23:50-56	19:38-42
Guard placed at the tomb	**27:62-66**			

WORD STUDIES

So Judas came to the grove, guiding a *detachment of soldiers* and some officials from the chief priests and Pharisees (18:3). The Greek *speira* is a translation of the technical Roman military term, "cohort." John thus fills out our picture of who was involved in Christ's arrest. In addition to an armed mob *(ochlos)* of ordinary people (Matt. 26:47; Mark 14:43) and a group of temple police (Luke 22:52) and temple officials, a few soldiers from the Roman garrison of Jerusalem had been assigned to aid the capture, undoubtedly at the request of the chief priests. This is important to John, who wants us to understand that Gentiles as well as Jews were responsible for Jesus' execution.

Just as the Gospel is universal, an open invitation to humanity that "whoever will" may come (3:16), so is responsibility for Jesus' death universal. Christ died for Jew and Gentile alike. How necessary then that even in this small detail we see Romans as well as Jews involved in His initial arrest.

Simon Peter and *another disciple* **were following Jesus (18:15).** Most assume that the other disciple was John himself. The text adds that he was able to follow Jesus into the courtyard because he was "known to the high priest" (18:15). Some speculate that since Salome, John's mother, was Mary's sister (cf. John 19:25 with Mark 15:40), she too would have been a cousin of Elizabeth, wife of Zechariah the priest (Luke 1:36), and thus may have had some family connection to the priestly class.

In any case, John's acquaintance with the high priest enabled him to witness and later report on the initial, secret questioning of Jesus (18:19-24).

Then the Jews led Jesus from Caiaphas to the palace of the *Roman governor* (18:28). What little is known about the governor, Pontius Pilate, is hardly flattering. *The Revell Bible Dictionary* reports:

> Pilate served first as prefect and then procurator of Judea. As such, he had vast authority, including command of the military forces that occupied the little land. He alone could order the death sentence. He appointed the Jewish high priest and even

exercised control over funds in the Temple treasury. His service in Judea is attested not only in the Gospels, but also by first-century historians Flavius Josephus and Philo Judaeus, and by recently discovered inscriptional evidence in Caesarea Maritima, the Roman administrative seat.

The Jewish sources that report on Pilate's decade in the Holy Land [A.D. 26-36] portray him as a hostile, insensitive person. One of Pilate's first acts was to antagonize the Jews by setting up image-bearing standards in Jerusalem [that were] considered idolatrous by the Jews. Due to determined demonstrations by the populace, Pilate was forced to take down the standards. Josephus and Philo also accuse him of slaughtering hundreds of Jews *(compare* Luke 13:1), as well as misappropriating Temple funds in order to pay for an aqueduct to bring water to Jerusalem from a distant spring. Yet Pilate served in Judea for ten years rather than the normal three or four, evidence that the Emperor Tiberius considered him an effective administrator. Interestingly, the only known mention of Pilate in pagan writings is a passing reference in Tacitus to Pilate's service at the time of the execution of Christ (p. 793).

It is interesting that Pilate, so often guilty of accepting bribes, of insulting the people he ruled, of outright robbery and of ordering numerous executions without trial, first hesitated to order Jesus' death—and then gave in to the Jewish leaders. For the fascinating "story behind the story," see the discussion of Jesus' trial before Pilate, in the Passage In Depth, below.

"But we have no right to execute anyone," the Jews objected (18:31). The governors of Roman provinces supervised the administration of criminal law in their jurisdiction, and they alone had the authority to inflict the death sentence. The fourth edict of Cyrene (A.D. 6-7) affirmed the duty of the governor to either judge capital cases personally, or to appoint a jury to perform this duty.

Pilate was among the most oppressive governors of Judea, and made frequent use of his power to order executions. The records show that even mild governors of Judea did not hesitate to execute those they considered "troublemakers." Thus while the Jewish high court could not order Jesus' execution, they have every reason to expect that Pilate would gladly order the death of the popular young prophet who had kept Jerusalem in turmoil. They were shocked and shaken when Pilate said, "Take Him yourselves and judge Him by to your own law" (18:31).

It is important to note that manipulating Pilate into executing Jesus had long been a goal of Christ's opponents. The Pharisees had attempted to trap Jesus by asking if it were right to pay taxes to Caesar; they intended to find grounds to accuse Jesus of fomenting rebellion against Rome.

Jesus said, "*My kingdom* is not of this world. . . . But now *My kingdom* is from another place" (18:36). When asked by Pilate if He is a king, Jesus responds by making a statement about His kingdom. A better rendering here would be "my kingship," for *basileia,* like the Hebrew *malkuth,* refers first to sovereign rule, power, or authority, not to geographical or ethnic boundaries. Jesus states that His kingship is not "of this world." It does not originate in the world and, without militant followers ready to form an army, it is clear that Jesus has no political power. Thus Jesus, although a king, is no threat to Roman authority.

Jesus' kingship is not *enteuthen,* "from here." That is, Jesus' authority does not have its origin in this world but in the spiritual realm. One day heaven's authority will be imposed on the whole earth and all its inhabitants. But that time is not now, and heaven's kingdom is not yet come. Pilate clearly understands Jesus' words about "My kingdom," and exclaims, "You are a king, then!" And Jesus is.

"What is truth?" Pilate asked (18:38). Man's kingdom is established on power. Jesus' kingdom is established on truth, and particularly the saving truth that Jesus' words and deeds proclaim. We can hear the scorn in Pilate's voice as he mutters, "Truth? What is that?" And then turns away without even waiting for an answer.

The sophisticated of this world raise their eyebrows along with Pilate, and politely ridicule the notion that "truth" exists, much less

can be known. And, like Omar Khayyam of Fitzgerald's Rubaiyat, Pilate dismisses the worth of seeking it:

With them the seed of Wisdom did I sow, And with mine own hand wrought to make it; And this was all the Harvest that I reaped—I came like Water, and like Wind I go. Into this Universe, and Why not knowing Nor Whence, like Water willy-nilly flowing; And out of it, as Wind along the Waste, I know not Whither, willy-nilly blowing. . . . Perplexed no more with Human or Divine, Tomorrow's tangle to the winds resign, And lose your fingers in the tresses of The Cypress-slender Minister of Wine. How easy to ignore the true issues of life, and refuse to be perplexed with human or divine.

But what Pilate never realized, in turning away from Jesus without waiting for an answer to his query, "What is Truth?" is that in failing to listen to Jesus' answer, he lost his best opportunity to find eternal life.

Give us Barabbas! (18:40) Now Barabbas had taken part in a rebellion. The Greek text simply identifies Barabbas as a *lestes.* This word was reserved for violent men—robbers, pirates, rampaging soldiers, and insurgents. While the general Jewish population might have viewed Barabbas as a "freedom fighter," first-century literature makes it clear that the high priests disowned the actions of such active nationalists, intent on accommodation with the ruling Romans. Thus when Pilate suggested he might release either Jesus or Barabbas, he assumed that the religious leaders who had accused Jesus would ask him to free Christ rather than risk freeing the notorious Barabbas.

How wrong Pilate was. And how unmistakably the choice displays the character of Jesus' enemies. Rather than seek the release of One who had healed God's people and cast out demons, the leaders chose freedom for a murderer and violent man (Mark 15:7).

Then Pilate took Jesus (19:1). One of the most interesting extra-biblical accounts of Christ's death was written by Josephus, shortly after the destruction of Jerusalem in A.D. 70. The Greek manuscripts of Josephus' *The Jew-*

ish War lack this extended passage, leading most scholars to believe it is a later addition. However, it contains an interesting, although unlikely, explanation of Pilate's uncharacteristic surrender to Jewish wishes in the matter of Jesus' crucifixion. The following is from a translation of Josephus' *The Jewish War* appearing in the Loeb Classical Library.

> At that time there appeared a man. . . . Some said of him, "Our first lawgiver is risen from the dead and hath performed many healings and arts," while others thought that he was sent from God. Howbeit in many things he disobeyed the Law and kept not the Sabbath according to [our] fathers' customs. Yet, on the other hand, he did nothing shameful; nor [did he do anything] with the aid of hands, but by word alone did he provide everything.
>
> And many of the multitude followed after him and hearkened to his teachings; and many souls were in commotion, thinking that thereby the Jewish tribes might free themselves from Roman hands. Now it was his custom in general to sojourn over against the city upon the Mount of Olives; and there, too, he bestowed his healings upon the people.
>
> And there assembled unto him of ministers one hundred and fifty, and a multitude of the people. Now when they saw his power, that he accomplished whatsoever he would by [a] word, and when they had made known to him their will, that he should enter into the city and cut down the Roman troops and Pilate and rule over us. And when thereafter knowledge of it came to the Jewish leaders, they assembled together with the high-priest and spake: "We are powerless and [too] weak to withstand the Romans. Seeing, moreover, that the bow is bent, we will go and communicate to Pilate what we have heard, and we shall be clear of trouble, lest he hear [it] from others, and we be robbed of our substance and ourselves scattered and our children scattered.
>
> And they went and communicated it to Pilate. And he sent and had many of the multitude slain. And he had that Wonderworker brought up, and after instituting an inquiry concerning him, he pronounced judgment: "He is a benefactor, not a male-factor, nor a rebel, nor covetous of kingship." And he let him go; for he had healed his dying wife.
>
> And he went to his wonted place and did his wonted works. And when more people again assembled around him, he glorified himself through his actions more than all. The teachers of the Law were overcome with envy, and gave thirty talents to Pilate, in order that he should put him to death. And he took [it] and gave them liberty to execute their will themselves. And they laid hands on him and crucified him contrary to the law of their fathers.

Jesus answered, "You would have no power over Me if it were not given to you from above. Therefore *the one who handed Me over* to you is guilty of a greater sin" (19:11). Pilate's claim to have power to crucify or free Jesus (19:10) is dismissed by the Lord. Since Pilate's power is "from above," Pilate should consider that he will have to give account to God for his actions. The person really on trial in this situation is not Jesus, but Pilate himself!

The identity of "the one who handed Me over to you" has been much debated. Some suggest Christ refers to Judas, since the same verb, *paradous*, is used of him in John 13:21. But Judas turned Jesus over to His Jewish enemies, not to Pilate. Some suggest that the one who handed Jesus over is God the Father, noting that Acts 2:23 says Jesus "was handed over to you by God's set purpose and foreknowledge." But the rest of Scripture testifies that this was not sin, but rather a demonstration of the righteousness of God (Rom. 3:25-26). The best suggestion is that Jesus is referring to the high priest, who as spiritual leader of his people announced the necessity of Christ's death (11:49-53), formulated the charges brought against Jesus (Mark 14:61-64), and as we will see, exerted the pressure on Pilate which forced him to pronounce the death sentence. Because of his position as Israel's spiritual leader and his clearer knowledge of Jesus' works and claims, his active participation in the judicial murder was by far a greater sin than that committed by the Roman governor. Yet perhaps the most significant expression here is Jesus' reminder to Pilate that whatever authority he had was "from above." It is the same with us today. It is God who gives us the freedom to make the significant choices in our life. And it is to Him that we must one day give an account.

Mary Magdalene went to *the tomb* and saw that the stone had been removed from the entrance (20:1). Today two sites in Jerusalem vie for the honor of recognition as the place where Jesus was buried. One lies under the Church of the Holy Sepulchre. The other is the "Garden tomb," a first-century tomb rediscovered in the 19th century. The Garden tomb site is regarded as doubtful by most contemporary archeologists, yet it fits both with the Gospel accounts and first-century burial practices.

Of course, the site is irrelevant, for Jesus was only passing through! Today it makes little difference just where Mary, Peter, John, and the others went to look for Jesus. It makes all the difference in the world that that tomb was empty, and Jesus gone! "And with that He breathed on them and said, 'Receive the Holy Spirit' " (20:22). How does John's account of the giving of the Spirit fit with the very different account in Acts 2? Calvin saw this event as a partial giving of the Spirit, writing in his commentary on John's Gospel that "the Spirit was given to the apostles now in such a way that they were only sprinkled with His grace and not saturated with full power." Others suggest John's account is predictive, intended to make it very clear that when the Spirit did come on Pentecost that He was unmistakably the gift of the risen Lord. Jesus spoke of reception of the Spirit as if it were a completed act because it was, in the sense of being guaranteed by Jesus' resurrection. One fascinating suggestion is that the phrase "He breathed on them" is an Aramaic idiomatic expression still used today, which means simply that He "encouraged them." If so, the rest of Jesus' saying here is to be understood as promise and prompting, letting the disciples know what will be done for them and what they are to do.

However one understands the text, two things are certain. The Spirit is Jesus' gift to His church. And, the Spirit has come, not only empowering us for service but also enriching our lives by His transforming power.

If you forgive anyone his sins, they are forgiven; if you do not forgive them, they are not forgiven (20:23). J.R. Mantey, in an article "The Mistranslation of the Perfect Tense in John 20:23, Matt. 16:19, and Matt. 18:18" in *Journal of Biblical Literature* 58 (1939), pointed out that our English versions render this verse wrongly. Today, over 50 years later, modern versions continue to make the same mistake. What the verse says literally is that "those whose sins you forgive have already been forgiven; those whose sins you do not forgive have not been forgiven." To grasp the significant difference this makes, check the Word Study of Matt. 16:19.

When they had finished eating, *Jesus said to Simon Peter* (21:15). We can imagine Peter, there by the shore, sitting behind the other disciples, almost out of sight. The memory of his denial of Jesus is almost overpowering, and although he loves his Lord and was ecstatic when he realized the identity of the figure bending over a fire by the side of the sea (21:7), he fell uncharacteristically silent as the others ate.

And then Jesus spoke to Peter. What the two said is discussed in the in-depth treatment of Jesus' denial found in the Word Study of Matt. 26:31-35. What is important for us to note here is simply that Jesus spoke first.

What a comfort to us, when we have failed God and ourselves. We have no need to hang back, uncertain. Christ still seeks us, eager to restore us to fellowship and empower us for service. Listen carefully, and you can hear His voice speaking today.

When Peter saw him [John], he asked, "Lord, what about him?" (21:21) We are to listen for God's voice speaking to us about our own life. Guidance isn't given on a party line, and we're not invited to listen in on Jesus' instructions to another.

THE PASSAGE IN DEPTH

Jesus Christ on Trial
After Jesus was arrested, He was subjected to a series of trials. Putting together the picture given in the several Gospels, we can trace the

events of that long night, as follows:

I. Preliminary Examination: nighttime
Before Annas   John 18:12-14, 19-23
Before Caiaphas John 18:24; Matt. 26:57,
                  59-68; Mark 14:53, 55-65;
                  Luke 22:54, 63-65

II. The Religious Trial: daybreak
Before the   Matt. 27:1; Mark 15:1;
Sanhedrin   Luke 22:66-71

III. The Civil Trial: early morning
Before Pilate   John 18:28-38; Matt. 27:2,
                  11-14; Mark 15:2-5; Luke
                  23:1-5
Before Herod   Luke 23:6-12
Before Pilate again John 18:39–19:1, 4-16;
                  Matt. 27:15-26; Mark
                  15:6-15; Luke 23:13-25

I. Preliminary examinations of Jesus: nighttime
BEFORE ANNAS (18:12-14, 19-23)
Annas had been high priest between A.D. 6 to 15, before being deposed by Pilate's predecessor, Valerius Gratus. However, his influence was undiminished, as he saw five of his sons and his son-in-law succeed him to the post. It is likely, since according to the OT the high priest was appointed for life, that many Jews considered him the only legitimate high priest despite the Roman's appointment of others to that post, an attitude that may be reflected in Luke's reference to the high priesthood of Annas and Caiaphas (Luke 3:2).

Edersheim, in his *Life and Times of Jesus the Messiah*, writes about Annas:

No figure is better known in contemporary Jewish history than that of Annas; no person deemed more fortunate or successful, but none also more generally execrated than the late High Priest. He had held the Pontificate for only six or seven years; but it was filled by not fewer than five of his sons, by his son-in-law Caiaphas, and by a grandson. And in those days it was, at least for one of Annas' disposition, much better to have been than to be High Priest. He enjoyed all the dignity of the office, and all its influence also, since he was able to promote to it those most closely connected with him. And, while they acted publicly,

he really directed affairs, without either the responsibility or the restraints which the office imposed. His influence with the Romans he owed to the religious views which he professed, to his open partisanship of the foreigner, and to his enormous wealth. The Sadducean Annas was an eminently safe Churchman, not troubled with any special convictions or with Jewish fanaticism, a pleasant and a useful man also, who was able to furnish his friends in the Praetorium with large sums of money. We have seen what immense revenues the family of Annas must have derived from the Temple-booths, and how nefarious and unpopular was the traffic. The names of those bold, licentious, unscrupulous, degenerate sons of Aaron were spoken with whispered curses.

Given the influence of Annas, it is understandable that Jesus was taken to his home first. The intent of this first interview was simply to determine how best to proceed in carrying out the priesthood's intent to cause Jesus' execution. As the text tells us, Christ saw no need to expand in private on what He had openly asserted in public, and so refused to answer.

BEFORE CAIAPHAS (John 18:24; Matt. 26:57, 59-68; Mark 14:53, 55-65; Luke 22:54, 63-65).
Annas ordered that Jesus, still bound, be taken to the house of Caiaphas. Matthew tells us that "the teachers of the law and elders" had already assembled there. It is clear from this that the plot to arrest Jesus secretly at night was well known to the whole Jewish leadership. The Mishna, in Sanhedrin 4:1, lays down rules for inquiry into capital and noncapital cases; rules which clearly were violated in this nighttime, "unofficial" trial of Jesus. The Mishna reads (4:1):

A. All the same are property cases and capital cases as to examination and interrogation.

B. As it is said, You will have one law (Lev 24:22).

C. What is the difference between property cases and capital cases?

D. (1) Property cases [are tried] by three [judges], and capital cases by twenty-three.

E. (2) In property cases they begin with the case either for acquittal or for conviction, while in capital cases they begin only with the case for acquittal, and not with the case for conviction.

F. (3) In property cases they decide by a majority of one, whether for acquittal or for conviction, while in capital cases they decide by a majority of one for acquittal, but only with a majority of two [judges] for conviction.

G. (4) In property cases they reverse the decision whether in favor of acquittal or in favor of conviction, while in capital cases they reverse the decision in favor of acquittal, but they do not reverse the decision in favor of conviction.

H. (5) In property cases all [judges and even disciples] argue either for acquittal or conviction. In capital cases all argue for acquittal, but all do not argue for conviction.

I. (6) In property cases one who argues for conviction may argue for acquittal, and one who argues for acquittal may also argue for conviction. In capital cases the one who argues for conviction may argue for acquittal, but the one who argues for acquittal has not got the power to retract and argue for conviction.

J. (7) In property cases they try the case by day and complete it by night. In capital cases, they try the case by day and complete it [by] day.

K. (8) In property cases they come to a final decision on the same day [as the trial itself], whether it is for acquittal or conviction. In capital cases they come to a final decision for acquittal on the same day, but on the following day for conviction.

L. (Therefore they do not judge [capital cases] either on the eve of the Sabbath or on the eve of a festival.)

A comparison with Matthew's account shows how deep the animosity felt against Jesus was, and how the leaders hypocritically violated the traditional rules they supposedly held so dear. Not only was this nighttime trial illegal, but the judges, rather than argue for acquittal "were looking for false evidence against Jesus so that they could put Him to death" (Matt. 26:59). In the end Jesus confirmed His claim to be "the Christ, the Son of God" (26:63). Triumphantly the high priest

shouted, "Now you have heard the blasphemy" (26:65) and called for an immediate guilty verdict and death sentence.

II. The Religious Trial: daybreak
BEFORE THE SANHEDRIN (Matt. 27:1; Mark 15:1; Luke 22:66-71)
The Sanhedrin reassembled at daybreak to confirm a verdict they had already (illegally) pronounced.

It is hard for us today to understand the extent of the authority exercised by the Sanhedrin in the first century. Research shows some nine different functions fulfilled by this assembly of 70 or so priests and rabbis.

(1) The Sanhedrin served as the supreme court for settling doubtful points of religion and law. (2) The Sanhedrin served as the supreme court to settle disputed issues. No local court was permitted to act contrary to a ruling of the Sanhedrin. (3) The Sanhedrin was empowered to impose discipline (Acts 9:1-3). (4) The Sanhedrin served as a legislative body with the power to establish *taqanot* (regulations) and *gezerot* (ordinances) that were binding on Jewish people everywhere. (5) The Sanhedrin had the responsibility of establishing the official calendar, important because this set the dates for religious festivals. (6) The Sanhedrin supervised the temple services. (7) The Sanhedrin alone had jurisdiction in cases that might involve capital punishment. (8) Politically the Sanhedrin was also empowered to act as representatives of the whole population of the Holy Land, as would our modern Senate, in matters such as giving consent to the ordination of kings or declarations of war. (9) The Sanhedrin also served as the political body which dealt with the Roman occupation forces, or with other rulers and nations.

Thus there is no question that the Sanhedrin was the true, officially constituted authority in Judaism and the Jewish homeland when its members met that fateful morning to ratify officially a verdict its members had [illegally] agreed to in the early morning hours. Officially condemned for blasphemy, the Sanhedrin now must bring Jesus before Pilate, for only Pilate had the authority to order execution.

III. The Civil Trial: early morning
BEFORE PILATE (John 18:28-38; Matt. 27:2, 11-14; Mark 15:2-5; Luke 23:1-5. See Word Study of 18:28, above.)

We must remember that "the Jews" (18:28) is a phrase used by John to designate the religious leaders, not the entire Jewish people. This is made clear here where Pilate says, "Take Him yourselves, and judge Him by your law" (18:31). "The Jews" here must be the Sanhedrin, which had the power to judge Him by Jewish law.

The Sanhedrin had convicted Jesus of blasphemy for claiming to be God. But this was not against Roman law, so the Jewish leaders had to find some other capital crime of which to accuse Jesus. Rather than bring a specific charge, they argue that the very fact Jesus is brought to Pilate proves Him to be a "criminal" or "habitual evil doer," *kakon poion*. We can almost sense panic in the leaders when Pilate seems to return Jesus to their jurisdiction: "But we have no right to execute anyone." (See Word Study of 18:31, above.)

The specific charge the Sanhedrin finally made is not stated, but is clearly implied in Pilate's questioning of Jesus about His kingship (see Word Study of 18:36, above). If Jesus were setting Himself up as king of the Jews, this would constitute rebellion and be punishable by death. In questioning Jesus, Pilate came to the conclusion that there was "no basis for a charge against Him" (19:38).

It is difficult to explain Pilate's subsequent actions. On the basis of what we know of his character, Pilate was not particularly concerned with what was right or wrong. Though he seems to often have taken perverse pleasure in violating the sensibilities of the Jews, the rather weak effort to free Jesus lacks the aura of disdain that marked many of Pilate's other acts. It seems from John's account both that Pilate is in some awe of Jesus—and that for some reason he is hesitant to offend the Jewish Sanhedrin.

BEFORE HEROD (Luke 23:6-12)

Luke adds an incident not found in the other Gospels. Pilate, still seeking some way out of condemning Jesus, discovers that Christ is a Galilean. This territory ruled by Herod, and so Pilate orders Jesus taken to Herod!

Herod is delighted, for he has heard much about Jesus and wants to see Him perform a miracle. But Jesus refuses to speak with Herod—despite the chief priests and teachers of the Law crowding around and shouting out accusations against Him the whole time. Disappointed and angry, Herod sends Jesus back to Pilate.

BEFORE PILATE AGAIN (John 18:39–19:1, 4-16; Matt. 27:15-26; Mark 15:6-15; Luke 23:13-25)

When Jesus returned from Herod, Pilate ordered Him flogged. This was a prelude to crucifixion, and the Roman flagellum was a fearsome weapon with stones or metal woven into leather strips.

Pilate, however, still seems dissatisfied, and again brings Jesus out, presenting Him to the Sanhedrin as an innocent man. When the members of the Sanhedrin see Jesus, they loudly demand He be crucified. Pilate, knowing very well that the Sanhedrin has no power to do so, says, "You take Him and crucify Him" (19:6). And again Pilate pronounces Jesus innocent.

Now the Sanhedrin suddenly blurts out the real reason they want Jesus executed. "He claimed to be the Son of God" (19:7). John says that when Pilate heard this, "he was even more afraid" (19:8).

What then is happening here? Pilate has already pronounced Jesus innocent. He clearly is in some awe of Christ. And he has no respect at all for the Sanhedrin, knowing very well that the charges they initially made had nothing to do with the real reason they want Jesus dead. Why then is Pilate wavering? He has the power to free Jesus if he wishes, and had frequently shown how little he cared for the Jews' complaints. But now Pilate shows weakness, and only "tried" to set Jesus free (19:12). Yet he was unable to bring himself to say the word that would release Him. Why?

The answer has been exposed in Harold Hoener's classic study of Pontius Pilate. The Emperor Tiberius had "retired" to a private island where he could engage freely in his notorious sexual perversions. In Rome the commander of the Praetorian Guard, an officer named Sejanus, actually ruled the Empire in Tiberius' name, promoting friends and executing enemies. After some years in power, accusations against Sejanus were smuggled to Tiberius, who ordered the Senate to condemn him to death.

The death of Sejanus created a panic among those who had owed their positions to him. Many committed suicide; others were executed. Only those far from Rome escaped the bloodbath. And Pilate had been a protégé of Sejanus!

The Sanhedrin was fully aware of the precarious political position of Pilate. As Pilate desperately sought a way to release Jesus, the Jews kept shouting, "If you let this man go, you are no friend of Caesar" (19:12). Already an object of the paranoid Tiberius' suspicions, with Sejanus' other remaining associates, Pilate did not dare release Jesus, whatever the truth about His guilt or innocence! Pilate's real fear was that somehow he would find himself accused if he turned Jesus loose.

Finally Pilate gave in and ordered Jesus crucified.

How tragic when the issues of right and wrong become irrelevant, and we make decisions on the basis of what is expedient rather than what is just.

SUMMARY

What do we see when we look back on the trials of Jesus? The first thing we see is that Christ was condemned by a Sanhedrin that violated its own rules in conducting an illegal trial. These religious leaders then deceitfully brought Him to Pilate on charges of which He had not been convicted in their court. And when Jesus was found innocent by Pilate, they exerted political pressures specifically intended to force him to render a verdict which was against his own conscience and against Roman law as well, which called for the innocent to be exonerated.

The second thing we see is a cruel and weak man, convinced that Jesus was innocent, completely aware of the vindictiveness and deceit of Jesus' accusers, who despite his power is too weak and fearful to do what he knows is right. Pilate finally surrenders to his fears and the political pressures brought to bear and condemns Jesus to death.

How clearly then the trials of Jesus reveal the weakness and sinfulness of human beings. And how clearly they reveal the grace of God. For as the role of the politics in far-off Rome that forced Pilate to condemn Christ remind us, Jesus was given up "by God's set purpose and foreknowledge" (Acts 2:23).

The world's greatest injustice ultimately displayed the justice, the grace, and the forgiving love of our God.

EXPOSITION

The resurrection of Jesus was greeted with shock by His followers, followed by a surge of excitement. As the author of the Gospel of Luke continues his carefully researched history, he captures the kindling of a flame that burned brightly in Jerusalem, and then spread swiftly through the whole Roman Empire.

The opening chapters of Acts lay the foundation for the explosive growth of the young church. For some 40 days the disciples are taught by Jesus "about the kingdom of God" and their responsibility to spread the message of Jesus "to the ends of the earth" (1:1-8). Christ's visible ascension into heaven was followed by a brief period of waiting, during which the disciples chose a faithful follower of Jesus to take the place of Judas Iscariot (1:9-26). That wait ended on the Day of Pentecost. Then, with unique visible signs, the Holy Spirit swept into Jerusalem, entering the little company of believers and forever bonding them to Jesus and one another as Christ's living body, the church (2:1-13). The visible signs accompanying the Spirit's coming drew a wondering crowd, and became the occasion for history's first Gospel message (2:14-41). That message contains every essential element of the apostolic proclamation of Jesus, and in this sense serves as a model for evangelistic preaching throughout our age. In the same way, the bonding together of converts to form the close fellowship described in 2:42-47 and 4:32-37 serves to model universal principles of congregational life.

Luke then reports another incident. Stimulated by the healing of a "man crippled from birth" (3:1-10), Peter preaches another powerful evangelistic message (3:11-26). This time Peter and John are brought before the Sanhedrin and questioned. The two apostles boldly confront the men who had conspired to have their Lord killed (4:1-12). Unable to punish men who had publicly performed such a notable miracle, the Sanhedrin threatened James and John and let them go (4:13-22). The two apostles, again setting a pattern which is to be followed by us today, reported what had happened to "their own people," and so called the church to prayer. God responded, providing a fresh filling of the Spirit and enabling them to continue to speak out boldly.

These early chapters of Acts introduce motifs that run throughout the NT epistles, and are vital for us today. The first motif is the Holy Spirit. His coming launches the church; His presence vitalizes Christ's people; His filling enables them to minister. The second motif is evangelism. The early Christians are driven to proclaim the Lord, absolutely convinced that "salvation is found in no one else, for there is no other name under heaven given to men by which we must be saved" (4:12). The third motif is fellowship. The members of the young church are drawn together by a shared commitment to Jesus. They worship, study, share, and pray together in a unity that inspires deep caring for one another. While we must approach the Book of Acts as a descriptive document that reports what happened in the first century, rather than as a prescriptive document which instructs us on how we are to live today, these three motifs remind us how vital a dependence on the Spirit, a passion for evangelism, and a commitment to fellowship are for any who seek to follow Jesus Christ in our day.

WORD STUDIES

In my former book, Theophilus, I wrote about all that Jesus *began* to do and teach (1:1). While Jesus is no longer physically present in this world, His work here is hardly finished! Acts launches the story of what Jesus *continues to do* through His followers.

Jesus is still "doing and teaching" in the world — through us.

He appeared to them over a period of forty days and spoke about *the kingdom of God* (1:3). The phrase "the kingdom of God" refers not only to God's sovereignty over the universe He created, but more particularly to how God expresses His rule in history, and in the lives of believers. This instruction was essential, for the death and resurrection of Jesus required a complete reorientation of the disciples' vision of what the future held. Steeped as they were in the OT's vision of an earthly kingdom ruled by the Messiah, they needed to understand Messiah's mission in its broadest sense, and sense their own vital role in the spread of the present, New Covenant form of God's kingdom.

Luke's specific quotes show how vital this instruction was. The disciples ask: "Lord, are You at this time going to restore the kingdom

Relationship between the Old and New Testament Visions of God's Kingdom

Unity: in ultimate goal, the "glory of God."
Divergence: in emphasis

Old Testament	New Testament
— theocratic purpose	*— soteriological purpose*
1. God will rule the world through the Jewish Messiah's reign.	1. God will save individuals and society through the Jewish Messiah's work.
2. The nation Israel is emphasized.	2. The believing individual and community (the church) are emphasized.

Harmony: in teachings

The theocratic emphasis of the Old does not rule out concern for individuals (see Dan. 4; Ezek. 18; Nahum 1:6-7; Jonah 4).	The revelation of the fullness of God's salvation as it relates to individual transformation does not abrogate the emphasis of the Old (see Acts 1; Rom. 9–11).

Unification: in Christ

Jesus, the promised King of the Old Testament prophets, is also the Redeemer of the New Testament! In His person all of God's purposes will be fulfilled.

to Israel?" (1:6) Clearly the disciples still have an OT perspective on the kingdom, a perspective shaped by the prophets' vision of a dominant Israelite kingdom ruled by the divine descendant of David — the Messiah. Note that Jesus does not reject this kingdom vision. In fact, He confirms their vision, saying "it is not for you to know" *when* (1:7). (See the following chart, showing the relationship between Old and New Testament expressions of the kingdom.)

But that form of God's rule is future, not present. And so, in what may be the most quoted of all verses in Acts, Jesus tells His disciples to "be My witnesses in Jerusalem, and in all Judea and Samaria, and to the ends of the earth" (1:8).

It is important to work for justice in our society, and to be activists for what is right. But we must remember that God's present kingdom finds its true expression in and through a people who believe in Jesus, whose first priority must be to give clear witness to Him.

John baptized with water, but *in a few days* you will be baptized with the Holy Spirit (1:5). The promise occurs early in each of the synoptics: Jesus will baptize His own with the Holy Spirit (Matt. 3:11; Mark 1:8; Luke 3:16). And the promise is repeated during the last week of Jesus' ministry, with the Spirit's coming still in the future (John 14:26; 16:7-11). And it is still future here, just a few days before Pentecost. Later Peter will look back on Pentecost and identify that day as the time of the Spirit's coming (Acts 10:45; 11:15-16).

We can debate the exact meaning of Pentecost and disagree over the role of tongues. But we dare not forget that the Holy Spirit is the source of spiritual power in this age. Nor forget that Christ's promise has been fulfilled, and the Spirit now is ours.

Judas . . . fell headlong, his body burst open (1:18). On the manner of Judas' death, see the Word Study of Matt. 27:3-5.

Then they cast lots, and *the lot fell* to Matthias; so he was added to the eleven disciples (1:26). Several things should be noted about the incident. First, before lots were cast, the disciples eliminated all but two candidates. The casting of the lots was a last resort taken after the personal qualifications of the candidates had been carefully examined and no clear "winner" emerged. Second, when the disciples could not decide, they bathed the casting of lots in prayer. They were not relying on chance, but expected God to express His will through the process, which was not unusual during the OT era (Prov. 16:33).

Most important, however, is the fact that this is the last time we read any decision being made by casting lots or any similar way. Why, if casting lots was an acknowledged OT way of discerning God's will? Most likely because just a few days after this event the Holy Spirit was given to the church. From that moment on the Spirit became our guide. Now we look to Him, and in faith commit ourselves to obey when He shows us the way (13:2).

How vital it is that we recognize the Spirit's presence in our lives. How vital to look to Him for guidance in all we do.

When the day of Pentecost came . . . (2:1). This festival was held 50 days after Passover, and marked the end of the grain harvest. It was intended as a thanksgiving festival, marked by the offering of sacrifices and the giving of voluntary contributions from the recent harvest (cf. Lev. 23:15-22; Num. 28:26-31; Deut. 16:9-12). Pentecost was one of three "pilgrim festivals" that adult males in Israel were expected to attend. In rabbinic tradition Pentecost also marked the date of the giving of God's Law to Moses. No wonder many thousands of pilgrims from the Jews scattered throughout the Roman Empire and the East were present for this, the most significant Pentecost of all!

Rabbinic writings report that as many as 12 million people gathered to celebrate Passover. Josephus estimates 3 million. These numbers are high, given the area in and around Jerusalem. Yet it is clear that the city's population of some 55,000 in the first century was doubled or tripled by visitors, many of whom came for Passover and stayed on through Pentecost.

Luke's reference to the "native" lands from which many of the Jewish pilgrims came (2:8-11) is in fullest harmony with what we know of the Jewish diaspora in the first century. Jews composed a significant minority in the Roman Empire, probably about 10 percent of the 60 million who lived there then. Nearly every major city had its Jewish population, and undoubtedly some from every nation were present when the Spirit came and Peter preached history's first evangelistic message.

Suddenly a sound like the blowing of a violent wind came from heaven and filled the whole house where they were sitting. They saw what seemed to be tongues of fire that separated and came to rest on each of them. All of them were filled with the Holy Spirit and began to speak in other tongues, as the Spirit enabled them (2:2-4). The sound, the visible flames, and the speaking with other tongues served together to mark the inauguration of the church.

There is a fascinating parallel—and contrast—with the giving of the Law to Moses, which rabbinic tradition said had taken place on the Day of Pentecost. Then, thunder rumbled and flames broke forth on the top of Mt. Sinai, and God's Spirit engraved the Ten Commandments on tablets of stone. Here there is also a sound and flames. But not on some distant mountain peak. Now the wind sweeps into a house in Jerusalem; the flame divides to rest on every believer. And, enabled by the Spirit, all were "declaring the wonders of God" (2:11), showing that God's Law is now being engraved on human hearts.

We frequently debate the role of "tongues" in Christian experience. But let's not miss the fact that the *combination of signs* here mirror, and yet transmute, signs associated with the giving of the Law on Sinai. The primary message of these signs is clear: a new age has come! The Old Covenant of the Law is superseded by the New Covenant of the grace that is poured out on all in Jesus Christ.

We hear them declaring the wonders of God in our own tongues! (2:11) This verse makes it very clear that the phenomenon described here is not the same as the *glossolalia* (gift of tongues) described in 1 Corinthians 12–14. There, an interpreter was needed when a person spoke in tongues; here everyone understood as the Christians spoke known languages. (See the commentary on 1 Cor. 12–14.)

But again, let's remember that Luke is not caught up in our debate about the nature and extent of the spiritual gift of tongues. Luke is

simply describing the signs that, on that Day of Pentecost launched the Christian era and marked the initiation of God's New Covenant community.

This is what was spoken by the prophet Joel (2:16). The original prophecy mentions spectacular physical evidences—blood and fire and billows of smoke, with the sun turned to darkness and the moon turned to blood. Yet these signs did *not occur.* To some, this is evidence that OT prophecy should be interpreted in a spiritual way rather than a literal way. However, neither the quote nor Peter's use of it requires complete fulfillment of Joel's vision.

It is good to remember that "the last days," which begin with the Spirit's coming and close with terrible signs just before the Lord returns, have already extended nearly 2,000 years. The more spectacular "signs" are associated not with the dawn of that day, but with its twilight.

Even this is not necessary to defend Peter's use of this passage. The Dead Sea Scrolls show that Peter quoted this passage as a *pesher* (an interpretation). This well-established rabbinic approach to an OT passage does *not* exegete details, but looks at the thrust of the passage to make a point. Peter is providing a biblical image which will enable his listeners to rightly interpret the phenomenon his critics witness. In essence Peter is saying, "Don't you remember that God through Joel spoke of a future pouring out of His Spirit? This is it!"

I will pour out My Spirit on all people. Your sons and daughters will prophesy (2:17). Peter does not exegete every detail of Joel's prophecy, and we should not either. But there is surely a promise and a warning for us in his words. God's Spirit is poured out on *all* believers, men and women alike. In this age of the Spirit, even that most excellent of spiritual gifts, prophecy (1 Cor. 14:1), is the providence of sons *and daughters.* Let's be sure that we do not place restrictions on women in ministry which the Holy Spirit does not!

This Man was handed over to you by God's set purpose and foreknowledge; and *you*, with the help of wicked men, put Him to death by nailing Him to the cross (2:23). The Bible maintains a careful balance between God's sovereignty and human responsibility. Both God's "set purpose" (*boule*) and "foreknowledge" (*prognosei*) determined Jesus' fate: God *willed* His death. But this does not relieve Jew or Gentile of their responsibility for the crime of nailing the Savior to the cross.

Every person, before he or she acts, is aware that he or she *can* choose. We may blame our parents. We may blame discrimination or poverty. We may blame society. But blame whomever or whatever we will, we know and God knows that every human being is responsible for the choices he or she makes.

Peter replied, "Repent and be baptized, every one of you, in the name of Jesus Christ for the forgiveness of your sins" (2:38). The Gospel of John and the Epistles of Paul teach that faith in Jesus is the sole key to salvation. Why then does Peter here call for repentance and baptism "for the forgiveness of your sins"? The reason is that, in this context, repentance *is* belief!

The Jewish people have failed to acknowledge Jesus as their Messiah. Now they must "repent "(*mentanoesate*), a word which indicates a complete change of both heart and mind about the One whom the Resurrection has demonstrated is Lord.

Earlier John's baptism served as a public confession of sin. Now Peter calls for baptism "in the name of Jesus Christ," to serve as a public affirmation of belief in Him.

Thus there is no discrepancy at all between Peter's call to the Jews of Jerusalem to repent and be baptized, and Paul's call to the Gentiles to believe in Jesus Christ. To change a mind marked by unbelief, and to give public evidence of that change by being baptized, *is* faith.

They were greatly disturbed because the apostles were teaching the people and proclaiming in Jesus the resurrection of the dead (4:2). The word is *diaponoumenoi*, meaning "worked up" or "indignant." The temple guard must have reported that two ordinary men had performed a miracle and were preaching about Jesus in the temple courts. Two things seem to have upset the religious leaders most at this point: Peter and John were teaching without authorization, and — and this would surely have upset the Saddu-

cees, who denied the possibility of a resurrection — they seemed to be trying to prove the doctrine of resurrection by an appeal to the case "of Jesus" (*en to Iesou*).

What a shock it must have been when, "the next day" (4:5), Peter and John asserted that they performed the miracle "by the name [power] of Jesus Christ of Nazareth, whom you crucified" (4:10).

Many have wondered why, in view of this accusation, the Sanhedrin did not act against Peter and John immediately. Verse 13, which says the Sanhedrin "realized that they were unschooled, ordinary men," provides a clue. The *'am ha'eres* (the people of the land) were not considered capable of understanding finer points of rabbinic law. Therefore they were not punished for a first offense, but rather were instructed that the act was unlawful and warned not to do it again. This is exactly what happened here: the disciples were instructed not to "speak or teach at all in the name of Jesus" (4:18) and then given "further threats" (4:21).

We cannot, however, give the Sanhedrin too much credit for following its own rules with Christ's disciples, after violating them so completely in condemning Jesus (see the commentary on John 18–21). Luke adds that "they could not decide how to punish them, because all the people were praising God for what had happened" (Acts 4:21).

How sensitive political leaders are to public opinion! And how quickly they ignore it when their own power seems to be at risk.

They raised their voices together in prayer to God. "Sovereign Lord," they said . . . (4:24ff). The picture of the church gathered for prayer in the face of official opposition is vivid. Their prayer serves as a model for us in similar situations. Note the pattern:

DEVELOPING PERSPECTIVE
■ Acts 4:24 We affirm God as Sovereign.

■ Acts 4:25 We remember how empty is every effort, and how powerless is every person who attempts to thwart God's purposes.

■ Acts 4:26-28 We acknowledge God's complete control of every circumstance.

DEFINING OUR NEEDS
■ Acts 4:29 We ask Him to empower us.

■ Acts 4:30 We ask Him to act through us. As a result of this prayer of great faith, "they were all filled with the Holy Spirit and spoke the Word of God boldly" (4:31). Circumstances had not changed. But God's people *were* — changed and empowered.

THE PASSAGE IN DEPTH

The Holy Spirit and Pentecost (2:1-13).

Background. The Word Study of 2:2-4, above, points out that three signs marked the coming of the Spirit on the day of Pentecost. Together these symbolize the superseding of the Old Covenant inaugurated on Mt. Sinai by the New Covenant, based on Christ's death. Sadly, this implication is all too often lost in modern debate about the role of one of the signs — tongues. A good summary of this often-divisive issue is found in The *Zondervan Dictionary of Christian Literacy*:

Tongues in the Bible. In the Old Testament the word *tongue* is used to indicate the physical organ and languages. It is also used symbolically, as the organ that expresses character by revealing the heart of the speaker. At times our New Testament uses the word *tongue* in each Old Testament way. For instance, when Acts indicates that the Spirit-filled disciples spoke in other tongues, the context makes clear that all the bystanders (Parthians, Medes, Elamites, Egyptians, Libyans, etc.) heard the message in their own native language (Acts 2:4-12).

In 1 Corinthians 12 and 14, however, where speaking in tongues is identified as a spiritual gift, something unusual is in view. A tongue is not an understandable language, and it calls for a person gifted with "interpretation of tongues" to make any message intelligible (1 Cor. 12:10). Paul himself claims the gift of tongues (1 Cor. 14:18) and speaks of it as "pray[ing] with my spirit" (1 Cor. 14:14-17). He does, however, warn against the misuse of this gift when the church is gathered. To guard against misuse, tongues are to be used in public worship only when the person speaking (or another person) can interpret so that the church will be edified (1 Cor. 14:6-17). Paul is particularly concerned that unbelievers might come in, for they will misunderstand what they hear as mere babbling and will "say that you are out of your mind" (1 Cor. 14:23-24). In contrast, Paul urges that church gatherings concentrate on prophecy, that is, on clear teaching in the congregation's own language of what God has revealed to His people. In this case the stranger "will be convinced by all that he is a sinner" and so "he will fall down and worship God" (1 Cor. 14:24-25).

It is certainly clear from these chapters that speaking in tongues is a spiritual gift, that it edifies or builds up the person who speaks in tongues, and that when there is an interpreter present, speaking in tongues can also edify or build up the gathered congregation. It is just as clear that this gift is not to become central in our gathered experience as the people of God, for clear, intelligible instruction is more important then.

How Christians disagree. Christians acknowledge the gift of tongues as described in the Bible. But the nature and role of that gift is disputed.

To some, speaking in tongues is the definitive evidence that the Holy Spirit has come into one's life. Those without the gift lack the Spirit — if not the Spirit Himself, at least that special link to the Spirit of which tongues is the sign. For them possession of the gift of tongues is foundational to deeper spiritual experience and spiritual power. Often those of this persuasion believe that the tongues of Acts 2 and of 1 Corinthians 12 are the same.

On the other hand, many Christians believe that the gift of tongues was temporary, limited to the age before the New Testament was complete. This and other extraordinary gifts were intended as signs, which were no longer needed when the whole Bible became available to the church. Typically quoted as proof of this view is 1 Cor. 13:8, which contrasts the unfailing nature of love with tongues that will be stilled. A stronger theological argument rests on pneumatology: This camp is sure the Bible indicates that the Holy Spirit enters all Christians on conversion. Thus, speaking in tongues was never intended as a unique sign of the Spirit's presence in the Christian's life.

These theological distinctions reflect deep emotional commitments. Those who speak in tongues testify to a deeper life in Christ than they had known before. They understandably resent others who deride their experience as either hysteria and self-delusion or as something demonic. On the other hand, the traditionalist has often felt threatened by pentecostal teaching, which has caused dispute and division in many congregations.

Today emotions are not as high as they have been, and mediating positions have developed. Those who speak in tongues recognize the reality of the Spirit's working in those who do not, and tongues is taking its place as one among many spiritual gifts, not "the" gift. Those who have not spoken in tongues are less ready to rule out the experience of brothers and sisters who have. This moderating of attitudes increasingly permits us all not only to hold our own convictions on what has been a sensitive issue, but also to affirm our unity with Christians who differ from us.

When we look at the many books written on the issue, it is clear that Christians are not likely to come to a single, common conviction. So we must agree to disagree in this area. It is more striking to realize that in the Epistles, only 1 Corinthians 12–14 deals with the question at all, and then it primarily tries to regulate the public misuse of the gift. The rest of the New Testament is silent about tongues, but rich with instruction on love. Admittedly many issues find their focus in the debates about tongues, but there is no debate at all about the fact that we owe one another love. We do not owe each other agreement, but we are obligated to accept and love each other. Whatever our convictions about tongues, we remain the children of God together, through faith in Jesus Christ (Gal. 3:26) (pp. 354–56).

Application. Let's keep the focus in our study of this text on what Luke intends to portray, the initiation of a new age: the age of the Spirit, the era of the New Covenant community.

Peter Addresses the Crowd (2:14-41); Peter Speaks to the Onlookers (3:11-26).

Background. These passages contain two of the three "evangelistic sermons" recorded in the Book of Acts. They have been studied intensely to define the essence—the kernel—of the apostolic witness to Jesus Christ in the Jewish community. C.H. Dodd, in his classic work, *Apostolic Preaching,* distinguishes six re-

curring themes in these sermons:

1. The age of fulfillment has dawned.
2. This has taken place through the ministry, death and resurrection of Jesus, of which a brief account is given, with proof from the Scriptures.
3. By virtue of the resurrection, Jesus has been exalted at the right hand of God, as Messianic Head of the new Israel.
4. The Holy Spirit in the church is the sign of Christ's present power and glory.
5. The Messianic Age will shortly reach its consummation in the return of Christ.
6. The *kerygma* always closes with an appeal for repentance, the offer of forgiveness and the Holy Spirit, and the promise of "salvation," that is, of "the life of the age to come," to those who enter the elect community (pp. 21–24).

One thing that Dodd's exposition does suggest is that Peter's messages were carefully contextualized. That is, they were shaped to the perceptual field of his listeners, and thus well suited to his Jewish audience. This is seen in Peter's use of "Christ" in the sense of "Jewish Messiah." This distinctive usage is underlined (1) by Peter's urging repentance in order that the time may come for Christ to return and to "restore everything, as He promised long ago through His holy prophets" (3:21); and (2) by the fact that Luke only refers to "Christ" as a title—and on every occasion when it is used it is in speech addressed to a Jewish audience! (2:31, 36; 3:18, 20; 4:26; 5:42; 8:5; 9:22; 17:3; 18:5, 28; 26:23)

Dodd's conclusions, then, do not provide us today with the "essential gospel" which we are to proclaim to people of our day. Yet that "essential gospel," which resonates throughout the rest of the New Testament, and which shapes our understanding of our mission today, is central to both of Peter's messages.

Interpretation. To say that elements of Peter's sermons define the "essential gospel" does not imply that anything else he says is either untrue or unimportant. The "essential" elements are, simply, those truths which so define Jesus and His work that, without them, the Gospel is emasculated. What are these essential truths on which our salvation hinges?

■ Christ was a true human being. "Jesus of

Nazareth was a man accredited by God" (2:22). Christ lived and died a true human being, fulfilling the "servant song" predictions of Isaiah (Acts 3:13).

■ Christ was crucified. The crucifixion was a historic event, part of God's eternal purpose, and yet also a witness against a humanity which hated and rejected God's Son (2:23; 3:13-14).

■ Christ was raised from the dead. Jesus was raised from the dead, in a historic event that took place in space and time, and exalted to God's right hand (2:24-33; 3:15).

■ All this is in complete harmony with the Scriptures. God confirms all that has happened by the Scriptures, which predicted all beforehand (2:25-36; 3:21-26).

■ We must respond to the Christ-event and its meaning in order to be saved. For the Jews who had rejected Jesus a faith-response took the form of repentance: of changing their minds about Him (2:38-41; 3:19). For all who hear the Good News, faith brings forgiveness.

Application. The core of the Gospel and the foundation of our faith is simply this: The historical Jesus died for us, was raised again, and is thus established both as Lord and Savior. These truths are confirmed by predictions in the OT Scriptures. Only through Jesus, and faith in His name, can salvation be found.

When we witness, it is these essential truths which we must keep in view—and communicate to all as clearly as we can.

The Fellowship of Believers (2:42-47); The Believers Share Their Possessions (4:32-37).

Background. The Teacher's Commentary (Victor) highlights a Greek word which provides a key to interpreting these Acts passages that describe fellowship in the early church. That word is *homothumadon*. The commentary says:

> A unique Greek word, used 10 of its 11 New Testament occurrences in the Book of Acts, helps us understand the uniqueness of Christian community. *Homothumadon* is a compound of two words meaning to "rush along" and "in unison." The

image is almost musical; a number of notes are sounded which while different, harmonize in pitch and tone. As the instruments of a great orchestra blend under the direction of a concertmaster, so the Holy Spirit blends together the lives of members of Christ's church.

The first use of *homothumadon* is found in Acts 1:14. There, in the Upper Room, the 11 disciples and a few women were united in prayer. Earlier strife and jealousies that marred their relationships were gone; the disciples were one, waiting for the Spirit's promised coming. Then in Acts 2:1 we see 120 believers gathered, focusing together on the Lord as they sensed the Spirit's first dynamic touch. The next occurrence is v. 46, as the community (then some 3,000), "continuing daily with one accord [*homothumadon*] in the temple, and breaking bread from house to house, did eat their meat with gladness and singleness of heart" (KJV). . . . As those who are Jesus' own make Him the common focus of their lives and seek to help each other find the Holy Spirit's freedom in their lives, *homothumadon* becomes the mark of Christian community (pp. 768–69).

Interpretation. How do we build that wonderful *homothumadon* that appears both so attractive and so distant?

It is striking that the first thing each paragraph above notes is that the community "had everything in common" and "gave to anyone as he had need" (2:44; 4:32-37). We should not read into these descriptions an early "Christian communism." As Peter pointed out to Ananias (5:4), who had sold property and only pretended to give all the proceeds to the disciples for distribution to the needy, "Didn't it [the piece of property] belong to you before it was sold? And after it was sold, wasn't the money at your disposal?"

In fact, this is the very point. There was no *obligation* to surrender personal or property rights. Instead, the values of the early Christians had shifted from possessions to persons. They chose to give, because they had learned to care deeply for others.

There can be no real *homothumadon* in our churches today unless we learn to care deeply for one another. When we do, we too will express our love in practical ways.

285

The second element in the early church's *homothumadon* is expressed in 2:46-47: "Every day they continued to meet together in the temple courts. They broke bread together in their homes with glad and sincere hearts, praising God and enjoying the favor of all the people." The source from which love for others wells up is love for God. The wonderful unity of Christians grows as we discover and continually affirm our oneness in shared worship of and enthusiasm for God.

Application. The Teacher's Commentary concludes:

> Sometimes we look back on these early chapters of Acts as though they picture a church that has been lost—as though unity and love and the experience of Jesus' pres-

ence are things that cannot really be ours today. Let's not make this mistake. God's Spirit is still a present reality. *Homothumadon* is still possible in today's shattered and impersonal world. If we look for a reason for emptiness in our own experience, let's look first to our hesitancy to share ourselves with our brothers and sisters. Or look to our failure to let others pick up the burdens of our lives, and bring them in confident prayer to God.

The church, the new community Christ formed, *is* here today. *We are the church.* And God, the Spirit, is able to take our 11s, and our 120s, and our 3,000s and, as we joyfully focus our shared life on Jesus, orchestrate our lives to His wondrous "one accord" (p. 769).

ACTS 5:1–11:18
Reaching Out

EXPOSITION

As the young church is established in Jerusalem it faces challenges from within and from without. Despite the stress these challenges cause, each results in the strengthening of the body of Christ, and in an ever-sharpening definition of its mission.

The first challenges come from within. Ananias and Sapphira are moved by Satan to introduce greed, hypocrisy, and sham into the fellowship, and so corrupt the purity of the church. Their deaths make it unmistakably clear that God is active among this people who are called to reflect His holiness, and stimulate a fresh wave of miracles and evangelism (5:1-16). A little later a conflict develops between Greek-speaking and Aramaic-speaking Christians over the distribution of food to the needy. This conflict, which has explosive potential, is resolved in a wise and godly way which demonstrates the unifying love that exists within the young church. This incident too stimulates spread of the Word, and "the number of disciples in Jerusalem increased rapidly" (6:1-7).

It is important for us today to note that, as internal challenges to the purity and unity of the Christian community are met, numerical growth takes place. To a great extent our effectiveness in evangelism depends on the purity and unity of our local congregations.

The early church also faces external challenges. The response of the people to the apostles' preaching fills members of the high priest's party with jealousy. The apostles are arrested, and only the moderating voice of Gamaliel, perhaps the most honored of Jewish sages even today, prevents the Sanhedrin from causing their deaths (5:17-42). Nevertheless, the rapid growth of the church creates intense hostility. Frustrated by the bold preaching of Stephen, members of one synagogue conspire to falsely accuse him of speaking against the temple and Moses' Law—high religious crimes. Hauled before the Sanhedrin, Stephen recounts God's historic efforts to reach a people determined to resist the Holy Spirit, a people who persecuted the prophets, and who have now betrayed and murdered the Righteous One Himself. In a fit of raw fury the whole company drags Stephen outside the city and stones him to death (6:8–8:1a).

The incident leads to an intense, open, and official persecution of the church, which forces a great exodus of Christians from Jerusalem. But this too has positive results. As the Christians stop in the small towns of Judea and Galilee they share their faith (8:1b-4). Then an unexpected result of the scattering takes place in Samaria. There, when Philip preaches Christ, great crowds respond to the Gospel. When Peter and John come to investigate, they realize that God intends to unite Jew and Samaritan in one church, and they too were "preaching the gospel in many Samaritan villages" (8:5-25).

A little later Luke tells of another incident that introduces yet another challenge for the church. Peter is sent for by a Roman army officer named Cornelius. God shows Peter he is to go, despite the fact that the man is a Gentile. At Cornelius' home Peter hardly begins to explain the Gospel when the Holy Spirit comes upon Cornelius and the other Gentiles, and they begin to speak in tongues. Later, in Jerusalem, when Peter is condemned for going into an "unclean" Gentile home, he is able to point to this sign as evidence that God has chosen to accept the Gentile as well as the Jew who believes in Jesus (Acts 10:1–11:18). The Jewish Christians accept this as evidence that "God has granted even the Gentiles repentance unto life" (11:18). Yet just how Jew and Gentile are to relate to one another as members of the same body poses a challenge that is not to be resolved for decades to come.

In the meantime, the Sanhedrin seems determined to stamp out the Christian movement wherever it has spread. A Pharisee named Saul, a fanatical persecutor of the church, is given letters authorizing him to arrest Christian Jews in Damascus. On the way he is confronted by Christ Himself. Stunned and blinded, Saul stumbles on into the Syrian city where he is healed and thoroughly converted to Christ (9:1-19). Rather than imprison Hebrew Christians, Saul baffles the Jewish community by powerfully proclaiming the Christian message! Saul's fervent advocacy of Christ so stirs up the Jews that they determine to kill him, and he is forced to flee to Jerusalem. There too he debates so boldly that his life is endangered, and he is spirited out of the city and sent home to Tarsus by fellow Christians (9:20-31). There he is destined to wait until his message and his character mature, and he reappears as Paul, the great apostle to the Gentiles.

The story Luke tells in these chapters is complex, and its themes are interwoven. Yet they are very clear. The young church grows, but at each stage faces fresh internal and external challenges. Dangers within threaten the purity and unity of the body of Christ. As these are overcome, the witness of the church is enhanced, and the church grows.

Threats from without take the form of persecution. Yet as persecution scatters the Jerusalem believers, the church's mission to spread the Gospel is more and more clearly defined. Not only Jews, but also Samaritans and even Gentiles, must be told the Good News that Jesus saves. The church is about to discover its mission, and so explode out of its tiny homeland and spread, like a flame, Empire-wide.

WORD STUDIES

With his wife's full knowledge he *kept back* part of the money for himself, but brought the rest and put it at the apostles' feet (5:2). The verb *nosphizo*, to "set aside for oneself," is used in the Septuagint to describe the sin of Achan, who took forbidden wealth from Jericho and who, like this couple, suffered the death penalty (Josh. 7). To some, each crime seems slight and not deserving of the penalty. Yet each is treated as most serious in Scripture (5:3, 9).

In each case God's people had just set out on a new course: in Joshua, the founding of a nation; in Acts, the founding of a new community of faith. Each mission required complete obedience and dedication to God. Both acts, that of Achan and that of Ananias and Sapphira, introduced an element of corruption that if it grew would drain God's people of spiritual vitality and power.

In each case too the act and its punishment served as a warning: God *was* present among His people, vital, active, and holy. Both Israel and the church expect God to act for them. And both must learn that they must remain faithful if God were to work through them.

Great *fear* seized the whole church and all who heard about these events (5:11). When the OT describes "fear of the Lord" as the "beginning of wisdom" (Prov. 1:7, KJV), it simply means that an awe of God as a real presence makes the critical difference in how we choose to live our lives. Those who are convinced that God is real, and that He is actively involved in human affairs, are aware that He watches all that happens with approval or disapproval.

The deaths of Ananias and Sapphira made God's real presence in the church unmistakably clear, and made a great impression on the church and the population of Jerusalem.

This, by the way, is the first use of "church" (*ecclesia*) in Acts. From now on this word will occur often, as a description both of local congregations and the entire body of believers.

The apostles performed many *miraculous signs and wonders* among the people (5:12). While 1 Cor. 12:9-10 lists "healing" and "miraculous powers" among the spiritual gifts given by the Holy Spirit, 2 Cor. 12:11 identifies such "signs, wonders and miracles" as "things that mark an apostle." While Acts describes notable miracles similar to those Jesus performed, there is no instruction in the epistles that suggests we should expect such miracles today.

THOUGHTS ON MIRACLES

Miracle. The naturalist insists that the material universe is all there is. Whatever happens *must* then be the result of natural laws, and miracles simply cannot happen. Reports of God's mighty acts in OT times and of Jesus' miracles are either rejected out of hand, or some energy is expended trying to figure out reasonable natural causes to explain them away.

The supernaturalist believes that there is a reality beyond our material universe. The Christian, basing his or her faith on God's self-revelation in Scripture, has confidence in the God who is Creator and Sustainer of the physical universe. We also realize that there is no uncrossable gulf fixed between the natural and the supernatural. God has bridged the gap often, and has shown that He is completely capable of acting in the material world.

Looking through history and Scripture we find two ways in which God has demonstrated this capability.

■ God has performed *obvious miracles,* which seem to involve suspension of natural laws.

■ God has performed *hidden miracles,* which involve shaping events using only processes that are apparently natural.

Obvious Miracles. These are events to which everyone agrees the word "miracle" should be applied. "Nobody has ever heard of opening the eyes of a man born blind" (John 9:32) argued one beneficiary of Jesus' healing. There was no question in the mind of the witnesses: something supernatural had happened here. Even Jesus' enemies, burning with frustrated fury, couldn't deny that something had happened that could not be explained by appeal to any natural process.

It is important for us to realize that obvious miracles are concentrated in specific periods of Bible history. There are obvious miracles associated with the Exodus period (1450–1400 B.C.). There are obvious miracles associated with the ministry of the prophets Elijah and Elisha (875–825 B.C.). There are many miracles associated with the ministry of Christ on earth and the early years of the apostles (A.D. 30–45). But apart from these three periods, miracles are *not* the commonplace experience of God's people. Overriding natural law, or acting against the flow of natural processes, just is not the typical way that God works out His will.

Hidden Miracles. What we do find in Scripture, and especially in prophecy, is that God is secretly at work in our world. The OT tells how God used even enemy invasions to discipline Israel when she sinned. At other times God used disease or rumors to save His people. The OT is full also of specific prophecies concerning Jesus' birth, life, and of the events surrounding His death and resurrection. All these came to pass just as foretold. While we must believe that God had a hand in guiding events to their foreordained conclusion, there is usually no hint of obvious miracle. Cause and effect follow in natural sequence; the persons involved act freely, moved by their own motives. No one looking on would have reason to point and say, "Look! There's evidence of God's intervention."

Hidden miracles then are recognized by the eye of faith, and easily dismissed by unbelief. Hidden miracles cannot be compared with the darkness that struck the whole land of Egypt, or the fall of the walls of Jericho. They can't be compared with the feeding of the 5,000, or the apostles' healings in Jerusalem. There is nothing obviously supernatural about hidden miracles. In fact, God's hand is disguised by the seeming natural flow of event following event. Yet these *are* miracles: God at work, gently guiding natural processes to keep us in the center of His will, or work out His plan for you and for me. God *can* perform the obvious miracle today. But He probably will not. Still we can rest assured. We are surrounded by the loving care of God who is quietly at work, performing His miracles in every detail of our lives.

When they heard this, they were furious and wanted to put them to death. But a Pharisee name *Gamaliel,* a teacher of the law, who was honored by all the people [intervened] (5:33-34). Gamaliel (referred to as "Rabban Gamaliel the First") is still honored as one of the greatest of the sages. One tradition identifies him as the *Nasi,* the learned judge who served as President of the Sanhedrin (see *Hagigah, Mishnah II:2*). This view, while debated, may be supported by a report in the Tosefta (*Sanh. II:6*), which portrays Rabban Gamaliel dictating to a scribe named Johanan an official letter to upper and lower Galilee and to the Diaspora of Babylonia and Media to designate a particular year as one in which 30 days were to be added in order to adjust the lunar to the solar year. The great respect in which Gamaliel was held is indicated further in this quote from the Mishnah (*Sotah 9:15 L.*): "When Rabban Gamaliel the Elder died, the glory of the Torah came to an end, and cleanness and separateness perished."

This background helps us realize that in every likelihood no other voice than that of this exceptional man could have calmed the fury of the priestly party and won the release of the apostles.

Opposition [to Stephen] arose, however, from members of the *Synagogue of the Freedmen* (6:9). "Stephen" is a Greek name, and he preached to Greek-speaking Jews who were part of the permanent population of Jerusalem. "Freedmen" is *Libertinoi,* a Latin term suggesting that the members of this synagogue were freed slaves or sons of slaves. This would not be surprising, as many Jews had been taken captive and enslaved in earlier rebellions in the Holy Land. Frustrated by their inability to defeat Stephen in debate, they finally brought charges against Stephen, distorting the intent of his teaching about Christ.

Stephen's lengthy defense turns the charge around. God *did* speak through Moses. But Stephen's accusers have not only followed the example of their forefathers in rejecting Moses, they have now murdered the One of whom Moses spoke! It is not Stephen who is impious; it is his accusers and judges. As for Stephen, he sees Jesus, exalted in heaven, standing at the right hand of God.

Mad with fury, members of the highest court in Judaism turned into a mob, swept Stephen out of the city, and killed him.

The death of this first Christian martyr launched a period of official persecution. Yet as Christians fled Jerusalem, they carried the Gospel message with them. In attempting to stamp out the Christian movement, the leaders only succeeded in spreading it! It has always been this way. The blood of the martyrs *is* the seed of the church. The more those in power try to suppress Christ, the more urgently Christians proclaim Him.

When they arrived, they *prayed* for them that they might receive the Holy Spirit (8:15). Luke adds a note of explanation because this is an extraordinary event, not a pattern in the first century or for today. They prayed and laid hands on them "because the Holy Spirit had not yet come upon any of them" (8:16-17). Why here, and here only, are prayer and laying on of hands associated with the coming of the Holy Spirit upon believers in Jesus?

We must remember that deep-seated hostility and religious competition had existed between the Jews and Samaritans for generations. By giving the Spirit through Peter and John the Lord made it clear (1) that the church was one, and (2) that the apostles were its authoritative leaders. Without this evidence of unity and authority, the Samaritans might very well have begun a splinter movement. And without it, the Jewish Christians might have been unwilling to accept the Samaritans as members with them of the body of Christ.

Today we need no such signs to remind us that faith in Christ unites us with every other believer in the world. That is taught clearly in the New Testament epistles (Eph. 4:1-7; Gal. 3:28). Yet the hostility and suspicion that *do* exist in the church today remind us that clear, supernatural evidence of unity and authority surely were essential when the Samaritans believed, and became members of the universal church.

Now an angel of the Lord said to Philip, "Go south" (8:26). How strange. God sent Philip away from a thriving evangelistic work to meet one man.

Let's never forget, in our pride in numbers: it is individuals who are important to God. The one person you or I reach is an eternal soul, as precious as each of the thousands preached to by famous evangelists.

"Surely not, Lord!" Peter replied. "I have never eaten anything impure or unclean" (10:14). In the OT community of faith, commitment to God was demonstrated by isolation from anything or anyone that was ritually unclean. Laws of ritual purity touched on every phase of a person's life—from conception and birth, to clothing that might be worn, food that might be eaten, and the treatment of the dead. The intent of these laws of separation was to constantly remind the Jewish people that they were set apart to God, and that they were to honor God in every aspect of their lives.

In Peter's vision the animals God showed him were all ritually unclean, and thus not to be eaten by a Jew (Lev. 11). In commanding Peter to kill and eat, God made a powerful affirmation both about the laws by which Peter had lived all his life, and about the essential nature of our new life in Christ.

The first message is expressed in 10:15. What makes a thing "impure" or "clean" is not the thing itself, but God's Word. Peter grasped the meaning of his vision, and when the Gentile Cornelius' messengers came, Peter did not dismiss them because they were Gentiles and thus "unclean." Peter's mission to the house of Cornelius opened the door of the Gospel to the Gentiles, and made it clear to Jewish believers that Christ's salvation extended to all.

The second affirmation implicit in Peter's vision took longer to assimilate. Holiness in the new community was no longer to be expressed by separation *from,* but by an active involvement *in* the world. Holiness in the new community is a dynamic and vital force that enables the believer to reject temptations to sin and, by exposure to all of Christ's love and righteousness, to draw others to the Savior.

While Peter was still speaking these words, the Holy Spirit came on all. . . . They heard them speaking in tongues and praising God (10:44, 46). Again Luke describes an event which is neither prescriptive nor normative for the church. This is no proof text for the notion that speaking in tongues is the essential evidence for the coming of the Holy Spirit to believers. Why then are the two associated here?

Peter explains. Speaking in tongues was compelling evidence that these Gentiles had been fully accepted by God, and were in fact members of Christ's church! Even those who proved most hostile to Peter's violation of the laws of separation (11:2-3) were forced by this evidence to acknowledge that God had accepted these Gentiles, and to realize that "God has even granted the Gentiles repentance unto life" (11:18).

THE PASSAGE IN DEPTH

The Choosing of the Seven (6:1-7).

Background. Rabbinic writings suggest that already established patterns of caring for the poor were adopted by the Jerusalem church, and are reflected in this passage. The Jewish system of poor relief involved *tamhuy*, the "poor bowl," and *quppah*, the "poor basket." The first was a daily distribution of food provided for the homeless. The second was a weekly distribution of food and clothing provided for poor families. In both cases help was provided in goods, not in cash.

Acts 6 describes Christian poor relief as also being provided in goods. The fact that it was provided daily suggests enough food was made available to the widows for the two daily meals eaten by the Jews. Since Acts 2:42-46 reports that the Christians gathered daily for worship, it seems likely that food for the poor was provided at a shared evening meal, with extra distributed for the next day.

Interpretation. The division between Grecian (Greek-speaking) Jews and Aramaic-speaking Jews in Jerusalem was reflected in the church. The old suspicion of those who were "different" was also carried over when these Jews were converted and became members of the new church. The Talmud reflects the fact that the Pharisees were openly contemptuous of Hellenists, and viewed the native-born Jew as superior. It is not surprising that fear of discrimination carried over as well, and was reflected in the feeling that "their widows were being overlooked in the daily distribution of food" (6:1). The charge may or may not have been true. What is important is that the apostles acted immediately to deal with this threat to the unity of the Christian community.

It is important here to note both the role of the spiritual leaders ("the Twelve") and the community ("all the disciples together") in solving the problem (6:12). Essentially the leaders (1) assembled the community, (2) defined their own role in the church, (3) established procedures to be followed in resolving the problem, (4) made the congregation responsible to resolve the dispute together, and (5) officially confirmed the choices of the congregation and ordained them to their task. We see each of these elements in Acts 6:2-3:

(1) So the Twelve gathered all the disciples together and said, (2) "It would not be right for us to neglect the ministry of the word of God in order to wait on tables. Brothers, (4) choose seven men from among you (3) who are known to be full of the Spirit and wisdom. (5) We will turn this responsibility over to them."

It is particularly notable to see the way the congregation fulfilled its responsibility. They chose men "full of faith and of the Holy Spirit" (6:5). And, strikingly, every person they chose has a Greek name — and thus represented the group that had initially charged discrimination! In essence the Aramaic speakers in the young church chose to become vulnerable to the ones who had criticized them, expressing an amazing trust that their critics — who had experienced discrimination — would not be guilty of discriminating against others.

This passage has been used in some traditions to give definition to the office of "deacon" in the contemporary church. It is interesting to note that the Greek text which uses the noun *diakonia* ("distribution") in 6:1, and the verb *diakoneo* ("wait on") in 6:2, never uses the noun *diakonos* ("deacon") as a title. At the same time, it is likely that the function per-

291

formed by the seven is much like that performed by those Paul does call deacons in 1 Tim. 3:8-13. What is more important than trying to justify our definition of modern church offices from this passage is to note that as problems arose in the church, those problems were met creatively by the invention of a role not established on the basis of Christ's recorded teaching or on the basis of a corresponding secular position. The Twelve simply acted to meet the need that emerged from the congregation's ongoing experience.

Certainly one thing we can learn from this passage is that *function* is more important than *office,* and that we too need to be flexible and responsible to the Spirit's leading as we seek to meet needs in our own day.

Implications. This passage is filled with implications for churches and church leadership today:

■ Paternalism. Perhaps the first lesson to be learned is that the spiritual leadership of the church must avoid paternalism. The way to develop a mature church is not to impose solutions from above, but to involve the congregation in problem-solving and to trust the membership with a significant role in decision-making.

■ Trust. It would have been so easy to become defensive and argue about who was or was not to blame. Instead the congregation focused on the problem, and the Aramaic-speaking Christians displayed their trust of their brothers by making Greek speakers responsible for distributing to all. In becoming vulnerable themselves, this segment of the congregation displayed a trust which allayed the fears of the Grecian members of the young church.

■ Priorities. The spiritual leaders of the church must give their attention "to prayer and the ministry of the Word" (6:4). Yet the material concerns of believers also must be addressed. And those who deal with the "practical" must themselves be persons "full of faith and of the Holy Spirit."

■ Flexibility. We must be ready to respond to needs. Too often our churches are locked into old programs or old offices. Rather than seek creatively to meet needs as they emerge, we

struggle to maintain church machinery. This incident in the life of the early church reminds us that *people* are more important than our church *constitutions,* and that innovation is not a four-letter word.

Saul's Conversion (9:1-31).

Background. Paul's conversion experience is critical in understanding this man whose total commitment to Jesus is reflected not only in Acts but also in his 13 letters found in our New Testament. Luke gives us no less than three versions of the conversion story (9:1-19; 21:37–22:21; 26:1-32), two of which represent Paul's telling of the story to a Jewish and then a Gentile audience. Clearly the appearance of the risen Christ to the apostle was foundational not only to his conversion, but his awareness that he had been set aside by God as a witness and apostle to the world.

Interpretation. The conversion story contains the following significant elements:

■ Saul's persecution of the church.
■ Saul's confrontation by Jesus.
■ Saul's commission as an apostle.
■ Saul's early zeal.

Each helps us understand more about this zealous Jew turned Christian missionary and theologian.

■ Saul's persecution of the church (9:1-2). The first time we meet Saul is at the stoning of Stephen. The text says, "Meanwhile, the witnesses laid their clothes at the feet of a young man named Saul. . . . And Saul was there, giving approval to his death" (7:58; 8:1).

The term *neanias,* "young man," was applied in the first century to individuals from about 24 to 40 years of age. This, plus the fact that Saul was given charge of the clothing of the witnesses (who, according to Jewish law, must cast the first stones) and that he was "giving approval" has been taken by some to indicate Saul was in fact a member of the Sanhedrin. Since, as Paul later tells us, he studied with Gamaliel, this may be possible, but it is still unlikely.

Saul's continuing hatred of Christians as heretics is reflected in his request for letters from the high priest commissioning him to arrest any believers that might be found in Damascus. But how would the high priest have jurisdiction over citizens of Damascus?

In the Roman Empire ethnic groups were

considered to be governed by the laws of their own nation, even when they moved to foreign lands. Thus the 6 million or so Jews scattered through the Roman Empire were still subject to rulings by the Sanhedrin in Jerusalem. Paul's letters from the high priest would be considered by the Damascus authorities and by the Jewish community as adequate authorization to imprison any Christian Jews and return them to Jerusalem for judgment.

But what is important in this passage is not the legalities, but the insight we have into the absolute zeal of the young Pharisee, Saul. He views those who follow Christ as traitors to Judaism and to God, and he is totally committed to stamping out this pernicious movement!

Let's remember Saul when we meet our own times' bitter enemies of Christianity. The most fanatical enemies of the faith are likely, on conversion, to become Christ's most ardent advocates.

■ Saul's confrontation by Jesus (9:2-6). Some have argued that Luke's accounts of Saul's conversion conflict. Luke tells us that Saul heard the voice (*phonen* [9:4]) and that his companions also heard the voice (*phonen* [9:7]). Acts 22:9 says that his companions did not hear the voice (*phonen*), while Acts 26:14 says only Saul heard the voice (*phonen*). The conflicting accounts have led some critics to suppose Luke is using different source materials and simply failed to notice that they disagreed.

The solution is found in the fact that *phone* can mean both "sound" and "speech." What first-century readers undoubtedly understood is that all traveling together heard the sound, but Saul alone understood the words the voice spoke.

Even more significant to the Jew is the fact that a "voice from heaven" in rabbinical thought was always God's voice—not the voice of an angel or other created being. Thus Paul was stunned when the speaker identified himself as "Jesus, whom you are persecuting" (9:5). Suddenly Saul's theology was shaken to its very foundation, as he realized that Jesus must indeed be God!

■ Saul's commission as an apostle (9:7-19). Paul was blinded in that confrontation on the Damascus road. For three days he walked in darkness, no doubt pondering the implications of what the voice had revealed.

In Damascus the Lord sent Ananias to Paul to return his sight, and no doubt to report words of commission: "This man is My chosen instrument to carry My name before the Gentiles and their kings and before the people of Israel" (9:15). His healing, in the name of the Lord Jesus, confirmed the truth he had begun to realize, and brought about his actual conversion. From that moment, sure both of Jesus' lordship and his own destiny, Saul set out to serve Christ and promote His cause.

■ Saul's early zeal (9:20-31). Saul had been converted. And now that same zeal that had led him to persecute the church was directed toward promoting the Gospel.

It is fascinating that Saul's approach to evangelism seems to have been just as abrasive and confrontational as his attacks on the believers. In Damascus "Saul grew more and more powerful . . . proving [from the OT Scriptures] that Jesus is the Christ" (9:22). After days of being confounded by the persistent evangelist, the Jews in Damascus conspired to kill him!

Saul escaped to Jerusalem. There, after finally being accepted by the believers, Saul again began to speak "boldly" (9:28) and "debated" (9:29) with the very Grecian Jews who had murdered Stephen. Again his aggressive witness aroused such hostility that his opponents tried to kill him. This time the Christians in Jerusalem "took him [Paul] down to Caesarea and sent him off to Tarsus" (9:30). The next comment, that "the church . . . enjoyed a time of peace" (9:31), may be a subtle comment on the impact of Saul's early ministry. Rather than win converts, the aggressive Saul seems to have had the gift of arousing intense hostility.

There is a difficult balance for us all to maintain as we witness. We must present compellingly the message that Jesus alone saves. And yet we must do so in such a way that others are won rather than offended. Given the increasing polarization of Jewish and Christian communities in Damascus and Jerusalem, it may not have been possible to achieve this ideal. And so we should not be overly critical of Saul. At the same time we may be reminded that zeal is no substitute for wisdom. Nor is the passion of the new convert a substitute for the patience of a mature believer.

Implications. According to the Dead Sea Scrolls, a righteous man is one who "bears unremitting hatred toward all men of ill repute" (IQS 9.22). Another scroll says, "The nearer I draw to You, the more I am filled with zeal against all that do wickedness and against all men of deceit. For they that draw near to You cannot see Your commandments defiled, and they that have knowledge of You can brook no change of Your words (IQH 14:13-14). Surely this "holy hatred" was felt by Saul the persecutor. And perhaps by Saul the new convert.

Yet how different this attitude from that we see reflected in Rom. 10:1: "Brothers, my hearts desire and prayer to God for the Israelites is that they may be saved." And how different from 1 Cor. 13:13: "And now these three remain: faith, hope and love. But the greatest of these is love."

We cannot expect a total change in attitude or maturity in a new convert. But as you and I mature in our faith, we surely will become the zealous and *loving* persons that Saul became.

ACTS 11:19–15:35
The Era of Evangelism

EXPOSITION

The church is now well established in Jerusalem, and smaller communities of believers have been planted throughout Galilee and even in Samaria. The first Gentiles have been converted and accepted, and a Gentile church has even been established in Antioch (11:19-30). Soon Luke will report Paul's stunning innovation—direct evangelism of Gentiles—an innovation which will usher in a stunning era of worldwide evangelism. But first Luke looks back, briefly, to make it very clear that while our attention is directed to the Gentile mission, God continues to work among His OT people.

Luke establishes this by relating two incidents of direct divine intervention on behalf of the Jewish church. James the brother of John is executed by Herod Agrippa, and Peter is taken prisoner and held for a show trial. An angel releases Peter, and he escapes (12:1-19). Shortly afterward Herod, who has shown himself an enemy of the church, is struck with a fatal illness (12:20-25). Luke may draw our attention away from the Holy Land, but God remains vitally involved in the experience of Christians there.

Meanwhile in Antioch, Barnabas and Saul are set apart by the Holy Spirit for the first missionary journey (13:1-3). Luke immediately establishes the fact that God will also intervene actively for the missionaries. On Cyprus God strikes an evil sorcerer with blindness at Paul's word, leading to the conversion of the Roman proconsul (13:4-12). Moving on to Pisidian Antioch, Paul presents the Gospels in the synagogue to the Jewish community, and is invited to speak again. The next Sabbath "almost the whole city" gathered to hear! (13:13-52) This overwhelming response to the Gospel by the Gentiles infuriated the Jews—and gave a new focus to Paul's missionary journeys. When he entered a new community, Paul would continue to share Christ with the Jews first. But at their synagogues he would also contact many Gentiles who had been attracted to Judaism. These Gentiles, rather than Jews, would become the core of a colony of believers in every Empire city. And, tragically, the Jews in these cities would often become active enemies of the missionaries and their message.

We see this pattern at Iconium and in Lystra. But in each of these cities we also see evidence that God is active on behalf of His representatives, performing miracles of healing, and restoring Paul after he was dragged from Lystra and left for dead (14:1-20).

Paul's experience on this first missionary journey unquestionably shaped his understanding of his mission. On the way back to Antioch, Paul revisited thriving new churches that had been established. Back in his home church he "reported all that God had done through them and how he had *opened the door of faith to the Gentiles*" (14:21-28, emphasis mine).

The sudden influx of Gentiles, and especially establishment of predominantly Gentile churches, led to theological debate. What is the relationship of these Gentile believers in Israel's Messiah to the Law of Moses? Many Jewish Christians sincerely believed that to please God, Gentiles who believe in Christ must adopt the way of life laid out so completely in the OT. In essence, Gentiles must become Jews to be good Christians. Paul, however, saw this as a distortion of the Gospel itself, a Gospel which affirmed that human beings were accepted and forgiven by God not on the basis of what they do, but on the basis of what Jesus has done for all. This troubling question was officially resolved in a council held at Jerusalem (15:1-35). There Paul's view prevailed, and the apostles, elders, and "the whole church" agreed that salvation is a gift received by faith by both Jew and Gentile. Neither Gentile nor Jew need surrender his cultural heritage to be a faithful Christian.

This affirmation by the first council in the history of the church was truly crucial. Yet throughout the early decades of this era, Gentile Christians would be troubled by zealous Jews claiming that only through obedience to OT Law could a NT faith be appropriately expressed.

WORD STUDIES

The disciples were called *Christians* first at Antioch (11:26). Antioch was the capital of the imperial province of Syria. It controlled the trade routes between Asia Minor, the Euphrates, and Egypt. The city enjoyed *liberties,* a status exempting it from paying tribute to Caesar or serving as a military garrison, and permitting an independent constitution. From the city's founding, Jews formed a large and influential segment of the population. Later on, during the Judean revolt of the Jews in A.D. 69, the Jewish population here suffered less persecution than in some other centers of the Empire.

Here at first the Gospel was preached "only to Jews" (11:19). But when some spoke to Greeks (Gentiles) about Jesus, a significant revival broke out in the non-Jewish population, and a separate Gentile congregation was established. Initially Christianity had been perceived as a sect of Judaism. The Jews called believers "Galileans" or "Nazarenes," and the believers thought of themselves as followers of "the Way." The designation *Christianous* re-

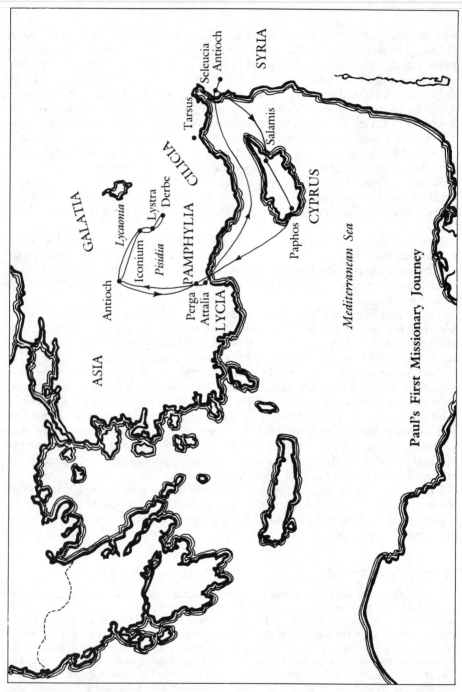

The Gentile Mission was launched from Antioch. The first missionary journey described in Acts 13–14 was to nearby Asia Minor.

flects common Greek usage and means a "follower of" or "belonging to" Christ. The name reflects the fact that here, for the first time, a truly Gentile church has come into being and is distinguished by the population of the city from the Jewish community.

It is that others be aware of who we are and think of us as followers of Jesus Christ.

It was about this time that _King Herod_ arrested some who belonged to the church, intending to persecute them (12:1). The ruler is Herod Agrippa, the grandson of Herod the Great. Herod was a close personal friend of the Emperor Claudius, who in A.D. 41 granted him all the lands held by his grandfather, including Judea and Samaria as well as lands in Galilee. Herod, whose family was hated by the populace, set out to win the favor of his new subjects by acting the part of a pious Jew. How well he succeeded is reflected in the Mishnah (Jewish writings dating from 30 B.C. to A.D. 200). One passage (_Sotah 7:8_) describes Agrippa's participation in the Festival of Sukkot, and the relevant segment reads:

> I. Agrippa the King stood up and received it and read it standing up, and sages praised him on that account. [Standing was a mark of respect. Other rulers appointed by the Romans had sat down when participating in this ceremony.]
>
> J. And when he came to the verse, _You may not put a foreigner over you, who is not your brother_ (Deut. 17:15), his tears ran down from his eyes.
>
> K. They said to him, "Do not be afraid, Agrippa, you are our brother, you are our brother, you are our brother."

There is little doubt that Herod Agrippa's active persecution of the church was part of his design to win over the Jewish leadership. Even the fact that James the brother of John was beheaded is suggestive, for _Mishnah Sanhedrin 9:1_ prescribes this form of death for "people of an apostate city." Since the execution of James was greeted so enthusiastically by "the Jews" (used here as in John as a synonym for the high priest and his associates in the Sanhedrin [12:3]), Peter was placed under especially heavy guard. Rather than be chained to one soldier, he was chained to two, with two addi-

tional guards posted at the door!

Herod's pseudo-pious efforts did win the approval of his subjects. But they did not win the approval of God. Luke tells us that shortly after, in A.D. 44, following a very brief reign, God struck Herod with a deadly disease. From Luke's description, commentators have supposed the king was infected with intestinal round worms. These worms can grow up to 16 inches long, clogging intestines and causing extreme pain as well as vomiting of the worms and death.

How much wiser Herod would have been to seek to please God rather than the influential among his subjects.

JOSEPHUS ON HEROD AGRIPPA'S DEATH

> After the completion of the third year of his reign over the whole of Judea, Agrippa came to the city of Caesarea . . . he celebrated spectacles in honor of Caesar.
>
> On the second day of the spectacles, clad in a garment woven completely of silver so that its texture was indeed wondrous, he entered the theater at daybreak. There the silver, illumined by the touch of the first rays of the sun, was wondrously radiant and by its glitter inspired fear and awe in those who gazed intently upon it. Straightway his flatterers raised their voices from various directions—though hardly for his good—addressing him as a god. "May you be propitious to us," they added, "and if we have hitherto feared you as a man, yet henceforth we agree that you are more than mortal in your being." The king did not rebuke them nor did he reject their flattery as impious. But shortly thereafter he looked up and saw an owl perched on a rope over his head. At once, recognizing this as a harbinger of woes just as it had once been of good tidings, he felt a stab of pain in his heart. He was also gripped in his stomach by an ache that he felt everywhere at once and that was intense from the start. Leaping up he said to his friends: "I, a god in your eyes, am not bidden to lay down my life, for fate brings immediate refutation of the lying words lately addressed to me. I, who was called immortal by you, am now under sentence of death. But I must accept my lot as God wills it. In

fact I have lived in no ordinary fashion but in the grand style that is hailed as true bliss." Even as he was speaking these words, he was overcome by more intense pain. They hastened, therefore, to convey him to the palace; and the word flashed about to everyone that the king was on the very verge of death. . . . Exhausted after five straight days by the pain in his abdomen, he departed this life in the fifty-fourth year of his life and the seventh of his reign (*Antiquities, XIX, 343–350*).

Peter knocked at the *outer entrance,* and a *servant girl* named Rhoda came to answer the door (12:13). Often little things can tell us so much. The "outer entrance" is *ten thyran tou pylonos,* a door opening onto a vestibule which led to living quarters well back from the street, indicating a large and wealthy home. Rhoda was probably a Gentile slave girl. At this time in Jerusalem no Jewish slaves were held by Jewish masters, and all male as well as female slaves mentioned in rabbinical or other literary sources were Gentile. Rhoda would have been expected to keep key biblical laws. If such slaves were freed by their Jewish masters, they were considered converts and became Jews. It was not unusual for freed slaves to remain in the family employ or even marry a member of the family.

Rhoda's utter excitement at hearing Peter call to her tells us much about her—and about how completely the young servant girl had been accepted into the family and the church. She shared the family faith; she shared the concern for Peter's welfare; and she shared the whole congregation's joy at his release. Let's always remember that social distinctions count for little in the body of Christ. What counts is sharing faith, concern for others, and joy at God's work in their lives.

Then Saul, who was also called Paul (13:9). The significance of the events on Cyprus is captured in this seemingly trivial remark. As a Roman citizen the apostle undoubtedly had a Jewish name (Saul) and a Greek name (Paul). Up until now the apostle has been called "Saul," Saul has been named after Barnabas (13:7), and the visitors have preached to Jewish populations (13:5). From this point on in Acts the name Luke uses is Paul, Paul is always listed first, and while

evangelistic efforts in every city are launched in the synagogue, the Gentiles soon become the focus of ministry and the core of the membership of new churches.

What happened here to cause this change? Sergius Paulus (quite possibly Lucius Sergius Paulus, mentioned in recovered inscriptions as a "curator of the Tiber" in the reign of Claudius) sent for the two preachers. This was undoubtedly an inquiry caused by disturbances that preaching Christ created in the Jewish community. His interest at this stage was official, not religious. Yet when the Jewish sorcerer was blinded by God at Paul's word, the proconsul believed.

This experience apparently had a great impact on the apostle. From this point on Paul became the leader of the missionary team—and his vision of carrying the Gospel to Gentiles shaped the direction of the ministry.

Brothers, if you have a message of encouragement for the people, please speak (13:15). Visitors were typically invited to share as Paul was at Pisidian Antioch (see map). His sermon was carefully shaped for his audience, as the summary Luke provides shows. Essentially Paul argues that God who acted in history past for the Jewish people has acted again. Both Judaism and the Christian outgrowth of that faith are confessional, rooted in God's acts.

Paul makes four points in summarizing the confessional basis of each faith: Judaism is rooted in the conviction that (1) God chose the people of Israel, (2) caused that people to multiply in Egypt, (3) led the people out "with mighty power," and (4) gave them the land of Canaan as a permanent inheritance (13:16-19).

After demonstrating that Jesus is in the messianic line (13:20-26), he summarizes the confessional basis of Christianity. (1) Jesus was crucified, (2) buried, (3) raised from the dead, and (4) seen alive by many witnesses (13:27-31). The God who acted in the past has acted again, and in fulfilling OT prophecy now offers forgiveness and justification to all.

Though we shape the message to the listener, we never *change* the message to suit the listener's beliefs or bias. Paul says bluntly to his Jewish audience that in Jesus we are "justified from everything you could not be justified from by the law of Moses" (13:39). We need to be just as clear that salvation is found in Christ alone.

Since you *reject* it (13:46). The Jews of Pisidian Antioch did not reject and then actively oppose the Christian message on its merits, but out of jealousy. Ultimately, however, neither the motives of those who reject our message or even their active hostility should matter to us. There are those who will respond. Those who reject harm only themselves.

The Jews who refused to believe *stirred up* the Gentiles and *poisoned their minds* against the brothers (14:2). The intense animosity of the Jewish community against the missionaries (the sense of the word "apostles" here) is reflected in nearly every city Paul visits. In a sense that hostility *contributed* to the evangelistic effort. No one in the city could have been unaware of the presence of the apostles or of at least the outline of their message.

Iconium was a Greek city with its government structured on a traditional Greek pattern. It is likely in this context that "the people" (*to plethos* [14:4]) refers to an assembly of leading citizens that met to conduct city business. If so, the official response to Paul's message was mixed. Until A.D. 64 Christianity was officially considered a sect of Judaism, and thus was a *licit* religion, protected by law. It would be difficult for city officials to take sides in what must have seemed an internal Jewish squabble, even though many Gentiles joined the Christian group.

The impression of confusion in the disorder is strengthened by the use of the word *horme,* translated "plot" here (14:5), which suggests a sudden or impetuous act rather than a carefully laid plan.

In many ways it is a shame that the Gospel creates so little controversy today. Despite airwaves filled with radio and TV preaching, despite towns and cities filled with churches, Christianity seems all too easy for most to ignore. Perhaps, unlike Paul, we have failed to be confrontational enough and failed to boldly warn scoffers: Take care! Today we must again proclaim that unless listeners believe, they surely will perish (13:41).

The *gods have come to us* in human form! (14:11) Geography and the use by the population of Lystra of the Lyconian language suggest that this was a "backwoods" area. Paul's miracle of healing led the Lyconians to identify the two as Zeus and Hermes. Why? Inscriptions from about 250 B.C. reveal these Greek gods were worshiped in the area, and Ovid (c. 43 B.C.) reports a legend that once these two gods had visited the area in disguise. A thousand families refused to accept them—and their homes were later destroyed. One older couple did welcome the two gods and were richly rewarded. In view of the familiar story, the conclusion that Paul and Barnabas were Hermes and Zeus was not surprising—nor was the eagerness of the population to welcome the two supposed deities.

How fascinating that this same population was shortly afterward swayed by Jews from Antioch and Iconium to stone Paul and leave him for dead.

Paul and Barnabas *appointed* elders for them in each church (14:23). The Greek word here is *cheirontonesantes,* a compound word from one term that means "extend the hand" and another that means "to stretch." It originally meant to vote by a show of hands. A.T. Robertson says that it finally came to mean "to appoint with the approval of an assembly that chooses," and at times in the sense of "to appoint without regard to choice."

We can best understand the apostles' act as one of ordination to local church leadership. In revisiting the young churches Paul and Barnabas undoubtedly sought out those whose progress in the faith and whose character (1 Tim. 3) were recognized by the congregation, and gave them official recognition.

Christian leaders are not created by those higher in the church hierarchy. Rather, Christian leaders emerge as some display a deep and total commitment to Jesus, and are recognized by the congregation as mature believers whose example others will wish to follow.

You are to abstain from *food sacrificed to idols,* from *blood,* from the *meat of strangled animals* and from *sexual immorality* (15:29). The Jerusalem council ruled that Gentile Christians were exempt, and not required to be "circumcised" and "obey the law of Moses" (13:5).

Yet the council went on to write a letter to Gentile churches specifying certain "requirements" (15:28). This word may be too strong, for the Greek phrase indicates the council asked for no more than "these necessary things" (*plen touton ton epanagkes*).

Two questions now must be answered. What are these things "necessary" for, and what is the relationship of these "necessary things" to the Mosaic Law? First, it's clear that these things are not necessary for salvation. Most commentators agree that the things specified were necessary to "do well" (*eu praxete*) between Jew and Gentile Christians. That is, the things mentioned were so offensive to the Jews that their practice would make it difficult or impossible to maintain fellowship between the two major groups that were united in the new Christian community.

A link between OT Law and the things "necessary" to maintain fellowship does exist. But it is the intensity of Jewish feelings about these issues that defines them. Basic morality is not at issue: Jew and Gentile agreed for the most part on what is morally right and, as James pointed out, "Moses has been preached in every city from the earliest times and is read in the synagogues on every Sabbath" (15:21).

What can we say about them? "Food sacrificed to idols" reflects on the Jewish utter horror of anything associated with idolatry. The eating of blood and of animals that were strangled and thus retain the blood in the meat, reflects a similarly deep abhorrence of consuming this most sacred of fluids (Lev. 17:11-12). The most difficult to define is abstaining from "sexual immorality" (*porneia*). This is difficult because, if general immorality is intended, this *is* a moral issue. It is hardly conceivable that basic sexual morality was not clearly understood and practiced by both Jewish and Gentile Christians. So it is most likely that the word *porneia* is used in a more technical sense (as in 1 Cor. 5:1) to indicate marriages that are forbidden in Lev. 18:6-18, some of which were not considered wrong in Greek culture.

In this one official request by the Jews to the Gentile churches, there is an implicit recognition that we do not have to be the same to have fellowship with other believers. We also need to be open enough to share those peculiar convictions that we hold which, if violated, would make it difficult for us to relate to our brothers and sisters in Christ. And we need to be willing to honor the convictions of others, and do what is necessary to live in fellowship and harmony with them.

THE PASSAGE IN DEPTH

The Council of Jerusalem (Acts 15)

Background. The mass conversion of Gentiles to Christ introduced tensions in the young church. Jewish Christian traditionalists insisted that the Gentile converts adopt the lifestyle the OT prescribed for the Jewish people. Paul saw this as a denial of the essential nature of the Gospel, and fought this view fiercely. When the issue was finally brought before the apostles and elders in Jerusalem, an "official position paper" was produced. Gentile converts were not required to be—or to live like—Jews.

This decision by the Jerusalem council, and battles fought against Judaizers in most of the Gentile churches during the following decades, had a significant impact on *Jewish* as well as Gentile Christians. Because the first Christians were Jews, and because these Jewish believers continued to live a life of piety according to Jewish law, the church was at first considered a sect (*min*) of Judaism. The fact that Paul was authorized by the high priest to make prisoners of followers of Jesus in Damascus (Acts 9:1-4) shows that even the church's enemies considered believers to be Jews. If they had not been considered Jews, the high priest and Sanhedrin would have had no authority to imprison the followers of Jesus in Damascus!

But now, with the emergence of predominantly Gentile churches throughout the Empire, and with the decision of Jerusalem council on record, it became increasingly clear that Christianity was a faith which, despite its OT roots, was distinct from Judaism. The result was increasing antagonism on the part of orthodox Jews toward Jewish Christians. That antagonism soon grew so intense that the sages ruled Jewish Christians apostate, not Jews at all!

Scholars have identified several different early Jewish Christian sects, designated Ebionites A, Ebionites B, Nazarenes (Notzrim), and Gnostic-Syncretists. Most interesting to us are the Nazarenes, who were observant Jews, yet believed in Jesus as the virgin-born Son of God, believed in the Holy Spirit as a distinct person of the Godhead, and who accepted Paul's letters as Scripture. The active animosity toward Jewish Christians is reflected in Justin Martyr, who charged around A.D. 150 that "you Jews pronounce maledictions on the Christians in your synagogues." His charge is supported by ancient liturgy to be used by pious Jews as "benedictions" some three times a day:

"May the apostates have no hope, and may You uproot the wicked government speedily, in our day. May the Nazarenes and the Minim (sectarians) disappear in a moment. Let them be erased from the book of life and not be inscribed with the righteous."

A second-century story retold in the Tosefta (*Hul. II:24*) further indicates the disposition of the sages toward Jewish Christians:

Rabbi Eliezer was arrested by the Romans and charged with being a *Min* (here the equivalent of "Christian"). They put him out on the stand to be tried. The governor said: "How does an old man like you come to be involved in such matters?" The Rabbi answered: "I put my faith in the Judge." Of course, he meant the Father in heaven, but the governor thought he was referring to him. So he said, "Since you put your trust in me—*dismiss*! You are discharged." When Rabbi Eliezer left the stand he was upset because he had been arrested for *minut*. His disciples came to him to console him, but he would not be comforted. Then Rabbi Akiba entered and said: "Rabbi, may I say something without giving offense?" He answered: "Say on." Said he: "Is it possible that one of the *Minim* once told you something of their teaching that pleased you?" He answered: "By Heaven, you have reminded me! I was walking once along the main street of Sephoris, and I met Jacob of Kefar Sikhnin, and he told me a bit of *minut* in the name of Yeshua ben Pantera (Jesus), and I enjoyed it! . . . That is why I was arrested for *minut*, because I violated the Scripture that says: 'Remove thy way from her, and come not near the door of her house' " (Prov. 5:8).

These and other similar items in the writings of the sages remind us that the Jerusalem church paid a price for its courageous pronouncement. In recognizing the independence of Gentiles from Judaism, these Jewish Christians also isolated themselves from the OT community of faith. Jew and Christian were now sharply distinguished from one another, despite their many similarities. And Jewish Christians, however observant of Moses' Law, would be denied any part in their ancient heritage by those Jews who rejected the claims of Christ.

Interpretation. The chapter breaks down into four sections: the issue raised, debate, conclusion, and the official position stated.

■ **The issue raised (15:1-4).** Those identified as "some men" from Judea were probably Jewish Christians identified in Paul's letters as Judaizers (Gal. 6:12-13). We can assume that they were convinced their position was right. Yet in view of the growing hostility to Christian Jews (see Exposition, above) they may have acted from mixed motives. If in fact conversion to Christ *transformed pagans into good Jews,* thus identifying them with the Jewish cause, the growing hostility of official Judaism might have been blunted! But Paul and Barnabas sharply disputed the notion that conversion to Christ required Gentiles to adopt Jewish customs and culture. The church quickly sent them and other delegates to Jerusalem to see if these visitors from Judea reflected the view of the apostles and elders of the mother church.

■ **The debate (15:5-12).** A significant group of Christian Pharisees supported the view of the Judaizers. *Of course* Christians must "be circumcised and required to obey the Law of Moses." This was not necessarily a salvation issue with these Pharisees. Support for this position most likely rested on the fact that Moses' teaching was in fact the revealed will of God. It followed that anyone who believed in God would by necessity (*dei*, "must" [15:5]) be subject to His revealed will.

In response, Peter recounted the story of the conversion of Cornelius, and noted that he and his household were accepted by God *as Gentiles.* God "made no distinction between us and them, for He purified their hearts by faith" (15:9). Certainly this experience provides a precedent for direct outreach to Gentiles as Gentiles, without insisting they become *Jewish* Christians.

Of particular note is Peter's gratuitous observation that the law has been "a yoke [here in the sense of burden] that neither we nor our fathers have been able to bear" (15:10). If due to human weakness, Law failed to accomplish what God's grace and faith in Jesus has now won, why force the Law upon Gentile converts?

Paul and Barnabas quickly followed up Peter's remarks. Peter had drawn his conclusion on the basis of God's working in one instance. Now the two apostles followed up by reporting multiplied stories of the miraculous signs God had performed among the Gentiles. The point was, of course, that God had clearly set His seal of approval on direct evangelism of Gentiles.

It is important to note that both Judaism and Christianity are faiths which are rooted in the conviction that God has acted for His people in history. The call and covenant with a real Abraham, God's mighty acts on behalf of Israel when that people were slaves in Egypt, the thunder and fire that shrouded the top of Sinai, the manna provided in the wilderness, the drying up of the Jordan—these acts of God were the foundation of Israel's understanding of God. Thus Paul's recitation of *how God had acted* for the Gentiles was especially compelling. These men fully expected to develop their theology on the basis of God's actions in history rather than by appeal to logic or philosophical argument.

■ The conclusion (15:12-21). While it was valid to develop theology from God's acts, the church's *interpretation* of those acts must meet another test. It must be in harmony with Scripture. Thus the decisive contribution in resolving the issue was made by James, who stood up and argued that "the words of the prophets are in agreement" (15:13) with the empirical evidence that God is in fact "taking from the Gentiles" a people for Himself.

James then states a conclusion that no one

in the council meeting could debate further. The Gentiles should not be asked to adopt Jewish culture, thus making "it difficult" (15:19) for those turning to God. They should, however, be asked to refrain from certain practices that would make it most difficult for Jewish Christians to fellowship with them (see Word Study of 15:29, above).

■ The official position stated (15:22-35). James' Holy-Spirit-led conclusion expressed the consensus of "the apostles and elders, with the whole church" (15:22). Delegates were sent with Paul to Antioch to authenticate a document that was then to be circulated to the new Gentile churches.

Application. In many ways this first church council can serve as a model for resolving disputed issues today. We note especially that:

(1) The issue was clearly defined.

(2) The issue was brought to the entire leadership for open discussion and debate.

(3) Differing positions were actively argued.

(4) Evidence from what God was currently doing was considered.

(5) The interpretation of what God was doing was tested for harmony with Scripture.

(6) Special concern was shown for the sensibilities of those who "lost" the debate.

(7) The "winners" were asked to surrender some of the rights they had won in view of some of the convictions of the "losers."

While this model of resolving disputes is helpful, it is important to remember that even in the first century the council action did not resolve the issue. Most Gentile churches were still troubled by a few itinerant teachers who persisted in teaching that Christians must submit to the Law of Moses. We cannot expect everyone to surrender convictions which are wrong, however clear the voice of God through church and Scripture.

What we can do is seek to hear the Holy Spirit's voice through our brothers and the Word of God. And, as we debate, remember always that we are one family in Christ, and that those who differ from us remain brothers and sisters whom we have a duty to love.

ACTS 15:36–19:41
The Gentile Church

EXPOSITION

The decision of the Jerusalem council (Acts 15) signaled a dramatic transition in the Christian movement. Initially Christianity had been viewed as a Jewish sect. But the council decided that Gentiles be granted full acceptance without being required to adopt a Jewish lifestyle. Now Christian missionaries could aggressively promote Christianity in the broader first-century culture as a truly independent faith, despite its acknowledged OT roots.

Acts 16–19 gives us a striking description of the disruptive impact of the Christian message on Hellenistic society, and of the confused and often hostile response of the Gentile world.

The shift of focus is signaled by Paul's call to leave Asia and cross into Europe (16:6-10). In Philippi Paul finds no synagogue. Instead he preaches in the marketplace, "advocating customs unlawful for us Romans to accept or practice" (16:21). When the missionaries are beaten and imprisoned, Paul claims the protection guaranteed by his Roman citizenship (16:11-40). Paul is now ministering in the Gentile world, not as a Jew but as a man of Rome. In Thessalonica Paul does go first to the local synagogue. But the Jews' hostility is aroused when the Gentile population shows intense interest in Paul's message. As this chapter develops, we sense a dramatic result of the missionary focus on Gentile evangelism: throughout the Empire Jewish communities become increasingly antagonistic to the Gospel and its messengers (17:1-15). But, as Paul's preaching in Athens shows, the most basic concepts about God, long established in Judaism, seem not only strange but ridiculous to those whose worldview has been shaped by the speculations of Greek philosophers (17:16-34). The Gospel message is in direct conflict with the pagan roots of first-century society.

Luke goes on to describe other incidents that illuminate the impact of Christianity's transition to a predominantly Gentile movement. While the Jewish community is divided over the Gospel, the majority actively oppose Christianity (18:1-11). And, increasingly, the secular government is drawn into the dispute (18:12-17), although with different results (16:22-24; 19:35-41). Perhaps even more revealing is the portrait that Luke gives of the impact of Paul's ministry in Ephesus (19:1-41). There the Gospel leads many to give up the practice of magic, which was deeply embedded in first-century pagan culture (19:1-20). But it also threatens the livelihood of those who make a living selling religious items to pilgrims visiting the world-famous temple of

Artemis that stands just outside Ephesus (19:23-41).

Taken together, the incidents that Luke describes in these chapters help us sense why many perceived Christianity as a threat to the peace of the Empire. Christianity's radical teachings antagonized the Jews, who in that age were probably about one-tenth of the Empire's total population. Intense hostility was aroused that created problems for governors charged with upholding law and order. What's more, the insistence of the missionaries that converts abandon the easy tolerance of paganism and commit totally to Jesus as Lord, led to serious economic disruptions. The loss of livelihood of the silversmiths of Ephesus is just one illustration of this phenomenon.

It is difficult for us, living in a culture where Christianity exerts a strong presence, to grasp how dramatically the emergence of a Gentile church challenged first-century beliefs and institutions. Yet the history of the next few centuries bears witness to the fact that because of missionaries like Paul, the world was launched on a course that led to dramatic and often disruptive change.

WORD STUDIES

Paul did not think it *wise* to take [Mark], because he had deserted them in Pamphylia (15:38). The Greek word is *exiou*, from the verb *axioo*, meaning "to consider worth, suitable." In this case Paul looked at how young Mark had behaved on their first missionary journey. In contrast Barnabas considered what Mark might become and wanted to give him a second chance. In this case Barnabas was proved right. Years later Mark wrote the Gospel that bears his name, and even Paul wrote concerning him, "Get Mark and bring him with you, because he is helpful to me" (2 Tim. 4:11).

Like Barnabas, we do well to see the potential in others, rather than dwell on their past failures.

They had such a *sharp disagreement* that they parted company (15:39). The Greek word is *paroxysmos*, "irritation, disagreement." The word is purposely neutral, and Luke seems careful not to assign blame. Actually, we must ascribe the best of motives to each person: Paul, who so valued total commitment to Christ; Barnabas, who so valued the nurturing of others.

At times even the best of Christians will fail to find common ground, and decide to move in different directions. In this case there was one immediate positive result: outreach was doubled as two missionary parties rather than one set out to share the Gospel.

Paul wanted to take [Timothy] along on the journey, so he circumcised him because of the Jews who lived in that area (16:3). Some have condemned Paul for this act of "compromise." Yet the text tells us that Timothy's "mother was a Jewess" (16:1). In Judaism racial identity is established by the mother rather than the father. Thus Timothy would be considered a Jew by the "Jews who lived in that area." It was thus appropriate to circumcise Timothy, for the Apostle Paul's consistent argument in the NT is that believers are to express their faith through the cultural forms they inherited. It was not appropriate for Jews to insist Gentile Christians adopt a Jewish lifestyle. Thus it followed that it was not appropriate for Paul to insist Jewish Christians abandon their Jewish lifestyle on conversion!

Paul is totally consistent then in having Timothy circumcised as a testimony to the Jews that commitment to Jesus did not require apostasy from their dearly loved Jewish customs.

We were met by a slave girl who had a *spirit by which she predicted the future*. She earned a great deal of money for her owners by fortune-telling (16:16). The Greek says she had a *pneuma pythona*, a "Pythian spirit." In Greek mythology the Python was a serpent/dragon that guarded the oracle of Apollo. The phrase Paul uses came to mean a demon-possessed person who served as the mouthpiece of the Python.

Paul's exorcism of the spirit destroyed the

slave's value to her owners, and led to a riot and Paul and Silas' imprisonment. The incident also illustrates a theme mentioned earlier in the Exposition. The "editorial" below might have appeared in any first-century newspaper, and helps us sense one aspect of the disruptive impact the spread of the Gospel had within the Roman Empire.

"HOLY SPIRIT" THREATENS EMPIRE-WIDE INDUSTRY

Reports from all over the Roman Empire indicate that a major industry, with sales in the many millions of dollars, may be threatened by a new Eastern religion.

■ In Samaria, the magician Simon is stunned by the ability of Christians to work real miracles. When Simon offers to pay for the "Holy Spirit" who gives this power, he is threatened by the Christian leader, Peter (Acts 8:9-25).

■ On Cyprus, the sorcerer Elymas tries to oppose a Christian named Paul—and is blinded by this man who calls himself an apostle (Acts 13:4-12).

■ In Philippi this same man, Paul, casts an evil spirit out of a slave girl used by her master to tell fortunes. "How can we make any more money off her?" the unhappy owners complained. When Paul is thrown into prison, an earthquake opens the cells and frees him. "Paul uses this 'Holy Spirit' magic," the owners say. "So why isn't it OK for us to make money off demons?" (Acts 16:16-40)

■ In Ephesus seven Jewish exorcists are beaten by a demon-possessed man they are paid to treat. They try using the name "Jesus" as a magic formula, but the demon, who claimed to know Jesus and Paul, beat them up anyway (Acts 19:13-16).

■ In Ephesus Paul influences the population to destroy $5 million worth of books on magic (Acts 19:17-20).

■ Still in Ephesus, Paul ruins the business of people who make and sell images of the goddess Artemis. Demetrius, head of one of the local unions, stirs up a riot among concerned businessmen. "We've got to stop this movement," Demetrius claims, "or we'll all be unemployed."

The concern expressed by the victims of this Christian missionary are real. Every day our citizens spend over $80 million on the occult. They visit fortune-tellers. They buy charms and amulets. They hire magicians to cure diseases or curse enemies. Why, our whole travel industry is based on people visiting cities like Ephesus where there are famous temples or shrines.

Simply put, the Empire can't afford to put up with people like Paul, who preach against witchcraft and idolatry. Our whole economy would crumble if these fanatics had their way.

Some may argue that Paul's message is true, and that the power of this "Holy Spirit" and "Jesus" is greater than the power of the spirits we depend on. That may be. But the bottom line is, we don't dare become Christians. Too many people make a living from the occult. It's an industry the Empire simply has to support.

These men are Jews, **and are throwing our city into an uproar (16:20).** This charge by the owners of the slave girl Paul healed reflects an incipient anti-Semitism which characterized most cities with Jewish populations. It is significant that the Jews in Philippi could not even muster the ten men required to establish a synagogue (16:13), and yet even here a strong anti-Jewish bias is revealed. Emil Shurer's *History of the Jewish People in the Age of Jesus Christ* (Vol. III.1, p. 132) points out that it is

quite consistent with the overall historical framework, that the Jews were persecuted by the cities, while the higher authority of the Roman *imperium* took them under its protection. Hatred against the Jews repeatedly broke out in the cities, and of course especially where the Jews had the most marked communal rights, as in Alexandria, Antioch, many cities in Asia Minor, and even in Caesarea in Palestine, where pagans and Jews had received equality of rights from Herod the Great. The central complaint was precisely that the Jews refused to worship the gods of the city. But it was always the Roman supreme authority which protected the religious freedom of the Jews.

History records many specific incidents which illustrate the antagonism of the general population to the Jews, which attitude is reflected in this verse. And history makes it equally clear that, very soon, a similar antagonism would be directed against Christians.

The reason was the same—refusal to worship the community's gods, and thus a significant withdrawal from community life. But as soon as it became clear that Christianity was not a Jewish sect, the protection of the state was withdrawn from followers of our Lord.

Believe in the Lord Jesus, and you will be saved—*you and your household* (16:31). One theological tradition sees in this phrase a unique covenant commitment. Those in this tradition see in Paul's words God's own promise to save the children of believers.

This doctrine of "household salvation" does not imply that a person can be saved by his or her parents' faith. Rather, it suggests that God will graciously grant the gift of faith to the children of those who believe and that the child will make a personal commitment to the Lord at some time during his or her life.

While we cannot doubt the grace God displays toward believers in dealing with our

---

PLINY'S CORRESPONDENCE WITH TRAJAN CONCERNING CHRISTIANS (A.D. 111–112)

Pliny requests guidance from Trajan:
I have never been present at an examination of Christians. Consequently, I do not know the nature or the extent of the punishments usually meted out to them, nor the grounds for starting an investigation and how far it should be pressed. Nor am I at all sure whether any distinction should be made between them on the grounds of age, or if young people and adults should be treated alike; whether a pardon ought to be granted to anyone retracting his beliefs, or if he has once professed Christianity, he shall gain nothing by renouncing it; and whether it is the mere name of Christian which is punishable, even if innocent of crime, or the crimes associated with the name.

Later, Pliny wrote again to report Christian rites were harmless:
They declared that the sum total of their guilt or error amounted to no more than this: they had met regularly before dawn on a fixed day to chant verses alternately among themselves in honor of Christ as if to a god, and also to bind themselves by oath, not for any criminal purpose, but to abstain from theft, robbery, and adultery, to commit no breach of trust and not to deny a deposit when called upon to restore it. After this ceremony it had been their custom to disperse and reassemble later to take food of an ordinary harmless kind.

Trajan replied in a letter preserved in a collection of Pliny's correspondence:
You have followed the right course of procedure, my dear Pliny, in your examination of the cases of persons charged with being Christians, for it is impossible to lay down a general rule to a fixed formula. These people must not be hunted out; if they are brought before you and the charge against them is proved, they must be punished, but in the case of anyone who denies that he is a Christian, and makes it clear that he is not by offering prayers to our gods, he is to be pardoned as a result of his repentance however suspect his past conduct may be. But the pamphlets circulated anonymously must play no part in any accusation. They create the worst sort of precedent and are quite out of keeping with the spirit of our age.

And so the principle was established: Christians were condemned simply for their faith. Later, under less civil rulers, the state did actively seek out the followers of Christ.

children, this verse imports a meaning to "household" that is foreign to the first century, and almost surely not intended here by Luke. That meaning *is* explored in the Passage In Depth of Acts 16:31, which follows.

They beat us publicly without a trial, even though we are *Roman citizens* (16:37). In *Studies in Roman Government and Law* (Praeger, p. 54), A.H.M. Jones notes that even Roman provincial governors were forbidden "to kill, scourge, torture, condemn or put in bonds a Roman citizen who appealed to the people, or to prevent a defendant from presenting himself in Rome." As a citizen Paul had rights which the magistrates had violated in responding hastily to the shouts of the crowd. This was a serious offense, a fact reflected in the city officials' "alarm" and their eagerness to "appease" Paul and Silas (15:38-39).

Christians do have a dual citizenship. We owe total allegiance to heaven. Yet even as we live by the laws of our earthly nation, so we can claim all the rights granted us here as well.

They are all defying Caesar's decrees, saying that there is another king, one called Jesus (17:7). It is interesting to note the variety of charges made to various city magistrates as reported in these chapters. In Philippi Paul and Silas were accused of being Jews "throwing our city into an uproar" and of advocating unlawful customs (16:20-21). In Thessalonica the Jews falsely accused Paul and Silas of defying Caesar's decrees and, in essence, asserting the sovereignty of a competing authority, Jesus.

Later, in Corinth, another group of Jews accused Paul of "persuading the people [*ho laos,* i.e., the Jewish people in distinction to Gentiles] to worship God in ways contrary to the law" (18:13). Later, in Ephesus, the implicit charge was they had "discredited" the goddess Artemis (19:27). Despite the angry shouting of the mob the charge was rejected, for "these men . . . have neither robbed temples nor blasphemed our goddess" (19:37).

These incidents further demonstrate the social disruption created in the Roman Empire by the preaching of the Gospel. They also reveal something of the frustration of both Christianity's enemies and government authorities. What valid legal charge could be laid

against the missionaries? And what basis in law could governors find to pronounce judgment?

Ultimately a solution was found, illustrated in the correspondence by a provincial governor name Pliny and the Emperor Trajan (see box below). Christianity simply was not a *licit* (legally sanctioned) religion. Thus, although Christians were guilty of no crimes *per se,* they were guilty of practicing a *superstition* — a foreign cult. This alone was a violation of Roman law, and sufficient basis to condemn Christians to death.

A group of Epicurean and Stoic philosophers began to dispute with [Paul] (17:18). These two major schools of philosophy, despite their differences, represented the best pagan culture could produce in terms of understanding man's place in the world. Stoics placed great confidence in rationality, self-reliance, and in moral duty. God infused all that exists, and thus the Stoics stressed living in harmony with nature.

The Epicureans believed that any gods which might exist had no interest in human affairs. While often misunderstood as hedonists, the true Epicurean held that *ataraxia,* a life of tranquility from pain, disruptive passions, and superstitious fears, was the ultimate in pleasure.

Despite their differences, adherents of the two groups both assumed the eternality of matter, denied the possibility of a personal God who intervenes in human affairs, and found the notions of future judgment and resurrection utterly ridiculous. The most basic assumptions of paganism and Christianity were in utter conflict, in the same way that the basic assumptions of Christianity and contemporary evolutionary theory are in conflict.

Paul then stood up in the meeting of the Areopagus and said . . . (17:22). Paul's sermon to the men of Athens has been analyzed again and again. What is perhaps important to us is to note Paul's effort to find some starting point from which to argue his case. As noted above, the basic assumptions — the worldview — of Christian and pagan were diametrically opposed. Yet even pagan thought has some insight into the true nature of the God the Athenian's own altar demonstrates they do not know (17:23). Here Paul quotes from pagan poets, not as authority for what he is about to say, but simply to illustrate that even pagan poets had realized God cannot be represented by material images. It is thus the true, immaterial God the pagans glimpse only dimly that Paul presents.

THE CONTEXT OF PAUL'S QUOTES

They fashioned a tomb for thee,
O holy and high one—
The Cretins, always liars,
evil beasts, idle bellies!—
But thou art not dead;
thou livest and abidest for ever,
For in thee we live and move
and have our being.
　　　Epimenides the Cretan, 600 B.C.

Let us begin with Zeus. Never, O men,

let us leave him unmentioned. All the ways
are full of Zeus, and all the marketplaces
of human beings. The sea is full of him;
so are the harbors. In every way we have all
to do with Zeus, for we are truly his offspring.
　　　The Phainomena
　　　Aratus, 310 B.C.

Did you receive the Holy Spirit when you believed? (19:2) The context makes it clear that these men were disciples of John the Baptist. They accepted John as a precursor of the Messiah, but had not as yet heard about Jesus. For a discussion of reasons for the unusual expedient of laying on hands, see the Word Study of Acts 8:15.

THE PASSAGE IN DEPTH

Paul and Silas in Prison (Acts 16:16-40).
Background. Everything about this passage shouts its cultural context. Luke is writing about the Gospel's penetration of the Gentile world, and its every feature reflects this orientation. The slave girl has a Pythian spirit; the crowds charge Paul with "advocating customs unlawful for us Romans" (16:21); the jailer is intent on suicide when he finds the prison doors open, for in that society an individual charged with the care of criminals would suffer the punishment intended for them if they should escape. As the story concludes, Paul is released by chastened magistrates after asserting his Roman citizenship.

Everything in this passage signals that the missionaries are operating in pagan rather than a Jewish society. As a result, we are driven to interpret significant terms used in the account *as they would have been used and understood within that culture.*

Interpretation. This leads us to an assumption which must underlie our understanding of Paul's promise to the Philippian jailer, "Believe in the Lord Jesus, and you will be saved—you and your household" (16:31). To interpret our verse we cannot import a Jewish understanding of "household." We certainly cannot import the modern idea that a "household" is the nuclear family. In fact, we should

not even suppose that later Christian uses of "household" are defining. Instead we need to understand what the *jailer himself* as a first-century pagan would have understood when Paul used this word. Simply put, the Roman "house" included the *pater familias,* his wife, his children and their wives, household slaves, and even others who owed him some social obligation, such as clients or freed slaves.

When Paul spoke to the jailer of *su kai o oikos sou,* "you and your house," he undoubtedly was understood to include more than the man and his wife and children! In fact, Luke uses this "house" terminology in five different locations in Acts, each time in reference to a person of high enough social status to have household slaves and/or retainers: Cornelius (10:2; 11:14); Lydia (16:15); the jailer (16:31); and Crispus, the synagogue ruler (18:8).

Paul's use of *oikos* (house) is similar, as is seen by comparing 1 Cor. 1:16; 16:15; and Phile. 2. Especially significant is Paul's mention of "Caesar's *oikias*" in Phil. 4:22. The apostle clearly does not mean Caesar's relatives, but rather members of the Praetorian guard or others in the administration of the Empire whom Paul contacted while imprisoned.

With this meaning of "house" or "household" established, the verse in question clearly *cannot* be understood as a kind of covenant commitment made to believers that their children will come to personal faith. The most likely alternative is the simplest one. The promise that Paul made to the jailer is a promise that is made to every member of the jailer's household: each and every individual who believes will be saved. The Gospel makes one great promise to all humankind, and each individual must choose whether or not to respond to that invitation. Those who do respond, and do believe, will surely be saved.

Application. One other interpretation has been suggested for this verse. Some point out that in Roman culture the head of the house had great influence over every member, whether immediate family, slave, or client. And so some understand Paul's promise to imply that the key to the family's salvation is the head of the family's act of faith.

Perhaps in our emphasis on salvation as an individual choice we overlook the importance of reaching those who have great influence with others. But be this as it may, Paul's words here remind us of two great truths. The whole household of humanity *is* included in the promise God makes us in Jesus. And yet each of us must, as an individual, make a personal choice of faith.

Paul in Ephesus (19:1-22).

Background. These few verses are notable for their reference to the occult. We catch a glimpse of Jewish exorcists at work, and read of books of magic worth perhaps some $5 million being destroyed. Here too we read of "extraordinary miracles" (19:11) performed by Paul; miracles which are notable because of their unusual character.

It is striking that Ephesus, the site of a magnificent temple to Artemis which drew pilgrims from all over the Mediterranean world, was also a center of occult practice. What a testimony to the fact that first-century public religion fell desperately short of meeting the spiritual needs of the city's populace! Much literature exists that gives us insight into the nature of first-century occult practices. Reading it today, we can sense something of the desperation of those who, finding no comfort in either public religion or philosophy, turned to superstition.

Notice the light shed on an incident that Luke reports:

Some Jews who went around driving out evil spirits tried to invoke the name of the Lord Jesus over those who were demon-possessed. They would say, "In the name of Jesus, whom Paul preaches, I command you to come out." Seven sons of Sceva, a Jewish chief priest, were doing this. One day the evil spirit answered them, "Jesus I know and Paul I know about, but who are you?" Then the man who had the evil spirit jumped on them and overpowered them all. He gave them such a beating that they ran out of the house naked and bleeding (19:13-16).

While magic practices were condemned by the sages, magic not only was practiced by the Jews, but Jewish exorcists were highly regarded by their pagan neighbors. This was in large part because both pagan and Jewish magic assumed that the ability to name a supernatural being gave an individual some power over that being. The awe in which the Jews held the name Yahweh, never even pronouncing it, gave rise to the common view that Jewish exorcists commanded vast supernatural powers. Luke's report in Acts makes it clear that some assumed that Paul performed magical cures by calling on the name "Jesus," and so enterprising Jewish exorcists added His name to their incantations.

An early book of Jewish magic, the *Sefer ha-Rasim* (*Book of Mysteries*) gives us this list of names of angelic beings invoked in various incantations, on the assumption that these "angels of the fourth step" have "power to do good or ill": SGR'L, MLKY'L, 'WNBYB, PGRY'L, PRYBY'L, KLNMYY', 'WMY'L, MPNWR, KWZZYB', 'LPY'L, PRYBY'L, S'QMYH, KDWMY'L, 'SMD1, HWDYH, YHZY'L. The same book provides the following interesting instructions for cursing and releasing an enemy:

I hand over to you, angels of disquiet who stand upon the fourth step, the life, soul and spirit of N son of N so that you may fetter him with chains of iron and bind him with bars of bronze. Do not grant sleep to his eyelids, nor slumber, nor drowsiness. Let him weep and cry like a woman in travail and do not permit anyone to release him.

Write thus [on a lead strip] and put in

the mouth of the dog's head. Put wax on its mouth and seal it with a ring which has a lion engraved upon it. Then go and conceal it behind his house, or in the place where he goes in and out. If you wish to release him, bring up [the head] from the place where it is concealed, remove its seal, withdraw the text and throw it into a fire. At once he will fall asleep. Do this with humility and you will be successful.

Most exorcisms relied on such formulas and the repetition of words with little or no meaning. The effectiveness of the spell depended more on correctly pronouncing the words than on the humility or other character traits of the exorcist.

There is a striking similarity between both Jewish and pagan magic/exorcism and practices, even then many thousands of years old. For instance, this incantation from ancient Mesopotamia, performed while circling a home's entrances with parched flour, would not have seemed strange to Jews or Gentiles in Paul's Ephesus.

Be off, be off, begone, begone,
Depart, depart, flee, flee!
Go off, go away, be off, and begone!
May your wickedness like smoke rise ever
heavenward!
From my body be off!
From my body begone!
From my body depart!
From my body flee!
From my body go off!
From my body go away!
To my body turn back not!

To my body approach not!
To my body near not!
On my body be not!
By the life of Samas, the honorable, be
adjured!
By the life of Ea, lord of the deep, be
adjured!
By the life of Asalluhi, the magus of the
gods, be adjured!
By the life of Girra, your executioner, be
adjured!
From my body you shall indeed be separated!

How tragic, when human beings must turn in anguish to such humbug, desperate to find some relief from sickness, or poverty, or pain. Desperate for a hope that can only be found in knowing and trusting the Living God.

Interpretation and Application. Luke tells us that in Ephesus Paul performed "extraordinary miracles" (19:11). Why in Ephesus, this center of the occult? We can only see in Paul's miraculous healings a wondrous display of the grace of God. For these miracles, out of the ordinary even for apostolic works, served as testimony to the power of Jesus.

Some mistook the nature of that power and attempted to wed the Lord's name to occult practices. But others who had practiced sorcery understood. Here at last was what they had been seeking all the time: hope!

"Jesus is the answer!" we can almost hear them cry, as they bring their scrolls and books of magic formulae and burn them publicly.

What no occult source can tap, Jesus provides.

ACTS 20–28
Paul's Imprisonment

EXPOSITION

In these final chapters of Acts, Luke leaves his description of the impact of the Gospel on contemporary society, to trace what happened to the first century's great pioneer missionary, Paul. "Compelled by the Spirit" (20:22), Paul begins a painful journey to Jerusalem—a journey that will tear him away from the congregations he loves and place him in personal peril.

Paul's farewell to the Ephesian elders (20:13-38), the only message Acts records that is delivered to believers, powerfully portrays the heartache caused by that separation. On the way, prophetic warnings help prepare Paul for what lies ahead (21:1-17)—captivity and the threat of death.

In Jerusalem Paul is urged to demonstrate his solidarity with his people by undergoing ritual purification (21:17-26). But while he is worshiping, Jews of the diaspora recognize him, and shout that he is desecrating the temple. Only Roman intervention saves Paul in the riot that follows (21:27-36). Yet the crowd quiets and listens to Paul's story of his conversion—until the apostle reveals that God has sent him to the hated Gentiles (21:37–22:21). Taken into the Roman fortress that stood next to the temple, Paul avoids examination by torture by asserting his Roman citizenship (22:22-29). Still, the Roman commander feels a duty to find out exactly why Paul is being accused by the Jews, and arranges for a meeting of the Sanhedrin. There, Paul's claim that the real issue is the doctrine of resurrection creates havoc, as the Pharisees, who believe in resurrection, and the Sadducees, who deny its possibility, fall into a loud and angry argument (22:30–23:11).

When a plot to assassinate Paul is uncovered, the Roman commander sends him with a military escort to Caesarea, the seat of the Roman governor (23:12-35). After an indecisive trial before the Roman governor, Felix, Paul is kept under house arrest for some two years (24:1-27). When Felix is replaced by Festus, the Jews renew their attempt to have Paul condemned. Festus decides to send Paul to Jerusalem for a new trial, leading Paul to exercise his right as a Roman citizen to be tried in an imperial court in Rome (25:1-12). Before Paul can be sent on Festus asks King Agrippa, who rules Jewish lands and is familiar with the Jewish/Christian debate, for advice on how to frame any charges that might be lodged in Rome against the apostle. This gives Paul an opportunity to tell his story once again, and powerfully argue for the Gospel not only before the governor and the king, but also before "the high ranking officers and

311

the leading men of" Caesarea (25:23–26:32).

Finally, after over two years of imprisonment in Rome, Paul, with Luke as his companion, is sent off to Rome under guard. Luke's graphic portrayal of the shipwreck has been called the most revealing written report on first-century ships and sailing practices extant (27:1-44). Yet in Luke's telling of the story, what is important is an angel God sends to Paul, who calms his fears and tells him that he will yet make his defense before Caesar (27:13–28:11). The imprisonment, the dangers, the anguish of isolation from the churches Paul had planted, all are part of God's larger plan to bring the Gospel to every element of Empire society.

The Book of Acts closes suddenly. Paul in Rome invites the leaders of the Jewish community to hear his views on the Christian movement, this sect "people everywhere are talking against" (28:22). After a full day of teaching, some are convinced, but the majority reject the Gospel message. Luke closes his book with Paul's "final statement." As Isaiah said, God's OT people have closed their hearts and minds to the Lord. And so God's salvation has been sent to a people who *will* listen: the Gentiles (28:17-31).

In a sense this also sums up the purpose of this historical work of Luke. He has traced the origins of the Christian movement from the resurrection of Christ to the flourishing of an enthusiastic messianic Jewish community within Judaism. Luke has traced events on to the church's stunning discovery that the Gospel is for Gentiles as well as Jews, and to the decision of the Jerusalem council that Gentile Christians are to be accepted as brothers without being asked to abandon their own customs or culture. Luke has then gone on to give us a glimpse of the disruptive impact of the Christian message, now divorced from its Jewish roots, on the wider Roman world—an impact that would lead ultimately to official condemnation of the new faith and its adherents.

In this context the report of Paul's trials serves several purposes. The report follows up the confusion city officials experienced in dealing with charges made against Christians (16–19). It shows that, when examined by the highest provincial authorities, Paul was shown to be innocent of any crime. In this sense Acts is an *apologia*—a defense against later charges that Christianity is a criminal movement.

But even more, the Book of Acts as a whole is an affirmation of God's intent to fulfill His purpose in Christ. Whatever hostile peoples or governments may do, the church and the individual Christian will surely triumph.

WORD STUDIES

And now, *compelled* by the Spirit, I am going to Jerusalem, not knowing what will happen to me there (20:22).

The Greek word is *dedemenos,* the past perfect participle of *deo,* "to bind." The Holy Spirit has communicated God's will to the apostle, with the result that Paul has been and is now bound to go to Jerusalem.

Someone has said: Never doubt in the dark what you were shown in the light. Despite the pain of parting and the uncertainty that masks the future, the apostle remains firmly committed to doing God's will.

The Holy Spirit says, "In this way the Jews of Jerusalem will bind the owner of this belt and will hand him over to the Gentiles" (21:11). Many have speculated that this and other messages given Paul by prophets on the journey to Jerusalem were "warnings." These commentators have speculated that Paul's determination to go to Jerusalem was generated by some personal desire, mistakenly or deceitfully ascribed to the Holy Spirit. But is this a warning or a sign of God's grace?

In 20:22 (above) Paul confessed to being in

the dark about what would happen to him in Jerusalem. How terrible a burden uncertainty is for any of us. How frustrating it would have been for the apostle to experience the hostility of his people, not knowing whether the next moment might be his last. But then came a word of prophecy! Paul would face hostility. He would be bound. But he would survive to be handed over to Gentiles, and so ultimately fulfill his mission to that world.

A warning? No, a word of grace, and a reminder that even men of great faith, like Paul, need encouragement from the Lord. As do we all.

Take these men, join in their purification rites and pay their expenses. . . . Then everybody will know that there is no truth in these reports about you, but that you yourself are living in obedience to the law (21:24). If commentators have criticized Paul for going to Jerusalem despite the Holy Spirit's warnings, these same writers have tended to excoriate Paul for his "hypocrisy" in undergoing Jewish purification rites. They have ascribed the meanest of motives to the apostle, and at the very least have charged him with deceptive practices.

Actually, such charges are unwarranted. The fact is that when Paul visited Jerusalem times were tough. Many were even starving, and the nationalistic movement that within a decade or so would lead to the first Jewish revolt and destruction of the temple was already strong. Paul had come with a large gift for the Jerusalem believers contributed by the Gentile churches. Yet politically it was hardly expedient for the Christian community to accept the gift, and so identify themselves with the hated Gentiles!

And so the leaders of the church came up with a wise suggestion. Paul would undergo the purification rites expected of any Jewish pilgrim, and pay the expenses of four men completing a Nazarite vow—considered a pious act in Judaism. This would demonstrate Paul's solidarity with his own nation, and perhaps silence the false rumor that Paul called on his Jewish converts to deny their cultural identity. Then the church would accept the gift, and in this show solidarity with the worldwide church dominated by Gentiles.

The plan was acceptable to Paul, for the simple reason that *no compromise was involved.*

Paul never taught "all the Jews who live among the Gentiles to turn away from Moses, telling them not to circumcise their children or live according to [Jewish] customs" (21:21). What Paul did teach was that Gentile Christians must not deny their cultural heritage, and assume that by becoming "Jewish" they would be more pleasing to God. To Paul, one's culture was irrelevant, and commitment to God could and must be expressed within the framework provided by one's own society.

Paul himself was a man of two cultures. And so, since culture *is* irrelevant to relationship with God, Paul freely lived as Gentile among the Gentiles, and lived as a Jew among Jews. Without hesitation Paul accepted the suggestion, on a principle he himself had earlier laid down:

> To the Jews I became like a Jew, to win the Jews. To those under the law I became like one under the law (though I myself am not under the law), so as to win those under the law. To those not having the law I became like one not having the law (though I am not free from God's law, but am under Christ's law), so as to win those not having the law. . . . I do all this for the sake of the gospel, that I may share in its blessings (1 Cor. 9:20-23).

Let's be sure, when we criticize others, or when we limit our own freedom of action based on others' perceptions of right and wrong, that our reasoning is not as superficial as that of those critics who here condemned Paul.

The crowd listened to Paul until he said *this.* Then they raised their voices and shouted, "Rid the earth of him! He's not fit to live!" (22:23) The crowd listened quietly as Paul told of his conversion, and told of hearing the voice of Jesus. But when he spoke the word "Gentiles," they exploded in utter fury. We need no further evidence of the extreme nationalism prevalent in that day, or of the wisdom of the church leaders who asked Paul to demonstrate his respect for Jewish customs by undergoing ritual purification.

The commander went to Paul and *asked,* "Tell me, are you a Roman citizen?" (22:27) It is strange to us that the army officer should simply ask about Roman citizenship, and then accept the word of a person accused of fomenting a riot that he really was a citizen. But in the first century no one carried passports, voter registration, or ID cards. At that time citizenship was a rarity, and the *diploma civitatis Romanae* given individuals newly raised because of some service or high social standing was kept in the family archives, and the new citizen's name was recorded at Rome, and he was listed as a citizen on the local municipal registration. But Roman citizens neither carried identification when traveling nor wore distinctive clothing.

The fact is that in the first century, a mere verbal claim of citizenship *was* taken at face value. Perhaps the reason is not so hard to understand when we look into Roman law and discover that a person falsely claiming citizenship or falsifying documents could be condemned to death.

I stand on trial because of my hope in the resurrection of the dead (23:6). Here again Paul has been accused by commentators of deception and insincerity. Certainly if Paul's words had been a ploy, it was successful, as the seventy-one men seated on the court divided along party lines, with the Pharisees defending Paul and the Sadducees attacking him.

But while we do not want to gloss over the human failings of any of history's great men and women of faith, neither do we impute flaws they may not have had. As a general principle it is best to accept an interpretation which casts any action in a positive light, unless something in the text makes it clear that action was in fact wrong or wrongly motivated.

In this case, we need to realize that Paul spoke and thought of the resurrection within the framework provided by Christ's rising from the dead. In a very real sense, the whole Christian Gospel is about resurrection—His and ours. As Paul had written earlier to the Corinthians, "If Christ has not been raised, our preaching is useless and so is your faith," and "If Christ has not been raised, your faith is futile; you are still in your sins" (15:14, 17).

The validity of Paul's entire ministry, as well as his understanding of the OT and his hope for the future, hinged on the resurrection of Jesus.

Thus Paul's statement, "I stand on trial be-

cause of my hope in the resurrection of the dead," was utterly true, and in a distinctive way pinpointed the issue that then faced not only the Jewish people, but the entire Roman world.

The text tells us that "*when* he said this" (23:7) the Pharisees and Sadducees fell into violent argument, for the two parties differed theologically. Perhaps the tragedy here is that rather than deal with the real question Paul's affirmation posed—"Has Christ been raised, so that we do have hope?"—the Sanhedrin returned to its ancient and acrimonious theological debate.

How often we see this in our own attempts to witness. We pose the issue—Christ. And quickly the person we're speaking with changes the topic, to some safe theological issue which we can debate without the necessity which always exists in any confrontation with the Gospel. The necessity is not of debating, but of making a personal, decisive, life-shaping choice.

We have taken a solemn *oath* not to eat anything until we have killed Paul (23:14). Numbers 30:2 states, "When a man makes a vow to the Lord or takes an oath to obligate himself by a pledge, he must not break his word but must do everything he said." But don't suppose that the 40 men who pledged before the high priest to assassinate Paul starved!

The Reference Guide to the Steinsaltz edition of the *Talmud* (Random House, 1989) describes a *halakic* (interpretive and applicational) concept called *se'elat lehakam,* "a request [made] to a scholar." The reference guide explains, "If a person makes a vow or takes an oath, or consecrates property and afterwards regrets having done so, he may go to a scholar and request of him that he release him from his vow" (p. 259).

The Jerusalem Talmud (*Avod. Sar.40a*) illustrates this principle with the following, which bears a striking similarity to Luke's story: "If a man makes a vow to abstain from food, Woe to him if he eats, and, Woe to him if he does not eat! If he eats, he sins against his vow; if he does not eat, he sins against his life. What then must he do? Let him go before the sages, and they will absolve him from his vow."

There is little doubt that, no matter what

Numbers commands, the unsuccessful 40 assassins hurried to one of the rabbis after Paul was escorted to Caesarea, for release from their vow.

He wrote a letter as follows (23:25). The Greek text says *echousan ton tupon touton,* "having this pattern." Luke is not claiming to have seen a copy of the transmittal letter, but rather makes it clear that what he is reporting is the sense of such a letter.

I appeal to Caesar! (25:11) Roman citizens had a right of appeal to the emperor (*provocatio ad Caesarem*). During the first century this right could be exercised by Roman citizens living outside of Italy only when the case was *extra ordinem,* beyond the normal competence of a provincial governor, and particularly when the possibility of capital punishment existed.

Later this right, like citizenship itself, was widely extended.

Festus interrupted Paul's defense. "You are out of your mind, Paul," he shouted.

"Your great learning is driving you insane" (26:24). The notion of a resurrection was as foreign to the practical Roman, Festus, as it was to the Sadducees. Festus concluded that Paul's intense immersion in his traditions had driven him over the edge (*mainomai,* "mad"). In essence Festus' charge is that Paul is being totally unreasonable; he has immersed himself in a religion that makes no sense at all.

Paul's answer is that his words and position are both *aletheias kai sophrosynes* (26:25): both true and reasonable. The words mean "in harmony with reality" and "rational, sober." Everything Paul affirms can be proven to the satisfaction of those with a sound mind.

Publius, the *chief official of the island* (28:7). Latin inscriptions of the era tell us that in the first century the Roman governor of Malta was called "the first man of the island." Here, as everywhere else in Acts, the text bears evidence of the firsthand, accurate knowledge of places and events reported in this trustworthy historical document.

THE PASSAGE IN DEPTH

Earlier Luke has given us revealing pictures of the reaction in various cities of the Empire to the Gospel and its messengers. In these chapters that trace Paul's journey back to Jerusalem, his imprisonment in Caesarea, and his trip to Rome for trial, Luke introduces us to several fascinating first-century personalities. If Luke's portrayal of Ephesus, the temple city corrupted by the practice of the occult, reminds us of the need of society for a spiritual renewal, a little knowledge of the leading individuals Luke introduces reminds us of every human being's *personal* need for salvation and the forgiveness of sin.

The high priest Ananias (23:2). Ananias the son of Nedabaeus was high priest from A.D. 48 to 58 or 59. Although very rich, he was known for his greed, and did not hesitate to use violence and assassination to gain his ends. Josephus says that his servants went to the threshing floors and seized tithes that should have gone to ordinary priests. Interestingly, the Talmud (*Pesahim 57a*) contains a parody of Ps. 24:7 that ridicules Ananias for his greed:

"Lift up your heads, O ye gates; that Yohanan ben Narbai, the disciple of Pinqai [meat dish], may go in and fill his belly with the divine sacrifices."

Ananias like many of the wealthy was strongly pro-Roman. This with his avaricious and brutal character made him extremely unpopular with the people, who were increasingly nationalistic. When the rebellion against Rome broke out in A.D. 66, Ananias was dragged from a hiding place by the crowds and put to death.

We see Ananias in Acts 23, acting in character, violating the law he was charged with upholding by commanding Paul to be struck. Paul's response was prophetic if hasty: "God will strike you, you whitewashed wall! You sit there to judge me according to the law, yet you yourself violate the law by commanding that I be struck!"

Governor Felix (Acts 24). If we took the words of Tertullus, the professional orator employed by the Jewish leaders to press their case against Paul, we would conclude that Felix was a most admirable man. After all, according to Tertullus,

"We have enjoyed a long period of peace under you, and your foresight has brought about reforms in this nation. Everywhere and in every way, most excellent Felix, we acknowledge this with profound gratitude (24:2-3).

In fact, this flattery could hardly have strayed further from the truth. Antonias Felix was born a slave in the household of Antonia, the mother of the Emperor Claudius. Claudius appointed him governor of Judea in A.D. 48, although such a post was traditionally reserved for Romans of at least equestrian rank. According to Josephus his time in office was marred by a number of uprisings and insurrections. He put these down with utter brutality; the Roman historian Tacitus called him "a master of cruelty and lust who exercised the powers of a king with the spirit of a slave."

It is interesting that this cruel and grasping man married three wives, each of whom was a princess. The last of these was Drusilla, the youngest daughter of King Agrippa I, who deserted her husband for Felix.

Certainly the average Jew hearing Tertullus' words about this man noted for his ferocity and brutality would have been stunned. A period of peace? Reforms? A ruler who won the gratitude of the governed? Certainly not Felix, whose years in office from A.D. 52 to 59 revealed how terribly corrupt the unregenerate human heart can be. Felix's misuse of his authority makes it abundantly clear how greatly he needed the Gospel and the inner transformation promised by Christ to all who believe.

Drusilla (24:24). Drusilla was Felix's third wife, and as noted above, the daughter of Herod Agrippa I. As a teenager she married Azizus, the ruler of Emesa, and Azizus converted to Judaism in order to win her. But Drusilla's beauty attracted Felix, even as his viciousness seems to have fascinated her. So Drusilla deserted her husband and became the wife of the pagan Felix. In this she seems to have been motivated by a desire for social advancement and power, even as Felix was motivated by love.

The text tells us that initially both Felix and Drusilla sent for Paul and listened as he spoke of "righteousness, self-control and the judgment to come" (24:24). This message that spoke directly to the lifestyle of the pair must have proven especially unpalatable to Drusilla. While Felix talked with Paul "frequently" during the next two years (24:26-27), there is no mention of Drusilla hearing the apostle again.

What happened to Felix and Drusilla after the governor's recall to Rome by Nero? We do not know, for they simply disappear from history.

Festus (25:1-12). Nothing is known of Festus before he became governor of Judea in A.D. 59 or 60. He inherited a hostile and troubled land, with deep-seated problems exacerbated during Felix's harsh rule. The impression Luke gives us is of a person who is well meaning, but uncertain as he struggles to come to understand the difficult people of this land he now governs. History tells us little of the kind of ruler that Festus became, for he died in office in A.D. 62.

King Agrippa (25:13). The ruler's full name was Marcus Julius Agrippa II, and he was the great-grandson of Herod the Great. He was brought up in Rome, as his father had been, but was only 17 when his father died in A.D. 44 (see the Word Study of Acts 12:1). Six years later, after the death of an uncle, Agrippa was appointed king of Chalcis by the Emperor Claudius. In A.D. 53, his little kingdom was exchanged for larger lands north of Judea, and these holdings were further expanded in A.D. 56 by Nero. Although he ruled lands populated mainly by Jews, Agrippa struggled to prevent the Jewish rebellion of A.D. 66 that culminated in the destruction of Jerusalem and its temple. During the war Agrippa remained steadfastly on Rome's side, and after the rebellion was suppressed he was rewarded by Vespasian with the lands he had earlier governed, plus more new areas. History records no offspring for Agrippa. On Agrippa's death, the Herodian line disappeared.

Perhaps Acts 26:25-32 gives us history's most revealing portrait of Agrippa. Festus interrupts Paul's presentation of Christ with the cry, "You are out of your mind!" Paul responds, "Not at all. What I say is both true and reasonable." He then looks at Agrippa, and says, "The king is familiar with these things" (26:26). Then, with a brief phrase, Paul makes Agrippa the focus of every eye. "King Agrippa, do you believe the prophets? I know you do" (26:27).

We can almost feel the tension generated by this affirmation. Everyone turns to look at Agrippa; Festus incredulous, others perhaps shocked, waiting to see what the king will say. There is a pause as Agrippa struggles for a reply. He *does* believe the prophets. The Talmud (*b. Pesahim 88b*) indicates Agrippa's mother was deeply interested in the Jewish religion, and the Romans looked on Agrippa as their expert in that obscure faith. Even so, how can Agrippa admit to giving any credence at all to a doctrine the Roman governor has just labeled insane? And then Agrippa blurts out words that the KJV so terribly distorts: "Almost thou persuadest me to be a Christian" (26:27). The NIV says it clearly: "Do you think that in such a short time you can persuade me to be a Christian?"

The joke is a weak one, but it is enough. Paul, seeing Agrippa's choice, says, "Short time or long—I pray God that not only you but all who are listening to me today may become what I am." And then, lifting his hands and looking at his fetters, adds ironically "except for these chains." With Paul's remark the tension drains from the room, and the important men and women of the governor's retinue file out of the room.

On the way out Agrippa remarks to Festus, "This man could have been set free if he had not appealed to Caesar" (26:32).

In fact, both Agrippa and Festus knew full well that the governor had authority to free Paul *after* the appeal. The authority he lacked was to condemn him. But in the remark Agrippa gave tacit approval to a politically wise course. There was no gain to Festus in freeing Paul, and so at the very beginning of his rule, alienating the population he would have to govern. Send Paul off to Rome! There he would no longer be a problem Festus had to deal with. And there, Paul would no longer challenge Agrippa to make a decision that the king wanted desperately to put off.

How great was Agrippa's need. From Paul's remarks we can conclude that he knew the claims of Christ were both "true and reasonable." Yet Agrippa considered the approval of Festus more important than the approval of God. Though a ruler, he was a weak man

unwilling to stand for the truth, and because of his weakness, eager to be rid of the man who had exposed his shortcomings to himself, and to the world.

Bernice (25:23). Today we would call Bernice Veronica, her name in Latin. In the first century she was called many things.

Bernice was the sister of Agrippa, just a year younger than the king. She had been married to her uncle Herod of Chalsis, but when he died came to live with her brother. Both the Roman writer Juvenal and the Jewish writer Josephus report persistent rumors that Bernice and Agrippa had an incestuous relationship. Apparently her brief marriage to King Polemo of Cilicia in A.D. 63 was an attempt to silence the rumors. But within three years she had returned to her brother. After the Roman war Bernice became the mistress of Titus, the army commander who later became emperor. She followed Titus to Rome in A.D. 75, but public opinion forced the two to break off their open affair, and Bernice was forced to leave the city. She hurried to Rome when Titus became emperor in A.D. 79, but again Titus was forced to ignore her. After this Bernice returned again to Palestine.

The nomadic life of Bernice suggests a search for a fulfillment that she never was able to find. It was not only the average man of the first century who lived a life of "quiet desperation." Strip away the palaces and the jewels, the pomp and fine clothes, and we realize that history's beautiful people are as frail and empty as the rest. They search among the world's treasures, but cannot find anything that will give their lives meaning, or give themselves a value divorced from material possessions. Bernice reminds us how desperately *every* human being needs to look beyond what the world has to offer, to find true fulfillment in a personal relationship with God.

Summary. It would be wrong to suggest that there were not sensitive and good men and women in the first century. The correspondence between Pliny and Trajan (see Word Study of Acts 17:7) suggests that in many people, a moderate and even admirable humanistic disposition characterized at least some of the powerful in the pagan world. Yet even "good" men and women fall far short of God's righteousness, just as much as the wicked need a Savior.

EXPOSITION

The Book of Romans has rightly been called Christianity's greatest theological treatise. Paul, presented in Acts as the prototype missionary, is here revealed as a premier theologian as well.

This second role was thrust upon the great apostle. As the Gospel spread, the make-up of the church rapidly changed from a predominantly Jewish fellowship to one that was predominantly Gentile. With that change serious questions were raised. How could the God who chose the Jews now welcome pagan Gentiles? How could He who revealed His Law through Moses build a community where that Law no longer served the foundation of community life? Didn't God's supposed offer of a "by faith" salvation to those outside of His ancient covenant with Israel imply inconsistency at best, and at worst a denial of His own Word? Forced to debate questions like this on his missionary journeys, Paul drew on his mastery of the OT and Holy Spirit guided insight into God's unfolding purpose, and provided Christianity's definitive answer.

In its simplest form the answer is this: Human beings must be righteous to fellowship with the holy God. But neither Jew nor Gentile is righteous. And so God acted in Christ to provide righteousness as a gift, which both must receive by faith.

While the answer is simple, it has multiplied implications. Paul sets out in Romans to spell out the impact of this "by faith" righteousness for the new faith-community. Paul's development of these implications is traced in the outline on page 319. The first three chapters of Romans launch Paul's argument and establish a critical point. Both Jew and Gentile lack righteousness, and so are objects of God's wrath.

Romans opens with personal greetings from Paul, an apostle of Jesus the Son of God, to the saints in Rome (1:1-17). After expressing his desire to meet the believers in this city he has never visited, Paul states his theme: God in the Gospel has revealed a righteousness that is "from God"; a righteousness that is "by faith" through and through (1:16-17). He immediately launches into his argument. Mankind's corruption demonstrates both its lack of righteousness and the wrath of God (1:18-32). This is true of Gentile (2:1-16) and Jew (2:17-29) alike; a reality established by Scripture's clear affirmation that "there is no one righteous, not even one" (3:1-18). Whether the moral light one has is derived from that which God planted in human nature, or which He revealed in Moses' Law, is irrelevant. Any law, natural or revealed, establishes standards which men may agree with, but which no human being lives by! Thus all any standard of righteousness can do is condemn the one who affirms it, and make that person conscious of sin and aware that he or she will be held accountable by God (3:19-20).

The conclusion "all have sinned" is much like the black velvet on which a magnificent diamond is laid so that its full splendor might be more fully appreciated. Against the dark menace of mankind's impotence Paul displays the jeweled centerpiece of God's grace. Yes, in Jesus Christ, God revealed His wrath against sin. Yet in stunning contradiction, the flame of wrath against sin that burned so bright at Calvary transformed that very act of judgment. Jesus, the Son of God, rose triumphant from the ashes, to become the channel through which God's grace and redemption flow to all who look to Him in simple faith (3:21-31). In Christ the bad news becomes the Gospel; the charge that all have sinned is transformed into a message of hope. For only those who acknowledge sin and abandon every effort to justify themselves will look to Jesus as their sole hope, and find in Him the gift of righteousness God freely gives to all willing to believe.

WORD STUDIES

Romans

Revealing Righteousness from God

I. Introduction (1:1-17)
  A. Salutation (1:7)
  B. Personal items (1:8-13)
  C. Theme (1:14-17)

II. Deliverance: Righteous Standing a Gift (1:18–5:21)
  A. Universal need of righteousness (1:18–3:21)
    1. Guilt of the Gentiles (1:18-32)
    2. Guilt of the Jews (2:1–3:8)
    3. Proof of universal guilt (3:9-20)
  B. Provision of righteousness (3:21-26)
  C. Harmonization: Justification and the Law (3:27-31)
  D. Illustration: Justification in the Old Testament (4:1-25)
    1. Abraham, David, and justification (4:1-8)
    2. Circumcision and justification (4:9-12)
    3. Inheritance and justification (4:13-17)
    4. Faith and justification (4:18-25)
  E. Exaltation: The certainty of justification (5:1-11)
  F. Summation: The universality of justification (5:12-21)

III. Victory: Righteous Living a Possibility (6–8)
  A. The basis for victory: Union with Christ (6:1-14)
  B. The principle: Enslaved to righteousness (6:15-23)
  C. The relationship: Freed from the Law (7:1-25)
    1. Law and the believer (7:1-6)
    2. Law and sin (7:7-12)
    3. Indwelling sin and the believer (7:13-25)
  D. The power: The Spirit within (8:1-17)
  E. The end: Glorification (8:18-39)

IV. History: Righteous Dealings a Certainty (9–11)
  A. Israel's present rejection is just (9:1-33)
  B. Israel's present rejection explained (10:1-21)
  C. Rejection not complete (11:1-36)
    1. It is not total (11:1-10)
    2. It is not final (11:11-36)

V. Community: A Righteous Reality (12–16)
  A. Christ's impact (12–13)
    1. In the community (12:1-21)
    2. In society (13:1-14)
  B. Christ's attitude incarnated (14:1–15:13)
    1. Uncondemning (14:1-13)
    2. Self-sacrificing (14:13–15:4)
    3. Purposive (15:5-13)
  C. Paul's farewells (15:14–16:27)

Romans. The book takes its name from the city to which it was sent. Earlier Rome had a large community of Jews; in the era of Augustus some 40,000, or 5 percent of the population, was Jewish. Suetonius reports that in the reign of Claudius riots broke out among the Jews at the "instigation" of a certain "Chrestus." Scholars debate whether this took place in A.D. 41, 46, or 49, but most see the likely cause of the riots as a dispute in the Jewish community between traditionalists and followers of Christ.

As a result of the riots, the emperor exiled a number of leaders from both groups (probably including Aquila and Priscilla: Acts 18:2; Rom. 16:3), and closed the synagogues. This undoubtedly stimulated a sharp break between the Roman church and the Jewish community. Yet when Claudius died in A.D. 54, the Jewish exiles were allowed to return. Thus when Paul wrote his letter to the Romans, probably in A.D. 57, many of the Jewish and Christian exiles had drifted back to resettle in the capital of the Empire.

It would hardly be surprising, even though the Christian house churches and the Jewish community were now sharply distinguished, if questions raised in the old debate continued to plague both Jewish and Gentile Christians. And to answer those questions there was no one more qualified than Paul, the Pharisee who was also a Roman citizen; the man of two cultures who thoroughly understood both Jewish and Gentile worlds.

Paul, a *servant* of Christ Jesus (1:1). The Greek word here for servant is *doulos,* "slave." In Hellenistic culture it was considered shameful to be a slave. Yet Paul is intent on making his identity clear. He is a slave to Christ, bound to do Jesus' will rather than his own. It was Jesus who summoned him to apostleship, and set him apart (*aphorismenos:* consecrated, commissioned) for the Gospel. Paul writes as Christ's representative, to serve Jesus' purposes rather than any purpose of his own.

How special it is to say "I am a *doulos* of Christ Jesus," to know that His will is more important to me than my own. There will never be another Apostle Paul. But the humblest Christian can affirm with Paul, "I am Jesus' *doulos.*" You can say it, and so can I. As long as we mean it and live it.

Jesus Christ our Lord (1:3-4). Paul has established his own identity. Now he establishes the identity of the One whose *doulos* he is. Jesus is demonstrably human through His descent from David. He is demonstrably God, "declared with power" (1:4) to be the Son of God by His resurrection. The phrase reads *"oristhentos uiou theou en dunamei."* The first word here is best understood as "officially designated." While the oldest son of a human king is in fact his heir, in nearly every society there is a ceremony at which he is officially designated as his father's successor. Jesus did not *become* God's Son by virtue of the resurrection. Instead that act of unimagined power was the public and official announcement by God of the position that Jesus always held by virtue of His eternal Sonship.

Let's not take this Book of Romans as the theologizing of a mere human being. Paul speaks as the apostle, the messenger, of Jesus the Son of God. Romans, with the rest of the NT, is the authoritative Word of God.

To all in Rome who are loved by God and *called to be saints* (1:7). The phrase is *kletois hagiois,* and is better rendered "called saints." We know the identity of Paul and the identity of Jesus. Who are the recipients of this letter? Paul says they are God's "called saints" — those who are saints by virtue of having been called.

The word "saints" has deep OT roots in a term that has the sense of "set apart for God's sole use." Just as the objects used in temple worship were not to be diverted to common or unclean use, so God has set those He calls in the Gospel apart for Himself and for His service.

That is, that you and I may be *mutually encouraged* by each other's faith (1:12). Paul is eager to minister to these believers in Rome (1:11). But his enthusiasm almost runs away with him. He has much to contribute, but he has almost implicitly denied a truth he will develop later. Christians are *interdependent.* How blessed the congregation where the pastor is as sensitive as the Apostle Paul to spiritual leadership's greatest danger: a pride that assumes that he or she instructs but need not learn from others, listens but never shares, advises congregants but never seeks their counsel.

I am not *ashamed* of the Gospel (1:16). "Shame" (*epaischunomai*) in the NT is the disgrace that comes to a person whom events show has put his confidence in an empty or worthless thing. Paul is convinced that his confidence in Christ is not misplaced, and has staked his entire life on the Gospel's trustworthiness.

Perhaps more important, if we too live and act as God's "called saints" in the conviction that Christ is real, God will have no cause to be ashamed of us!

I am not ashamed of the Gospel, because it is the *power of God for the salvation* of everyone who believes (1:16). Power is *dunamis*. This is not, as some would have it, the explosive force (dynamite) of God, but rather the unquenchable energy that enables Him to transform human beings from within.

The concept underlying "salvation" keeps our focus on the internal. In the OT "salvation" is primarily deliverance from foreign enemies; in the NT it is primarily deliverance from the corrupting power and dread eternal consequences of sin. Here Paul perhaps expects his readers to think also of the everyday use of the word in the first century, where *soteria* meant "health, safety, preservation." The Gospel is the power of God — power that flows to all who believe, to deliver us from every ruinous consequence of our sin and make us spiritually healthy at long last.

For in the Gospel a righteousness from God is revealed, a righteousness that is by faith from first to last, just as it is written, *"The righteous will live by faith"* (1:17; Hab. 2:4). See the article below for a discussion of the nature of righteousness. Here in this theme statement it is important to note that Paul goes back to the OT to establish the essential link between righteousness and faith.

Many in the Jewish community would understand this verse from Habakkuk to teach that the righteous man would live by his faith(fullness) to the Law of Moses. Paul, however, is about to demonstrate that what the OT verse really means, and the OT consistently teaches: the righteous man is one who lives by his *trust* in God.

RIGHTEOUSNESS

The Hebrew words translated "righteous" and "righteousness" are constructed on the root *SDQ*. Each of these words reflects the conviction that people are *righteous* when their actions are in accord with an established standard, and presuppose that standard is the will of God as revealed in His Law. Yet in praising the Lord as a "righteous God" (Ps. 4:1; Isa. 45:21) whose acts are "always righteous" (Jer. 12:1; Ps. 71:24), the OT makes it clear that beyond this, absolute righteousness belongs only to God. Thus God Himself is the standard man must match, for God's will expresses His essential character.

The OT identifies two special ways that God displays His righteousness in His relationship with human beings. God hates wickedness, and His character required He create a moral universe and accept the role of its Judge. Thus the OT says, "He will judge the world in righteousness" (Pss. 9:8; 96:13). Yet the OT also identifies God's role as Savior as another expression of His righteousness (Ps. 31:1; Isa. 45:21). This thought, that God's righteousness is expressed in these two seemingly contradictory ways, is basic to Paul's argument in Romans.

Yet the OT speaks also of the "righteous" man. It is easy to compare man with man, and say one is "more righteous" than another (1 Sam. 24:17). But if God Himself is the true measure of righteousness, how can a human being be considered righteous in comparison to Him? Paul will argue that this is impossible. While in a limited sense the individual who lives in conformity to Moses' Law is "righteous" *by that standard* (Deut. 6:25), such human righteousness does not merit God's favor (Deut. 9:4-6). Only that personal, trusting response to God's revelation of Himself that both Testaments know as "faith" can bring any human being a righteous standing before God (Gen. 15:6).

What Paul is about to explain in Romans is that the imputed righteousness of which the Old Testament speaks is now available to all humankind through faith in Jesus Christ. That righteousness owes nothing to the Law (Rom. 3–4), but instead is offered to sinners on the basis of Christ's substitutionary death, and is received by faith alone (4–5). Yet imputing to human beings a righteousness that we do not by nature have is no mere cosmic bookkeeping entry. The God who imputes righteousness to the believer enters the believer's life! United to Jesus by a work of the Holy Spirit and empowered by that same Spirit, the Christian who lives by faith rather than law is actually enabled to live a truly righteous life! (chaps. 6–8) Ultimately, in the resurrection, God's transformation will be complete and every taint of sin will be removed. In that glorious day and throughout eternity "we shall be like Him [Jesus], for we shall see Him as He is" (1 John 3:2).

And so in the Gospel we discover the stunning extent of the eternal plan of our righteous God. He has stooped in Christ to lift up fallen humanity, not just from the morass of sin into which we have plunged, but up and up until, cleansed and transformed, we will fully share His moral character.

Thus in this letter any reference by Paul to the believer's "righteousness" will have one of these emphases. There is an *imputed righteousness,* credited to our account on the basis of Christ's work so that we are pronounced innocent in God's heavenly court. There is an *active righteousness,* based on our link with the risen Lord, that infuses our present life as we remain open to the Holy Spirit, and enables us to live truly good lives here and now. And there is a *promised righteousness,* an eternity won for us by Jesus during which we will at last be like our righteous Lord.

Since what may be known about God *is plain to them,* because God has made *it plain* to them (1:19). The root in each case is *phaner,* as a verb a distinctive Christian term affirming revelation. As an adjective it describes its subject as "visible, clear, plainly seen, evident." This verse affirms more than might appear. All mankind has been given a revelation of God in and through His Creation. Even more, God has shaped humanity so that this revelation is understood! The universe is God's transmitter (1:20), and humanity was created with built-in radios, pre-tuned to its wavelength. Yet we willfully turned down the volume, suppressing God's message and pretending not to recognize Him in His handiwork. Paul rightly concludes that "men are without excuse" (1:20).

In the same way the men also abandoned *natural relations* with women and were inflamed with lust for one another (1:27). Neither OT nor NT know homosexuality as

an "alternate lifestyle." In every biblical text the gay way is unnatural, "indecent," and a "perversion" of God's will.

***You,* therefore, have no excuse, you who pass judgment on someone else (2:1).** The Greek is a vocative, *ho anthrope.* It immediately tells us that Paul uses a diatribe style in Romans: he pauses to address a representative listener. This listener has set himself aside from the rest of humankind, and mocks the foolishness of those Paul describes in 1:18-32.

But Paul closed his argument there with a list of vices broad enough to include everyone — including the scrupulous Pharisees! One might scoff at idolatry and reject homosexuality and yet be in the grip of greed, deceit, malice, faithlessness, or arrogance. And how easy it is for the best of us to stoop to gossip, slander, or boastfulness. The fact is that Paul's description of the ways of fallen man is broad enough to include all. How then can we judge; we who "do the same things"?

To those who by persistence in doing good . . . He will give eternal life (2:7). Paul here is not teaching salvation by works. Instead he contrasts two approaches to religion: one that seeks God's glory and honor by persistently doing what is good, and the other that is essentially selfish, and so quickly slips away from truth into wickedness. Strikingly, Gentile as well as Jew would understand the broad framework Paul intentionally lays out here. The Jew might claim sole possession of the Law, but could not claim exclusive possession of the *attitude toward religion* that Paul is describing! Later Paul will make it clear that only the person who lives in faith's utter dependence on the Lord is capable of the life of persistent goodness that true religion demands.

Indeed, when Gentiles, who do not have the law, *do by nature things required by the law,* they are a law for themselves (2:14). The Jew claimed that possession of Moses' Law gave them a spiritual advantage over Gentiles. Here Paul points out that God gave all human beings a moral nature, and that all have standards of right and wrong. While specific rules may differ, the same kinds of things are viewed as moral issues in every society. While what is considered sexually illicit varies, no society assumes a man may have any women he wants at any time. While rules vary, every society identifies some areas in which persons have personal rights and social responsibilities. Thus the fact that Gentiles "by nature" act in accord with standards established in the very areas regulated by Moses proves that non-Jews have *not* been left without law!

Paul then goes on to observe that this is not an advantage at all. Why? No person in any society has ever lived in full accord with his own standards! What natural law, like Moses' Law, does is make human beings vulnerable to judgment! (2:12) Because conscience requires a person to live by the standards he or she accepts, and condemns when he or she falls short, laws witness to every human being's failure to live that life of persistent doing of good which alone can please God.

If you are convinced that you are a *guide for the blind,* a light for those who are in the dark (2:19). The basis for Jewish religious pride lay in the conviction that they were chosen by God to receive His Law. This made the Jew superior to all other peoples—a conviction that in the end Paul shows stimulated a pride and boasting that was ridiculous in view of (1) the fact that Gentiles too have light (see 2:14 above), (2) the fact that Jews broke their law even as Gentiles violated their standards (2:21-24), and (3) the fact that law is given to be kept, not to be "possessed."

We can find modern examples of the attitude of well-meant but definite superiority that Paul critiques. In his *Studies in Jewish Law, Custom and Folklore* (KTAV Publishing, 1970), Jacob Z. Lauterbach writes:

> Thus, the very doctrine of the selection of Israel (by God), far from making the Jew particularistic and unfriendly to other people, has made him universalistic, broadminded, tolerant, and friendly towards all other people. For, if he is to help in the education of the younger children of his Father in heaven, he can do so successfully only by loving kindness and sympathetic understanding of the younger children and not by an overbearing and unfriendly attitude. For "an impatient and ill-tempered person cannot be a successful teacher."
> And the relation of Israel to the other

nations, according to this very doctrine of the selection of Israel, is precisely the relation of teacher and pupil. There can be no enmity or ill-will on the part of a teacher to his pupil, especially when the teacher undertakes to teach voluntarily and without compensation. Naturally, even such a teacher may occasionally get a little impatient with his pupils. He may, at times, be provoked to anger and righteous indignation by the indifference and lack of appreciation manifested by some pupils or the misbehavior and bad conduct of others. . . . Yet he does not abandon his task. He knows well that he himself has attained to the position of teacher only by receiving the precious doctrine his great teachers gave to him and by assiduously training himself to follow the instructions and carrying out the commandments of his Master (pp. 166–67).

How difficult to convince a people so confident that possession of the Law made them humanity's teacher that they, like the rest of humankind, were in fact sinners who needed to turn from reliance on the Law to simple faith in Jesus in order to be saved!

A man is not a Jew if he is only one *outwardly,* nor is circumcision merely outward and physical (2:28). The Greek word means "visibly," and helps sum up Paul's critique of the religion in which he was trained. It placed too much stress on appearances, on the external, the ritual, the physical. Ultimately what makes a true Jew is a matter of the heart, not the flesh, and cannot be measured as the observant Jews measured piety.

What does all this mean? Simply that the Jew, like the pagan, rejected the light God gave him. Rather than deteriorate into licentiousness and open sin, Judaism deteriorated into pride and superficiality. The conclusion is that both Gentile and Jew lack that righteousness that God's own righteousness demands that He require.

What advantage, then, is there *in being a Jew?* (3:1) The Greek is *to perisson tou Ioudaiou,* literally "the advantage of the Jew." This issue is racial rather than individual. Paul's answer is "Much in every way!" for the Jew was entrusted with the *logia* of God. The thought is not so much the "very words" as the NIV has, but as in ordinary Greek usage the "inspired utterances," the "oracles" of God. Israel *was* chosen, and although throughout history and at the present moment "some did not have faith" (3:3), God is faithful to His utterances.

Paul here has shifted from the Jews' approach to the OT as laws describing what man must do, to the OT's character as divine promise describing what God most assuredly will do. God remains faithful to His covenant promises, a faithfulness that is stunning in view of Israel's persistent refusal to respond to Him with trust.

But if our unrighteousness brings out God's righteousness more clearly (3:5). At Kaddish, Israel rebelled and refused to attack Canaan. Only two of that generation, Joshua and Caleb, lived to enter the Promised Land. Yet despite the near universal rebellion of God's people, He was faithful to His promises. The unrighteousness of the Exodus generation "brings out" God's righteousness in keeping His covenant promises "more clearly."

But this is no excuse for the unrighteous! They cannot say, "See, what we did really glorified God after all!" Sin is sin, and the condemnation of all who do evil is deserved. And assured!

There is no one righteous, not even one (3:9-18). Paul has argued that Jew and Gentile alike have sinned and fallen short of God's glory. Now he proves his point by quoting from several psalms. His Jewish readers might reject his argument. But they can hardly reject the verdict of words they *know* are God's own.

Whatever the Law says, it says to those who are under the Law, so that every mouth may be silenced and the whole world *held accountable* to God (3:19-20). The word is *hupodikos,* used in its legal sense of "liable to punishment." The moral law in which the observant Jew and the moral Gentile hope has proved to be not a source of hope, but rather the standard by which their failure has been established! Thus law is no road sign directing us to divine reward, but rather a mirror, which when used correctly, shows us our sin.

THE PASSAGE IN DEPTH

God's Wrath against Mankind (1:18-32).
Background. Many Christians have been brought up short by challenges to God's fairness. "What," they say, "about those who have never heard? Is it fair for God to condemn the pagan who never has a chance to hear of Jesus?"

The question is hardly new. In the ancient world as well as in our own, "What about those who have no chance to know God?" was posed as a serious objection to Christianity. Celsus, in the second century, wrote, "Is it only now after such a long time that God has remembered to judge the life of men? Did He not care before?" (*Cels.* 4.7) Porphyry argued that the God of all the world would hardly reveal Himself only to a specific people, and asked what would become of the ancient Romans who knew nothing of Jesus because they lived before His lifetime? The emperor Julian the Apostate scoffed at Jesus, asking why God sent prophets to the Jews "but to us no prophet, no oil of anointing, no teacher, no herald to

announce His love for man which should one day, though late, reach even unto us also? . . . If He is the God of all of us alike, and the creator of all, why did He neglect us?"

There is an answer to this question. And it is found in this passage in a powerful argument developed by the Apostle Paul.

Interpretation. It is important to note immediately that our text says that the wrath of God "*is being revealed*" (1:18). This passage is not, as some have supposed, a listing of sins which merit eschatological judgment. Paul writes of a wrath that "is being revealed" against a race that willfully suppresses what it knows about that God who has, from the beginning, revealed Himself to all through His creation.

The thought is repeated several times in the passage: "What may be known about God is plain to them" (1:19); "although they knew God" (1:21); "they exchanged the truth of God for a lie" (1:25); "they did not think it worthwhile to retain the knowledge of God" (1:28). The Jews alone may have had the

Scripture. But God made Himself available to all, speaking to them through His creation, and God was in fact known by all — to the extent that He could be known through this channel of revelation.

However, what men did with this revelation was to reject it, and the God who presented Himself to them in it. They suppressed the truth. They "neither glorified Him as God nor gave thanks to Him" (1:21). They "did not think it worthwhile to retain the knowledge of God."

The failure of the pagan world to worship the God of Scripture is not God's fault, for He did not withhold Himself. The failure is theirs for not responding to the God who does make Himself known!

Yet Paul's purpose here is not to argue God's fairness, but to explain why and how wrath against "all the godlessness and wickedness of man" (1:18) is even now being revealed from heaven. Man's basic attitude toward God is revealed in suppression and rejection of their knowledge of Him. Now Paul shows that God's wrath is revealed in the sins in which mankind cut off from God indulges itself!

Three times, in 1:24, 26, and 28, Paul says that God "gave them over" (*paredoken autos*). The verb here means "to hand over control of or responsibility for." Since man did not want to glorify or respond to God nor thank Him, God handed him over to the control of his own "sinful desires" (1:24). Because people worshiped and served created things, God handed them over to the control of their own "shameful lusts" (1:26).

Because they did not think it worthwhile to retain the knowledge of God, God handed them over to the control of their own "depraved mind" (1:28). *This deliberate act of "handing over" is an act of judgment, which has resulted in a continuous revelation of the wrath of God from heaven.* Here we have to make the important point that the acts Paul lists in this passage are not presented as sins for which man must face eschatological judgment. They are themselves the evidence that mankind is the present object of God's wrath!

Science fiction of the 1940s often explored the question of what would result from an atomic war. Writers seemed fascinated by the idea that mutants would be caused by rampant radiation. Stories and even movies were popu-lated by ugly, misshapen, hostile beings with distorted faces and extra limbs, mere brutes who fought and fed on their victims. One would only have to look at the misshapen mutant men and women and observe their ways to know that atomic warfare had corrupted human civilization.

This is Paul's argument here! The society we know is corrupt and rife with sin. Human beings are mutants, misshapen men and women twisted by depraved minds and sinful passions. Society is corrupted by "every kind of wickedness" (1:29) as men and women filled with "envy, murder, strife, deceit and malice" feed upon rather than love one another selflessly. The sin we see in ourselves and all around us is unmistakable proof that God even now is judging a humanity that has rejected and abandoned Him.

Application. Today we can hardly turn on TV news or pick up a newspaper without being confronted by more evidence that human beings and our society lie under the wrath of God. Yet the spiritual mutants who inhabit our lost planet have forgotten what humanity once was before the Fall — and what humanity could be again if only each of us would reorient our lives to the Lord our God.

Righteousness through Faith (3:21-31).

Background. The major debate over this passage focuses on the Greek word translated in the NIV as "a sacrifice of atonement" (3:25). There is no question in a reader's mind that these powerful verses present the hope of a salvation available to all which has been won for humankind by Jesus Christ on Calvary; a salvation which is appropriated by faith. The question is: *how* did Jesus' death make it possible for God to not only acquit sinners but also impute a righteousness that is foreign to fallen human nature?

The answer hinges on our understanding of the Greek word *hilasterion.* Is "sacrifice of atonement" a satisfactory rendering, or do we need to go back to older versions and their rendering of the word as "propitiation."

The translators of the Septuagint used the verb *hilaskesthai* to translate the Hebrew *kipper.* C.H. Dodd concluded that when the subject was human, it had the meaning of making expiation (payment, satisfaction), but that when God is the subject, the concept is simply one of forgiveness. Thus the verse would simply affirm that Jesus' death was a sacrifice through which God offers salvation to believing sinners, without in any way defining how or why that sacrifice was efficacious.

Not everyone agrees. There is no doubt that the ordinary meaning of the word in the first century identified a sacrifice as *propitiatory*. That is, that the sacrifice was intended to serve as a gift intended to propitiate (appease, satisfy) an angry deity. Yet the Septuagint often has this word in contexts where it is very clear that God's anger with His sinning people is a definite factor. More important, the whole flow of argument in this section makes it clear that Paul is writing *about* the "wrath of God . . . being revealed from heaven against all the godlessness . . . of men" (1:18). Wrath (*orge*) is spoken of four times (1:18; 2:5, 8; 3:5), in ways which make it plain that a righteous God not only intends to but already is judging a sinful humanity. God is not free to figuratively shrug His shoulders and say "I forgive," thus ignoring sin. Somehow, in some way, the death of Jesus must meet the requirements of justice and so turn aside the wrath of God, so that forgiveness may flow. Only if Jesus' sacrifice is understood as a *hilasterion* in the classic sense of propitiatory sacrifice can we truly understand the teaching of these verses.

Interpretation. Paul has shown in Rom. 1–3 that "all have sinned and fall short of the glory of God" (3:23). Man has no righteousness, but rather lies under the wrath of God. Yet in the Gospel God offers a "righteousness [that comes] from God" (3:22) and is received "through faith in Jesus."

But how can a God whose righteousness is expressed by *judging* sin acquit sinners "freely by His grace"? (3:24) Paul's answer is that this is possible because Jesus provided redemption, in that He was presented by God as a *propitiatory sacrifice*. Jesus' death was necessary if God were to forgive, for God was required by His very nature to punish sin. By punishing sin in Jesus as our substitute, God has *demonstrated His justice*.

Suddenly the mystery of how God could act in harmony with His own righteous character and still forgive OT saints is solved. God from eternity intended to uphold the requirements of moral law, both natural and revealed, which laid on the Creator the obligation for punishing sin. He has taken that punishment upon Himself in the Person of the Son.

In this act, God became totally free to extend His grace to humanity, and provide a forgiveness that has nothing to do with law, but is appropriated simply by trust in the Promise of the One who presents His Son as the object of our faith, as well as the basis of our salvation.

Application. Let's remember that Christ's death was no gesture on God's part. It was not, as some have said, merely His way of showing love. The death Jesus died must not be trivialized. It was a costly death, a death in which the Son took our sins upon Himself and experienced the full weight of the Father's wrath against unrighteousness. Only that kind of death could have met the demands God's nature imposed upon Him. Only that kind of death could have won us the freedom which we now have in Him.

ROMANS 4–6
The Righteousness of Faith

EXPOSITION

Paul has shown that all people stand condemned by God, with no righteousness of their own (chaps. 1–3). How then can history record that some men and women of old were close to God? Paul's answer is, only because "[an unrighteous] man is justified by faith apart from observing the Law" (3:28).

For proof Paul points to Abraham. Contemporary Jewish sages often suggested that it was Abraham's obedience that caused God to bless him and grant him a covenant relationship. But the Scripture says Abraham "believed God" and that his faith was "credited to him as righteousness" (4:1-5). David agrees in Ps. 32:7-8. What's more, since Abraham was uncircumcised at the time God spoke these words, the Gentile has as great a right as the Jew to call Abraham "Father"! What God considers is whether or not a person has a faith like Abraham's (4:10-17). And what characterized Abraham's faith was simply that, when he heard God's "impossible" pledge to give him a son by Sarah, he was "fully persuaded that God had power to do what He had promised" (4:18-25).

It is to those who rely on God's promise, not those who seek to establish their own righteousness through the Law, that God grants the blessings of peace, access, and personal transformation (5:1-5). It's those who acknowledge their ungodliness and powerlessness, and realize that Christ died for them, who have hope and joy (5:6-11).

Still, how does it happen that all are sinners? The answer is that in Adam's fall the race became corrupt. But now God has acted in Christ to redeem us and make us righteous. Sin reigned, but through Jesus, grace now rules! (5:12-21) That rule finds expression in every believer's life. Through our union with Jesus, the grip that Adam's Fall gave sin on our personalities is broken, and the new life to which Jesus Himself was raised flows through us (6:1-7). If we daily count on this promise, refuse to respond to sin's demands, and offer ourselves and our bodies to God as instruments of righteousness, we will no longer be mastered by sin! (6:8-13)

Paul closes this chapter with an important point. The chains sin forged have been broken by Jesus, but all this means is that we who are unchained are now free to choose our master. No human being is truly independent, and so the only choice we have is one of whom we will serve. Let's always remember that Christ set us free in order that we might choose to serve God, and reap the rewards of holiness and eternal life (6:19-23).

WORD STUDIES

What shall we say that *Abraham*, our forefather, discovered in this matter? (4:1) Commentators have been quick to note that this chapter is a tightly reasoned *Midrash* — that is, an exposition of an OT text (4:3; Gen. 15:6) developed on a rabbinical model. Thus some insight into the expository principles of rabbinic Judaism is helpful to us.

In this opening verse Paul calls on his Jewish readers to look back to Abraham. Why would Abraham's experience be relevant? It was the conviction of the rabbis that Scripture is not time-bound. That is, the Bible is a book of the present and not just the past. In sacred history God speaks authoritatively to people of the present. Thus what happened to Abraham is as significant existentially as historically.

Thus Paul is able to argue that what Abraham found in his relationship with God establishes a pattern for all who claim a relationship with God like his.

How important it is to approach Scripture as God's living, present Word. In *A Midrash Reader* Jacob Neusner sums up one common bond that has always linked committed Christians and religious Jews: "We and they share the conviction that Scripture is God's word not then alone but also now, spoken not in time long gone but in and to our own age: to me, here and now" (p. 163).

And so Paul invited God to speak through His words to Abraham to Paul's contemporary readers then, and to you and me.

If, in fact, Abraham was justified by *works*, he had something to boast about — but not before God (4:2). In the tapestry of first-century Jewish religion "faith" was simply one strand, interwoven with works, law, obedience, merit, and blessing into a whole that confused rather than distinguished their roles. Paul, however, has begun to separate these threads, and insists that they must be kept apart if God's message is to be understood.

"Works" here is to be understood as piety, that reverent obedience to God's Law which the Jew assumed to *be* faith. Thus, in Judaism, blessing was something a believer merited *because of* his piety. This view shaped even the interpretation of the events of Abraham's life, as seen in the second-century B.C. writings of Ben Sira (44:19-21):

ABRAHAM, father of many peoples,
kept his glory without stain.
He obeyed the Most High's command,
and *entered into a covenant* with him;
In his own flesh the ordinance was incised,
and when tested, he *was found steadfast.*
For this reason, God promised him with
an oath
to bless the nations through his descendants,
To make him numerous as the grains of dust,
and exalt his posterity like the stars,
Giving them an inheritance from sea to sea,
and from the River to the ends of the Earth.
(italics mine)

Knowing full well the view expressed by Sira, Paul challenges the interpretation as he asks, "What does the Scripture say? 'Abraham *believed* God' " (4:3). Blessing was in response to faith, not works. It was a gift, not wages (4:4-8). The righteousness God credited Abraham with was granted 13 years before his circumcision, not because of it (4:9-12). It had nothing to do with Law, for God's words to Abraham were of promise, not obligation (4:13-18). Abraham was credited with righteousness on the *basis of faith and faith alone!* Rabbinic Judaism has lost the way to blessing by failing to make these distinctions, and thus losing sight of the saving grace of its God.

Abraham was *justified* (4:2). The Greek word *dikaioo* means "to acquit," "vindicate," "pronounce righteousness." Paul showed in Rom. 1–3 that all have sinned. Thus, already guilty before God, the question is not how one might remain in His good graces, but how one already condemned might be acquitted!

The Gospel still makes no sense to those who assume that somehow they are on probation, and that their destiny hinges on what they will do in the future. Only those who realize they are already condemned have hope, for only such will turn from works to that faith which relies solely on God's grace expressed in Jesus Christ.

David says the *same thing* when he speaks of the blessedness of the man to whom God credits righteousness apart from works (4:6-8). This is hard to understand when we read the verses Paul quotes from Psalm 32. What correspondence is there between "it was credited to [Abraham] as righteousness" and "the man whose sin the Lord will never count against him"?

The answer is found in another Midrash principle of interpretation called *gezerah shavah,* "verbal analogy." The Stienmetz Talmud's article on hermeneutics (p. 150) calls this:

A fundamental Talmudic principle of Biblical interpretation, appearing in all the standard lists of exegetical rules. If the same word or phrase appears in two places in the Torah, and a certain law is explicitly stated in one of these places, we may infer on the basis of "verbal analogy" that the same law must apply in the other case as well. . . . In its simplest form, then, *gezerah shavah* is a type of linguistic interpretation by means of which the meaning of an obscure word or phrase is inferred on the basis of another occurrence of the same word or phrase in a clearer context.

What Gen. 15:6 and Ps. 32:7-8 have in common is the Greek word *logizesthai,* found in the Septuagint of both verses though translated in our NIV by two English words, "credits" (4:6) and "count" (4:8). What Paul has done is use the established principle of verbal analogy to argue that the sense of Gen. 15:6 can be carried over to Ps. 32, to explain what David is saying about the forgiveness of sins. The person who is forgiven by God is at the same time credited with righteousness, and this blessing is a consequence of faith.

Is this *blessedness* only for the circumcised? (4:9) Paul now uses "blessedness" to tie together his argument (4:6-9). It is clear that in this context the blessedness the Scripture speaks of is a complete and full salvation summed up in essentially synonymous phrases: "reckon righteous," "forgive transgressions," "cover sins," and "not count sin against" the man who believes. "Blessedness" is not a reward, but a gift given to those with faith. And this gift is available to Gentile as well as Jew (4:9).

Against all hope, Abraham in hope *believed* (4:18). See the discussion of 4:1-25 in *The Passage in Depth* (below).

Therefore, since we have been justified through faith, *we have* peace with God (5:1). The manuscripts disagree whether the word here, *echomen,* is spelled with a long or a short "o" — two different though similar letters in Greek. Taking the "o" as long, some versions read "let us have [or continue at] peace with God." The context, however, supports the NIV, for Paul goes on to list benefits that are ours through Jesus.

As we look at the list of benefits it is important to remember that phrase, "We have." This is no catalog of "pie in the sky bye and bye." Everything on this list is ours, now, to be claimed and enjoyed. And the list?

- We have peace with God (5:1).
- We have access to God and His grace (5:2).
- We have justification (5:9).
- We have present-tense salvation (5:10).
- We have reconciliation (5:11).
- We have the capacity to live a righteous life now (5:17).
- We have life itself (5:18).
- We have eternal life! (5:21)

Not only so, we also rejoice in our *sufferings* (5:3). It seems strange to find "suffering" mentioned in a passage that lists benefits believers enjoy through Jesus. But then, looking at the list above, we realize that every benefit listed is spiritual, not material. Jesus did not die to make us wealthy, to guarantee physical health, or to immunize us to suffering during our earthly life. Jesus died to give us gifts far richer than these!

Here Paul reminds us that through Christ we are given the privilege of *understanding the purpose of God in permitting those things which bring us suffering.* Simply put, our faith provides a perspective that enables us to experience joy despite pressures and disappointments that every human being must experience. Through suffering the Lord will enrich us by developing our perseverance and our character. Suffering will help guard us from the error of fixing our hopes on what me may gain here tomorrow, rather than on God.

So when we hear the radio or TV preacher claim that "God wants His children to be rich," let's remember: What God really wants is for us to realize that we *are* rich. God may well use poverty, sickness, unemployment, loss, and pain to keep our eyes fixed on the spiritual wealth that we already possess, and our hopes fixed on Him.

God *demonstrates* His own love for us in this: While we were still sinners, Christ died for us (5:8). The verb *sunistesin* means "puts together." It's hard to sense God's love when we experience suffering. Yet Christ's death is the act which puts everything together for us — history's great, decisive, totally certain demonstration of the depths of the love God has for us.

That act of love is utterly amazing when we remember that we for whom Christ died were powerless, ungodly, and still sinners. Remembering what we were when Jesus died for us, how can we doubt God's love for us now that Jesus' death has brought us back into harmony with God, and He has showered us with spiritual blessings? No wonder we rejoice in God! In Jesus we know God and are assured of His love.

Don't you know that all of us who were baptized into Christ Jesus were baptized into His death? We were therefore buried *with* Him (6:1). Romans 5 speaks of benefits believers receive *through* Jesus. Now Paul turns to the benefits that are ours *with* Him.

Paul is not writing here of the rite of water baptism. Instead he is speaking of a spiritual reality explained in 1 Cor. 12:13, which uses the word *baptizo* to define that work of the Holy Spirit by which He unites the believer to Jesus as a member of Christ's body.

"Baptism" here is clearly explained in the context: it is being "united with" Jesus by an unbreakable spiritual bond.

Perhaps the closest analogy to the meaning of this relationship is drawn from the laws governing marriage in a "community property" state. Imagine a young woman with nothing who is courted and won by a multimillionaire. The moment they wed, the wife is considered to have an equal share in her husband's property. When a couple is united in marriage in such a state, their lives and possessions are merged.

This is what Paul says happens when we believe. Our lives and possessions merge. We

bring our sin . . . and Jesus takes it upon Himself. Christ brings His resurrection life . . . suddenly in Jesus that power for holiness flows into our lives. In Paul's terms, we died with Christ. We were raised with Christ. And it is this, our union with Jesus, that gives us freedom to reject the tug of the sin that still taints our personalities, and to choose to live righteous lives that honor our Lord.

For sin shall not be your master, because you are not under law, but under grace (6:14). Paul has explained in 6:1-13 that we are no longer under the mastery of sin. But why the "because" here? And what does "law" have to do with sin's mastery in the human heart?

For the answer to these troubling questions we will need to look at Rom. 7–8, which explores the question of whether "law," which Paul has shown cannot be treated as an aid to winning salvation, has any role at all in the life of the Christian.

Don't you know that when you offer yourselves to someone to obey him as slaves, you are slaves to the one whom you obey? (6:16) The whole passage (6:15-23) is a digression from Paul's argument. But it is an important one. Paul has shown that Christ sets believers free from the power of death, and urges readers to "offer the parts of your body to [God] as instruments of righteousness" (6:13). Now Paul responds to an imagined reader who misunderstands, and shouting "Free at last!" mistakes grace as a license to do whatever he or she wants.

Paul's answer is that for human beings there is no such thing as "freedom" from the powers that vie for our allegiance. We will either use our freedom to choose to do wrong, or to choose to do righteousness. In either case we become slaves, either to the sin that pulls us toward wrong, or the God whose spirit woos us toward righteousness.

For the wages of sin is death, but the gift of God is eternal life in Christ Jesus our Lord (6:23). Paul does not warn us that if we choose to sin God will condemn us. In Rom. 8:1 he is quick to correct any such impression, affirming that there is now no condemnation for those who are in Christ Jesus. Instead Paul reminds us of the nature of the lands into which the two paths between which we much choose lead.

Sin is a pathway which leads to death. We need to understand death here in its fullest, most exclusive sense. The *Zondervan Expository Dictionary of Bible Words* sums up the NT's teaching on death in this way:

Death, then, is a biological concept that is applied theologically to graphically convey the true state of humankind. The death that grips mankind is moral and spiritual. Death warps and twists man out of the pattern of original creation. Every human potential is distorted, every capacity—for joy, for relationships, for harmony with God, for true goodness—is tragically mis-shapen. And because each ugly twist and turn gives expression to sin, man—intended to reflect God's image and likeness—falls instead under God's condemnation (p. 409).

The believer *can* use his or her freedom to sin, and still go to heaven. But the sinning saint like the lost sinner will wander through life empty, frustrated, and unfulfilled. For the path of sin leads deeper and deeper into the land of death.

How much richer our lives will be if we choose to be slaves of righteousness, and find each step we take leads us into a richer, fuller, more blessed and satisfying experience—benefits of God's life within us today.

THE PASSAGE IN DEPTH

Abraham Justified by Faith (4:1-25).

Background. Earlier we noted that first-century Jewish religion treated faith, works, law, obedience, merit, and blessing as a whole, without making clear distinctions between their roles or defining the relationships between these vital elements of OT religion.

It is fascinating to look today at the *Mishnah,* that tremendous work of the sages of A.D. 30–200 which was intended to codify the Oral Law—traditional rules for daily life and worship—that even in Jesus' time dominated the outlook of the Pharisees. In repetitious, tedious detail the sages examined and defined the religious duties of the Jew, to produce a book that in rabbinic Judaism has the same standing as the OT, God's revelation to man. In doing this the sages struggled to define things which were similar and things which were different, creating lists and then making rulings based on their lists. What is fascinating is that in this intense drive to define, no attention is paid to the issues that Paul raises in Romans. There is no examination of assumptions about the nature of faith, or the relationship of faith to the law, or faith to obedience. No one asks the questions Paul asks about the nature of man and the damage wrought by the Fall. Instead the sages seem to proceed on the assumption that Israel has special standing with the Lord by virtue of God's covenant with Abraham, and that by obeying God's laws a pious Jew merits blessings here on earth and (if orthodox) wins the reward of entry into heaven. Thus all that really counts is defining as carefully as possible what constitutes an obedient life, so that a pious Jew might understand what God requires.

But in Romans Paul calls his readers to examine their assumptions, and to define not laws but critical theological concepts. In the process Paul is forced to revise his own understanding of the OT, and driven to make distinctions that no Jew of his generation even imagined might exist.

Interpretation. As we read through this passage we see that Paul carefully *sorts* the theological concepts with which he deals into two opposing categories. In this his approach is distinctly within that taken by rabbinic Judaism. He seeks to group things which are the same together, and carefully distinguish them from things which differ. However, as noted, Paul applies this *Midrash* approach not to *halakah* (laws for living) but to *aggadah* (the theological, philosophical, ethical).

Paul comes up with two lists in this passage, each of which he argues is mutually exclusive. While the items on each list are tightly linked to each other, none can be associated with an item on the other list—*as long as what we are talking about is God's act of freely justifying sinners.*

List #1
- Works (pious acts, obedience)
- Wages

- Circumcision
- Law
- Wrath
- Death

List #2
- Faith (trust in God's promise)
- Justification
- Blessedness
- The crediting of righteousness
- The forgiveness of sins
- Gift
- Promise
- Grace
- Abraham's heirs
- Life from the dead

In reading through this passage, it is clear that "faith" is the key word on the second list. It is the person with faith who steps out of the realm characterized by elements on the first list, into a realm characterized by elements on the second. It is no wonder, then, that Paul in 4:18-25 returns to Abraham, to provide both a definition and an example of this "saving faith" about which he is here concerned. (For "faith and works," see the discussion on James 2:14-26, pp. 577–80.)

Here Paul looks at the historical context in which Abraham exercised that faith which Gen. 15:6 says "believed the Lord" so that "He credited it to him as righteousness." God promises Abraham, now 100 years old, with a 90-year-old wife who has long since ceased menstruation, that the two of them will have a child together. Abraham *knew*, humanly speaking, this was impossible. But rather than "waver through unbelief" (4:20), Abraham believed God.

He heard the word of promise, and trusted the God who gave it.

The analogy is clear. To us too God makes a promise in Christ: a promise of forgiveness and acceptance, a promise of acceptance and life. Humanly speaking it is impossible for us to change our nature or our state as sinners, rightly subject to the wrath of God. When like Abraham we hear the word of promise, and trust the God who gave it, we too are credited with righteousness, and given all that this entails.

In the OT a complex mix of concepts was expressed by *'aman* in Hebrew, and was carried into the Greek Septuagint as in the word

Paul uses here, *pistis*. The underlying idea is one of "certainty, assurance." In its various forms the root is applied to various relationships, and so denotes faithfulness, fidelity, truth, steadfastness, faith, certainty, and firmness. The strong tendency in Judaism was, and is, to emphasize the faithfulness dimension. God was honored for His faithfulness to His covenant. And "faith" was in effect the faith(fulness) of the pious Jew who lived up to his obligations under Mosaic Law.

In returning to Abraham, Paul argues that the *pistis* which is credited for righteousness is in fact simple trust—the heart's joyous response to God's word of promise, a conviction that although God offers the impossible, He will surely do what He has said.

Israel's perception of "faith" as the Jew's faith(fulness) to the law's requirements was in error, for it failed entirely to consider the fact that all have sinned and fallen short of God's glory, and lie under His wrath. The only hope of Gentile or Jew is a word of promise, by which God will commit Himself to do for us what no human being can do for himself.

Application. While the first-century Jew saw *pistis* as faith(fulness), and thus practical, the modern American tends to think of *pistis* as belief, and thus intellectual. "Do you believe in God?" to most of our day means little more than "Do you think God exists?" or "Do you think Jesus is God's Son?" Taken this way, "faith" is supposing something to be true.

Both ancient and modern perceptions of faith are tragically flawed. Saving faith is something entirely different: it is to hear God's word of promise in Jesus, and in response, to trust ourselves to Him completely. In the final analysis *pistis* is not concerned with acts or intellect. It is a word that describes our basic attitude toward God. Until a person's attitude toward God changes, and he or she abandons independence and self-reliance to rely completely on God's grace, that person remains trapped and lost.

Death through Adam, Life through Christ (5:12-21).

Background. In Rom. 1–3 Paul argued that all humankind is lost in the grip of sin, Jew as well as Gentile. In Rom. 4 Paul showed that justification by faith is also universally available to all who trust God to keep His promise in the Gospel—Gentile as well as Jew.

Paul now steps back a moment to ask how can this be? How did it happen that all men became sinners? And how can life now be offered to all?

As background we need to understand something important about the relationship between "sin" and "sins." While "sins" are acts of wickedness or violations of God's Law, "sin" is something else again. "Sin" refers to that essential flaw in human nature which distorts man's moral character, darkens his intellect, and bends his will toward evil. In biblical terminology, this condition is frequently spoken of as "death," not in its biological but in its spiritual sense.

The Jew of Paul's time saw "sins" as discrete acts by which a person violated the Law given through Moses. Paul points out that even when there was no law, and so no one could be charged with a "sin," human beings were spiritually dead. They lived in a *state of sin,* for they were spiritually dead. Thus Paul says that "death reigned from the time of Adam to the time of Moses" (5:14).

The wonder of the Gospel is that in its good news God comes to us all with the promise of a gift of *life.*

Interpretation. Paul begins his exposition by stating that "sin entered the world through one man, and death through sin, and in this way death came to all men, because all sinned" (5:12). *Humanity's relationship with Adam* is the source of sin in our race and in every individual.

This is not an insight unique to the Apostle Paul. The Book of 2 Esdras, a first-century Jewish work found in the Roman Catholic Bible's Apocrypha, says

[Adam] transgressed. . . . Thou didst appoint death for him and his descendants. . . .

For the first Adam, burdened with an evil heart, transgressed and was overcome, as were also all who were descended from him. Thus the disease became permanent (3:7, 21-22).

O Adam, what have you done? For though it was you who sinned, the fall was not yours alone, but ours also who are your descendants (7:118).

Other apocryphal works do not quite support this view. The second-century Apocalypse of Baruch says, "Adam is therefore not the cause, save of his own soul, But each of us has been the Adam of his own soul" (2 Baruch 54:19). But Paul is clear. In some awful way sin so corrupted Adam's essential nature that the taint bred true, and every human being since has been born spiritually dead. It is our relationship with Adam that makes us sinners.

Now Paul compares and contrasts. As one man's act of sin brought death to the race, so one Man's act of obedience now brings life. Jesus is the Second Adam, the founder of a new race of men and women in whom life has been restored. In establishing a new relationship, with Jesus the Son of God, we step out of the realm of sin and death into the realm of righteousness and life, where grace reigns, and we are at last able to become what God always intended humankind to be.

Application. The exact why and how all this is true is difficult to grasp. Yet we cannot doubt that Adam's sin caused a great mutation in our race, and is the source of endless sin and suffering. Adam's fall changed his relationship with God, and shaped our innate attitude toward God as well.

Ultimately "sin" and "death," and also "life" and "righteousness," are all *relational* terms, for their deepest meaning reflects truth about the nature of our relationship with God. It is not what we do that makes us sinners. It is the fact that we are alienated from God. It is not what we do that saves us. All that can save is a personal relationship with God. And in the Gospel, through Jesus Christ, this is now available to all.

Dead to Sin, Alive in Christ (6:1-14).

Background. Paul's reasoning has now led him to an exciting conclusion. All people are sinners (chaps. 1–3). God justifies sinners by a "faith" which has nothing to do with faith(ful) obedience to God's commands, but rather exists as an unhesitating trust in God (chap. 4). God's saving promise is Jesus Christ, and through faith in Him all who believe receive a multitude of benefits—peace with God, access, hope, reconciliation, righteousness, and life (5:1-11). Earlier Paul has shown that a faith relationship with God is available to Gentile as well as Jew. Now he shows the reason: all men are related to Adam, and that

333

relationship is the source of racial death. But now faith opens to all the door of relationship with Jesus, and *that* relationship is the source of our new life.

Exposition. Paul now probes the implications of the relationship we have with Jesus. As the Word Study of 6:1 points out, that relationship is one of *union with.* Our bond with Jesus is so intimate and close that in God's sight we died with Jesus on Calvary, and when Jesus was raised from the dead to new life, we were raised with Him.

The implications of our identification with Jesus are stunning. If we died to sin, then sin—as distorted human nature—has no more power over us.

This does not mean that sin—again as distorted human nature—has no *influence.* We still are tempted. We still feel sin's pull. We are often all too aware of our desire to do what we know is wrong. But when the urge to sin comes, we do *not have to* commit sin! We cannot say, "The devil made me do it," or, "I just couldn't resist the temptation." In Jesus our freedom of choice between what we know to be good and what we know to be evil has been restored!

What's more, if we have been raised to life in Jesus, that same resurrection power which raised Him lifts us to life as well. *We are not left alone to struggle with sin.* We are called to choose. In our choice of obedience it is His life that flows through us, His will that animates us, His strength that enables us to be "instruments of righteousness" for our God.

It is at this point that Paul begins to answer the question that has troubled many Christians. "I know that union with Jesus makes it possible for me to live a godly life. But what do I *do?*" Paul's answer is summed up in a series of active verbs: know (6:6), count (6:11), offer (6:13). Paul's prescription can be summed up in three steps.

1. Know: grasp what union with Jesus means. Our crucifixion with Jesus ended sin's dominance, and our resurrection with Him provides power for righteous living.

2. Count: consider what God says to be true. Count on God to make real in our experience what He promises.

3. Offer: or as other versions more appropriately say, "present yourselves to God." That is, act in accord with what you understand to be His will.

Application. So often we make the simple difficult. It is God's genius to make the difficult simple.

This is certainly true when it comes to living the Christian life. Some pray desperately for strength. Some emphasize commitment. Some struggle to find and follow rules. Some seek a special word of direction from God. Some speak of strengthening our will. But Paul reminds us that all living in harmony with Jesus requires is the simplest of simple faiths.

Are we simple enough to take God at His word, and believe we do not *have* to sin? Are we simple enough to believe that God will do what He has promised in our lives today? If we are, then all we have to do is step out in faith, act on what we know is right—and Christ's power will lift us beyond ourselves, and His righteousness will be lived out in our daily lives.

ROMANS 7–8
Righteousness Now

EXPOSITION

In Rom. 6:14 Paul made a statement that shocked every Jewish reader: "Sin shall not be your master, because you are not under law, but under grace." He digressed in the next verses, but now returns to answer the objections that would have burst from every Jewish throat. The dialogue between the outraged Jew and Paul goes something like this.

Objection: "How can you say we're not under law?" Answer: "We died with Christ. Death brings release" (7:1-3).

Objection: "But *why* would anyone want to be released from God's wonderful Law?" Answer: "Because the Law stirs up our fleshly nature and produces sin. God wants us to relate to Him in the way of the Spirit" (7:4-6).

Objection: "How can you speak so against God's own Law!" Answer: "The Law as an expression of righteousness is holy, righteous, and good. The problem lies in the way we sinners react to Law. In fact it was the Law that made me realize my terrible spiritual condition as spiritually dead" (7:7-13).

Objection: "But Paul, doesn't the fact that now you're a Christian make any difference?" Answer: "Now I *want to* do what the Law commands. But when I try to relate to God through the Law, I find myself still powerless" (7:14-25).

Cry: "O Paul, is it hopeless, then?" Answer: "Thank God, no! Christ died to condemn sin in the flesh, and now the same Spirit who raised Him lives in me, to enable me to live a truly holy life. When we live 'according with the Spirit' and 'controlled by the Spirit' we are enabled to please God, and fully meet every requirement of the Law" (8:1-11).

Objection: "Paul, I just don't understand." Answer: "I know, it's difficult. But the key is this. You now have a totally different relationship with God. Your obligation is to 'Daddy,' not a distant master. You are His heirs, not His slaves. When He speaks to you through the Spirit respond fearlessly, as a son, and you'll learn by experience what I mean" (8:12-17).

With this imaginary dialogue finished, Paul is filled with a holy awe and enthusiasm. In one of the most powerful passages in the NT Paul goes on to exult in the cosmic impact of the resurrection of Jesus. Christ's resurrection means transformation, for the universe as well as for us (8:18-25). It means power in prayer today, conformity to the likeness of Jesus tomorrow (8:26-30). And *this* means that we live our human lives today totally secure in the unshakable confidence that God loves us, and that nothing "in all creation will be able to separate us from the love of God that is in Christ Jesus our Lord" (8:31-39).

WORD STUDIES

I am speaking to men who know the Law—that the Law has authority over a man only as long as he lives (7:1). One of the most difficult issues in this passage is Paul's use of *nomos,* "law." The reason lies in the complexity of the term rather than the complexity of Paul's argument.

The background for Paul's use is, of course, the Hebrew concept of *Torah.* The word means "teaching," or "instruction," and is most broadly applied. *Torah* may refer to God's revelation in a general way. It may point to a specific set of instructions—as in Rom. 7:2, the "law of marriage." *Torah* may indicate the moral or ceremonial codes, or the first five books of Moses. However, whatever its specific referent, *Torah* always *assumes divine instruction.* Law is a gift from God revealing what is right and good, the path that will lead to blessing as man lives his life in this world.

The Greek word *nomos* as used in the NT frequently reflects the meanings of *Torah.* Yet Greek culture added its own complexities to the term. *Nomos* encompassed the traditions and norms of society. The term also reflected the conviction of the Hellenistic philosophers that there were universal principles which operate in the world, and that man must learn to live in harmony with them. Many of Paul's references to "law" in Romans 7–8 are frequently taken in this sense: when Paul speaks of a "law of sin and death" (8:2) he means sin which operates as a universal principle in fallen human beings. In contrast "the law of the spirit of life" in Jesus Christ (8:2) is understood to be another universal principle operating in the believer by which the Spirit of Jesus vitalizes and empowers.

The interpretative approach that seeks to trace shifts in this passage between Torah-Law (Law as God's revelation) and *nomos*-law (law as a universal principle) has a long and respectable tradition. It may be the best way to deal with the passage.

However, we need to remember that the apostle's issue here arises out of the fact that the OT Law *is* a divine revelation. His full attention is given to analyzing that Law and its relationship to Jew and Christian. So it may be wiser if we attempt to trace the thought of the passage while keeping Torah-Law meanings as our major focus.

If we do take this approach, we quickly see that the central issue for Paul is a simple one. *How we relate to Torah is the key to failure or success in the Christian life!* If we read Torah (God's revelation) as servants, bound to keep the rules established by our exalted master, sin takes advantage of our weakness and condemns us. But if we read Torah (God's revelation) as children, gladly responding to our Father in the full confidence that we are heirs of His promise, the Spirit empowers us even in our mortality, and we are enabled to live godly and holy lives.

By Law a married woman is *bound to her husband* as long as he is alive (7:2). The Greek word is the rare *hupandros,* meaning "under a husband." In Jewish law only the husband had the right to a divorce. Only if a divorcee's husband died could a woman be freed "from the obligations of the marriage law" (NEB) to marry another.

In this illustration Paul acknowledges the Jew's point that no human being can release himself from the obligations Mosaic Law imposed on the Jews. But he then points out that our union with Jesus in *His* death really *is* our death. Thus death has freed the believer from "Torah-as-obligation," even as the death of a husband to whom the wife is united frees him! Paul is correct, legally speaking, to affirm "you are not under Law"! (6:14)

When we were *controlled by the sinful nature,* the sinful passions *aroused by the law* were at work in our bodies, so that we bore fruit for death (7:5). This is undoubtedly one of the most important verses on this whole subject in the entire NT.

The phrase that the NIV translates "controlled by the sinful nature" is actually *en te sarki,* "in the flesh." Paul uses the phrase to describe the unsaved, but also of his own experience as a believer (Gal. 2:20; Phil. 1:22; 1 Peter 4:2). In its broad character, *en sarki* or *kata sarki* (according to the flesh, Rom. 8:8), the word indicates the attitudes, perceptions, and motives of fallen man. Thus Paul in this passage intends to look first at Torah as fallen man approaches it, and later will contrast the way the believer who possesses Christ's spirit will approach it.

The phrase "aroused by the law" is *dia tou nomou energeito* (7:5). The law, as approached by fallen man, energizes, or stimulates, the sin

nature! The result is that the works human beings perform under the law are flawed, and must necessarily lead to death!

Paul's view is utterly at odds with the Jews' view of Torah—obligations (see the quote from Josephus). But it is utterly basic to Paul's teaching on the way to victory in the Christian life. Paul is convinced that there is a different way to approach *Torah*, not as obligation but as promise. And if the believer adopts this "new" way, he or she will experience a victorious Christian life.

JOSEPHUS ON THE JEWS' VIEW OF LAW

Starting from the very beginning with the food of which we partake from infancy and the private life of the home, he [Moses] left nothing, however insignificant, to the discretion and caprice of the individual. What meats a man should abstain from and what he may enjoy; with what person he should associate; what period should be devoted respectively to strenuous labor and to rest—for all this our leader made the law the standard and rule, that we might live under it as under a father and master and be guilty of no sin through willfulness or ignorance. For ignorance he left no pretext. He appointed the law to be the most excellent and necessary form of instruction, ordaining not that it should be once for all or twice on several occasions but that every week men should desert their other occupations and assemble to listen to the law and to obtain a thorough and accurate knowledge of it, a practice which all other legislators seem to have neglected (*Against Apion*, 2:173–175).

We have been released from the law so that we serve in the **new way** of the Spirit, and not in the old way of the written code (7:6). The Greek says *en kainoteti pneumatos*, "in newness of spirit." The word for "new" here does not mean "recent" as much as "fresh, vigorous, and superior." In Christ a new epoch has begun; the old and inferior way of approaching Torah by the "letter of the law" has given way to coming to Torah through the Spirit in discovering not obligation, but promise.

Paul charts the difference this makes in 7:4-6, as we see in comparing the elements of these verses below:

LAW		THE SPIRIT
↓	energizes	↓
sinful nature		new nature
↓	producing	↓
fruit to death		fruit to God

What a wonderful relief to come to God's teaching, our Scriptures, and to hear not the Torah of obligation, but the Torah of promise, and so in the Word of God to find freedom and release.

Sin, *seizing the opportunity* afforded by the commandment (7:8). The phrase was a favorite of military writers, and described the base from which an aggressive expedition was staged. Sin not only has a foothold in our lives; it is eager to strike deep into our personalities.

Paul's thought here is that when we read Torah-as-obligation, its very prohibitions stir up the sin nature by identifying an opportunity to strike. We have all experienced this as a psychological phenomenon. To be told "Don't cut the cake" makes it seem even more desirable. To be told "Wait till marriage," rather than quieting youth's desires, seems to enflame them.

But Paul has more than the psychological in view here. He is describing an awful reality. Sin always twists our response to Torah-as-obligation. Those who remain chaste become critical and condemn those who fail, or feel a pride that is in itself just as much sin as immorality. Approach God's Word with the attitude and perspective of fallen humanity, and in every case the consequence will, in some form, involve sin.

Once *I* was alive apart from law; but when the commandment came, sin sprang to life and I died (7:9). One of the confusing elements in this passage is Paul's use of "I." Is he speaking of his own personal experience? Is he speaking of himself as a representative Jew, or a representative of the human race? Is the "I" universal, used in the sense of "every man"?

The confusion is perhaps reduced when we realize two truths. First, Paul is a human being, who shares a common nature with all of us. Thus when we read his "I" we can rightly understand him to be dealing with the case of "everyman." If we remember that Paul has shown in Rom. 2 that the Gentile as well as the Jew has *Torah in the sense of divine teaching through revelation,* we realize that Paul the Pharisee can speak out of his own experience for everyman, Jew and Gentile alike.

Second, in analyzing his experience Paul is aware that as a Christian he is a deeply divided man. Living only *en sarki* (as a fallen human being) Paul had felt "I was alive" (7:9). Later he will say of his early life in Judaism "as for legalistic righteousness [I was] faultless" (Phil. 3:6). After his conversion Paul became terribly aware of his sinful nature. And he found that while he still loved God's Torah and wanted to obey, something deep within his personality battled him constantly, and the perfect obedience he so passionately desired regularly escaped him.

The division Paul senses within himself corresponds to the division he sees within the Law. There is an "I" of the flesh, even as there is a Torah of obligation. And there is an "I" made alive by the Spirit, even as there is a Torah of promise. What Paul is doing in this passage is describing how approaching Torah with a perspective shaped by the "I" of the flesh, even when one desires holiness, must utterly fail.

Therefore, there is now *no condemnation* for those who are *in Christ Jesus* (8:1). Paul has described the condition of those who are *en sarki,* in the flesh. Now he focuses attention on what it means to be *en Christo.* First it means that for us there is "no condemnation."

Katakrima is a legal term that means "to give judgment against." Here the word has both a forensic and practical implication. Because of Jesus God has acquitted us, and there is no judgment entered against us in the records maintained in heaven. What is more, there is "no condemnation" *now* for those who relate to God in Spirit. The flesh Torah-as-obligation has no relevance to the believer. With a stunning jolt the epoch of the Savior has transformed all.

For what the law was powerless to do in that it was weakened by the *sinful nature,* God did by sending His own Son in the likeness of sinful man to be a sin offering. And so He condemned sin in *sinful man,* in order that the righteous requirements of the law might be fully met in us, who do not live according to the *sinful nature* but according to the Spirit (8:3-4). The NIV is a dynamic translation. That is, rather than giving a word-for-word version of the original, it seeks to communicate the meaning or intent of a passage. Here the translators have chosen to render a basic term Paul uses in Rom. 7 as a reference to "sinful man" or the "sin nature." That Greek word is *sarx,* or flesh. Perhaps the translation does drive home Paul's point. But it is important to understand that in these chapters *en sarki,* "in flesh," characterizes humanity as related to Adam, fallen and in the grip of a sin that twists and distorts desires and perceptions as well as deeds. Paul is saying here that Christ, in taking on the *likeness* of a human being related to Adam, through His own death as a real human being, put an end to the old and introduced a new epoch. The believer is now *in Christ,* and now relates to God through Christ's Spirit. As we live and relate to God with the perspective of the new "I" rather than the perspective of the old "I," we discover that "righteous requirements" of Torah are in fact "fully met" in us.

You, however, are controlled not by the sinful nature but by the Spirit, *if* the Spirit of God lives in you (8:9a). This is not the "if" of uncertainty, but the "since" of glorious realization. Paul is quick to say that *every* believer possesses the Spirit of Christ (8:9b).

We now have the capacity to relate to God in the Spirit rather than in the flesh, and as we do "He who raised Christ from the dead will also give life to your mortal bodies through His Spirit, who lives in you" (8:11).

The phrase "mortal bodies" is important. In 8:3 Paul points out that Torah-as-obligation was powerless to shape a holy people because our weakness as fallen creatures held our "I" in an unbreakable embrace. Here Paul reminds us that now the Spirit of God lives in us to vitalize us in our mortality, energizing the new "I" that is ours through rebirth so that we now can please God.

For you did not receive a spirit that makes you a *slave* again to fear, but you received the Spirit of *sonship*. And by him we cry "Abba, Father" (8:15). Ultimately the critical difference between the old and the new epochs remains one of relationship. As fallen, men were slaves, and the Torah expressed the obligations each person as creature owed the Creator. As redeemed, believer is an heir, and the Torah expresses the promised blessings that God has in store for we who are His sons and daughters.

The person operating in the flesh cannot help but look at Torah-as-a compilation of duties to be performed, and will somehow assume that the human being who works merits some reward from the Lord. But the person operating in the Spirit cannot help but look at Torah-as-a loving explanation of what God intends to do within and through His dearly loved children. The flesh looks at Torah-as-obligation and fears; the honest man knows that he falls short. The spirit looks at Torah-as-promise, and cries out *Abba* ("Daddy!"), just like a child whose father, returning from a trip, has brought him a very special gift.

The creation itself will be *liberated* (8:21). The word means to "set free," here from "slavery to corruption." Paul intends us to realize that the new epoch, like the old, has cosmic as well as personal implications. In Adam's fall the very fabric of nature itself was ripped and torn, forced into a mode characterized by corruption and decay (Gen. 3:17-18). In Christ, the original state of the natural universe will surely be restored.

We ourselves, who have the *firstfruits of the Spirit*, groan inwardly as we wait eagerly our adoption as sons, the redemption of our bodies (8:23). Mosaic Law called for Israelites to bring the first ripe produce of the land to the Lord as an offering (Ex. 23:19; Neh. 10:35).

The ritual was an expression of thanks, and of confidence in God's blessing for the harvest soon to come. Here Paul casts the Spirit, given to every believer, as God's pledge that at the final adoption ceremony we who have now been welcomed in Christ as God's heirs will receive the full benefits of that relationship, and be fully conformed to Jesus Himself.

We know that in all things God works for the *good* of those who love Him (8:28). Not everything that happens to us is "good" in the way we tend to think of good. But the Greek here makes distinctions we do not see. *Kalos* suggests "good" in the sense of "beautiful and pleasing." *Agathos,* the word used in this verse, suggests "good" in the sense of "useful and beneficial."

God never promises that we will like the "all things" that happen in our lives. But He does promise that, in His supervision, God will permit nothing to touch those who love Him that cannot be beneficial or useful in their lives.

For those God foreknew He also *predestined to be conformed* to the likeness of His Son (8:29). While Christians will continue to debate the issue of whether or not God predestines some to be saved, this verse cannot be appealed to as evidence for either side. The apostle's subject is the meaning of a new epoch for those "in Christ." The wonder of this verse is that, just as nature will be rescued and restored from the corruption caused by sin, so will we who believe. And even more! Lifted even beyond Adam in his innocence, we are destined to be transformed, to be like Jesus Himself!

THE PASSAGE IN DEPTH

Struggling with Sin (7:1-25).

Background. No one who reads this passage carefully, and compares it with Rom. 8, can help but notice a dramatic shift in terminology. In Rom. 7 Paul uses "law" (*nomos*) 20 times. He speaks of "I" some 22 times, and "I do" no less than 14! On the other hand, in Rom. 8 Paul uses "law" only four ti.nes, and "[Holy] Spirit" 20 times!

It is obviously critical to our understanding of this passage to come to some conclusion as to what Paul means by *nomos* in Rom. 7, and what he means by "I."

As discussed in the Word Study of Rom. 7:1, above, it is best to take *nomos* in this critical section of Romans in the most basic sense of the OT term, *Torah.* "Law" is teaching (revelation) given by God to human beings—whether in nature, to the Gentiles, or in written form, to the Jews. The critical issue in Paul's discussion is that fallen man (the man *en sarki*) perceives God's revelation as a Torah-of-obligation. When God's Word comes to fallen man, it is seen not only as an obligation but an opportunity. Fallen man assumes that he is called to try to obey God, he can obey God, and his obedience places God under some obligation to him. For fallen man, the Torah seems to offer a way of salvation, and the best intentioned of men find satisfaction in the works they do.

What Paul is concerned about in Rom. 7 is Torah-as-obligation, Torah as fallen man seeks to relate to law, and through law, to God. Paul's conclusion is that this approach is as fruitless for the believer as it is for the unsaved!

Similarly, the Word Study of Rom. 8:9, above, explored Paul's use of "I" in this passage. Here we note a parallel between his divided "I" and the two ways of viewing Torah. Paul is aware that as a believer he is influenced by the flesh (his fallen nature) as well as by his new nature. When he approaches God with the flesh's mind-set, perceiving a Torah-of-obligation, the believer finds himself unable to do the good he so eagerly desires to do. He wants to please God, but when he tries to obey, he fails!

And so Rom. 7 ends with a cry of despair. But a cry which Paul transforms in Rom. 8 into an exultant shout of victory.

Interpretation. The flow of Paul's argument is not difficult to break down, however obscure its details.

■ The Paradox: The holy, righteous, and good nature of law vs.its terrible consequences (7:7-13).

■ The Implications: A "spiritual" law cannot benefit fallen human beings (7:14-21).

■ The Frustration: Even a converted man under law is turned into a prisoner of sin (7:21-25).

The Paradox (7:1-13). The Jewish believer, still enthusiastic for God's Law, would immediately see Paul's teaching in 7:4-6 as an attack on God's OT revelation. The Gentile Christian, who also revered the OT, would be confused as well. And so Paul takes pains to clarify his thinking.

He agrees wholeheartedly that the Torah, in itself, is "holy, righteous, and good." God's revelation reflects His own nature and character; how could it be anything less?

But human beings do not experience Torah as a distant abstraction. *Man and Law necessarily interact.* In this interaction, Paul says, that which is holy, righteous, and good, "kills"!

Paul does not retreat here from his teaching in Romans 5:12-21 that all human beings are born spiritually dead. Instead he is examining the fallen man's interaction with the Law, and its impact on him. Fallen man (man "in the flesh") finds his nature rebelling against the standard revealed in the Law. So when the Law says "Do not covet," what is "produced in me" is "every kind of covetous desire" (7:7-8).

We've all seen little children in stores, running from Mom and Dad who insist "Stay here" or cry out "Come back." Somehow the parent's insistence that the child stay makes him want to wiggle or run all the more. Thus the dreadful paradox of "Law" as it is experienced by fallen man. Although holy and righteous and good in itself, Law when approached in the flesh becomes a stimulant to sin!

And the result of this is that when we hear Law speak, sin stirs within us. And this is in fact *intended by God,* "in order that sin might be recognized as sin" (7:13).

Here Paul explains what he meant earlier when he asked if "faith" didn't really "nullify the law" (3:31). Remember his answer? "Faith" enables us to "uphold the law." By making salvation a matter of faith rather than Law, the Christian puts Torah-as-obligation in the very place God intended it to be, not a marker pointing us toward a salvation to be earned by works, but as a mirror revealing us to be sinners in need of a salvation we can never merit on our own!

The Implications (7:14-21). Paul now leads us to an awful realization. When "I" approach the Law as a fallen human being perceives it, as a Torah-of-obligation, I experience sin as an overpowering force within myself, a force that shapes my experience. I agree with the Law's demands and want to do what it requires, but instead "what I hate I do" (7:15). And Paul repeats himself: "no, the evil I do not want to do—this I keep on doing" (7:19).

In a sense it is not the "I" that desires to please God who acts, but rather, the cause of our frustration and failure lies in the fact that "sin living in me" controls my actions (7:20).

The Frustration (7:21-25). Paul's conclusion may well be drawn from his early personal experience as a believer. Yet in writing he speaks for all of us. Inner warfare takes shape as an endless struggle between my delight in God's Law, and the "[principle of] sin at work within my members" (7:23).

Looking back, and ahead. In interpreting this passage we need to remember that this agonizing description is found between two passages with a very different tone. Romans 6:1-14 celebrates our union with Jesus, and promises "sin shall not be your master, because you are not under law, but under grace" (6:14). Romans 8:1-11 announces that there is "no condemnation" for us now. Christ's death dealt with our sin nature, and the Spirit who raised Jesus from the dead vitalizes even our mortal bodies. As we walk according to (in accord with, in harmony with, controlled by) the Holy Spirit, fully aware of our new position as God's heirs, the sons of a loving Father, we *are enabled by the Spirit* to live righteous and holy lives!

How do we explain the tone of Rom. 7,

then? By noting that in our passage Paul is explaining *why* the believer must shrug off the old way of looking at Torah-as-obligation. That is lost humanity's perspective on God's Word, and destructive for us as well as them. We Christians are to look at Scripture as a Torah-of-promise, and *rather than try to keep God's Law, expect the Holy Spirit to make real in us what Scripture says is now our heritage as God's children.*

Whenever we come to Scripture as Torah-of-obligation, our sin nature will be stimulated by the Law to acts of sin. But when we come to Scripture in the Spirit, and hear God's Word as a Torah-of-promise, our new natures are stimulated by God's Word of promise to trust and to obey.

Application. Romans 7 does not tell us how we come to Scripture as a Torah-of-promise. But Rom. 6 did tell us.

■ Know: Grasp what union with Christ means.

We died with Jesus, and were raised with Him to new life. The old epoch and the old ways of looking at relationship with God are totally replaced.

■ Count: Consider what God says to be true.

When God speaks to us now it is with the promise of what will be, not with a demand that we do what is impossible. Torah-as-promise tells me not to try, but to trust God.

■ Present yourself to God: Step out and act.

Act in the full conviction that the Holy Spirit can and will act in and through you.

The simple secret to righteousness really is faith. Trust brings us forensic righteousness: the declaration by God that we have been found innocent because of Jesus. And trust brings us practical righteousness. When we simply trust God to make real in us what the Word of God reveals, He will.

More Than Conquerors (8:28-39).

Background. What frees us to discover God's Word as a Torah-of-promise rather than perceive it as a Torah-of-obligation?

The answer lies in realizing the true nature of the new relationship with God that we now enjoy in Christ. Fallen human beings have an innate awareness of alienation from God. Law is perceived as a standard established to enable a man to approach God. Fallen human beings, driven by fear, assume that if they honestly try to live by the standard, they will merit at least some consideration for their acts. Even when condemned by conscience for failures, fallen man hopes that his good works will outweigh the bad.

Then the Gospel comes, and in Christ we hear the good news that God loves us despite our awful flaws. We discover that Christ died for our sins; rather than condemning us, He has pronounced us innocent. What is more, we learn that God has made us His heirs, and provided His own Spirit to transform and enable us. Suddenly the Torah-as-obligation becomes totally irrelevant to our relationship with the Lord! We no longer need to fear, or try to merit a salvation we have received as a gift.

When this realization grips us, and in every loving Word revealed by God we see Torah-as-promise, then in total trust we throw ourselves into his arms. Then the Law describes not what we must be but what is *already ours.* It is not to be earned, but is given. It is not what we try to do, but what we trust Him to do in us. And it is this, ours in the full confidence of God's love, that frees us.

And so Paul ends this magnificent chapter with a great reminder of how complete God's love for us is. For when we at last learn to perceive God's Word in view of our new nature as God's sons and heirs, what we will

sense there is promise alone. And as promised, God *will* fulfill His Word in our lives.

Consider, then, the powerful description of the love of God with which Paul concludes. And consider how assurance of God's love for us frees us from fear, and from the burden of reading His Word as duty to be performed.

What, then, shall we say in response to this? If God is for us, who can be against us? He who did not spare His own Son, but gave Him up for us all—how will He not also, along with Him, graciously give us all things? Who will bring any charge against those whom God has chosen? It is God who justifies. Who is he that condemns? Christ Jesus, who died—more than that, who was raised to life—is at the right hand of God and is also interceding for us. Who shall separate us from the love of Christ? Shall trouble or hardship or persecution or famine or nakedness or danger or sword? . . .

No, in all these things we are more than conquerors through Him who loved us. for I am convinced that neither death nor life, neither angels nor demons, neither the present nor the future, nor any powers, neither height nor depth, nor anything else in all creation, will be able to separate us from the love of God that is in Christ Jesus our Lord (8:31-39).

ROMANS 9–11
Righteous in History?

EXPOSITION

Paul's exposition of righteousness has concluded in a paean of praise. The righteousness of God that comes by faith transforms not only our standing with God, but our experience. We are declared righteous (chaps. 4–5), we are enabled to live righteous lives (6–8:17), and ultimately, we will be made perfectly righteous as, in the resurrection, we are conformed to the image of God's Son (Rom. 8:18-39). To the Jew, who viewed righteousness as faithful adherence to the Mosaic Law, Paul's presentation of the righteousness that comes from God, through Christ, as a gift to all who believe, was stunning indeed.

Yet Paul's argument to this point has left one great problem unresolved. In speaking about a "righteousness of God" (1:17; 3:21-22) that is mediated by faith, hasn't Paul made himself vulnerable to the charge that God Himself is acting unrighteously? Doesn't the welcome now extended to Gentiles mean that God has gone back on His Word to His covenant people, Israel? If Paul is right in his view, how can it be fair of God to turn His back on Israel in favor of this new community of faith, Christ's church?

To answer this objection, Paul turns again to the OT, and to a carefully reasoned argument developed from the biblical text. First Paul shows that the covenant promise is not extended automatically to all the *physical* descendants of Abraham (9:1-9). From the very beginning, God demonstrated His freedom to extend mercy to whomsoever He chose (9:10-21). God is thus not being inconsistent now in calling out a people from the Gentiles (9:22-26). Nor is God being inconsistent toward Israel, for in the church He is preserving a remnant of a people who rejected faith in favor of works (9:27-33).

As far as being fair is concerned, Christ is available to all, Jew as well as Gentile, and He "richly blesses all who call on Him" (10:1-15). Certainly throughout history Israel heard God's message, yet history shows that generation after generation was "disobedient and obstinate" (10:16–11:8). The blindness of Israel in history past and in the present age is a divine judgment on an unbelieving people (11:9-10). But this does not mean that God has rejected His people, or broken His covenant promises to Israel! The Gentiles are branches, but the root into which they have been grafted is Jewish. One day God will act to restore the natural branches. In that great day when the prophet's vision is fulfilled and the "deliverer [Messiah] will come from Zion," "all

343

Israel will be saved" (11:11-27).

The one great and utter certainty that underlies all history is that "God's gifts and His call are irrevocable." The Gospel age may show that God's plan is more complex than His OT people, or even we, can grasp. But we must never interpret events in such a way that we make God the least unfaithful to His Word (11:28-32).

And so Paul concludes his defense of God's righteousness with a doxology of praise to one whose judgments are unsearchable, and whose paths are "beyond searching out" (11:33-36).

WORD STUDIES

My brothers, those of my own race, the people of Israel (9:3-4). For Paul the people of Israel pose both an emotional and a theological problem. On a personal level Paul feels unceasing grief and anguish as he sees those of his own race turn their backs on salvation by faith. On a theological level Paul must deal with this charge: if Christ is for the Gentiles, then God has gone back on His word to Abraham's seed, and broken His covenant promises. Paul's sorrow for his own people persisted lifelong. But in Rom. 9–11 he is able to resolve the theological tension.

Yet as we read these chapters we can hardly grasp how difficult it was for a person steeped in Judaism to hear what the apostle is saying.

The reason is that to the ordinary Jew and to the sages, Israel is unique. The many privileges granted the race (9:4-5) were most often perceived as *merited*. This view is illustrated in a quote from *Leviticus Rabba,* found on p. 345. Although completed about A.D. 450, this exposition of Leviticus reflects the persistent view of the sages concerning Israel and her relationship with God, from at least the first century onward. In the passage quoted, the rabbis argue that when a word is applied to Israel, it expresses praise by drawing attention to Israel's excellencies. But when the same word is applied to the nations, that word condemns and draws attention to their flaws.

There is nothing here but the expressed assumption that God not only loves His people, He is also pleased with them. And the assumption that Israel's faithfulness to God's Law merits God's favor!

It is good to be sure that God loves us. It is disastrous to assume that He loves us because we deserve it!

It is not as though God's Word had *failed*

(9:6). The word is *ekpipto,* and means to "fall off" or "fall from." It is used in Acts 27:17, 26, and 29 to portray a ship that fails to hold its course. Paul is saying that despite the creation of the church, the influx of Gentile believers, and the rejection by most Jews of their Messiah, the course set in God's Word has not been abandoned.

However things may *look,* God has not changed, nor will He go back on His Word.

It's so easy for us too, when we are faced with tragedy or loss, to wonder if God has turned away and now neglects us despite His promise of unshakable love. We may find it difficult to understand our circumstances, just as first-century Jews were stunned by events. But at such a time we are to trust God, not doubt Him. We are to seek a fresh understanding of His ways, not insist that God adjust to our old ideas of how He must behave.

For not all who are descended from *Israel* are Israel (9:6). Despite the tendency of some to see physical descent from Abraham as a guarantee of salvation, there were in the first century many who were troubled by the failure of fellow Jews to be fully committed to God's Law. This laxity bothered those Jews who identified themselves and their party as the devout, the "righteous," or "the elect of righteousness."

They must have been well aware of the point Paul argues here. Not everyone who is an Israelite *physically* is one *spiritually.*

It is important to note that Paul is not contrasting the OT's physical (Jewish) Israel with a supposed NT spiritual Israel (the church). He is leading us back into the OT to make it very clear that within the larger circle of the physical descendants of the patriarchs there is a smaller circle drawn. And within that smaller circle are the spiritual descendants who make up the true family of Abraham and of God.

To be born a Jew was a happy accident of birth. But to be born again was, from the very beginning, no accident but a personal, con-

LEVITICUS RABBA V:VII

1.B. [Since, in laying their hands on the head of the bull, the elders sustain the community by adding to it the merit they enjoy], said R. Isaac, "The nations of the world have none to sustain them, for it is written, 'Those who sustain Egypt will fall' " (Ezek. 30:6).

C. But Israel has those who sustain it, as it is written: "And the elders of the congregation shall lay their hands [and so sustain Israel]" (Lev. 4:15).

1.A. Said R. Eleazar, "The nations of the world are called a congregation, and Israel is called a congregation."

B. The nations of the world are called a congregation: "For the congregation of the godless shall be desolate" (Job 15:34).

C. And Israel is called a congregation: "And the elders of the congregation shall lay their hands" (Lev. 4:15).

D. The nations of the world are called sturdy bulls and Israel is called sturdy bulls.

E. The nations of the world are called sturdy bulls: "The congregation of [sturdy] bulls with the calves of the peoples" (Ps. 68:30).

F. Israel is called sturdy bulls, as it is said, "Listen to me, you sturdy [bullish] of heart" (Isa. 46:12).

G. The nations of the world are called excellent, and Israel is called excellent.

H. The nations of the world are called excellent: "You and the daughters of excellent nations" (Ex. 32:18).

I. Israel is called excellent: "They are the excellent, in whom is all my delight" (Ps. 16:3).

J. The nations of the world are called sages, and Israel is called sages.

K. The nations of the world are called sages: "And I shall wipe out sages from Edom" (Obad. 1:8).

L. And Israel is called sages: "Sages store up knowledge" (Prov. 10:14).

M. The nations of the world are called unblemished, and Israel is called unblemished.

N. The nations of the world are called unblemished: "Unblemished as are those that go down to the pit" (Prov. 1:12).

O. And Israel is called unblemished: "The unblemished will inherit goodness" (Prov. 28:10).

P. The nations of the world are called men, and Israel is called men.

Q. The nations of the world are called men: "And you men who work iniquity" (Ps. 141.4).

R. And Israel is called men: "To you who are men I call" (Prov. 8:4).

S. The nations of the world are called righteous, and Israel is called righteous.

T. The nations of the world are called righteous: "And righteous men shall judge them" (Ezek. 23:45).

U. And Israel is called righteous: "And Your people—all of them are righteous" (Isa. 60:21).

V. The nations of the world are called mighty, and Israel is called mighty.

W. The nations of the world are called mighty: "Why do you boast of evil, of mighty men?" (Ps. 52:1).

X. And Israel is called mighty: "Mighty in power, those who do His word" (Ps. 103:20).

scious choice to trust in God's Word of promise.

Not only that, but Rebekah's children had *one and the same father* (9:10). The Greek phrase is even more explicit, and says that Rebekah "conceived [Jacob and Esau] by the one act of sexual intercourse."

Why is this important? Paul has earlier cited God's choice of Isaac and rejection of Ishmael as evidence that the deepest meaning of "Israel" cannot be established by mere physical descent from Abraham. However, the Jewish reader might argue that Ishmael was the son of a slave woman, not of Sarah. So Paul's argument is invalid.

"All right," Paul seems to say. "Look at Jacob and Esau." Not only did they have the same mother, but the fact that they were twins—conceived by the same act of intercourse—is indisputable proof that they had both parents in common. And yet God chose Jacob and rejected Esau! However exalted one's genealogy, physical descent simply is no guarantee of God's favor!

It's great to be born into a Christian home. But mom's or dad's faith cannot save anyone.

Before the twins were born or had done anything good or bad (9:11). What then about the argument of the elite, that they were the true Israel because they, unlike their lax brothers were faithful to God's Law?

With these words Paul slams another door in his readers' faces. You can't establish relationship with God on the basis of physical descent. Nor can you establish it on the basis of works—for God announced His choice of Jacob before the twins were born!

Paul's point is simply this. When we examine the sacred history, we simply *must* conclude that God has always operated on principles that in some way Israel has misunderstood completely!

How dangerous it is to be dogmatic. We need to study and develop sound beliefs; beliefs which are deeply rooted in Scripture. Yet we must never be dogmatic, but always willing to submit what little we do understand to the Word of God for correction and reform.

In order that God's purpose *in election* might stand (9:11). This phrase, which has caused so much theological turmoil and still

troubles many, is *kat' eklogen,* literally, "in terms of His free choice."

Paul is not arguing in this passage for a predestination which determines the eternal destiny of passive individuals, thrusting some helplessly into perdition and snatching others out of the fires. Paul is not arguing that human beings have *no* choice. What Paul *is* arguing is that for Israel to suppose that either their descent from the patriarchs, or their observance of the Law *limits God's freedom of choice* is demonstrably wrong!

The sacred history itself reveals again and again that God is free to make those choices that will best suit His good purposes. The clear implication is that, if God now chooses to offer His salvation to Gentiles and to bring a new covenant community into existence, He is certainly free to do so!

How foolish of us to try to fit God in some conceptual box. How foolish when we hear the testimony of a brother as to what the Lord has done in his or her life to object, "But God *can't* do that." God is freer than we may suppose and makes choices that reflect His purposes, not our own; His perception of His Word, which all too often is not quite ours.

Jacob I loved, but Esau I hated (9:13). The phrase is legal rather than emotional. It is an OT way of saying that Jacob was chosen, while any claim of Esau to covenant promises was decisively rejected.

The apostle does not teach that Jacob was predestined to salvation, or Esau predestined to be lost. The implications of the statement are limited by Paul's theme, which is the total freedom of God to choose.

Therefore God has mercy *on whom He wants* to have mercy, and He hardens whom He wants to harden (9:18). The quote that indicates God "hardened" Pharaoh is even more troubling to many than the words that express God's "hatred" of Esau.

But again, we must understand the emphasis as one that is appropriate to Paul's theme of God's utter freedom of choice—and we must not assume that if God acts so freely that we human beings have no freedom of choice at all!

In fact, it is possible to show from Exodus that this exercise of God's freedom did *not* affect Pharaoh's own responsibility for his choices. *The Bible Reader's Companion* (Victor, 1991) observes that many feel

> if God made Pharaoh resist Him, it wasn't fair to punish the ruler and Egypt for that sin! And the text does say God hardened Pharaoh's heart (4:21; 7:3; 14:4). But it also says Pharaoh hardened his own heart (8:32; 9:34-35). Also, how God hardened Pharaoh's heart is important. God did not change Pharaoh's natural tendency, nor did God force Pharaoh to act against his will. It was God's act of self-revelation that hardened the heart of Pharaoh. A similar self-revelation caused the Hebrew elders to believe (4:30-31).
>
> God still hardens and softens hearts—by the same means. He reveals Himself to us in Christ. Those who choose to believe are softened, and respond to the Lord. Those who choose not to believe are hardened, and refuse to respond. Each freely chooses his or her reaction to God's self-revelation. And each, like Pharaoh, is fully responsible for his own choice (p. 56).

The freedom of God must not lead us to assume that human beings are puppets. Nor must the responsibility of human beings for their own actions lead us to assume God is limited in His freedom of choice by anything that you or I may do.

Does not the potter have the right to make out of the *same lump* of clay some pottery for noble purposes and some for common use? (9:21) The image looks back to Jer. 18:1-11. There God the Creator is described as a potter, who takes a marred pot in His hands, crushes it into a lump again, and "formed it into another pot, shaping it as seemed best to him" (18:4).

So what real objection can the Jew have if God the Creator now chooses to refashion marred Gentiles and shape them into a noble vessel, the church? The creation cannot question the Creator.

Of particular note is the phrase "the same lump of clay." Israel saw itself as unique, special, utterly different from the rest of humanity. Yet to God all mankind is "the same lump of clay," not two. Neither Jew nor Gentile has exclusive claim on the grace, the goodness, or the love of God.

What if God, choosing to show His wrath and make His power known, bore with great patience the objects of His wrath? (9:22) The phrase is better rendered, "What if it is the case that. . . ." God's exercise of His freedom of choice is not arbitrary or capricious. What He chooses to do is guided by His purpose in Creation and in salvation.

Paul does not attempt a total explanation of the choice God makes. He simply illustrates from a principle established in Rom. 1–2. God has great patience. While the sin that mars human society shows both God's wrath and His power, God delays final judgment in order that today the "riches of His glory" (9:23) might be made known to both those Jews and Gentiles whom He has chosen to "call . . . 'My people' " (9:25).

Though the number of the Israelites be like the sand by the sea, only *the remnant* will be saved (9:27). The remnant (*to hupoleimma*) is a constant theme of the OT prophets, and is a most positive doctrine. However terribly the nation Israel may apostatize and its population turn from God, the Lord remains committed to preserve a core of true believers. The *Zondervan Expository Dictionary of Bible Words* notes,

> The theme of "a remnant" runs through the OT. This is an important theme, for it affirms that however great Israel's apostasy and God's judgment, a core of the faithful will still exist (e.g., 1 Kings 19:18; Mal. 3:16-18). It is prophetically important, for it pictures the fulfillment of the divine purpose in only a part of the people of Israel. Apostasy, even by the majority of the Jews, could not nullify the divine promise. Over and over the prophets pictured contemporary or coming judgments in which the majority died, and only a believing minority remained. Thus the doctrine of the remnant underlines the OT teaching on faith. It is not mere physical birth that brought a personal relationship with God. Those who were born within the covenant still needed to respond personally to God and to demonstrate an Abraham-like trust by their response to God's Word (p. 521).

Understanding the significance of "the remnant," we can see the force of this quote in

Paul's argument. God *has been consistent* from the very beginning. He has always distinguished between physical and spiritual Israel. He has always demonstrated that He is totally free to choose to show mercy to those who believe, whether they be Jew or Gentile. And God has from the very beginning demonstrated His commitment to accomplish His stated purpose—not through the "people" Israel, but through the believing remnant.

The Gentiles, who did not *pursue righteousness,* have obtained it (9:30). The phrase does not mean that the Gentiles as a people were unconcerned with moral issues. What Paul means is that the Gentiles did not look at righteousness as the Jews did, as a thing to be pursued within the framework established by the Mosaic Covenant. How strange! The Jews, who hungered for God, saw Law as a great flight of stairs they must mount to reach Him; they had stumbled and been left behind by Gentiles who simply responded to His promise with faith.

It's not enough to be sincere, or even to be "zealous" (10:2). With God the only thing that counts is trust in the promise He has made to us in Jesus Christ.

Christ is the *end of the Law* so that there may be righteousness for everyone who believes (10:4). Paul's point is that Christ's coming puts an end to the Jewish *misunderstanding of the Law as a way of salvation*—the subject of 10:1-3. No one can hear the Gospel of God's grace in Jesus, and at the same time hold on to the view that what we do compels God to save or bless us.

If you *confess with your mouth,* "Jesus is Lord," *and believe in your heart* that God raised Him from the dead, you will be saved (10:9). Paul is not alone in seeing Deut. 30:11-14, from which he quotes, as a critical OT source. The apocryphal book of Baruch and the writings of Philo in the first century see in Deuteronomy's allusion to the commandment as "up in heaven" and "beyond the sea" a reference to some cosmic revelation rather than discrete regulations. So here Paul's Jewish readers would understand some precedent for his exposition.

To Paul, the cosmic intent can only be to refer to Christ, and the "commandment" of the OT must be understood as its true nature is revealed in Jesus—a call to faith which begins in the heart and is expressed in action. Once again the utter harmony between the Testaments is revealed—when the OT is rightly understood as a Torah-of-promise rather than a Torah-of-law.

Thus the present rejection of Israel is fully explained. In the words of Deut. 29:25 they "abandoned the covenant of the Lord, the God of their fathers"—as that covenant must be understood.

Did they not hear? Of course they did (10:18-21). The faithful Jew may still argue that the cosmic message of the OT, a Torah-of-promise, just isn't clear. Paul rejects this argument out of hand. Didn't they hear? Of course they did! The problem is that Israel was not willing to *listen,* and as a "disobedient and obstinate people" turned its back on faith in favor of works.

THE PASSAGE IN DEPTH

The Remnant of Israel (11:1-32).

Background. What has and will happen to Israel remains a deeply divisive issue in theological circles. The question also has practical implications for Jewish-Christian relationships.

The traditional Christian position in regard to the Jewish people is called *supersessionism.* It is the teaching that the church superseded (replaced) Israel as God's Covenant people. The central conviction of supersessionism is that no one is saved apart from a personal faith in Jesus Christ. The old distinctions once drawn between Jew and Gentile have been erased as far as the way of salvation is concerned!

Recently supersessionism has been challenged. Many, seeking a closer relationship between Christians and Jews, have postulated a *two-covenant* approach. That approach notes that Jew and Christian *do* worship the same God, and so concludes that the Jew establishes a valid personal relationship with God through the Old Covenant (Mosaic Law), while the Christian bases his equally valid and equally personal relationship with God through faith in Jesus Christ.

Basic teachings are lightly tossed aside: the

universal testimony of the NT that salvation is by faith and not works, Paul's careful demonstration that all are sinners in need of a righteousness which God provides as a gift to those who believe, even Jesus' statement that "no one comes to the Father except through Me" (John 14:6). How amazing! There is *no way* that a "two-covenant" theology can be supported from the Word of God.

The problem, however, is that some of the *conclusions* drawn by those who rightly hold the supersessionist view are wrong! Some conclusions that have been drawn from supersessionist belief but do not necessarily follow are these:

■ The church has taken Israel's place in God's plan.

■ The church has inherited the blessings that God promised to Israel.

■ The Jews have been rejected *as a people,* and the covenant promises made to them have been revoked.

Paul, in Rom. 11, is going on to ask the question, in view of what he has taught before, "Did God reject His people?" Does the sudden unveiling of the church as a New Covenant people of God mean that the purposes and promises of the OT have been set aside? Paul's answer is extremely clear.

Exposition. Has God rejected His OT people? Paul responds with a simple, logical outline.

Has God Rejected His Old Testament People?

A. GOD'S ACCEPTANCE OF A SPIRITUAL ISRAEL (11:1-6)

B. GOD'S REJECTION OF RACIAL ISRAEL (11:7-32)
* It is deserved (11:7-10)
* It is beneficial (11:11-17)
* Digression: a warning against arrogance (11:18-24)
* It is temporary (11:25-32)

God's Acceptance of Spiritual Israel (11:1-6). The first proof that God has not rejected Israel is an obvious one. Paul himself is a Jew and a Christian. Even more, although by the time Paul wrote this letter Gentiles predominated in the church, Jewish Christians were present in significant numbers. These Jewish Christians had responded with faith to God's promise in Christ, and *they* now represent that faithful remnant of which the OT so often speaks.

Paul then points to biblical and historical precedent. In the time of Elijah the apostasy marked every facet of Israel's national life. Yet when Elijah cried out to God, the Lord told him of 7,000 hidden believers who had not bowed down to Baal. In grace, God preserved His OT people in that faithful remnant during an age of awful apostasy.

And now? Rather than reject Israel, God has again displayed His amazing grace toward Israel by preserving a remnant of that people within the church of Jesus Christ!

God's Rejection of Racial Israel (11:7-32). It is undoubtedly true that the church *has* superseded racial Israel as the people of God. But Paul has a number of things to say about this rejection.

■ Israel's rejection is deserved (11:7-10). Racial Israel did not obtain the standing with God it so eagerly and earnestly sought. In seeking a relationship with God based on works rather than on faith (10:1-4), Israel has fallen under the wrath of God. There is no doubt that racial Israel's present state is a divine result of divine judgment, just as Isaiah and David display.

■ Israel's rejection is beneficial (11:11-16). It has helped the rest of humanity. Israel is not "beyond recovery" (11:11). And because Israel did not welcome its Messiah, the door to salvation has been thrown open wide to the Gentiles.

In speaking of Israel's rejection as the "reconciliation of the world" (11:15), Paul is clearly thinking of the prophets' vision of a world dominated by the nation Israel, ruled over by God's Messiah. While "what if" speculation is futile, clearly Paul suggests that *if* Israel had accepted Christ immediately after His resurrection the divinely revealed program of the ages could have marched to immediate fulfillment. Instead the continued refusal of Israel to acknowledge Christ has meant the "reconciliation of the [Gentile] world" to God through the Savior.

What is the reference in 11:16 to "firstfruits"? Here as in Rom. 8 the imagery is of the first-ripe produce of the land, which serves as a promise of the future harvest. Spiritual Israel, Christian Jews who have accepted God as the Messiah, serve as God's clear promise to redeem His ancient people in His own harvest time.

Interestingly Paul makes it clear in 11:15 that, while the temporary rejection of national Israel has benefited mankind, the restoration of national Israel will bring even greater benefits to the world. "If their rejection is the reconciliation of the world, what will their acceptance be but life from the dead?"

Thus while national Israel's rejection is a divine judgment on unbelief, all that God has done and will do is, ultimately, for the blessing of all. In spite of national Israel's rejection, spiritual Israel is blessed, and the world of the Gentiles is granted an opportunity to experience the grace of God.

■ Digression: a warning against arrogance (11:18-24). Here Paul introduces a warning. The ultimate cause of Israel's rejection was her people's arrogance. They assumed that they possessed a privileged position, and so twisted God's Torah-of-promise into a Torah-of-law. Rather than trust, and by faith claim a righteousness God is eager to give, Israel insisted on working, and in pride assumed that pious acts could make them righteous before God. Paul reminds us that the root and trunk of salvation are Jewish. Israel's present rejection is simply the breaking off of Jewish branches from that still-standing tree, and the grafting in of Gentiles. Those Jewish branches were broken off because of unbelief, "and you stand [only!] by faith" (11:20). How easily God could cut off the Gentile branches and graft the Jewish back in again. After all, it is *their* tree!

We must be careful here not to read this passage as if Paul were talking about an individual and his personal salvation. This is no warning that once saved, an individual is in danger of being cut off from the Savior. Paul is talking about *peoples,* not individuals. The supersessionist, who despises Israel and sees the church as taking Israel's place in God's eternal plan is on dangerous ground. It is certainly easier for God to graft Israel back into life-giving relationship with Him than it was for Him to graft in Gentiles, who lived as strangers to God outside of His ancient covenants!

■ Israel's rejection is temporary (11:25-32). Paul makes his last point: God *will* restore national Israel! Quoting from promises recorded in Isa. 27:9 and 59:20-21, Paul foresees a day when Christ will "come from Zion," fulfilling the role assigned Him as Messiah in the OT. The Jewish people as a people are still God's elect. And when that day comes, "all Israel will be saved" (11:26).

Application. Paul gives a summary statement that helps us define that element of supersessionism which is correct, and associated conclusions which are not. "As far as the Gospel is concerned, they are enemies on your account; but as far as election is concerned, they are loved on account of the patriarchs" (11:28).

There is no salvation for any human being, Gentile or Jew, apart from the Gospel of faith in Jesus Christ. And "two covenant" theology which postulates two ways of salvation is wrong. Yet it does *not* follow that God has rejected Israel or turned aside from His commitments to Israel. As far as election is concerned, Israel is loved. And "God's gifts and His call are irrevocable" (11:29).

As history rushes to its close there will be a restoration of Israel, first to faith and then to prominence, as every prediction concerning the Covenant people is fulfilled. We do not know the details. And it is unwise to be too confident with our prophetic charts that diagram every detail of tomorrow's end-time news. Yet the unexpected present and temporary rejection of national Israel, an event not clearly foreseen by the prophets, reminds us that God's plan is more complex than we often assume.

And it is with this thought that the apostle

closes this section of Romans (11:33-36). His review of sacred history has shown clearly some of the hidden depths of God's wisdom and knowledge, and made it plain that His judgments are "unsearchable" (11:33). We do not, cannot, know the mind of God. But we can, in utter awe, praise and glorify Him for the complexity, the grace, the beauty, and the glory of His plan.

ROMANS 12–16
A Righteous, Loving Church

EXPOSITION

The final chapters of Romans have been called its "practical" section, in contrast to its "theological" core. In fact these chapters are the final development of what is throughout a theological argument. Paul has shown that Jew and Gentile alike have no righteousness of their own (chaps. 1–3), but that God credits righteousness to those who believe (chaps. 4–5). This righteousness from God is not simply forensic, for in saving us God unites us with Christ, providing a channel through which the Holy Spirit's power can flow to actually enable us to live righteously here and now. And in fact, the Spirit's presence is God's guarantee of our ultimate redemption and our final perfection in Christ's own image (chaps. 6–8). With his exploration of this righteousness which is "by faith from first to last" complete (1:17), Paul paused to answer the objection of those who saw in this the apparent setting aside of Israel. God has not acted unrighteously, for sacred history demonstrates His freedom to make such choices, the principle of mercy that underlies His acts, and His commitment to His promises. Sacred history also establishes the principle of the remnant, that spiritual Israel is always preserved despite the apostasy of national Israel, and thus Paul assures his reader that ultimately "all Israel will be saved" (chaps. 9–11).

But now there is one issue left. "Righteousness" is more than a forensic issue. It is more than an individual issue. Throughout Scripture we see that righteousness is also a corporate issue. God is intent on creating a just, moral community, a people whose lives together will bear witness to His character as well as to His grace. And so in Rom. 12–16 Paul invites us to visualize the shared lifestyle of a righteous, loving church.

How then does the community of faith express and experience righteousness? First, each individual must be committed to God's will (12:1-2). Then each must commit to the body, using whatever gifts he or she has for the others' benefit (12:3-8) while daily expressing real and practical love (12:9-21). Members of God's righteous community

351

will live as good citizens of the secular state (13:1-7), always acting in accord with the principle of love, for the outsider as well as the brother or sister in Christ (13:8-14).

Christians will also extend each the freedom to be responsible to Christ for many personal convictions. By refusing to condemn or look down on one another over "disputable" matters, the church will maintain its spirit of unity and glorify God. Acceptance, not conformity, is to be the norm in the community of faith (14:1–15:13).

In conclusion, Paul shares on a more personal level, speaking about his motives and future plans (15:14-33). Of special interest are the many greetings recorded in the last chapter, where in the list of names we find several women and a mix of Jewish, Greek, and Roman names (chap. 16). Christ's church truly is a new community, drawn from every human strain, and bonded together in Him to live—together—a life of love.

WORD STUDIES

Offer your bodies as living sacrifices, holy and pleasing to God—this is your *spiritual act of worship* (12:1). Paul purposely adopts the language of the OT in order to show the contrast with the Christian's calling. Rather than bodies burned on an altar, Christian worship calls for daily surrender of our living members to do God's will. This, Paul says, is our *logiken latreian,* better understood as "reasonable religion." *Latreia* is usually translated "serve," and refers to the practice of worship at the OT temple. What Paul is saying is exciting.

In view of the fact that God has given us righteousness, appropriate worship will take the form of living out that gift in our daily lives.

Our every act of obedience is worship!

Be transformed by the *renewing of your mind* (12:2). The word used here for "mind" is *nous,* and should not be confused with either "knowledge" or "reason." What Paul has in mind is more appropriately expressed in English as "perspective," or "way of thinking."

Believers are to resist the pressures exerted by the world to squeeze us into its way of thinking, and instead to have our every perspective on the issues of life renewed and transformed. The only way you or I can ever *do* the will of God is to recognize it. And we can only recognize God's will if we learn to see life's issues from God's perspective.

How great a gift Scripture is. And how great a gift the Spirit, who uses the Word to renew our minds and transform our lives.

So in Christ we who are many form *one body,* and each member belongs to all the others (12:5). Paul knows there must be a corporate expression of God's work in individuals. Here he suggests a unique way of looking at Christian interpersonal relationships. The church is a "body." Christians are this spiritual body's limbs. How intimately then we Christians are bonded to one another.

In this passage Paul emphasizes one implication of the "body" relationship. The church *functions* as a body when each member uses his or her gifts to serve the others. (For a discussion of spiritual gifts, see the commentary in 1 Cor. 12–14, pp. 383–90.)

This Rom. 12 emphasis serves as an important reminder. Too often Christians look at local churches as "service organizations." What programs does the church have for my children? What programs does it have for me? Is the choir good? Is there a youth group?

While these may be legitimate concerns, this is not really God's way of looking at the church. We must open our hearts to God's Word, and let the Spirit renew our perspective. We must begin to see the church as a closely knit fellowship of men and women who are dedicated to caring for and serving one another. And we must come to our churches seeking to share one another's lives.

Love must be sincere. . . . Be devoted to one another in *brotherly love* (12:9-10). In every NT passage dealing with the church as a body, the context emphasizes love. The word for love here is *agape.* In secular Greek this was the least distinctive of the common terms. So the writers of the NT took this word and filled it with a unique Christian meaning.

This is the word the early church chose to

use when speaking of God's love expressed in Jesus. God's love is no response to our goodness or beauty. Instead God's love is an expression of the character and will of the One who chose to love us sinners.

Agape-love is a commitment to caring. Even more, *agape*-love is a commitment to act for the welfare of the person(s) loved.

In sending Jesus, God filled a common word with uncommon meaning, and defined forever the way you and I are to relate to one another in Christ's church. When we do love one another with *agape*-love, committed to caring and committed to acting for one another's welfare, then and only then will Jesus' church function as the body that it is.

Share with God's people who are in need (12:13).
In *The New Testament in Its Social Environment* (Westminster Press, 1986), Stambaugh and Balch write:

Perhaps the most conspicuous quality of Christians was their charity, their generosity toward the poor. Matthew's Gospel is especially emphatic on the necessity of clothing the naked and visiting the sick (5:42–6:4; 19:16-22 and parallels; 25:31-46), and in Acts we see individual acts of charity (3:1-10; 9:36; 10:2-4) as well as more institutionalized provision for the poor — the distributions to the widows at Jerusalem (6:1) and the collection for victims of famine (11:27-30; 24:17). There are many exhortations to charity (Acts 20:33-35; Rom. 12:13; Eph. 4:28; 1 Tim. 5:3; Heb. 13:1-3; James 2:14-17; 1 John 3:17-24), which in the following generations *was recognized by outsiders as one of the characteristic qualities of the Christian community* [emphasis mine] (cf. Lucian, *Passing of Peregrinus* 12–13; Julian, *Misopogon* 363a-b; *Letters* 430d, ed. Spanheim).

It remains true that Christian love can be measured by our concern for others.

In doing this, you will *heap burning coals on his head* (12:20).
This saying from Prov. 25 has puzzled commentators through the ages. The view of Chrysostom and others, that Paul suggests we do good to an enemy so that his final punishment will be all the more severe, does not seem at all in keeping with Paul's tone here. The view of Augustine and Jerome seems more likely, that Paul uses the verse to suggest a "burning shame" that may lead to repentance.

Our only real help in understanding the metaphor of "heaping burning coals" on a person's head is found in the Jewish Targum on Prov. 25:21-22. There the image is understood in a positive sense, for the text adds "and the Lord will reward you" (i.e., make him your friend, enable you to win him over). We can conclude that, whatever the image meant to the first-century reader, the intent is positive. By doing good to those who seek to harm us we do in fact "overcome evil with good."

Let no debt remain outstanding, except the *continuing debt* to love one another (13:8).
The Greek has *opheilete,* a word which expresses a sense of moral obligation and personal responsibility. Paul expands this obligation beyond the church ("one another") by making reference to "his fellowman." As God loved us when we were His enemies, so we Christians are to love all.

But why does Paul suggest that love is the *only* thing we owe others? For the simple reason that love *includes everything!* Since *agape*-love seeks only to benefit its object, there is no need for the Law's list of don'ts. A person who truly loves won't use the body of another to selfishly commit adultery, won't kill, steal, or even covet another's possessions!

Love does no harm to its neighbor. Therefore love is the fulfillment of the Law (13:10).
Paul does not suggest, as did proponents of situation ethics, that *love replaces law* as a moral guideline. Rather Paul argues that a person who loves will choose the path that law marks out.

Augustine put it succinctly. "Love God, and do as you please." A person who loves God will do nothing to displease Him. And a person who loves others will do nothing to harm them.

So whatever you believe about *these things,* keep between yourself and God (14:22).
The "these things" of this passage are practices which are not forbidden in Scripture, but which some Christians felt were not appropriate for believers. In the first century

353

some felt strongly that keeping one day a week "sacred," and significantly limiting activities on that day, was an important expression of Christian faith. Similarly some believers were horrified that other Christians ate meat. The problem was, and is, that Christians who "don't" condemn and criticize those who "do," while the Christians who "do" look down on the "fanatics" who "don't."

Paul's advice in this verse is striking in its simplicity. After arguing that each Christian must be given freedom by the faith community to make up his or her own mind about such things, Paul sets out this very practical principle: "Keep your convictions to yourself."

How many divisions in our families and in our churches would be healed if we would only keep what we believe about disputable matters between ourselves and God—and focus on paying that debt of love that we owe to all.

I commend to you our sister Phoebe, a *servant* of the church in Cenchrea (16:1). The same Greek word is translated "deacon-(ess)" elsewhere in Paul's letters, as the NIV note acknowledges.

Scholars studying first-century sociology have developed a number of insights that bear on this reference, and are suggestive when we consider Phoebe's—and other women's—role in the first-century church. A sample of their views is found in the box on p. 354. While this background hardly constitutes "proof" Phoebe held the church office of deacon, it does help us answer the question of whether or not a woman might have been accepted as a leader in first-century society.

THE PASSAGE IN DEPTH

Submission to the Authorities (13:1-7).

Background. The church came into being as a community of faith, scattered throughout a hostile pagan world. It was vitally important if the church were to be the righteous community envisioned by Paul for the relationship between church and society, and particularly church and government, to be defined.

The roots of the original uncertainty can be traced back to the church's Jewish roots. In Babylon the Jewish community adopted as a guiding principle the rule that "the law of the sovereign is law for us." But in the West an intense and unshakeable hostility toward Rome was generated in Judea/Palestine, and influenced Jews throughout the Empire. In Judea Rome was viewed as "Rome the Guilty," the "kingdom of wickedness," whose overlordship must be resisted. What a contrast this was to the perspective of other subject peoples, who celebrated Rome as "eternal and divine," and who praised her emperors as "saviors." It is interesting that while the Jewish populations of Empire cities constantly agitated for civil rights, they also, for religious reasons, isolated themselves from the political life and responsibilities of other citizens. Thus the Jews were resented throughout the Empire, and were frequently the target of charges, even as their section of the city was a not infrequent site of riots.

Much of this hostility was a natural outgrowth of the first-century view that every responsible citizen should participate actively in the life of his community. Later this conviction generated major criticism of Christians. Yet public life in the cities of the Roman Empire was *pagan* life. Public events led by city and provincial officials involved the worship of the society's traditional gods and goddesses and, in time, honored the emperor as a deity. Like the Jews, Christians were unwilling to participate in what they considered idolatry.

And so pagan thinkers like Minucius complained that Christians "do not understand their civic duty" (*Octavius 12*), and Celcius argued that Christians ought to "accept public office in our country . . . for the sake of the preservation of the laws of piety" (*c. Cels. 8.75*). He ridiculed the Christians' reason for their withdrawal—that public service demanded involvement in pagan worship and thus denial of the true God. To Celcius, "where God is concerned it is irrational to avoid worshiping several gods." After all, the "man who worships several gods, because he worships some one of those which belong to the great God, even by this very action does that which is loved by Him. Anyone who honors and worships all those who belong to God does not hurt Him since they are all His" (*c. Cels. 8.2*).

PHOEBE THE "DEACONESS": INSIGHTS FROM CULTURAL BACKGROUND

The *thiasoi* that met in Greek cities and the *collegia* in Roman cities resembled Christian communities in several significant ways. They all worshiped some god. The professional, social, and burial societies all adopted a patron deity, to whom sacrifice was made as a central ceremony of the regular (usually monthly) meeting. . . . Most of these societies depended on the generosity of one or several patrons to supplement the more modest contributions of ordinary members. These patrons were expected to provide more elaborate banquets, for example, or to pay for the construction of a new temple. The host of Christian house churches functioned in a way analogous to that of such patrons. At Corinth, Stephanas seems to have been such a patron (1 Cor. 16:15-18), and at nearby Cenchreae, Phoebe is identified as *diakonos* and *prostatis* (Rom. 16:1-2). The latter term probably denotes a woman who functions as patroness to some society (Stanbaugh and Balch, *The New Testament in Its Social Environment*, Westminster, p. 140).

For some women the traditional roles were too confining. Not surprisingly, the most conspicuous examples come from the upper classes, whose situations gave them greater freedom. Even Philo, a firm believer in the spiritual and mental inferiority of women, granted that the formidable empress Livia was an exception. The instruction (*paideia*) she received enabled her to "become male in her reasoning power." Nor were opportunities altogether wanting for women of lower standing. Inscriptions show that women were active in commerce and manufacture and, like their male counterparts, used some of the money they made in ways that would win them recognition in their cities. Pomeroy observes that freed women from the eastern provinces often traded in luxury goods, "such as purple dye or perfumes"—a fact to be remembered when we meet Lydia, "a dealer in purple cloth," in Acts 16:14. In Pompeii a woman named Eumachia, who made her money in a brick-manufacturing concern, paid for one of the major buildings and donated it to a workmen's association. She held the title of *sacerdos publica*. Another woman there, Mamia, built the temple of the Genius of Augustus. Women with status and in business of all sorts are attested in Pompeii. Moreover, MacMullen points out that women appear more and more frequently as independent litigants, although the greatest activity begins just after the period of our primary concern. Throughout Italy and in the Greek-speaking provinces, MacMullen finds a small but significant number of women mentioned on coins and inscriptions as benefactors and officials of cities and as recipients of municipal honors therefore (Wayne A. Meeks, *The First Urban Christians*, Yale, p. 24).

In Romans 16:1 Phoebe is described as the *diakonon tes ekklesias* of the Corinthian port city of Cenchreae, a person who has helped Paul and many others (16:2). For that reason the community which Paul is addressing ought to help her *en hoo an humoon chreze pragmati*, "in whatever she may require from you." The term *pragma* frequently means "business" in the economic sense of that word, and the generalizing relative clause all the more hints that something more than just congregational matters are involved. At the least, the statement could be understood as a recommendation to support Phoebe in her "worldly" business. This support would reciprocate Phoebe's service to Paul and others. Thus her services too consisted of "earthly" things, *sarkika*. (Gerd Theissen, *The Social Setting of Pauline Christianity*, Fortress, p. 88)

Thus it was that, while the early Christians did not share the *hostility* of Palestinian Jews toward Rome, the nature of Roman society did force the Christian community into a course of action which was perceived as disloyal and hostile by the Roman government and people.

In essence, the church of Jesus Christ was

forced to try to live out God's righteousness in a situation where there was constant tension between believers and the state. And so the issue of how the Christian was to relate to an essentially hostile government was extremely difficult for the church, and Paul's teaching here was of critical importance.

Interpretation. Paul's principle for relating to secular government is essentially that of the Babylonian Jews. "Everyone must submit himself to the governing authorities" (13:1-7) is clearly parallel to "the law of the sovereign is the law for us."

Paul, however, is careful to give a theological basis for submission to secular authorities (13:1). He argues that God Himself has ordained government. This does *not* mean that God has ordained a *particular* government, such as the "government of the United States." What Paul argues is that God has so structured the world of human beings that there will be authorities and subjects, governments and citizens. The person who finds himself a citizen must respond appropriately to government, or he violates the divinely ordained ordering of society. One who does this will find himself in rebellion against God.

Paul goes on to explain *why* God ordained this state of affairs (13:3-4). He did it to promote the public peace. A government's mission is to "bear the sword." In this government is "God's servant, an agent of wrath to bring punishment on the wrongdoer."

This does not imply either that the government is the *conscious* servant of God, or that government is responsible to establish laws which are in conformity with biblical standards. Instead Paul argues that the very nature of the government-governed system God has ordained leads rulers to punish evildoers—for their own self-interest.

Because in our fallen world human beings have great potential for wickedness, the restraint imposed by human government is absolutely essential. The fact is that any government must punish evildoers to survive. It cannot afford to let its citizens be victimized and murdered, for a prosperous citizenry is essential to the well-being of the state. Thus, enlightened self-interest requires rulers to punish evildoers, and a side benefit of this is the protection and well-being of their subjects.

Paul argues that in submitting to rulers, the Christian supports the system which God has

ordained and so participates in one of God's gracious purposes in our present world. This is what Paul means when he says we are to be subject for conscience' sake, not just because the government has the power to punish us. Conscience demands that we actively support the workings of a system God has instituted for the benefit of humankind.

As Paul concludes, "This is . . . why you pay taxes" (13:6-7). It is to support a system God has ordained—even though that system, like the Roman Empire, misuses its power to persecute Christians! And, these verses clearly imply, our support of government is to be active and wholehearted.

The principle of submission that Paul laid down was followed rigorously by the Christian church even in times of persecution. But, as pointed out above (see *Background*), Christians were unable to *participate in governing.* Christians failed, out of a religious conviction that their pagan neighbors could neither understand nor appreciate, to make many of the civic contributions expected of citizens in the first century. In time Christians came to be viewed with a deeper hostility than the Jews had been. Christian withdrawal from public life was such a betrayal of the Hellenistic ideal that believers were accused of hating mankind, and the Christian refusal to worship the deities of the larger society led to charges of atheism.

Even so the average Christian concentrated on living a good life within the framework of human as well as divine law. Athenagoras, the second-century Christian writer, makes this defense: "Among us you will find uneducated persons, and artisans, and old women, who, if they are unable in words to prove the benefit of our doctrine, yet by their deeds exhibit the benefit arising from their persuasion of its truth; they do not rehearse speeches, but exhibit good works; when struck, they do not strike again; when robbed, they do not go to law; they give to those that ask of them, and love their neighbors as themselves" (*Plea,* chap. 11). In short, Christians were the best of citizens in a state that despised, misunderstood, and mistreated them.

Application. A critical question in our day revolves on how rigorously we Christians are to apply Paul's principle of submission to rulers. No one takes Rom. 13 to teach that the believer is to obey the ruler when to do so would mean disobeying God. No one takes Rom. 13 to suggest that the ruler's will is, *ipso facto*, the will of God.

But often issues are not clear-cut. Does Rom. 13 mean, for instance, that the Colonies had no right to rebel against the British crown in the 1770s? Does Rom. 13 mean, for instance, that those who marched during the 1960s in defiance of racist laws were wrong? That a person convinced that war is immoral had no right to resist the draft in the 1970s? That in the 1990s it is wrong to picket abortion clinics? Given Rom. 13, can civil disobedience ever be right?

While obedience to God must always take precedence, we may often find ourselves in a moral dilemma, where no clear-cut "this is right" stands in contrast with a clear-cut "this is wrong."

How do we resolve an issue when we come to a Scripture that says, "Submit . . . to the governing authorities," and our conscience seems to shout out that this time, at least, we must *not* submit?

To answer we must return to the core of Paul's teaching. Paul has said that *government as a system* is ordained by God. The Christian's submission to rulers is a matter of conscience, and expresses an intent to support government as a structure which God has ordained for the benefit of mankind. Thus *whatever we do should support the government in its rightful function.*

One way we support and submit to government is by obeying the laws of our land. But it is also possible to support and submit to government while *disobeying* the laws of our land. We submit by obeying, but we also submit by *refusing to resist government in its lawful role of punishing those who break its laws.*

For instance, if I picket an abortion clinic and my conscience requires me to unlawfully block access to it, then I must also in conscience support the government's right to punish me for my action. I can't refuse to show up for trial, or flee to Canada. I may have broken a law by blocking access, but *I uphold the rule of law* by accepting any punishment the courts then impose.

What Rom. 13 teaches us is that we must always act in good conscience to uphold the rule of law, even when my commitment to God's law compels me to break a law of my society.

It is never easy to live with the tension we feel as Christians between our commitment to a God whose values often are vastly different from the values of our society, and our commitment to live as good citizens in the world of men. And yet we are called to live with just this tension, and as we do so to either obey human laws, or to demonstrate our submission to the rule of law by accepting punishment when conscience calls us to disobey.

The Weak and the Strong (14:1–15:7).

Background. There's really one issue raised in this passage. That is, "What is the price of acceptance in the Christian community?"

Acceptance is important to everyone, Christian or not. The question of acceptance is overwhelmingly important during the teen years, when self-concept is fragile and self-doubts surge. Teens try to find a group of others they can identify with, a group to which they can belong. No wonder it's so important to wear what the other kids wear, to like the same music, and to do whatever others do. By acting like the others in their group, teens win acceptance and feel that they belong.

It's the same for most adults. We dress the same as our coworkers. When asked out to dinner the first question is, "What should we wear?" Underneath the obvious patterns of dress are more subtle rules. To fit in one crowd you need to play tennis and belong to the club; to belong to another you need to become involved in a common cause.

In every human society there's a price to pay for acceptance—conformity. Conformity in dress, conformity in activities, conformity in values and lifestyle. If we are like others, we assume we'll be accepted by them and will finally feel that we too belong.

Too many Christians have adopted this system and, squeezed into the world's mold, often have set up their own standards for belonging. We too put a price tag on acceptance. For some the price tag is doctrinal: to be accepted you must believe in an inerrant Bible, or Jesus' return before the Millennium. But for most, the price is conformity in lifestyle rather than belief. You mustn't smoke or drink. You must meet in church rather than a home Bible study—or you must be in a house church rather than a church building. You must be a political conservative or liberal; take a strong stand on abortion. None of these things is directly forbidden in Scripture. Yet if you fail the test of conformity that the local Christian community establishes, you may be tolerated, but you won't be accepted. In subtle ways you'll be informed that you don't really belong. We may not advertise our prices, but in all too many churches the price of acceptance is there, and people do read our prices.

It is this, the price Christians demand from others for acceptance, that Paul deals with in our passage.

Interpretation. When we understand acceptance as something that the world offers in return for conformity, we can understand how jolting the Bible's teaching is. Paul writes extensively on this topic here, and begins his instruction with these words: "Accept him whose faith is weak, without passing judgment on disputable matters" (14:1).

The passage goes on to explain. As in Christian communities today, believers in Paul's time had begun to put the price tag of conformity on belonging. One group accepted only vegetarian Christians. Another accepted only those who agreed with them on which day of the week is most sacred. A person would be truly accepted only if he believed in Jesus *and* conformed to the splinter group's distinctives.

But Paul speaks out boldly for the freedom of the Christian. He reminds the Romans that each individual belongs to the Lord now, and that "Christ died and returned to life so that He might be the Lord of both the dead and the living" (14:9). In areas open to dispute (i.e., where the right thing to do is not clearly established by a direct teaching of the Word of God), we are not to judge or look down on our brothers. Jesus alone is qualified to pass judgment (14:10-12). Released from our self-imposed responsibility to live others' lives, we are free simply to love them. Paul puts it this way: since God has accepted our fellow Christians, who are we to set up additional tests of fellowship? (14:3-4)

There is a wonderful freedom that we have in Christ. In the world, human beings may fearfully insist on setting up tests others must meet. In Christ, we can open our hearts to others warmly, welcoming even those whose faith is weak. Paul concludes his explanation with these challenging words: "Accept one another, then, just as Christ accepted you, in order to bring praise to God" (15:7).

Application. In this passage Paul has clarified the divine perspective on "disputable matters." In the process he established several principles that we Christians must learn to live by:

■ We are not to stand in judgment or look down on others whose convictions differ from our own.

■ We are to recognize the lordship of Jesus as a practical reality. This means we must protect the freedom of individual Christians to make up their own minds about "disputable matters." Jesus, not *my* conscience, is my brother's Lord.

■ The "disputable matters" about which we differ are neither wrong nor right *in themselves.* But, any act which violates conscience is wrong for that person.

■ In the exercise of our freedom we are to remain sensitive to the convictions of others. Choosing to act in ways that benefit our brothers is more important than asserting our freedom to do something which violates another's conscience.

■ We are better off if we all agree to keep our convictions on doubtful things to ourselves, and get on with the business of loving and serving each other.

Let's always remember the example of Christ. How did Jesus accept you and me? He welcomed us in our imperfection. He welcomed us in our ignorance. He welcomed us while old practices still clung to us like the linen wrappings of the grave clung to a raised Lazarus (John 11:44). Jesus welcomed us to a transforming experience of love, confident that the power of God's forgiveness would cleanse and purify us. It is our privilege as Christians to reach out, with this same loving welcome, to all who confess Jesus as Savior.

Accepting others doesn't mean that we must agree with all they believe just now. It doesn't mean that we approve of all they do. In the world, acceptance means that there must be conformity. In Christ, acceptance means that, in the company of Jesus' people, there is welcome and warmth and love—a love which tells brothers and sisters that, at last, they have found the people to whom they belong.

1 CORINTHIANS 1–4
A United Church Family

The letter to the Corinthians has been called the NT's "problem epistle." It contains Paul's response to reports of conflict in the local body and confusion over Christian practice and doctrine. Each new topic is introduced by the Greek phrase *peri dei,* "now concerning," making it relatively easy to outline the book and to follow Paul's discussion. Yet commentators have not agreed on a unifying theme, other than to note that throughout the book Paul seems intent on defending his apostolic authority, which factions in Corinth have challenged.

Yet there does seem to be a unifying theme, an underlying problem that is reflected in several of the issues with which Paul deals. That underlying problem is simply this: through one means or another, members of the Corinthian church seem intent on establishing their spiritual superiority. The issue is prestige: who within the church has higher status, greater influence, more power, a better right to rule?

In their drive for position the various Corinthian groups asserted their claim in different ways. One group claimed superiority because its allegiance was to a more impressive human leader (chaps. 1–4). Another claimed to be more spiritual because its members abstained from sex in marriage (chap. 7). Another because its members did not eat meat from pagan temple meat markets (chap. 8). Still others claimed superiority because of higher rank in city society (chap. 11), while another group protested that its members were obviously more spiritual because they spoke in tongues (chaps. 12–14). Again and again we sense the struggle of the Christians in Corinth to establish a hierarchy within the faith-community: a hierarchy which, on this group's or that group's scale of values, would make *them* superior to the rest!

No wonder Paul's writing here is so vigorous! The church is to be one, the living body of Christ on earth. To fulfill its divinely ordained purpose the church must be one in experience as well as in reality. So Paul sets himself to the task, not only of defending his apostolic authority, but also of correcting the thinking of those who supposed that their particular doctrine or practice was a basis for a claim of superiority over their brothers and sisters.

And so we come to the opening chapters of this important epistle. There, after initial greetings (1:1-9), Paul addresses those who sought to build their own prestige by claiming to be followers of a more impressive human leader than the others (1:10-17). Paul goes on to show that this worldly kind of thinking may seem "wise" by human standards. But God's wisdom, which men count "foolish," has revealed all such thinking to be vain. The Gospel focuses our attention on Christ, not human leaders (1:18-31); its appeal is to faith, not persuasive argument (2:1-5). The content of God's wisdom is ours by revelation, and every person who has the Spirit has access to the mind of Christ (2:5-16). In view of this, the Corinthian quarreling over human leaders shows they operate like "mere men," not mature Christians (3:1-4). Human leaders are just workers in the field God is cultivating; it is His people that are important and not their leaders. What counts is that you are Christ's — not that you follow Apollos or Paul or anyone else (3:5-23).

However, the church is to regard apostles as "servants of Christ" and to realize that they have been entrusted with "the secret things of God" (4:1-7). Despite the low regard Paul would be held in by those of the Hellenistic world (4:8-13), he is their "father through the Gospel," the founder of their church, and God has granted him a spiritual authority to which the arrogant among them must submit, or experience the consequences (4:14-21).

CORINTH

The city of Corinth lay on an isthmus controlling access to two seas, the Aegean on the east and the Ionian on the west. This prosperous ancient city, called "the bridge of the seas," had been destroyed by the Romans in 146 B.C. It was reestablished in 46 B.C. by Julius Caesar and populated with army veterans and freedmen. The city's strategic location quickly drew a large population, and about the time of Christ's birth Strabo wrote that "Corinth is said to be 'wealthy' on account of trade." Another source of prosperity was the banking industry which flourished there. A third factor was the large colony of artisans who settled in Corinth. For instance, Corinthian bronze was prized throughout the Empire, and Corinthian lamps were exported to every land. Finally, in Paul's day Corinth was also the capital of Achaia, and government activity brought both population and wealth into the city. The picture we derive is that of a bustling, active, prosperous community, populated by ambitious women and men, anxious to prosper and succeed.

Much has been written about the sexual mores of Corinth, and the erroneous report of a temple to Aphrodite served by 1,000 temple prostitutes. There is no doubt that morals were lax in Corinth, as in any ancient port city! But the phrase "to Corinthianize," a euphemism for indulging in promiscuity, was coined before the ancient city was destroyed in 146 B.C., and did not refer to first-century Corinth.

What seems more significant is the general tone of the city: its drive and enthusiasm, its focus on success and personal achievement. As we look into the epistle which Paul wrote to his "problem congregation" there, we quickly sense that these qualities have infected the church, and are reflected in the drive of its members to establish their own prestige within the fellowship of faith.

Surely in our own society we value the traits of hard work, enthusiasm, and commitment to personal success that marked the men and women of Corinth. And yet those very traits, as we will see, may be destructive to the unity we must learn to develop as we live together as members of the one body of our Lord Jesus Christ.

WORD STUDIES

Paul, called to be an apostle of Christ Jesus by *the will of God* (1:1). Paul typically begins his letters by identifying himself as an apostle. Here, however, he lays stress on his calling "by the will of God." Those in Corinth who arrogantly discount the apostle's appearance, and compare him unfavorably to better orators, ignore the real issue. Paul is God's man; it is by God's will that Paul has the rank of apostle. For this reason, the church must respect Paul and listen attentively to his teaching.

It is important that we too look beyond superficial things in our relationships with those who have spiritual authority in our churches. An attitude of disrespect or antagonism can do more harm to the local body than any leader's weaknesses, or even errors in judgment a leader may make.

To the church of God in Corinth . . . called to be holy *together* with all those everywhere who call on the name of our Lord Jesus Christ (1:2). This letter is addressed to the whole church, not to any factions within it. Christians have been called, as a people, to be set apart together for God. We are called in Christ to be God's holy people together: we are not to set an independent course, as the Corinthians have, setting up our own criteria by which to judge one another's spirituality.

Christians who seek to establish their own superiority within the church abandon the church's calling to be a holy, unified community of faith.

You do not lack any *spiritual gift* as you eagerly wait for our Lord Jesus Christ (1:7). It's not our spiritual potential that counts. It is whether or not we strive to realize our potential.

At the same time, Paul shares an important perspective here. He "always thank[s] God" (1:4) for this divided, flawed church, for he knows that potential exists. Later Paul will show us that God grants every believer spiritual gifts. So the potential for growth and change exists in everyone. Looking at the problems in the Corinthian church Paul might well have become discouraged. Yet Paul chose to focus on the promise that possession of God's Spirit brings to every person in Christ.

When we're discouraged with others, let's remember Paul's example. Let's join him in thanking God for the potential that, in His time, God will help even the dullest Christian realize.

So that there may be no divisions among

you (1:10). The Greek word is *schismata*. The literal meaning is "tear" or "crack." Paul is not thinking here of such phenomena as denominationalism. Rather his concern is for conflict in the local body which sets Christian over against Christian, and destroys the unity "of mind and thought" that is essential as we bear vital testimony to Jesus.

Again, this does not mean Christians should not have different opinions. What it means is that our differences must not be allowed to tear the fabric of unity that enables us to give witness of our essential oneness in the Lord.

For the message of the cross is foolishness to those *who are perishing*, but to us *who are being saved* it is the power of God (1:18). Paul is intent on making it clear that the Gospel is not a form of "wisdom." In the Greek world "wisdom" involved a rational effort to make sense out of what man observed and experienced. In Judaism "wisdom" demanded a visible miracle, the direct intervention of God to fulfill the end-time promises (cf. 1:20 with 1:22).

But Paul makes an important point in using the present participle when setting believer and unbeliever in contrast. Those who "are being saved" have rejected human approaches in order to rely on a wisdom of God as expressed in the message of Christ. It is those who "are perishing" who disparage the message of Christ as foolishness and reject out of hand the wisdom of God.

The implications are obvious. If we have set out on faith's life by considering the foolishness of the cross to be the true wisdom, we must certainly continue in our Christian walk by fully committing ourselves to God's wisdom and ways.

***Not many of you* were wise by human standards; not many were influential; not many were of noble birth (1:26).** The fact of the matter is that in the first century only about 1 percent of the population could have been characterized as wise by human standards, influential, or of noble birth. The fact that at least some from this extremely small upper class were Christians is very significant.

Even so, Christians as a class were scorned by the elite. The pagan writer Celsus is quoted by Origen (*Contra Celsus* 3:44) in a passage that distorts, yet sneers at this statement by

Paul. Celsus wrote,

> Their injunctions are like this. "Let no one educated, no one wise, no one sensible draw near. For these abilities are thought by us to be evils. But as for anyone ignorant, anyone stupid, anyone uneducated, anyone who is a child, let him come boldly." By the fact that they themselves admit that these people are worthy of their God, they show that they want and are able to convince only the foolish, dishonorable and stupid, and only slaves, women, and children.

The self-appointed elite of our day also tend to sneer at Christianity. Yet in God's time those who believe will be shown to be the truly wise.

I did not come with *eloquence* or *superior wisdom* as I proclaimed to you the testimony about God (2:1). In chapter 1 Paul called attention to the content of the Gospel, and identified it as an expression of God's wisdom. Here Paul calls attention to the manner of presentation of Christian teaching. Neither "eloquence" (*hyperochen logou*: overpowering oratory) (2:1) nor "superior wisdom" (probable meaning of *sophia* here is "philosophical discourse") are relevant.

This point is important, for in Hellenistic culture the skill of an orator was often judged of greater significance than the content of his speech, and in many a court case the verdict went to the advocate whose oratory was overpowering, rather than to the person with right on his side.

When it comes to the presentation of the Gospel, however, the message is more important than the messenger. It is the truth of the Gospel that compels. The validity of our witness does not stand or fall on either our looks or our speaking skills.

Modern Christians can also give more weight to the messenger than the message. "I just enjoy his preaching so" can seem far more important to some than whether the sermon challenges us, teaches us, and calls us to a transformed way of life.

We speak of *God's secret wisdom,* a wisdom that has been hidden (2:7). What characterizes God's wisdom? Paul has four

important things to say about it.

■ It is contained in a *mysterion*; it is "secret" wisdom. The term refers to truth inaccessible to human beings, but now revealed to all in Christ.

■ It "has been hidden." This phrase explains "secret." Until the Incarnation, God hid rather than disclosed that part of His eternal plan which has been now revealed in Jesus.

■ "None of the rulers of this age understood it" (2:8). Paul's point is that God's wisdom remains hidden to those who will not believe. Even though unveiled, those committed to man's way of looking at the universe simply cannot "see" the Gospel.

■ Finally, although out of order, God's wisdom has been "destined for our glory" (2:7). In taking our stand with the divine wisdom, we are assured of the ultimate salvation promised us, for we will stand, transformed and in Christ's own image, before our God.

What a contrast with human wisdom, restricted as it is not only by our puny powers but also by our inability to see the reality that lies beyond the physical and social world in which we live.

How foolish we are if we let the arguments of mere human beings sway us in any way from our commitment to God's revealed truth!

However, as it is written, "No eye has seen, no ear has heard" (2:9). Commentators have struggled with the question of what Paul is citing here, for no OT passage really resembles the quote, either in Hebrew or in the Greek Septuagint. Since the closest parallels that have been found are Isa. 64:4 and 65:17, tortuous arguments have been developed to show how Paul derived what must be an exceptionally free paraphrase.

However, Paul in this passage is contrasting human wisdom with God's secret wisdom. It is possible that he is quoting from a secular source, not as proof of his position, but to illustrate the limits of humanity's ability to grasp reality. If so, Paul may very well have been referring to a passage in the writings of the fifth-century B.C. Greek, Empedocles, whose words so strikingly resemble Paul's! (see the italicized portion in the quote from

Empedocles below) Surely the Empedocles passage makes exactly the point Paul is driving home here, as he contrasts the wisdom of God with the wisdom of man.

EMPEDOCLES

Weak and narrow are the powers implanted in the limbs of man; many the woes that fall on them and blunt the edges of thought; short is the measure of the life in death through which they toil. Then are they borne away; like smoke that vanished into the air; and what they dream they know is but the little that each hath stumbled upon in wandering about the world. Yet boast they all that they have learned the whole.

Vain fools! For what that is, *no eye hath seen, no ear hath heard, nor can it be conceived by the mind of man.*

The *spiritual man* makes judgments about all things, but he himself is not subject to any man's judgment (2:15). In this passage the *pneumatikos* is "the man with the spirit." It's important to Paul's argument to know that he consistently teaches every Christian has been given God's Spirit. On the one hand, then, Paul reminds the Corinthians that no faction can claim spiritual superiority over another, for all possess the Spirit!

Some take the phrase "is not subject to any man's judgment" to mean that the Christian is not subject to judgment by any man without the Spirit. In view of Rom. 14, and in view of the divisions in Corinth, it is more likely that Paul here is warning the Corinthians not to stand in judgment on one another. Each believer has access through the Spirit to the mind of Christ, and is responsible to Him as Lord. And, since we do know the mind of Christ, we must certainly acknowledge that the unity of the body on earth is His will!

You are still *worldly* (3:3). The word here is *sarkikos,* "fleshly," "of the flesh." Although they possess the Spirit, the Corinthians do not live by the Spirit; their outlook and behavior expresses the sinful nature of mankind.

While the NIV translation of "worldly" is unfortunate, it does remind us of an important truth. All those "don'ts" Christians have tended to list—smoking, drinking, whatever—are not really "worldliness." Worldliness is "acting

like mere men" (3:3), moved by the selfish impulses that drive lost humanity.

I gave you *milk,* not *solid food,* for you were not yet ready for it (3:2). The Gospel is both milk and meat, so suggests 1 Cor. 2:6-16. Salvation is the milk; solid food is the realization that the Christian life must be lived in the light of God's wisdom rather than the wisdom and ways of human society.

If *it is burned up,* he will suffer loss; he himself will be saved, but only as one escaping through the flames (3:15). God's wisdom calls for each of us to build with materials that will survive when the material universe is consumed (2 Peter 3:5-7). Our salvation is not at issue here. What is at issue is whether or not our behavior will stand scrutiny in the day when God rewards those who have done His will.

Unfortunately, some who line up for inspection in that day will, in Paul's image, quickly leap away from the perishable wooden structure of their deeds, as its flames turn to ashes.

If anyone destroys God's temple, *God will destroy him;* for God's temple is sacred, and you are that temple (3:17). It is important to note that Paul's awesome warning concerns destruction (*phtheiro:* ruin, corruption) of the church as a true Christian community. The reason for this warning is that God's temple is holy, set apart for His own purposes. Again no loss of salvation is implied. But the warning is extremely serious. The person, persons, or faction who corrupt the Christian community and ruin it in sofaras its ability to reflect God's wisdom is concerned, themselves face ruin by the Lord.

I care very little if I am *judged* by you or any human court; indeed, I do not even judge myself. My conscience is clear, but that does not make me innocent (4:3-4). Paul is a servant of Jesus, entrusted with a mission, well aware that those granted such a trust must be found faithful. The Corinthians have scorned Paul and attacked both his conduct and his teaching.

Yet faithfulness is something that only the Lord can evaluate. While we need to maintain a clear conscience, we are not competent even to judge ourselves, for we may well be unaware of motives and desires that deflect us from God's path. What then do we do? We simply commit ourselves to do God's will as we understand it.

This age is not the time to criticize others. It is not even the time for agonizing introspection. It is time to concentrate every effort on serving the Lord.

For who makes you *different* from anyone else? What do you have that you did not receive? And if you did receive it, why do you boast as though you did not? (4:7) The word is *diakrino,* to evaluate, judge, make distinctions. Paul here challenges the individuals who are causing the schisms in Corinth: What distinguishes you? What makes you different?

Whatever distinction a Corinthian might claim—whether wealth, whether a particular spiritual gift, whatever—that Christian is now confronted with the fact that who he or she is, and whatever gifts or abilities he or she may have, come from the Lord.

This truth is double-edged. There is no room to be puffed up or proud about something we have been given. At the same time there is great comfort here. You and I realize our gracious and loving God made us as we are. He supervised the development of our bodies in the womb. He chose the cultures and families into which we were born. And all that He has done is a gift, for His shaping has fitted us for the role in life—the role in His church—that we are now able to play.

So let's thank God for who we are, without taking pride in those things which may distinguish us from others. And let's thank God for what distinguishes others as well, for they like we are God's gifts to His whole people.

Up to this moment we have become the scum of the earth, the refuse of the world (4:13). These are strong words. *Perikatharmata* is dirt or filth removed by washing; *peripsema* is embedded dirt removed by scraping after the bath. What a powerful image Paul presents, and how sharply the great apostle draws the distinction between the wisdom of the world and of God.

The cultured in the Hellenistic world scorned Paul and his fellow evangelists as scum. Yet history has validated them as not only the shapers of Western culture, but bearers of a Good News which has transformed billions.

He will remind you of my way of life in Christ Jesus, which *agrees with what I* teach everywhere in every church (4:17). The words in italics are not in the Greek. That text simply says "my way [of life] which I teach."

Let's never suppose that Christian teaching is doctrine divorced from practice. Teaching believers to live godly lives is as much the mission of the pastor or missionary as instructing them in doctrine. But to truly teach a godly way of life, the Christian leader must live it as well as talk it. For Christians, Gospel living is a necessary adjunct to Gospel words.

The kingdom of God is not a matter of talk but of *power* (4:20). The word is *dunamis,* a freedom of action which cannot be thwarted by anything man may do. The power that Paul relies on is not his own, but that of the Holy Spirit. God will deal with the arrogant unless they submit to His words to them through the apostle.

THE PASSAGE IN DEPTH

Wisdom from the Spirit (2:6-16)

Background. As the quotation from Celsus (see Word Study of 1 Cor. 1:26, above) shows, the educated in the Roman Empire looked at Christianity, and scornfully dismissed it as a religion of and for fools.

Even though the Empire was ruled by Rome, the Empire's culture was essentially Greek. The Greek language, and Greek

thought, dominated in the cities of the Empire and shaped the perspective of the upper classes. The Greek worldview, shaped over hundreds of years by notable philosophers and poets, celebrated human achievement. The successful athlete who had sculpted his body to perfection, the great orator, the thinker whose speculations about the nature of the universe fascinate the mind—these were the admired and idolized. Even the common people had access to the wisdom of the age, as itinerant teachers traveled from city to city, collecting fees from students who gathered around them as they propounded the theories of Plato or argued for the ethical stance of the Stoics or Epicureans.

Underlying every school of thought, however, was an unstated but universal assumption. Human beings, using their rational faculties, could penetrate the deepest secrets of the universe and grasp its underlying reality. Philosophers might differ about the nature of that reality. Yet all agreed that wisdom (*sophia*, the exercise of intellect and insight was the means by which mankind could understand the universe and could learn to live in harmony with universal laws.

In view of this deeply ingrained outlook, we can understand why Celsus and others so scornfully dismissed Christianity. Christians did not rely on *sophia*. Their religion was rooted in the superstitious (i.e., irrational) belief that a dead Jew had come back to life. And their leaders even demanded that this incredible message be taken on faith. This new religion with no basis in *sophia* (rational argument) was in fact against all *sophia* (reason). Christianity simply must, then, be a religion of fools and madmen, of the ignorant who have abandoned reason for irrationality.

As we better understand the intellectual climate of the first-century world, we sense the importance of Paul's teaching in 1 Cor. 2:6-16. For here he argues that there is another *sophia*—a divine wisdom that is drastically different in nature from the *sophia* of man.

Interpretation. Paul's argument, that Christianity is rooted in a divine wisdom which stands in contrast to mere human wisdom, can be outlined as follows:

The nature of God's *sophia* (2:6-8).
The limitations of human *sophia* (2:9).
The revelation of God's *sophia* (2:10-11).
Our access to God's *sophia* (2:12-14).
The import of our access to God's *sophia* (2:15-16).

The Nature of God's *Sophia* (2:6-8). Paul begins by asserting that he does speak "a message of *sophia*" (2:6). This is a message he speaks among the "mature," here to be understood as those who have been enlightened by the Spirit.

This *sophia* of God stands in sharp contrast to "the wisdom of this age" and its rulers. Worldly wisdom is useless, for its proponents are "coming to nothing." The "rulers" are to be understood as those influential persons who set the tone of the age: the thinkers, the movers, the secular and religious leaders. The great problem with human wisdom is that it is a dead end. More than that, it is a pathway which dissolves under the feet of mankind as people follow it; it becomes more and more gossamer until it dissolves completely, leaving those who tried it suspended in nothingness.

What a contrast with God's wisdom, which is "destined for our glory" (2:7). Those who follow the path of God's wisdom are not only on solid ground, but that path will bring them safely to glory.

What are the contrasting characteristics of God's wisdom and man's wisdom?

■ God's wisdom is *mysterion*, "secret."

■ It has been hidden prior to Christ's arrival.

■ It cannot be understood by human beings without the Spirit.

■ It leads to glory.
In contrast:

■ Man's wisdom is apparent.

■ It reflects on what can be touched and seen.

■ It fits the natural (lost) person's way of thinking.

■ It leads to nothingness.
God's wisdom and man's are of completely different orders, as distinct in nature as in content.

The Limitations of Human *Sophia* (2:9). The essential problem with human wisdom is that its conclusions are necessarily flawed. First, humans can only reason from evidence that they can access by the senses. Only what the eye has seen or the ear has heard can be considered by humans who speculate about the true nature of the universe.

And there is another problem. The human mind, even in its wildest flight of fancy, is unable to conceive of that reality which God knows.

There is thus no way that man could ever discover "what God has prepared" (2:9) by the exercise of rational faculties (*sophia*).

It is interesting that Paul seems to quote here not from Scripture but from Empedocles. Yet how appropriate that quote is. For the fifth-century B.C. poet clearly stated the fatal flaw in human *sophia*; he knew full well that those who "boast . . . that they have learned the whole" are "vain fools!" (Empedocles) Unaided man wandering about the world, at best, may stumble on fragments of the truth, but can never, ever, learn the whole (see the entire quote in the Word Study of 2:9, above).

The Revelation of God's *Sophia* (2:10-11). How then can human beings, limited as we are, have access to God's secret *sophia*?

The answer is revelation. God's Spirit, who as God has access to the mind of the Father, knows the very thoughts of God. And the Spirit has revealed these thoughts in words (2:13).

Thus the Christian has no need to rely on his or her limited human abilities. Instead the Christian looks to revelation, and in revelation gains access to knowledge about "all things" (2:15), which no mere human could ever discover on his or her own.

Our Access to God's *Sophia* (2:12-14). But don't all people now have access to God's *sophia* through Scripture? The answer is yes and no. Because the Spirit's words have been "enscripturated"—written down—anyone can read them. But reading, or even hearing this secret wisdom expounded, does not mean that the natural man will understand or accept the divine wisdom! It is only those who possess the Spirit who will understand, for the Spirit who inspired the words must reside within to interpret them appropriately if God's wisdom is to profit us.

This does not mean that only the Christian can understand the Gospel well enough to explain it to others. It does mean that only those with the Spirit will take God's Word to heart, sense its implications for their lives today, and follow the path that it marks out.

The Importance of Our Access to God's *Sophia* (2:15-16). The first implication is that

the "spiritual man" (i.e., the person with the Spirit [2:15]) is able to see the issues of life from a completely different perspective than the rest of mankind. With access to God's Word and with the Interpreter of those words dwelling within, the Christian "makes judgments about all things" without being "subject to any man's judgment" (2:16).

The world may scorn the Christian and call his beliefs and way of life foolishness. But our Spirit-led judgments about the issues of life simply are not subject to human judgment. Lost men and women, blind to the realities that we understand through revelation, have no basis from which to judge you and me. Through the Word and the Spirit you and I have access to the mind of Christ Himself!

Application. Paul's exposition has a dual application. In the first place his exposé of the flaws in man's approach to wisdom reassures us in our commitment to God's Word. We have no need to cringe when the sophisticated of this age attack our faith. No person without the Spirit of God can possibly understand reality as God has shaped it. But you and I, with the written Word and its Interpreter within, have access to ultimate truth. Let us stand fast, and affirm the truth of God undaunted by any ridicule or attack from the lost.

In the second place, in the context of the factionalism that was destroying the unity of the Corinthian church, Paul's discussion of the two wisdoms reminds us that we must commit fully to God's wisdom if we are to live in harmony with others in Christ's church. The access to the mind of Christ that our faith provides is not only ours, but our brothers' as well. We are not to stand in judgment on others' convictions, nor they on ours. The way of God's wisdom is the way of unity—a unity forged by the realization that God has called us to love one another, and in love to discover a oneness that will remain forever a mystery to mere humans.

When I recognize that my brother too has the Spirit to guide him, I will no longer insist on imposing my convictions on him or seeking to exalt myself as better than he. Then I will at last realize that the Spirit has been given to me, not that I might judge or control others, but that I might discover the path God wants me to walk, with Him.

1 CORINTHIANS 5–6
Church Family Discipline

EXPOSITION

In the Corinthians' competition for position and prestige the church had abandoned God's wisdom in favor of the bankrupt wisdom of mere men. Paul now moves on to deal with reports that the church actually tolerates sexual immorality, and that believers are carrying their disputes before secular courts. The relationship of these matters to the argument of chapters 1–4 is clear. The Corinthians are "worldly," for they have abandoned application of God's wisdom to issues that bear on the purity of the church.

The first evidence of worldliness is their church's toleration of immorality. Paul passes judgment on the sinner and insists that the church "hand this man over to Satan" (5:1-5). It is essential that the church "get rid of" malice and wickedness that the community may be marked by "sincerity and truth" (5:6-8). Paul then goes on to clarify his words. His instruction not to "associate with sexually immoral people" (5:9) relates only to relationships *within the church.* Christians are not to withdraw from unbelievers who are immoral. It is no business of ours to stand in judgment on the lost, but most surely it is the business of the church to discipline believers who live immoral lives (5:9-13).

Paul then turns to the issue of disputes within the church, disputes which in some cases have been taken before secular courts. If disputes do arise, why not have other believers—with access to God's wisdom—judge between the disputants? (6:1-6) The very existence of lawsuits shows a failure to live by the wisdom of God. The kind of disputes reported to Paul involve charges of cheating and wronging others. Surely no one committed to the wisdom—the way of life laid out by God for His people—would ever perpetrate such wrongs (6:7-8). Aggravated and angry, Paul states the obvious. Too many relationships in Corinth reflect the ways of the wicked, who will never "inherit the kingdom of God" (6:9). All this should lie in the past for the Corinthian believers, who have been washed and sanctified and justified in Jesus' name (6:9-11).

Again Paul pauses to explain. In one sense the Corinthians who claim that "everything is permissible for me" (6:12) are right. The Christian is saved by Christ's sacrifice, and neither past nor present works have any bearing on a person's salvation. But this is not the issue. We have been joined to Christ, and are linked to Him in the most intimate of unions by the Spirit of God. How can anyone imagine that Jesus would willingly be involved in sexual immorality? Yet when the Christian sins, he makes Jesus a party to his wickedness (6:12-17). How unthinkable, then, sex sin is. Don't these Corinthians who prate about permissibility realize their bodies are temples of God's *Holy* Spirit? Don't they realize they were bought with a price, and as God's own people now, are bound to honor Him with their bodies?

We can sense Paul's intense disgust as he deals with moral corruption in the Corinthian church. These self-important people, who are so puffed up in their own eyes, have not just turned their backs on God's wisdom. They have repudiated His call to holiness and to a life that honors their Lord.

WORD STUDIES

It is actually reported that there is sexual immorality among you, and *of a kind that does not occur even among pagans* (5:1). While we may tend to view first-century pagan society as grossly immoral, this is not necessarily the case. The Greek romance novels of the era, unlike the romance novels of our day, developed their plot around the faithfulness of the hero and heroine to each other! A good example is seen in the Ephesiaca of Zenophon of Ephesus, in which Habrocomes and Anthia pledge "that you will abide chaste unto me and never tolerate another man, and that I shall never consort with another woman" (1.11.3-5). The popularity of such novels with ordinary people suggests that faithfulness was widely admired. This attitude is also attested in many epitaphs of the time praising women as *monoandros,* "a one-man woman."

It is striking that the immorality tolerated by the Corinthian church was of a kind that "does not occur even among pagans." That immorality is defined in the next phrase, "A man has his father's wife" (5:1). The verb "has" is a present infinite; it indicates a continuing immoral affair. Since the "sexual immorality" is *porneia,* a general term rather than the more specific term for incest, it is most likely that the case involved a man engaged in an affair with a woman who had been his father's wife, although now the two were either divorced or the father was dead. Not only was such a relationship illicit by OT Law (Lev. 18:8), but it was also forbidden in Roman law, at least as stated in the Institutes of Gaius.

Yet this immoral sexual relationship, scandalous in the eyes of both Jew and Gentile alike, was ignored by the leaders of the early church.

Shouldn't you rather have been *filled with grief* and have *put out of your fellowship* the man who did this? (5:2) What is the appropriate reaction when a fellow believer falls into the regular practice of sin? Our first reaction should be grief—a deep anguish of soul over not only our brother's sin but our own failure to help him keep to the right paths.

This attitude is set over against the pride of the Corinthians. And it reminds us that whenever it is necessary to exercise church discipline, we dare never do so in a spirit of pride or condemnation. Our brother's failure is to some extent our own.

In calling on the church to put the man "out of your fellowship," Paul prescribes how we are to deal with those who continually practice sin. The rationale is important. Sin interrupts the fellowship between the believer and the Lord. When a Christian continues in sin, he or she clearly does not understand or care about his present spiritual condition.

It then becomes the responsibility of the church to act out the reality of that spiritual separation in the body here on earth. We put those who persist in practicing sin out of our fellowship in order that they may sense the pain of separation from the Lord through their enforced ostracism from His people.

***Hand this man over to Satan,* so that the *sinful nature may be destroyed* and his spirit saved on the day of the Lord (5:5).** Again the NIV translation is unfortunate. The Greek text says hand him over "for the destruction of the flesh." The translators *interpreted* rather than translated this text.

There are a variety of interpretations of handing over to Satan. Some take it as turning someone out into Satan's sphere. Others say it is an Aramaic idiom meaning, "Let them suffer with their own evil devices," or "Let them stew in their own juice."

One alternative suggestion that has merit is that Paul does intend to make a distinction between participation in the fellowship dominated by the Spirit and participation in a world dominated by demonic forces. Confronted by the reality of this difference, the ostracized believer may experience the pain that living in the flesh causes, and its attractiveness to him may be extinguished.

What commends this interpretation is the simple fact that church discipline is not designed to punish sinners, but to bring them to their senses and restore them to fellowship with the Lord and His body.

Get rid of the *old yeast* (5:7). Paul uses OT imagery to make an important point. When a first-century housewife made bread she used yeast to make the dough rise. Most of the dough was cooked, but a small portion was kept and mixed with new ingredients. Overnight the yeast permeated the new mixture, and the process was repeated again and again.

At Passover time, every bit of the old leaven was cast out, and Israel again celebrated its redemption and a new start. And so Paul reminds the Corinthians. Christ is our Passover Lamb. He has given us a totally new beginning, and by ridding ourselves from such "old" things as malice and wickedness, we are to become what we are — new men and women, renewed in Jesus to live a life of sincerity and truth.

Not at all meaning the people of this world who are immoral, or the greedy and swindlers, or idolaters (5:10). How strange that Christians are quick to scorn and withdraw from the unbeliever who is immoral, but are tolerant of fellow believers. Paul reminds us that we are not to withdraw from contact with unbelievers. Nor are we to judge them. After all, when the lost show themselves to be sinners, they are simply "doing what comes naturally." They don't need us to condemn or criticize their behavior. They need Jesus to forgive their sins and set them on a new way of life!

Witnessing isn't convincing others that they are sinners. Witnessing is telling them the Good News that Jesus loves them despite their sins. And, witnessing is showing them Jesus' love by truly caring for them, despite their sins.

Expel the sinning believer, yes. But don't withdraw from the unbeliever who is a sinner. After all, you are a sinner's best hope!

Everything is permissible for me (6:12). Paul is not expressing his own view, but the assertion of some in Corinth that they have unrestricted freedom to act any way they please as far as the physical body is concerned. Their argument? "Food for the stomach and the stomach for food" (6:13). One college student expressed the same argument in challenging Billy Graham: "Eating a ham sandwich isn't a moral issue. Sex is just as natural, and isn't a moral issue either."

Since food and hunger complement each other, why shouldn't we be just as free to satisfy our sex drives through those bodily structures God created to complement them?

In horror Paul rejects this view, and sets out four tests that Christians should apply to any issue.

■ Is the action being considered beneficial (*sumpherei*)? Does it make a positive contribution to our own Christian development and to the development of others?

■ Is the action being considered something that will master us (*exousiasthesomai*: overpower and dominate [6:12])? Clearly man's sexual nature, twisted by sin, dominates all too many of us.

■ Is the action being considered in harmony with the fact that the body is "for the Lord"? (6:13) Paul consistently makes it clear that we have been redeemed in order to "offer the parts of your body to [God] as instruments of righteousness" (Rom. 6:13). The argument that sex is "natural" is empty and irrelevant. What counts is that all we do in our bodies is to serve the cause of righteousness. And sexual immorality is not righteousness. It is sin.

■ Paul's final test is: Is the action contemplated in harmony with the truth that the Lord is "for the body"? (6:13) Paul means that Christ has redeemed our bodies. He has raised us from the corruption of the grave that marked our old life, and united Himself to us in an unbreakable bond. In this union all we do should be an expression of Jesus; we are channels through which Jesus is embodied today in our world.

No wonder Paul has such a horror of sex sins. A horror that he wants us to share. As the living temples of the living God, we must flee sexual immorality as the plague! For a plague it is, and utterly dishonoring to our Lord.

THE PASSAGE IN DEPTH

Expel the Immoral Brother (5:1-13).

Background. In 1 Cor. 4:5 Paul instructed the Corinthians to "judge nothing before the appointed time." Yet in this passage Paul is sharply critical of the church for failing to judge an immoral brother.

Paul is not being inconsistent. A survey of passages on "judging" helps us make important distinctions. In general we are not to "judge" in the sense of condemning others. But we are to "judge" in the sense of evaluating.

Even more important is to make distinctions between what Christians are *not* to attempt to evaluate, and those areas in which evaluation is important.

What We Are *Not* to Judge.

■ We have no right to condemn others, but rather are to forgive (Matt. 7:1-2; Luke 6:37-38).

■ We are not to judge others for practices which are not specifically condemned in Scripture. When doubt exists about whether or not a particular practice is appropriate for Christians, we must extend to each brother and sister the right to follow their own conscience—and we must follow ours (Rom. 14:1-18).

■ We are not to judge the faithfulness of another believer to his or her calling in the Lord (1 Cor. 4:3-5).

■ We are not to relate to non-Christians in a judgmental way. Their morality or immorality is not the issue. The only issue is that they need to know Christ (1 Cor. 5:12).

■ We are not to use condemnation or criticism in an attempt to force others to conform to our consciences (Col. 2:16).

■ We are not to talk against, "slander,"

our brothers. When we do we exalt ourselves as judges rather than doers of the Law. Only God who gave the Law can condemn (James 4:11-12).

In each of these passages "judging" has a quasi-legal force. The person judging calls the motives or choices of others into question, and then condemns them. Yet each element of this process is ruled out, first of all by the fact that mere human beings are not competent to evaluate others' motives or "doubtful" practices. Even when an action is clearly wrong, our role is not to condemn but to forgive and seek to restore. Judgmental attitudes and attempts to punish or condemn are simply not appropriate in the Christian community.

What We Are to Judge.

■ Human beings are to judge violation of criminal and civil law. God established human government to restrain evildoers (Rom. 13:1-7).

■ We are to make "judgments about all things." Here *anakrino* means to exercise discernment, to examine. Because we have the Word and the Holy Spirit we can see the issues of life from God's perspective (1 Cor. 2:15).

■ The church is to judge the brother or sister who persists in the practice of immorality or other sin (1 Cor. 5:12-13).

■ Believers are to serve on panels established to resolve disputes between Christians (1 Cor. 6:2-5).

■ "Judge for yourselves" on issues clearly established in Scripture, and to develop convictions based on principles established in the Word of God (1 Cor. 10:15; 11:13).

■ We are to judge ourselves, in the sense of being aware when our actions fall short of God's will. Recognizing sins, we confess them and are restored to fellowship with the Lord. When we judge ourselves, no discipline by the church or by the Lord will be required (1 Cor. 11:31-32).

Awareness of the NT's teaching on judging provides significant background as we approach the question of church discipline, and the necessity that discipline imposes on us of judging the actions of a brother or sister in the Lord.

Interpretation. The most important issue is established in the simple statement that "there is sexual immorality among you" (5:1). Paul is referring to the persistent practice (see Word Study of 5:1, above) of something that is unquestionably immoral. But why is it "unquestionably immoral"? Certainly not because Paul or even the church calls it to be immoral. Paul knows that the practice is sexually immoral because that behavior has been identified as immoral in Scripture. Thus Paul and the church are not judging another's motives or faithfulness to the Lord. They are agreeing with God's Word that the behavior being practiced is wrong.

This is the first distinctive of church discipline. It is appropriate only in cases where the matter being judged is sin, as clearly defined in the Word of God.

Rather than approach this passage verse by verse, we may note the following elements in the case with which Paul is dealing. From these we can establish principles that guide us in our own application of church discipline today. The relevant elements are:

■ A fellow-believer's personal choice to practice what the Bible identifies as sin—this is what necessitates church discipline.

■ The goal of discipline is not punishment, but restoring the brother to fellowship with God and the church. In the case of the Corinthian brother, his expulsion led to repentance and full restoration to fellowship (2 Cor. 2:6-8).

■ The rationale for the particular discipline a church imposes (expelling) is a basic spiritual reality. Sin breaks our fellowship with the Lord (1 John 1:6). It is thus appropriate for Christ's body on earth to act out that reality on earth, helping the sinning believer experience the separation his practice of sin imposed.

■ The occasion for church discipline is moral fault, not an isolated act of sin, but a continuing practice of sin. It is important to note here that the church does not discipline for differences in conviction or differences in doctrinal viewpoint. Only the practice of what Scripture clearly identifies as sin is subject to church discipline.

■ The local Christian community bears the responsibility of imposing discipline on sinning members. Most believe that what we see in this passage is a final rather than first step in seeking to restore a sinning brother, and look to Matt. 18:15-17 to develop a step-by-step process. Yet when the brother persists in sinning, then the church "assembled in the name of our Lord Jesus" (1 Cor. 5:4) is to act in concert to expel him.

There is a vast difference between the "judging" involved in this exercise of church discipline and the judgmental attitude we see reflected in passages that warn against judging others. In the case of church discipline the Christian does not make an independent determination of right and wrong, but rather agrees with God in His judgment of a particular practice as sin.

Application. Underlying the teaching of this passage is the conviction that the church of Jesus Christ is, and must be, holy. There is no room in our fellowships for a lax attitude toward sin. To some extent, at least, the purity of the church is related to its power. We are unlikely to see revival without also seeing a fresh, total commitment on the part of God's people to both personal and corporate holiness.

Lawsuits among Believers (6:1-11).

Background. A little later than Paul wrote this the orator Aristides praised the Roman justice system for its fairness throughout the Empire and to all classes of people (*Orations,* 26.94).

> There is an abundant and beautiful equality of the humble with the great and of the obscure with the illustrious, and, above all, of the poor man with the rich and the commoner with the noble.

His claim, while flattering to the government, was hardly in accord with reality. Roman law codes, in fact, made a sharp distinction between the treatment to be given "the illustrious" and the treatment to "the humble." The upper classes, only about 1 percent of the population, had a distinct advantage in the courts. Not only were they able to hire orators to sway judges to their cause. They were favored in the very structuring of the laws.

It is interesting that the phrase Paul uses to describe the disputes taken to Gentile law courts is *pragma echon* (having a lawsuit). The term indicates that the civil cases taken to the courts were property cases (*pragma*), and this may well imply that those appealing to the courts were members of the upper class who might well expect a favorable judgment.

Whether or not this is the case, Paul's construction indicates intense revulsion at the practice: the word order in Greek suggests we might better translate v. 1, "Dare anyone, having a case against another, take it for judgment before the ungodly and not before the saints!"

Paul's conviction that disputes between Christians should be settled within the fellowship of believers reflects both a long tradition in Judaism and also a unique aspect of Roman law. The Romans showed great tolerance of the customs and beliefs of those peoples which conquest brought into the Empire. This meant that various races and nationalities were allowed to apply their own laws and customs in settling disputes that arose between members of their own group.

This right had long been exercised by the Jews, who were committed to the Law of Moses and whose sages sought to apply it in every area of life. In Palestine panels of sages served as judges, and difficult cases were brought to the Sanhedrin in Jerusalem. Frequently sages were sent out by twos to inform the Jewish communities scattered throughout the Empire of important decisions affecting the religious calendar, and to serve as judges settling cases in the places they visited.

This tradition of using Jewish judges to settle disputes between Jews was deeply ingrained, as was a horror of appealing to Gentile courts. On the basis of Ex. 21:1 the rabbis held that it was unlawful for a Jew even to appear before a Gentile court. A ruling based on that verse found in b. Git. 88b says

R. Tarfon used to say: In any place where you find heathen law courts, even though

their law is the same as the Israelite law, you must not resort to them since it says, "These are the judgments which thou shalt bring before them," that is to say, "before them" and not before heathens.

But it would be a mistake for us to assume that Paul's horror is shaped by the outlook of contemporary Judaism. His reaction is shaped by a far deeper understanding of the issues involved. Ultimately, his concern is that *the church has failed to take responsibility for the settling of disputes between believers,* disputes that must by their very nature cause hurts and division.

Interpretation. Our passage raises a variety of issues, issues that are far more complex than many suppose. While a verse here is often used as a "proof text" to condemn Christians who even think of suing another believer in court, that application of what Paul teaches may well be tragically wrong! To explore the complex issues that our passage introduces, we need to examine both Paul's words to the individuals involved, and his words to the Christian community.

PAUL'S WORDS TO THE DISPUTANTS

Rather than take civil disputes into pagan law courts, Paul instructs the Corinthians to bring such issues "before the saints" (6:1). Certainly the saints, whom Paul reveals will one day have a part in judging the fallen angels, are competent to judge "trivial cases" (6:2), further defined as "the things of this life" (6:3).

In so classifying the matters in dispute, Paul makes it clear that, compared to our calling to live as citizens of God's kingdom, mere money issues are hardly worth disputing. Yet the issues are not trivial in another sense. By becoming embroiled in conflict Christians go "against another" (6:6). Rather than seeking the other's welfare, each seeks to win his case, without concern for the harm or hurt his actions may cause.

Later Paul will say that "the very fact that you have lawsuits among you means you have been completely defeated already" (6:7). If the issues in dispute had been approached in a Christian manner, with each person concerned about what is fair and right for the other, no such conflicts could exist! The very fact they do exist shows that members of the local body have abandoned the most basic principle of brotherly love that is to govern Christians' interpersonal relationships.

What does Paul mean then when he says, "Why not rather be wronged? Why not rather be cheated?" (7:7) Is he really proposing that we adopt the role of victim, and let the carnal Christian exploit the spiritual one? The answer here is both yes—and no.

On an individual level Paul, addressing the plaintiff (the one who feels defrauded) challenges this defensive action. Christ taught that a person is to love his enemies, and pray for those who misuse him (Matt. 5:43-48). Paul himself wrote the Romans that believers are not to "repay anyone evil for evil" (12:17). On the contrary, "If your enemy is hungry, feed him" (12:20). Mistreated, the Christian's appropriate response is to "overcome evil with good" (12:21). Thus in bringing the lawsuit, rather than enduring the wrong and returning good, the plaintiff has departed from Christ's principles for godly living. Whether he wins the suit or loses it, he has already suffered a significant spiritual defeat.

With this said Paul addresses the defendant, whose wrong precipitated the suit. In cheating and doing wrong to a brother (6:8), the defendant has acted in the spirit of greed and selfishness that motivates those who have no part in the kingdom of God (6:9-11). Whether or not he succeeds in gaining some temporal advantage, he too has suffered defeat, for his action threatens his eternal reward.

On an individual level, then, both the victim and victimizer have failed to act as saints who have been washed, sanctified, and justified in the name of our Lord Jesus Christ.

PAUL'S WORDS TO THE CHURCH

With this judgment passed on the individuals involved in the suits brought before unbelievers, we need to go back to the beginning of the passage and note that there is a message here for the church. When disputes do arise, *it is the responsibility of the body to resolve them.* And so Paul asks, "Is nobody among you wise enough to judge a dispute between believers?" (6:5)

The fact of the matter is that, because we have been given the Spirit and thus have access to the mind of Christ (1 Cor. 2:15-16), Christians *alone* are competent to work out disputes that arise between believers. Indeed,

there are far greater issues at stake here than who wins and who loses, who gains financially and who suffers loss. The process of evaluating must not only consider the matter in dispute, but must also resolve the conflict in such a way that harmony is restored between the parties. Until each party comes again to that place where he or she truly cares for, and gladly serves, the other, the dispute has not been settled at all.

There is another aspect to disputes between believers as well. Looking at the issue again from the point of view of the faith community, it is essential that the victimizing behavior *is* dealt with. The framework of OT law suggests that, while a person can bring suit from a wrong motive, in some cases a believer *should* bring wrongdoing before the church, in ministry to the wrongdoer as well as in fulfillment of each Christian's responsibility to maintain the purity of the body of Christ.

The Old Testament concept of responsibility is expressed in the criminal justice system of Mosaic Law. The OT established no police or criminal court system. Instead, each community was responsible to enforce the biblical code of law. Within the community, elders served as judges of the facts, and each member of the community was responsible to serve as a witness in any case concerning which he had personal knowledge (Lev. 5:1). More importantly, any citizen who witnessed a crime was responsible to come forward with his information, and to take the role of prosecutor (Lev. 24:11; Num. 15:33).

This responsibility was so significant that Deut. 13:6-11, speaking of idolatry, says, "If your very own brother, or your son or your daughter, or the wife you love, or your closest friend" should privately urge you to worship false gods, "show him no pity." The evil must be exposed and, in the case of idolatry, the idolater put to death. The passage goes on, "Your hand must be the first in putting him to death, and then the hands of all the people."

The underlying idea here is that Israel is to be holy, for God is holy. And each Israelite was made responsible to maintain the purity of the believing community.

This OT principle is picked up in the NT and applied by Jesus. Matthew 18:15-17 records Christ's teaching:

If your brother sins against you, go and

show him his fault, just between the two of you. If he listens to you, you have won your brother over. But if he will not listen, take one or two others along, so that "every matter may be established by the testimony of two or three witnesses." If he refuses to listen to them, tell it to the church; and if he refuses to listen even to the church, treat him as you would a pagan or a tax collector.

Note that the principle expressed in both Testaments remains the same. An individual with direct knowledge or experience of a wrong is responsible to act. The goal of his action in both Testaments is to confront wrong, restore harmony between the wrongdoer and his victim, and thus maintain the purity of the believing community.

What Paul is concerned with in 1 Cor. 6 is first of all the wrong attitude of both parties to the disputes. But we would be wrong if we tore this passage out of the wider context of teaching justice and holiness provided by both the Old and the New Testaments. A person who is wronged may, with the right attitude, bring the wrongdoing before the church. And many feel that the last phrase in Matt. 18:17, "If he refuses to listen even to the church, treat him as you would a pagan or a tax collector," indicates that lawsuits before secular courts are a valid and even necessary option if the wrongdoer will not respond to arbitration by the church.

Application. Our passage has both personal and corporate application.

It speaks to us as individuals with the reminder, first of all, that the most important thing in life is learning to evaluate every experience from God's perspective—a perspective which vastly differs from the perspective of mere men. It is agonizingly difficult when others wrong us, to first of all deal with our own attitudes toward them. Rather than seek to defend ourselves or our rights, we are to commit ourselves to doing only good to the person who has hurt us.

Even when this is our attitude it's difficult to take the next step. We must confront the wrong, first for our brother's benefit, and then to maintain the purity of the community of faith. This means going to the one who has wronged us, and involving other Christians in a process of confrontation that is intended to heal rather than divide.

Ultimately, if our brother fails to respond to us or to the church, it is conceivable that he should be brought into the secular courts and forced there, publicly, to confront his wrong.

Yet the implications of this passage for the Christian community may well be even more important. For the community of faith is to be a self-cleansing community, committed to doing whatever is necessary to maintain its purity and minister to its members. Tragically, the modern church seems not only hesitant, but also unwilling, to become involved in the process of cleansing.

Paul tells us to bring disputes "before the saints [the church]" (6:1). And yet the church throws up its hands, backs away, and refuses to become involved. All too many Christian leaders would rather "paper over" disputes. They urge the wronged to forgive, without calling for the person committing the wrong to confess and ask forgiveness. They tell the wronged to suffer in silence rather than to confront. And, in taking this course, such Christian leaders permit the wrongdoer to suffer his or her own spiritual loss, and they permit the church to exist in a blemished rather than purified state.

It is not easy to live by the teachings of our Lord. It is not easy for individuals. It is not easy for the Christian community. But ease is hardly the issue. The issue is: are we willing to commit ourselves to live by Christ's teachings? Or will we go on, living like mere men?

1 CORINTHIANS 8–10
Church Family Disputes

EXPOSITION

All too often fellowship between Christians becomes strained when a practice one group of believers finds perfectly acceptable shocks another. Their first thought, "How could a (true, dedicated) Christian do that?" creates hesitancy, then suspicion, and then a spirit of judgmentalism and division in the church. Those with differing outlooks may be one in Christ, but cracks develop in their unity over the issue that divides them.

In Corinth one issue that divided the church was whether or not a believer could eat food that had been offered to idols in heathen sacrifice. The one group was horrified: "How could a (true, dedicated) Christian do *that!*" The other group was amused: "There's no such thing as pagan 'gods.' So why not?"

This issue touched on several areas of Corinthian life. In biblical times most people seldom ate meat. When city people did, the meat was generally purchased from a market associated with a pagan temple, and represented the third of the animal that was the priest's portion. If a Corinthian wanted a roast for a special dinner, the temple meat market was the place to buy it. But some Christians felt strongly that having anything at all to do with paganism, even indirectly, was terribly wrong.

There was another, even more significant problem. When first-century pagans held a dinner party or banquet, whether for a few friends or a large group, it was traditional to dedicate the meal to some god or goddess. Therefore, many Christians refused all social invitations to the homes of pagans, unwilling to eat a meal that was even loosely linked with idolatry. Other Christians saw no harm in participating. After all, "An idol is nothing at all in the world and . . . there is no God but one" (8:4). And, for those in business, or for clients of a more powerful patron, attendance at such social occasions was important.

Many commentators suggest a third problem. Apparently some Christians were actually participating in meals sponsored by friends at pagan temples. These Christians laughed at the notion there was anything wrong with the practice, again because "an idol is nothing at all in the world."

In our passage Paul gives the Corinthians several guiding principles that are specific to the issue of food offered to idols. In the process he also develops principles that can guide you and me in *any* issue where there is a conflict between some Christians who claim freedom to engage in a practice that troubles a group of brothers and sisters within their church. Paul teaches that love for one's brother in Christ is more important than the right to exercise Christian freedom (8:1-13).

As the passage develops we see that Paul himself has gladly surrendered many of his own "rights" as an apostle (9:1-18). He has shown his love and commitment to the Lord by adopting the social and cultural patterns of groups to whom he has witnessed and taught (9:19-27). In contrast, ancient Israel exercised no self-control at all, and actually adopted idolatry and engaged in the immorality associated with it (10:1-13). So be warned, Paul concludes. It remains dangerous to toy with idolatry in any form. Thus the Christian should not participate in activities which involve overt heathen religious practices.

Still, as far as normal social occasions are concerned, it is all right to join in. But if the host publicly announces that the meat was dedicated to an idol, don't eat it for the sake of *his* conscience. And as far as buying meat at a market associated with a pagan temple, don't make this an issue. Enjoy your steak as a gift from God—but be sensitive to the conscience of your brothers and let love, not your "rights," serve as the guiding principle (10:14-22).

WORD STUDIES

Now about *food sacrificed to idols* (8:1). The word is *eidolothuton,* and the issue was more significant than we can imagine. Only the very rich in the first century ate meat regularly. Nearly every social occasion at which 99 percent of the population would eat meat had some association with a deity, who might be viewed as guest of honor or as the host. This meat was normally purchased from butchers who had obtained it from pagan priests.

While difficult for us to understand, up through the third century A.D. there was really no formal social activity that was completely secular. All such occasions had some kind of religious association.

The Jewish position on eating such meat was clear. Rabbi Akiba ruled, "Meat which is about to be brought into heathen worship is lawful, but that which comes out from it is forbidden, because it is like the sacrifices of the dead" (Avod.S.ii.3). Yet no Jew would have sat down at a Gentile table to share meat from any source.

It's clear that the majority of the early Christians agreed with Akiba. Pliny the Younger, writing late in the first century, reports that conversions to Christianity seriously affected the market for meat in many parts of the Empire! (Letters 10.96.9-10)

We know that we all possess knowledge. Knowledge *puffs up* (8:1). The NIV translates the first sentence better in the footnote,

reading " 'We all possess knowledge,' as you say."

In more than one place in 1 Cor. Paul's words represent a position taken by one side or the other in one of this church's many debates. This quote points up the fact that each party to the dispute argued its point based on some known truth. Thus the one side might argue, "We know idolatry is wrong," while the other argues, "Yes, but we know the gods and goddesses of the pagans are nothing."

What's the problem with taking this approach to resolving disputes? Paul says that "knowledge puffs up." The word here is *phusioi* (to puff up, or blow up like a billows). What an image: such arguments are all wind, with no substance. Appealing to what we "know," and trying to argue others into accepting our conclusions, is an exercise in futility.

Paul explains further in v. 2: "The man who thinks he knows something does not yet know as he ought to know." Our "knowledge" of spiritual truth is limited and imperfect. Every attempt to resolve difficulties by appeal to what we "know" is destined to fail.

Knowledge puffs up, but love *builds up* (8:1). The word here is *oikodomeo.* The building metaphor is important in the NT, and frequently is used to portray the strengthening of God's people, and the spiritual development of the individual.

Paul's point is basic to his argument in this entire three-chapter passage. When approaching an issue from the point of view of knowledge, believers take opposite sides and argue. Neither is open to hear the other; each is thinking up new ways to support his own position and "win" the argument. The result is much wind, but no resolution. And no spiritual growth!

When approaching an issue from the point of view of love, believers stand together. Love enables them to hear each other, and as they consider each point of view they open their hearts to the Spirit of God, who is the Teacher of Christians. The result of giving priority to love is that we nurture each other, and grow not only in understanding but spiritually.

Our first goal in seeking to resolve differences with other Christians is not to try to "win," but to maintain a spirit of unity and love which will enable us to explore issues without interrupting our fellowship.

The man who loves *God* is known *by God* (8:3). Some of the best early Greek texts do not have the italicized words. In these texts the passage reads "If anyone loves, this one truly knows (or, is known)." This seems a better rendering for this context. The person who really understands how to deal with this issue is the one who loves, not the one who "knows."

What a reminder for us today. The truly wise and godly person in our congregation today is not marked off by superior knowledge, but by greater love (1 Cor. 13).

We *know* that an idol is nothing at all in the world (8:4). It is best to understand Paul here as quoting a position taken by one group in Corinth. He admits that they do have a point. The fact that there is only one God means that pagan gods and goddesses are unreal. Paul seems to suggest that a person who is convinced of this truth might very well eat "food sacrificed to idols" without a twinge of conscience.

But what does Paul mean when he says, "Indeed there are many 'gods' and many 'lords,' yet for us there is but one God the Father"? (8:5) Paul is saying that while pagan gods have no objective reality, they still have a subjective effect on those who believe in them. Later Paul will show that paganism also has

a behavioral impact on those who participate in social affairs linked with idolatry.

So to say, "We know . . . there is no God but one" (8:4) is true, but is not the whole truth. And thus the apostle points out the limitations of approaching an issue like this from the standpoint of "knowledge."

Be careful, however, that the *exercise of your freedom* does not become a stumbling block to the weak (8:9). "Freedom" here is *exousia*, which means "authority," "power," "freedom of action." Paul does suggest here that those believers whose faith is strong enough to both recognize the objective unreality of pagan deities and be subjectively unaffected are authorized to eat meat sacrificed to idols. He then appeals to love and the concern for the welfare of others that is love's identifying mark.

If a "strong" Corinthian evaluates his choice on the basis of knowledge, he concludes he has a right to eat. But if the same Corinthian evaluates his right to eat on the basis of love, he will refrain in order not to do possible harm to a "weak" brother.

If what I eat causes my brother to fall into sin, I will never eat meat again, so that I will not cause him to fall (8:13). Paul's conclusion is very strong. Speaking for himself, Paul is totally committed. His every act will be guided by love.

Don't we have the *right* to food and drink? *Don't* we have the *right* to take a believing wife along with us, as do the other apostles and the Lord's brothers and Cephas? (9:3-5) Paul has come down strongly in favor of surrendering a right (the freedom to act in a particular way) when an exercise of that right might harm a fellow believer. Now he takes pains to show that he has consistently lived by this principle himself.

He gives several illustrations of surrender of his personal rights. Paul has an apostle's right to material support by those he teaches (9:4, 7-14). He has a right to the companionship of a wife (9:5). Yet Paul did not use "any of these rights" (9:12, 15). He was intent instead on making the Gospel "free of charge" (9:18). Paul wanted to leave not the slightest doubt that the Gospel is, through and through, an expression of God's love.

We who teach and encourage others to live love can hardly charge them to make sacrifices that we ourselves are unwilling to make.

WORK, OR ACCEPT SUPPORT?

Some suggest that Paul may have been criticized for choosing not to accept support. After all, didn't Jesus instruct His followers to go out without purse, and accept the hospitality of those who would welcome them? (Matt. 10) Did not his decision to work "defraud" the churches of the opportunity to aid him in his mission?

Perhaps. Yet there was clear precedent in both Jewish and Greek society for the position that Paul took. Of the rabbis quoted in the Talmud, more than 100 are identified by their trade! Among the most famous first-century rabbis, Shammai was a carpenter, and Hillel was a day laborer even as he studied. Rabbi Eleazar b. Zadoq and Abba Saul b. Batnith kept shops in Jerusalem during the whole of their teaching years. Paul's work at a trade thus would seem both natural and "right" to his own people.

On the other hand, a long tradition in Hellenistic culture might work against him. Epictitus, the Cynic, reflects the view of most of the many itinerant philosophers who wandered the Empire and taught for food and fees. In Dissertations III, 22, pp. 46–48, he wrote,

> Behold, God has sent you one who shall show by practice that it is possible (to be happy with the Cynic way of life). "Look at me, I have no house or city, property or slave; I sleep on the ground, I have no wife or children, no miserable palace, but only the earth and sky and one poor cloak.
> Yet what do I lack? Am I not without pain and fear, am I not free?"

In working to support himself and his mission, Paul might have seemed to some not only to violate this tradition, but even to be overly concerned with worldly things, rather than being free of such concerns to serve his God.

Paul's explanation here, then, puts this whole issue in perspective. He is free to accept support. But he does not exercise that right, not because he cares about money, but because he does not want anyone to miss the point that the Gospel truly is free.

We can be sure of one thing: Paul was often misunderstood. People are sure to misunderstand our motives too, whatever we do. So what we must do is follow Paul's example: do what we believe to be right, and share our motives with others who doubt us, without any defensiveness at all.

To the Jews I *became like a Jew*, to win the Jews (9:20). Paul refers to three groups to further illustrate his willingness to surrender personal rights for the benefit of others. Among the Jews Paul embraces Jewish customs, although he is not bound to keep the OT rulings and traditions which defined Jewish lifestyle throughout the Empire. Among the Gentiles he is under no obligation to live like a Jew, although Paul claims no "freedom" from his responsibility to live by Christ's will.

Paul also adapts his behavior so as not to offend the conscience of the weak. In all of this, his goal is to "save some" (9:22).

Some have accused Paul of compromising his own convictions to appear to hold convictions that are not really his. But there is no compromise here. Paul is exercising his freedom to surrender his personal rights for the benefit of others. In this Paul serves as an example for you and me. So many things that some people treat as important are really irrelevant. Paul wrote, "Food does not bring us near to God; we are no worse if we do not eat, and no better if we do" (8:8). His goal in adapting to the culture of those among whom he worked was to put no obstacle in their way that might keep them from attending to the real issue—Jesus, and the salvation God offers all of us in Him.

Everyone who *competes in the games* goes into strict training (9:25). Paul's reference is to the Isthmian games, held in Corinth every other year. His point is clear. Athletes gladly surrender their "right" to an easy life and go into "strict training" to prepare themselves for the games. As a Christian, who seeks a prize far greater than the crown of leaves awarded victors in running and boxing, Paul's surrender of his rights is more than wise in view of "the crown that will last forever" (9:25) which he will win for faithful and loving service.

So that after I have preached to others, I myself will not be *disqualified* from the prize (9:27). The word is *adokimos,* "unqualified." It is used here in an athletic context: self-control is necessary, not for salvation, but to live that disciplined life that keeps us on course for eschatological rewards.

This final reminder is important. Letting love guide us, and being willing to surrender our "rights" when this will benefit others, really is important. The Corinthians may insist on their rights and enjoy a steak at the temple market. Or they can realize how irrelevant such "rights" are, exercise self-control, and seek those rewards for faithful service which God will grant when Jesus returns.

They were all baptized into Moses in the cloud and in the sea (10:2). The phrase refers to the initiation of Israel into covenant relationship with God under Moses' leadership. Paul's argument is that, like the Corinthians, ancient Israel also received spiritual blessings, including sustenance and protection from Christ. He was with the Israelites as well as with his NT people (10:3).

Paul's point is that despite their blessings, that generation did not please God—and rather than enter the Promised Land their bodies were "scattered over the desert" (10:5).

The point is very clear. God's blessings are not a license to ignore Him or His ways. We are to respond to the God who blesses us with a wholehearted commitment to His ways.

These things occurred as *examples* to keep us from setting our hearts on evil things as they did (10:6). The word is *typoi,* which means a figure or pattern which can serve as a model, an example. Paul looks back, and sees patterns in the Exodus generation's relationship with God which should serve to warn the Corinthians today. The patterns are:

	ISRAEL	GOD
10:7-8	Worshiped idols; were sexually immoral.	Destroyed 23,000 in one day.
10:9	Tested God.	Were killed by snakes.
10:10	Grumbled.	Were killed by destroying angel.

The blessings God gives us make it even more certain that He will not tolerate our sins. We must not be proud or arrogant. Instead God's gifts should make us humble and responsive.

If you think you are standing firm, be careful that you *don't fall!* (10:12) Here Paul uses the common verb *pipto* to represent committing sin. Paul is speaking here to those "strong" Christians who assume that the blessings they have received (10:1-4) make them invulnerable to the dangers involved in pagan worship. While idols may be "nothing at all in the world" (8:4), Israel's history shows that idolatry is dangerous! To those who are so sure of themselves, Paul says: Watch out! Overconfidence is all too often a prelude to sin.

No *temptation* has seized you except what is common to man. And God is faithful; He will not let you be tempted beyond what you can bear. But when you are tempted, He will also provide a way out so that you can stand up under it (10:13). The word is *peirasmos,* which means "test" or "trial." It is often translated "temptation," for under both internal and external pressures many persons tend to sin.

One of the best-known verses in the Corinthian letters, it has encouraged Christians throughout the centuries when life becomes difficult. In context it serves as a warning as well as promise. Paul sees testings as "common to man." The Corinthians are vulnerable to the sins associated with idolatry, whatever they may say about idols being "nothing at all in the world." In affirming the faithfulness of God, Paul makes it clear that no one has to sin when testing comes. But note that Paul says God will "provide a way out."

What is the "way out" that the Corinthians are to seek? The next verse, 10:14, says it succinctly: "Flee from idolatry." Don't stay in a situation where you experience temptation to sin.

This is an important principle for us to remember. God's "way out" is often quite simple. We are to "get out!"

Do not those who eat the sacrifices *participate in* the altar? (10:18) Here *koinonoi* means "partners," "those who share." In Judaism part of the sacrifice was returned to the worshiper, who ate it with his family and friends. The host for this meal was considered to be God, who provided the meal and who, as host, took those who participated under His protection. The great first-century Jewish scholar Philo refers to this in spec.leg. 1.221, saying that this food must be eaten in three days because it belongs to God, not the one who made the sacrifice. He, "the benefactor, the bountiful . . . has made the convivial company of those who carry out the sacrifices partners (*koinonon*) of the altar whose board they share."

It follows that those who participate in similar meals sponsored at pagan temples and dedicated to pagan gods, become partners to idolatry. And, while idols may be nothing, "The sacrifices of pagans are offered to demons" (10:20). There are hostile spiritual powers that operate on human beings through pagan worship.

Clearly, then, "You cannot drink the cup of the Lord and the cup of demons too" (10:21). The Christian must not participate in any public or social event which is openly dedicated to a pagan deity.

Eat anything sold in the *meat market* without raising question of conscience (10:25). On the other hand, meat sold at a market (*makellon*) no longer had religious significance, whether or not it had been earlier sacrificed to an idol.

If some *unbeliever* invites you to a meal and you want to go, eat whatever is put before you without raising questions of conscience (10:27). The word is *apistos,* "without faith." Paul is consistent in his position on relationships with non-Christians: such relationships are encouraged rather than discouraged (5:9-13). How then is the Christian to react when invited to dinner? Paul's guidelines are simple.

Enjoy the meal without worry about the source of the main dish. Meat in itself has no religious significance, and is not a matter for the Christian's conscience (*suneidesis,* as a moral abater).

But if anyone says to you, "This has been offered in sacrifice," then do not eat it, both for the sake of the man who told you and for *conscience' sake* (10:28). Here "conscience" (*syneidesis*) is used in the usual sense of "moral consciousness." Our understanding hinges on a question. Why would anyone make a point of saying that the meat has been "offered in sacrifice"? The answer seems to be that the host assumes Christians, like Jews, would not eat meat sacrificed to a pagan deity. So the unbeliever's warning is a moral act, an act which the Christian should honor, and so not cause the host to worry that by eating the Christian might have done something "wrong."

Food isn't a matter for the Christian's conscience (8:8; Rom. 14:5, 14). But concern for the conscience of others—whether Christian or non-Christian—is a matter of conscience. And "whatever you do" (10:31) the Christian is to act for the glory of God, being careful "not [to] cause anyone to stumble, whether Jews, Greeks or the church of God" (10:32-33).

THE PASSAGE IN DEPTH

The Rights of an Apostle (9:1-27). Paul launches this chapter with a rhetorical question: "Am I not free?" The question introduces an issue that underlies not only what Paul teaches the Corinthians, but his teaching in Rom. 14–15 and other NT passages as well. Thus it is important to our interpretation of the passage to understand the NT's perspective on freedom. When the Corinthians claim the right to eat at pagan temples, buy meat that had been earlier sacrificed to idols, and join pagan friends in their homes for dinner parties

that, according to custom, were likely dedicated to some pagan deity, they too were saying: "Am I not free?" "Now that I'm a Christian, and see that the gods of the pagans are nothing, can't I do what I want as far as food sacrificed to idols is concerned?"

In affirming this right, the "strong" in Corinth, who were freed from any superstitious awe of idols, claimed exactly what Paul said: "Am I not free?" And often today Christians who are "strong," and whose consciences are not troubled by the irrelevant things that trouble some brothers and sisters, make the same claim. "Why shouldn't I do this or that? Am I not free?" Certainly that question, "Am I not free?" deserves an answer. And to answer, we must grasp the nature and the limits of Christian freedom.

Freedom in the Old Testament.
Several different Hebrew words are translated *freedom* in English versions. Among them are *salah, 'azab, naqi,* and *hapsi.* A survey of their use in the OT indicates a view of "freedom" as released from internal or external restrictions as imposed by others or society. These words, however, are applied only to specific situations, and none suggests an abstract concept of "freedom," or a doctrine of "freedom" such as we find in the NT.

The Greek Words.
In contrast to the Hebrew, Greek culture did speak of "freedom" in the abstract. *Elutheria* meant freedom in the sense of being "independent of others." *Elutheros* meant "free," "not bound," and implied that a person was his own master, able to act without reference to limits others might try to impose. *Elutheroo* was "to free, set loose, or release."

Originally these were political terms, and made a distinction between the freedoms of full members of a community and those not enjoyed by slaves or outsiders. As the centuries passed it became clear that political "freedom" did not release the individual or the community from such tragedies as war, injustice, or famine. And so the philosophers of the Hellenistic world began to look within, and seek a personal freedom from the pain man suffered in the world. To the Stoic, deeply concerned with the issue, freedom could only be found in detaching oneself from worldly concerns.

Common man took up the terms for "freedom" and applied them in a very different way. To the ordinary person "freedom" spoke of the opportunity to do whatever he or she wished. The free man was his own master, unfettered by lack or by limits imposed by others. The person who was truly free could do whatever he wished, whenever he wanted to. Free from external limits, the free man was able to follow his own desires.

Nowhere in the NT are any of the words for freedom used in the political or Stoic sense. Nor is freedom ever viewed as the license to do whatever a person wants without hindrance or consequences. The NT develops a new concept of freedom, one that is rooted in Scriptures' deep conviction that all human beings are locked in bondage to sin—a bondage that no one is able to overcome.

The New Testament on Human Bondage.
Human bondage is complex and complete. Human beings are subject to forces of evil marshaled by Satan and his minions (Luke 13:16; Eph. 6:12; 2 Tim. 2:26).

Human beings are in bondage to their own sin nature; a swirling complex of passions that masters rather than serves the unsaved. In this condition people are spiritually dead, dominated by an "old self" which is utterly corrupt and impels them to use their "freedom" to sin (Rom. 6:6; Eph. 4:22; Col. 3:9; Gal. 5:1; 2 Peter 2:19).

In addition, human beings are in bondage to law. This is because the law, though holy, righteous, and good in itself, stimulates the sin nature to sin (Rom. 7:1-4). It sets up moral standards. Man the sinner is never able to live by the standards. As a result, law looms over human beings, demanding without enabling, condemning rather than offering hope (Rom. 3:19-20; 6:14; 7:7-25).

While human beings cry out for freedom to do what they want, because of bondage to Satan, sin, and even law, freedom is an illusion. For sinful man will only use his freedom to sin, and the consequences—the wages—of sin is death.

THE FREEDOM OF GOD'S CHILDREN
Then, to man in his desperate state, comes the Good News of the Gospel. And carrying it, Paul announces "Christ has set us free" (Gal. 5:1). And Paul says to the Corinthians, "Am I not free?" expecting the sure answer, "Yes!"

What then is the nature of the freedom Christ has won for the Christian? Several key passages help us see.

■ John 8:31-36. Jesus promises that those who hold to His teaching "will know the truth, and the truth will set you free." Here "truth" refers to reality as God knows it. Mere human beings stumble through life, unable to separate truth from illusion. Those who commit themselves to follow Jesus' teachings cut through the illusions and experience reality. By following Christ we are led away from what harms, to what helps. Away from what is bad, to what is good.

Why is this so important? Jesus explains: "Everyone who sins is a slave to sin" (John 8:34). The freedom Jesus gives is release from the power of sin, the ability to experience life as God reveals it to be.

■ **Rom. 6:15-23.** Paul picks up on Jesus' point. We are "slaves" to the one we obey. Man is never free in the sense of *independent*. Instead each of us must choose a master. And that master will either be sin—which pays as its wages death—or God—who guides His slaves into righteous living and blesses them with eternal life.

■ **Rom. 8:2-11.** Paul points out that even the Christian is subject to the pulls and limitations of a body still infected by sin. But God has given us His Holy Spirit, and the Spirit's vivifying power is the source of a new dynamic for holy living.

■ **Gal. 5.** Old Testament Law offers the believer neither salvation nor power for holy living. But the "freedom" that Christ gives does provide a power that enables us to ignore the impulses of our sin nature and live to please God. What is vital is that we make a choice. For, since no person is independent, he or she must decide whether to serve sin or to serve God.

If we choose to serve sin, our lives will be marked by hatred, jealousy, fits of rage, envy, etc. If we choose to serve God, we will be freed to live loving, patient, kind, faithful, and good lives.

Christian freedom is not freedom to do as we please. It is freedom from the domination of sin; it is freedom to commit ourselves to God and live to please Him. And, in the context of 1 Corinthians, it is freedom to surrender our rights in consideration for others and for their spiritual well being. Whether they be Jews, or Greeks, or members of the church of God.

THE LIFE OF
A TRULY FREE CHRISTIAN

What Paul does in Romans 14–15 and 1 Cor. 8–10 is give us a sketch of the lifestyle of the truly free.

The Christian is aware that rules concerning doubtful things have nothing to do with him. The free man knows that such rules as "Don't eat this," and "Don't buy meat at public markets" are not matters of conscience, and neither eating nor refraining from eating have anything to do with pleasing God. Thus the Christian has a "right" to eat or not eat, without judging others or being judged by them.

The Christian is also aware that consideration for others is a matter of conscience. The truly free man is just as free *not* to exercise his "rights" as to exercise them. And, when refraining from an action which might cause another person to stumble, the Christian exercises the freedom God has granted him to serve the Lord by doing good.

The Christian who successfully distinguishes between actions which are and are not matters of conscience will refrain from making irrelevant matters issues within the Christian community. He will act on his conscience without making his choices a matter of public debate. And always the Christian will seek to be sensitive to others who may not share his perspective, yet whose welfare he or she is committed to serve.

1 CORINTHIANS 12–14
Church Family Gifts

EXPOSITION

Paul has dealt with a number of the problems that have emerged in the Corinthian church. In a drive for prestige, some have claimed superiority because they followed superior leaders (chaps. 1–4). Others assumed they were better than their brothers because they were "strong," and thus free to eat food sacrificed to idols (chaps. 8–10). Now Paul looks at another claim. "We're more spiritual than you," some insisted. "And we can prove it. We speak in tongues—and you don't!"

As we examine 1 Corinthians 12–14, it is important to realize that the issue Paul discusses here is not "spiritual gifts." Rather he is concerned with the broader topic of spirituality. What is spirituality, anyway? What do spiritual gifts have to do with spirituality? How do we recognize the truly spiritual among us? And, finally, what about this gift of "tongues," which some claim makes them better than others?

Once we understand that the issue here is spirituality rather than spiritual gifts, it becomes relatively easy to trace Paul's argument. The great apostle begins by noting that what makes a person "spiritual" is the Holy Spirit (12:1-3). But the Spirit expresses His presence in different ways in different Christians. Every spiritual gift, not just "tongues," is a manifestation of His presence (12:4-11). A good analogy is provided by the way the human body is formed and functions. Each body part is different, but each is essential if the body is to function as a whole. Just as no body of all "eyes" or all "feet" is whole, so no church could be whole if every believer had the same gift. Thus every spiritually endowed believer is essential to the body of Christ. The more spectacular gifts, such as "tongues," are not evidence of spiritual superiority at all (12:12-31).

Here Paul pauses to make an important point. If the church wants a test of spirituality, Paul will provide one! That test is a simple one, yet devastating to those who in arrogance and pride assert their superiority over their brothers and sisters in the Lord. The truly spiritual person is marked by love. And "love is patient, love is kind. It does not envy, it does not boast, it is not proud" (13:1-4). In short, the spiritual person displays qualities in every relationship that are in direct contrast to the attitudes and behaviors of those who seem so driven to establish their own prestige in the community of faith!

Now Paul returns to the question of spiritual gifts and their exercise. Every spiritual gift is important to the body. Still, if gifts were to be ranked, "prophecy" (instruction)

383

is definitely more important than "tongues." Why? As far as the church is concerned, the person who instructs in intelligible words builds up others, while the person who speaks in tongues may edify himself but makes no contribution to others (14:1-19). As far as outsiders are concerned, "tongues" may serve as an initial sign alerting them to God's presence. But if outsiders then visit the church and everyone is speaking in tongues, that initial impression will soon give way, and the visitor will simply conclude that these folks are all crazy! If the visitor hears the Word of God being taught in his own language, he will be convicted and converted (14:20-25). At best, then, the gift which the Corinthians exalt as a sign of spiritual superiority is a minor one, which makes very little contribution to the spiritual well being of Christians, and even less contribution to evangelistic outreach.

In closing, Paul provides some very practical instruction on how to conduct meetings of the church. Apparently the competitive exaltation of tongues had led to complete disorder in congregational meetings. So Paul emphasizes order: an order which gives every member an opportunity to contribute according to his or her gift; an order which requires members of the body show each other the courtesy of listening (14:26-33).

Paul's final words are addressed to specific groups in the church, groups which apparently have been most involved in the dispute over tongues. Those women who have disrupted the church's meetings are to "remain silent" and learn "submission" (14:33b-37). Those who have claimed to be "spiritual" are now to acknowledge that what Paul writes has the force of a divine commandment (14:38). But what about tongues? The church is not to forbid speaking in tongues, for it is a valid spiritual gift. What the church at Corinth must learn, and the church of our own day as well, is to structure its meetings so that order is maintained, and those with spiritual gifts are provided a structure within which to minister to all (14:39-40).

WORD STUDIES

Now about *spiritual gifts*, brothers, I do not want you to be ignorant (12:1). The Greek does not have "gifts." The phrase is *ton pneumatikon,* "the spiritual." Commentators disagree whether the phrase implies spiritual "gifts" or spiritual "people." In view of the wide range of Paul's discourse, each of these renderings seems too narrow. It is best to take this phrase as "Now about the things of the Spirit," or perhaps even better, "Now about spirituality, brothers, I do not want you to be ignorant."

It's not surprising that the Corinthians were confused about spirituality. Today, some 2,000 years later, many Christians are still confused. This extended passage is important to us, because here Paul gives us a simple test by which we can recognize the truly spiritual among us. And a goal toward which each of us can strive.

When you were pagans . . . you were *influenced and led astray* by dumb idols (12:2). The combination of verbs (*'egesthe 'apagomenoi*) is unusual in Greek, and suggests that the two indicate a singular phenomenon, and should be translated together rather than separately. Most likely Paul is referring to the "inspired utterances" or "ecstatic speech" of those who were supposed in Greek culture to be inspired by one of the "mute idols" of the pagans.

This sheds much light on the problem in Corinth. Some of the Christians there carried over into their new faith the assumptions of paganism. Those who spoke in tongues seemed to them to have a special endowment of the Spirit, even as the oracles associated with pagan temples, who fell into similar ecstasies, were supposed to be especially close to their gods or goddesses.

But this view is rooted in an ignorance that Paul is about to dispel. An ignorance about the Spirit of God and His relationship to believers that marks too many of God's people today.

No one who is speaking by the Spirit of God says, "Jesus be cursed," and no one can say, "Jesus is Lord," except by the Holy Spirit (12:3). Paul has just taught that ecstatic utterances are not evidence of the Spirit's vital presence. What, then, is? The answer is, a person's relationship to Jesus is evidence of the Spirit's presence.

No one who rules Jesus out as *anathema* (an object of divine wrath) has the Spirit. In contrast, one who acknowledges Jesus as *kurios,* "Lord" (the eternal God, the Yahweh of the OT), does so by the Spirit and thus demonstrates His presence.

The verse has nonetheless troubled some, who point out than anyone can say, "Jesus is Lord." This phrase is an early Christian confession of faith. To publicly confess that "Jesus is Lord" was to commit to Jesus as the exalted one, God in the flesh, the One raised from the dead who is the source of eternal life to all who believe in Him.

Paul's statement here also sets an important matter in perspective. Throughout church history some have focused attention on the Spirit of God, and claimed that certain of His gifts make them more spiritual than other believers. Paul reminds us that Jesus is Lord. Christ is the One on whom we are to focus, the One on whom the Spirit Himself focuses! As Jesus said, "He [the Spirit] will testify about Me" (John 15:26).

Anyone who shifts the focus in his spiritual life from Jesus to the Spirit has most surely missed the mark.

Now to each one the *manifestation of the Spirit* is given for the *common good* (12:7). Paul has said that the person who confesses Jesus as Lord "speaks by the Holy Spirit" (12:4). That is, that person possesses the Spirit.

Now the question is: how does the Spirit manifest His presence in the believer's life? Paul's answer is that the Spirit gives "gifts," *charismata.* These gifts are manifestations, expressions, of the Spirit through the believer. Paul emphasizes three things in this verse and its context. (1) The gifts, though of "different kinds" (12:4-6), are the working of one and the same Spirit. (2) Each believer has a spiritual gift (12:7). And (3) the gifts are intended to promote the "common good" (12:7). That is, the *charismata* are to be used to strengthen and build up individual believers and the believing community. They are not tests or measures of spirituality.

We learn several things from this verse. Perhaps the most important is that every brother and sister in the Lord has something to contribute to his or her church. Every believer is a minister; every believer has an ability to contribute to the welfare of others. We need to learn to see ourselves and others as ministers, not just as those who receive ministry from professional Christian leaders. And we need to reach out to care for our Christian brothers and sisters. As we do, the Spirit will work through us, and others will be blessed.

SPIRITUAL GIFTS

There is much debate over the nature of the gifts listed in 1 Cor. 12, Rom. 12, and Eph. 4. A typical set of definitions is found in Charles C. Ryrie's book, *The Holy Spirit* (Moody Press, 1965). Here, adapted, is Ryrie's view of the gifts and their function.

■ **Administration.** The ability to guide, direct, lead, and care for the church.

■ **Apostleship.** The ability to serve as a missionary, or other special representative of God.

■ **Discernment.** The ability to distinguish true from false sources of revelation.

■ **Evangelism.** An exceptional ability to win others to the Lord.

■ **Exhortation.** The ability to encourage, comfort, and admonish others constructively.

■ **Faith.** The ability to believe in God's power to meet special needs.

■ **Giving.** The ability for exceptional contribution of one's material resources to other believers.

■ **Hospitality.** The ability to provide a welcome to travelers in need of food and shelter.

■ **Mercy.** The ability to provide comfort and kindness to the distressed.

■ **Miracles and Healings.** The ability to perform acts of healing and restore health without the use of natural means.

■ Pastor/teacher. The ability to lead, protect, guide, teach, and care for members of the body of Christ.

■ Prophecy. The ability to understand and communicate an immediate message of God to His people.

■ Service. The ability to identify the needs of others and help meet them.

■ Teaching. The ability to understand the implications of God's revelation for daily life, and to guide others to understand and live God's truth.

■ Tongues. The ability to speak in an unknown [spiritual] language.

■ Interpretation of Tongues. The ability to understand and explain the words of one who speaks in tongues.

It is important to look at this list as a *representative* rather than *exhaustive* itemization. In fact, anything that a believer might do that strengthens or contributes to the development of another believer is a "manifestation of the Spirit," the exercise of a gift which contributes to "the common good" (12:7).

The body is a unit, though it is made up of many parts; and though all its parts are many, they form one body. *So it is* with Christ (12:12). The "so it is [also] with" (*houtos kai*) alerts us to perhaps the NT's primary metaphor intended to help us understand the nature of the church. In Romans, Paul taught that by faith the believer is joined to Jesus in an indissoluble union. Now he teaches that those united to Christ are also united to one another, in as organic a relationship as that which obtains between the limbs and organs of a body.

The image conveys several realities. We cannot be Christians alone; we must function with others. We cannot fulfill our mission in life separated from a church; we must be close enough to others to exercise our gifts by loving and serving them. And we cannot permit strife and schism in the local congregation; we must be united by a shared commitment not only to Jesus but also to one another.

We were all *baptized by one Spirit* into one body (12:13). The contribution of this verse is its biblical definition of the phrase "baptism of the Spirit." Spirit baptism is that work of the Spirit by which all who believe are united to Jesus, becoming members with all other Christians of that church which is the one body of Christ.

Some in the charismatic tradition give a theological rather than biblical definition of "baptism of the Spirit." In that tradition, the baptizing work of the Spirit is understood to be a work that the Spirit performs in the believer subsequent to conversion, a work which many hold is proved only when the person who receives this "baptism" begins to speak in tongues. Without making any judgment about the validity of this theological position, we are forced by 1 Cor. 12:13 to note that *biblically* the "baptism of the Spirit" is a very different thing.

But in fact God has *arranged* the parts in the body, every one of them, just *as He wanted them to be* (12:18). The Greek verb *etheto* in Hellenistic times meant to "set" or "arrange." Here it emphasizes God's active role in determining the part each Christian is to play within the church. Along with 12:11, which emphasizes that the Spirit gives gifts to each one "as He determines" (*bouletai,* "chooses," or "wills"), the phrase makes an important point.

God is the One who chooses our gifts. They are not indicative of spirituality, but rather of the role God has for us to play within the body. It is hardly appropriate for us to either "seek" gifts we lack, or to exalt those with one gift over those with another. Instead let's rejoice that each of us is equipped by God for the role he or she is expected to play within the body of Christ.

God . . . has given *greater honor* to the parts that lacked it (12:24). The Greek play on words in vv. 23-25 is impossible to render in English. The point however is clear. We cover parts of the body we consider "unpresentable" (i.e., our sexual organs [12:22]) and we give special attention to "weaker" parts (for instance, the stomach, by providing it with food [12:23]). Similarly the church should pay special attention to persons whose gifts are not as visible as tongues, or as "desirable" as the gift of pastoring.

The fact is that every part of the body is indispensable, and merits equal concern. If any suffer, the whole is harmed. If any are honored, all share in the glory. Clearly then each member is worthy of equal concern, and the Corinthians, who exalted tongues as *the* spiritual gift, have completely missed the point!

But *eagerly desire* the greater gifts (12:31). A similar thought is expressed in 14:1: "Follow the way of love and eagerly desire spiritual gifts." But how does this exhortation fit with Paul's stress on the fact that God distributes spiritual gifts according to His own sovereign will? (12:11)

The answer is that Paul is speaking to the Christian community, not to individuals, as the second person plural of the Greek verbs indicates. He reminds the church that rather than emphasize tongues they are to give priority to the "greater," *mallon*, gifts (14:5). According to chapter 14 such gifts as prophecy (14:3), which strengthens, encourages, and comforts the church, thus contributing directly to the common good.

But before Paul goes on to give this explanation, he pauses to explain the "most excellent" (12:31) way of love. Not "love rather than gifts," but love as the context within which spiritual gifts must be exercised.

If I speak in the *tongues* of men and of angels, but have not love, I am only a resounding gong or a clanging cymbal (13:1). It is likely that the Corinthians did think of the gift of tongues in terms of angelic language. In the Jewish *Testament of Job* (48-50), Job's three daughters were given sashes which enabled them to speak "ecstatically in the angelic dialect." Some have suggested that some in Corinth rejected sexuality (1 Cor. 7) because they assumed the gift of tongues initiated them into the realm of angels, so that they assumed they had "arrived" at spiritual perfection.

Yet the behavior of this very group showed a distinct lack of love! And living a life of love is the "most excellent way"; the way of true spirituality.

Paul's critique here is devastating. Even if a Corinthian did speak "in the tongues of men and of angels," without love that person is

only *chalkos echon,* "a resounding gong." What Paul refers to here are large, empty bronze vessels placed at the back of stone amphitheaters which served as an amplification system. Far from being models of spirituality, those who speak in tongues but lack love are empty, hollow men and women.

If I give all . . . but have not love, I *gain nothing* (13:3). Tongues and "faith" (13:2) are not sufficient evidence of spirituality. How about such total dedication that a person gives everything he or she possesses to the poor, and even welcomes martyrdom? Without love the giver will "gain nothing" (13:3).

Certainly the poor who received food gained. Good works certainly profit their beneficiaries. But the giver gains nothing. Without love there is no inner satisfaction. Without love there is no personal spiritual growth. Without love there is no eschatological reward.

In all of this Paul does not criticize tongues, that faith which works miracles, or those good works that benefit others. Instead he reminds us that love has primacy in the Christian life. Without love the Christian is empty; without love there is no benefit for us in whatever we may do.

Love *is* . . . (13:4-5). How often we forget that God expresses Himself in the simple, human things. Christ did not come with a stunning flash of light, but as a baby born in a manger in an obscure corner of the civilized world. Nor is "spirituality" a matter of a spectacular gift. Instead it is discerned in the most modest of actions and the commonplace of our daily lives.

If we want to discern the truly spiritual among us, and if we wish to be spiritual men and women, we need first of all to understand the definition Paul gives us here of the nature of love.

Now we see but a *poor reflection* as in a mirror; then we shall see face to face (13:12). The Greek phrase, *en ainigmati,* probably does not mean "poor reflection." Corinth was famous for its bronze mirrors and the excellent image they reflected. What Paul is saying is that, as well as we see God revealed today, it is nothing compared to how well we will know Him when we stand in His presence, and see Him face to face. Our knowledge now is indirect and partial, and therefore may well fail us at times. But love will never fail (13:8). So let's commit ourselves to love.

And remain humble about that which we believe we "know."

THE PASSAGE IN DEPTH

Gifts of Prophecy and Tongues (14:1-25).
Background. An awe of the ecstatic marked pagan religion. The oracle at Delphi breathed in the volcanic fumes that rose to her cubical and uttered the often unintelligible message of the god, which was then interpreted by priests. A person with epilepsy was said to suffer from the "divine disease," and was thought to be especially close to some deity. It is not surprising then that the young Christians in Corinth were deeply impressed by those who spoke in tongues, and viewed them as especially spiritual. Given the belief of many Jews that charismatic speech was the language of angels (see Word Study of 13:1, above), the awe in which those with the gift of tongues were apparently held in Corinth would not have been challenged by any Jewish believers in the church.

While we can understand the fascination of the Corinthians with this unusual spiritual gift, we have considerable difficulty in defining that gift. There are only two passages in the NT which deal with speaking in tongues: 1 Cor. 12–14 and Acts 2. And many commentators argue that these two accounts deal with different rather than the same spiritual phenomenon.

We can understand why. In Acts 2 "all of them" were filled with the Spirit and "began to speak in other tongues" (2:4). Each member of the crowd "heard them speaking in his own language" (2:6). In Acts 2 speaking in tongues served an evangelistic purpose.

Reading through 1 Cor. 12–14 we are struck by the fact that only some, rather than all, Corinthians spoke in tongues. We are also impressed by the fact that rather than being filled by the Spirit, those who spoke in tongues are like the others "worldly" and "acting like mere men" (1 Cor. 3:3). Further, those who speak in tongues in 1 Cor. cannot be understood by anyone. Rather than being a recognized foreign language, here tongues is unintelligible speech that requires an interpreter. Finally, while Paul sees tongues as a gift that edifies, builds up, the speaker (14:17), the gift neither edifies other Christians nor is useful for evangelism (14:23).

While none of these observations provide compelling evidence that two different phenomenon are involved, it seems clear that the exercise of the gift of tongues in the Corinthian congregation created a variety of problems. To resolve those problems Paul first explained that a person's spiritual gift is not evidence of his or her spirituality, for each gift is a "manifestation of the Spirit" who dwells in every believer (chap. 12). Paul then put "love" forward as the true measure of spirituality, and a quality which is essential as the context within which any spiritual gift must be exercised (chap. 13).

Now Paul is ready to deal explicitly with the problems created in Corinth by the unrestricted exercise of the gift of tongues.

Interpretation. Paul is about to instruct the church to regulate the exercise of the gift of tongues. But rather than simply lay down rules, the great apostle carefully explains the reasons for the guidelines he intends to establish. We can outline discussion as follows:

Tongues Is a Lesser Gift (14:1-25).
■ Tongues are inferior to prophecy (14:1-5).

■ Tongues does not nurture believers (14:6-19).

■ Tongues does not win the lost (14:20-25).

Regulating the Gift of Tongues (14:26-40).
■ An interpreter must be present (14:26-28).

■ Order must be maintained (14:29-33).

■ Disruptions must cease (14:34-36).

■ Tongues are not to be forbidden (14:37-40).

Tongues Is a Lesser Gift (14:1-25). The church's acclaim of tongues as the ultimate spiritual gift, and prime evidence of spirituality, is totally misplaced. The Corinthians have in fact fastened on a minor gift and made it a major issue. But what makes tongues a lesser gift? Paul carefully explains.

■ Tongues is inferior to prophecy (14:1-5). Spiritual gifts are given "for the common good" (12:7). That is, their primary function is to nurture and build up individuals and the church. But when speaking in tongues a person directs the exercise of the gift to God, not men (14:2). In contrast, a person who prophesies (in the sense of speaking the word of God, communicating or explaining God's message to man) speaks to men "for their strengthening, encouragement, and comfort" (14:3). The gift of tongues is minor in comparison with a gift like prophecy. Tongues as a gift cannot stand on its own, for tongues must be interpreted if it is to play that role in the church for which gifts are intended.

■ Tongues does not nurture believers (14:6-19). Paul develops the implications of the fact that tongues is unintelligible speech. Even musical instruments must play recognizable tunes. Trumpets that call a troop to battle must sound a recognizable signal. Even the language of foreigners has meaning to those who speak it. How obvious it is that for something to have meaning (14:10-11), it must have some recognizable pattern. It must be intelligible.

Strikingly, because tongues is unintelligible speech, it even makes very little contribution to the spiritual life of the speaker, much less listeners (14:14-15). It is obvious that tongues can make no contribution to other believers, unless the speaker or another member of the congregation can interpret. Those who hear a person speaking in tongues can't even say "Amen" to the speaker's expression of thanksgiving, "since he does not know what you are saying" (14:16).

Paul puts the value of tongues to the church in perspective when he, as one who himself speaks in tongues, says, "I would rather speak five intelligible words to instruct others than ten thousand words in a tongue" (14:19).

■ Tongues does not win the lost (14:20-25). The paragraph seems rather confusing, a fact often attributed to a minor transmission error of the Greek text. Yet Paul's thought seems clear enough.

The OT seems to indicate that even though God speaks through "men of strange tongues," this phenomenon will not cause people to "listen to Me [God]" (14:20-21).

Given the view of ecstatic utterances in the Hellenistic world, a believer's public exercise of the gift of tongues may create an initial impression that he or she has a special relationship with God (14:22). But if a non-Christian follows up that initial impression, and comes to a church meeting where everyone is speaking in tongues, "will they not say that you are out of your mind?" (14:23) Given an overdose of tongues, non-Christians will simply dismiss these people as crazy, and go away shaking their heads in disgust.

On the other hand Paul argues that if a non-Christian comes to a Christian meeting and he hears members of the congregation speaking the words of God in intelligible speech, he will "be convinced by all that he is a sinner. . . . So he will fall down and worship God, exclaiming, 'God is really among you!' " (14:24-25)

Put plainly, tongues has almost nothing to contribute to the gathered church, and very little to contribute to the person who speaks in tongues. Clearly the church should give priority to gifts like prophecy, which does contribute to all.

Regulating the Gift of Tongues (14:26-40). Paul does not forbid the exercise of this gift in church meetings. He does, however, set down guidelines which are intended to regulate its use.

■ An interpreter must be present (14:26-28). The congregational gathering is a time when each brother and sister has an opportunity to exercise his or her gift "for the strengthening of the church." Because tongues, as unintelligible speech, can make no such contribution, this gift is to be exercised only when the speaker or someone else who is present is able to interpret the tongue.

■ Order must be maintained (14:29-33). The fact that Paul makes this point suggests that those who spoke in tongues had been in the habit of interrupting others, supposedly carried away by the Spirit. All too often meetings of the church had apparently deteriorated into shouting matches, with several speakers in tongues competing to see who could rant the loudest. Paul says that "the spirits of prophets are subject to the control of prophets" (14:32). That is, God does not turn His people into puppets and jerk their strings in ways that rob them of control! The excuse "I couldn't help myself. I was possessed by God!" simply won't wash.

The meetings of the church then are to be marked by courtesy and order, not confusion and competition. God is not a God of disorder.

■ **Disruptions must cease (14:34-36).** This instruction to women to "remain silent in the churches" has caused considerable debate, particularly in view of Paul's apparent recognition of women as "prophets" in church meetings in 11:4-5 of this very letter. The question of women in the church will be explored in greater depth in the next study, of 1 Cor. 7 and 11. However, the fact that these words of Paul about women are found in this context seems to indicate that a group of women was perhaps the most vocal and disruptive in the use of tongues in gatherings of the church in Corinth.

■ **Tongues are not to be forbidden (14:37-40).** Paul has carefully explained the limitations of the gift of tongues. Now he reminds the Corinthians, and us, that while this gift is a relatively minor one, it *is* a spiritual gift. As such the gift of tongues is not to be forbidden by the church.

Application. Paul's whole purpose in this extended passage has been to provide perspective on the gift of tongues. That gift is not a sign of spirituality, for every believer has the Spirit, and every gift is an endowment of the Spirit. A far more sure indicator of spirituality is love, which is essential as the interpersonal context in which every gift is to be exercised. As for tongues, it is a very minor gift. As unintelligible speech, it makes very little contribution to the edification of the church or to winning the lost. Five words of prophecy in understandable speech mean more than 10,000 words in a tongue.

Thus when the church gathers, while an exercise of this gift is not to be forbidden, its exercise is to be limited—and regulated.

What wonderful balance 1 Cor. 12–14 brings to a dispute which continues into our own day. Those who do speak in tongues are not to be arrogant, as if their gift somehow makes them special. And those who do not speak in tongues are not to feel threatened, nor to

reject the exercise of this gift out of hand. Instead we are to realize that God's "most excellent way" (12:31), the way of love, is to govern our relationships with those who are like us in their Christian experience and view of tongues—and with those who are unlike us in their Christian experience and their view of tongues.

If we proceed in the spirit of love, neither the exercise of the gift nor its absence need divide our local expression of the living body of Christ.

Orderly Worship (14:26-33).

Background. The house church. For the first three centuries A.D. Christians assembled for weekly worship in houses. This passage gives us some insight into what happened at these meetings: there was apparently a free interchange in which each person contributed according to his gift. In Paul's words, "When you come together, everyone has a hymn, or a word of instruction, a revelation, a tongue or an interpretation" (14:26). Only a few passages describe the gathering of a first-century congregation, but each reflects this atmosphere of mutual ministry. Heb. 10:24-25 says "let us consider how we may spur one another on toward love and good deeds. Let us not give up meeting together, as some are in the habit of doing, but let us encourage one another." And Col. 3:16 adds this to the developing picture: "Let the word of Christ dwell in you richly as you teach and admonish one another with all wisdom, and as you sing psalms, hymns and spiritual songs with gratitude in your hearts to God."

How many people assembled for the weekly meeting of the church? An article in the *Biblical Archaeologist* of September 1984 (vol. 47: No. 3) provides this perspective on "The Corinth that Saint Paul Saw" by Jerome Murphy-O'Connor.

As the number of Paul's converts grew it became necessary to find a place where they could assemble. The strained relations with the Jews excluded the synagogue, and Christianity's lack of status put any other public meeting-place out of the question. Private houses, therefore, became the centers of church life.

The villa at Anaploga, one of the four houses of the Roman period excavated at

Corinth, can be dated to the time of Paul. It is, therefore, the sort of house in which Gaius acted as host, to Paul and the church (Romans 16:23).

Given the social conditions of the time, any gathering that involved more than very intimate friends of the family would be limited to the public areas of the house, the *triclinium* [dining room] and the *atrium*. In the Ana-pologa villa the *triclinium* measured 5.5 by 7.5 meters, but the floor space of 41.25 meters was diminished by the couches that lined the walls. The *atrium* located just outside measured 5 by 6 meters, but once again the amount of usable space was reduced by the 2 by 2 meter pool in the middle.

Such figures go a long way towards explaining the problems that arose in the celebration of the Eucharist at Corinth (1 Corinthians 11:16-34). At a minimum the community numbered between forty and fifty, which means that the overcrowding would have been uncomfortable, and everyone could not be accommodated in the same room (p. 157).

The point that is important to us here is simply this. Gatherings of what we today would call the "local church," where several hundred or even a thousand assemble to sit in pews, does not reflect gatherings of the first-century church. In house churches scattered throughout a city 30 or 40, or at the most 50, met to minister to each other. There, in the relative intimacy of what was surely a "small group," the gifts of the Spirit were exercised, as each in Paul's words, contributed for "the strengthening of the church" (1 Cor. 14:26).

1 CORINTHIANS 7, 11, 14
Women in the Church Family

EXPOSITION

James Thurber captioned one of his *New Yorker* cartoons, "I love the idea of there being two sexes, don't you?" Reading 1 Corinthians, it seems unlikely Paul would have agreed. Not because Paul was anti-woman, despite what some say. Simply because a number of the problems in the church in Corinth involved interaction between the sexes. In chapter 5 Paul spoke out strongly against sexual immorality. In chapter 7 he writes to correct misunderstandings about sex in marriage and divorce. In chapter 11 Paul addresses a worship issue that involves women's dress, and moves on to further correct the Corinthians who had corrupted the celebration of the Lord's Supper. Then in chapter 14 the question of women in worship is again raised, although briefly (14:33b-36). Because these passages are linked, it's helpful to explore in one chapter the issues each raises.

Paul condemned sexual immorality, undoubtedly as sternly when he lived in Corinth as in chaps. 5 and 6 of this letter. But what is this dedicated, single apostle's real attitude toward sex? Some in Corinth apparently believed that Christian commitment required celibacy, and went so far as to refuse normal relationships with their spouses or to divorce them. So Paul discusses the larger issue of sex (7:1-9). He then looks at divorce, and notes that the Christian is not to initiate separation even from a nonbeliever (7:10-16). As a general principle, converts should seek to live a Christian life in that state in which they came to know the Lord, without striving for a change in condition (7:17-25). Paul then returns to the question of sexuality, and notes that while marriage is certainly authorized for virgins and widows, Paul sees great advantages in the single state (7:26-40).

Marriage is a primary social context within which men and women interact. The church is itself another primary social context in which the two sexes must interact. And so Paul looks at two very specific situations in which conflict between the sexes has developed. In one case, some women have become so excited by their new freedom to participate in worship that they refuse to dress in church in a way that is considered appropriate for women (11:2-10). Paul rebukes them, but then goes on immediately to put to rest any suggestion that women are inferior. In fact men and women are interdependent, and the right of women to participate, as women, in ministry in the church must be preserved (11:11-16).

Later Paul calls for women to limit their participation in meetings of the local church, a limitation which must be understood in the context of Paul's discussion of the misuse of the spiritual gift of tongues (14:33b-36).

But Paul's comments on propriety in worship have reminded him of another problem in Corinth (11:17-31). This church, so marked by division, has distorted its celebration of the Lord's Supper itself. The religious celebration has been turned into a common meal, where upper-class friends of the host are provided with food, and ordinary members are left out or relegated to standing outside in the *atrium*, hungry, while others feed themselves in the *triclinium* (dining room). The failure of the Corinthians to recognize the significance of this observance is serious, and their insensitivity to their brothers and sisters is a cause of the illnesses from which some of them suffer.

In these passages, again, we see what is certainly the major underlying problem of Corinth. Corinth is a church divided, corrupted by a drive for prestige, marred by efforts of individuals and groups to establish their primacy at the expense of others. This spirit of competition and antagonism is seen in every interpersonal relationship, including relationships between husbands and wives, and between men and women within the fellowship. And the spirit of competition and antagonism is certainly revealed as those in the upper social classes claim privileges which put the more poor in their place as second-class citizens of God's kingdom as well as the kingdom of man.

WORD STUDIES

It is good for a man *not to marry* (7:1). Here as in other places (8:1) the apostle is not giving his considered judgment, but rather quoting a view expressed by some in Corinth. This is even more clear when we realize the original Greek reads "not to touch a woman," that is, not to have sexual intercourse. The real issue here is not marriage but celibacy.

As the passage develops Paul will treat celibacy within marriage, as well as the issue of whether or not those with a strong sex drive should marry in the first place.

The question of marriage is a uniquely Gentile one. The Jews, whose heritage Paul shares, took their stand on Gen. 2:18: "It is not good for the man to be alone." In Judaism marriage was considered a prime responsibility of every man. But some Corinthians were converted out of the general culture, with loose attitudes toward sex, and uncertain about the extent of the moral purity to which they were called in Christ, went to the other extreme. It is also likely that for some, forebearing from sexual relationships had become a matter of pride, a basis for the claim to that higher spirituality which many were driven to claim in their drive for prestige in the body of Christ.

Paul's response is to reject this view, and argue for full and normal sexual expression within marriage (7:2-3).

In the same way, the husband's body does not *belong to him alone* but also to his wife (7:4). Paul uses the verb *exousiazo*. The husband does not have exclusive claim to his body, but each partner in the "one flesh" relationship of marriage (1 Cor. 6:16) has sexual rights of which he or she is not to be deprived.

The language is pointed. Those persons who have opted for celibacy in marriage are not spiritually superior at all. Their withdrawal has deprived their spouses of something that is rightfully important. Rather than act in love, the celibates have made their choices without reference to the needs or desires of their marriage partners!

But if they *cannot* control themselves, they should marry, for it is better to marry than to burn with passion (7:9). The NIV here misses the point. Paul is writing of those with a strong sex drive who, according to the verb he uses, *"do not"* control themselves. This is further supported by the first-class conditional ("if" with the present indicative), which assumes the condition to be met. Paul then is writing to single persons who are having sexual relations. It is of note that Paul does not insist, "Just say 'No.'" He is more practical than that. The antidote is marriage, within which individuals may give legitimate expression to their sex drive.

"To the married I give this command (not I, but the Lord): A wife must not separate from her husband" (7:10). In the first century the distinction we make between "legal

separation" and "divorce" did not exist. What Paul means here is divorce.

Paul introduces this command as one directly from the Lord, undoubtedly referring to the tradition recorded in Matt. 19 and Mark 10. Paul is not introducing a new theme here. He continues to speak to those who exalt celibacy, withholding themselves from their spouses, and even going to the extent of divorcing on ascetic grounds. Certainly Christ's words about divorce apply in this situation.

While many appeal to this text as a basis for a "no Christian divorce" position, we should remember that Paul is dealing here with a very specific problem in Corinth. Before we take his words as a universal principle, binding on all Christians in every situation, we need to hear what he says within its historical context.

But if she does, she must remain unmarried or else be reconciled to her husband (7:11). The phrase, *ean de kai*, represents a present general condition. Rather than representing a hypothetical situation, Paul is describing an alternative possibility which, while not ideal, is permissible.

This is striking in view of the "command" just given. Yet, unlike the immoral brother of 1 Cor. 5, no expulsion from the church is prescribed for the person who has divorced, even for this unacceptable reason.

Paul does, however, make it very clear that he is not, in providing this alternative, giving a general license to those who divorce *in order to remarry*. The person who has divorced in order to live a celibate life must do just that: either remain unmarried, or be reconciled to her husband.

There is more, however, on divorce in this passage, for soon Paul considers a very different situation, and draws a very different conclusion (see Word Study of 7:15, below).

The unbelieving husband has been *sanctified* through his wife. . . . Otherwise your children would be unclean, but as it is, they are *holy* (7:14). The two words in question are *hagiazo*, "to sanctify, set apart" and *hagia*, "holy, set apart for God." These terms are not used in a moral but a relational sense. In OT law a person who came in contact with something or someone unclean became unclean himself. Now, the dynamic of Christ's presence transforms the situation. The presence of the believer in the family unit brings the children and the unsaved spouse into the sphere of that divine influence exerted by the Spirit through the believer.

Paul's point is that a person who has been converted need not separate himself or herself from a spouse who has not yet come to know Christ—as long as the unsaved person is willing to continue living with the Christian.

But if the unbeliever leaves, let him do so. A believing man or woman *is not bound* in such circumstances (7:15). Paul is still dealing with practical problems faced by young Christians in Corinth. Some have accepted Paul's teaching and not initiated divorce. But their non-Christian spouses have left them! What is their situation? Are they to remain unmarried, and wait for their spouses to be converted and hope for a future reconciliation?

Arguing that this hope is unrealistic (7:16), Paul announces full release from the marriage bonds. The believer in this situation is "not bound" (*ou dedoulotai*; not under bondage [7:15]). Some argue that Paul means the believer is not obligated to attempt to maintain a marriage with the unwilling spouse. It seems more likely, however, that Paul means that in this case the believer is not obligated to follow the guidelines he has earlier set down: do not divorce (7:10), but if one does divorce remain unmarried or be reconciled to one's spouse (7:11). In the case of desertion or abandonment by a spouse no longer willing to maintain the marriage, the person who has been abandoned is, in reality, "unmarried."

Paul does not deal here with the question of remarriage. And, throughout this passage he strongly recommends the single life (7:25-26), and just as strongly urges his readers not to seek a change in state, whatever their present state may be (7:27-28). However, a strong case can be made that the once-married person whose spouse refuses to maintain the marriage, who is not bound by Paul's earlier rulings, is as free as any unmarried individual to marry if he or she is so led by God.

DIVORCE AND REMARRIAGE

Few issues are more painful, and few more divisive, than the debate over whether and under what conditions Christians may divorce and remarry. A recent title, *Four Views on Divorce,* (InterVarsity Press), thoroughly explores all relevant passages and their various interpretations. The author's own view is developed in another book, *Remarriage: A Healing Gift from God* (Word).

Were you a *slave* when you were called? Don't let it trouble you—although if you can gain your freedom, do so (7:21). In the Roman Empire a change in status from slave to free, or vice versa, was fundamental. In fact there were three levels involved: slave, freedman, and free. The freedman was a person who had been a slave, but had purchased or been given his freedom by his master.

The significance of these categories is reflected in epitaphs from the period. In fact these categories seem often to override other considerations of status, such as sex or position in the family. The name of a woman who had been freed would be placed before that of her slave husband. And the name of a freeborn son might be placed ahead of both father (slave) and mother (freed).

The change in status from slave to freedman, offering the even higher status of freeborn to the children, was greatly desired. And many in the Empire moved up this pathway. Research by Gordon on Italy's lesser aristocracy showed that as many as a third of the officials in commercial centers like Ostia and Capua were sons of freedmen.

In view of this, Paul's advice to "remain in the situation" in which a person was called, seems stunning (1 Cor. 7:20). Why shouldn't a Christian try to better himself? Why not seek a path that will provide a better life for one's children?

Paul's "although" in 7:21 helps us understand. Paul is not against advancement, per se. Paul is against focusing so intently on worldly goals that the believer is distracted from his or her calling to live as "Christ's slave." The Christian's goal should be to do God's will in each situation—not to concentrate on trying to change the situation.

What an appropriate word this is for us today. How often we think that, if only we had more money, or more time, or if only we did not have a wife and children, then we could be more devoted to God. Paul reminds us that this kind of thinking is wrong. We are not to concentrate on what we would do if things were different. We are to concentrate on serving Jesus in the situation that exists today. In this and in this alone will we experience peace.

A woman is *bound to her husband* as long as he lives. But if her husband dies, she is free to marry anyone she wishes, but he must *belong to the Lord* (7:39). The word translated "bound," *dedatai,* is the same word found in 7:15, where Paul says a woman is not bound if her unbelieving spouse is unwilling to live with her. It is clear then that here Paul is stating the ideal that governs marriage, but which does not rule out the exceptional situations he has written about earlier.

The most important contribution here is not the restatement of an ideal with which all Christians agree. The most important contribution is Paul's comment that a Christian widow who remarries must do so in the Lord.

Marrying a fellow-Christian does not guarantee immunity from heartache, disappointment, or even divorce. But it does mean that we have a chance for that harmonious, loving, Christian home that every adult and child needs.

Now I want you to realize that the head of every man is Christ, and *the head of the woman is man,* and the head of Christ is God (11:3). Despite the efforts of some to impose hierarchical implications, Paul is clearly not using "head" in a superior/ subordinate sense. Head, *kephale,* was not generally used in Greek literature in the sense of "chief" or "highest in rank." Although the Hebrew word *ro'sh* did carry this sense, the translators of the Septuagint almost never use *kephale* to translate *ro'sh* when "ruler" is intended, although they did use *kephale* if the physical "head" were intended. Paul's first-century readers would have understood his metaphor to indicate "source of life" rather than "ruler" or "superior vs. inferior."

Why does Paul begin this way, and what is he saying? Soon Paul will deal with the specific problem, which has to do with head coverings. But before he does, Paul wants to construct a framework for his remarks. That framework is at once theological, historical, and relational. Christ is the source of man's life (John 1:4). Adam (*ho aner;* "the man") is the source from which woman was formed. God Himself is the source from which the incarnate Christ came. What we do, then, re-

flects on the source from which we spring, to its honor or dishonor.

From time to time we hear someone argue from this passage that men, the "head," are superior and women are inferior, so women must obey men. But how is Christ inferior to the Father, who is His "head"? From eternity Father, Son, and Holy Spirit existed as One God, coequals although with different roles in carrying out the plan of salvation. We might much more logically argue for the *equality* of men and women from this verse than for woman's subordination. In fact, Paul does exactly this in stressing the interdependence of the sexes in 11:11-12.

Yes, the roles of men and women do differ: in the family, in society, and in the church. But role differentiation must not be distorted to suggest superiority/inferiority. And Paul's use of "head" here must not be taken to support a hierarchical view of male/female relations in home or church.

Every woman who prays or prophesies *with her head uncovered* dishonors her head (11:5). Paul does not object here to women "praying and prophesying" in church meetings. What he objects to is women who do so with their heads "uncovered."

Despite intense research and discussion it is not possible to say exactly what Paul means by an "uncovered" head, or just why this was inappropriate. Views of the head covering range from veils, such as those worn by women of the Middle East, to scarves, to wearing the hair loose and uncombed, to cutting the hair short. Unfortunately, we are so far removed from the first century and particularly from the practices of the early Christians that we simply have no way of knowing just what these words refer to.

What we do know, however, is enough. The Corinthian women were apparently excited about the new freedom they experienced in Christ. It is true that in the first century, women did have a role in synagogue worship. But that role was limited, as T. Megillah 23 defines: "All may come forward to make up the quorum of seven, even women and minors. But the sages say a woman should not read Scripture, out of respect for the congregation."

But in Corinth women not only led in prayer, they prophesied, serving as agents of

God's ongoing revelation to His people!

What apparently happened is that some of the Corinthian women chose to assert their equality with men at worship by adopting a male way of wearing their hair. If they now had the privilege once reserved for men at worship, they would assert that privilege by adopting male dress and styles!

It is this that bothered Paul. In adopting an extreme feminist position, the women in Corinth in effect denied Creation truth, for God Himself created men and women different, not the same.

But the woman is the glory of man (11:7). Paul develops his original argument. God is the source of male/female differences (11:7-9). The difference is not demeaning, for "woman is the glory of man."

This phrase helps us see that in saying woman was created "for" man Paul is not saying woman was created for man to dominate, or for man to have authority over. Instead, Paul is saying that woman, coming from man, completes man, and with man makes the human race a realizable possibility. The excellencies of the female reflects credit on the male, from whose rib she was formed as his partner and equal.

For this reason, and because of the angels, the woman ought to have a *sign of authority* on her head (11:10). Paul now drives his argument home. The authority, *exousia*, Paul speaks of is not some supposed authority of the man over the woman, as some have taught. Instead it is the new freedom—the authority, the right—that women as women have within the church to pray and prophesy. By proudly dressing their hair as women,

these Corinthians will demonstrate to men and angels that women are not second-class citizens and do not have to deny their feminine nature to win equality. It is as women that Paul wants these Corinthians to take their place beside, rather than beneath, the men of the congregation, as equal partners and equal participants in the worship of God.

The message of this passage has a contemporary ring. Today too some women have come to feel that they must dress, act, and behave like men if they are to achieve equality. The good news of the Gospel is that, in Christ, women are accepted and valued as women. And that they have authority to participate fully in ministry as they exercise the spiritual gifts they have been given by our God.

And, today, the church must learn what Paul knew and taught, and so open doors to ministry that have too long been closed.

As in all the congregations of the saints, women should *remain silent* in the churches. They are not allowed to speak, but must be *in submission* (14:33-34). After studying Paul's affirmation of the freedom and authority women are to enjoy as women both praying and prophesying in the church, this verse just three chapters later comes as a shock. Is Paul inconsistent? How can women pray and prophesy, and at the same time remain silent. How can they have authority, and not be allowed to speak? How can women be spoken of as equals in chapter 11, and here be cast as subordinates who are to be "in submission"?

For a discussion, see the Passage in Depth discussion of the role of women in the church.

THE PASSAGE IN DEPTH

The Lord's Supper (11:17-34).

Background. While on the subject of worship, Paul writes to correct practices in Corinth that are associated with the Eucharist, the celebration of the Lord's Supper. Three matters cause him concern. (1) The church is abusing the *agape* (the love-feast) accompanying the celebration, vv. 17-22. (2) The church is not taking the celebration seriously, or following the form established by Jesus, vv. 23-

26. Paul restates the form, emphasizing the fact that the ceremony is a "remembrance" (11:24, 26), an opportunity to stand again at the foot of the cross and sense as well as affirm the meaning of Christ's death for us. (3) Some in the church are partaking "unworthily," vv. 27-34. Here the fault is the "unworthy manner" (11:27) of partaking. The problem here is not the form of celebration, but the attitude of the celebrant. Those who approach

the service cavalierly, ignoring unconfessed sin, risk God's displeasure and even sickness and physical death. The Lord's Supper honors a sacrifice made to free us from the grip of sin. We can hardly participate worthily if we wallow happily in sin's grip, and thus deny the purpose of Christ's death.

It is, however, the first matter that reflects the overall theme of this letter. "When you come together as a church, there are divisions among you" (11:18). Here the divisions are apparently social ones, as the host provides for upper class members and social equals, and ignores the poor.

Murphy-O'Connor's description of the homes in which the Corinthian Christians met made it very clear that little room was available (see Orderly Worship [14:26-33] in Passage in Depth for 1 Corinthians 12–14). Some by necessity were welcomed into the *triclinium* (dining room) while others would by necessity be outside in the *atrium*. Much attention has been given in the last 30 years to the sociology of the church at Corinth, and much of the stress within the body has been traced to preexisting social stratification. As far as shared meals are concerned, those of different social classes at the same dinner would normally be provided with very different quantities and qualities of food. Apparently this common practice had been carried over by some in Corinth who hosted meetings of the church, with divisive results! In following this practice "you despise the church of God and humiliate those who have nothing" (11:22).

An interesting section of one of Pliny's letters suggests greater sensitivity to the impact of this treatment than was shown by the Corinthian Christians toward their brothers.

I happened to be dining with a man — though no particular friend of his — whose elegant economy, as he called it, seems to me a sort of stingy extravagance. The best dishes were set in front of himself and a select few, and cheap scraps of food before the rest of the company. He had even put the wine into tiny little flasks, divided into three categories, not with the idea of giving his guests the opportunity of choosing, but to make it impossible for them to refuse what they were given. One lot was intended for himself and for us, another for his lesser friends (all his friends are graded) and the third for his and our freedmen. My neighbor at table noticed this and asked me if I approved. I said I did not. "So what do you do?" he asked. "I serve the same to everyone, for when I invite guests it is for a meal, not to make class distinctions; I have brought them as equals to the same table, so I give them the same treatment in everything." "Even the freedmen?" "Of course, for then they are my fellow-diners, not freedmen." "That must cost you a lot." "On the contrary." "How is that?" "Because my freedmen do not drink the sort of wine I do, but I drink theirs."

So, Paul says, it must be in the church. For when believers gathered for a love-feast and to celebrate our Lord's death, it was not to make social distinctions. All alike were guests of the risen Lord, all alike His freedmen, whose freedom had been purchased at the cost of the Savior's blood.

Women in the Church (11:2-16; 14:33-36).
Overview. In order to understand any single passage touching on this theme, it is necessary to place it in a wider context. For this reason, I here quote an extended article from the *Zondervan Expository Dictionary of Bible Words.*

1. Evidence of the Significance of Women. Despite the reality of life in a male-dominated culture, women played a surprisingly significant role in the early church. The reason is undoubtedly that, in Christ, women as well as men are the recipients of spiritual gifts for ministry. Thus, the contribution of women to the total ministry of the body of Christ is basic to the health and growth of the whole congregation.

Specific lines of NT evidence show that an important place was given to women in the life of the church. A few facts are worth noting.

■ Women played a critical role in the establishment of several NT congregations (Acts 16:13-15, 40; 17:4, 12).

■ Women are identified by name and called "fellow workers" by Paul (especially Rom. 16, where seven women are identified by name). This inclusion of women in a ministry team is a significant departure from Jewish practice. The naming of Priscilla before her husband Aquila is also extremely significant (Rom. 16:3).

■ Women are seen participating through prayer and prophecy in church meetings (1 Cor. 11:5). Although the OT foretold a day when sons and daughters would prophesy as the Spirit was poured out on "both men and women" (Joel 2:28-32; Acts 2:17-18), the participation of women in church gatherings again violates OT tradition.

■ Phoebe is identified in Rom. 16:1 as a deaconess, and other evidence suggests that women may have participated with men in the diaconate.

Despite the clarity of evidence in each of these areas, suggesting that women participated freely in the life of the early church and were recognized as significant contributors of ministry, there are problem passages which are difficult to interpret.

2. Women in Church Office.
The offices mentioned in the NT were ordinarily filled by males. This seems true whether one speaks of apostles, elders, or overseers (bishops). This is not true, however, of the office of deacons. Phoebe is identified in Rom. 16:1 as a deaconess of the church in Cenchrea. The word means "servant" and is so rendered in most English versions, but it is the same word used in 1 Tim. 3:8, where "deacons" are supposed to be (among other things) "men worthy of respect, sincere, not indulging in much wine." Then verse 11 says, "In the same way, their wives [*gyne*] are to be women worthy of respect, not malicious talkers" (3:11). The NIV and some other versions interpret *gyne* as "their wives," but the NIV adds a footnote: "Or . . . *deaconesses*." The lack in the original of a possessive ("their") suggests that the better translation is "women" not "wives." The passage may well be speaking of those women who, like the men Paul referred to, were deacons and bore the responsibility of that office.

While there is evidence that women served as deacons in the early church, there is a lack of evidence concerning their serving in any other office. We should be careful how we

argue from silence. Whatever role deacons had in the church, we have positive indications that women served among them.

3. Women in the Worship Service.
The most controversial NT passages regarding women have a common context; they deal with issues related to worship. However we understand these passages, we need to interpret them in the total context of a gathering in which women *did* (at least in the church at Corinth) take part, for Paul wrote about women praying and prophesying when the congregation gathered (1 Cor. 11:5). Within this framework of participation, the passages and the most likely interpretations follow.

According to 1 Cor. 14:34-36, women are to "remain silent in the churches" to the extent that they "are not allowed to speak." Any questions should be held till they are at home and can "ask their own husbands." This very blunt instruction has been interpreted in several ways. (1) It decisively rules out female participation. (2) It was added by someone other than Paul. (3) It is an example of Paul's inconsistency and reflects his culture-bound, antifeminine view. (4) Paul's statements in chapter 11 are misunderstood, and women are not to speak in church. (5) The prohibition in chapter 14 must be seen in a narrow view, as dealing with some specific problem rather than reflecting a pattern in church meetings as a whole.

This last option is most in keeping with a high view of Scripture and with careful attention to the text. In 1 Cor. 14:26-40, Paul is dealing not only with disorderly meetings but also with the question of prophetic revelation (14:30). Paul has indicated that "two or three prophets should speak, and the others should weigh carefully what is said" (14:29). The Greek verb rendered "weigh" is *diakrino* ("judge," "discern"). It is in this immediate context that Paul gives his instructions about the silence of women. Thus, it is best to take the passage to mean that in the process of weighing prophets, women are to remain silent and not participate.

This interpretation is in harmony with an understanding of the other critical passage, 1 Tim. 2. In writing to Timothy, Paul again turns to the congregational meeting. Here he says of women, "A woman should learn in quietness and full submission. I do not permit a woman to teach or to have authority over a man; she must be silent" (2:11-12). Paul then gives a theological argument from Creation and the Fall as basis for his ruling (2:13-14).

There is a difference between this and the 1 Cor. 14 passage. Here "quietness" and "silent" are both translations of *hesychia,* whereas in 1 Cor. 14 the word is *sigao.* This latter word is used nine times in the NT (Luke 9:36; 20:26; Acts 12:17; 15:12-13; Rom. 16:25; 1 Cor. 14:28, 30, 34) and means "Be silent," with the force of "Shut up." But *hesychia* is used only four times in the NT (Acts 22:2; 2 Thes. 3:12; 1 Tim. 2:11-12) and indicates a restful but attentive receptiveness. That attitude, which promotes learning, is further set in contrast with "teaching" or "having authority" over a man. It is best not to separate the concepts of teaching and authority, though this is possible grammatically. Rather, we need to see in the whole discussion the issue of "authoritative teaching." Authoritative teaching in the church is thus viewed as incompatible with the woman's appropriate role of *hesychia* and submission.

The parallelism between the two passages is thus made clear. Women did participate to some extent in the gatherings of the church at Corinth in the form of prayer and prophesying. But any prominent or dominant role was specifically forbidden, especially the judging of prophets and uttering of authoritative teaching for the church body.

4. Implications for Today.
The two limitations on women's ministry that the Epistles specify are the roles that most believe were filled by elders or bishops (overseers) in the early church.

Essentially, these offices seem directly linked with guarding the health of the local body by protecting those processes that make for spiritual healthiness in the church. Included might well be the judging of the message of a contemporary prophet and the giving of an authoritative teaching (interpretation of the Scripture) intended to guide the local body.

If this view is correct, it seems clear that the early church did not include women among its elders or overseers. It seems possible that, since Paul's arguments for his position are rooted in theology rather than in contemporary custom, this limitation is intended for the church today as well.

We must remember that much debate continues to go on over these passages. Certainly whatever conviction one develops must be held humbly and balanced by a strong affirmation of the significance of women as persons in the church of Jesus Christ (pp. 631-33).

1 CORINTHIANS 15–16
Resurrection: *This Family Is Forever*

EXPOSITION

As Paul's letter nears conclusion, he turns to a final issue: the teaching of "some of you" (15:12) that no resurrection lies ahead for believers. Paul's response is in three parts. First he reminds the Corinthians of foundational truth: *Christ was raised from the dead* (15:1-11). Clearly resurrection is an objective reality, and indeed the source of the believer's new life in Christ. Second, Paul shows the absurd consequences of their denial of resurrection (15:12-34). If there is no resurrection of the dead, then Christ was not raised, and Christianity itself is a hoax (15:12-19). If Christ is raised, then that resurrection is evidence that death has been conquered, and that the dead in Christ will be raised (15:20-28). Paul then notes practical implications of denial of the resurrection. In such a case, suffering for Christ is foolishness, and believers might as well live for the flesh—as some apparently are doing (15:29-34).

With the issue put to rest, Paul turns to another question: *how* are the dead raised? (15:35-58) This more than anything else seemed to pagans contrary to reason. Later Celsus argued, "what sort of body, after being entirely corrupted, could return to its original nature and that same condition which it had before it was dissolved? As they have nothing to say in reply, they escape to a most outrageous refuge by saying that 'anything is possible with God.' But indeed neither can God do what is shameful nor does He desire what is contrary to reason" (c. Cels. 5.14). Indeed, Paul's careful attention to *how* suggests that Celsus expresses the view of doubters in Corinth. Paul's answer avoids the "outrageous refuge," by using analogy to show that resurrection does *not* restore the body to "its original nature" or "that same condition" it had before dissolution. Men do not think it strange that a new life springs from a seed planted in the ground, although the original seed suffers dissolution. Why be surprised that the earthly body undergoes a transformation, from perishability to imperishability, from dishonor to glory, from weakness to power, from natural to spiritual? We are related now to Christ, not Adam, and when Christ returns the dead in Christ will be raised and living believers will be transformed with them. Then the glad cry will ring out through the universe, "Death has been swallowed up in victory!" (15:54)

Chapter 16 seems an anticlimax after the triumphant shout that concludes Paul's defense of resurrection. Yet it reminds us that while glory lies ahead, we must in the meantime deal with the mundane—and that the mundane is important. So Paul reminds the Corinthians about a collection they are making for the poor (16:1-4), which reminds him that Timothy may soon arrive (16:5-11), although Apollos is unwilling to return to Corinth soon (16:12). And then, with a series of concluding exhortations and wishes, Paul ends his letter to Corinth. Truly Corinth was a problem church. But its members remained dear to the great apostle, and his last words express an attitude which, if not always evident in the strong words he uses in this letter, certainly pervade all he has written: "My love to all of you in Christ Jesus. Amen."

WORD STUDIES

For what I received I passed on to you as of first importance (15:3). The Greek permits taking "first" in a temporal sense. But the context makes it clear; Paul is emphasizing the centrality of what he "passed on to you" as the Gospel message. What are Christianity's central doctrines? The next verses tell us

> that Christ died for our sins
>   according to the Scriptures,

> that He was buried,
> that He was raised on the third day
>   according to the Scriptures,
> and that He appeared (15:3-5).

God foretold in the Scriptures what happened in space and time, to which the apostles and others were eyewitnesses. The resurrection is thus a historical reality.

Some have tried to relegate the Resurrection to a "spiritual" realm in a salvation history which is different in kind from space/time history. They see the story of Jesus' resurrection as a creative way of expressing the conviction of the apostles that even after the cross Jesus was "real" to them. How different this theology is from the simple affirmation of Paul that the death, burial, and resurrection of Jesus were equally real, attested by both Scripture and eyewitnesses. As Peter so plainly says, "We did not follow cleverly invented stories when we told you about the power and coming of our Lord Jesus Christ, but we were eyewitnesses of His majesty" (2 Peter 1:16).

"That He was raised on the third day according to the Scriptures" (15:4). Commentators differ as to whether the phrase "according to the Scriptures" refers to the Resurrection alone, or to a third-day Resurrection.

The popular first-century Jewish view held that corruption of a corpse began only on the third day. Thus Paul may have been making an oblique reference to Psalm 16:10: "You will not abandon me to the grave, nor will you let your Holy One see decay."

It is more likely, however, that Paul refers to the Scriptures simply as a witness to the fact that Messiah was to die and be raised again. While Psalm 16:9-11 does refer to Jesus' resurrection (Acts 2:25-31), Paul may have been thinking of an even clearer passage.

By oppression and judgment, He was taken away.
And who can speak of His descendants?
For He was cut off from the land of the living;
for the transgression of my people He was stricken.
He was assigned a grave with the wicked, and with the rich in His death,
though He had done no violence, nor was any deceit in His mouth.
Yet it was the Lord's will to crush Him and cause Him to suffer,
and though the Lord makes His life a guilt offering,
He will see His offspring and prolong His days,
and the will of the Lord will prosper in His hand.
After the suffering of His soul,
He will see the light of life and be satisfied;

by His knowledge my righteous servant will justify many,
and He will bear their iniquities.
Therefore I will give Him a portion among the great,
and He will divide the spoils with the strong,
because He poured out His life unto death,
and was numbered with the transgressors.
For He bore the sin of many,
and made intercession for the transgressors.

Isa. 53:8-12

These words, written by the Prophet Isaiah some 700 years before Jesus was born, constitute powerful testimony to both the death and resurrection of Jesus. Neither can be discounted or dismissed. Both death and resurrection are central to the Christian Gospel, fully attested as real events that took place in space-time history.

THE OLD TESTAMENT ON OUR RESURRECTION

The doctrine of personal resurrection is not developed in the OT. Yet it clearly is present, and was taught by the Pharisees of Jesus' day. Undoubtedly, the clearest statement in the OT is found in Dan. 12:2: "Multitudes who sleep in the dust of the earth will awake; some to everlasting life, others to shame and everlasting contempt." But the OT doctrine does not rest on a single verse. Isaiah looked forward to a day when "He will swallow up death forever (Isa. 25:8) and proclaimed, "Your dead will live; their bodies will rise. You who dwell in the dust, wake up and shout for joy" (Isa. 26:19). Both Enoch and Elijah were taken directly to heaven (Gen. 5:24; 2 Kings 2:11), events which suggest the continuation of life beyond our world, although their cases are obviously unusual. Other verses which hint at a deliverance that extends beyond this life include Job 14:14; Pss. 17:15; 49:7-12; 73:23-26.

While the doctrine is not developed, it is clear enough so that Jesus could justly condemn the Sadducees, who ridiculed the idea of a personal resurrection, saying, "You are in error because you did not know the Scriptures or the power of God" (Matt. 22:29; Mark 12:24).

And that He *appeared* to Peter, and then to the Twelve. After that He *appeared* to more than five hundred . . . (15:5). The verb is *ophthe,* which here simply means Jesus was visible to those who served as witnesses of His resurrection. The list of witnesses is impressive, especially in view of the fact that when Paul wrote most of them would have still been alive. A complete list of post-resurrection appearances includes the following:

Peter	Luke 24:34;
	1 Cor. 15:5
Two disciples	Luke 24:13-31
Apostles (not Thomas)	Luke 24:36-45;
	John 20:19-24
Apostles (with Thomas)	John 20:24-29
Seven at Lake Tiberius	John 21:1-23
500 in Galilee	1 Cor. 15:6
James in Jerusalem	1 Cor. 15:7
Many at the Ascension	Acts 1:3-11
Paul, near Damascus	Acts 9:3-6;
	1 Cor. 15:8
Stephen when stoned	Acts 7:55
Paul in the temple	Acts 22:17-21; 23:11
John on Patmos	Rev. 1:10-19

As many have pointed out, we have more historical evidence for the bodily resurrection of Jesus than for nearly any other event that happened in the ancient world. Those who reject the Gospel cannot validly argue that its claims cannot be authenticated historically.

Then those who have *fallen asleep* in Christ are lost. If only for this life we have hope in Christ, we are to be pitied more than all men (15:18-19). "Sleep" here is *koimaomai,* frequently used in the NT as a euphemism for death (Matt. 27:52; 28:13; Luke 22:45; John 11:11-12; Acts 7:60; 12:6; 13:36; 1 Cor. 7:39; 11:30; 15:6, 18, 20, 51; 1 Thes. 4:13-15; 2 Peter 3:4). Paul has reviewed the evidence for Christ's physical resurrection. Now he looks at the implications of denying it. If Christ was raised, we will be raised. But if Christ was not raised, and resurrection is a hoax, then Christianity is futile, we are still in our sins, and the dead are lost. For the Christian, hope requires a resurrection. Without resurrection all is meaningless.

The Christian emphasis on resurrection is particularly significant in view of the fact that no such hope was offered by ancient paganism or the mystery religions of the East. Christ's resurrection was proclaimed as evidence of the effectiveness of His death in procuring our salvation, and as evidence that one day the believer too would be raised.

ROMAN FUNERALS

Roman funeral rites looked backward rather than forward. The rites of famous men emphasized a brief biography, with emphasis on the virtues and character of the deceased. Polybius (6.54.2) saw them as a "way the good repute of noble men is constantly renewed; the fame of those who have achieved something grand is kept immortal, and the glory of the benefactors of the country becomes familiar to the people and is handed on to posterity." Tacitus (*Agric.*1, 46) saw the biographical emphasis as a way to "bequeath to posterity a record of the deeds and characters of distinguished men" and so enable them "to live forever."

Yet there was no doubt in any pagan mind that while the memory or fame of "distinguished men" might live forever, the individuals themselves were dead and gone beyond recall. Not until the Gospel light began to shine in the first-century world did pagans dream that the dead could live again.

No wonder Paul reminds the Thessalonians, concerned about those who "fall asleep," that the Christian does not "grieve like the rest of men, who have no hope" (1 Thes. 4:13). The Gospel does bring hope. And the hope of resurrection is one to which we all gladly cling.

Christ *has indeed* been raised from the dead, the *firstfruits* of those who have fallen asleep (15:20). Earlier Paul posed hypotheticals: "If Christ has not been raised" (15:14, 17). Now the hypotheticals are set aside, and Paul affirms a certainty. Christ indeed is raised. What is more, Jesus' resurrection is like the first fruits of a harvest; it serves as a guarantee that a complete harvest is to follow. In this sense Jesus' resurrection serves as God's personal guarantee that we too will be raised when harvest-time comes.

Then *the end will come,* when He hands over the kingdom to God the Father after He has destroyed all dominion, authority and power (15:24). Paul's point is that our resurrection is one event, albeit an important one, in a sequence of culminating events. The first event was Jesus' resurrection, which transformed the course of history and made the believer's resurrection sure. Yet this must be placed in a framework reflecting God's overall plan. There is

Christ,	the firstfruits
When He comes,	those who belong to Him
Then the end	when He turns over the kingdom to God when all other dominions are brought to an end: i.e., demonic powers death itself

The resurrection of Christ is thus more than a guarantee of our resurrection. It is the critical event of history itself; the event which introduces the eschatological ruler who will accomplish God's purposes and abolish Satan and death, thus restoring the universe to its original pure state, and reversing the flow of destructive power unleashed when Adam fell.

No wonder Paul says that "if Christ has not been raised, your faith is futile; you are still in your sins" (15:17). Everything—for us individually, for our race, for our universe, and for the accomplishment of God's plan—depends on the resurrection of Jesus Christ.

Then the Son Himself will be *made subject* to Him who put everything under Him, so that God may be all in all (15:28). The language is functional rather than ontological. That is, Paul does not suggest the inferiority of Christ, who from eternity has been with God as God. Paul is saying that with His own role as Savior and Messiah fulfilled, Jesus will have restored the universe to full harmony with God the Father's will, for the Father to again administer.

Now if there is no resurrection, what will those do who are *baptized for the dead?* (15:29) The reference is puzzling, in view of the fact that there is no reference to such a practice in church history, and no hint in Scripture of any doctrine vindicating the practice. The best solution seems to be that some in Corinth, feeling baptism was necessary if a person were to enter God's future kingdom, practiced a vicarious baptism on behalf of

loved ones who had died.

Paul's mention of the practice does not suggest an endorsement. Rather, he points to the Corinthian's inconsistency. How can they claim on the one hand that there is no resurrection, while anxiously practicing baptism on behalf of the dead? Either there is a future life, or there isn't. If there isn't, why this compulsion to undergo baptism for the dead?

As for us, why do we *endanger ourselves* every day? (15:30) The Greek phrase is strong: Paul risks his life daily to promote the Gospel. But unlike the Corinthians, Paul is not being inconsistent! He knows that resurrection lies ahead, and so he commits himself fully to a way of life that would make no sense at all if there were no resurrection.

Most of us have never asked of ourselves the question that Paul clearly has asked and answered. Because resurrection does lie ahead, we too would do well to commit ourselves to wholehearted service, whatever material sacrifices may be involved.

Come back to your senses as you ought, and *stop sinning* (15:34). Is the "sin" here denial of the believer's resurrection, or elements of a loose lifestyle lived as though no resurrection lies ahead? The best answer is suggested by the quote in v. 33 from the Greek poet Menander's *Thais,* "Bad company corrupts good character." The word translated "company," *homilia,* can mean "conversation" as well as "companionship." What Paul may be saying is that "evil talk [such as that denying resurrection] has a corrupting influence on Christian commitment." The Corinthians need to "come back to your senses" (15:34), keep their eyes on that future resurrection guaranteed by Christ's own return to life, and stop committing those sins of the flesh that no one looking expectantly for Christ's return would commit.

John makes the same point in his first epistle, writing, "Dear friends, now we are children of God, and what we will be has not yet been made known. But we know that when He appears, we shall be like Him, for we shall see Him as He is. Everyone who has this hope in Him purifies himself, just as He is pure" (1 John 3:2-3).

How are the *dead* raised? With what kind

403

of *body* **will they come? (15:35)** As pointed out in the Exposition, above, "how" was a matter of great concern in the first century. The focus of the question is made clear by the interaction of two words found in this verse. *Nekros,* "dead," is found 11 times in vv. 1-34, but only 3 times in the rest of the chapter. On the other hand *soma,* "body," is found 10 times in the last part of the chapter, but not once in vv. 1-34. The concern then is how can the body be raised? How can something that has undergone complete decay in the grave be reanimated? And, perhaps even more, who would want to return to such a disgusting thing? We can understand—if the Corinthians thought of raising the dead body as a zombie-like return to animation—why the notion seemed repugnant.

Paul points out that while there is a correspondence between the body that dies and the body that is resurrected, they are not exactly the same. The mortal body is perishable, dishonorable, weak, and "natural." In contrast the resurrection body will be imperishable, glorious, powerful, and "spiritual" (15:42-44). Rather than likeness to Adam, the resurrection body corresponds to Christ's (15:49).

How foolish! What you sow does not come to life *unless it dies.* **When you sow, you do not plant the body that will be, but just a seed, perhaps of wheat or something else (15:36-37).** Paul's statement has been criticized as unscientific, for, technically, the planted seed does not die. But Paul is not writing a biology text. Instead he is pointing out that nature itself answers the "foolish" objection of those who suppose that resurrection of the body means the reanimation of the corrupt. When a seed is planted something new emerges! This pattern is followed in the supernatural as well as in the natural order. The body of the believer is buried, but in the resurrection that which emerges from the grave will be renewed and transformed.

We will not all sleep, but we will all be *changed* **(15:51).** When Jesus returns living believers will undergo a transformation of their bodies as well. The Greek word is *allasso,* which is not normally used to indicate such a transformation. Its meaning, however, is clear, for Paul says "the perishable must clothe itself with the imperishable, and the mortal with immortality" (15:53), for "flesh and blood cannot inherit the kingdom of God" (15:50). The transformation to be effected by our resurrection is not optional; it is essential. In its present form the body simply cannot "inherit the kingdom."

Then the saying that is written will come true: "Death has been swallowed up in victory" (15:54). Paul quotes two OT prophecies, the only predictions he ever quotes that have not yet been fulfilled. Isaiah 25:8 says, "He will swallow up death forever. The Sovereign Lord will wipe away the tears from all faces." And Hosea 13:14 says, "I will ransom them from the power of the grave; I will redeem them from death. Where, O death, are your plagues? Where, O grave, is your destruction?"

Yet in another sense these prophecies have been fulfilled in Jesus, and we simply await their full realization. In His own death and resurrection Jesus has rendered helpless the one who held the power of death, and won eternal victory for you and me (Heb. 2:14-15; Col. 2:15).

The sting of death is sin, and *the power of sin* **is the law (15:56).** In triumphing over death, Jesus also overcame the enemies that brought death to humanity. The first enemy is sin, which Rom. 6 shows us no longer holds its corrupting power over the person who is united by faith to Jesus. The second is the law, which according to Rom. 7:1-4 is the "power of sin" in that the law's "Do not" in fact energizes or stimulates the sin nature to acts of sin.

In defeating death, Jesus put an end to the power of death's associates, that we might even now live godly lives. No wonder Paul concludes, "My dear brothers, stand firm. Let nothing move you. Always give yourselves fully to the work of the Lord" (15:58-59).

Each one of you should set aside a sum of money in keeping with his income (16:2). Many of Paul's letters mention collections gathered for the relief of Jewish believers in the Holy Land. The cause is never mentioned, but perhaps by A.D. 55–56, the time of Paul's third missionary journey, the attitude toward Christians had hardened and believers in the Holy Land had difficulty earning a living. At any rate, Paul mentions the Galatians here, and writes of the collection in Rom. 15:26 as well as in 2 Cor. 8–9.

While Paul's major teaching on giving is included in his second letter to Corinth, the emphasis here on regularly setting money aside "in keeping with [one's] income" is an important adjunct to that larger passage.

THE PASSAGE IN DEPTH

The Resurrection.
Paul argues in this passage that the resurrection, both of Christ and of the believer, is utterly basic Christian truth. He also makes it very clear that "resurrection" is dramatically different from those miracles of the past by which the dead were restored to earthly life.

There are a number of OT and NT incidents of restoration to mortal life. Among them are the return of two women's sons (1 Kings 17:17-24; 2 Kings 4:8-37). Jesus' raising of the daughter of Jairus (Matt. 9:18-26; Luke 8:41-56) and the spectacular raising of Lazarus after three days in the grave (John 11) demonstrate God's power over death. But each of these persons who were restored died again. Unlike the resurrected, they did not pass beyond the power of death to experience an endless life.

The resurrection of Jesus is never compared to these resuscitations. Instead the resurrected Jesus "lives forever" (Heb. 7:24) and therefore "has a permanent priesthood. Therefore He is able to save completely those who come to God through Him, because He always lives to intercede for them" (7:24-25). Christ's resurrection is proof of all His claims to deity, for He was "declared with power to be the Son of God by His resurrection from the dead" (Rom. 1:4).

It is no wonder then that the resurrection of Jesus was a keystone in apostolic preaching (Acts 2:24-36; 3:15-26; 4:10; 5:30; 10:40; 13:34, 37; 17:18-32). What is more, His resurrection is the guarantee that believers too will be raised to eternal life (1 Cor. 15:20).

There are three aspects of resurrection teaching that are important to us: its nature as transformation, its characteristics, and its power.

■ Resurrection as transformation. While the Bible teaches that all the dead must appear before God for judgment (Heb. 9:27; Rev. 20:11-15), resurrection to a transformed state of being is for believers only. John writes that the God who has made us His children intends us to be like His Son (1 John 3:2; Rom. 8:29).

In 1 Thes. 4 Paul explains that when Jesus returns those who have "fallen asleep" (4:14) in Him will come with Him, and those left alive will meet them in the air. The "dead in Christ" (4:16) will be raised before the living believers are caught up. Together the whole family will meet Jesus in the air, and "so we will be with the Lord forever" (4:17).

Our passage adds more details. Here Paul simply notes that while the resurrection body will correspond to our present body it will, in contrast, be imperishable, glorious, and infused with power (4:42-44). Transformed into the "likeness of the man from heaven" (4:49) through a transformation that takes place "in the twinkling of an eye, at the last trumpet" (4:52), the "dead will be raised imperishable, and we will be changed."

Resurrection, then, means an utter transformation of our mortal bodies into something beyond our capacity to imagine.

■ Characteristics of the resurrection body. While we know very little about the resurrection state, it is fascinating to discover clues as to its characteristics in the NT's description of the resurrected Jesus. Christ spoke of His body as being "flesh and bones" (Luke 24:39), perhaps in contrast to "flesh and blood" (1 Cor. 15:50), as "the life of a creature is in the blood" (Lev. 17:11). We also note that Jesus was able to suddenly appear among His disciples in a locked room (John 20:26). Is the resurrected body free of the material limitations under which we are forced to live? This subject, while fascinating, is not really developed in either Testament, and so we are left with John's "What we will be has not yet been made known" (1 John 3:2). Yet we do know that when our resurrection comes the weakness with which we mortals live will be replaced by strength and immortality. And we shall live forever.

■ Resurrection power. One of the most important but often neglected aspects of the NT's teaching is that the raising of Jesus made available to believers a flow of resurrection power. After initial despair as Paul tried to live a Christian life in his own strength, Paul discovered the life of faith, and writes exultantly, "If the Spirit of Him who raised Jesus from the dead is living in you, He who raised Christ from the dead will also give life to your mortal bodies through His Spirit, who lives in you" (Rom. 8:11). The Holy Spirit, who was the agent of Christ's resurrection, lives within you and me. This means that, even though we live today in mortal bodies, the Spirit lifts us beyond our limitations and enables us to live godly lives.

At times a failure to realize this truth has led to misinterpretation of other passages. In Phil. 3 Paul is not expressing uncertainty about his own resurrection when he speaks of yearning "somehow, to attain to the resurrection from the dead" (3:11). Instead Paul is eager "to know Christ and the power of His resurrection [now!] and the fellowship of sharing in His sufferings [now!], becoming like Him in His death [now!], and so, somehow, to attain [now!] to the resurrection from the dead [in the sense of experiencing the new life the Spirit is able to give to us even in our mortality] (3:10-11).

While Paul looks forward to his future resurrection, and encourages the Corinthians to have perfect confidence that they will one day be transformed and raised, Paul's own focus is on the present rather than the future. What he wants to do is live his present life drawing on the Spirit, the source of resurrection power, and so experience in his daily routine a quality of life that will be fully realized only in eternity.

What a goal for you and me! We know that one day we will be like Jesus. Let us rely on the Spirit of God to enable us to live our life here as Jesus lived. In the power, and for the glory, of God.

2 CORINTHIANS 1–3
The Inadequate Man

EXPOSITION

Second Corinthians was written sometime between 6 and 18 months after 1 Corinthians. Apparently most of the problems Paul dealt with there, such as lawsuits and abuse of the Lord's Supper, were now corrected. Even so Paul's relationship with the Corinthians continued to deteriorate, perhaps requiring a quick but "painful visit" by the apostle (2:1; 12:14, 21; 13:1-2). This failed to resolve the problem, and the anti-Paul clique continued to attack the apostle and his representatives (2:5-8, 10; 7:12), encouraged by Judaizers from Palestine (11:4, 22).

Although this is debated, many commentators believe Paul then wrote a brief but severe letter (2:3-4, 6, 9; 7:8, 12) that was delivered by Titus (2 Cor. 8:6a). Meanwhile, Paul himself left Ephesus to minister in Troas (Acts 19:23–20:6; 2 Cor. 1:8-11) and in Macedonia (2:16; 7:5). There Titus joined Paul and reported good news: the Corinthians had responded positively to the severe letter he had delivered (7:5-16). But before long Paul heard of still other problems in Corinth. Frustrated, and yet strangely confident, Paul then wrote the letter that we call 2 Corinthians; a letter which is perhaps the most personally revealing of any of Paul's epistles. For despite his continuing conflict with critics in Corinth, Paul with great honesty shares his weaknesses as well as his strengths as he explains the principles of his New Covenant ministry.

Paul's utter honesty is revealed in the first chapter. After typical greetings (1:1-2), Paul praises the Lord as the "God of all comfort," and goes on to confess his own deep distress and need for comfort (1:3-11). This is striking indeed. Rather than defend himself by reciting his credentials as an apostle, Paul exposes his weakness as a man "under great pressure, far beyond our ability to endure, so that we despaired even of life." This self-revelation has a purpose: only a man of weaknesses who has experienced the comfort that God provides is able to identify with others who are weak and communicate God's comfort to them. Paul's letters have exposed the weaknesses of the Corinthians. Now he exposes his own, to reassure them that God is able to deliver them both.

Paul then answers the charge that despite his promises to spend time in Corinth he has gone back on his word. Paul's answer is simple: he has shared his intentions, but as a servant of Christ he has been responsive to God's will. And the Lord has had other plans (1:12-22). What's more, Paul's delay is no evidence of a lack of love for the Corinthians. He hesitated, in order to spare them another "painful visit," and in great distress wrote instead (1:23–2:4). Apparently Paul's letter was effective, and the church disciplined those who led the attack on the apostle. Paul encourages the body to forgive the now penitent individual and welcome him back into fellowship (2:5-11).

At this point Paul launches into what has been called a "digression" that extends from 2:12 to 7:16. Digression or not, these chapters contain a stunning explanation of the principles of ministry under the New Covenant, in contrast to ministry under the Old Covenant of Mosaic Law.

Paul begins by picturing himself marching in a victory procession celebrating the triumph of Jesus over all God's enemies (2:12-3:6). As that procession winds its way through the world, the Gospel message is like the fragrance of thank offerings wafting through the world, a fragrance that to the lost is like the stink of death, but to the saved "the fragrance of life." The impact of that ministry is seen in the human beings who are changed by it, as God's Word is written by the Holy Spirit "not on tablets of stone, but on tablets of human hearts."

Paul's thoughts are drawn to a further comparison (3:7-18). The Old Covenant had a kind of glory, but a glory that faded, even as the radiance that shined from Moses' veiled face faded whenever he left the presence of God. But the New Covenant has a far greater glory. Israel, still fixing its eyes on Moses, cannot see Christ's glory, for the real meaning of the Law remains veiled. How different for Christians! Through Christ, God is at work within us accomplishing an ever-increasing rather than fading transformation. As we unveil, sharing ourselves freely and honestly, we see Christ reflected in the transformation He is working in each of us.

What a basis for confidence Paul has, despite his own admitted weakness and the obvious flaws in the Corinthians. Christ is at work within every believer. As the Spirit continues His work, and the members of the body learn that openness and honesty that Paul displays, Christ will continue to perform His transforming work within them. And they will see, and know, His glory.

WORD STUDIES

The Father of compassion and the God of all *comfort,* who *comforts* us in all our troubles (1:3-4). These verses introduce a central theme of chapters 1–7. "Comfort" is *paraklesis,* a word that can mean "encourage" as well as "comfort" or "consolation." The word occurs ten times in verses 3-7, with *thlipsis* ("trouble," "affliction," three times) and with *pathema* ("suffering," four times). Life is filled with pressures and distress for Paul, but the encouragement he receives from God strengthens and enables.

No life is without troubles and distress. But only the Christian experiences divine encouragement in "all our troubles."

Who *comforts us* in all our troubles (1:4). Paul uses the first-person, plural pronoun or verb with a variety of referents, ranging from (1) Paul himself, (2) Paul and his coworkers, (3) Paul and his addressees, (4) all Christians, (5) all men in general, and (6) even all Jews.

Here the reference is not to Paul himself, but to Paul as a representative Christian.

How good to be included in that class of persons whom God the Father, source of all comfort, stoops to encourage and renew.

We were under great pressure, far beyond our ability to endure, so that we *despaired* even of life (1:8). The word here is *exaporethenai,* a rare word that means literally "no exit." Here Paul's "we" is "I," and his confession of despair is wrenched from him by an experience of "great pressure." The RSV translates "utterly, unbearably crushed."

The confession seems to be a great risk. Paul is already under severe attack from critics in Corinth. Doesn't this admission of weakness make him more vulnerable to his enemies?

While this is the fear that moves many to hide their weaknesses and emphasize their strengths, Paul is far wiser in the ways of the

Lord. All men are weak, easily overwhelmed by circumstances. Only a confident hope in God's continuing intervention, and an appeal to the help others give by their prayers, can help when "great pressure" builds and there seems to be no way out.

Especially in our relations with you, in the *holiness* and sincerity that are from God (1:12). Many of the best Greek text traditions read *haploteti* ("integrity") rather than *hagioteti* ("holiness"). Paul is answering the charge of some with being inconsistent and fickle. His answer is that no, he has always acted with integrity.

The problem is that Paul had planned to revisit Corinth. In 1 Cor. 16:2-8 he mentions two options: After Ephesus he would go to Macedonia and then Corinth on his way to Jerusalem. In 2 Cor. 1 he mentions another route: Ephesus, then Corinth, then Macedonia, back to Corinth, and on to Judea. The problem was not just this change in plan, but the likelihood that he made a quick "painful visit" to Corinth from Ephesus, and afterward reverted to his original travel plan (Acts 20:1-3, 16). Paul's opponents not only charged the apostle with being unable to make up his mind. They also charged him with being fickle and deceitful. Thus the claim that despite these changes Paul has always dealt with the Corinthians with *haploteti* (integrity).

When I planned this, did I do it *lightly?* Or do I make my plans in a worldly manner so that in the same breath I say, "Yes, yes" and "No, no"? (1:17) Paul admits he did not fulfill his original plan (1:23). But this was not because his character is flawed and he vacillates (*elaphria*, acts "lightly"). In fact he does not make plans *kata sarka* ("according to the flesh," and thus "in a worldly manner").

Paul's point is important. He is no salesman planning an itinerary. Paul is a servant of Christ. God says yes and no, and always keeps His promises. One implication of this is that God has the right of yes and no over the plans made by His servants (1:18-20).

God's Spirit within our hearts is His guarantee of our future redemption. Paul's reference to the Spirit as the one who anointed us is important. The word *chrisas*, found here, is always used figuratively, and indicates a special anointing or commission by God. But a similar word, *chrisma*, is also used of the Spirit's anointing. The first term emphasizes the Spirit's commissioning work; the second, the work of the Spirit in the believer as teacher and guide (1 John 2:20, 27; John 16:12-15).

The passage contains a vital truth we each need to apply in our own Christian walk. We are to make plans. But at the same time we need to remain sensitive to the Holy Spirit, who may very well lead us in a different direction than we have planned to go.

Our yes today may reflect the limited light we have, and may well become no tomorrow as the Spirit shows us God's will. Let's not become so trapped by our plans that we become unresponsive to the Spirit's leading.

It was in order to spare you that I did not return to Corinth (1:22). Paul has just suggested that his change of plans was not capricious, but a response to God's leading. Isn't Paul now inconsistent in giving his own reason for not returning?

Again there is an important lesson for us. The Spirit speaks in many different ways to us, and as we live in tune with Him we recognize His voice. In this case the Spirit spoke through Paul's concern for the Corinthians and his desire not to make "another painful visit" (2:1) to them. As the conviction grew that a visit as originally planned would be a poor way to express the love he felt for the Corinthians, he sensed the Spirit's work and so changed his plans.

Don't expect the Spirit to write bold messages on the bathroom mirror, or interrupt a radio program to speak aloud. The Spirit speaks within us, through our minds and hearts, and through our love and concern for others. Let's learn to look within, and be sensitive to what the Spirit whispers there.

The *punishment* inflicted on him by *the majority* is sufficient for him. Now instead, you ought to forgive and comfort him (2:6-7). Some have felt that the person mentioned here is the immoral brother of 1 Cor. 5, who has now repented under the censure (*epitimia*) by the community. Here *ton pleionon*, "the many," most likely indicates the whole community, rather than a majority who supported discipline in contrast to a minority which did not.

Modern commentators find little evidence

for the view that the immoral brother of 1 Cor. 5 is in view, and instead argue that Paul is speaking of someone who actively opposed Paul. After the apostle's stern letter they suggest he was disciplined by the Corinthians.

The primary problem with the contemporary view is theological. Church discipline is directed against one who consistently practices sin. One might argue that resisting apostolic authority is sin. But there is no suggestion elsewhere in the NT that such action is to be taken against those who disagree with or even resist Christian leaders.

While this debate will probably never be satisfactorily resolved, a most important principle is clearly expressed in the passage. The ultimate goal of church discipline is not punishment, but rather restoration. The repentant are to be forgiven and welcomed home. And so Paul reminds us that we too are to be eager "to reaffirm . . . love" (2:8) for those who stray by welcoming them back when they demonstrate their sorrow.

In order that Satan might not *outwit* us. For we are not unaware of his *schemes* (2:11). A failure to extend forgiveness and re-affirm love for a disciplined brother or sister opens the door to Satan, who will use the occasion to *pleonektethomen* (defraud, cheat, outwit) the congregation. It is not simply that Satan will gain a hold on the brother under discipline. The entire church will be affected and hardened by a failure to extend love and forgiveness.

When Paul says we are not "unaware of Satan's schemes" he uses the word *noemata*, "thoughts," "evil designs." It is God's thought to forgive sinners. It is Satan's thought to keep men trapped in their sins by blocking experience of God's forgiveness and cleansing power.

If we err in the matter of discipline and restoration, let's be sure that we err by leaning toward God's ways rather than Satan's.

God, who always leads us in *triumphal procession* in Christ (2:14). The imagery is drawn from the Triumphs voted victorious generals by the Roman Senate. The general, riding in a chariot, led a parade of soldiers guarding captives and other spoil taken in a notably successful military campaign.

What is Paul's role in this procession? He is

at once booty, spoil won by Christ in His conquest at Calvary, and a member of Christ's conquering army, through whom God "spreads everywhere" (2:14) the good news of the Gospel.

Today we march in the same procession. We are displayed by Jesus as precious items won by conquest. And we are soldiers in His army. May our lives display the beauty He sees in us, and may we be as bold in ministry as Paul.

Unlike so many we do not *peddle* the word of God for profit (2:17). The term *kapelos* was used by Plato to mock philosophers who "hawked wisdom," as if knowledge could be retailed or wholesaled. One of the things that set Paul apart was the purity of his motives. Paul argues in 1 Cor. 9:9-12 that those who minister full time have a right to support. But this is very different from those whose motive for ministry is to win an offering from those whom the true minister of Christ is called to serve.

He has made us competent as ministers of a new covenant (3:6). The Greek says God *ikanosen hemas*, "has qualified us." The aorist tense suggests Paul is thinking of his call to ministry by God. No innate capabilities qualify anyone for ministry. It is God's call that qualifies, for with His call He provides enablement.

He has made us competent as ministers of a new covenant—not of the letter but of the Spirit; for the letter kills, but the Spirit gives life (3:6). The controlling theme of Paul's letter is exactly this: New Covenant ministry.

The Old Covenant is the Law of Moses, which governed the relationship between each generation of Israelites and the Lord. Paul demonstrated in Rom. 4–5 that the Law was never intended to be a way of salvation, even though Israel tended to view it in that way. Thus Jeremiah predicted a day when the Lord would make a New Covenant with Israel, different in essence from the Old, in that it offered God's people both forgiveness and a new heart. God's moral standards, recorded in stone at Sinai, would then be engraved on the hearts of His people. In the era of the New Covenant men respond not to external demand but rather to the Spirit's inner stimulus to godliness.

Paul has used the language of the New Covenant in describing the Corinthians as a "letter from Christ" (3:3). Now he moves on to further explore the differences between Old and New Covenants. The New Covenant is the realm of the Spirit. The Old Covenant, the realm of the letter. The Spirit vitalizes; the letter kills.

But what does Paul mean by the letter, the *gramma?* Both Old and New Covenants are divine revelation. Both, rightly understood, call forth faith and invite those who hear to rely on God for salvation. But Israel missed this saving message, seeing only the letter of the Law. In treating the OT as letter, as a word intended to evoke self-effort rather than faith, Israel was killed rather than made alive.

But now, approaching the same Scriptures in the Spirit, the believer discovers that the Law points beyond itself to Christ, and calls for that complete reliance on God's grace that constitutes saving faith.

THE PASSAGE IN DEPTH

The God of All Comfort (1:3-11).

Background. Second Corinthians truly is the most revealing of Paul's letters. At the same time it is the most important of the NT's epistles in shaping a philosophy of New Covenant ministry, a philosophy of ministry as relevant to the lay believer as well as to the ordained.

It does not seem that Paul's goal is to define ministry principles. Rather what he seems to do is to share, and it is his sharing that gradually helps us understand not only the man, but also the nature of New Covenant ministry itself.

Interpretation. As noted in the Word Study of 1:3 above, Paul's focus in these paragraphs is on troubles, sufferings, and distress—and on the comfort or encouragement that God freely provides.

Thlipsis, rendered by both "trouble" and "distress," is frequently used in the NT to describe intense spiritual and emotional distress, caused by either external or internal pressures. Every human being who ever lived is vulnerable, for none of us can exercise control over all the circumstances of his life.

This reality is expressed more strongly in the word used in the passage for suffering, *pathema.* In Greek culture this root expressed the common view that mankind is afflicted, forced to undergo experiences beyond human control, which yet cause great physical and mental anguish. Typically the root is used by suffering and distress. First, he experiences God as a source of comfort or encouragement. No matter how great the distress God "comforts us in all our troubles" (1:4).

Second, such pressures have taught Paul a vital lesson. He must rely on God, not on himself or his ability. God has delivered Paul from such circumstances in the past. Thus rather than let pressures cause him to give up, Paul looks ahead with "hope" (1:10).

That word, "hope" (*elpizo*), is used 70 times in the NT epistles, where it is always the expectation of something good. If we looked only at the present, and the difficulties under which we live, we might very well be trapped in permanent despair. But Paul reminds us to look expectantly to tomorrow, and to rely on God to make tomorrow bright with expected deliverance.

But Paul has even more to say about our common experience of distress and suffering. God not only comforts us and gives us hope—God makes suffering meaningful. Our difficulties are not weavings of indifferent Fates, but part of the plan of a loving God, who will use our sufferings not only for our good but to benefit others.

Such sufferings are in fact part and parcel of our calling to be the body of Christ in this world. This is expressed in v. 5, which says that "the sufferings of Christ flow over into our lives." One interpretation suggests Paul here reflects a Jewish doctrine known as *heble hammasiah,* "the afflictions of Messiah." This is not suffering by the Messiah, but suffering experienced by those who associate themselves with Him prior to His coming into His kingdom.

But it is better to give the phrase a more distinctly Christian meaning. Christ in His redemptive work committed Himself to live as a human being, subject to suffering. Now we, Christ's body on earth, continue His mission and experience the same antagonism from natural man. Our willingness to live as Jesus lived, in service to God and our fellowman, guarantees that Christ's sufferings will overflow and encompass us as well.

But there is an even more striking reason why God permits us to suffer. Suffering and distress are not simply concomitants of following in Jesus' steps. Suffering and distress are essential qualifications for ministry to others. As we experience distress and realize our vulnerability, we turn to the Lord and experience His comfort. And the experience of both our humanness and of God's grace are required for effective ministry. As Paul says, we are able to "comfort those in any trouble [only] with the comfort we ourselves have received from God" (1:4).

To comfort others, we must suffer as they do, for only as we show ourselves vulnerable to suffering will others accept us as valid witnesses to the comfort provided by God. Simply put, if others are to accept our testimony to God as the source of comfort, they must see us as enough like them so that they can identify with us. The only person who can give others hope in God must be one who is recognized as a fellow victim of circumstance, who knows the same distress and pain as they experience.

No wonder then that Paul is willing to risk making himself vulnerable to his critics. Temporarily casting aside his cloak of apostleship, Paul opens his heart to show the Corinthians a very human man, a man who hurts and doubts and fears as others do. The "unspiritual" (James 3:15) folk in Corinth could hardly identify with Paul as a "super-apostle" (2 Cor. 11:5; 12:11). But they can identify with Paul the inadequate man, who suffers in his vulnerability even as they do. And, from Paul the vulnerable man, the Corinthians can hear the message of God's comfort they might never have accepted from Paul the Great.

Application. Perhaps one of the most important contributions of this passage is the guidance it provides for what, in another book (*Youth Ministry,* Zondervan), I have called "identification counseling." This approach to helping others recognizes that a common experience of trouble provides the basis from which we can speak meaningfully to the troubles of others, and share what has comforted and encouraged us. Many who attempt to

minister adopt a directive approach. The hurting person is expected to reveal his problem. The helper suggests a (hopefully) biblical solution, and the hurting person is expected to accept this solution and act on it. Others who attempt to minister adopt a nondirective approach. The hurting person is again expected to reveal his problem, the helper listens and reflects feelings and thoughts. This process is supposed to clarify the problem so that the hurting person can find his own solution, and then act on it.

Paul's approach, as seen in this passage, is very different. He, as helper, learns about the pressures under which the others labor, shares his own similar conflicts, and with them shares his own solutions—the comfort and the hope he finds in relying on God. Out of this process of sharing, the hurting person discovers God's solution and is motivated by the example of the helper to choose, and act on it.

The key to this approach to ministry is the willingness of the person ministering to humble himself, to reveal his or her vulnerability as a human being, and after disclosing his vulnerability to share "the comfort we ourselves have received from God" (1:4).

The Glory of the New Covenant (3:7-18).

Background. We are immediately struck by Paul's constant use of the word "glory," which appears 12 times in these 11 verses. The Old Covenant had a glory of its own, but the New Covenant has a greater glory. Before looking at the contrasts Paul develops between Old and New Covenants, it is helpful to trace the significance of "glory."

Concerning this term, the *Zondervan Expository Dictionary of Bible Words* says:

> In the OT, the glory of God is intimately linked with the Lord's self-revelation. There is much imagery: a blazing splendor and flaming holiness mark His presence (e.g., Ex. 16:10; 40:34, 35; 2 Chron. 7:1, 2). But neither raw power nor burning holiness adequately express God. Thus Exodus links God's glory with an unveiling of His loving character. When Moses begged God to show him His glory, the Bible reports: "The Lord said, 'I will cause all My goodness to pass in front of you, and I will proclaim My name, the LORD, in your

presence. I will have mercy on whom I will have mercy, and I will have compassion on whom I will have compassion. But,' He said, 'You cannot see My face, for no one may see Me and live' " (Ex. 33:19-20). In the same sense of unveiling, God says, "I will gain glory for Myself" in the case of Pharaoh's refusal to let Israel go (Ex. 14:4). God's great redemptive power was displayed in the Exodus (Num. 14:22), even as His creative power is displayed when "the heavens declare the glory of God" (Ps. 19:1).

But "glory" implies more than a disclosure by God of who He is. It implies an invasion of the material universe, an expression of God's active presence among His people. Thus, the OT consistently links the term "glory" with the presence of God among Israel in tabernacle and temple (e.g., Ex. 29:43; Ezek. 43:4-5; Hag. 2:3). God's objective glory is revealed by His coming to be present with us, His people, and to show us Himself by His actions in our world (pp. 310-11).

Now Paul argues not that the Old Covenant possessed no "glory," but that the glory of the New Covenant far surpasses that of the Old. In arguing this point Paul fixes our attention on how God's glory is displayed in His coming to be with His people under the Old and under the New Covenants. In doing so he also shows us how the Christian truly is free to adopt the "risky" approach to New Covenant ministry that Paul has himself displayed in making himself vulnerable in chapter 1.

Interpretation. Paul has indicated that God the Holy Spirit has written on the living hearts of the Corinthians, making them a "letter from Christ." This is the essence of New Covenant ministry: God displays His glory through His presence within the believer. Yet a moment's consideration suggests this is a poor display of God's glory! After all, the Corinthians are surely a poor rather than good expression of God's glory! Why, the Corinthians displayed the quarreling characteristic of "mere men" (Rom. 2:3; 1 Cor. 3:3-4), tolerated immorality, went to law in pagan courts, were divided over whether to eat meat offered at idol temples, and were marred by many other obvious flaws. How can Paul say that

they are "a letter from Christ"? Surely reading that letter reveals nothing of the glory of God!

Even Paul is a poor example. Doesn't Paul admit that he has experienced distress "beyond our ability to endure, so that we despaired even of life"? (2 Cor. 1:8) Surely the Old Covenant, delivered by Moses, a truly admirable man, displays a far greater glory than this New Covenant Paul praises!

Paul agrees that Moses is the central human figure associated with the Old Covenant. And so he asks his reader to compare the glory of God as displayed in Moses to the glory of God displayed in the New Covenant believer. To do this Paul selects an incident reported in Ex. 34:29-35, and using only established principles of Jewish *midrash* (exegesis, commentary), shows that the glory of the Old—that era's visible evidence of God's presence—was a fading glory, in contrast to the glory of the New—today's visible evidence of God's presence—which is an "ever-increasing glory" (3:18). The passage that Paul develops in 2 Cor. reads:

> When Moses came down from Mount Sinai with the two tablets of the Testimony in his hands, he was not aware that his face was radiant because he had spoken with the Lord. When Aaron and all the Israelites saw Moses, his face was radiant, and they were afraid to come near him. But Moses called to them; so Aaron and all the leaders of the community came back to him, and he spoke to them. Afterward all the Israelites came near him, and he gave them all the commands the Lord had given him on Mount Sinai.
>
> When Moses finished speaking to them, he put a veil over his face. But whenever he entered the Lord's presence to speak with Him, he removed the veil until he came out. And when he came out and told the Israelites what he had been commanded, they saw that his face was radiant. Then Moses would put the veil over his face until he went to speak with the Lord.

In looking back to this passage, Paul sees it as a vivid illustration of the difference between the admitted "glory" of the dispensation of the Old Covenant, and the far greater "glory" of the New Covenant era.

Paul notes that when Moses went in to

speak with the Lord, his face became radiant. Being in the presence of God transformed Moses' aspect. But Paul notes something else. When Moses came out of the Lord's presence, he spoke to the people unveiled. But soon he put a veil over his face, leaving it there until he again entered God's presence. Why did Moses behave in this way? Surely it was not to spare the people the awesome sight, for on returning from God's presence Moses spoke to the people unveiled. The real reason for the veil, Paul says, was to hide the fact that the radiance, the glory, was temporary and fading! So Moses put the veil over his face "to keep the Israelites from gazing at it while the radiance was fading away"! (3:13) It is clear, then, that the Old Covenant, as exemplified in the lawgiver himself, offers no permanent transformation!

Now, Paul says, compare the impact of the New Covenant. Rather than go up to Sinai or into the tent of meeting to appear before God, the New Covenant brings the Holy Spirit to the believer! And with the Spirit comes a glory that, rather than fading, increases! For, as Paul says, "we . . . all . . . are being transformed into His [Christ's] likeness with ever-increasing glory, which comes from the Lord, who is the Spirit" (3:18).

The Jew who looked back to Moses and saw in his radiant face evidence of God's glorious presence in the Old Covenant, looks at the Christian and sees no such thing. But, Paul says, the Jew has missed the point! The veil still remains, so he does not realize that the glory of the Old Covenant is a fading, impermanent glory, while that of the New Covenant is a transforming, ever-increasing glory!

The real and unmistakable display of God's living presence in the Christian is the process of transformation which we experience.

And so Paul readily admits that the Old Covenant did have a glory of its own. God did reveal Himself through those letters engraved in stone. But the New Covenant has a far greater glory, for today the Spirit of God dwells in those who know Christ, and actively writes on their living personalities that holiness which displays God's presence in a glory far greater than that of the Old.

Application. Paul weaves the application of this truth into his argument. The Christian, with this sure expectation ("hope") of continuing transformation, is "very bold" (3:12). In this we are "not like Moses, who would put a veil over his face" (3:13). He goes even further. "We," Paul says, "with unveiled faces all . . ." (3:18).

Moses covered his face, so the Israelites could not see what was happening in his life. In contrast, Christians take the veil off, so others can see exactly what is happening in their lives! This, of course, is exactly what Paul did when in chapter 1 he revealed his vulnerability, and spoke of the great pressure he felt, his own inability to endure, and the sense of despair that gripped him (1:8).

But, someone is sure to say, "Paul, that's weakness. Don't you open yourself up to criticism?" And Paul's answer to this is, "Of course!" That is why it takes "bold[ness]" to be a Christian (3:12). We do make ourselves vulnerable to criticism and misunderstanding. And it is scary, to really be ourselves with others by taking off the veils most men hide their weaknesses behind.

But, someone else will object, "Paul, you're supposed to preach Christ. You're supposed to tell others how sufficient and powerful He is, and how great it is to be a Christian. Doesn't this kind of boldness you suggest undercut your message, and make being a Christian less attractive?" And Paul's answer to this is an unqualified "No!" The Gospel message is not: Believe in Christ, and be perfect now. The Gospel message is: Christ saves sinners. He comforts and enables inadequate men. The Gospel is that Jesus understands us in our weakness, meets us where we are, and undertakes to make us new. What is more, His work within us is displayed over time. We look back, and we make the wonderful discovery that, while we are not yet all we will be, we are not what we were! God's Spirit has been at work in our lives, and we are growing into Christ's likeness.

To Paul, this is why we Christians must be very bold. It is "with unveiled faces [that we] all reflect the Lord's glory." The Greek word the NIV translates "reflect" is *katoptrizomenoi* ("reflecting" or "beholding"). To behold is to be preferred. Paul is saying that, as we remove our veils, we do necessarily show our present imperfections. By removing our veils we also enable others to witness the process of transformation that is going on within us. As Christians live together unveiled, vulnerable and weak as we are, we will discover that God is at work in one another's lives. We will see Jesus in the unveiled faces of those we come to know and love, for the Spirit of God, who gives us the freedom to be real with one another (3:17), is performing His transforming work within our lives.

No wonder Paul says "since we have such a hope, we are very bold" (3:12). The confidence that God the Spirit is at work within us gives us the freedom to be real with one another. And as we exercise that freedom, we see a glory that so far surpasses the glory of the Old Covenant that "what was glorious has no glory now in comparison with the surpassing glory" that is ours in Christ (3:10).

---

2 CORINTHIANS 4–7
The Ministry of Reconciliation

EXPOSITION

Paul has provided a powerful example of openness and vulnerability and laid the foundation for a New Covenant ministry (chap. 1). The Gospel's good news is that God is present in the believer's life, giving us all hope of a gradual transformation toward Christ's likeness (chap. 3). Building on this reality Paul twice affirms, "Therefore . . . we do not lose heart" (4:1, 16). New Covenant ministry rejects the use of "deception," to preach the perfections of Christ, not "ourselves" (4:1-6). We are like clay jars that contain a great treasure; what counts is not what is seen, but what is unseen; not the temporary that is passing away, but the kernel of eternity within 4:7-18).

Paul pauses to note that our mortality will surely be "swallowed up by life." Life here means being trapped in imperfection, but it does not change our goal of seeking to please the Lord, whether now or in glory (5:1-10). Again Paul states a basic principle of ministry. Unlike those who take pride in what is seen, Paul counts on that which can't be seen: the reality of Christ in the heart of the believer, and the fact that love will motivate the believer to live for the Lord. Paul is utterly convinced of this. The purpose of Christ's death was that "those who live should no longer live for themselves but for Him who died for them and was raised again." It is unthinkable that Christ's sacrifice should fail to accomplish its purpose (5:11-15).

With this perspective Paul no longer regards anyone "from a worldly point of view." It is not appearances, but the spiritual reality. It is not present flaws, but the promise of the future that is most real to the apostle. Since the believer is now in Christ, the new has come. And the new will most surely renew the believer. Thus Paul's mission to

Christians is to urge reconciliation—that is, a life that is in complete harmony with Christ, and with the fact that in becoming sin for us, Christ enabled us to "become the righteousness of God" in Him (5:16-21). And to become that today! (6:1-2)

With his theological foundation laid, Paul returns to more personal sharing. In all his hardships Paul has spoken freely to the Corinthians, opening his heart to them (6:3-13). In complete integrity Paul can urge the Corinthians to avoid intimacy with unbelievers, and rely on God's promise that the person who purifies himself from sin will be welcomed by God as His own (6:14–7:1). As for the Corinthians, Paul's criticisms were never intended as condemnation. Paul continues to have great confidence in these believers and loves them intensely. Yet he is not sorry for words that may have seemed harsh, for those words were heard with a "godly sorrow" that led to repentance. Their response to his harsh words has demonstrated just what Paul knew all along: the unseen Jesus in their hearts truly is the controlling influence in their lives. And their response has brought joy to the apostle and to others who love them as he does (7:2-16).

WORD STUDIES

Therefore, since through God's mercy we have this ministry, we do not lose heart (4:1; cf. 4:16). The Greek is *ouk egkakeo*, do "not behave weakly," and indicates perseverance. Paul understands the nature of the Spirit's transforming work in believers, and this keeps him on track whatever setbacks may occur.

How important that we too understand. It's so easy to become discouraged when our children disappoint us, or when someone in whom we've invested much time and prayer turns back to an old way of life. Like Paul, we need to realize that we have a New Covenant ministry—a ministry which acknowledges human weakness, and yet relies on the Spirit of the Lord to work that gradual inner transformation which will in time enable every believer to better reflect our Lord's glory.

We have this treasure in *jars of clay* to show that this all-surpassing power is from God and not from us (4:7). The vivid image of the clay pot (*ostrakinon skeuos*) has attracted the attention of many commentators. Such vessels, often used as oil lamps in the first century, were both fragile and inexpensive. In our frail mortal bodies the Spirit's flame burns, revealing a glory that is all the more amazing in view of the commonness of its container.

The fact that God revealed Himself in the incarnate Christ was a great miracle. It is perhaps an even greater one that God is able to reveal Himself in you and me.

So then, death is at work in us, *but life is at work in you* (4:12). The NIV translators supply "at work" from the first clause, leading to a misunderstanding. The phrase *en humin* here is a dative of advantage, and the phrase should read "but it is life for you."

Paul has recounted the constant pressures under which he ministers (4:7-9). To Paul this experience of constant dying (suffering) is not only his lot, but is also proof of his calling. His constant exposure to suffering and his evident weakness means only that in him the resurrection life of Jesus is "revealed" (*phanerothe* [4:10]). Paul suffers willingly because his continuing commitment despite his "dying" displays the power of Jesus. He also suffers willingly because his "dying" is of great advantage to the Corinthians, for his suffering has brought them the new life in Jesus they now enjoy.

There is a sense in which all of us who know Jesus are called to suffering, even as Jesus was. Only in our weakness can we really display the strength of Jesus. And, all too often, only in sacrificing something dear to ourselves can we bring the gift of life to others. Yet how good it is when we can make our sacrifices with that joy which Paul expresses when he writes, "all this is for your benefit, so that the grace that is reaching more and more people may cause thanksgiving to overflow to the glory of God" (4:15).

So we *fix our eyes* not on what is seen, but on what is unseen. For what is seen is temporary, but what is unseen is eternal (4:18). The word is *skopounton,* usually used in the sense of "setting one's sight on." It indicates a careful examination, a penetrating gaze that determines the worth of the thing examined and keeps that worth in view.

This verse is critical in understanding Paul's argument in these chapters. He clearly sees the flaws in the Corinthians, and just as clearly sees the distress and sufferings that are associated with his commitment to serve Christ. But these things are dismissed as *proskaira,* "temporary" (4:18). Paul looks beyond mere sensory phenomena, realizing that everything he can touch and see and feel is passing and, in an ultimate sense, unreal. Paul is concerned with the eternal, with a reality which is beyond the power of our senses to discover. It is that reality, which he has discovered in Christ, on which he has fixed his gaze, which determines his course.

The better we understand the ways of God, and the more firmly we are committed to them, the better we will see our own way through life. Keeping our gaze fixed on the eternal is the best way to guard against life's disappointments and distress.

Now we know that if the *earthly tent* we live in is destroyed, we have a building from God, an *eternal house* in heaven (5:1). A bewildering profusion of interpretations make this passage one of the most debated in the NT. Most, however, equate "earthly tent" to mortal body, and "eternal house" to resurrection body or to some intermediate body with which the believer will be "clothed" until the day of resurrection comes.

While this debate will never be adequately resolved, we do see here a basic theme in Christian thought. Many in the first century believed that the "naked" (5:3) soul could approach God "unclothed" (without a body). To them "resurrection" was spiritual rather than bodily. Paul settled that question in 1 Cor. 15, but returns briefly to it here. That death of which Paul himself is so aware (4:7-15) is no more a loss than physical death will be, for the loss of the mortal body will simply mean stepping beyond the seen to a realm in which, though unseen by us now, we will be clothed again and this time by life! (5:4) And this

wonderful transition from the seen to the unseen, from mortality to a full experience of eternal life, is guaranteed by the Spirit who is present in us (5:5).

How petty our speculations about whether or not Paul has a temporary, transitional body in view in these verses. The real message of the passage we are sure of: Beyond time eternity exists. And the return of this present body to dust is an utterly meaningless event, for a glorious heavenly body awaits those who die in Christ.

Confident of this wonderful truth "we make it our goal to please [God], whether we are at home in the body or away from it" (5:9).

For we must all appear before *the judgment seat* of Christ (5:10). The *bema* in Corinth was a raised platform located near the center of the city. While it was from the judgment seat that city officials announced judicial sentences, the imagery was not frightening to Paul's first-century readers. It was from the *bema* that all public proclamations were made, those commending individuals as well as censuring them.

What Paul writes of here is not final judgment, but that evaluation of the believer's works referred to in 1 Cor. 3:10-15. On Christ's return believers will not only experience the fullness of salvation, but will appear before the Lord *hina komisetai,* "that each one may receive what is due him" (5:10). Christ's return is harvesttime for us as well as for the Lord. We are God's harvest, while we each reap "what is due him for the things done while in the body."

Let's be sure to live so that our harvest is bounteous, and the words Jesus speaks from heaven's *bema* are words of commendation rather than rebuke.

For *Christ's love compels* us (5:14). "Christ's love" is most often understood as an objective rather than subjective genitive. It is the love Christ has for us and has expressed on Calvary, rather than our love for Christ that exerts compelling force in the Christian's life. "Compel" is *sunechei,* to "hold in one's grip." More is implied than moral influence. Christ's love has unleashed a force within us that cannot be denied. That love is transforming in character, and most surely will renew the believer as it had transformed Paul, once an enemy of the Lord, into His most dedicated servant.

Because we are convinced that one died for all, and therefore all died. And He died for all, that those who live should no longer live for themselves, but for Him who died for them and was raised again (5:14-15). The connectives here drive home Paul's meaning. Why does Christ's love compel us? Because that love found expression in His dying for "all" (here, clearly all believers). Therefore the believer, in union with Jesus, died as well, and in union with Jesus was raised to new life (Rom. 6:1-14). "That" is *hina*, which here expresses purpose rather than result. Paul's point is that through the death of Jesus and our union with Him, God intends to so work in our lives that we will come to the place where Paul now is — a place where we live for Jesus rather than for ourselves!

What Paul has done here is to lay out the theological foundation on which he builds his ministry — the great truth which shapes the way he relates to the Corinthians and others. Paul does not lose heart, even when the Corinthian church is split by disputes and immorality. He continues to minister with confidence, because he is totally convinced that nothing in the world will be able to thwart God's purpose in the atonement! God will surely accomplish in every believer's life what He intended to do when He gave His Son for us.

How will God accomplish His purpose? By uniting us to Jesus, so that we share both His death and His resurrection. This work accomplished by Christ's love will exert a compelling force in the believer's life, and so the believers in Corinth too will most surely grow toward the likeness of their Savior.

What a vital truth for us to keep in mind. At times it seems we take one step forward in our Christian life, only to fall back two. And all too often those we love seem indifferent, unaffected by Christ's call to full commitment. When discouraged we can take heart. God most surely will accomplish His purpose in us and in them. Jesus' death will not, cannot, be meaningless. Through His great love a power has been introduced within us that will move us as it moved Paul to "no longer live for

[ourselves] but for Him who died for [us] and was raised again" (5:15).

So from now on we regard no one *from a worldly point of view* (5:16). The world evaluates people on the basis of performance, on what they do or do not do. From a worldly point of view, the Corinthians themselves might well be regarded as failures — flawed Christians at best, indistinguishable from "mere men" (1 Cor. 3:3). But Paul sees Christ, alive in their hearts, a compelling influence who will reshape their every motive until they gladly choose to live for Him alone.

Though we once *regarded* Christ in this way, we do so no longer (5:16). The verb is *egnokamen*, "to know," used here in the sense of a way of looking at or understanding Christ. The thought is introduced to clarify the importance of not viewing others in a worldly (fleshly) way. Judging by appearances, Jesus was a total failure — a Messiah rejected by His own people and delivered up by them for crucifixion. From the world's point of view, Jesus was either a tragic or ridiculous figure. But how different the reality! The Crucifixion, far from marking His mission a failure, has proven to be the keystone of its success. And the Resurrection has demonstrated that He Himself is the ever-living Son of God.

What a reminder to us that spiritual things are seldom what they seem to be. We must learn to look beyond appearances, and we must base our lives on beliefs which, despite a frequent lack of visible evidence, we know to reflect reality.

Therefore, if anyone is in Christ, he is a new creation; the *old* has gone, the new has come (5:17). The "old" is *archaias,* that which comes from an earlier time. The new act of creation accomplished in the believer has put the old order of sin, death, and the flesh which is associated with Adam in our past. From now on we are to view others and ourselves in a perspective shaped by the reality of Christ's work in our lives. Paul is not teaching perfectionism here. Nor is he saying that we experience now a freedom from the influence of the old in our lives. What Paul is saying is that the old is "gone" in the sense that its power over us is broken. The new dynamic of life in Christ promises us a transforming freedom — the freedom to become.

All this is from God, who *reconciled* us to Himself through Christ and gave us the ministry of reconciliation (5:18). Paul continues his argument by noting the tension between our present reconciled state and our experience of reconciliation.

"Reconcile" (*katallasso*) is a critical theological term in the NT, and indicates a change in personal relationships between human beings, and especially between human beings and God. *Zondervan Expository Dictionary of Bible Words* notes that several vital truths are expressed in passages where this word is found.

(1) It is human beings who need to be reconciled; their sinful attitude toward God must change. (2) God has acted in Christ to accomplish reconciliation, so that with our sins no longer counted against us, believers no longer have a basis for counting God an enemy. (3) When we come to believe the Gospel, we experience a psychological and spiritual change, as our attitude is brought into harmony with the divine reality (p. 515).

This passage affirms the objective work of Christ in accomplishing reconciliation. It also focuses our attention on the psychological and spiritual. Paul's "ministry of reconciliation" is directed toward believers, not unbelievers (5:18-20). The goal of this ministry is to effect that change in perception and attitude toward God which will enable the Christian to truly become new. With our outlook in full harmony with God's own, we will "in Him . . . become the righteousness of God."

God was reconciling the world to Himself in Christ, not counting men's sins against them (5:19). Paul's argument in this passage is closely and tightly reasoned. Jesus' death was a propitiation, in the sense that He paid the price sin requires. Jesus' death was redemption, in that the price He paid bought our freedom. And Jesus' death is reconciliation, in the sense that it displays the grace of God, and constitutes proof that God truly does forgive rather than count our sins against us.

The phrase *me logizomenos autois,* "not count-

ing [their trespasses] against them" reflects a truth emphasized in Rom. 4. God does not charge sins to the account of anyone who has faith in Jesus (Rom. 4:3; Ps. 32:2). The Gospel of Christ emphasizes forgiveness, not condemnation! Let the law and our conscience condemn and make us uneasy about our standing with God. Jesus puts all that behind and invites us to come to God freely, assured that sins are no longer an issue in our relationship with the Lord.

What makes this point so important is that Paul's New Covenant "ministry of reconciliation" maintains this same emphasis! In his dealings with the Corinthians he does not seem inclined to count their sins against them! Instead he is positive and optimistic. Looking beyond the present problems he says with total honesty, "I have great confidence in you; I take great pride in you. I am greatly encouraged; in all our troubles my joy knows no bounds" (7:4).

Paul is absolutely convinced that the love of Christ is the controlling influence in their lives, and that they will come to that place where they, like Paul, gladly live for the Lord rather than themselves. Paul's role is not to fix blame or condemn, but to continue to express the confidence he has in Christ's work within them — and by expressing this confidence to help the Corinthians live more and more in harmony with the Lord.

Again, what a lesson for us. The parent or pastor who relies on constant criticism, whose words produce guilt, hinders rather than helps the spiritual growth. But the parent or pastor who says, "I have great confidence in you," and refuses to let that confidence be shaken by even repeated failures, performs a reconciling ministry that will produce fruit. Christ is in the heart of every believer. The Spirit is present to do His transforming work. We are to believe in God for our children's growth and transformation, until through the example of our faith, they come to rely on Him for themselves.

Rather, as servants of God we *commend* ourselves in every way (6:4). The word is *sunistanein,* "to prove or show." Paul is drawing on his own experience to provide a sketch that will enable the reader to recognize a true servant of God.

That picture, developed in the next verses,

reminiscent of Rembrandt's paintings, is a study on light against darkness. Against the background of afflictions (6:4-5), the servant of God displays inward qualities through which the light of Jesus shines.

The nine background afflictions are presented in groups of three: general trials ("troubles, hardships, and distresses"); persecution ("beatings, imprisonments, and riots"); and the natural consequences of commitment ("hard work, sleepless nights, and hunger"). Yet the gloom cast by these difficulties serves to emphasize rather than extinguish the "purity, understanding, patience and kindness" along with the "sincere love" and "truthful speech" that the Holy Spirit and the power of God work in the willing servant of Christ's life (6:6-7).

Do not be yoked together with unbelievers (6:14). The word is *heterozygountes,* "in double harness," and is found only here in the NT. Commentators agree that the instruction draws on the OT prohibition against plowing with mismatched animals (Deut. 22:10), and perhaps also against mismating two kinds of domesticated animals (Lev. 19:19).

The problem is determining just how this principle applies. Paul has already told the Corinthians not to withdraw from association with even immoral non-Christians (1 Cor. 5:9-13). And he has told Christian spouses to stay with their non-Christian husbands or wives as long as that person is willing to live with them (1 Cor. 7:12-14). Yet it is clear that Paul expects Christians to contract new marriages only with one who "belong[s] to the Lord" (1 Cor. 7:39).

Paul stated a general principle, which we might paraphrase: Don't get yourself into any relationship with unbelievers that might involve compromise with Christian standards or witness. Just what those relationships might be — social, business, or other — Paul knows each of us has to rely on the Spirit's guidance to help us determine.

Later Paul does give us an additional word of guidance. Let's remember that God calls us to a life of purity, purging from our lives anything that "contaminates body and spirit" (7:1). If a relationship which we are considering does not promote the "perfecting of holiness out of reverence for God," then it should be avoided.

***Make room* in your hearts (7:2).** The word *choresate* has been paraphrased "make a place for me." The word carries the thought not just of opening, but of expanding. Paul is saying: enlarge your hearts; enlarge your capacity to respond.

Too often when we react to some real or imagined slight we can almost feel our hearts close. Paul reminds the Corinthians that no matter what charges some have laid against him, he has "wronged no one . . . corrupted no one . . . exploited no one" (7:2). And even his request that they now make room for him in their hearts is not uttered in a spirit of condemnation.

The best way to help another person open his or her heart to us is to follow Paul's example and reaffirm our own love, being careful not to attack, criticize, or condemn.

Godly sorrow brings repentance that leads to salvation and leaves no regret, but worldly sorrow brings death (7:10). The word translated "sorrow" is *lupe* in each case. This Greek word, also rendered "grief" and "pain" in the NT, is a broad term encompassing all sorts of physical and emotional distress. Interestingly, the translators of the Septuagint used it to translate some 13 different Hebrew terms which display subtle shades of meaning not found in the Greek.

Here, however, Paul's emphasis is on whether a person's response to *lupe* is "godly" or "worldly." When sorrow leads to repentance — that change of heart and mind that sets us on the path leading to salvation — that sorrow falls into the category of "godly." It is important here to remember that "salvation" is frequently used in the sense of present deliverance. Here Paul's point is that repentance reverses our rush toward disaster, and redeems the situation so that we are delivered from the consequences associated with the earlier, wrong choices we made.

On the other hand sorrow is worldly if all it produces is grief, or even a recognition that we've been wrong — without leading to repentance. A good example of ungodly sorrow is seen in Saul, who seems to have felt regret when admitting to David, "I have sinned. . . . Surely I have acted like a fool and have erred greatly" (1 Sam. 26:21). Yet despite this admission Saul did not repent — and his failure to do so led shortly afterward to his death.

Sorrow, grief, or pain, however we take *lupe* here, is God's gift to us. Repentance signifies our acceptance of it as a gift, and transforms sorrow into something that benefits us despite the hurt.

I am glad I can have *complete confidence* in you (7:16). The verb "complete confidence" is *tharrein,* "to have confidence, courage." Paul looks ahead without fear, confident in the Corinthians' continuing progress in the faith.

Earlier we saw that Paul's confidence is based on his conviction that Christ died in order to bring believers to that place of commitment where they live for Him rather than themselves (5:15). He does not base his evaluation on what can be observed, but on the fact that Christ is in the heart, and His love will

"compel" transformation.

And so Paul's emphasis, seen in the prominent place given the word at the very beginning of the sentence, is not on the Corinthians' reaction, but on his own! *Chairo!* "I rejoice!"

• How good it is to see in others evidence that even now they are responding to that inner compulsion and taking steps toward godliness. How good to see that our confidence has not been misplaced!

So it is with Paul. He is not confident because they have been "obedient," receiving Titus with "fear and trembling" (7:15). Instead their response was expected, a confirmation of the confidence Paul already had. What that response creates is not added confidence, as though there had been doubt, but joy!

THE PASSAGE IN DEPTH

The Ministry of Reconciliation (5:11-21).

Background. Paul has stated that he fixes his eyes "not on what is seen, but on what is unseen. For what is seen is temporary, but what is unseen is eternal" (4:18). This is a basic principle of New Covenant ministry, one which Paul develops in his important exposition on the nature of his "ministry of reconciliation" to the Corinthians.

This emphasis is in striking contrast to Judaism. On the one hand, Judaism does have a definite creed. Perhaps the best representation of Judaism's creed is expressed in the "Thirteen Principles of Faith" developed by Moses Maimonides (A.D. 1135–1204). That creed, preserved in the daily prayer book, begins, "I believe, in perfect faith, that the Creator, may His Name be blessed" and goes on to enumerate the following tenets: (1) God is the sole Creator, (2) uniquely One, (3) beyond all conception and form, (4) the First and the Last, and (5) the true God of prayer, and (6) that the words of the prophets are True, (7) that Moses is the True and First prophet, (8) that the whole Torah was given to Moses; (9) that there is no new covenant, (10) that the Creator is Omniscient, and (11) rewards and punishes for observance of the commandments; (12) that in His own time God will yet bring the Messiah, (13) and resurrect the dead.

Yet while Judaism is a theological system, it is essentially a ritual system, which places its practical emphasis on 11 above: the belief that what is seen is important, for God rewards and punishes for observance of the commandments.

In a helpful little book entitled *Judaism,* Michael A. Fishbane, Samuel Lane Professor of Jewish Religious History at Brandeis University, writes of Judaism as a ritual system.

> In traditional Judaism, all aspects of life are ritualized through halakhic regulations — from the first thoughts and prayers in the morning through the final prayers upon one's bed at night, from permitted to unpermitted foods to permitted and unpermitted business practices, from the obligations of daily prayer to the requirements of festival celebration and personal mourning. Accordingly, all aspects of life take on the legal character of *mutar* and *asur,* or "permitted" and "forbidden," acts; and such other categories as *hayyav* and *patur,* or "obliged" and "free" (not obligated), and *qodesh* and *hol,* or "holy" and "profane," also dominate the daily religious consciousness and experience of the traditional Jews. Accordingly, the observant Jew will be typically scrupulous in performing his halakhic obligations, that is, highly

attentive to the proper times and manner of performing the commandments (p. 83).

This, of course, was Paul's background as a Pharisee, one of the most strict of the first-century Jewish sects. For Paul to say, as a minister of the New Covenant—dismiss the seen as temporary and transient, and thus essentially unimportant—is striking indeed.

In fact, the statement must have amazed the first-century pagan as well. Like all men of every era who had even the vaguest notions of morality, or of a deity who measured man's actions by some moral standard, they would have evaluated themselves and others strictly on performance—on what they did, and thus not on the unseen but on what could be observed.

Why has Paul moved to the radical position he now takes? Because, as he has said in chapter 3, he is a minister of God's New Covenant—a covenant which Maimonides' creed explicitly denies. The Old Covenant work of God was an external Law, written on stone. The New Covenant work of God is an internal transformation of the believer's character, written on the heart. Man's works under the Old Covenant were visible; God's work through the New Covenant is unseen. Yet the former is transitory and essentially useless, while the latter is eternal, filled with the promise of salvation.

Paul's ministry of reconciliation is rooted in this New Covenant perception of reality, a perception which shapes the way he relates to the Corinthians and to every believer in the churches he or others have founded throughout the Empire.

Interpretation. Many of the Word Studies (above) analyze the key terms and thoughts developed in this passage. Thus here, to avoid repetition, it is only necessary to briefly trace the apostle's argument.

Paul, in awe of the Lord, is fully committed to the mission of persuading men. He rejects the charge some have laid against him of presenting an "easy" way of salvation in order to win the Corinthians' and others' favor. And he feels it necessary to explain again the ministry principle on which he operates, "so that you can answer those who take pride in what is seen rather than what is in the heart" (5:12). Here we see again the contrast between seen and unseen. Paul's critics base their claims on

visible results; Paul bases his hopes on something that cannot be seen and measured, on what is in the heart. While this might seem madness to some, it is not to the apostle, who counts on the love of Christ to energize ("compel") a transformation that flows from the heart outward.

But will such an inside-out transformation actually take place? It must, since Christ died for all (believers), and believers "therefore died." God's intent in this great act was to transform enemies not simply into friends, but into followers. He died, "that those who live should no longer live for themselves but for Him who died for them and was raised again" (5:15).

This has totally changed Paul's perspective on spiritual realities. No longer does he evaluate others from a "worldly point of view" (5:16). Again we return to the contrast between the seen and the unseen. The world, without spiritual perception, can only form judgments on evidence available to the senses. Paul looks beyond, into the heart, and realizes that "if anyone is in Christ, he is a new creation" (5:17). The old tie with Adam which held a person in helpless bondage is broken; the new has burst forth in his heart!

What Paul thus has is a "ministry of reconciliation." Even as a seed is watered that it might grow, so Paul encourages the growth of the new which, like a seed waiting to burst forth and bud, lies in the heart. As far as legal standing is concerned, the believer has been brought into harmony with (reconciled to) God by Christ. Now, it is simply a matter of bringing one's way of life into harmony with Christ; simply a matter of encouraging the new life to express itself in lifestyle.

Here again we see the stark contrast between the Old and New Covenants. The one focuses on externals; on ritualized behavior. The other looks beyond even present failures and flaws, to focus on the "new creation" within. The one demands conformity. The other encourages transformation.

But how does a New Covenant ministry of reconciliation encourage transformation? Paul sees the key in God's own demonstrated attitude toward humankind. God was in Christ, reconciling the world, not counting people's trespasses against them. In the same way Paul refuses to count the trespasses of the Corinthians. And he refuses to hold their failures against them! Rather than condemn them for their many flaws, Paul simply keeps on imploring, asking, entreating (*parakalountos,* 5:20) the Corinthians to bring their lives into harmony with Christ.

And he does so with a confidence and assurance that must have encouraged the Corinthians to risk just such a commitment. After all, the great transaction has taken place. God placed the full weight of our sins on Jesus, and in a matching transaction planted new life within our hearts, "that in Him we might become the righteousness of God" (5:21).

Application. It is all too easy to fall into the trap of evaluating on the basis of the seen. It happens in churches, which tend to measure success and failure in terms of numerical growth. It happens in families, where parents tend to measure their success more in terms of their children's present flaws than in terms of their future potential. It happens in our own lives, as we find ourselves at times so weighed down by guilt over our failures that we are unwilling to risk stepping out in some new venture of faith.

Yet Paul's insight reflects reality as God knows it, and as God wants us to know it too. The things that are seen are transitory. However discouraging the present may be, every today is not only subject to change, but is sure to change! The wonderful message of the New Covenant is that the direction of that change, because Christ is in the believer's heart, will be toward the likeness of our Savior.

2 CORINTHIANS 8–9
New Testament Principles of Giving

EXPOSITION

At the end of his first letter to the Corinthians (16:1-4), Paul mentioned a "collection for God's people." Now he takes up in detail the theme of giving. The NT Epistles and Acts make it clear that between about A.D. 52 and 57 much of Paul's energy was devoted to raising money for "the poor among the saints at Jerusalem" (Rom. 15:26; Gal. 2:10). But why was there so much poverty among Christians in Jerusalem? One reason undoubtedly was that many were ostracized by the Jews, who would refuse to employ or even purchase goods from persons who by this time were viewed not as members of a Jewish sect but as apostates. Another factor was a food shortage caused by overpopulation, which resulted in a famine in A.D. 46 during the rule of Claudius (Acts 11:27-30). The problem for the poor would have been exacerbated by the heavy taxes imposed in Palestine by not only the Romans but also by local rulers. Some have also suggested that the willingness of those with larger estates to sell their possessions to support the poor, while it might have met immediate needs, would have had the long-range impact of impoverishing all (Acts 2:44-45; 4:32-35).

Whatever the causes, Christians in the Holy Land were nearly destitute during this period, and Paul dedicated himself to raising funds among the Gentile churches to meet what was a truly desperate need. In many ways, the contributions Paul so earnestly encouraged were a vivid demonstration of central Christian truths. How appropriately the concern of the Gentiles symbolized not only the oneness of Jew and Gentile in Christ (Eph. 2:11-22), but also acknowledged the debt these one-time pagans owed to the people among whom the Gospel originated (Rom. 15:19, 27). Perhaps it also had a special personal meaning for Paul, as a way in which he could repay in part saints who, as Saul, he had once persecuted (Acts 8:3; 9:1; 26:10-11; 1 Cor. 15:9; Gal. 1:13). Yet, most of all, both Paul's emphasis on giving, and the eagerness of the Gentile churches to help (2 Cor. 8:3-4), displayed that commitment to others that the NT calls "brotherly love": a willingness to make personal sacrifices for the well-being of others in the family of our Lord.

Against this background Paul writes glowingly to the Corinthians of the example set by the churches of Macedonia (8:1-5), to urge them to also excel in this "grace of giving" (8:6-7). Paul is careful not to command: NT giving must flow from a willing heart rather than a command to set aside a set percentage of income (8:8-12). He is also careful to point out that the goal is "equality": the meeting of every present need, fully aware that one day the recipient may well supply the need of the giver (8:13-15).

After some personal remarks about himself and Titus (8:16–9:5), Paul continues to develop what is in fact a NT theology of giving. Each person is to "decide in his heart" what to give, looking to Jesus as God's model for every relationship with others. Each is also to remember that what is sown determines what is reaped (9:6-7), and that no one can outgive God, who supplies us with all we need that we may be generous toward others (9:8-11). Such giving will stimulate praise as well as prayer in the hearts of the receiver (9:12-15).

WORD STUDIES

They urgently pleaded with us for the privilege of sharing in this service to the saints (8:4). The Greek has *ten charin,* "the grace" of sharing.

Charis ("grace") appears no less than 10 times in chapters 8–9, and is translated in several different ways. Here it is the honor or privilege of participating in service. In 8:1, 9:8, and 9:14 *charis* is used of God's gift enabling the Corinthians to take part. In 8:6 and 8:19 *charis* is the collection itself, as an expression of love and goodwill. In 8:7 giving itself is described as a "grace," emphasizing the virtue of the act. In 8:9 *charis* is God's own generosity, while in 8:16 and 9:15 *charis* is the thanksgiving that wells up in those who receive the love offering.

Underlying each of these uses is the basic idea embedded in the term. Grace (*charis*) is a favor or benefit bestowed, and at the same time the response of gratitude that is appropri-ate to what has been received. The multiple use of the term in these chapters underlines the fact that giving is through and through a gracious act. Giving is our grateful response to the great gift given us in Christ. Giving is the bestowal of a benefit on others, that in turn stimulates their response of praise to God and prayers for the giver. The very freedom we have to give generously is itself a gift, and a recognition of God's own gracious commitment to supply all our needs that our plenty might overflow to meet the needs of others.

What a privilege to see giving, not as a duty or a burden, but as a grace. How freeing to understand that our weekly offering at church, and our regular support of missions and the needy, is truly a source of joy.

I am not commanding you, but I want to test the sincerity of your love (8:8). Here *epitagen* has the sense of "an order." Paul does not misuse his apostolic authority to command an action which must, in order to please God, be a genuine expression of sincere love rather than an obligation or duty.

One way that we rob our fellow Christians of the joy of giving is by insisting "you must" rather than inviting "you have the opportunity." Some fear giving would fall off if Christians were not told they are "required" to tithe their income. But something more important is involved here. When we impose a percentage requirement, which Paul is careful not to do, we in fact limit giving, for love is a far more powerful motive than obligation in the Christian's life.

NOTES ON TITHING

The basic passage on tithing is found in Lev. 27:30-33. It reads:

A tithe of everything from the land, whether grain from the soil or fruit from the trees, belongs to the Lord; it is holy to the Lord. If a man redeems any of his tithe, he must add a fifth of the value to it. The entire tithe of the herd and flock—every tenth animal that passes under the shepherd's rod—will be holy to the Lord. He must not pick out the good from the bad or make any substitution.

Other passages further explain. Numbers 18:21-32 instructs that tithes be used to maintain the Levites, the tribe set apart to serve God, and in consequence not given its own province when Canaan was conquered by Joshua. Deuteronomy 12:5-14 and 14:22-26 teach that the tithes were to be brought to the central sanctuary, which was later established at Jerusalem. Deuteronomy 14:27-30 and 26:12-15 introduce another tithe, to be collected every third year. This tithe was to be stored locally and distributed to the needy. While some see three tithes in the OT, it seems more likely there were two: the annual 10 percent set apart for those who served the Lord, and the third-year tithe intended for the relief of widows, orphans, and destitute strangers.

It is important to understand that the tithe was on all that the land produced, not on income derived from trade. The tithe was in fact rent that God charged the people of Israel to

whom He granted the privilege of living there (Deut. 1:8; 3:2). The tithe was also intended as an opportunity to express faith. God had promised to bless His people's work (14:29). Those who trusted Him set aside their tithe gladly, sure that He would supply their every need in future bountiful harvests (Mal. 3:10).

But why doesn't the NT require a tithe from Christians, and rather reflects Paul's refusal to command? To answer we must remember that the tithe was imposed on Israel, a faith community that was also a nation. Israel had a land of its own, and civil structures governed by Moses' Law. Israel's primary tithe supported the nation's worship center, and a special levitical and priestly class dedicated to service there. What is more, the tithe served as God's portion of the produce from the land He permitted Israel to occupy.

In contrast the NT faith community exists as small, scattered fellowships distributed in every nation. Our faith community has no central worship center to support. Rather than a priesthood on the OT model, every believer is now seen as a priest. Thus in the NT, while Paul argues for the right of "full-time" Christian workers to be supported by those to whom they minister, neither the rationale for giving nor the use to which contributions were put are the same in the two Testaments. The only real parallel that exists is seen in that concern for the poor expressed in Israel's third-year tithe and in Paul's collection for the poor in Jerusalem.

We can hardly justify importing the tithe into this era. The roots of that practice are as much a part of Israel's life under Law as any ritual sacrifice. And the NT's teaching explicitly states each is to give, not some set amount, but as the individual "has decided in his heart to give, not reluctantly or under compulsion, for God loves a cheerful giver" (2 Cor. 9:7). As an expression of love and of confidence in God's ability to supply our every need, Christian giving truly is a gracious thing. It is our love response to God's wonderful gift to us, as our response of love for brothers and sisters in need.

For if the *willingness* is there, the gift is acceptable according to what one has, not according to what he does not have (8:12). The word is *prothumia,* "eagerness," "willingness to act." It is not the size of the gift that pleases God, but the attitude of the giver.

How do we measure attitude? Paul says it is "according to what one has." The widow's gift of two tiny coins (Mark 12:41-44) far outweighed the gold and silver coins contributed by the rich, for she gave all. Let's not fall into the trap of thinking how much we would give if we were wealthy. Instead, let's simply give as we are able, eager to offer what help we can.

Our desire is not that others might be relieved while you are hard pressed, but that there might be *equality* (8:13). The Greek word, *isotetos,* means more than equality. It also means fairness, or fair shares.

Paul explains in the next verse. His intention is that those needy now might be supplied, with the expectation that those who are able to give now may in the future be in a position where their own needs will be met by those with whom they currently share.

Perhaps the image of the church as the body of Christ best helps us understand. Money is like the oxygen and nutrients carried in the blood to cells throughout the body. "Giving" is simply a way of distributing resources so that every member of the body has his or her basic needs met, and is able to function within the whole. It is hardly fair for one leg to be bloated and fat, while the other is wasting away from starvation. This is not the way things work in the human body. And it is not to be the way things work in the body of Christ.

Each man should give what he has *decided* in his heart to give, not reluctantly or under compulsion, for God loves a cheerful giver (9:7). The word *proeretai* should perhaps have been translated "determined" in his heart. It emphasizes the consciousness and deep conviction which is to be reflected as each of us considers how much to give.

It is no wonder that so many Christians are uncomfortable with the freedom that we have been given in Christ. Perhaps we realize that with freedom comes responsibility, and this we are not ready to accept.

Certainly the church has generally failed to teach freedom and responsibility in the area of giving. We try instead to import an Old Testament standard that, while it relieves us of the responsibility to "determine in our hearts," also robs us of the joy of freely choosing to express our love for the Lord and our commitment to our brothers and sisters. Paul, at least, while urging generosity, is careful to impose no false demands or set up percentage standards for others. He protects both freedom and responsibility, convinced that once freed, Christians will be responsible.

May we have this same confidence in God, in ourselves, and our brothers.

You will be made rich in every way so that you can be generous on every occasion (9:11). God blesses us not that we might be comfortable, but that we might be generous.

Your confession of the Gospel of Christ, and for your generosity in *sharing* with them and with everyone else (9:13). The word is *koinonias,* an expression of that common bond which makes every Christian a participant with every other believer in Christ. Strikingly, *koinonia,* rather than other terms, is typically used to describe Christian giving (Rom. 15:26; 2 Cor. 8:4; 1 Tim. 6:18). The message in this is important. Christian giving is not "taking" from ourselves to "transfer" to another. It is a far warmer transaction than this, a sharing that enriches rather than impoverishes both giver and recipient.

Thanks be to God for His indescribable *gift* (9:15). The word *anekdiegetos* is unusual, and describes a gift that is beyond our capacity to measure. Our first thought is that Paul must be referring back to Christ's gift of Himself (8:9). Yet it is more likely that the doxology is stimulated by the grace that Paul senses infuses everything: the example of Christ, the abundant provisions provided by God, the freedom to give responsibly and cheerfully, the privilege of sharing with others, the gratitude and the praise that giving arouses in the hearts of those who receive. Everything is touched by grace, and giving, which seems to all too many of us a burden, is made golden indeed.

THE PASSAGE IN DEPTH

New Testament Principles of Giving (2 Cor. 8–9).

Background. It would be all too easy to read these chapters and draw a false dichotomy between Paul's NT emphasis on personal responsibility in giving and the OT necessity of paying God's tithe. The temptation is great, especially when we see so many Christians who urge the OT obligation as a standard for today. Certainly if we would, we could point to a great difference in tone between this passage and the writings of the sages who sought to define the exact nature and limits of the righteous Jew's responsibility.

For instance, the Mishnah (Maaserot 3:10) examines the case of a fig tree standing in a garden, with one branch extending into a neighbor's courtyard. A person in that courtyard is allowed to eat the figs one by one as he pleases. But if he gathers figs together (picks a basketful), he must tithe them.

Or take the tractate Maaser Sheni, which discusses the second tithe. There in 4:6 the sages examine a situation in which a purchaser takes possession of produce in the status of the second tithe. What are his obligations if, before he can pay for it, its price rises to two selas? And what happens if it is worth two selas when he buys it, but the price falls to one sela before he can pay for it?

The motive in asking and answering questions such as these was to put a hedge around the Law. That is, the sages were deeply concerned that every implication of Moses' be explored, so that a person committed to obedience might not violate the Law inadvertently. But whatever the motive, there is a clear and vast difference in tone between this approach to giving and the approach Paul takes in 2 Cor. 8–9.

Yet, as I noted, there is a sense in which this contrast creates a false dichotomy. The reason is that there is no real parallel between the OT tithe and NT giving! The tithe was an obligation laid on Israel, a rental due God for the use of His land until His promise to give the land to Abraham's Seed (Christ) would be fulfilled at history's end (Gen. 12:7; 3:15). The sages were intent on defining the extent of that obligation, and setting out rules that would guide the pious Jew in meeting it. In contrast, Paul is talking about voluntary giving to help the poor, which was always distinguished in the OT and in Judaism as a separate issue from the tithe.

Thus Ben Sira, writing 150 years before Christ, encourages the pious to respect the priest and "give him his portion as you have been commanded" (7:31), and then moves immediately from the tithe to speak of generosity to the poor.

> To the poor also extend your hand,
> that your blessing may be complete.
> Give your gift to anyone alive,
> and withhold not your kindness from the dead;
> Avoid not those who weep,
> but mourn with those who mourn;
> Neglect not the care for the sick—
> for these things you will be loved. (7:32-35)

In the *Book of Jewish Knowledge,* Nathan Ansubal notes that the ancient rabbis

> believed that when God gave wealth to the rich, He did not give it to them outright, nor did He do so to reward them for their actions or for any special merit. He merely gave it to them in trust for the poor. Thus they—the rich—were only, so to speak, God's fiscal agents on earth for the poor. To extend *tzedakah* 'with a full hand': to the poor, therefore, fulfilled its true inner meaning as an act of 'righteousness.' From this was developed the axiom that, if the rich were really honest and God-fearing, they would eagerly distribute the wealth they were holding in trust from God to God's innumerable creditors—the poor, the sick, the helpless, the needy, etc. (p. 82).

In his delightful book, *The Joys of Yiddish,* Leo Rosten notes that there is no word for "charity" in Yiddish, but rather giving is *tzedaka,* the obligation to be upright, and above all to help one's fellowman. He writes:

> Every Jewish community placed great stress on helping the poor, the sick, the handicapped—and refugees, who have always been a saddening part of the history of the Jews. Every community had a spe-

cial fund for the needy; every holiday included philanthropic activities; and every home contained little boxes into which coins, for variously designated charities, were dropped. Every Jewish child was told and taught very early in life to feel a duty to help those who needed it; children were often given coins to give to medicants who came to the door (pp. 420-21).

Giving to help the poor, then, was and is as great a virtue in Judaism as it is in Paul's great exhortation to the Corinthians (and us!) to be generous to the needy.

We can, of course, argue that there is a great difference in the motive for giving made explicit in the writings of the sages and the writings of Paul. Paul sees giving as a response to God's grace; the rabbis saw giving as a meritorious act. Thus the story is told of Rabbi Akiba's debate with Tineius Rufus, the Roman governor of Judea. Rufus challenged the rabbi: "If, as you say, your God loves the poor, why then does He not support them?" Rabbi Akiba is said to have replied that God left the care of the poor to the Jew "so that we may be saved by giving's merits from the punishment of Gehenna."

Even so, our basic distinction remains. The giving described and encouraged in the NT is not comparable to the OT tithe, but is in fact more closely related to the principle established in Deut. 15:10-11: "Give generously to him and do so without a grudging heart; then because of this the Lord your God will bless you in all your work and in everything you put your hand to. There will always be poor people in the land. Therefore I command you to be openhanded toward your brothers and toward the poor and needy in your land."

It is on this kind of giving that the NT too focuses our attention. In that era there were no buildings with large mortgages to pay, and few salaried ministers. Yet there have been Christians in various parts of the world who at different times have needed help in order to survive and function as members of the body of Christ. Without criticizing the brick-and-mortar orientation of much contemporary giving, we can certainly agree that the real needs of human beings must have priority as we prayerfully consider how God wants us to direct the resources He leads us to set aside for His work.

Interpretation. Embedded in these two important chapters are a number of basic concepts that shape our understanding of Christian giving. Rather than attempt to outline this passage, the best way to explore it is to identify and discuss these basic concepts. They can be listed as follows:

- Giving is a privilege (8:4).
- Giving flows from commitment (8:5).
- Giving is voluntary (8:8).
- Giving is purposeful (8:13-16).
- Giving has personal consequences (9:6).
- Giving involves head and heart (9:7).
- Giving has spiritual as well as material results (9:12).

As we look at these concepts one by one, we begin to build a distinctive NT theology of giving that can guide us individually and in our churches.

Giving Is a Privilege (8:4). Paul describes participation in the offering he is collecting for the poverty-stricken saints in Jerusalem as "the privilege of sharing in this service to the saints" (8:4).

It's clear that the Macedonian churches Paul refers to viewed giving as a privilege. Despite undergoing "most severe trial" and despite their own "extreme poverty" (8:2), the Christians in this province were eager to participate. It is important here to note that Paul describes these believers as also knowing an "overflowing joy." They had a vital, satisfying relationship with Jesus that gave them inner joy despite their difficult circumstances.

It is impossible to look at "giving" in isolation from the rest of one's Christian experience. No one whose love for Christ has cooled, no one who is oriented to the world rather than heaven, no one whose happiness is tied to what he possesses, no one who fails to experience a welling up of joy as he senses Jesus' daily touch, will find giving a privilege or sense the grace that infuses the opportunity God gives us to share with those in need.

Giving Flows from Commitment (8:5). Paul continues to describe the Macedonians, and notes that "they gave themselves first to the Lord and then to us in keeping with God's will."

The Macedonians' experience of God's

grace caused an overflowing joy (8:2). The early Methodists were criticized by the then staid Church of England from which they sprang as "enthusiasts." All that emotion was deemed inappropriate. Yet emotion plays a vital role in true Christianity. Religion is never enough, however. Joy in Jesus must be coupled with commitment to the Lord, and that commitment must be expressed by living a life that is "in keeping with God's will" (8:5).

If Christian giving is to be as generous and spontaneous as Paul seems to describe here, the joy we have in Jesus must lead us to dedicate ourselves to the Lord, and to consciously commit ourselves to do God's will.

Again we're reminded that "giving" cannot be considered in isolation from the overall spiritual experience of an individual or congregation. If we give our first attention to nurturing spiritual growth, people will respond generously when confronted with a need.

Giving Is Voluntary (8:8). One truth that many find hard to accept is that giving truly is voluntary. The Christian is not obligated to tithe. The Christian is not required to contribute. Thus Paul says, "I am not commanding you."

One of the most difficult truths for us to grasp is that the grace that releases us from obligation in our relationship with God actually frees us to do far more than we otherwise would have. When Paul says he wants to "test the sincerity of your love," he alerts us to the ultimate and necessary motivation for giving and for every act of service.

Unlike the Rabbi Akiba, who saw giving as a way to gain merit that would save a person from the torments of Gehenna, Paul says "you know the grace of our Lord Jesus Christ" (8:9). Rather than seek a merit that accrues through our actions, we understand that through Christ's self-emptying we who were utterly destitute have "become rich." Christ here is not presented so much as an example for us to follow, but as the source of a salvation which has already won us the ultimate prize—salvation—and enriched us with every spiritual blessing.

What then is left for us to do? Nothing! But what does the knowledge of this grace of Christ create within us? Love! And the sincerity of our love is demonstrated in voluntary acts of service—acts of service, whether giving

or other, that we do, not because they are a duty and not because we expect to gain by them, but simply because we love the Lord, and find it a joy and a privilege to do His will.

Giving Is Purposeful (8:13-16). There is a distinct difference here between the rationale for giving in the NT and in first-century Judaism. In Judaism the poor of the land were the socially deprived: the widow, the orphan, the homeless, the day-laborer who could not find work. Generosity to such persons was encouraged, for God had expressed special concern for such persons. Besides, Prov. 19:17 taught, "He who is kind to the poor lends to the Lord, and He will reward him for what he has done." Certainly there was a similar compassion for the poor, as such, in the early church (Acts 4:32-37; 6:1-3; James 1:27). But in this case Paul presents a very different purpose for giving than relief of individual need.

Back in Jerusalem and Judea the entire Christian community was nearly destitute, for reasons explored in the Exposition (above). Paul sees this as a special problem, a church problem, in that in a significant part of the world conditions made it impossible for the believers to survive and function. Paul's gift is not only intended to meet the very real human needs that exist, but also to provide the resources required to enable a vital witness to Christ in Jerusalem and Judea.

Here we see the appropriateness of the analogy between the church and a body. Each member must be supplied with whatever is needed for health and vitality if the work of Christ in the world is to be done. The contribution Paul is soliciting is intended not only to meet the needs of the poor in Jerusalem, but to enable the church there to survive and function.

This analysis suggests two primary purposes in Christian giving. We give to meet human need simply because God does care for the poor and oppressed. We also give to enable Christians to function as the church, witnessing to Christ in multiplied ways within society.

In regard to this second purpose, which is paramount in this passage, Paul reminds us that such giving is not to be viewed as endless. Deuteronomy bluntly stated that there would always be poor people who need help (15:11). But Paul says give now, "so that in turn their plenty will supply what you need" (2 Cor.

8:14). The church scattered across the world is interdependent, and as history moves on, first one area and then another will prosper or decline. It is the responsibility of those who prosper now to give generously to supply needy believers in the lands in decline, fully aware that in time their situations may well be reversed.

Giving Has Personal Consequences (9:6). While the believer's salvation in no way hinges on any meritorious acts, and while the Christian is not under obligation to give, there are personal consequences to every choice we make. Paul, unwilling to command giving, nevertheless feels completely free to spell out some of the implications of the Corinthians' decision to give or not to do so. Thus Paul says, "Whoever sows sparingly will also reap sparingly, and whoever sows generously will also reap generously."

This verse should not be turned into a promise of financial blessing now. God gives us no guarantee that an "investment" of $50 in Brother so and so's TV ministry will give us a $500 return within three months! The promise is eschatological. We sow material things here and now, and in doing so we store up treasures in heaven (Matt. 6:19-21). It is a simple fact that one who sows few material things will have little stored up in heaven when Jesus returns and our harvesttime comes.

This is not and should not be a primary motive for giving. But it is a reality we should keep in mind, to give us perspective on the relative insignificance of material wealth. If we hold back, it may well be because things are precious to us. Paul wants us to remember that things are not precious; people are. In giving generously to help God's people in need we show that our priorities are in harmony with God's, and display a love that will, by God's grace, be richly rewarded when Jesus returns.

Giving Involves Head and Heart (9:7). As the Word Study of 9:7 pointed out, we are to carefully evaluate and "decide" what we will give. This not only emphasizes personal responsibility, but also careful and rational evaluation.

But what principle should we use in evaluating? The answer is suggested in 8:13. We are to look at what we have, and look at what others need. And then, balancing what we have against what others need, make our choice.

But the kind of giving Paul is exploring here is not simply a matter of the head. It is also a matter of the heart. Once we have decided what is appropriate, we are to make our contribution cheerfully, "for God loves a cheerful giver." The word "cheerful" (*hilaron*) is the source of our word, "hilarious." Giving is to be joyful, a delight. When our heart is in the gift, all sense of obligation or begrudging is absent, and the act of giving is purified, a sacrifice which God approves and whose maker He loves.

It would be wrong to discourage any offering which is made without a sense of joy. If we did, the recipient would be defrauded of the gift. But it would be just as wrong to fail to remind one another that any gift not motivated by love and given cheerfully has no profit for the giver! (1 Cor. 13:3)

Giving Has Spiritual As Well As Material Results (9:12). The receiving of the gift stimulates praise to God and prayers for the giver. Giving thus has direct spiritual as well as direct material consequences. We give not only to meet others' needs, but because in giving we deepen their relationship with the Lord, and cause them to sense His constant love and concern.

Application. Paul's two great chapters on giving help us as individuals to reexamine our attitude toward wealth and our sensitivity to the needs of others. But his teaching here also suggests that those in church leadership should reexamine not only their teaching on giving, but also the ways in which the church seeks to raise funds. By presenting clearly the needs for which contributions are sought, and by instructing them in the concepts Paul presents here, an even greater generosity can be stimulated, and God receives even more praise.

2 CORINTHIANS 10–13
Spiritual Authority

EXPOSITION

Paul's unmatched exhortation to Christian giving (chaps. 8–9) ends on a note of praise. Then, almost suddenly, the tone of his letter changes. Although he still appeals rather than commands, his tone now is stern. He wraps the mantle of apostolic authority around him, and confronts those in Corinth who, claiming a higher authority, challenge his.

These chapters are not so much a defense of Paul's position as they are a judgment on the Corinthians. The evidence Paul presents has always been available to them, yet many have chosen to listen to "super-apostles" (11:5; 12:11) who have promoted themselves rather than Christ.

Paul begins his defense with an appeal and a warning (10:1-6). The Lord gave Paul the authority that he has, and the criticisms that "in person he is unimpressive" does not change the fact that his critics' claims are rooted only in self-commendation (10:7-12). God has given Paul Corinth as part of his *kanon,* that territory for which he is responsible, and so Paul is intensely concerned with the welfare of the Corinthians (10:13–11:3). No wonder Paul is concerned when someone comes to Corinth and preaches a different Gospel, and then attacks Paul on flimsy grounds (11:4-12). Such men are "false apostles," who serve Satan rather than righteousness (11:13-15).

Against his will Paul is driven to "boasting," here presenting evidence of his apostleship (11:16-21). Strikingly, Paul's "boasting" diametrically opposed that of the false "super-apostles." They point to their strengths; Paul points to his sufferings (11:22-29) and his weakness (11:30–12:10). Paul has learned that human weakness is the secret of spiritual strength, for it is the man who is weak who relies on the Lord, and it is through our weaknesses that His strength is most vividly displayed. All this, accompanied by miracle-working power, is evidence of Paul's apostleship (12:11-13). The Corinthians' failure to respond is of great concern, for Paul fears that when he visits them he will find the community marred by unspirituality and sin (12:14-21).

Paul concludes with a warning. If the faults he has identified are not corrected he "will not spare those who sinned earlier or any of the others." If the Corinthians do not "examine [themselves]" Paul may have to be "harsh in the use of [his] authority" (13:1-10). Paul then closes the book with a request that the church "listen to my appeal," and a benediction (13:11-14).

Paul's extended defense of his authority is important to us today. This is not because the modern church hesitates between his words and those of his first-century opponents. History has established Paul's writings as Scripture, and the "super-apostles" who opposed him have long been forgotten. Yet these chapters provide vital insights into the nature of spiritual authority, and into the delicate balance Christian leaders today must maintain between protecting the freedom of believers to be responsible to the Lord, and their own responsibility to guide and protect the body of Christ.

WORD STUDIES

By the meekness and gentleness of Christ, I *appeal* to you (10:1). The word *parakalo* reminds us that even as Paul is about to assert his apostolic authority, he does not command but instead tactfully reminds the churches of their personal responsibility to exercise moral judgment.

Christian leadership is less concerned with gaining conformity than commitment. Paul does not want to make the church do what he says. Paul instead seeks to influence the church to recognize his instruction as God's will, and want to respond to it.

The *weapons* we fight with are not the weapons of this world (10:4). The word is *strateias,* a military term further developed in this and the next verse. The arguments of Paul's opponents are like a wall of words, erected not against Paul but "against the knowledge of God."

What are the worldly (*sarkinos,* "fleshly") weapons that Paul eschews? Probably the very things his opponents emphasize: impressive looks, oratorical skills, things that seem appealing, but only "on the surface" (10:7). We will see more clearly the nature of Paul's "weapons" as he continues his defense. But they can be summed up as weaknesses which enable Christ to speak more clearly through him.

The less we depend on our own strengths in ministry, the more we will depend on Christ. And the more we depend on the Lord, the better He will be able to work through us.

We will be ready to punish every act of disobedience, once your obedience is complete (10:6). "Punish" here is *ekdikesai,* a legal term that blends the ideas of taking vengeance and doing justice. The word "your" in "once your obedience is complete" is plural, indicating that Paul is addressing the church as a whole. Thus Paul has two groups in mind,

intruders who commend themselves as "super-apostles" (11:5) and lead the Christian community astray, and the community they have influenced. Paul will deal with the false apostles. But he wants the community to first reject the false gospel, and reunite in its commitment to the Gospel of which Paul is an apostle.

Again we see Paul's awareness that Christians are responsible, and must act responsibly. Paul writes rather than visits, in order to give the Corinthians an opportunity to purify themselves.

Even if I *boast* somewhat freely about the authority the Lord gave us for building you up rather than pulling you down (10:8). The theme of boasting, introduced here, is expanded in 10:15-18 and also in chapters 11–12. The verb *kauchaomai* means "to boast, glory, take pride in." Here the word is used with some irony: Paul's critics are boastful, comparing their strengths with Paul's supposed weaknesses, and thus commending themselves as superior. Paul, on the other hand, glories in one thing: it is God who has given him authority in the church, and that authority is exercised not to tear down the church, but to build it up.

The same should be true of Christian leaders today. They serve because they were called by God to a ministry of serving others. And they are intent, not on their own positions, but on building up the body of Christ.

If this is our attitude, the false pride and arrogance reflected in the boasting of Paul's opponents will be replaced by the humble boasting of those who glory in the Lord Jesus Christ.

Even if I boast somewhat freely about the *authority* the Lord gave us for building you up rather than pulling you down

(10:8). The word *exousia* means "freedom of action," and thus power or authority. As God's apostle, Paul has been given authority, or freedom of action, in regard to the church in Corinth. But Paul is very much aware that his freedom of action is limited by the purpose of his commission: he is to build up rather than tear down.

This awareness is undoubtedly a major reason why he appeals rather than commands, and waits for the church to respond before descending upon them. All too often by forcing obedience parents and church leaders weaken rather than strengthen the young. Paul teaches, encourages, appeals, warns, and explains, seeking to influence the congregation to freely choose what is right. Paul knows that choosing right strengthens character, while being forced to do right against one's will may weaken it.

We do not dare to classify or compare ourselves with some who commend themselves (10:12). The problem with Paul's opponents is that their claims are based on *heautous sunistanonton,* self-commendation. Their approach is to contrast their supposed strengths with Paul's supposed weaknesses. Paul, somewhat sarcastically, says in effect that he isn't able to play at comparisons. As Paul goes on we see that he does not emphasize his strengths, but the very weaknesses which his opponents disparage.

Before that, however, Paul rests his case on something more important. He has been commissioned by God, and the Lord has given him authority within a territory for which Paul has been made responsible.

This is always the issue. Not whether we are wiser, better speakers, more knowledgeable, or skilled, than others. The issue is whether God has called us to be leaders, and given us a "territory" for which we are to be responsible.

We . . . will confine our boasting to the field God has assigned to us, a field that reaches even to you (10:13). The word here is *kanon,* which in other contexts means "rule" or "standard." Its use here is technical, illustrated in an inscription found in Galatia in 1976, an edict dating from A.D. 13–15 which defines the services a city was required to perform. That inscription reads in part,

Sextus Sotidius Strabo Libuscidianas, legate of [Tiberius] Caesar Augustus, acting as praetor, declares: . . . that no one would make use of transport free, but, since the license of certain people demands immediate action, I have promulgated in the individual cities and villages a kanon of what I judge desirable to be supplied, it being my intention to maintain it, or, if neglected, enforce it, not merely by my own powers, but by the divinity of the excellent savior Augustus, from whom I accepted this very thing in my mandate.

Here *kanon* is a list of what things traveling officials may requisition, and, important for our passage, the prescribed territory within which those subject to the decree are responsible to see the edict is carried out.

Paul's claim, then, is that God has granted him a *kanon,* a prescribed territory for which he is responsible, and that this territory includes the Corinthians. The debate over strengths and weaknesses is thus totally irrelevant, for whatever his opponents may say, the responsibility to God for what happens in Corinth is Paul's. And Paul has been granted commensurate authority.

Again, this business of self-commendation based on comparison with others is totally irrelevant to spiritual leadership. The first and most important question is, what *kanon* has God assigned to leaders, and what are their responsibilities within it.

I am jealous for you with a godly jealousy. I promised you to one husband, to Christ, so that I might present you as a pure virgin to Him (11:2). Paul's role is not that of a father, as in modern weddings, but as a "friend who attends the bridegroom" (*philos tou numphiou,* John 3:29). Edersheim, in *Sketches of Jewish Life,* notes that in Judea one "friend" was assigned to the bride and one to the groom. These acted as intermediaries and served as "guarantors of the bride's virgin chastity." After marriage the friend of the bridegroom continued to serve the couple, seeking to maintain good terms between them, and also defending the reputation of the bride against any criticisms.

Using this imagery Paul makes it clear that while Corinth is Paul's *kanon* from God, his ministry is motivated by an intense love for this people who are Christ's bride, and by a burning desire to see the church maintain an intimate relationship with her Lord.

Leaders must not only be faithful to their responsibility. They must love.

Was it a sin for me to *lower* myself in order to elevate you by preaching the Gospel of God to you free of charge? (11:7) The word here, *tapenion,* means "to humble," but suggests more. In Greek culture words from this root conveyed contempt; a person who was *tapeinos* was socially powerless, a condition viewed as shameful in the Hellenistic world.

But why should Paul's willingness to support himself be a cause for criticism? One interesting suggestion is that his critics charged that by working Paul demonstrated a lack of faith. After all, when Christ sent His disciples out two by two He told them to take no purse, but depend on the generosity of those who received their ministry! (Matt. 10) So those "super-apostles" who boasted that their speaking was superior (11:6) also boasted that they were more spiritual, because they took money from the Corinthians and let the church support them!

The argument should have been hard to sustain in view of Paul's earlier explanation that, while he had a "right" to support, he surrendered that right (1 Cor. 9), sacrificing it in favor of an eternal reward. Paul's opponents have distorted Paul's motives, so that they, who are "false apostles," "masquerade as servants of righteousness" when in fact they serve Satan's ends (2 Cor. 11:13-14).

Anyone in spiritual leadership is sure to experience what Paul faces here—criticism based on distortion of his motives and misrepresentations of his acts. It is frustrating. But it is part of the cost of serving Christ.

What anyone else dares to boast about—I am speaking as a fool—I also dare to boast about (11:21). Paul has been forced into a foolish contest, one of comparing credentials. In fact Paul's credentials are better. He too is a Palestinian-trained Jew (a "Hebrew" [11:22]); he has worked harder than his opponents (11:23a); he has suffered more (11:23b-27); he cares more (11:28-29).

Having said this, Paul introduces a stunning note he will develop in chap. 12. Paul is weak-er than his opponents, and this is in fact one of the secrets of his strength. In developing this theme he will display a "foolishness of God" which is far wiser than the wisdom of men! (1 Cor. 1:25)

I know a man in Christ who fourteen years ago was caught up to the *third heaven* (12:2). The passage has caused untold speculation. Why does Paul, obviously speaking of himself, use the third person? What is this "third heaven"? What does Paul mean "whether in the body or apart from the body"? (12:3) And what, later, was his "thorn in [the] flesh"? (12:7)

As far as the use of the third person is concerned, the best suggestion is that Paul adopts it in order to avoid any suggestion that he takes personal credit for the visions or the revelations granted him (12:1).

The mention of "third heaven" is usually thought to assume a cosmology which views earth's atmosphere as a first heaven, the realm of the heavenly bodies as a second heaven, and the spiritual realm inhabited by God and His angels as the third heaven. However, intertestamental writings also mention a sevenfold division of the heavens (2 Enoch 8-22 and the Ascension of Isaiah), and a fifth heaven (3 Apocalypse of Barnabas 11:1) and even suggest a tenfold division of heaven (2 Enoch 20:3b). Since the NT is silent on the matter, speculation as to Paul's cosmology seems useless. But the intimation remains: he was caught up into a realm accessible only to God.

Paul's uncertainty about whether his vision was received in or out of the body (12:3) has been quoted by those who argue for "astral projection," a phenomenon in which the soul is supposed to leave the living body. This parenthesis hardly supports that theory. Paul simply says that while the vision was real, he does not know whether or not he was physically present in that paradise where he experienced such wonders and was told things he is unable even now to reveal.

At this point Paul is quick to introduce his "thorn in my flesh" (12:7). God permitted Satan to send this "messenger," but for His own purposes. After pleading with God three times for its removal, Paul realized that the "thorn" was a gift, intended to make him weak in man's eyes, that God's power might be "made perfect" (12:8) in his weakness.

No one will ever know what that thorn was, despite much speculation. The word *skolops* means "stake" as well as "thorn," and suggests severe torment. While some suggest that the "thorn" is Paul's opponents, most take it as some chronic, debilitating illness. In the latter case this would surely be ammunition for Paul's enemies. How could a true apostle, with any real power, be unable to heal himself?

For when I am weak, then I am strong (12:10). Weakness is *astheno*, a word that indicates more than frailty; it suggests an incapacitating disability. In contrast, strong is *dunatos*, not healthy, but powerful. Paul is strong in his weakness, because God works in and through human frailty.

This is a theme totally foreign to the thinking of Paul's critics. But, after all, their weapons are worldly, of the flesh (10:4). In his lengthy defense Paul has offered the Corinthians a striking alternative. They can measure a person's authority by criteria which Paul's critics put forward—or they can acknowledge the criteria which Paul has advanced. Criteria which exalt Christ, not any human being. Criteria which display a wisdom of God which stands in utter contrast to the wisdom of this world (cf. 1 Cor. 1:18–2:16).

Have you been *thinking* all along that we have been defending ourselves to you? (12:19) The word *dokeite* here is better taken as "assumed" or "supposed." As the Corinthians—and modern Christians—read these chapters, many "assume all along" that what Paul is doing is defending himself and his apostolic authority.

In fact, Paul has been providing a standard that will enable the Corinthians to reevaluate—a standard which, if they fail to acknowledge its validity, will provide a basis for their judgment as well!

This will be my third visit to you. "Every matter must be established by the testimony of two or three witnesses" (13:1). Paul here quotes Deut. 19:15, but dropping in this verse puzzles commentators. What "witnesses" does Paul refer to? Is he referring to his visits themselves? Is Paul threatening to hold court when he comes, and call witnesses who can unmask the sinners there? Perhaps we should understand the witnesses as the words of this letter, words which have expressed spiritual truths "in the sight of God" (12:19), and which His Spirit authenticates in the hearts of His own (1 Cor. 2:12).

Certainly this understanding is in harmony with Jesus' words to the Jewish leaders who opposed Him. "Do not think I will accuse you before the Father," He warned. "Your accuser is Moses, on whom your hopes are set" (John 5:45). The very Word of God which frees those who respond to it condemns those who will not. Every word Paul has penned in the defense of his apostleship has the potential to free his readers—or to serve as the basis of their judgment when he visits again.

Let's remember this double-edged nature of Scripture. It invites yet warns, frees yet binds, vindicates yet judges. Let us be careful to respond to God's Word, lest that same Word serve as a witness against us when we appear before our Lord at His return.

Examine yourselves to see whether you are in the faith; *test yourselves* (13:5). "Examine" is *peirazo*, usually meaning test or tempt, but here used in the neutral sense of "discern." This is followed up immediately with an exhortation: *dokimazete*, "test yourselves." The word carries the expectation of approval: examine and test yourselves, and you will discover that you truly are in the faith.

Careful self-examination will uncover the Christ who is within the Corinthians, and they will recognize His voice speaking through the apostle, for the Lord truly has given Paul authority to build them up (13:10).

How much better it is to look within and listen to Christ's inner voice, than to fix our attention on the supposed weakness of leaders God has placed in our churches. Or be swayed by the complaints of critics who carp on every real and imagined weakness to destroy rather than enhance the ministry of the local church.

THE PASSAGE IN DEPTH

Paul's Defense of His Ministry (chaps. 10–13).

Background. The problems Paul addresses in 1 Cor. were created by members of the local congregation. The problems addressed in 2 Cor. were created by outsiders, by Palestinian intruders who preached "a different Gospel" (2 Cor. 11:4) and who sought to tighten their grip on the young congregation by vigorous attacks on Paul's authority. Murray J. Harris, in his commentary on *2 Corinthians* (Zondervan), gives an excellent summary.

Paul, they alleged, was a double-minded [apostle] who acted capriciously (2 Cor. 1:17-18; 10:2-4) and lorded it over his converts (1:24; 7:2), so restricting their spiritual development (6:12). He carried no letters of commendation (3:1; 10:13) because he commended himself (4:2, 5; 5:12; 6:4; 10:12, 18; 12:11; cf. 1 Cor. 9:1-3; 14:18; 15:10b) as would a madman (5:13; 11:1, 16-19; 12:6, 11) or imposter (6:8). Just as his gospel was obscure (4:3; 6:2-3), so also the letters he wrote were unintelligible or devious (1:13) and written with

the perverse aim of condemning and destroying (7:2-3; 10:8; 13:10) and causing pain (2:2, 4-5; 7:8). He was impressive at a distance but weak and contemptible when he deigned to make a personal appearance (10:1-2, 9-11; 11:6; 13:3-4, 9). His refusal to accept remuneration from the Corinthians proved that he cared little for them and that he was aware of being a counterfeit apostle, not the mouthpiece of Christ (11:5, 7-11, 13; 12:11-15; 13:3a, 6). Yet he exploited the willingness of the church to support him by having his agents organize a collection, ostensibly for the saints at Jerusalem but in reality for himself (12:16-18). Such were some of the charges made by Paul's calumniators (p. 314).

Perhaps the most significant insight into these competitors of the apostle is provided in 11:22: "Are they Hebrews?" All agree that the term here means "Palestinian Jew," in distinction to "Israelite," or Jewish in racial origin. These were individuals who were or claimed to be Christians who claimed a special authority, perhaps derived (1) from personal ac-

AUTHORITY IN RABBINIC JUDAISM

A wide range of ancient and modern writings helps us understand the view of authority prevalent in first-century as well as contemporary rabbinic Judaism. Michael Fishbane explains that in Judaism "God, the Torah, and the interpretation of Torah by qualified sages" are intersecting structures of authority. Jacob Neusner in his excellent book, *Foundations of Judaism,* develops the implications of this view on pp. 119–121.

It was not the case that one component of Torah, of God's word to Israel, stood within the sacred circle, another beyond. Interpretation and what was interpreted, exegesis and text, belonged together. . . . Scripture and the Mishnah govern what the rabbi knows. But it is the rabbi who authoritatively speaks about them. The simple fact that what rabbis were willing to do to the Mishnah is precisely what they were prepared to do to Scripture—impose on it their own judgment of its meaning. . . . The rabbi speaks with authority about the Mishnah and the Scripture. He therefore has authority deriving from revelation. He himself may participate in the process of revelation (there is no material difference).

If Paul's Palestinian opponents approached the church with this view of authority, they in effect claimed the right to authoritatively reinterpret the Gospel message that Paul had preached as the Word of God. And, in making this claim, the intruders implicitly required the Corinthians to submit to their words as to the Words of God Himself!

quaintance with Jesus during His life, which some think is implied in 5:16, (2) from the 12 Apostles or Peter, or (3) from the Jerusalem church.

What is interesting is that it was customary for the Sanhedrin to send delegations to Jewish communities throughout the Empire, with letters attesting to their authority, to give official notice of the dates of annual festivals and to serve as judges to settle disputes. These men, sages themselves, acted with unquestioned authority, for not only was the Sanhedrin the supreme authority for all Jews everywhere, but Palestinian rabbis were thought to have a superior holiness and greater authority.

What apparently happened is that Christian Jews from Palestine appeared in Corinth, and claimed the same kind of authority over that congregation that Jewish rabbis sent out by the Sanhedrin exercised over the Jews of the diaspora! When many in Corinth resisted, appealing to Paul's authority, these intruders mounted a vigorous attack against the absent apostle which succeeded in seriously undermining his authority. This led to the writing of 2 Corinthians, in which Paul does far more than defend his apostleship. He explains the nature of New Covenant ministry, and in the chapters now under consideration contrasts the approach to spiritual leadership represented by his "super-apostle" opponents with his own approach.

Interpretation. Chapters 10–13 present Paul's specific response to the Palestinian intruders whose claims of authority have confused the Corinthians. While these claimants call themselves "apostles," it is clear that they use this word as a functional equivalent of "rabbi" or "sage," and that underlying their claim is a distinctive concept of spiritual leadership. Paul's response develops three vital concepts, concepts which certainly apply to the modern church, because they are central to an understanding of spiritual leadership, whatever title we may give our leaders. We can examine these concepts under the follow titles:

■ The Marks of an Apostle.
■ The Ministry of an Apostle.
■ The Authority of an Apostle.

THE MARKS OF AN APOSTLE

The claim of the intruders to spiritual authority over the church at Corinth was supported by several claims. They possessed superior knowledge and eloquence (11:6). They claimed to have visions and revelations (12:1, 7). They possessed letters of commendation (3:1). They took money in payment for spiritual services (11:12). Moreover, they were from Palestine, the seat of primitive Christianity (5:16; 10:7).

If we take 2 Cor. 12:12 as it is rendered in the NIV, we might suppose that the marks of an apostle are the ability to perform miracles. That verse reads, "the things that mark an apostle—signs, wonders and miracles—were done among you with great perseverance" (12:12). But the NIV translation is unfortunate, implying as it does that miracles are the essential authenticating mark of an apostle. This translation is unlikely theologically, as Paul has just provided an extended defense in which he lists a variety of other things as evidence of his apostleship. The translation is unlikely logically, for if miracles were "the things that mark an apostle," his opponents would have rested their case on their ability to perform miracles, and Paul could have argued his case simply by listing miracles he performed while in Corinth. The translation is also unlikely grammatically. The phrase "signs, wonders, and miracles" is in the dative case, rather than the nominative, which would be expected if the NIV's rendering were correct.

What then is Paul saying? Simply that "the marks of an apostle were displayed among you in all persistence, [along with] signs and wonders and mighty works." Paul's hard work, his sufferings, his deep concern for the churches, and the fact that God worked mightily through him despite his evident weaknesses—these are the compelling evidences that Paul has been commissioned by God.

It is the same today. The marks of leaders whom we can trust and respond to remain a persistent commitment to servanthood. A servanthood that today too is displayed in hard work, in suffering, in deep concern for God's people, and in evidence that God is at work despite the human weakness that is all too present in each of us.

THE MINISTRY OF AN APOSTLE

Twice in this letter Paul speaks of the "authority the Lord gave us for building you up rather than pulling you down" (10:8; 13:10). Paul does more here than affirm that the Lord (not

Palestine!) is the source of his authority. He both defines and limits his authority. His *kanon*, that realm for which he has been made responsible, includes Corinth (10:13). He is responsible for "building you up," yet he is specifically limited as well, for in his ministry he is to do nothing that might "pull you down."

The question then is: how does Paul the apostle minister so that he might buiid up the Corinthians and avoid pulling the church down? Several characteristics of Paul's ministry are shown throughout 2 Corinthians. In chapters 1–3 Paul modeled self-revelation, and showed that Christ is seen in the process of transformation that takes place in believers, not in some claim to sinless perfection that affirms strengths. In chapters 4–7 Paul showed that a ministry of reconciliation rests on the conviction that Christ's love is a compelling force within the heart of the believer. Because Paul knows that God will surely accomplish in believers that purpose for which Christ died, the apostle relies on the unseen working of the Spirit; he both has and expresses complete confidence even in flawed saints. In chapters 8–9 Paul has further shown this confidence in refusing to command the Corinthians to give, but rather emphasized their personal responsibility to consider giving carefully, while making clear various reasons why cheerful, generous giving is wise as well as right.

This same spirit pervades our present chapters. Paul "appeals" to the believers to respond (10:1), and his apparent self-defense has in reality been a revelation of ministry based on weakness rather than strength, on service rather than superiority.

On the basis of this stunning explanation of the nature of New Covenant leadership, Paul calls on his readers to "examine yourselves," and expresses confidence that when they do they. will pass the test by recognizing that Christ indeed has been speaking through him. Not through the false apostles from Palestine, who base their claims on a completely different view of ministry and of the leader's authority.

THE AUTHORITY OF AN APOSTLE

The problem with the interpretation advanced here is that it seems to be denied by the fact that Paul very sternly warns the Corinthians.

Paul says very clearly, "I already gave you a warning when I was with you the second time. I now repeat it while absent: On my return I will not spare those who sinned earlier or any of the others" (13:1-2). A little later he says, "I write these things when I am absent, that when I come I may not have to be harsh in my use of authority" (13:10).

Reading these verses it seems that Paul has abandoned his earlier commitment to modeling, teaching, and appealing, and has turned to threats of punishment (cf. 10:6). So it would appear that spiritual authority does include the right to demand compliance as well as exist as a position from which to influence God's people.

At least, it would appear this way, if Paul had not added a final clause to his warning, and then an explanation. Paul has said, "On my return I will not spare those who sinned earlier or any of the others," but then adds "since you are demanding proof that Christ is speaking through me." Paul then says, "He [Christ] is not weak in dealing with you, but is powerful among you" (13:2-3).

What will Paul do to punish those who refuse to respond to his gentle instruction? Nothing! He does not have to! The fact is that as an apostle, appointed by the Lord, whose *kanon* includes Corinth, Christ is speaking through him. If the Corinthians fail to respond it is not Paul they reject, but the Lord! Thus, Paul says, it is Christ who will deal with the sinners, and He is not weak in dealing with you, but is powerful among you.

The true spiritual leader does not need coercive powers. The true spiritual leader, called by God, appointed to a ministry, and responsible to guard and guide a people, is one through whom Jesus is working. The person who remains unresponsive as that leader shares God's enscripturated truth must answer to Jesus, not to the leader.

And he or she most surely will.

Application. Spiritual leadership in the church of Jesus Christ is a challenging role not only for the leader but for the congregation. All too often our view of leadership is worldly, having far more in common with the approach of Paul's critics than with the approach Paul outlines in this epistle.

There are other passages that we must also explore to develop an appropriate theology of leadership. Jesus' words on servanthood found in Matt. 20. Paul's instruction to Timothy and Titus on selecting leaders, which in so many ways mirrors Acts 6. The words of the writer to the Hebrews about how we are to respond to the leaders God gives. The insight into the role of gifted individuals in the body found in Eph. 4. The exhortation in 1 Peter 5 to those who shepherd God's flock.

But surely the entire book of 2 Corinthians is critical in understanding not only the role of the leader, but how the leader is to minister in order to call out the very best in God's people. And how the leader who is in touch with the nature of New Covenant ministry is not to relate to a congregation he or she is called to build up, and not tear down.

GALATIANS 1–2
The Gospel

EXPOSITION _____

Galatians is a brief, powerful defense of the Gospel as Paul preached it. His opponents are Judaizers—men of Jewish background who insisted that to be Christian a person must not only accept Christ but must also accept circumcision and keep the Law of Moses. Almost as quickly as evangelists spread Christianity among the Gentiles in the wider Roman Empire, Judaizers visited the young churches and introduced their corrupting teachings.

This letter was probably written to churches that Paul founded in the Roman province of Galatia on his first missionary journey—cities like Pisidian Antioch, Iconium, Derbe, and Lystra (Acts 13–14). Although the time of writing is much debated, it seems most likely Paul wrote shortly after the Jerusalem council reported in Acts 15. In this brief book Paul answers three sets of charges raised by the Judaizers: (1) that Paul was not one of the original apostles and does not reflect the view of those who knew Jesus personally, chapters 1–2; (2) that Paul's Gospel is not the true Gospel, because he sets aside God's Law, chapters 3–4; (3) that Paul's Gospel must lead to loose living, for law is man's bulwark against immorality, chapters 5–6. None of these charges is true. And Paul's response, particularly to the latter two charges, constitutes with Romans Scripture's clearest exposition of the nature of the Good News of salvation in Jesus Christ.

Paul answers the first set of charges by telling the story of his life and relationship with the 12 Apostles. After a brief greeting (1:1-5) and expression of shock that the Galatian churches have been so quickly swayed to a "different" Gospel (1:6-10), Paul begins his defense. The major point he makes is that rather than be dependent on any human authority, he received both his call and his Gospel directly from the Lord (1:11-24). Paul then goes on to tell of his relationship with the other apostles. In the private meetings that were held alongside the public sessions of the Jerusalem council, the apostles set before the Twelve "the Gospel that I preach among the Gentiles." The Twelve neither added to nor subtracted from Paul's teaching, but acknowledged his commission to spearhead the work among the Gentiles, even as Peter was commissioned to spearhead work among the Jews (2:1-10).

Then Paul tells a story that dramatically illustrates his claim to have equal standing with the Jerusalem Twelve. When Peter himself, visiting Antioch, failed to "act in line with the truth of the Gospel," Paul confronted Peter "in front of them all." And he confronted Peter on the very issue the Judaizers were raising: forcing Gentiles to follow Jewish customs, as though salvation were a matter of observing the Law! (2:11-15) Quoting his own words, Paul affirms Christianity's central truth and greatest wonder: "I have been crucified with Christ and I no longer live, but Christ lives in me." Any retreat to Law from this great reality in effect sets aside the grace of God, and makes Christ's death meaningless (2:16-21).

Paul's letter is more brief than we might wish. And certainly these first two chapters leave many biographical questions unanswered. Just when did Paul go up to Jerusalem? What happened in these private meetings with the Twelve? What did Peter say and do after Paul confronted him? But Paul is not concerned here with answering our questions. He has a clear purpose in mind, and he sticks to it. Paul *does* preach the true Gospel. He received it from God, it was affirmed by the Twelve and the Jerusalem elders. And rather than being subordinate to the Twelve, he is their equal in apostleship, as shown in his bold confrontation of Peter when he erred.

WORD STUDIES

Paul, an apostle—sent not *from* men nor *by* man, but by Jesus Christ and God the Father (1:1). The first preposition, *apo*, indicates source, while the second, *dia*, denotes means or agency. Paul's very first words then strongly assert his apostleship, and in effect affirm: The risen Lord and God the Father directly commissioned me as an apostle, and I neither owe this position to men, nor am I dependent on men for the content of my Gospel.

It's true that Paul was unique, as was the particular apostleship he alone shared with the Twelve. But Paul's confidence that it was God who called and equipped him is something each of us can share, as long as we are conscious of walking in God's will.

Who gave Himself for our sins to *rescue us from the present evil age* (1:4). "Rescue" here is *exeletai*. Paul does not mean we are to be taken out of society, but instead are to be rescued from corruption by its evil influence. The present age—suggesting that it is passing and temporary—is characterized by *poneros*, "evil." This word, in contrast to the more philosophical *kakos*, denotes wickedness and active rebellion against God's will. *Poneros* is used to describe the character of Satan (Eph. 6:12) and also the character of a humanity that is not only lost but also depraved (Matt. 15:18-19; Mark 7:21-23).

Consider then how great a salvation Jesus offers. Jesus rescues us, not only from the corrupting influence of the society in which we live, but also from the *poneros* within! How wrong the Judaizers' charge that the Gospel Paul preaches leads to immorality. Moral transformation depends on Christ's work within us, not on laws and rules that anyone may erect outside.

Christian Experience: Past, Present, Future.

■ Past: "As for you, you were dead in your transgressions and sins, in which you used to live when you followed the ways of this world and of the ruler of the kingdom of the air, the spirit who is now at work in those who are disobedient. All of us also lived among them at one time, gratifying the cravings of our sinful nature and following its desires and thoughts. Like the rest, we were by nature objects of wrath" (Eph. 2:1-3).

■ Present: "But because of His great love for us, God, who is rich in mercy, made us alive with Christ even when we were dead in transgressions—it is by grace you have been saved. And God raised us up with Christ and seated us with Him in the heavenly realms in Christ Jesus" (Eph. 2:4-6).

■ Future: "In order that in the coming ages He might show the incomparable riches of His grace, expressed in His kindness to us in Christ Jesus" (Eph. 2:7).

And are turning to a *different gospel*— which is really no gospel at all (1:6-7). In

Greek there are two words frequently translated "different" or "another": *allos,* which indicates another of the same kind, and *heteros,* which indicates another which is essentially different from that to which it is compared. The Galatians, in listening to the Judaizers' version of the Gospel, were deserting the truth for a system which is "no gospel at all." What Paul is dealing with in this letter is *essential truth* — truth which is central to the meaning of Christ's death for us, and central to our rescue from the power of evil.

Confusion about the true nature of the Gospel is one of the most serious threats to modern Christianity as well. Any "gospel" which mixes works with faith, or which confuses freedom with license, is a powerless gospel which will disappoint those who accept it.

Even if we or an angel from heaven should preach a gospel other than the one we preached to you, let him be eternally condemned (1:8). The word is *anathema.* The word is generally translated "accursed," and is closely related to the OT concept of dedicating captured cities or loot to destruction. Thus the word indicates turning an object or person over to God for a judgment which will surely bring its or his condemnation.

This most forceful expression is used not only once, but twice (1:9), indicating the intensity of Paul's reaction to the "gospel" preaching by the Judaizers. This is no minor issue. Again we see that confusion about the essential character of the Gospel is utterly destructive, and must be cleared up at all costs.

How important then this little book must be. If anyone is confused, Galatians will surely define the issues and make the true Gospel plain.

Am I now trying to win the approval of men, or of God? Or am I trying to *please men?* (1:10) This verse serves as a transition. Paul has been accused of shading the truth, of making the Gospel "easy" and thus more pleasing to his hearers. In essence, the Judaizers argued that *they* were interested in God's approval — as proven by their insistence that the Galatians must keep a Law from which Paul lightly released them. Paul's present words to the Galatians, blunt and some might think even harsh, make it clear that he is not

"now" (a touch of irony) tilting toward trying to please men rather than God. As Paul goes on to write about his background, it will become more and more clear that Paul has always been committed to pleasing the Lord, and fulfilling his apostolic commission.

I did not *receive it* from any man, nor was I *taught* it; rather, I received it by *revelation* from Jesus Christ (1:12). The issue raised here is one of how truth is transmitted.

"Receive" is *parelabon,* which Paul may use here in a technical sense. If so, it describes the way in which the rabbis carefully memorized the traditional interpretations and expansions of the Law by earlier sages — the "traditions of the elders" which Jesus had so strongly criticized (Matt. 15:1-9). In the Hellenistic world, antiquity was widely viewed as a test of a religion's validity. Many Romans, while ridiculing some Jewish practices, still viewed Judaism as a valid religion because it could trace its roots back for two millenniums. Undoubtedly one of the Judaizers' bases for the claims would be that the rules they insisted Paul's converts follow had been "receive[d]" in a valid historical process.

"Taught" is *edidachthen,* which looks at present rather than historic transmission. The Galatians had been taught the Gospel by Paul. A human agent was involved. But, Paul is about to claim, no human agent was involved in transmitting the Gospel to him!

"Revelation" is *apokalupsis,* the most significant of the Bible's terms for God's communication with human beings. In the first century this word had little religious significance. Thus, as frequently happened, the early Christians took a religiously neutral term and filled it with unique theological meaning. While this term has several different applications, the defining phrase is *Iesou Christou.* The name is in the genitive case, and may be either objective or subjective. Thus the text may read "revelation *of* Jesus Christ," indicating He was the object of the revelation, or, if a subjective genitive, "revelation *from* Jesus Christ." The NIV correctly chooses "from," for the issue Paul raises here is the source of the Gospel being preached.

Paul puts the issue very plainly. These Judaizers may appeal to the traditions of their people. They may claim to have learned their

Gospel from the teachers in the Jerusalem church. But the Apostle Paul received *his* Gospel from Jesus Himself!

How early was this recognized by the churches, and how early were Paul's writings accorded the status of Scripture—that same status enjoyed by the canonical books of the OT? Testimony not only comes from the earliest writings of the church fathers, but from the Apostle Peter as well! For, writing in 2 Peter 3:15-16, that apostle mentions the writings of "our dear brother Paul" and speaks of those who distort his letters "as they do the other Scriptures, to their own destruction."

I was *advancing in Judaism* beyond many Jews of my own age and was extremely zealous for the traditions of my fathers (1:14). All Jewish boys were expected to learn basic Bible passages and memorize chapters from the books of Moses. Thus knowledge of the Bible was widespread. But this was only the first stage of study, and was followed by other levels. We can calculate the proportion who advanced by the following proverb, reflecting a later age but still significant, quoted in the introduction to the *Steinsaltz Edition* of the Talmud: "A thousand enter to study the Bible, a hundred to study Mishna, ten to study Gemara, and one to teach."

In the first century, for Paul to study with Gamaliel, founder of one of the two major first-century interpretive schools in Judaism, indicates that he truly was "advancing in Judaism beyond many Jews of [his] own age"!

How important was this within Judaism? We can sense something of what underlies this claim by noting the extreme hierarchial structure of Judaism in Palestine during the Talmudic period (A.D. 200–500), which had its roots in the earlier Mishnaic period (30 B.C.–A.D. 200). Only a select minority of students were ordained as rabbis and joined the scholarly aristocracy. Even within this small group a rigid hierarchy existed. For instance, when meeting as a Sanhedrin of 23 or 71, the scholars sat in a fixed order, defined by place within the hierarchy. It was common for such scholars to sign their correspondence indicating their place in the row: "the third," or "the sixth."

Paul, a "Hebrew of Hebrews; in regard to the law, a Pharisee; as for zeal, persecuting the church; as for legalistic righteousness, fault-less" (Phil. 3:5-6), would surely have reached the highest rank within Judaism—a point he does not hesitate to make in refuting the Judaizers who are corrupting the Galatian churches.

But when God, who set me apart *from birth* and called me by His grace (1:15). The Greek word is *koilias,* "from the womb." The thought is that God set Paul apart *before his birth.* The same thought is expressed even more clearly in Jer. 1:5, where God says, "Before I formed you in the womb I knew you, before you were born I set you apart; I appointed you as a prophet to the nations."

Paul undoubtedly draws a *conscious* parallel here between his call and that of Jeremiah. Not only did the Gospel he preaches come from God, but he himself was chosen by God for the mission of preaching it!

In our day there is another vital implication to this passage. Despite the medical evidence that a fetus is a totally independent being, with its own unique chromosomal identity, pro-abortionists continue to cast abortion as the right of a woman to do what she chooses "with her own body." But from the womb, long before birth, God recognized Jeremiah and Paul as unique individuals, and He chose each of them for a special mission in life.

How many potential servants of God are today brutally torn from the womb, their rights as independent human persons violated, for what are all too often totally selfish reasons? God knows the unborn as individuals, as persons who will one day have names that acknowledge their independent existence. We need to pray that one day soon the unborn will be similarly recognized by our courts and our people.

Fourteen years later *I went up again* to Jerusalem (2:1). Scholars disagree about the chronology of the visit. It seems most likely that Paul is referring to the trip he took to Jerusalem to pose the issue he discusses in this letter before the Jerusalem council.

While he does not mention the public meetings described in Acts 15, there were undoubtedly private meetings with the church's leaders, as described here. The fact that the decision of the council is not quoted is also understandable, in view of the fact that the concessions the council asked for might well be misinterpreted by Galatians at this point in time.

443

Paul does not want to introduce an extraneous issue, but to keep the focus on the central issue: both Christian experience and salvation are matters of faith and not law.

Assuming that the visit mentioned here is the same as Paul's trip for the Jerusalem council, we can give the following general outline of his life and ministry:

A.D. 34	Conversion
A.D. 36	To Tarsus for "silent years"
A.D. 46	To Antioch
A.D. 47-48	First missionary journey
A.D. 48	Jerusalem council (Acts 15)
A.D. 49	Writes Galatians
A.D. 50-51	Second missionary journey
A.D. 53	Third missionary journey begins
A.D. 59	Journey to Rome
A.D. 64	Martyrdom

Again, the chronology is uncertain. But chronology is not the issue here. What Paul is intent on showing is that, although his Gospel is in no way dependent on the other apostles, they have heard and affirmed his teaching, and have affirmed his divine commission as apostle to the Gentiles.

Yet not even Titus, who was with me, was compelled to be *circumcised,* even though he was a Greek (2:3). Circumcision was the physical sign of inclusion within the Abrahamic Covenant, and predated the Law (Gen. 17:14). The Judaizers insisted that con-verts to Christ first be circumcised, and then keep the Mosaic Law. In essence their teaching was "Believe in Jesus, become a Jew, and keep Moses' Law, and you will be saved." Paul will deal with the Law in the next chapter. Here he refutes the notion that the Jerusalem leaders teach that Gentile converts must be circumcised. The proof? They didn't even require that of Titus—one of Paul's missionary team! How then could they demand that the Galatians and other Gentile Christians be circumcised?

It is important to see in this paragraph the three groups that Paul defines. There is Paul and Barnabas and Titus, representing the Freedom Party. There are "false brothers" (2:4) who infiltrated the movement with the intent of making "us slaves," the Slavery Party. And there is also "them" (2:5), defined in 2:9 as "James, Peter and John, those reputed to be pillars."

What happened was simply that, when the dispute was aired, the apostles and pillars of the Jerusalem church sided totally with the Apostle Paul.

This does not prove Paul to be right or wrong, for the very simple reason that Paul's commission is from God, not Jerusalem. But that experience cuts the ground out from under the Judaizers in Jerusalem. The leaders of the Jerusalem church have never agreed with them, but from the first great explosion of the Gospel in the Gentile world have sided with Paul!

THE PASSAGE IN DEPTH

Paul Opposes Peter (2:11-21).
Background. It is difficult for us to understand the intense pressure that would have been placed on Peter and Barnabas by the Jewish Christians from Jerusalem. The fact that they were "from James" (2:11) suggests they can hardly be classed with the "false brothers" (2:4) who opposed Paul at the time of the Jerusalem council.

It is more likely that these representatives "from James" were a committee much like the one headed by Peter himself which had gone to check on the reports of a great revival in Samaria (Acts 8:14). There is no indication in the text that this delegation *opposed* the revival in Antioch. Instead we see that these men were members of the "circumcision group"—observant Jews who before their conversion would have been among the *haber,* those dedicated to keep the law in every traditional detail, in contrast to the *am haares,* the general Jewish population which was observant, but not as scrupulously so.

There is no doubt that persons with this background would have been unwilling to eat with Gentile converts to Christ, not necessarily because they doubted their conversion, but because they were Gentiles.

This is driven home by rulings in the Mishnah which deal with the relationships between a Jewish *haber* and an *am haares.* For instance, according to *Tohorot 7:4* if the wife of a *haber* should leave the wife of an *am haares* grinding grain in her house, the house is unclean—if the sound of the millstones ceased. On the other hand if the sound did not cease, the house is only unclean as far as the *am haares* can reach out and touch.

Of course, if there are two *am haares* grinding and the wife of the *haber* leaves them alone, the house is unclean even if the sound does not stop for, according to Rabbi Meir, "one grinds, and one snoops about."

Given this mind-set, we can see why members of this party would sternly disapprove of any Jewish believer who dared to actually eat with a Gentile Christian. Without necessarily saying a word, but with shocked and condemning looks, such persons would exert tremendous pressure on Jewish Christians in the basically Gentile church in Antioch.

And of course this is exactly what did happen. Under that pressure Peter, the other Jews, and "even Barnabas" (2:13) were led astray and so withdrew from their Gentile brothers and sisters in Christ.

In one sense this was petty and irrelevant. In another sense it was vitally important, an act that symbolically distorted the Gospel message itself, and disrupted the unity of the body of Christ, potentially introducing those same hierarchical distinctions which divided contemporary Judaism into often hostile and competing parties. Perhaps even more serious, this symbolic act, so far out of "line with the truth of the Gospel" (2:14), would surely lead in time to a denial of justification by faith alone, and transmute Christianity from a Gospel of grace to a Gospel of works, even as the OT had been transmuted in Judaism from a religion of faith-based righteousness into a religion falsely promising a righteousness supposedly achieved by works of the Law.

It is no wonder then that Paul, who saw the issue clearly, openly opposed Peter, and argued that believers must *live* as well as *believe* a justification that comes by faith alone.

Interpretation. Paul's brief account of the incident covers only the highlights of his confrontation of Peter.

■ Peter "separate[s] himself" from Gentile Christians (2:11-13).

■ Paul affirms justification by faith (2:14-16).

■ Paul defends justification by faith against the charge of antinomianism (2:17-21).

Peter "Separate[s] Himself" from Gentile Christians.

The Background, above, helps us understand the peer pressures that led not only Peter but also other Jewish Christians in Antioch to "draw back" (2:12) from Gentile believers.

Paul's observation that Peter was "afraid" (*phoboumenos*) of them and his charge that Peter was hypocritical in withdrawing from the Gentile brothers and sisters has upset Catholic theologians. Some have supposed that Paul is talking about a different Peter, or that the confrontation was "staged" to drive home Gospel truth to the believers in Antioch. After all, hadn't God Himself shown Peter that the Gentiles were now "made clean" (Acts 10:15), and hadn't Peter boldly affirmed this truth in the face of severe criticism after entering the house of Cornelius? (Acts 10–11) It just doesn't seem possible that Peter, the Prince of Apostles and the acknowledged leader of the Twelve, would surrender that position!

Actually, something very different is involved. The tense of the verb tells us that before the men came from James, Peter used to eat *regularly* with the Gentile believers. It was one thing for the early Jewish church to agree that Gentile believers were free from obligation to Moses' Law. It was another point entirely for the early church to agree that *Jewish* believers were no longer obligated to keep Moses' Law.

It was this issue that Peter, the "apostle to the Jews" (Gal. 2:8), was unready to face. In private he was willing to eat with Gentiles, thus violating the contemporary understanding of Jewish Law. But when *haber* from Jerusalem came to Antioch, he drew back "afraid."

It is not necessary to put the worst face on Peter's fear and suppose he was simply unwilling to face criticism. We can credit him with the best of motives: concern that the rumor might spread that he was *not* observant of the Law, he would lose all credibility in the Jewish community, and that thus his future ministry would be hurt. Whatever Peter's motives, his withdrawal led the other Jews in the Antioch church, and even Barnabas, to follow his example and to separate themselves from the Gentile believers.

Whatever Peter's motives, his actions created a division in the body of Christ, and not only that, were not in "line with the truth of the Gospel" (2:14).

445

The incident serves as an important reminder. If Peter was so vulnerable to fear of what others might think and do that he acted hypocritically, you and I certainly are vulnerable too. How vital it is that we test our every action, to make sure that we are "acting in line with the truth of the Gospel." We must practice truth as well as believe and proclaim it.

Verse 13 makes it clear that Peter's action had an impact on the Gentile Christians in Antioch as well as on the Jewish believers there. While Peter was living "like a Gentile" (2:14) his example made it clear to the predominantly Gentile church that the Jewish Law was irrelevant to life in Christ. Later, when he separated himself from them he reversed his moral influence, and in effect "force[d]" (*anankazo*, "insisted, compelled") the Gentiles to follow Jewish customs. His actions not only implied that Jewish ways were spiritually superior, but also that the unity of the church could be preserved only if the Gentiles adopted them too.

Paul Affirms Justification by Faith (2:14-16). Paul now gives a brief summary of what he said when confronting Peter "in front of them all." Peter and the other Jews know very well that no one is "justified by observing the Law, but by faith in Jesus Christ" (2:16).

This truth is affirmed no less than three times. "We, too, have put our faith in Christ Jesus that we may be justified by faith in Christ and not by observing the Law." And again, "By observing the Law no one will be justified."

There are three key terms here: justified, faith, and law. "Justified" is a legal term, which in the language of the courts meant to be declared innocent, or found not guilty. Its opposite is to be found guilty, or to be condemned.

"Faith" is a religious term which in its Christian sense means to "put one's trust in." Fully convinced of the trustworthiness of God, a person believes "into" (*eis*) Christ, committing himself or herself to the Lord and relying fully on Jesus for salvation.

"Law" here is primarily the Law of Moses, but more than that is Israel's *understanding* of that Law, which assumed that by keeping it a person could justify himself before God.

Paul now reminds Peter and the other Jews that they *know* a man is not, and cannot be, justified by observing the Law, while a person can and will be justified by faith in Jesus

Christ. What is more, and here again Peter is speaking to the believing Jews who joined Peter in his hypocrisy, "we, too, have put our faith in Christ Jesus."

To retreat to observing Jewish customs in this context of a Gentile church is bound to confuse the truth of justification by faith alone, and imply that keeping Moses' Law is somehow essential to Christianity.

How important is the principle of justification by faith alone? So important that Peter himself had to be confronted when his actions even *implied* that Law had something to do with salvation.

Paul is not anti-Law. In Rom. 7 he makes it very clear that the Law, in its role as a revealer of God's character, is holy, righteous, and good. But Law has nothing to do with justification, and we must be careful to do nothing that implies it does!

Paul Defends Justification by Faith against the Charge of Antinomianism. It is uncertain whether Paul continues to quote the gist of his words with Peter, or at this point closes his quote and addresses his words to the Galatians. It is clear, however, that Paul has shifted from attack to defense, and that what he defends against is the charge—heard over and over again through the centuries of our era—that justification by faith must lead to loose living.

Commentators have advanced a number of interpretations of v. 17. The verse might be taken to argue that even if Christians should sin after being justified by faith, this does not make Christ a promoter of sins. But this seems irrelevant to Paul's theme in Galatians and the argument he has developed. The best interpretation keeps the focus on the issue of justification by faith rather than Law, and the assumption of the Judaizers that without the Law those who seek justification by faith *would* sin, and thus the doctrine makes Christ a promoter of sin. Paul's answer to the charge is that the legalist completely misunderstands the implications of justification!

In v. 18 Paul points out that a person justified by faith, who abandons the faith principle to return to Law as a way of relating to God, *would* "prove that I am a lawbreaker." After all, as Paul will write later in Romans, the person who tries to keep the Law is destined to fail and thus demonstrates himself to be a sinner

(Rom. 7:21-24). Only the one who lives "according to the Spirit" (8:4) is able to fulfill the "righteous requirements of the Law," and thus break out of the web sin has woven around every human being.

With this understood Paul presents the positive dynamic which enables the believer and the believer alone to live a righteous life. It is not Law, but Christ that frees us. The person who believes in Christ is able to live for God, because the believer is crucified with Christ, and now Christ lives in him or her. Faith not only justifies, faith vivifies, so that "the life I live in the body, I live by faith in the Son of God." The Christian *must* live by faith, for a return to Law as a basis either for justification or as an aid to Christian living sets aside and would make irrelevant God's grace.

Concluding his summary Paul makes a final, compelling point. If righteousness could be achieved through the Law, Christ's death would have been unnecessary. The very fact that Jesus had to die makes it clear that law is powerless to save or sustain.

As Galatians develops we will see that Paul's report of this incident is central to his argument. Paul is not telling the story just to support his claim of apostolic independence and equality with the Twelve. The story serves as a transition into the heart of Paul's defense of his Gospel against the Judaizers.

Peter's retreat to Jewish customs clouded basic Gospel truths that must be affirmed. And Paul will go on to affirm them powerfully. In chapters 3 and 4 Paul will explore in depth the nature, and the inadequacies, of Mosaic Law as a way of salvation and as an aid to Christian living. In chapters 5 and 6 Paul will confront directly the charge that freedom from the Law must result in sin. As Paul will show, the issue is not the Law, but the sin nature. The solution is not to enforce any law, but to "live by the Spirit" (5:16). Only a change within, and only that change worked by God in the hearts of those who believe in Jesus, can free a person to live a righteous life.

Application. For most of us, the most immediate application of Paul's story of his confrontation with Peter is personal. We are reminded of how vulnerable each of us is to the pressures imposed by our peers, and to fears about how others will react if we behave in ways they do not expect.

But there is perhaps an even greater lesson here. Peter acted apparently without being aware that his behavior was in effect denying truths that he himself believed. Paul, however, saw the implications of Peter's actions, and the distortion of the Gospel implicit in what he was doing.

GALATIANS 3–4
The Good News of Faith

EXPOSITION

Paul has briefly told of a time when he challenged the Apostle Peter for failure to "act in line with the truth of the Gospel" (2:14). Under pressure from a newly arrived group of Christian Jews from Jerusalem, Peter hypocritically adopted a lifestyle governed by Mosaic Law. His action was bound to send the wrong message about the role of the Law in Christianity.

Paul reports how he confronted Peter, provides a capsule statement of his position, and uses this as a springboard into a careful analysis of the role and limitations of the Law.

Paul begins this analysis by an expression of his frustration. As J.B. Phillips' translation puts it, Paul bursts out with "O you dear idiots of Galatia!" It seems incomprehensible to Paul that the Galatians have so quickly abandoned reliance on the Spirit who has done so much for them, in favor of attempting to reach spiritual goals by human effort (3:1-5). Paul draws attention to Abraham, and reminds his readers that the principle of faith too is rooted in the OT (3:6-9). And that same OT makes it clear that Law brings a curse, not a blessing. Christ assumed that curse for us, that He might make the blessings given Abraham available to the Gentiles through the same avenue that Abraham received them—God's promise, which is appropriated by faith.

The Judaizers will be quick to react against this understanding of the OT. And so Paul directs their attention to severe limitations that Scripture itself ascribes to Moses' Law. While "faith" is a basic and persisting principle, Law, according to the OT itself, is temporary (3:19-20). What's more, Law is limited in its ability, for Law has no capacity to give spiritual life (3:21-22). Of course, Law was never *intended* to save. Law was nothing more than a household slave, keeping track of God's underage children (3:23-24), until Christ could come, and faith would induct all who believe into full sonship in the household of God. As God's *pedagogue*, commissioned to lead His people to Christ, Law's mission was ended when Christ came. Thus Law is no longer in force, and its authority is nullified as far as the believer is concerned (3:25–4:7).

There is more at stake here than a point of theology. In turning back to Law, the Galatian Christians risk being trapped in a way of life that has already robbed them of their joy and delayed the formation of Christ within them (4:8-20). To drive home his point Paul returns to the OT, and using an established principle of rabbinic interpretation, applies a story found there to the present situation. God Himself told Abraham to send Ishmael, the offspring of the slave Hagar, away from the tents inhabited by Abraham, Sarah, and Isaac, who was born to that couple "as the result of [God's] promise." The story illustrates Paul's point: there is no way for Old and New Covenants to coexist in the same house. As God's New Covenant people, the Galatians must "get rid of the slave woman and her son (Law)" and live only with and by promise (4:21-31).

Paul's argument is complex, but complete. Experience, example, the explicit teachings of Scripture, and even allegorical interpretation of sacred history, all testify to the fact that Law has no contribution to make to Christian life. Even more, Law is detrimental, and the entire way of thinking shaped by Law must be gotten rid of if we are to experience joy and grow in our faith.

WORD STUDIES

You foolish Galatians! (3:1). Paul does not use *moros*, which indicates a person who is morally or spiritually deficient. The word here is *anoetos*, which indicates a person who fails to exercise his powers of perception.

The Christian believer has the capacity to successfully evaluate the issues of life in the world. The problem is that too often we don't bother to think things through to their logical end.

Life Versus Law

GALATIANS 3–5

Why isn't the Law for us now?

I. The Law is opposed to life (3:1-18). This is demonstrated by:
  A. Experience: How did you first receive and live your spiritual life? (3:1-5)
  B. Example: How did Old Testament saints receive spiritual life? (3:6-9)
  C. Exposition: What does the Scripture teach about how life is to be received? (3:10-18)
II. The Law's role (3:19–4:7) is shown in Scripture to be severely limited:
  A. In extent: It is temporary (3:19-20).
  B. In ability: It cannot make alive (3:21-22).
  C. In function: It was a custodian (3:23-24).
  D. In force: It is nullified today (3:25–4:8).
    1. Because we are "in Christ"
    2. Because we are now sons
III. The Law is an inferior way that now leads to tragic results for the believer (4:8–5:12). Law leads to:
  A. Dissatisfaction: It robs us of joy (4:8-19).
  B. Bondage: It robs us of freedom (4:20–5:1).
  C. Powerlessness: It turns us from expectant faith to hopeless effort (5:2-12).

Did you receive the Spirit by observing the law, or by believing what you heard? Are you so foolish? After beginning with the Spirit, are you not trying to *attain your goal* by human effort? (3:3) The word is *epiteleisthe*, "to bring to completion," used here in the sense of "reach the end," to contrast with "beginning."

Paul is surprised at the spiritual ineptness of the Galatians because the issue is so clear-cut. The choice lies between the Spirit and the flesh ("human effort" here is *sarx*, "flesh"), between faith and works.

It shouldn't take much thought to realize

that no human effort brings us spiritual life. Why in the world would anyone suppose then that human effort, even effort guided by God's Law, would having anything to do with living the Christian life?

Does God give you His Spirit and work miracles among you because you observe the Law, or because you *believe what you heard?* (3:5) The Greek reads *ex akoes pisteos*, where the preposition *ex* indicates a direct causal relationship. Use of the present participle for both "give" and "work miracles" indicates that Paul continues the contrast of "beginning" and "attaining" introduced in v. 3. Both salvation and vital Christian experience are functions, not of observing the Law, but of "believ[ing] what you heard."

Neither *akoes* or *pisteos* are independent here. Each is an element in an ongoing process—a process of hearing which is linked to and carried out in faith.

Understand, then, that those who believe are *children of Abraham* (3:7). One of the strongest arguments advanced by the Judaizers is reflected in words of the Pharisees reported in John 9:29: "We know that God spoke to Moses."

Starting from this certainty, the Judaizers argued that since the Law was given to Moses by God, the Law *must* be binding on all those who seek to please God or relate to Him.

Paul, however, calls on the Galatians to "consider Abraham" (3:6). Moses is honored as the lawgiver, but Abraham is honored as father of God's people. Abraham, a pagan when God spoke to him and when he first believed, is the man God started with. Thus Paul points to Abraham rather than Moses as the valid prototype to whom his pagan converts are to look.

What then was Abraham's experience? Long before Law was introduced, Abraham believed God, and his faith was credited to him as righteousness. But in what sense are those who believe *children* of Abraham? "Children" is *huioi*, "sons." In addition to identifying male offspring, *huios* can mean "descendant" and, figuratively, a spiritual relationship. Here Paul says that a spiritual link exists between those who believe today and Abraham.

So those who have faith are *blessed* along

with Abraham, the man of faith (3:9). The present indicative passive participle here emphasizes that they "are being blessed." Paul's point is that those with faith *share the blessing* that Abraham enjoyed. What blessing does Paul have in mind? The text makes it clear that Paul focuses our attention on the blessing of justification by faith apart from works. This is further supported by the use of the singular, "the blessing," *he eulogia,* in 3:14.

We enjoy many spiritual blessings in Christ. But the ultimate blessing is that of a salvation that is freely granted to all who believe.

All who *rely on* observing the law are under a curse (3:10). The text says *ex ergon nomou,* "of works of law." Paul contrasts two different approaches to salvation: one seeks God's blessing by faith; the other claims God's blessing on the basis of performing that which the Law requires.

Paul points out that everyone who takes this second approach to religion receives the opposite of Abraham's blessing—God's curse.

The curse is unavoidable for the Law demands *perfect* obedience (3:10). That is, we must approach Law as a whole, not as an aggregate of separate and distinct rules. Just as a person who uses a pin to puncture a balloon breaks the whole balloon, so a person who breaks any statute has broken the whole Law.

Given the unitary nature of the Law, it is impossible for the person who seeks to relate to God through Law to avoid being under the curse as a lawbreaker.

Christ *redeemed* us from the curse of the law by becoming a curse for us (3:13). The word is *exagorazo,* to buy out of slavery by the payment of a price.

But how does Paul arrive at the relationship between the curse on those who violate the Law and Christ's death? By using a basic principle of rabbinic interpretation, called *gezera savah,* "verbal analogy." In its simplest form this principle means that if the same word or phrase appears in different passages in the Torah, inferences may be drawn on the basis of the verbal similarity rather than on conceptual correspondence.

Here Paul has quoted two verses from Deut. (21:23; 27:26), each of which begins with a word based on the same verbal stem ("curse"). Paul uses "verbal analogy" to link

the verses, and shows that in Christ's death on the cross, to which a curse was attached, He took on Himself the curse pronounced on those who failed to perfectly keep God's Law.

Why did He do this? So that the whole matter of relationship with God might be shifted from an issue of Law to one of faith; from an issue of obedience to God's commands, to a faith response to God's promise.

What a stark and utter contrast Paul develops between two approaches to salvation. On the one side Paul sets Law, reliance on works, and God's curse. On the other side he sets promise, hearing with faith, and God's blessing (see also 3:18).

What Paul is telling the Galatians is that none of these principles is interchangeable. The Galatians have been listening to men who have linked Law and reliance on works with blessing, and have failed to realize that what must always accompany Law and reliance on works is not blessing, but cursing.

The promises were spoken to Abraham and to his Seed. The Scripture does not say "and to seeds," meaning many people, but "and to your *Seed,*" meaning one Person, who is Christ (3:16). In both Hebrew and Greek "seed" frequently functions as a collective noun. Why then does Paul say God's intent in Genesis is singular, and that the reference actually is to Christ?

If the original verse were taken as "offspring," some might argue that the promise was fulfilled in Abraham and the patriarchs, prior to the giving of the Law. But now Paul shows that the promise is made to Christ, and thus spans the ages *before* and *after* the Law, and by implication operated as well *during* the era of the Law.

And there is even more. Since Abraham's true Seed is Christ, the Son of God, and those who believe are brought into union with Christ by faith—then we become sons of God through Him, and Abraham's spiritual offspring, inheriting with Christ the blessings promised Him by God.

The law was put into effect through angels by a mediator. A mediator, however, *does not represent just one party;* but God is one (3:19-20). Galatians 3:20 has been called the "most obscure" verse in the Bible, and something between 250 and 300 different interpretations of it have been advanced. The main point, however, seems clear. Law was a multiparty instrument, and thus the contract involved depended on the performance of both parties.

On the other hand, the promise made to Abraham and his Seed was a unique covenant: it had the character of an oath or promise made by God, and did not depend in any way on Abraham's or the Seed's performance.

Is the law, therefore, opposed to the promises of God? (3:21) Paul has shown that Law, reliance on works, and God's curse is a distinctly different system than that of promise, hearing with faith, and God's blessing.

It might seem that these two systems, none of whose elements can be interchanged, are opposed to each other. Here the Greek has *kata,* "against." The two systems are utterly different, but are they incompatible? Could the same God have possibly been the source of both Law and promise?

Paul's response is that they are *not* incompatible. Law has no ability to impart life (3:21), so Law clearly does not function in the same realm governed by promise, which *does* have the capacity to impart life. How then is Law compatible with promise?

Paul argues that all humanity is a "prisoner of sin" (3:22), and then goes on to say that "before . . . faith came" we were "held prisoners by the law" (3:23). The word *synkleio,* "to lock up together," to "be shut in on all sides," occurs in each verse. But the phrase "held prisoner by the law" is *upo nomon ephrouroumetha,* "guarded by the law." The question here is whether the guard is set to *protect* those who are shut up by sin, as some argue the Greek word *phroureo* implies, or to

hold them prisoners, as the NIV has it.

The answer is suggested by Paul's reference to a *paidagogos,* a "boy leader," often a family slave, who was put in charge of a child until he reached the age of responsibility. How galling it was for a child, eager to go out and play, to be "guarded" by his pedagogue and forced into a pattern of behavior which the boy himself often hated. The image here is not one of the Law gradually educating a child toward recognition of Christ, but of the Law forcing the child into patterns of behavior that were contrary to his nature, and thus demonstrated again and again the reality of sin (4:1).

What the Law does then is constantly remind the sinner that he *is* "a prisoner of sin." The Law shouts again and again that there is no escape — until one turns away from self-effort to faith, and suddenly realizes a freedom that releases him from the supervision of the Law.

But when the time had fully come, God sent His Son, born of a woman, born under the law, to redeem those under the law, that we might receive the *full rights of sons* (4:4-5). The Greek word is *huiothesian,* which generally means adoption. See the discussion of this image in *The Passage in Depth* (below).

What has happened to all your joy? (4:15) The word here is *markarismos,* which means blessedness or happiness. The usual word for "joy" in the NT is *chairo.*

Paul's point is an important one. The subjective experience of those who are objectively blessed (3:9-14) should be one of overflowing happiness. The Galatians have abandoned faith as the wellspring of Christian experience, and as a result have lost their sense of joy.

THE PASSAGE IN DEPTH

Sons of God (3:26–4:7).

Background. In this passage Paul uses two images to convey the tremendous impact of establishing a relationship with God on the basis of faith. The first of these images is that of an heir coming of age. And the second is that of a person being adopted into a Roman family.

Coming of age in the first century was ex-

tremely significant in both Jewish and Hellenistic societies. In Judaism a boy passed from childhood to adulthood about the age of 12. In the Hellenistic world an adolescent became an adult about the age of 18. In both cultures rites of passage underlined the importance of the event.

In Judaism a boy became a "son of the Law." Prior to that time he was responsible to his parents, and they were responsible for him. After his *bar mitzvah* the boy accepted full responsibility for his own actions, and pledged himself to be obedient to God's Law.

In the Hellenistic world the minor came of age during the festival of *Apatouria*. Here too the event symbolized entry into full adult responsibilities, and passed from the charge of his parents to that of the state.

It was Roman custom to mark the passage with a sacred family festival, the *Liberalia*. This took place on March 17, and included formal adoption of the child by the father. The ceremony marked the father's acknowledgment of the child as both son and heir, and the father had the prerogative to set the age of a son's *Liberalia*.

What is important in all these cultures is that as a child, as Paul emphasizes in our passage, even a son had no more *legal standing* than did a slave. What is more, the child had no freedom and no right to make independent decisions. But *afterward* the adult child enjoyed both responsibility and freedom of choice.

It might be argued that Paul is thinking only of the coming of age ceremony in developing his argument. After all, "adoption" was part of the Roman ceremony. At the same time, it is helpful to us to understand something of adoption from outside the family as well as from within. For each adoption provided the new "son" with the same wonderful rights!

In Roman law, when a person was adopted his old relationships were severed, and past debts and obligations were canceled. The adoptee was transferred to the authority of the father of his new family. On the one hand the father was now considered owner of the adoptee's possessions, and gained the right to guide his new son's behavior. In addition, since the father became liable for the adoptee's actions, the father also had a right to discipline him.

On the other hand, the son became an heir and thus in one sense a legal owner of all the father possessed. While he owed his adopted father obedience, the father accepted responsibility for his new son, and was committed to support and maintain him.

What a wonderful image this is for Paul to use. It reminded the believers in Galatia that as God's sons now, they owed no allegiance to their old masters. All they had and were belonged to God, but in return all God's resources became theirs! God is fully committed to all who become "sons of God" through faith in Jesus Christ, and in return we commit ourselves to live as His children, so that in all we do we might reflect credit on Him.

Interpretation. In Gal. 3:7 Paul introduced the thought that through faith believers become the spiritual offspring of Abraham. Now he goes further. Through faith in Jesus Christ all believers become sons of God!

The term "son" here does not imply gender, but is used in a distinct *legal* sense. In the first-century world "sons" enjoyed a well-defined and vital legal standing that was *not* conveyed simply by biological relationship. This was, of course, familiar ground to Paul's first readers. It is not familiar ground to us, for our legal system has no close parallel.

Understanding the first-century background, however, does permit us to outline the passage so that Paul's major points are emphasized.

- Sonship Defines Our Identity (3:26-29).

- Sonship Establishes Our Rights (4:1-5).

- Sonship Explains Our Access (4:6-7).

Sonship Defines Our Identity (3:26-29). When Paul writes that "there is neither Jew nor Greek, slave nor free, male nor female, for you are all one in Christ Jesus" (3:28), he is not suggesting that these important first-century social distinctions no longer exist. Certainly Jewish Christians, the majority of whom continued observing Jewish practice, were distinct from Gentiles in many ways. And there was no way that conversion wiped out the social chasm that yawned between the slave, who was essentially without human rights in the Roman Empire, and the free man, who did have rights. Similarly, especially in view of 1 Cor. 11, Paul is not suggesting that all social distinctions between male and female are to be wiped out.

Paul is saying that no longer can any of these social distinctions be used to establish the *identity of Christians.* There are Jewish Christians and Christian slaves. There are Christian men and Christian women. But these are now merely descriptive terms, none of which is relevant when we ask the central question, "What is a Christian?" Paul asserts now that the one thing which sums up the identity of *all* Christians is the relationship each enjoys with God the Father. Through Jesus Christ "you are all sons of God" (3:26).

As noted, "sons" indicates something more important in the Roman world than biological descent. "Sons" is a legal term, and denotes the standing enjoyed by an individual after he or she has been formally acknowledged by a natural or adoptive father.

In the context of Paul's argument this argument caps his insistence that Christians are not subject to Moses' Law. He has gone to great lengths to show the inadequacies and limits of the Law, and to prove that the Law was never intended by God to fulfill the function ascribed to it by the Judaizers who were troubling the Galatians. Here he reminds his readers that Law, never more than a household slave charged with making an underage child do what the head of the household requires, has no authority at all over one who has been formally recognized by the Father as His son and heir.

Established in our new identity as sons, our old relationship with Law has come to a complete and final end, and Law no longer has any authority over us.

Sonship Establishes Our Rights (4:1-5).
Paul drives home his point by clearly stating the central legal point: Even a child who is potentially heir to his father's estate has no more legal standing than a slave until he is formally adopted as his father's son.

Now Paul abandons the image of the pedagogue to speak of guardians (*epitropos*) and trustees (*oikonomos*), words which are used synonymously in first-century documents. While the pedagogue watched the child and governed his behavior, guardians and trustees watched over his inheritance. It was *they* who made the day-to-day fiscal decisions and managed the estate. And the child, even though the whole estate belonged to him, had no right to make any decision in regard to it. Again the analogy is powerful. The minor child under guardians and trustees has as little control over himself and his inheritance as the human being without Christ has over "the basic principles of the world" (4:3) under which the unsaved lived. Even though God created man to live in fellowship with Him

and to be heirs of creation, when sin entered, mankind lost all control over himself and his inheritance, surrendering it up to the "basic principles" which operate in our lost and twisted world.

But all this changed when God sent His Son to redeem those who were "under the law." It would be a mistake to read this as "under Moses' Law," and limit Paul's focus to the Hebrew race. The Gentile as well as the Jew is "under the law," both in the sense of being responsible to a divine revelation of moral principles (Rom. 2), and in the sense of approaching relationship with God as if it were a matter of works. God sent His Son to redeem all of us, with the goal that through Christ we might "receive the full rights of sons" (4:5).

Christ then is the key to a dramatic *change in legal status* for all who believe. The believer becomes a son of God, and as such his or her inheritance passes out of the control of trustees and managers, and the believer is given direct access to it. Suddenly we are free to live as responsible individuals; free to make responsible choices; and perhaps most important, we now have access to the vast resources of God, which are our inheritance in Jesus Christ.

Sonship Explains Our Access (4:6-7).
The Judaizers who promoted their false "gospel" in Galatia claimed that the Law was a resource intended by God to aid righteous living. Paul now reminds the Galatians of that access to their inheritance in Christ which is the true resource for holy living. Because we are now sons, God has sent "the Spirit of His Son" (4:6) into our hearts. The Spirit provided immediate and direct access *to* God, and He Himself serves as the conduit through which enablement flows to us *from* God.

Much has been made of the use of "Abba," a diminutive that suggests intimacy and might be rendered "Daddy." However, even more should be made of the phrase, "Abba, Father." A servant might possibly address his master as *Pater* (Father), as a term of respect. But only a child of the master would dare address Him familiarly, as "Abba, Father."

Paul's point is thus driven home decisively. Through faith we have a relationship with God which could never have been established by reliance on works. A master might determine his relationship with a slave on the basis of the slave's works. But a son has a relationship with his father that is established by the father's choice, defined by law, and assures the son both of access to his father and of his father's full support.

Application. How could anyone who truly understands the relationship between father and son ever imagine that God wants to relate to us through law, or that the blessings that are ours to be earned rather than received by faith?

Truly the Galatians were foolish. And so, all too often, are we.

Hagar and Sarah (4:21-31)
Background. The Bible seldom interprets the stories of the patriarchs allegorically. But in giving a figurative interpretation of the story of Ishmael and Isaac (4:24), Paul does not depart from established Jewish *midrash* (interpretation). It is not at all uncommon for the sages

to see in the stories of the OT direct application to a present issue.

For instance, *Genesis Rabbah 47 XLVII:V* (about A.D. 400-450) looks at the same incident Paul examines, and sees the Jewish people in Isaac and, as established in other passages, sees Christian Rome in Ishmael. (The discussion is reproduced in the box below.)

The point the midrash makes is that while Jews (Isaac) and Christians (Ishmael) trace their origins to Abraham, it is Israel which possesses enduring covenant promises, while the Christian ascendancy is temporary and will pass. This point is made subtly, in a typical rabbinic play on words, for the root letters in "princes" are also the root letters in "vapor" (2C), while the root letters in "tribe" are the same root letters as are found in "rod" or "staff" (2D).

Paul, of course, sees other implications in the story. Paul says that Sarah and Hagar represent the New and Old Covenants. The de-

---

GENESIS RABBAH ON GENESIS 16

1. A. "God said, 'No, but Sarah your wife [shall bear you a son, and you shall call his name Isaac. I will establish My covenant with him as an everlasting covenant for his descendants after him]. As for Ishmael, I have heard you. Behold, I will bless him and make him fruitful and multiply him exceedingly. He shall be the father of twelve princes, and I will make him a great nation.' "
   B. R. Yohanan in the name of R. Joshua b. Hananiah, "In this case the son of the servant-woman might learn from what was said concerning the son of the mistress of the household:
   C. " 'Behold, I will bless him' refers to Isaac.
   D. " '. . . and make him fruitful' refers to Isaac.
   E. " '. . . and multiply him exceedingly' refers to Isaac.
   F. " '. . . As for Ishmael, I have informed you' through the angel."
   G. R. Abba bar Kahana in the name of R. Birai: "Here the son of the mistress of the household might learn from the son of the handmaiden:
   H. " 'Behold, I will bless him' refers to Ishmael.
   I. " '. . . and make him fruitful' refers to Ishmael.
   J. " '. . . and multiply him exceedingly' refers to Ishmael.
   K. "And by an argument *a fortiori*: 'But I will establish my covenant with Isaac.' "

2. A. Said R. Isaac, "It is written, 'All these are the twelve tribes of Israel' (Gen. 49:28). These were the descendants of the mistress.
   B. "But did Ishmael not establish twelve?
   C. "The reference to those twelve is to princes, in line with the following verse: 'As princes and wind' " (Prov. 25:14).
   D. "But as to these tribes [of Isaac], they are in line with this verse: 'Sworn are the tribes of the word, selah' " (Hab. 3:9).

tails that support this view are that while Hagar gave birth in a normal way, Sarah's womb was dead, and the birth came as a result of promise.

Similarly Law, the Old Covenant, rests on the efforts of the natural man to please God, while the New Covenant executed in Christ rests entirely on promise.

With this established, Paul looks back at the story and asks what happened to the son of the slave woman? The answer is that the son of the slave woman persecuted the son of the free (i.e., law was and is hostile to promise), and God commanded Abraham to "get rid of" (4:30) the slave woman and her son, "for the slave woman's son will never share in the inheritance with the free woman's son."

Law and promise cannot coexist.

Therefore the Galatians must get rid of law, and rely completely on God's promise, heard and responded to with faith.

GALATIANS 5–6
The Good News of Freedom

EXPOSITION

Paul was deeply concerned at reports that the churches of Galatia had been influenced by Judaizers, men claiming Jerusalem's authority to correct Paul's "distortion" of the Gospel message. The Gospel according to the Judaizers was: Believe in Jesus, be circumcised, and keep Moses' Law. In essence they insisted that to be a Christian a person must convert to Judaism, accepting Jewish customs, and keep Jewish law in order to have a relationship with the Jewish Messiah. They attacked Paul's "easy" Gospel by disputing his authority, by emphasizing that Law was an historic revelation, and by charging that Paul's lawless Gospel promoted loose living.

As we come to Gal. 5, Paul has already responded to the first two of these charges. He received his Gospel by direct revelation, and while his teaching and commission as apostle to the Gentiles has been affirmed by the leaders in Jerusalem, the message he preaches requires no human being's stamp of approval (chaps. 1–2). As for the Judaizers' insistence on observing the Law, this shows a complete misunderstanding of God's OT revelation. Law has no capacity to bring life, is associated with curse rather than blessing, and was always intended to be temporary (chap. 3). What has now happened is that, through faith in Christ, God formally grants believers the "full rights of sons" (4:5). This frees us from our past slavery to sin and to Law. Thus, as God told Abraham to "get rid of" Hagar and Ishmael, who symbolize human effort and who must not inherit with Isaac who symbolizes promise, believers must "get rid of" Law if they are to live a successful Christian life (chap. 4).

But how important is this new freedom we enjoy as formally recognized "sons" of God? Paul says Christians must stand firm and claim the "freedom [for which] Christ has set us free" (5:1). The person who accepts circumcision, which here symbolizes reliance on the flesh, derives no present benefit from his relationship with Jesus. Only faith opens the channel through which God's empowering grace flows to us (5:1-12).

Again Paul reminds his readers that they have been called to freedom. But Christian freedom is not a license to indulge the flesh, and thus wallow in a life of sin (5:13-21). What Christian freedom really involves is freedom *from* sin, a freedom that releases the Holy Spirit to produce in our personalities those qualities which we all acknowledge characterize goodness and holiness.

When these qualities exist and grow in us, Law is irrelevant. The issue for the Christian, then, is not struggling to keep Law, but rather living by the Spirit (5:22-26).

Paul closes with several thoughts loosely related to his theme. Although not governed by Mosaic Law, we are still responsible to and for each other (6:1-6). One must never suppose that release from the Law indicates that God shrugs His shoulders at sin. Every person reaps what he sows, and the harvest of those who sin is destruction, while the harvest of those who sow to please the Spirit is a full experience of eternal life (6:7-10).

Finally Paul sums up his message. The Judaizers are urging a way of life which has nothing to do with Christianity. One's cultural heritage, whether Jew or Gentile, is irrelevant, for all that counts is that in Christ we are God's new creation. The power of the Gospel hinges, not on what any man does in an effort to win God's approval, but on what God has done in and for us through Jesus Christ (6:11-18).

WORD STUDIES

It is for *freedom* that Christ has *set us free* (5:1). This has been called Galatians' key verse. It sums up what has gone before, and orients us to the rest of Paul's brief letter.

In Judaism taking up the yoke of the Law was considered the heart of religion. But Paul has shown that promise, not Law, is central in God's revelation, and that Christ died to free us from both sin and the Law that defined it.

But what *is* the "freedom" for which Christ has set us free? The Greek word is *eleutheria,* which in secular society generally indicated a person who was his own master. Not so in Scripture, where Christian freedom is understood against the background of humankind's bondage to sin and, later, to Law. Paul is saying that Jesus Christ has released us from everything that hindered the living of a righteous life, in order that we might fulfill our intended destiny as children of God, called to reflect the character of our Heavenly Father.

To bring our experience in harmony with our standing as the sons of God, we must stand firm in our freedom, and not weigh ourselves down by voluntarily accepting again a "yoke of slavery" (5:1).

Christian Freedom
Galatians 5:1 and 5:13 describe Christians as those who are called to freedom. These passages help us better understand the freedom we are to claim and to enjoy.

■ John 8:31-36. A person who lives by Jesus' words comes to "know the truth, and the truth will set you free." Here "truth" is God's revelation of reality, a revelation that enables us to cut through competing notions of what life is about. Unsaved human beings live in a world of illusion, never able to see the truth, never able to tell what is really right and good, what is helpful and what harms. The person who is guided by God's Word makes good choices, and avoids the perils that stalk those who stumble about in the dark.

So "freedom" is release from the spiritual blindness and obstinacy that are inherent in fallen humanity's tragic condition. Faith's ability to hear and respond to Jesus' words enables us to know by experience a reality which others can never glimpse, much less grasp. This is freedom indeed.

■ **Romans 6:15-23.** Paul develops a theme Jesus introduced in John 8:34, "Everyone who sins is a slave to sin." Freedom is release from the hold sin has on us—the ability to place our every member at God's disposal in the service of righteousness.

Far from independence, Christian freedom involves *a change of masters*. We are released from the dominion of sin, and transferred to a realm where God's will is supreme.

The passage emphasizes the end result of the service rendered to each master. Those who serve sin experience shame and death. Those who serve righteousness become holy.

Romans 8:2-11. Romans 8 explains how a person with no ability to keep the Law can experience freedom. The answer is the Holy Spirit, who breathes life into and energizes believers who turn themselves over to His control despite their mortality.

Here too freedom is the divinely aided ability to do what is right and good.

■ **Galatians 5:1-26.** Paul has made it clear that Law is neither a means of salvation nor a path to spiritual achievement. Christ has freed us from the Law, granting those who believe the "full rights of sons." But what is the nature of this freedom? It is freedom to "serve one another in love" (5:13). This is freedom: to so relate to the Holy Spirit that, rather than have our attitudes and actions shaped by the promptings of our sin nature, we and our way of life are transformed by God from within.

Here Christian freedom is freedom to live such good lives that "law" becomes totally irrelevant, for nothing in our way of life is proscribed by law.

Summary. Clearly Christian freedom is not independence, or the right to do anything we want. Christian freedom is a dependence on the Spirit which releases us from our bondage to the power of indwelling sin, and the exercise of our freedom is to live a disciplined life, both doing—and being—good.

If you let yourselves be circumcised, Christ will be of *no value to you at all* (5:2). Circumcision symbolized identification with God's OT people, descent from Abraham and the patriarchs, and participation in the Covenant. It meant "being Jewish," and being subject to the Law God gave to the Chosen People. Here Paul uses "circumcision" to indicate acceptance of the position upon which the Judaizers insisted: a Christian must voluntarily choose to live under the Old Covenant after his conversion.

But why does Paul say that Christ "will be of no value to" (literally, "will not profit") the Christian who voluntarily adopts Law as a way of relating to God? Paul is not speaking here of salvation, but of Christian living. It is as if a person has been given a lamp, but is given the choice of two electric sockets into which to plug it. One socket is energized, but no power flows through the other. A person who plugs into the dead socket receives no benefit, no matter how good his lamp may be.

As long as the believer seeks power for Christian living by plugging into Law, knowing Christ makes no difference in his daily life.

You who are trying to be *justified* by law have been alienated from Christ; you have fallen away from grace (5:4). The NIV text obscures Paul's point by giving *dikaiousthe* its usual rendering of "justified." The reason why this rendering obscures is that we tend to take "justification" in its legal sense, as that judicial declaration by God that those who believe in Jesus are innocent. We thus assume that "justification" is always to be read as equivalent to "salvation," and so conclude that this verse is talking about salvation. But this is simply is not the case!

Kittel's *Theological Dictionary of the NT* (Vol. II, p. 216) rejects the forensic meaning in Gal. 5:4, and gives an alternative which reflects a use of *dikaioo* common in ordinary first-century speech. It renders the Greek phrase, "you who would be righteous by law." That is, Paul is not talking about justification/salvation, but about the fact that some in Galatia had adopted the Judaizers' point of view and attempted to achieve *experiential righteousness* by means of the Law.

Paul has not shifted his focus from Christian experience to salvation, but continues to explain why Law is of no value to the believer. The reason is that in trying to "be righteous by law" (Kittel), the believer has "been alienated" (*katargeo,* "cuts himself off") from that sphere in which Christ operates, a sphere characterized not by Law but by grace.

Paul's "fall from grace" then implies no loss of a believer's salvation. It simply describes a Christian's experiential disconnection from the source of power for righteous living.

In Christ Jesus neither circumcision nor uncircumcision has any value. The only thing that counts is *faith expressing itself through love* (5:6). Paul sums up his argument. Neither Jew nor Gentile has any advantage. What makes the difference in Christian experience is not Law, but "faith expressing itself in love."

Why this phrase? Perhaps in part to refute the Judaizers' claim that faith can express itself through Law. But even more, perhaps, to focus our attention on the primary evidence of the work of the Spirit in our hearts.

Soon Paul will tell us that the "fruit of the Spirit" is love (5:22). Certainly here we have an echo of Paul's teaching in 1 Cor. 13. There he says that true spirituality is not indicated by possession of any particular spiritual gift, but rather by that love which is so beautifully portrayed in vv. 4-7 of that great chapter.

Here Paul says the same thing. The Christian does not demonstrate his faith by the rigor with which he keeps Moses' Law, but by the love he or she shows in every relationship, with God and with others.

You, my brothers, were called to be free. But do not use your freedom *to indulge* the sinful nature; rather, serve one another in love (5:13). The word translated "to indulge" is *aphorme*. The word originally indicated a base of operations from which to launch an expedition. Paul is saying: affirm your freedom in Christ, but don't let the flesh use that freedom as a base from which to operate. Rightly understood, freedom is a base from which to launch out upon a life of love and service.

The person who says, "I'm saved now, so I can do what I want" has misunderstood Christian freedom, and uses freedom to justify actions which he or she knows are wrong. The person who says, "I'm saved now, so I can dedicate myself to loving God and others" is the only one who has rightly understood the nature of his or her freedom in Christ.

The entire law is summed up in a single command: "Love your neighbor as yourself" (5:14). This theme is developed in Rom. 13:8-10. Paul's point in each passage is that love and Law are both related to righteousness. They are not in conflict in this respect. In fact, the statutes of OT Law were in effect operational definitions of love: they described how a person who loved God and others would—not just should!—behave.

The problem with Law, of course, is that while it describes the loving thing to do in some detail, it has no capacity to create loving human beings. Yet Law's entire thrust was summed up in the command: Love your neighbor as yourself. What a tremendous advantage we have now that Law is no longer an issue. Now, through Christ, we are freed to really love others. When we do love, we find ourselves living that righteous life which love as well as Law requires.

So I say, *live by the Spirit,* and you will not gratify the desires of the sinful nature (5:16). The original has "walk (*peripateite*) by the Spirit." The phrase reflects a common Hebrew idiom, in which "walk" means "conduct one's life."

The Judaizers have told the Galatians to conduct their lives by looking to Law. But Paul has argued that Law has no role in the Christian life. The person who seeks to "be righteous by law" (5:4) falls from grace, and cuts himself off from Christ as a resource for righteous living.

In Rom. 7:4-6 Paul goes even further, and says that the sinful nature (*sarx,* the flesh) is actually energized (stimulated) by the Law.

What then is the Christian to do? The Christian is to conduct his or her life by looking not to the Law, but to the Spirit of God. For, Paul promises, the person who does look to (rely on) the Spirit "will not gratify the desires of the sinful nature [*sarx,* the flesh]."

The acts of the *sinful nature* are obvious (5:19). Again the word is *sarx,* used theologically to portray fallen human nature. Paul's point is that the Law wasn't really needed to define what everyone recognizes as harmful, hateful, and wrong. No one should ever suppose that, law or no law, persons who "live like this" (5:21) will have any part in ["inherit"] the kingdom of God.

Paul then goes on to describe the fruit the

Spirit produces, and points out that Law has no value to the believer, for Law merely defines what is *wrong*. No one would ever think of passing a law against the loving ways of those who live by the Spirit.

Our challenge, again, is not to try to keep the Law, but to remain sensitive and responsive to the Holy Spirit of God (5:25).

Those who live like this will not inherit the *kingdom of God* (5:21). The "kingdom of God" is that realm in which God's power and authority operate without hindrance. Christians who live by the Spirit enjoy the "full right of sons" to participate now in their ultimate inheritance.

The participle *prassontes* emphasizes habitual behavior. Those whose lifestyle is dominated by the flesh have no access to the blessings and power that are available to us in Christ.

Carry each other's burdens and in this way you will fulfill the *law of Christ* (6:2). The Law of Moses is characterized by rules and regulations. The rabbis in fact counted some 614 "do's" and "don'ts." Paul has reduced these to one: love (5:14), which is what he means in 6:2 by the "law of Christ."

Each one should *carry his own load* (6:5). At first glance this seems in direct conflict with what Paul has said in 6:2, "Carry each other's burdens." However, the first readers of Paul's letter would have understood perfectly. The Greek word translated "burdens" in Gal. 6:2 is *bare*, an unusually heavy load, while Gal. 6:5 has *phortion*, a load which is appropriate to the ship designed to carry it or the soldier's normal pack.

Love calls us to help others in distress. But protecting others from the normal pain or responsibilities of life is not love.

The one who sows to please his sinful nature, from that nature will *reap destruction;* the one who sows to please the Spirit, from the Spirit will *reap eternal life* (6:8). The image of the "harvest" in Scripture generally has an eschatological reference. But Paul is not warning his readers that if they fail to live to please the Spirit they will be lost. His point is that however we look at them, flesh and Spirit are opposing principles.

Earlier Paul wrote flesh and Spirit "are in conflict with each other" in their *essential nature* (5:17). Paul then showed that flesh and Spirit contrast with each other *in the lifestyle they generate* (5:19-23). Now Paul completes his analysis by showing that the flesh and spirit *yield contrasting harvests*.

In view of all this, why then would any Christian want to live a fleshly life? How much better to do good, confident that "at the proper time we will reap a harvest if we do not give up" (6:9).

THE PASSAGE IN DEPTH

Galatians, a Study in Contrasts.

Background. The earliest Christians were Jews who recognized Jesus as the Messiah. Deeply committed to a lifestyle governed by the Law, they saw no conflict between their commitment to Jesus and their observant way of life. Even the discovery that Gentiles responded to the Gospel message, and that those who believed were given the Holy Spirit, seemed irrelevant to the first Jewish Christians' continuing commitment to a way of life governed by Law and tradition.

A problem did arise, however, when some in the early church argued that Gentile Christians should also submit to circumcision and be required to keep the Law of Moses. On the surface, this point of view seemed reasonable. After all, God Himself did give Israel her Law. How could one who acknowledged God fail to submit to that Law that God Himself revealed? Even more, what alternative existed? Wouldn't Gentile Christians look to their own traditional moral and cultural values if they were not taught to look for guidance to God's historic revelation to Israel?

In the normal course of events antithesis between any two positions tends to be resolved by synthesis. The tension between two poles is gradually reduced by building bridges between them, and something new emerges. But Galatians takes a different approach. Paul seeks no synthesis which Jew and Gentile can both comfortably accept. Instead he argues that an essential conflict exists. No synthesis can be achieved, but an absolute distinction must be maintained—between Law and Promise, between slavery and freedom, between living by the flesh and living by the Spirit.

In Galatians Paul develops his theme by rejecting synthesis completely, and by more and more sharply describing antitheses. A most helpful way of looking at Galatians and understanding the power of this brief book, is to

Galatians 1:1–2:21

Paul's Gospel	Another Gospel
★ freedom	★ slavery
	★ requires all to "follow Jewish customs"
★ faith	★ observing the Law
★ justified	★ no one justified
★ crucified with Christ	
★ Christ lives in me	
★ live by faith	
★ affirms grace	★ sets aside grace
★ brings righteousness	★ cannot bring righteousness

trace the introduction and development of the various antitheses Paul sets out for us to consider.

Galatians 3:1–5:12

Faith	Observing the Law
★ receive the Spirit	
★ attain goal	
★ justified (declared righteous by God)	★ no one justified
★ makes us sons of Abraham	
★ provides us with Abraham's blessings	★ brings a curse
★ related to promise	★ related to works
★ depends on God alone	★ depends on human performance
★ imparts life	★ cannot impart life
★ agency by which we become sons of God with full rights	
★ freedom	★ slavery
★ expresses itself through love	★ expresses itself through works
	★ denies grace
	★ cuts off from Christ as a source of power

Interpretation. As this brief letter develops, Paul, in more and more detail, defines the elements of Christian life and experience, not by synthesis, but by antithesis. Here is an outline of how these contrasts are developed.

The Gospel Paul preached among the Gentiles was received by direct revelation from God. Both Paul's commission from God and the content of the Gospel he proclaims were affirmed by the leaders of the Jerusalem church.

The Apostle Paul's Gospel is one of salvation by faith alone, with no contribution at all made by observing the Law. The Gospel establishes a union between Jesus Christ and the believer, so that the Christian participates in Christ's crucifixion and also shares in Christ's new life, so that Christ lives in him or her. This Christ-life is lived by faith, and because it has nothing to do with observing the Law serves to display the wondrous grace and mercy of our great God.

Paul's Gospel is a Gospel of faith, with no room for reliance on observing the Law. Salvation is by faith, and the goal of the new life imparted by the Spirit is as much a matter of faith as receiving the Spirit in the first place. The Law requires human effort to be achieved. But no one can be justified by observing the Law. All the Law brings is slavery and a curse.

On the other hand, faith relies solely on the promise of God. One who exercises simple faith in God's promise is given life, and with life the Holy Spirit. Through faith in God's promise we become not only Abraham's sons, but also are adopted into God's family, with the full rights of sons to both intimacy with the Father and all the access to the abundant blessings that are part of our inheritance.

What is more, our formal recognition as God's sons brings with it freedom from the Law, which before Christ served as a pedagogue, in charge of our every action, granting us no more freedom than was enjoyed by a slave.

That freedom is important, for the person who steps back under Law obligates himself to obey the whole Law, and in taking on this obligation rejects grace, and cuts himself off from Christ as a source of daily enablement.

Galatians 5

The Spirit	The sinful nature
★ *Love*	★ *Law*
★ *In conflict with the sinful nature*	★ *In conflict with the Spirit*
★ *If led by Spirit, not under Law*	★ *Law is "against" its acts*
★ *The Spirit produces good and righteous fruit*	★ *The sinful nature produces acts of obvious sin*

Paul has denied that "Law" has any place in Christian experience. But isn't this a denial of the importance of righteousness? Paul now shows that in ruling out Law he has *not* opened the door to license. The reason is that the principle of love underlies all the Law's righteous requirements. And the Spirit of God produces love in the heart of the believer!

The antithesis that counts is the one that exists not between Law and faith, but between the flesh and the Spirit. For as soon as a person seeks to relate to God through Law, he must necessarily turn to his own resources, and this will activate the flesh. In contrast, a person who seeks to relate to God by faith turns to the Spirit, and the Spirit creates love in his heart, which spills over into every attitude and action which is right and good.

Application. In describing these sets of opposites Paul reminds us of vital and wonderful truths. What we cannot do God can and will do, in us as well as for us. We will never become the truly good persons we yearn to be by trying to obey God's Law. But we will become progressively more and more righteous as we trust God's Spirit to guide and enable us.

Life by the Spirit (5:13-26).

Background. The contrast Paul develops between the fruit produced by the Spirit and the acts of the flesh is the culmination of his teaching in Galatians. God did not free us from Law that we might behave lawlessly, but so that by relying completely on the Spirit, He might be unleashed to transform us from within. This is especially clear when we compare the two lists in this brief passage: the list of the acts of the flesh, and the list of the fruit of the Spirit.

The first list contains four distinct categories of acts of the flesh. Each is a behavior, an overt act rather than a character trait. The categories Paul's list falls into are:

■ *Sex sins:* immorality, impurity, debauchery (sensuality).

■ *Religious sins:* idolatry, witchcraft.

■ *Interpersonal sins:* hatred, discord, jealousy, fits of rage, selfish ambition, dissensions, factions, envy.

■ *Intemperate sins:* drunkenness, orgies.

In contrast, the list Paul gives of the fruit produced by the Spirit includes no specific acts or behaviors at all! Everything on this list is internal, a trait of character.

Why doesn't Paul make the two lists strictly parallel and contrast godly actions with sinful actions, or contrast godly character traits with sinful character traits?

Perhaps the best explanation is that Law, which the Judaizers praised, deals *only* with externals in its approach to righteousness. It relates to what a person *does,* not what a person *is.* On the other hand, God approaches righteousness in a totally different way. At best what we do is only a reflection of what we are. The way to produce righteousness is to make a change *within,* so that a person is a truly loving and good person. When this kind of transformation is effected, one's actions will be truly good and loving too.

The Judaizers of the first century, and those who would today mix Law and grace, seem unable to grasp this most basic of truths.

Ephesians is one of several letters that Paul wrote while imprisoned in Rome (Acts 28:30). Some believe Ephesians was originally an encyclical letter, intended for circulation among all the churches, rather than directed to the Ephesians. The question seems irrelevant, however. Like Paul's other collected letters, this epistle is for *us*. And, clearly, this marvelous letter is different from 1 and 2 Cor.'s responses to specific problems that emerge in one congregation. Rather, Ephesians shares an exalted vision of Christ's church. In Ephesians we discover our identity as the body of Christ, as a temple under construction by the Holy Spirit, and as the family of God. Here we see the marvels of God's work of grace, as He takes twisted sinners who are antagonistic toward Him, saves and unites them to Jesus as Head, and then creates from this raw material a "new man." A new man who not only serves God gladly, but experiences a growing transformation, becoming "mature, attaining to the whole measure of the fullness of Christ" (4:13). Throughout, Ephesians exalts Christ, for it is His cosmic role and purposes which are being fulfilled in the world today through His body here on earth, that church of which you and I are integral parts.

After a very brief introduction (1:1-2), Paul begins his letter with one of the clearest and most powerful trinitarian passages in the Bible (1:3-14). We have been blessed with "every spiritual blessing in Christ" as the direct result of the work of the Trinity. The Father chose us before the creation of the world and poured out His grace upon us in Christ (1:3-7). The Son redeemed us, purchasing the forgiveness of our sins, choosing us in Him to "be for the praise of His glory" (1:8-12). And, being included in Christ, the Spirit serves as God's seal and guarantee of our ultimate redemption (1:13-14). The church, then, is no afterthought, but central to God's eternal plan. The church is no shanty, but a construction that has involved the dedicated effort of each Person of the Godhead.

Having penned this, Paul is moved to a wonder that spills over in prayer and praise, ending in a doxology to the resurrected Christ. Our Lord is not only exalted above every cosmic power, but in a special way is "head over everything" for the church. And, wonder of wonders, we, His body, are "the fullness of Him that fills everything in every way" (1:15-22).

This initial revelation of the importance of the church to God is particularly stunning when we consider, as Paul now asks us to do, the inferior raw material which

God used in its construction. God took beings who were spiritually "dead in your transgressions and sins," deserving of nothing but God's wrath. And, because He loved us anyway, God "made us alive with Christ." He then raised us up "and seated us with Him in the heavenly realms." And none of this was in response to any good work we might have done: it was all of grace, all an expression of the unmerited favor of a God who has re-created us in Christ. Only now, as His workmanship, can we perform the good works, and now they will reflect to *His* credit and glorify Him (2:1-10).

This, then, is the church. It is a new creation, a new creation in which old distinctions between "Jew" and "Gentile" are irrelevant. For we all come to God through Christ, whose death destroyed the old barrier of Law and commandments by making peace for all humanity with God. Suddenly all that counts is Christ, for in Him all humankind is united in "one new man." United at last in Christ, a diverse and often hostile humanity at last has a single foundation on which to stand. On this foundation, joined together by and in the Lord, we "are being built together to become a dwelling in which God lives by His Spirit" (2:11-22).

All too often we tend to think of salvation in individualistic terms: He is saved and going to heaven. She is saved and committed to the Lord. I am saved as well. Ephesians calls us to look beyond ourselves as individuals, and catch God's vision of the church as Christ's body; as a people united in Christ, called together to those good works that glorify the One who created us; called to be together a dwelling in which God lives by His Spirit.

WORD STUDIES

Praise be to God . . . who has blessed us in the *heavenly realms* with *every spiritual blessing* in Christ (1:3). Don't suppose that Paul intends to contrast spiritual with material blessings. Paul is not suggesting that the material is irrelevant. Rather he reminds us that the truly significant blessings granted us by God are spiritual, communicated to us by the Holy Spirit.

Why the phrase "in heavenly realms"? Because Christ, exalted in heaven over all principalities and powers, is the One who has secured them for us, and guarantees them to us.

For He *chose us* in Him before the creation of the world to be holy and blameless in His sight (1:4). The verb here is *exelexato,* "to choose out." This verb is usually used in the Septuagint to translate verbs which speak of God's choice of Israel as His covenant people.

One of the greatest of Greek scholars, Bishop Lightfoot, states that the use of this word implies three ideas: the stem of the word (*leg*), "telling over"; the preposition in the compound (*ek*), to choose some out of a group while not choosing others; and the middle voice God's "taking to (for) Himself."

The implication that God "before the creation of the world" chose some *for salvation* has troubled many, who view any form of predestination as a threat to God's "fairness." Such folk suggest that God's "choice" is not for salvation at all, and note that the verse asserts He chose "us" (those who have believed) "to be holy and blameless." According to this view, the divine choice is limited to fulfilling God's purpose in those who trust in Christ.

See The Passage in Depth for a discussion of God's choice, foreknowledge, and predestination in Eph. 1:1-14.

In Him we have *redemption* through His blood, the forgiveness of sins, in accordance with the riches of God's grace (1:7). This is one of the great theological terms used in the NT to describe the meaning of Christ's death. That death was necessary, for Christ's blood is the price of redemption; only thus could God offer sinners forgiveness and freedom.

Redemption. The concept is introduced in the OT, with various shades of meaning expressed by three different Hebrew terms. Implicit in each term is the conviction that human beings are helpless, captive of external or internal forces they cannot overcome without the intervention of a third party. Redemption, the solution, is:

■ *Padah,* a commercial term that indicates a transfer of ownership though payment or some equivalent. This is the word used in Deut. 15:15 of God's Exodus deliverance of Israel from slavery in Egypt (Ps. 78:42-43). Of all the uses of this verb in the OT, only in Ps. 130:7-8 does its use suggest redemption from sin.

■ *Ga'al,* a relational term, means "to play the part of a kinsman" and act to relieve a relation who is in trouble or danger. The emphasis here lies on the necessity of a relationship existing between redeemed and redeemer. A close relationship was required to give the redeemer his right or to obligate him to act on the other's behalf. This word too is used of God's deliverance of Israel (Ex. 6:5-6).

■ *Koper* is usually translated "ransom." It is a form of the verb *kapar,* "to make atone-ment."

The OT records God's acts on behalf of Israel, and frequently interprets them using words which emphasize God's kinship with His Covenant people. Both love and duty moved God to deliver His people from enemies before whom they were utterly helpless. Whatever the price, God was willing to pay it to win His people's safety.

The NT has two words translated "redeem" or "redemption." They are to be understood within the framework established in the OT, rather than by their reference to their use in Hellenistic pagan culture.

■ *Lytroo,* means to "redeem or ransom," and focuses attention on both the release won and the means by which release is accomplished. This root is found only a few times in the NT epistles, in Titus 2:14, 1 Peter 1:18, Heb. 9:12. However, a stronger noun, *apolu-trosis,* translated "redemption," occurs in Eph. 1:7 and in eight additional NT passages. The application of these terms in the NT makes it clear that Jesus' blood was the price of redemption. It took Christ's death to release us from the "empty way of life" of the past that "we may serve the living God."

There is an interesting parallel here with Roman law. A person captured in war, and later ransomed by another Roman citizen, was obligated to his ransomer until the price had been repaid. You and I can never repay the Lord the price of our redemption. Thus we are eternally indebted to Him, and in gratitude we gladly surrender all we have and are into His hands.

■ *Agorazo,* "to purchase," is another word used to clarify the meaning of redemption. A compound, *exagorazo,* is an allusion to the slave market, and has been taken to imply not only the purchase of a slave, but a purchase intended to take the slave permanently off the market. Thus redemption is a purchase that takes us permanently *out of* our old state as slaves to sin, self, and Satan.

While the OT terms define the concept of redemption, it is the NT that applies this concept to personal salvation. Human beings are revealed as helpless, locked in sin's unbreakable grip. Only the blood of Christ can redeem, breaking sin's bonds and guaranteeing us a place in the family of our God.

In Him we have redemption through His blood, the forgiveness of sins, in accordance with the riches of God's grace (1:7). This same verse uses another of the great theological terms of the NT, "grace." The concept is closely related to that of redemption, for "grace" too operates against the background of human helplessness.

Grace. The Hebrew word closest to the developed NT concept is the verb *hanan,* "to be gracious, to be merciful," and the noun *hen,* "grace," "favor." The emphasis in each is on the compassionate response of one who is able to help another person in desperate need.

In the NT "grace" is *charis.* In ordinary speech and in the Gospels the verb indicates a favor or benefit bestowed, and also gratitude appropriate to what has been received. But *charis* is developed as a technical theological term in the epistles. Here it is used by Paul to communicate a truth lying at the heart of God's saving work in Christ. In fact, "grace" provides the perspective which enables us to sense the meaning in God's past and present acts.

For instance, in Rom. 3 Paul shows all are sinners, but then describes God's decisive act of setting Christ forth as a propitiating sacrifice that we might be forgiven. This, Paul says, is grace.

In Rom. 5:15-21 Paul portrays salvation as a gift coming to us through Jesus, that reverses the destructive impact of Adam's initial act of sin. This, Paul says, is grace.

In Eph. 2:1-11 Paul sums up the helpless condition of the human race. We are born dead in sins, following the ways of this world and Satan, gratifying the desires of our sin nature. Yet God reached down to us in our utter impotence to give us the gift of life. This, Paul says, is grace.

What is most wonderful of all is that at the source every gracious act lies in the character of God. He reaches out to us because of who He is, loving, compassionate, and merciful — and *despite* rather than *because of* who we are. Because grace is rooted in God's character we are freed from any fear that our sins will alienate Him from us. God approaches us with the promise of forgiveness, telling us that He loves and accepts us anyway, and inviting us to receive the gift He offers us so freely in Jesus Christ. And this, the Bible tells us, truly is grace.

Having believed, you were marked in Him with a *seal,* the promised Holy Spirit (1:13). "Seal" is the aorist passive of *sphragizo,* to seal. In the Hellenistic world a man's seal, a carved insignia pressed in wax, had legal significance. Stamped on possessions the seal indicated ownership and served as a ward against theft. On a document, the seal authenticated the message it contained, and symbolized the full authority of the person who sent it. Further, a sealed document could be opened only by the one to whom it was addressed.

Paul here portrays the Holy Spirit as God's seal, stamped on the heart of the believer. The Spirit marks us as God's own, and places us under His protection, guaranteeing that we can be delivered to God, the One who in Christ has destined us as His own.

The promised Holy Spirit, who is a *deposit guaranteeing* our inheritance until the redemption (1:13-14). The Holy Spirit is a promise which has been kept. He is with us now. Paul now uses an analogy to help us understand further the implications of the Spirit's presence within us.

God's spirit is an *arrabon.* The word is drawn from the world of commerce, and means a deposit made on goods, which serves as a guarantee that full payment will be made and the goods will be collected by the buyer.

God has purchased us in Christ to be His own precious possession. The Holy Spirit is with us as an *arrabon,* assuring us that at history's end God will surely collect us as His own.

Even more, this particular deposit guarantees us *our inheritance.* All those "spiritual blessings" of which 1:3 speaks will overflow to us in their fullest extent when we join Jesus in the heavenly realms.

That the eyes of your heart may be enlightened in order that you may know *the hope to which He has called you* (1:18). "Heart" is often used in Scripture in the sense of the "whole inner person"; the center of perception, emotion, and will. The "hope" Paul has in view here is not our future, ultimate salvation, but rather the "riches of His glorious inheritance in the saints" (1:18) and "His incomparably great power for us who believe" (1:19).

There is a question about the first phrase. Does Paul mean we are to appreciate how precious we are to God — and thus gain confidence, knowing the value God places on us? Or does Paul mean we are to appreciate the vast resources that are our inheritance now as children of God?

While either reading is possible, the second is more likely. We have hope today because we have received the Spirit. He is the seal and the guarantee that we belong to God. More, He is the One through whom we access God's riches, which are now *our* inheritance. When we understand the vast resources available to us, we face tomorrow as well as eternity with confidence and hope.

And His incomparably great power *for us who believe* (1:19). Paul is eager for us to grasp just what we can expect ("hope for") *now* because of our relationship with God's Spirit. The Spirit is the conduit of God's incomparably great power, which operates *eis hemas,* "for us." Paul's thought is that God's incomparable power is channeled *toward us,* to flow in us and through us.

Paul piles up synonyms to emphasize the

overwhelming nature of that divine power which had its fullest demonstration in the raising of Christ from the dead and His exultation over every competing authority in the universe. The words Paul used include *dynamis* (intrinsic capability), *energeia* (effective power in action), *kratos* (power exerted to control and overcome resistance), and *ischys* (the vital power inherent in life, but usually used of physical strength).

Too many Christians feel weak, and live as weaklings. They expect spiritual failure and so either are unwilling to try, or try halfheartedly. Paul prays that the eyes of our hearts will be opened, to realize that all the vast power of God is available to us now, channeled to us by the Holy Spirit.

We are to approach the challenges of life as victors, not as victims. For the power that flows to us is Christ's own power, and He is supreme over all.

God placed all things under His feet and appointed Him to be *Head over everything for the church,* which is His body (1:22). This one whom God has exalted "far above all rule and authority, power and dominion" (1:21) has been given to us as "Head over everything for the church." We have the power to overcome because the One who is our Head is supreme.

But what does the term "Head" suggest here? In the OT "head" is frequently used in an institutional sense, to indicate authority, as head (commander) of the army. But Ephesians views the church as a living organism, and the relationship between Jesus and each believer is organic in nature. A study of the passages which use this metaphor, portraying Jesus as head of the church as a living organism (Eph. 1:22; 4:15; Col. 1:18; 2:10, 19), emphasize Jesus' role as the source, sustainer, protector, and organizer of the church's life.

We need the eyes of our hearts enlightened to see one important implication of this truth. Jesus is the *living* Head of the church. We as the people of God must learn to look to Jesus as the organizer of our lives, and not surrender to human leaders a guiding and directing role that rightly belongs to Jesus alone.

His body, the *fullness of Him* who fills everything in every way (1:23). The relation of *to pleroma* to other elements in the sen-

tence is debated. The NIV takes it in apposition to the preceding noun, "body." In this case the body can be thought of as complementing on earth Christ's role as Head in heaven.

But the participle translated "who fills" might be either middle, "He who fills," or passive, "the one being filled." Thus Paul may be saying that the body is being filled by Christ, infused with His life and attributes and power.

Whichever thought is intended, this final statement sums up the uniqueness of our relationship with Jesus. We, together, complete the resurrected Jesus, and His presence within completes us.

As for you, you were *dead* in your transgressions and sins (2:1). "Death" and "life" are basic metaphors in the NT, taking us beyond the biological to expose the spiritual state of the unsaved. Ephesians 2:1-4 is perhaps the Bible's most powerful description of the impact of spiritual death on the present experience of human beings.

Death is characterized by a lifestyle of transgressions (*paraptomata,* "falling aside") and sins (*hamartia,* "falling short") (2:1). Lost man is morally feeble, totally inadequate to the challenge of living God's way.

Death is characterized by following the ways of this world (*kosmos*). Here "world" is used theologically, to describe a society whose mores and morals are anchored in time rather than eternity, and reflect distorted human values rather than the values of God (2:2).

Death is characterized by following the ways of "the ruler of the kingdom of the air" (2:2), a metaphor for Satan. Human beings eagerly rush down the trail Satan has blazed, ignoring the way God has marked out for us in His Word.

Death is characterized by "gratifying the cravings of our sinful nature, and following its desires and thoughts" (2:3). The worst in human nature, rather than the best, captures our allegiance. The problem is greater than one of inadequacy; human beings are in rebellion against God.

Death is characterized by living under the cloud of God's wrath, sensing our guilt, knowing that a holy God must surely punish us.

What an appropriate image, for human beings are so completely ruined by sin that they have as much hope of pleasing God as a corpse laid out in its coffin has of responding to a neighbor's shout.

This brief but powerful description of spiritual death serves two purposes. It reminds us that we truly are helpless apart from God's grace. And it drives home the fact that the building materials from which God constructs His church are shoddy indeed. Only a true miracle can vitalize and transform us, or make us fit participants in the body of Christ.

For it is by grace you have been saved, through faith — *and this* not from ourselves, it is the gift of God — not of works, so that no one can boast (2:8-9). Grammatically *kai touto*, "and this," might refer to "saved," to "faith," or relate to the entire process that Paul has described. It's best to take it in this third sense.

The argument over whether "faith" can be conceived of as "work" (something generated by or from within a lost human being) is not at issue here. Paul's point is that since human beings are dead in their trespasses and sins, there is simply nothing a person can do to contribute to his or her own salvation. Salvation must be a work of God, from first to last.

In this case our appropriate response is one of humble gratitude for a grace-driven salvation that is offered us as a free gift — not argument over whether or not the "nothing" that human beings can do does or does not include "believe."

For we are God's *workmanship*, created in Christ Jesus to do good works, which God prepared in advance for us to do (2:10). Paul reminds us that as Christians now we are the Lord's *poiema*, His works of art. But the beauty of God's workmanship is not displayed in posing. That beauty can only be displayed when we are put to work fulfilling His purpose in us.

Is there any conflict here between the "good works" the unsaved attempt, and the "good works" that Christians are called to do. There is a vast difference between seeking to win God's favor by our performance, and fulfilling the purpose God has in having granted us His favor. Doing "good works" before salvation, undertaken to earn God's blessing, is like trying to build a road to the moon by piling up heaps of dirt here on earth. Doing "good works" after salvation, as a grateful response to God for what the Lord has done for us, is simply walking along a highway God has constructed for us.

For He Himself is our peace, who has made the two one and has destroyed the barrier . . . by *abolishing in His flesh the Law* (2:14-15). Many words and phrases in 2:11-22 remind us of the vast difference between Jew and pagan (Greek) in the first century. In the eyes of the Jew humanity was divided into two races: Jew, and all the rest of mankind, the Gentiles. Gentiles were cut off from all the privileges granted the Jews by God (2:11-13), but these people who had been "far away" from God (*makran*) were now "near" (*engus*) in Christ.

Not only were the Gentiles near, but for Christians the old religious barrier was shattered, and the two constituted, religiously speaking, one "new man." Thus Clement of Alexandria would later quote a work called the *Preaching of Peter*, saying "We who worship God in a new way, as the third race, are Christians."

Here then Paul points to Christ as "our peace," not only the One making peace, but the One in whom we experience a peace and harmony between the "races" which could not exist before. What Christ did was to "abolish" (*katargeo*, "to annul," "to make of no effect, irrelevant") the Law that in Jewish eyes set them apart from all other men. Paul's point is that since the believing Jew no longer relates to God through the Mosaic Law, there is no cause for the ancient antagonism on either part. Now the believing Gentile participates in all those blessings that once were available only to the believing Jew, and together we are fellow citizens with God's people and members of God's household.

If you and I relate to others on the basis of our joint participation in Christ, none of the social or ethnic differences that divide us now will be able to stand.

THE PASSAGE IN DEPTH

Spiritual Blessings in Christ (1:3-14).

Background. The OT portrays a God who acted freely in choosing Israel and in giving Israel her land. God's total freedom of action is underlined in a variety of ways. Thus God said to Moses, "I will have mercy on whom I will have mercy, and I will have compassion on whom I will have compassion" (Ex. 33:19). The same truth is asserted in another way in Deut. 9:6. There God warns the Exodus generation not to assume that His gift to them of the land is based on any merit of theirs. "Understand, then, that it is not because of your righteousness that the Lord your God is giving you this good land to possess, for you are a stiff-necked people."

In Rom. 9–11 Paul carefully develops this very theme. A review of sacred history demonstrates again and again that God's freedom of action in no way was restricted by any human act, nor does any human act obligate God to any course of action. Paul argues there that certain historic events, such as God's announcement to Rebekah before her twins were born that the elder (Esau) would serve the younger (Jacob), took place "before the twins were born or had done anything good or bad—*in order that God's purpose in election might stand*: not by works but by Him who calls" (9:11). Paul's argument throughout this passage is that *God's acts are determined internally, and proceed from His mercy. They are not determined externally, as a response or reaction to man's behavior.*

Paul might well have multiplied illustrations from the OT. But his point is established. And, strikingly, that point was utterly missed by first-century sages. They assumed God's sovereignty. Yet at the same time it was unthinkable to them that God, the Moral Judge of His universe, who rewards good and punishes evil, would not respond to the good in accord with their merits.

In fact the writings of the sages and their successors frequently extend this assumption, and portray God acting in a certain way *on account of the merits of Israel.* For instance, Genesis Rabbah 29, commenting on Gen. 6:8, "Noah found favor," quotes Rabbi Simon, who argues from the use of "found" in Hosea 9:10—"I found Israel like grapes in the wilderness"—that Noah found grace "on account

of the merit of the generation of the wilderness"! (XXIX:III 1.H.)

And this despite the fact that God was angry with this unbelieving generation and condemned it to wander until every adult who participated in the great disobedience had died!

It is even more suggestive to look through the index to Emil Shurer's massive, three-volume *History of the Jewish People in the Age of Jesus Christ,* and find no reference to election, foreknowledge, predestination, sovereignty, or other concepts associated with the relationship of God's freedom of choice to man's supposed merits! Simply put, such issues were ignored because the sages assumed both that a person zealous for the Law could please God and that God was bound to reward such a person both now and in the world to come.

But this assumption is not reflected in the NT. Rather, the NT epistles present a vision of a lost humanity, totally cut off from God by sin, and without any merit acceptable to the Lord. The Law given to the Jews is no help, because Law condemns those who fall short, and all have fallen short. The moral law implanted in pagans is no help, for though they recognize right and wrong, they too fall short of the standards imposed by their own consciences (Rom. 2). Thus all have sinned and fallen short of the glory of God, and all stand before God without merit and condemned (Rom. 3). The Law is no help at all, because sinful human beings are spiritually dead, and Law cannot give life (Gal. 3:21-22).

With every human being totally helpless, our only hope is an appeal to God's mercy. And that mercy is offered to all in Jesus Christ, who died for all. Because of God's great mercy extended to us in Jesus, all who believe will be saved.

But now Ephesians seems to push the issue back even further. Is the saving act of faith something that is generated within the heart of a lost human being? Or is that saving act of faith itself a gift of a merciful God? And, if faith itself is a gift, that gift clearly is given to some but not to all. Does God then by acting choose some for salvation, and by not acting destine the rest for perdition?

It is against the background of this question—a question not raised in first century or contemporary Judaism simply because in that religion salvation is perceived as a matter of merit—that most read Eph. 1:3-14. And find it troublesome.

Interpretation. Paul begins with a doxology, in the form of a traditional Jewish blessing (1:3). He then moves to describe the role of each person of the Godhead in bringing us the blessings we now enjoy. The passage can be outlined:

■ The role of the Father (1:4-6).

■ The role of the Son (1:7-12).

■ The role of the Spirit (1:13-14).

The Role of the Father (1:4-6). The role of the Father overflows these verses to dominate the whole passage. Even the work of the Son was according to God's purpose and choice (1:11). What specifically did the Father do?

■ God chose us in Christ before the creation of the world to be holy and blameless.

■ God predestined us to be adopted as His Sons through Jesus Christ.

■ God did this "according to His good pleasure" (1:9).

The word translated "chose" (1:4) is *exelexato,* the aorist middle indicative of *eklego,* which means to select, and implies choosing some from many. The choice is described as having taken place before the Creation, and thus could hardly be dependent on anything the chosen had done. The choice is also described as having taken place "in Christ." Calvin, in his commentary on Ephesians, observed that "if we are chosen in Christ, it is outside ourselves. It is not from the sight of our deserving, but because our heavenly Father has engrafted us, through the blessing of adoption, into the body of Christ. In short, the name of Christ excludes all merit, and everything which men have of themselves; for when He says that we are chosen in Christ, it follows that in ourselves we are unworthy."

The word "predestined" is *proorisas.* The word means to "mark out ahead of time," and is found six times in the NT. It is helpful to compare other uses of the word to sense the way in which it is used in Scripture. Acts 4:28 says that the events associated with and culminating in Jesus' death were exactly what God's "power and will had *decided beforehand* should happen." First Corinthians 2:7 speaks of God's plan to redeem us through Christ as something "destined for our glory before time began." An examination of these passages indicates that the whole process of salvation—including specifically Jesus' death, our adoption into God's family, our transformation into Jesus' likeness—all this was planned and carried through as God had decided beforehand.

Another phrase makes this emphasis even more clear. All He did was in "His will according to His good pleasure" (1:11). Here "pleasure" is *eudokian,* a verb used 21 times in the NT, of which no less than 15 express either a human being's or God's pleasure regarding a choice one has made. God, at least, is completely satisfied with His choices.

Finally, "will" here is *thelematos.* Like its synonym *bouloumai,* when used of the purposes of God *thelo* indicates fixed purpose and absolute determination (Luke 7:30; Acts 4:28; Heb. 6:17).

In the case of a despot these terms would seem harsh and heartless indeed. But we must remember that the character of the Person who chooses, predestines, and wills colors the connotation of these terms. Paul does not hesitate to present God as totally sovereign in distributing His blessings. But Paul reminds us that God's choice must be understood in view of His love (1:4) and His grace (1:6).

The Role of the Son (1:7-12). Christ was commissioned to carry out the Father's grand design. Paul speaks of "redemption through His blood, the forgiveness of sin" that are ours because of Christ's self-sacrifice.

But here too Paul looks back beyond time to isolate the origin of the blessings we have received. The root cause is not in ourselves, but in God's will and His "good pleasure" (*eudokeo* again, 1:9), which God "purposed in Christ." The word translated "purposed" is *proetheto,* "to set before Himself." From eternity itself the Father not only turned this plan over in His mind, but cherished it, returning to it again and again as an ultimate demonstration of good, which will be made clear when He acts "to bring all things in heaven and on earth together under one head, even Christ" (1:10).

But here too Paul reminds us that you and I have also always been on God's heart and in His mind. Using now familiar terms, Paul says, "In Him *we* were also *chosen,* having been *predestined* according to the *plan of Him* who works out everything in conformity with the *purposes of His will*" (1:11, italics mine). And all this God has done that we "might be for the praise of His glory" (1:12).

The Work of the Spirit (1:13-14). Here for the first time Paul portrays human beings as actors in the drama of salvation. "You also were included in Christ when you heard the word of truth, the Gospel of your salvation. Having believed. . . ." If we assume that "hear[ing] the word" connotes, as it frequently does in the OT as well as the NT, *responding* to the Word, we can understand Paul to say that we were included in Christ *when we believed.* This is supported by the immediately following participle, "having believed."

Thus Paul views God's choice, plan, and purpose as originating in eternity, but our participation as something that takes place in time, and only when we believe.

The apostle immediately returns to his theme, and describes the work of the Holy Spirit in bringing us the blessings of salvation here and now. This return to his theme reminds us of an important interpretive principle. We must make sure that we do not extend the range of any passage beyond the purpose of the writer. Paul is praising God for what He has done for us, and in this bright accolade leads us to consider in awe and wonder the investment of each person of the Godhead in our salvation. We are not some minor, relatively insignificant concern of a God whose attention is focused on cosmic issues. Our salvation has been the focus of His concern long before the act of creation, and each person of

the Godhead has stepped forward to invest His energies — and His pain — in accomplishing our redemption.

Paul simply is not asking whether faith is itself something that God causes in the hearts of those who believe. Logically "God is sovereign" and "man has free will" are contradictory. But biblically the teaching that God chooses, predestines, and wills is set beside the invitation — whosoever will may come — with no contradiction at all.

Application. We human beings will undoubtedly continue to wonder, and some of us will be disturbed by the words Paul uses in Eph. 1 to describe God's role in planning and providing our salvation. I suspect Paul was not bothered, however, for one simple reason. The great apostle understood and counted on the love and the wisdom of God.

"It doesn't seem fair" is perhaps the worst of all reasons for being disturbed about Eph. 1 or Rom. 9–11. Whenever that statement is made, we must in all honesty supply the words "to me." What we are really saying is "It doesn't seem fair *to me.*" And in making such a statement we act foolishly, as if you and I, with our limited understanding and ignorance of the ultimate reality, had some basis for standing in judgment on God!

But the second reason is most compelling. Whether or not any conclusions we rightly or wrongly draw from these passages pose a moral dilemma, the fact remains that *we know the God who chooses.* And the ultimate recourse in dealing with any such paradox is to remember and rest in the character of a God we know, in Christ, as a God of infinite love and compassion.

Is predestination, as we posit it, unfair? We simply have no basis on which to judge. But can God act unfairly? Of course not! And in this wonderful truth we take refuge from all doubt — and abandon the dispute.

EPHESIANS 3–4
One Family, One Body

EXPOSITION

Paul continues his exploration of the corporate implications of salvation. The OT makes it clear that from the beginning God intended to save Gentiles as well as Jews. But God's intention to make Gentile and Jew "members together of one body" was purposely not disclosed in the earlier revelation (3:1-9). This amazing turn of events must not be viewed as a change in God's plans, or as a rejection of Israel. Rather it is a demonstration of God's "manifold wisdom"; the unveiling of a new facet of "eternal purpose" far more complex than had earlier been imagined (3:10-13). It is in this context that Paul prays for the church as family (*patria*). It is only as the disparate elements who make up Christ's one church are rooted and established in love for one another that, together, they come to know the love of Christ—a love which while beyond our comprehension is not beyond our capacity to experience (3:14-19). But how is this possible? In a grand doxology Paul praises God as the One who is able to do "immeasurably more than all we ask or imagine" through that power of His which is at work within us, bringing Him glory throughout all generations (3:20-21).

Paul has now established the fact that the church is a "mystery": a technical term indicating a previously hidden but now revealed aspect of God's purpose. In Eph. 4, Paul focuses our attention on the unity of the body and explains something of God's purpose in this unexpected creation of a truly new community of faith. Believers are to "make every effort" to maintain the unity of a body which is indeed one: indwelt by one Spirit, won by one Lord, owing allegiance to one Father (4:1-6). Within the context of a unity maintained by such expressions of love as humility, gentleness, patience, and forebearing, gifts distributed by Christ the Victor at His ascension are exercised, and Christ's purposes in and for the body are realized (4:7-10). Strikingly, that purpose is not realized in the leaders Christ gives the church but in the laity. Leaders are servants, whose role is to equip God's people for *their* "works of service." Through the efforts of all its members the body of Christ is built up (4:11-13), and through active participation in a growing, ministering body the individual believer matures (4:14-16).

And what a wonderful transformation takes place within the context of Christ's body. Those who lived in darkness and impurity are taught to put off their former way of life and put on the new self that God creates in Christ (4:17-24). Here is a practical

471

theology indeed, for with an experience of the dynamic realities that give Christ's church its shape and form, a totally new way of living emerges. Once lost and hostile human beings become imitators of God, and live lives of love (4:25–5:2).

WORD STUDIES

You have heard about the *administration* of God's grace that was given to me for you (3:2). The word is *oikonomia,* usually "task" or "stewardship." Here Paul presents himself as the one entrusted by God to carry out the strategy implicit in the doctrine of grace by serving others (see Word Study on Grace for 1:7).

You will be able to understand my insight into the *mystery* of Christ (3:4). A *mysterion* is an aspect of God's purpose unrevealed in the OT, but unveiled in Christ and the preaching of the Gospel. The prepositional phrase "of Christ" may be taken in one of several ways: as a mystery which Christ authors, a mystery which *is* Christ, or a mystery relating to Christ. This last option is preferable. The Gospel of Christ involves a stunning revelation of the unexpected extent of divine grace (3:2), a grace which reaches out to encompass Jew and Gentile on equal terms.

This mystery is that through the Gospel the Gentiles are *heirs together* with Israel (3:6). Paul uses three terms with the prefix *syn-* to express the stunning fact that Gentiles are welcomed into Christ's body as equals with the chosen people. Gentiles and Jews are coheirs (*sygkleronoma*), co-members in a common body (*syssoma*), and co-partners (*symmetocha*). To understand something of the truly astounding nature of this new revelation to both first-century Jew and Gentile, see discussion in this chapter's The Passage in Depth.

This mystery, which . . . was *kept hidden* in God (3:9). Again this section emphasizes the unexpectedness of the present unity of Jew and Gentile in Christ. God's failure to mention this aspect of His purpose in the older revelation was deliberate. Now, however, the church has come into existence, and angelic beings as well as we human beings can begin to appreciate something of the complexity of God's eternal purpose, and glorify Him in awe and wonder.

For this reason I kneel before the Father, from whom *His whole family* . . . derives its name (3:14-15). When Jesus taught His disciples to pray "Our Father," the intent was to emphasize the stunning intimacy with God which individuals can now experience. Here Paul has a different intent. The church is a "family" (*patria*) deriving its identity from One who is Father (*pater*).

While rendered "whole family" here, in the first century a *patria* was any group united by descent from a common ancestor. Thus the *patria* might be a family, or a tribal group, or as in the case of Israel, an entire nation. Yet the essential which united members of any *patria* was its common origin, an origin which gave it its very identity.

Clearly Paul is continuing to reinforce his teaching on the unity of Jew and Gentile in Christ's church. We are co-members in Christ's body. Even more, through Christ we now trace our genealogy back to a common Father, God, and thus have been constituted a *patria,* a family.

So as Paul prays for the church, he approaches God as the *pater* (Father) who has given us our shared identity. And in his prayer he asks that we might experience the reality of that unity which he has described.

I pray that you, being rooted and established *in love,* may have power, together with all the saints, to grasp how wide and long and high and deep is the love of Christ, and to know this love that surpasses knowledge (3:17-19). Our understanding of this prayer hinges on how we take the phrase "in love."

Are we to be rooted and established in *Christ's love for us?* Are we to be rooted and established in *love for Christ?* Or are we perhaps to be rooted and established in *love for one another?* The grammar holds no answer, so we must refer to context. And here context seems determinative. The entire passage is an exploration of the church as a mystery, in which Jewish and Gentile believers are united as equals. As members of a *patria* now, we must develop relationships rooted and established in love. Only thus will we have power "together with all the saints" to experience what cannot really be grasped intellectually: the love Christ has for us.

The point is vital for us to grasp. Christ's love is far too wide, long, high, and deep to comprehend. Yet that love can be known experientially. And it is communicated to us within the church as the new community of faith becomes rooted and established in love for each other.

The principle of incarnation remains valid. We know God, because He became incarnate in Christ. And we come to know Christ as our Lord continues to express Himself through our brothers and sisters, who are members of His living body here on earth.

I urge you to live a life *worthy* of the calling you have received (4:1). The word *axios* means to "bring up the other beam of the scales." The image is one of balance; the Christian's way of life must harmonize with the truths he professes to believe.

Be completely *humble* and *gentle*; be *patient*, *bearing with* one another (4:2). Paul now introduces four graces which are essential elements in that "worthy" life which is appropriate to the Christian's life. These four are not exhaustive. Like the rest of this passage they target traits which are critical if the church is to experience love and oneness.

"Humble" is *tapeinophrosyne*. In Greek culture the root served as an expression of contempt applied to the social inferiors. In the NT the term is positive, representing a person's proper estimate of himself in relation to God and to others. The humble person sees others as persons of great value because they are loved by God, and finds satisfaction in serving them.

"Gentle" is *prautes*, which might be rendered as considerateness. Words constructed on this root suggest a mild, soothing quality. Rather than generate strife, a gentle person tends to generate a peaceful and harmonious climate around him or her.

"Patient" is *makrothymia*, a capacity for self-control that enables an individual to keep on loving and forgiving despite provocation.

"Bearing with" is *anechomenoi*, which might

be rendered "put up with" until a provocation is past.

In essence Paul has given us a clear explanation of the love he calls church members to exhibit. If we live with each other in these ways, we will learn what love is, and experience the love that Christ has for each one of us.

There is *one* body and *one* Spirit (4:4-6). Paul continues to emphasize the unity of the church. As in Eph. 1, he sees each Person of the Godhead as vitally involved. In Eph. 1 Paul focused on the involvement of Father, Son, and Holy Spirit in the work of salvation. Here in Eph. 4 Paul reverses the order, and focuses on the involvement of Spirit, Son, and Father in creating and maintaining the unity of church.

The Holy Spirit is the agent of unity; the Son is the One to whom we are united; the Father is the One whose purposes are expressed through the unity of the body.

With this great affirmation Paul concludes this section of his letter, which has again and again emphasized the unity of the church as a truly new community of faith, and shifts his attention to the question of how individual members of this community are to live.

When He ascended on high, He led captives in His train and *gave gifts to men* (4:8). Paul's use of this psalm has troubled many, as Psalm 68:18 reads, "When you ascended on high, you led captives in your train; you received gifts from men, even from the rebellious." How do we reconcile the OT and NT versions of this verse?

One suggestion is rooted in the fact that the Targum, which is the Aramaic paraphrase of the Hebrew original, reads "Thou ascendest up to the firmament, O prophet Moses, thou tookest captives captive, thou didst teach them words of the Law, thou gavest them as gifts to the children of men." Thus one assumption is that Paul may reflect this paraphrase rather than the original.

A more satisfying suggestion is rooted in the imagery of a conqueror's triumph. Christ the Victor returns to heaven with the captives in His train. Then, enthroned in glory, He shares with His followers on earth the spoils which He has won. The OT and NT thus look at a common event, Christ's Triumph, and emphasize two different but harmonious consequences. The Victor receives the spoils — and generously distributes them to His followers.

It was He who gave some to be apostles, some to be prophets, some to be evangelists, some to be pastors and teachers, *to prepare God's people* **for works of service (4:11-12).** The 1906 Papal Encyclical *Vehmenter Nos,* asserts, "As for the masses, they have no other right than of letting themselves be led, and of following their pastors as a docile flock." How different Paul's emphasis! Whether the leaders have wide areas of responsibility (apostles, prophets, evangelists) or only local (pastors and teachers), they are ordained to serve the laity. It is the laity who perform the "works of service" that build up the body of Christ.

From Him the whole body, joined and held together by every supporting ligament, grows and builds itself up in love, as each part does its work (4:16). Paul sums up. Maturity for individuals and for the corporate church comes through the active participation of "each part."

So I tell you this, and insist on it in the Lord, that you must no longer *live as the Gentiles do* **(4:17).** It is only now that Paul shifts our attention from the body and our participation in it to focus on the individual believer. Christianity calls for a radical reorientation of life; the putting off of an "old self" and the putting on of a "new self" which was created to be like God in righteousness and holiness.

Paul here urges the Ephesians not to fall back into their old way of life. It is a Gentile way of life, first in that the church at Ephesus was predominantly Gentile, and second in that the sins described here were more characteristic of a Gentile than a Jewish lifestyle. Paul warns specifically against:

■ "The futility of their thinking" (4:17). The word is *mataiotes,* often associated with idolatry, but here indicating the foolish beliefs underlying their behavior.

■ "The ignorance that is in them" (4:18). Their views are an expression of utter igno-

rance about reality.

■ "The hardening of their hearts" (4:18). That ignorance is as much moral as mental. The Gentiles chose not to respond to the light they had, and in hardening their hearts against it condemned themselves to wander in darkness, the captive of beliefs rooted in falsehood.

Paul further describes the Gentiles as:

■ "Having lost all sensitivity" (4:19). The word is *apelegkotes.* Their hardened hearts are no longer capable of distinguishing between right and wrong, leaving them vulnerable to the passions that surge unchecked within.

■ "Have . . . given themselves over to sensuality" (4:19). Sensuality is *aselgeia,* unrestrained abandonment to sexual and other debauchery.

■ "Have given themselves over . . . to indulge in impurity" (4:19). Here the word is *akatharsia,* uncleanness or filthiness.
"*With a continual lust for more [impurity]"* (4:19). Here the word is *pleonexia,* which indicates an insatiable desire. The Gentile's life of utter self-indulgence does not bring satisfaction, but rather fans the flame of an unquenchable desire that drives the individual further and further from God, and further and further from what God intends human beings to become.

Put off **your old self . . .** ***put on*** **the new self (4:22, 24).** The imagery of putting off and on clothing is common in Greek literature, and also frequently found in Scripture. Here is another reminder that both old and new potentials exist within the personality of the believer. God has given us a new self. It is our responsibility to choose to put on that self, and live by its promptings.

In your anger do not sin; Do not let the sun go down while you are still angry (4:26). We derive two principles from these brief proverbs. First, anger is not in itself sin as long as it remains an emotion. But anger is likely to move us to actions which are sin. Second, we must take this danger so seriously that we deal with our anger before the sun goes down. That is, do not hold anger, or let it turn to bitterness. In fact we must "get rid of all bitterness, rage and anger" (4:31).

Our goal is to "live a life of love," willingly giving ourselves for others, even as Christ gave Himself for us (5:1-2).

HUMAN ANGER

The Hebrew words translated "anger" tend to be descriptive, describing the physical symptoms of anger. The flared nostrils, the burning sensation, the fierce and hostile look, are all reflected in Hebrew terms. This, of course, is because anger is in fact a physical and emotional reaction to what appears to us to in some way seriously violate a relationship.

A survey of OT passages makes it clear that in some cases anger is justified, as was Moses' reaction to Aaron's manufacture of the golden calf (Ex. 32:19; cf. 1 Sam. 20:34). In many cases anger while understandable cannot be justified (1 Sam. 17:28; 18:8).

Another important teaching is that anger can be expressed righteously or sinfully. The furious Potiphar felt justified in condemning Joseph to prison, and in fact reacted with restraint rather than taking personal revenge. While the anger Simeon and Levi felt over the rape of their sister was justified, their plot to murder all the men of Shechem was not, and

is sternly condemned (Gen. 34; 49:6-7). Whatever the justification, the angry individual has no right to take revenge. As Ps. 37:8-9 says, "Refrain from anger and turn from wrath; do not fret—it only leads to evil. For evil men will be cut off, but those who hope in the Lord will inherit the land."

In view of the tendency of anger to lead to evil, the OT contains many warnings against it (cf. Prov. 27:4; 29:22; 30:33; etc.).

Ultimately the Bible makes it clear that we are responsible for our own anger. Anger is *our* reaction to circumstances, and we can choose to react in other ways. Thus Ps. 37:8 tells us to "refrain from" and "turn away from" anger, and not to "fret" over situations that might stimulate our anger. Rather than accept the burden of anger we are to turn the unfair situation over to the Lord. Because God is the moral Judge of His universe, we can be sure that "evil men will be cut off." Psalm 37:7 puts it this way: "Be still before the Lord and wait patiently for Him; do not fret when men succeed in their ways, when they carry out their wicked schemes." Rather than fret, we release the situation to the Lord, thankful that the burden of appropriate response is His and not ours.

THE PASSAGE IN DEPTH

Paul the Preacher to the Gentiles (3:1-21).

Background. Paul is very careful to admit that the church is a completely unexpected entity. While the OT makes it clear that God has always intended to extend the blessings of salvation to the Gentiles, there is no hint in the older revelation that God ever intended to make salvation available to Jew and Gentiles on the same basis, and to place them on the same footing within the community of faith.

The first-century Jew, in fact, struggled with and never quite resolved this deeply emotional issue concerning Jewish/Gentile relations. On the one hand Israel saw herself as one who carried the knowledge of God to the Gentiles, and was convinced that one day Judaism would become a world religion. When the Gentiles at last acknowledged God, they would be accepted by the Lord. But on the other hand the basic attitude of the Gentile

world toward the Jews was one of contempt and aversion. Recognizing this, the Jews understandably took comfort in OT passages that spoke of God's judgment of the Gentiles. Thus later Jewish commentators tended to interpret the sayings of Scripture about the Gentiles in a negative way, arguing that even when the same terms were applied to Israel and the Gentiles, the identical terms still implied the blessing of Israel and the cursing of the Gentiles. Thus Leviticus Rabbah V:VII notes:

J. "The nations of the world are called sages, and Israel is called sages.
K. "The nations of the world are called sages, 'And I shall wipe out sages from Edom' (Obad. 1:8).
L. "And Israel is called sages, 'Sages store up knowledge' (Prov. 10:14).
M. "The nations of the world are called unblemished, and Israel is called unblemished.
N. "The nations of the world are called

unblemished: 'Unblemished as are those that go down to the pit' (Prov. 1:12).
O. "And Israel is called unblemished: 'The unblemished will inherit goodness' " (Prov. 28:10).

Given this ambivalence, and the fact that the church *is* a mystery unrevealed in the OT, it is understandable that Jew and Gentile alike should feel uncomfortable about the notion that the two races were now one, a third race of humankind fashioned in Christ by the working of the Holy Spirit. And it was not easy to set aside the old prejudices, and learn to live that life of love which alone is able to maintain a unity which exists as a theological reality, but yet must also be experienced as a practical reality.

TYPICAL OLD TESTAMENT PASSAGES ON GENTILE SALVATION

The Abrahamic Covenant

All the peoples on earth will be blessed through you (Gen. 12:3).

Isaiah's Servant passages (which Israel applied to herself rather than Messiah)

Here is My servant, whom I uphold, My chosen One in whom I delight; I will put My Spirit on Him and He will bring justice to the nations. He will not shout or cry out, or raise His voice in the streets. A bruised reed He will not break, and a smoldering wick He will not snuff out. In faithfulness He will bring forth justice; He will not falter or be discouraged till He establishes justice on earth. In His law the islands will put their hope (42:1-4).

And now the Lord says — He who formed me in the womb to be His servant to bring Jacob back to Him and gather Israel to Himself, for I am honored in the eyes of the Lord and My God has been My strength — He says: "It is too small a thing for you to be My servant to restore the tribes of Jacob and bring back those of Israel I have kept. I will also make You a light for the Gentiles, that You may bring My salvation to the ends of the earth" (49:5-6).

Let no foreigner who has bound himself to the Lord say, "The Lord will surely exclude me from His people." And let not any eunuch complain, "I am only a dry tree." For this is what the Lord says. . . . "Foreigners who bind themselves to the Lord to serve Him, to love the name of the Lord, and to worship Him, all who keep the Sabbath without desecrating it and who hold fast to My covenant — these I will bring to My holy mountain and give them joy in My house of prayer. Their burnt offerings and sacrifices will be accepted on My altar; for My house will be called a house of prayer for all nations." The Sovereign Lord declares — He who gathers the exiles of Israel; "I will gather still others to them besides those already gathered" (56:3-8).

Interpretation. There is a marked emphasis on the unity of the body of Christ in the Book of Ephesians. Ephesians 2:14-22 affirms that Christ destroyed the "dividing wall of hostility" that separated Jew and Gentile in order to create "one new man out of the two."

As a result Gentiles are "fellow citizens with God's [Old Testament] people," elements in a single building that God is now constructing from living persons as a holy temple in which He will dwell.

In Eph. 3 Paul admits that this is a mystery — a surprising element of God's plan that was not revealed in the OT. Yet this element is consistent with God's grace, and consistent too with His "manifold wisdom." We should not expect God's design to be simple or simplistic. And so although unrevealed before, the church is now displayed to all as a *patria* that takes its identity from God who is the Father of us all.

Typically Paul cannot resist drawing practical implications of his doctrinal teaching. God has constituted us a family, and it is in and through loving family relationships that we will, together, experience something that none can understand—the very love of Christ.

As Paul moves on to chapter 4, he returns again to his central theme. We are one body in Christ. The unity exists. However, it must be maintained by the consistent effort of each member of the body to relate to others in humility, gentleness, patience, forbearance. As we do we discover another wonder: Christ "gave gifts to men" (4:8). In His triumph the Victor shares the spoils with us, enabling every believer to contribute to the growth and maturity of the body and its members!

Again, full experience of the unity which does exist is essential. It grows as "the whole body, joined and held together by every supporting ligament" builds itself up, and this happens only "as each part does its work" (4:16).

While the rest of the chapter shifts our attention to the individuals who together make up the body, it is clear that even here the individual is considered in respect to his or her relationship with other members of the body.

Application. The teaching of Ephesians on the unity of the body of Christ has direct application now, as it has throughout the history of the church. Whatever social barriers may exist within any society, those barriers have become irrelevant in Christ. And they must be irrelevant to Christ's people.

This is far more a practical than theoretical issue. Within the body we must live a life of love. Within the body we must be completely humble and gentle; patient, bearing with each other in love. Within the body we must acknowledge the primacy of love in our interpersonal relationships and love actively. And we must also acknowledge our dependence on one another. No segment of society is superior, called to "minister" while other segments are "ministered to."

In a fascinating work by George H. Gallup, Jr. and Timothy Jones (*The Saints Among Us,* Morehouse, 1992), the authors concluded those they classified as "saints" are more likely to be found among the powerless of society: the nonwhite, female, uneducated poor. Today as in NT times we need to learn that God does not work in the ways of human society. As Paul wrote in 1 Cor. 1:26-29, "Not many of you were wise by human standards; not many were influential; not many were of noble birth. But God chose the foolish things of the world to shame the wise. . . . He chose the lowly things of this world . . . so that no one may boast before Him."

EPHESIANS 5–6
One in Love

EXPOSITION

Paul has called upon those who are in Christ, who compose mankind's third race, to "be imitators of God" and so "live a life of love" (5:1-2). The verse looks both back to

4:17-32 and forward to 5:3–6:9. Initially Paul continues with a call for individual believers and the church to remain committed to sexual morality (5:3-14), temperance (5:15-18), and shared worship (5:19-20). At this point, however, Paul takes a significant turn, to describe how to live a life of love within the framework of the rigid social structures which marked the world of the first century.

Hierarchy was implicit in the social structures of the first century. The emperor stood alone at the peak of the pyramid. Just below was the senatorial order of some 600 men. Below them were the *equites,* wealthy landowners and businessmen. Below them were local aristocracies in the provinces and cities of the Empire who possessed some political power or influence due to their wealth. Within these classes women were expected to stay in the background, to bear children and remain faithful to their husbands, and to lead totally uneventful lives. It was understood that the husband was to rule, the wife was to be subordinate. The status of women is reflected in the general rule that a Roman woman could not inherit more than 10 percent of her husband's estate.

The great mass of the population occupied the lower classes—small landholders, craftsmen and shopkeepers, and the poor who supported themselves as day laborers. Below them, lowest of all on the social scale, were the slaves, regarded in law as mere property despite the fact that many slaves were highly educated, talented individuals. Within this highly stratified society social standing and privileges were assumed and fiercely guarded.

The NT does not directly challenge existing social structures. Instead, as exemplified here, the NT speaks directly to Christian persons and calls them to live a life of love *within* the structures of society. Thus while the wife is urged to submit to her husband, the husband is called on to love his wife enough to put her needs first in their relationship (5:23-33). While the child is urged to obey parents, parents are urged not to "exasperate" their children (6:1-4). And while slaves are told to obey their earthly masters, Christian masters are charged to treat their slaves well and with respect (6:5-9). Ultimately the life of love to which Christians are called must break down all artificial barriers erected by society. Initially, the life of love would enable God's people to be together what Paul has shown that we are—one body, one *patria* in the Lord.

The Book of Ephesians concludes with a unique review. Paul looks back over what he has written, and visualizes the truths he has emphasized as the equipment of a Roman soldier. Armed with the great realities of our faith, the Christian is enabled to stand, confident and assured (6:10-20, 21-23).

WORD STUDIES

But among you there must not be even a hint of *sexual immorality* (5:3). The word is *porneia,* a general term encompassing sexual looseness. It was as common in Paul's day as it is in our own. And as wrong.

Nor should there be *obscenity, foolish talk* or *coarse joking,* which are out of place, but rather thanksgiving (5:4). This is the only place in the NT where these three terms occur. Obscenity is *aischrotes,* "filthy language." Foolish talk is *morologia,* stupid, silly

chattering. Coarse joking is *eutrapelia,* which suggests the approach of the sophisticated who treat sex with flip arrogance. Such talk is not suitable for Christians, whose mouths are much better employed in uttering thanksgiving to God.

You were once darkness, but now you are light in the Lord. Live as children of light (5:8). Paul does not say that the believers were *in* darkness, but that they *were* darkness. What that means is powerfully portrayed in Eph.

2:1-3 and 4:17-24. Similarly, now believers do not simply walk in the light, we *are* light. Our calling in this world is to be what we have become in Christ.

Be very careful, then, how you live—not as unwise but as wise, *making the most of every opportunity,* because the days are evil (5:15-16). Here *kairon,* which usually indicates time, is appropriately rendered as "opportunity." The circumstances in which we live are difficult, but as any sharp businessman realizes, difficult times often present unusual opportunities for profit. Rather than become despondent, the Christian is to be even more alert, ready to seize each opportunity that presents itself to let Christ shine.

Do not get drunk on wine, which leads to debauchery. Instead, be filled with the Spirit (5:18). We are to be under the influence of the Spirit of God, not of alcohol.

The analogy may rest on the power of each to lower natural inhibitions. However, when our inhibitions are lowered by wine, this "leads to debauchery." This thought is reflected in a passage in the pseudepigraphical writing *The Testament of Judah* (see below). In contrast, filling with the Spirit relaxes those inhibitions which cause us to hesitate to speak out for the Lord.

TESTAMENT OF JUDAH 14:1-4

And now, my children, I say to you, be not drunk with wine; for wine turns the mind away from the truth and inspires the passion of lust and leads the eyes into error. For the spirit of fornication has wine as a minister to give pleasure to the mind; for these two also take away the mind of man. For if a man drinks wine to drunkenness, it disturbs the mind with filthy thoughts leading to fornication and heats the body to carnal union; and if the occasion of the lust is present, he does the sin and is not ashamed. Such is the inebriated man, my children, for he who is drunken reverences no man.

This is a profound *mystery*—but I am talking about Christ and the church (5:32). In Paul's letters a *mysterion* is the current revelation of a truth unrevealed in the OT. Its use here is unexpected until we realize that Paul's teaching on husband/wife relationship truly is a stunning and unexpected unveiling of the true nature of God's intent for marriage. Genesis 2:24, to which Paul refers, lays the foundation for the marriage union. But the implications of that union only became clear when Christ appeared and modeled marriage for us in His relationship with His bride, the church.

As discussed later in The Passage in Depth, the model for marriage seen in Ephesians is in stark contrast to the view common in the first-century world—and all too often to the view held by many Christians today.

Children, obey your parents in the Lord (6:1). The exhortation is addressed directly to children. Apparently Paul expects children to be present in the congregations where his letter will be read!

The phrase "in the Lord" is not intended to release children whose parents are unbelievers from the obligation of obedience. Rather the phrase suggests the transformation of the family initiated by Christianity. In Roman society the *paterfamilias* was supreme. The phrase "in the Lord" is an explicit recognition that both children and parents are subject to Christ. It is His authority that is supreme in the family as in the church.

Honor your father and mother—which is the *first commandment with a promise* (6:2). The phrase is puzzling for this fifth commandment is not the first of the ten associated with a promise. One suggestion is that *protos* ("first") here is used anarthrously in order to indicate that "honor your father and mother" is *a primary commandment.*

Perhaps, however, the rabbis who viewed this as the weightiest of the commandments were correct. Psychologically at least this would be the first commandment to have meaning to a young child. And a child who learns to relate appropriately to his or her parents is far more likely to later relate properly to God.

Fathers, do not *exasperate* your children (6:4). The Greek word is *parorgizete,* which suggests such unreasonable treatment of children that they become discouraged or resentful. Even more significant, however, is the fact that Paul makes fathers responsible for the treatment of their children. Under Roman law the father was supreme within the household. While his children owed him respect and obedience, he was under no obligation to consider their feelings or well-being. The extent of this right is illustrated in the fact that if an owner sold a slave, and the slave later purchased his or her own freedom, the first owner had no further claim. But if a father sold a son or daughter into slavery, and that child purchased or won his freedom, the father could sell his child again and again.

Thus in the context of the times, Paul's indication that living a life of love obligates Christians to family and social inferiors as well as obligates Christians to respect their families and social superiors was truly revolutionary.

Slaves, obey your earthly masters with respect and fear. . . . And masters, treat your slaves in the same way (6:5, 9). The same stunning theme of *mutual obligation* is here introduced into the most oppressive of first-century social institutions. At that time slaves were property, with few personal rights. Paul calls for slaves to "live a life of love" by giving their human masters wholehearted service. And then he calls for Christian masters to view their slaves as fellow human beings, and to live their life of love within the framework of that social institution by showing consideration for their slaves. This theme of mutual obligation is found in several NT passages, reproduced here.

Slaves, obey your earthly masters with respect and fear, and with sincerity of heart, just as you would obey Christ. Obey them not only to win their favor when their eye is on you, but like slaves of Christ, doing the will of God from your heart. Serve wholeheartedly, as if you were serving the Lord, not men, because you know that the Lord will reward everyone for whatever good he does, whether he is slave or free.

And masters, treat your slaves in the same way. Do not threaten them, since you know that He who is both their Master and yours is in heaven, and there is no favoritism with Him (Eph. 6:5-9).

Slaves, obey your earthly masters in everything; and do it, not only when their eye is on you and to win their favor, but with sincerity and reverence for the Lord. Whatever you do, work at it with all your heart, as working for the Lord, not for men, since you know that you will receive an inheritance from the Lord as a reward. It is the Lord Christ you are serving. . . .

Masters, provide your slaves with what is right and fair, because you know that you also have a Master in heaven (Col. 3:22-25).

Slaves, submit yourselves to your masters with all respect, not only to those who are good and considerate, but also to those who are harsh. For it is commendable if a man bears up under the pain of unjust suffering because he is conscious of God. But how is it to your credit if you receive a beating for doing wrong and endure it? But if you suffer for doing good and you endure it, this is commendable before God (1 Peter 2:18-23).

Put on *the full armor of God* so that you can take your stand against the devil's schemes (6:11). *The Teacher's Commentary* interprets the armor passage, noting:

Many different interpretations of the armor have been given, and its equivalents in the panoply of the Roman soldier of Paul's day have been discussed. But what is most important has often been overlooked: Paul here describes the armor *which enables us to stand against attacks on our life together as Christ's new community.* Viewed from this perspective, what are the divine resources we have been given? (p. 932)

■ The belt of truth. "Put off falsehood and speak truthfully [with your] neighbor," Paul has warned, "for we are all members of one body" (4:25). Openness and honesty gird us together; misunderstanding and hidden motives divide.

■ The breastplate of righteousness. "There must not be even a hint of sexual immorality, or of any kind of impurity, or of greed" (5:3) among God's holy people. Righteous living is essential, guarding the very heart of our shared lives.

■ Feet fitted with the Gospel of peace. More than once in this letter Paul has stressed how the Gospel brings peace, reconciling us to God and making us one. In Ephesians, peace is the bond that holds the unity created by the Spirit. When unity is maintained, Christ's church is enabled to move in full responsiveness to its Head.

■ The shield of faith. We maintain a confident hope in the reality and power of God. This trust extinguishes doubt. We are inade-

quate in ourselves, yes. But our trust is in God, who "is able to do immeasurably more than all we ask or imagine, according to His power that is at work within us" (3:20).

■ The helmet of salvation. Salvation has brought us to a new life and identity. By keeping our identity as Christ's living church constantly before us, our perception of life is transformed. Satan's dreams of distorted relationships cannot cloud the mind of a person who grasps the full meaning of the salvation we enjoy in Christ.

■ The Spirit's sword. Why does Paul explain here that the sword is "the Word of God"? (6:17) It is because, in all of Eph., Paul has not discussed Scripture as he has the other elements of our armor. This vital tool is needed for us to wage our spiritual warfare.

"And pray in the Spirit on all occasions with all kinds of prayers and requests. . . . Be alert and always keep on praying for all the saints" (6:18).

THE PASSAGE IN DEPTH

Wives and Husbands (5:21-33).

Background. It has been suggested that no one living today can grasp the beauty of this famous passage on husband/wife relationships. In order to understand, one would have to reproduce the attitude toward women that existed in the first century. Perhaps even more significant, one would also have to reproduce the attitude toward personal significance. For in the highly stratified social world of the first century, status was fiercely guarded, and the rights of the superior were asserted whatever the expense to an inferior.

Thus as background to Eph. 5 we need to look at (1) the general attitude toward women in society, and (2) the assumptions about personal significance which were reflected in every social institution, including marriage.

ASSUMPTIONS ABOUT WOMEN

Lefkowitz and Fant in their anthology on *Women's Life in Greece and Rome* (Baltimore: Johns Hopkins University, 1982) provide a variety of quotations on women from ancient writers. Together they portray an attitude that would hardly be shared by even the most

chauvinistic men today. Two typical examples suffice. The Greek Simonides, writing *On Women* in the sixth century B.C., says:

Yes, this is the worst plague Zeus has made — women; if they seem to be some use to him who has them, it is to him especially that they prove a plague. The man who lives with a woman never goes through all his day in cheerfulness. . . . Just when a man most wishes to enjoy himself at home, she finds a way of finding fault with him and lifts her crest for battle. The very woman who seems most respectable is the one who turns out guilty of the worst atrocity.

In the first century A.D. the Roman Valerius Maximus comments on historic relationships between great men of Roman history and their wives. He writes:

Egnatius Metellus . . . took a cudgel and beat his wife to death because she had drunk some wine. Not only did no one charge him with a crime, but no one even

481

blamed him. . . . Gaius Sulpicious divorced his wife because he had caught her outdoors with her head uncovered: a stiff penalty, but not without a certain logic. "The law," he said, "prescribes for you my eyes alone to which you may prove your beauty. . . . If you, with needless provocation, invite the look of anyone else, you must be suspended for wrongdoing." Quintus Antistius Vetus felt no differently when he divorced his wife because he had seen her in public having a conversation with a common freedwoman. For, moved not by an actual crime but, so to speak, by the birth and nourishment of one, he punished her before the sin could be committed, so that he might prevent the deed's being done at all, rather than punish it afterwards. . . . And so, long ago, when the misdeeds of women were thus forestalled, their minds stayed far from wrongdoing.

This easy assumption of a man's right to treat a woman however he wished is reflected in the writings of Ben Sirah as well. In 9:2 he warns, "Give no woman power over you to trample upon your dignity." While Ben Sirah's writings frequently praise marriage and describe a good wife as a great blessing, those same writings make it clear that the relationship between husband and wife in Judaism as in the secular world was not conceived of as a relationship between equals. Thus Ben Sirah writes:

> Depressed men, saddened face,
> broken heart—these from an evil wife.
> Feeble hands and quaking knees—
> from a wife who brings no happiness to her husband.
> In a woman was sin's beginning;
> on her account we all die.
> Allow water no outlet,
> and be not indulgent to an erring wife;
> If she walks not by your side,
> cut her away from your flesh with a bill of divorce (25:23-26).

By the first century Judaism did define 10 duties that a husband owed to his wife. These included such things as providing medical treatment, a respectable funeral, food, the support of her daughters till they married, etc. However, the "something indecent" (Deut.

24:1) over which a man might divorce his wife was, according to Edersheim, interpreted then to include "every kind of impropriety, such as going about with loose hair, spinning in the street, familiarly talking with men, ill-treating her husband's parents in his presence, and even speaking to her husband so loudly that the neighbors could hear" (*Sketches of Jewish Social Life*).

There is no question that marriage was viewed far more positively in Judaism than in secular society. Even so, the orientation to marriage as reflected in Ben Sirah was male, reflecting on how the wife benefited her mate, and not on how he might serve or benefit her. Thus Ben Sirah writes:

> Though any man may be accepted as a husband,
> yet some women are better wives than others.
> A woman's beauty makes her husband's face light up,
> for it surpasses all else that charms the eye.
> And if, besides, her speech is soothing,
> his lot is beyond that of mortal men.
> A wife is her husband's richest treasure,
> a help like himself, a staunch support.
> A vineyard with no hedge will be overrun,
> a man with no wife becomes a homeless wanderer.

ASSUMPTIONS ABOUT PERSONAL SIGNIFICANCE

The world of the first century was rigidly stratified. Persons with higher status assumed that they were intrinsically superior to their social inferiors. Thus an individual's personal significance, in his own eyes and in the eyes of others, was determined largely by his social position.

Stambaugh and Balch, in *The New Testament in Its Social Environment,* observe that "the 'honorable ones' regarded the 'humble' with disdain and without apology across the great gulf fixed between them." The authors go on to note that "classical literature is filled with upper-class sneers, unrelieved by any sense of compassion, at the disgusting laziness and squalor and servility of the poor. . . . Even at meals, whether private dinner parties to which a rich patron invited some of his clients or public banquets given by an aristocrat for his fellow citizens, your place and even what you got to eat depended strictly on your status" (p. 114).

This orientation to status was reflected in the honorifics of which the Greek language was full. But, as the NT letters illustrate, Christianity mounted a powerful challenge to this way of thinking. Paul, in speaking of the "administration of God's grace that was given to me" (3:2) claims no exalted title, but instead speaks of himself as a mere "servant of the Gospel" (3:7). When he mentions the church's apostles, prophets, evangelists, and pastor/teachers he stuns the first-century reader by casting them in the role of preparing God's people for *their* works of service—an educational task typically performed by slaves or freedmen, lowest in the social order despite their intelligence or talent (4:11-12). When defining the church as a *patria* in which Jew and Gentile are heirs together, members together, and sharers together in one body (3:6), Paul sets forth an egalitarian model which literally had no parallel in ancient cultures. As Paul affirms elsewhere, having clothed ourselves with Christ there is "neither Jew nor Gentile, slave nor free, male nor female, for you are all one in Christ Jesus" (Gal. 3:28).

As we come to Eph. 5:21-33, then, we can only discern the powerful truth he affirms if we see that passage against the background of the first-century society. A society where women were valued, but only insofar as they contributed to the happiness of men. And where men assumed, without ever imagining an alternative view might possibly exist, that the husband's status so totally overshadowed that of the wife that, while a man might care for his wife, he owed her little or no duty beyond that of physical maintenance. It was literally unthinkable to initiate any discussion of husband/wife relationships as Paul does here, with the statement, "Submit *to one another* out of reverence for Christ" (5:21).

Interpretation. The controlling principle in this discussion of husband/wife relationships is 5:21, unfortunately isolated from 5:22 by a heading and paragraph in the NIV. That "submit to one another out of reverence for Christ" is the controlling principle is illustrated in two ways.

First, Paul moves to discuss interpersonal relationships in three settings: husband/wife, parent/child, and master/slave. Each situation involves relationships in which culture assumed the absolute authority of one party, and the total submission of another. In each situation Paul affirms the responsibility of the "subordinate" to be responsive to the "superior."

And in each situation Paul calls on the "superior" to show a concern for the "subordinate" which was *not* expected culturally. In fact in each situation what Paul calls for would have been considered not only inappropriate, but in fact would have been considered a shameful *subordination of a superior to an inferior.* While to us today the injunctions to "love your wives," "do not exasperate your children," and "treat your slaves [considerately]" seem almost commonplace, in the first century these injunctions were radical indeed.

The second reason to view "submit to one another" as the controlling principle in each of these situations is grammatical. In the Greek, v. 22 reads *Hai gynaikes tois idiois andrasin hos to kurio,* "Wives to your own husbands as to the Lord." The verb "submit to" is not in the original text, but is assumed by the translators from v. 21.

The issue that Paul is discussing in Eph. 5:22-23, then, is how a husband and wife *submit to one another* out of reverence for Christ. In developing this theme Paul is careful not to suggest that a wife should adopt a mode of relating to her husband which violates cultural norms for the institution of marriage. Nor does Paul suggest slaves rebel and violate the norms of that institution. The wife is to be responsive to her husband, as the church is responsive to Christ. Slaves are to obey their earthly masters.

The radical change is that within the context of each institution, the tyrant is to *learn to submit* by coming to see and to treat the wife, child, or slave as a human being with feelings, needs, and concerns that the "superior" is responsible to meet!

What does this mean within marriage? We can summarize by noting three charges which Paul gives to the husband:

■ Husband, love your wife (5:25).

■ Husband, love with Christ's intent (5:26-28).

■ Husband, love your wife as you love yourself (5:33).

Husband, Love Your Wife (5:25). If this phrase had been penned by a classical writer, he would surely have chosen one of three words for "love." *Erao* expressed sexual passion, and it is appropriate for the Christian husband to have a continuing, maturing desire for his wife. *Phileo* and *storgeo* were terms often used to express family affection. And it is appropriate for husbands to feel a warm affection for their wives. Paul, however, chooses to use *agapao,* a mild term in secular Greek, but a word infused with unique Christian meaning by its use in the NT. Here *agapao* expresses unselfish love—a love that consciously commits itself to see to the welfare of the beloved, whatever the personal cost.

In choosing to put the wife's welfare first, for this is what *agapao* implies, the husband willingly subjects his own interests to the needs of his wife, and thus submits to her, out of reverence for Christ.

Husband, Love with Christ's Intent (5:26-28). Paul reminds us that Christ loved the church and gave Himself for her "to make her holy." Our Savior's intent was that through His ministry to us we might become all that we can be. His intent was to lift us up. His intent was to enable us to become.

In the first century the upper classes saw marriage as significant to advancing the man's wealth or standing. The family from which his wife came, the dowry she brought, these were important because of their impact on *his* status in the community. The idea that a husband should concern himself with the needs, the ambitions, the potential of his wife, never crossed the mind of the first-century male.

But this is just what Paul is arguing for. The husband must love his wife, see her as a person, and concern himself with meeting her needs and helping her achieve her potential.

Husband, Love Your Wife as You Love Yourself (5:33). In marriage the husband and wife are united as one. A wife is not to be viewed as a piece of property, but as an extension of the husband himself. We devote ourselves to maintaining our health and wholeness, and promote our own development. This same concern must be lavished by the husband on the wife.

And with this said, Paul returns to the wife.

The husband must love the wife, and the wife owes her husband appropriate respect.

Application. All too often the debate in modern times has focused on the wrong questions. How much authority does the husband possess? How is the wife to submit? Can a wife work if her husband disapproves? Does the man have the right to disciple (or beat) his wife? Can women be doctors or lawyers?

Paul himself refuses to become involved in this kind of debate. In every culture certain patterns of behavior are considered appropriate within the context of its institutions. Paul is not calling for the overthrow of marriage or the family, or even for the abolishment of slavery. He is not critiquing the expectations his society imposes on wives, or children, or masters. Paul is arguing that, within the church, each person, whatever his role in society, owes a debt of mutual submission to others. This debt can only be paid by infusing every relationship with *mutual commitment.* The wife owes duties to her husband. But the husband owes his wife a love which puts her needs on a par with his own, and puts her growth and development ahead of his own. The child owes duties to his father, but the father owes his child careful consideration and training. The slave owes duties to his master, but the master must learn to see and treat the slave as a person of worth and value, and not simply as property.

What has happened, of course, is that the Christian ideal has gradually, and over the centuries, so transformed cultural expectations that most of us assume the way of life Paul calls for here. We read these verses and say, "Of course," and never realize how revolutionary these words are.

For some, of course, they remain revolutionary. For the man who appeals to Scripture as an excuse for mistreating his wife, the words still must be heard. Paul is not speaking about the institution of marriage, but about the relationship of marriage partners. When the husband loves with Christ's love, and with Christ's intent, and cares as much for his wife's well-being as he does his own, the issues so often debated are easily resolved. Where the husband does not love, or seek to live in mutual submission, the issues cannot be resolved, and the marriage will fall far short of God's ideal.

PHILIPPIANS
Called to Joy

EXPOSITION

Paul's letter to the Philippian church was written while he was imprisoned in Rome, awaiting trial. Paul's warmly personal missive is notable for its emphasis on joy and rejoicing despite difficulties.

Paul's letter adopts the standard form for a letter, but introduces an invention which later became standard. After a brief *salutatio* (greeting, 1:1-2), Paul moves to the *captatio benevolentiae* (1:3-11). In this section, traditionally intended to secure the good will of the reader, Paul shares his deep affection for the Philippians and reaffirms the mutual commitment they share to the Gospel, as well as a specific prayer he offers on their behalf. It is at this point that Paul introduces his own invention, which by the second and third century became a convention: he shares information on his own present situation and feelings about it (1:12-27). Paul is frustrated by his imprisonment and uncertain about the future. But he sees evidence that what has happened to him has "served to advance the Gospel" (1:12), and in this he rejoices.

The rest of the letter is more complex, as Paul shifts several times between *narratio* and *petitio* (specific request or demand) before reaching his brief *conclusion* (4:21-23). Within the body of the letter are several sets of exhortation intermixed with various narrations and a striking hymn concerning Christ. Paul urges a life worthy of the Gospel (1:27-30), marked by a unity (2:1-4) which can only be achieved by a Christ-like humility in relating to others (2:5-17). In an aside Paul asks the church to welcome back Epaphroditus, and to be responsive to the ministry of Timothy (2:18-30). At the same time they must "watch out for" Judaizers, who would turn the Gospel of grace into a religion of human effort (3:1-11). Again Paul urges his readers to keep their focus on Christ, and follow his pattern of committed living while looking forward to the Lord's return (3:12–4:1).

The letter then introduces a series of brief exhortations of both personal (4:2-3) and universal (4:4-9) nature before thanking the Philippians for a financial gift, and putting their generosity in spiritual perspective (4:10-20).

In part because of its complexity and the various topics taken up, some commentators have argued that Philippians is a composite of several different letters rather than a single composition. However, there is no compelling reason to assume that Philippians is not what it purports to be: a letter written by Paul during his imprisonment, and carried personally to Philippi by Timothy and Epaphroditus, filled with warm personal

485

notes and exhortations that are totally appropriate from the apostle to a congregation he holds in such warm regard.

WORD STUDIES

Because of your *partnership* in the Gospel from the first day until now (1:5). The Greek word *koinonia* means "to have something in common with." This word is used 13 times by Paul, and is the term he uses to describe what we today call "giving." In view of this, and the parallel of the construction here with Rom. 15:26 and 2 Cor. 9:13, it suggests that Paul is referring to the fact that the Philippians have, from the first, contributed financially to enable Paul to continue his evangelizing ministry.

So that you may be . . . *pure* and *blameless* until the day of Christ, *filled with the fruit of righteousness* that comes through Jesus Christ — to the glory and praise of God (1:10-11). Paul prays that the Philippians might be the best Christians possible, and uses three adjectives to describe what is involved in achieving that goal.

"Pure" is *eilikrineis,* "to discern by the light of the sun." The imagery suggests living a life so open and transparent that all will be aware of the individual's moral integrity.

"Blameless" is *aproskopoi,* a compound meaning "not causing someone to stumble" or "not stumbling." Paul may mean for us to take the adjective in both senses. The Christian is to be equally careful to avoid obstacles intended to trip him up, and to avoid any action which might trip others up.

The "fruit of righteousness" is an image commonly used in Scripture to portray the qualities of character produced by God's work within the believer's personality (Amos 6:12; Gal. 5:22). This fruit can only be produced by an inner transformation worked by God's Spirit through Christ.

It is for this reason that a Christian's pure, blameless and fruitful life truly is "to the glory and praise of God." Only God is able to make us the best that we can be.

It has become clear throughout the whole *palace guard* and to everyone else that I am in chains for Christ (1:13). Since Paul had appealed his case to the emperor, he was guarded by shifts drawn from the emperor's Praetorian Guards (the meaning of *praitorio* here). How striking that whatever happens to us the Lord truly does turn to good. How else would the members of this elite military force have had the opportunity to hear the Gospel?

Some preach Christ out of envy and rivalry, but others out of good will (1:15). Later Paul will turn his attention to the Judaizers, who distort the Gospel by insisting on works as essential for salvation (3:2-11). Here the tension is personal rather than doctrinal. Some become more active evangelists out of a competitive spirit, taking a perverse pleasure in the thought that Paul is in bonds and unable to reach out. Others become more active evangelists out of love, in an effort to relieve Paul of the concern that expansion of the Gospel will be set back by his enforced idleness.

It is fascinating to see how Paul refuses to judge motivations, and is delighted in the fact that for whatever reason the Gospel is being preached. Few of us are this mature. Paul's critics might bitterly resent his success, but the apostle will not resent theirs! Instead he will rejoice that Christ is being preached, and leave the question of motives to the Lord.

What has happened to me will turn out for my *deliverance* (1:19). Paul does not refer here to his release from prison. The most serious danger any of us faces is the discouragement that difficulties often create. Paul does, however, "eagerly expect" and "hope" that through the experience "Christ will be exalted in my body, whether by life or by death" (1:20).

"Eagerly expect" (*apokaradokia*) is found only in Christian literature after Paul and suggests a concentrated focus on what is ahead. "Hope" is the family *elpis,* which indicates the confident anticipation of future contingency sure to be realized. The secret of deliverance from any current threat to our spiritual health is to focus on the future that is assured to us by and in Jesus Christ.

Who, being in very nature God, did not consider equality with God something *to be grasped* (2:6). The word *harpagmon* is used only here in the NT, and is rare in other literature. In this context the argument makes it clear that Paul uses it to provide the ultimate example of humility. Christ, who existed as God, equal with the Father, did not see maintaining His status as something that must be held on to at all costs. Rather than insisting on the status that was appropriate to His essential nature, Christ willingly emptied Himself and took on human form. If this was Christ's attitude, how foolish we are to struggle to maintain the scraps of status offered us in human society!

For more on this exalted hymn and its role in the argument of Philippians, see The Passage in Depth below.

Continue to *work out your salvation* with fear and trembling, for it is God who works in you to will and to act according to His good purpose (2:12-13). Paul assumes that the Philippians are saved. Thus it becomes important to "work out" the experiential dimension of that new life which the believers now possess.

Even this does not depend on us, but rather on the fact that the God who grants us salvation works in us. His working transforms our wills and our actions, so that our desire and drive is channeled into performing God's will.

Salvation is not won by works. But the salvation which God gives us is so dynamic a reality that it will necessarily work itself out in our lives.

But even if I am being *poured out like a drink offering* on the sacrifice and service coming from your faith, I am glad and rejoice with all of you (2:17). In both pagan and Jewish rites sacrifices typically involved pouring wine on top of the sacrifice or at the foot of the altar. This libation generally completed the sacrifice.

The Apostle Paul's use of the present tense here suggests that he sees his present suffering as something of a seal stamped on the sacrificial giving and works of service of the Philippian believers. What Paul is saying is that he is truly glad and thankful to be able to share with them in this way in their own ministry and service to God.

He almost died for the work of Christ, risking his life to make up for the help you could not give me (2:30). Paul commends Epaphroditus because of his willingness to *paraboleusamenos te psuche*. The image here is a strong one that suggests a reckless act. Lightfoot suggests it might be used of "persons who risk their lives to nurse those sick with the plague." In fact, the word was unknown outside the NT until it was found in a second-century A.D. inscription near the Black Sea, where it means "to daringly expose oneself to danger."

We know little about Epaphroditus. We know he was a member of the Philippian church. We know he brought Paul a contribution from them. We know he was desperately ill while with Paul, and that the apostle was deeply concerned about him. And, from the participle *paraboleusamenos* we know that his decision to reach Paul with aid was made in the full awareness that to do so was to risk his life. The commitment Paul felt to the Philippians was reciprocated, at least by this man who came from them.

***Finally,* my brothers, rejoice in the Lord! (3:1)** The use of *to loipon* here has been taken by some as evidence for later additions to this book. However, a survey of contemporary literature suggests that the phrase was also used to introduce new topics, and thus might as well be rendered "furthermore." In this case the paragraph heading is misleading, for the exhortation to "rejoice in the Lord" goes with what follows, and stands in contrast with Paul's warning against depending on the flesh (human works).

Watch out for those dogs, those men who do evil, those *mutilators of the flesh.* For it is *we who are the circumcision* (3:2-3). Paul very consciously calls the men he describes dogs (*kuon*). This is a word for unclean street mongrels, used in contrast to the diminutive affectionately applied to house dogs (*kunarion*). "Dog" was a term of contempt frequently applied by the Jews to Gentiles. Here Paul turns the epithet back against the Jews, who "do evil" and "mutilate the flesh." This last phrase involves a play on words, contrasting *katatome* (to cut for religious purposes) with *peritome* (circumcision). Paul's point is that the Jews practice a rite which is meaningless because rather than rejoicing in the Lord as the source of salvation, they cut the flesh in the expectation that this rite will have saving value. Because circumcision in contemporary Judaism has lost its spiritual significance, and because that significance is understood by the ones who believe in Jesus, it is the Christians who are truly "the circumcision" — that is, the covenant people of God.

For whose sake I have lost *all things*. I consider them rubbish. Paul's use of *panta* here is significant. He has listed those things emphasized by Judaism which he himself once considered of value in his effort to establish his own righteousness. If such things had any value, Paul's claims to spiritual superiority were at least as firmly based as those of the Judaizers who now trouble the church. In fact, however, Paul has turned his back on them, and not only on them, but on "all things" upon which any human being anywhere might rely to establish a claim on God's favor.

Simply put, all such things are rubbish, of no value at all. Only Christ, and the righteousness which God gives to those who are found in Him, has any meaning at all.

And so, somehow, to *attain to the resurrection* from the dead (3:11). It is surprising that so many commentators persist in seeing Paul's remark as eschatological. Paul is eager to experience the power unleashed and made available to believers in Christ's resurrection (3:10). He continues in the same vein with the unusual phrase, *ten exanastasin ten ek nekron:* a resurrection "out from" the dead. What Paul is deeply committed to is to live his life in Christ so that the lifestyle which emerges will be that truly stunning expression of Christianity — godliness from the spiritually dead. The phrase "and so, somehow" expresses not doubt but wonder. And the train of thought reflects a truth that Paul not only grasps, but has clearly expressed in Rom. 8:11: "And if the Spirit of Him who raised Jesus from the dead is living in you, He who raised Christ from the dead will also give life to your mortal bodies through His Spirit, who lives in you."

Life, emerging from the dead, indeed! Life,

emerging not by any human effort but by the supernatural working of God within.

Forgetting what is behind and straining toward what is ahead, I press on toward the *goal* (3:13-14). Paul's powerful analogy is drawn from athletics. It enables us to sense the intensity with which the runners drive themselves toward the goal, muscles straining.

Actually "goal" is *skopos,* "goal marker." This was a post at the end of the course on which the runner would fix his eyes and by which he could measure his progress. Paul doesn't define what serves as goal markers in our Christian experience. Perhaps the answer is self-evident, the model of Christ who made it His purpose to fulfill the will of God and whose resurrection power enables us to choose that same will as our own.

I plead with Euodia and I plead with Syntyche to *agree with* each other in the Lord (4:2). "Agree with" can't explain the breadth of *to auto phronein.* The Greek phrase, "to have the same mind," emphasizes a harmony in attitude and emotions as well as of outlook.

It's not enough for Christians to agree on doctrine, or even on practice. We are called to a unity rooted in a love that overcomes hurts as well as disagreements, and that dissolves grudges.

Whatever you have learned or received or heard from me, or seen in me — put it into practice (4:9). This verse is perhaps the classic summary of the Christian teaching, for both instructor and learner. The two pairs of verbs describe the instructor's role. "Learned" and "received" describe instruction; "heard from" and "seen in" describe the example set by the instructor. Christian teaching involves the description of a reality which the believer is called to experience. Thus the teacher must both describe and demonstrate Christianity.

The learner, however, has a single responsibility. He or she is to "put into practice" that which is taught. One can be said to have learned only when one *does,* not when one *knows* in the sense of mastering words and concepts.

THE PASSAGE IN DEPTH

Imitating Christ's humility (2:1-11).

Background. The idea that God could or would become a man was a major stumbling block to thoughtful pagans. Celsus, a Greek who wrote about A.D. 170, considered the doctrine of the incarnation "shameful," and argued that "God is good and beautiful and happy, and exists in a most beautiful state. If then He comes down to men, He must undergo a change, a change from good to bad, from beautiful to shameful, from happiness to misfortune, and from what is best to what is most wicked" (Cels. 4:14).

In Hellenistic/Roman culture it was not unthinkable that a human being might be raised to divinity. Some critics of Christianity even granted that Jesus might be such a person, although they were averse to considering the Jewish wonder-worker on a par with some of their own ancient heroes, or even with Jewish heroes like Daniel. But for the One God that the enlightened pagans of the first century did believe in to leave that "good and beautiful and happy state" in which He must exist to become a mere human being? Never! Such a transformation would not only be against God's nature; it would be against His best interests as well!

For Paul too the thought is stunning. Yet the Incarnation had happened. And thus rather than deny its possibility on theological/philosophical grounds, Paul invites us to reevaluate our perception of God, and to reevaluate our notion of what is "good and happy and beautiful," in view of what the Incarnation necessarily involved.

This is exactly the force of Paul's opening call to the members of the Christian community at Philippi to maintain their unity by doing "nothing out of selfish ambition or vain conceit, but in humility consider others better than yourselves. Each of you should look not to your own interests," Paul writes, "but also to the interests of others" (2:3-4). In adopting this attitude the Christian follows the example set by Jesus Christ in His incarnation. The good, happy, and beautiful are not found in looking out for one's own interests, but in spending oneself in the interest of others.

Interpretation. Philippians 2:6-11 is generally agreed to be a hymn of the early church, whether written by Paul or simply quoted by

him here. The exact structure of the hymn is debated, but its dual theme is clear. Jesus voluntarily chose incarnation, and subsequently Jesus was exalted by God's sovereign action.

Jesus' Voluntary Act (2:6-8).

The phrase "being in very nature God" (2:6) is literally "existing in the form [*morphe*] of God." The word *morphe* implies a harmony between appearance and essential nature, so that the one reflects the other. Paul's emphasis here is not so much on Christ's essential nature as it is on the status which Christ rightly enjoyed because He was God in that essential nature. Every outward sign and symbol, every privilege of deity, belonged to Christ because Christ *is* God.

When Paul says Christ did "not consider equality with God something to be grasped" it is the *status* associated with deity, rather than Godness itself, that he has in mind. Christ's underlying attitude was displayed in His act of emptying or making Himself "nothing," and in "taking the very nature [again, *morphe*] of a servant, being made in human likeness" (2:7).

On the one hand the grammar indicates that Christ always existed in the form of God, while in the Incarnation He also took on, as a new thing, the form of a servant. Here too *morphe* implies both essence and image, but again emphasizes image. In becoming a human being, Jesus did not cease to be God in His essential nature. But He did abandon the status and deity, exchanging it for the status of a "servant."

The word translated "servant" is *doulos*, a bond-slave. Paul's point is: as a slave has no social advantage but is in fact disadvantaged by the absence of all status, so Jesus totally abandoned His status as God to live as a "nothing" among men.

But Paul goes on. Living among us as a human being Jesus humbled Himself even more, and permitted Himself to suffer the most shameful and painful of all ancient forms of execution: crucifixion (2:8). Thus Christ's attitude was *totally* selfless, totally self-sacrificial, solely directed toward the interests and needs of others. And thus in the Incarnation we discover truths about God and His love for human beings that no one could imagine before.

489

God's Sovereign Act (2:9-11). The voluntary humiliation of Jesus was followed by His exaltation by the Father. Christ was not only raised from the dead and restored to a status appropriate to His nature; Christ was "exalted . . . to the highest place" and given a "name that is above every name" (2:9). The Greek word is *huperupsosen,* a word occurring only here in the NT, which means literally to "super-exalt."

In this act God gave to Jesus a name, Lord (2:11), at which every knee must bow and which every tongue must confess (2:10). Thus God's restoration of Jesus is to a higher status—that is, a higher *visible* position and rank—than He enjoyed before.

Before Christ voluntarily chose the path of self-emptying He existed as God, but in unbelief human beings could and did ignore Him. Now, raised and super-exalted and given the name Lord, Christ will return in glory and in that great denouement will be acknowledged by all, believer and unbeliever alike. The believer recognizes Jesus today and gladly chooses to kneel before Him. The unbeliever will recognize Jesus when He comes and against his will shall be forced to kneel and confess Christ as Lord of all.

The pattern seen in the passage then is as follows:

	Pre-Incarnation	Incarnation	Post-Incarnation
Essence	God	God/Man	God/Man
Form	Deity	Human	God/Man
Status	Equality with God	Rightless-slave	Super-exalted
Name	God the Son	Jesus the Christ	Lord

Application. While this great hymn of the early church has tremendous theological impact, Paul introduces it in order to make an ethical point. What is right and good and beautiful is to "consider others better than yourselves" (2:3) and to look "to the interests of others" (2:4). This is a position which ran counter to cultural values, for in Hellenism the right and good and beautiful thing to do was to consider yourself and your interests always, and strive for personal fulfillment. No wonder pagan thinkers objected to the notion that God would choose to become incarnate. Their view of God was shaped by their values,

and they could not believe that God would act in a way so foreign to their own outlook.

In contrast Judaism and Christianity call us to accept God as He reveals Himself to us, and then to shape our values to fit Scripture's revelation of God. Rather than argue that God would not choose humility because we would never willingly do so, the Christian looks at the example of Christ and decides to choose humility because by doing so Christ revealed humility as a virtue.

Rather than consider position and status to represent that which is good and happy and beautiful, we look at the example of Jesus and realize that the good and happy and beautiful life is a life lived for others.

There is, of course, another aspect of this hymn which is important to us. Jesus chose the way of self-humbling, and the result was that God super-exalted Him. God *is* a rewarder of those who live out His values. Because we hold God's approval a far greater good than anything we might gain here, we gladly choose to abandon status for servanthood. And because we hold happiness in eternity of greater benefit than any pleasures enjoyed during our brief existence here on earth, we treasure the opportunity to share in the sufferings of Christ.

Paul's great hymn in praise of Christ makes unmistakably clear the implications of several rather enigmatic statements recorded in the Gospels. "Whoever exalts himself will be humbled, and whoever humbles himself will be exalted" (Matt. 23:12; Luke 14:11; 18:14).

"Whoever wants to save his life will lose it, but whoever loses his life . . . will find it. What good will it be for a man if he gains the whole world, yet forfeits his soul?" (Matt. 16:25-26) And so the great paradox is explained. For the Christian, the way up leads down. And giving is the path to gain.

Joy in Philippians.

Background. Everyone wants to be happy. This was as true in the first century as it is today. And, in that era, a variety of philosophies offered ethical systems which promised to guide students to a whole and happy life. These systems were far too sophisticated to mistake "feeling happy" for happiness. And so the philosophers set about redefining the term, for while they could not help anyone feel happy, it was certainly possible to convince them that their state was a happy one, however they might feel!

Most of the philosophies of the day, each of which had roots going back some hundreds of years, had its own notion of happiness and how to achieve it. The Stoics and Platonists generally agreed that it was necessary to be happy to live a moral life, and that such a life could be achieved only when reason dominated the emotions and guided the soul. The Cynics were convinced that they had found a shortcut to happiness. This was living a simple life; in practicing to be "in need of only a few things." A person who wants little is self-sufficient, and free from the wants and worries of those caught up in the drive for possessions. To the Epicurians, happiness seemed absurdly easy to attain. They simply distinguished "happiness" from "pleasure," and filled life with a few austere activities which were as isolated as possible from pain. Happiness is to be found in "sober reasoning" which leads to an "understanding of the ultimate good of the flesh and its limits" and so "supplies us with the complete life" (Diogenes Laertius).

The philosophers considered joy (*chara*) a subdivision of pleasure (*hedone*). As an emotion *chara* was viewed with suspicion by the Stoics, who under the pressure of common opinion later did classify it as a "good mood" of the soul. While the other schools had a more positive view of joy, they still saw it as something reserved for the wise, who approached obtaining it as they approached the search for happiness.

What is striking in the NT use of this concept, whether in the form of a noun (*chara*) or verb (*chairo*), is that it retains its basic secular force. Yet how one experiences this strong, positive, confident, and exalted mood is directly linked with another of faith's paradoxes. Even as the way to exaltation is by voluntary humiliation, illustrated in Phil. 2:6-11 (see above), so the Christian's joy is often experienced in circumstances that no one would consider happy! Joy, a grace produced in us by the Holy Spirit (Gal. 5:22), can be experienced in and despite of tribulation. The joy we Christians know lies ahead for us somehow spills over from the eschatological future into our present, and we know joy.

Interpretation. The words "joy" and "rejoice" occur 14 times in this brief letter. *Chara,* "joy," is found in 1:4, 25; 2:2, 29; 4:1. *Chairo,* "to

rejoice," is found in 1:18; 2:17, 18, 28; 3:1; 4:4 (twice). In addition *sugchairo,* "to rejoice with," is found in 2:17 and 18.

■ Occurrences of *chara*:
1:4-5: "I always pray with joy, because of your partnership in the Gospel from the first day until now."
1:25: "I will continue with all of you for your progress and joy in the faith."
2:2: "Make my joy complete by being likeminded."
2:29: "Welcome him [Epaphroditus] in the Lord with great joy."
4:1: "Therefore, my brothers, you whom I love and long for, my joy and crown. . . ."

Chapter 2 of this great book contains Paul's appeal for the Philippians to adopt the outlook of Christ and to put the interests of others first. The christological hymn in this chapter makes it clear that those who voluntarily humble themselves will be exalted by God. Thus there is an eschatological reward in store for those who adopt Christ's attitude.

But even a quick reading of those verses in which *chara* appears makes it evident that this lifestyle brings *present* as well as *future* reward. As we Christians become involved in one another's lives, we find that a sense of joy infuses us. A sense of partnership binds us together; observing one another's growth in the Lord thrills us; and the others who have become dear to us become a source of constant joy whatever our circumstances.

■ Occurrences of *chairo*:
1:18: "Whether from false motives or true, Christ is preached. And because of this I rejoice. Yes, and I will continue to rejoice."
2:17 "But even if I am being poured out like a drink offering on the sacrifice and service coming from your faith, I am glad and rejoice with all of you."
2:18 "So you too should be glad and rejoice with me."
2:28: "Therefore I am all the more eager to send him, so that when you see him again you may be glad [*chairo*]."
3:1: "Finally, my brothers, rejoice in the Lord!"
4:4: "Rejoice in the Lord always. I will say it again: Rejoice!"

Here 1:18 suggests that a focus on communicating the Gospel to others is a source of joy for the Christian. Both 2:28 and 4:4 return to the theme of mutual bonding within the fellowship as a source of joy, while 3:1 calls for a focus on one's personal relationship with God.

■ Occurrences of *sugchairo*:
2:17: "But even if I am being poured out like a drink offering on the sacrifice and service coming from your faith, I am glad and rejoice with all of you."

2:18: "So you too should be glad and rejoice with me."

Here Paul blends the themes of ministry and of relationships. Joy comes as we participate with others in serving Christ, and any sacrifices we may make or suffering we may endure takes on new meaning as the commitments that move us are shared.

EXPOSITION

Colosse is the least significant of the cities to receive one of Paul's letters. Although once a great city, when Paul wrote it was an "insignificant market town" outstripped in importance by both Laodicea and Hierapolis, some 10 and 12 miles distant. Yet Paul's letter to Colosse is a critical and powerful statement of the centrality of Jesus Christ, written to a church apparently confused about His primacy. While the population of Colosse was primarily Phrygian and Greek, 2,000 Jewish families had been settled in the district by Antiochus III over 200 years earlier. Thus the cultural roots of Colosse itself were diverse—a factor in the development of a "Colossian heresy" which seems to have involved a synthesis of pagan, Greek, and Jewish ideas. The details of the system of thought Paul challenges remain undefined. But the central issues are clear, as Paul writes to assert the primacy of Jesus Christ, and to describe the life those who follow Jesus are to live in this world.

After a brief greeting (1:1-2) Paul expresses his appreciation for the Christian community at Colosse (1:3-8), and shares the prayer for them which has long been on his heart (1:9-14). Having assured the Colossians of his appreciation and concern for them, Paul moves immediately to the critical issue which concerns him: their view of Jesus Christ. Because of who Jesus is in His essential nature, and because of what He accomplished for us in His death, Christ must in all things be granted the supremacy which truly is His (1:15-23). Paul's whole life since his conversion has been focused on just one thing: explaining the hope that "Christ in you" brings. For whatever fine-sounding arguments others may advance, "all the treasures of wisdom and knowledge" are summed up in Christ (1:24–2:5).

Paul now reminds his readers that "just as you received Christ Jesus as Lord," so we are to "continue to live in Him." Power for Christian living is not found in any "human tradition" but rather in the new life to which we have been raised with Christ (2:6-12). We Christians live in a new world—a world not characterized by the now-canceled IOUs collected under the Law (2:13-15), or by rules and rituals imposed by those in Colosse who have lost sight of the significance of Christ. What counts in Christian experience is that vital relationship which Jesus maintains with members of His body—an organic relationship, in which growth depends on maintaining close connection with Christ our Head (2:16-19). The retreat of so many in Colosse to ascetic practices may have an "appearance of wisdom," but in reality these disciplines are "self-imposed" and have no value in countering the passions that surge in the flesh (2:20-23).

Soon Paul will go on to describe the lifestyle that will emerge as the Colossians refocus their faith on Christ. But that lifestyle is only made possible by a relationship with a Person who truly is God, from whom both the pattern and power for holy living can be drawn.

WORD STUDIES

The faith and love that spring from the hope that is stored up for you in heaven (1:5). "Hope" in Paul's letters can refer either to a settled confidence about the future (the act of hoping) or to the thing which is hoped for (the content of the hope). Here the emphasis is on the thing hoped for—a future which God has already prepared and keeps safe for the believer in heaven. This "future orientation" of true Christianity may have been criticized by the false teachers of Colosse. It has certainly been criticized by scoffers since then, who have characterized our faith as offering "pie in the sky by and by." Yet for those of us who realize that the years we spend here are less than the blinking of an eye compared with the endless extent of the eternity toward which all men are propelled, that "by and by" is rightly given priority.

Whatever any human philosophy may seem to promise, only Christ can guarantee our eternal future.

Commercials Nothing New

Today's advertisements that feature "before" and "after" pictures of men and women who have lost 40, 50, or 100 pounds on "diet X" really are nothing new. The philosopher Porphyry, a disciple of Plotinus, produced this testimonial to the value of his master's views:

There was also Rogatianus, a senator, who advanced so far in the renunciation of public life that he gave up all his property, dismissed all his servants, and resigned his rank. When he was on the point of appearing in public as praetor and the lictors were already there, he refused to appear or to have anything to do with the office. He would not even keep his own house to live in, but went the round of his friends and acquaintances, dining at the house of one and sleeping at another (but he only ate every other day). As a result of this renun-

ciation and indifference to the needs of life, though he had been so gouty that he had to be carried in a chair, he regained his health and, though he had not been able to stretch out his hands, he became able to use them much more easily than professional handicraftsmen. Plotinus regarded him with great favor and praised him highly and frequently held him up as an example to all who practiced philosophy (*Vita Plotini* 7).

Certainly Rogatianus' commitment to the philosophy of Plotinus led to significant improvement in his physical health. But only commitment to Christ offers eternal life.

He *has rescued* us from the dominion of darkness *and brought* us into the kingdom of the Son He loves (1:13). "Rescue" (*errusato*) is to deliver, to liberate. The imagery harkens back to the OT and the suffering of Israel under Egyptian tyrants. What is perhaps more significant is the verb tense: God "has rescued" us in Christ from the tyranny of darkness, and "has brought" us into Christ's kingdom. The verb here is *metestesen*, used to describe moving a group of people from one country and resettling them in another. God has delivered us from the tyranny of darkness. And unlike the Exodus generation, we are not doomed to wander for years in an empty wilderness. We have been resettled in "the kingdom of the Son He loves," where Christ rules, and where we can experience a new life, *now*.

So Christianity is *not* simply a religion of "pie in the sky by and by." Relationship with Jesus has an overwhelmingly powerful impact on our life now, liberating us from the old and freeing us to live out the new.

And through Him to *reconcile to Himself all things,* whether things on earth or

things in heaven (1:20). This verse has sometimes been interpreted to teach universalism — the belief that ultimately everyone, including Satan, will be saved. That argument depends on identification of the "all things" of v. 20 with the "all things" of v. 16, which clearly includes angelic beings, combined with a soteriological understanding of *apokatallaxai*, "to reconcile."

If we accept the phrase "all things" in its widest and most likely meaning, two strong alternatives to universalism are available, each of which has the advantage of being in harmony with Scripture's unmistakable teaching that Satan and those who follow him are destined for eternal punishment.

The root *allasso* means "an alteration of things" and in the NT indicates a change in relationships. The form we have here, *apokatallasso*, emphasizes the completeness and finality of the change in view. Whenever the relationship between God and human beings is in view, the particular change in relationship is the restoration of harmony between God and man, God's enemy. And that restoration is always viewed as accomplished by Jesus Christ in His death and resurrection (Rom. 5:10-11; Eph. 2:16; etc.).

Here, however, the "all things" said to be reconciled by Christ are not human beings at all, but as defined in 1:19 either focus our attention on the whole creation, or on those fallen angelic beings referred to there as thrones, powers, rulers, and authorities. It seems best then to ask the question: Just what "alteration" of relationship does the rest of Scripture teach was accomplished by Jesus between (1) God and the whole creation, or (2) God and fallen angelic beings.

If (1) the "all things" encompasses the total creation, personal and impersonal, material and immaterial, it would seem best to understand the verse to teach that Christ accomplished a reordering of a universe run wild, corrupted in every aspect by Satan's and then by human sin. Christ's death and resurrection, followed by His exaltation to the throne of God, was that cosmic act on the basis of which God will bring the universe back into complete harmony with goodness and with His perfect will.

If (2) the "all things" in view are fallen angels, then the change effected by Christ was subjugation. Their rebellion was effectively put down, for in the cross Christ "disarmed the powers and authorities," and "made a public spectacle of them, triumphing over them by the cross" (2:15).

However we understand this verse, its place in Paul's argument is easy to see. The Colossian heresy was eroding the place rightfully owned by Christ in Christian faith. And so Paul responds. Christ is not only God, the Creator and sustainer of the universe; Christ's incarnation and death on the cross were central in God's plan for salvation — and in a cosmic as well as personal sense. In His death Christ saved those who believe, and once and for all established God's Sovereign control of the entire universe. Christianity is Christ, for Christ truly is supreme.

Now I rejoice in what was suffered for you, and *I fill up in my flesh what is still lacking in regard to Christ's afflictions, for the sake of His body, which is the church* (1:24). It is clear that Christ's suffering for us on the cross is totally efficacious. As the writer of Hebrews says, "we have been made holy through the sacrifice of the body of Jesus Christ once for all" (10:10). In what sense then did Paul's suffering supply "what is still lacking" in regard to Christ's afflictions *(thlipseon)*? Two popular views have held that (1) Paul means he is suffering *for the sake of* Christ, or that (2) Paul's sufferings *resemble those of* Christ. There is, however, a better solution: we are Christ's body, and Christ is present in us. Thus Christ continues to suffer with us as we Christians know pain and difficulty. So on the road to Damascus Christ said to Paul, who was actively persecuting Christians, "Why do you persecute *Me?*" (Acts 9:4) In persecuting Christians, Paul was persecuting Christ!

Now Paul is one of those who experienced suffering as a Christian, and the great apostle is deeply aware that Christ feels his every pain. Yet the apostle takes great joy in suffering "for you [the Colossians]." As vulnerable human beings living in a corrupt world, we are subject to suffering of many kinds. But Paul's suffering is the specific consequence of his commitment to Christ and the Colossians. Paul has identified himself with Christ's mission, and can rightly view his sufferings as something voluntarily undertaken for the sake of the church, and thus view them as afflictions which help "fill up" (complete?) what Christ must yet suffer for the sake of His people here on earth.

See to it that no one takes you captive through *hollow and deceptive philosophy*, which depends on human tradition and the basic principles of this world rather than on Christ (2:8). In the first century "philosophy" was not so much a system of speculative thought as it was a perspective which provided guidance for living one's life in this world. Each contemporary "philosophy" was rooted in notions about the nature of the universe and man's place in it. And each propounded to define a path for life that was assumed to be in harmony with the underlying reality.

According to Paul, the problem with such philosophies is that they are *kenes apates*, "empty deceit." Like a highly decorated balloon, human philosophies may appear attractive, but they are empty, without any substance to support their appearance. Paul even explains. Human philosophies depend on the "tradition of men"—and man is fallible. Simply because a viewpoint is ancient doesn't make it correct. Human philosophies also rest on "the basic principles of the world." The Greek term translated "basic principles," *stoicheia*, originally indicated the alphabet, and later the physical elements. In the sense chosen by the NIV it means the elementary; the ABCs. By nature man is so limited that he can never gain more than a kindergartener's grasp of reality.

The final flaw in the philosophies which have distracted the Colossians is that they ignore Christ. Rather than depending on Christ as the foundation of our understanding, they depend on old and worn-out ideas developed by people who by nature are so limited that they can never get beyond the ABCs in their grasp of reality.

How foolish we are today if we allow ourselves to become impressed by the wise of this world, and fail to remember that however far their intellect may be beyond our own, their best is as nothing compared to wisdom of God revealed in Christ and recorded in the Word of God.

Having *canceled the written code*, with its regulations, that was against us and stood opposed to us (2:14). The "written code" is *cheirographon*, "handwriting." All understand this as a reference to the Mosaic Code, but debate in what sense it is intended. *Cheirographon* may describe the Law as an indictment drawn up against us, the accused. Or it may describe the Law as a list of charges which we, the accused, have read and signed, indicating the charges are accurate.

This second sense is preferable, and reminds us that divine Law indicts Jew and Gentile alike. As Paul points out in Rom. 2, while the Jew affirms the validity of God's Law, conscience serves a similar function among the Gentiles by testifying that right and wrong do exist—and that each individual has knowingly done that which he or she believes to be wrong.

This Law consists of regulations ("legal demands," RSV). These are "against us" in that all are subject to Law through the Mosaic Code or conscience, and "stood opposed to us" in that when we could not satisfy its requirements, the Law necessarily became our accuser. But because of Christ, Law and its handwritten bill of indictment have become irrelevant! Christ "canceled" the indictment: He "took it away"; He "nailed it to His cross."

The Greek word for "canceled" means to blot out, to wipe away, or in the case of a law, abolish. In Christ every obligation we have had to God because of the Law is wiped away, and we are freed to live our new lives without reference to the past.

And having *disarmed* the powers and authorities, He made a public spectacle of them, triumphing over them by the cross (2:15). The Greek verb is *apekdusamenos*, intensive here in the middle voice, and meaning "having stripped." Just what Christ stripped from the hostile angelic rulers of the "dominion of darkness" (1:13) is not specified. Some assume the imagery is military, and the angelic rulers were stripped of the weapons which gave them power over humanity. However, the kingdom context suggests a political rather than military setting, and the reference to making these beings a "public spectacle" indicates another fascinating possibility.

In the Roman Empire those intangible assets which persons in power possessed, and through which they dominated others, were *auctoritas* and *dignitas*. Colleen McCullough, in the glossary of her fascinating bestseller *The*

Grass Crown, describes these qualities as follows:

> *auctoritas.* It carried nuances of pre-eminence, clout, leadership, public importance, and—above all—the ability to influence events through sheer public reputation (p. 993).

> *dignitas. Auctoritas* was public, *dignitas* personal, an accumulation of clout and standing stemming from a man's own personal qualities and achievements. Of all the assets a Roman nobleman possessed, *dignitas* was likely to be the one he was most touchy about; to defend it, he might be

prepared to go to war or into exile, to commit suicide, or to execute his wife and son (p. 1101).

What Paul may very well be saying in this verse is that through the Cross Christ stripped demonic powers of their *auctoritas* and *dignitas.* They are no longer able to influence events through sheer reputation. And the reputation gained by past achievements has crumbled into dust, as in the Cross Jesus publicly exposed their ultimate powerlessness.

Supernatural powers and authorities can now be ignored, for the one with real *auctoritas* and *dignitas* has been revealed. And we gladly shift our total allegiance to Him.

THE PASSAGE IN DEPTH

Christ and the Colossian Heresy (1:15–22).

Background. The theory that Paul wrote this letter to attack an emerging heresy was strongly advanced by Bishop Lightfoot in his 1875 commentary on Colossians. Since then scholars have debated not only the nature of but also the existence of such a heresy. While it has not been possible to give a clear definition of the heretic system, it does seem clear that Paul did write to combat a heresy, and that its major elements can be discerned.

In part, evidence for the existence of a heretical system is found in a number of words and expressions associated with ancient religious ideas and mystery religions. Paul speaks of teachers of a "philosophy," which they present as ancient (and therefore to the first-century person, trustworthy). These teachers use catchwords like "fullness" (*pleroma*) and catch phrases like "things seen upon entering" (*ha heoraken embatteuon*). The false teachers also insisted on "voluntary worship" (*etheloth-reskia*) of angelic beings (*threskei ton angelon*) who were placated by strict observance of taboos (cf. 2:21) and by "severe treatment of the body" (*apheidia somatos*).

Again, the details of the heresy which had taken root in Colosse are debated. Does Paul write against Essene Judaism, a pagan mystery cult, a syncretism of gnosticized Judaism and paganism, or Jewish Christian mystical asceticism? Yet while the exact nature of the Colossian heresy is uncertain, it is clear that Paul writes to combat a specific threat to the

church. And, as we examine what he says in the light of known philosophic systems of that time and the next few centuries, the basic tenets of the Colossian heresy can be discerned.

First, it is clear that the Colossian heresy was rooted in *dualism.* That is, those who troubled the church in Colosse made an assumption common in Greek philosophy that both the material and immaterial universes were co-eternal. That is, matter had not been created by God. Matter existed from the beginning, and God—or a lower deity—had simply *shaped* already existing matter to "create" our world.

Another ancient tradition held that God existed at a distance from and unaffected by what happens in the material world. Later Plotius would refine the work of Plato and present a complex argument to show that between the immaterial God and the material universe a series of "emanations" must exist.

Plotius developed the theme already present in some philosophies that only the immaterial God was truly "good." He argued that in this case, in contrast, the material must be "evil." It followed that God could not contaminate Himself by any contact with the material universe. How then was the material universe shaped in its present form? To solve the problem Plotinus postulated a series of beings standing between God and the material universe. Those closer to God were more "immaterial" and more "good." Those closer to the universe were more "material" and "evil."

The god who actually shaped the universe, the *demiurge* of Plato, simply could not possibly be "God," but must be one of the lower-ranking, more "material" angelic powers.

While we should not read the developed philosophy of Plotius (A.D. 207-260) back into the first century, the basic elements of his philosophy surely did exist within the culture, and the mystic tendencies exhibited in Plotinus were also present both in Judaism and in oriental mystery cults. Thus as we read Colossians and see the themes Paul emphasizes, we can reconstruct the basic beliefs held by the false teachers who were corrupting this early church. And we can appreciate why Paul responds to their teachings as he does.

The first reason for Paul's vigorous response is that the Colossian heresy *completely undermines the central role in Christianity of Jesus Christ.* Even if Jesus is recognized as a deity, He must by definition be a *lower* deity, for no being higher in the ordered ranks existing between the universe and God would deign to contact the "evil" material world. Jesus could even be acknowledged as Plato's demiurge, or Scripture's Creator, and still be relatively insignificant.

And so the proponents of the Colossian heresy may have given lip service to Jesus, but urged the Christians to go beyond Christ to find the "fullness" of God. This they might achieve by voluntary humility and the worship of powers supposedly higher in rank than Jesus, and by carefully following taboos defining what they might and might not touch, what religious celebrations they must observe, and what they could or could not eat and drink (cf. 2:16-18).

Interpretation. After those preliminaries which marked polite correspondence in the first century, Paul immediately launches his critique of the Colossian heresy with a paragraph that makes perfectly clear the true nature of Jesus Christ and His work.

■ 1:15. "He is the image of the invisible God, the firstborn over all creation." The word "image" is *eikon,* which implies both likeness and manifestation. God's nature is stamped on Christ as the face of the emperor is stamped on a coin: Jesus is *recognizably* God, and thus is the revealer of God. The "invisible God" is not masked by serried ranks of angelic beings. He is present, available to the eye, in Jesus Christ.

The word "firstborn" is *prototokos,* which suggests both priority and supremacy. As far as time is concerned, Christ existed before the universe. As far as supremacy is concerned, Christ has the highest possible rank in the family of God. As God's heir Christ is the One who has the master's right over control of the entire universe. There is no way in which Christ is subordinate to "higher" angels.

■ 1:16-17. "For by Him all things were created: things in heaven and on earth, visible and invisible, whether thrones or powers or rulers or authorities; all things were created by Him and for Him. He is before all things, and in Him all things hold together." Here Paul makes a vital assertion. The material and immaterial universe are *not* coeternal. In fact, only God is eternal. Both the material universe and the immaterial universe were *created,* and by Christ!

This means that whatever angelic beings exist do so only because Jesus Christ created them! They are totally subordinate to Christ, and could not possibly be superior to Him. And yet there is more. It is only by Christ that "all things hold together." The word *sunesteken* means to "sustain." Paul's thought is that not only did Jesus bring the visible and invisible universe into existence, but it is only by the present continuous exercise of His power that the universe maintains its shape and form. If for a moment Jesus ceased to exercise that power, the cosmos would fall into chaos.

■ 1:18. "And He is the head of the body, the church; He is the beginning and firstborn from among the dead, so that in everything He might have the supremacy. For God was pleased to have all His fullness dwell in Him." Christ is supreme not only in the material and immaterial universe, but also in the church. In His resurrection Christ established a new humanity, responsive and responsible to Him alone. Rather than being a "lower" religion, Christianity is the highest faith, for the Christian is in an organic relationship with the one in whom all God's fullness dwells.

■ 1:20. " . . . and through Him to reconcile to Himself all things, whether things on earth or things in heaven, by making peace through

His blood, shed on the cross." For insight into this verse, see the Word Study on Col. 2:15, above.

■ **1:21-22.** "Once you were alienated from God and were enemies in your minds because of your evil behavior. But now He has reconciled you by Christ's physical body through death to present you holy in His sight, without blemish and free from accusation." Paul has established the supremacy of Christ in both spiritual and material realms. Now he shows that Jesus, the one in whom all the fullness of God dwells, entered the material universe and accomplished a spiritual purpose in His "physical body through death." The material and spiritual are *not* realms that are isolated from each other. Instead what happens in one realm can and does affect what happens in the other. Even as man rebelled in the physical universe by eating a forbidden fruit, and thus became "alienated" and "enemies in your minds," so God by dying in the physical universe has reversed the spiritual condition of those who believe the Gospel's good news.

Application. Jesus is the central and supreme figure in Christianity. He is utterly unique: God in His fullness, and yet truly human, master of material and immaterial universe.

Today we are unlikely to be drawn into the kind of religio-philosophical system to which those in the first century were vulnerable. But we are likely to make a similar dichotomy in our thinking. We are all too likely to relegate Jesus to the realm of the supernatural and unseen, and fail to realize that He exercises full control over the details of our ordinary lives as well, and that because of our relationship with Jesus we can influence events through prayer.

Christian Living
and the Colossian Heresy (2:6-23).

Background. The dualistic assumptions which lay at the heart of the Colossian heresy had practical as well as philosophical/theological implications. Dualism led to a denial of the full deity and primacy of Jesus Christ. Dualism also led to the view that man's nature had both "spiritual" and "material" aspects, and that the two were essentially unrelated. The inner, spiritual man was "good" and the physical, material man was "evil." It was the immaterial that could sense

and approach God. And this must be done through the mind or spirit.

Two different lifestyles grew out of dualism. The one lifestyle was characterized by licentiousness. If the physical is intrinsically evil, whatever sensual indulgence a person engages in is only what might be expected of the physical man. What is more, since there is no direct link between the immaterial and material, what the physical body does has no real impact on the spiritual part of man. A person can be a mystic, whose spirit reaches out to seek God, and at the same time a lecher whose body indulges in the grossest of sins.

The second lifestyle is characterized by asceticism. The good human spirit is trapped within an evil physical body. One way to strengthen the spiritual is to deny or punish the body by "harsh treatment." Here, it is discipline that counts—rigor in following rules that govern eating, sleeping, and touching. Rules that call for strictly observing hours and days of prayer or fasting.

While there is little or no indication in Paul's letter that the church was influenced toward licentiousness, there is significant evidence that a pattern of asceticism was being imposed by the heretical teachers. Paul warns about letting others judge you "by what you eat or drink, or with regard to a religious festival, a New Moon celebration or a Sabbath day" (2:16). He speaks of rules: "Do not handle! Do not taste! Do not touch!" (2:21) And he speaks of "harsh treatment of the body" (2:23). Taken together it seems clear that those who introduced false teaching in the Colossian church imposed not only a false theology but also insisted on an ascetic way of life that supposedly promoted spiritual advancement.

Interpretation. Paul has established that Christ Jesus truly *is* Lord. Now he calls on the Colossians to "continue to live in Him" (2:6) and to do so "just as you received Christ Jesus as Lord"—by faith. It is only as the believer is "rooted and built up in Him" that spiritual growth takes place (2:7).

The ascetic approach to spirituality advanced by the false teachers is "hollow and deceptive," a mere "philosophy" that is rooted in "human tradition and the basic principles [ABCs] of this world" (2:8). Paul then goes on to contrast the two approaches to the spiritual life.

■ The Christian approach: internal trans-formation (2:9-15). God gave His own fullness to us in Christ. Jesus exercises His power to go beyond that external and ineffective operation in the flesh which men call circumcision, and which served as an external sign of covenant relationship with God. Jesus reached deep into our personalities and performed an operation which *excised* the "sinful nature" (lit., "the flesh," *sarx*). He did this by uniting us to Christ (which is the sense of "baptism" here, as it is in 1 Cor. 12:13 and Rom. 6), taking the death we deserved and giving us His own new life. So, Paul says, when we were dead, "God made you alive with Christ" (2:13). And stripping all those powers which once dominated the lost of their *auctoritas* and *dignitas,* Christ freed the believer to live out a personal relationship with God.

■ The false teachers' approach: ascetic self-denial (2:16-23). In place of dynamic personal relationship with Jesus the false teachers offer only an empty system of regulations—do's and don'ts undertaken to win the favor of angelic beings supposedly standing between Christ and God, who demand self-denial as a sign of "voluntary humility." Paul, although describing the disciplines that the false teachers have imposed, calls their pretentions of humility and their "harsh treatment of the body" of no "value in restraining sensual indulgence" (2:23).

This is an important point. Rather than subduing the body, asceticism simply *redirects* expressions of the sin nature. Ascetics may not indulge in promiscuous sex, but their pride and the contempt they feel for those less disciplined is just as much sensual indulgence—just as much an expression of the flesh—as promiscuity would be.

Application. It would seem at first glance that Paul, while contrasting the externalism of the pseudo-Christian teachers who have infiltrated the Colossian congregation with vital Christianity, does not explain *how* to live out this inner life he commends.

In fact, however, Paul has already explained the secret. It is contained in the prayer which he offers regularly for the Colossians, as recorded in Colossians 1:9-12.

There Paul asks that God will fill the Colossians with a knowledge of that which God has willed (*tou thelematos autou* [1:9]). But this knowledge of the content of God's will, which we have in Scripture through revelation, must be held in "wisdom and understanding" (*sophia* and *sunesin* [1:9]). Each of these directs our attention to the ability to see the practical implications of God's revelation, "that you may live a life worthy of the Lord and may please Him in every way" (1:10).

What happens when we see the implications of God's revelation for life in this world, and respond by choosing to live a life worthy of Him? A series of participles tells us. We bear fruit in every good work. We grow in the (personal, not theoretical) knowledge of God. And we are strengthened by His own glorious might.

COLOSSIANS 3–4
A New Life to Live

EXPOSITION

In Colossians the Apostle Paul confronts a heresy that had captured the allegiance of many in the church there. The heresy was rooted in dualism: the view that the spiritual and the material worlds were opposed and coeternal. A spark in man participated in the spiritual, the realm of God and good, even though the body was material, a part of the "evil" physical universe.

The acceptance of these assumptions totally corrupted Christianity. Jesus Christ simply could not be identified with the ultimate God, for God could have nothing to do with the material universe. Jesus at best was a low-ranking member of that series of angelic beings which filled the gap between the material and the spiritual realms. Given the same basic assumptions, the "spiritual life" must be inner and intellectual, having little or no relationship to a human being's daily life. One might justify a life of sensual self-indulgence by shrugging off what the "evil" body did, or one might argue for a life of ascetic self-denial as an attempt to strengthen the inner person by denying the desires of the flesh.

In Col. 1–2 Paul confronts both the heretics' basic assumptions about reality and their conclusions. The reality is that Jesus created both the material and spiritual universe. Rather than being forever isolated from each other, they find their basis of unity in Christ, who stands now as Lord in each realm. In Christ, God the Son entered the material universe and through His death in a physical body reconciled "all things" to God, bringing both realms back into harmony with God. Thus Christ is exalted in Christianity to His rightful place of supremacy, a place denied Him in the "hollow and deceptive" philosophy seized upon by the heretics.

The Colossian heresy also has a faulty view of spirituality. Human beings do not have a dual nature: a "good" spiritual or inner man, and an "evil" physical or outer man. Human nature is totally corrupt, for by nature human beings are "alienated from God and . . . enemies in your minds because of your evil behavior" (1:21). But Christ has met our need. He bore our sins on the cross, and through faith's union with Jesus the old in us is put to death and we are given new life by God. This inner transformation is the basis for the spiritual life, and all those "regulations" followed by the ascetic with the intent of subduing the flesh are totally irrelevant to spirituality. In fact, "they lack any value in restraining sensual indulgence" (2:23).

With this established, the apostle now moves on in Col. 3–4 to describe the life lived by a person who has experienced inner renewal through Christ. Here we again see a striking contrast between the approach of the heretics in Colosse and the approach of biblical Christianity. In Christianity the life we live in the body is *not* irrelevant to spirituality. In fact, *true spirituality is expressed by the life we live in the body.* Thus the person who has experienced inner renewal will "put to death" sins that grow out of bodily passions (3:1-7) and egotistical pride (3:8-11). That inner renewal will be practically expressed by the compassion, kindness, humility, gentleness, and patience of the believer. That renewal will be expressed in the peace and harmony which marks the local Christian body as God's own (3:12-17). That renewal will be expressed in the positive way in which all persons relate to others within the structures established by their society (3:18–4:1). Thus true Christianity, far from supporting a dualistic view of reality, presents a unitary view of reality, in which the spiritual and material universes are united in Christ, and the Christian life is nothing less than Christ's life within us expressing itself in every act and relationship.

Chapter 4 of Colossians is essentially the letter's closing. Paul gives a few brief closing instructions (4:2-6), and adds personal greetings to a number of individuals in Colossae, and in nearby Laodicea (4:7-17). His last remark is a request to remember the apostle in his chains (4:18).

WORD STUDIES

Since, then, you have been raised with Christ, *set your hearts on* things above (3:1). The Greek word is *zeteite,* literally "seek." The word indicates both focus and urgency. Its present imperative tense indicates continuing action. Thus, keep your life focused on and keep on pursuing things above.

Since, then, you have been raised with Christ, set your hearts on *things above,* where Christ is seated at the *right hand* of God (3:1). The phrase "things above" (*ta ano*) has an ethical as well as a spatial connotation. Paul's point is not that all things of earth are intrinsically evil, but that we must be willing to evaluate all things in the perspective provided by eternity.

The further definition of "above" as that place where Christ is seated at the "right hand of God" makes a special contribution. In biblical times a position at the right hand of a powerful person was viewed as the place of honor, influence, and power. When the Christian evaluates by those things that are above we evaluate all things by Christ.

Set *your minds* on things above, not on earthly things (3:2). The Greek word is *phroneite,* which means to "consider" in the sense of "judge," "give your mind to," "be intent on," or "be sensible and reasonable." Christian spirituality is not simply a passion for holiness, but is a way of thinking; an orientation to life that is not earthly in nature but rather constantly takes Christ and His perspective into account.

When Christ, who is your life, *appears,* then you also will *appear with Him in glory* (3:4). The realities which the Christian knows by revelation and experience are "now hidden with Christ in God" (3:3). The gap between the invisible and visible worlds remains during this age, even though the gap was bridged by Christ and is even now being bridged in the believer who has died and been raised to new life in our Lord. But the time is coming when the unification of the two worlds achieved by Christ on Calvary will be realized by all. This will happen when Christ "appears." The Greek verb *phaneroo* means to manifest or make visible. When Christ visibly returns, at the same time our position "with Him in glory" will also become apparent to all.

***Put to death,* therefore, whatever belongs to your earthly nature (3:5).** The word *nekrosate,* "make dead," is very strong. And the aorist tense indicates a decisive act. This is very different from the approach taken by the Colossian heretics, who attempted to suppress the body by "harsh treatment." What Paul calls for is a decision to exterminate those things that are associated with the old, by shifting our allegiance totally to those things associated with the new life we have in Christ.

Paul is careful to define what "belongs to your earthly nature." He does not want us to mistake the morally neutral needs and desires associated with life here on earth as intrinsically sinful. And so he adds in apposition, "sexual immorality, impurity, lust, evil desires and greed, which is idolatry" (3:6). The first four all are linked with sexual vice. The last, greed (*pleonexian*), indicates a fierce and ruthless passion for material things.

It is this kind of thing that the believer is to decisively reject, "putting to death" and burying these expressions of the sinful nature.

Now you must *rid yourself* of all such things as these: anger, rage, malice, slander, and filthy language from your lips (3:8). The Greek verb *apothesthe* means to "put away." Both literally (Acts 7:58) and metaphorically (Rom. 13:12; Eph. 4:22), the word is used of taking off clothing. Together with "put to death" in 3:5 "rid yourself" is an image of decisively rejecting any expression of the old self in favor of the new (3:9–10).

In 3:5 the characteristics of the old self in view were essentially the sensual, growing out of fleshly passions. In 3:8 the characteristics are essentially attitudinal, growing out of one's psychological orientation.

"Anger, rage, malice" suggest a hostile disposition toward others. When directed against other persons "slander" (*blasphemia*) indicates insult and slanderous accusation, while "filthy language" (*aischrologia*) is more likely in this context to mean "abusive speech." Taken together they picture the ego run wild: self-absorbed, contemptuous, and hostile toward others in disposition and in action.

What Paul has done here, of course, is to provide two lists which represent, in 3:5, sins associated with the physical body, and in 3:8, sins associated with the psychological or inner man. Again Paul drives home the fact that the dualism of the false teachers in Colosse is truly an empty deceit. The corruption of human nature in the Fall defiles the whole person, and the renewal that is ours in Christ is intended to cleanse the whole person. Anything less is unworthy of Christ, and a denial of the new self the Christian becomes.

***Do not lie* to each other (3:9).** The form of the verb *pseudesthe*, with the negative particle, means "stop lying." The separate treatment given lying here tends to give it special emphasis. Why should this be? Perhaps because lying and deceit are the means by which most people express the hostility and malice toward others. The person who is openly antagonistic and verbally attacks those he comes in contact with drives others away, and is soon isolated from normal society. Many a person disguises his basic hostility with a veneer of sociability.

Since you have taken off your old self with its practices and have put on the new self, which *is being renewed* in knowledge in the image of its Creator (3:10). Paul has used images which might be misunderstood. "Put to death" and "rid yourself" seem to be single, decisive, once-for-all acts. Now Paul reminds us that while turning to Christ is a single act, and that conversion is a taking off of the old and a putting on of the new, *the renewal we experience is gradual and progressive.* We know this, for "being renewed" (*anakainoumenon*) is in the present tense, indicating a continuous process.

There are several reasons for hope in this truth. First, we are not forced to expect perfection of ourselves. When a new or a mature Christian fails, he or she need not question his or her salvation. Second, in Christ we *have* put on a new self. A vital newness exists for us. Third, this new self "is being renewed . . . in the image of its Creator." As Christians we are on a pathway that definitely leads upward!

It is possible for Christians to fail *temporarily.* But ultimately the new self given to us by God will find expression in our lives.

Therefore, as God's chosen people, holy and dearly loved, *clothe yourselves* (3:12). The call to "clothe yourselves" (*endysasthe*) is parallel to Paul's earlier calls to "put to death" and "rid yourselves." The present urgent call expresses the positive aspect of the Christian's personal responsibility, while the earlier calls express the negative aspect of the Christian's responsibility.

What Paul does in these exhortations is

remind us that, while the transformation we experience within is God's work in its entirety, you and I are responsible to make the moral choices which determine whether or not that work of God will find expression in our daily life. (See The Passage in Depth.)

Let the peace of Christ *rule* in your hearts, since as members of one body you were called to peace (3:15). The word is *brabeuo,* used only here in the NT. In earlier Greek it had a sporting connotation and meant "to umpire." It is possible that by the first century the word simply meant to decide or rule.

The critical question here is whether Paul is continuing to discuss relationships within the church, and thus the "peace" is interpersonal, or whether Paul introduces a new subject, and the peace is internal. The NIV translators favor the second view, in which case "peace" is a confidence that comes as we make choices within God's will. A lack of peace may well indicate that we need to rethink a decision or put it off for a time.

And whatever you do, whether in word or deed, do it all *in the name of the Lord Jesus* (3:17). In the first century to act "in the name" of another person was to act as his representative. All we say or do will help shape the impression others have of Jesus.

THE PASSAGE IN DEPTH

Rules for Christian Households (3:18–4:1).

Background. In the first century, as in our own day, most people unquestionably accepted the "rightness" of existing social institutions. They also unquestionably accepted the established expectations for those who fulfilled the roles within these institutions. Thus a Roman senator would never engage in trade, but must derive his income from land holdings or from wealth won (or extorted) while holding office in one of Rome's distant provinces or territories.

It was not that there is anything immoral about trade in any objective, biblical sense. But within that society engaging in trade was not considered appropriate for a senator, and in fact would have been deemed scandalous.

The fact is that in every society sets of expectations, usually unwritten but nevertheless understood by all, exist for every role. There may be nothing intrinsically "right" or "wrong" about these expectations. But to live harmoniously within a society, and to have influence within it, a person cannot violate the expectations associated with his or her role.

In certain things, the early Christians *were* radical, for they did violate the expectations of those within their community. For instance, the well-to-do who were "good citizens" were expected to take part in public affairs. But all public activities involved sacrifice to state gods or, later, the emperor as a god. This was simply not possible for Christians, and in time Christians were scorned as unpatriotic and even misanthropes.

Similarly Roman soldiers were expected to venerate the eagles that served as the symbol of their legion. Christian soldiers refused to take part in what they viewed as an act of idolatry but what their officers viewed as disloyalty. History records that many Christians in the Roman army were executed because of the stand they took to worship Jesus only.

Yet most often there was no compelling moral reason for Christians to violate the expectations of society. A Christian wife could be a "good" wife according to first-century views of marriage without denying Christ. A Christian father could be a "good" father without violating first-century views of the role of fathers. And a Christian slave could be a "good" slave according to first-century views of the role of slaves without violating his commitment to Christ.

It is important to recognize this fact as we read Paul's exhortations to wives and husbands, children and parents, and to slaves and masters. *What Paul says does not require us to accept the first-century view of marital roles, of parent/child relationships, or of slavery.* What Paul teaches here is simply that Christians are to fulfill the expectations that society has for them — so long as to do so does not involve a violation of the loyalty we owe to Jesus Christ.

Interpretation. Paul begins with the exhortation, "Wives, submit to your husbands, as is fitting in the Lord" (3:15–4:12). The series of exhortations introduced by this verse parallels instructions Paul gives in Eph. 5:21–6:9, and a discussion of that longer passage is included in the chapter on Eph. 5 and 6.

What we want to observe here are several principles that govern Paul's treatment of three sets of relationships: the relationship between wives and husbands, children and parents, and slaves and masters.

First, this series of exhortations grows out of the command in 3:17 to "do it all in the name of the Lord Jesus." As Christ lived His life here on earth within the framework provided by the expectations of His society, so we are to live within the framework provided by our society. This does not necessarily imply, for instance, that God places His stamp of approval on slavery. It does mean that a slave in the first century was to be guided by first-century norms governing the relationship of a slave with his master. As a representative of Christ within his society, the slave should be an *ideal* slave. Similarly as a representative of Jesus the master should be an *ideal* master.

Again Paul is not saying that slavery, or the behavior expected of a slave, is "right." This is not the issue at all. The issue is that to represent Christ the Christian needs to win the admiration of those within his society by excelling in those qualities of which the society approves.

We can draw a similar conclusion for wives. In the first century wives were expected to be submissive to their husbands, a quality expressed in a variety of ways. The Christian wife, to represent Christ, should set about winning the admiration of her husband and peers by excelling in those qualities of which the society approves.

Second, Paul emphasizes the duties expected of persons in each role he discusses. He does not discuss the rights of a wife or child or slave under the law. This is not surprising in view of other letters in which Paul urges Christians to voluntarily surrender rights in favor of duties. The classic example is found in 1 Cor. 9, where Paul outlines his rights as an apostle (9:1-12), and goes on to explain that he did not use (claim) any of his rights, preferring to "make myself a slave to everyone, to win as many as possible" (9:13-19). Paul goes on then to comment that "to the Jews I became like a Jew, to win the Jews" and "to those not having the law I became like one not having the law" (9:20-23). What Paul is saying is that when among Jews he made

himself subject to them in that he lived by *their* expectations, and when among Gentiles he lived by *their* expectations.

This was not "compromise," but rather duty—the same duty he urges on husbands and wives and children and parents and slaves and masters here in Colossians. The duty to serve as Christ's representative by being the very best in whatever role we may be asked to fill, as that role is defined by our society.

In this Paul *must* emphasize "duty," for there it is our calling as it was Paul's calling to "make myself a slave to everyone, to win as many as possible" (1 Cor. 9:19).

Third, in his description of how to live in society "in the name of the Lord Jesus" (Col. 3:17), Paul emphasizes the fact that duties are reciprocal. Every role in society has a complementary role. Employees have employers. Wives have husbands. Children have parents. Slaves have masters. While the person in the (socially) subordinate role has a duty to the person in the (socially) superior role, the person in the superior role also owes a duty to the person in the subordinate role.

This principle is more important than we might suspect, for it means that *ultimately social roles are irrelevant.* That is, for Christians, a social role is neither superior nor inferior. All a social role does is define *how* the Christian is to serve others.

Being a first-century wife meant serving a husband by submitting. Being a first-century husband meant serving a wife by loving.

Being a first-century child meant serving a parent by obeying. Being a first-century parent meant serving children by giving them gentle rather than harsh guidance.

Being a first-century slave meant serving a master by sincere hard work. Being a first-century master meant serving the slave by treating the slave fairly.

In Christianity, the role does not make any individual superior or inferior, for each of us is a slave called by God to serve others. In Christianity all the role does is define the duty we owe others, and *define how we serve them.*

Implications. The stunning implications of Paul's teaching here and in Ephesians are frequently overlooked. We make the mistake of the secular person by thinking of social roles as defining significance. But to the Christian, neither a male nor a female, a master nor a slave, is more significant than the other. Each is called to live within his or her role as a representative of Jesus Christ, so that whatever he says or does reflects the presence of Jesus within.

To this end we need to focus not on the prerogatives of our social roles, but on their duties. The central question becomes: How, given that I am a wife, a husband, a child, an employer, etc., can I now serve others? What unique opportunities does my role, as my role is understood in my society, give me for doing good?

It is also important to note the impact of this understanding of Paul's teaching on the continuing debate concerning women. Why does Paul call on the wife to "submit"? Is it because in the divine order women were created to be subject to men? Or is it because in the framework of first-century society women were expected to be submissive?

Many would argue that the basis for women's "submission," as they understand submission, is ontological and rooted in the creation order. But, in the context of Paul's teaching here and in Ephesians, serious consideration should be given to the possibility that Paul is consciously instructing first-century wives to live within the framework of society's expectations, in order to best fulfill the duty required of every Christian to "do it all in the name of the Lord Jesus, giving thanks to God the Father through Him" (3:17).

1 THESSALONIANS
The Word: Heard and Lived

EXPOSITION

Thessalonica was a vital, cosmopolitan city in the first century. From 146 B.C. it had served as the Roman administrative center for its province, winning the title "the mother of all Macedon." Paul arrived in the city early in A.D. 49. After a brief ministry in the synagogue there, described in Acts 17:1-9, Paul worked for a time with the predominantly Gentile converts he had won, until he was driven from the city. We do not know how many months Paul ministered in Thessalonica, but he was there long enough to engage in his trade (1 Thes. 2:9; 2 Thes. 3:8), for at least two special gifts to be sent from Philippi, and for the members of the young church to come to know Paul well (2:4-12). This letter, written from Corinth in A.D. 50, was written to express his enthusiasm for the vital nature of their faith and to encourage living to please God.

The letter begins typically, with thanksgiving for the Thessalonians' eager response to the Gospel. Not only did they receive the Word, the Word has sounded forth from them, so everywhere people are talking about what God is doing among them (1:2-10). Paul also reviews his ministry there, perhaps to counter the critics who followed him everywhere and attacked the faith by attacking Paul. Paul reminds them of how he ministered among them (2:1-12), of their own response to his teaching God's Word (2:13-16), and speaks of his continuing interest in their welfare (2:17–3:13). At this point Paul reminds them of his earlier teaching and urges them to live pure, holy, and loving lives (4:1-12). Paul also deals with an aspect of eschatology on which the Thessalonians are confused. Those who die as Christians will participate with living saints in the resurrection to take place when Jesus returns. It is appropriate to grieve for lost loved ones. But the future awaiting them and us introduces an encouraging element of hope (4:13–5:11). Four brief exhortations follow (5:12-22), and lead to the relatively brief conclusion which features a prayer Paul offers for the Thessalonians and requests for himself (5:23-28).

WORD STUDIES

Your work produced by faith, your labor prompted by love, and your endurance inspired by hope in our Lord Jesus Christ (1:3). Paul takes great comfort in remembering the tremendous progress in faith members of this young church have made in such a brief period of time.

Paul specifies three evidences of progress,

each of which is paired with a quality of character which produces it. Thus:

Quality		Expression
Faith	produces	Work
Love	produces	Labor
Hope	produces	Endurance

Note: "Work" (*ergou*) is the product of effort, "labor" (*kopou*) is unusual effort. Love moves us to do more than might normally be expected to serve others.

By pairing Paul reminds us of an important truth. Those inner Christian qualities, if they truly exist, will surely find expression in the way we live.

We know . . . that He has chosen you, because our gospel came to you not simply with words, but also with power (1:4-5). Paul has just noted that inner Christian qualities find expression in the way the believer lives his or her life. Now he makes a similar point. The Gospel comes as words, but not simply *with* words. The Holy Spirit infuses these words with power, and the two have a visible impact.

In this passage the words "came" (1:5), were "welcomed" (1:6), and then "rang out" (1:8) from those who were so powerfully affected by them that they became "imitators of us and of the Lord" (1:6).

They tell how you *turned to God* from idols to serve the living and true God (1:10). The Gospel message focuses our attention on Christ and the salvation God offers us in Him. Early Christian evangelists did not attack idolatry, but rather presented Jesus. Conversion was not a turning from idols to God, but a turning to God from idols. That is, the decision to turn to God was critical; the decision to reject idolatry followed.

We sometimes lose sight of this conversion order. We agitate for prayer in school, or against abortion, and urge social change. We confront an alcoholic or child abuser, and urge personal reformation. But salvation is not a matter of turning from alcohol to God. It's a matter of turning to God (and then) from alcohol.

They displease God and are hostile to all men in their effort to keep us from

speaking to the Gentiles so that they may be saved. In this way they always *heap up their sins to the limit*. The wrath of God *has come upon them* at last (2:15-16). Paul's reference is to Jewish opponents who in effect followed up their killing of the prophets and Jesus by continuing to oppose God by persecuting Christians. The phrase "heap up their sins to the limit" reflects a similar saying by Jesus found in Matt. 23:32. Paul's point is that God has established a limit, a line which when crossed makes judgment inevitable. The phrase *ephthasen de ep' autous he orge eis telos* might be rendered "wrath has overtaken them for good and all," indicating that not only has the line been crossed, but God has begun to execute the judgment which He has decreed.

It is important not to generalize this statement to incorporate the Jewish people as a whole. Paul makes it clear in Rom. 11 that even now a believing remnant of Israel is being preserved. Paul's words are directed against those Jews of Thessalonica who, like the leaders in Jerusalem, violently oppose Christ and His representatives.

That each of you should learn to *control* his own *body* in a way that is holy and honorable, not in passionate lust like the heathen, who do not know God (4:4-5). The word translated "control" is *ktasthai*, which usually means "acquire," while "body" is *skeuos*, "vessel." While *skeuos* is used metaphorically of the body in the LXX and in the NT as well, in 1 Peter 3:7 both a husband and wife are referred to as *skeue*, and the woman as the "weaker vessel."

An NIV footnote acknowledges this by giving as an alternative reading, "learn to acquire a wife, not in passionate lust, like the heathen."

Whichever rendering reflects Paul's intent, the apostle is intent on reminding the Thessalonians that they are not to be dragged about by their sex drive.

Perhaps it is more needful, in our society, to emphasize the alternate rather than the accepted meaning. Too many young (and older!) people have been programmed to see love and marriage primarily in terms of sex, and to seek a mate among those who are most arousing sexually. Not surprisingly, marriages based on "passionate lust" seldom last.

Make it your ambition to lead a quiet life, to mind your own business and to *work with your hands,* just as we told you (4:11). Paul's instruction suggests that many in Thessalonica were idle and needed to concentrate on getting their own affairs in order. However, his call to "work with your hands" suggests much about the social strata making up this church.

In the Roman world working with one's hands was considered demeaning—an activity suited only to slaves and those freedmen at the bottom of the social order. In contrast Judaism exalted working with one's hands, and the Jewish ideal was a man who was trained in both the Scriptures and in a trade. Christianity shared this view of work, and to set an example the Apostle Paul himself followed his trade of tentmaking (leather working) whenever possible.

Paul's call to "work with your hands" strongly suggests that most Christians in Thessalonica were drawn from the lower classes (1 Cor. 1:26-31).

For God did not appoint us to *suffer wrath* but to receive salvation through our Lord Jesus Christ (5:9). This verse has been used by some as a proof text to show that the Christian will not go through the time of tribulation which the OT prophets and Christ Himself associate with the Second Coming and history's end. However, wrath (*orge*) here, as in 1:10, is better understood as the wrath to be expressed at rather than preceding Jesus' return.

Do not *put out the Spirit's fire* (5:19). Older versions read "Quench not the Spirit," which is the literal meaning of *to pneuma me sbennute.* The figure of fire is related in both Testaments to the Holy Spirit and His activities (Jer. 20:9; Matt. 3:11; Luke 3:16; Acts 2:3). This very brief verse is followed immediately by a reference to prophecies (5:20-21a). Thus many conclude that "quenching" the Spirit is refusing to speak out when the Spirit prompts you to share His message.

THE PASSAGE IN DEPTH

Paul's Ministry in Thessalonica (2:1-12).

Background. Chapter 1 of this book relates what happened when the Word of God came to Thessalonica. In that chapter Paul emphasizes the supernatural, the power of the Gospel, and the role of the Holy Spirit.

In chapter 2, Paul gives us a fascinating insight into the *human dimension* of evangelism. In essence, Paul shows us evangelism at its best, in which the supernatural and the natural, the divine and the human, work together to win others to Christ and nurture their growth in the Lord. In fact, nearly every verse in this section helps us better understand the nature of effective personal ministry.

Interpretation. Paul's description of evangelism at its best features three powerful elements. These are:

- Integrity (2:3-6)
- Investment (2:7-9)
- Involvement (2:10-12)

Integrity (2:3-6). Paul begins by reminding the Thessalonians of the kind of person he is—and proved to be among them. Paul doesn't expect disagreement. He says, "You

know we never used flattery" (2:5) and later "You are witnesses. . . . For you know that we dealt with each of you as a father deals with his own children" (2:10-11). Paul had established a relationship with the Thessalonians which was so intimate that the apostle was certain the members of the church would never doubt him when he spoke of his motives.

How many people in our churches today do we know well enough to be confident of their motives? How many know us that well? It is important to act with integrity. But it is also important to be close enough to others that they know us well enough to be *sure* of our integrity.

What, then, does integrity in an evangelizing relationship involve? Paul says the following:

> For the appeal we make does *not* spring from *error* or *impure motives, nor* are we trying to *trick you.* On the contrary, we speak as men approved by God to be entrusted with the Gospel. We are *not trying to please men* but God, who tests our hearts. You know we *never used flattery, nor* did we put

on a *mask to cover up greed* — God is our witness. We were *not* looking for *praise from men*, not from you or anyone else (2:3-6).

The passage is filled with what we might call "negative description." Paul's integrity is seen first of all by understanding what his motives and methods do *not* involve.

■ Not spring from error (2:3). The Greek word for error is *planes*, used here in the passive sense of self-delusion. Although apparently an intellectual trait, Paul may see in this word a reflection of the Hebrew words for "fool," which do have a moral dimension. Paul's ministry does not spring from error, for in his integrity Paul is not morally corrupt. He knows the purifying truth of God, and presents it to others.

■ Not impure motives (2:3). The word *akatharsia* typically denotes sexual impurity. It is likely that the itinerant teachers who traveled from city to city in the first century promoting their philosophies frequently exploited others sexually. Paul states what all in Thessalonica knew: he was not a "user," and in his integrity he refrained from exploiting others sexually or in any other way.

■ Not trying to trick you (2:3). The word here is *dolo*, "guile" or "trickery." At times Paul was accused of this by his enemies (2 Cor. 4:2; 12:16). But he refused to rely on the oratorical techniques to which persons in the first century were so responsive. Referring to this in 1 Cor. 2:4, Paul says, "My message and my preaching were not with wise and persuasive words." There was not the slightest dishonesty in Paul's approach to ministry, in his heart, or in the way in which he presented the Gospel to others.

■ Not trying to please men (2:4). Paul was often accused of adjusting his lifestyle or his message to his audience, and so compromising his integrity (Gal. 1:10). But the phrase "trying to please men" implies trying to please men *for his own advantage.* Paul ministers with integrity. The only glory Paul seeks is God's, and the only one's benefit Paul seeks is the person he is trying to reach with the Gospel.

■ We never used flattery (2:5). The Greek

word, *kolakeias,* is found frequently in classical writings, where it describes saying nice things to gain some selfish advantage. The love and affection that Paul has frequently expressed for the Thessalonians has no element of *kolakeias* in it. In all such expressions the apostle has been utterly sincere.

■ Not put on a mask to cover up greed (2:5). "Greed" is *pleonexias.* The term is more inclusive than another Greek word which indicated a passion for money. Here "greed" involves any and all sorts of self-seeking.

Paul ministered with integrity for, as we would say, he was not in the ministry for what he could get out of it.

■ Not looking for praise from men (2:6). Here "praise" is *doxan,* honor or glory. What Paul is saying here is that he was not in the ministry for any prestige, or for the awe which the philosophers and magicians of the time so craved.

And so in a few brief words and phrases Paul describes the integrity required of one who would minister for the Gospel of God. An integrity which we not only are to possess, but also must communicate by living such open lives with those to whom we minister that they know us — well.

Investment (2:7-9). The second element in Paul's approach to ministry is investment. By that I mean his willingness to invest himself heart and soul in those to whom he ministered. We see it in the following:

> But we were *gentle among you, like a mother caring for her little children.* We *loved you so much* that we were delighted to *share with you* not only the Gospel of God but *our lives as well,* because you had become *so dear to us.* Surely you remember, brothers, our toil and hardship; *we worked night and day* in order not to be a burden to anyone while we preached the Gospel of God to you (2:7-9).

Again Paul uses a number of brief phrases and powerful images to remind his readers of how deeply Paul invested himself in the relationship he developed with them.

■ Gentle among you (2:7). Gentle is *nepioi,*

which suggests thoughtfulness and consideration. Just as significant is the phrase "among you" (*en meso hyumon*), where *en meso* indicates moving among the church members as equals. Paul and his team rejected every opportunity to domineer and instead sought to develop mutuality as a context within which real caring could take place.

■ **Like a mother caring for her little children (2:7).** Again the words are significant. "Mother" is *trophos*, "nurse," which suggests here a nursing mother. "Her" is intensive; these are her very own little ones.

Perhaps the most fascinating thing about this description is that Paul applies the image to himself—a man who according to an early description was a small, bent man, who peered up at others from under heavy eyebrows from which jutted a nose which almost met his chin. How unlike a nursing mother the great apostle appeared. But despite it all the image fit, because all knew his *heart* was that of a nursing mother which delighted in his little ones.

We loved you (2:8). The word here is an unusual one, *homeiromenoi*. It means to yearn for. Paul is not speaking here of the selfless *agape* love which every Christian owes another. He is speaking of that yearning to be with the beloved which comes only as we come to know another person as an individual and come to care for someone deeply.

■ **We were delighted to share with you . . . our lives (2:8).** The yearning Paul has mentioned is powerful evidence of his investment of himself in the Thessalonians. Here he provides further evidence. "Delighted" is *eudokoumen*, which indicates intense pleasure. Ministry was a pleasure for Paul, not a duty, and all because he had come to care in a deep, personal way for the Thessalonians. "Our lives" is *psychas*, which goes beyond sharing experiences to share as well Paul's total being—his feelings, thoughts, attitudes, beliefs—all that makes him the person he is.

■ **So dear to us (2:8).** Here we at last have *agape*, that root used in the NT to express the deepest kind of commitment—love.

■ **We worked night and day in order not to be a burden (2:9).** Is Paul's love for the Thessalonians not only deeply emotional but also characterized by selfless commitment? Paul mentions just one indicator. Rather than accept support from the Thessalonians, Paul worked at his trade "night and day" in order to support himself.

The thrust of this section of Paul's letter is quite clear. The apostle truly has invested himself in the deepest possible way in those to whom he ministers. Moved by growing love, the apostle has generously shared himself with them and sacrificed himself for them.

Involvement (2:10-12). The final section summarizes and gives a fascinating description of just how Paul became involved in the lives of the Thessalonian Christians.

> You are witnesses, and so is God, of how holy, righteous, and blameless we were among you who believed. For you know that we *dealt with each* of you *as a father* deals with his own children, *encouraging, comforting* and *urging* you to live lives worthy of God, who calls you into His kingdom and glory (2:11).

Paul's ministry had a goal. All he did among the Thessalonians was focused on nurturing these young believers to "live lives worthy of God" (2:12). How?

■ **Dealt with each of you (2:11).** It is a wonder how the apostle found time to deal individually with his converts. We know that he worked at his trade to support himself in Thessalonica. We know from Acts 17 that he quickly gathered a band of followers and taught them on the Sabbath. We can assume from other descriptions of Paul's ministry in Acts that he spoke to groups in many different settings. Yet despite his busy schedule, Paul writes to those who most surely would have known the truth of how "we dealt with each of you" (2:11).

■ **As a father deals with his own children (2:11).** Several of the church fathers pointed out that Paul likens himself to a nursing mother when he speaks of cherishing these believers, but to a father when he speaks of training them. Two thoughts may be implied. First, it is the father who accepts responsibility to oversee the training of his, literally, "very own" children. And second, a number of years pass before the father becomes personally involved in a son's instruction. As far as love is concerned, Paul is eager to wrap these young believers up in his arms. As far as nurture is concerned, Paul steps back and treats each individual with the respect due to a person who is a responsible individual. No matter how much we love others, we cannot baby them when it comes to nurture.

■ Encouraging (2:12). The word is *parakalountes* which can also mean "admonish." It probably has this sense here, indicating that Paul spurred individuals on to commitment to Christian conduct. Thus the phrase should probably read "exhorting and encouraging."

■ Comforting (2:12). The word is *paramuthoumenoi,* which is better understood as encouraging. It conveys a warm sense of support for the person who is discouraged, intended not to excuse failure but to put it in perspective as a prelude to success.

■ Urging (2:12). Here the word is *martyromenoi* which has a tone of authority. It implies giving strong direction and guidance.

What is perhaps most significant is that the apostle demonstrates here that he knows "each of you" (2:11) well enough to be able to give each what he needs to progress in living a worthy life, whether what an individual needs is encouragement, comfort, or urging.

In his integrity, Paul invested himself in building a truly loving relationship with the Thessalonian believers, and became significantly involved in their lives.

Application. Perhaps little more needs to be said. Effective evangelism does involve the communication of a powerful, supernatural, and efficacious Word of God. But Scripture shows us that those who minister are called to prepare the hearts of those who hear as well as to proclaim.

Today, as in the first century, effective ministry calls for building a community of love. In that community God's Word *will* be heard. And from such a community, the Word of God will spread.

The Coming of the Lord (4:13-18).

Background. It is difficult for us to grasp how the men and women of the first century viewed death. For us as for them, of course,

death remains an enemy, and the ache experienced at the death of a loved one is painful indeed. Yet our perspective on death has been shaped by two factors not present then. The first of these is that our perspective has been shaped by centuries of a Christian tradition which affirms the certainty of resurrection. The second is that our perspective is also shaped by the long lives which most people live. Based on the ages recorded in epitaphs inscribed on tombs from two to three centuries before and after Christ, the life expectancy of a male was 29 years and that of a female only 27 years. For most of us death comes at what is deemed an appropriate time—after a long and productive life. For the man or woman of the first century, death was a dark specter who insisted on visiting human beings long before their time.

One of the fascinating side roads in archaeology has been the collection of epitaphs from Jewish tombs from just before and during the first centuries of the Christian era. The first collection was published by Jean-Baptiste Frey in the 1930s, and the most recent, *Ancient Jewish Epitaphs,* by Pieter W. Van Der Horst in 1991. Most of these were inscribed in Greek rather than Hebrew, and many express something of the dark despair about death felt by Jew and pagan alike. Three inscriptions drawn from Frey's work illustrate:

> Theodorus, the foster father, to his most sweet child. Would that I, who reared you, Justus, my child, were able to place you in a golden coffin. Now, oh Lord, [grant] in your righteous judgment a sleep of peace to Justus, an incomparable child.

> Here I lie, Justus, 4 years 8 months, who was sweet to my foster father.

> This is the tomb of Horaia; wayfarer, shed a tear. The daughter of Nikolaos, who was unfortunate in all things in her thirty years. Three of us are here, husband, daughter, and I whom they struck down with grief. My husband died on the third, then on the fifth my daughter Eirene, to whom marriage was not granted. I then with no place or joy was here after them under the earth on the seventh of Choiak. But, stranger, you have already all there is to know from us to tell all men of the swiftness of death.

This is the grave of Arsinoe, wayfarer. Stand by and weep for her, unfortunate in all things, whose life was hard and terrible. For I was bereaved of a mother when I was a little girl, and when the flower of my youth made me ready for a bridegroom, my father married me to Phabeis. And Fate brought me to the end of my life in bearing my firstborn child. I had a small span of years, but great grace flowered in the beauty of my spirit. This grave hides in its bosom my chaste body, but my soul has flown to the holy ones. Lament for Arsinoe.

Reading epitaphs like these helps us sense the frustration and despair associated with death at the time Paul wrote this great paragraph about the Christian's hope in 1 Thes. *Interpretation.* Paul writes to clarify an aspect of his resurrection teaching which had not been explained during his relatively brief time in Thessalonica. The believers there knew Christ would return, and looked forward to that event eagerly (1:10). But what would the Christian who died before Christ's return miss? And what happened to the believer who was now "asleep"? (4:13) The common pagan view is expressed in a poem by Catullus:

> The sun can set and rise again
> But once our brief light sets
> There is one unending night to
> be slept through.

Given the general sense of despair associated with death in the first century, uncertainty would have weighed heavily on the hearts of those Christians who lost loved ones. And so Paul is quick to reassure them. Death is a tragedy, and the Christian like the pagan will grieve when a loved one dies. But unlike the pagan, the Christian has a hope. A hope that when understood brings tremendous comfort—and further sets Christianity apart from paganism.

Paul starts by affirming a central doctrine: "We believe that Jesus died and rose again" (4:14). Resurrection is an established fact. So the question is not whether or not there is a resurrection, but (1) What happens to the believing dead? and (2) What is the relationship of the believers who have died to those who are alive when Jesus does come?

The first question is answered indirectly. "God will bring with Jesus those who have fallen asleep in Him" (4:14). Although the body has died and been buried, the believer himself or herself—his consciousness—is now "with Jesus" and will accompany Jesus on His return.

Clearly the Christian may grieve in view of his own loss when a loved one dies. But if that loved one is a believer, we cannot grieve for him or her! As Paul wrote to the Corinthians, "As long as we are at home in the body we are away from the Lord" (2 Cor. 5:5) and "would prefer to be away from the body and at home with the Lord" (5:8).

Thus the "sleep" of death in Christianity is limited to the body. The believer's conscious self is awake, alert, and "with the Lord."

The second question is answered more directly. What is the relationship of the dead to the living believer? How will their resurrection take place? Will the person who has died miss out on the Second Coming? What *will* happen?

Here Paul is quite explicit. Those living at Christ's return "will certainly not precede those who have fallen asleep" (4:15). The living believer enjoys no special advantage over the person who has died in the Lord.

What then will happen? "The Lord Himself will come down from heaven" (4:16). When He comes He will speak *en keleusmati,* "a word of command." This is a military term, and emphasizes the authoritative nature of the word by which Jesus calls the believing dead to life. As John 5:25 says, "the dead will hear the voice of the Son of God and those who hear will live." At that same time archangel voices and God's trumpet call will echo Christ's command (Matt. 24:31; Rev. 11:15). And the dead will respond. Paul writes "the dead in Christ will rise first," and then together with "we who are still alive and are left will be caught up . . . to meet the Lord in the air" (4:16-17).

The word translated "meet" the Lord is *apantesin.* It is frequently used in a technical sense, to describe a delegation of citizens who formally meet an important visitor outside a city, and escort him within its walls. Some have concluded that the resurrected and transformed saints meet Christ "in the air," and then accompany Him back to execute the judgments described in 1:5-10, and in other passages. Others argue that the saved meet Christ and return with Him to heaven. However, Paul clearly identifies the point he wishes to make, saying "so we will be with the Lord forever" (4:17). Wherever Jesus is, we will be. And it is this truth, that those who die before us and we who are alive at Christ's coming have the same wonderful hope, that Paul wants his readers to understand. And with this point made, Paul concludes, "Therefore encourage each other with these words" (4:18).

Application. This passage in 1 Thes. has stimulated several theological debates. Why, for instance, does Paul say "*we* who are still alive" when Christ returns? Did Paul expect Jesus to come during his lifetime? If so, doesn't the fact that he was mistaken cast some doubt on the rest of his teaching about the Second Coming? There are, of course, several possible solutions to the original question that make the suggested conclusion totally unnecessary. Paul may simply be identifying two categories, the dead and the living. He must place himself among the living, for clearly he has not died. More likely, however, Paul did hope Christ would come during his lifetime. Jesus made it very clear that no person knows the date of a return that the Father holds as His own secret (Matt. 24:36). Thus Christ could conceivably return at any time, a point driven home by Jesus in Matt. 25. Given then that Jesus' return is imminent, Paul in fact sets us an example. Like the apostle, we see ourselves as members of that last, fortunate generation who will not see death but will be living when our Lord returns.

The passage has also been pivotal in eschatological debates. Some argue that the event described, given the name "Rapture," proves a premillennial view of the future. They note that Paul does not describe a *general* resurrection, but a resurrection only of the dead "in Christ." Fitting this description together with other descriptions of resurrection in the Old and New Testaments, they find support for their dispensational view that Israel and the church are distinct, complementary aspects of a divine plan far more complex than most believe.

While we can grant the theologian the right to speculate, and the student of prophecy the right to try to fit this passage here or there in his charts, we must remember that Paul's concern here is neither to clarify nor confuse eschatological sequence.

Paul's concern is *pastoral,* and it is as a pastor that Paul draws our attention to this one aspect of the future. The dead and the living share a common hope in Christ. We will both be transformed; we will be caught up together into heaven; we will alike be with our Lord forever.

It is this wonderful truth that comforts us, and transforms grief to confidence and even joy.

2 THESSALONIANS
The Day of the Lord

EXPOSITION

Paul's second letter to the Thessalonians was probably written within a few weeks of the first. News from Thessalonica alerted the apostle to a significant increase in persecution there. Under this pressure some members of the church, confused by a letter supposedly from Paul (2:2), were convinced that the intensity of their suffering proved that the Day of the Lord was at hand, and Christ was about to appear. A number of Christians reasoned that if Jesus were about to return, there was no use working, and were living off their fellow-believers. Each of these issues corresponds to themes found in 1 Thessalonians (1 Thes. 4:9-12 with 2 Thes. 3:12; 1 Thes. 4:13–5:11 with 2 Thes. 2:1-12), further indication of the close relationship between the two letters.

After a typical greeting (1:1-2), Paul reassures the Thessalonians that their sufferings have a purpose (1:3-5) and that when Christ returns, God will repay those who trouble them (1:6-12).

Then Paul goes on to correct a serious misunderstanding. Their present suffering is not evidence that the "Day of the Lord has already come." Various events, including the open appearance of a "lawless one" supported by counterfeit miracles, which will be associated with the Day of the Lord, have not taken place (2:1-12). Until that day the Christian is to stand firm and be of good hope (2:13-17). It is clear from this brief word of correction that despite the brevity of Paul's stay in Thessalonica he had instructed the congregation there in eschatology. They were well aware that a time the OT prophets and Jesus identify as a period of "Great Tribulation" is to come at history's end. In view of the despair many felt at the intense hostility and persecution they were experiencing, the rumor spread that Paul himself had said their troubles were evidence that this was the end time, and Jesus must be about to appear.

This misunderstanding generated a false hope, and also led to destructive practices. After requesting prayer (3:1-5), Paul warns against idleness. The belief that Christ might return at any time is no excuse for idleness: those who are unwilling to work have no right to financial help from other Christians (3:6-15). Having dealt with these three issues, Paul concludes (3:16-18).

WORD STUDIES

Among God's churches we boast about your perseverance and faith in all the persecutions and trials you are enduring (1:4). The word *diogmois* ("persecutions") is used of sufferings incurred for the sake of Christ, while *thlipsesin* ("trials") encompasses all sorts of troubles that human beings might experience. Paul does not boast about the Thessalonian church because it is suffering, but because in spite of persecution and trials the church was growing in faith and love (1:3).

There is no benefit in suffering itself. It is how we respond to suffering that is praiseworthy.

All this is *evidence that God's judgment is right,* and as a result you will be counted worthy of the kingdom of God, for which you are suffering (1:5). The faithfulness of the Thessalonians in the face of suffering did not make them "worthy of the kingdom." Instead God pronounced them worthy on the basis of Christ's sacrifice when they believed. Their faithfulness truly is evidence that God is right in justifying those who believe; they *are* different now, and one day their worthiness will be displayed to all.

God is just: He will *pay back* trouble to those who trouble you (1:6). The doctrine of divine retribution is well established in Scripture (Ps. 137:8; Isa. 66:6; Rom. 12:19; Heb. 10:30). It is also a major thread in Jewish intertestamental writings, as in the following quote from 1 Enoch, dating from about 200 B.C.

The Great Holy One will come forth from His dwelling and the Eternal God will tread from thence upon Mount Sinai.
And He will appear with His army,
yea, He will appear with His mighty host from the heaven of heavens.
And all the watchers will fear and quake, and those who are hiding in all the ends of the earth will sing; and trembling and great fear will seize them unto the ends of the earth.
And the high mountains will be shaken and fall and break apart,
and the high hills will be made low

and melt like wax before the fire;
And the earth will be wholly rent asunder, and everything on the earth will perish, and there will be judgment on all. . . .
Behold, He comes with the myriads of His holy ones,
to execute judgment on all,
and to destroy the wicked,
and to convict all flesh,
for all the deeds of their wickedness which they have done, and the proud and hard words which godless sinners spoke against Him (1:4-7, 9).

This will happen when the Lord Jesus is *revealed from heaven* in blazing fire with His powerful angels (1:7). The word here is *apokalypsei,* a term with a variety of applications in the NT, but always with theological significance.

Here it is used of the visible return of Christ at history's end — a return which is visible to all humankind for it involves all. Here the reference to Christ's "powerful angels" is reminiscent of Matt. 24:30, which reports Jesus' teaching: "At that time the sign of the Son of Man will appear in the sky, and all the nations of the earth will mourn. They will see the Son of Man coming on the clouds of the sky, with power and great glory." In each context Christ's accompaniment by "angels" is described as visible to the world of men.

Christ's return means one thing for the saved: we will appear with Him in glory. It means something else entirely for those who reject the Gospel and persecute God's people.

He will punish those who do *not know God* and do *not obey the Gospel* of our Lord Jesus (1:8). Some see in the two phrases reference to Gentiles (those who do "not know God") and to the Jews (those who do "not obey the Gospel").

The distinction seems unnecessary. All human unbelief is marked not by ignorance about God but by a rejection of what is known about Him (Rom. 1:18-20), which finds its clearest expression in the refusal of those who do hear to respond to the Gospel.

Don't let anyone deceive you in any way, for that day will not come until *the rebel-*

lion occurs and *the man of lawlessness* is revealed (2:3). In 1 Thes. 4, Paul wrote of Jesus' return for those "in Christ." The dead were to be resurrected, and the living transformed, before together launching up to meet the Lord in the air. In 2 Thes. 2, Paul writes to remind the members of this church that the "Day of the Lord" could not be already present because two conditions are unfulfilled. The Day of the Lord is characterized by (a) "the rebellion," and (b) the revelation of the "man of lawlessness."

"Rebellion" is *apostasia*, which was used in contemporary literature of either political rebellion or rebellion against divine authority. The latter sense is primarily intended here: mankind will become openly hostile to God and to God's own.

"Lawlessness" is *anomias*. The *Zondervan Expository Dictionary of Bible Words* says words on this root "are active concepts. They reflect actions that are not outside the governance of law, but are in active violation of either divine or innate moral principles. The apostle John says, 'Everyone who sins breaks the law; in fact, sin is lawlessness' " (1 John 3:4) (p. 399). The "man of lawlessness" is further described here as a man "doomed to destruction" and one who "will oppose and will exalt himself over everything that is called God" (2:4). The added note that he even "sets himself up in God's temple, proclaiming himself to be God" clearly identifies this event with a prediction about the end times made by Daniel in his prophecy (11:31-32) and confirmed by Jesus Himself (Matt. 24:15).

Paul's argument seems to give weight to what is called the "pre-tribulation Rapture" view of history's end: that Christians are caught up in the air to be with the Lord (1 Thes. 4:13-18), followed by a great rebellion led by the "man of lawlessness" (2 Thes. 2:3), which is finally put down by the return in power of Jesus to earth (1:5-10). The Thessalonians are reminded that "the Day of the Lord" — God's great end-time plan — could not possibly have been instituted. Not only are they unraptured and suffering persecution, but the second stage of the end-time program which involves a worldwide rebellion led by one we call the Antichrist, has not begun either!

What a temptation to suppose, when our society is crumbling and Christians suffer, that Christ *must* return soon to rescue us. He very well may. But let's remember that for many generations of Christians God's purpose has been to develop our "perseverance and faith in all the persecutions and trials" we must endure (1:4).

And now you know *what is holding him back*, so that he may be revealed at the proper time (2:6). The Greek is *to katechon*, neuter here, but masculine in 2:7, where it is rendered "the one who now holds it back." A host of suggestions has been made concerning the identity of this restraining power. These range from the preaching of the Gospel, to the church, the existence of a Jewish state, the Roman Empire, and even human government. Perhaps a more likely argument favors the Holy Spirit, partly because in Jesus' Upper Room discourse references to the Spirit show a similar alternation between neuter and masculine. The thought here is that the Holy Spirit, who is present in the world in believers, will be "taken out of the way" at the Rapture of the church (cf. John 16:7-11; 1 John 4:4). It is only then that "the lawless one will be revealed" (2:8).

All kinds of counterfeit miracles, signs and wonders, and in every sort of evil that deceives those who are perishing (2:9). Miracles have never been commonplace, despite our fascination with them. The Bible records only three periods marked by the performance of multiple miracles: the time of the Exodus, the age of Elijah and Elisha, and the time of Christ and the apostles. Each of these periods extended some 40 years; each came at a pivotal period of sacred history. Strikingly, while the miracles that were performed fulfilled God's purposes — winning Israel's freedom from Egypt, turning back the move in Israel to Baal worship, and authenticating Christ and His disciples — not one of these ages of miracles produced universal revival. Miracles confirmed the faith of those who believed, but did not create faith in unbelievers.

The fourth great age of miracles lies ahead. It is described here, and its wonders ascribed not to God but to Satan. This time miracles do work, and "those who are perishing" (2:10) line up behind the man of lawlessness en masse!

Faith in God comes in a response to His Word. Those who will not believe God's Word are terribly vulnerable to any and every religious counterfeit.

For this reason *God sends them a powerful delusion* so that they will believe the lie and so that all will be condemned who have not believed the truth but have delighted in wickedness (2:11-12). Paul is not teaching that God is responsible for the unbelief of those who follow the "man of lawlessness," whom we often call the "Antichrist." The "powerful delusion" which leads those living at history's end to eagerly follow the man of lawlessness is part of God's judgment on those who "refused to love the truth and so be saved" (2:10).

God did not cause their unbelief. He is responsible, as a judge is responsible for the sentence he imposes on criminals, for the powerful delusion which moves the lost to acclaim the Antichrist.

From the beginning God *chose* you to be saved through the sanctifying work of the Spirit and through belief in the truth (2:13). For a discussion of the role of God's choice in salvation, see The Passage in Depth discussion of Eph. 1:3-14.

So then, brothers, *stand firm* and hold to the teachings we passed on to you, whether by word of mouth or by letter (2:15). Paul's exhortation to "stand firm" (*stekete*) focuses on the present situation in Thessalonica. By holding to the teachings (*paradoseis*, literally, "traditions," that Paul has given concerning the future, the Thessalonians can avoid becoming "unsettled or alarmed" by the events of the day.

If anyone does not obey our instruction in this letter, take special note of him. Do not associate with him, in order that he may feel ashamed. Yet do not regard him as an enemy, but warn him as a brother (3:14-15). For more on church discipline, see The Passage in Depth commentary on 1 Cor. 5:1-13.

THE PASSAGE IN DEPTH

The Day of the Lord (2:1-12).

Background. Paul refers here to "the Day of the Lord" (2:2) in a context which clearly associates that day with the "coming of our Lord Jesus Christ" (2:1). In writing, "Don't you remember that when I was with you I used to tell you these things?" (2:5) Paul makes it clear that despite the brevity of his stay in Thessalonica he was careful to instruct these new believers about eschatology. Paul's use here of the phrase "the Day of the Lord" also makes it clear that his teaching incorporated the vision of the future revealed in the OT prophets, for this phrase has deep roots in the older revelation.

Along with "that day," "the Day of the Lord" is frequently, but not always, used to signify that the prophet is in fact conveying a message about history's end, and the culmination of God's plan for the ages. The *Zondervan Expository Dictionary of Bible Words* notes however that "the key to understanding the phrases is to note that they always identify a span of time during which God personally intervenes in history, directly or indirectly, to accomplish some specific aspect of His plan" (p. 211). To understand Paul's discussion of the "rebellion" and the "man of lawlessness" we must then set these within the context of the OT's vision of "the Day of the Lord" and "that day."

The *Expository Dictionary* describes the events most often linked to this "day."

Briefly, the day of the Lord is seen as a day of terror, during which Israel would be invaded and purged with an awful destruction. Amos warned those of his day who hoped God would intervene soon: "Woe to you who long for the day of the Lord! Why do you long for the day of the Lord? That day will be darkness, not light" (5:18).

Zephaniah adds, "The great day of the Lord is near—near and coming quickly. Listen! The cry on the day of the Lord will be bitter, the shouting of the warrior will be there. That day will be a day of wrath, a day of distress and anguish, a day of trouble and ruin, a day of darkness and gloom, a day of clouds and blackness" (1:14-15). The dark terror of divine judgment was to be poured out on unbelieving Israel (Isa. 22; Jer. 30:1-17; Joel 1–2; Amos 5; Zeph. 1) and on the unbelieving peoples of the world (Ezek. 38–39; Zech. 14).

But judgment is not the only aspect of that day. When God intervenes in history, He will also deliver the remnant of Israel, bring about a national conversion, forgive sins, and restore His people to the land promised Abraham (Isa. 10:27; Jer. 30:19–31:40; Micah 4; Zech. 13) (p. 211).

We can better grasp the context within which Paul writes if we look at some of the passages with which Paul apparently familiarized the Thessalonians. To that end, a number of passages dealing with both the dark and bright aspects of the Day of the Lord are included below.

When we look them over, we can understand why the Thessalonians may have identified their sufferings with the persecutions of what has been called the end times' "great tribulation." And, if we assume that Paul taught them that the Rapture of the church would occur prior to that period, we can see why the believers in Thessalonica would become "unsettled" and "alarmed" about what was happening to them.

ISAIAH 2:10-13
Go into the rocks,
   hide in the ground
from the dread of the Lord
   and the splendor of His majesty!
The eyes of the arrogant man will be humbled
   and the pride of men brought low;
the Lord alone will be exalted in that day.
The Lord Almighty has a day in store
   for all the proud and lofty,
   for all that is exalted
   (and they will be humbled).

JOEL 1:13-15
Put on sackcloth, O priests, and mourn;
   wail, you who minister before the altar.
Come, spend the night in sackcloth,
   you who minister before my God;
for the grain offerings and drink offerings
   are withheld from the house of your God.

Declare a holy fast;
   call a sacred assembly.
Summon the elders
   and all who live in the land
to the house of the Lord your God,
   and cry out to the Lord.
Alas for that day!
   For the day of the Lord is near;
   it will come like destruction from the Almighty.

JOEL 2:1-2
Blow the trumpet in Zion;
   sound the alarm on My holy hill.
Let all who live in the land tremble,
   for the day of the Lord is coming.
It is close at hand—
   a day of darkness and gloom,
   a day of clouds and blackness.
Like dawn spreading across the mountains
   a large and mighty army comes,
Such as never was of old
   nor ever will be in ages to come.

AMOS 5:18-20
Woe to you who long
   for the day of the Lord!
Why do you long for the day of the Lord?
   That day will be darkness, not light.
It will be as though a man fled from a lion
   only to meet a bear,
as though he entered his house
   and rested his hand on the wall
   only to have a snake bite him.
Will not the day of the Lord be darkness, not light—
   pitch-dark, without a ray of brightness?

MATTHEW 24:15-21
So when you see standing in the holy place "the abomination that causes desolation," spoken of through the prophet Daniel—let the reader understand—then let those who are in Judea flee to the mountains. Let no one on the roof of his house go down to take anything out of the house. Let no one in the field go back to get his cloak. How dreadful it will be in those days for pregnant women and nursing mothers! Pray that your flight will not take place in winter or on the Sabbath. For then there will be great distress, unequaled from the beginning of the world until now—and never to be equaled again.

AMOS 9:11-15
"In that day I will restore
David's fallen tent.
I will repair its broken places,
restore its ruins,
and build it as it used to be,
so that they may possess the remnant of Edom
and all the nations that bear My name,"
declares the Lord, who will do these things.
"The days are coming," declares the Lord,
"when the reaper will be overtaken by the plowman
and the planter by the one treading grapes.
New wine will drip from the mountains
and flow from all the hills.
I will bring back My exiled people Israel;
they will rebuild the ruined cities and live in them.
They will plant vineyards and drink their wine;
they will make gardens and eat their fruit.
I will plant Israel in their own land,
never again to be uprooted
from the land I have given them,"
says the Lord your God.

Interpretation. By referring to the Day of the Lord, Paul identifies the specific concern of the troubled Thessalonians. They are experiencing intense persecution, and the wicked in their city seem to be running wild. Can this be the end time? How do current events relate to the future about which Paul has taught them so carefully?

Paul gives their concern careful attention. He explains that the present cannot be the end time of prophecy, because that period is marked by open, worldwide rebellion and the appearance of the Antichrist, a world leader called here the "man of [characterized by] lawlessness" (2 Thes. 2:3). While lawlessness finds expression in every generation's present, it does not find *full* expression because evil's full expression is restrained by the Holy Spirit.

Application. It is important to note, whatever one's eschatology, that Paul himself is not really concerned with diagramming God's plan for the future. What Paul is concerned about is settling the uncertainty and the fears of the believers in Thessalonica who have become

alarmed by their present sufferings. Rather than go into details, Paul simply clarifies two major prophetic themes, without making specific reference to their relationship with each other, or even the Rapture he described in a letter sent to Thessalonica a few brief weeks before. Paul wants the Thessalonians to understand, first, that those who trouble them will be dealt with by God (1:5-10), and that their troubles cannot be identified with the end-times period of terrible tribulation predicted by the prophets and confirmed by Jesus Himself. With this confusion resolved, the believers in Thessalonica will again be freed to fix their hope in Christ and His return — and leave the details of that Coming to the Lord.

Warning against Idleness (3:6-15).

Background. Paul's instructions to the Thessalonians about those idle members of the church who have stopped work in expectation of Christ's return seem blunt and almost harsh. "If a man will not work, he shall not eat" (3:10) is not an easy precept.

The injunction, however, can be understood against the background of the Bible's teaching on the nature and the function of work.

The Old Testament on Work.

A number of words for "work" are found in the OT. Several portray work as toil and drudgery. *'Mal* conveys the frustration and drudgery of labor that fails to produce satisfaction. *Yaga'* emphasizes the exhaustion that comes from hard work, while *mas* and *sebalah* are forced labor. Yet, despite the OT's recognition that work has its dark side, other Hebrew words also portray a bright side.

'Abad means to serve, and while sometimes used of forced service is frequently employed to describe service to God. Whether work is a joy or a pain often depends on for whom we are working. *'Asah* means "to do, make, accomplish." The derivative noun *ma'eseh* looks at the process and the product of our labors. God takes great satisfaction in His works; when our work is productive we can take satisfaction in our works too. *Po'al* is another term for "work" that incorporates the idea of recompense. Work, whether physical labor or moral deeds, merits an appropriate reward.

The darker words for "work" in the OT remind us that sin has so impacted our universe that often work is a struggle with an unresponsive nature. Yet work, which can be frustrating and fruitless, has the potential of being productive and satisfying.

What is more, the whole idea of work has intrinsic meaning. We human beings derive our identity from God. Since God by His work brought our universe into existence and continues to work out His good purpose through history, we can never say that work is meaningless. Work is in a deep and real sense fulfillment: we are created to be like God, and in our work we can glorify God as well as participate in His good purposes for us and the world.

The New Testament on Work.
The Greek of the NT reflects many of the meanings found in Hebrew words for work. *Ergon* and related terms speak of labor, activity, achievement. *Poiema,* a form of the verb "to do," can refer to the product of labor as well as work itself. Both Creation and salvation are spoken of as God's works. *Praxis* is another group of words that describe acts and accomplishments.

The word *kopos* suggests labor, and reflects the realization that work is often difficult and unrewarding. Yet this is the word Paul uses to describe his own tentmaking (1 Cor. 4:12) and the honest toil that Paul calls on former thieves to engage in (Eph. 4:28). Work is not always easy. But it need not be easy to be rewarding, satisfying—or right. It is true that *mochthos* moves beyond toil to hardship. But it appears only three times in the NT: in 2 Cor. 11:27, 1 Thes. 2:9, and here, where Paul describes himself as setting a model for the Thessalonians by working "night and day, laboring and toiling so that we would not be a burden to any of you" (3:8). Clearly we cannot measure work by its difficulty for often the most costly labor is the most meaningful.

Undoubtedly Paul is the best example of the NT's work ethic. He chose to work rather than accept support that he might make the Gospel free to all, and so that he might set an example. Idleness and dependence on others is not godly. Christians are to accept responsibility to provide for themselves, and to earn money they can share with the truly needy. In a unique sense the NT sees work not as an end in itself, but rather as an opportunity for Christians to provide an example of right behavior, as an opportunity to minister directly by the way in which our work benefits others, and as an opportunity to minister indirectly by sharing extra funds with those in need.

Against this background we can better understand Paul's insistence that those who have become idle in Thessalonica mend their ways. Other Christians must stop enabling them to be idle by providing even the food they need to meet their basic needs. If a Christian is unwilling to work because of an unclear vision of the role of work in God's plan, hunger will see to it that he changes his ways.

1 TIMOTHY
Church Life and Leadership

EXPOSITION

The Books of 1 and 2 Timothy along with Titus are normally considered together. These "pastoral epistles" are directed to younger men who served with Paul and represent the next generation of church leaders. To some extent the term "pastoral" is misleading, for Timothy and Titus were, like Paul, itinerant leaders who traveled from place to place as needed to guide and to correct local congregations. Second Timothy was written during Paul's second imprisonment in Rome and shortly before his execution. The other two letters were probably written within three or four years of this date, probably A.D. 66 or 67.

This first letter to Timothy is rich in wise advice on the structure of church life, and insight into the challenges of church leadership. Paul begins by urging the suppression of false teachers (1:3-7), and reminding Timothy that the proper use of the Law is limited to establishing the fact that the behavior of the ungodly and sinful truly is sin (1:8-11). Yet, as Paul's experience shows, God's transforming grace extends to the worst of sinners (1:12-17). In view of God's grace, Timothy is to "fight the good fight, holding on to faith and a good conscience" (1:18-20).

The heart of Paul's instruction to Timothy focuses on the lifestyle that is appropriate within the church. His instructions touch on prayer (2:1-8), women (2:9-15), the choice of "overseers" (3:1-7) and "deacons" (3:8-13), and concludes with a liturgy of praise (3:14-16). These instructions are intended to help Timothy "know how people ought to conduct themselves in . . . the church of the living God."

Paul then shifts his focus to Timothy himself. It is apparent that although Paul dearly loved Timothy, and sent him on important missions, Timothy by nature was shy and hesitant. Thus Paul's words seem at times to go beyond encouragement to exhortation. Paul reminds Timothy that he can expect to find false teaching infecting the churches, and that his duty is to "point . . . out" the truth to the brethren (4:1-10). But Timothy is to do more. He is to "command and teach" the truth, and is not to "let anyone look down on you because you are young." And the exhortations continue: Timothy is to "be diligent in these matters," "give yourself wholly to them," and "persevere in them" (4:10-16).

Paul then returns to the issue of Christian conduct within the church, with instructions for several specific groups. He touches on the relationship between the older and the younger (5:1-2), on the ministry of widows (5:3-16), on the respect due elders

(5:17-25), and on the duty slaves owe believing masters (6:1-2). Paul then warns against false teachers, who are exposed by their behavior and unhealthy attitude toward money (6:3-10).

Paul begins to bring his letter to a close by charging Timothy "Fight the good fight of the faith . . . without spot or blame," and to "command" God's people to do good (6:11-19). Even Paul's farewell contains exhortations, reminding us again that Paul remains concerned not about Timothy's commitment but about his "toughness" and his ability to stand under pressure (6:20-21).

WORD STUDIES

Nor to devote themselves to *myths* and *endless genealogies* (1:4a). The Greek *mythos* originally meant a story or narrative, but by the first century the meaning had shifted to imply fable or fiction. Some see the mention of genealogies as a reference to the gnostic belief in a series of angelic beings supposed to stand between God and man. It is more likely that Paul refers to the endless, speculative interpretations of biblical genealogies engaged in by some Jewish teachers.

In contrast to the encoded truths the rabbis sought in the names of OT heroes, the Gospel's good news is in plain sight, producing faith rather than promoting controversies.

The *goal of this command* is love, which comes from a pure heart and a good conscience and a sincere faith (1:5). "Goal" is *telos*, the "end" or intended consequence. Unlike the false doctrines which produce only useless speculation and controversy, the Gospel produces love, which can flow only from a pure heart, a good conscience, and sincere faith.

Never imagine that the goal of teaching Christian doctrine is to produce people who know the truth. The goal of teaching Christian doctrine is to purify the human heart so that believers will be truly loving.

We know that *the law* is good if one uses it properly. We also know that *law is made not for the righteous* but for lawbreakers and rebels (1:8-9). Since Paul has been speaking about self-proclaimed religious leaders (1:6-7), it is clear that "the law" here is the divine law, either as revealed to Moses, or as implanted by God in the consciousness of pagans (Rom. 2). Paul says that law is good (*kalos*; balanced and beautiful) if used "proper-

ly" ("lawfully," *nomimos*).

He then goes on to point out that law is "made not," is *ou keitai,* not enacted or established. Laws are enacted because of evils men do. If no one stole, no law would be enacted against stealing. And even more, after a law has been enacted, it remains irrelevant to the man who does not steal.

Paul's point is important. The life that is in harmony with "sound doctrine" (1:10) is a good life. And since the person living the good life does not do the things laws are enacted against, law simply is not useful to those who live in harmony with the Gospel.

For further discussion of the believer and the Law, see the chapters on Rom. 6–7 and Gal. 3–4.

Fight the good fight, holding on to faith and a good conscience. Some have *rejected* these and so have *shipwrecked their faith* (1:18-19). The word translated "rejected" is *apotheomai,* to push away or repudiate. Commentators suggest the word indicates a decisive, violent rejection. The image of a shipwreck is appropriate. When violent storms struck the ships that sailed the Mediterranean, the fragile wooden vessels were often driven against the rocky shores. In such cases those on board lost everything, and were thankful to escape with their lives.

Those who reject the faith also lose everything of worth, and themselves as well.

Whom I have *handed over to Satan* to be taught not to blaspheme (1:20). For a discussion of this phrase, see the Word Study of 1 Cor. 5:5.

This is *good,* and pleases God our Savior, who *wants* all men to be saved and to

come to a knowledge of the truth (2:3-4).
Paul describes peaceful and quiet lives lived in
godliness and holiness as "good." Here the
word is *kalos,* which means "beautiful" in contrast to *agathos,* good in the sense of "useful."
Paul's point here is that the beautiful life of
godliness and holiness lived by Christians is a
significant factor in seeing nonbelievers come
to knowledge of the truth.

"Wants" is *thelei,* which expresses God's
wish, but in no way implies that God has
determined to save all. It may be difficult for
us to realize, but even God is not free to do
anything He wants, in that He cannot act
against His nature. His love can only be exercised in harmony with His holiness and His
justice. How wonderful that God has devised
a way that His love can be expressed and His
justice satisfied.

**Christ Jesus, who gave Himself as a *ran-
som for all men* (2:5-6).** The word for ransom is *antilytron.* This is the only place the
word appears in the NT. In the first century,
lytron was a price paid to free a slave. The
compound we have here means what is given
in exchange as the price of freedom.

This ransom price was paid on behalf of all
humankind (4:10). It surely is not God's fault
that not all will be saved. The problem lies
with human beings who reject the Gospel, and
refuse to accept the title deed to emanci-
pation from sin's grip offered everyone in
Jesus Christ.

**A woman should learn in *quietness* and
full submission. I do not permit a woman
to teach or to have authority over a man;
she must be *silent* (2:11-12).** "Quietness"
and "silent" renders the same Greek word,
hesychia. The word is used only four times in
the NT, and indicates a receptive attitude. It
does *not* imply a surrender of a woman's intellectual abilities or what has been called the
"duty of private judgment." It also should not
be taken to imply that a woman should offer
no comment during church meetings: a right
of participation that is established in 1 Cor.
11:5.

Paul seems to intend us to understand 2:11
in association with 2:12, which throws both
"quietness" and "submission" into the context
of church leadership rather than participatory
membership.

Here "to teach or to have authority" are
best understood as "authoritative teaching," as
might be done by an elder of the local church
or an itinerant leader of the larger church like
Timothy or Titus or Paul himself.

Many try to avoid the implications of these
difficult verses by suggesting that Paul writes
out of sensitivity to the then existing view of
the role of women, and that this passage therefore does not really speak to the modern
church. However, the next verses make it
abundantly clear that Paul cites a *theological*
base for his judgment. It seems most likely
that Paul does here restrict women, not from
participation in church meetings, or even from
prophesying (1 Cor. 11:5), but from a role
that involves authoritative teaching binding on
the church.

**But women will be *saved through child-
bearing,* if they continue in faith, love
and holiness with propriety (2:15).** The
verb here is *sozo,* "save." The word is used in
the NT in two senses: to describe physical
healing and spiritual salvation. The problem is
that many godly women have died in childbirth, making that rendering unlikely. But at
the same time it is difficult to connect childbirth to the spiritual dimension of salvation.

This is undoubtedly one of the most difficult of the Bible's verses to interpret. Three
primary interpretations have been advanced.
(1) The Greek word for childbirth is accompanied by the article "the." Some commentators thus argue that "the childbirth" is a reference to *Christ's* birth, through which women
as well as men are saved. (2) A second view
sees this verse as a reference to Gen. 3:15, and
the prediction that a woman's seed would
crush Satan's head and bring salvation to all
mankind. (3) A third, suggested by Vine,
holds that Paul is teaching that in accepting
motherhood as the woman's appropriate role,
a woman will be saved from falling prey to
first-century social evils and be able to add her
testimony to that of the other believers in the
church.

**Now the *overseer* must be above re-
proach, the *husband of but one wife*
(3:2).** The NIV uses the word "overseer"
where other English versions have "bishop."
The Greek *episcopos* is very likely a synonym of
presbyteros, which is rendered "elder" (Titus

Qualifications for Leadership

Scripture	Qualification	Explanation
Titus 1:5-9	1. Above reproach	Not open to censure; having unimpeachable integrity.
	2. Husband of one wife	A one-wife kind of man, not a philanderer (doesn't necessarily rule out widowers or divorced men).
	3. Having believing children	Children are Christians, not incorrigible or unruly.
	4. Not self-willed	Not arrogantly self-satisfied.
	5. Not quick-tempered	Not prone to anger or irascible.
	6. Not addicted to wine	Not fond of wine or drink.
	7. Not pugnacious	Not contentious or quarrelsome.
	8. Not a money-lover	Not greedy for money.
	9. Hospitable	A stranger-lover, generous to guests.
	10. Lover of good	Loving goodness.
	11. Sensible	Self-controlled, sane, temperate.
	12. Just	Righteous, upright, aligned with right.
	13. Devout	Responsible in fulfilling moral obligations to God and man.
	14. Self-controlled	Restrained, under control
	15. Holding fast the Word	Committed to God's Word as authoritative.
	16. Able to teach sound doctrine	Calling others to wholeness through teaching God's Word.
	17. Able to refute objections	Convincing those who speak against the truth.
Additional from 1 Timothy 3:1-7	18. Temperate	Calm and collected in spirit; sober.
	19. Gentle	Fair, equitable, not insisting on his own rights.
	20. Able to manage household	A good leader in his own family.
	21. Not a new convert	Not a new Christian.
	22. Well thought of	Good representative of Christ.
Additional from 1 Peter 5:1-4	23. Willingly, not under compulsion	Not serving against his will.
	24. According to God (in some Greek texts)	By God's appointment.
	25. Not for shameful gain	Not money-motivated.
	26. Not lording it over the flock	Not dominating in his area of ministry (a shepherd is to lead, not *drive* the flock).
	27. As an example	A pleasure to follow because of his Christian example.
	28. As accountable to the Chief Shepherd	Motivated by the crown to be gained—authority to reign with Christ.

1:6-7; Acts 20:17-28). This was the premier local leadership role in the early church, but was a shared role, as the Acts passage and others indicate that local churches were guided by teams of elders, rather than by a single "pastor."

Paul provides a checklist against which to measure those who aspire to this office, a list which emphasizes the importance of character rather than the gifts or training of spiritual leaders (see list).

Probably the most debated qualification is the one quoted in this verse: "the husband of but one wife." By the end of the second century this qualification was interpreted to mean "married only once." However, most commentators hold that "the husband of one wife" emphasizes monogamy and total faithfulness. The spiritual leader is to be a one-woman kind of man.

Deacons, likewise, are to be men worthy of respect (3:8). The English "deacon" is from the Greek *diakonos,* "servant." Most see the seven deacons of Acts 7 as prototypes for the office in the local church. By the time Philippians was written "overseers and deacons" were distinct church offices (Phil. 1:1). The distinction is made even more clear in the pastorals, although the specific duties of each office are not defined. In general, however, commentators agree that the overseers/elders were responsible for the spiritual oversight of the local congregation, while deacons administered its practical ministry to members and others.

In the same way, *their wives* are to be women worthy of respect (3:11). The Greek simply says *gyne,* a word used with the meaning of "woman" as well as "wife." The possessive pronoun, "their," is not in the Greek text. For this reason many scholars hold that Paul means women *deacons* are to be women worthy of respect, an interpretation given weight by Paul's identification of Phoebe as a *diakonon* of the church of Cenchrea (Rom. 16:1).

They forbid people to marry and order them to abstain from certain foods, which God created to be received with thanksgiving by those who believe and know the truth (4:3). While OT law called for abstaining from certain foods, that law has none of the spirit of asceticism exhibited by the false teachers who plagued the early church. (For a discussion, see the chapter on Col. 1–2.) Paul says the trend toward asceticism, which in effect replaces dependence on God with self-effort, is encouraged by demonic forces which work through "hypocritical liars" (4:2). The phrase implies that the false teachers know better. Their persistence in doing wrong has made them insensitive to sin.

The tendency toward asceticism was very strong in the early centuries of our era. Its impact is reflected in the church's veneration of "saints" who adopted its ascetic ideals. Simon the Stylite stood upright for decades on the top of a pillar, eating tiny meals only on Tuesdays and Saturdays. Other saints retreated into the wilderness, and rolled in brambles to punish themselves when moved by any sexual thought or desire. The same tendency toward asceticism is partly responsible for the development of a celibate priesthood within Roman Catholicism.

Yet asceticism and self-denial simply are not Christian. Paul argues that the Christian's outlook must be shaped by the realization that "everything God created is good" (1 Tim. 4:4), and is to be received with thanksgiving. The reference here to consecration "by the word of God and prayer" (4:5) does not mean that God's good gifts need to be cleansed. Paul's thought is that by receiving God's "everything" in faith and with a prayerful attitude, we are able to enjoy His gifts with a clear conscience.

Don't let anyone look down on you because you are *young,* but set an example for the believers in speech, in life, in love, in faith and in purity (4:12). The Greek word is *neotes,* which indicates a person who is grown up, but not yet 40. In the ancient world, a person Timothy's age, probably in his early 30s, was not expected to have gained the discernment and wisdom required in leaders.

A passage in the Mishnah quoting Rabbi Judah ben Tema (*Abot 5:21*), reflects a similar view as it characterizes 14 periods in a man's life:

(1) At five to Scripture, (2) ten to Mishnah, (3) thirteen to religious duties, (4) fifteen to Talmud, (5) eighteen to the wedding

canopy, (6) twenty to responsibility for providing for a family, (7) thirty to fullness of strength, (8) forty to understanding, (9) fifty to counsel, (10) sixty to old age, (11) seventy to ripe old age, (12) eighty to remarkable strength, (13) ninety to a bowed back, and (14) at a hundred—he is like a corpse who has already passed and gone from the world.

Given the cultural milieu, in which pagan and Jew alike expected a person to be 40-60 years old before being qualified to understand and counsel, we can understand why a 30-year-old Timothy may have been hesitant to assert his authority.

What is significant here is that Paul introduces new criteria by which the church is to evaluate its leaders. What qualifies a person for leadership responsibility in the church of God is not age, but character. Timothy and leaders today are to set an example for the believers in speech, in life, in love, in faith, and in purity.

Why was Timothy's youth troubling? Did it make a difference in the first century who one received teaching from? Absolutely! The higher the status of the teacher, the greater the status of the doctrine and the more secure socially a follower of that doctrine would be. It is interesting that even in the late fourth century the Roman writer Libanius ridiculed Christians of his own upper class, saying that they had received their doctrine from "your mother, your wife, your housekeeper, your cook."

Watch your life and doctrine closely. Persevere in them, because if you do, you will *save both yourself and your hearers* (4:16). It is essential that what one believes and how one lives be in complete harmony. Thus we are to pay close attention to both. All too often in our own day scandal has ruined not only the reputation but also the ministry of well-known Christian leaders. Holding to sound doctrine while drifting from a committed Christian lifestyle is the surest way to lose yourself—and your hearers.

But the widow who *lives for pleasure* is dead even while she lives (5:6). In biblical times widows generally had no way to earn a living. Those who were without children or grandchildren to support them were quite lit-

erally destitute. The Jews and the early Christian church showed great concern for such women and were careful to provide for them. This letter to Timothy suggests that Christian widows were not simply placed on a dole. Those who had demonstrated Christian character were given quasi-official roles within the church (5:9-10), and an active ministry to younger married women (Titus 2:3-5).

Paul, however, further limits membership on this official role, although without limiting the rights of widows who have no families for financial support. He encourages younger widows to remarry. And he warns that "the widow who lives for pleasure is dead while she lives." The phrase "who lives for pleasure" is a single word in Greek. That word, *spatalao*, means to live self-indulgently or luxuriously. Paul is not accusing such widows of sexual misconduct, but of materialism, of a self-absorbed perspective which contrasts with that of the widow who "puts her hope in God and continues night and day to pray and to ask God for help."

Such a woman is "dead" in the sense that she is insensitive to the realities which mark others as spiritually vital and alive.

Do not be hasty in the *laying on of hands* (5:22). The reference is probably to ordination (Acts 14:23 where the word translated "appointed" means literally "to stretch out the hand"). Apparently the role of itinerant leaders of the wider church, whether a Paul or a Timothy, officially confirmed the local church leaders chosen (elected?) by local congregations. Paul thus warns Timothy about extending this official recognition in a "hasty" manner. In doing so Timothy would to some extent be vouching for the character of the person he ordains, and if they proved corrupt he would appear to "share in the sins of others."

Stop drinking only water, and *use a little wine* because of your stomach and your frequent illnesses (5:23). Timothy seems to have concluded from various teachings in Scripture that drinking alcohol was wrong, and so drank "only water." It is interesting that Paul does not tell Timothy to claim or even pray for healing. Instead he advises the medicinal use of "a little wine."

The use of wine in countering the effect of

impure water was common in the ancient world. Both Jewish and Greek authorities, including Hippocrates, recommended a moderate use of wine to treat patients with chronic stomach problems.

For the love of money is *a root of all kinds of evil* (6:10). This may be the most misquoted verse in the Bible. Paul does not say that "money is the root of all evil," but that a love of money is a root from which all evils spring. Those who are motivated by a love for money will be vulnerable to the temptation to take any path—however evil—to get it.

THE PASSAGE IN DEPTH

Portraits of the Early Church.

It is always difficult to picture life in an earlier age. We come to history with ideas shaped by our experience within our own culture. As a result we tend to read our perceptions back into the past. This is perhaps particularly true when it comes to thinking about the church. In our experience church is where we go on Sunday mornings to sing and listen to preaching. The meeting takes place in a church building, where educational and social activities are also scheduled on Sundays and other evenings during the week. Often this building is the site for meetings of committees or boards which have responsibility for ministry to the larger community, or responsibility for doing the work necessary to maintain the church as a building and institution. Somehow we never realize that our experience of church life is very different from the experience of first-century believers as reflected in the NT.

That experience was shaped by very different cultural forces, and perhaps a very different view of the nature of the church itself. To understand, we need to consider something of the nature of the early church as a community, and something of the nature and functioning of leaders in the NT age.

The Church As Community.

The social needs of the average person in the first century were met in part by a variety of clubs, or *collegia*. There were clubs for workers in various occupations, clubs for adherents of different religions, clubs who promised their members a decent burial, etc. Most of these clubs were small neighborhood groups, which met in the home of a better-off patron.

The early church was patterned after these smaller, neighborhood groups, primarily because the existing model fit the society. Most of a person's life was lived within his or her neighborhood: a 30-minute trip in a car might represent a day's journey in the first century. In the crowded cities of the first century there were no large auditoriums available where hundreds could meet. House-church membership was limited by the space available. The proximity of members to each other, and the limits on congregational size, permitted a level of intimacy that is seldom experienced by moderns who sit passively Sunday mornings, listening with others who like them have often traveled 10 or more miles to "attend church."

The early church's organization into smaller groups had definite advantages. The NT portrays the church as a living body, composed of individuals whose spiritual gifts make it possible for them to contribute to the growth of each other. In the intimacy promoted by the structure of the early church these gifts were more likely to be exercised as "each one" contributed his or her hymn or word of instruction or revelation, or tongue, or interpretation (1 Cor. 14:26). Rather than be passively dependent on the ministry of a pastor, the form of the church promoted the responsibility of all members for ministry in the church. This is not to suggest that lay ministry cannot or does not take place in the church of our time. It is simply to point out that the form of the first-century church—a form that persisted for perhaps 250 years—*encouraged* mutual ministry, while the institutional forms prevalent in our day do not.

Similarly, the neighborhood nature of the smaller first-century congregation, along with the relative intimacy encouraged by its house-church setting, made it much easier for the early Christians to be as involved in each other's lives as the NT's constant call to "love one another" requires. For biblical love of neighbor is not abstract, but practical, and is expressed within the warp and woof of lives that are shared significantly.

The neighborhood "club" form in which the first- and second-century church existed promoted community in ways that modern church forms do not and cannot.

The Church's Leaders.

Two basic types of leaders existed in the early church. These were local leaders and itinerant leaders.

It is important to note that by the time Paul wrote the letters to Timothy and Titus, a distinction had emerged between local church leadership offices and the spiritual gifts. While one might argue that a person ordained as an elder should have the gift of teaching (1 Tim. 3:2), it is clear spiritual maturity and character are the basic qualifications required for this premier local leadership post, and for the lesser post of deacon.

Perhaps the most significant aspect of the first-century local leadership structure is that the NT consistently speaks of elders, plural. It is clear that the oversight of churches was placed in the hands of a team of elders rather than in the hands of a single elder. Although we have no clear evidence, in view of the small size of the first century's neighborhood house-churches, it seems likely that elders supervised all the house-churches in a city or a district of a city.

The ministry of local leaders was further supported and supervised by itinerant leaders like Paul, Timothy, and Titus. Itinerant teachers of philosophy were a familiar sight in the first century. And traveling pairs of sages from the Sanhedrin in Jerusalem visited Jewish communities in cities across the Empire to inform them of that body's rulings and to serve as judges of disputes between Jews.

Thus this network of itinerant leaders also reflected patterns that already existed within first-century society.

Application. We are not to look back at the form and leadership patterns of the early church with the notion that these must be normative for the church of every age and society. It is clear from the fact that the church adopted patterns already existing in that time that culture will always have an impact on the forms which congregations take.

However, looking back does serve to remind us of two vitally important truths. First, the forms taken by our own churches and all too often unquestioningly accepted truly are *not* normative at all. They too reflect contemporary society, and have roots in our own Western culture. They are far from sacred, or from having biblical sanction.

Second, whatever forms our churches take should be evaluated by theological rather than cultural criteria. Does the form of the local church you attend facilitate the exercise of members' spiritual gifts? Does it promote the development of intimacy and the growth of mutual love?

Similar questions can and should be asked about church roles and offices. Is local leadership multiple, or do we exalt individuals? Do we emphasize the importance of character over gift or ability when selecting leaders? Is there some network of support and accountability that extends beyond the local congregation to the wider church?

It may be impossible, and even unnecessary, to try to duplicate the form of the first-century church in our day. But we must seriously consider how to encourage the development of those dynamic processes so essential for spiritual formation that the form of the first-century church did support so well.

2 TIMOTHY
A Look Ahead

EXPOSITION

Second Timothy is Paul's last letter. It was written during a second imprisonment in Rome—an imprisonment which culminated in his execution in Rome. As such it has special weight, the weight typically given the last words of a dying man. In this letter Paul looks ahead and describes challenges to the Christian movement which he foresees. He gives young Timothy, and us, critical advice concerning how to meet these challenges.

Yet the themes developed in this short letter are not new. In fact most are also developed in Paul's earlier letter to Timothy (see comparison chart below). In order to meet the challenges of the future the Christian must remain committed to a holy life (1:3-12) and to sound doctrine (1:13-14). This truth with which Timothy has been entrusted must be communicated intact to the next generation through faithful men (2:1-7). After a brief reminder of Paul's own commitment to the Gospel (2:8-13), Paul returns to his theme. In the future it will be increasingly important for leaders to live godly lives and minister wisely (2:14-26), for sin will become even more entrenched in society and false teachers will worm their way into the church and corrupt the faith of many (3:1-9). How can we resist such attacks from without and within the church? Paul's prescription is simple but profound. We continue to live godly lives and preach the truth, being ready and willing to suffer any hardship our commitment may cause (3:10–4:5).

Paul's letter reminds us of both our weakness and our strength. There are forces within society and within the church that often seem about to overwhelm us. But our calling is to faithfulness. As we remain faithful to the great truths of the Gospel, and continue to live godly and loving lives, we are sure to triumph. For the truth we believe is God's truth, and the life we live is Christ's life, and our God will triumph in the end.

Parallel themes in 1 and 2 Timothy:

1 Timothy
1:3-7   Goal of *ministry*: love from pure heart.
1:8-11   Lifestyle contrary to *sound doctrine* described.
1:18-20 Timothy to *hold to the faith*.

2:8-10 Examples of *godly life.*
3:1-15 *Leaders'* qualifications.
4:1-5 *False* lifestyle.
4:11-16 Need to set example in *faith, life.*

2 Timothy
1:3-12 Called to a faithful life of *ministry.*
1:13-14 Must guard *sound doctrine.*
2:1-7 Timothy to entrust truth to *faithful men.*
2:14-19 Leaders must live *godly lives.*
2:14-19 How *leaders* live, teach.
3:1-9 *False* ministry.
3:10-4:5 Need to continue in godly *life, teaching.*

WORD STUDIES

For this reason I remind you to fan into flame the *gift of God,* which is in you through the laying on of my hands (1:6). Gift here is *charisma.* It is the same word as is used for the "ordinary" spiritual gifts distributed by the Holy Spirit to every believer. This, however, is an unusual gift, intended to enable Timothy for ministry. For the significance of laying on hands, see the Word Study of 1 Tim. 4:14.

Perhaps more important is the reminder implicit in the call to "fan [the gift] into flame." God freely gives His gifts to us—but leaves us free to use or abuse them.

For God did not give us a spirit of *timidity,* but a spirit of power, of love and of self-discipline (1:7). The word *deilia* means "cowardice." In context with other passages in these two letters it hints at Timothy's shy and hesitant nature. But Timothy is not limited by his weaknesses, even as you and I are not limited by ours. God has given us His own Spirit—a Spirit who breathes power, love, and self-discipline into the believer's life.

TIMOTHY

Timothy joined Paul's missionary team on the apostle's second journey (Acts 16:1). Paul's exhortation to Timothy not to let anyone look down on him because of his youth (1 Tim. 4:12) suggests either that Timothy had a shy and retiring nature or reflects that culture's prizing of age in leadership. Yet Paul's commendation of Tim-othy to the Philippians conveys this young disciple's strengths and commitment. Paul says, "I hope . . . to send Timothy to you soon. . . . I have no one else like him, who takes a genuine interest in your welfare. For everyone looks out for his own interests, not those of Jesus Christ. But you know that Timothy has proved himself, because as a son with his father he has served with me in the work of the Gospel (Phil. 2:19-22).

Timothy may well represent many young Christians who remain uncertain and hesitant despite a history of faithful service. He also represents a reality in the church. The leaders of each generation must pass the ministry on to others, who in turn will train still others to take up the burden of leadership. Timothy might appear young, but an early commitment to Christ and a genuine concern for others had effectively equipped him for ministry (*The Revell Bible Dictionary,* p. 960).

I know whom I have believed, and am convinced that He is able to guard what I have *entrusted* to Him for that day (1:12). This is one of those great verses in Scripture which cries out to be memorized, in this or that earlier version which read: "I know whom I have believed, and am persuaded that He is able to keep that which I have committed unto Him against that day" (KJV).

Here "entrusted" (NIV) or "committed" (KJV) is *paratheke,* "deposit," found only here and in 1 Tim. 6:20. The image is of a person who has to take a lengthy journey and leaves his valuables with a friend, to guard them for him until he returns. Paul reminds us that our life on earth truly is a journey. How glad to know that all that is valuable and lasting has been deposited with the Lord, who keeps it safe for us until we come home.

The things you have heard me say in the presence of many witnesses entrust to reliable men who will also be qualified to teach others (2:2). Transmission of the Gospel was and remains a person-to-person kind of thing. Justin Martyr, who lived from about A.D. 100 to 167, studied all his culture's philosophical systems, convinced that philosophy alone could produce happiness. In his *Dialogue with Trypho* Justin records a conversation with an "old man" that totally changed the direction of his life—and that illustrates the human dimension of the transmission of the Gospel from generation to generation. The old man began:

A long time ago, long before the time of those reputed philosophers, there lived blessed men who were just and loved by God, men who spoke through the inspiration of the Holy Spirit and predicted events that would take place in the future, which events are now taking place. We call these men the prophets. They alone knew the truth and communicated it to men, whom they neither deferred to nor feared. With no desire for personal glory, they reiterated only what they heard and saw when inspired by the Holy Spirit. Their writings are still extant, and whoever reads them with the proper faith will profit greatly in his knowledge of the origin and end of thing, and of any matter that a philosopher should know. . . . Above all beseech God to open to you the gates of life, for no one can perceive or understand these truths unless he has been enlightened by God and His Christ.

When he had said these and many other things which it is not now a fitting time to tell, he went his way, after admonishing me to meditate on what he had told me, and I never saw him again. But my spirit was immediately set on fire, and affection for the prophets, and for those who are

friends of Christ, took hold of me; while pondering on his words, I discovered that his was the only sure and useful philosophy. Thus it is that I am now a true philosopher. Furthermore, it is my wish that everyone would be of the same sentiments as I, and never spurn the Savior's words, for they have in themselves such tremendous majesty that they can instill fear into those who have wandered from the path of righteousness, whereas they ever remain a great solace to those who heed them.

Here is a trustworthy saying:
If we died with Him,
  we will also live with Him.
If we endure,
  we will also reign with Him.
If we disown Him,
  He will also disown us;
If we are faithless,
  He will remain faithful,
  for He cannot disown Himself
    (2:11-13).

Most believe these verses are drawn from an early Christian hymn. We should link the hymn with Paul's preceding reference to "the salvation that is in Christ Jesus" (2:10). As far as salvation is concerned, Christ *is* the issue. And there are only two possible responses when a person is confronted by Christ in the Gospel.

The first response is positive. Those described have "died with Him." The verb *synapethanomen* is an aorist, referring to that union with Christ which faith effects (Rom. 6). "Endure" (*hypomenomen*) is a present tense, showing continuous action. But "endure" does not quite capture the meaning of the Greek word. In English "endure" suggests bare survival; the Greek *hypomeno* is an active, positive term. It suggests a believer who has died with Christ and been raised again, and who now faces difficulties and transforms them into triumphs, even as Jesus transformed the cross into a crown. This is one choice which all people have: to come to Christ, exchanging spiritual death for spiritual life, and living that life triumphantly.

The other choice we have is to disown Christ. Here "disown" (*arnesometha*) is also in the aorist, indicating a decisive decision, or one which reflects a permanent disposition of mind. This is not a matter of wavering or doubt. It is a decision made by persons who are *apistoumen*, "without faith." This alone makes it clear that the "we" in view here is the human race, and the hymn reflects on the choices available to all mankind.

But what then does the ancient hymn intend to affirm by the statement that God remains faithful, "for He cannot disown Himself"? It is to take this as an affirmation of God's commitment to a Gospel which some men foolishly reject. Whatever man's reaction to the Gospel, Jesus remains the one way by which human beings may be saved. He has committed to Himself to provide salvation in Christ. He will keep His commitment, whatever men may say or do.

In 1992 the International Council of Christians and Jews produced a theological statement intended to build what the August 22, 1992 *Jerusalem Post* called a "working alliance" between Christians and Jews. It is interesting to evaluate the following quote from the theology papers developed at that congress in the light of this early Christian hymn, and such verses as John 3:16 and John 14:6.

The Torah, as the expression of the covenant of Sinai, remains valid for the Jews as a gift to them that was never revoked. Accordingly, mission to the Jews is theologically unacceptable. The church . . . is not the successor or heir of God's covenant with Israel but a new universal way to enter into communion with the God of Israel alongside the people of Israel.

Do your best to present yourself to God as one approved, a workman who does not need to be ashamed and who correctly handles the word of truth (2:15). The Greek word *orthotomounta* means to "hold a straight course." The KJV translation as "rightly dividing" led some to see this verse as a support for dispensationalism, which "divides" sacred history into a number of discrete ages, or dispensations. It is, however, clear Paul has frequently defined the "straight course" in Scripture and also the "off course" use of the Word. Scripture's "sound teaching" is intended to lead to a life of love and holiness. The false teachers Timothy must confront misuse the Word of God, devoting themselves to "meaningless talk," misusing the Law and

engaging in empty arguments about the hidden meanings of its genealogies (cf. 1 Tim. 1:4-7; 2 Tim. 2:16-18; 3:1-9).

Nevertheless, God's solid foundation stands firm, sealed with this inscription: "The Lord knows those who are His," and "Everyone who confesses the name of the Lord must turn away from wickedness" (2:19). Salvation, like a coin, has two sides: God's, who knows His own by looking into their hearts; and man's, as we demonstrate that we are God's own by our determination to live a holy life.

The Lord's servant must not *quarrel* (2:24). The Greek *machesthai* is a strong word, used of armed warfare and hand-to-hand combat. It came to be used of a "war of words," or constant wrangling. Arguing and quarreling is no way to win others to Christ. On the human level, the more strongly we confront or condemn others, the more likely we are to harden them in their opposition to the faith. On another level, "quarreling" fails to take into account the fact that the unsaved are in the grip of Satan. We might paraphrase with Thayer, that the unsaved need "to be set free from the snare of the devil and to return to a sound mind."

There is no use insisting that a person spiritually blind see our point of view. Instead we can only "gently instruct" (2:25) such persons, relying on God to "grant them repentance leading them to a knowledge of the truth."

There will be terrible times in *the last days* (3:1). The phrase comes from the OT (cf. Isa. 2:2; Micah 4:1; Joel 2:28). The question here is whether, as many think, Paul intends to identify the *present age* as "the last days," or whether "the last days" refers to the end times. Paul's grim portrait of people during this period certainly suggests what he called "the rebellion" in 2 Thes. 2:3.

On the other hand, most passages where this phrase is found seem to indicate that "the last days" are now (Acts 2:17-18; 3:24; Heb. 1:2; 2 Peter 3:3; 1 John 2:18). If history involves a progressive unfolding of God's purposes in Creation and redemption, and "the Day of the Lord" is the culminating period, then "the last days" may very well be the epoch prior to the Day of the Lord.

If we take this view, the "last days" extend from the Resurrection of Jesus to His Second Coming. While the full expression of the evils Paul describes in 3:1-5 are restrained, they are all clearly evident in our society now.

However we understand "the last days," we must be aware that modern society is hostile to God and to His values. And the description Paul gives of men and women of that time all too aptly describes many in our own day.

Having a form of godliness but denying its power (3:5). Appearances can be deceiving, and an outward piety can mask any or all of the traits Paul has been describing in 3:1-4. Paul's further description of the *modus operandi* of these corrupt individuals in 3:5-9 indicates that he expects these persons to appear *within* rather than outside of the church! This in turn suggests that Paul does think of "the last days" as present, then and now.

Church history provides an interesting example of the kind of person Paul seems to describe. A man named Peregrinus joined the church in order to exploit Christians. When he was finally imprisoned by secular authorities, the Christians remained deceived and treated him as a hero, bringing him money and food. His contemporary, Lucian, commented:

> The poor wretches have convinced themselves . . . that they are going to be immortal and live for all time. . . . They despise all things indiscriminately and consider them common property, receiving such doctrines traditionally without any definite evidence. So if any charlatan and trickster, able to profit by occasion comes among them, he quickly acquires sudden wealth by imposing upon simple folk (Peregrinus 13).

Just as *Jannes* and *Jambres* opposed Moses, so these men oppose the truth (3:8). These men are not mentioned in the OT, but a long Jewish tradition identified them as the magicians in Pharaoh's court who opposed Moses (Ex. 7:11).

All Scripture is God-breathed and is useful for teaching, rebuking, correcting and training in righteousness, so that the man of God may be thoroughly equipped for every good work (3:16-17). The Greek word translated "God-breathed" (*theopneustos*) is found only here in the NT. The image suggested is that of a ship carried along by the winds that fill its sails. Yet this word tells us little about the *process* of inspiration. Instead the focus is on the product: a "Scripture" which carries the meaning God intended without in any way blocking out the writer's freedom or individuality.

However, Paul's emphasis here is on the value of Scripture. The word for "useful" is *ophelimos*, "profitable." Again as throughout the pastorals the apostle focuses our attention on how we are to *use* Scripture in living our Christian lives. How does Scripture touch our lives?

"Teaching" (*didaskalia*) is a general word for instruction. "Rebuking" (*elegmos*) has the sense of conviction of sin in the Septuagint. "Correcting" (*epanorthosin*) means to "restore to a right state." "Training [*paideia*] in righteousness" is the kind of guidance given by a parent who rears a child. When we approach Scripture to learn, letting God's Word indicate areas in our lives where we are out of step with God, and responding so that God's Word restores us to a right state, we will be guided — as a parent guides a child — to live a righteous life. As a result of this kind of involvement with God's Word we are equipped "for every good work."

Now there is in store for me the *crown* of righteousness (4:8). Crown here is *stephanos,* the wreath of leaves given the victors in one of the Greek athletic games. "Of righteousness" can mean "the crown appropriate for a righteous man," or "the crown which is won by righteousness," depending on how one understands the genitive. Paul goes on to state that this crown awaits "all who have longed for His appearing" (4:8). If we connect this statement to 1 John 3:3, "Everyone who has this hope in him purifies himself, just as He [Christ] is pure," we find support for the idea that the crown Paul has in mind is won by righteousness.

The more you and I long for Christ's return, the less concerned we will be with those things which might hinder us from living righteous lives.

THE PASSAGE IN DEPTH

Paul's Charge to Timothy (3:10–4:5).

Background. Jacob Neusner writes in *A Midrash Reader* (Fortress Press, 1990):

We and they share the conviction that Scripture is God's word not then alone but also now, spoken not in time long gone but in and to our own age: to me, here and now. . . . All Christians and Jews must begin by bringing themselves to Scripture, and Scripture to their own time and place. For study of those words of God, the Bible to Christians, the whole Torah to Jews, is the one palpable, this-worldly, and concrete testimony we have, and I think, all we have and all we shall ever have, to tell us what God means" (p. 163).

In this we perhaps hear an echo of Paul's words to Timothy, that "all Scripture is God-breathed and is useful for teaching, rebuking, correcting, and training in righteousness, so that the man of God may be thoroughly equipped for every good work" (3:16-17).

All with a high view of Scripture would certainly agree. The Bible is God's Word, not then alone, but now. Not alone to inform us, but to transform us. All do not, however, agree how to *use* God's Word.

This is, in fact, one of the major themes of the pastoral epistles, which frequently mirror conflicts over the approach to Scripture taken by the apostle and by various schools of false teachers. Here are some of the passages which reflect an inappropriate approach to the Scriptures:

Inappropriate Uses of Scripture.

■ Mythological approach (1 Tim. 1:3-8). First Timothy opens with Paul's charge to Timothy to "command certain men not to teach false doctrines any longer" (1:3). These doctrines were apparently generated by the false teachers' devotion to "myths and endless genealogies" (1:4). The word "myth" (*mythos*) which originally meant "story" came to mean "fable." Today we think of fables as made-up stories with a moral. Since in this same passage Paul says they "want to be teachers of the law" (*nomos*, the Greek word for *torah*: used here with the meaning of "the divine revelation"), it is apparent that these teachers approach the Bible's stories as *mythos*, seeking to draw out and apply hidden meanings, and approach its genealogies with endless speculation about their hidden meanings.

This approach to Scripture is mentioned a number of times in the two letters to Timothy. In 1 Tim. 4:7 Paul says, "Have nothing to do with godless myths and old wives' tales," and the same letter speaks of the person who teaches "false doctrines" as an individual "with an unhealthy interest in controversies and quarrels about words that result in envy, strife, malicious talk, evil suspicions and constant friction between men of corrupt minds" (6:3-5).

■ Legalistic approach (1 Tim. 1:8-11). Closely associated with the mythological approach is a misunderstanding of OT law. Paul notes that law is good (useful, beneficial) if a person uses it properly. This means first of all recognizing that the Bible's "Do nots" are promulgated "not for the righteous but for law-breakers and rebels, the ungodly and sinful, the unholy and irreligious" (1:9). The believer does not search Scripture for rules to follow, as though "do's" and "don'ts" win him or her merit with God or advancement in the Christian life.

Yet not only do many treat Scripture primarily as a source of rules to be followed; many go beyond its laws to impose additional requirements. Paul describes some of this, when describing false teachers who "forbid people to marry and order them to abstain from certain foods, which God created to be received with thanksgiving by those who believe and who know the truth" (1 Tim. 4:3).

■ Rebellious approach (2 Tim. 3:1-9). In this paragraph Paul describes persons who reject the Scripture as an authority. These are "lovers of themselves" (3:2), who give priority to the satisfying of their own selfish desires rather than to seeking and pleasing God. "Having a form of godliness but denying its power" (3:5)—Paul reminds us that even the most corrupt want to appear upstanding. They are eager to cloak their motives, even as a purveyor of smut attempts to wrap himself in the mantle of a defender of freedom of speech!

Rather than misuse Scripture by mythologizing or legalizing its message, they reject its message although they may very well use its language as a cloak for their own evil desires. Such persons do not distort, but "oppose" the truth (3:8).

While passages in 1 and 2 Timothy suggest several different ways that Scripture is misused, there is also an emphasis on being "a workman who does not need to be ashamed and who correctly handles the word of truth" (2 Tim. 2:15). There is also considerable indication of how Scripture is to be handled by believers.

Several principles are implicit in what Paul writes.

Appropriate Use of Scripture.

■ Approach Scripture as a witness to salvation. First and most important, Scripture is a witness to the salvation God has provided for us in Christ. Paul reflects on this in 1 Tim. 1:15, when he writes, "Here is a trustworthy saying that deserves full acceptance: Christ Jesus came into the world to save sinners." Scripture witnesses to Christ because God "wants all men to be saved and to come to a knowledge of the truth. For there is one God and one mediator between God and men, the man Christ Jesus, who gave Himself as a ransom for all men — the testimony given in its proper time (1 Tim. 2:3-6). The Gospel is woven throughout this as through the other letters of Paul (cf. also 2 Tim. 1:8-11; 2:8-10; 3:15). In a very real sense Christ and the Gospel are the lens through which all must come to Scripture to discover *anything* of value. For all else that Scripture has to say is valueless for anyone who ignores or misses God's message about His Son.

■ Approach Scripture as "sound doctrine" and as a guide to Christian living. In this phrase, found in 1 Tim. 1:10 and 2 Tim. 4:3, the adjective is *hygiainouse,* which means to be "healthy" or "sound." The thought is that Christian teaching is not only wholesome, but also promotes spiritual health. Paul notes that the end in view in stopping false teaching is to teach sound doctrine which will produce a love "which comes from a pure heart and a good conscience and a sincere faith" (1 Tim. 1:5).

What Paul has in mind is the fact that the Christian is not seeking conformity to Scrip-

ture as an external standard, but rather seeks transformation by an experience of the "truths of the faith" (1 Tim. 4:6). Thus when we read the Scripture we seek to discover realities which with God's help we can experience. Thus Paul reminds Timothy to "set an example for the believers" (4:12) and to "watch your life and doctrine" (4:16).

It is within this context that Paul in 2 Tim. 3:10–4:5 gives a specific prescription, showing us how to read Scripture to avoid the errors of mythologizers, legalists, and those who reject Scripture's teachings out of hand.

Interpretation. Paul nowhere suggests that coming to Scripture as God's Word and really listening to it makes for an easy life. In fact, in 2 Tim. 3:10–4:5 Paul makes it perfectly clear that using Scripture correctly will set the Christian on a course which will involve hardship and conflict. For God's ways are not appreciated in man's world. And the Christian who follows the pathway Scripture defines will find himself at variance with human culture.

The following outline illustrates:

■ The Cost (3:10-12)
■ The Conflict (3:13-15)
■ Scripture's Value (3:16-17)
■ The Charge (4:1-5)

■ The Cost (3:10-12). Paul writes very plainly to Timothy. "You . . . know all about my teaching, my way of life, my purpose, faith, patience, love, endurance." The fact is that Paul's understanding of Scripture has shaped His whole "way of life," from its wellsprings in his motives and trust in God, to its visible expressions in patience, love, and endurance. Timothy cannot possibly suppose that Scripture, rightly understood, can produce the selfishness, the quarreling, or the rigid legalism that is produced by the false teacher's erroneous approach to the Word of God.

Paul goes on. Timothy also knows that Paul's understanding of Scripture and his commitment to live according to God's Word has led to "persecutions, sufferings" (3:11). There is a cost associated with following the path God's Word defines.

■ The Conflict (3:13-15). Paul quite bluntly states that "in fact, everyone who wants to live a godly life in Christ Jesus will be persecuted"

(3:12). The more closely we follow Jesus, as following Him is defined in God's Word, the further our path diverges from that of the "evil men and impostors [who] will go from bad to worse." This inevitably brings us into conflict with the world. We should not read "persecution" as the life-threatening hostility of some governments to Christians. We should understand "persecution" as any active hostility: as teens' ridicule of the moral standards of a peer, or an employer's refusal to promote an active Christian, or a non-Christian spouse's anger at his or her partner's new desire to follow Jesus.

Whatever the conflict involves, like Timothy we are to "continue in what you have learned and have become convinced of" (3:14). Timothy's learning and conviction grew out of confidence in the integrity of the persons who first taught him the Scriptures, and from knowing the Scriptures themselves as the source of God's saving message.

■ Scripture's Value (3:16-17). Having heard the saving word the new believer, who is now a "man of God," needs to be thoroughly equipped for every good work. At this point Scripture takes on this challenging role. The Word of God is "useful" (profitable, *ophelimos*). So how do we approach Scripture to hear it as God's equipping Word?

Paul states that Scripture is profitable for "teaching, rebuking [convicting], correcting [restoring to a right state], and training in righteousness."

There is a pattern here. "Teaching" is a general word that we can take as information concerning reality as God knows and has revealed it. On one hand, this revelation convicts us, by showing us where our ways are in conflict with God's. On the other hand, this same revelation corrects us, restoring us by guiding us back to what is right. Restored again to harmony with God, this same revelation trains us in righteousness, teaching us daily how we are to please and live for the Lord.

Thus as we read Scripture we are to let it speak to us in these different ways, and respond as we hear and understand.

■ The Charge (4:1-5). In view of the preceding, Paul charges Timothy with preaching the Word "in season and out of season." There is a fascinating parallel, and distinction, made between the ministry of Scripture in rebuking and correcting, and the ministry of Timothy. Timothy is to rebuke (*epitimeson*), which means to censure or reprove. But Scripture is able to rebuke (*elegmos*), which means to convict of sin. Timothy is to correct (*elenxon*), which means to reprove. But Scripture is able to correct (*epanorthosin*), which means to restore to an upright position. The person ministering the Word draws the listener's attention to his or her need, but only Scripture can effect the change required.

So Timothy is rightly charged to preach the life-changing Word. He is to minister with great patience and careful instruction, despite the resistance of the hearers, or their eagerness for teachers who will say what they want to hear rather than preach the truth.

But neither Timothy nor you or I are to become discouraged. Recognizing that there is and always will be a conflict between God's way and man's way, Christians fulfill their charge from God as Timothy is to fulfill the charge given him by the Lord: "Keep your head in all situations, endure hardship, do the work of an evangelist, discharge all the duties of your ministry."

And live the Word.

TITUS
Teaching for Results

EXPOSITION

The brief letter of Paul to Titus is significant chiefly for three characteristics. It provides a succinct summary of NT truth. It provides a similar sketch of Christian lifestyle. And it describes the teaching by which truth is translated into daily experience.

Merrill Tenney provides this summary of the theological topics touched on in Titus: the personality of God (2:11; 3:6); God's love and grace (2:11; 3:4); His title as Savior (2:10; 3:4); the Holy Spirit (3:5); His triune being (3:5-6); the deity of Christ (2:13); the vicarious atonement of Christ (2:14); the universal offer of salvation (2:11); salvation by grace, not works (3:5); the incoming of the Holy Spirit (3:5); justification by faith (3:7); sanctification by God of His people (2:14); separation from evil (2:14); inheritance of eternal life (3:7); and the return of Christ (2:13).

In another work I identified a similar list of characteristics of a Christian lifestyle: godliness (1:1); faith (1:2; 2:2); qualities of leaders (1:5-9); ministry of leaders (1:8-9); temperance(2:2); love (2:2, 4); self-control (2:2, 5-6); endurance (2:2); dedication to doing good (2:7; 3:1, 8, 14); personal integrity (2:7, 10); seriousness (2:7); subjection to authority (2:9; 3:1); trustworthiness (2:10); rejection of sin (2:12); humility (3:2); considerateness (3:2); peaceableness (3:2); harmony (3:10).

Yet perhaps the most striking element in this short letter is its emphasis on teaching, not as mere communication of information about God, but as instruction intended to produce a lifestyle that is in harmony with revealed truth. This theme, developed on Titus 2, is one of the most significant passages in the NT for developing a biblical philosophy of ministry, whether pulpit ministry, classroom ministry, or a nonformal ministry within the Christian community and the home.

In addition commentators often point to three brief gems nestled in Titus, rich summaries of truths central to our faith. These are found in 1:1-3 (foundations of faith), 2:11-14 (the fruit of grace), and 3:3-7 (the transforming power of grace).

WORD STUDIES

At His *appointed season* He brought His word to light (1:3). The Greek is *kairois idiois*, "His own time." Paul frequently refers to the Incarnation as an event which God carefully "timed" to take place at an exact moment in history's flow. The thought is found in Acts 17:26; Rom. 5:6; Gal. 4:4; 6:9; Eph. 1:10; 1 Tim. 2:6, and 1 Tim. 6:15. Certainly the early years of the first century were uniquely suited to God's purpose. The Roman world was at last unified and at peace; a common language made communication of the Gospel message easy; open borders, with an excellent system of roads and shipping lanes facilitated missionary travel; recognition won by Judaism as a licit religion in the Empire protected the new faith emerging from it in its early decades; even the wide distribution of the Jews throughout the West and the East were all vital elements in the explosive spread of the Gospel. It is safe to say that at no time in history, before or since, were so many conditions favorably arranged for the spread of the message of Jesus.

Brought His word to light through the preaching entrusted to me by the command of God our Savior (1:3). In recent decades theologians have tended to see the word *kerygma* as a technical theological term, for the Gospel message itself. This emphasis on the content of the Gospel has been at the expense of an alternative meaning, the act of preaching. The NIV translators have chosen an appropriate middle ground. Rather than implying that we must choose either the message preached or the act of preaching it, our version combines the two: Paul has been entrusted with the mission of preaching the message of God.

This is appropriate, especially when we realize that "preaching" is not the pulpit ministry we suppose it to be today, but the act of a herald or town crier, commissioned to publicly announce the good news in the streets or wherever the people were.

I left you in Crete that you might ... appoint elders in every town (1:5). The word *kathistemi* does not indicate "ordination" as we understand it. The use of this word in Acts 6:3 suggests that it signified giving one's approval to local leaders selected or put forward by the congregation. That is, the congregation, which knows its members better than itinerant leaders, evaluates its members using criteria Paul lists in 1 Timothy and this epistle. Paul or his representatives then *kathistemi*, gave their approval to the congregation's choice.

There is a healthy check and balance system at work here. No congregation is simply "as-signed" its leaders. Yet the necessity of ecclesiastical approval makes it clear a veto power existed, so that unwise choices could be reversed.

Appoint *elders* in every town, as I directed you. . . . Since an *overseer* is entrusted with God's work, he must be blameless (1:5, 7). Two Greek words are translated by "elder" in these verses: *presbuteros* and *episkopos.* This latter word is translated "bishop" in many English versions. However, the NIV rendering is appropriate, and the two titles are probably used interchangeably. Thus Jerome, in the fourth century, wrote, "Among the ancients, bishops and presbyters are the same, for the one is a term of dignity, the other of age." And, "The Apostle plainly shows that presbyters are the same as bishops." Again, "If anyone thinks the opinion that the bishops and presbyters are the same, to be not the view of the Scriptures, but my own, let him study the words of the apostle to the Philippians." Most of the rest of the church fathers took Jerome's position.

The husband of but *one wife* (1:6). This phrase has been distorted in two different ways. Some have argued that it indicates an elder/bishop must be married. But in this case it would have been more natural for Paul to write "the husband of a wife," not "one" wife.

On the other hand, the verse has been taken to mean that no one who has remarried can serve as a church elder. Typically this interpretation has been applied inconsistently. Some exclude a person who has divorced and remarried from the elder's office, but accept those who remarry after their first wives die. Some resolve this problem by suggesting Paul means one living wife. Others by noting that *gynikos* is "woman" as well as wife, and *aner* is "man" as well as husband. In a sexually loose era, Paul insists that church leaders set an example of purity by being "a one-woman kind of man."

Since an overseer is entrusted with God's work, he must be ... (1:7-8). These two verses give sets of contrasting negative and positive qualities of persons who are to be entrusted with God's work. Several are direct contrasts; others flesh out powerful images of personal character.

Negatives	Positives
Not . . .	But
Overbearing	Hospitable
Quick-tempered	Self-controlled
Given to much wine	Disciplined
Violent	Holy (seeking
Driven by profit	to please God)
	Lover of good
	Upright

However closely we may examine the individual terms, taken together they provide a sharp and clear portrait of the character required by anyone in Christian leadership.

Even *one of their own prophets* has said, "Cretans are always liars, evil brutes, lazy gluttons" (1:12). The Greek is better rendered, "Even one of them, their own prophet." Here "prophet" is used in the sense of religious leader or reformer. The reference is to Epimenides, the fifth-century B.C. poet honored by the people of Crete. The contemptuous evaluation of the Cretans is reflected in pagan writings and even in the Greek language itself, where the word *kretizo*, "to Crete-ize," came to mean "to lie" or "to cheat."

How striking that this letter to Titus envisions a complete transformation of those Cretans whose dishonesty, brutality, and sensuality had made them objects of contempt throughout the Mediterranean world.

To the *pure*, all things are *pure*, but to those who are corrupted and do not believe, nothing is pure (1:15). The enigmatic verse has a dual impact on us. Following Christ's teaching (Matt. 15:10-11; Luke 11:37-41), Paul reminds us that purity is not an attribute of objects. Purity is a matter of the heart, so that objects and activities take their character from the intent of the person who uses or engages in them. Conversely, the notion of the false teachers that by engaging in certain activities or refraining from touching certain objects an individual becomes holy is nonsense. For a person who has not been saved and transformed within by Jesus, nothing is pure: all is corrupt.

Pay no attention to *Jewish myths* (1:14). See the Word Study of 1 Tim. 1:4.

To be *busy at home* (2:5). The Greek word is *oikourgos*, which means literally a "worker at home." It's found only here in the NT. The context suggests that older women are to help newlyweds learn how to make their home and their new family a priority.

To be *subject* to their husbands, so that no one will malign the Word of God (2:5). The verb may be taken in the middle voice, to "subject herself," and so stress the voluntary nature of submission within the context of Christian marriage. Of greater significance is the explanatory phrase added by Paul: "so that no one will malign the Word of God."

Paul's point, consistently underlined in his other epistles, is that while all human beings are equal in the sight of God, society assigns each of us different roles. Thus human governing authorities are to be not only obeyed but also shown appropriate respect, masters are to be obeyed by slaves, and wives are to be submissive to husbands. No one is demeaned or lessened as a person or a believer by fulfilling his or her social role appropriately.

So that those who oppose you may be ashamed because they *have nothing bad to say* about us (2:8). The Greek word here is *akatagnostos*, "not open to just rebuke." Note the distinction. We can't keep others from saying bad things about us. But we can be sure that nothing we do *justifies* any bad thing they may say.

THE PASSAGE IN DEPTH

Background. By NT times "philosophy" had shifted focus from speculation on the nature and origin of the universe to lifestyle issues. Even the Greek word used to describe philosophic schools was *bios*, "way of life." While each school's roots were sunk in the soil of a particular view of the nature of reality, the emphasis of each was placed squarely on what that view implied concerning the nature of a life of virtue. The philosopher Musonious Rufus described the object of philosophy as "to find out by discussion what is fitting and proper and then to carry it out in action."

This emphasis may seem surprising to moderns, whose study of ancient philosophers tends to concentrate on their metaphysics. It may also be surprising to Christians, who put great stress on doctrine and theology. In fact this stress on Christian belief has had a significant impact on our assumptions about the nature of teaching and learning. If what is distinctive about Christianity is its system of beliefs—its unique understanding of reality—then teaching Christianity must emphasize the transmission of truth. But Paul reminds Titus and us that Christianity is "truth that leads to godliness" (1:1). It follows then that Christian teaching must do more than communicate true information. It must promote Christian living.

The implications of this fact have not been fully understood by the church or its leaders. While information can be transmitted in formal, classroom settings or by preaching, neither of these settings is particularly effective in shaping lifestyle. Even when a preacher does explain the practical application of a truth, verbal explanations alone seldom facilitate significant change.

Against this background the second chapter of Titus takes on particular significance. For here Paul describes a "teaching" which does not rely on talk alone, but integrates a variety of activities which are specifically designed to develop a way of life which is "in accord with sound doctrine" (2:1).

Titus 2

You must *teach* what is in accord with sound doctrine. *Teach* the older men to be temperate, worthy of respect, self-controlled, and sound in faith, in love and in endurance. Likewise, *teach* the older women to be reverent in the way they live, not to be slanderers or addicted to much wine, but to *teach what is good.* Then they can *train* the younger women to love their husbands and children, to be self-controlled and pure, to be busy at home, to be kind, and to be subject to their husbands, so that no one will malign the Word of God.

Similarly, *encourage* the young men to be self-controlled. In everything *set them an example* by doing what is good. In your *teaching* show integrity, seriousness and soundness of speech that cannot be condemned, so that those who oppose you may be ashamed because they have nothing bad to say about us.

Teach slaves to be subject to their masters in everything, to try to please them, not to talk back to them, and not to steal from them, but to show that they can be fully trusted, so that in every way they will make the teaching about God our Savior attractive.

For the grace of God that brings salvation has appeared to all men. It *teaches* us to say "No" to ungodliness and worldly passions, and to live self-controlled, upright and godly lives in this present age, while we wait for the blessed hope—the glorious appearing of our great God and Savior, Jesus Christ, who gave Himself for us to redeem us from all wickedness and to purify for Himself a people that are His very own, eager to do what is good.

These, then, are the things you should *teach. Encourage* and *rebuke* with all authority. Do not let anyone despise you.

Interpretation. Paul was concerned with communicating doctrine, mercy, commitment, conduct—truths *plus* a whole new way of life. *Christian communication is to touch the entire person;* to shape beliefs, attitudes, values, and behavior. To teach the whole person, instruction must go beyond processing information. Even true information.

If we study the pastoral epistles carefully we see that Paul's stress on instruction typically focused more on shaping lifestyle than passing on truth. These second-generation Christians knew and accepted the basic doctrines of our faith. What they needed most was to learn how to live lives that were in harmony with the truths they knew. We might summarize Paul's view of teaching by using his own words: teaching is helping the people of God learn how to "conduct themselves in God's household" (1 Tim. 3:15).

Titus 2 helps us understand what is involved in this kind of teaching. To see it, we need to examine each of the bold-faced words.

"Teach" in Titus 2:1 is *laleo,* "to speak, assert, proclaim." What is to be the subject of this vocal instruction? Not "sound doctrine" itself, but a lifestyle that is in harmony with the revealed truths that shape our understanding of God and the meaning of our life in this world.

There is no word for "teach" in the original

of Titus 2:2. The Greek does, however, use a common grammatical construction which implies imperative, urgent communication. What is to be given such urgent attention? Again, it is lifestyle: a way of life which is "temperate, worthy of respect, self-controlled, and sound in faith, in love, and in endurance."

"Teach what is good" in Titus 2:3 is *kalodidaskalous,* used only here in the NT. The older women are responsible themselves to be admirable persons, and then to instruct the younger women in how to develop such a character.

"Train" in Titus 2:4 is *sophrontizo.* It means "to encourage, advise, urge." In NT times the word implied teaching morality and good judgment. In essence the older women were to show concern for the moral development and improvement of the younger women.

"Encourage" in Titus 2:6 is *parakeleo,* which means to "encourage or exhort." It suggests a coming alongside, a close and personal relationship, a true friendship in which one can learn and draw strength from another.

"Example" in Titus 2:7 is *typon.* This word means more than a "visible impression." It implies "a pattern or example to follow." We teach others God's ways by showing them by our own way of life what these ways are.

"Teaching" in Titus 2:7 is *didaskalia,* the act of (usually verbal) instruction. It is important that example and instruction go together.

"Teaches" in Titus 2:12 is a different word, *paideuousa.* This word implies giving guidance, as a parent might guide or correct a young child. Others see our way of life. We explain that way of life in words. And as others then seek to imitate us, we remain alongside, to guide and correct their initial steps toward godliness.

In Titus 2:15 "teach" is again *laleo,* "to speak." And "encourage" is again *parakaleo.* But "reprove" is a new word, *elencho,* which means "to bring to light, to expose." In context it means to convince, and if necessary to reprove in order to convict.

When we integrate all these terms and concepts into our notion of teaching, we find the concept is far broader than is generally recognized in our society. First, a teaching ministry is one of shaping lives, not simply one of passing on even true information. Second, Christian teaching deals with every aspect of our lives. The tasks and tensions of daily life, relationships with others—all are concerns on which Christian teaching must focus. Third, we must conclude that teaching is a very complex task, which actively involves the teacher with the learner in a relationship which includes instructing, modeling, encouraging, advising, urging, exhorting, guiding, exposing, and convicting.

Implications. If we are to take Paul's portrait of Christian teaching seriously, we need to rethink many aspects of contemporary church life. We need to take the relational far more seriously, for effective communication of a life that is in accord with sound doctrine requires more than speaking to a passive audience on Sunday, whether in a pew or classroom. We need settings in which lives can be shared, the lived meaning of Christian truths explored, and together we can support one another as we seek to follow Jesus Christ.

EXPOSITION

This brief letter contains only 335 words in the original Greek. It is a personal note: Paul's request to a wealthy church leader named Philemon to welcome back a runaway slave named Onesimus. From allusions in this note it appears that Onesimus had not only run away, but had also stolen from his master. Onesimus headed for Rome, apparently intending to lose himself in the crowded capital of the Empire. While in Rome, Onesimus encountered Paul, who was awaiting trial, and the runaway slave was converted. Onesimus apparently stayed with Paul for some time, and grew in his new faith. But the time finally came when it was necessary for Onesimus to return to his master. He went, carrying this note from Paul, in which the apostle appeals to Philemon to accept him "as a man and as a brother in the Lord" (16).

This brief note is fascinating in two regards. First, it reflects Paul's commitment to servant leadership. Rather than command, Paul seeks to persuade. The Christian leader cannot be satisfied with grudging obedience. Only by extending to others the right to refuse to serve Christ can their choice to respond to the Lord be made freely. The wise leader's goal is not to require conformity, but to encourage commitment.

Second, this brief note highlights what some have seen as a moral conflict in Paul's teaching. On the one hand the apostle affirms that since all believers are members now of God's own family, "there is neither Jew nor Greek, slave nor free, male nor female, for you are all one in Christ Jesus" (Gal. 3:28). Yet on the other hand Paul consistently urges Christians to accept their roles within the rigidly stratified world of the first century. Citizens are to submit to rulers. Wives are to submit to their husbands. Slaves are to serve their masters faithfully. In each case, the institution referred to was seriously flawed, if not morally repugnant. How then can the apostle, who on the one hand affirms the equality of all men and women in Christ, on the other hand call for Christians to submit to rather than resist injustice?

This latter issue seems to concern Paul not at all as he writes this personal note, appealing to Philemon "on the basis of love" (9) to welcome back a once "useless" (11) slave "who became my son while I was in chains" (10). The letter is especially warm for it is filled with evidence of the trust Paul has in Philemon's generous nature, as well as confidence that Philemon likewise will trust Paul's judgment and honor his request. What a privilege we have as Christians, and what bonds of affection and mutual support grow out of a shared commitment to Jesus Christ.

WORD STUDIES

And to the church that meets in your home (2). In the phrase *kat' oikon sou, sou* (your) is singular, and reminds us that it wasn't until the third century A.D. that any record of separate church buildings can be found. This, plus the fact that Philemon owned slaves, indicates that he was both well-to-do and probably an influential man.

Other references to house churches in the NT also mention their owners: Priscilla and Aquila in Rom. 16:5, Nympha in Col. 4:15.

I always thank my God as I remember you *in my prayers* (4). The Greek construction indicates "at the time of" my prayers. This suggests that Paul set aside specific times during the day for prayers, a practice followed in Judaism.

While prayer is frequently a spontaneous act, there is great value in Paul's practice.

Formerly he was *useless* to you, but now he has become *useful* both to you and to me (11). This verse would surely bring a chuckle to the reader, for in that era plays on words were a major element in humor. And this is a double play on words. The name Onesimus, a common name given to slaves, means "profitable" or "useful." While a different root, *chrestos,* is used here, the two words clearly play off the runaway slave's name. Onesimus, "profitable," was formerly *a-chrestos,* "useless" to his master. Now, as a Christian, he will be *eu-chrestos,* "of good use."

The humor, intended to bring a smile, does lighten the tone of the note, and further indicates Paul's own trust in Philemon as one with whom he can freely share his concern.

No longer as a *slave,* but better than a slave, as a dear brother (16). This verse has been taken by some as an indication that Paul is suggesting that Philemon grant Onesimus his freedom. This is possible, but not necessarily Paul's intent. In 1 Cor. 7:21 Paul urges slaves not to be dissatisfied by their state. "Don't let it trouble you," he says, and then adds "although if you can gain your freedom, do so." More significantly, in Eph. 6:9 Paul urges Christian masters to treat their slaves well. He does call for Christian slave owners to free them.

Again we see the peculiar tension that exists in the NT between the affirmation of equality for all in Christ, and apparent support of present social institutions, despite the fact that these institutions seemingly violate the rights of individuals whom God sees as equals.

No longer as a slave (16). This phrase deserves one other comment. There is no doubt that in the world of the first century, transition from slave to freedman marked an extraordinary rise in status. However, the freedman, a *libertas,* continued to be bound by both legal and informal ties to his previous master, who now became his patron. Even if Onesimus had been freed by Philemon, as a freedman the ex-slave would have been obligated to Philemon as his patron, and thus might very well have been "useful" in either state.

If he has done you any wrong or owes you anything, *charge it* to me (18). The word is *elloga,* an accountant's term. The way in which Paul approaches this question seems to many to indicate that, like many runaway slaves, Onesimus financed his flight by stealing something of value from his master. However, the very act of running away constituted theft. A slave in the first century was property, of value in and of himself. A slave purchased for manual labor was cheap, bringing only about 500 denarii. This amount is put in perspective by remembering that a free laborer earned a single denarius for one day's work. On the other hand, Cicero speaks of a slave trained by a well-known comedian who was worth over 100,000 denarii, and several writers of the era mention 50,000 denarii as the price of a slave trained in medicine, philosophy, or rhetoric.

Thus whether or not Onesimus stole money from his master, he undoubtedly robbed Philemon of himself. And in the first-century world Onesimus was undoubtedly a commodity with monetary value. A commodity that Philemon as his owner had every right to sell into far more onerous service than service in his own household.

Paul's appeal then is that Philemon accept Onesimus back into his household, and the apostle's guarantee is to indemnify Philemon for any monetary loss Philemon may claim for the loss of Onesimus' service during the period of his desertion of his post.

The offer is a generous one. But there is no doubt that Paul, knowing Philemon's charac-ter, knows very well that this Christian gentleman will refuse his offer but, moved by it, welcome Onesimus back and "do even more than I ask" (21).

THE PASSAGE IN DEPTH

Background. Slavery was an accepted institution in the first-century Roman Empire. The massive work edited by S. Safrai and M. Stern, *The Jewish People in the First Century*, notes that slavery was characteristic of Jewish as well as secular society. Ben Sira, writing some two centuries before Christ, includes advice on how to deal with slaves. While generally kindly, this Jewish writer suggests

Fodder and whip and loads for an ass;
    food, correction, and work for a slave.
Make a slave work and he will look for his rest;
    let his hands be idle and he will seek to be free.
Yoke and harness are a cure for stubbornness;
    and for a refractory slave,
    punishment in the stocks.
Force him to work that he be not idle,
    for idleness is the teacher of much mischief.
Give him work to do such as befits him;
    but if he fails to obey you, load him with chains
(33:25-30a).

While Ben Sira also advises kindness, the basis for his suggestion is both benevolent and practical.

Yet never lord it over any human being,
    and do nothing that is not just.
If you have but one slave, treat him like yourself;
    you would miss him as though it were you who was lost.
If you have but one slave, deal with him as a brother;
    your life's blood went into his purchase.
If you mistreat him and he runs away,
    in what direction will you look for him?
(33:30b-33)

In contrast Philo praises the first-century Essenes who refused to practice slavery. In *De vita contemplativa* (*The Contemplative Life*) Philo writes,

Not a single slave is to be found among them, but all are free, exchanging services with each other, and they denounce the owners of slaves, not only for their injustice in outraging the law of equality, but also for their impiety annulling the statute of Nature, who mother-like has borne and reared all men alike, and created them genuine brothers, not in mere name, but in very reality though this kinship has been put to confusion by the triumph of malignant covetousness, which has wrought estrangement instead of affinity and enmity instead of friendship.

Philo's impassioned words reflect a revulsion for the institution of slavery which is clearly absent from the New Testament. Yet the very existence of the sentiments Philo expresses in the world of the first century, and in an Essene community which was well established in Palestine in the time of Christ, makes the silence of the NT even more puzzling. Surely Philo's argument, which turns on the assumption of exploitation on the one hand, and on a philosophic affirmation of the innate natural equality of all human beings, is far weaker than arguments which could have been mounted by the Apostle Paul. And yet Paul, rather than rebuke the slave owner Philemon, clearly assumes his right to deal as he wishes with Onesimus. And rather than critique the institution of slavery, Paul speaks directly to slaves and, again and again, urges them to submit to their masters.

The following passages from Paul and from Peter demonstrate the consistent approach to slavery of the NT writers.

Slaves, obey your earthly masters with respect and fear, and with sincerity of heart, just as you would obey Christ. Obey them

545

not only to win their favor when their eye is on you, but like slaves of Christ, doing the will of God from your heart. Serve wholeheartedly, as if you were serving the Lord, not men, because you know that the Lord will reward everyone for whatever good he does, whether he is slave or free.

And masters, treat your slaves in the same way. Do not threaten them, since you know that He who is both their Master and yours is in heaven, and there is no favoritism with Him (Eph. 6:5-9).

Slaves, obey your earthly masters in everything; and do it, not only when their eye is on you and to win their favor, but with sincerity of heart and reverence for the Lord. Whatever you do, work at it with all your heart, as working for the Lord, not for men, since you know that you will receive an inheritance from the Lord as a reward. It is the Lord Christ you are serving. Anyone who does wrong will be repaid for his wrong, and there is no favoritism.

Masters, provide your slaves with what is right and fair, because you know that you also have a Master in heaven (Col. 3:22–4:1).

Slaves, submit yourselves to your masters with all respect, not only to those who are good and considerate, but also to those who are harsh. For it is commendable if a man bears up under the pain of unjust suffering because he is conscious of God. But how is it to your credit if you receive a beating for doing wrong and endure it? But if you suffer for doing good and you endure it, this is commendable before God. To this you were called, because Christ suffered for you, leaving you an example, that you should follow in His steps (1 Peter 2:18-21).

In none of these passages does the NT even imply any moral objection to slavery. In fact, the words of Paul seem to imply support for this institution which, on any grounds, we must judge morally reprehensible.

And so the question must be asked, "Why?" "What is Paul thinking?" And, "What underlies the position taken in the New Testament?"

Interpretation. A first step in interpreting any passage of Scripture is to examine it in its context: both the immediate context in which the passage appears, and the larger context of the message of the Gospel itself.

If we look at the immediate context of the two Pauline passages, we note that his prescription of submission is not addressed only to slaves. It applies equally to the husband/wife relationship. Peter follows his exhortation to slaves by saying, "Wives, in the same way be submissive to your husbands" (3:1). And this is directed not only to wives with Christian husbands, but specifically to those whose husbands are pagan.

It is common for some interpreters to conclude that the NT writers are both cowardly and chauvinistic. On the one hand Paul and Peter are blamed for failing to confront such evils as slavery out of fear that if they did, the Roman authorities might stamp out their movement. On the other hand the apostles are portrayed as blinded to the rights of women by the spirit of an age in which women were assumed to be inferior.

The problem here of course is that, in the case of women, the NT radically breaks out of the mold of first-century Jewish as well as Hellenistic and Roman thought. Luke takes great pains to describe Jesus' frequent contacts with women, something quite out of the ordinary for a rabbi of that time. As the age of the Spirit dawns, Peter proclaims that young men and young women alike will prophesy (Acts 2:17; 1 Cor. 11:5). In Paul's letters he frequently mentions women whom he identifies as "fellow workers" (Phil. 4:3) and one even as a "deaconess" (Rom. 16:1, NIV note). While in Judaism husbands were held to owe their wives a weekly marital duty, this falls far short of Paul's assertion in 1 Cor. 7:4 that while the wife's body belongs to the husband, "in the same way, the husband's body does not belong to him alone but also to his wife."

All this, and other evidence, invalidates the easy assumption that Paul's call to "submit" can be used to convict him of insensitivity at the least, and at worst of a callous chauvinism.

Clearly we must search deeper for an explanation of Paul's surprising call for the submission of slaves and wives within the framework of first-century institutions which as then constituted were repugnant to principles of equality which Christians rightly hold dear.

The answer is found in what moderns

might label a unique "social invention." To understand it, we must remember that in the rigidly stratified world of the first century, identity was solely a function of social status. One's person was defined by the role he or she filled in society. The wealthy Roman citizen was "someone" because he held citizenship and had wealth. Slave and freedman alike were nothing in the estimate of the elite and middle class. Women were defined by their relationship to men, as mothers or wives or daughters. As noted in an earlier study (Passage in Depth for Eph. 5–6), the inherent status of women is reflected in the fact that in Roman law women were disqualified from inheriting more than 10 percent of their husbands' estates. While some couples surely loved one another, the wife remained largely restricted to her home and unquestioningly obeyed her husband.

Christianity exploded into this rigidly stratified world with the good news that no individual's identity is defined by race or sex or wealth or social position. The Christian who has clothed himself or herself with Christ has entered a realm where there is "neither Jew nor Greek, slave nor free, male nor female, for you are all one in Christ" (Gal. 3:28). What's more, within the fellowship of this new community a unique equality exists. Each believer has a spiritual gift that enables him or her to minister to others. When the church at Corinth attempts to ascribe status on the basis of which gifts an individual possesses, Paul rebukes them. Every gift is an expression of the Holy Spirit. The community of faith is a body, which although it has many parts, maintains an essential unity. In this body/community every part is indispensable, so that those that seem to be less in man's eyes are honored by God and are to be treated with equal concern by others. Even spiritual leaders are cast, not as authorities over the body, but rather as servants, who model their ministries on that of a Christ who was willing to give His all for us.

Suddenly and decisively all those criteria on which human society ascribed status are seen to be irrelevant. They simply do not apply to Christians, for we are a people whose identity is established by our relationship with Jesus Christ, and by the fact that God in Christ loves us not for our position but for ourselves.

Paul's stunning social invention is nothing less than the separation of identity from social role and social status. Thus a woman or a slave can stand tall. However society may view either, each is assured of personal significance to God and within the Christian community.

We return then to our question. How can Paul ignore the institution of slavery, which Philo and others recognized even in the first century as intrinsically evil? How can Paul fail to challenge the demeaning of women that is undoubtedly reflected in the dominant first-century view of marriage?

He ignores them on three grounds. First, they are irrelevant to the Christian's real concern: to be Christ's man or Christ's woman. One's social role no longer defines the Christian man or woman. The slave does not need freedom to be personally significant. Nor does the wife need a job to be "liberated."

Second, one's social position is a gift from God. This is implied in 1 Cor. 7:20 where Paul says "each one should remain in the situation which he was in when God called him." A moment's thought helps us see why it is important to view one's role as a gift. If only slaves were Christians, no master would welcome the Gospel. If only the wealthy elite of the Empire were believers, those 600 families who in the first century composed the senatorial class, Christianity would have become a religion of the few. If only women converted, it would have become a faith for women only, like more than one of the Empire's mystery religions. In fact, however, Christianity spread across the social barriers. Masters and slaves, men and women, Jews and Gentiles, all became believers. And clearly for the message to spread, its most natural channel must be from wealthy slave-owner to wealthy slave-owner, not from slave to owner. Ultimately being a Christian slave meant that one would have a unique opportunity to reach other slaves, tradesmen with whom one dealt daily for food, or even the children of the family whose upbringing was then entrusted to slaves. Christians were needed in every strata of society if all were to hear the Gospel. And it is in this sense that whatever social position a first-century Christian held must be seen as a gift: as a divine commission to a ministry to others that only a person in his or her particular position could perform.

The third reason is closely linked to the second. Each person is to fulfill any obligations required by his or her social position as a witness to the healing of God's grace. Christianity does not directly threaten the social order of the society. Christianity instead strengthens it, for it develops responsible, caring individuals who are better wives, better husbands, better slaves, better masters, than the pagans around them. Thus Paul tells young Titus to encourage the older women to train the younger to love their husbands and be subject to them "so that no one will malign the word of God" (2:5). The ability of the Christian to live a godly life *in any circumstance,* even be it unjust, is a shining witness to the power of Christ to satisfy and to fill the heart with joy.

Application. In modern society Christians both understand, and fail to understand, the great social invention that underlies the radical spirit of the NT. We no longer believe, in the same way that the ancients did, that social status actually defines us and provides identity. Yet the frustration felt by many women in our society does reflect a failure to truly understand. That failure is first on the part of men, whose limited view of women's roles in the home and in the church reflect a persistent attempt to stratify by sex. And it is second a failure on the part of women, whose frustration shows that they have similarly failed to grasp that the limits imposed by society are irrelevant to either their identity or their significance as Christian persons.

Paul's solution will not sit well with many. Yet it is truly godly and wise. In calling on slave and master to love and serve each other, the apostle laid a foundation for the ultimate rejection of an unjust institution. And in calling on slave and master to fulfill their roles responsibly, he released them to live as free individuals. Free, not from restrictions imposed by society's institutions, but free within the framework of those institutions to live a life of joyful service to Jesus Christ.

No one is ever free from restrictions imposed on him or her by our institutions, whether they be the institutions of secular society or the institutional accretions that history has imposed on the church. The unique freedom of the Christian is found in living triumphantly within those limitations, seeing in them ever fresher ways to further the spiritual kingdom of our Lord.

HEBREWS 1:1–4:13
Jesus, The Living Word

EXPOSITION

Properly speaking, the Epistle to the Hebrews is more a tract than a letter. Its author is unknown, but its intent is clear. While itself untitled, the appellation "to the Hebrews" is ancient, reported in the East by Eusebius and in the West by Tertullian. The group to which this tract is directed does not consist of Jews, but Jewish Christians. Keeping strictly within the context of OT thought and imagery, the writer demonstrates to those who apparently feel the pull of the old ways that Christ is, in every respect, both a fulfillment of the Old Covenant, and the author of a new and better covenant relationship with God. While the identity of the writer is unknown, it seems most likely from his failure to refer to the destruction of the temple by Titus in A.D. 70 — an event which would have strengthened his argument concerning sacrifice and the levitical priesthood — that this book was written prior to that date. The author's reliance on the Septuagint in his OT quotes, his pure and beautiful Greek, combined with his familiarity with distinctively Jewish principles of interpretation, suggest that he was himself a Hellenistic Jew, perhaps directing his letter to Jewish Christians in Palestine whose close association with those who still practiced the ancient traditions exerted a strong pull on their hearts.

Yet to the writer of Hebrews there can be no turning back. The whole of the older revelation points directly to Christ, not only as its fulfillment, but as its original object. And so the author launches immediately into a powerful, sevenfold affirmation of who Jesus is (1:1-4), followed by a scripturally rooted comparison of the Son of God with angels who, in Jewish tradition, were mediators of the Old Covenant (1:5-14). Since the New Covenant is mediated by the Son Himself, it follows that the believer must "pay more careful attention" to it than to the Old (2:1-4). Indeed, the Son of God became a true human being and suffered in order to make human beings the spiritual children of God — a purpose which indeed required He take on flesh and blood, for only as a human being could He serve in a priestly capacity and make atonement for our sins (2:5-18).

The writer will return to the themes of priesthood and sacrifice soon. But first he returns to the issue of covenant relationship itself. The Jews saw angels as mediators of the Old Covenant, and the writer has shown that the Mediator of the New Covenant is God the Son. But he has also argued that Jesus is a true human being. How does He compare then with Moses, revered by Israel as the lawgiver and greatest man in sacred history? The writer's answer is this: Moses was a great man, a faithful servant in the house of God. But Jesus was faithful too, and not as a servant, but as a son "over God's house." Moses served, but he served within the framework of a house that Christ created. Clearly, the Son who owns the house and the Builder who conceived and constructed it is superior to one who serves in it, however great a servant he may be (3:1-6).

Now comes one of the greatest warnings, and greatest invitations, in all of Scripture. The writer looks back to the Exodus generation and notes that they were unable to enter Canaan because of unbelief. They heard God's voice calling them to go up and conquer the land, but hardened their hearts and refused to respond to His call. Rather than experience rest in the Promised Land, they were doomed to years of restless wandering in the wilderness (3:7-19). Using a long-established principle of Jewish interpretation the writer turns to a key phrase, "today," to show that the "rest" God promised is timeless and available to every generation. But no generation which refuses to hear God's word to them, and is corrupted by an evil heart of unbelief, can know this rest. The apparent unwillingness of those to whom the author writes to turn to Christ completely, and trust absolutely in Him, places them in danger of recapitulating the destiny of those wilderness wanderers who could never know peace because in their unbelief they disobeyed the voice of God (4:1-13).

To the writer of the Book of Hebrews there is no two-covenant option: one way of salvation for the Jews found in the Old Covenant made by Moses at Sinai, and another way of salvation for the Gentiles found in a New Covenant faith in Christ as Son of God and Savior. There is one option alone: to recognize the voice of God in the Gospel, to acknowledge Christ as the object and fulfillment of the older Testament, and to unhesitatingly place one's trust and confidence in Him alone.

WORD STUDIES

In the past God spoke to our forefathers (1:1). Pagan writers raised a number of objections to Christianity. One of the most serious was expressed by Celsus, writing in the second century, "Is it only now after such a long age that God has remembered to judge the life of men? Did he not care before?" (cf. Cels. 4.7)

The answer of the writer to the Hebrews is that God was not silent in ages past. He did speak, in many different ways, to "our forefathers." Paul would have added that God spoke not only to the Jews through special revelation, but also to all Gentile people through nature (Rom. 1:18-21). The fault is not in that revelation which God has granted to all human beings, but in mankind's response to revelation. The history of Gentile and Jew alike demonstrates all too clearly man's basic unbelief and refusal to respond to God's voice.

But now, the writer of Hebrews will say, God has spoken to us in a strong, unmistakable voice, "by His Son" (1:2). That is a voice we *must* hear, for there is truly no excuse if we ignore or reject the message so clearly conveyed by the Living Word.

And again, when God brings His *firstborn* into the world, He says, "Let all God's angels worship Him" (1:6). This is the only NT passage in which Jesus is directly described as God's *prototokos*, "firstborn." Many cultists argue that this word shows that Christ is a created being, not God from all eternity as John 1:1-3 and other passages clearly teach. However, the author's intent in this passage is to compare the *status* of Christ with that of angels. In this context *prototokos* is used in a quasi-legal sense, to indicate that Jesus has the same relationship to God the Father that a firstborn son had with his earthly father. As "heir of all things" (1:2), Jesus the Son of God is worshiped as God the Father is, by all God's angels.

Far from bringing Christ's essential deity into question, *prototokos* here affirms it in the strongest possible way.

Are not all angels *ministering spirits* sent to serve those who will inherit salvation? (1:14) This is a final contrast in a series comparing Christ and angels. Christ is enthroned in glory; all angels, without exception, are servants. Although "spirits," and thus of a higher order now than man, angels are servants not simply of God, but those who express their allegiance to God (*leitourgika,* "ministering") by serving saved human beings.

We must *pay more careful attention,* therefore, to what we have heard, so that we do not *drift away* (2:1). The verb *prosechein* means not only to focus our attention on something, but also to act on what we learn. "Drift away" is *praryomen,* a familiar word used of a ring that slips unnoticed from a person's finger, or a ship that slips its anchor and drifts from its secure harbor. Those who fail to act on the message delivered by God's Son are in serious danger of slipping away from the truth.

Yet at present we do not see everything subject to Him (2:8). Having defined the relationship between Christ and angels, the writer begins to review the place of human beings in God's plan. Man was to have dominion over God's creation. Yet it is clear that at present this destiny has not been realized.

Why? Before humankind could realize its destiny Jesus had to taste death for us, that by His suffering we might be lifted up to glory as children of God.

What our passage provides is a special insight into the relationship between Jesus, angels, and human beings. A relationship we can diagram as follows:

Original	Incarnation	Resurrection
Jesus		Jesus/us
angels	angels	angels
us		Jesus/us

Jesus is not only exalted above the angels, but has lifted us up with Him. Our destiny is fulfilled in Christ, through whom God's origi-nal intent to make all things subject to humankind will at last be realized.

It was fitting that God, for whom and through whom everything exists, should make the *Author* of their salvation *perfect* through suffering (2:10). The word translated "author" is *archegos,* which has been variously rendered as "pioneer" or founder. The thought here is clearly that Christ is the One in whom salvation originates; He personally not only went on ahead to show the way, but through His suffering He became the Way.

In what sense could God "make [Christ] perfect"? The word is *teleios,* and is most often used in the sense of completion. Suffering could add nothing to Christ's essential nature; He did not change or become different. But the actual act of suffering in space and time was necessary for Jesus to become the Author of a salvation which required His death and resurrection. The cross perfected Jesus in the sense of fully qualifying Him to serve as the Savior of humankind—a work which He could not have accomplished apart from His suffering and death.

And that He might *make atonement* for the sins of the people (2:17). The word is *hilaskesthai,* and means "to propitiate," not to "make atonement." The distinction is important, for propitiation relates to the righteous wrath of God which is aroused by sin. In His death Christ took the punishment that justice decreed "with respect to [accusative case] the sins of the people."

Let us, therefore, *make every effort* to enter that rest, so that no one will fall by following their example of disobedience (4:11). The Greek word is *spoudazo,* which suggests "diligent, concentrated effort." It seems almost contradictory that one must struggle to enter into rest. But the writer is making an important point. Rather than wrestle with life's challenges on our own, we are to concentrate our efforts on being obedient to God, confident that His voice will guide us in every "today."

Key Concepts Chart

Hebrews	Theme	Concept	Key Verses	Key Words	Meaning
Chap. 1	Jesus' identity	Jesus is God	Heb. 1:1-2	whole, complete	Jesus is enough . . . there is nothing more I need.
2	Our identity	We are Jesus' brothers	Heb. 2:11	mastery, dominion	I need to see myself raised to mastery of life in Jesus.
3 & 4	Life-principle	Experience our position	Heb. 4:10	rest, faith, response	When I trust and obey God, I enter His rest.
5	High Priest	Jesus links us with God	Heb. 4:16	weakness, link	When weak, I can come confidently to Jesus for forgiveness and aid.
6	Maturity	Security stimulates growth	Heb. 6:18	insecure, foundation	I can forget myself and launch out in reckless trust that the Atonement is complete.
7	Priesthood	Relationship is assured	Heb. 7:25	guaranteed relationship	I can have assurance of salvation: Jesus is my Guarantee!
8 & 9	Law	Righteous-ness is necessary	Heb. 8:10	command-ment law, inner law	I can trust Jesus to make me progressively more righteous as I trust and obey Him.
9 & 10	Sacrifice	Holiness is ours	Heb. 10:14	guilt, cleansed	I can see myself in Jesus as a holy, not a guilty person.
10	Warning	Maturing takes time	Heb. 10:35-36	process, persevere	I can know that daily commitment to God's will produces maturity.
11	Faith	Faith enables	Heb. 11:6	enablement, obedience	I can meet any challenge enabled by faith in God.
12	Discipline	Faith becomes commitments	Heb. 12:10	patience, holiness	I can discipline myself to full commitment to faith's life.
13	Love	Faith produces love	Heb. 13:20-21	externals, grace	I can find life's real meaning in others and in Christ.

THE PASSAGE IN DEPTH

The Sevenfold Identification of Jesus Christ (1:1-3).

Background. Both Jew and Gentile were troubled by the Christian's belief in Christ's deity, but for very different reasons.

The notion that a god might appear as a human being was a common element in many pagan religions. So the possibility existed that Jesus might have been a god. But surely He could not have been *the* God whom the higher philosophies postulated must exist. For, while the higher Greek philosophies assumed the existence of one supreme Being, the philosophers also believed that each people created its own local, subordinate deities, each of whom expressed some, although not precise, truth about God. What's more, enlightened pagans believed that when they worshiped these deities they in fact through them worshiped the one, High God.

What's more, to thinkers like the Emperor Julian the Apostate, it was unthinkable that the high God should reveal Himself only to one people, the Jews, or though one Person, Jesus Christ. At best the God of the Jews, and the God of the Christians, was a regional deity, like other regional deities' imperfect representations of the High God, yet beings through whom the hidden One might be worshiped.

The Jews had a very different objection to Jesus. For them it was unthinkable that the transcendent Yahweh of the OT should become a human being. Whoever this Christ might be, prophet, rabbi, or even Messiah, He could not possibly be the Creator, the God of Abraham, the God of Moses.

These first verses of the Book of Hebrews confronts the beliefs of pagan and Jew alike with a bold, clear affirmation of just who Jesus is.

Interpretation. The following three verses from the beginning of Hebrews contain seven statements about Jesus Christ, which are numbered:

In the past God spoke to our forefathers through the prophets at many times and in various ways, but in these last days He has spoken to us by His Son, (1) whom He appointed Heir of all things, and (2) through whom He made the universe. The Son is (3) the radiance of God's glory and (4) the exact representation of His being, (5) sustaining all things by His powerful word. After He (6) had provided purification for sins, He (7) sat down at the right hand of the Majesty in heaven.

What, then, does each of these statements about Christ affirm?

■ *Christ is appointed "Heir of all things."* In our society an "heir" is a person who gains possession of something by the death of another. In the world of the first century "heir" emphasizes lawful possession, without implying how a person gained possession—as the Son of God Christ holds rightful title to the universe itself and all that it encompasses. He is no regional deity of the pagans, nor is He inferior in any way to the God of the OT, for He is that God enfleshed.

■ *Christ is the One "through whom [God] made the universe."* The phrase "the universe" is actually *tous aionas,* "the ages." It is clear from other passages that Christ Himself was the Agent of Creation (John 1:3; 1 Cor. 8:6; Col. 1:16). Here the writer may very well reflect the deeply rooted Jewish conviction that God is the God of history, who directs the flow of history as well as brings the material universe into being. Christ, the Son, has from the beginning supervised all that happens on earth, channeling events from generation to generation so that all moves purposefully toward God's appointed end.

■ *Christ is "the radiance of God's glory."* The term *apaugasma* can mean "radiance" or "reflection." Jesus shines with the brightness of God's own "glory," a term which is frequently used in the OT to signify the presence of God. Unmistakably, the writer says, God is present in Jesus, and that presence shines forth from within Him.

■ *Christ is "the exact representation of His [God's] being."* The key term here is "exact representation," *character.* It is used literally of the image stamped on a coin by a die. The writer's point is that in Jesus God's essential nature is revealed to us, for Christ "bears the very stamp of His nature" (RSV).

■ Christ even now is *"sustaining all things by His powerful word."* The word *pheron* means to "carry along." The image is one of dynamic action: only Christ's active support enables the universe and all processes in it to continue operation. Here again "universe" is *aionas,* ages. It is not simply that Christ supports and sustains what we call the processes of natural law. Christ is actively involved in the flow of this present age, seeing to it that God's purposes are being achieved.

■ Christ *"provided purification for sins."* Now suddenly the writer changes the direction of our gaze. Rather than looking upward in wonder to contemplate who Christ is in His essential nature, he focuses our attention on the fact that it is this awesome One who has stepped into space and time to personally put away our sins. "Purification" is *katharismos,* "cleansing." And soon the writer will turn his attention to this work, showing us that the incarnate Christ became both High Priest and Sacrifice, the only One in the universe able to restore a sinful humanity to right relationship with God.

■ Christ *"sat down at the right hand of the Majesty in heaven."* The phrase is rich in OT symbolism. Sitting signifies rest, and work completed. The right hand signifies the place of honor. This final image shows us a Christ restored to His original, eternal glory, but more than restored—honored eternally for completing the work of salvation which was set before Him.

Implications. Thus the writer concludes his introduction of Jesus Christ. How far Christ is from the regional deity of the pagan; He is the transcendent deity of the OT. To know Christ, to recognize Him for who He is, both pagan and Jew, and modern "scientific man," must surrender personal assumptions about God, and bow before Jesus Christ as Lord of all.

Hearing God's Voice (3:7–4:13).

Background. This is the second of four warnings found in Hebrews. The first (2:1-4) is a warning against drifting away from God by failing to pay close attention to the Gospel message.

The second warning, found here, is a warning not to ignore God's voice when He speaks to us in our "today." Ignoring God's voice is

at heart unbelief, for true belief is expressed by obeying God whenever He speaks to us. Only by responding to God's voice can anyone find the rest that is promised to every generation of the people of God.

The third warning (6:1-12), one of the most misunderstood passages in Scripture, concerns maturity. The Christian is not to return in constant panic to the foundational issues of our faith, but rather "go on" (6:1) to build his or her life on confidence in what Christ has done.

The fourth warning (10:26-39) contrasts those who shrink back when difficulties come with those who stand fast and persevere in doing the will of God.

Each of these warnings is appropriate for Hebrew Christians who feel themselves drawn back to their OT roots. In view of the superiority of Christ and the New Covenant He administers, the writer warns his readers. They must pay close attention to this Gospel, respond as God speaks to them, go on to maturity rather than back to foundational truths and, in spite of pressures within and without, they must persevere in doing the will of God as that will is revealed in Jesus Christ.

These warnings to first-century Hebrew Christians all have relevance to us today. Perhaps the second warning contains the greatest truths for us to grasp. This passage shows us the way to a life of inner peace. A way that leads us to a life of true rest, despite any inward or outward struggles we may have.

Interpretation. Quoting Ps. 95:7-11 the writer focuses our attention on an attitude which characterized the relationship of God to a particular OT generation. It is the generation of those who, freed by God's power from slavery in Egypt, were led by Moses toward the Promised Land. These men and women heard God's voice, first in a timeless revelation at Sinai, and then in a timely revelation at Kadesh Barnea. At Sinai God revealed the general principles through which His will might be discerned. At Kadesh Barnea God spoke a unique word: a word which was uniquely for that moment and that generation. His people were to enter the land and take it.

But God's people hardened their hearts and refused to obey. As a result God was forced to declare, "They shall never enter My rest" (3:11). In this context, *rest* clearly refers to the land of Canaan, promised to Israel by God, here. In the six days of Creation God foresaw and resolved every problem that might arise. He has already planned each solution, for the end is assured in the beginning. And it is God's rest (4:5) that believers are invited to enter! We are to come to the place where we appropriate fully what God has done and, while never becoming inactive, are to stop *laboring*. The Christian life that so many experience as an exhausting struggle is not God's intent for us. The life of rest God has for us is experienced only as we respond to His "today" voice, showing us the way we should go to tread pathways He has marked out ahead of time for us. Fear of the future, uncertainty, are taken from us when we realize that our whole duty is to let God guide, and respond when He speaks to us in our "today."

■ Entering rest. The analysis of that early generation's failure has specific application to our experience. "There remains, then, a Sabbath-rest for the people of God" (4:9). The Bible tells us that we are to rest from our own work, just as God did from His (4:10). The lifestyle of the person who is raised to mastery of life in Christ is not to be one of ceaseless struggle. We are to experience rest.

In chapter 3's final analysis of the early generation, we saw that the critical problem was one of attitude toward God. The people heard what He said. But they hardened their hearts and would not respond. Unwilling to trust God, they were unable to obey.

Modern psychology describes an "attitude" as a disposition or tendency to respond. Attitudes are always linked to behavior. To say a person has a critical attitude implies that in many situations he will tend to criticize rather than appreciate others. The rebellious attitude exhibited by the men and women Moses led out of slavery had behavioral consequences. When God spoke to them, their tendency was, first of all, to fail to trust His word, and second, to disobey.

In Scripture these two characteristics, trust and obedience, are always linked. Trust in God leads us to believe that what He says to us is prompted by love. This attitude is critical to the kind of obedience that God desires. A person who does not trust, but fears, might outwardly conform to the orders of a tyrant. But only trust and love enable us to make a willing, inner commitment to follow the instructions of our Heavenly Father. When we trust God, we are freed to obey God from the heart.

Thus the writer tells us to make every effort to enter God's rest. He does not tell us to struggle to obey God, for this would be useless. But if we make every effort to love God and develop that attitude of simple trust, then when we hear His voice in our "today," we *will* obey. And in this kind of obedience we will find rest.

■ God's Word. The passage concludes with a promise often mistaken for a threat. God's Word, the writer says, is living and active. Sharper than any double-edged sword, it penetrates even to dividing soul and spirit, joints and marrow; it judges the thoughts and attitudes of the heart. Nothing in all creation is hidden from the eyes of Him to whom we must give account (4:12-13).

Some see these words as a threat, as though God were described examining *them*, eager to highlight every hidden fault. But this is not the point at all! The writer has just explained rest. That rest goes back, beyond the promise of Palestine to Israel. God's rest is a rest of the soul and spirit, a rest of thought and attitude. The inner person is to be at rest as well. And we can rest, for nothing is hidden from God's gaze. He knows our deepest, most secret needs. And through His Word we hear His voice in our "today," and as we respond, He guides us to His solutions for our needs.

And we know rest.

HEBREWS 4:14–8:13
Jesus, Our High Priest

EXPOSITION

It is hard for us today to grasp the role the high priest played in first-century Judaism. As the writer of Hebrews continues his demonstration of the superiority of Christianity, he asks his readers to compare the High Priesthood of Jesus with the high priesthood under Mosaic Law. The writer begins by affirming that we have a "great High Priest," a superlative in itself as the Jews described the High Priest as the "great priest." Through Jesus, our "great High Priest," we approach God's throne itself, and find both mercy and grace (4:14-16). While only One who is appointed by God can serve as High Priest, Jesus was uniquely designated by God as the source of an eternal salvation, modeled not on the priesthood of Aaron but on the priesthood of Melchizedek (5:1-10).

Now again the author digresses to incorporate his third warning. His readers have been believers long enough to be teachers, yet have not advanced beyond elementary revelation. They need to move beyond Scripture's ABCs and become mature (5:11–6:3). Within the context of this call to maturity, the writer raises a hypothetical question. They have experienced relationship with God through Christ (6:4-5). If they fall away and return to Judaism, where do they expect to find salvation? Do they expect the Son of God to be crucified all over again? (6:6) The illustration of the field picks up the context of growth. God has provided in Christ that "rain" which is essential to fruitfulness. It is His intent that His people go on, not that they become useless, weed-choked fields (6:7-9). And surely, despite the tone of his warning, fruitfulness is what the author expects from these hesitant, yet still faithful Christians (6:10-12).

On what basis then does the writer expect vitality and spiritual growth? First, he expects them to go on because the salvation we have in Christ is secured by that promise and oath of God—a promise and oath by which Jesus was ordained to Melchizedekian priesthood (6:13-20). This priesthood is of a higher order than the Aaronic (7:1-10). More importantly, the shift from Aaronic to Mechizedekian priesthood indicates a radical change in the entire, interlinked OT approach to faith as defined by the Mosaic Covenant (7:11-22). As High Priest, Christ lives forever to guarantee us an eternal salvation (7:23-28). Under the New Covenant which He provides, we are granted inner transformation, an intimate relationship with God, and the forgiveness of all our sins (8:1-12). The New and better Covenant initiated at Christ's death has made the Old obsolete (8:13). Surely, then, there is no reason for

557

the uncertain Jewish-Christians to whom Hebrews is addressed to go back to the Old. Rather they can make a full commitment to the New, and go on to maturity.

WORD STUDIES

Since we have *a great High Priest* (4:14). The whole argument of this section of Hebrews hinges on the significance of the high priest. It is appropriate then that we begin with a brief survey of the attitude of the Jews toward the high priest.

His role in OT faith is established in its documents. The high priest alone entered the holy of holies once a year to make the sacrifice that atoned for "all the sins" of God's people (Lev. 16). Even his death was thought to have power to atone, for when a high priest died, all who had killed others accidentally and fled to a city of refuge (Num. 35:9ff; Deut. 19:1ff) were released and free to return home (Num. 35:25). The scribes agreed that their guilt was so fully expiated by the high priest's death that they might assume their former positions.

Ben Sira, writing about 200 B.C., composed the following hymn to the high priest Simon II, which suggests something of the awe with which OT believers regarded the holder of this office.

How splendid he was as he looked forth from the Tent,
  as he came from the house of the veil!
Like a star shining among the clouds,
  like the full moon at the holy-day season;
Like the sun shining on the temple of the King,
  like the rainbow appearing in the cloudy sky;
Like the blossoms on the branches in springtime,
  like a lily by running waters;
Like the verdure of Lebanon in summer,
  like the blaze of incense at the sacrifice;
Like a vessel of beaten gold
  studded with an assortment of precious stones;
Like a luxuriant olive tree thick with fruit,
  a plant whose branches run with oil;
Wearing his splendid robes,
  and vested in sublime magnificence,
As he ascended the glorious altar
  and lent majesty to the court of the sanctuary.

When he received the sundered victims from his brother priests
  while he stood before the sacrificial hearth,
His sons ringed him about like a garland,
  like young cedars on Lebanon;
And like poplars by the brook they clustered about him,
  all the sons of Aaron in their dignity,
With the offerings to the Lord in their hands,
  in the presence of the whole assembly of Israel.
     The Wisdom of Ben Sira (50:5-13)

A further indication of the intense feeling in Israel concerning the high priest is reflected in an interesting historical sidelight. In the first century the power of the office was viewed as transmitted to a living high priest by his investiture with the eight parts of the truly splendid high-priestly garments. Thus as a safeguard against rebellion, Herod the Great and later the Romans kept these garments locked up in the Fortress Antonia, and handed them over to the high priest only on feast days.

The Jews agitated for decades for the release of the high priest's garments until finally, in June of A.D. 45, the Emperor Claudius personally ordered the vestments turned over.

In a significant way, then, the high priest summed up the central elements of OT religion. The Law might condemn, but it also offered a way to approach God through an atoning sacrifice which could be offered only by the high priest. Thus the high priest was a bridge between man and God, and an avenue through which the grace of God might flow toward a people who, however unworthy, were yet the objects of God's affection.

It is no wonder, then, that the writer to the Hebrews takes such great pains to show that, while Judaism had its high priests, Christ, Christianity's "great High Priest" (4:14) is far more glorious, and offers an even greater, more awe-inspiring salvation.

For we do not have a high priest who is

unable to sympathize with our weaknesses, but we have one who has been *tempted in every way, just as we are*—yet was without sin (4:15). The Greek *kath' homoioteta* can mean "in the same way" we are tempted, or tempted "by reason of His likeness to us." The writer's point is that Christ was a true human being, who shared all the weakness inherent in being a creature limited by His physical nature. Since Christ has "walked in our shoes," so to speak, He understands by experience rather than simply intellectually what it means to be tempted and so can sympathize with us.

Some might argue that since Christ was God He was untroubled by the limitations that trouble us. The writer disagrees: Christ was fully human. The phrase "yet without sin" reminds us that in fact Christ knows even more about temptation than we do. After all, who understands pressure better? The person who caves in under it after a few minutes? Or the person who never gives in?

Let us then approach the throne of grace with confidence, so that we may *receive mercy* and *find grace to help us* in time of need (4:16). Christ's sympathy extends both to those who have surrendered to temptation, and those who still resist it. For our failures He has mercy. For our trials, He has grace to help us in our time of need. Whatever our situation, Jesus understands and cares.

He is able to *deal gently* with those who are ignorant and going astray (5:2). The verb *metriopathein* reminds the readers that the high priest is to take a position between indignation and indifference. He must not condemn the sinner nor condone the sin. This was possible only because every high priest was "selected from among men" and thus sensitive to human frailties as well as to the requirements of God's Law. For the Aaronic priesthood, this meant each must "offer sacrifices for his own sins, as well as for the sins of the people" (5:3).

The author then goes on to distinguish Christ's ministry from that of the OT priestly line. Like Aaron, Christ was called by God to the position of high priest (5:4-5). Unlike Aaron, Christ was both God's own Son and also a "Priest forever" (5:6). Unlike flawed Aaron, who under pressure surrendered to sin, Christ

"learned obedience from what He suffered" (5:8). Here the phrase "once made perfect" (5:9) has the meaning of "being now fully qualified for His role." Christ became the source of eternal salvation for you and me.

He offered up prayers and petitions with loud cries and tears to the One who could save Him from death, and He was heard because of His reverent submission (5:7). Commentators agree that this is a reference to Christ's experience in Gethsemane. What the writer means by the reference to being saved from death, however, continues to puzzle everyone. Some say Christ did not ask to be saved from dying, but from death, and that the Resurrection is God's answer to His prayer. Some suggest what God delivered Christ from was the fear of death. Others say Christ was concerned that under the pressure of that stress which caused Him to sweat blood Christ feared He might die there in the garden, and not complete His work.

Perhaps it's best to remember that the report of Christ's prayer in the garden emphasizes His words, "Yet not as I will, but as You will" (Matt. 26:39). Jesus' prayer was heard. God's will was done. And through His suffering then, as throughout His life, Christ's feet marched steadfastly along the path of obedience.

Solid food is for *the mature,* who by constant use have trained themselves to distinguish good from evil (5:14). Maturity doesn't come cheaply. It's not enough to know God's Word. We have to put it to constant use as a guide for making daily choices, and so train yourself in godliness. Scripture alone can't make us mature. Committing ourselves to practice God's Word constantly, will.

Men swear by someone greater than themselves, and the *oath* confirms what is said and puts an end to all argument (6:16). This passage is significant in that it reminds us of the character of the OT covenant, or *brit,* as it relates to the definition of God's relationship with human beings. Used in the context of business, *brit* can be rendered as "contract." Used in the context of national politics, *bĕrît* can translated "constitution." Used in the context of international politics, *bĕrît* is a "treaty."

In each of these contexts, the *bĕrît* can be broken by either party, and typically the penalties for violation are listed in the *bĕrît* document. But when used of God's relationship with human beings, *bĕrît* is to be understood as an "oath"; a solemn statement of what God commits Himself to do. Even the Law Covenant has this character, for the penalties imposed should God's people violate the Law, and the blessings promised for keeping it, are themselves statements of what God firmly intended to do.

This "oath" character of the divine covenant is clearly understood in the OT, as reflected in the prayer of Moses recorded in Ex. 32:13: "Remember Your servants Abraham, Isaac and Israel, to whom You swore by Your own self; 'I will make your descendants as numerous as the stars in the sky and I will give Your descendants all this land I promised them, and it will be their inheritance forever.' "

So the writer of the Book of Hebrews reminds his readers that throughout all of sacred history God's oaths have been unbreakable. Strikingly, the designation of Jesus Christ as a "High Priest forever" is reported in Scripture itself (5:5-6), giving it the force of an oath and covenant commitment. Thus the writer concludes that "we have this hope [in Jesus] as an anchor for the soul, firm and secure" (6:19).

It is significant that the warning of Heb. 6 is encapsulated in this exalted presentation of Jesus as our high priest. If our salvation is secured by God's oath, then the author's talk of "fall[ing] away" (6:6) *must* be hypothetical, for anyone who is the beneficiary of Christ's high priestly ministry is guaranteed an "eternal salvation" (5:9).

For more on the warning passage, see The Passage in Depth on page 561.

He has become a high priest forever, in the order of Melchizedek (6:20). The Greek word translated "order" is *taxis*. It is used six times in the NT of the priesthood, and refers to a particular group or class. Thus the writer is saying that Christ's priesthood is to be classified as Melchizedekian rather than Aaronic. Chapter 7 is dedicated to developing the significance of this classification. In brief, the author argues that the superiority of the Melchizedekian priesthood is demonstrated in the OT by the fact that:

■ He blessed Abraham rather than vice versa, demonstrating that Melchizedek was greater (7:1).

■ Abraham paid him tithes, implicitly acknowledging Melchizedek's superiority (7:2).

■ Melchizedek was "without beginning of days or end of life" (7:3). This need not imply that the original Melchizedek was an angelic being or a preincarnate appearance of Christ. It does reflect a typical rabbinic approach, which held that much may be inferred from the silences of Scripture as well as from its statements. The point is that Christ is not qualified for His priesthood by His genealogy, but by His personal qualities. The silence also implies that Christ's priesthood is not terminable by death.

■ Christ is "declared to be living" (7:8). This thought is further developed in 7:23-24. The Aaronic priests died, but since even death cannot prevent Christ from continuing in office, He has a "permanent priesthood" (7:24) and is able to "save completely" (7:25) those who come to God by Him.

■ Even Levi, then in the loins of his father, paid tithes to Melchizedek (7:9), decisively showing the superiority of the priest-king's priesthood.

This seems a strange argument to us. But it is not so unusual in the context of a culture where one's personal identity was rooted in his genealogy. To understand Aaron, one must place him in the line of Levi his father, Israel his grandfather, Isaac his great-grandfather, and Abraham his great-great-grandfather. Only in the context of this line can Aaron's identity be established, and only by descent from Aaron can any subsequent priest's identity be established. In a very real sense then, Levi and Aaron did participate in every defining act of Abraham's life. In that sense, Aaron himself did pay tithes to Melchizedek, which act demonstrates again the superiority of the Melchizedekian priesthood over the Aaronic.

What then is the inescapable conclusion? That Christ truly is "a High Priest who meets our need" (7:26). How majestic Christ is seen to be. He is set apart from and high above an Aaronic priesthood, which was forced daily to offer the repeated sacrifices for themselves and others. For Christ offered sacrifice once and for all for men's sins when He offered Himself. And the fact that His sacrifice was never repeated proves it accomplished the purpose for which it was intended: our salvation.

For when there is a change in the priesthood, there must be a change of the Law (7:12). This is one of the most significant verses in this section of Hebrews. It reminds the author's readers that *torah* is one. The Mosaic revelation portrays an interlinked system in which God's relationship with Israel is defined; a covenantal system which defines God's requirements, and which balances man's failures by sacrifices offered by the Aaronic priests.

What the author points out is that a change in the priesthood destroys the balance of the OT system, and clearly implies a change in every other aspect of it as well—a change in Law, and a change in sacrifice.

As we move on from chapter 7 we see the author develop this very point: there has been a dramatic change in Law (chap. 8), and a change in sacrifice as well! (chaps. 9–10)

They serve at a sanctuary that is *a copy and shadow* of what is in heaven (8:5). The author lays a further foundation for his argument by reminding his readers that the tabernacle and temple of the old order displayed but did not constitute heavenly reality. Everything about the Old Covenant promulgated through Moses was a mere reflection, pointing beyond itself to heavenly realities.

Christ, who entered heaven itself, is the Mediator of a new and far better covenant than that mediated by Moses.

If there had been nothing wrong with that *first covenant,* no place would have been sought for another (8:7). In context the "first covenant" is the Mosaic. In arguing that something was "wrong" with it, the author simply points out that God Himself found fault with the fact that the Mosaic system was unable to perfect Israel, as history demonstrates (8:9).

The Christian emphasis on the New Covenant aroused furious opposition in Judaism. This continuing hostility of Israel to this teaching is reflected in the work of the great Jewish scholar/philosopher of the Middle Ages, Moses Maimonides. His "thirteen principles of faith," found in many Jewish prayer books today, include among them the statements that Moses is the True and First prophet, and that "there is no new covenant."

Yet the writer of Hebrews quotes God's promise of a New Covenant from Jer. 31, "It will not be like the covenant I made with their forefathers when I took them by the hand to lead them out of Egypt" (Heb. 8:9). Under the New Covenant the Law once written on stone will be transcribed within the living believer. Man's uneasy relationship with the Lord will be transformed into intimacy. And the sins covered by the sacrifices of the old economy are at last fully and freely forgiven, to be remembered no more.

By calling this covenant *"new,"* He has made the first one obsolete; and what is obsolete and aging will soon disappear (8:13). The Greek word is *kainos,* which in the NT as in first-century secular Greek, focuses attention on quality. It is not that the New Covenant is more recent. The important thing is that the New Covenant is superior.

The *Zondervan Expository Dictionary of Bible Words* notes:

> Christ's death initiates a new covenant between God and man—a covenant that is vastly superior to the old Mosaic Code (Mark 14:24; Luke 22:20; 1 Cor. 11:25; 2 Cor. 3:6; Heb. 8:8). Through Christ, human beings themselves become new creations (2 Cor. 5:17) and discover a realm of life in which all things become new (2 Cor. 5:17). These new creations wrought by Christ Himself live as new people, God's renewed humanity (Gal. 6:15; Eph. 4:24). The believers form a new community (Eph. 2:15) in which Jesus' new commandment, to love as He loved us, is enfleshed (John 13:34; 1 John 4:7-8; 2 John 5). One day God will complete His new work of creation and call into being new heavens and a new earth (2 Peter 3:13; Rev. 21:1-25) (p. 458).

Thus "new" in the qualitative sense makes the strongest possible statement about the impact of the Good News that comes to us in Jesus. The Gospel message is not a message of reform but of transformation. It is a fresh, powerful word from God. In contrast to all that God does in Christ, the "old" is obsolete and inferior indeed.

THE PASSAGE IN DEPTH

Warning against Falling Away (5:11–6:12).

Background. Over the centuries this passage has probably been the most frequently turned to by those intent on proving that a believer can lose his or her salvation. Yet through those same centuries a variety of interpretations has been advanced.

Tertullian, followed by others, believed that Heb. 6 teaches that there is no repentance for a Christian who sins after baptism. More recently, K.S. Wuest dismisses the passage as irrelevant, saying that the conditional participle shows the writer intends us to see that the "danger" he warns against is unreal. Others, with Calvin, have suggested that the writer's reference to "tasting" (6:4) indicates one who has had only a partial experience of God's grace, and not that full experience associated with salvation. To others the words of reassurance in v. 9, that "we are confident of better things in your case," indicate that the writer is speaking hypothetically. To others the words "it is impossible" (6:4) are proof positive that the writer is speaking of a very real danger of a person becoming so hardened by a return to the Old Covenant that there is no possibility of a return to a relationship with God governed by the New.

It is indisputable, given these varied and strongly argued interpretations, that this is a difficult passage. One which we can understand appropriately only by reference to the main thrust of the book, the nearer context of this warning within its argument, and the development of the writer's theme within the warning itself.

Insofar as the book is concerned, it is best to understand it as addressed to Christians of Jewish origin. As we have seen, the pull of the old remains strong in this Jewish/Christian community living three decades or so after Christ's death. They believe in Jesus as Savior, yet are strongly attracted to their OT heritage. Thus the writer sets out to reinforce their commitment to Jesus and the burgeoning Christian movement by a thorough exposition of the superiority of Jesus Christ. To demonstrate that superiority, the writer compares the Old and New, point by point. The Old was mediated by angels, the New by God's own Son. The Old featured Moses, an honored servant in God's house. The New features Jesus, the Builder and Owner of the house in which Moses served. The Old had a glorious high priesthood. The New has a far more glorious high priest, Jesus Himself. And at every point Jesus' Melchizedekian priesthood is vastly superior to the Aaronic priesthood.

It is within this discussion of the two priesthoods that the Hebrews warning passage is found. The implication is clear. How could one think of turning back to seek relationship with God through a priesthood whose shortcomings are so clearly displayed in contrast to the "eternal salvation" (5:9) that is guaranteed to us through the high priesthood of Jesus Christ?

In the middle of this argument the writer pauses to examine the present experience of those to whom he writes, and urges them to trace with him the implications of the choice they are even then considering.

Interpretation. The warning is developed with a logic of its own. We can summarize it this way:

■ Inaction has left the readers immature (5:11-14). They have not applied the principles of Christian faith to their daily lives, which alone is able to bring them to maturity.

■ They have focused their attention on elementary, foundational truths (6:1-3). The things they stress are the underpinnings of the Judeo-Christian heritage. These are things Christians are to build on, not constantly return to.

■ They have failed to see the implications of the choice they are considering (6:4-6). Here the argument does become hypothetical. The writer asks, "What would a Christian who has turned his back on the cross do to return? Crucify Jesus all over again?"

■ Returning to the theme of maturity, the writer uses the familiar image of a field (6:7-

8). As rain is to a field, so grace is to the believer. Each is intended by the giver to produce a crop. The field that produces only weeds is burned, that its ashes might fertilize the ground. Instead of pondering a return to the Old Covenant, the readers must soak in the grace that flows to them through Jesus, their High Priest, and become mature so that they can produce fruit.

■ The writer reassured his readers. Despite his warning, he is confident that God will produce the "things that accompany salvation" (6:9) in their lives. To that end they are to continue their good works, and "show this same diligence" (6:11) along with those others whom "through faith and patience inherit what has been promised" (6:12).

The logic of the warning, then, expresses the writer's concern for his brothers. He does not fear that they will be lost. This is really not what he is warning about at all. He is fearful, however, that these Hebrew believers will fail to grasp the real issue, and as a result will be trapped in a way of life which cannot bring them to spiritual maturity, or make their lives fruitful for God.

Without commenting on every word in this argument, we do need to give close attention to the three critical verses over which so much debate has raged.

It is impossible for those who have once been enlightened, who have tasted the heavenly gift, who have shared in the Holy Spirit, who have tasted the goodness of the Word of God and the powers of the coming age, if they fall away, to be brought back to repentance, because to their loss they are crucifying the Son of God all over again and subjecting Him to public disgrace (Heb. 6:4-6).

The first thing to admit is that the writer has unquestionably identified the persons he has in mind as Christian believers. They are described by four participial phrases, the first of which is further defined by the next three. The writer is speaking of people who:
Have been enlightened: [that is, they have]

■ tasted the heavenly gift
■ shared in the Holy Spirit
■ tasted the goodness of the Word of God.

In John's and in Paul's writing (Eph. 5:14), "light" comes with acceptance of the Gospel message. All others walk in darkness. In the NT particularly "taste" is used metaphorically of the conscious experience of a relation. One who "tastes" death is dead (John 8:52; Heb. 2:9). There is thus no contrast implied here between "taste" and "full experience." These are true believers, who have experienced the gift of salvation, received the Holy Spirit, and participated in the goodness of the Word of God. They are Christian believers, in every sense of the word.

What then about the argument that "it is impossible . . . if they fall away, to be brought back?" (6:4, 6) The word *adynaton*, "impossible," is strong and absolute. In this very letter it is used of the impossibility of God proving false (6:18), the impossibility of the blood of animals removing sin (10:4), and the impossibility of pleasing God without faith (11:6). Clearly the writer holds that should a Christian apostatize there would be no way back. Note however that he does not imply that a Christian can or will apostatize. The argument, "It is impossible if . . . then," is by its very form necessarily hypothetical. Should a true Christian apostatize (and this neither implies one can or one cannot) then he or she could never repent and return to the lost relationship.

But why not? The answer is that turning from Christ involves a rejection of the efficacy of the sacrifice He offered as our High Priest. And what would anyone who rejects that do? Ask that Jesus be crucified again? Unthinkable! For to do this would put Christ to public disgrace, being an open admission that His sacrifice of Himself was inadequate to do for us what God has promised.

We might paraphrase these verses (6:4-6) this way:

What would you want to do? Leave faith's foundations and return to Judaism? How then would you ever be restored to New Covenant relationship with the Lord—you who have been enlightened, tasted the heavenly gift, shared in the Holy Spirit, and known the flow of resurrection power? Would you crucify Jesus all over again, and through a new sacrifice be brought back to repentance? How impossible! What a disgrace, this hint that Jesus' work for you is not enough.

And so the writer's warning is intended to show his readers that there *is* no viable way back to the old. Christ lives now as High Priest for all who believe in Him. To return would be to deny Him. And should one deny Christ and His work, there is no hope.

Implications. Today it's popular to seek a betterment of Jewish/Christian relationships by affirming a "two covenant theology." The Mosaic Covenant, some say, is still in force for Israel. The New Covenant, these same persons say, opens up a way of salvation for the Gentile that the Jew does not need.

How strange this argument sounds as we hear again the words of the writer to the Hebrews. Christ has been appointed High Priest to represent all who come to God through Him. Christ is the Mediator of the New Covenant, a covenant which has replaced that older way which "is obsolete and aging [and] will soon disappear" (8:13). And disappear it has, for today no High Priest offers sacrifices on the Day of Atonement. No temple stands to contain an altar where sacrificial blood once was shed. Today the only hope of all mankind, Jew and Gentile alike, is to be found in Jesus Christ.

HEBREWS 9–13
Jesus, Our Sanctification

EXPOSITION

The writer of Hebrews set out to demonstrate the superiority of Christ and the New Covenant which He administers. He has shown Jesus to be superior in His Person (chaps. 1–2). Jesus is also superior to Moses as lawgiver, for He speaks as the Son with the authoritative voice of God (chaps. 3–4). The writer has also shown Christ's superiority as High Priest (chaps. 5–6), and argued that the change in the priesthood which Jesus represents implies a change in the whole system of religion through which the OT believer related to the Lord (chap. 7). Specifically, Christ introduces the promised New Covenant, which the OT itself predicts will supersede the Mosaic. Through the New Covenant ministry of Christ, sins once merely covered are now fully forgiven, human beings are transformed, and a new, more intimate relationship with God is established (chap. 8).

The writer now goes on to show that, while only sacrificial blood can win forgiveness, the animal sacrifices offered under the Old Covenant, and the tabernacle where their blood was spilled, were but shadowy images of a heavenly reality (9:1–10:18). That blood offered on earth cleansed the earthly things, but was not able to cleanse the conscience of human beings. The sacrificial blood of Christ is infinitely superior, for His blood was offered to heaven. Christ's blood not only obtained eternal salvation for us, but even cleanses our consciences so that we might experience inner transformation here and now. The animal sacrifices that were offered repeatedly reminded us of our sinful state, for they could not take away sins. In contrast the blood of Christ was offered once for all, and that one sacrifice cleanses us forever from our sins, for it guarantees full and complete forgiveness.

The author has now completed his great comparison between the Old and New Covenants. And so he pens what some see as another warning. If those who rejected the Law of Moses "died without mercy" (10:28), how much more certain is the punishment of those who reject the grace offered under a New Covenant that was instituted with the life's blood of the Son of God? (10:19-39) But this reminder is not meant as a threat to the author's Jewish-Christian readers. It is meant as encouragement. God now as then is the Vindicator of His Word. Indeed, in the early bloom of their faith these Christians stood their ground in the face of intense suffering. Certainly they will not "throw away your confidence" (10:35), but rather, after doing the will of God, "will receive what He has promised" (10:36).

With his great exposition on Old and New Covenants complete, the writer briefly reviews the role of faith (chap. 11). Rather than argue, as Paul does in Romans, this writer simply illustrates the fact that faith in God (rather than keeping the Law) has been the key to every accomplishment of saints under the Old Covenant as well as under the New! And now we have received, in the New Covenant instituted by Christ, something that is not different in essential character, but far, far "better" (11:40). In view of this testimony of generation upon generation of saints, we need to fix our eyes on Jesus as "Author and Perfecter of our faith" and, persevering, follow Him (12:1-3).

How then are the Hebrew Christians to understand the persecutions which, this next section may suggest, led to their hesitation in the first place? For history tells us that Palestinian Jewish Christians were severely persecuted by their Jewish brethren, not only being ostracized but also impoverished, and "publicly exposed to insult and persecution" (10:33). Such experiences, the writer says, are to be seen as discipline, imposed by a loving Heavenly Father in order to "produce a harvest of righteousness and peace for those who have been trained by it" (12:4-13).

Understanding this, every Christian is to concentrate on holiness, ever sensitive to the grace of God and to the fact that in committing to a New Covenant relationship with the Lord, the believer must turn away from earth and earthly things to be loyal to the hidden kingdom of God. The created universe will soon be shaken into nonexistence, and then only the heavenly realities now unseen will remain. And we, who worship God acceptably in reverence and awe, will remain with them (12:14-29).

The writer's last chapter (13:1-25) contains a number of brief exhortations, and what is perhaps the greatest benediction of all: "May the God of peace, who through the blood of the eternal covenant brought back from the dead our Lord Jesus, that great Shepherd of the sheep, equip you with everything good for doing His will, and may He work in us what is pleasing to Him, through Jesus Christ, to whom be glory for ever and ever. Amen."

WORD STUDIES

Now the first covenant had regulations for worship and also *an earthly sanctuary* (9:1). The author looks back in history to the tabernacle, the pattern of which was duplicated in the Jerusalem temple. He argues that though it was patterned on heavenly realities, it was at best an earthly shadow cast by those realities, serving as "an illustration for the present time" (9:9). The fact that the writer does not refer to the destruction of the Jerusalem temple, which made it impossible for Israel to offer the sacrifices called for by Moses, suggests that this book was written before A.D. 70. That destruction, however, later posed a most significant question. How can the Jews possibly relate to God under the Old Covenant when the basic requirements of that covenantal system cannot possibly be fulfilled?

The sages of rabbinic Judaism struggled with this issue after the destruction. To whom should tithes be paid, if the Levites no longer served at the temple and thus required a tithe in return for their service? (Num. 18:21) The answer of the sages was that the tithe should be given to a priest, but only one who is learned (a *haverim*), and then as a favor.

But how about the sacrifices that were central to the OT system, and through which atonement was made for the sins of God's people?

The following, from the Midrash compilation called the *Pesiqta deRab Kahana,* reveals the sages' solution:

2. B. "Said the Holy One, blessed be he, to them, 'Since you engage in studying about them, it is as if you actually carried them out.' "

3. A. R. Huna made two statements.

B. R. Huna said, "All of the exiles will be gathered together only on account of the study of Midrash-teachings."

C. "What verse of Scripture makes that point? 'Even when they recount [Mishna-teachings] among the gentiles, then I shall gather them together' " (Hosea 8:10).

D. R. Huna made a second statement.

E. R. Huna said, "From the rising of the sun even to the setting of the sun my name is great among the nations, and in every place offerings are presented to my name, even pure offerings" (Mal. 1:11). Now is it the case that a pure offering is made in Babylonia?

F. "Said the Holy One, blessed be he, 'Since you engage in the study of the matter, it is as if you offered it up.' "

4. A. Samuel said, "And if they are ashamed of all that they have done, show them the form of the house and the fash-ion of it, the goings out and the comings in that pertain to it, and all its forms, and write it in their sight, that they may keep the whole form of it" (Ezek. 43:11).

B. "Now is there such a thing as the form of the house at this time?"

C. "But said the Holy One, blessed be he, if you are engaged in the study of the matter, it is as if you were building it."

The sages, after the destruction of the Jerusalem temple, rejected the Christian contention that Christ's sacrifice fulfilled and made irrelevant the sacrifices required under the Old Covenant. Yet it was impossible for any high priest to serve in a nonexistent temple or to carry out the law regarding sacrifices. All that was left for adherents of the OT faith was the OT itself. And so the sages concluded what we have seen, that *studying* about sacrifices and offerings must now be the same as making them. And that *studying* about the temple must now be the same as going up to that house of God to worship the Lord there.

The solution is a creative one, but again substitutes the teachings of men for requirements established in the Word of God. The destruction of the Jerusalem temple in fact validated every argument developed by the writer of the Book of Hebrews. The "earthly tabernacle" (9:1) has been shaken to the ground. But Christ, our High Priest, has taken up the ministry once performed by the sons of Aaron, and through the sacrificial offering up of His own life has opened the way for us into the true holy of holies in heaven itself.

This is an illustration for the present time, indicating that the gifts and sacrifices being offered were not able to *clear the conscience* of the worshiper. They are only . . . *external regulations* applying until the time of the new order (9:9-10). Several times in Heb. 9–10 the writer refers to the conscience, and contrasts the effect of the blood of Christ with the effect of the OT's animal sacrifices. The blood of Christ purifies the believer *inside.* The sacrifices of the OT were *external* in effect, cleansing only material things, and even that fleetingly, for those sacrifices were repeated day in and day out.

The *Zondervan Expository Dictionary of Bible Words* comments on the cleansed conscience (9:14) emphasized in this two-chapter section by the author of Hebrews:

The Book of Hebrews shows us another aspect of conscience. The writer looks back at the OT sacrificial system, with its repeated sacrifices for sins, noting that they were "not able to clear the conscience of the worshiper" (9:9). The endless sacrifices were in fact an "annual reminder of sins" (10:3), constant testimony to the worshiper that his past was with him and that he stood guilty before God. All of an individual's acts of sin were stored up in his conscience, shouting out his guilt and draining away any confidence in the possibility of a different future.

Guilt does this to us. It saps our strength and makes us unwilling to take a risk. It robs us of the hope that our future will be different from our past.

Hebrews presents this argument to show a contrast. What the OT sacrifices could not do, the blood of Jesus accomplishes. That blood, offered to God, does "cleanse our conscience from acts that lead to death, so that we may serve the living God" (9:14). Through Christ we are cleansed "once for all" (10:2, 10, 14). With our sins forgiven and ourselves cleansed, we have the assurance that God Himself no longer remembers our lawless acts (10:17).

Cleansing is both objective, accomplished by Jesus' sacrifice, and subjective, experienced increasingly as we appropriate what Jesus has done for us. There will be times when our conscience will still drag our glance back to the past and shout out accusations. Then we must remember that our sins are forgiven (and the past gone). We must forget them (and it) and look ahead to how we can serve the living God.

As we continue to have confidence in God's Word and to act on the promise of a fresh future, our confidence will be rewarded. And we will be freed to look only ahead, enthusiastic about our opportunities to serve the Lord (pp. 186–87).

In the case of a will, it is necessary to prove the death of the one who made it, because a will is in force only when somebody has died; it never takes effect while the one who made it is living (9:16).

The word translated "will" is *diatheke,* used in the Septuagint and the NT to communicate the idea of covenant. The flexibility of *diatheke* permits the writer to shift easily between the concept of covenant and that of a will. The main point of comparison is that in each case, a death makes the terms of the document final. When a person dies, no one can modify the terms of his will: once in force, it is irrevocable.

The Greek word translated "prove the death of" is *pheresthai,* which means to "bring forward," and is perhaps used here in the technical sense of "be registered" or "demonstrated by evidence." The death of Christ instituted the New Covenant; He was "sacrificed once to take away the sins of many people" (9:28). The New Covenant is now, irrevocably, in force, and the Old Covenant has been made obsolete (8:13).

But those sacrifices are an annual *reminder* of sins (10:3). The Greek word is *anamnesis,* "remembrance." The author's point is that the sacrifices of the Mosaic system stimulated remembrance of sins. An analogy may help. A person with faulty kidneys may be forced to consistently use a dialysis machine to cleanse his blood. Even though the machine keeps him alive, each use also reminds him of his deadly disease.

The very fact that the sacrifices of the Old Covenant had to be repeated constantly reminded the worshiper of his sinful state. In contrast, the fact that Christ offered one sacrifice and then "sat down at the right hand of God" (10:12) shows that His sacrifice was efficacious. The glorious news is that sin is no longer an issue! For under the New Covenant God has said, "Their sins and lawless acts I will remember no more" (10:17).

Where these [sins] have been forgiven, there is no longer any sacrifice for sin (10:18). This verse sums up the teaching of these chapters. In accord with God's will "we have been made holy through the sacrifice of the body of Jesus Christ once for all" (10:10).

God permitted the destruction of the Jerusalem temple in A.D. 70 because the services there had become totally irrelevant! The real answer to the problem with which the sages of rabbinic Judaism struggled is not studying the regulations governing sacrifices and offerings. The real answer is that the Old Covenant has been superseded by the New Covenant. And through the death of Jesus Christ salvation has been secured for all who are willing to come to God through Him.

If we deliberately keep on sinning after we have received the knowledge of the truth, no sacrifice for sins is left (10:26). "Truth" (*alethia*) here stands for the content of the Gospel. The writer is not referring to those who have received the Person of the Savior, but who have become acquainted with New Covenant truth and rejected it. They are surely liable to far more serious punishment than the death penalty imposed on those who rejected the way marked out in the Old Covenant. There are three reasons. The one rejecting Christ has:

■ "Trampled the Son of God under foot" (10:29). This strong expression goes beyond rejection to viewing with hostility and utter contempt.

■ "Treated as an unholy thing the blood of the covenant" (10:29).

■ "Insulted the Spirit of grace" (10:29). The word for insult is *enybrizo,* and suggests an arrogant indifference to the Spirit who ministers God's grace to us.

Again we are reminded of a basic truth emphasized in the NT, but all too often compromised in modern time. There truly is only one way of salvation. To lightly turn aside from Jesus Christ and attempt to approach God in any other way, merits "only a fearful expectation of judgment and of [the] raging fire that will consume the enemies of God" (10:27).

Now *faith is* being sure of what we hope for and certain of what we do not see (11:1). This famous chapter is frequently taken as a set of general observations on the nature of faith. But what role does the chapter have in the overall argument of the writer?

The author does make several significant statements about faith. Faith provides the perspective which enables us to realize that God is distinct from and yet the source of the material universe (11:1). Faith's perspective is also essential to relationship with God, for it en-

ables us to sense Him not only as a present reality, but to see Him as Person—who rewards those who earnestly seek Him (11:6). But the author's intent is not really to philosophize about either God or faith. His intent is to show us that "faith," so central in the relationship of a New Covenant believer with the Lord, was also central to the relationship of OT saints who lived in the time of the Old Covenant.

In Rom. 4 the Apostle Paul does something similar. After showing that Law is unable to save, he turns to the OT to prove that faith has always been the key to personal relationship with God. While Paul refers to Abraham and David in that chapter, he carefully exposits the texts associated with each to build a carefully reasoned and biblical argument.

In Heb. 11 the writer does not argue: he shows. Again and again he points out that it was "by faith" OT heroes and heroines accomplished great things (11:4-35a). Even more, those who by human standards failed, and suffered or even lost their lives, were all "commended for their faith" (11:39).

It is hardly surprising, then, that the "something better" (11:40) God has provided for us in the New Covenant should also be grasped by faith. And the Mosaic system, now obsolete, should have no relevance to those whose faith is firmly fixed in Jesus Christ.

Therefore, since we are surrounded by such a great *cloud of witnesses* (12:1). The word cloud (*nephos*) was at times used metaphorically in classical Greek of a large crowd. "Witnesses" here is *marturon.* The "therefore" suggests that the author does not have "spectators" in mind. He seems to be thinking of the hosts referred to in chapter 11, who have given witness to us of what it means to run life's race by faith.

Yet his next words remind us that we draw the strength we need to run by looking to Jesus. Perhaps the witnesses, living still with the Lord they trusted, not only inspire us, but even now cheer us on.

Do not forget to *entertain* strangers, for by so doing some people have entertained angels without knowing it (13:2). In v. 1 of this chapter the author calls for "brotherly love" (*philadelphia*). Here he calls for hospitality, using a Greek word which means literally "love of strangers" (*philoxenia*).

It's important to remember that while our faith calls us to love one another deeply, it also calls us to show hospitality to strangers. God's love isn't limited to our little circle of friends. In Christ, that circle expands to encompass all humanity.

Keep your lives free from the love of money and be *content* **with what you have, because God has said, "Never will I leave you; never will I forsake you" (13:5).** The word is *apkoumenoi,* and means "to have enough." Most NT uses focus our attention on the attitude of contentment, which lets us be satisfied with whatever is available (1 Tim. 6:6-8).

Here the writer sets out a significant contrast. On the one hand a person may love money, focusing attention on it as the basis of his or her security. Or a person may focus attention on God, and find the basis of his or her security in the Lord.

No OT verses read exactly as the author's quote. However, the first-century Jewish philosopher Philo uses exactly the same words in one of his works, which suggests that each is quoting a version of the Septuagint which has been lost. The thought, however, is reflected in a number of OT passages:

■ I am with you and will watch over you wherever you go, and I will bring you back to this land. I will not leave you until I have done what I have promised you (Gen. 28:15).

■ Be strong and courageous. Do not be afraid or terrified because of them, for the Lord your God goes with you; He will never leave you or forsake you (Deut. 31:6).

■ No one will be able to stand up against you all the days of your life. As I was with Moses, so I will be with you; I will never leave you nor forsake you (Josh. 1:5).

■ The poor and needy search for water, but there is none; their tongues are parched with thirst. But I the Lord will answer them; I, the God of Israel, will not forsake them (Isa. 41:17).

Throughout sacred history God has been the one stable element in the experience of His people. Those who look to Him feel secure despite life's uncertainties. Those who seek security in material things remain ever discontent.

Remember your *leaders,* **who spoke the word of God to you. Consider the outcome of their way of life and imitate their faith (13:7).** The Greek word here is the present participle of the verb *hegeomai.* This is a very general term, and does not distinguish position, as would "elder" or "bishop" or "apostle." We only know that these leaders spoke the word of God to the Hebrews, either at first, or recently. The "outcome of their way of life" is probably not, as some suggest, martyrdom. The outcome is rather the Christian character that faith's way of life produces.

This word for "leader" is used three times in this short chapter. Here, in v. 17, and in v. 24. Verse 17 is particularly important—and often misunderstood. *Church Leadership* (Zondervan) discusses this verse in depth:

The Book of Hebrews first exhorts believers, "Remember your leaders, who spoke the word of God to you. Consider the outcome of their way of life, and imitate their faith" (13:7). Shortly after, the writer says, "Obey your leaders and submit to their authority" (v. 17). It would seem that here we have a clear-cut case of the very kind of authority that this chapter suggests spiritual leaders must reject. Here is a demand for obedience. Leaders seem to have at least some right to control. And here is a reference to an "authority" that leaders have.

But let's look more closely at this verse. In the original the phrase reads, *Peithesthe tois hegoumenois hymon kai hypeikete.* Each word here is significant and conveys a much different message from its English equivalent.

Peithesthe is from *peitho,* which literally means "let yourselves be persuaded, or convinced." A fair translation would be, "Be open to the persuasion of your leaders."

Tois hegoumenois hymon is translated "your leaders." It is a term used of rulers and princes, but the original word means "to lead, or guide." Here we see the spiritual leader in the church as one who has traveled along the road toward godliness and, as a valid model, is able to point out that way to others.

Hypeikete is the single word translated by the English phrase, "submit to their authority." The word is at times so translated. Originally, however, it was used, as in classical Greek, to describe soft and yielding substances. The root idea is not "give in" but "be disposed to yielding."

The whole instruction, therefore, focuses on the attitude that members of the body are to maintain toward their leaders. We can paraphrase the instruction and so capture the underlying thought of the verse as it would have been understood by a Greek reader of the NT: "In your relationship with those who are your leaders and guides to godliness, be sure you maintain a yielding disposition, and remain open to their persuasion." The passage goes on, "For they keep watch over you as men who must give an account. Be responsive to them so that their work will be a joy, not a burden, for that would be of no advantage to you."

With this insight, the whole tone of *obey* changes. The "authority" of the leader is seen not to be some right to control, but only a right to influence the choices of brothers and sisters over whom the leader keeps watch (p. 140).

The high priest carries the blood of animals into the Most Holy Place as a sin offering, but the bodies are burned outside the camp. And so Jesus also suffered outside the city gate to make the people holy through His own blood. Let us, then, go to Him *outside the camp,* **bearing the disgrace He bore (13:11-13).** The phrase casts multiple images. The first use refers to the disposal of the bodies of the sacrificial animals whose blood was presented to the Lord on the Day of Atonement. But there is also a reminder that, in the days of Israel's wilderness experience, those considered unclean were sent outside and isolated from the people of God. The fact that Christ died on a wooden cross ("tree," Gal. 3:13) forever disqualified Jesus from participation in that community formed by the Law. Yet the very thing which made Him accursed in the eyes of Israel makes those who believe in Him holy.

The conclusion is inescapable. Christ Himself stands forever outside the Old Covenant community of faith. These Jewish Christians can hesitate no longer. They must accept what to Old Covenant friends and neighbors appears to be shame, and must step outside, separating from that community in order to show their solidarity with Christ and commitment to the New Covenant which supersedes the old.

THE PASSAGE IN DEPTH

God Disciplines His Sons (Heb. 12:4-15).

Background. In its early decades the Christian movement was considered a sect of Judaism. This view was initially held by the Jewish leaders as well. This is clearly reflected in the words of the Palestinian Christian community to Paul, reported in Acts 21:20: "You see, brother, how many thousands of Jews have believed, and all of them are zealous for the Law."

Yet reports of Paul's ministry to Gentiles outside of Palestine led to serious concerns. It was not so much that the Christian community objected to the message of salvation by faith. At that time, in the A.D. 50s, Jewish Christians in Palestine were concerned that "you teach all the Jews who live among the Gentiles to turn away from Moses, telling them not to circumcise their children or live according to our customs" (Acts 21:21).

This commitment to "our customs" was not rooted in any effort at compromise. It grew out of and expressed the commitment Jewish-Christians felt toward the OT, and their sense that their faith in Christ was a further development of that earlier revelation rather than a repudiation of it. Yet even in these early days Christians were discriminated against within the larger Palestinian Jewish community. One of Paul's reasons for frequently urging the Gentiles to collect offerings for the saints in Palestine is that in times of distress the Jewish-Christian minority was the first to lose work, and was overlooked in the distribution of charity which was such an important obligation within Judaism.

Apparently by the time the Book of Hebrews was written, in the late A.D. 60s, the chasm between the Jewish and Jewish-Christian communities in Palestine had widened. Indeed, one of the most interesting side-lights on early church history is the report that, before the destruction of Jerusalem, Christian prophets warned those who believed in Jesus to flee the city. Despite the shared commitment to customs rooted in the OT, Old Covenant and New Covenant communities had become increasingly distinct.

This separation of the communities took place much more rapidly outside of Palestine. Shortly after Paul's first missionary journey Jewish opposition developed, and the NT frequently speaks of Judaizers who tried to impose an Old Covenant lifestyle on Gentile converts.

A developed hostility of Jews toward Christians is reflected in Revelation's letter to Smyrna, dating from about A.D. 90. That letter warns and encourages:

> I know your afflictions and your poverty—yet you are rich! I know the slander of those who say they are Jews and are not, but are a synagogue of Satan. Do not be afraid of what you are about to suffer. I tell you, the devil will put some of you in prison to test you, and you will suffer persecution for ten days. Be faithful, even to the point of death, and I will give you the crown of life (Rev. 2:9-10).

All of this gives us some further insight into the situation facing those to whom the Book of Hebrews is addressed. The split between Old and New Covenant communities has widened. Now, at last, the Hebrew Christians must consider whether or not they are willing to "go to [Jesus] outside the camp, bearing the disgrace He bore" (13:13). To help them consider this choice, the writer has carefully compared the features of the Old and New Covenants, to demonstrate the superiority of the New. He has shown that throughout sacred history faith, not "our customs" (Acts 21:21), has been the key.

Now, in Heb. 12, the writer deals with one more issue. His readers' present commitment to Christ has brought them suffering. And more suffering surely lies ahead. How can suffering be explained within the context of the New Covenant?

Interpretation. As Heb. 12 opens the writer uses the image of a race. In 12:4 the image shifts. The believer is still in a contest, but this time it is a boxing contest, with the Christian's opponent sin itself. Unlike Christ, these Christians have not yet been bloodied by their struggle. Whatever sufferings or persecutions full commitment may bring, their distress cannot be compared to the Lord's.

With this point made, the writer goes on to explain the role of suffering in New Covenant experience. He makes several points:

■ Suffering is discipline motivated by love (12:5-6).

■ Discipline is a father's right and obligation (12:7-10a).

■ God's discipline is directed toward producing righteousness and peace (12:10b-11).

■ Our response to discipline is critical (12:12-15).

Within the framework of these few verses we have a satisfying answer to that question which has troubled believers from the time of Job and surely before: Why do the righteous suffer? Why do bad things happen to good people? The answer this writer advances is: It is because God loves us as sons.

■ Suffering is discipline motivated by love (12:5-6). This basic point is established by quoting Prov. 3:11-12. Rather than lose heart when suffering, we are to encourage ourselves by remembering that "the Lord disciplines those He loves."

"Discipline" is a difficult word for us, because it connotes punishment. But the Hebrew word *yasar* and its derivative, *musar*, denote "correction that contributes to education." At times this may involve punishment. But always attention is directed to the goal. At times the means may be painful. But the outcome is always intended for the disciplined person's good.

This is brought out strongly in the Greek word used throughout this passage, *paideuo.* The word means "to bring up," or "to train." In all but four occurrences of this root in the NT it has the sense of corrective guidance as a means of training or educating. Thus the difficulties we undergo as Christians are not to be perceived as retribution or punishment. They are not to be seen as expressions of anger. And they are not to make us cringe, fearful that somehow we have offended God and caused Him to strike back at us. Everything that happens to us is to be seen as an expression of divine love.

■ Discipline is a father's right and obligation (12:7-10a). Each child recognizes his human father's right to discipline him or her. In fact, discipline leads a child to respect his father, despite the fact that our fathers, in view of human limitations, can only do as they think best. The wording clearly suggests that human fathers make mistakes. And despite this, their children continue to respect them.

God, our Father, makes no mistakes. How much more then we should accept difficulties as God's discipline, and by our attitude under trial show respect for Him.

■ God's discipline is directed toward producing righteousness and peace (12:10b-11). The writer reveals the end toward which God's discipline is directed. No matter how unpleasant the difficult experiences of our lives, or how painful our sufferings, we can take comfort in the fact that "later on" such experiences will produce "a harvest of righteousness and peace."

The outcome, however, is not automatic. The word translated "trained" in v. 11 is *gegymnasmenois*. It is drawn from athletics, where it means to continually exercise ourselves. The body-builder says, "No pain, no gain." He means that only by breaking down muscle tissue and rebuilding stronger strands can his goal be reached. The discipline that God imposes gives us ever fresh opportunities to exercise ourselves spiritually, and so move closer to God's goal for us of truly righteous lives and inner peace.

■ Our response to discipline is critical (12:12-15). What are we to do when difficulties come? Give up? Sink down in despair? Abandon hope, and turn away from the future in fear? Not at all. Rather than let suffering paralyze us spiritually we are to stand up, mobilize our resources, and keep moving on (12:12). And in what direction should we move? Toward peace in our interpersonal relationships. And toward holiness in every area of our lives.

The passage concludes with a fascinating reminder. "See to it that no one misses the grace of God and that no bitter root grows up to cause trouble and defile many" (12:15). It's easy under the stress of suffering to turn inward, and wallow in self-pity. It is easy then too to grow bitter, consumed by thoughts of the unfairness of it all. What the writer of Hebrews wants us to remember is that even our trials are a grace gift from God.

Grace surrounds us in our suffering. Grace comes to us not only through, but in, our pain. For in His wonderful grace God has determined to treat us as sons, and so is personally involved in our training. What we receive we receive at His hands. And what we receive at His hands truly is good.

Personal application. Few passages in Scripture have such unmistakable relevance to the author's first-century readers, and at the same time such clear relevance to you and me as well. The words of Heb. 12 remain a comfort and inspiration to every believer who experiences suffering of any kind.

How we need to sense God's love and grace flowing to us in the painful things that happen. They are, as we continue on, God's doorways to righteousness and peace.

JAMES
Faith's Lifestyle

EXPOSITION

James remains one of the most practical and interesting books of the New Testament. It has also been one of the most controversial, particularly during the Reformation when emerging Protestant leaders stressed the Pauline doctrine of salvation by faith alone. James frequently mentions faith. But his emphasis on faith's expression in the believer's life seemed to the Reformers to tread dangerously close to suggesting a works-based salvation. To Martin Luther this book was "an epistle of straw," and only its authentication by the early church kept some from seeking to expunge it from the canon.

The book was written by James, the half brother of Jesus, in the early days before Christianity's aggressive missionary movement led to that explosive growth marked by a great influx of Gentiles. Thus James writes in a time when the church was distinctively Hebrew-Christian, and its members lived as observant Jews. The Book of Acts portrays James as a prominent leader of the Jerusalem church, a position confirmed by the Apostle Paul in Gal. 2:9. Early traditions ascribe to James the nickname, "the Just." An interesting sidelight illustrates his piety within the framework of Jewish customs. Early traditions tell us that James was executed in A.D. 62, during the three-month period between the death of Porcius Festus and the arrival of L. Lucceius Albinus to take up the Roman procurator's office. This was done at the instigation of the high priest, Ananus II. But James' reputation for piety was such that the Pharisees openly expressed their regret, and secretly petitioned to have Ananus removed from office.

It is very clear, then, that the Book of James reflects early Palestinian Christianity, before emerging issues in the 60s and beyond sharpened the distinction between the Jewish and Christian faith communities. Many would date James as early as A.D. 45-50. And, in that day, James' concerns were clearly pastoral rather than polemic, personal rather than theological. His deep concern is that those who follow Jesus live lives that are fitting for men and women of faith. With this theme in mind, we can easily trace the development of this little, yet most practical book of the NT.

James begins with a call to practice faith's lifestyle (1:2–2:13). He develops this theme by looking first at individual issues: how the believer is to respond in the face of trials (1:2-4); how to apply to God for wisdom (1:5-8); how to handle riches and poverty (1:9-11); how to view and respond to temptations (1:12-18).

James then looks at interpersonal issues: There is no room for a quick temper or

573

immorality, but rather believers must live the Word (1:19-25). Piety is to be shown in caring for the needy (1:26-27), in rejecting favoritism (2:1-7), and by loving in practice rather than in word only (2:8-13). Then, in what is the most controversial passage in the book, James explains the principles which underlie the believer's lifestyle of faith (2:14-26). See The Passage in Depth on page 578.

James then turns to problems that will continue to plague any person who seeks to express his faith in daily life. Even the most committed Christian will struggle to tame his or her tongue (3:1-12), to apply God's rather than worldly wisdom (3:13–4:10), to stop judging others (4:11-12), and to restrain natural arrogance (4:13-17).

Nevertheless, the man or woman of faith has expectations that are simply not available to others. The believer looks forward to future redress by God of all wrongs done to him (5:1-6). He foresees a personal harvest of future blessings despite present suffering (5:7-11). And he experiences answers to prayer here and now (5:12-18).

The book closes with a compassionate reminder (5:19-20). Those who have strayed from faith's way of life are not to be condemned, but restored.

Throughout the book, then, James keeps our eyes fixed on what it means to live as a Christian. To those who argue that this emphasis implicitly contradicts Paul's teaching on faith as "simply believing," John Calvin replies, "It is not required that all handle the same arguments." If you wish to know how to be saved, read Paul. But if you wish to know how the saved should live, read James.

WORD STUDIES

Consider it pure joy, my brothers, whenever you face *trials* of many kinds (1:2). The word *peirasmois* includes moral tests, such as temptations, and also tests from outside, such as persecution. The fact is that human beings are vulnerable to both sources of stress. But the person of faith is to view this situation in which we find ourselves positively and with joy. Why? Because if we meet testing with "perseverance" (1:3) we will become mature as Christians, thus reaching God's goal for us.

"Perseverance" is *hypomonen*, a word which suggests determination and persistence. Stress alone has no therapeutic value. It is our faith-driven response to stress that produces maturity.

If any of you lacks *wisdom*, he should ask God, who gives generously to all without finding fault (1:5). Here as in the Book of Proverbs "wisdom" is knowing how to respond to the trials and challenges we face in daily life. James makes two important points. First, God isn't upset when we don't know what to do, but is eager to show us our next step. Second, when we ask God for guidance, we must do so responsibly. That is, our motive in seeking guidance must be obedience, not curiosity. We can't approach God saying, "What should I do?" unless we are willing to do what God shows us.

This is brought out in the description of the "double-minded" man (1:8). The Greek has *dipsychos*, "double-souled." He's the man on the fence, tilting first one way ("I will") and then the other ("I won't"). God doesn't reveal His will to this kind of person.

Perhaps withholding knowledge from the double-souled is an act of grace. With knowledge comes responsibility. The person who knows what to do, but will not do it, is guilty of disobedience. But similarly revealing His will to one who is committed to do it is also an act of grace. For the person who does God's will is blessed in his obedience.

Let's ask God for wisdom. But only if we are truly ready to do whatever God shows us we're to do.

The brother in humble circumstances ought to take pride in his *high position*. But the one who is rich should take pride in his *low position* (1:9-10). The first word is *hupsos*, "exaltation." The second is *tapeinosis*, "lowliness." The danger of poverty is that a person might envy the wealthy and feel inferior, while the danger of wealth is that a person might become proud and arrogant. Each danger is balanced by the perspective on life that is shaped by faith. The poor finds comfort and identity in the realization that in Christ he has been exalted to the position of a child of God. The rich recovers humility by contemplating the fact that material wealth is fading, and that in order to come to the Lord he abandoned reliance on his possessions to approach God as a beggar seeking a salvation rooted in grace.

When *tempted,* no one should say, "God is tempting me" (1:13). "Tempted" here is *peirasmos,* which can refer to external circumstances or to a pull toward sin. Here references to "evil" (v. 13), "evil desires" (v. 14), and "sin" (v. 15), make it clear that James is dealing with the second issue. He begins by reflecting on the common response of those without faith when tempted to do wrong. They look around for something to blame. If they cannot blame circumstances, they blame others, the devil, or even God. The *Word Bible Handbook* sums up the Bible's teaching on temptation, with special reference to this passage:

> Several Hebrew and Greek words express the idea of trial, test, or enticement, and thus of temptation. Temptation is not always viewed as bad in the Bible. Temptation may lead to acts of sin. But temptation is also an opportunity for obedience and thus a chance to affirm our personal commitment to God.
>
> There are two aspects of testing and temptation. One aspect is external, involving pressure situations in which we find ourselves. James and Peter both view suffering and persecution in this light. A difficult decision to make may fit in this category. Even desire for a good goal which can only be achieved by questionable means sets up tensions and can be described as a temptation. We are never deserted even in the most difficult of circumstances. James writes that whatever the temptation, we can ask God for wisdom and be sure that He will give us guidance.
>
> There is also an internal aspect of temptation. James describes what happens within us: "each one is tempted when, by his own evil desire, he is dragged away and

enticed. Then, after desire has conceived, it gives birth to sin" (1:14-15). That inner pull toward sin is an expression of man's sin nature and is always with us. No attraction we feel to evil comes from God, but from within us. God may place us in a situation where great pressure is felt. But God is never responsible when our impulse is to respond wrongly.

It is at this point that temptation provides us with opportunity. We can follow the sinful tendencies pressure situations bring out, or we can choose to be responsive to God. The Bible says that "no temptation has seized you except what is common to man. And God is faithful; He will not let you be tempted beyond what you can bear. But when you are tempted, He will also provide a way out so that you can stand up under it" (1 Cor. 10:13). By drawing on God's wisdom and making godly choices, in spite of external circumstances or internal pressures, we grow to maturity (James 1:4). It is by godly choices that we demonstrate the genuineness of our faith, and so bring "praise, glory and honor" to God and to ourselves (1 Peter 1:3-9).

It is helpful for us to remember that Jesus too suffered temptations. His testings came directly from Satan and yet were permitted by God so Jesus might be seen to be a perfect man. When our testings come, they too are permitted. For God wants you and me to know the joy of victory, and the satisfaction that comes from remaining true to Him (pp. 767-68).

Any one who listens to the word but does not do what it says is like a man who *looks at his face in a mirror* and, after looking at himself, goes away and immediately forgets what he looks like (1:23-24). The verb translated "looks" is *katanoounti,* which indicates "attentive scrutiny." This little allegory describes a person who finds a mirror and looks at himself intently.

The allegory hinges on a simple question. Why do people look in the mirror? While some might simply wish to admire themselves, in most cases we look in a mirror to guide our actions. How should I comb my hair? Back, or to the left? Do I need more makeup? Is my face dirty? And we act based on what we see in the mirror. But what if we look intently, and then go away, simply forgetting the smudge on our cheek or that cowlick that sticks out so wildly? Why, then, the mirror has proven totally irrelevant and our look into it utterly meaningless.

Similarly, James argues, to look into the Word of God and not act on what we see there means that what we have found in Scripture is meaningless to us. It is not the person who knows what the Bible says who will be blessed. It is the person who *does* what the Bible says.

Religion that God our Father accepts as pure and faultless is this: to look after orphans and widows in their distress and to keep oneself from being polluted by the world (1:27). The word *threskos* is found only here in the Bible. Its meaning, established in Jewish writings and early Christian writings, is "belief and/or worship expressed in religious observances." What God cares about is not ritualistic observance, but a concern for people in need.

This theme is hardly new. It could hardly be expressed more clearly than in Micah 6:8: "He has showed you, O man, what is good. And what does the Lord require of you? To act justly and love mercy and to walk humbly with your God."

Have you not *discriminated* among yourselves and become judges with evil thoughts? (2:4) The Greek word, *diekrithete,* is constructed on the same root as "judges." In showing favoritism to the rich some in the church showed they valued certain human beings over others. We may differ from each other in many ways: wealth, intellect, social skills, status, or position. But in God's sight we each have infinite value as persons, and must learn to value and treat one another as brothers and sisters—equals.

Interestingly, the Talmud (*Niddah* 9:16) makes this same point, noting that "Formerly, a *dargash* was used for the burial of the rich and a *klivas* for the poor, and the poor felt shamed: it was ruled that out of respect for the poor, all burials should be in *klivas.*"

For whoever keeps the whole *Law* and yet stumbles at just one point is guilty of breaking all of it (2:10). Here *ton nomon*

refers to the commandments which express God's will for human beings. His argument seems strange to us, for clearly, showing favoritism is not the same as adultery or murder.

But James' point is that the Law cannot be understood in its parts, but must be viewed as a seamless whole. Human beings like to soothe their consciences by thinking, "Well, I lied. But I never committed adultery." Or, "Yes, I cheated on my taxes, but I never killed anyone." This makes sense only if we dismantle the whole, and rank its parts into such categories as "not too bad," "bad," and "really bad."

But what if we approach the Law as a seamless whole? In this case, violation of one of the Law's rulings makes us a "lawbreaker" as much as violation of any other ruling. Suppose we blow up a balloon, and write each of the Ten Commandments on a different section of its surface. Try however much we may, it is impossible to take a pin and break only one section of that balloon. The balloon is a whole. Whatever part we break, we break the whole.

There is no consolation for those who argue that "he or she is worse than I am." Or for those who argue that "I've done more good things than I've done bad." Because the Law is a seamless whole, violating the Law in one point makes a person a lawbreaker.

Speak and act as those who are going to be judged by the *law that gives freedom* (2:12). James refers to what he has called the "royal law" (2:8) of love. This law gives freedom, in part because it reaffirms the unitary nature of God's will for us, and releases the Christian from the burdens imposed by rabbinic Judaism's view of *torah* observance. Love also gives freedom, for when we act in love we find ourselves fulfilling the Law (Rom. 13:10). But even more significantly, love frees us to receive and extend mercy when we fall short. In this way love triumphs over judgment now and at history's end.

With the tongue we praise our Lord and Father, and with it we curse men, who have been made in God's *likeness* (3:9). The word is *homoiosin,* the Greek term used in the Septuagint and intertestamental Hebrew literature to translate references to man's creation in the image of God (Gen. 9:6; Sir. 17:3).

James points out that this is inconsistent, and "should not be" (3:10).

Of particular note is the indication here that the "image of God," as distorted as that image may be, nevertheless persists in fallen human beings. Clearly the image cannot be, as some have suggested, innocence or sinlessness. The best answer is that man was created a person, with all those divine attributes which distinguish human beings from the animals.

The *wisdom that comes from heaven* is first of all pure; then peace-loving, considerate, submissive, full of mercy and good fruit, impartial and sincere (3:17). James is speaking here of a basic orientation to life, a divine perspective which guides relationships and choices. This is contrasted with a human "wisdom" which is not wise at all. How do we know? We know each kind of wisdom is distinguished by unmistakable *signs* which mark the character of the person who lives according to that wisdom.

How clear it is that those whose lives are marked by envy and selfish ambition, by disorder and evil practices, have nothing at all to do with heaven.

You do not have, because you do not ask God. When you ask, you do not receive, because you ask with wrong motives, that you may spend what you get on your *pleasures* (4:2-3). The Greek word is *hedonais,* from which we get "hedonism." James' point is that, despite many a sermon illustration referring to our account in the "bank of heaven," prayer is not like going to the bank to draw out funds for what we want. Prayer is instead the avenue by which those eager to do God's will seek the means which will enable them to do it.

Or do you think Scripture says without reason that the spirit He caused to live in us envies intensely (4:5). The NIV footnote captures the meaning of this difficult verse: "that God jealously longs for the spirit that He made to live in us." The context helps us understand. James is writing to those whose attachment to this world and its pleasures have caused them to stray from full commitment to the Lord. When this happens, God jealously longs for us to turn back to Him with that first love that Christ awakened in our hearts.

Submit yourselves, then, to God (4:7). God has promised grace to the humble. Submit is *hupotagete.* Submission is not obedience, but rather the decision to place oneself under the authority of another. This attitude leads to obedience. But only one who has humbled himself and sworn to be loyal only to God will stay on that path.

"Submit" is the first of 10 imperative commands in vv. 7-10. Each command is forceful, calling for immediate response. There is no room for delay in one who seeks to live by faith. Faith must express itself, not in words, but in such actions as: submit, resist, come near, wash, purify, grieve, mourn, wail, change, and humble.

Brothers, do not *slander* one another (4:11). The word *katalaleite* means "do not speak against one another." Slander suggests false charges. This term is broad enough to incorporate things that may be true, but are spoken with unkind intent. In essence, the speaker takes it upon himself or herself to punish a brother or sister, despite the fact that God alone is Judge.

Paul's words in Eph. 4:15 are very much to the point: we are to speak the truth in love. If what we have to say falls short of either truth or love, we are to remain silent.

Instead, you ought to say, "If it is the Lord's will, we will live and do this or that" (4:15). It is all too easy for us to develop independent attitudes, and forget that in all things we are in fact dependent on the Lord. There is no great value in uttering the words, "God willing," whenever we speak about our plans for the future. But it is essential that in our hearts we reject the arrogant assumption that we have any way of foreseeing or controlling the future. We, and all we have and are, remain in God's hands.

He should call the elders of the church to pray over him and anoint him with oil in the name of the Lord. And the prayer offered in faith will make the sick person well (5:14-15). James sets suffering in the context of suffering and troubles in general, for the same root, *kakopath-,* is used in vv. 10 and 13. The response of the believer is first of all patience and perseverance. But the believer's greatest resource in any extremity is prayer.

James points to sickness as a circumstance in which prayer is especially important. He also gives careful instructions to the elders. They are to pray over him, and anoint him with oil. The prayer is preeminent, for "pray" is the main verb. Anointing is secondary, for *aleipsantes* is a subordinate participle.

There should be no debate over whether the anointing is ritual or medical in character. The word used of ritual anointings is *chrio*, while *aleipho*, which means "to smear," is commonly used when a medicinal application of oil is in view. Further, smearing with oil was undoubtedly one of the most common medical treatments of ancient times. What is significant here is that, while encouraging the use of medical treatments, James gives full credit for subsequent recovery to the faith and prayers of believers.

If he has sinned, he will be forgiven. Therefore confess your sins to each other and pray for each other so that you may be healed (5:15-16). The conditional phrase suggests that while some sickness is a divine discipline imposed because of persistent sin, sin is not the cause of all sickness. The "therefore" suggests that, since there is some connection between sins and sickness, it is wise for us to "confess [our] sins to each other." It seems best to take *exomologeisthe*, "confess," in its basic sense of acknowledge. We are to live such open and honest lives with one another that we will be sensitive to each other's temptations, and thus able to pray for one another.

THE PASSAGE IN DEPTH

Faith and Deeds (2:14-26).

Background. It is difficult to find references to "faith" in intertestamental or rabbinic writings, or in modern commentaries on these works. This does not mean that rabbinic Judaism is devoid of doctrine. But "faith," as it is understood in the NT, simply is not a major theme in that religion. For instance, in Emil Schurer's massive three-volume work on *The History of the Jewish People in the Age of Jesus Christ,* "faith," in its NT sense, does not appear in the index. In part this is because rabbinic Judaism has no clear doctrine of resurrection or personal salvation. But another reason is that developed Judaism assumes that keeping God's Law is the way to blessing, here, and should there be a hereafter, hereafter. In vol. IIIa, p. 194, Schurer comments as follows on an intertestamental work, "The Psalms of Solomon": They attest belief in the hereafter and that the future fate of a man is determined by his present way of life. It lies within his own free choice to do right or wrong (cf. esp. 9:7). If he does the first, he will rise to everlasting life; if the latter, he will go down to everlasting destruction (3:16; 13:9-11; 14; 15).

In a work simply titled *Judaism* (Harper and Row, 1987), Michael A. Fishbane writes that "through devoted obedience to the prescriptions of the Torah and its rabbinic elaborations, Judaism has taught that one might lead a life of divinely guided sanctity and ascend along just this path to religious perfection and communion with God" (p. 16).

If we look at the Book of James against this background, we note something very dramatic. James' writings bear a clear resemblance to the teachings of many of the OT prophets, and those of Christ Himself. His frame of reference is that of a man whose roots are those of a Palestinian Jew. Yet "faith" is one of James' persistent themes, and in fact he uses that word more often — 16 times — in this little book than Paul used it in Galatians — 15 times!

Clearly James has stepped outside the framework of rabbinical thought in this little book, and squarely into that unique view of relationship with God which affirms the ruin of every human being by sin, and firmly holds faith to be the only basis for renewed and continuing relationship with the Lord.

Why then the concern of Luther and other reformers that James' little book suggests a salvation by works in contrast to salvation by faith alone. The following chart may help to distinguish the concerns of each writer, and thus clarify the reason for differences in their approach.

James wrote:

To explore how faith finds expression in the life of the believer.

Out of concern that those with faith produce fruit (2:20), so that no one confuses creeds with vital Christianity.

Shortly after Jesus was raised, when the church was still Jewish, and OT truths were known by all.

Paul wrote:
To explain saving faith in relation to the work of Christ on Calvary.

Out of concern that faith be placed in Jesus alone, unmixed with any reliance on law or on any supposed "works of righteousness."

When the conversion of individual Gentiles had raised many theological questions never before explored.

It is in this context that James penned this section on "faith" which so troubled the reformers, and has confused others as well. We need to remember that James, like Paul, makes a distinction between *faith* which exists as "a belief about," and *faith* which exists as "trust in." To those who cry, "I believe that there is one God," James responds with a classic turn of the sarcastic knife, "Good! Even the demons believe that—and shudder" (2:19). In contrast, James will say, there is a faith which is truly reposed in God, and we will recognize this faith by the fact that it produces deeds which are performed as a response to God's Word.

Interpretation. Perhaps the best way to trace James' argument in this passage is to quote it, with titled sections.

Mere Words Are Hollow (2:14-17).

What good is it, my brothers, if a man claims to have faith but has no deeds? Can such faith save him? Suppose a brother or sister is without clothes and daily food. If one of you says to him, "Go, I wish you well; keep warm and well fed," but does nothing about his physical needs, what good is it? In the same way, faith by itself, if it is not accompanied by action, is dead.

Faith and Deeds Cannot Be Separated (2:18-19).

But someone will say, "You have faith; I have deeds." Show me your faith without deeds, and I will show you my faith by what I do. You believe that there is one God. Good! Even the demons believe that—and shudder.

Abraham Demonstrates the Unity of Faith and Deeds (2:20-24).

You foolish man, do you want evidence that faith without deeds is useless? Was not our ancestor Abraham considered righteous for what he did when he offered his son Isaac on the altar? You see that his faith and his actions were working together, and that his faith was made complete by what he did. And the scripture was fulfilled that says, "Abraham believed God, and it was credited to him as righteousness," and he was called God's friend. You see that a person is justified by what he does and not by faith alone.

Rahab Demonstrates the Unity of Faith and Deeds (2:25).

In the same way, was not even Rahab the prostitute considered righteous for what she did when she gave lodging to the spies and sent them off in a different direction?

Summary Statement (2:26).

As the body without the spirit is dead, so faith without deeds is dead.

Mere Words Are Hollow (2:14-17). James begins his discussion of faith by describing a person who "claims to have faith but has no deeds." This present subjunctive used in a third class conditional sentence indicates a pattern. James is speaking about people who "keep on saying they have faith, and yet keep on having no works." Again, it is faith's *lifestyle* that so concerns this pious leader of the Jerusalem church. James immediately poses a question: Can *that kind* of faith save him? Immediately we see that James is speaking about "faith vs. faith," not "faith vs. works" or even "faith and works." One kind of faith exists as mere words, without any accompanying actions.

To show how empty words can be, James draws a homey illustration. Suppose a fellow believer is destitute, and you smile and wish him well. Now, what good are such empty words to anyone—to you or to the destitute brother? And so James lays down a principle which he will take pains to prove. When considering faith vs. faith, the only kind of faith that counts is that which is "accompanied by action." Any other kind of faith is dead, in the sense that it is useless and ineffectual.

Later James will conclude, having proven his point: any "faith" which stands alone is no more true faith than a body without breath is a living person (2:26).

Faith and Deeds Cannot Be Separated (2:18-19).

James then responds to someone who argues that faith and works must, by their very nature, be dealt with in isolation. This is implicit in the challenge, "You have faith; I have deeds."

It's best to take 18b, as the NIV translators do, as James' reply to this challenge. "Show me your faith without deeds" is in fact a challenge issued in response. As Jesus once pointed out to some Pharisees, it is easier to say, "Your sins are forgiven," than to say, "Get up and walk" (Matt. 9:4-7). There is no way to demonstrate either the forgiveness of sins or the claim of a person to "believe." But, James points out, while you must struggle to show me your faith without deeds, I certainly can "show you my faith by what I do" (2:18).

But there is an even more serious flaw in the "faith" of those who claim to believe but whose faith remains unaccompanied by works. Even if we accept their claims, in a creedal, intellectual sense, we must remember that even the demons believe that God is One. Their "belief," however, causes them to shudder, for they know that one day God will judge them!

Implicit in James' response is the affirmation that that kind of faith can do nothing for the person. He remains vulnerable to judgment, and so like the demons, rather than debate what he should do, he shudders! For that kind of faith cannot save!

Abraham Demonstrates the Unity of Faith and Deeds (2:20-24).

James had argued that true faith in God cannot be isolated from actions. If anyone truly believes, it will be reflected in his or her behavior.

Now he turns to the Old Testament for scriptural evidence and asks, "Was not our ancestor Abraham considered righteous for what he did?" (. . . *ouk ex ergon edikaiothe*) When used by Paul this root, *dikaio-,* is clearly used in the sense of God's declaring the person who believes in Jesus righteous in His sight.

At first glance, then, it would seem James *is* contradicting Paul—that James proposes here a salvation by works. However, this Greek root does not only mean to "declare righteous." It can also mean "to justify" in the sense of vindicating. Here James' point is that our view of Abraham, and God's pronouncement that Abraham is to be considered righteous, is demonstrated by his actions. It is important to note here that James points to an incident in Gen. 22, the sacrifice of Isaac, to prove his point. This incident took place long after Gen. 15:6 reports that God accepted Abraham's faith as righteousness. Thus *subsequent to his salvation by faith Abraham demonstrated his faith* by responding immediately when God called on him to bring his son to Mount Moriah and present him as a sacrificial offering!

So, James concludes, "you see that a person is justified by what he does and not by faith alone." That is, "faith" in isolation from works is not the kind of faith that the Christian is speaking of when he says that we are saved by faith and declared righteous by God.

Rahab Demonstrates the Unity of Faith and Deeds (2:25).

First-century Judaism was fascinated by Rahab, and looked at her as a prime example of the pious individual. And so James draws attention to Rahab and makes the same point. We consider Rahab righteous because of what she did, not because of any mere verbal claim to "faith."

Summary Statement (2:26).

James concludes his argument. You can no more isolate faith and actions than you can isolate the spirit from the body. "As the body without the spirit is dead, so faith without deeds is dead."

Simply put, "faith" without works doesn't work. Saving faith is not that kind of "faith."

Application. The issue that James explores remains a practical one for the modern church. It's not that God has appointed any of us as fruit inspectors, commissioned to examine the lives of our brothers and sisters to see if they have a faith that works.

What's more important is to listen carefully to what James has to say—and examine ourselves. It is so easy to go to church and to "believe." But Christian faith calls for commitment as well as confession.

1 PETER
Submission and Suffering

EXPOSITION

This First Epistle of Peter was probably written about A.D. 64 or 65. But its theme of submission despite unjust suffering remained particularly relevant to the church for several hundred years. During this period Christians experienced significant persecution. A letter written about A.D. 110 by the younger Pliny, a provincial administrator, asks the Emperor Trajan "whether it is the mere name of Christian which is punishable, even if innocent of crime, or rather the crimes associated with the names." Trajan's answer instructs Pliny not to accept anonymous charges against anyone as a Christian, or to "hunt them down." But he says that "if [Christians] are brought before you and the charge against them [that they are in fact Christians] is proved, they must be punished." Less than 50 years after Peter wrote, to bear the name "Christian" in the Roman Empire was considered a capital offense. What a need for Peter, aware of growing hostility even in the 60s, to write and show believers how to live in times when maintaining allegiance to Jesus means suffering, discrimination, ridicule, and even death.

Peter begins by laying a vital foundation. To stand up to suffering the Christian must have a strong sense of his or her identity in Christ (1:3–2:10). This is rooted first of all in a salvation granted to us by God (1:3-12), a salvation through which we embark on a life of holiness, reverence, and genuine love (1:13-25). In that life we serve our God as His chosen priesthood (2:1-10).

Our response to suffering must be made in view of who we are as God's people, for privilege brings with it responsibility. And that responsibility is to "live such good lives among the pagans that, though they accuse you of doing wrong, they may see your good deeds and glorify God in the day He visits us" (2:12). That "good life" is one characterized by a submissive respect for others and human institutions, despite the fact that they may treat us unfairly (2:13–3:12). Should persecution come even though we do nothing but good, we are to trust God and remember that Christ also suffered unjustly—with blessed results (3:13–4:11).

Now Peter turns to another, related subject. We've seen how individuals are to respond to suffering. What are the responsibilities of the church and its elders in times of trial (4:12-19) and judgment? (5:1-11) For the elders the challenge is to shepherd God's flock. For the congregation, it is to remain humbly responsive to God's will, self-controlled and alert. And to wait for God to restore us after we have "suffered a little while." The letter closes with brief greetings and a benediction (5:12-14).

581

Throughout church history this letter has spoken to thousands who have remained committed to Christ despite persecution. Peter has more to say about suffering than any other NT or OT book. He reminds us that God uses suffering to purify our faith, and help us experience His own presence in our lives. And, Peter teaches, God uses our suffering as a witness to the world—a witness which will bring God, and us, glory when Jesus comes again.

WORD STUDIES

To God's elect, *strangers* in the world, scattered (1:1). The word is *parepidemois*, and together with the phrase "God's elect" defines the believers' identity. Theologically they are the chosen of God, linked eternally with Him. Sociologically they have become strangers, living in a society where they not only have no roots, but which is hostile toward them. The following extended quote from Pliny's letter to Trajan helps us sense what it had begun to mean to be a Christian when Peter wrote to the scattered church.

The method I have observed towards those who have been denounced to me as Christians is this: I interrogated them whether they were Christians; if they confessed it I repeated the questions twice again, adding the threat of capital punishment; if they still persevered, I ordered them to be executed. For whatever the nature of their creed might be, I could at least feel no doubt that contumacy and inflexible obstinacy deserved chastisement. There were others also possessed with the same infatuation, but being citizens of Rome, I directed them to be carried thither.

These accusations spread, as is usually the case, from the mere fact of the matter being investigated, and several forms of the mischief came to light. A placard was put up, without any signature, accusing a large number of persons by name. Those who denied they were, or had ever been, Christians, who repeated after me an invocation to the gods, and offered adoration, with wine and frankincense, to your image, which I had ordered to be brought for that purpose, together with those of the gods, and who finally cursed Christ—none of which acts, it is said, those who are really Christians can be forced into performing—these I thought it proper to discharge. Others who were named by that informer at

first confessed themselves Christians, and then denied it; true, they had been of that persuasion but they had quitted it, some three years, some many years, and a few as much as twenty-five years ago. They all worshiped your statue and the images of the gods, and cursed Christ.

They affirmed, however, the whole of their guilt, or their error, was that they were in the habit of meeting on a certain fixed day before it was light, when they sang in alternate verses a hymn to Christ, as to a god, and bound themselves by a solemn oath, not to any wicked deeds, but never to commit any fraud, theft or adultery, never to falsify their word, nor deny a trust when they should be called upon to deliver it up; after which it was their custom to separate, and then reassemble to partake of food—but food of an ordinary and innocent kind. Even this practice, however, they had abandoned after the publication of my edict, by which, according to your orders, I had forbidden political associations. I judged it so much more necessary to extract the real truth, with the assistance of torture, from two female slaves, who were styled deaconesses; but I could discover nothing more than depraved and excessive superstition.

Who have been chosen according to the foreknowledge of God the Father, through the sanctifying work of the Spirit, for obedience to Jesus Christ and sprinkling by His blood (1:2). Against the hostility of the world as reflected in the letter of Pliny, a man who for his time was both mild and conscientious, the Christians are immediately reminded that each Person of the Godhead is personally involved in their salvation. The Christian may be treated with casual cruelty by his society. But no believer is treated casually by God!

Who through faith are shielded by God's power until the coming of the *salvation* that is ready to be revealed in the last time (1:5). Salvation (*soteria*) is a major theme in the first section of 1 Peter. It is salvation that establishes our relationship with God; it is by being saved that we gain our new identity in Him.

This term occurs here, in 1:9-10, and in 2:2. These verses remind us that salvation is something we experience as well as look forward to. The fullness of all that salvation means will be revealed "in the last time."

Even today, Peter says, we are *komizomenoi* (1:9), (receiving) salvation. We experience salvation now as a growing love for Christ, and as an "inexpressible and glorious joy" (1:8) which exists despite external circumstances. In this we experience the flowering of a promise made in ancient times—a promise the prophets puzzled over, which through Christ is now fulfilled.

Finally, Peter challenges his readers to "grow up in your salvation," and so mature in the faith (2:2).

Understanding our identity as persons who are "saved" is vital in times of persecution, for it provides us with essential perspective. In 1 Peter 1:3-9 Peter reminds his readers that the saved have:

■ A new birth.

■ A living hope of resurrection to come.

■ An inheritance kept in heaven.

■ Security, as those shielded by God's power.

■ A genuine faith, which is burnished to a bright splendor by the trials which bring us present grief.

■ A genuine faith, which by enduring will result in "praise, glory and honor" when Jesus returns (1:7).

■ A Spirit-generated love for Jesus, even though He has not yet been seen.

■ An "inexpressible and glorious joy" (1:8) which wells up despite persecution and pain.

How much those believers gained who refused to bow before images of the emperor and Roman gods and who spurned the demand to curse Christ, despite the fact that they lost their lives. We do not know the names of the two deaconesses that Pliny tortured before he killed. But we will see and honor them in glory.

They knew their own identity in Christ. And they rejoice with Him this very day.

Trying to find out the *time and circumstances* to which the Spirit of Christ in them was pointing when He predicted the sufferings of Christ and the glories that would follow (1:11). The phrase *tina e poion kairon* is a healthy reminder for students of prophecy. The major elements of God's plan for the future have been revealed through the prophets. What is uncertain is the "time and circumstances." The sequence of events, the relationship of one to another, the time required for or between events, all this was unclear to the prophets themselves. Let's not be too confident that those charts which propose to represent the sequence of events still future to our time are accurate. Yes, prophecy does show us what lies ahead. But the "time and circumstances"? No.

Therefore, prepare your minds for action; be self-controlled; *set your hope fully* on the grace to be given you when Jesus Christ is revealed (1:13). This is the main emphasis of the verse. *Elpisate* is an aorist imperative; it sets and sums up the course Christians are to follow. In view of our identity as Christians, we are God's elect, strangers in our society. Thus our hopes, our expectations, must not be focused on anything this world might offer. Wealth, fame, acceptance, even survival—all are meaningless when compared to the inheritance which is to be ours when Christ comes. If we hope for nothing here, if every expectation is fixed on the Second Coming, then nothing that happens can move us to act in any way that might imply denial of our Lord.

But just as He who called you is *holy,* so be holy in all you do (1:15). Holiness here is moral purity. Just as fixing our hope on the grace to be ours strengthens us to live in society as strangers, so fixing our hope in Him insulates us from the power of those "evil desires you had when you lived in ignorance" (1:14).

Now that you have purified yourselves by obeying the truth so that you have sincere love for your brothers, love one another *deeply,* from the heart (1:22). The command is modified by the adverb, *ektenos,* "unremittingly." The Christian facing persecution is not expected to withstand the pressure of pagan society alone. In troubled times we have a special need for the unremitting support of others in the faith community.

The command is placed in a strongly theological setting. Such love is possible because believers have "purified [themselves] by obeying the truth." "Obeying" here as often in the NT has the sense of "believing." Faith has made a difference in the character of believers, enabling them to love. Now the Christian must exercise that new ability, and gather around to provide unremitting support for those who are being persecuted.

It is significant that Peter emphasizes the "imperishable" nature of the seed which, now planted in our hearts, sets us on a totally different course from those who, mere flesh and blood, wither away like grass (1:23-25). We die, but are immune to death. We suffer, but in suffering experience joy. We love, and in loving offer others the support they need to remain faithful to who they are—Jesus' own people, born again of His imperishable Word.

You also, like living stones, are being built into a spiritual house to be a holy *priesthood* (2:5). In the first chapter of this letter Peter portrays the Christian as an individual chosen by God, but a stranger in this world, who is enriched by the experience of salvation and supported by others in the loving faith community. Now, 1 Peter 2:1-10 concludes the first section of this letter, and Peter's definition of our identity in Christ. Here, he says, we are God's chosen priests, called to serve Him here and now. We are in fact a "royal priesthood," for as well as being High Priest, Jesus Christ is King.

What does it mean to be a believer-priest? It means first of all that we serve God personally, and praise Him in word and deed. It means that we have direct access to God. It means that we minister to others, bringing God's Word to them, and their needs to the Lord. It means that each of us is called to serve, not to be served, even as Christ gave Himself for us.

One of the great tragedies of church history is that the doctrine of the priesthood of all believers, rediscovered during the Reformation, has never been fully implemented. For "ministry" encompasses far more than preaching and teaching; it is to infuse our every relationship with others and with the Lord.

Live *such good lives* among the pagans that, though they accuse you of doing wrong, they may see your good deeds and glorify God on the day He visits us (2:12). The phrase is *anastrophe . . . kalen,* which might be rendered "beautiful conduct," or "noble lifestyle." It was common as hostility to Christianity grew to accuse believers of being atheists and antisocial. In time wild tales of orgies at Christian love feasts, and rumors that Christians drank the blood of murdered victims, spread through the Empire. The Christians could only respond by "living beautiful lives" among the pagans. Ultimately, when Christ returns, those pagans who persecuted believers will be forced to admit that all they ever witnessed in Christians was a beauty, a purity, a simplicity of life that reflects glory on our God.

Live such *good lives* (2:12). Verses 11-12 are pivotal in Peter's letter. They refer back to our identity as God's "aliens and strangers in the world" (2:11), and they direct our attention ahead. For Peter is about to describe what constitutes the "beautiful life" that he urges his readers to live.

The writings of Greek moralists frequently exhorted readers to live better lives by including lists of virtues and vices. Paul and other writers of the New Testament do the same thing. Here we see Peter adopt this approach, in a lengthy list of *haustafeln,* duties expected of members of a household.

In the ancient world the household was seen as a microcosm of society. If the household, composed of its male head, family members, slaves, and others, was orderly, moralists believed that the state would be orderly also. Thus the *haustafeln* detailed the duties a family member owed to the gods, to the state, to spouses and children.

It's helpful to see 1 Peter 2:13-3:7 as just such a list, directed to the household of God, describing the pattern of life that is beautiful in God's sight.

Submit yourselves for the Lord's sake to every authority instituted among men (2:13). Rather than "every authority," the Greek *ktisis* is better understood as "creature." Peter calls on Christians to submit to every *person* in authority, whether kings, husbands, masters, etc. "Submit" here is the common word *hypotasso*, "to subordinate oneself," and implies being responsive and obedient.

Several things are significant in Peter's list. First, it lacks the mutuality found in similar instructions in Paul's letters. In both Col. 3:18–4:1 and Eph. 5:21–6:9 the command to the socially inferior submission is balanced by a command given the socially superior, thus:

■ Wives, be subject. vs. Husbands, love.
■ Children, obey. vs. Parents, don't anger.
■ Slaves, obey. vs. Masters, treat fairly.

Here, however, Peter's list of responsibilities is directed *only* to the socially inferior. What's more, he frequently assumes that the socially superior will be unfair! Thus slaves are to submit "to those who are harsh" (2:18), and wives are to be submissive even to husbands who "do not believe" (3:1).

The second difference explains the first. Paul is speaking about relationships between Christians. The husbands and wives, the slaves and masters, are assumed to have faith in Christ in common. But Peter explicitly writes about living good lives "among the pagans" (2:12). The point is, of course, that despite the fact pagans owe no reciprocal duty to Christians, Christians still owe a duty to pagans who are their social superiors.

Third, Peter says we are to submit "for the Lord's sake" (2:13). The phrase *dia ton kyrion* means, literally, "because of the Lord." It is God's desire that our lives be visibly beautiful. We submit, not because human institutions are in themselves binding on those who are citizens of heaven, but because if our lives are to reflect praise on the Lord we must do what is good *as those in our society understand good.* In choosing to submit voluntarily we demonstrate to all that, whatever they may think of our faith, we cannot rightly be charged with antisocial or seditious behavior.

To this you were called, because Christ suffered for you, leaving you an *example*, that you should follow in His steps (2:21). The word is *hypogrammon,* a pattern to be copied in writing or drawing. The verse calls us to remember, when we are troubled by the unfairness of others, that Christ was treated unjustly by His contemporaries. Despite the fact that He did nothing wrong, He evoked the hostility of the religious leaders of His people, and was not only persecuted but judicially murdered. Peter's call to a life marked by submission is a call to a "beautiful lifestyle" simply and solely because this is the way Jesus chose to live in our world. And this is the way that we will in the end reflect glory upon our God.

Husbands, in the same way be considerate as you live with your wives, and treat them with respect as the *weaker partners* and as heirs with you (3:7). Peter's list of household duties does conclude with a reciprocal thought, as he addresses Christian husbands who live with believing wives. Perhaps this is intended to guard against a tendency seen throughout history—for men to insist on submission in their wives, without the balancing emphasis Scripture places on love and consideration.

The phrase "as weaker" *(hows asthenestero skeyei)* uses the common word for weakness, and does not define what Peter means. This is, however, defined by the overall context. Peter clearly is not speaking of physical weakness, but he is looking in these chapters at issues of social power. In the first century women were, in every legal and other sense, far weaker socially than their husbands. But in the Christian community recognition of such weakness is to be responded to with increased respect in contrast to exploitation. Only as the Christian husband honors his wife, as Paul defines in Eph. 5, can the husband maintain a right relationship with God and so be in a position where his prayers can be answered.

They think it *strange* that you do not plunge with them into the same flood of dissipation, and they heap abuse on you. But they will have to give account to Him who is ready to judge (4:4-5). The Christian's lifestyle of submission is in stark contrast with that of the pagan, who is driven by passions and selfish ambition. The pagan thinks our way of life is "strange" *(zenizontai).* The word is unusual and connotes shock, disappointment, and even anger. We can understand the reaction. The Christian's way of life exposes corruption of the way of life of the pagan, and evokes hatred. The pagan chooses his way because he does not believe in judgment to come. But judgment surely lies ahead.

In view of the fact that we know "the end of all things is near" (4:7), we choose lives of self-control, love, hospitality, and ministry to one another.

Dear friends, do not be *surprised* at the painful trial you are suffering, as though something strange were happening to you (4:12). The entire sentence summarizes the situation Peter and his readers face in society. This outbreak of persecution is not to cause surprise. This is the same root that we find in 4:4 above: the surge of persecutions that swept the church in Peter's time and for centuries after, should not cause Christians to be upset or angry. Indeed, we are to rejoice in them, for they enable us to "participate in the sufferings of Christ" (4:13). In such a circumstance our sufferings, like His, come because we are committed to the will of God in a society where those who live godly lives evoke the antagonism of those who do not believe.

For it is time for *judgment* to begin with the family of God (4:17). God judges sin. Why be surprised if that judgment involves us in suffering? An innocent Christ felt the weight of that judgment. Why be surprised if a redeemed people participate in His sufferings, not in any propitiatory way, but rather as partners with Christ in an experience of the consequences of sin that has warped each human being. Surely if we who have been redeemed still experience the consequences of God's

judgment on sin, "what will become of the ungodly and the sinner?" (4:18)

Be *shepherds* of God's flock that is under your care (5:2). Peter's words here recall for us Christ's saying about the Good Shepherd. He is One who lays down His life for His sheep. Peter writes in an age where it was becoming dangerous to be a Christian, much less a leader in that movement. These early Christians served, "not because you must, but because you are willing, as God wants you to be" (5:2).

We need only recall Pliny's letter, quoted at the beginning of this study, to understand something of the possible cost of being a leader. "I judged it so much the more necessary to extract the real truth, with the assistance of torture, from two female slaves, who were styled deaconesses." A measure of the faithfulness of martyred leaders in the church is reflected in Pliny's conclusion. "I could discover nothing more than depraved and excessive superstition."

And the God of all grace, who called you to His eternal glory in Christ, after you have suffered a little while, will Himself *restore you* and make you strong, firm and steadfast (5:10). The Greek word is *katartisei,* "to mend, or make whole," and implies the full development of one's potential. Peter's promise is that God will intervene *now.* Yes, we suffer, but only for a brief moment, which pales to insignificance when compared to the eternal glory that awaits us. And, even as we wait we experience God's work in our lives, mending us, strengthening us, that we may face life as firm and steadfast followers of our Lord.

THE PASSAGE IN DEPTH

Suffering for Doing Good (3:8–4:2).

Background. Peter laid down rules which those in God's household are called to live by in a pagan society. His goal is clear: he describes a way of life which is "good," in the sense of beautiful and attractive.

The striking thing about this way of life is that it is patently *unfair* to the one who adopts it! Peter goes so far as to indicate that it is to our credit if you "suffer for doing good and

you endure it" (2:20). He reminds us that Christ chose us to live in this same way, and that we are to follow in His footsteps.

Yet this raises a very basic question about the nature of God. How can a just God permit His people to suffer unjustly? Doesn't the mere fact that we are called to submit to injustice indicate a moral flaw in God's character?

That question has been raised frequently, and a variety of answers has been suggested.

Books like Granger Westberg's *Good Grief,* Rabbi Harold Kushner's *Why Do Bad Things Happen to Good People?* and C.S. Lewis' classic *The Problem of Pain,* all examine this issue. But Peter gives what is undoubtedly Scripture's clearest and most satisfactory analysis.

Interpretation. Many elements in this passage have troubled interpreters. But if taken in the flow of the argument, the meaning is clear. That argument is as follows: God's way of life leads to blessing, for the Lord Himself supervises the consequences of our choices (3:8-13). However, if the unusual thing should result, and we suffer for doing what is right, we are actually blessed (3:14-17). This truth is demonstrated by Christ, who also suffered unjustly, but as a result brought us to God (3:18a).

Here Peter introduces a rather complex illustration which will develop a secondary point. Through Noah God's spirit spoke to the people living in that distant day. In that time only a few were saved, being carried through the waters of judgment to later be deposited in a new world. In the same way we have been carried safely through the waters of judgment in Christ, and deposited in a spiritual realm, resulting in a commitment to live the rest of our earthly lives fulfilling God's will rather than fulfilling earthly human desires (3:18b–4:2).

The thrust of the entire passage is, simply, that if when we do right and troubles follow, this happens according to God's express will and is intended, in the end, to bring a blessing to both us and others.

Before going into the major argument of the passage in depth, it is perhaps best to look at the troublesome and complicated analogy that the Apostle Peter draws between the Christian's experience and that of Noah. The following chart explains the comparisons that Peter makes.

Passage. "Spirits in prison, who disappeared long ago" (3:19-20).

"Eight [people] in all" (3:20).

"Water" (3:20).

"Baptism" (3:21).

"Symbolizes" (3:21).

Identification. Men of Noah's day who rejected the message God announced through Noah (cf. 1:11).

Noah's family, who did believe and entered the ark.

The Genesis Flood, the means of judgment.

Union with Christ (1 Cor. 12:13). The water is an image of judgment, not of salvation.

The two pictures of deliverance are what correspond, point by point. The correspondence is *not* between water and water baptism.

Parallel. The "unrighteous" (3:18) who rejected Jesus' message and had Him crucified.

"You" (3:21), who believe in Christ.

God's coming judgment on sin.

In Christ we are carried through judgment to salvation.

As Noah was given a new world to live in, so in Christ we entered a new world too, and live by new principles.

To become a Christian thus is not simply to be forgiven, but to be transported through judgment into a new world, in which we are expected to govern our lives by new and totally different principles (God's will) than governed us in the old, lost world which we have abandoned in order to follow our Lord.

With this *outcome* of salvation understood, we can return to the main argument and Peter's answer to the problem of pain, and particularly to the reason why we are called by God to live submissively even when those with authority in our particular society treat us unjustly.

God Supervises the Results of Our Choices (3:8-12). Peter tells us that, despite his call to submit even to unjust treatment, that God has called us "so that you may inherit a blessing" (3:9). In the normal course of affairs our commitment to His beautiful lifestyle will result in just this. Why? Going to the OT, Peter quotes from Ps. 34:12-16, to demonstrate that "the eyes of the Lord are on the righteous" (3:12). This phrase means more than "God is watching." It means that He is actively observing, with a view to being involved in the life of the righteous. You and I can never control the results of any action. But God is the God of Providence: He is always working out His hidden will through chains of cause and effect that seem to the unbeliever either random chance or a necessary result of actions taken. The Christian sees God's hand in all things, and recognizes that while we act, it is God who determines the results of any action.

If, then, God is ever vigilant to supervise the outcome of our choices, it follows that if we do what is right and good, in most cases good will follow, and we will be blessed. Even looking at it from a human point of view, Peter asks, "Who is going to harm you if you are eager to do good?" (3:13)

Yet at Times We Do Suffer for Doing Good (3:14-17). Here Peter uses a conditional which makes it clear that he is speaking of the unusual: "even if you should suffer for what is right" (3:14). He quickly adds a phrase he will explain later: even then, "you are blessed."

Before explaining, however, he looks at how you and I should respond to this kind of unusual, yet frightening experience. When we do right, and something terrible happens, we must (1) not be frightened, (2) in your hearts set apart Christ as Lord, (3) be prepared to give an answer to everyone who asks you to give the reason for the hope you have, and (4) keep a clear conscience (3:14-16).

Fright is the all-too-normal feeling that surges when something goes terribly wrong and we feel deserted, wondering if God has removed His protecting hand. There is an antidote to fright, partly found in understanding how what is happening can fit with God's announced intention to bless us. And found partly in our conviction that Jesus Christ *is* Lord.

This is why Peter tells us, "in your hearts set apart Christ as Lord." We must always remember that Christ is Sovereign. However great the trial, nothing can or has happened that is beyond His control. Our present and our future rest securely in His hands.

This conviction enables us to deal with tragedy in a totally unexpected way. We continue

to have "hope." Here as in the rest of the NT hope exists as the confident expectation that good things lie ahead. While others commit suicide in despair, the Christian who in his heart sets Christ apart as Lord remains upbeat and positive, eager to see what lies hidden beyond tomorrow. This attitude is one which amazes the pagans who know us, and provides a unique opportunity for witnessing. So Peter says to be ready to explain to those who ask, "How come?" But to do so in a gentle, positive, and respectful way.

Then Peter reminds us of the importance of keeping a good conscience. How tempting it might seem to try to escape our sea of troubles by doing something expedient but wrong. Instead we are to remain committed to doing good.

Finally Peter reminds us that "it is better, if it is God's will, to suffer for doing good than for doing evil" (3:17). The clear implication is that when we do suffer for doing good, it is by God's *express* will, a unique and unusual event quite unlike suffering that comes as a consequence of doing evil.

Christ Is the Prime Example of the Principle (3:18). Any who doubt that blessing can come through injustice is invited to look to Christ. He "died for sins once for all, the righteous for the unrighteous, to bring you to God" (3:18).

The verse is often misunderstood. Peter's point is not that Christ died *for* us, the unrighteous. Peter is saying that Christ, the truly righteous man, died *instead of* the unrighteous men who plotted His murder! Viewed from a mere human standpoint, this was a terrible injustice. The Son of God, the Gift of God's love, bowed His head and permitted corrupt and sinful human beings to manipulate a total miscarriage of justice.

But you and I do not view Christ's death primarily as an injustice. Instead we see it as it was, an act of self-sacrifice, through which God reconciled a lost humanity to Himself and brought forgiveness down to earth. Thus, Peter says, using a *hina* of result rather than of purpose, Christ died. Not "to bring you to God," but rather "with the result that He brought us to God."

And suddenly we see it. Through history's greatest injustice, God brought eternity's greatest blessing to you and me!

If we ever wonder whether unjust suffering can be a blessing, we need look only to the Cross for proof.

And so we have God's Word to comfort us when trials come. Whatever we experience as a consequence of doing good, it is God's will. And, if that consequence should be suffering, then we can know that through our pain God intended to bless. Not only others. But, when Jesus comes, the sufferer as well.

Application. Today we live in a land where society, though hardly Christian, is not overtly hostile to our faith. We do not as yet risk the loss of our job because of our faith. We do not risk homelessness, or the loss of our life. We hardly risk ridicule.

And yet each of us has had the experience of doing what we believed to be right, and having things go tragically wrong. For all such experiences, 1 Peter 3–4 has a comforting word. Yes, suffering is a part of the normal Christian experience. But it is not a sign of unspirituality, not necessarily the result of sin, and surely not an indication that God no longer loves us.

He does.

And He intends to use any suffering we may experience as we seek to follow Him to bless us.

2 PETER and JUDE
Danger! Danger!

EXPOSITION

There are so many similarities between 2 Peter and Jude that many commentators have suggested an oral or literary dependence. Certainly each writer is deeply concerned about the danger to the church from false teachers. And the language they use to describe and denounce false teachers is nearly identical. Whatever the personal links between the two writers, one the Apostle Peter, and one the brother of James and half brother of our Lord, it's clear that from the late A.D. 60s and beyond Christianity was under attack from without and from within. Intensifying persecution from the government, which Peter deals with in his first letter, was matched by a corruption of true Christianity introduced by teachers who distorted the Gospel of God's grace. And so two men, each a recognized leader, felt burdened to deal with the danger of truth's contamination by men who masqueraded as Christian teachers for their own selfish ends.

Peter's letter ranges over more subjects. After a brief greeting (1:1-4), Peter affirms the essential virtues which are to mark individual believers as well as leaders (1:5-15), and reaffirms the divine majesty of Jesus Christ (1:16-21). Peter then devotes 22 verses to an extended and intense warning against false teachers (2:1-22). This is followed by a reaffirmation of the certainty of Christ's return (3:1-18). In view of the coming destruction of all things, God's people are to "make every effort to be spotless, blameless and at peace with Him" when Christ returns, and to grow in God's grace.

Jude, who set out to write about salvation (1:1-3a), found himself led to utter a fervent call to believers to contend for the faith. Here "the faith" means that body of truth delivered to the church once for all through the prophets and apostles. This call is necessary because the faith is already being corrupted by false teachers. Like Peter, Jude sets out to describe these men and to characterize their teaching—and to warn that they are doomed to face God's judgment.

Jude then appeals directly to true Christians to persevere and to "build yourselves up in your most holy faith" (1:20-23). The book concludes with a doxology which praises God's power and ability to keep His people from falling (1:24-25).

WORD STUDIES

Who through *the righteousness of our God* and Savior Jesus Christ have received a faith as precious as ours (1:1). The Greek is *en dikaiosune,* through the righteousness or, perhaps better, the "justice" of our God. In acting to save us God chose the morally just path: He punished sin, by Himself taking its penalty.

As Peter moves on he will often use *dikaosune* in its moral sense (1:13; 2:5, 7, 8, 21; 3:13), setting up a strong contrast between the Lord and God's true people and false teachers and those who follow them.

He has given us His very great and precious promises, so that through them you may *participate in the divine nature* and escape the corruption in the world caused by evil desires (1:4). Peter is not suggesting here that Christians become gods. Rather he teaches that through God's promises as expressed in the Person and work of Jesus God works a radical change within us. He cuts us off from the world and its corruption, and transforms our desires, turning our hearts toward heaven. In 1 Peter the apostle puts it this way: "You are not just mortals now; the live, permanent Word of the living God has given you His own indestructible heredity" (1:23, PH).

For if you possess these qualities in increasing measure, they will keep you from being *ineffective and unproductive* in your knowledge of Jesus Christ (1:8). Here *argos* is idle, inactive, while *akarpos* is unfruitful. Peter is affirming a positive result by describing its opposite. A Christian who possesses the qualities he has listed above will experience vital, constant growth and will produce spiritual fruit.

Peter's description of a chain of virtues, each of which leads to and enhances another until reaching a climax, is a familiar literary device called *sorites* or *gradatio.* An example from the apocryphal *Book of Wisdom* (6:17-20) reads

> The beginning of wisdom is the most sincere desire for instruction, the concern for instruction is love of her, and love of her is the keeping of her laws, and giving heed to

her laws is assurance of immortality, and immortality brings one near to God; so the desire for wisdom leads to a kingdom (RSV).

Another example, from about A.D. 90, is this list in *m. Sota 9:15,* composed by R. Phineas ben Jair:

> Zeal leads to cleanness,
> and cleanness to purity,
> and purity leads to self-restraint,
> and self-restraint leads to sanctity,
> and sanctity leads to humility,
> and humility leads to the fear of sin,
> and the fear of sin leads to piety,
> and piety leads to the Holy Spirit,
> and the Holy Spirit leads to the resurrection of the dead.

Peter's *sorites* begins with faith, and describes those qualities growing out of faith which culminate in love (2 Peter 1:5-7). What a contrast between the virtues described here, and the passions which consume the false teachers Peter will soon describe.

Be all the more eager to *make your calling and election sure.* For if you do these things, you will never fall . . . (1:10). The key word here is *bebaian,* "sure." In law *bebaian* means to validate, as of a will. In general speech it means to confirm. Peter does not suggest that God's calling or election depend on man's response. But he does remind us that it is by responding to God's grace by living a life filled with the graces he has described that the reality of our election is confirmed for all to see.

What, on the other hand, will we see when we look at false teachers and those who follow them? Clear evidence in their lives and character that God has *not* called or elected them. Their corrupt way of life confirms that they are destined only for judgment.

And we have the word of the prophets made more certain (1:19). The key term is *bebaioteron.* This word is a strong comparative, meaning "more certain," "more reliable," which is frequently used as a superlative. It is best to take it in this latter sense here. In that case Peter, who has testified to his personal vision of Christ's glory (1:16-18) is saying that he himself, despite confidence in the authenticity of his vision, places very great reliance on the prophetic word.

We do not simply have the testimony of the apostles who witnessed Christ's glorification and His resurrection, despite the fact that all they relay is trustworthy. We have the most reliable witness of all: the witness of prophets who spoke of Christ and His glory long before the Incarnation.

For prophecy never had its origin in the will of man, but men spoke from God as they were carried along *by the Holy Spirit* (1:21). How can we place such reliance on the words of the prophets? We can do so because the prophets are not the origin of their message. Rather the Holy Spirit is the source of prophecy, and the words of the prophets are truly messages from God.

Again there is an implied contrast here. False teachers, like false prophets, *are* the source of their own messages, as well as the interpreters of what they say. So there is a strong correlation between the OT false prophets and the false teachers who trouble and torment the church (2 Peter 2:1). How much wiser to place "very great reliance" on the prophetic word, and reject the muttering of those who diverge from that sure Word.

They will say, "Where is this 'coming' he promised? Ever since our fathers died, *everything goes on as it has since the beginning of creation" (3:4). The Greek phrase is *panta autows diamenei ap' arches ktiseos,* which can be translated "everything remains just as it has been since the beginning of the world."

The scoffers who laugh at the doctrine of the Second Coming base their ridicule on an assumption which underlies much of the modern "scientific" worldview. The universe and all that is in it can be explained by natural processes which have themselves operated from the beginning. There is no need to invent a "God" to explain the origin of the universe or the development of living creatures. Man is just another animal which has evolved accidentally.

Peter answers by pointing to the Creation, and to the cataclysmic judgment of the Genesis Flood. God created, and He has intervened in the flow of history.

When Peter charges that the critics "deliberately forget" this, he reflects an argument advanced by Paul in Rom. 1. What can be known of God has been revealed to mankind from the Creation. But, unwilling to acknowledge God, human beings "hold down the truth," and in its place invent and affirm explanations for the way things are which are patently ridiculous.

The Lord is *not slow* in keeping His promise, as some understand slowness. He is patient with you, not wanting anyone to perish, but everyone to come to repentance (3:9). The Greek *ou bpaduvei* is better rendered "not late." God has not defaulted on any of His promises. In fact, the measured pace He has adopted is motivated by patience. God is waiting, to extend the opportunity for human beings to repent.

The meaning of the phrase "not wanting anyone to perish" has been a bone of contention between Calvinists and Arminians. However, the verse proves neither position, for the expression simply reminds us that God's love encompasses all. It is His desire that none perish, despite the fact that Scripture teaches those who remain estranged from Him must.

Be on your guard so that you may not be carried away by the error of lawless men and *fall from your secure position* (3:17). The word *sterigmou* represents a stable position, like that of the planets in the heavens. Like the sun, revealed truth is the center around which we orbit. It is tragically possible for even true believers to be deceived and drawn into error as promoted by false teachers. When that happens, our "orbit" becomes unstable, and our whole lives are affected by the "wobble."

But this is not something that Peter expects his readers to experience. Instead, he expects them to "grow in the grace and knowledge of our Lord and Savior Jesus Christ" (3:18).

***Keep yourselves in God's love* as you wait for the mercy of our Lord Jesus Christ to bring you eternal life (Jude 21).** Like Peter, Jude closes his warning about false teachers with an exhortation. The exhortation raises a question. How can we "keep ourselves" in God's love? The answer is found in John's Gospel. There Christ tells us to "remain in

My love" (John 15:9). And the next verse explains that we remain in God's love by obeying His commandments.

Yes, false teachers still threaten the church.

But if we maintain our stability by relying completely on God's Word, and remain in God's love by obeying it, we will surely be secure.

THE PASSAGE IN DEPTH

False Teachers and Their Destruction (2 Peter 2); The Sin and Doom of Godless Men (Jude 3-19).

Background. We saw in our study of 1 Peter that Christians were viewed with increasing hostility by the Roman people and government. By the early 100s it was a capital offense to be a Christian, whether or not convicted of any crime. The response of Christians was to follow the way defined by Peter in that letter: to live submissively, as blameless citizens, blameless wives, and/or blameless slaves.

At the same time we must recognize that some of the rumors of strange or base practices has some basis in fact. It is clear from reading 2 Peter and Jude that so-called Christian teachers, whom we might today call cult leaders, did gain followings among loose adherents of the faith. It is not surprising if pagans, who could hardly be expected to know the differences, ascribed to Christians in general the excesses of the few.

But what were some of the practices that were associated with false teaching? Looking into 2 Peter and Jude we see intimations of the immorality and corruption reflected in this quote from the writings of Epiphanius of Cyprus, who describes the practices of a so-called Christian group called Phibionites (*Panarion* 26.4-5).

When they thus ate together and so to speak filled up their veins from the surplus of their strength they turned to excitements. The man leaving his wife says to his own wife: "Stand up and perform the agape with the brother." Then the unfortunates unite with each other, and as I am truly ashamed to say the shameful things that are being done by them, because according to the holy apostles the things that are happening by them are shameful even to mention, nevertheless I will not be ashamed to say those things which they are not ashamed to do, in order that I may

cause in every way a horror in those who hear about their shameful practices. After they have had intercourse in the passion of fornication they raise their own blasphemy to heaven. The woman and the man take the fluid of the emission of the man into their hands, they stand, turn toward heaven, their hands besmeared with the uncleanness, and pray as people called *stratiotikoi* and *gnostikoi*, bringing to the father the nature of all that which they have on their hands, and they say: "We offer to thee this gift, the body of Christ." And then they eat it, their own ugliness, and say: "This is the body of Christ and this is the Passover for the sake of which our bodies suffer and are forced to confess the suffering of Christ." Similarly also with the woman when she happens to be in the flowing of the blood they gather the blood of menstruation of her uncleanness and eat it together and say: "This is the blood of Christ."

Epiphanius' description is both vivid and revolting. But it does reflect rumors about Christian practices that were current in the Roman Empire by the end of the first and through the second centuries of our era. It surely depicts an excess perhaps implied in Jude's warning against "godless men, who change the grace of our God into a license for immorality" (v. 4), and who according to Peter appeal to the "lustful desires of sinful human nature" (2:18) and are themselves "slaves of depravity" (2:19).

Undoubtedly many of the false teachers that plagued the early church led groups that looked more like modern congregations than the dissolute group Epiphanius describes. Yet a false teacher, whether disguised as an "angel of light" (2 Cor. 11:14-15) or openly depraved, always constitutes a serious threat to Christ's church. A threat against which both Peter and Jude warn their first-century readers—and us.

Parallel Passages in 2 Peter and Jude

2 Peter 2:1-22

But there were also false prophets among the people, just as there will be false teachers among you. They will secretly introduce destructive heresies, even denying the sovereign Lord who bought them — bringing swift destruction on themselves.

[2]Many will follow their shameful ways and will bring the way of truth into disrepute. [3]In their greed these teachers will exploit you with stories they have made up. Their condemnation has long been hanging over them, and their destruction has not been sleeping.

[4]For if God did not spare angels when they sinned, but sent them to hell, putting them into gloomy dungeons to be held for judgment, [5]if He did not spare the ancient world when He brought the flood on its ungodly people, but protected Noah, a preacher of righteousness, and seven others; [6]if He condemned the cities of Sodom and Gomorrah by burning them to ashes, and made them an example of what is going to happen to the ungodly; [7]and if He rescued Lot, a righteous man, who was distressed by the filthy lives of lawless men [8](for that righteous man, living among them day after day, was tormented in his righteous soul by the lawless deeds he saw and heard) — [9]if this is so, then the Lord knows how to rescue godly men from trials and to hold the unrighteous for the day of judgment, while continuing their punishment. [10]This is especially true of those who follow the corrupt desire of the sinful nature and despise authority.

Bold and arrogant, these men are not afraid to slander celestial beings; [11]yet even angels, although they are stronger and more powerful, do not bring slanderous accusations against such beings in the presence of the Lord. [12]But these men blaspheme in matters they do not understand. They are like brute beasts, creatures of instinct, born only to be caught and destroyed, and like beasts they too will perish.

[13]They will be paid back with harm for the harm they have done. Their idea of pleasure is to carouse in broad daylight. They are blots and blemishes, reveling in their pleasures while they feast with you. [14]With eyes full of adultery, they never stop sinning; they seduce the unstable; they are experts in greed — an accursed brood! [15]They have left the straight way and wandered off to follow the way of Balaam son of Beor, who loved the wages of wickedness. [16]But he was rebuked for his wrongdoing by a donkey — a beast without speech — who spoke with a man's voice and restrained the prophet's madness.

[17]These men are springs without water and mists driven by a storm. Blackest darkness is reserved for them. [18]For they mouth empty, boastful words and, by appealing to the lustful desires of sinful human nature, they entice people who are just escaping from those who live in error. [19]They promise them freedom, while they themselves are slaves of depravity — for a man is a slave to whatever has mastered him.

[20]If they have escaped the corruption of the world by knowing our Lord and Savior Jesus Christ and are again entangled in it and overcome, they are worse off at the end than they were at the beginning. [21]It would have been better for them not to have known the way of righteousness, than to have known it and then to turn their backs on the sacred commandment that was passed on to them.

[22]Of them the proverbs are true: "A dog returns to its vomit," and, "A sow that is washed goes back to her wallowing in the mud."

Jude 4-16

⁴For certain men whose condemnation was written about long ago have secretly slipped in among you. They are godless men, who change the grace of our God into a license for immorality and deny Jesus Christ our only Sovereign and Lord.

⁵Though you already know all this, I want to remind you that the Lord delivered His people out of Egypt, but later destroyed those who did not believe. ⁶And the angels who did not keep their positions of authority but abandoned their own home—these He has kept in darkness, bound with everlasting chains for judgment on the great Day. ⁷In a similar way Sodom and Gomorrah and the surrounding towns gave themselves up to sexual immorality and perversion. They serve as examples of those who suffer the punishment of eternal fire.

⁸In the very same way, these dreamers pollute their own bodies, reject authority and slander celestial beings. ⁹But even the archangel Michael, when he was disputing with the devil about the body of Moses, did not dare to bring a slanderous accusation against him, but said, "The Lord rebuke you!" ¹⁰Yet these men speak abusively against whatever they do not understand; and what things they do understand by instinct, like unreasoning animals—these are the very things that destroy them.

¹¹Woe to them! They have taken the way of Cain; they have rushed for profit into Balaam's error; they have been destroyed in Korah's rebellion.

¹²These men are blemishes at your love feasts, eating with you without the slightest qualm—shepherds who feed only themselves. They are clouds without rain, blown along by the wind; autumn trees, without fruit and uprooted—twice dead. ¹³They are wild waves of the sea, foaming up their shame; wandering stars, for whom blackest darkness has been reserved forever.

¹⁴Enoch, the seventh from Adam, prophesied about these men: "See, the Lord is coming with thousands upon thousands of His holy ones ¹⁵to judge everyone, and to convict all the ungodly of all the ungodly acts they have done in the ungodly way, of all the harsh words ungodly sinners have spoken against Him." ¹⁶These men are grumblers and faultfinders; they follow their own evil desires; they boast about themselves and flatter others for their own advantage.

Interpretation. A glance at the two passages side by side quickly reveals that Peter and Jude are in complete harmony in their description of false teachers. We note the following common themes:

Theme	2 Peter	Jude
(1) Infiltration	2:1	4, 12
(2) Immorality	2:3, 10, 14 18-19	4, 7
(3) Deny Christ	2:1	4
(4) Greed motive	2:3, 14-15	15-16
(5) Reject authority	2:10	8-10
(6) Unreasoning beasts	2:12	10
(7) Dominated by sinful desires	2:10, 14-15, 18	12, 16, 18
(7) Empty, useless	2:17-19	12-13
(8) Retribution sure	2:1, 3-6, 13	5-7, 14-16

Looking at each of these themes in turn, we see:

■ Infiltration (2 Peter 2:1; Jude 4, 12). False teachers gain entrance by pretending to be believers. Jude says they "secretly slipped in among you" (v. 4). Initially their agenda is unclear as they hypocritically take part in the church's worship. It is only when they are accepted, and have gained some influence in the congregation, that their true nature and motives are unveiled.

■ They practice and teach immorality (2 Peter 2:3, 10, 14, 18-19; Jude 4, 7). One characteristic of false teachers which comes up again and again is their immoral lifestyle. They justify their behavior on the basis of grace. The argument is that since the Christian has been freed from the Law, he or she is

595

freed to do whatever he or she pleases. Jude says this is to "change" (*metatithentes*, to transpose, make into something else; here with the clear connotation of "corrupting") the grace of God into something it isn't—license to sin. And to drive home God's attitude toward immorality each writer looks back in history to describe God's judgment on Sodom and Gomorrah for the same kind of sins.

It is important to note that much of the appeal of false teachers rests in the fact that their teaching seems to validate immoral behavior. It is by mouthing "boastful words and, by appealing to the lustful desires of sinful human nature, they entice people who are just escaping from those who live in error" (2 Peter 2:18). The false teacher presents this as freedom, while in fact it is the worst sort of bondage: bondage to one's own baser instincts, and captivity to sins which all too soon master us (2 Peter 2:19-20).

■ Their teaching denies Christ His place as Sovereign Lord and Savior (2 Peter 2:1; Jude 4). John's epistles further develop the nature of this denial. It is essentially rejecting the Scripture's teaching that Christ is the eternal God, come in the flesh (1 John 2:22-23; 4:2-3).

■ False teachers are motivated by selfishness and greed rather than by a desire to serve (2 Peter 2:3, 14-15; Jude 15-16). "Greed" (*pleonexia*) can be used of sexual lust, but in this context it is most likely a reference to finances. False teachers exploit those they deceive for personal gain. Jude's image is explicit; they are "shepherds who feed only themselves" (12). What a contrast to the true shepherds described in 1 Peter 5, who serve as overseers "not because you must, but because you are willing, as God wants you to be; not greedy for money, but eager to serve" (5:2).

■ False teachers reject authority (2 Peter 2:10; Jude 8-10). The authority which the false teachers reject is not that of the apostles, but that of God Himself. The illustration each uses involves angels. In part this reflects the Jewish belief that the Law of Moses was mediated by angels, and angels carefully observed its practice. Thus Paul encourages appropriate behavior in church "because of the angels" (1 Cor. 11:10). It would seem that the false teachers here might have been rebuked for

offending the angels with their immoral behavior. Their reaction was to ridicule angelic beings. The point made by Jude and Peter is that even if they *were* as righteous as Moses or had the spiritual authority of Michael, they would not be above the moral law which is expressed both in the Old Testament and the New.

What a lesson for churches now struggling with the demand of homosexuals for recognition as a valid "alternative lifestyle," and even for ordination to the ministry. To even consider such a thing is to reject God's authority, and find oneself not in the company of the saints but of the heretics against which Peter and Jude warn us all.

■ False teachers react as unreasoning beasts (2 Peter 2:12; Jude 10). The *Zondervan Dictionary of Bible Words* explains the significance of this imagery.

> The animal mind (brute beast) is locked into present experience and must react to the present without awareness of the spiritual universe and without ability to project from the present to the future. An animal may learn from past experience, but it cannot draw on information beyond experience, nor can it reason from information to the end of a chain or probable cause-effect events.
>
> A similar point is made by both Peter and Jude. They describe false teachers as being "like brute beasts, creatures of instinct" (2 Peter 2:12) who "understand by instinct, like unreasoning animals" (Jude 10). The animal mind is capable of understanding. But its understanding is of a different order from that of human understanding. Animal experiences are interpreted by instinct, and animals lack the capacity to reason from experience to a deeper understanding of the past or of the future (p. 53).

■ False teachers are dominated by sinful desires (2 Peter 2:10, 14-15, 18; Jude 12, 16, 18). Those desires drive them into acts which pollute the body (2 Peter 2:10). Why not the soul? The answer is that within they are already polluted with, literally, "eyes full of adultery" (2:14). The expression suggests that they are always on the lookout for a woman with whom they can commit adultery. As

Jude adds, they are driven to "follow their own ungodly desires" (Jude 18).

■ The false teachers and their teachings are empty, useless, and without any value (2 Peter 2:17-19; Jude 12-13). A series of vivid similes portrays the hollow men and their hollow teachings. Clouds without rain and springs without water are unable to nurture growth. Uprooted autumn trees are dead and fruitless. Waves of the sea, and wandering stars, are purposeless and valueless.

But it is not just that false teachings are void of value. They are destructive, for they promise freedom while in fact adding links to the chains that make lost human beings the slaves of sin.

■ The fate of the false teachers and their followers is sure: they face the retributive judgment of God (2 Peter 2:1, 3, 4-6, 13; Jude 5-7, 14-16). This theme echoes again and again through these brief warnings. The appeal of false teachers to man's baser desires may be momentarily attractive, but each step taken in the path marked out by false teachers is a step toward judgment.

Application. Jude and Peter both express a deep concern that believers not be led astray by false teachers. Tragically, there are false teachers in the church today—often holding high positions. It remains for us, and for our institutions, to beware.

and toward which God had led His people from the moment of their redemption (Ex. 3–11).

The Application Made (3:12-15). The writer immediately makes his point. We have been raised to take a possession in Christ. Our share in Him makes us new men and new women, and opens up the possibility of a victorious Christian life. But our share in Christ can be of no practical value to us if we permit the same attitude to develop in us that was displayed by Israel of old. This attitude, characterized here as sinful and untrusting (3:12), can harden us and keep us from responding to God's voice when He speaks to us.

The writer is saying that the primary issue we face as believers, and the focus of our daily concern, must be to keep our hearts open to God. We must be eager and ready to respond when we hear His voice speaking to us in our own "today."

A Tragic End (3:16-19). The writer returns to the OT generation, to identify them clearly, and to mark off the tragic results of hardening our hearts to God. Who were the rebels? They were actually men and women who had experienced the mighty acts of God by which He freed them from slavery in Egypt! With whom was God angry? Those very people who sinned—and whose bodies ultimately fell in the wilderness, never to know the rest found by entering the Promised Land. And who does God declare can never experience His rest? Those who disobey. All who disobey.

A "Rest" Remains (4:1-11). This section of Hebrews is complicated by a multiple use of the word "rest," and by a complex argument. We can best follow the thought if we sort out some of the elements, rather than study the passage verse by verse.

■ The promise stands. This is the thought with which the chapter begins (4:1). Even though a later, obedient generation did enter the Promised Land, that entry did not completely fulfill the promise of a "rest" for God's people. In fact, much later, in the time of David, the promise and the warning were repeated! "Today, if you hear His voice" (4:7). If God's full blessing for His people had been achieved when Joshua led Israel into Canaan,

then the promise of a rest would not have been repeated much later to the people of David's day. Nor would it have been repeated by the writer of Hebrews to first-century Christians, and through this NT book, to you and me.

■ The nature of rest. The word "rest" is used in Heb. 3–4 in three distinct ways. First is the usage we've just seen: entry into the Promised Land is a portrait, a tangible example, of the concept of rest.

It is an appropriate portrait. God had promised the land to Abraham and his descendants. During the years of Israel's slavery in Egypt, pagan peoples populated and improved the land. They built houses, planted vineyards and orchards, and tamed the wilderness. Yet their lifestyle more and more evidenced the grossest of sins. The time of their judgment by God corresponded with Israel's release from slavery. In coming into Canaan, Israel would be God's instrument of judgment on their sin—and Israel would inherit riches for which the people had not labored. The people would sit under trees they had not planted and drink wine made from grapes of vines they had not cultivated. They would come into a land where the work had been done for them—and they would rest.

Like Israel of old, you and I in Jesus have been delivered from slavery. Sin's power in our lives has been broken, and we are called by God to enter a spiritual "Promised Land" where we will find rest. We are to enjoy the benefits of the work Christ has done for us. The Christian life is not one of struggle to carve out a bare living in some wilderness. The Christian life is one of appropriating all the benefits of the spiritual abundance that Jesus so richly provides.

A second connotation of "rest" is seen in the application of the term to God's own rest, taken on completion of Creation. Jewish teachers noted a fascinating feature of the Genesis account. For each of the first six days, the text speaks of "evening and morning." The beginning and the end were clearly marked off. But the seventh day has no such demarcation. The rabbis took this to mean that God's rest has no end. With His creative work complete, God is not inactive. But He no longer *works,* for His work is done.

There is a wondrous thought expressed

1, 2, and 3 JOHN
Walking with God

EXPOSITION _____

The Epistles of John, with Revelation, are the latest of the NT writings. All were written late in the life of the beloved apostle, who survived his companions by some three decades. Irenaeus (c. A.D. 130-200) wrote that "all the presbyters, who associated in Asia with John, the disciple of the Lord, testify that John handed down [these things]. For he remained with them until the times of Trajan [A.D. 98-117]. . . . And also the church in Ephesus founded by Paul—John having remained with them until the times of Trajan—is a faithful witness of the tradition of the apostles."

It is important to compare John's letters to the later letters of Paul, Peter, and Jude. In Peter's first letter he writes of persecutions to come. In his second letter, like Paul's 2 Timothy and Jude, the apostle warns of the danger posed by false teachers. John, living through the challenges the other three foresaw, writes in a warm, pastoral way, of the church's response to those challenges. That response is to reaffirm the basic truths of the faith, and to emphasize the positive lifestyle of love and obedience that grows out of a personal relationship with Jesus Christ. As long as Christians remain committed to Him, and live lives of love and obedience, the church will be strong and safe.

John's first letter is undoubtedly the most difficult of any biblical book to outline. It is filled with recurrent thoughts and themes, as John returns again and again to his emphases on fellowship with God, on truth, love, righteousness, and faith. This pattern has led most commentators to believe that the book is without a logical plan and marked rather by association of these basic ideas. Others have struggled to identify a structure they believe must be there, but without compelling success.

Still, it may be most profitable if we simply read this beautiful and compelling book paragraph by paragraph and thought by thought, without concern for overall structure. John's letter is first of all pastoral, and indeed devotional. As we meditate on each thought we learn how to live in fellowship with Jesus and with one another in a community bonded together by love, and by an eagerness to respond to the living words of Jesus Christ.

A thoughtful outline which can help those who feel more comfortable reading within a proposed structure for this book is provided by Stephen S. Smalley, in his volume on 1, 2, 3 John in the *Word Biblical Commentary*.

1 John

WORD STUDIES

We proclaim to you the eternal life, which was with the Father and has appeared to us (1:2). The first four verses of John are a single sentence in Greek. The main verb, "we proclaim" (*apangellomen*) appears here in the Greek, and was added by the NIV translators to v. 1 to make the thought more intelligible to English readers. But why the complicated construction? Perhaps because the subject is itself such a mystery. The eternal God has become flesh, and has been experienced through the senses (heard, seen, touched) by mortal men! This stunning message—a message rejected by the false teachers that infect the church (cf. 1 John 4:2-3; 2 John 7)—is the central truth of the Gospel. Only those who respond to Jesus as the very Son of God will have fellowship with the Father and with the Son.

We write this to make *our joy* complete (1:4). John's writings contain frequent references to the joy that is generated by fellowship with Jesus (cf. John 15:11; 16:22-24; 17:13). Here the "our" is more than individual experience. It reflects a joy shared by the whole community of faith; a magnification of individual experience that comes when those who know Jesus love one another and walk in fellowship with each other and the Lord.

Let's never forget the community character of joy. We can only know joy's full meaning when it is shared.

If *we claim* to have fellowship with Him yet walk in the darkness, we lie and do not live by the truth (1:6). The phrase *ean eipomen*, "should we claim," is repeated three times in this short section. In each case the "claim" is set against a reality which exposes the claim as false, and which reveals God's true way to deal with the vast disparity between God's nature and man's.

Only by acknowledging that gap and dealing with our failings in God's way can we experience true fellowship with God.

If we *walk in the light,* as He is in the light, we have fellowship with one another, and the blood of Jesus, His Son, *purifies us* from all sin (1:7). John frequently sets light and darkness in contrast with each other. Here light and darkness represent an honest vs. a dishonest appraisal of one's own self. The person who walks in the light is not sinless, for the text says such a person still needs forgiveness and purification. Instead the person who walks in the light sees things in the light of God's Word, and accepts the verdict of that Word on what is right and what is wrong; what is good and what is evil; what is righteous and what is sin. As long as a person

The Counterfeit		**The True**	
1 John 1:6 We claim to have fellowship while walking in darkness.	1 John 1:7 We are lying. Not practicing the truth.	We walk in the light as God is in the light.	We have fellowship with each other. The blood of Christ purifies us from all sin.
1 John 1:8 We claim to be without sin.	We deceive ourselves. Truth is not in us.	1 John 1:9 We confess [acknowledge] our sins.	He forgives us our sins. He keeps on purifying us from all unrighteousness.
1 John 1:10 We claim we have not sinned. God's word has no place in us.	We make God out to be a liar.	1 John 2:1 When we sin.	We have Jesus as our Intercessor, to defend us.

accepts the verdict of God about himself and his action, there is hope. He or she is walking in the light, and will seek God's forgiveness acknowledging his or her sins to the Lord (1:9).

Because of Christ, God is fully capable of dealing with our sins. But God can do nothing for the person who refuses to admit that he or she has sinned and needs God's help.

"Purifies us" is *katharise*, to cleanse or purify. The tense indicates an ongoing, continuous process by which God deals not just with acts of sin but with the very principle of sin in our lives. John's point is that when we walk in the light, and are honest with God and with ourselves, we open up our personality to the Lord so that He can work within us to change our inner orientation toward sin, to an inner orientation toward righteousness. Paul put it this way in 2 Cor. 3:18: We "are being transformed into His likeness with ever-increasing glory, which comes from the Lord, who is the Spirit."

If we claim to be without *sin*, we deceive ourselves (1:8). The phrase *harmartian echein*, "to have sin," draws attention not to acts of sin, but to the principle of sin residing in fallen human nature. Any claim that a believer is unaffected by sin, or that sin has no presence within the believer, is utterly false. Such a claim draws one into the shadowy realm of self-deceit, for anyone who holds this belief must explain away sinful emotions such as lust or anger, often by relabeling one's feelings as

"righteous indignation," or "natural attraction." In the grip of such a delusion it is impossible for a person to acknowledge sins to God that he or she might be forgiven. And it is impossible for anyone in the grip of such a delusion to open his or her life to the Holy Spirit that He might perform His cleansing work.

If we *confess* our sins, He is faithful and just and will forgive us our sins and purify us from unrighteousness (1:9). "Confess" (*homologeo*) means "to acknowledge." The point is well expressed by Augustine, who says "he who confesses and condemns his sins already acts with God." To confess sins is to condemn our sins by labeling them for what they are, sins. When we take this step, we take our stand with God and against our own actions. It is this, not feeling sorry or promising to "never do it again," which makes it possible for us to experience forgiveness and the cleansing work of God in our lives.

He is the *atoning sacrifice* for our sins, and not only for ours but also for the sins of the whole world (2:2). The Greek is *hilasmos,* which means "to propitiate or expiate," and draws attention to the fact that in His death Christ satisfied the justice of God, which demanded sin be punished. It is on the basis of Christ's work that we experience the forgiveness and cleansing that John has just described.

600

But what does it mean when it says that His is the atoning sacrifice for "the whole world"? Simply that Christ's sacrifice was sufficient in God's eyes to pay for all humanity's sins, not just for those of believers. However, the consistent teaching of Scripture is that the merit of Christ's sacrifice is applied to the account only of those who believe.

We know that we have come to *know Him* if we obey His commands (2:3). In Judaism obeying God's commands was a condition for relationship with God. In Christianity, obeying God's commands is a *characteristic* of the person who knows God, in that intimate sense of "knowing" that represents personal relationship in the Bible.

The importance of obedience as a characteristic of true Christianity is emphasized again and again in 1 John, along with the quality of a practical love for others.

One who keeps on saying "I know Him" but does not habitually practice obedience *pseustes estin*, "is a liar" (2:4).

Whoever claims to live in Him must *walk* as Jesus did (2:6). Walk is *periepatesen*, frequently used as an image for "way of life." Anyone who maintains an intimate relationship with Jesus Christ will demonstrate the reality of that relationship by living a Christlike life. The tenses of the verbs make it clear that John is speaking of lifestyle. The claim being made is not that one is saved, but that one is living in fellowship with the Lord—"living in" Him. The proof of that claim, not proof of the claim to be saved, is that one maintains a Christlike lifestyle.

Here, as in v. 1, John deals with a trilogy of claims, diagrammed below.

THREE FALSE LIFESTYLE CLAIMS

	2:4		2:5
"I know Him"	Does not do what He says.	We know we know Him if . . .	We obey His Word.
			A liar. The truth is not in him.

	2:6		2:6
"I live in Him"		Must live as	Jesus lived.
"I am in the light"	Hates his brother.	Lives in the Is still in darkness.	If loves brother. light . . .

Anyone who claims to be in the light but *hates his brother* is still in the darkness (2:9). "Hate" here is not so much an emotion as an attitude or failure to respond. John is not so much describing active animosity as he is an indifference to the needs of others, which is expressed by a failure to respond to them with love.

Love demonstrates itself by feeding the hungry, clothing the naked, sheltering the homeless, and caring for the sick. Any lack of this kind of love, or failure to respond to the needs of the brothers, is in John's vocabulary, "hate."

Do not *love the world* or anything in the world (2:15). The command not to love uses the NT's strongest word for love, *agape*. It implies more than having an affection for. *Agape* implies a choice—a decision to set one's heart.

"World" here is *kosmos*, which originally meant "order" or "system." In one sense the world is the ecosystem as God has created it. In another it is the arena in which human beings experience life. However, *kosmos* is also a theological concept, and it is in this sense that we find it here. Of this sense the *Zondervan Expository Dictionary of Bible Words* says *kosmos*

portrays human society as a system warped by sin, tormented by beliefs and desires and emotions that surge blindly and uncontrollably. The world system is a dark system (Eph. 6:12), operating on basic principles that are not of God (Col. 2:20; 1 John 2:16). The entire system lies under the power of Satan (1 John 5:19) and constitutes the kingdom from which believers are delivered by Christ (Col. 1:13-14). Its basic hostility to God is often displayed (1 Cor. 2:12; 3:19; 11:32; Eph. 2:2; James 1:27; 4:4; 1 John 2:15-17; cf. John 12:31; 15:19; 16:33; 17:14; 1 John 2:1, 13; 5:4-5, 19) [p. 639].

John makes it clear that the principles which drive the world are in direct conflict with God and all that He stands for. Thus no one who is caught up in the world's approach to life will do the will of God. Or enjoy the eternal blessings known by those who live forever.

CHARACTERISTICS OF THE *KOSMOS* (1 John 2:16)

NIV phrase	Meaning	Expressed in
"The cravings of sinful man"	Desires of the flesh, i.e., selfish, sinful impulses	Materialism, selfishness, egotism, injustice, racism, etc.
"The lust of his eyes"	Greed, sexual passion, awakened by appearances	Superficialism, materialism, covetousness, avarice, etc.
"The boasting of what he has and does"	Ostentatious pride	Defining oneself and others by possessions, status, reputation, income, etc.

Dear children, this is the last hour; and as you have heard that the *Antichrist* is coming, even now many antichrists have come (2:18). The Greek is *antichristos*; "Christ" with the prefix *anti-*, meaning "against" or "in place of." The word is used only by John, and only five times by him. As this verse illustrates, in the singular, "Antichrist" identifies a specific individual destined to come at history's end, while in the plural it identifies persons contemporary to any generation who are moved by the spirit of the Antichrist, and thus hostile to Christ and His people. Most likely the antichrists of John are the same as the false prophets of Paul and Peter.

For if they had belonged to us, they would have remained with us; but *their going* showed that none of them belonged to us (2:19). The word is *ekelthan*; to withdraw. It is clear that initially the "antichrists" or false teachers John writes of presented themselves to the congregation as believers. When the differences in their character and teachings became clear, they no longer pretended, but withdrew from the church, undoubtedly drawing some believers they had deceived with them.

This verse is a comforting one for Christians who are concerned when those they thought were true Christians fall away, or even show hostility to the faith they once verbally espoused. Are we to explain this by saying that they were saved, but are now lost? Or that they are backsliding now, but will be restored before they die? John provides another way to understand such events. They withdrew from us because they didn't really belong to us. If they had, they would have stayed. By going, they showed that they did not belong in the first place.

But you have an *anointing* from the Holy One, and all of you know the truth (2:20). The Greek word is *chrisma*, an "anointing" or "consecration." John's point is that the Holy Spirit has acted in a unique, spiritual way to set the true believer apart, so that he or she is able to perceive the truth.

This understanding is supported by Christ's teaching as reported in John's Gospel. "When He, the Spirit of truth, comes, He will guide you into all truth" (16:13; cf. 14:17; 15:26).

This same thought is expressed a little later in 1 John 2:27. Because of the Spirit's presence, the Christian is not dependent on human teaching. Instead, the Spirit guides and interprets.

The concept is important, and consistent throughout the NT (1 Cor. 2:10-15). There is an objective revelation of God available to human beings in Creation, and especially in

God's written revelation. But to understand and appropriate the truth of God requires subjective enablement granted only to those who believe and who are endowed with the Holy Spirit.

Who is the liar? It is the man who denies that *Jesus is the Christ.* Such a man is the Antichrist (2:22). The phrase "Jesus is the Christ" links the two natures of Christ in a way that was and is unacceptable to cultists. Jesus, of true human birth, is at the same time "the Christ," God eternally existent.

No one who denies the true humanity and full deity of Jesus can have any access to the Father, or any chance of personal relationship with God. Christ truly is the one and only way, the one and only truth, and the one and only life. No one comes to the Father except by Him (John 14:6).

If you know that *He is righteous,* you know that everyone who does what is right has been born of Him (2:29). John has used "righteous" (*dikaios*) in describing both God (1:9) and Jesus (2:1). Here either may be in view. Again John is looking at the lifestyle characteristic of the true believer. The lifestyle does not make one a believer; belief is the source of lifestyle. Clearly anyone who has been born of God, and shares his heredity, will be like his righteous Heavenly Father and do right.

Everyone who has this *hope* in Him purifies himself, just as He is pure (3:3). Here again "hope" (*elpis*) is confident expectation in something which is sure to come to pass.

What the Christian expects is the return of Christ, and a personal transformation into Christ's likeness. With our eyes fixed on that wonderful day, we are unmoved by the cravings, lusts, and boasting that energizes people of the world, and so are freed to concentrate on that which makes us pure, just as Jesus is pure.

Everyone who sins breaks the Law; in fact, sin is lawlessness (3:4). The present participle indicates John is again looking at lifestyle. He is concerned about the one habitually practicing sin. In calling this "lawlessness" John expands on the idea of "break[ing] the Law." It is not simply a matter of violation

of a specific ruling in the code. Rather it is a matter of a rebellious attitude. It is God who gave the Law, thus lawlessness is at heart rebellion against God.

John looks at the purpose of Christ's appearance in 3:5. Christ came to deal with mankind's rebellious attitude, and He succeeded! Thus it is inconceivable that anyone who has appropriated Christ's finished work "keeps on sinning" (3:6).

Again we must be careful. John does not teach that it is impossible for believers to sin. Indeed, earlier in 1:8 he makes it clear that believers will sin at times, and must be ready to acknowledge it when they do. But when we look at lifestyle, at the whole pattern of a person's life, we realize that it is impossible for a true believer to make sinning a habit. The attitude of rebelliousness that keeps us practicing sin has been dealt with by Christ. We may stumble at times and even fall. But Christ will lift us, and see to it that we stand. Rather than lawlessness our lives will reflect a respect for and commitment to doing what is right.

Thus John concludes that "no one who is born of God will continue to sin, because God's seed remains in him; he cannot go on sinning, because he has been born of God" (3:9).

If anyone has material possessions and sees his brother in need but has no pity on him, how can the *love of God* be in him? (3:17) God's kind of love (*he agape tou theou* here is best taken as a subjective genitive) is giving, compassionate, practical. It responds to the needs of others with a compassion that moves a person to reach out a helping hand.

The person who "has no pity," who literally "closes his heart" to his brother in need, lacks the love of God. And, as John says, "we know that we have passed from death to life, because we love our brothers" (3:14).

John does not write this to cause the uncertain to agonize over whether they are saved or not. He writes it to reassure those who do love that the presence of a caring spirit is evidence of the reality of God's presence within.

Dear friends, *if our hearts do not condemn us,* we have confidence before God (3:21). Here *kardia* is used with the meaning of conscience. The whole phrase (*ean . . . me kataginoske*) should be rendered "if our consciences *no longer* condemn us." John has just argued that a failure to help needy brothers creates an inner moral tension and a troubled conscience. There is divided love: love for God and love for possessions. One who resolves this tension by giving himself or herself up to the love of God, and freely responding to meet the needs of destitute brothers and sisters, no longer has a troubled heart. His conscience no longer condemns him. And, John says, in this case such a person can "have confidence before God." Nothing now interrupts our fellowship with the Lord, or hinders our prayers.

This is how you can recognize the Spirit of God: Every *spirit* that acknowledges that *Jesus Christ has come in the flesh* is from God, but every spirit that does not acknowledge Jesus is not from God (4:2). Here "spirit" is used in a general sense, as in the phrase "the spirit of the age." John is describing the basic outlook of the antichrists and false prophets against which he is warning his readers: they are moved by a religious spirit which refuses to recognize the true humanity and full deity of Jesus Christ, and thus are in conflict with the Holy Spirit who affirms that Jesus is God enfleshed.

Again we see that Christianity is Christ. No faith which calls itself "Christian" but refuses to acknowledge Jesus for who He truly is, is of God.

Love is *made complete among us* so that we will have confidence on the day of judgment, because in this world we are like Him (4:17). The Greek phrase is *teteleiotai . . . meth' hemon,* and introduces John's summarizing explanation of how love reaches its goal among God's people. When we are like Jesus in this world, living in fellowship with the Lord and loving one another, we have a confidence that will carry through to the day of judgment itself.

There is *no fear in love.* But perfect love drives out fear, because fear has to do with punishment. The one who fears is not made perfect in love (4:18). The love John writes of in this chapter is first of all God's love, which moved Him to redeem us. But it is also our response to God's love, experienced as love for Him, and as love for and

from others in the family of faith. In a real sense the believer lives life in a realm permeated by love. The love we experience is so overwhelmingly real that there is no room left for fear.

A person who does fear has not yet reached the goal of being made perfect in love. He or she still has much to learn about God's love for the individual, and much to learn about opening his or her heart to love others and accept love from them.

This is the one who *came by water and blood*—Jesus Christ (5:6). The phrase has been interpreted in many different ways. Augustine saw here a reference to the blood and water that came from Christ's side on the cross (John 19:34). Calvin and Luther both saw a reference to the sacraments. Other commentators have suggested it alludes to the OT sacrificial system, where water stands for purification and blood for the sacrifice itself. Most commentators agree with Tertullian and take the verse to refer to Christ's baptism and death.

Perhaps the verse is intended to refute a persistent early heresy which suggested that Jesus became the Christ in His death. John says that Jesus was always the Christ, the same in His earthly ministry and suffering launched at His baptism, the same in His death on the cross.

For there are three that testify: the Spirit, the water and the blood; and the three are in agreement (5:6). This verse has, like 5:5 above, stimulated a variety of interpretations. Sacramental churches have seen here a reference to the rites of baptism and communion through which the Spirit continues to witness to Jesus. Other traditions have seen a reference to the historic events of Christ's baptism and His crucifixion, and understood the Spirit's ministry as taking the biblical record of these events and making their meaning subjectively clear to the reader. In either event, the witness of these three harmonize and become God's own testimony to His Son. A testimony sensed to be true by those who believe. A testimony so real that when rejected by those who will not believe the rejection is tantamount to calling God a liar (5:10).

If we ask anything according to His will, He hears us (5:14). Peter Marshall comments, "When we learn to want what God wants, we have the joy of receiving His answer to our petitions."

If anyone sees his brother commit *a sin that does not lead to death,* he should pray and God will give him life (5:16). There is no satisfactory answer to several questions that 5:16 and 5:17 raise. What does "death" mean here? What is a sin that does not lead to death in contrast to a sin that does lead to death? What specific sins does John have in mind? Why shouldn't we pray for those whose sins are in the "lead to death" category? Don't they need our prayers even more than others?

It is probable that no NT passage raises so many questions that commentators agree are, in the last analysis, unanswerable.

Perhaps the best suggestion is that John is thinking of his whole exposition of the Christian lifestyle as one of love and obedience. A person who claims to be a believer, but who resolutely refuses to conform to the Christian way, has set his or her feet on a path which is characterized by death. Christians may slip and fall, and be rescued by our prayers. But the person who adamantly refuses to submit to the Christian way of life shows by his choice that he is beyond redemption, and should not be prayed for as a brother.

Many *deceivers,* who do not acknowledge Jesus Christ as coming in the flesh, have gone out into the world (2 John 7). The word is *planoi,* and is a reference to false prophets who consciously try to lead others astray. Here as in 1 John the key to recognizing the heretical teacher and his teachings is his view of Jesus Christ. Is Jesus the Christ, God come in the flesh? Any failure to affirm the full deity and true humanity of Jesus marks teacher and teachings as false and deceitful.

Anyone who *runs ahead* and does not continue in the teaching of Christ does not have God (2 John 9). The verb *proagon,* "is advanced," is found only here in the NT. It was favored by early gnostics, who claimed

to have "advanced" knowledge beyond that of ordinary Christians. John here uses it contemptuously of those who claim to have "advanced beyond Christ" in approaching God. What an impossibility! We may advance *in* Christ, growing up in Him. But there is no way that one can advance beyond Him.

My dear friend *Gaius* (3 John 1). Like 2 John, 3 John is a brief note penned by John to a church leader. And, like many overlooked books of the Bible, it is a rich source of material for meditation and preaching.

The following outline is from a sermon preached by Richard Schmidt, of Hudson, Florida's First Methodist Church. It captures the teaching of this little book, and illustrates its practical value for us today.

I. ANALYSIS OF 3 JOHN
An outline easily forms around the three men whose names appear. Gaius is the recipient of Encouragement; Diotrephes is the subject of Criticism; Demetrius is an example of Testimony.

A. Gaius . . . Encouragement (vv. 1-8)
  1. He was in poor health (v. 2)
  2. He was faithful to Christ (v. 3)
  3. He was one of John's converts (v. 4)
  4. He was devoted and friendly (vv. 5-6)
B. Diotrephes . . . Criticism (vv. 9-10)
  1. Loved to be first (v. 9)
  2. Rejected John's counsel (v. 9)
  3. Unjustly accused John (v. 10)
  4. Rejected the brethren (v. 10)
  5. Forbade others to entertain (v. 10)
  6. Excommunicated the brethren (v. 10)
C. Demetrius . . . Testimony (vv. 11-12)
  "Dear friend, do not imitate what is evil but what is good."
  Demetrius was all that Diotrephes should have been.
II. APPLICATION OF 3 JOHN
  A. Hospitality . . . Caring for others.
  B. Generosity . . . Giving to others.
  C. Honesty . . . Sharing with others.
  D. Purity . . . Cleanliness within ourselves.

REVELATION
The Apocalypse

EXPOSITION

Revelation is a book that fascinates and troubles readers. Its powerful yet obscure images puzzle us, yet at the same time clearly present us with a great, irresistible realization. The gentle Jesus of the Gospels is the Mighty God who will display His Majesty in terrible judgments on sin. And history marches surely toward that great denouncement.

Four traditional ways of looking at Revelation have emerged. The *Futurist* view sees the great events described after Rev. 1–3 as associated with the future return of Christ, and the beasts of Rev. 13 and 17 identified with the Antichrist. This is the view of the early church, reflected by such church fathers as Justin Martyr, Irenaeus, Hippolytus, and others. This view is also held by many evangelical Christians today. The *Historicist* view, which originated in the late 1100s, saw Revelation as a prophetic survey of events taking place between the first and second advents. Luther and Calvin adopted this view, and saw the pope and the Catholic church in the beasts who withstood God. Few today would take a historicist approach to interpreting Revelation. The *Preterist* view sees Revelation as a disguised polemic against the Roman Empire and Roman religion of John's own day. This approach was not suggested until A.D. 1614, and has little or no support today. The *Idealist* view of Revelation sees the book as poetic and spiritual in nature. That is, rather than relating to any historical events at all, Rev. 4–22 affirm great and timeless truths concerning the sovereignty of God, and the struggle between good and evil. Ultimately, Revelation affirms, God will surely triumph, for time and eternity are in the hand of the Creator, and Jesus Christ will emerge victorious in the end.

In asking which approach is the correct one we must ask: Correct for what purpose? If we look at the apocalyptic literature which flourished in Judaism in the two centuries before Christ, we realize that all such books are constructed on a particular view of history. That view is that history must be understood as a series of events which progress from a beginning to an end preordained by God. The powerful and obscure images that characterize apocalyptic works are intentionally eschatological: they are intended to portray future history. If Revelation is rightly classified as apocalyptic literature, and clearly it was so defined by the early church, then it must be interpreted from the standpoint of the futurist.

There is another answer to the question: Correct for what purpose? While early and modern commentators believe that they can construct at least an outline of events associated with the return of Christ from this book, especially when taking into account the 278 reflections of the OT found in Revelation's 404 verses, it is wrong to assume that John expected the typical reader to use Revelation to construct prophetic charts. Instead the visions which John saw and records fulfill the function ascribed to this great work by the Idealist. In reading Revelation, in absorbing its imagery, you and I are lifted up with John and overwhelmed by the realization that God *is* history's Lord. No matter what our circumstances may be today, Christ will triumph. Evil will be judged, the wicked punished, and God's righteousness will be fully vindicated in the end.

For this reason, while we might rightly study Revelation from a Futurist standpoint, it is more rewarding for us to simply read this great book through, and let its imagery saturate our hearts and minds. The vivid descriptions of the praise that echoes before God's throne in heaven (Rev. 4), the reaction of the terrified and yet unrepentant wicked as God's judgments begin to unfold (Rev. 6:9-17; 9:20-21), and the vision of the woman "drunk with the blood of the saints" (17:6), all convey more powerfully than any prose the significance of the events described. And far more powerfully reassure us of the ultimate triumph of our God.

Revelation divides naturally into three sections. Revelation opens with a focus on the present as, about A.D. 98 living in exile on the Island of Patmos, the Apostle John is confronted by the glorified Christ and told to convey His message to seven churches in Asia (Rev. 1–3). John is then caught up and given a vision of "what will take place later" (1:19). What follows is an extended vision of onslaughts of divine judgment directed against sinful humanity and the spiritual powers of wickedness that have led the rebellion against God from evil's beginning (Rev. 4–20). The last section of the book portrays the triumphant return of Jesus, an era of peace on earth followed by a final rebellion, and then the last judgment. The book closes with a vision of eternity, and what we call "heaven," when the saved enter into the fullness of that eternal life given to those who believe in Jesus Christ (Rev. 21–22).

THE SECTIONS IN BRIEF

Letters from Christ to Seven Churches (chaps. 1–3)

Context. The Apostle John identifies this book as the "revelation of Jesus Christ" (1:1). While the Greek construction permits us to take the phrase to mean a revelation *from* Jesus, it is better to take it as "revelation of," meaning an unveiling of Jesus as He was then and is now, glorified with the Father in heaven.

It is striking here to see the reaction of John. This "disciple whom Jesus loved" (John 13:23), who took every occasion to be close to his Lord, is stunned at the vision of Christ undisguised. He falls at Jesus' feet "as though dead" (1:17), awestruck and terrified by the awesome display of Jesus in His deity.

Christ lifts John up and commissions him to write "what you have seen, what is now and what will take place later" (1:19). Futurists see this as the key verse in the book, defining its contents. "What you have seen" is Jesus glorified, described in 1:9-18. "What is now" is the condition of the seven churches to whom John is told to write, recorded in chapters 2–3. And "what will take place later" is the rest of the book, recorded in chapters 4–22. Thus the visions of John are placed squarely within the Jewish apocalyptic tradition, as prophetic, symbolic descriptions of history's end.

The focus of this section of the book, however, is on "what is now." Here we have a series of seven letters to seven extant churches in Asia Minor. Each letter describes the church addressed, presents a particular aspect of Christ, and encourages a specific response.

While these letters undoubtedly address the current situation in John's time, they have been taken by generations of preachers as typical of churches of every age. The typology, with the characteristics of the church, John's description of Jesus, and the desired response, are summarized on the following chart.

Church	Characteristic	Jesus	Response
Ephesus, the Steadfast (2:1-7)	Works hard, perseveres, rejects wicked, endures, but left first love	Walks among the seven lamps in heaven	Return to first love
Smyrna, the Persecuted (2:8-11)	Undergoing suffering, poverty, persecution	The One who died but is alive again	Remain faithful
Pergamum, the Immoral (2:12-17)	Remains true, faithful to death, but does tolerate immorality	Holds sharp, double-edged sword [the Word]	Repent of evil ways
Thyatira, the Compromising (2:18-29)	Doing more than at first, but tolerates immorality, false teaching	Eyes of fire, feet of bronze (bronze speaks of judgment)	Hold to the truth
Sardis, the Counterfeit (3:1-6)	Has reputation as alive, but is dead; deeds incomplete	Holds the Spirit, angels, in His hand	Wake up, obey what has been heard
Philadelphia, the Obedient (3:7-13)	Has little strength, yet kept the Word; patiently endures	Holds key of David (speaks of royal authority)	Hold on to what you have
Laodicea, the Materialistic (3:14-22)	Neither cold nor hot; wealthy, but poor spiritually	Ruler of creation	Be earnest, repent under discipline

Pattern of the Notes to the Seven Churches. The messages sent to the churches follow a common pattern:

■ Each note is addressed to the "angel" of the church, perhaps best understood as a reference to the "prevailing spirit" of the congregation rather than to any supernatural guardian or human leader.

■ Each note then identifies Christ with a specific but different phrase. To Ephesus the speaker is "Him who holds the seven stars in His right hand and walks among the seven golden lampstands" (2:1), while to Philadelphia the speaker is "Him who is holy and true, who holds the key of David" (3:7). It is clear that in each case the identification points out an aspect of Christ's character or role which corresponds to His evaluation of the church, or His call to it for reformation.

■ Each note then reports what Christ "knows" about that church. That is, the characteristics of the congregation are defined, as in the letter to Ephesus where the speaker says, "I know your deeds, your hard work and your perseverance. I know that you cannot tolerate wicked men, that you have tested those who claim to be apostles but are not, and have found them false" (2:2). In essence this is an evaluation of the church's accomplishments and serves as a commendation, except in the case of the churches of Sardis and Laodicea where no hint of commendation can be found.

■ Each note then announces the speaker's verdict concerning flaws that require correction, except now for Smyrna and Philadelphia.

■ Each note then contains a sharp and clear command, defining what the church must do to correct the flaws in its lifestyle or the errors which have crept in to corrupt it.

■ Each note also contains the exact same exhortation, "He who has an ear, let him hear what the Spirit says to the churches." The reference to "churches," plural, suggests that each of these letters has application to every first-century reader—and to us today.

■ Each note closes with the promise of reward to those who overcome. Christ, the Ruler of the universe, is fully capable of keeping His promise of blessing to those who remain loyal to Him, and express that loyalty in full commitment to His ways.

Judgments Associated with the Return of Christ (chaps. 4–18).

Background. The section begins with a voice calling John to "come up here" and the promise "I will show you what must take place after this" (4:1). This is yet another repetition of the "past, present, future" framework so often made explicit in this book.

Vv.	Past	Present	Future
1:1	God was	God is	God is to come
1:5-7	Jesus freed us from our sins	Jesus has made us priests	Jesus is coming and all will see Him
1:8	The Lord was	and is	and is to come
1:19	John to write what he has seen	what is now	what will take place later
4:1			shown what must take place after this

It is important to understand the perspective from which John now continues his report. The apostle has been caught up into heaven. Standing there, he is able to observe what is happening in two realms: the spiritual realm of God and His angels, and the material realm of the biosphere, where human beings live their lives. In a sense he is backstage, able to observe the play, but able also to see all those behind-the-scene activities that are required if the play is to go on.

What John does, then, is from the standpoint of heaven, to simply *describe what he sees happening in heaven and on earth.*

Two aspects of this section of Revelation seem particularly important. First, the description of the judgments that befall the earth and its population. And second, the description of the praise offered to God and Jesus in heaven.

The judgments are portrayed in a characteristic way: they are described without interpretation. It is this that makes Revelation so difficult to understand. For, as powerful as the images John uses are, we are hard put to rephrase them in more mundane terms.

I've discussed the reason in another book (*The Teacher's Commentary*, Victor) as follows:

Imagine that one of our great great grandfathers, who lived 150 years ago, was suddenly transported to our time. He witnesses a traffic jam, sees a TV football game (replete with replays), is taken in a 747, and goes to an air-conditioned movie. Then he is returned to his own age, and given the task of explaining it all to his contemporaries.

He lacks all the terms and images we use to describe what are to us commonplace events. He has experienced something that no one else in his day can even imagine. How terribly difficult it must be for him to struggle for words to communicate what he has seen.

Well, this was exactly John's situation. What he saw are real events. And John reported what he witnessed. But he had to struggle with an inadequate vocabulary, and use imagery that may communicate something of his vision to the people of his day—even though his imagery did not exactly describe what he saw.

Look, for instance, at this passage. What, really, is John describing? The events are real, surely. And they will happen. But just *what* is he talking about?

"The first angel sounded his trumpet, and there came hail and fire mixed with blood, and it was hurled down upon the earth. A third of the earth was burned up, a third of the trees were burned up, and all the green grass was burned up.

"The second angel sounded his trumpet, and something like a huge mountain, all ablaze, was thrown into the sea. A third of the sea turned into blood. A third of the living creatures in the sea died, and a third of the ships were destroyed.

"The third angel sounded his trumpet, and a great star, blazing like a torch, fell from the sky on a third of the rivers and on the springs of water—the name of the star is Wormwood. A third of the waters turned bitter, and many people died from the waters that had become bitter" (8:7-11).

It is clear from this description that John described terrible cataclysms that will strike our earth. Some imagine that what he saw and tried to describe was a terrible atomic war, or perhaps a space war. But the fact is, we can't tell just what it was that John saw.

We know that it was terrible, and associated with worldwide divine judgment. We can also be sure that when it does happen, we'll recognize the events. But till then there is much uncertainty. . . . We sense the power and terror of the last days that John described. But we dare not be dogmatic in our interpretation of them (pp. 1065-1066).

Despite this difficulty, there is great value in reading the awe-inspiring portrayal of judgments to come. Though terrifying, they remind us that God is dedicated to justice, and that ultimately evil will be punished and put away. The wicked will not triumph, and the righteousness of God will be displayed to all.

FUTURIST VIEW OF REV. 4–22

Chapter Basic understanding

4   The focus of the spiritual realm is God Himself, constantly being praised as "holy, holy, holy," the Creator who is worthy of glory, honor, and power.

5   A sealed scroll, the deed to the OT's messianic kingdom (Dan. 7:13-14), is taken by Christ, who is proclaimed worthy to open it, for He purchased men for God with His own blood.

6   As the seals that secure the scroll are opened, terrible judgments are unleashed on earth. Futurists link this with the Great Tribulation predicted in the OT and described by Jesus in Matt. 24:5-8.

7   The predicted conversion of the Jews to the Messiah result in 144,000 missionaries from Israel's ancient tribes preaching across our planet. At the same time, the souls of those martyred during this period worship God.

8   The time of terrible tribulation continues as earth's population is devastated by a series of natural disasters.

9   Now man's hidden enemies, the demon minions of Satan, are unleashed, and their persistent hostility to humankind is revealed in vicious attacks on humankind.

10   The scene shifts back to heaven, where after a brief interlude the culminating events at history's end will be acted out.

11   Two witnesses, often identified as Moses and Elijah (Matt. 17:10-11), preach for 3-1/2 years in Jerusalem, before being killed near the end of the Great Tribulation. Their return to life and to heaven prefaces the culminating judgments.

12   A dragon and a woman symbolize Satan's efforts to exterminate the Jewish people during the reign of the Antichrist.

13   The Antichrist and false prophet emerge from the sea of humanity, and impose an authoritarian regime which exercises control over every aspect of human life.

14 All of humanity is called now to make the clear choice that exists between Christ and Antichrist. Now the judgment that falls is administered directly from heaven by angelic beings.

15–16 The Great Tribulation judgments continue as angels pour out disaster after disaster on unrepentant humanity.

17 An angel now announces the fall of Mystery Babylon, representing the false religion imposed by the Antichrist.

18 The announcement continues, with the description of the fall of another aspect of "Babylon"; the commercial, civil, and military power of the Antichrist.

19 Now, at last, the personal return of Christ is announced with "Hallelujahs" in heaven. That return marks the end of the rebellion, as the Antichrist's armies are slain. And the Antichrist and the false prophet are cast alive into a "lake of burning sulfur."

20 For 1,000 years Satan is restrained, and peace reigns. At the end of this time Satan is released, and again finds ready followers among man. This final rebellion is put down by Christ. Satan is cast in the lake of fire, and the unbelieving revived to face final judgment. John says that "if anyone's name was not found written in the book of life, he was thrown into the lake of fire."

21–22 The scene now shifts to heaven, and we are given a glimpse of what God has in store for those who believe. The beauties of the new creation pale before the fact that from now on "the dwelling of God is with man, and He will live with them" in perpetual harmony.

The second major characteristic of this extended apocalyptic section is its frequent explosions of praise addressed to God or to Jesus. The judgments that strike terror on the earth provoke an entirely different reaction in heaven. Below there are cries of consternation; above, paeans of praise. The acts experienced by the unrepentant on earth as calamities are, in heaven, revelations of God's righteousness, and full vindication of His holy love.

Great and marvelous are Your deeds,
    Lord God Almighty.
Just and true are Your ways,
    King of the ages.
Who will not fear You, O Lord,
    and bring glory to Your name?
For You alone are holy.
All nations will come
    and worship before You,
    for Your righteous acts have been revealed (15:3-4).

And so we sense again the great value of this book to the church throughout the ages. It stands as testimony, pointing clearly to the judgments which lie ahead at history's end, yet placing those terrible acts in perspective as the vindication of our glorious and utterly righteous God.

REVELATION 21–22
The New Jerusalem

Background. History's march toward judgment concludes in Rev. 20. There, after 1,000 years of peace imposed by Jesus as reigning Messiah, Satan is released. There is no question that the earliest teachers in the church were convinced that such a millennial kingdom would be established, during which the OT prophets' promises to Israel would be fulfilled. Yet the question arises: Why? Aside from the fact that such a period would enable God to keep the prophets' promises in a literal way, why should such an era be part of His eternal plan?

The fact that after his release Satan so quickly gathers followers is suggestive. In one sense, all of human history is a demonstration of the truth of God's words to Adam, warning him not to eat the forbidden fruit: "when you eat of it, you will surely die" (Gen. 2:17). That reality was demonstrated in the murderous rage of Cain against Abel. It was demonstrated in the plunge of prediluvian society into a corruption so great that only a devasting Flood could purge that world of evil. The reality of man's fall was demonstrated in the idolatry which ruled till the days of Abraham; in the unwillingness of the Exodus generation that benefited from God's miracles to trust Him enough to enter the Promised Land. The reality of man's fall was displayed in the refusal of Israel to live by God's Law, and in the failure of Christians to fully live out the transformation God's Spirit has now come to enable.

Again and again, era after era has shown the dread effect of sin on human beings. Yet one question remains: What if human beings lived in a perfect environment? What if a just moral society became a reality, and for hundreds upon hundreds of years every evil influence was removed? What if good infused every human institution, and only good was modeled to the young as they matured? According to many a modern social scientist, in such a utopia human beings would be different. Would the tendencies toward sin which we sense in ourselves and see in every other person be eradicated?

How fascinating to view the millennial kingdom as the behavioral scientist's laboratory, and as God's ultimate demonstration of the terrible impact of sin. Even after 1,000 years of Christ's beneficent reign, unregenerate human beings still rush to follow Satan when he is released. They joyfully turn their backs on Christ, and rush toward the promise of "freedom" to follow the impulses that have earlier been forcefully restrained.

Now, at last, the truth is undeniable. Human beings have been totally corrupted by sin. Only personal faith in the saving work of Christ can suffice to write any name in the Book of Life. As every man divorced from Christ is called before God's great white throne to face final judgment, each is found wanting and is condemned. Condemned, in John's stark words, to a "fiery lake of burning sulfur" (19:20) where, with Satan and the Antichrist, "they will be tormented day and night forever and ever" (20:10).

The Book of Revelation, in harmony with the rest of the New Testament and the Old, affirms the uniqueness of human beings. Created in God's image, no individual's identity can be simply snuffed out. Each one of us is destined to remain ourselves, self-conscious and aware, for all eternity. For the lost, this means eternal punishment. For the saved, what it means is sketched in Rev. 21 and 22.

Preview of Eternity for the Saved. Revelation 21–22 describe a new heaven and earth, created by God to be the home of righteousness. The most important thing about this new creation is that here, at last, God and a redeemed humanity live together in fellowship and harmony.

For us this means that "God Himself will be with them and be their God. He will wipe every tear from their eyes. There will be no more death or mourning or crying or pain, for the old order of things has passed away" (21:3-4). For God, it means fulfillment of the possibilities inherent in the original creation of an innocent Adam and Eve. For in the new world there is no room for "the cowardly, the unbelieving, the vile, the murderers, the sexually immoral, those who practice magic arts, the idolaters and all liars" (21:8). The new world is populated by the redeemed and made-righteous alone.

These two chapters also describe something of the characteristics of the new universe. Like our present universe it contains a planet called earth, but a planet not bound to any sun. As John says, "The city does not need the sun or the moon to shine on it, for the glory of God gives it light, and the Lamb is its lamp" (21:23).

One of the most striking features of the new world is the "new Jerusalem" (21:2) described as a cube some 1,500 miles on each side, with gates of precious jewels. Some, misreading the passage, have ridiculed the idea that "heaven" could be so small. How could all the believing dead be contained in such a space? But the New Jerusalem is no more the whole heaven than the old Jerusalem was the whole of the first creation. God's glory always expands far beyond our ability to comprehend. And thus the New Jerusalem is but the capital of new earth, which itself is the center of a vast universe of starry hosts. As powerful as human imagination has proven to be, what God has prepared for us is far beyond our capacity to conceive or fantasize.

And it is here that Scripture leaves us. With a warning and a promise. Let those who do wrong continue to do wrong. God will be vindicated in the end.

And let those who have chosen to follow Jesus look forward eagerly. In the near distance we can hear His voice echoing: "Behold, I am coming soon! My reward is with Me, and I will give to everyone according to what he has done" (22:12).

INDEX

C

632